The Ultimate
Multimedia Handbook

The Ultimate Multimedia Handbook

Jessica Keyes
Editor

Second Edition

McGraw-Hill

New York San Francisco Washington, D.C. Auckland Bogotá
Caracas Lisbon London Madrid Mexico City Milan
Montreal New Delhi San Juan Singapore
Sydney Tokyo Toronto

Library of Congress Cataloging-in-Publication Data

The Ultimate multimedia handbook / Jessica Keyes, editor. — 2nd ed.
    p.   cm. — (McGraw-Hill series on visual technology)
   Includes index.
   ISBN 0-07-034530-9 (pbk.)
   1. Multimedia systems. I. Keyes, Jessica, (date). II. Series.
QA76.575.U48   1997
006.7—dc21   96-47090
                                                        CIP

First edition published under the title *The McGraw-Hill Multimedia Handbook*.

McGraw-Hill

A Division of The McGraw-Hill Companies

   2 3 4 5 6 7 8 9 0   DOC/DOC   9 0 1 0 9 8 7

ISBN 0-07-034530-9

*The sponsoring editor for this book was Jennifer Holt DiGiovanna, the editing supervisor
was Andrew Yoder, and the production supervisor was Suzanne W. B. Rapcavage. It was
set in New Century Schoolbook by Jana Fisher through the services of Barry E. Brown
(Broker—Editing, Design and Production).*

Printed and bound by R. R. Donnelley & Sons Company.

 This book is printed on recycled, acid-free paper containing 10% postconsumer
waste.

McGraw-Hill books are available at special quantity discounts to use as premiums and
sales promotions, or for use in corporate training programs. For more information, please
write to the Director of Special Sales, McGraw-Hill, 11 West 19th Street, New York, NY
10011. Or contact your local bookstore.

This book is most appreciatively dedicated to my clients and friends, old and new, my family and my editors. In particular, I would like to dedicate this book to my Uncle, Seymour Harrison, who passed away during final edits. He was an inspiration to us all.

Contents

Part 2 Authoring

Part 3   Animation, Video, and Sound

Part 4   Advanced Topics in Multimedia

Part 5   The Internet

Contributors

Phil Abram *Eastman Kodak Company, Rochester, New York* (Chap. 50)

Rex J. Allen *Allen Communication, Salt Lake City, Utah* (Chap. 13)

Chris Ammen *Television Associates, Mountain View, California* (Chap. 63)

Barbara Baker *Starlight Networks, Inc., Mountain View, California* (Chap. 48)

Mel Baiada *Bluestone, Mt. Laurel, New Jersey* (Chap. 21)

Glenn Becker *NuMedia Corporation, Alexandria, Virginia* (Chap. 39)

Bob Bennett *Autodesk Multimedia, Sausalito, California* (Chap. 26)

Pam Berger *Byram Hills High School, Armonk, New York* (Chap. 14)

Peter B. Blakeney *IBM, Atlanta, Georgia* (Chap. 44)

Alan Briggs *Producer, London, England* (Chap. 52)

Tim Brock *St. Petersburg Junior College, St. Petersburg, Florida* (Chaps. 25, 51)

Red Burns *New York University, New York, New York* (Chap. 2)

Steven Bussard *Bussard & Associates, Pasadena, California* (Chaps. 56, 61)

Julie Capsambelis *St. Petersburg Junior College, St. Petersburg, Florida* (Chap. 51)

Alton Christensen *CoSA, Providence, Rhode Island* (Chap. 30)

John Colligan *Macromedia, San Francisco, California* (Chap. 43)

Cross-Industry Working Team *Reston, Virginia* (Chap. 67)

Kevin Daniel *NeoSoft Corp., Bend, Oregon* (Chap. 59)

Les Dunaway *Technology Helping People, Inc., Kennesaw, Georgia* (Chap. 40)

Joseph Dunn *Macromedia, San Francisco, California* (Chap. 43)

Dr. Schahram Dustdar *University of Art, Linz, Austria* (Chap. 54)

Mike Evans *National Semiconductor, Santa Clara, California* (Chap. 41)

Joseph Fantuzzi *Macromedia, San Francisco, California* (Chap. 43)

Jeffrey P. Geibel *GEIBEL Marketing Consulting, Belmont, Massachussetts* (Chap. 65)

Ken Gerlach *Hewlett-Packard, Cupertino, California* (Chap. 4)

Lewis Gruskin *IBM, Atlanta, Georgia* (Chap. 24)

Konstantin Guericke *Caligari Corp., Mountain View, California* (Chap. 67)

Satish Gupta *Media Vision, Fremont, California* (Chap. 9)

Harry Hallman *Corporate Media Communications, Atlanta, Georgia* (Chap. 11)

Guy Hancock *St. Petersburg Junior College, St. Petersburg, Florida* (Chap. 12)

Ray Harris *Optibase, Dallas, Texas* (Chap. 31)

David E. Hartman *St. Petersburg Junior College, St. Petersburg, Florida* (Chap. 25)

Donna Hefner *Macromedia, San Francisco, California* (Chap. 43)

Christine Hemrick *Cisco Systems, Inc., San Jose, California* (Chap. 45)

Josh Hendrix *CoSA, Providence, Rhode Island* (Chap. 30)

Jeff Hooks *St. Petersburg Junior College, St. Petersburg, Florida* (Chap. 8)

Lynn Jones   *Digital Equipment Corporation, Marlboro, Massachusetts* (Chap. 64)

Roger Karr   *Digital Equipment Corporation, Marlboro, Massachusetts* (Chap. 19)

Michael Kellner   *Apple Computer, Santa Clara, California* (Chap. 20)

Richard V. Kelly, Jr.   *Digital Equipment Corporation, Marlboro, Massachusetts* (Chap. 46)

Jessica Keyes   *New Art/Techinsider, New York, New York* (Chaps. 1, 15, 68, 69)

Susan Kinnell   *UCSB, Santa Barbara, California* (Chap. 14)

Paulina Knibbe   *Cisco Systems, Inc., San Jose, California* (Chap. 45)

Cliff Kondratiuk   *Sierra Semiconductor, British Columbia, Canada* (Chap. 27)

Lucy Lediaev   *Philips Interactive Media of America, Los Angeles, California* (Chap. 22)

Claude Leglise   *Intel Corporation, Santa Clara, California* (Chap. 33)

James Long   *Starlight Networks, Inc., Mountain View, California* (Chap. 48)

Kirk Mahoney   *Engaging Media, Houston, Texas* (Chap. 60)

Mike McGonagle   *Computer Corporation of America, Los Angeles, California* (Chap. 22)

Rob Morris   *V_Graph, Westtown, Pennsylvania* (Chap. 58)

Glenn K. Morrissey   *Asymetrix Corporation, Bellevue, Washington* (Chap. 18)

Ken Morse   *Kaleida Labs, Inc., Mountain View, California* (Chaps. 32, 47)

Kurt Mueller   *Dataware Technologies, Campbridge, Massachusetts* (Chap. 23)

Jay Murray   *Gateway 2000, N. Sioux City, South Dakota* (Chap. 57)

Eric Nahm   *Verbex Voice Systems, Edison, New Jersey* (Chap. 55)

Jeffrey V. Nickerson   *Coopers & Lybrand, Edison, New Jersey* (Chap. 50)

Mike O'Berry   *St. Petersburg Junior College, St. Petersburg, Florida* (Chap. 51)

Amy Pearl   *SunSoft, Mountain View, California* (Chap. 34)

Tim Picraux   *Unisys Corp., Blue Bell, Pennsylvania* (Chap. 34)

Marco Pinter   *Digital Media International, Sunbury, Pennsylvania* (Chap. 37)

Rudy Prokupets   *Lenel Systems International, Fairport, New York* (Chap. 6)

Steven L. Raber   *IBM, Atlanta, Georgia* (Chap. 3)

Bruce A. Rady   *TouchVision Systems, Chicago, Illinois* (Chap. 38)

Gary Robbins   *St. Petersburg Junior College, St. Petersburg, Florida* (Chap. 51)

John Sievel   *Gnomon, Inc. Ashford, Connecticut* (Chap. 53)

Deborah Slater   *Verbex Voice Systems, Edison, New Jersey* (Chap. 55)

Lex van Sonderen   *Philips Interactive Media of America, Los Angeles, California* (Chap. 22)

Larry Strickland   *St. Petersburg Junior College, St. Petersburg, Florida* (Chap. 51)

Valerie Taylor   *Independent Multimedia Producer, Mountain View, California* (Chap. 63)

Serge Timacheff   *Logitech, Fremont, California* (Chap. 28)

Bill Tonnies   *St. Petersburg Junior College, St. Petersburg, Florida* (Chap. 51)

Prem Uppaluru   *Fluent, Natick, Massachusetts* (Chap. 42)

Vince Wallsko   *The Walisko Group, Washington, D.C.* (Chap. 39)

Rob Wallace   *Wallace Music & Sound, Glendale, Arizona* (Chap. 36)

Joseph Weintraub   *Thinking Software, Woodside, New York* (Chap. 10)

J. Alan Whiteside   *Multimedia Learning, Inc., Irving, Texas* (Chaps. 7, 29)

Mary F. Whiteside   *Southwestern Medical Center, University of Texas, Dallas, Texas* (Chaps. 7, 29)

Frederic M. Wilf   *Elman, Wilf & Fried, Media, Pennsylvania* (Chap. 17)

Lee Wilson   *National Semiconductor, Santa Clara, California* (Chap. 49)

Wing F. Wong   *Coopers & Lybrand, Edison, New Jersey* (Chap. 50)

Andrew Young   *Young Minds, Inc., Redlands, California* (Chap. 16)

Foreword

It's unbelievable, but true. This book has grown by hundreds of pages. Many chapters have been added to a book already brimming with great food for thought.

The first edition of this book, *The McGraw-Hill Multimedia Handbook*, quickly became a best-seller. Some even called it the "bible" of the multimedia industry. And it was. Chock full of "hands-on" advice from the multimedia industry's most notable experts, the Handbook provided developers, managers and those just interested in the topic everything they needed to develop technically perfect and artistically creative multimedia systems.

In this second edition, renamed *The Ultimate Multimedia Handbook*, I've invited a handful of new multimedia experts as well as two fistfuls of Internet gurus to join the fray.

From where I sit, the Internet is multimedia. It's got text, imagery, video, sound, interactivity—all the elements of multimedia. Add to that a couple of high-capacity telephone lines, thousands of computers and millions of potential users, and you've got the formula for ultimate multimedia. Funny, that's the name of this book.

Preface

Multimedia and the Internet are both hot topics. But that's not the whole reason for this book. As a technologist with some 18 years experience, I can't remember a time when a set of technologies caught the minds and hearts of so many people. Myself included.

True, multimedia started life on the consumer side of the house with Nintendo and Sega taking a huge chunk out of our kids' allowances. But then something funny happened. People began to realize the potential of "sight and sound" on business.

For more than two decades we've been at the mercy of the computer's flat representation of data. Precious little insight can be gleaned from a myriad of rows and columns of multi-digit numbers. But even though a bit of multidimensionality was introduced to the process with the advent of the spreadsheet and various and sundry graphics programs, information visualization requires much more. A complete immersion of the senses.

The term *multimedia* is familiar to most. After all we used it almost everyday in grade school. That was back when multimedia meant nothing more than going to the audio-visual department to gather up the projector to view the requisite film on health for hygiene. But wait. This sounds eerily like what we're doing today. It couldn't be that Mrs. Applegate, our fourth grade teacher, was on the cutting edge of the multimedia revolution?

Well, maybe she was. For Mrs. Applegate knew full well the value of involving all of the senses in a learning experience. Information visualization isn't so very far afield from Mrs. Applegate's fourth grade classroom.

By using any combination of video, sound, graphics, and animation presents us with an unlimited vista in making the world understandable, not only to children, but to businesses, academia, and the sciences.

The human body interprets input from the five senses in parallel. A combination of sight, sound, smell, touch, and hearing enables us to react intelligently to the current situation. If multimedia is to be successful, then multimedia productions must follow this lead.

This implies some rather dramatic capabilities of the hardware and software that multimedia producers utilize. For those readers who thought that multimedia was just a presentation with some sound or animation piped in, think again.

Multimedia requires a fluidity between system resources that, to be frank, is barely possible today. Just ask your systems administrator about the vagaries of LAN systems response and you'll begin to understand just what I'm talking about. Today most system users suffer silently at the hands of what we optimistically refer to a client/server environment. Too many users slow the system. Too much data being routed between client and server slow the system down even more.

Fortunately, our senses can easily accommodate variable speeds in populating a textual data screen. But just try that when populating a display with a video and you'll wind up with what looks like a movie made by a three-year old on a tricycle!

It's good that technology (as ever) is moving rapidly to accommodate multimedia's intense requirements. But it would be erroneous to think that "computing" is leading the way. For multimedia is actually a convergence of many industries. Publishing, consumer electronics, computing, cable and broadcast television, telephone, communications, and film have been referred to as "seven octopuses," all with tentacles in each others' pockets.

Bill Gates, Microsoft's perennially innovative chairman, has created a company whose goal is to develop a technology that will merge moving images with text and art with history. Continuum Productions, Inc. is out to create a database that combines the art, music, photographs, and historical information giving new meaning to the term *performance art*.

Where Gates' artistic vision might seem pure whimsy, the Post Office has embarked on the ultimate in practical applications of multimedia (especially for those of us who have to wait more than five minutes to get a roll of stamps). The U.S. Postal Service has introduced some high-tech multimedia kiosks that offer stamps, address-change services, and custom printing. And they're not even rude.

Perhaps the most intriguing of all multimedia applications are the ones that virtually breath. At Carnegie Mellon's Studio for Creative Inquiry, a virtual gallery is underwraps that, when completed, will permit people to take a stroll through ancient Egypt. Even more interestingly, Digital Equipment Corp. is one of the organizations whose Artificial Life & Virtual Reality Applications Group is working on something called a "virtual cadaver." Virtual cadavers provide a "body" to surgeons-in-training, where they would normally fear to tread. Dick Kelly, one of the contributors to this book, expounds on this subject in more depth later on.

But for those business users or technologists, who don't have much of a taste for cadavers, or art for that matter, and who still have multi-billions invested in enterprise systems, fear not. Multimedia is coming your way.

Oracle is one of the mostly used of all database management systems. Thousands of payroll systems, personnel systems and the like are run using Oracle's relational database model. There was a time when relational was considered "old-hat"—it just stored data. But times change. Today's Oracle incorporates interactive multimedia services, such as electronic libraries, multimedia messaging as well as audio and video. So, even enterprise users can perform such esoteric multimedia functions as video conferencing, video on demand, and even home shopping.

All this comes at a great time because, in the past year, graphical use of the Internet is at an all-time high. Although the Internet has been around since the year of the flood (counting in computer years), it's only been the last few that graphical Web browsers have been available.

Mosaic and Netscape have changed the shape of the world. Where once Internet access meant dull text, it now means graphics, hyperlinks, JPEG, MPEG, and much more. Current estimates put its user base somewhere between 22 and 30 million end-users.

So, how do you get on the road to information visualization through multimedia and the Internet? Easy. Just turn the page. Inside you'll find the answers to the perennial questions, "where, what, when, how, and why."

The Ultimate Multimedia Handbook is not meant to be read cover to cover. You'll get more mileage out of it if you turn to the part(s) of particular interest. It is configured in a logical manner, of sorts.

In the beginning, there was a beginning. All books have one. And this book is no different. So, in part one, you'll find the basic introduction to the salient issues of multimedia: what it is and how it's used (or should be used). Don't be turned off by the word "introduction." There's some real heavy-hitters who've contributed to this part. Even the multimedia aficionado would do well to peruse this part.

In part two you'll find chapters on creating and authoring a multimedia system. Producing an effective multimedia system takes a lot more than sound and video dumping. Dumping aside, those interested in attaching sound, speech or music, or video or animation would do well to flip to part three where you'll benefit from widely diverse expertise. We've even got a composer for you.

Part four is where we tackle the heady issues of networking, virtual reality and standards. Even if you're an expert in multimedia, you'll find worthy nuggets of information here.

To use current 'Net vernacular, part five contains some really cool information on the Internet. Everything from Web design to VRML. So, surf on over.

Finally we come to part six. Although there are several compendiums of products out there, I find them overwhelming. So, in this part I've provided an "annotated" version. That is, in this part you'll find a wealth of resources that I find intriguing. Resources in the areas of authoring software, sound boards, CD-ROMs, consultants, publications, associations, clip art, clip sound and clip videos. In other words, I've sifted through tons of literature from scads of vendors and the ones listed are the ones I found to be of interest to me.

So, read on and multimediate.

Acknowledgments

This book wouldn't have been possible without the help and encouragement of many people. First of all, I'd like to thank my husband Robert without whose unwavering support this book would never have been finished. Of course, special kudos go to Debra Nencel and Andrew Pisko, my trusty assistants.

But I'd also like to thank the many contributors to this book who gave willingly of their time and expertise. These are the real heroes. I know they, as I, hope that this book will become the wings that makes multimedia fly on the wings of the Internet.

JK, New York City

Multimedia Issues

Getting Started in Multimedia

Jessica Keyes

How Is Multimedia Different from Traditional Data Processing?

When computers first made their entrance into the corporate arena some three decades ago, they were thought of merely as numerical processors (i.e., number crunchers). In fact, the very first commercial application (albeit governmental) was to count the census. But monumental change was in the offing. Largely due to staggering advances in chip technology, no longer are computers relegated to the basements of large organizations. Today, (personal) computers can be found in millions of organizations on an equal number of desktops.

When the computer migrated from the basement to the desktop, precepts about programming migrated as well. As any professional programmer will attest to, no longer are monolithic systems developed. Instead, systems are composed of a series of distributed modules, some running on the PC and some running on the mainframe (or server), which taken together are collectively referred to as *client/server*.

Dispersion of system components to the PC, or client, required a change in the way programmers think about user interfaces. Where mainframe-based systems were largely character-based, these newer PC-based systems were much more icon-, or image-, based.

Even though image-oriented processing is a step in the right direction, multimedia, for the most part, has not yet caught on to any great degree in the corporate arena. There are several possible reasons for this.

The primary reason is that multimedia is so "different" from traditional systems development. Even though so much of today's PC-based development sports enhanced imagery as a user interface, there the similarity ends. For traditional systems simply do not (usually) handle audio, video, or animation. And these are the three key components of multimedia.

The majority of corporate systems, in spite of their colorful GUIs (graphical user interfaces) are numerical or text-oriented. Even though the advent of client/server has added an additional layer of complexity to the process, development of traditional systems is largely a straightforward process. One requests a record. One transfers this record to the client. The client processes the record and then transfers it back to the source from whence it originated. The "source" is usually a database, often relational in nature, that stores simply numbers or characters.

But even here things seem to be changing. Developing these GUIs saw the increase in new software development tools that enable programmers to quickly build user interfaces from a set of building blocks. Programmers had just discovered a mode of programming that had long been popular in the rarefied environments of artificial intelligence labs and in the domain of the vendors themselves. Object-oriented programming made its entrance in a big way and continues, to this very day, to have a radical effect on how systems are built.

Perhaps the biggest change is in the way we *think* about systems. Instead of a kluge of code which serves the purpose of building a system from top to bottom, we now tend to think in terms of *objects*. Objects are discrete, for lack of a better term, *things* that are self-contained and independent. They contain all the data and logic they need to carry out their designated functions. In essence, then, systems are built simply by connecting one or more objects.

Objects, of course, can be anything. No longer are we confined to the world of numbers or characters. An object can just as easily be a picture of a house as the number 23. Or a video clip as well as the text string, "123 Main Street." And because objects can be a number, a character, an image, a video clip, or sound, the world of multimedia is, for the first time, readily available to anyone who cares to dabble.

In essence, the technical skillsets needed to build a multimedia system are not dissimilar to those required to build any object-oriented system. One just uses a different set of tools. But in this era of a cacophony of different toolsets, systems developers have grown used to this diversity.

The biggest difference is in handling the three-dimensionality of multimedia. Where traditional systems present one view of the information, multimedia systems are "alive" with many views of the system—its sight as well as its sound. No longer are we confined to a rather one-sighted and very flat view of information. With multimedia we can look at information from all sides, sort of take a walk around it surveying it from all sides. And with virtual reality, we can even talk a walk inside of it.

In essence, one could describe traditional systems as "static" and multimedia systems as very much "dynamic" in nature. The big question then becomes, especially for those just getting involved in multimedia development, *"Just when and where do you add those elements of multimedia (i.e., animation, sound, video, imagery) to make the largest impact?"*

A Question of Content

Aside from the technical aspects of developing a multimedia application, perhaps the biggest bugaboo for system developers, when presented with their first multimedia project, is content. But how to best integrate sound, video, animation, graphics, and text is largely in the domain of the content specialist. It is usual in the case of development of traditional systems to actively solicit the involvement of an expert from the area being automated. Why should the development of multimedia systems be any different?

User experts are natural content specialists. It is their understanding of the "business" that will enable them to direct (which is an appropriate verb here) the multimedia production. Essentially, their expertise should be able to accurately dictate the most logical placement of text, graphics, sound, and video.

Indeed, many of the consumer CD titles on the market today have been directed by just these content experts. *The Family Doctor,* authored and edited by Dr. Allan Bruckheim, is one of many examples. But even the good doctor needed a goodly dosage of technical expertise to put his production together.

Unless the title being produced is about computer topics, where the content and technical expert may be one and the same, the minimal human resource requirement for a multimedia production should always be at least one technical expert and one content expert.

Similar to other data processing applications, a multimedia application has a systems life cycle. And it should be followed. Some get the impression, because multimedia is infinitely interactive, that this type of system can be thrown together in one great kluge. Actually, there is nothing to prevent this sort of "development by chaos." But as in any software system, the end result really does reflect the hard work and organization of the software development process.

For those just getting started in multimedia, the difficulty is compounded by the unfamiliarity of the terrain. As already mentioned, the tools (both hardware and software) are quite different from traditional data processing tools. But this should not really faze the hardy stock of techno-gurus that have cut their teeth of late on such esoteric technologies as client/server, object-orientation, and even artificial intelligence. Ultimately, multimedia is just one more tool for the system developer's toolbox.

A Quick Jump Start into Multimedia

Getting started in multimedia will be one of the more eye-opening experiences of your career. I know it was for me. Even though I already had 15 years of experience and had built a multiplicity of systems, multimedia was (and is), well...different.

Right off the bat, I had to make a slew of decisions about what software and hardware I would use. Because my experience is largely in the IBM PC–compatible arena, this last decision was already premade for me. A mere five years ago, the platform of choice was the Apple or the Amiga. And these are still wonderful platforms. However, the surge toward multimedia in the IBM PC (and clones) arena is nothing short of staggering. There are probably few hardware vendors who don't sell multimedia PCs. And even if you bought yours years ago, there's a plethora of upgrade kits to choose from. Just perusing the annotated appendix at the end of this book will make your head spin with the number of choices available.

The remainder of this chapter will take you through a typical multimedia "getting started" process. Although not everyone will make the same choices given their individual environments, this chapter will give you an excellent overview of what you need to get quickly started in building your very first multimedia title.

Choosing your hardware

As was true in my case, part of your decision may already have been made for you. If your organization is predominantly IBM PC compatible–based, then this should be your delivery platform. Alternatively, if you're Apple-based, then a Mac it is. Or Amiga. In other words, you first need to find out who you're delivering the system to. And it's insufficient to presume that, since the data-processing group is IBM PC–based, the entire organization is IBM PC–based.

There are many organizations who offload development to the PC, but ultimately deploy on a mainframe, midrange, or workstation. The delivery platform of the ultimate end user, then, is of prime importance in making any hardware decision.

In some cases, especially where the multimedia system is marketing-oriented, the ultimate hardware platform is not known. In other words some users may have Macs, some PCs, and some only mainframes.

First let's address the mainframe issue. Developing multimedia applications on a mainframe is, as of this writing, nearly an impossible feat. Mainframe resources are highly leveraged and, as a result, operational folks would frown mightily at the mere mention of such a resource-intensive operation. With often hundreds (and sometimes thousands) of users sharing slices of time, resource allocation becomes an art form in these environments. Given that even 1 minute of compressed video gobbles up somewhere around 9 Mbytes, you can envision a rather nice traffic jam (although chapters in Part 4, Advanced Topics, will show you how to get around this—at least from a workstation or PC perspective).

Another nail in the mainframe coffin is the lack of available authoring software. Although it's not impossible to "grow your own" multimedia application using any number of traditional programming languages, authoring software has those "hooks" that make the development of multimedia software...if not a breeze, then at least a lot easier.

Finally, mainframes that use purely dumb terminals, as opposed to PCs, are for the most part precluded from the element of sound altogether.

That multimedia appears to be excluded from the mainframe domain is really an anomaly, as far as I'm concerned. In spite of the reasons stated above, the mainframe is really a natural platform for multimedia. With its nearly unlimited storage capacity, the storage of even 60 minutes of video (or sound) is only a drop in the bucket.

It really wouldn't take much to make the mainframe a multimedia server. It certainly has the capacity, and the network is already in place. In fact, a variant of multimedia has been practiced for years in just this fashion. *Imaging* is the convergence of two very different forms of media: text and graphics. Literally thousands of organizations are already using their mainframe to view documents along with their associated images. So adding video and sound is just two giant steps forward in the game of multimedia.

There's no reason why multimedia-enabled PCs can't be tethered to mainframes that act as the repository of the database, which stores not only text but sound, imagery, and video. While object-oriented databases are a natural for this task, some relational database vendors (such as Oracle) are moving quickly to provide these very capabilities.

For those organizations that rely on "dumb" terminals as clients of their mainframes, I can only hope that these terminals become not so dumb in the near feature. There's just no reason why these terminals can't be sound-equipped.

But even if your organization decides not to deploy on the mainframe, there's still the sticky wicket of the possibility of a diversity of hardware platforms. Fortunately, there are some software vendors who see this as an opportunity. One of them, Lenel Systems, markets MultiMedia Works, which is a universal player that supports 40 file formats including AVI, Quicktime, DVI, FLC, FLI, CD-Audio, Wave, and Midi. What this means is that you can write one smart system that determines the runtime environment and acts accordingly.

Upgrading your hardware

The majority of PCs out in the field are IBM PC–compatible. But not all of them are multimedia-enabled. What this means is that few of them have enough hard-disk capacity, the ability to reproduce sound, a CD-ROM drive, a super VGA graphics card, or enough memory or speed to put it all together. Of course, it is entirely possible to successfully create and run a multimedia application without any of the above features—but the result may be less satisfactory. However, I've created and run very small applications without benefit of a sound card (I used a Windows driver to enable the speaker that comes with the PC—tinny, but usable) or CD-ROM. One caveat here is that if the application fits on a high-density diskette, then that should be the deployment media, since not many organizational PCs with a few years on them have a CD-ROM drive.

One thing you'll discover sooner rather than later is that there's a plethora of standards to consider (see Chap. 15 for much more on this). But why should multimedia be any different from any other technology? After all, proprietary standards are what sells hardware.

Whereas IBM calls their entry Ultimedia, the rest of the world has labeled it *multimedia*. The Multimedia Marketing Council (MMC) has developed a specification for a PC that ensures quality playback of multimedia productions. While it relies heavily on Microsoft's Windows as an operating system (whereas IBM bases its standard on its very own OS/2 or DOS), Ultimedia and the Multimedia Marketing Council's MPC (multimedia PC) are so similar as to be nearly indistinguishable.

The MPC Level 2 Specification is as follows:

25-MHz 486SX microprocessor

4 Mbytes of memory

3.5-inch floppy drive

160-Mbyte hard disk

16-bit sound

Two-button mouse

Windows 3.0, plus Multimedia Extensions or Windows 3.1

Color monitor with 640 × 480 resolution with 65,536 colors

Serial port, parallel port, MIDI I/O port, joystick port

But this is a specification for new PCs. If you need to upgrade the one already on your desk, then the MMC has graciously accommodated you with the following:

CD-ROM drive with a 300 kbyte-per-second transfer rate
   CD-ROM XA–ready (Photo CD)
   Multisession-capable
   Average seek time of 400 milliseconds
16-bit sound

MIDI I/O port and joystick port

You'll notice that nowhere do you see a reference to a video card (I don't mean a VGA card here, but one that processes digital video feeds). That's because part of the standard is the use of Microsoft's very own AVI (audio/video interleaved) video file format. AVI files require no special adapter card to play back video. This is its strength. Its weakness is that to get a superior video image, you really do need a digital video adapter.

The MPC standard actually provides the minimum requirements you need to "do good multimedia" at the lowest cost. Scratching the need for a video adapter greatly reduces the cost and enables multimedia applications to be more widely disseminated.

The first thing that people usually purchase when they decide to go multimedia is a CD-ROM drive. These greatly vary in price (see the appendix). You can buy very inexpensive CD-ROM drives ($199) at most computer stores—or even through catalogs. Of course, the cheaper the drive, the slower it'll be. And a slow speed is something you may regret later on.

From an organizational perspective, there are several alternatives to be considered when planning a department- or company-wide implementation. Purchasing a CD-ROM drive for each and every corporate PC (even at the low price of $199) can be very costly. You might want to consider networking those PCs (if they aren't already) and then networking a series of CD-ROM drives at the server.

If we remember that one rather small CD disc can hold somewhere around 250,000 pages of information, just think how much information a series of 3 or 4 or even 10 CD-ROM drives can handle. Just be sure to buy the very fastest CD-ROM drives if you're thinking of stacking them together.

While networking CD-ROM drives will require the expertise of a specialist (again, see the appendix), installing a single CD-ROM drive just requires perseverance. It's really no different from installing any other adapter card, except that in this case you must also install a drive. For those who are fainthearted at the prospect of installing another drive, or haven't the room for another, consider installing an external CD-ROM drive. It takes up some space on the desk, but it's a fairly easy installation process.

Multimedia loses much of its pizzazz without sound. And even though it's possible to get sound from the PC's built-in speaker if you install the right drivers (in the Windows control panel), there's nothing quite as exciting as good quality sound coming out of your PC through either attached headphones or speakers. For this you need a sound card.

There are many on the market. If you're planning on using pure voice annotation (no music), an 8-bit sound board will be sufficient and the least expensive solution. There are also several external devices available, such as Logitech's Audioman, which simply connect up to the PC's parallel port and voilà, sound!

If you're considering sound clips and/or music along with pure voice annotation, then a 16-bit card will provide about the same quality as the CD audio in your stereo system. But as you'll soon find out, there are great variations. A rule of thumb: the more expensive the sound card, the better the quality. And don't expect your local PC dealer to even stock some of the high-end cards.

Most sound cards come complete with a microphone and software that lets you "edit" the sound file. In a Windows-compatible environment, sounds are generally captured as .WAV files. Non-Windows systems store sounds in completely different formats. Although both store sound, they are incompatible without translating one to the other.

There's really no nice neat way to sum up what you'll need. Perhaps the following list from the June 1993 *Windows Sources* (p. 392) does the best job of explaining the requirements—and expenditures—of multimedia:

If you want to run authored multimedia titles, then use a 20-MHz 386SX-based PC with 2–4 Mbytes of RAM, a 256-color VGA display, an 80-Mbyte hard disk, a sound board, and earphones or speakers. It will cost between $1000 and $2000.

If you want a system for authoring applications, then upgrade to a 25-MHz 486DX-based PC with 8 Mbytes of RAM, 200-Mbyte hard disk, and a CD-ROM drive that transfers 300K or 600K of data per second. It will cost between $2500 and $3500.

If you want to author full-motion video applications, then upgrade to either a 33-MHz 486DX-based PC or a 66-MHz 486DX/2-based PC with a 300- to 500-Mbyte hard disk. It will cost between $4000 and $5500.

If you want to master applications for CD-ROMs, then upgrade your 66-MHz 486DX/2 to include a 1-GB hard disk, 16 Mbytes of RAM, and a 24-bit color board. Cost is between $3000 and $8000.

If you want to play commercial CD titles, then add a CD-ROM player with audio output that's controlled by a sound card. It will cost between $350 and $700.

If you want to record sound, then add a studio-quality microphone and high-end sound board. It will cost $150 for a good microphone, $300 to $600 for a sound board.

If you want to compose music, then add a MIDI keyboard. It will cost between $350 and $800.

If you want to digitize photos, then add a color scanner. It will cost between $1200 and $1500.

If you want to add video, then add a camcorder, VCR, and a video capture card. The video capture card will cost between $550 and $1200.

Yet another caveat is called for here. Windows-based systems are nowhere near as robust as either the Mac or (especially) workstations, in spite of the PC's popularity. The more you put inside of your computer, the higher the risk of incompatibility. For example adding sound, video, and a scanner requires three additional adapter boards. Each adapter board uses a system interrupt (IRQ) and a memory location. Conflicts, which arise when more than one device is configured for the same interrupt or memory location, are ticklish at best to sort out and fix.

If you intend to do heavy-duty multimedia development on your PC, then the minimum MPC requirement that I've listed above actually is insufficient. My advice is to double the memory and hard-disk storage requirements at a minimum, and to make sure your PC is as fast as they come. Also, be sure to spend a good deal of time with your Windows manual, figuring out ways to optimize the way Windows runs.

Perhaps the best advice I can give, and it's advice that I've taken myself, is to split development across more than one PC. I wouldn't be exaggerating if I told you that digital video work can hog all of the horsepower of a fairly high-end PC—and then some. By offloading your digital video work to a separate PC, you'll leave yourself plenty of room on your main PC for authoring, graphics, and sound. *And* you won't experience the memory conflicts that seem to be standard multimedia fare in the PC arena.

A question of peripherals

Of course, all of this software and hardware means little if you have no way of "inputting" your multimedia element of choice into your application. While most sound cards come with a microphone, no digital video cards come with camcorders or VCRs (it's a pity). And while the microphone in question is quite functional, it is not of high quality.

Sound. On the sound side you'll need a high-quality microphone as well as some extension cabling if you want to plug your stereo system into the back of the sound card. This last item lets you feed the music from your CDs, LPs, cassettes, and even radio directly into your computer through the "line in" port of your sound card, without the ambient noise a microphone picks up. So if you have some great background music for your multimedia production, this is the way to go. Use the microphone only when you want to add the "human" element to your production—that is, a voice-over.

Figure 1.1 shows the real bargain you're getting by buying a sound card. The one I'm using for the purposes of this chapter is Creative Labs' Sound

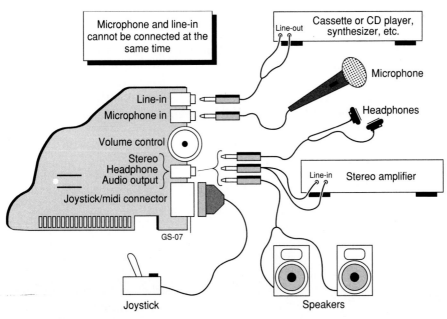

Figure 1.1 Sound board connectors.

Blaster 16ASP. As its name implies, it's a 16-bit sound card that enables me to get some pretty good audio fidelity in spite of the card's fairly low cost. Actually I'm quite pleased with it, and I don't see any reason why you should spend a cent more on a higher-quality sound board (unless, of course, you're a musician).

Probably the connection that is the biggest mystery to first-time multimedia developers is the one for MIDI. Because it's explained in infinite detail in other chapters of this book, I'll just provide you with a quick peek into this musician's dream.

In general there are two types of sound files, Wave and Midi. Wave files capture the entire sound, which is why they take up so much space. Just 7 seconds of sound, recorded in stereo at 16 bits and sampled at 44 kHz, takes well over one million bytes of disk storage. As shown in Fig. 1.2, you can minimize disk storage by changing some of the recording parameters.

Soundo'LE, bundled with the Creative Labs sound cards, gives you just this capability. For example, recording in mono, in 8 bits, and at a sampling rate of 11 kHz will take less than 75K—a big difference. And if you apply one of the compression algorithms, even less space is required. Using Creative's ADPCM (Adaptive Differential Pulse Code Modulation) algorithm will reduce the disk requirement to a mere 36K.

Whereas Wave files store the actual (digital version) sound, MIDI files store instructions for MIDI devices. Actually MIDI is an acronym for Musical Instrument Digital Interface, which is an industry-standard connection for computer control of electronic musical instruments and devices. Perhaps the most popular is the synthesizer.

If you don't have a MIDI instrument then, depending on the software you have installed you can still take advantage of the power of MIDI. Figure 1.3 shows the full range of capabilities of this type of software. Turtle Beach Systems' Turtle Tools comes with several applications. One of them, KeyPlayer, lets you use your own computer keyboard to "create" anything from a new symphony to rock music. Even rap. Starting with a base of MIDI files supplied with the product, you can become an instant Madonna.

Since Windows-based systems play either MIDI or Wave files, the inexpensive software and hardware that I've just described can really enhance your multimedia production, making it look and "sound" a lot more professional than it really is.

Images. Although you can buy ready-made "clip art" and even photographs from any number of multimedia (and desktop publishing) vendors, there are times when you want to do your own. Sure, you can use a high-end paint package to draw your own, but not everyone is artistically gifted. That's where a good scanner comes in.

There are probably as many scanners on the market as there are printers. Even facsimile machines have gotten into the act by "claiming" that you can use a faxed image as input to a design or paint program. Actually they're quite right. Before I bought my scanner that's exactly what I did (and was

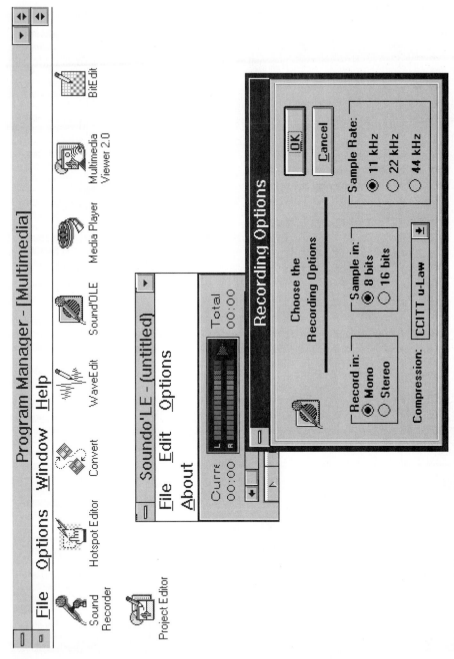

Figure 1.2 Recording options for WAVE files.

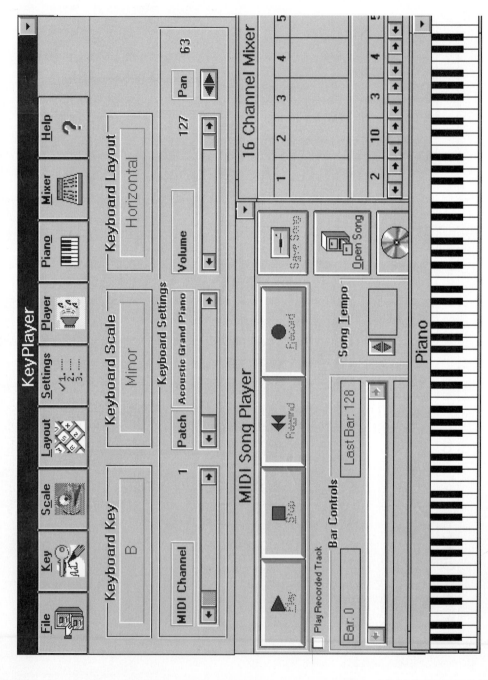

Figure 1.3 Turtle Beach Systems MIDI interface.

quite smug about it). Faxed images are of extremely low quality, so the best advice I can give you is to search out a better alternative.

And as mentioned, there are plenty of options. For the most part, even though handheld scanners are quite reasonable in price, unless your eye-hand coordination is perfect, opt for a flatbed. Since there are variations even here, you'll want to look at the competitors carefully.

If you're like me, you'll want the best ratio between price and functionality. I wanted a flatbed, color, the highest possible DPI (dot per inch) when scanning, and a bunch of bundled-in software.

That's just what I got with the Microtek Scanmaker IIXE. It scans in full color, lets me set the resolution (it can scan to a virtual 1200 dpi), and came bundled with Aldus's PhotoStyler. About a month after I purchased the scanner I saw an ad that indicated they were now bundling it with Adobe's PhotoShop. After I wrote them a letter indicating that I had just purchased mine, they sent me a copy of PhotoShop. What a deal! I got both PhotoStyler and PhotoShop.

PhotoShop has much more functionality than PhotoStyler. But PhotoStyler is easier to use and takes a lot less memory. The rule of thumb here is don't overindulge on the software. Buy the capability that you actually need. Although PhotoShop has some great features, I really don't need them. Of course, *you* may!

Having a scanner means being able to take your own pictures (Ansel Adams, beware) and input them directly into your multimedia project. This is why having a *color* scanner is so important, since vivid color is the base of all multimedia. Figure 1.4 shows that just by putting a photograph inside the scanner and setting a few variables you can easily scan a picture.

Once the picture has been scanned, the software (in this case PhotoStyler) provides plenty of options that you can use to alter your image, as shown in Fig. 1.5. You can even crop out parts of the image and just use a section of it. This, in fact, is the method I used to build the graphics for the sampler multimedia applications that we'll be building in just a few minutes.

There are alternatives to scanning, such as the new digital video cameras, but from my perspective owning a scanner is one smart move. Not only will it permit you to scan images but you can also use it to scan text, along with some robust OCR (optical character recognition) software.

For this purpose, I use Caere's OmniPage. I simply put my sheet of text facedown on the scanner, open my word processor, and scan, as shown in Fig. 1.6. What comes out the other end is an editable file.

Of course, this is imaging from a PC perspective. Imaging has had a long life of its own, even before multimedia became a household buzzword.

There are literally thousands of organizations that have incorporated imaging as a major component of their "paperless" office plans. Even the government is doing it. The U.S. Customs Service uses imaging to transmit information about would-be drug smugglers.

Video. Perhaps the multimedia element that gives developers the biggest "twinkle in the eye" is video. It's fun. It's as simple as that.

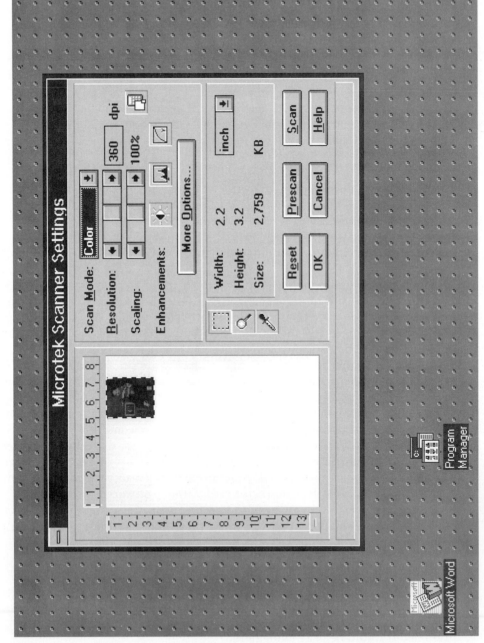

Figure 1.4 Scanning with Microtek.

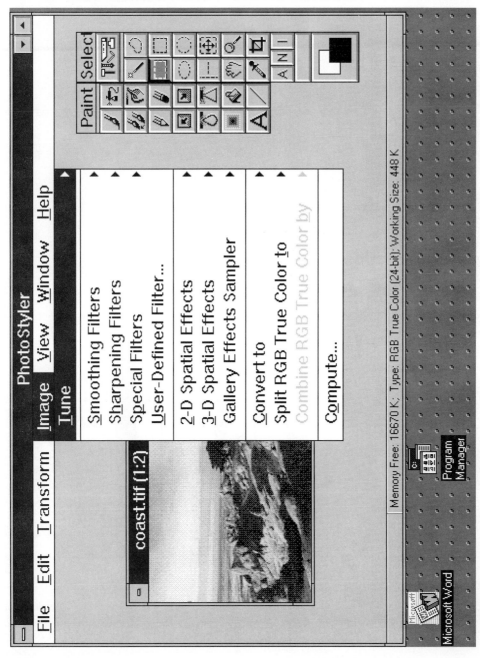

Figure 1.5 PhotoStyler lets you alter images.

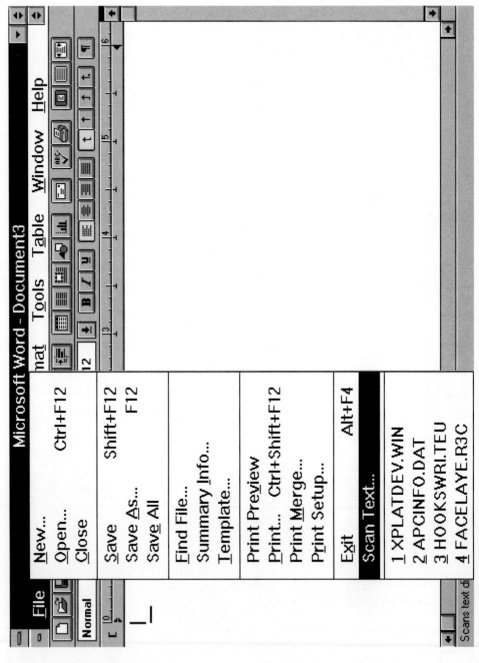

Figure 1.6 OmmiPage embeds itself into your word processor—scan text.

It's quite possible to add video to a multimedia production without ever having a digital video card. If you're creating in a Windows environment, video is stored as AVI (Audio Video Interleave) files. Although the quality is far less than other digital delivery mechanisms, AVI does have a distinct advantage. That is, it permits the playback of video segments without a digital video adapter. In other words, AVI is a software-only solution. And because you can purchase literally thousands of minutes of video clips from dozens of multimedia vendors, you can add video to your production without getting your hands dirty.

Of course, if you want to tailor video to your own specifications you will need some additional software to do this. And if you want to shoot your own videos, not only do you need a camcorder or VCR as an input source, but a video capture card as well.

The card I used for the purposes of this chapter is the VideoSpigot. Originally developed by SuperMac Technology, the Windows version has since been sold to Creative Labs, leaving SuperMac free to concentrate on the market they like best: Macintosh.

The VideoSpigot itself is no more than a board and some compression software. The software that actually enables you to capture, import into your computer, and then edit the video image is Microsoft's very own Video for Windows, as seen in Fig. 1.7.

VFW is easy to use, but it's not nearly as robust as some of the higher-end digital video packages listed in the appendix. Additionally, it's not as popular as Microsoft had hoped it would be. As I write these words, Microsoft has sold only 50,000 copies of VFW. Perhaps this is because the original standard for video, Quicktime, now runs on the PC as well as on its original Mac platform.

If video is a central part of your multimedia project and you need to do some fancy footwork, then VFW is not the package for you. However, if all you require is the ability to capture a stream of video and then clip out only the frames you really need, then VFW is a most cost-effective choice.

Video is perhaps the most storage-intensive of all the multimedia elements. One minute, uncompressed, takes about 50 megs of hard disk. It doesn't take a mathematician to figure out that you'll quickly run out of storage space at this rate. Fortunately, VFW enables you to store the video clip you've created in a compressed format—and it enables you to select the best compression method for your needs.

VideoSpigot loads VFW with several compression methods (called *codecs*). One of the most popular is Intel's Indeo, which will trim that 50 megs down to an almost manageable 9 megs.

Animation.   Simply put, animation is the process of creating, usually graphically, a series of frames, and then having them display rapidly to get a sense of movement. Sort of like Bugs Bunny. In the world of multimedia, especially on a PC platform, multimedia and video overlap somewhat. It is quite possible to run an AVI (video) file that was created via animated means rather than through a camera.

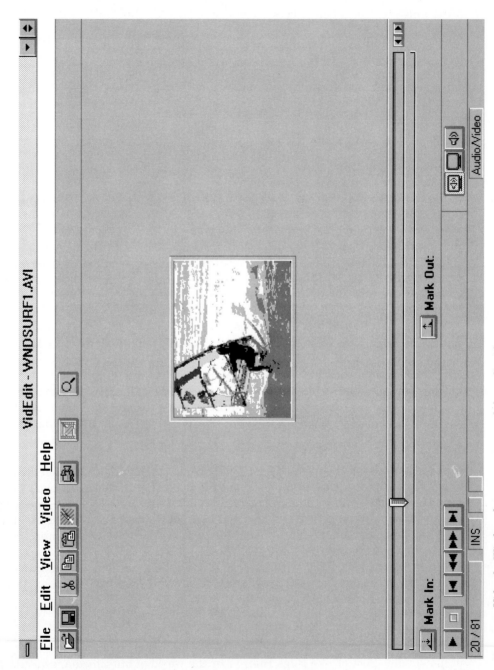

Figure 1.7 Video for Windows lets you capture and then edit video.

There is a plethora of software packages that provide wonderful abilities to draw and then animate objects. Sometimes even the authoring tool provides the ability to animate objects created within the context of the authoring package. Asymetrix's Toolbook lets you create an object and then "drag" it around the screen. Toolbook monitors the direction in which you are moving and then creates an animation from it.

Other packages, such as IBM's Storybook Live, give you a series of animated sprites to use inside your multimedia titles.

Video display adapters

Most developers, especially those who have never worked with interactive systems, fail to consider the ramifications of the video card that they're using either in development or production. When you're working with text there is little difference between adapter boards, but it's an entirely different matter when you're dealing with graphics.

The following table clearly illustrates the differences between the four categories of video cards. Note that the higher the resolution, the more colors you can display. However, you'll also notice that the higher the resolution, the more memory you'll need.

Board	Pixel resolution	No. of colors	Memory for 1 image
CGA	320×200	4	16,000
EGA	640×350	16	112,000
VGA	640×480	256	224,000
SuperVGA	512×480	16,777,216	983,000

Even though the majority of multimedia developers will work on a SVGA-enabled platform, where graphics are riveting in all their full-blown colorful glory, developers should be cognizant of the fact that not all delivery platforms are so well endowed. Believe me when I say that graphics that look wonderful under SVGA will look somewhat paltry in an EGA mode. Therefore, developers must "plan" their systems accordingly.

If the ultimate implementation platform is known beforehand, then all development work should be done (or at least well tested) on that particular platform. Unfortunately, there are many occasions when the developer knows only that the ultimate implementation platform will be a generic PC. Since the video adapter may well be SVGA or VGA—or even EGA—the development team has some hard decisions to make.

One method for solving this problem is to choose only those graphic images and digital video clips that display equally well on all platforms. Alternatively, different imagery can be used on the different platforms. The system can be programmed to "detect" the graphic adapter and then display those images targeted for that device.

Unfortunately, this last piece of advice is seldom followed, even by many of the makers of multimedia products. The result? When first-time users load up that demo disk, they invariably are disappointed. In the end, sloppy miscasting of target hardware can only do damage to the professional image of the industry.

Building a Multimedia System

Now that the stage has been set, it's time to get down to the nitty-gritty of building your multimedia application. Although it's entirely possible to simply add a little video here and a sound clip there, you'll soon find out that the very best multimedia productions are those that have been carefully planned and executed.

The very first step of the planning process, however, is budgeting, and here Steve Bainbridge of the Wilson Learning Corporation, located in Eden Prairies, Minnesota, has thoughtfully provided a good rule of thumb for this process. By his estimate, a 2-to-4-hour interactive multimedia system will cost about $150,000, with the following distribution of resources:

Document design	2%
Research and writing	10%
Video and audio production	56%
Graphics and text	6%
Programming	9%
Project management	8%
Mastering/check disc	6%
25 copies of videodisc	5%

Andersen Consulting's Ed Smith, who is based in San Diego, uses a consulting model approach to budgeting. The following example was calculated for development of a half-day of multimedia instruction.

Design and development (300 days × $500/day)	$150,000
Administration and management (60 days × $600/day)	36,000
Video subcontract (40 finished minutes)	80,000
Direct reimbursable (travel, mastering, etc.)	11,500
Total	$277,500

Smith uses two yardsticks when developing multimedia budgets:

1. The ratio of development hours to user contact hours:

Low	400:1
Medium	800:1
High	1200:1

2. Cost per finished minute:

Low	$1000 to 1500
Medium	$1500 to 2200
High	Over $2200

Start with a plan

All professional system developers use the system requirement and specification as their starting point. These documents are the blueprint of the deliverable system. Nothing less should be done for a multimedia application.

In the case of multimedia, though, a requirements specification contains much more than programming instructions. It also contains the overall graphic layout of the system, including the placement of any and all video, sound, imagery, and hypertext.

For the remainder of this chapter, we are going to use the example of the development of a first aid system. The system will contain text and graphics, as well as some sound and video. Even though this example is rather simplistic, it will serve a useful purpose as a demonstration of the steps one takes to design and develop a working multimedia system.

The purpose of the *First Aid Manual* (we'll call it FAM for short) is to provide end users with specific information about how to handle emergency first aid situations. The user should be able to do the following:

1. Choose a topic from a Table of Contents

2. Use the capability of hypertext to get a clarification of relevant topics and terms

3. Perform a word search to "find" any words or phrases of interest

4. See relevant graphics and videos, as well as hear relevant sound clips

The makeup of the developmental team is reflective of the problem at hand. A team can consist of from 1 to n members, with the lower number indicating a simple problem with the source information readily available and the higher number indicating a complex system—both hardware- and information-wise. For example, a multimedia system for stock market trading that incorporates live digital video feeds, sound, and graphics and is distributed to a thousand locations worldwide will call for a fairly large developmental team. This team will be composed of content specialists (i.e., experts in trading) as well as a multitude of system development experts (i.e., a specialist in digital video, a specialist in distributed systems, programmers, etc).

FAM, on the other hand, is a rather simple system (for the purposes of this chapter). Our purpose is to take a manual that has already been written and translate it for a multimedia platform. Because the information is already available we won't need a content specialist, unless we want to verify the currency of the information.

Many multimedia titles on the market today have been developed in just this manner. This seems to be the modus operandi for organizations that are already publishers of huge amounts of information. Quite a large number of the technical trade magazines and newspapers have dusted off their back issues and republished them on CD-ROM. Packaged with robust retrieval software, the final product lets the user search for any title or author name, or virtually any key word or phrase, for up to 10 years of back issues.

When developing a multimedia title in this manner, you must make absolutely sure that the project is legally within bounds. That is, you can't just pick a title and decide to multimediate it (see Chap. 17 on legal issues in multimedia). You must either already own the copyright or secure it from the person or organization that does. In our case, the text of the first aid manual comes from the *First Aid Book,* published by the U.S. Department of Labor. And most of what is published by the government is copyright-free—that is, you can use it free and clear without worrying about infringing on anyone's copyright. In fact, I recently saw an advertisement for a CD-ROM that contains the full text of all the pamphlets published by the government's Consumer Information bureau.

Because the government did not thoughtfully provide me with their first aid manual on disk, I had to take the preliminary step of converting the printed page to something a computer can work with. Although there is always the option of rekeying the manual into a word processor, a far simpler method is to use your scanner.

As I already mentioned, I find a scanner indispensable. But a scanner is only as good as the software that you use with it. For the purposes of OCR (optical character recognition), I have been using Caere's OmniPage. In spite of some peculiar installation problems (which I will discuss in my next book, *The Productivity Paradox*), the software works like a charm. I merely place a page of text facedown on the scanner (much the same as with a copier), click on the "scan text" item in my word processor's file menu, and lo and behold: editable text.

Picking an authoring tool

As you browse through the appendix at the back of this book you will notice that there is no dearth of choices in the area of authoring tools. Not all of these tools have the same functionality, so you'll want to spend some time assessing a selection of tools before you make your final decision.

Most organizations seem to "centralize" on one tool for each software category. For example, they prefer to use one CASE tool, one programming language, and so on. Unfortunately, not all business problems fit so neatly into such a unitary approach. This is especially true in the multimedia arena. There are tools for DOS, tools for the Mac, tools for Unix, scripting tools, hypertext tools, and on and on.

To narrow the field, you'll first have to decide what platform your final product will run on. In our case, FAM will run under Windows on the PC. Therefore I can ignore all authoring and other types of products that run on the DOS-only Mac or Unix platforms.

The characteristics of the product you want to develop should dictate the type of authoring tool you will use. FAM is extremely text-oriented; will require the ability to easily navigate around the text; requires the ability to use "hot words" to enable the user to get more detailed information about a particular area of interest; will not require a high level of interactivity in the use of selectable buttons; and will require the ability to integrate sound, video, and graphics.

As you review this attribute list, you may come to the conclusion that a hypertext-type product would be the best fit for your system. Those of you who are regular Windows users have no doubt had occasion to use the Windows Help function. Windows Help is a hypertext module that rather nicely enables the user to easily navigate through a lot of textual information. Microsoft's Multimedia Viewer (which is purchased separately from Windows itself) gives developers the very same functionality.

Since FAM's target end users are already Windows-literate, I've decided that the best authoring tool for the project is Multimedia Viewer.

A Quick Tour of Multimedia Viewer

Microsoft's Multimedia Viewer is really a set of eight different tools. There is a ninth tool, Microsoft Word for Windows, that doesn't come with the toolkit, although many of us already have it. In fact, this is one of the reasons I decided to use Viewer. Given the confusion factor that this product presents to first-time users, I'm not sure I would have selected Viewer over some of the other hypertext tools on the market. In other words, Viewer is less than intuitive. But it does let you create robust multimedia systems, as shown in Fig. 1.8.

Viewer's eight tools can be described as follows:

Viewer Project Editor	This is used to create the user interface, to configure the search features, identify the external files you'll be using, run the program that builds (compiles) your title, and also give you test capabilities.
Viewer Topic Editor	This module, which is activated through Word for Windows, is used to add features such as sound, graphics, digital video (in the form of Microsoft's AVI), hypertext links, etc.
Hotspot Editor	This is used to add "hot spot" regions to pictures so that the user can click on a picture, for example, and jump to another topic.
Viewer Compiler	Used to build your titles.
WaveEdit	Used to record, play, edit, and add special effects to sound files.
BitEdit	Used to edit bitmapped graphics.
PalEdit	Used with BitEdit to change the colors in an image or apply a particular palette. If you're going to use a large number of graphics for your title, you'll be using this a

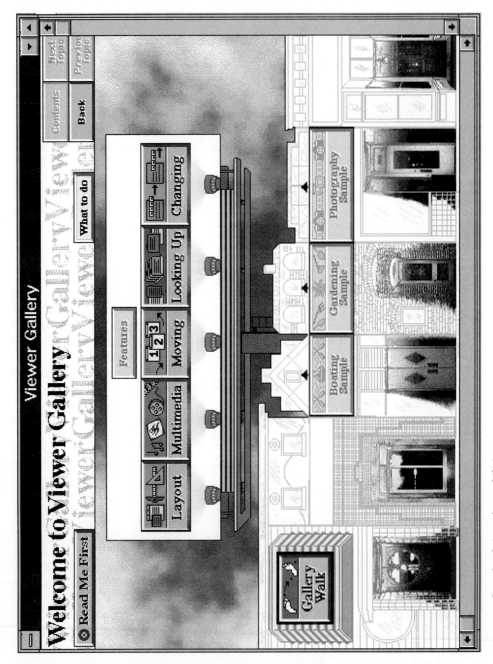

Figure 1.8 Sample of viewer's capabilities.

great deal, since you'll want to have a certain consistency in the colors you use in your title. Also, the more colors you use, the more memory it takes.

Convert   This is used to convert audio and graphics file formats into formats that can run under Viewer.

The Multimedia Viewer development kit also comes with a royalty-free run-time viewer also called, quite confusingly, Multimedia Viewer.

The nice thing about Viewer (and most other multimedia authoring tools) is that you can develop simple systems or incredibly complicated systems by using basically the same steps. Figure 1.8 shows the startup screen of one of the titles that Microsoft ships with their product. The intent of "Viewer Gallery" is to walk developers through the many capabilities of the Viewer development tool. Although the picture is reproduced here in black-and-white, the actual screen is in full, vivid color—chockful of graphics.

The FAM system will be much simpler. We merely want to build a hyper-text version of the paper manual and throw in a few multimedia elements for good measure. But the steps we take to build FAM are also the steps that we would take to build a system as complex and graphical as the Viewer Gallery. So we're getting off to an excellent start.

The first step

The very first step in creating a Viewer title is to create a project file using the Project Editor. In essence, a project file is a collection of pointers that point the way to the text file, sound file(s), graphic file(s), and video file(s), with the text being stored in the RTF section of the project and everything else being stored in the colloquially named "Baggage" section as shown in Fig 1.9.

The RTF section is actually a Word for Windows file, stored in Rich Text Format (RTF). Although many word processors have the ability to store text as RTF files, there actually is (believe it or not) no set RTF standard. So if you think you can get around the requirement to install a copy of Word for Windows, think again. Microsoft is smarter than that.

When setting up Viewer, you have an opportunity to indicate the drive/directory location of Microsoft Word, so getting to the appropriate file is as simple as entering the appropriate file name if the title is new, or "point-and-clicking" to the file name from a list. Since we've already scanned a file into the system and saved it in the RTF format, all we need to do is click on the file name. In all cases, we need to make sure that we maintain this file in RTF format. This adds an additional query from Word every time we want to open our file, as shown in Fig. 1.10.

Developing a title in Viewer is largely an exercise in word processing. Viewer relies on hidden text and footnotes to embed the commands that the run-time system interprets. Unfortunately, this plethora of footnotes is less than intuitive.

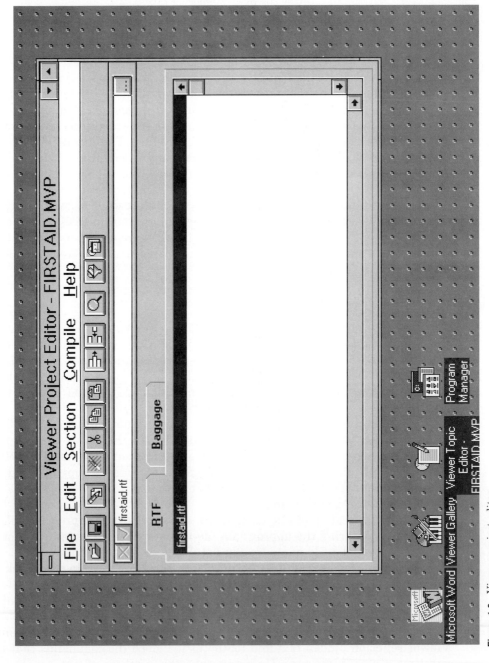

Figure 1.9 Viewer project editor.

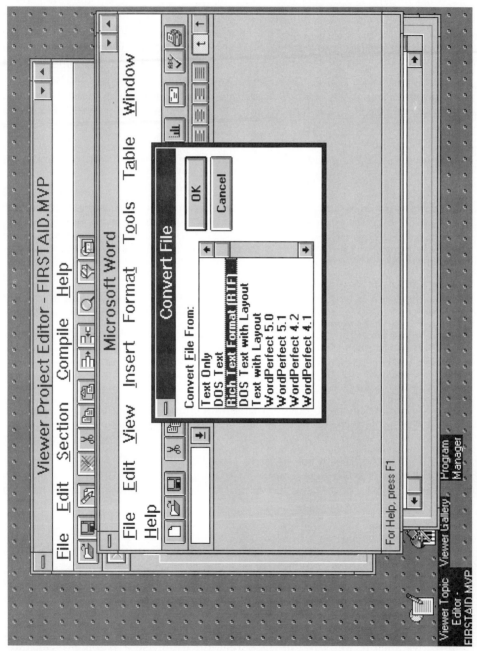

Figure 1.10 Converting to the RTF format.

The table of contents

Most hypertext systems start from the base of a Table of Contents. The Table of Contents is the jumping-off point for the user to select and "jump to" any of a wide variety of topics. As you'll see later on, one of Viewer's nicer features is its starter menu and push-button bar. Without any programming whatsoever, your users have a built-in help function as well as the automatic ability to immediately return to the Table of Contents (the Contents button), return to the prior topic (Go Back button), see a list of all topics viewed in the order they were chosen (History button), as well as perform a search for a word or phrase (Search button).

Figure 1.11 shows a Microsoft Word screen with FAM's Table of Contents screen, which is heavily annotated. To get this far required much use of Viewer's Topic Editor, as shown in Fig. 1.12.

The Topic Editor enables me to select in English a programming attribute, such as add a picture, which the Topic Editor will then convert to one or more footnotes as shown in Fig. 1.13.

Dividing text into topics

Essentially, the developer (and/or content expert) has to review the text to determine the beginning and end of each topic. In our example (Fig. 1.11), you can see that there are quite a few topics: "Introduction to First Aid," "Importance of First Aid," "The Anatomy of the Human Body," and so on. Each of these is considered a topic and starts on a new page. Since a hard carriage return (CTRL + Enter key) is the dividing line between topics, multipage topics are easily done using the standard page break (i.e., automatic paginating).

Each topic needs to have a title and a context string, which is essentially a shorthand way of getting to the topic. For example you'll notice that in Fig. 1.11, the topic "Introduction to First Aid" has the word "Intro" next to it. This tells Viewer that should the user click on this line in the Table of Contents, the action should be to "jump to" the topic with the context string value of "Intro." If you take a quick look at the footnotes shown in Fig. 1.13, you see that the first two lines read as follows:

$Introduction to First Aid

#Intro

Translating the $ (Fig. 1.12), we discover that this first line indicates that it is a title. And the # sign indicates a context string (see, I told you it was a bit convoluted!).

Because Viewer is a true Windows product, I have the ability to designate things such as the color of the screen (or even use a graphic background, as Microsoft did in Fig. 1.8), the font and size of the text, as well as the color of the text. I can even give my system a title. Figure 1.14 shows (although in black-and-white) the Table of Contents in the finished product.

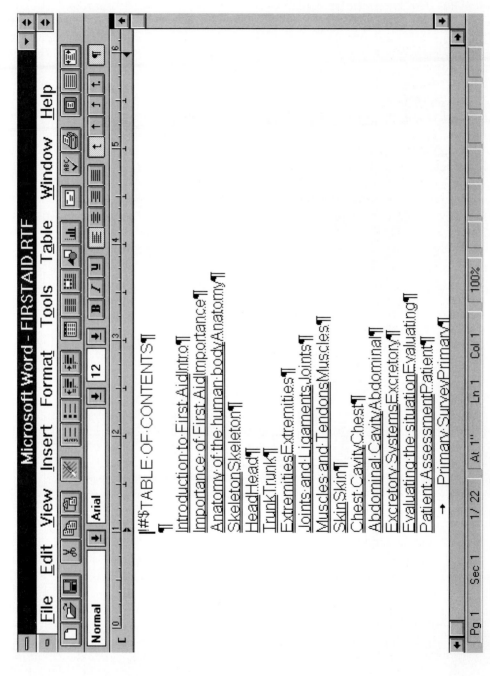

Figure 1.11 RTF version of the table of contents.

1.31

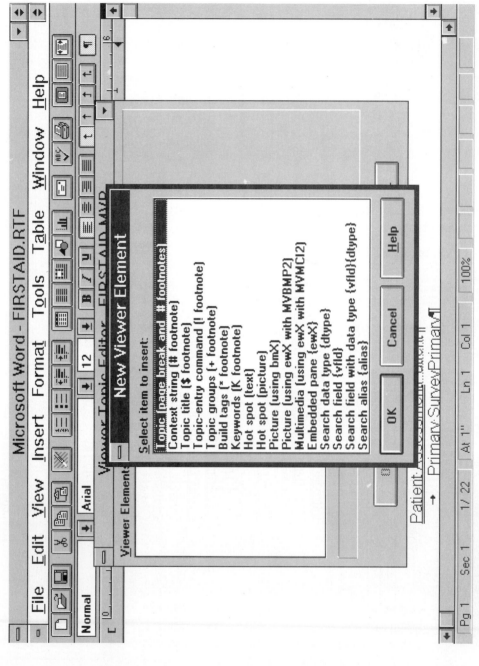

Figure 1.12 Viewer's Topic Editor.

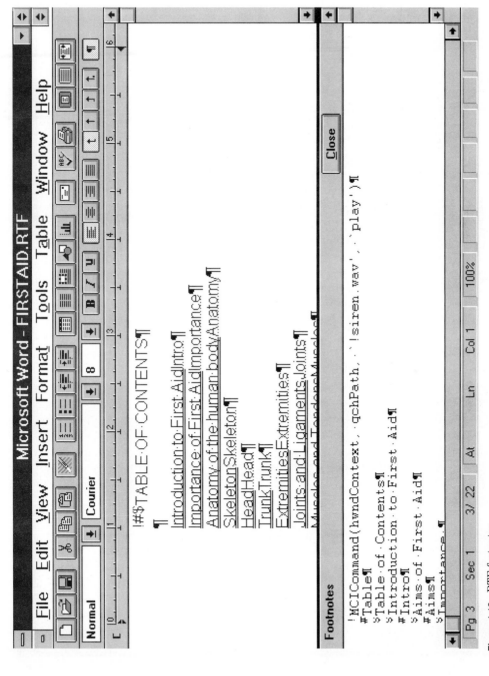

Figure 1.13 RTF footnotes.

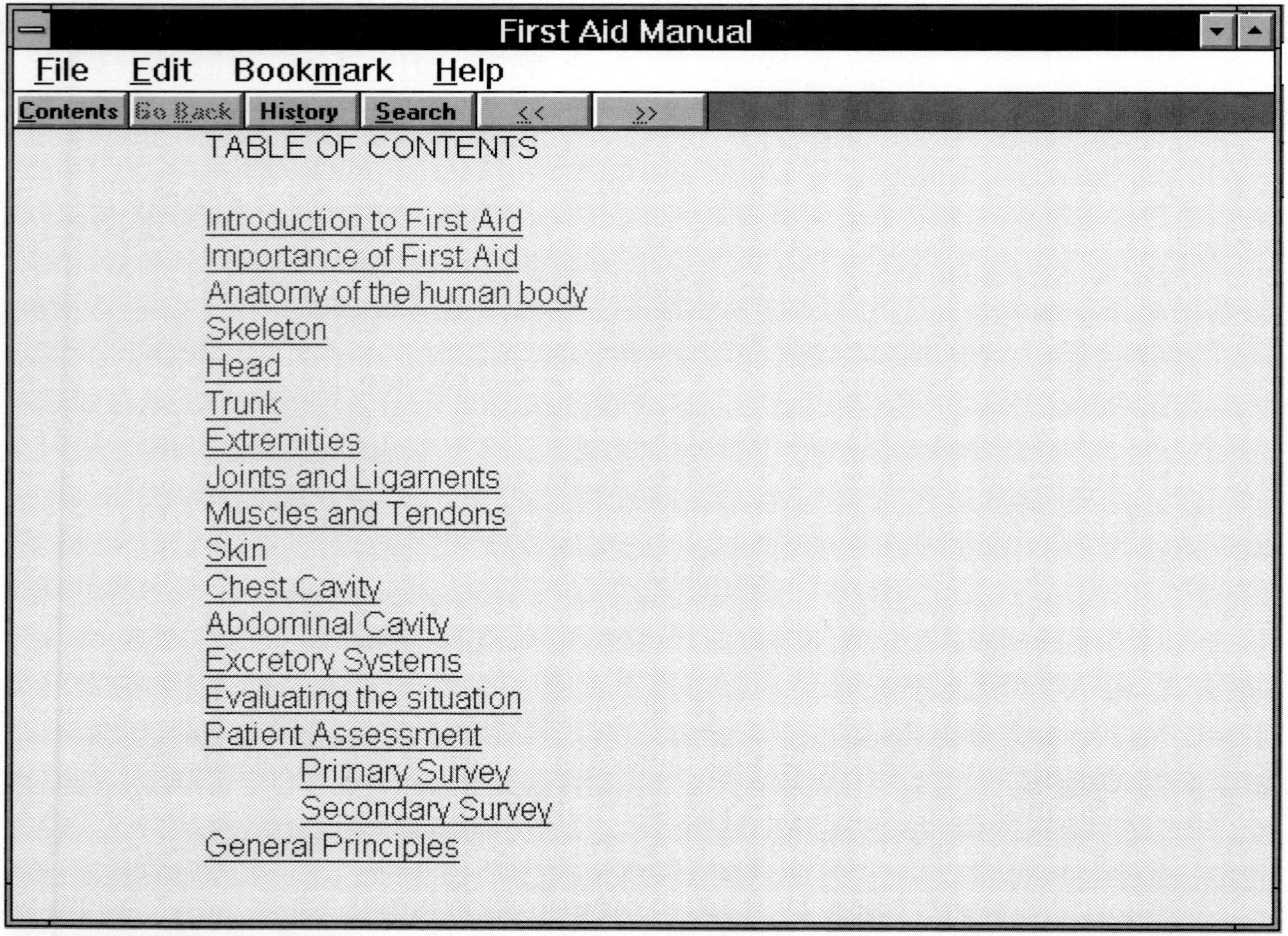

Figure 1.14 Finished table of contents.

The interface shows the "First Aid Manual" window with menu items: File, Edit, Bookmark, Help, and a toolbar with Contents, Go Back, History, Search, <<, >>.

TABLE OF CONTENTS

Introduction to First Aid
Importance of First Aid
Anatomy of the human body
Skeleton
Head
Trunk
Extremities
Joints and Ligaments
Muscles and Tendons
Skin
Chest Cavity
Abdominal Cavity
Excretory Systems
Evaluating the situation
Patient Assessment
Primary Survey
Secondary Survey
General Principles

Because Viewer is hypertext-oriented, I have the ability to display text in one or more windows or panes—or I can display text in pop-up windows.

In the topic "Introduction to First Aid," I want to add a sort of disclaimer. I want the user to know the philosophy of first aid. To do this I can create a hot key out of either a picture or some text. I'll choose the later. In Fig. 1.15, you'll see the text of the topic "Introduction to First Aid." The third paragraph down starts with the phrase, "First aid does not replace the physician...." Note that this is underlined. That's because I designed it as a hot key. In this way the user knows that there's more information to be found if he or she scrolls over to this sentence. Clicking the hot key displays a pop-up screen that discusses the aims of first aid.

Adding multimedia

Up to now we've worked only with the hypertext capabilities of Viewer. Now it's time to add some multimedia.

The government's publication on first aid had graphics as well as text. I scanned these separately, storing the graphics in several TIF files. In order to use graphics, though, I must first convert these files into a graphical format that Viewer can use. Figure 1.16 demonstrates the Convert capability that comes bundled with Viewer.

I must associate each of the graphic images, once converted, with its proper location in the RTF file. To do this I merely scroll to the correct location in the RTF file and press the hot key to get into Viewer's Topic Editor. From Topic Editor I choose "Picture (using ewX With MVBMP2)". Figure 1.17 displays the interactive screen the developer is presented with. Here you get to indicate the file name of the graphic, store it in Baggage (in the Project File), and dictate the placement of the image.

Figure 1.18 shows how FAM looks when it's all put together. While all "commands" are actually a series of footnotes, and therefore it is possible to bypass Topic Editor altogether and just code it yourself, unless you're really experienced and do this sort of thing frequently, I wouldn't hazard it.

Adding digital video and digital sound is done in much the same way as with pictures. I happened to have a digital sound file in Wave format of an ambulance siren, so I added it to the Table of Contents. Unfortunately I can't show you sound, but I *can* show you what the embedded command (located in the footnotes) for sound looks like:

```
!MCICommand(hwndContext, qchPath, '!siren.wav', 'play')
```

Sound and video require use of the Media Control Interface (MCI). MCI is a platform-independent multimedia specification that was published in 1990 by Microsoft and other vendors to provide a consistent way to control devices such as CD-ROM and video playback units. In the example, I simply loaded the file "siren.wav" into Baggage and used the Topic Editor to "place" the sound in my text file.

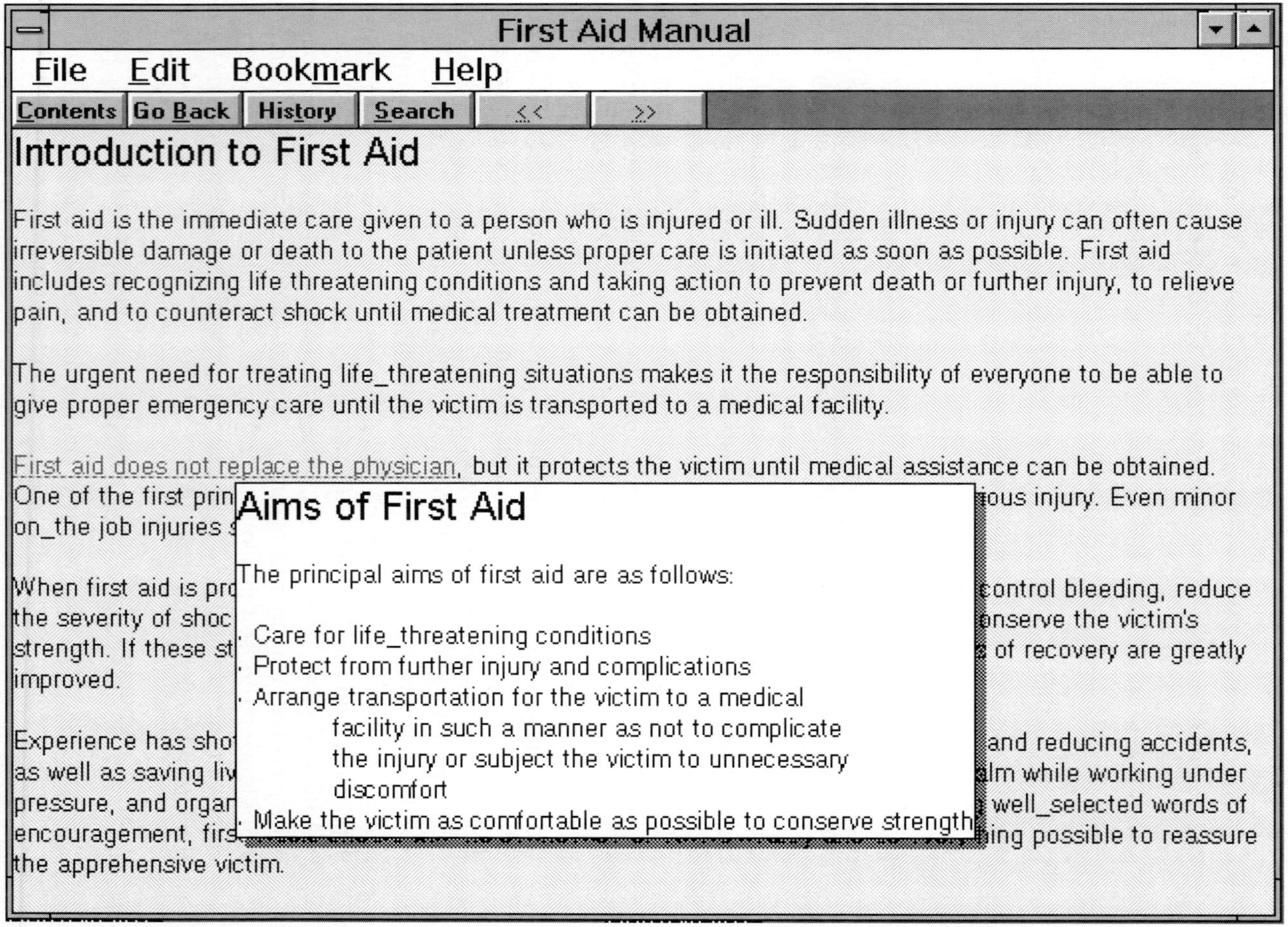

First Aid Manual

File   Edit   Bookmark   Help

Contents | Go Back | History | Search | << | >>

Introduction to First Aid

First aid is the immediate care given to a person who is injured or ill. Sudden illness or injury can often cause irreversible damage or death to the patient unless proper care is initiated as soon as possible. First aid includes recognizing life threatening conditions and taking action to prevent death or further injury, to relieve pain, and to counteract shock until medical treatment can be obtained.

The urgent need for treating life_threatening situations makes it the responsibility of everyone to be able to give proper emergency care until the victim is transported to a medical facility.

First aid does not replace the physician, but it protects the victim until medical assistance can be obtained.
One of the first prin... ious injury. Even minor
on_the job injuries ...

Aims of First Aid

When first aid is pro... The principal aims of first aid are as follows: ...control bleeding, reduce
the severity of shoc... onserve the victim's
strength. If these st...   Care for life_threatening conditions   of recovery are greatly
improved.   Protect from further injury and complications
                       Arrange transportation for the victim to a medical
Experience has sho...   facility in such a manner as not to complicate   and reducing accidents,
as well as saving liv...   the injury or subject the victim to unnecessary   im while working under
pressure, and organ...   discomfort   well_selected words of
encouragement, firs...   Make the victim as comfortable as possible to conserve strength ing possible to reassure
the apprehensive victim.

Figure 1.15 Pop-up screen.

1.36

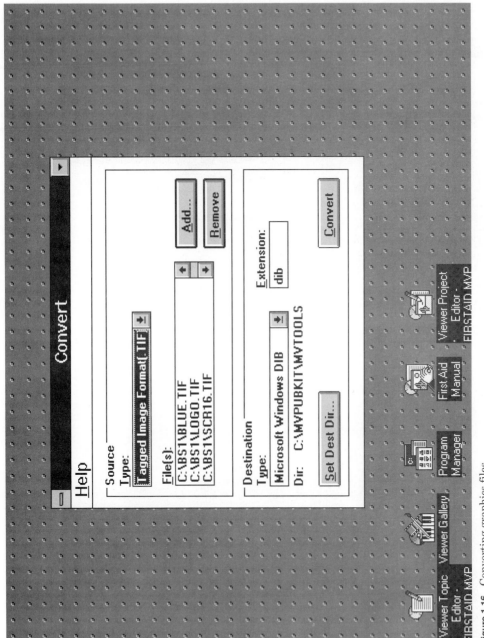

Figure 1.16 Converting graphics files.

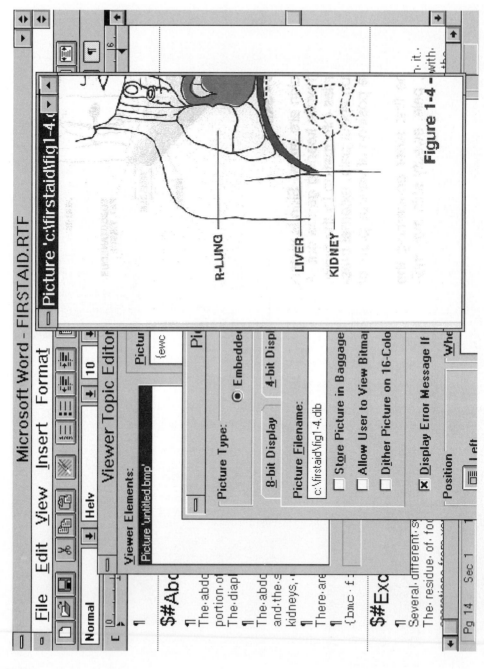

Figure 1.17 Adding a graphic.

1.38

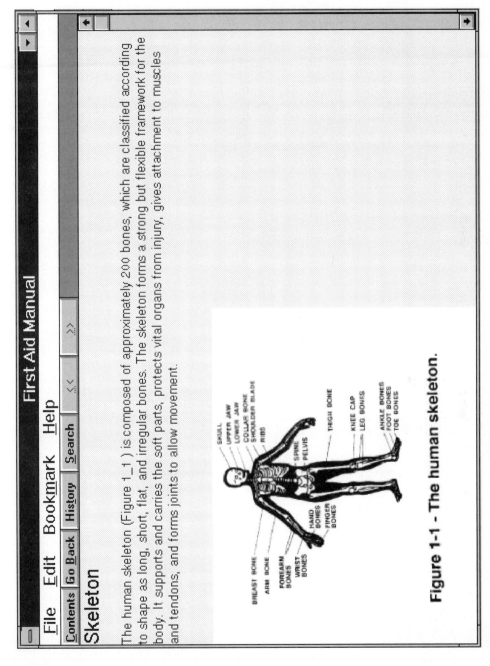

First Aid Manual

File **Edit** **Bookmark** **Help**

Contents | Go Back | History | Search | << | >>

Skeleton

The human skeleton (Figure 1_1) is composed of approximately 200 bones, which are classified according to shape as long, short, flat, and irregular bones. The skeleton forms a strong but flexible framework for the body. It supports and carries the soft parts, protects vital organs from injury, gives attachment to muscles and tendons, and forms joints to allow movement.

SKULL
UPPER JAW
LOWER JAW
COLLAR BONE
SHOULDER BLADE
RIBS
SPINE
PELVIS
THIGH BONE
KNEE CAP
LEG BONES
ANKLE BONES
FOOT BONES
TOE BONES
BREAST BONE
ARM BONE
FOREARM BONES
WRIST BONES
HAND BONES
FINGER BONES

Figure 1-1 - The human skeleton.

Figure 1.18   Viewer title with graphic added.

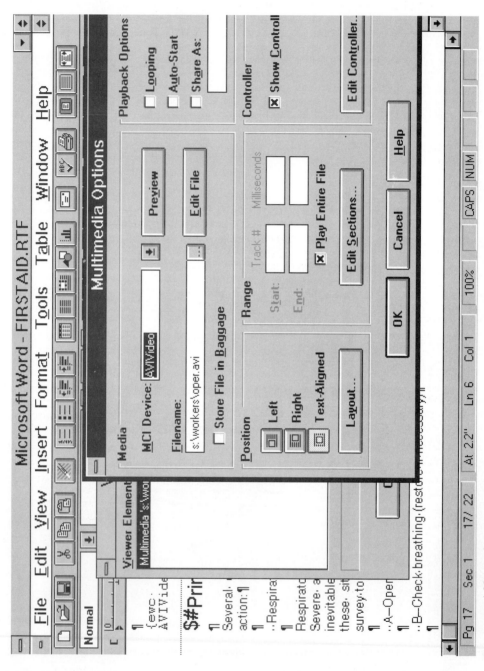

Figure 1.19 Adding video to a viewer title.

Video is done in a like manner. Figure 1.19 shows the development environment at the point in time the developer has told the Topic Editor that he or she would like to add video to the text file. In the upper-left-hand corner, you'll see the image itself. It's a color image of doctors in an operating room. Viewer utilizes the AVI file format that was developed by Microsoft to allow playback of video files without any video hardware. Also note how small the video clip actually is. The quality of video is dependent upon a lot of things. For most systems, the limited amount of memory and hard-disk space precludes the use of full-screen video—hence tiny video clips like "oper.avi."

You'll also notice the multitude of options the video MCI driver gives the developer. And of course, you can take a gander at the convoluted command structure of the MCI command.

Putting it all together

Although so far I haven't mentioned compiling the title at all, I really wouldn't wait until you've added everything before you compile for the first time. It's best to test the system continually. Both Build (compile) and Test are available as items on the Project Editor menu.

Although FAM is a small and simple system, it clearly demonstrates how to combine hypertext, graphics, and audio as well as video to produce a fairly interactive system.

Once you've tested your system thoroughly, you should be ready to package and distribute it. The distribution medium, however, is largely dependent upon how big your system is. FAM has a limited amount of text, only five graphics, one video clip, and one sound clip. But even such a limited system may be too big to deliver on one floppy diskette. Because even 1 minute of compressed video can take up 9 Mbytes of storage, the delivery medium of choice for most multimedia systems is CD-ROM. And here I'll direct you once again to the appendix, from which you can get a list of vendors who will gladly transfer your system to CD-ROM, or where you can find one or more vendors who will be more than happy to sell you your very own CD-R drive that will enable you to create your own CD-ROMs.

No matter which route you take, remember to test, test, and test again. You should especially make sure that your system runs on a PC other than the one on which it was created. For instance if you created it on an ALR machine, then test it on a Compaq, a Dell, or an IBM.

Conclusion

The multimedia developer should be prepared to master a number of tools. And as the market is changing rapidly, it's a good idea to keep abreast of these changes. For example, over lunch the other day I heard that there is a company in Norway that has just about perfected a compression algorithm that will permit the storage of up to 90 minutes of video on just a floppy. Steven Spielberg, move over!

2

Cultural Identity and Integration in the New Media World

Red Burns

In the last 50 years there has been an overwhelming change in communications. This change has not yet been fully understood by any of us who are in the middle of it. It is of the order of change occasioned by the introduction of writing and the printing press. Knowledge, power, and material relationships are changing radically as a result of the new forms of communications.

The electronics revolution in communications is multifaceted. On the surface there are the startling convergences of computing, audio, video, graphics, and text. To these convergences we can add the expanding temporal and spatial reach of the new distribution networks.

As each new form of communications develops, it promises new opportunities and resulting benefits to society. Yet there is enormous potential for abuse. And one of these abuses is an antiseptic technological world that cannot easily handle human paradox.

The New Media

These new communications technologies have an almost irresistible allure, and their promise surrounds us. Extravagant claims are everywhere. And in fact there is much to be excited about. Yet we need to avoid becoming blindly seduced if we are to create desirable and equitable applications that justify our efforts and investment.

For individual users, it won't be long before a single wire comes into the home providing access to local as well as international information. This wire will serve as the link for voice, data, and video transmission.

This mode of communication and expression can be used by one voice or by many. Determining whose voice gets heard, determining an equitable use of this new power, is an important issue to consider.

The technology itself is as straightforward as a mathematical equation. The applications, however, are myriad. In the end it is people, not machines, who design applications.

My own engagement with communications technologies began a long time ago in documentary film at the National Film Board of Canada. At that time a filmmaker went into a community, took notes, wrote a script, shot a film, edited it, and sent it off to be distributed. A most worthy occupation—telling other people's stories. We, the filmmakers, felt quite comfortable with our interpretation of others—their values, their lives, their aspirations. We were the professionals. We created a world about others. We selected material we thought was important to represent them, rather than letting them represent themselves. In some cultures, it might be said that we were robbing others of their identity. At the time, I believed we were performing a valuable communications service: telling people's stories. The professional framed the message; this was an accepted practice.

A current example of this kind of representation can be seen on Cable News Network. CNN is broadcast to almost every major city in the world. During the Gulf War, CNN reached Israel, Saudi Arabia, and Iraq, as well as my home in New York City. Each viewer regardless of her/his culture received the same information at the same time. CNN is representing the world to us not only in America, but internationally. After the Army censors, the editors at CNN were essentially editing the war for all of us. That is very powerful!

As electronic media become the main mode of communications between peoples, the danger is that we may recreate the kind of colonialism found in classical literature where only one voice was represented. Interactive networks can provide a means for different voices, and certainly for more than one.

An example of a global interactive network was seen during the August 1991 activities in Russia. Computer conferencing provided an electronic link between Russia and the outside world. While it is estimated that there are only 1.5 million personal computers in the Soviet Union—and probably only 2 percent have modems—the personal and public communications they make possible didn't exist a few years ago. It has been reported that many Muscovites received scanned images of *The Washington Post* and *The New York Times* during the attempted coup, describing the reaction of the West to the events unfolding in Russia.

In one instance, NATO officials wanted to send a message of support to Boris Yeltsin and could not communicate directly from Brussels to Moscow. They sent their message through the Sovam teleport in San Francisco to Nikolai Kapranov, a top adviser to Yeltsin. Kapranov had an account on the computer mailbox. He sent a message back saying he had translated the NATO message and distributed it in the form of leaflets. He reported that the people inside the parliament building were grateful to know that they had a connection with democratic countries.

In the field of video, one of the first technologies I found that offered the possibility of this kind of self-representation was a Sony Portapak reel-to-reel $\frac{1}{2}$-inch video, which I witnessed a demonstration of in 1970. I was astounded! The skills required to operate the camera were not out of reach for nonprofessionals. The cost was not prohibitive, and for the first time it was possible for ordinary people to make their own video documents. Interpreters became unnecessary. An option was available that had not existed before. The feeling of empowerment was thrilling to those who chose to use this new means of communications. By thinking about how they presented themselves, people learned about themselves and their community. Often that learning process was as important as the documentary ultimately produced. This modest-looking advancement was quite revolutionary in its potential to allow people to tell their own stories and control their information. Combined with a cable distribution system, people were able to present their own point of view in the dominant medium of American society: television.

This was an important time in the history of television in the United States. Broadcast television had always been a medium of scarcity, using a great deal of bandwidth and expensive equipment. Television production clearly was not available to ordinary people. The development of cable television changed all that. Not only were over-the-air television signals transmitted, but new origination opportunities arose.

The convergence of the low-cost, portable video equipment and an equally low-cost distribution network—cable television—created an unusual opportunity in the United States in the 1970s. At the time, cable television reached about 20 percent of American homes (now it reaches an estimated 60 percent). While the initial purpose of cable was to bring television reception to areas blocked by physical obstructions, the cable carried with it much more bandwidth than was then available to broadcast stations. With very little investment, small communities and cable systems could originate programming. No spectrum space scarcity here! You could originate channels as well as retransmit over-the-air television.

Empowerment through Media

My research group, The Alternate Media Center at New York University, was set up in 1971 to examine possible relationships between communities, video, and cable. We set out to train people to develop and distribute their original documents locally on new cable channels. We set up models of Public Access Centers in partnership with cable systems in several U.S. cities from New York to California. We provided equipment and training for community members to shoot and edit videotapes of local concern.

People who were not media professionals, but who had community interests, were offered training and time on the cable systems on a first-come, first-served basis. City council meetings and protests were videotaped, interviews were conducted, conditions in schools and neighborhoods were recorded. Discussions of community problems were raised. It was an extraordinary political opportunity. Ultimately these access centers were absorbed by the cable systems and mandated by the Federal Communications Commission. Public Access in the United States is now established in communities across the country.

While this is an enticing story of empowerment through technology, there are important lessons to be learned from it. Many of the programs, on these channels, were ignored by the communities. Producers anxious to imitate the broadcast style of commercial television but with none of its resources or professional know-how lost their audiences quickly.

When communities stopped trying to mimic broadcast television and found their own voice, their own appropriate use for the video technology and the distribution channel, their audiences returned. Authenticity—a real and original voice—made community cable appealing. When people were themselves, not what they thought they should be, they were far more interesting than they had realized. There was now an alternative. It clearly pointed out the difference between access to a communications channel and access to an audience.

The flip side of the access issue is CNN. In the late seventies CNN exploited cable and combined it with satellite technology to distribute news worldwide from Atlanta, Georgia.

While this service is available worldwide, it is not distributed to many individual homes in many countries because the requisite satellite dishes are still very expensive. So outside of the United States, CNN usually is found in hotels and government offices and newsrooms. Its influence is even more powerful under these circumstances, since many of those who have access to it are members of government or the local press—in other words, the most influential people.

Interactivity

Marshall McLuhan's global village may be too simple a model for today's complex interactions of culture, politics, technology, and media.

One way to better navigate the course of the future global technologies might be to examine these complex issues and international situations in terms of smaller, local ones.

With technological change comes the widening opportunity for interactivity. One of the attributes of interactivity is two-way communication. Television broadcasting is an example of one-way communication.

One-way media as we know them originate from one source and go to many. Interactive media create very different opportunities. They allow exchange and origination from many different sources.

Two-way communications and one-way communications are as different as a conversation and a lecture.

Interactivity has the potential to provide a new perspective on the issues of access to an audience, access to technology, and access to information. It can give a voice where one was not heard before. How we use it is a question of some significance.

Earlier I spoke of projects developed by the Alternate Media Center, which demonstrated to me the importance of allowing users to design their own systems, of allowing the content to create the application. In the mid-seventies, we responded to a National Science Foundation question about whether two-way television could deliver social services in a cost-effective manner. We chose to work with old people, because we knew they are large consumers of social services. We believed that the key was to design a communications system that would be used by senior citizens and programmed by them for their own use. The technology had to be transparent and unthreatening. The real job was to find a way to have the users make the system their own. There are many ways to communicate information. One way is to push the information out and the other is to pull the information out. We chose to organize a system that would have people pull the information out.

We began in 1975. One of our first efforts was to set up a governing board of community members to help us design and implement a two-way interactive television system for senior citizens in Reading, Pennsylvania. Using a return band of the local cable system, we originated from three neighborhood communication centers in existing senior citizen facilities. These were our permanent origination points. We also set up several mobile origination points from different city agencies such as City Hall, the social security office, schools, and the county commissioner's offices. These locations were introduced once a week.

Four separate origination sources were sent to the head end of the cable system. Only one channel was transmitted to cable subscribers. This was done by combining two locations on one split screen with a simple switcher. Switching was determined by who was talking. Because the cameras were placed directly beside the receiving signal, people were able to look at each other while talking from different locations. Those at home could participate by way of a telephone patched in at the head end and heard by everyone on the cable system.

While I have briefly described the technical grid, this project was not about technology. Communications technology does not exist apart from the people who create and use it. This was not broadcast television, although initially everyone wanted to emulate what they saw on television. Our analogy was the telephone. We said, "You don't make a program when you call someone on the telephone—you begin with the reason for the call, and the content is the dialogue that follows."

The important aspect of the programming was exchange and interaction.

A few examples. We found a woman in her eighties who had been active in local politics. She was a natural to "host" the weekly "live" exchange between the mayor and city council members. Other people hosted discussion programs that took place in four different locations at the same time. Those who hosted were in fact producers, but we avoided the jargon of television and instead used the metaphor of a telephone to suggest conversation rather than one-way television. Presenters determined the topic of the day, invited the participants, and stimulated discussion in four different locations.

Another woman who was interested in nursing homes took a camera person to various homes in the area and brought back a "taped" report for others to share. Her questions to the nursing home staff were far more relevant to the needs of older people than any questions we might have come up with. The videotape and the organizer's accompanying live commentary provided a lively exchange of questions and answers about the nursing home from people who didn't have the opportunity to visit.

Research and planning of programs was required, and many of the old folks became completely engaged in the process. I suspect the benefit of the activity kept many a mind agile. Voluntary committees that were responsible for the programming developed original ideas. The programming these folks created could never have been developed by a program director who didn't share their interests and problems. As a result of the broadcasts, people who hadn't seen each other in years discovered each other on television. When they waved to each other on camera, some thought it would trivialize the system; it turned out to be an unexpected benefit because our intent all along had been to encourage communication.

As familiarity and comfort were the order of the day, we needed to have open microphones at each of the centers. People had to be able to jump up and get involved in the discussion easily. The engineers advised that we could not have open audio with 14 microphones, because of feedback, but we knew that if the system was not spontaneous and easy to use people would reject it. So we found an engineer who listened to our concerns. He designed a feedback suppressor to solve the problem. The difficulties we encountered strengthened our conviction that users ought to drive the technology—not the other way around. It is a point I feel very strongly about. Too often technology drives an application because users are intimidated by the technology and do not have a hand in its design.

This project demonstrated that if people are given the tools, the environment, and the encouragement, they can create something that reflects them.

I remember vividly the day I was driving in Reading, Pennsylvania, and on my car radio a local news announcer referred to a comment that someone had made on one of the programs. I knew then that the channel had been accepted and become a permanent fixture in the community. The board of elders that we left in place in 1977 still operates to this day. They found the funds to sustain the system and manage the governance of what is now a model program in the United States. They don't remember that we were ever there, and we consider that our greatest success.

What global networks can learn from this model

The global reach of television has made *globalization* a current buzzword in media. And multinational companies are rushing to serve new markets, with the promise of profit not far behind.

There are many options. Nowhere will issues of design and transparency be more important than in the interactive global networks now being formed. They are facing multinational issues of control, ownership, intellectual property, and transborder dataflow. But if, as these networks develop, these issues overshadow user issues such as accessibility and ease of use, we will lose an extraordinary opportunity to create interesting and exciting new forms.

The same factors that proved to be crucial at Reading apply to global networks. Transparency and clear and simple design are essential to demystifying technology and making it accessible to its users.

The telephone is a wonderful example of interactive applications designed by users. The telephone company provides an empty pipe and a universal interface, and the telephone is easy to use. Adults discuss business, teenagers discuss whatever teenagers discuss; some use it to combat loneliness, others to order groceries; some to make appointments, still others to make love. It is truly a user-generated medium.

The June 27, 1991 issue of *The Washington Post* featured a story about the telephone. A sociologist with Bellcore, the research arm of the Baby Bells, was quoted:

> When the Eskimos in remote northern Canada first got direct-satellite telephone communications about 20 years ago, the Canadian government figured they would just use it to talk to each other. Instead, the Eskimos started calling Seattle to check the market for seal meat and started cutting their own deals. That kind of thing has happened all over the Third World.

The historic landscape is littered with technologies that were developed for one purpose but used for vastly different ones. If flexibility is included in the design, users are able to adapt technology to their own needs.

Initially, when Bell developed the telephone, Western Union refused to invest in the new company. Western Union was convinced that people would not conduct business on the telephone because they needed information in writing. But the convenience of use, the transparency of the technology (we don't know whether a phone call is carried on terrestrial lines or through a satellite), ease of use (you don't need a manual), and most important, the opportunity to use it for a variety of communications, has made it an indispensable part of our lives.

Tomorrow's high-speed networks will have the capacity to carry multimedia in real time. The same need for transparency and ease of use applies to these networks. If a doctor is about to operate on a critically ill patient and needs to consult with doctors elsewhere, whether the distance is small or great a CAT scan can be sent down the network quickly. Museums and libraries can use these same networks to increase their distribution and availability to many more people in distant locations. Physical distances can be cut dramatically. As with the early days of the telephone, we can now only imagine applications. But once the empty pipe has been laid and is accessible, imagination and need will drive new uses.

The People, Not the Technology

It is startling how quickly virtually any discussion of the future of computing, entertainment, publishing, broadcasting, office technology, and education evolves into speculation about the technology. But the technology is as straightforward as a mathematical equation. What *isn't* clear is how we can benefit from these new and powerful developments.

Now that users and artists can use these new tools because of lower costs and less obtuse interfaces, something new has been added to the mix. I use the term *artists* in a general sense. Art traditionally has shown us new ways to look at the world. The sensitivity and sensibility of the artist can temper a singular technological approach.

There is no question that we will have the ability to move large amounts of digital information across space and time. Fiber optics, digital switching, compressed video, direct satellite transmission, will take us to this electronic nirvana. Broadband digital switched networks will be accessible almost anywhere in the industrialized world, television receivers will be computers, imaging technology will get cheaper and smaller, and improved displays will incorporate graphics chips capable of decompressing full-motion video. High-resolution video will merge with computer displays. This new digital technology translates images, graphics, text, video, and sound into a common language.

But it is still *people* who lead the development of applications, *people* who bring humanity to the machines, *people* who will speak this common language. How we train people, how we encourage people to recognize a moral as well as an aesthetic responsibility, are serious considerations.

Training the new technology designers

In 1979, the Alternate Media Center developed a graduate program in the Tisch School of the Arts at New York University: the Interactive Telecommunications Program. Its focus is telecommunications and the production of multimedia applications. The fact that the program is in the School of the Arts is significant. We are not housed in schools such as those of Computer Science, Social Science, Education, Business, or Journalism. We are in the School of the Arts because our primary interest is in creative communication.

The focus on interactivity requires that we look to the new technologies as the engine; that we look at technology as the verb, not the noun; that our commitment is to people, not technology. There is a new community of disciplines. Today fields that were once worlds apart are converging.

Our students and faculty come from a wide range of backgrounds. Computer scientists work with students from the fine arts, sound engineers, video makers, musicians, writers, journalists, architects—all are in the mix. What can they teach other? A great deal, and perhaps most importantly, that there is no one way to create, rather many different ways. Skills and approaches are exchanged. This is an environment with no fixed circumference, fluid enough to move with the acceleration of technological change.

The field has yet to be defined. The ability to communicate must be combined with creative vision. This is not an inherent attribute of the technology, however; it comes about when the technology is accessible to talented and imaginative people.

We believe that a new kind of communications professional is needed, one who can adapt to changes, who is aware of issues of power, control, representation, interface, and aesthetics, one who is able to demystify technology and yet has enough knowledge of its attributes to put it in perspective.

This new kind of professional is comfortable with both creative and analytical modes of learning. Our curriculum is set up for the student who wants to *learn* rather than for the student who merely wants to acquire a skill. This student is a new breed of person. One who understands the value of pictures, words, critical thinking, judgment, understanding, technology, and aesthetics. One who has the ability to manipulate tools, and the critical capacity to sort out information. In short, a student who reflects the knowledge shift from static knowledge to a dynamic, searching paradigm.

We believe that technology is not value-free. It takes on the values of the designers. How do you provide an environment where diverse talented people can harness these technologies so that they add to the human spirit?

We encourage collaboration rather than competition. The emphasis on collaboration creates a kind of collegiality that is exciting in any learning environment. Group projects allow students to add their particular skills to a project even as they learn about other disciplines. Students are encouraged to fail, to try out ideas and concepts that may or may not work and to learn from their mistakes. We prefer to ask questions rather than look for solutions.

Along with classes, students work on projects—experimenting with pushing the technology to the edge of the possible, combining tools and ideas in new ways. The tools are personal computers, video, graphics, sound, animation, and text—the medium is transmission. These new convergences of technologies are providing capabilities to individual users that once were reserved for highly skilled technicians operating very expensive equipment.

Labs are the heart of our graduate program, a crucible in which a mix of ideas and talents creates new forms and applications. Students in the Interactive Telecommunications Program developed and produce a program called *Window* which is cablecast each evening over Manhattan Cable, the local cable television company. The topics ranges from homelessness, racism, and sexism to other community issues.

Interactive videodiscs and telephone call-ins allow viewers to choose portions of a videodisc produced by students. The telephone interface was designed by one of our students—he is not an engineer, but was interested in experimenting with interactivity in a mass medium. The opportunity to control a television program is appealing to people who watch *Window*. We know that the audience is involved, because the call-in lines are constantly in use during the cablecasts.

The tools to mix and edit audio and video and electronic text are now accessible to a broad range of creative professionals—producers and artists—who want to take direct control of the process. Computer technology was once the domain of the computer scientist. Now, because of miniaturization and less obtuse interfaces, artists are working with computers. This may prove to be one of the most exciting developments, because artists will bring a new dimension and creative investigation of the possibilities of communications technology.

The computer can be a creative partner, but it can't do anything by itself. Only a talented and imaginative creator can make it *sing*.

We are now able to move beyond traditional linear exposition to explore interactivity, a nonlinear presentation of information. Parallel, even concurrent story lines are possible in this new medium.

This is an entirely new art form. We are freeing the music, film, video broadcast, and publishing industries from the limitations and practices imposed by previous generations of technology.

Our students are joining the ranks of the experimenters and the "imaginers." We expect them to raise the ethical questions, the aesthetic requirements, and the empowerment issues, and to address the design needs we emphasize when they go out and create the technology applications of our future.

Many of our graduates have set up their own companies, while others work in many different areas for both profit and nonprofit corporations such as the Nynex Media Lab, Apple Computer's Advanced Technology Group, the American Museum of Natural History, Chase Manhattan Bank, Educational Testing Service, the Telecommunications Office of the City of New York, Philip Morris, IBM, Optical Data, HBO, and ABC News Interactive, to name only a few.

In our graduate program, we try to maintain a balance between the excitement and allure of potential new and enhanced forms of communication and the responsibilities and pitfalls inherent in technological advances. We walk a tightrope, learning as we go.

Sometimes a technology's use is not obvious, and it needs to be introduced into a community of users who can design one themselves. Sometimes a technology can be adapted by a creative team or an event. Often a need creates an application.

However a communications technology comes to life, it is sure to take on the values of its creators and the users. It is important to remember that there is no one way but rather many different ways. In a time when big popular, centralized media can control how a person, a political point of view, or a cultural group is represented, it is crucially important that we come up with ways to provide alternate means for people to create their own media and, as a result, their own ways of representing themselves.

A Zen monk once asked a Zen teacher, "What is the way?" The teacher answered, "Ordinary mind is the way." The monk asked, "Then should we direct ourselves toward it, or not?" The teacher replied, "If you direct yourself toward it, you go away from it." The monk said, "If I don't direct myself toward it, how can I know the way?"

The teacher said, "The way is beyond knowing or not knowing."

This chapter was originally presented at the Cultural Identity and Integration in the New Media World conference at the University of Industrial Arts, Helsinki, Finland, November 1991.

Tapping the Power of Multimedia

Steven L. Raber

Introduction

A Michigan power company replaces a grueling, 12-hour standup training class with a self-paced multimedia training program that is more consistent, accurate, and detailed. A museum uses multimedia to teach the rigors of seventeenth-century maritime life to youngsters raised on microwave dinners and MTV. An NBA team immediately translates floor action into crowd-inspiring music with a multimedia system that responds to a touch on a screen.

These are just a few of the thousands of multimedia applications currently in use in homes, schools, and businesses, with thousands more under development. These applications are being used to teach, entertain, persuade, document, sell, and communicate in more powerful and exciting ways than anything that's ever existed before. And the power of multimedia is spreading rapidly. Less than three years ago, a multimedia system cost more than $10,000. Now the price has fallen to less than a fifth of that, and before long every PC will come equipped with multimedia capabilities. In fact, a McGraw-Hill poll of Fall 1992 Comdex attendees discovered that 41 percent believe that multimedia will have the greatest practical impact on computing during the next five years. Portability, wireless communications, and other technologies ranked far behind.

Multimedia represents a technological crossroads at which increasing PC power, digital technology, and video access have converged, personalizing, for the first time, the information revolution. Multimedia takes yesterday's training film, PC graphics presentation, audio tape, and other common media and merges them into impactful presentations that are much, much greater than the sum of their parts. It incorporates such information-handling technology as hyperlinking, which allows nonlinear navigation through data, and object orientation, which simplifies complex operations with point-and-click utility.

As a result, multimedia heralds a new way of learning and communicating as it moves from being a programmer's playground to a technology as familiar as the VCR and as necessary as the fax. In other words, if the eighties spawned PCs and networking belongs to the nineties, then multimedia will be the technological breakthrough of the millennium.

But exactly what is this revolution called "multimedia," and how can you put it to work for you? Is it another one of those technological fantasies that never seem to make the transition into everyday life, like videophones or intra-city "people-movers"? Is it one of those technologies where it pays to be cautious until the market has matured, like the early days of the VCR? Or is it more like today's telephone, a once-revolutionary technology that no one can now live without?

The answer is that if multimedia is not already having an impact on your life, it soon will be (see Fig. 3.1). That's why it's important to know not only what multimedia is, but how you can make it work for you. Don't be put off by unfamiliar buzzwords like DVI and MPEG, or fears of making irremediable mistakes. Instead, think of using multimedia as being similar to driving one of today's cars: a lot of advanced technology is hidden under the hood, but driving is still easy enough for everyone to learn.

Using Multimedia at Home

Look at many of today's top-selling multimedia titles—*Sherlock Holmes,* National Geographic Society's *Mammals,* and *Where in the World Is Carmen*

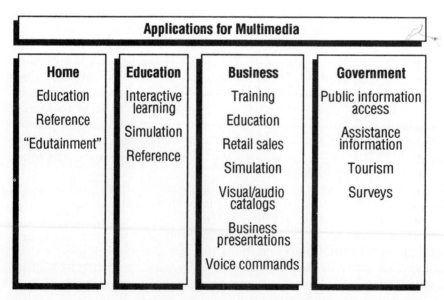

Figure 3.1 Applications for multimedia.

Sandiego?—and you'll see how multimedia impacts the home. If your kids think Nintendo is awesome, then wait till they learn how multimedia immerses them in intergalactic space battles, rock 'n' roll theme parks of the future, and danger-packed voyages to the bottom of the sea. As one observer put it: MTV to the max.

Mad Dog McCree, for example, brings home the old action movies we watched at theaters as kids. Shoot the bad guy, and he keels over. Miss him, and you risk being plugged by the outlaw.

But, fortunately, home applications of multimedia are not limited to shoot-'em-ups. National Geographic's *Presidents* lets children explore timelines of history and experience famous presidential speeches at a click of the mouse. *The New Grolier MultiMedia Encyclopedia* combines the depth of traditional encyclopedias with exciting visualization of the moonwalk and other events. And *The 1991 Time Magazine Compact Almanac* captures the twentieth century, with over 10,000 articles and video footage ranging from Henry Ford's Model T to Boris Yeltsin and the Soviet coup.

Undoubtedly slowing the spread of multimedia into the home is the cost of commercial multimedia applications, which can range from less than $30 to several hundred dollars. Few consumers are willing to make that kind of entertainment investment, sight unseen. To help consumers overcome this hurdle, a major multimedia publisher and distributor has introduced a multimedia "test-drive" program. The publisher is entering into agreements with video rental stores to let consumers rent a new title for $3 per day, then buy it if they like it. Other major publishers are rumored to be looking at similar programs, which means that, before long, multimedia franchises may fill every shopping mall.

Multimedia Goes to School

In the classroom, multimedia also can bridge the chasm between theory and practice by giving students the opportunity to practice what they have learned in a safe and controlled environment. And by making the theory real, multimedia engages students, turning them into active rather than passive learners.

Multimedia in the schools can be used to enhance learning and aid simulations. Seventh- and eighth-graders in a Rhode Island high school created a multimedia presentation that explored the historical significance of the *Titanic,* its tragic fate, the long search for the wreckage, and the technology used to find it. The students used IBM's LinkWay and Storyboard Live!, two programs that can combine text, graphics, animation, still photographs, and motion video into one document on the computer. In the process the students not only learned about geography, history, and math, but also developed higher-order thinking skills and problem-solving abilities.

Simulation also unlocks the power of multimedia. For example, a major midwestern university uses multimedia to teach introductory chemistry to more than 2000 students per semester. Students perform such experiments as the ionization of salt in water or determining the acidity of unknown solutions. The lessons allow students to perform procedures and make decisions about experiments that would be much more difficult with traditional instruction. The benefits include allowing students to study reactions that are too hazardous, expensive, or time-consuming to be completed in the standard chemical laboratory. Less hazardous waste is generated, and teachers can spend more time one-on-one. Instructors report that students seem to be better prepared for actual lab work and more motivated to study chemistry, perhaps because multimedia gives them the opportunity to learn from mistakes in a hazard-free setting.

High schools nationwide are using a class of multimedia that IBM calls "knowledge systems." These systems include *The Illuminated Books and Manuscripts* and *Columbus: Encounter, Discovery, and Beyond,* each incorporating 180 hours of interactive learning. *Illuminated Books* studies five classic works of literature, including Shakespeare's *Hamlet* and Alfred Tennyson's "Ulysses," while *Columbus* is a cross-disciplinary study of the Renaissance and the Age of Discovery.

Getting Down to Business

The power of multimedia has been recognized by business and government as well. Already multimedia is having a significant impact in training/education, retail sales, business presentations, communications enhancement, and even public information access.

Training

It's every manager's nightmare: overhearing an employee tell a customer, "I don't know. It's not my area."

Training employees so as to eliminate this problem is expensive. But the cost pales next to the price of untrained or poorly trained employees on customer relations, safety, or internal efficiencies. As a result businesses, always looking for ways to cut costs and improve productivity, have embraced multimedia as enthusiastically as an investment tax credit.

It's easy to understand why. Multimedia has the power to teach and train according to an individual's ability, without the intrinsic handicaps of classroom training, videos, and instructional manuals. An oft-quoted study says that people remember about 25 percent of what they see, 40 percent of what they see and hear, and almost 75 percent of what they see, hear, and do. While other forms of instruction are often merely variations on one-time show-and-tell, multimedia is see-and-do, with multiple opportunities to repeat if the information is not understood. The learning process is greatly accelerated when the user is in control.

Therefore, multimedia represents the best tool for business to bring what is commonly acknowledged to be an underskilled work force up to the demands of the twenty-first century.

Just open a copy of *BusinessWeek* or *The Wall Street Journal* to learn about multimedia in action. Before, the best one of the nation's largest telecommunications companies could offer trainees were flip charts and prerecorded videotapes and audiotapes. Now it's taking multimedia to its 43,000 employees, providing everything from technical training to simulated customer encounters to creative problem solving and decision making. The payoffs: employees learn more in less time with longer retention, while the company ensures consistent training nationwide and keeps employees on the job and out of the classroom longer.

Companies nationwide report similar benefits. A major steel company reported a 20 to 40 percent reduction in training time and a 20 to 40 percent increase in retention. A retail sporting goods chain cut average training time per employee from 8 to 4 hours. An overnight express company slashed instructor-led classroom time from 7.5 to 2.6 hours without cutting content. Multimedia courses save a Big Six consulting firm $10 million annually.

Currently, this business training occurs at stand-alone stations, each equipped with the necessary add-ons. But if companies put multimedia training programs on a network, the costs of current decentralized approaches will decline dramatically even as the benefits expand exponentially. The power of multimedia to teach and train will increase even more as courseware increasingly incorporates pattern-recognition features that automatically adjust information according to individual responses.

Retail

Businesses also are using multimedia to extend their sales reach through multimedia "kiosk catalogs" and "kiosk sales representatives." These kiosks—stand-alone multimedia devices that look like ATMs and feature touch-screens, color images, video, and audio—are being placed in high-traffic areas, delivering accessible information to targeted prospects when they are in a buying mood. Information can be accessed through a touchscreen and viewed on the monitor, or even printed out. With the right communications links, kiosks can even be programmed and updated from a central facility.

Kiosks not only represent low-cost (less than $15,000), high-return sales tools but also can distinguish a business from its competition. Companies can collect information about their customers, either by recording the options chosen or by asking questions directly. Consumers benefit from reduced costs, since a manufacturer or retailer has no human, inventory, or operating costs.

With multimedia kiosks, customers can browse through colorful presentations of products before placing orders. Multilingual audio can serve a heterogeneous population, or even support a beachhead in international markets. A telephone link could allow the prospect to speak to a sales representatives while a credit card reader takes the order. A major Ohio bank is even testing videoconferencing on its kiosks, which will allow customers to see the customer service representative "live."

At the current rate, multimedia kiosks soon will be as ubiquitous as ATMs. Major league baseball teams are using kiosks that permit ticket buyers not only to buy game seats with a credit card, but also to see a view of the playing field from that particular seat! A major computer company plans to sell software for its palmtop computers via kiosks. Another company has used kiosks to provide sheet music to customers in whatever score, key, or arrangement they desire.

The benefits of multimedia just begin with consumer sales. Architects and engineers can use multimedia to transform blueprints and drawings into simulations of buildings and products, complete with interior visualizations including furnishings and decorations. Other companies can use multimedia to demonstrate those hard-to-inventory items such as handmade furniture, industrial equipment, or earthwork. Real estate agents can show prospects the interiors and exteriors of homes that meet their pricing, location, and other criteria, eliminating wasted trips to unsatisfactory sites. In fact, one Denmark agency used such a system to increase prospect traffic by 400 percent while reducing the number of house visits per purchase by almost 50 percent.

Waves gently kissing palm-shrouded shores...the ethereal chimes of medieval cathedrals...mountain panoramas ringing pristine ski trails—nothing can sell a vacation or trip like multimedia. Plus, multimedia can provide all of the extra details as to lodging, tours, special attractions, and all that really makes a trip. And when the entire family needs persuading, travel agencies can even "print" a custom videotape for the client to take home.

Business presentations

But multimedia is not limited to special business needs such as sales or training. It can also deliver benefits every day in your office. You can improve every PC application with business audio, taking advantage of voice recording, annotation, and even supplementing other input devices. For example, you can eliminate all of the yellow "stickies" that grow on every business document by embedding audio comments, suggestions, or explanations in the spreadsheet, letter, or other document. This technology is easily networkable, which means that voice files can be moved around and shared on the network like any other type of computer data. The productivity benefits are obvious. You can speak faster than you can write, plus you can more easily convey nuance or feeling.

Other applications of business audio include checking the clarity of your grammar or thought process by having the computer "read" back documents. Or you can even train your PC to be a faithful servant, teaching it to "save file" or "print" with a spoken command.

Documentation

Multimedia has proven to be a highly effective form of documentation for three reasons. First, it provides a visual means to show complex events, such as the routing of a phone call; second, it can rapidly access information required for installation or repairs; and third, it can show events chronologically in real time. For example, a major telephone firm now uses 90 seconds of visual animation to convey information that once took 20 pages to explain.

Multimedia documentation offers other benefits as well. It can provide examples of warning bells and lights, a capability no written documentation can provide. It can be much more current that old-fashioned manuals, since information stored on a server can be updated daily, if necessary.

Public information access

Government touches our lives in so many ways—through our schools, taxes, and services—yet the most common citizen complaint is that you can't get information out of governmental agencies, as anyone who has every tried to call the Division of Motor Vehicles can testify. But multimedia kiosks offer governments a new avenue to communicate with citizens and help build a sense of community—24 hours a day. They can easily be placed in lobbies, shopping malls, public parks and facilities, convention centers, airports, museums, art galleries, and anywhere else people congregate and need information.

For example, the "L.A. Project" used multimedia to help citizens recover from the devastating 1992 Los Angeles riots. The multimedia kiosks, located in central community sites, offered citizens information on "Where Can I Get Help?" or "What Can I Do To Help?" The information connected victims with resources concerning financial aid, legal rights, food and clothing, shelter, small business assistance, and other categories. The information, displayed in English, Spanish, or Korean and reinforced with an audio recording, made the system accessible to persons with limited literacy. A similar system was used in Florida to help citizens recover from the devastation of Hurricane Andrew.

Other locales presently linking government to multimedia include Hawaii, which offers residents health, human services, and employment information; California, which is planning to provide vehicle registration renewals via touch-screen transaction kiosks; Oregon, which uses multimedia kiosks to give drivers' tests; and the Long Beach, California, Municipal Court, which allows violators to pay for traffic citations at an "Auto Clerk" kiosk.

Collaborative multimedia computing

Multimedia can help to provide a new solution for work-group productivity that is best termed *collaborative multimedia*. Using advanced videoconferencing technology, collaborative multimedia allows real-time interaction between people who need to work together but who can't be in the same place at the same time. This permits "multimedia meetings" to occur as spontaneously as a phone call. As a result organizations can reduce travel costs and the non-productive time spent traveling, allow work groups to span wider geographies, and improve productivity through work-group interaction.

The IBM Person to Person/2 is a videoconferencing system that incorporates a camera placed beside a computer so that participants can see each other as if they were in a face-to-face meeting. All desktop applications—spreadsheets, graphics, text—become de facto groupware because they are shared simultaneously among all participants. Once these applications have been moved into an open window called a "chalkboard," participants can use a set of drawing tools to highlight some points or delete others as if they were all standing together at a blackboard.

How to Get Started with Multimedia

The benefits of multimedia are clear. But how can you turn the promise into reality? It's easier than you think. In fact if you can program a VCR, you can probably build a cutting-edge multimedia application.

Essentially, there are three avenues you can go down to get into multimedia on PCs (see Fig. 3.2):

1. Buy a complete, ready-to-go system based on standardized platform.

2. Upgrade your current system.

3. Use a "best-of-breed" approach, assembling a customized system with individual components optimized for specific needs.

Which avenue you will take depends on several factors: your budget (of course), potential applications, technical and/or programming skills, and your choice of operating systems.

In many ways the choice of an operating system for PCs is the most fundamental, since it will shape your choice of applications, upgrade paths, and total functionality. The three choices are DOS, Windows, and OS/2.

DOS was once the powerful engine that propelled the PC revolution, but now it's showing its age. Other operating systems long ago surpassed DOS in terms of power and functionality. However, although one day it may be as hard to find a DOS-based PC as it is now to find a car running on leaded

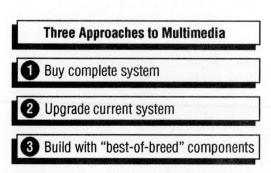

Figure 3.2   Three approaches to multimedia.

gasoline, there are still millions of users worldwide whose PCs provide all the functionality they need. These users can take advantage of some multimedia training applications that offer interactive response, some animation, and links to a VCR, videodisc player, or other analog device. Additionally, DOS-based PCs can be linked in a network that contains more powerful multimedia capabilities in a central repository.

Microsoft's Windows opened the door to graphical user interfaces in the PC world, and has consequently been incorporated into many multimedia applications. Windows permits a computer's additional memory to be tapped, thus giving multimedia applications the extra "room" to strut their stuff. Windows 3.1 incorporates multimedia extensions, which essentially means that it provides the necessary "hooks" to synchronize and orchestrate the sound, video, and other capabilities of most multimedia applications. As a result, Windows is heavily used for education and "edutainment" applications.

IBM's OS/2 is a 32-bit operating system, which is nothing more than a fancy way of saying that it provides a much wider "data highway" than the 8- or 16-bit capabilities of DOS and Windows. OS/2 can incorporate all the capabilities and functionality of DOS and Windows, plus provide the capacity for preemptive multitasking, which manages multiple streams of data (or applications) simultaneously. OS/2 with Multimedia Presentation Manager/2 (MMPM/2) provides a consistent platform for applications to incorporate sound, graphics, video, and images through the use of any easy-to-program, high-level interface. MMPM/2 is device-independent, which means that applications and tools can be written independently of the wide variety of multimedia devices and formats. MMPM/2 also allows multimedia hardware to be more fully exploited through device-sharing. Eventually, all advanced operating systems will be able to exploit the power of today's 32-bit microprocessors.

The stand-alone path

The easiest way to get into PC multimedia is to buy a complete system from IBM, AST, Advanced Logic Research, or other manufacturers. For maximum functionality, make sure the system includes MPC Level 2 certification. This MPC specification is the electronic equivalent of the Good Housekeeping seal of approval, which means that the computer has been tested to ensure compliance with an industrywide minimum standard for enhanced multimedia computing.

To receive Level 2 certification (see Fig. 3.3), computers must have: 486 25-MHz or compatible processor; 4-Mbyte RAM; 160-Mbyte hard drive; double-speed (which means it has a data-transfer rate of both 150 and 300 bytes-per-second), XA (extended architecture)-ready, multisession-capable CD-ROM drive; 16-bit sound; and a monitor that offers a display resolution of 640 × 480 with 64K colors. (If some terms are unfamiliar, don't worry; they will be explained later in the chapter.) Buying an MPC Level 2 certified computer ensures compatibility with a wide range of powerful off-the-shelf multimedia software.

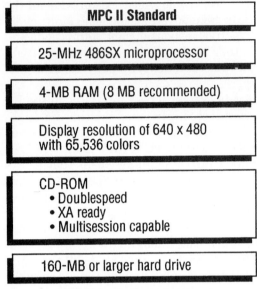

Figure 3.3 MPC II standard.

Upgrading a PC

If you're not ready to turn your current system out to pasture, then a multimedia upgrade kit may be best for you. In fact, upgrade products currently constitute the majority of multimedia hardware sales.

Before you take this path, first be sure that your existing system has sufficient horsepower. Pass those outdated IBM PC/XTs and ATs down to the kids; effective multimedia requires at least a 386SX with 4 Mbytes of memory. A 486 with 8 Mbytes of memory is even better. Add Windows to the mix, since it (or its equivalent) not only provides a graphical user interface (GUI) but also serves as the umbrella that lets such disparate elements as CD-ROM drives and video capture boards work together. The larger the hard-disk capacity, the better.

Multimedia upgrade kits usually contain a compatible CD-ROM drive and sound board, along with some bundled multimedia applications. For example, one popular upgrade kit that includes the sound board and drive comes with Compton's Multimedia Encyclopedia, Lotus 1-2-3 Multimedia for Windows, Nautilus Multimedia magazine, MacroMedia Action!, the Deluxe CD-ROM version of Carmen Sandiego, and Sierra's King's Quest V. As a result, these kits can represent a tremendous bargain, since buying these titles separately could cost thousands of dollars or more. Some even buy upgrade kits based not on the technology but solely on the type of titles they will receive.

"Roll your own"

Or you might want to "roll your own" multimedia system, adding one kind of CD-ROM drive and a top-of-the-line sound card. But remember that you may pay a price for such freedom of choice. Compatibility becomes a problem, and it may be troublesome getting the individual components to work with one another. But if you do decide to go this route, it's time to get down to multimedia basics.

Getting Down to Basics

A CD-ROM drive, either internal or external, is often the heart of a multimedia system. CD-ROM drives access the information contained on CD-ROM disks, which are just like audio CD disks except for special error-correction coding to ensure accuracy. CD-ROM disks hold about 650 Mbytes of data (the equivalent of 300,000 pages of information) or about 70 minutes of audio.

The two most critical specifications for choosing a CD-ROM drive are data-transfer rate and access time. Look for a continuous data-transfer rate of at least 150K per second. Slower rates will turn video and animation into herky-jerky screen stutters and may cause compatibility problems with the rest of your system. The newest—and most expensive—drives can wear two hats, spinning the disc at 300K per second for text or graphics, and slowing to 150K per second so that music and speech sound normal.

Access time is determined by how fast a drive scans a CD-ROM disk for information. Older drives take a half-second (500 milliseconds) or more to find data, while newer ones have access times as fast as 150 milliseconds. (Still slow compared to hard drives, which have access times of about 10 to 20 milliseconds.) The faster the better, but don't get one with an access time of less than 400 milliseconds, especially if you are going to depend on your PC for search-and-retrieval applications.

Look for a drive that meets the ISO 9660 standard data format, and avoid those with the older High Sierra (named after the Nevada hotel where the standards committee met in 1983) format. To avoid potential obsolescence down the road, get a CD-ROM player that can accommodate the emerging extended architecture (XA) format. The XA technology allows interleaved audio, video, and data streams on a CD-ROM disc. The standard is also compatible with Kodak's Photo CD technology, which lets you store photo images on CD.

Internal or external? Like modems, both offer the same functionality, so the choice essentially depends on your pocketbook and how handy you are with a screwdriver. Internal CD-ROM drives cost about $100 less than external drives, but require installation of drive rails and power-supply cabling inside a $5\frac{1}{4}$-inch half-height drivebay. (Check the documentation to make sure it explains installation clearly enough.) If you typically set your computer on its side to save space, then make sure the CD-ROM can operate in this position.

For external drives, just install an interface card (also called an *adapter* or *controller* card) in an empty slot and connect a cable to the drive. Remember that some external drives plug into proprietary interface cards while others use industry-standard SCSI connections. The interface makes no difference in performance, but SCSI-compatible CD-ROM drives will let other SCSI devices such as hard drives or tape drives "daisy-chain," or share the same adapter. On the other hand, using proprietary interface cards usually is cheaper, and it eliminates potential configuration headaches. If you do choose a proprietary card, make sure a controller is included. Buying one separately could add several hundred dollars to the cost.

Portable drives are small, lightweight external drives that plug into the parallel port through an adapter. They are usually used with portable computers. Remember, however, that all CD-ROM drives will run more slowly when connected to the parallel port.

Some drives permit disks to be directly loaded into the machine; others require CD-ROM caddies. There's no difference in performance, but caddies will help keep fingerprints and foreign matter from affecting the integrity of your disk. Handle with care! If dust does get inside the drive, it can interfere with the optical mechanism's ability to "read" information on the disk. Ideally, the CD-ROM drive also will have front-access controls for headphones and volume control.

All CD-ROM drives should come with an installation disk that will add Microsoft's CD-ROM extension drivers (MSCDEX Version 2.2 or later) and a device driver to your system's CONFIG.SYS file, ensuring that the computer recognizes that a read-only drive is attached. Changes to your AUTOEXEC.BAT file may also have to be made so that your computer knows how to handle the new drive.

The type of application will determine whether you need a buffer or not. For text search and retrieval, a buffer isn't necessary, although it can speed up searches. However, smoothly displaying graphics, video, and animation requires a consistent transfer rate of 150 kbytes per second. To ensure this type of performance, look for a drive with a 32K to 54K buffer.

Of course, other important criteria that apply to all the components of a multimedia system include reliability, ease of setup, pricing, and technical support.

Sound boards

Yes, all PCs do come with audio capabilities, but most can do no more than deliver one-note hoots and toots. Sound boards (Fig. 3.4) give your PC the ability to talk, sing, and entertain. Better sound boards can take sounds from a microphone, stereo, CD disk, or even a hard drive and mix them all together before outputting the result through speakers and headphones. This comes in handy, for example, if you want soft background music behind a travelogue narration.

The heart of a sound board is an analog-to-digital (ADC) chip that digitizes audio so it can be handled by your computer, and a digital-to-analog converter (DAC) chip that can turn computer output into sound. Almost every sound board will advertise compatibility with Creative Labs' Sound Blaster.

Minimally, a sound board should support CD Audio (so you can play the same CDs used in your stereo), MIDI files, and "waveform audio," better

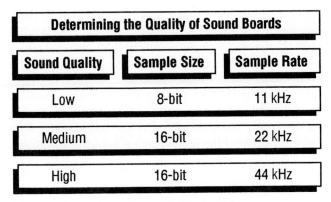

Determining the Quality of Sound Boards		
Sound Quality	**Sample Size**	**Sample Rate**
Low	8-bit	11 kHz
Medium	16-bit	22 kHz
High	16-bit	44 kHz

Figure 3.4 Determining the quality of sound boards.

known as the WAV file format supported by Windows 3.1. WAV files are just a way to capture, store, and play back audio with a computer.

The quality of digitized audio is directly dependent on the "sample size," or how much data the ADC and DAC chips can process at once, and the "sample rate," or how fast the ADC and DAC chips can process the data. The sample size and sample rate seem like obscure terminologies until you know your specific application. Buy a sound card with an 8-bit sample size and a 22.05-kHz sample rate, and the audio output is going to sound like AM radio in an older car. In truth, this probably is adequate for games, but it may handicap more sophisticated business presentations or many newer multimedia titles.

For typical CD player output, look for higher-level cards with 16-bit sample sizes and a higher, FM-quality, 44.1-kHz sample rate. However, there's a price to be paid for higher fidelity: greater storage requirements. Sound sampled at 16 bits and 44.1 kHz takes 16 times as much disk space as the same sound sampled in 8-bit mono at 11 kHz. Of course compression can relieve the burden on your hard disk, but remember that the more you compress, the worse it sounds. There also currently aren't any standards for compression, which means that files compressed with one board and its software may not be readable by another board. Again, determine your entertainment, business audio, CD-ROM, and input requirements before you buy. 8-bit mono is fine for spreadsheet annotation, but probably inadequate for wooing prospects or making presentations.

Also consider cards with a MIDI interface, which means you can connect a computer to such electronic instruments as keyboards and drum machines. The MPC specifications call for MIDI support, although you can probably get along without it for most multimedia applications.

Almost all sound boards come with bundled software that let you record, edit, play MIDI and digital audio, or even author a multimedia presentation. For sound editing, check to see if the software supports Windows' OLE links. Most also include text-to-speech programs that read what you type.

Remember, however, that bundled software often has minimal capabilities, and serious applications may require software with additional capabilities.

If you already have a CD-ROM drive, check for compatibility. Several popular sound boards come with a CD-ROM connection, but some of these have a proprietary interface. For the widest—and safest—selection, look for a sound board that includes a SCSI connector. Better boards also will come with a microphone input jack and RCA output jacks for headphones or stereo speakers as well. When installing the sound board inside your computer, place it as far as possible from the power supply and hard drive so as to minimize potential interference.

Video (still images)

Mention multimedia, and inevitably it will be defined in terms of "video." However, multimedia experts often stretch the word *video* to cover two meanings (see Fig. 3.5). The first is a series of static images, much like those seen in a slide show, and the other is "full-motion" video, which is comparable to watching TV or a movie.

Getting static images into a computer requires a video capture board, sometimes called an *NTSC/VGA board.* This expansion board digitizes an analog video signal from a VCR, camcorder, TV, or other NTSC source so that it can be stored and manipulated by a computer. With the proper software you can then shrink, edit, or crop the image, and augment it with text and graphics. Often this software is bundled with the board, but separate applications will offer greater functionality. More sophisticated boards provide the additional capability of controlling hue, contrast, and brightness and letting you crop, pan, and zoom in on a single image before saving it to disk in a popular graphics file format.

Unfortunately, getting the right video board is more complicated than buying a sound board. Video boards use a variety of signals and connections and follow different standards, and even the digital output can differ. And that doesn't include the differences in color-handling, resolutions, and file format

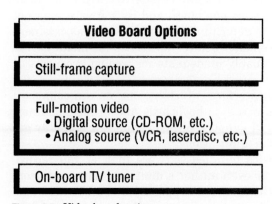

Figure 3.5   Video board options.

support. This means that you often have to adjust DIP switches or jumpers on both the expansion board and the motherboard to match signal type and monitor usage. For example, if your video capture board has VGA capabilities, you must switch off the system-board video to avoid interference from the add-in VGA.

Video (full-motion)

Full-motion video can come from two sources: a CD-ROM disk or other digital storage device, or from such familiar items as VCRs or laserdiscs. Full-motion video—defined as 30 frames per second—from a digital source has a great deal more potential. You can, for example, add new images or clips to existing video as easily as inserting a sentence in a word processing document, eliminating the endless back-and-forth tape winds required for analog editing.

But at the same time, digital video is much more difficult to accomplish, mainly because full-motion video requires an extremely large data-transfer rate (up to 30 Mbytes per second) to display on the typical monitor. This means the average hard disk with dozens of applications and hundreds of files can support about 3 seconds of full-motion video. There are two approaches to reducing the vast burden digital video places on PCs: reducing the image (often to one-quarter of the monitor's size) or number of colors displayed, and compression.

JPEG, MPEG, P*64, DVI, and C-Cube are the best-known compression methodologies that permit digital video. All have their strengths and weaknesses, and each is best suited to particular applications. But the technology used most often in today's multimedia presentations is DVI (Digital Video Interactive), a proprietary, programmable compression/decompression technology based on the Intel i750 chip set. DVI can compress full-motion (30 frames per second) video at ratios between 80:1 and 160:1 and play it back in full-frame size and color. The IBM PS/2 ActionMedia II, an adapter card available for Micro Channel PS/2s, PS/ValuePoint, and other ISA-compatible computers, incorporates DVI technology and can support two modes of real-time compression and write to any digital medium.

Systems with DVI technology allow up to 72 minutes of full-screen, full-motion video playback from a CD-ROM disc, which can be produced for significantly less cost than laserdiscs. Images can also be easily edited or combined on-screen with computer-generated text and graphics. DVI technology, incorporated on IBM's PS/2 ActionMedia II adapter card, also permits you to capture, digitize, and compress multiple images and store them on disk or tape. While typical analog multimedia technology cannot produce laserdiscs in real time, DVI-based ActionMedia II applications can be created "on the fly" and stored on hard discs and other media.

Playback also is available from software-only compression, although there are some tradeoffs involved. Intel Indeo software can let any 486 computer with OS/2 or Windows play back video, although you'll only see 24 frames per second on one-quarter of the screen. Other software-only compression applications include IBM's PhotoMotion. This software, used in National Geographic's *Mammals, The New Grolier's MultiMedia Encyclopedia,* and many of the leading consumer/education titles on the market today, provides full-motion video playback with synchronized audio from a hard drive, and permits more than two hours of quarter-screen motion video, complete with audio.

Because of digital's storage and compression requirements, many people use a graphics board that allows full-motion video to be displayed from a VCR or laserdisc player. Laserdiscs look like large CD-ROM disks but incorporate analog—not digital—recording. As a result they provide high-quality video, exceeding the resolution of broadcast TV by about 40 percent.

VCRs and laserdisc players require an adapter board to be installed in the computer, which allows graphics to be mixed with video "windows." These boards, exemplified by the IBM M-Motion Video Adapter/A adapter card or VideoLogic's DVA4000 board, essentially let a PC serve as the brains of a VCR or other player. Some boards have two-way capabilities, allowing you to record computer-altered images on videotape.

Other components

Of course the better the speaker, the better the audio. Make sure they are magnetically shielded to prevent interference with your PC. Some sound boards have enough power to drive loudspeakers directly. However, you'll get better sound by using speakers with built-in amplifiers or by linking the speakers to your stereo system. Most stereos and sound boards use pin plugs—also called *RCA* or *phono* plugs—although adapters may be required for different kinds of speakers and sound boards.

Many retail applications require touchscreen technology. It is a direct and intuitive way to control a computer, and extends the power of multimedia to those who may be uncomfortable with using a mouse or a keyboard. Some monitors, such as the 8516 Touch Display, offer integrated touchscreen capabilities, or use add-on touch panels to bring touchscreen technology to existing monitors.

Getting into Multimedia—Software

Once the system has been set up, you need the necessary software to create and run multimedia presentations. This software will fall into one of five categories:

1. Authoring tools, which bind text, sound, graphics, and video into a coherent whole while adding interactive capabilities

2. Graphics tools, which are used to create still graphics, images, and special effects

3. Animation tools, which add motion to graphics and text

4. Audio tools, to capture and edit sound

5. Video tools, which capture and/or edit digital motion video.

Unfortunately, no one piece of software can do it all, which has its advantages and disadvantages. On the plus side, you can get software optimized for each particular application, but you risk incompatibility and the constant need to "shop around" for suitable applications (see Fig. 3.6).

To solve this problem, IBM, working with independent software vendors, developed the Ultimedia Tools Series, which represents the best-of-breed in multimedia software tools, all designed to work together. Currently, there are more than 80 applications that are part of the Ultimedia Tools Series, including MacroMedia's Authorware Professional (authoring software); Fractal Design's Painter (graphics); Turtle Beach Systems' Wave for Windows (audio); Autodesk's Animator Pro (animation); and other applications.

All the UTS-certified applications share a common architecture, which means that compliant applications running under DOS, Windows, or OS/2 will look and act as similarly as possible and be able to exchange data. Depending on the programs, you can manipulate multimedia objects across programs, use a clipboard to copy and paste items from one application to another, and use DDE (Dynamic Data Exchange) techniques across Windows applications. The eventual goal of the Ultimedia Tools Series architecture is to offer seamless interoperability among all multimedia applications.

Clip media

If you, like many others, believe it's video that gives multimedia its punch, then you had better start assembling all the useful video images you can. Start taping those customer demonstrations or training sessions. Record your company president when he sets goals. Ask employees what they like about your company, and record the results.

And it doesn't have to be just video. Start taking digital photos with the Canon Xapshot, or have pictures digitized with the Kodak Photo CD system.

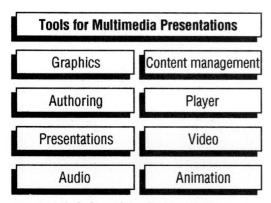

Figure 3.6 Tools for multimedia presentations.

Another alternative is to use a scanner, which looks like a desktop copy machine. The scanner digitizes your photo or artwork, allowing it to be imported into a computer application and manipulated like any other piece of art.

But be careful of what you copy. You don't want to run afoul of copyright law by illegally copying and using video, audio images, or text that belongs to someone else. That's why it's safest to generate your own multimedia material, or rely on the large library of material that producers permit to be used at will.

For example, Jasmine Stock Video offers a collection of video and production music for multimedia producers using Video for Windows. The Jasmine Stock Video Library can be used in the same way that "clip art" collections are used in desktop publishing. Using Indeo video software and these clip art CD-ROMs, PCs can show everything from Neil Armstrong's walk on the moon to the Great Wall of China, even to parachuting dogs and human cannonballs.

Conclusion

Soon after Alexander Graham Bell invented the telephone in the late 1800s, companies rushed to connect homes to this wonderful new technology. Unfortunately, these companies weren't linked together, and often a homeowner couldn't call his neighbor across the street because they were on different systems. The situation was resolved only after all the phone companies had been unified into a single company.

In some ways, that situation is mirrored in the multimedia world of today. Multimedia is still in its infancy, which means there is a variety of competing standards. This is a minor problem if you have standardized on a multimedia platform within your firm, but it does inhibit your ability to write a best-selling application for the mass market. Ultimately, many of the problems will be resolved when full-blown multimedia standards and capabilities are integrated into operating systems.

But that shouldn't stop you from getting into multimedia, any more than the lack of automatic guidance systems for your car keeps you from driving to work each day. Multimedia can produce significant paybacks for you at home, in school, and in your business, for a relatively small investment of time and money. Now, for the first time, you have the power to capture the promise of the information revolution and make it work for you.

4

The Virtual Classroom—
A Business Necessity

Ken Gerlach

The Training Challenge

The training gap

Corporate educational and training programs face serious obstacles and are not keeping pace with the reality and needs of a changing work force. As John Naisbitt writes, "We have essentially the same education system we had for the industrial society and we are trying to use it to equip us for the information age."[1]

In the past decade we have seen constant, revolutionary change in products, technology, and customer requirements, and in the skills and knowledge needed by companies' employees. As a consequence, corporate America must confront the huge challenge of retraining its work force to compete in a new and changing world economy. The American Society for Training and Development estimates that 55 million Americans, about 45 percent of the work force currently employed, will need to be retrained in the next decade in technical, executive management, supervisory, customer service, and basic skills training. Moreover, "it is estimated that corporations will have spent in excess of $30 billion in 1992 to train employees,"[2] but that has not been sufficient to solve the problem.

Training can be accomplished through traditional courses (over half of America's corporate training takes place in a traditional classroom), tutorials, or informal, "grapevine" learning. Structured, formalized training is more productive than informal training, and much more effective when done in house. The average U.S. company invests less than 2 percent of its payroll in formal training, reaching only one-tenth of the work force. The average amount of time corporations spend on training their employees each year varies by industry, ranging from 5 days per year for industries with established technologies to 10 days per year for industries with rapidly changing technologies. At Hewlett-Packard Company, the average for technical people is between 22 to 27 days per year. The surplus trained labor force of a few years ago has been considerably reduced, so each employee's current skills are especially crucial if a company is to remain competitive.

The typical corporate training environment is comprised of a face-to-face class, either in a central facility or in field offices to which a trainer is sent in each location. But traditional training cannot keep pace in an era when technical obsolescence of an employee's skills can occur within 5 years of graduation from training. Increased competition, driven by accelerated product obsolescence (decreasing product life due to shorter development and marketing cycles) also impacts the necessity for constant and ongoing training. For instance, the average shelf life of a personal computer is less than 9 months. At HP, 50 percent of revenues are generated with products introduced within the last 2 years—a very rapid turnover of products. With limited product life and rapid product development, the pressure to accomplish training goals within a limited time frame is enormous.

HP's field engineers became vulnerable during the 1980s, when the accelerated development of new products was coming faster than technology updates could be transmitted. The interval between new product release and the accomplishment of marketing/training functions had to be cut dramatically. Training was struggling to keep up with the technology—field engineers were required to learn more in less time, but there wasn't enough time.

Traveling trainers, sent from corporate headquarters to the company divisions and field offices, can take months to deliver training to all sites. The optimal solution is to bring the training to all the employees at the same time—have the subject expert or panel of experts deliver the same information to all company sites simultaneously via some reliable and proven technological delivery system such as satellite. Tom Wilkins, an R & D manager for Distance Learning products at HP, says, "Between completion of course materials and delivery, a critical gap develops, sometimes as long as six months. The longer it lasts, the more likely it is that the training will be outdated before it can be delivered to the students."

Traditional classroom training will become increasingly less viable in terms of delivery time, cost, and user downtime, since rapid changes in technology and product obsolescence are becoming the norm across industries. A company needs to train its people on new products or communicate new strategies in a way that collapses time and distance. The challenge will be to retrain employees while maintaining competitiveness, reducing soaring costs, and managing limited time.

Training to compete

If companies are to remain competitive, it is necessary that they plan for and quickly identify opportunities in a world that is truly becoming a global village. Local, parochial markets are disappearing, forcing organizations to either be responsive to changing market conditions or perish.

It is impossible for most corporations to be successful today without a worldwide strategy. In the 1960s, only 6 percent of U.S. business was exposed to international competition—today it's more than 70 percent, and increasing. At HP, more than half of its revenues come from overseas markets.

Frequent training and effective communication are fundamental if a company is to be responsive to changing markets and products and achieve a competitive advantage. Owing to evolving technology, collaborative management, and market-responsive production, a premium is now placed on employees who are multiskilled, multitrained, and who can be easily reassigned as needed.

"America's competitors in other countries commit significant resources to building a well-trained work force," but the United States has the "lowest percentage of spending on training compared to all the nations we...compete with" in Europe and in Japan.[3] In the United States the amount spent on upgrading employees' skills is only about 3 percent of what is spent on capital improvements to plant and equipment. Yet "the gains in productivity from workplace learning exceed the gains from capital investment by more than two to one."[3]

In today's global economy, the United States can no longer compete on the basis of mass production alone. We must respond faster to market needs and dramatically shorten product life cycles, bringing products to market in record time. Time-to-market will be crucial, with companies dependent on a smaller work force that must continually revise skills and use more technology in order to compete.

The Training Solution

In spite of the traditional classroom's inability to keep pace with growing training requirements, there has been a serious underutilization of available technology that could be used to solve the training/education dilemma.

For a company that needs to update and quickly train geographically dispersed employees, delivering a consistent message worldwide, there is one technology that will enable them to quickly and efficiently respond to the training challenge: distance learning. Distance learning (DL) is an electronically assisted teaching/learning environment in which teacher and student are geographically separated, rely on electronic devices, and interact within a format that closely resembles the traditional classroom.

In the past, technology has focused on improving discrete instructional tools and access to outside information. The new generation of technology is aimed at creating a "virtual classroom" where artificial or physical boundaries are removed. Students in different locations across the country not only observe and listen but participate and become involved in subject matter that is delivered by the most knowledgeable and effective learning facilitators available and flavored by applicable, real-world case studies.

An effective DL environment creates a virtual classroom by using a telecommunications channel (i.e., satellite telecast) to link people at a number of locations. Interactive, two-way communication and real-time feedback is provided, which encourages the users' active participation. Given this technology, class size is unlimited, time and distance boundaries are removed, and the student has direct access to experts. Corporate training can be conducted quickly and cost-effectively.

Training via HP's Interactive Network grew out of a strategic need to provide a cost-effective and rapid delivery system for continuous information transfer from the factory to worldwide field sales and support groups. Sixty percent of HP's technical field people now participate in DL (see Fig. 4.1).

In adopting a new training technology, a valid criterion to consider is whether it lowers cost and decreases time while maintaining or exceeding quality. HP has found that DL can deliver more training simultaneously to all locations, for lower cost with consistent quality. Instead of sending instructors to the field, one expert presents the same message to everyone, at the same time, across multiple sites. It certainly is more efficient than physically moving people across the country to training classes. The ability to share resources through technology is also a viable alternative to building more buildings and individual classrooms. DL can maximize resources and combine assets with other groups to produce programming.

DL is a strategic solution for corporations—an effective means to train employees quickly, cost-effectively, and with enhanced quality, for the training is delivered undiluted by an expert. DL can be a crucial part of an enterprise's strategy to better manage and continually improve its competitive position.

A Distance Learning System

Description

In the virtual classroom that a DL system creates, specially designed hardware and software enable real-time interaction between an instructor at a host site and students who may be located at multiple global remote sites. It employs two-way interactive telecommunications and electronic devices to teach from a distance.

There are various delivery technologies for DL to choose from: satellite, fiber optics, cable, codecs over telephone lines, and microwave. Computer-response units, scanners, facsimile machines, CD-ROM, videodisc, and radio also are utilized. For the purposes of focusing on larger numbers of students and widely dispersed receiving sites, satellite delivery best meets the objective.

Transmission via traditional analog satellite signals broadcasts audio and video to multiple receiving sites, with return audio and two-way data communication supported over conventional land phone lines. High-quality audio is paramount in learning environments; important considerations are speech delivered without excessive reverberation, noise, feedback, distortion, or the returning echo characteristic of a satellite transmission delay.

Figure 4.1 Participating in distance learning.

Video compression eliminates the redundant part of the analog signal, taking the analog video transmission and converting it to digital. With digital, there is no degradation of signal as it is retransmitted; and an additional benefit is that it requires significantly less bandwidth. Advances in digital compression will lower transmission costs, but more importantly will double or triple channel capacity (the number of channels that can be sent over any transmission medium).

A total distance learning solution (production, video, audio, and control system) is pulled together from various suppliers. A full integration of components requires expertise in audio, video, data, and control. This integration has been a barrier to market acceptance, because users do not have all the necessary expertise. Outside services usually are required for hardware/software installation and for test, design, production, training, and prototyping of the specific training/educational programming.

Let's consider the various configurations of communication technology presently available, and how they are applied.

Synchronous mode

One-way audio: radio program
Two-way audio: telephone conferences, radio talk show
One-way audio/one-way video: television program and videotape distribution

Asynchronous or virtual classroom

Two-way audio/two-way video: videoconferencing with compressed digital over telephone lines

The most economic and effective configuration for training environments is

Two-way audio/one-way video: DL transmitted over a high-quality analog satellite to multiple sites over a vast area

The virtual classroom simulates the feeling of a large number of students sitting in one classroom together, even though they are physically dispersed. Technology is applied seamlessly, and it is the most transparent to learners and instructors when the TV-quality image is maintained and the two-way questioning/answering process is unimpeded. Interaction is supported through computer-assisted response devices and communication technologies that enhance further feedback.

System configuration

For simplicity, DL configurations include a host site, mode of signal transmission, and receiving sites, as shown in Fig. 4.2.

Host site.   The program originates from the host site, a studio classroom from which the session is broadcast. This teleclassroom includes a lectern/console where an instructor has the ability to either take complete control of the console features or have the production crew handle them. The lectern is equipped with a computer-based console that facilitates interaction between the instructor and students at remote sites through voice or electronic question-and-answer, as shown in Fig. 4.3.

The broadcasting facility, or uplink, is equipped with a control room where a technician has duplicate controls to assist the instructor if needed. It may

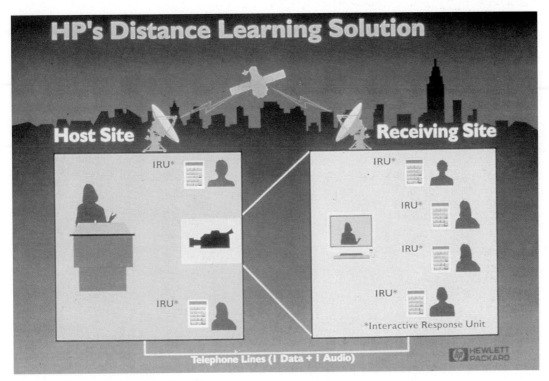

Figure 4.2   Distance learning configuration.

also include a director's console, various special-effects generators including VideoShow, stillstore, animation, chromakey (for displaying and annotating one image in combination with another), and camera and sound system controls. Video editing and duplicating equipment might also be included in this facility.

Transmission chain.   The first mile of communication link between the studio and satellite uplink usually consists of cable, fiber optics, microwave, laser, or telephone land line. The program signal is delivered to an uplink antenna or dish, then transmitted to a geosynchronous satellite in a fixed position 22,300 miles above the equator. Satellites have transponders (video channels) that receive and retransmit the video signal. If a broadcast is encrypted, the encoder or scrambler is colocated with the uplink and each receiver location needs a decoder to unscramble a broadcast.

Receive sites.   A satellite downlink receives and decodes the satellite signal into channels. Equipment configurations may include satellite dish; low-noise block converter; satellite video receiver; decoder for encrypted, scrambled code to maintain confidentiality and security; connectors; power supply; and video display.

Figure 4.3   Electronic Q & A. (*Source: Hewlett-Packard Company.*)

Interactivity.   This distinguishes DL from one-way, passive, instructional television. Interactivity allows each student to join in with the instructor and with the other students, giving a sense of being connected with the remote class members and facilitating their active involvement. Interaction is accomplished via telephone, two-way audio, video, and two-way electronic text and/or graphics interactivity. Interactive response units (IRUs) or keypad devices allow remote and local students to interact electronically with the instructor and among themselves during live classes. With IRUs, students can receive quick and meaningful feedback and actively participate when directly linked with the instructor. Instructors also receive immediate feedback from compiled student responses to numerical or multiple-choice questions via the interactive keypad system, and are able to immediately assess the students' comprehension of the material and thereby modify the content, rate, or presentation style in real time. A database can be used to gather all the transactions for later evaluation and analysis.

Instructor Preparation

When instructors are under pressure to improve efficiency in training, their choices typically are either to change the technology, change the way they teach, or some combination of the two. The task at hand involves putting the technological pieces together via system integration—bringing proven hardware and software into the mainstream of training.

The first obstacle for instructors to overcome is the paradigm shift from traditional, central training to DL, and one determining factor for acceptance is whether the technology is transparent to the learning. If the technology overwhelms the instructional process instead of serving as an effective teaching tool, then this approach will be resisted. Technology must be practical and easy for students and instructors to use. The goal is to take the face-to-face training environment and make the technology "invisible" so both the instructor and students can be actively involved in the learning process.

Production staff

There are production staff who can aid the instructor and ensure that the technology does not inhibit the process. The instructor is then free to concentrate on content and leave the production to the experts, who might include

Administrator.   Schedules the facilities and satellite time, organizes timely distribution of materials to all remote sites.

Remote site (field) coordinator.   Communicates directly with each receiving site coordinator. Reserves room and equipment, sets up a room for satellite signal receiving, troubleshoots technical problems, arranges participants' question procedure, and follows up with student evaluations.

Producer.   Oversees the entire production. Conducts initial meeting to define what is needed and to advise the instructor on techniques, resources, media, and production methods. The producer facilitates the process and makes sure the instructor's teaching aides (e.g., live product demonstrations, videotapes) are properly integrated into the class.

Director.   Works with instructor and directs the crew during rehearsal and broadcast to plan and select the best way to "shoot" the program, timing and pacing, camera angles, placement of graphics.

Additional crew (when necessary).   Videotape recorder operator, additional camera operator, character generator/graphics operator, production assistant.

Instructor skills

Televised teaching requires skills different from traditional teaching. Instructors need to familiarize themselves with the studio environment, the control room, and computer console, and learn new teaching skills for telecourses. An array of electronic educational tools including stored graphics, animation, videotape (roll-ins), drawing tablets, and remote cameras will need to be mastered so that they can be effortlessly incorporated in the program, as shown in Fig. 4.4.

Since timing is critical, there must be detailed organization of the class and explicit preplanning of the presentation. You should

- Develop a script to ensure that broadcast time constraints are adhered to.
- Establish procedures for course administration (e.g., fielding student questions and distribution/retrieval of materials).
- Foster new presentation skills suited to the medium, such as responding to camera movement, cueing, and speaking directly to the camera in an unhurried fashion while occasionally varying the tone of voice.

Figure 4.4 Learning console. (*Source: Hewlett-Packard Company.*)

- Select clothing with bright and bold colors but avoid plaids, stripes, and patterns that cause video interference.

- Orchestrate frequent interaction with students through predefined questioning strategies that stimulate discussion.

- Practice and rehearse in order to perfect timing and transitions, and to become comfortable with the technological tools. This is an extremely important objective; the instructor should be comfortable enough to easily focus on the student and use the technology to modify the course pacing or content to meet students' needs.

Benefits of Distance Learning

Using technology for technology's sake can often prove less than optimal. However, a new training methodology or technology should be adopted if it meets two objectives:

1. Reduces costs associated with conventional training by reaching more students in less time

2. Provides effective learning as well as, or better than, conventional face-to-face training

Distance learning fulfills these needs by offering the following benefits:

1. *Time savings.*   Content presented by a single source is received in many locations simultaneously and instantly. Information is disseminated to all employees at once, not just to a few at a time. Travel is reduced, there is less "down" time, and productivity is maintained without travel disruption or the need for "catch-up" time. DL can greatly reduce the time required to retrain a large, geographically diverse population and deliver time-critical messages immediately.

2. *Larger audiences.*   More people can attend. The larger the audience, the lower the cost per person. Delivery to the workplace at low cost provides the access to training that has been denied lower-level employees. A company can increase the number of students trained without increasing training resources and can eliminate or minimize trickle-down training, road shows, and information "gate-keepers."

3. *Lower costs.*   Travel, meals, and lodging costs are reduced by keeping employees in the office. In addition, lost opportunities for revenue generation are diminished, since field sales personnel get the necessary training with minimal disruption to their time spent with customers. HP continually has experienced significant cost reductions in delivering DL (compared to centralized training), with an average return on investment of $20 million per year over the last 5 years. The initial cost to install the entire studio and control room was paid for with the first two-week teleclass delivered to 750 students worldwide.

4. *Improved learning.*   HP surveys students to evaluate DL teleclasses, and results show that consistently more than 70 to 80 percent select interactive teleclasses as the optimal method for instructional delivery—students felt they learned more than in a conventional classroom. This is further supported by institutional and business studies which demonstrate that training at a distance is as effective as face-to-face training.

5. *Limited expertise leveraged across locations.*   The expertise of the best instructors can be delivered to thousands of people without sending trainers to conduct numerous training sessions at various locations. Topical experts spend more time in the office doing research and productive work rather than traveling. Each student, no matter how large the class, has direct access to the experts rather than to another representative instructor "trained by the trainer."

6. *Accessibility and flexibility.*   With a remote transmit or receive truck, a transmit or receive site can be located anywhere in the world; a benefit of the pervasive nature of satellite delivery.

7. *Usability.*   Useful for business, associations, hospitals or universities to present, inform, train or educate. Company updates, training, meetings, and other events can be broadcast live to multiple locations.

8. *Security.*   Encryption keeps out unauthorized outside viewers and protects confidential data.

9. *Interactivity.*   This defeats the boredom and passivity of one-way television classes. DL requires greater emphasis on involvement strategies and methods than traditional, teacher-centered strategies. A condition of effective learning is an environment where ideas can be freely communicated. Students receive not only visual and audio stimuli, but through interactivity (i.e., quizzes, telephone dialogue, and surveys) they participate in active, experiential ways. With distance learning the students can interact with the instructor when they need more discussion, enabling the instructor to respond to questions in real time, which is critical to students' learning and retention. Interactive keypads provide for immediate response and feedback, a crucial element since a student who does not receive feedback in a timely fashion quickly becomes demotivated. The dynamic exchange of ideas and questions keeps students alert, makes them feel they are involved and participating, and increases information retention and comprehension.[4]

Future Directions

The next decade promises greater access to and expansion of national and international education and training networks utilizing interactive telecommunications. The traditional classroom at a central location, or alternatively "train-the-trainer" strategies, are being displaced by real-time interactive virtual classrooms at regional locations where instructor and students no longer need to be in the same place at the same time.

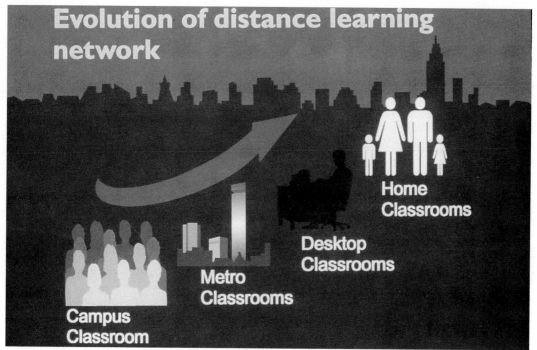

Figure 4.5   Distance learning network. (*Source: Hewlett-Packard Company.*)

The next major step will be toward workstation-to-workstation training and education that will replace DL studio-to-receiving-sites classroom training. Multimedia, interactively manipulating text, images, animation, graphics, sounds, digitized voice, and video, will enhance the desktop as the premier delivery vehicle.

Eventually, encapsulated training packages will be delivered on demand—individualized training that is self-paced and delivered when and where a student needs it. Students will have the ability to acquire new skills and knowledge when they need them, where they need them, and in as much depth as they need them, as shown in Fig. 4.5. Responsive training, delivered to the workstation, will enable employees to meet the demands of an increasingly competitive global marketplace.

Given rapid product development and changing worker skills requirements, it is critical that a training system be (a) distributed and (b) just-in-time. Training will be responsive to the individual's needs, taking place when and where needed. Multimedia will provide the necessary visual and auditory stimuli and facilitate interactivity. The components will be modular, so that the student need select only those training elements that are demanded for the immediate task.

The virtual classroom returns full circle, focusing once again on the individual student's needs. The future promises to be a time of individual freedom and control, in which the important skills required to efficiently compete in an ever-changing world economy can be easily revised and enhanced as needed.

References

1. Naisbitt, John and Aburdene, Patricia, *Reinventing the Corporation,* Warner Books, New York, 1985.
2. Roelandts, Willem P., "Distance Learning Solution," keynote address to Telecon XII, San Jose, CA, October 1992.
3. Portway, Patrick S. and Lane, Carla, "Corporate Training," in *Technical Guide to Teleconferencing and Distance Learning,* Applied Business Telecommunications, pp. 279–315, 1992.
4. Lane, Carla, "What is Teleconferencing?", in *Business Television and Distance Education: Partnerships in the 90s,* An ITVA Industry and Education National Videoconference Resource Manual, pp. 10–12, Feb. 12, 1992.

Imaging as a Corporate Multimedia Tool

Tim Picraux

Paper versus Images

Most organizations use some form of micrographics (i.e., microfilm or microfiche) as their archival storage medium of choice. Popular for well over a decade as an efficient and cost-economical storage medium for seldom-used but still important company documents, micrographics was seen as the perfect solution for historical or "passive" paper. But passive paper accounts for only a small percentage of an organization's paper flow. For there to be a discernible increase in productivity and quality, organizations must somehow be able to manage their "active" paper as well.

Managing active paper flow is perhaps the key component of the work-flow analysis process. Although a technique that has been practiced for years, the current emphasis on business reengineering has brought work-flow analysis to the fore.

Work-flow analysis examines the organization and the processes within it to find ways to significantly improve productivity and/or quality. In short the analyst, or a team of analysts, studies the various interdepartment and intradepartment business processes to pinpoint areas of improvement. Interestingly, the precursor to this technique was born of micrographics' younger cousin: imaging.

Imaging as a Work-Flow Paradigm

Whereas micrographics is limited both by its storage medium (i.e., fiche or film) and its relatively unsophisticated software and hardware environment, imaging suffers from neither limitation. Whereas micrographics was limited solely to the passive archiving of paper, imaging can be an active participant in the day-to-day interactivity of the typical work process.

This robustness alone accounts for the dramatic growth in the imaging market. According to BIS Strategic Decisions in Norwell, Massachusetts, the imaging market doubled in 1992 to $2.35 billion. And in a recent member survey by the Association for Information and Image Management, 56 percent of those responding said they were using imaging today, while another 29 percent said they were investigating it.

The benefits of imaging are manifold: work reduction and elimination; reduced costs; improved customer service; improved utilization of resources; better use of information; faster and more informed decision making; reduced time to market; expanded revenue opportunities; enhanced corporate image; increased flexibility; higher quality; and, ultimately, increased control by management and staff alike.

When imaging vendors first entered the organizational fray, what they found was a web of interconnected business processes that were largely unstructured, sometimes irrational, and always less than efficient. To sell their wares, vendors were forced to "prove" the worthiness of their products by implementing not only imaging systems but more efficient work flows as well. And although the concept of work-flow analysis was by no means invented by imaging vendors, these same vendors are largely responsible for fine-tuning the technique and perhaps even making it a part of the popular vocabulary.

Today, work-flow analysis is a subset of reengineering and is performed by a wide variety of professionals, from systems integrators to work-flow consultants to the imaging vendors themselves. The dramatic growth in the numbers of this breed of professional is at least partially attributable to the newer, faster, and more robust imaging environments now available.

The Imaging Environment

Imaging shares some of the basic features of the older micrographics systems. Systems consist of at least four components: a scanner (facsimile machines are often used as well), a printing device, an end-user workstation, and a storage medium. But there the similarity ends.

Whereas micrographics systems merely captured the "still" image of a document, imaging systems are powered by robust environments that permit a wide range of "interactivity" with the document. This feature set includes

- Rapid retrieval of document
- Retrieval and simultaneous viewing of a document by multiple viewers
- Ability to "zoom in and out" on any level of magnification
- Ability to "pan" the document in any direction
- Ability to rotate the displayed image
- Ability to display one or more overlays, or electronic transparencies, for a single document
- Ability to mark up imaged documents with text and graphical annotations

- Extensive editing capabilities, including the capability to copy, cut, paste, merge, and erase documents or portions of them, as well as manipulate document graphics

- Permanent storage of revised documents

- Ability to print on a wide variety of devices, including plotters, located throughout the organization

But today's very highly automated organizations require even more. They require that today's imaging systems be well integrated with the organization's existing applications, systems, and networks. This means that integration goes well beyond providing accessibility to the imaged document base across a wide range of heterogeneous hardware platforms. Integration also extends to enabling the end user to merge an image document to the very application that he or she is working with. For example, if an end user is working with Microsoft's Excel spreadsheet, there should be no barrier to being able to store the spreadsheet along with one or more complementary documents.

The Folder Metaphor

Vendors, for the most part, have tailored their generic systems to specific vertical industries (e.g., insurance, engineering), such that end users are provided an electronic desktop with familiar tools using the vocabulary of their particular industries. However, the concept of the "folder" can serve as an apt metaphor to explain how imaging works in general. But we must explain the concept of the automated folder in the context of the entire imaging process.

Scanning the document

In this first step of the process, scanners or fax machines can be used to convert hard copy into what is referred to as *raster data*. In selecting an input device, organizations should be aware that there is some variability in the quality of the output, which is largely dependent on the scanner used as input. Documents imaged with simple facsimile devices have a lower-overall-quality image than those imaged with a high-resolution scanner device. Measured in dots per inch (dpi), a rule of thumb is that the higher the dpi the better the resolution. In general, high-quality scanners scan at a resolution level of between 200 and 400 dpi. Additionally, different models of scanners vary in their speed anywhere from 8 pages a minute up to 50 pages a minute. Since scanners can be networked, several staff members working in tandem can scan quite literally thousands of documents a day.

Converting it to text

Although not all organizations require this functionality, today's robust imaging environments have the ability to convert imaged text into usable text through optical character recognition (OCR). What this means is that an end user can import text from a scanned document directly into his/her word processor.

Storing the document

Whereas micrographics systems stored documents on off-line microfilm and microfiche, imaging systems store documents directly on-line; therefore, these are always immediately available to the end user. Although magnetic disk (sometimes referred to as *hard-disk*) technology has been available for quite some time, newer advances in optical technologies have provided greater storage capacity at vastly reduced prices (i.e., an optical disk contains approximately 5.6 Gbytes of data, which translates roughly to 120,000 to 150,000 pages and costs just a few hundred dollars). Optical disks, which physically resemble CDs but can be as large as an LP record, use the light of a laser to etch information bits onto the surface of the platter. Although there are other, more expensive, technologies that permit both multiple-reads and multiple-writes, the preponderance of imaging systems use what is referred to as *WORM* (write once, read many).

Indexing the document

Whereas storage of the document relies on the attributes of the hardware, success in indexing the document very much relies on the sophistication of the software. Indexing itself can be viewed as a means to an end. The ultimate goal of indexing is to provide the organization with the ability to quickly retrieve the document by its important attributes. For example, a loan application might be indexed by loan identification number, name of applicant, geographic location, and so on. Although most imaging systems do offer the ability to browse, the availability of indices quickens the search process dramatically. Since indices are crucial to the ultimate success of the imaging system, it follows that determining what they are is an important process. This is truly the domain of the work-flow analysts. Performed by in-house staff, consultants, or systems integrators who know the business the organization is in, the critical task is to analyze the document in the context of the entire organization, not just look at it in its own right. For example, in our loan example above, a work-flow analysis could conceivably determine that loan documents should also be indexed by the loan officer, providing management with oversight capabilities.

Retrieving the document

While the document itself is stored on optical media, the indices can be stored on a database located in the organization's computer. If the imaging environment adheres to either de facto or de jure standards, organizations will have a variety of means to access their information. Whereas a standards-oriented imaging environment adheres to the CCITT (Consultative Committee for

International Telegraph and Telephone) Group 3 and Group 4 standard for facsimile transmissions, the same imaging environment should follow set standards that enable organizations to access documents outside of their imaging software. For example, indices stored in a proprietary database preclude organizations from using the index database in any of their applications. But an index database using the SQL (Standard Query Language) standard is immediately accessible to all. In nonopen, or proprietary systems, the imaged document often cannot be accessed by other systems or applications. An open system stores documents in an easily readable format such as TIFF (Tag Image File Format), which is a de facto standard file format designed to promote the interchange of digital image data and which easily provides access to the images from other systems and applications.

But if the imaging environment is truly robust, organizations need never go outside of it to access their document data. Using a folder metaphor, these systems contain advanced functionality for document management fully integrated within the automated environment with which the user is fully familiar. The end user need never leave his or her desk to walk over to an "imaging workstation." Instead, he or she could access the document(s) in question right at the PC on the desktop. The features of a robust imaging-integrated desktop environment include

- Compliance with the predominant windowing standards of a workstation, including Windows and Unix.

- Direct access at the user's desktop to information on existing mainframe computers.

- Storage of applicable documents and corresponding word processing documents and spreadsheet documents in an automated folder similar to the paper folders of yore. For example, a loan image would be stored in an automated folder alongside a spreadsheet that contained the loan worksheet and any letters that were sent to the customer.

- Ability to perform index searches and nonindex browsing, as well as boolean logic. Boolean search logic provides the organization with sophisticated exception reporting. Using our loan example, we could use boolean search logic to find those documents "where loans were over $70,000, customers were located in New York, and the loan was for a secondary residence."

- Ability to attach annotational notes to documents.

Controlling the Work Flow

Most imaging systems provide the organization with the technology to ably process the work flow within the organization. Some more robust imaging environments, however, provide management and control capabilities as well. Over and above basic routing of paperwork, advanced imaging systems provide event management. This ultrasophisticated software provides the bonus of being able to create site-specific work flows; represent the work flow graphically; test the work flow with a simulation capability; route work loads; set priorities; query the status of work-in-progress; as well as provide supervisor control to manage and reallocate work loads.

Imaging solutions are applicable to any type of industry, although banking, insurance, government, and manufacturing tend to be the technology leaders. But the attributes of these four industries are really generic to industry-at-large. Most organizations suffer from too-large paper flows, interdependent business processes, and a requirement for real-time access to their information resource. Ultimately, organizations that implement an imaging solution will increase productivity and quality—and also gain entry into the very heady world of multimedia.

A Short Imaging Glossary

Archival.   Readable (and sometimes writable) for a long time; "long" can mean from 5 to more than 100 years.

Boolean capabilities.   A feature of document-indexing software that permits the logical coordination of two or more index search specifications.

Browsing.   A system's ability to find an undefined feature or set of features in a database.

CCIT Group 3 and Group 4.   International compression/decompression standards for black-and-white images specified by the Consultative Committee for International Telegraph and Telephone (CCITT); the international standard for facsimile communications.

COLD (Computer Output to Laser Disk).   A system used to control the transfer of computer-generated output to optical disk for on-line or off-line storage.

Compression.   Conversion of a digital image to a lower number of bits for storage.

Compression algorithms.   Procedures according to which digital data sets representing images are compressed. Some of the most successful of these are contained in the CCITT Group 3 standards for digital facsimile.

Decompression.   Reconstruction of a compressed image for display or printing.

DPI (dots per inch).   A measurement of resolution referring to the number of pixels per inch on a workstation display monitor.

Folder management system.   A computer-based system that provides for the electronic capture, storage, distribution, annotation, display, and printing of images previously available only on paper or other hard-copy media. The emphasis of a folder management system is on the file folder, which contains multiple documents of varying numbers of pages and for which the tracking of work flow is important.

Jukebox.   An automatic selection-and-retrieval device that provides rapid, on-line access to multiple optical disks.

Optical disk.   A platter-shaped medium coated with an optical recording material.

ODSR (Optical Disk Storage and Retrieval).   A mechanical device that manages multiple WORM (Write Once, Read Many times) optical disks.

Optical storage.   Technologies, equipment, and media that use light—specifically, light generated by lasers—to record and/or retrieve information.

Platter.   A large, round disk for storing information.

Scanner.   A device that resolves a two-dimensional object, such as a business document, into a stream of bits by raster scanning and quantization.

TIFF (Tag Image File Format).   A de facto standard file format designed to promote the interchange of digital image data.

WORM (Write Once, Read Many times).   An attribute of certain optical disks. Once information has been "burned" into a sector of the disk it cannot be deleted or overwritten, but can be read any number of times.

Multimedia at Your Fingertips

Issues and Practical Implementations for Managing Multimedia Information

Rudy Prokupets

Multimedia is fundamentally changing the way we use information on our desktops. Personal computers traditionally presented information as text and graphics. Only very recently have certain breakthrough technologies evolved to become affordable and usable by personal computers. Audio technology has matured such that, with current hardware and software, users can record, play, and edit high-quality music, sound effects, and voice. The ability to play full-motion video in a scalable window on a desktop computer brought an array of video overlay boards to replace the very expensive still frame capture boards of yesterday. Newer boards added the ability to record compressed full-motion video onto a computer's hard disk, and new software integrates compression to minimize file size requirements. The capability now exists to take an analog video signal and convert it to a digital file, in real time and on a desktop. It will soon be possible to create high-quality digital movies on computer. In short, the era of inexpensive video on a desktop PC is now arriving.

At Your Fingertips

With the explosive growth of the new market for multimedia, many end users, application developers, and content providers face the problem of how to effectively organize, manage, and instantly access the vast amount of multimedia information they accumulate. One major stumbling block is the tremendous diversity of incompatible file and media formats for audio, digital and analog video, animation, graphics, and text. Another problem is the growing number of incompatible multimedia peripherals and "computer-ready" consumer devices, such as full-motion video boards, camcorders, VCRs, and laserdisc players.

Software developers wishing to create new multimedia applications, or to incorporate multimedia into existing applications, usually must work in authoring environments. Typically these development environments are closed, requiring the developer to learn a proprietary scripting language. Even then, authoring environments sometimes offer only limited capabilities. Many developers would prefer to create applications using more familiar software tools. End users, too, would like to be able to add vitality to documents, spreadsheets, or presentations, and multimedia offers that extra dimension.

What's needed is software that can satisfy the requirements of users at all levels: casual users with home computers, software designers, business professionals. All of these people need software that can not only simplify working with multimedia information but also enable them to use that information in new and productive ways. If these fundamental user requirements are to be met, such software must allow the user to

- Organize, manage, and find when needed all sorts of multimedia information
- Retrieve and access all of his/her multimedia data, without having to move among several software packages
- Simplify working with a diversity of formats and peripheral devices
- Add multimedia to other software applications without having to become a multimedia expert

Multimedia Object Manager

The phrase "object-oriented" has become a buzzword in the computer industry; as such, it is often misused by many multimedia companies. Essentially, a multimedia object is any discrete piece of information that can be represented—displayed or played—by a computer. In a truly object-oriented environment, all information—regardless of its format, type, or location—is accessed by the user in the same manner. It doesn't matter if the object is a graphic element, an animation, or an audio file, a digital video clip or a video clip from an analog device.

This generic approach has distinct advantages for both software designers and end users. Developers can use object-oriented programming to create a library of reusable objects. Once tested, these objects do not need to be retested for use in other applications, and they provide a consistent object-oriented interface from application to application. End users benefit from the developers' ability to quickly and efficiently respond to customer needs with upgrades and new products.

Because multimedia deals with real-world objects, it lends itself well to object orientation. Many users who work with multimedia quickly encounter the problem of managing the great quantity of data that they accumulate. Whether you have a CD-ROM with tens of thousands of art clips, or just a hard disk full of audio segments, locating files pertaining to a particular subject or stored in a specific format can be a nightmare. If you are a Windows user, you can use File Manager to search by file extension, file name, or directory; or you can rely on your own recollection. Each of these approaches can be extremely time-consuming.

Fortunately, multimedia content- and object-management software has emerged to address this need. By simplifying the processes of organizing, retrieving, displaying, and using important information, these products maximize user productivity. An example of a *content manager* is Aldus's Fetch, designed for the Macintosh computers. By contrast, MpcOrganizer and MediaOrganizer from Lenel Systems are *object managers* for the Windows platform. Lenel's approach has been to develop products that integrate user-critical functions, are truly object-oriented by design, and provide a consistent, user-friendly interface.

The ideal multimedia object manager is a highly integrated, object-oriented software package with three important functional components (see Fig. 6.1). The Multimedia Cataloging Database organizes all information as objects, enabling the user to quickly locate and retrieve them when needed. Once objects have been retrieved, they can easily be displayed by the Universal Multimedia Player. Finally, the Universal Multimedia-Enabling Server simplifies the process of incorporating the objects into other applications. These capabilities will be described individually in the following sections.

Multimedia cataloging database

There are a number of features that make multimedia cataloging database software powerful, flexible, and simple to use. Most importantly, it should be able to organize and manage all media types and all popular formats. It should, for instance, be capable of cataloging

- Analog and digital video, including full-motion segments and still frames

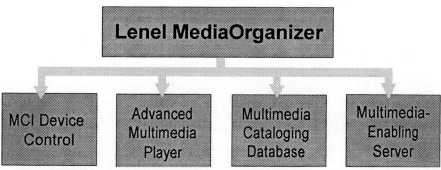

Figure 6.1 Integrated multimedia object manager.

- Scanned photographs, artwork, slides, and negatives
- Animation files
- Bitmap and vector graphics
- ASCII text and a variety of word processing documents
- Digital audio data from both audio CDs and audio files
- Data stored on hard-disk drives, diskettes, CD-ROMs, videotapes, and laserdiscs

It should even provide a method for cataloging nonelectronic reference materials: three-dimensional objects such as printed documents and magazine articles; folders containing hard-copy information; and artifacts.

The software should combine the power of a full-functioned relational database engine with a superimposed object-oriented layer. This will enable the user to create object records, collections of records, and databases with user-definable fields and free-text descriptions. It should support pointing device shortcuts such as drag-and-drop and double-click, to simplify record creation.

It should provide the ability to browse through records using visual representations such as object thumbnails. A *thumbnail* is a miniature view of an object. When organized into collections called *galleries,* multiple thumbnails can be quickly retrieved and simultaneously displayed. For optimal flexibility, galleries should not be limited in size.

Some software applications create thumbnails that each require 10 to 20 kbytes of disk storage. When such large thumbnails are embedded in a collection of object records, the results are very large records, excessive memory requirements, and a virtually unmanageable database. Keeping this in mind, we see that a cataloging database's object thumbnails should need no more than 5 kbytes to be useful in large database applications.

A user should be able to supply information to narrow the search for desired objects. The user should be able to locate objects using a single search criterion or multiple search criteria. Comparative searches specifying an *either/or* or an *and* condition should also be supported.

The software should support the use of thesauruses—collections of keyword synonyms enabling the user to search for and retrieve desired objects. With this feature, the user can create a thesaurus containing, for example, the synonyms *blue, lake, sea, river, liquid,* and *well* for the keyword *water.* Even a disorganized user would then be able to search the database for the keyword *water* and retrieve objects that were cataloged in association with *blue, lake, liquid,* etc. The user should also be able to generate reports of keyword and thesaurus search results.

Once an object has been located, the cataloging database software should provide automatic object playback. This implies that, as long as the computer has the capabilities to provide it, the user will be able to see a graphic or document, hear an audio clip, or see and hear full-motion video or animations. On-screen device controls should enable the user to adjust video attributes, sound volume, and size and position, if applicable.

Finally, well-designed cataloging database software should be flexible enough to allow access by multiple users on a network. If you work in a corporate environment, it's very important for you to be able to organize your data for use by your project team, department, or entire organization. This implies the ability to create, access, and update shared records, thesauruses, and databases, and the ability for multiple users to simultaneously play the same object on a file server.

Universal Multimedia Player

Whether you're a casual user with a computer that contains a little bit of everything, or a professional artist dealing with volumes of graphics and animations, if you work with multimedia, one of the first difficulties you encounter is how to display all of your files on your computer. For many of us, that means acquiring all of the necessary software and moving from package to package to view each type of file. This approach can be both costly and very time-consuming. Programs called *viewers* can display multiple formats of a single media type, but they don't address the great need for application software that can handle all formats—animations, audio, graphics, video, and documents—in a single environment.

This problem is compounded by the fact that virtually every industry-leading program has its own proprietary file format or formats. There are, for example, more than 20 widely used formats for graphics. Paint programs create files in formats such as BMP and PCX. Drawing packages work with formats such as CDR, DRW, AI, and WMF. Scanners often create files in TIFF format. Some on-line services and bulletin boards provide graphics in GIF format. None of these formats has become the industry standard, but many have become very popular. Even now, new formats, such as the Kodak Photo CD format for images, are being introduced. As a result, users frequently find themselves accumulating a large variety of files.

As new computer-based technologies have reached the commodity level, a growing number of incompatible multimedia peripherals and "computer-ready" consumer devices such as full-motion video boards, camcorders, VCRs, and laserdisc players have become available. Although some vendors provide device drivers with their equipment, such software often is designed with the technical end user in mind, making it difficult for others to use.

Some companies have understood these problems and have brought Multimedia Player software to the marketplace. Microsoft Windows includes Media Player. It's a good player but, unfortunately, it supports a very limited number of formats.

Lenel introduced the concept of a Universal Multimedia Player. With support for over 40 file formats, it can play graphics, documents, video from analog and digital sources, animations, and audio clips in all of the industry-leading formats.

A well-designed multimedia player should be intuitive enough to allow the user to play media objects using simple drag-and-drop or double-click methods.

In addition to all popular industry formats, it should fully support the Windows Media Control Interface (MCI) specification for controlling time-based objects and peripheral devices, such as analog and digital video, audio and VCR/laserdisc, and animation. This will enable the user to, if pertinent, adjust video attributes and sound volume on-screen as the object plays. The user should also be able to adjust the size and on-screen positioning of the object display window. The user should be able to make these adjustments quickly and easily, using features such as scroll boxes, radio buttons, and drop-down lists.

The user should be able to create a new object from an existing one—a portion of a video clip or audio segment—without having to make a copy of the original. Instead, the new object should include a reference to the original, thereby minimizing the new object's size. Furthermore, if the original object is an analog file, the new object could be digital and could be manipulated as such.

As an integral component of content management software, the universal multimedia player should provide auto playback of an object once the object has been located and retrieved by the cataloging database function.

Once a user has the capability to catalog, locate, retrieve, and play multimedia data, as well as the ability to control peripheral devices on-screen, it should be straightforward to string together a series of object plays to create dynamic multimedia presentations. A multimedia show combining text, graphics, analog and digital video, animations, and audio achieves greater message impact. The final component of an integrated multimedia content management package, a multimedia-enabling server, makes it easy for you to embed multimedia objects and shows into other applications.

Universal Multimedia-Enabling Server

The use of multimedia-enabling technology implies the ability to incorporate multimedia elements into other horizontal application software, such as documents, spreadsheets, and databases. You can bring an animation file into a word processing document, embed full-motion digital video in a graphic file, or add CD-quality audio to a spreadsheet. Multimedia can add vitality to an otherwise static file, increasing the effectiveness of your message.

There are a number of methods by which applications can be multimedia-enabled. These include object linking and embedding (OLE), cut-and-paste using the Windows clipboard, application macros, dynamic data exchange (DDE), a command line interface, and an application programming interface (API).

The two most powerful and flexible of these are OLE and an API (Fig. 6.2). An API has open architecture and is a set of functions. The functions can be accessed using traditional C function calls, or via the more innovative object-class libraries and visual controls. API functions provide high- and low-level device and data controls, resulting in much tighter integration than OLE. However, working with an API is strictly a programmer's task.

Figure 6.2 Multimedia-enabling technologies.

By contrast, object linking and embedding is interactive and doesn't require programming. A computer-literate end user can use OLE to add multimedia elements to other applications. When you *link* an object, you create a reference (link) to the source document in the destination document. When you *embed* an object, you make a copy of the object in the destination document. Embedding an object calls for a simple cut-and-paste operation.

OLE release 2.0 provides advanced features such as In-Place Editing and Automation, which enable users and developers to seamlessly integrate different object components—even entire applications—into new applications in very little time.

Applications that support OLE fall into two categories. *Servers* are applications whose objects can be embedded or linked into other applications. *Clients* are applications that can accept embedded or linked objects. An application can be both client and server. Most applications are being developed as OLE clients; very few are OLE servers.

Microsoft's Video for Windows and Gold Disk's Add Impact are multimedia-enabling servers. MultiMedia Works, from Lenel Systems, brought to the marketplace the first Universal Multimedia-Enabling Server, which allows you to integrate *any* multimedia objects into OLE-client applications and also includes API, Macro, and DDE interfaces.

A well-designed multimedia-enabling server should be flexible enough to allow users to integrate multimedia objects into other Windows applications using a variety of methods. This universality enables users to incorporate multimedia data into other commercial or custom applications using their method of choice. Novice users may prefer the cut-and-paste simplicity of the Windows clipboard and OLE. A software developer may prefer the flexibility and control of API functions.

A multimedia-enabling server should support all industry-leading formats for animation, audio, analog video, digital video, graphics, and text. It is especially important for the server to have a consistent user interface for all media types. Millions of individuals and corporations have video information stored on videotape devices, such as VCRs and camcorders. These devices essentially become information storage devices. The server should be able to control these analog devices, embed information from them into other applications, and treat that information the same way that it does digital information. Users should be able to incorporate analog objects into other software quickly and easily, without having to worry about the intricacies of device control and file manipulation.

Integrated solution

A recent poll by a leading personal computing publication found that a majority of users intend to use the forthcoming generation of computers for the following purposes (in order of preference):

1. Multimedia or video production
2. Database management
3. Application development
4. Personal productivity

If this is a reflection of typical needs, what then should a user look for to put multimedia at his or her fingertips?

The ideal multimedia management solution is an object-oriented, tightly integrated package that provides all of the capabilities just listed (Fig. 6.3):

- Content management with thumbnails
- Universal multimedia playback
- Universal multimedia server
- External device control

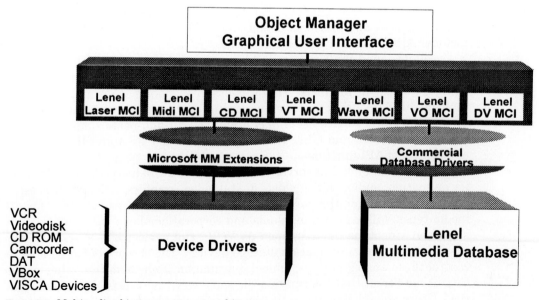

Figure 6.3   Multimedia object-management architecture.

Multimedia object-management software should be an integrated solution—the single solution to multimedia productivity. For this to be so, it must have a low cost/performance ratio. It must be capable of working with all industry-leading formats and media types. Furthermore, it must be positioned to proactively employ the emerging technologies and de facto standards of tomorrow. In short, it must be able to maximize the user's investment in hardware and software, even to the extent of adding multimedia elements to otherwise static software such as spreadsheets and documents.

It must be based on standards, avoiding proprietary interfaces. For the Windows user, this means supporting leading-edge technologies such as object linking and embedding (OLE) and media control interface (MCI). It must be powerful enough to give the user control over peripheral devices right from within the object management software.

Such a product should have a simple, intuitive, graphical user interface, employing flexible features such as a toolbar, context-sensitive help, "hotkeys," scroll bars, and buttons. The software should be simple enough such that users at all levels can immediately start to use the product's capabilities. It should be powerful enough to provide full relational database functions, yet intelligent enough to enable the user to execute these capabilities by simple mouse clicks or drag-and-drop actions.

A wise investment translates into long-term benefits for the user. For the casual user, high-quality object-management software takes the mystery out of working with multimedia, and provides a tool to organize and use information in new ways. For the professional, choosing well-designed multimedia object-management software can maximize hardware and software investment, provide a dramatic increase in productivity, create more effective business applications, and enhance message impact.

The Successful Multimedia Development Team

Expertise and Interaction

Mary F. Whiteside

J. Alan Whiteside

Expertise and Interaction: Components of a Successful Interactive Multimedia Project Team

Gone are the days when one or two individuals—usually a programmer and a designer or content expert—could create an interactive training program, especially if it involved multimedia. Creating an instructionally sound, sophisticated multimedia application requires individuals with a wide variety of talents and competencies to collaborate as a team. In other words, the way to meet clients' demands for technical and content sophistication in a multimedia program within today's amazingly short development time frames is by facilitating interaction among the members of a team who possess the required types of expertise for the project.

The skills required to execute a high-quality interactive multimedia project in today's business climate span a number of disciplines and departments or organizations. The development organization must be able to make smooth transitions from initial marketing contacts and project definition to analysis and design, through prototyping and actual development, to implementation and evaluation. The successful team should include one or more members of the client organization or department. Demonstrated expertise in a number of critical areas is essential if a project is to meet its objectives and stay within budget and time frame.

The field of multimedia is simply too broad and deep for one person to sufficiently comprehend it. Also the playing field changes almost daily, as new development approaches and technical functionalities leap onto the scene.

Generalists (those who have a working knowledge of several areas) are a mainstay of a team, because they can help to identify issues, synthesize information, ask insightful questions, and keep a team headed in the right direction. In fact, successful teams are composed of individuals who are continually gaining experience and knowledge in related areas.

A superior multimedia project team, however, will draw upon the collective knowledge and experience of "experts" in various fields related to the development of interactive applications. Expertise is here defined as *proficiency in or mastery of a given skill,* often combined with experience in using that skill in various circumstances. For an even relatively sophisticated project to be successful, the team should either include as members, or have access to, experts in a number of areas. The second half of this chapter lists many of the types of "experts" that a successful project team should include, along with their specific responsibilities.

Assembling a group of experts is not enough. If they are to succeed, the individuals must be unified as a team. Decisions made by one individual invariably affect many other team members. The very fact that there are more than one or two people developing the multimedia application means that more conscious communication among the individuals is required. Schedules must be agreed upon and set, with appropriate assignments made. The failure of one individual to meet the schedule can mean that a milestone is missed. Whenever more than one person is creating interactive sequences, consistency of style and approach is a concern. Another issue is whether some portion of content has been duplicated in another part of the program or whether sections of content have "fallen through the cracks" and haven't been included at all. From a positive perspective, when a group of individuals acts collaboratively as a team, productivity can be increased markedly, the voice of the customer can be more accurately discerned, and creativity can be enhanced.

This chapter cannot address the principles and practice of team building, interpersonal communication, or empowerment of employees. These topics are vital to an understanding of the "team of experts" approach to multimedia development, but they are the subjects of many enlightening articles and books. Instead, this chapter will focus on the need or rationale for both expertise and interaction on a successful project team.

The need for expertise

The need to have individuals with expertise in various areas either on or accessible to a multimedia development team can be substantiated from many perspectives. The situation is similar to that of an individual who needs medical attention. Generalists (in this case, primary-care physicians) play an integral part in the treatment of the individual, but specialists (experts in specific fields, such as orthopedists, surgeons, allergists, cardiologists, and radiologists) are called upon to consult with the principal physician in their specialty areas when necessary. In this way, needed expertise is brought to bear upon a problem. A similar relationship exists between experts in various disciplines and members of a successful multimedia development team.

The expertise required to develop multimedia applications can be broken down into three broad categories: (1) business/administrative, (2) instructional and artistic, and (3) technical. The business/administrative skills include, e.g., client relations; contract interpretation and negotiation; project scheduling; and team leadership. This type of expertise is provided mainly by the account representative, the project lead, and the program manager. (Specific responsibilities of all team members are detailed in the second half of this chapter.)

The instructional and artistic skills include, e.g., assessing end user/learner characteristics; specifying appropriate instructional strategies; defining and describing the subject matter or technical content for multimedia developers; evaluating courseware; importing, creating, and manipulating images of all types; and developing courseware with specified authoring tools. Instructional designers, multimedia developers, subject matter experts, and graphic artists typically provide these skills.

A multimedia development team also relies upon technical expertise, such as is required to: produce audio, photographic, and video elements for inclusion in the application; create software tools to facilitate the development of multimedia applications. Audio-video specialists and programmers or software engineers bring their skills to bear in this category.

Reasons are now given for including on a multimedia development team experts from each of these categories.

Client sophistication varies greatly.   Clients and potential clients span the spectrum of literacy about multimedia. Many have become well informed about the design, development, and delivery of multimedia, including issues in both the technical and instructional design domains. Other client contacts with little or no experience in this area have assumed, perhaps owing to the effects of downsizing, the responsibilities for implementing instructional or training programs.

An education effort on the part of the development team is therefore necessary to ensure that (1) the client understands the benefits and limitations of the technology solution being proposed; (2) the client's expectations match the services and products to be developed; and (3) the provisions of the contract are clear, especially with regard to ownership of the materials produced, client changes, and missed milestones. This education process typically is begun by the account representative. However, the program manager and project lead are, to the greatest extent, responsible for the business/administrative task of dealing with client expectations and ensuring that all come out of the project feeling successful.

Clients' expectation levels are rising.   Clients are expecting increased levels of sophistication and entertainment value in their final products. The artistic and technical members of the team are constantly challenged to be more creative and create added value in the multimedia products. For instance, we all have become accustomed to seeing intricate and engaging computer graphics on television and in films. Once clients have been tantalized by what they see and intrigued by reports of the latest breakthroughs in computer-delivered presentations, their expectations for a multimedia program are set. While some clients are coveting compact-disc-quality audio and full-motion video for their applications, this is not the full extent of their wish lists.

Individuals with expertise are required to implement other features, such as elaborate user or learner performance-measuring and -tracking systems that link to existing client databases. Creation of such tracking or monitoring systems requires programming or authoring system expertise, or both. Some multimedia applications (such as electronic performance support systems) require real-time links between the main program and external tools, such as the spreadsheets or databases that end users access as part of their jobs. Again, a programmer or authoring system specialist must be involved with the team. The development of specialized animation sequences, the creation of photorealistic graphics, and the incorporation of certain instructional strategies (such as giving a learner the ability to record and play back verbal responses to the program) also require distinctive expertise.

Multimedia demands new instructional approaches.   The instructional designer is responsible for designing effective informational or instructional programs. With the advancements being made in the hardware and software that support multimedia (e.g., increased desktop computing speed and power; wider bandwidths for increased transmission over networks; decreasing costs for storage space), new instructional approaches and solutions must be developed that will make use of the new opportunities while still ensuring that the program's objectives are met. The limitations of a few years ago have disappeared (remember CGA graphics, a maximum of 16 colors, and the single computer "beep"?). Technology has advanced to the point where we can now produce the kinds of informational and instructional applications that designers and developers knew should be created but that were unattainable, given the state of technology.

Also, the audiences who interact with a multimedia program have become more diverse, and multimedia solutions must speak to that diversity. Multimedia programs must be carefully designed to accommodate users who speak different languages, have different learning styles, reading levels, and years of experience with computers. Instructional designers also must keep in mind individuals with disabilities and cultural perceptions that may be different from the designers' perceptions (Schneiderman, 1992, pp. 26–31).

Given the new technological capabilities and the increasing instructional requirements, instructional designers and courseware developers must leverage the resources available and find new ways of ensuring that learners develop the required competencies. This will require using new types of interaction, such as having learners click and drag objects on the screen or record, play back, and critique their oral responses to questions. Leveraging the technology also means increasing the use of realistic simulations, scenario-based learning, and performance tracking, as well as a move toward techniques such as adaptive instruction/testing and intelligent tutoring.

Multimedia is a technically complex field.　More technical disciplines than ever before are represented within a successful multimedia development effort, and those disciplines are becoming increasingly complex. For instance audio, video, and sophisticated animation are relatively new to interactive programs, especially instructional applications. While instructional designers, content specialists, and programmers know something about each of these areas, expertise in them is rarely a part of their repertoire.

Similarly, graphics software has become both more functional and more complex, calling for additional skills from the graphic artist. The skills required of an artist to previsualize and then sculpt a three-dimensional object are different from those required for two-dimensional drawings. While new tools facilitate the construction of photorealistic three-dimensional graphic objects, artists must bring to bear on a project advanced visualization skills, as well as learn to use the new tools.

New authoring tools abound.　The range of multimedia authoring tools has expanded on every hardware platform, with each touting certain benefits. Sometimes a client specifies that multimedia development must be done with a certain tool (so that the client's own personnel can maintain the courseware). Not all projects will be completed on the same platform, and even on a given platform, some tools are more appropriate for certain projects than others. For instance, some multimedia tools are designed specifically for creating hypertext applications or linear presentations, while others are more appropriate for developing simulations or tutorials. Some tools create applications that will run under DOS, while others require the client to have Microsoft Windows installed on the delivery computer.

To be prepared for projects that fall into such different categories, the development group must be comprised of individuals who have technical expertise with different authoring tools. These individuals must not only be able to move efficiently from one tool to another depending upon the project, but often they must be able to understand the features, benefits, and limitations of each tool well enough to coherently explain them to clients and potential clients.

An integrated multimedia system is necessary.　The hardware and software components of sophisticated multimedia solutions are becoming so numerous and complex that it requires real dedication to read and assimilate all that is written, even about a relatively narrow topic. Only the systems analyst or integrator with a high level of expertise can recommend a complete and integrated system of hardware and software components that matches a client's needs.

Individuals with this type of expertise are also called upon to recommend or create special-purpose hardware or software tools for a multimedia application. For instance, new types of interaction devices (beyond the typical keyboard) have made dramatic appearances in the last few years. Pointing devices, once limited to function keys and alphanumeric keys, now include light pens, mice, touchscreens, trackballs, joysticks, and even voice input.

Occasionally, a unique interaction or pointing device is required to bring a higher level of fidelity to the program. The task of integrating such a device would most certainly fall to a systems analyst and/or software engineer.

The need for interaction

A successful team is much more than a group of individuals. Coordination and interaction are required to arrive at a successful solution within today's typical development time frames. Interaction among the various types of experts (including members of the client organization) is necessary because of the interrelatedness of the disciplines required for effective interactive program development. Several examples of the overlap will illustrate this requirement.

Changes in the workplace have meant that workers often need more than the one-shot training of a few years ago. Given the advent of electronic performance support systems (EPSSs), the need for a melding of technical and instructional design expertise has never been greater. Determining the types of supportive resources a user might need (such as database access, reference materials, glossaries, and coaching systems, as well as minitutorials on very specific topics) requires interaction between client representatives (most likely subject matter experts and master performers), instructional designers, and system analysts. Only with input from these sectors can the development of an effective multimedia program be ensured.

Other examples abound of tasks requiring the expertise of systems analysts and instructional designers. Consider how delivery platform choices have expanded since the term *multimedia* first gained prominence. A multimedia system can be configured with an internal or external hard drive. It may or may not be accompanied by a laserdisc player or a CD-ROM drive. The solution may not involve a computer at all, as in the case of CD-I or 3DO. Printers and audio speakers increasingly are becoming typical elements of a multimedia solution. Integrating all these components to reach a certain level of functionality often requires a skilled systems analyst or integrator.

The disciplines of graphic art and instructional design also must be correlated. For instance, a multimedia developer cannot request that a certain graphic be produced for a lesson without entering into the domain of the graphic artist. If the artist who receives the request is isolated from the project team, the resulting graphic may either be inappropriate for the program or not at all what the developer had in mind. The likelihood of this problem occurring is lessened if the artist is assigned to the project team, included as an integral member of the design meetings, and even physically colocated with the team.

Similarly, if the subject matter expert(s) from the client organization is (are) not made a functioning part of the development team, the content may not be represented accurately in the final program. The client's representatives also are less likely to "buy into" design decisions made by the team without substantive input and consideration of their perspectives. The subject matter expert is a prime protagonist for "the voice of the customer," and the administrative skills of the team must be used skillfully to bring to bear on the project the SME's technical skills.

The options for implementing multimedia programs are expanding with each new technology advance. For example, users may access multimedia programs via LANs (local-area networks), WANs (wide-area networks), or in a stand-alone mode. Decisions about implementation and maintenance of the application involve at least the business/administrative and the technical skills represented on the team.

Similarly, the methods of providing updated courseware or applications to the users have changed. No longer is it feasible for a single individual to have the responsibility of ensuring that all users have the latest version of the software. This process may be done via modem, over a company network, by sending users a new CD-ROM, or by various other means. The decision about which of these methods is best in a given situation must incorporate input from individuals who thoroughly understand the technical benefits, limitations, and constraints of each method, as well as from persons who understand the business implications of each option and can explain them to the client.

It is important to note that integrating a group of experts not only is essential to successful multimedia development, it also provides several important benefits for the development organization. These include: (1) enhanced productivity; (2) greater ease in discerning the "voice of the customer"; (3) formulation of more creative solutions; (4) the positioning of team members for professional growth.

Working smarter rather than harder is essential to a department's or company's profitability and viability. While it may seem at first that the "collaborative approach" requires more time to complete an interactive program than the "assembly line approach," interaction among members of a project team can result in significant productivity gains. When team members take joint responsibility for every major decision, there is less chance for confusion or for individuals to recklessly "do their own thing" at the team's expense. Also, barriers between functional areas can be reduced or eliminated when everyone has been identified as part of the project team. The process then becomes more important than departmental affiliations. As issues are discussed, various areas of expertise can be tapped to find creative approaches to problems and to keep individuals, and the team as a whole, from pursuing inappropriate or unproductive approaches.

For instance, while the graphic artist and the instructional designer may agree that the use of motion video would be beneficial at a given point in the program, if the team has been wise enough to include the systems analyst in the discussion he or she may object that the delivery platform specified by the client is not adequate to accommodate this type of solution. Similarly, an authoring system specialist who has been made part of the team may be able to construct a template that will automate the development of a certain type of interaction that the instructional designer wants to implement. This will save course developers a significant amount of time, since they will not have to recreate a particular sequence of code or icons in the authoring system every time that type of interaction is called for.

Hearing and understanding the voice of the customer throughout the project is crucial in multimedia development, just as it is in other business ventures. When a whole team (including members of the client organization) is involved in a give-and-take process, a clearer understanding of the desired outcome is achieved, and, very importantly, shared by all who contribute to the project. The inclusion of the client representatives goes a long way toward ensuring that the final outcome of the development process is a product that matches the expectations and needs of the customer. All members of the development team should first listen to their counterparts on the client's side or to the client representatives in general. Then they should provide input, based on their areas of expertise, about how best to use technology and sound instructional-message design principles to produce a product that is well received and effective in meeting the client's goals.

Taking the project team approach to interactive program development fosters creativity among the team members, and this is an important issue in multimedia development. Creativity by itself is not sufficient, but without it even the best instructional design may result in a dull, dry program. The informational goals or instructional objectives may even be compromised without an appropriately creative approach. An infusion of creativity among the developers can often make the difference between an adequate or mediocre program and an exceptional one.

Existing theoretical literature maintains that a person's level of creativity is directly related to his or her own interest in the work (intrinsic motivation). One organizational development consultant set up a research project in an effort to prove that "settings that encourage and promote individualized, unforced, even autonomous production boost intrinsic motivation and, accordingly, promote creativity" (Plunkett, 1988, pp. 68–71). In the experimental group (which received a participative management intervention), the participants showed an increase in feelings of input and participation. As determined by objective, independent judges, only the experimental group showed a definite and dramatic increase in creativity. Neither the placebo nor the control group showed a significant increase in creativity.

This study suggests that having a team of people shoulder the responsibility for a project is beneficial, in that more creative ideas are generated. Many organizations employing a project team approach could likely provide anecdotal support for this conclusion. Where participation and commitment to a project are increased, the creativity of the team members is likely to increase also.

One final benefit of having a collaborative, integrated multimedia development team is that each member is naturally positioned for professional growth as the group takes on issues, works through alternatives, and makes decisions that must be implemented. Each individual has a chance both to hear and to be heard in an open exchange of ideas, which can lead to a deepening and an extension of competencies as diverse perspectives are brought to the table. As multimedia screen design considerations are being discussed, for instance, graphic artists, instructional designers, subject matter experts, and others will have input. As differing opinions and views are expressed, team members should be evaluating their assumptions and biases about the new ideas, as well as the ideas themselves.

Summary of the case for experts and interaction

Without deliberate interaction among a team of experts charged with producing a multimedia product, several negative outcomes are likely. First, inappropriate multimedia solutions may be created that will not match the client's specifications, needs, or desires. These "solutions" may not be solutions at all; they may fail miserably to meet the program's stated goals and objectives. Second, productivity may suffer from lack of communication. If an expert doesn't know that an issue needs resolution, no solution is likely to be forthcoming, and the project schedule, budget, or both may suffer. Third, even if the application nominally meets the intended goals (e.g., the audience is adequately informed about a topic, or passes a posttest after a training intervention), the application may lack the cohesiveness, unity, and sparkle that a dedicated project team can provide.

On the positive side, designating a project team helps to ensure that all members are responsible for setting and meeting the schedule. Such an arrangement helps to bring focus to each individual's work efforts; he or she is part of a team whose goal is to complete a project they can be proud of on time and within budget. From a practical standpoint, project teams can contribute to higher-quality interactive solutions, individual growth of team members, and organizational productivity. From the perspective of client satisfaction, the creativity generated by interactions among a talented group of individuals is invaluable.

This approach to multimedia development may require a fundamental reorganization of a development organization's resources (physical and personnel). Internal shops that do not have in house all the expertise needed to complete a sophisticated multimedia project may have to rethink their approach to working with outside vendors and consultants. The project team is definitely the most efficient way to produce effective informational and instructional software that meets the client's needs, because it focuses everyone's attention and efforts on the "whole" rather than on isolated portions of the whole. Side benefits of the project team approach are that team members expand their horizons and learn new skills (thus becoming more productive and valuable to the company), and tend to bring more creative solutions to the design table. Furthermore, they can be genuinely proud that their input helped to shape a successful product.

Typical Team Roles and Responsibilities

Depending upon the scope and nature of the interactive multimedia project being considered, different types of expertise should be represented on the project team. The titles or designations described next are likely to differ from organization to organization, and responsibilities may be distributed differently. To a certain extent, the size of the development department or organization determines how the responsibilities are divided. Some individuals may "wear more than one hat." However, the key is to have all the functions covered by individuals who possess expertise in these areas.

While this is not an exhaustive list, each job discussed next is potentially important to the successful outcome of a multimedia project. The roles and responsibilities listed for each are recommendations. Since each multimedia development entity is different, modifications to the roles and responsibilities descriptions are likely.

Project lead/manager

The project lead is responsible for overseeing each phase of the project, from kickoff to completion and delivery. Planning, scheduling, and allocating resources are in the project lead's domain. This individual must be skilled in dealing with the administrative and business aspects of a project as well as the personnel and team-related issues. The project lead must also manage communication well, both among team members and between the team and the client representatives. Specific responsibilities of the project lead include

- Facilitating meetings between the client and the multimedia development organization
- Creating and monitoring

  Project schedule and budget
  Approval and sign-off process
  Roles and responsibilities
  Hardware and travel requirements
  Project team roles and responsibilities

- Managing the client review process and approval of each deliverable
- Acting as primary contact between client and multimedia development organization for project-management-related issues
- Communicating project status to multimedia development organization's management
- Setting project milestones and managing project to that schedule
- Coordinating approval/sign-off of materials with clients
- Selecting vendors for outsourced efforts

Program manager

The program manager brings business and administrative expertise to the team. While usually not a part of the everyday development activities, the program manager serves an integral function nonetheless by attending to contract-related issues, budgets, schedules, and resource requirements. In some organizations, especially those in which only a small number of projects are under way at one time, this function may be handled by the project lead or manager. Specific responsibilities of the program manager include

- Coordinating with all the development team project leads on

    Personnel assignments
    Milestone status vs. billing schedule
    Project personnel, and equipment resources and requirements

- Maintaining communication with client, especially on topics such as

    Overall project status
    Billing status
    Contract modifications

- Managing development-team budgets

Account representative/marketing representative

This individual's role in the multimedia development process also relates to the business/administrative aspects. The account representative initiates contact with a prospective client and provides the contact person(s) with the first glimpse of the development organization.

For outside vendors, it is important to communicate the salient features about one's company and why it should be the vendor of choice for a given project. While this process is begun by the marketing representatives, it often requires reinforcement from team members with expertise in the various technical disciplines.

Once an initial contract with a client has been secured, each member of the team becomes a selling agent, reinforcing the client's choice of vendors and assisting in the education process so that additional contracts will come with less intensive marketing efforts.

The account representative usually is responsible, throughout the life of the contract, for ensuring that effective communication is maintained with the client and that the "voice of the client" is heard and understood by the development team. When wearing this hat, it is important that the account representative not "oversell" the organization's capabilities or underestimate the time and budget required to produce what the client has in mind. Typical responsibilities of the account representative in this area include

- Ensuring that funding for the project being considered exists in the client organization

- Providing to the client sufficient background information about the development organization

- Describing for the client the types of services available to it through the development organization

- Gaining an initial determination of the type of need and/or project in which the client is interested
- Communicating to the development organization's management the scope of the project under consideration and the degree of probability that it will be funded

Instructional designer

The instructional designer (sometimes there is more than one) is the cornerstone of a multimedia development team. This individual's educational and experiential background is crucial in bringing together into a unified whole from the seemingly disparate fields represented on a development team, the team's principles, approaches, and ideas. The fields of graphic art and instructional design, and the various technical domains, should be given equal consideration in the multimedia application to be developed, and the instructional designer is key to this effort.

In general, this person is responsible for the processes used to develop the multimedia program and, if it is to be an instructional piece, for the effectiveness of that program. More specifically, the tasks of the instructional designer include

- Directing the technical activities of course developers, graphic artists, and other team members assigned to the project
- In technical meetings, leading the discussion related to content and instructional approaches
- Keeping in close touch with individuals from the client organization
- Having final responsibility for

  Definition of training issues
  Assessment of learner characteristics
  Definition of instructional strategies and approaches
  Analysis of end-user tasks
  Review of existing training materials and/or relevant documentation
- Having final responsibility for the development of

  Performance objectives
  Learning strategies
  Courseware styles and standards document
  Evaluation criteria
  Quality-control processes (jointly with project lead)
  Multimedia authoring procedures (jointly with project lead)
  Implementation plan
- Creating and securing agreement on the instructional approaches applied to the project
- Reviewing products of the instructional design process to ensure instructional integrity and consistency in style, organization, and level of detail

■ Planning and conducting formative evaluation of the program, including data analysis

Multimedia developers/courseware developers/courseware authors/instructional specialists/technical writers

The multimedia developers are charged with implementing the design for the application agreed to by the team. Reporting to the lead instructional designer, these individuals must produce a sound informational or instructional program, following the styles and standards delineated for the project.

Staffs are becoming leaner, individuals are acquiring new skills, and authoring tools are becoming easier to use. Thus, multimedia or courseware developers are becoming responsible for actually creating the on-line materials that end users interact with. This trend is a departure from the approach that divided the development process into writing/storyboarding on the one side and, on the other, "packaging" or manipulating the authoring system to put materials on line. Specific responsibilities of multimedia developers include

■ Conducting instructional analysis with subject matter experts (SMEs), software developers, and other resources as required

■ Researching the content related to the project in order to determine how to structure the multimedia

■ Detailing any procedural steps for the completion of tasks that audience members will need to perform

■ Participating in review meetings

■ Developing instructional materials that are consistent with the styles and standards agreed to by the team

■ Specifying for the artist the graphics to be included in the multimedia program

■ Authoring assigned multimedia modules, using the authoring tool(s) selected for the project

■ Providing first-level quality control for assigned on-line modules and print materials (if applicable)

Graphic artists

Visuals provide one of the most effective and efficient means of communicating. The graphic artist, whose sphere of interest and expertise often extends beyond visuals per se, brings invaluable benefit to the multimedia development team. He or she does so not only by creating graphic materials to complement other media, but also by introducing an insightful dose of creativity to discussions about the project.

It is important to ensure that at least one graphic artist is included in the design process from the beginning of a project. Not only will the team benefit from the artist's input, but the artist needs to be informed about factors affecting final artwork, such as purpose and tone of the program, the intended audience characteristics, and the technical constraints within which the visuals are to be created.

The graphic artist or artists may work strictly within the realm of original graphics, or they may also have responsibility for manipulating existing images (such as digitized photographs and so-called "clip art"). In addition, graphic artists are not limited to creating visual materials with computer-based tools. In some instances it may be appropriate to create a graphic manually and scan it into the computer for manipulation. The graphic artist's specific responsibilities include

- Working closely with other team members to formulate graphical approaches and strategies for the program
- Creating visuals that concisely and effectively convey information
- Producing visuals that provide a consistent look and feel throughout the application

Art director

When a multimedia development organization is large enough to warrant having an art director, his or her primary role is to ensure that the graphic artist(s) assigned to a multimedia project produce visual materials that are consistent with the purpose, style, and tone of the application. The art director may also serve as a graphic artist on the project, and should be involved at least in the initial team meetings. As the project matures and changes, the art director must be kept abreast of changes that could affect the number, type, or level of sophistication of the visuals being produced. Informal interaction between the project lead and the art director may be sufficient, or the art director may want to join the artist(s) assigned to the team at the regularly scheduled team meetings.

On a project that involves more than one graphic artist, the art director usually will be called upon to make assignments and track the progress of visuals as they move from the "request" stage to the "completed" stage. Specific responsibilities of the art director include

- Ensuring that project standards are maintained (from a visual perspective)
- Ensuring that graphic requests are appropriately assigned to the team's artists
- Tracking the flow of visual material production from graphic request through completion

Subject matter experts/content specialists/reviewers

Subject matter experts (SMEs) play a vital role in the instructional design process. These individuals not only supply knowledge of the content to the development team, they also often provide them with valuable insights concerning the target audience, pertinent examples to include in the program, and guidance about effective presentational strategies.

In short, SMEs help to ensure that the multimedia application reaches the desired goals. Most often they are employees of the client organization, but they also may be full-time employees of the multimedia development organization, or consultants hired for the duration of the project because of their special expertise. The subject matter experts for a project should be selected as soon after the start of the project as possible, in order to involve them in the audience and content analysis as well as the initial design process. Since SMEs for a project may have little or no experience with multimedia applications, each member of the team should consider spending a little extra time with the SMEs explaining how his or her part of the work effort is accomplished. The better the SMEs and developers understand each other's contributions to the process, the more smoothly the project will move forward and the more valuable will be the information the SMEs are likely to provide.

On some projects, other individuals besides the primary SMEs will serve as reviewers. These individuals may represent the actual target audience, or they may represent various technical disciplines within the client organization that have a stake in the content and/or the success of the multimedia program. Thus, specific responsibilities of subject matter experts/reviewers include

- Helping the development team understand and structure the content of the multimedia program

- Helping the development team understand the target audience characteristics and how they will relate to the multimedia program

- Supplying to the development team specific, relevant examples and anticipated common errors and misinterpretations likely to be made by the target audience

- Reviewing the multimedia program at interim stages and submitting written corrections and/or suggestions related to content accuracy, completeness, and relevance to the target audience

Systems analyst/integrator

When informational and instructional programs were first delivered by computer, they consisted mostly of text on the screen, with an occasional low-resolution graphic. Today's requirements for successful multimedia programs demand hardware and software that can present sophisticated animations, video-like effects, motion video, and audio. If users need to be able to access different types of peripherals (such as printers, CD-ROM drives, and modems), the ante is raised again. Even more complex multimedia challenges are becoming common, such as electronic performance support systems

(EPSSs) that are coupled with a client's existing software application, and training programs that will be accessed by users with different types of computers over local-area and wide-area networks. In these situations, planning and implementing solutions calls for a level of expertise beyond an ability to attach the right cables to the right equipment.

The systems analyst or integrator is responsible for planning and constructing a cost-effective system for the client. It goes without saying that the system recommended for the client must actually reach the objectives of the multimedia program. All the components must work together without manipulations by the client. Further, the systems analyst must adequately communicate to the team any constraints or limitations within which the multimedia program must be developed. Specific responsibilities of the systems analyst include

- Ensuring that a cost-effective system can be constructed that meets program objectives

- Ensuring that the features and benefits of the system are described (in understandable terminology) in such a way that the client can make an educated decision as to possible implementation of the specified configuration of hardware and software

- Communicating to the multimedia development team any constraints or limitations (as well as features and benefits) of the hardware/software platform

- Ensuring that all multimedia materials developed for the project will work with the proposed system

- Loading the multimedia program and any other required software onto the client's hardware, and installing the equipment at designated locations

- Troubleshooting any problems that seem to be hardware- and/or software-related

- Maintaining the hardware and software (this includes handling equipment failures and software upgrades) if this service has been contracted for

Authoring systems specialist

Depending upon a number of factors, an authoring systems specialist may be part of the multimedia development team and may play different roles. If the authoring tool being used is not very complex and the multimedia developers are experienced in the use of it, then the authoring systems specialist may be of more use to another development team. If, as is often the case with sophisticated multimedia programs, the authoring tool is a powerful one and some of the instructional or informational interactions have a number of branching options, the authoring systems specialist will serve as a primary resource for team members.

This individual should have mastered the system used by team members in order to troubleshoot very quickly any difficulties they might have. The authoring systems specialist also should perform a quality-control check on each segment of the program to ensure complete technical functionality. More specifically, the authoring systems specialist is responsible for

- Ensuring that the same version of the authoring system is installed on the computer of each team member who will be developing lessons on-line

- Creating and modifying as necessary any authoring system models or templates that increase productivity and facilitate consistency among the developers

- Troubleshooting any problems that arise related to the authoring system or when implementing the types of interactions the developers want to use

- Coordinating with the systems analyst on such issues as how the authoring system should be configured to meet the program objectives, and how the runtime versions of the multimedia program should be installed on the client's equipment

- Instructing users as to the procedures associated with putting multimedia materials on-line with the specified authoring system

- "Programming" any special or difficult sequences (such as a complicated animation or a branching structure)

- Ensuring that each segment of the multimedia application has full technical functionality

Quality assurance specialists

No products should leave the multimedia development organization without significant input from these guardians of quality. The quality assurance specialists should be involved early in the project so as to enable the sharing of design issues and potential areas of concern. It is sound business practice to proactively include individuals who can look for potential inconsistencies among developers and questionable instructional approaches, as well as pounce on the "typo" that no one else has found.

While the quality assurance specialists may not review all the materials themselves, their oversight of the review process is vitally important. More specifically, quality assurance specialists' responsibilities include

- Coordinating with the project lead to ensure that an adequate plan of reviews and sign-offs is in place when the project begins

- Ensuring that each part of the multimedia application undergoes appropriate review and testing (e.g., congruence of on-line materials with supporting paper-based materials; consistency of content across the application; soundness of instructional approach; technical functionality)

- Coordinating with the project lead as to the process for making changes to multimedia materials and documenting that appropriate changes have been made

- Checking the consistency, instructional approach, and technical functionality of at least a subset of the materials

- Checking to ensure that the established review process is being followed and that it is effective
- Managing the pilot test procedures

Audio/video specialist

The functions of the audio/video specialist may be performed by one or more individuals. These persons may be employees of the multimedia development organization or they may be consultants, called upon when their services are required. In reality, if complex audio or video requirements are part of a given project, the necessary staff is usually contracted for through a vendor who specializes in audio and/or video. For less demanding applications, an in-house expert can be called upon to perform one or both of these functions.

For a moderately sophisticated project, the audio/video specialist may be required to acquire and insert audio and video segments into the application. In other projects, an expanded team is required that might include, among others, a professional narrator, a sound engineer, a video producer, and one or more videographers. For a moderately sophisticated multimedia application, the responsibilities of the audio/video specialist include

- Providing the multimedia development team with input as to the types of audio and video that will best capture the "look and feel" the team is after
- Acquiring and/or shooting video clips that will be incorporated into the program
- Acquiring and/or recording audio clips that will be incorporated into the program
- Troubleshooting any technical problems related to the use of audio and video in the application
- Coordinating with the project lead about production schedules, so that the appropriate media are ready when they are needed during development
- Negotiating with vendors for the rights to media that are to be used in the program
- Serving as liaison between the multimedia development organization and those vendors selected to provide services such as narration, sound recording, and video production/editing
- Ensuring that the audio and video selected for the project blend with the established style and tone of the program, and that the media help the team to reach the program's objectives
- Helping to inform the team about issues related to copyright infringement and fair use laws

Software engineer/programmer

Not every project calls for the expertise of a software engineer or programmer. However, on certain projects, this individual is indispensable. Broadly speaking, the software engineer's domain is the planning and implementing of software tools that facilitate the development of multimedia programs. The scope of such tools ranges from the development of an entire authoring system to a few lines of code to add new functionality to an existing authoring system.

In the case of a multimedia-based electronic performance support system (EPSS), the software engineer may be called upon to program an interface between the client's software system and the EPSS itself. This interface enables data to be passed between the two systems so that the end user can access context-specific help, advice, coaching, reference, and instruction without leaving the main software system. Some typical responsibilities of the software engineer include

- Collaborating with the multimedia team to determine what software tools are necessary for success
- Collaborating with the client's technical staff (usually programmers) to determine how best to couple the multimedia application and the client's software system (applies to the development of an EPSS)
- Programming specialized pieces of code to accomplish certain functions that are required for the future by the development team
- Ensuring that extensions to an existing authoring system function correctly and do not adversely affect any other function

Client's project lead

The client's project lead represents the multimedia project to the client's management and serves as liaison to the development organization, whether internal or external to the client organization. This individual is often the development organization's main contact with the client, although the individual may or may not have the authority to officially accept the program as complete. In many cases a member of the client's management team is ultimately responsible for signing off on a completed project.

The role of the client's project lead is quite similar to that of the development team's project lead, but in this case as seen from the perspective of the client. It is a role that is crucial to the success of any multimedia project, because this person is usually charged with ensuring a successful product. It pays to take pains to ensure that the client's project lead is an integral part of the multimedia development team, since this person can be either the team's advocate or its adversary.

Since this person represents the client, and the team's approach should always be to please the client, the team certainly needs to listen to and act upon the input provided by this person. Note the crucial responsibilities of the client's project lead, and consider how they can impact the multimedia project, either positively or negatively:

- Securing corporate approval to begin each phase of the program
- Providing the needed logistical and economic support when the involve-

ment of SMEs and other reviewers necessary for project success is being solicited

- Providing the development team with access to the most current resource materials and information about the target audience

- Providing the development team with equipment and space if some of the development effort will take place at the client's site

- Securing a commitment from the client's team members (such as SMEs and other reviewers) concerning time frames and schedules

- Monitoring project activities from the client's perspective

- Serving as the client's point of contact for the multimedia development team members

- Providing feedback to the multimedia development team as to the progress and quality of project activities and deliverables

- Consolidating and communicating the inputs from SMEs and other reviewers about the multimedia program

- Providing consultation to the project team about the client's technical, schedule, and budgetary constraints

- Providing information to the development team about such issues as corporate culture and previous training efforts, issues that may affect the development team's recommendations about this project

- Making final decisions for the client in review meetings

- Supervising/managing the pilot testing and roll-out of the multimedia application from the client's perspective

- Making arrangements for the facilities and with the test participants for pilot testing of the new application

- Approving and signing off on each deliverable through final completion date (optional)

Other potential team members

As seen from the broadest perspective, many other individuals could be considered part of a multimedia development team. For instance, if the multimedia application is to be used as part of an instructor-based training program, those instructors need to become part of the team, much like SMEs, not only to provide input about the audience and the content but also to understand how the multimedia program will be used in their classrooms.

Before an application is delivered in its "final deliverable" form, it needs to be thoroughly tested. While much testing is done by the development team members (including quality assurance specialists), members of the target audience usually are asked to pilot-test the new application. Input from these individuals can be invaluable in ensuring that the program meets the expectations of the eventual audience and has adequately considered the audience's entry-level skills and knowledge.

Other client representatives or consultants also may be called upon for their unique expertise. Corporate culture really does differ from entity to entity, and it is important to know how the culture of an organization should be reflected in a multimedia program, lest the program run counter to that prevailing culture. Many companies have an almost hallowed set of technical terminology and/or stylistic conventions that must be accommodated or adhered to. Others have policies and procedures that may affect the development and delivery of the application. Having an "insider" provide this type of information can greatly increase the likelihood of success for the final product.

If the client's project lead cannot provide sufficient information about the culture in which the multimedia application will be fielded, then perhaps someone else within the organization can share that information with the team. Taking pains to integrate that person into the development team, and then to share ideas about the tone and style of the multimedia program, can prevent those culture clashes that make a project less than successful or cause portions of it to have to be redone.

Equally important when it comes to understanding the corporate culture is understanding the specific *international* culture in which the multimedia application will be fielded. Within most organizations that do business overseas, there are knowledgeable individuals who can advise the team both on technical matters (e.g., what form of electrical power is typical) and on content-related issues (e.g., whether a golf analogy is appropriate). It is prudent for the project lead to explore with the client's project lead what types of resources on international issues are available to be consulted before moving ahead too quickly with the design of the application.

Last, perhaps, but not least, are those individuals who provide the team with administrative services. The people who perform these services or keep equipment operational often do not get the credit they deserve. On any given project there is a wealth of tasks, such as photocopying and securing couriers for materials, that must be accomplished. Computers, printers, and copiers seem to require service at just the wrong moments. But the individuals who gain visibility only when things go awry also must be considered part of the multimedia development team.

References

Schneiderman, B., *Designing the User Interface: Strategies for Effective Human-Computer Interaction,* 2d ed., Addison-Wesley Publishing Company, Reading, MA, 1992.

Plunkett, D., "Intervention for Creativity: An OD Approach," *Training and Development Journal,* 42(8), 68–71, 1988.

8

Virtual Reality as Multimedia: A Teacher's Pet

Jeff Hooks

Anecdotally...

An old joke about testing the nature of reality tells of some empiricists walking down a railroad track and finding an object. Each uses a different sense to examine it: the first looks, the second touches, the third smells, and the last tastes. After they have determined the nature of the object, the last empiricist declares, "I'm sure glad I didn't step in it."

Defining Virtual Reality

Virtual reality (VR) is a technology that provides one with sensations and the control of perspective so that one experiences the illusion of being in the presence of an object, within a situation, or surrounded by a place. The illusion seems more real if different kinds of sensations are provided by media.

Combined with audio/video

Today, VR relies on audio and video technology augmented by a computer interface that reads the movements of a participant's body. These act as triggers that change the direction of sounds and the perspective of sights so that one sees and hears an artificial world that appears to respond in relation to one's body movement, just as the real world does. In the future, researchers can be expected to refine olfactory and tactile media to the point where they give users of VR the opportunity to rejoice over not having stepped in it, even though "it" is not really there.

VR as an Industry

Howard Rheingold's *Virtual Reality,* an encyclopedic account of the origins of VR, introduces the technology that, since the book's publication in 1991, has more than doubled in size and become a significant industry.

In the military

During the Persian Gulf War, the U.S. military used VR applications to allow pilots and tank commanders to experience a computer model of the Kuwaiti landscape.

In the premiere issue of the slick periodical *Wired,* cyberpunk author Bruce Sterling reported on his visit to the U.S. Army's Combined Arms and Tactical Training Center at Fort Knox, Kentucky: "The Pentagon has a virtual Kuwait on a hard disk—SAKI, the Saudi Arabia-Kuwait-Iraq database. It has the country mapped out meter by meter, pixel by pixel, in 3-D, with weather optional" (p. 95).

American soldiers used SAKI to give them a virtual experience of driving tanks and flying planes. It gave them skills in maneuvering over the terrain—skills as good as, and sometimes (especially during sandstorms) better than, the skills of the country's residents.

Today, the VR technology developed during that war has created a new standard for digital terrains, a standard for all American armed forces, called "Project 2851." Sterling: "Project 2851 is about the virtual reproduction and archiving of the entire planet. Simulator technology has reached a point today in which satellite photographs can be transformed into 3-D virtual landscapes" (p. 98).

In the marketplace

VR also has entered the marketplace in the form of video games, performance art, and telepresence. (Telepresence is similar to VR, but different in that it creates experiences by using actual sounds and pictures transmitted from distant locations rather than a computer-generated model.) Thanks to VR, arcade and home video games now can give players the sensations of climbing over 3-D cartoon landscapes, launching bombs from handheld guns, and avoiding capture by flying dinosaurs.

Bringing people together

Earlier this year, performance artists Billy Idol and Thomas Dolby were preparing tours of concert performances around the United States in which audiences would be transported into virtual worlds, i.e., live 3-D music videos (Thomas, p. 18). With telepresence, musicians and audiences, lecturers and students, conference participants, even lovers soon will meet together from distant locations without the difficulties of travel because sophisticated cameras and microphones will bring people together virtually.

VR in Education

Most revolutionary, however, is the transforming power this technology will have in education.

Known uses

Multimedia combined with interactive computer technology already has enabled students and teachers to bring the world into their classrooms. Soon students will don headsets with stereo video screens and stereo speakers that will enable them and their teachers to explore virtual volcanoes or medieval cathedrals. Medical students will practice on virtual patients, permitting them to perfect their techniques without endangering lives. Students of language will virtually join in on native-tongue conversations in foreign countries.

Uses unknown

So many possibilities exist that creative teachers will discover ways of using VR that are inconceivable today.

Adaptations and ramifications

VR can be implemented on computers that already are in many classrooms—especially when combined with videodisc players, CD-ROM players, and digitized recordings. Multimedia packages can be adapted so that, as students move mice or click keys, they look, listen, and control their perspectives while viewing a video screen that has become a window on a world—a window that looks into a remote location or a remote possibility.

Whatever the equipment, the result of VR in the classroom—the result of multimedia combined with interactive computer technology—will be an unprecedented enhancement of the educational experience in terms of creativity and efficiency.

An Early Experience

My first project using virtual reality as a classroom tool was the Virtual Library (Fig. 8.1), a HyperCard stack that I used in a classroom of networked Macintoshes, a CD-ROM player, and a modem. I had little computer experience outside of word processing when I developed the Virtual Library as part of St. Petersburg Junior College's Project Flamingo (the plan by which all seven campus sites are being computer-networked). SPJC provided training, equipment, and release time for teachers to develop Macintosh applications for classroom use.

A persistent problem

Most of my previous education had been in literature, and I had taught college classes, primarily in writing, for about 15 years. One task that had

Figure 8.1 The virtual library.

always presented me with problems was introducing students to library research. Because each student confronted different challenges in the library, I found the best method for teaching research was to physically visit the library with the students individually, offering suggestions and asking questions as they sought information.

Although this worked very well, the time it took was an impossible obstacle. Teaching an average of five classes of 25 to 35 students made this method unworkable, simply because there were not enough hours in a week.

A HyperCard solution

Solution: I created a model of the library as a HyperCard stack. The students would access the class model, which automatically dialed and connected with LUIS, the databank of Florida's university library system. Using this computer catalog, I could stay in the classroom and help students to sort through the lists of library materials displayed on their Macintosh screens. Then they could access some CD-ROM disks that contained a variety of bibliographical materials.

Lastly, the students were presented with the Virtual Library. I had scanned graphic representations of the interior architecture of the library as seen from a variety of angles and distances. I pasted these onto a series of coded HyperCard cards so that as the students moved the mouse, an appropriate view of the library's architecture was displayed on the screen. Thus, the students saw an animated representation of the library as if they were looking through a window and controlling a vehicle while they traveled in it inside the building.

When the students clicked the mouse following display of a book on a shelf, the book floated off the shelf and opened before them. With another click, the pages turned. Bibliographical data about the book was placed automatically in the students' virtual notebooks, where they also could take notes. A virtual photocopy machine could copy text and graphics from displayed books and then store them in the students' notebooks.

Upon leaving the Virtual Library, the students would be prompted to decide whether they wanted to print their notebooks. If they did, the classroom laser printer provided hard copies of the material they had gathered.

The material in the Virtual Library was extremely limited, of course. Only a few books could be opened, and only a few pictures in the books contained words and pictures. Other library resources, such as audio recordings, videotapes, and computer software, were included and could be viewed and listened to by the students, but for only the briefest duration.

Some advantages

One difference that made the Virtual Library a better teaching tool than an actual library, however, was that HyperCard enabled the texts, images, and sounds in the library sources to be electronically cross-referenced. They were *hypertexts* (Figs. 8.2, 8.3, and 8.4).

Figure 8.2 Frame 1 of book opening.

Figure 8.3 Frame 2 of book opening.

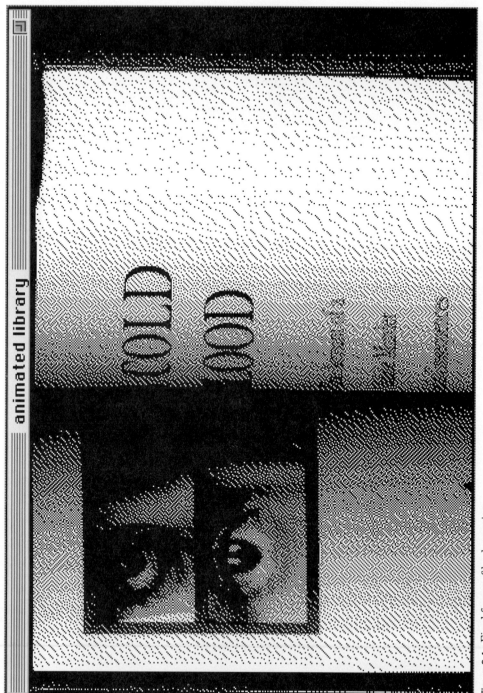

Figure 8.4 Final frame of book opening.

For example, a passage from Truman Capote's *In Cold Blood* contained words and phrases that acted as hot spots. When students clicked on the appropriate spots in the text, their view would be shifted automatically to a *National Geographic* map of Kansas, an entry in the *Oxford English Dictionary,* a photo of a grain elevator in an encyclopedia, or a sequence of dialogue from director Ken Russell's film version of the novel.

Positive fallout

The advantages of the Virtual Library actually amounted to more than time, efficiency, and ease. Students using the tool acted as if they were playing an exciting video game. Instead of exhibiting the yawning and foot-dragging behavior that I am sure most teachers recognize when announcing "the library tour," my students were eager to learn. They came to class early, and it was difficult to get them to leave so the next class could begin.

A Final Word

This experience made me a convert. Now, no matter what I am teaching, I try to find a method to use multimedia packages and interactive technology. In the future, I hope that all my teaching will be an exploration within a virtual world instead of a lecture in a conventional classroom.

References

Rheingold, Howard, *Virtual Reality,* Summit Books, New York, 1991.
Sterling, Bruce, "War Is Virtual Hell," *Wired,* 1.1 (Premiere Issue), pp. 46–51, 94–99, 1993.
Thomas, Wes, "VR Update," *Mondo 2000,* pp. 18–19, February 1993.

The Multimedia Odyssey

Satish Gupta

Introduction

Nations and companies are being called upon to speed up the development of products so as to remain competitive in a global, fast-paced economy. They need more rapid dissemination of the latest research information, and faster training and retraining of design, production, and service (human) resources. But today's communications methods already are being pushed to extremes. In short, if we are to succeed, we need more effective communications capabilities than those we've relied on until now.

We need not start from scratch, however. Print, audio, and video have a panoply of benefits upon which we can draw. The challenge is to combine them in such a way as to obtain the greatest advantages of each in a cohesive and coordinated way. That is the essence of multimedia.

Multimedia, like other new technologies, is progressing through a variety of developmental stages, each of which has implications for *applications, cost and justification, infrastructure,* and *standards.* We can chart multimedia's present location and course quite precisely. This information is essential for planning at which stage of its development one is prepared to adopt this technology. We can also identify some of the rocky shoals around which multimedia may have to navigate. Be assured, however, that multimedia has been established, is progressing, and will become pervasive.

Starting the Journey

In making our way from traditional communications methods to multimedia, we need to address the differences among those methods and the obstacles keeping us from combining them effectively.

Print and graphics

Different media have widely different information-transfer properties. Print, for example, requires the reader to scan coded sequences and decode them into cognitive constructs—words, sentences, paragraphs. Vision is our highest bandwidth sense, but it is hamstrung by the decoding speed required of reading. By their natures, writing and reading are sequential access methods. Indices may offer a reader some degree of random access, but always at the risk of loss of context or perspective.

Graphics (pictures, diagrams, charts, tables, etc.) can often replace many words and make it easier to describe a concept or idea. Like a snapshot, however, a graphic is static. It offers no inherent clues about the temporal relationships of its elements. Also, most graphics require captions to assist readers in understanding the ideas they are meant to convey.

On its positive side, print (with or without graphics) is a mature technology and requires no special systems on the part of the reader. It is portable, requires no batteries, and is very durable.

Animation

No one is sure who first drew simple sequences of pictures on the pages of a pad, then flipped through them rapidly to create an animated effect. We do know that nickelodeons had hand-cranked animators before the turn of the nineteenth century.

Animation offers the temporal juxtapositions that graphics lack. Unlike print or graphics, animation is a dynamic medium. We get a sense of relative timing, position, direction, and speed of action. We need no captions, because the message is conveyed by the motion and the scene.

Audio

We can assume that early man's first forms of communication were gestures and sounds. Oration was a revered art form among some of the earliest civilizations. Spoken words have power not only to convey meaning but to add subtleties, as well. For example, a person's "tone" may be more important than his or her actual words in understanding the importance of something. One need only watch film footage of Roosevelt, Mussolini, or Hitler to feel the emotional effect that voice can wield.

Like animation, audio is a dynamic medium. It depicts sounds and their sequences and give us a sense of their chronology. Also like animation, voice or music can be synthesized artificially.

The telephone and radio permit us to "carry" (electrical) voice signals over great distances. Of course, audio is more than spoken words. It provides the alternative to attending a live concert if one wishes to hear music. It also permits us to use music as a communication vehicle in conjunction with words and images. Hollywood has long recognized the value of background music for manipulating an audience's emotions. Consider the shrieking violins in

Hitchcock's *Psycho,* the ominous-sounding bassoons in *Jaws,* the tubular bells in *The Exorcist.*

Images

The term *image,* here, refers to reproductions of real objects that reflect light through lenses onto film or photoelectric transducers. A photographic snapshot of a statue, for instance, would fit this definition; a drawing of the statue would not. A picture is a high-speed information-transfer medium. The eyes can take in great amounts of information in an instant. Even the pattern-recognition processing that serves to identify the objects is much faster, say, than the processing rate of reading written words and phrases.

An image is reproduced in a static medium. It is a moment in time, captured, with no ability to convey what preceded that moment or what followed it.

Video

Video (e.g., motion images) both provides high-speed information transfer and shows temporal relationships. Video is produced by successive capture and storage of images as they change with time. In addition to the high-speed information-transfer properties of images, video adds more information by incorporating the element of time along with the images.

Like animation and audio, video is dynamic. For example, an entire service operation can be viewed from beginning to end, showing each step in sequence. The viewer sees exactly where each part is located, exactly how to make the adjustments, and exactly how long it should take. This is information that it is impossible to convey fully with any type of written material.

Artificial-world media

Words, graphics, animated graphics, and synthesized sounds allow us to create within an imaginary or artificial world. Using words, we can describe things that are not real, or real yet. We can draw pictures of atoms with electrons orbiting the nuclei—scenes we will never see of real atoms. With animation, we can make those electrons move. These media provide us with important tools for communicating about abstractions and conceptualizations.

Real-world media

Since audio, images, and video all involve reproduction of real sounds or physical objects, they are categorized as *real-world media.* In conjunction with *artificial-world media,* real-world media offer ways of reinforcing conceptual ideas with actual examples that are similar. Together, the two categories of media (artificial- and real-world) offer a powerful combination of communications capabilities (see Fig. 9.1).

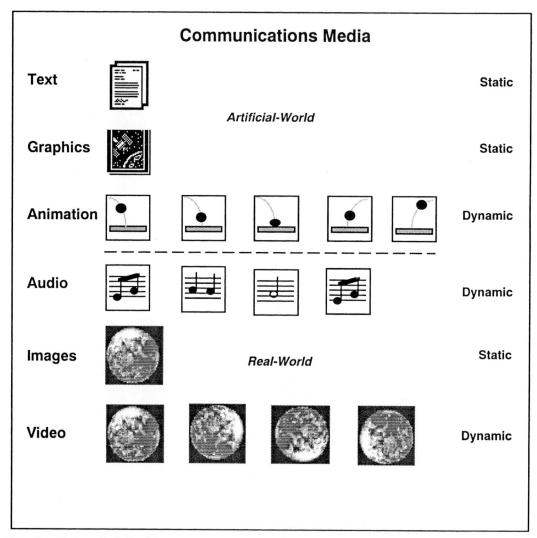

Figure 9.1 Temporal relationships.

Obstacles to combining the various media

The processing speeds, storage capacities, and input/output data-transfer rates needed to support text and static graphics are far different from those needed to support animation, digitized audio, and digitized video.

A system that meets the minimum requirements for digital audio and video could support text and graphics; however, one that meets the minimum requirements for text and graphics would be unable to support digital audio and video. Also, systems that can handle digital audio and video have proved much more costly than those that handle only text and graphics.

Also complicating things are the differences in the technologies used to support text, graphics, audio, and video. In computer systems, artificial-world variables (e.g., alphabetic characters, primitive graphic features) are all represented and processed using digital encoding and decoding of electrical signals. Digital electrical signals representing a page of text look much like those representing a page of graphics. What's more, the same circuits and components can be used to process either signal.

Audio and video have traditionally been represented and processed using analog technologies. The electrical signal's properties (voltages and frequencies) were made to vary in direct accordance with the physical variable's properties (e.g., loudness and pitch of sound; brightness and color of light). Mixing digital and analog signals has been a bit like mixing oil and water. Digitizing the audio and video is necessary before they can be fully integrated with text and graphics.

Fortunately, two factors are helping us to overcome these obstacles. Affordable personal computers and their related technologies are now being built that can handle the requirements of digitized audio and video. And all communications technologies are rapidly moving toward digital representation and processing.

Moving All Information toward Digital Encoding

Although analog systems appear simpler, digital systems generally provide better quality and more functions, and at a lower cost. For example a phonograph, which is an analog system, converts the movement of a stylus in a record's groove directly into an analog electrical signal. This is amplified and converted directly into a physical vibration by a loudspeaker.

A compact disc (CD) player, on the other hand, is a digital system. Instead of a groove, the surface of the CD is patterned with tiny "pits" or laser-burned holes, each representing a digital bit. As the CD turns, an infrared light source and detector detects and encodes these surface-reflection variations as digital 1's and 0's. The 1's and 0's are combinations of bits representing the magnitude of a sound's original analog signal at some sampling interval. A CD, for example, contains digital data sampled at a rate of 44,000 samples per second.

A microcomputer in a CD player processes the digital samples and controls their conversion into analog voltage levels. Each sample produces a voltage level, and the varying levels are sequenced at the sampling rate. Using signal processing techniques, the CD player connects the sequential analog levels together into a smooth representation of the original analog signal. This processed signal is then amplified and reproduced by a loudspeaker.

Comparing the phonograph to the CD player, it is obvious that the latter is a more complicated system. Yet sophisticated CD players can now be purchased for about $100, or less than the cost of an inexpensive phonograph. And the CD player provides nearly perfect resolution, without surface noise, wow and flutter, and other characteristics of phonograph reproduction. Logic says the CD system should cost much more than the phonograph, but digital microcircuit technology has literally turned this logic upside down.

The move to digital is unstoppable

When signals representing text, sound, and images are all digital signals, they can all be carried on a single network, stored using digital mass-storage techniques, and processed using digital microprocessor technology. This capability is essential for communication when people are separated in time and space.

Every communication approach is rapidly shifting to digital. Music in digital form on CDs has already been described. The telephone industry is using its Integrated Services Digital Network (ISDN) to transport voice and data. Photographs are becoming digitized, too. Kodak now makes it possible to get a Photo CD containing digitized versions of one's photographic images for display on a television. And television, too, is moving toward an all-digital, high-definition format.

The shift to digital makes multimedia practical

If text, graphics, animation, audio, and video were all done digitally, then combining them into a multimedia communications technology would immediately go from feasible to practical. The architectures of present-day personal computers are inherently capable of handling digital versions of text, graphics, animation, audio, and video. By plugging in innovative accessory circuit boards, a present-day PC can be suitably equipped to support multimedia for an additional $500 to $1000.

From Information to Communication Processing

We are witnessing a transition of computing from information processing to communication processing. Communications, once only an option for early PCs, has become a standard feature of contemporary PCs.

Since the first IBM PC was introduced in 1981, personal computers have rapidly shifted from being stand-alone personal productivity tools to being networked systems sharing peripherals, storage, and messages.

Current Macintosh computers, from the lowest (even the notebook models) to the highest end, come equipped with networking capability built in. Other PCs are easily configured for networking. Built-in and add-on modems permit PCs to participate in wide-area networks supporting public e-mail services (e.g., MCI and EasyLink) and more sophisticated networks, such as Apple's AppleLink.

Just as information processing evolved from a text-only orientation to text and graphics, so communications processing is now passing through a text-only stage to one of compound "documents" containing text, graphics, audio, and video. The proof that these multiple media are serious components of today's and tomorrow's personal computers is to be found in the changes taking place in computer operating systems. The Macintosh operating system includes QuickDraw and QuickTime, modules that support images and motion images. Microsoft's Windows and Windows NT include Video for Windows, its QuickTime counterpart (see Fig. 9.2).

Telecom-, Television-, and Computer-Centered Multimedia

Multimedia is not solely the province of computers. It is a technology that will be present in telecom, television, and computer systems. However, there

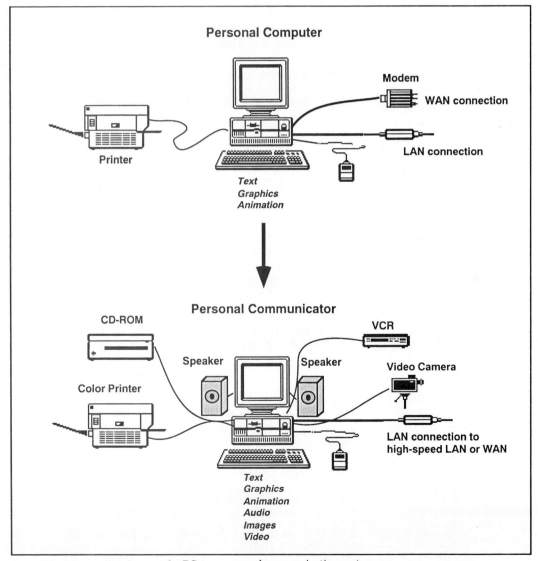

Figure 9.2   Multimedia changes the PC to a personal communication system.

are several distinctions that set these multimedia implementations apart, and there will be distinctions in how each is applied.

Telecom and television

Looking first at telecom and television, these two communications technologies are based on established infrastructure standards. There are very specific formats for signals meant to travel over telecom circuits, and for those that travel to television receivers via RF transmissions and via cable. These infrastructure standards are templates within which the multimedia technologies for telecom and television must conform.

The signals presently carried by telecom circuits are analog signals. However, switching and many other supporting functions have been done digitally for more than two decades. The Integrated Services Digital Network (or ISDN) is the telecom industry's current, fully digital network. ISDN provides end-to-end connectivity to support a wide range of both voice and nonvoice (e.g., data) services.

A Broadband Integrated Services Digital Network (BISDN) standard was proposed and accepted in 1992 that will operate at bandwidths of 1.5 Mbits per second and higher. Unlike ISDN, which is designed to make use of the existing copper-wire telecom infrastructure, BISDN will require fiber-optic transmission media.

The point, however, is not the type of media nor the data-transfer rates. The point is that the telecom industry does not first create an innovative technology, then permit a standard to emerge; it first creates a standard, then builds technologies that comply with that standard. We will see the same approach taken with telecom-centered multimedia. The limits of multimedia capability will be determined not by innovative design but by constraints imposed by preestablished standards.

Television, like telecom, also tightly conforms to standards. In the United States, television signals conform to the National Television Standards Committee (NTSC) standard. This calls for 525 lines of resolution transmitted at 60 half-frames (odd and even lines, interlaced) per second. The composite signal transmitted from a broadcast television facility includes the RF carrier plus video signals containing color and luminosity information, audio signals containing sound information, and a Modular Television System (MTS) signal for deriving stereophonic audio separation. The composite signal minus the carrier is used for direct connection (i.e., wired connection) of video and audio signals. As with telecom, today's television signals are analog signals. The proposed standard for high-definition television (HDTV), however, is likely to be a fully digital one.

Personal computers

In complete contrast with telecom and television, computer systems and technologies have evolved by first building innovative systems, then letting the market drive standards.

We've seen this scenario with peripheral interface standards, such as the Small Computer System Interface (SCSI), Shugart Associates System Interface (SASI), Centronics' parallel port for printers, and the like. We've also seen it with software standards, such as MS-DOS, and network standards, such as IEEE 802.3 (Ethernet) and IEEE 802.5 (Token Ring). Hayes Microsystems' AT Command set is the de facto standard for computer control of modems. What all of these have in common is that they were deployed long before they became standards. That is the way in the computer industry.

As a result, computer-centered multimedia can proceed apace without the constraint of standards such as those of telecom and television. One would therefore expect that the pace and degree of innovation would be highest in computer-centered multimedia. And it is.

Different strokes

Aside from the differences in infrastructure standards, telecom-, television-, and computer-centered multimedia will be applied in different ways. This is a function not only of technology but of a precedent, as well.

Teleconferencing

To some degree, telecom is already applying multimedia in an application called *teleconferencing*. Here we have essentially a closed-circuit connection linking two or more specially equipped conference rooms, permitting those in each room to see and hear those in the other room(s). Today's videoconferencing is generally a preplanned, orchestrated, televised meeting of people held in locations equipped for that purpose. Teleconferencing, on the other hand, can combine audio, video, text, and graphics, as well as people. Microphones capture the voices; television cameras capture images; and scanners are used to capture and transmit text and images that were initially on paper.

Despite the cameras and scanners, the primary focus of teleconferencing is verbal communication. Image motion is usually confined to the proverbial "talking heads." Rapid motion cannot be supported, because it causes differential data bursts that exceed the typical telecom channel capacity. Hence, waving hands disappear from the screen and reappear in jerky rather than smooth motion.

Further developments in multimedia are likely to make teleconferencing simpler and less costly, but they are not likely to change the nature—that is, formal organized meeting with a verbal-communication focus—of that application. By contrast, teleconferencing in a computer-centered context would likely result in more informal "meetings" pulled together in a much more spontaneous fashion.

Interactive television

So far, all attempts to establish an interactive television presence that is appealing to viewers and profitable to providers have been failures in the

United States. This is not to say that interactive television will never succeed, just not in the ways it has been implemented thus far.

Advances in multimedia technology will make it less costly to support interactive television—of sorts—but do not count on using your television for buying tickets to the theater or making reservations on airlines. Like telecom and teleconferencing, television and television-centered multimedia will have a focus closely related to its current success factor. For telecom, that factor is verbal communication; for television, the success factor is entertainment.

This is the lure attracting such notables as Time Warner and its alliance partner, U.S. West; Tele-Communications, Inc., the United States' largest cable operator; News Corporation, owner of the Fox Cable Network; and Sony, owner of Columbia's huge studio library. Each has different visions of interactive television, but entertainment is solidly at the core of them all.

Computer-centered multimedia—no limits

Computer-centered multimedia will be as multifaceted as computers themselves. What has shaped and continues to shape the implementations, applications, and costs of computer-centered multimedia is technology itself. More specifically, the four technology areas that are key to continued progress in computer-centered multimedia are *audio, high-capacity mass storage, video,* and *networking.*

As mentioned earlier, computer-centered multimedia can be viewed as an ongoing voyage whose present position and future course are both clearly discernible. This ship's sails are filled not with wind but with technology innovation. With each fresh breeze of innovation, the ship moves faster and covers a wider area.

We can look at where computer-centered multimedia was, where it is, and where it is going. We can see what effect the levels of technology have had, and will have, upon applications, costs, and justifications, infrastructure and standards. This will be very helpful in deciding at what point, and to what extent, one wishes to embrace multimedia.

The Voyage

Virtually every new technology, in becoming a success, passes through evolutionary phases. These correspond roughly to a market's adaptation sequence. The *enable* phase occurs early in the evolution and is utilized by the market's early adopters. During the *enhance* phase, many of the early technology's rough edges have been smoothed and a more mainstream group of users begins to adopt it. In the final stage, *pervade,* the technology becomes so well integrated and affordable that it has mass appeal and brings in the late adopters.

It took over four decades for mainframe computers to make this journey, but less than one for personal computers to do it. In the process, personal computers have revolutionized the way we live and work, and multimedia is creating a revolution of its own within that personal computer revolution.

Global problems provide the push and pull

Multimedia is being pushed and pulled into the business market by a combination of global problems. The developed nations of the world are in a state of information overload. The average U.S. citizen is exposed to thousands of items of information every day. This leads more to confusion than to increased understanding.

In today's globally competitive economy, knowledge has become one of the most valuable assets, but unlike most other assets, knowledge has a very short shelf life.

Technology markets have been a lifeblood for most of today's developed nations, but current markets are rapidly saturating, causing worldwide recessions and their related problems.

Another global problem is the changing-societal-work-ethic model. There are now many more things to enjoy when one is not working, and employees covet their leisure now as never before. Thus, if companies are to raise employees' collective productivity while giving them the leisure time they demand, they must find more effective ways of training them and having them do their jobs.

While they do not constitute a panacea, multimedia technologies, suitably applied, do promise to make a significant dent in these seemingly intractable problems.

The Enable Phase

The enable phase occurred during multimedia's infancy. This was the period during which analog and digital media were combined in rather inelegant ways, with rather cumbersome implementations. Nevertheless, to those early adopters who began using enable-phase multimedia, it made their applications cheaper, faster, and better. This was the case despite the high cost of employing dynamic media and the lack of tools to be used by those who were expert in the subject matter to be presented.

During the enable phase, a number of application areas depended upon the interactive use of multimedia. Computer-based training, for one, used this technology, when the objective was to train an employee in the repair of a specific piece of equipment. It permitted the student to view the repair process as often as desired and in the sequence preferred by the trainee.

In such a case, a trainer would have used a videotape that showed an expert making the repair. Student and trainer could then review the tape as often as necessary to achieve the required level of comprehension. In the absence of videotape or laserdisc, the repair would have had to be a live demonstration. Indexing signals on the videotape in conjunction with computer-based control functions would have made the viewing and reviewing process more precise and efficient.

Seeing and hearing information leads to greater retention than when simply reading it. Being able to interact with the information adds even greater retention. People generally retain about 20 percent of what they hear, 40 percent of what they see and hear, and up to 75 percent of what they see, hear, and do. Therefore, the interactivity afforded by a multimedia computer can significantly increase the effectiveness of training.

The value of this solution during the enable phase was so great for some applications that it was easy to justify the use of new and expensive technology. Even spending $100,000 to develop an hour's worth of interactive video training was acceptable, because it allowed more students to be trained in less time, reduced travel expenses, and kept students off the job for shorter amounts of time. Trainers were able to handle more students and with greater scheduling flexibility. The training pace was also very flexible, resulting in even more effective retention and learning.

Cost and justification

Multimedia during the enable phase was targeted at a few well-defined vertical applications and user groups. Justification was fairly straightforward, involving cost reductions, productivity improvements, and/or revenue increases as a consequence of adopting this technology.

Infrastructure

During the enable phase, multimedia equipment was relatively expensive, software tools were not mature, and the number of skilled users was limited. Those who were experts in training subject matter could not wield the tools themselves. Instead, they had to work in conjunction with those who were multimedia experts.

Standards

During the enable phase, each application was for all intents and purposes a custom implementation. Very little of what was used for one application could be adapted for use in another. What standards existed were related to individual media (e.g., VHS or Beta). Integrating the media into a multimedia application, however, proceeded with virtually no standards to speak of.

Results

Current multimedia applications developed during the enable phase are almost exclusively in the areas of training, education, and merchandising, and all are mostly interactive presentations.

The Enhance Phase

Multimedia is currently in the enhance phase. Here, the technology has become significantly less expensive, faster, and easier to use. Enable-phase applications have prompted development of new products and tools, creating an infrastructure capable of sustaining more growth.

The lower cost of multimedia makes it more appealing to those developing a broader spectrum of applications. While not critical to these applications, multimedia enhances their functionality and distinctiveness. Such applications include spreadsheets, word processors, electronic mail systems, groupware, document imaging systems, and database management systems.

Spreadsheets and word processors, for example, can be enhanced using voice annotation. Help functions in any application can be more effective when they make use of voice and/or video sequences. As hardware support for multimedia proliferates, software vendors will enhance their products with multimedia features. This will allow them to differentiate their products and gain competitive advantage.

The rate of growth and acceptance during the enhance phase rests on two factors: the number of systems capable of supporting multimedia, and the number of applications that employ multimedia. These factors are also mutually dependent. Obviously, multimedia hardware solutions that require an installed base of new systems will slow down the process. On the other hand, solutions that can take advantage of affordable upgrades for existing systems can catalyze the multimedia adoption process.

Cost and justification

Justification for using multimedia is harder to come by in the enhance phase than it was in the enable phase. Multimedia's contribution to horizontal applications such as spreadsheets, word processors, and the like is not critically important. In this case, "demand" means something like "want to have" rather than "need to have."

As it becomes easy to voice-annotate individual cells in a spreadsheet or a particular paragraph in a document, communication between coworkers will improve and information interchange will happen much faster. As the new technology continues to have a positive impact, its evolutionary growth becomes even more irreversible.

Infrastructure

In this phase of development, new tools are emerging that enable large numbers of people, unskilled in multimedia technologies, to perform simple, necessary functions (such as voice annotation or video-clip insertion) that are supported by many different horizontal applications.

As compared with earlier tools, these new tools will be lower-cost and therefore more appealing to a broader and larger group of users.

Standards

With the shift from vertical to horizontal applications, standards become much more important. A Pulse Code Modulation (PCM) standard for digitized voice is already part of the Multimedia Personal Computer (MPC) standard. Adaptive Delta PCM is the emerging standard for audio compression in the Compact Disc Read-Only Memory Extended Architecture (CD-ROM XA) definition.

For images and video, the Joint Photographic Experts Group (JPEG) and Motion Pictures Expert Group (MPEG) are in the process of meeting on compression standards. Intel, with its Digital Video Interactive (DVI), is seeking, as of this writing, to have it become a de facto standard.

These standards, however, have a different focus than the requirements of personal-computer-centered multimedia. As such, they do not appear to be compatible with the large number of existing 80386-based PCs.

Another candidate standard is currently called "Captain Crunch" and was developed in 1993 by Media Vision Inc. This video compression standard is significantly different from MPEG and DVI, making it much simpler to implement. As a result, Captain Crunch could provide the necessary full-motion-video multimedia support to tens of millions of existing PC systems. Media Vision foresees upgrade costs of only a few hundred dollars.

Candidate standards like Captain Crunch that can extend multimedia backward into the large installed base of current systems should help to propel multimedia much more quickly to the next development phase.

The Pervade Phase

By 1995 or 1996, virtually all personal computers will have multimedia capabilities. By then the cost of designing in multimedia, and the popularity of the technology, will have made it a standard feature. Concomitantly, personal computers will have become personal communications systems. On these systems, text, graphics, sound, voice, images, and motion images will be as easy to produce and manipulate as text and graphics are now. Application developers will include multimedia features as routinely as they now include *Help* and graphical-user-interface features.

Multimedia will be seen as the most effective way to communicate information in any business environment. It will be part of operating systems, networks, and database management tools. Product developers will have the benefit of a fundamental multimedia standard set.

We see evidence of these changes already in Microsoft's Multimedia Extensions (MME) to Windows, and in IBM's OS/2 Multimedia Presentation Manager and Apple's QuickTime.

Networks and networking software will also undergo changes that make them capable of supporting computer-centered multimedia applications and files. Local-area networks will be enhanced to support the transport of dynamic media. Wide-area networks will have the benefit of ISDN and BISDN running on the Synchronous Optical Network (SONET), or Asynchronous Transfer Mode (ATM). ATM is an international standard developed by CCITT for transporting voice, data, image, and video independent of rate, media, or services.

Cost and justification

At this phase of development, cost justification for multimedia will be irrelevant. All new computers will come equipped with basic multimedia capabilities, and software products will use those capabilities to create new applications and raise the value of the computers themselves.

Multimedia technology, like the graphical user interface, will become part of the user interface. Applications will use audio and video wherever they are best suited to the delivery of particular information.

Infrastructure

Multimedia capabilities will be built into system software, and improved user interfaces will make using multimedia both easy and intuitive. The skill issue will evaporate as users become more accustomed to working with audio and video, just as they now are to working with text and graphics.

Standards

Today, when one hits a key on a keyboard and a character appears on a computer display screen, no one cares that between the keystroke event and that of the displayed character, all kinds of encoding and decoding may have taken place.

Similarly, in the pervade phase of multimedia, users will not need to know or care about what happens to the voice spoken into the microphone, or the images captured from the camera or other video source. Multimedia files created on one platform will be readily movable to another platform, just as ASCII text files now move easily over WANs from platform to platform (see Table 9.1).

TABLE 9.1   Phases of Multimedia Evolution

	Enable	Enhance	Pervade
Applications	Vertical, training-oriented	Horizontal, included in popular personal productivity tools	Multimedia used virtually everywhere
Costs	High but justifiable	Much lower cost due to emerging standards and higher volumes	Irrelevant, because multimedia is standard part of all systems
Infrastructure	Hybrid analog and digital systems	Moving toward all-digital implementations	As easy to use as today's mouse and keyboard
Standards	None, except for individual subsystem standards	Standards for audio and video emerging	Comprehensive and transparent

Moving One "Byte" at a Time

The move from the personal computer of today to the personal communications system of tomorrow will be a giant step accomplished by making a sequence of smaller steps. These smaller steps relate to the four technologies at the core of computer-centered multimedia: *audio, high-capacity mass storage, video,* and *networking.*

Audio

Adding audio to personal computers meant handling a dynamic medium for the first time in an environment geared to static media. The requirements for handling audio, however, are easier to meet than those for video. Thus, audio was the first small step.

Computer games and applications such as Microsoft's Flight Simulator take advantage of a computer's audio-processing capabilities. Computer games have been the most prolific users of computer sound, and their popularity helped to drive the cost of add-in sound boards down well below $100.

The availability of sound for little or no extra cost is enticing software developers of business products to add sound to their wares. Lotus Development Corp., for example, was among the first to offer a software product—Lotus Sound—that enabled users of office applications (e.g., word processors, spreadsheets, and e-mail) to add voice annotations.

Microsoft has enhanced its Windows system to support sound, and both OS/2 and the Macintosh operating system have also been modified to support sound capabilities.

High-capacity mass storage

Digital sound and video consume huge quantities of data storage. For example, audio CD–quality stereo sound is sampled at 44.1 kHz with 16 bits per sample. This translates into a data-transfer rate of 705,600 bits per second per channel. At that rate, a 1.44-Mbyte flexible diskette can store 8 seconds of CD-quality sound.

Lower-quality sound can be sampled at 22 kHz with 8 bits per sample requiring a 176,000-bits-per-second-per-channel transfer rate. The flexible diskette could then store up to 32 seconds of stereo sound or 64 seconds of monaural sound. An hour's worth of monaural sound (sampled at 22 kHz with 8 bits per sample) would practically fill up an 80-Mbyte hard disk. Obviously, magnetic storage technologies, such as flexible and hard-disk drives, were a poor match for audio storage.

CD-ROM technology, on the other hand, offers inexpensive, removable, high-capacity (e.g., 650 Mbytes) storage. Audio CDs have largely displaced vinyl phonograph records as the medium of choice for music distribution and reproduction. CD-ROMs are becoming the primary medium for storing huge volumes of text, static images, and sound. As shown next, with suitable compression, CD-ROM technology is also the right medium for video.

Full-motion video

Real-color, full-motion video is incredibly memory-intensive. For example, a display screen with a picture element (pixel) array of 640 × 480 pixels, each pixel requiring 24 bits of data, represents over 7 million bits of data! If the screen were redrawn 30 times per second, the data rate would be greater than 200 million bits per second. One second's worth of video (e.g., 30 frames) would require more than 27 Mbytes of storage. Thus, an 80-Mbyte disk drive would be more than filled by 3 seconds' worth of video data, and a CD-ROM would hold about 24 seconds' worth!

Both the data-transfer rate and storage capacity requirements can be mitigated by choosing a smaller display area, using a 256-color scheme (e.g., 8 bits per pixel), or lowering the frame rate from 30 to 15. Each compromise, however, downgrades the quality of the video image.

The standards proposed by MPEG and Captain Crunch would compress the raw video data output into a much reduced amount of data, while preserving much of the video information. The end result of such compression is the ability to store more than an hour of video on a CD-ROM.

With MPEG, the raw video data must first be stored temporarily, then compressed, then stored in compressed form. Thus even though the final stored result is compressed, a large-capacity storage system is required for the interim data. Captain Crunch, however, performs real-time compression on incoming video data. Thus there is no need for a large-capacity buffer storage system. This real-time compression makes it feasible to process video on an affordable desktop.

Both video compression methods (MPEG and Captain Crunch) provide on-the-fly video decompression and display.

Multimedia networking

The fourth and final step in multimedia evolution involves networking. Today's networked personal computers are usually connected to local-area networks, or LANs. These networks allow users to share information, access data from on-line services, and handle transactions on corporate databases.

Today's LANs are designed for static media (e.g., text and graphics) and are optimized for use where data traffic is bursty rather than lengthy or continuous. This is not a good match for dynamic media, which need to preserve the time relationships very precisely.

Tomorrow's LANs, however, will be modified so as to efficiently manage audio and video data streams, thus forging multimedia into a pervasive business resource.

Wide-area networks are well along the path toward handling multimedia data. BISDN running on SONET or ATM is capable of supporting text, graphics, animation, audio, and compressed full-motion video.

The Pieces Fall into Place

With audio and video joining text and graphics as all-digital technologies, the way is now open to combine these multiple media within a common system and over a common network.

Personal computer technology keeps advancing, and with each advance another step is taken along the path of multimedia evolution that leads from feasibility to practicality. Once, audio on an 8-bit machine with 16-bit data paths and flexible diskette drives was feasible; today, audio on a 32-bit machine with 32-bit data paths and a CD-ROM drive is practical.

Video, because of its data intensity, called for the most in the way of computing resources, and a practical solution to the data-compression requirement. The computing resources are here, and so is the practical data-compression solution.

We will now begin to see an increase in the development of multimedia authoring tools, and a particular surge in those applications that employ multimedia. This will be due in part to the increasing number of systems capable of supporting multimedia, and in part to the communications value provided by this technology.

With systems capable of quickly and easily mixing text, graphics, sounds, and moving images, we can begin to meet the needs of twenty-first-century communications by using the right choices of communications media to their best advantages.

Multimedia on a Budget

Joseph Weintraub

Getting Started

True multimedia, with full-motion video, can be fantastically expensive today. The high-end JPEG video accelerator boards alone are currently $2000, about the price of a new 486DX33 PC with 200-meg hard drive. In addition, just 60 seconds of this high-definition video can consume more than 52 Mbytes of hard-disk space. A ten-minute MPC video production would require 10×52, or an astounding 520 Mbytes. How big is your hard drive right now? As a user you can get somewhat over 520 Mbytes on a single CD-ROM, but as an MPC Developer you would need several gigabytes of hard disk to work with and to store this video before it is converted to CD-ROM. Gbyte hard drives are available, and in fact a 2.1-Gbyte SCSI hard drive and controller would add just about $3000 to the cost of this hypothetical 486, now hovering around $8000 or $9000.

Our first multimedia disk was produced on a very tight budget, on a 386 PC with just a 120-meg hard drive, yet it is still a visually exciting and powerful half-hour presentation. It can be viewed on almost any DOS Machine with a color monitor, giving a potential audience of over 200,000 users, compared with the current installed MPC Base of under 12,000.

In this article I will show you, step-by-step, how we produced this sophisticated and professional automated VGA Slide Show on a 3.5-inch high-density diskette for the IBM/PC for under $2500 and how we can sell it profitably for just $29.95.

Step 1.   Prepare your slides and photographs

The easiest way, by far, to create your first multimedia presentation is to adapt a slide show or video for playback on the VGA or Super VGA Monitor of your PC. That way you don't have to worry too much about "creating" the presentation, and can concentrate on the technical details associated with getting it onto your PC's hard drive.

If you are creating a new presentation from scratch, you might consider shooting a few hundred Kodachrome slides with your Nikon, then selecting and arranging them in sequence in a slide projector tray till they do a good job of presenting your ideas visually. Later you will bring that slide presentation into your computer room and digitize it! Of course if you can afford a Fotoman Digital Camera from Logitech, you will save a good deal of time, not to mention film. (It uses magnetic disks.)

Step 2.   Write your narration

Present your slide show to a roomful of people, or even just one other person. As the slide show proceeds, narrate in a loud, clear voice so as to emphasize and explain your ideas fully. Capture the narration on a quality tape recorder!

Later, you can have this tape typed onto the computer, or perhaps even digitized directly into a MPC soundtrack on your hard drive. (Note that digitized voice also takes up a lot of hard-disk space. Do not plan to digitize more than 20 minutes of voice and music. If your narration is longer than 20 minutes, plan on presenting the text as bright-white on a blue background, or some other eye-pleasing combination.)

Step 3.   Install software and study the manuals cover-to-cover

At a minimum, you will need some sort of digitizer board installed in your computer, some sort of video camera to capture your slides, and the software that comes with your digitizer board that "takes the digital picture" and stores it on your hard drive. In addition you will probably want PC Paint or Aldus's PhotoStyler to touch up and perhaps add text to your digitized images.

If your slides, photos, video camera, or digitizer are black-and-white, you can "colorize" the images effectively once they are on your hard drive, and often come up with a more creative presentation than if you had started with perfect high-resolution color.

You will also need a multimedia run-time program or "slide show" software package so as to present your finished images with sophisticated wipes and dissolves between screens. We used Show Partner from Brightbill-Roberts with extremely good results. You will actually learn to use your software by working with it, but you can save yourself a lot of trouble by *reading the manual from cover to cover!*

Step 4.   Get your hardware installed and ready to use

We purchased a very simple but effective b & w Digitizer board with a b & w video camera. The total outlay for hardware and software was under $500. While the board we used is no longer available, you can still get a low-resolution board from Video Eyes for under $300.

Instructions for installing your hardware will vary with the board, but in general you just turn off your 386 or 486 computer, slip the board into an open slot, and secure it in place with just one screw. If no jumper switches have to be set, this should take you all of 10 minutes.

Step 5.   Prepare your work environment and try the tutorial

Someone once said to me, "When you work, *ONLY* work!" and I consider this very good advice. Get the family out of the house or office. Put out the dog and feed the cat. Turn off that darn TV and put on your "creativity music," which should not be so loud that you can't hear yourself think! Forget about your diet, your doctor, your spouse, your kids, your income, your taxes, your health, and any other worries that might be sabotaging your creative impulses!

Why is creative thought like meditation? Because they both require a certain mental discipline, solitude, and quiet time and space. What is the sound of one hand clapping? How many angels can dance on the head of a pin? How many pixels are there on a Super VGA Screen? What is the secret of a successful PC slide show or multimedia presentation? For me, the secret is in keeping my use of unusual special effects to a minimum. For you, it may be something else. Working with your specific hardware and software in a "loose" experimental way, without worrying too much about perfect results, may allow you to create moods and styles that are effective and very new!

Step 6.   Go through a minipresentation with just three slides

Don't mechanically record every slide in your tray just to get it done, only to find out after days of work that you have repeated the same mistake 300 times. Instead, take just your first three slides all the way to a finished presentation. Save your results on a floppy disk. Turn off your PC and leave the room. Go have a beer and a few pretzels...maybe a pastrami sandwich...or some brussels sprouts with garlic and butter...whatever...then come back, turn on the PC, make believe you are the audience, and start your three-slide presentation. Does it work? If not, fix it. If it does work, you are on the right track. Go on to slide number four.

My work consisted of a lot of mental leaps and bounds, but basically came in two flavors:

1. Grunt work
2. Creative play

The grunt work involved turning on the slide projector, focusing the next slide, focusing the b & w video camera on the projected image, endlessly adjusting the size of the image, observing the image on the PC screen, and pressing some keys to save it to the hard disk.

The creative play involved colorizing the image in PC Paint and trying out the seemingly endless variety of wipes, drips, weaves, and dissolves available in Show Partner! That's the most fun I've ever had.

Step 7.   Prepare your full visual presentation. Add text where appropriate.

Now that you know what works and doesn't, continue until you have completed your full presentation. Don't be afraid to continue to experiment with timing, color, text, dissolves and wipes, and other special effects. The longer your presentation, the more you must do to hold the viewers' interest through the entire show. You may be adding text to the bottom of screens or you may be alternating screenfuls of text and VGA images.

Be sure your screens don't zip by so fast that your audience can't finish reading the text. Since machines vary so much in speed, it is safest to ask the user to "press any key" to continue to the next screen. A show that drags along on an old 286 may zip by about 10 times too fast on a new 486.

Of course if you're using a soundtrack with digitized speech, you will want to keep text to a minimum—perhaps just titles and credits.

Step 8.   Check your spelling and continuity

Nothing destroys your professional image like a misspelled word. If you know you can't spell, use a spellchecker (or a literate friend) to check the spelling of your text. Don't get too fancy with fonts. Two or three font styles in bright-white against blue is just perfect! Blue on white or yellow is also quite readable. Avoid tiny type that older folks won't be able to read. Old English is tempting for some applications, but can be difficult to read on a PC screen.

Step 9.   Add voice or music as a planned part of your presentation

Add any special effects, but in moderation, please—this is not a psychedelic light show for a rock concert!

A good presentation does not require digitized voice, music, or special-effect sounds, but if you have the time and equipment, a soundtrack can add a lot. However, not all of your customers will have a SoundBlaster Pro with stereo speakers, so be sure your show stands on its own, even if no sound system is available to the viewer. Don't count on the PC speaker to deliver intelligible speech. It varies too much in quality from one PC to another, and some laptops have no speaker at all.

It is best to create your soundtrack on a high-quality multitrack tape recorder, for later translation to a variety of digital formats.

Step 10.   Make backup copies of all your work

How would you feel if you had worked for 48 straight hours, completed the first multimedia presentation of your life, and then had a fatal hard disk *CRASH* that Wiped out all of your work with no hope of recovery of even one single screen?! You'd feel pretty sick, right? So backup, backup, backup, backup! We now have a Jumbo Colorado Tape Backup that backs up the entire 212-meg hard drive in under 20 minutes, just by pressing F1.

But even if you can't afford a tape backup, you can afford a stack of floppy disks! It only takes five minutes to copy your presentation to a floppy, but it can save you *days of work.*

Step 11.   Prepare your "Silver Master"

You are getting down to the short strokes now. Your presentation is almost complete. Arrange all your PIC Files neatly in a single directory with your runtime software. View it from start to finish. Does it look good? Yes? Then *copy it to a floppy* and stash it securely in your bottom drawer! That is your *extra insurance backup.* Now copy to *another* floppy. That is your "Silver Master."

Step 12.   Alpha-test your Silver Master by yourself

Modify it if required. If you can sleep on it, this is a good time to do so. When you wake up the next day, view your Silver Master. Any required changes will stick out like a sore thumb. Make those required changes. Update your backups and Silver Master with the changes.

Step 13.   Show your Silver Master to a friend

Your first exposure to the world should be to a friendly part of the world: a friend or a loved one.

Step 14.   Ask for honest criticism, then revise as required.

You don't want false praise, you want honest, constructive criticism. You must learn to accept criticism from others, and develop the knack of seeing your work through their eyes. What sings to you may not sing to everyone.

Ask yourself: How general is my intended audience? Am I aiming my work at a special group? If so, show it to a representative member of that special group. If you feel that anyone could enjoy and learn from your multimedia presentation, then grab anyone off the street and show it to anyone! Communication involves you, your medium, your creation, and your audience! Check it out before you try to sell it.

Step 15.   Prepare your "Golden Master"

Your Golden Master is the master from which all sale copies will be reproduced. It should be perfect. I like to use Norton Utilities VL (volume label) to give my Golden Master a special unique volume name, and then use Norton FD (file date) to revise the file date and time so that they are the same on every file. These two steps add that small professional finishing touch you will find on many professional disks. You will notice that every file is dated 01/01/94, and every file was created at 12:00 am. This is of course impossible, yet it has become the mark of a professional multimedia disk.

Step 16.   Beta-test your Golden Master with a coworker or other person whose opinion you respect

I know you think you have tested more than enough, and everything is perfect, but there is always one more bug. Now is the time to enlist the help of a coworker and find that last misspelled word or other tiny error that will be so irritating after it has been copied onto your first 100 labeled diskettes!

Step 17.   Ask for honest, constructive feedback; make final revisions.

If you still have to make a few creative changes or clarifications, now is the time to bite the bullet and do so. There will not be another chance like this to get it right. Once it is right, if you are unfortunate enough to have a boss, this is when you show it to your boss.

Step 18.   Make a small production run of about 100 disks and manuals.

Wow! You have "published" your first multimedia presentation. If it is unusual and wonderful, perhaps your next run will be 5000 or 10,000 copies! Or maybe a few hundred thousand! Or maybe you will have a million-seller on your hands, and get rich and famous!

Step 19.   Run ads in *PC* magazine, *BYTE, PC Computing,* and *Computer Shopper.* Damn the expense!

Also send review copies to every reviewer in the world. Install an 800 number for orders. Get credit card vendor status. Your phone is ringing off the hook! Wealth, freedom, more creative time, and a visit from the bluebird of happiness!

11

The Competitive Edge

Harry Hallman

Introduction

Athletes train for it! Students learn for it! Governments go to war for it! But perhaps the most fiercely fought battles for obtaining a competitive edge are waged on the international playing fields of business and industry. The complexity and fast-changing business environment of today's world has wreaked havoc with organizations that were considered to be, just 10 years ago, the most formidable marketing forces on the face of the earth.

Now they, along with thousands of new startups, are scrambling to gain what little advantage they can. Cost-cutting, redesign of products, "right-sizing," and a host of other modern business techniques are being employed in order to allow these companies not so much to prosper as simply to survive.

An organization's ability to accurately and effectively communicate has never been more important. And any tool that allows companies to communicate better with their customers, employees, and stakeholders is or at least should be valued. Multimedia is one such technology.

What *Is* Multimedia, Anyway?

It's interesting that the most promising communications tool ever to be invented has started its life with such a confusing name. The term *multimedia* has different meanings to different groups of people.

To the advertising community, multimedia means the use of various media, such as print ads, broadcast television and radio, to conduct an advertising campaign. To schoolteachers in the 1950s and 1960s, multimedia was the use of audio, film strips, and books to help in the teaching effort.

In 1970, the term *multimedia* was invented to describe the use of multiple slide projectors synchronized with audio and shown on the same screen. That was changed, in the United States, to the term *multi-image*.

Then came the late eighties and early nineties. Multimedia now means the use of computers to communicate, inform, and educate through an interactive mix of graphics, video, text, and audio. The term has become so confusing that IBM created its own brand by renaming it Ultimedia. Others have decided that an appropriate name for this media should be *new media*.

Whatever you want to call it, multimedia is audiovisual communication with one important distinction—interactivity. And it is the interactive part of these media that offers to provide companies with a competitive marketing edge.

The advantages interactive audiovisuals offer in the field of training are fairly self-evident, but it is in marketing that we may see these media truly excel. Virtually all current marketing communication tools are linear in nature. That is, they make a specific statement and cannot deviate from that statement. They move in a straight line.

Unfortunately, prospects' minds very rarely move in straight lines. As they view a video or listen to a live presentation they get thoughts, have questions, develop concerns. Most salespeople correctly view these interactions as opportunities to move the sale closer to a close. Yet how many times have you heard a presenter tell a prospect that he or she will answer all questions at the end of the presentation, simply because he or she didn't want to deviate from the order of the slides in the tray? By then most of the good questions—and the sale—may have been forgotten.

Clearly, the more interactivity you create, the better. And the only tool better at this important task than interactive audio-visuals is prone to miscues, affected by the physical and mental atmosphere of the meeting place, and requires thousands of dollars in shipping costs just to get it in front of the prospect. That tool, of course, is the salesperson.

This is not to say that the salesperson will ever be replaced. That simply won't happen, but we can make them more productive, more articulate, more professional, and more knowledgeable. And that can be accomplished by using this new audiovisual tool we are now calling "multimedia."

Two Multimedia Success Stories

Thousands of people are using multimedia to help them in their marketing efforts and to create marketing successes. But two stories stand out as testimonies to the real power of multimedia. One involves the selling of a city, and the other netted a $110 million contract.

Atlanta's bid for the 1996 Olympics

How do you convince an international committee to consider your city for the Olympics? First you assemble a great team of city leaders, then you devise a method for that team to portray the city as a modern metropolis capable of handling millions of visitors. That's exactly what some citizens of Atlanta did.

Once the team of leaders had been put together, its members went to Fred Dyer of Georgia Tech University to help them develop some marketing tools that could show what the city would look like in 1996 when the Olympics came to town. Dyer and his group came up with a plan to create two different multimedia presentations. The first was a kiosk using full-motion video and sophisticated animation, all controlled by a roller ball.

Using the roller ball, the viewer visually flies in any selected direction across the metro Atlanta area. The rate of speed is controlled by how fast the viewer moves the ball. As he or she comes upon a part of the city that will house a specific building, the computer switches to 3-D animation of that facility. Again using the roller ball, the viewer tours the facility, receiving information on the go.

The second presentation the Georgia Tech group put together was a three-screen projected-video, computer-controlled extravaganza, all located in a minitheater. The theater houses a small grouping of chairs and a control panel that is a model of the city covered in Plexiglas. The panel is a sort of multimedia presentation of its own. Cars, trucks, and other vehicles move through the city streets as the viewer is asked to start the show and select one of two languages available.

The show was an interactive sight-and-sound extravaganza that provided the viewer with a realistic glimpse of what the 1996 Olympics would be like if held in Atlanta.

Of course the city of Atlanta *was* selected as the site for the 1996 Summer Olympic Games. While the effort to attract the Olympic Games and the millions of dollars that go with it was a major team effort, the leaders of that effort are quick to tout the power that their multimedia tools provided.

ETS expected excellence, and got it

In 1992, Educational Testing Services, the world's largest testing organization, was asked to bid (along with two competitors) to help a prestigious medical council computerize their current paper-and-pencil certification test. ETS was given three months to create a plan and present it at the council's national meeting.

Each competitor would make a two-hour presentation to the entire council of over 125 people. They also would be given the opportunity to operate a week-long technical center, where council members and their staff could see firsthand the type of work ETS was doing in the field.

While the ETS staff worked on the actual proposal, it turned to Lynn Tumulty of ETS's communications department to help it create the necessary materials needed to convince the council to select ETS for the project.

Tumulty devised a plan that included a mixed-media presentation of slides, video, audio, and live speaker for the two-hour presentation to the council. She then designed a strategy for the technical center that included the use of multimedia.

To help her in the creation of both the presentation and the multimedia, Tumulty asked Michael Olenski, Vice President of Corporate Media Communications of Philadelphia, PA, to create all the audiovisual materials, including the multimedia, and set them up on-site at the hotel where the event was to take place.

Olenski's staff created several free-running multimedia animated kiosks for the event. But perhaps the most powerful use of multimedia was in the creation of a simulated management software package. ETS wanted to show the council how the computer software that would manage the testing process would work. There simply were not enough time or resources to create a real working copy of this custom package.

Olenski's staff used Autodesk's Animator Pro animation software to create the computer software simulation. The program used standard graphic effects and interactivity to give the Council a realistic view of how the software would work. Both ETS and CMC staff helped to make over 150 one-on-one presentations of this simulation during the week-long event.

On Friday, as the council meeting came to a close, council members voted on their vendor of choice. ETS was selected to implement the five-year, $110 million effort. Both ETS and the council management acknowledged the impact that both the more traditional presentation materials and the multimedia software simulation had had on the selection process.

Other Practical Applications

Not all marketing opportunities are million-dollar babies. In fact, most are simple day-to-day events that lead in time to millions of dollars. Let's explore some possible uses of multimedia in helping to increase the effectiveness of communications in several important marketing efforts, including

1. Lead generation
2. Sales presentations
3. Proposals
4. Point of sale
5. Customer education
6. Customer satisfaction
7. Marketing/advertising research

These ideas are meant only to stimulate your own thought processes. It is the marketer's own imagination that will, of course, create unlimited uses for interactive audiovisuals.

Lead or sales generation

Multimedia kiosks placed in high-traffic areas, such as malls and trade shows, can collect names and addresses of interested prospects. They can issue coupons to be redeemed later at a business location. Through the proper collection of data, these devices can even help you to qualify the prospects.

While in the past this task has been taken care of with relative ease by standard computers, it is the advent of the colorful and exciting combination of graphics, sounds, and motion, all provided at reasonable prices, that makes multimedia so attractive for lead generation.

Sales presentations

Salespeople complain that the more traditional presentations, using slides and overheads, distract from the selling process. Those types of media are bulky and cumbersome, and because they are linear, the salesperson cannot always take advantage of the power of total interaction with the customer.

Perhaps one of the most powerful forms of multimedia for use in presentation is *compact-disc interactive* (CD-I). Imagine being able to store thousands of images, numerous full-motion, full-screen videos, all linked to high-quality sound, on one 5-inch compact disc. Now imagine opening your briefcase, plopping a small presentation unit onto the customer's desk, inserting the disc, and making a presentation you had programmed just hours before. No cumbersome trays and projection units. No changing from the slide projector to the videotape player and back again. And most importantly, when the customer asks a question that may deviate from the formal presentation, you will be able to immediately interact with your presentation media to answer that question.

Using standard computers and multimedia can provide the same benefits for conference-room or large-audience presentations.

Proposals

One of the most difficult aspects of the proposal presentation is making the ideas you are presenting come alive for the prospect. In the case of ETS, mentioned above, it was necessary to show how a specific software would function. Multimedia made that possible. If you were selling a new construction project, you might want to show what the building would look like when it was completed. And if you were an ad agency seeking a multimillion-dollar contract, you would certainly need to show and let the prospect hear your ideas. Multimedia makes all of these concepts come to life, and it can do this for virtually any product or service.

Point of sale

Audiovisuals have been used as point-of-sale tools for years, and have proven to be very effective. With multimedia you can add the dimension of interactivity (at a reasonable cost), and allow customers to see and hear exactly what they desire. They won't have to sit through a five-minute videotape to learn what they want to know. Instead they will go directly to the subject and get the answer quickly. That in turn will get them to the checkout counter faster.

Customer education

One of the most powerful tools a marketer has at its fingertips is customer/prospect education. The concept is simple. You, as a supplier, provide critical information that educates the customer or prospect so that they can make a logical buying decision. In doing this, you show your trust and your willingness to provide service, and this predisposes the customer to buy from you. One large telecommunications company has traced over $250 million in sales to a two-year customer education program they conducted.

Creating customer education materials in the form of CD-ROM or CD-I discs, and making them available to prospects and clients, will help to cut the cost of the more traditional approaches to conducting seminars. While seminars are extremely valuable for one-on-one interaction, and do facilitate sales, it is not always practical to have seminars in every city or to fly every prospect to your location. In such cases, an interactive multimedia customer education program could be sent to the prospect.

In the case of CD-I, a company could send the playback unit and disc to the prospect and it would be less expensive than the average air fare to fly a prospect to a location. And in those cases where seminars are practical, the multimedia can be distributed to the attendees so that they can share the important information with colleagues back home.

Customer satisfaction

Imagine getting a multimedia instruction disc every time you purchased one of those "impossible-to-put-together" toys for your child. Surely it would increase your satisfaction to be able to put the toy together faster and more easily. While packaging a multimedia instruction disc with every hard-to-put-together toy may not be practical, the $2 or so it would cost is certainly practical for automobiles, lawnmowers, manufacturing equipment, and thousands of other products that require assembly or special knowledge to operate.

Not only will you help to create satisfied customers, you may even attract new customers who see the multimedia as added value.

New products

Most companies have intellectual assets they have gathered over their years of being in business. Often this knowledge can be turned into new information-based products. The product could be a training program useful in other industries, or a database of facts that have value to others. In either case this information could be turned into multimedia programs offered for sale within the industry or even to the consumer market.

This is, of course, not a new idea, in that many companies already have done this successfully. But with the advent of multimedia and especially the new compact-disc technology, the creation of CD-I titles for now paper-intensive information may be more practical for many smaller organizations.

Is Computer Technology the Competitive Edge?

There are those who do believe that computer technology provides a competitive advantage for companies that are able to buy it. But study after study has proven that simply "buying" this type of technology has little effect on those factors that make a company a better competitor. In fact, in some cases productivity, customer service, and profitability have suffered, thus making the company *less* competitive.

It is the manner in which the technology is implemented that is the most important factor. Applications, applications, applications! A word that should be thrice emblazoned on every multimedia product. Every user, every provider, and every manufacturer of multimedia products and services should be thinking in terms of the applications, not just the features of a product.

"Build it and they will come" only works in the movies. In the real world of business you must first find out what the customer wants and needs, then build it better than your hundreds of competitors, and finally get up on the highest mountaintop you can find and shout to the world that you have an application that will fill their wants and needs. And you need to do it *often*. Multimedia can help companies do just this.

Virtual Anesthesia

Guy Hancock, DVM

Virtual reality can be understood as a substitution of man-made input for natural input to one or more of the senses, usually sight and sound. At the extremes of imagination are virtual environments, which provide complete immersion through coordinated stimulation of the senses of touch, proprioception, and even smell. Multimedia can be used to approximate a virtual environment by including recognizable visual, audio, and other cues that help the viewer/user suspend disbelief and become engrossed in the virtual experience.

Multimedia simulations can include many aspects of virtual reality to enhance believability for the user. In education, the simulations are designed to teach the student in preparation for real-life situations. Although they are not primarily entertainment, they must be entertaining enough to keep students interested if they are to be used more than a few times.

Interactive multimedia can use real or model instruments and controls connected to the computer. The most common example is the joystick for flight simulators. A more exotic example is found in advanced flight trainers that tilt and bump to give realistic proprioception sensations.

Elements relatively easily available to an author wishing to create a computer simulation include graphics, still video, video, sound, interactivity, and sequencing. Certain techniques and principles of applying each of these elements contribute to making the multimedia simulation more like virtual reality.

A project under development at St. Petersburg Junior College is an anesthesia tutorial and simulation for veterinary technology students. While designing More Anesthesia, Please!, we repeatedly examined and revised the use of graphic images, sound, video, timing, and interactivity.

Anesthesia was chosen as an appropriate subject because it is one of the most costly laboratory experiences to provide for students. In spite of the time and resources devoted to it, students lack confidence and want more practice.

Some experiences we cannot (or will not) provide in the laboratory, such as cardiac or respiratory arrest. A simulation of these emergencies is an excellent way for students to practice their responses. Anesthesia laboratories are, by necessity, conducted in small groups so that students do not get to be solely responsible for an anesthetic procedure. They also must progress through the anesthesia labs according to a schedule. This schedule is always too slow for the advanced students and too fast for some others. The anesthesia simulation can address or overcome all of these limitations and problems. It serves as a cost-effective complement and supplement to the anesthesia laboratories.

More Anesthesia, Please! is authored in SuperCard and runs on any Macintosh with a color monitor. SuperCard has many similarities to HyperCard, but it allows full use of color. The student goes through the steps, from picking a case and making choices about the equipment to inducing and maintaining anesthesia. Examples from this project are used to illustrate the application of these elements to enhance both the realism and engagement of the user.

There are two alternatives for storing the media; laser disc or CD-ROM. For a laser disc, the computer is connected to a laser disc player with a separate monitor. A script in the software directs the player to show particular still frames, video segments, or play audio from the laser disc. The scripts are activated by various events, such as mouse clicks or cards opening or closing. The laser disc version has the advantages of full-screen video at good resolution and 30-frames-per-second display. The disadvantage is in requiring the laser player and monitor.

In the CD-ROM version, the audio and video segments from the laser disc or other source are first recorded as QuickTime movies. The scripts then call these movies, which appear on the computer monitor. The advantages of CD-ROM are that the software and all the movies are on a single disc, and the discs are less expensive. CD-ROM players are becoming more commonplace and cost less than laser disc players. The disadvantages are a smaller window to view the movies, reduced frame rate, and lower resolution. The image must overlay and temporarily obscure part of the computer screen. The ideal solution is to make both versions available to the intended audience and let individuals pick the version that best fits.

Graphic Images

Graphic imagescan enhance a simulation if they realistically convey some aspect of the environment modeled by the simulation. The arrangement, size, colors, position, textures, and shading can all contribute to increasing the realism. Graphic images can complement video images when using a separate monitor to display video in a two-monitor system. Graphic images also can trigger recognition and familiarity if they closely resemble real objects the student has seen or will see (Fig. 12.1).

Figure 12.1 Opening sequence for virtual anesthesia. (*Source: Michon Pratt.*)

We created graphic images for a floor plan of the hospital, patient monitors, and chart. Graphics were used in floating palette windows, for button icons, and an anatomical diagram. We used a cartoon in the opening sequence, which was scanned from the artist's drawing.

Still Video Images

Still video images most enhance the realism of a simulation when the pictures are taken from real-life situations. Further enhancement occurs if the pictures are taken from the perspective of the participant in the real-life experience. For example, the picture that most closely simulates driving a car is taken from the driver's seat looking through the windshield. It is even more realistic if the car's location at the time is appropriate to the simulation, and if the car is actually moving so that objects at the sides are blurred slightly.

For More Anesthesia, Please!, still video images were taken from the video disc itself and in a clinical lab using a still video camera. Pictures of drug bottles, patients, and the anesthesia machine were used (Fig. 12.2).

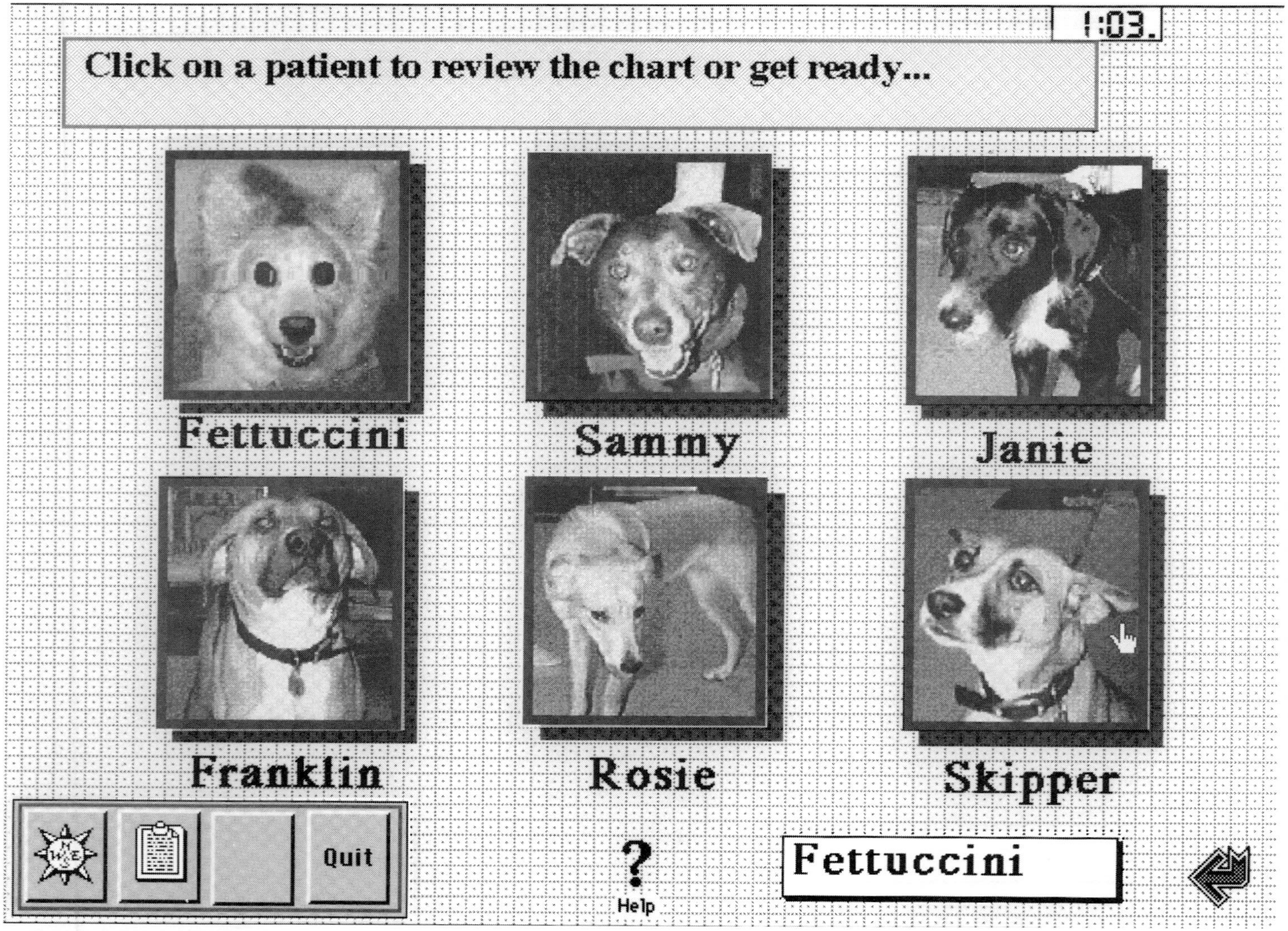

Figure 12.2 Still video imagery.

Video

Video offers much potential to draw the viewer into a virtual world. We are accustomed to watching television, to the degree that it might have become a reality of its own. A lot of TV is live video of real events, so video might make us more willing to imagine that simulated events are real. Video usually includes sound, and combining the two media gives a more powerful representation of reality.

People are very attuned to the sounds that accompany actions, activities, and events. Seeing motion, shadows and colors as we hear the expected sounds helps us enter the virtual world. The disbelief caused by the smaller-than-life-size screen, lack of depth perception, two-dimensional image, and colors that are not quite true is more easily overcome by the combination of sound and motion video.

For More Anesthesia, Please!, the video disc was repurposed. Our video selection was limited to what the original author filmed. The particular disc was well thought out, of good quality, and very complete. Some video scenes relevant to our purpose (not the same as the author's) are not on the disc. The challenge was to use as much of the available video as possible, as long as it enhanced the project. QuickTime video can be added for essential missing scenes. The tradeoff is that the storage size for the project increases dramatically as more QuickTime is added. However, video is so compelling in creating the virtual environment and engaging the user that it might well overcome this disadvantage.

Sound

Sound by itself can contribute to a more realistic simulation of reality. It has been found that the combination of wire frame visuals and sound are very effective in helping people to suspend disbelief. With the use of sound, it is not necessary to have fully realistic visual images in order to achieve immersion of the user in the virtual environment. Although people are not necessarily highly conscious of the many sounds that accompany daily activities and actions, they normally do expect to hear these sounds. The absence of real-life concurrent sounds would be noticed immediately. Conversely, the presence of these sounds, coordinated with graphics or video images in a simulation, adds a lot to the perception of reality.

Some of the sounds used in the project include a cow's moo, the click of knobs being turned on the anesthetic vaporizer, the click of switches on monitors, the sound of gas filling the rebreathing bag, and the beep of ECG monitors in surgery.

Music is another aspect of our auditory experience that is very familiar because of movies and television. Music is used to enhance these virtual experiences. In real life, no orchestra plays foreboding music to alert us to the next downturn of events. But we are so attuned to the uses of music in movies and television that, without concentration, it isn't consciously perceived. Music is used to emphasize storyline transitions, to reflect or influence the mood and emotion, to forewarn, and to reduce or enhance the surprise of the unexpected or shocking. Merely recall the soundtrack from the movie *Jaws*, with the play of its "heartbeat" theme each time the shark is about to appear. The music volume—and our tension levels—rise simultaneously, warning us unmistakably of some terrible impending development.

Using music effectively as a supporting element in a multimedia or virtual reality project is a challenge. It must be used consistently and in the proper places. If it is overdone or badly done, it detracts from the experience. The desired moods and emotions of the user must be the guiding principle in selecting music. The designer has to be conscious of the tempo, volume, and style of music used. Other elements to consider are the choice of instruments or voices, the melody, and duration. User control is another important consideration. It is very irritating to have the software lock up the computer, blaring out some long musical selection that cannot be shut off or turned down. You want your software to be used repeatedly. Keep asking yourself if the music you are using will sound as good to the user on the 20th playing as it does the first time.

For a good discussion of the technical aspects of using sound, refer to Cliff Kondratiuk's chapter, "Technical Aspects of Multimedia Audio," and Ken Morse's "Introduction to Digital Video and Audio." In other chapters, Serge Timacheff discusses "Bringing the Senses to Multimedia" and Mary and J. Alan Whiteside discuss the design considerations of "Using Audio in Multimedia Applications."

Interactivity

Interactivity means that the user receives appropriate and expected feedback in response to actions taken. In a simulation of doing a blood cell count under the microscope, the student might wish to change magnification from 10× to 40×. In real life, she would move an objective mounted on a turret. In a computer simulation, she might click on a button with the mouse, or click on a picture of a microscope objective. As the view changes to the larger magnification, the sound of the new objective clicking into place is heard. The sound reinforces the realism of the simulation because it is familiar, but also because it occurs in response to a user's action. Building more interactivity into a multimedia program helps it achieve a virtual reality.

Sequencing and Timing

The sequencing and timing of a multimedia program or simulation are important in creating a virtual reality. People are accustomed to events occurring in predictable sequences, and to having actions cause other actions or reactions. The multimedia program faithfully represents reality by not violating the beliefs and expectations of the users. The designer of a multimedia program has to make many decisions about which events in a sequence of A-Z are important, and which ones can be modeled or represented effectively. Not every step will be included. If enough of the important steps are represented effectively, the program will come closer to creating a virtual reality. Another aspect of sequencing is allowing the user to control the sequence of events. This mimics real life, and the consequences and feedback given to the user can further enhance the sense of realism.

The interactive canine anesthesia tutorial and simulation provides more examples of the various aspects of multimedia used to enhance the reality of the program. Veterinary technicians must examine each patient's chart for information that affects the administration of anesthetics. In developing the simulation, we attempted to make the on-screen chart look as much like a real patient chart as possible. Lots of information is in the chart, just as in a real one, forcing the technician to review the entire record and pick out the relevant items. To calculate drug doses, the student must recall chart information or go back to it for another look. Sometimes the units must be converted from pounds to kilograms before the calculations can be done—another real-life complication.

In another section of the program, the student will change the setting of the anesthetic vaporizer. The video disc being repurposed has a segment showing a close-up of a hand turning the vaporizer knob to the new setting. The parallel soundtrack includes the sounds of the vaporizer clicking into the new setting. When the anesthesia machine flush valve is pushed, a soundtrack segment from the video disc plays the sound of oxygen filling the rebreathing bag (Fig. 12.3). In surgery, the video is shot from the perspective of the anesthetist at the head of the table. Whenever something needs adjustment, the head technician turns and looks straight at the viewer, waiting for a response. This technique gets the student involved in the tensions and emotions of doing anesthesia.

Hardware and Software

The development of More Anesthesia, Please! has proceeded on a Macintosh IIcx and a Quadra 950. It is very helpful to have 8 to 12 (or more) megabytes of RAM memory so that multiple applications can be open simultaneously. VideoSpigot, QuickImage 24, and MoviePak Presenter video digitizer boards have been used. Video sources used are the laser player, video camera, Canon XapShot! still video camera, and videotapes. Sound was incorporated by using MacRecorder and SoundEdit to record and edit sounds, and by directing the laser player to play one or the other of the audio tracks. The laser player audio can be played either through the speaker in the monitor or through amplified speakers. It is helpful to have paint and draw programs to create graphics and edit pictures.

In repurposing a video disc, a major task is to index all the video and audio segments. We used a HyperCard stack designed for this purpose. It includes player controls to start and stop the disc, as well as find to specific frames. It took approximately six hours to create the index for one side of the laser disk for More Anesthesia, Please!. This work paid off when searching for each audio or video segment to include in the project. The lower the hardware

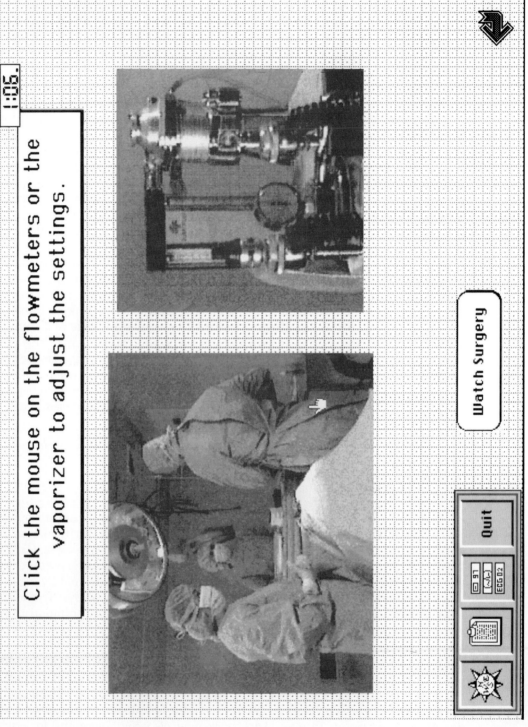

Figure 12.3 Watching the surgery.

requirements for running the project, the more units it will be able to play on. This was one reason for our choice to plan for a separate monitor with the laser player. Some video digitizer boards are capable of playing external video in a window on the Macintosh screen. However, these boards are not in most machines and are more costly than a video monitor. We decided that color was an essential aspect for this project. By making that choice, we gave up the potential to run the project on monochrome Macintoshes.

In summary, by involving more senses and more closely reflecting the real world, you can simulate a virtual reality in the mind of the viewer. Learning via multimedia virtual reality has the potential to be very memorable and influential. The advantages are that it can be much less costly to provide, can be repeated, and can allow the student to gain experiences that cannot be provided in real life.

Who Had Better Be on First

Getting Optimal Results from Multimedia Training

Rex J. Allen

The Great Irony

There is great irony in a book about multimedia—but it's not what you think.

You might think the irony lies in hefty chapters of printed matter that speak dryly of magnificent media in living color. But the chief irony is not in the contrast of digital video animations and dull chapter headings. A very good book, combined with a fertile imagination, can still grow mental media that not even Hollywood can afford to produce.

Or you may be thinking of the ironic contrast between a *passive* book and the exciting *interactive* technologies of multimedia of which we write. Actually, I found Hugo's *Les Misérables* to be profoundly interactive, and anything but passive.

So wherein lies the great irony? I have spent every working day of the past 14 years "in" multimedia—hardware, software, courseware. For me, the irony of this chapter in this book is that I don't know *you*. I don't know why you bought this book, or why you are reading this chapter. I don't know what you plan to do with multimedia technologies, or what motivates you, or what you knew before you began reading, or what TV shows you watch, or your background in instruction. Aye, there's the rub! You see, we at Allen Communication have enjoyed some remarkable successes with multimedia instruction *because* we worry incessantly about these very questions. We've learned that *who* must be on first.

Get to the point, you say. Okay, look at it this way. You are walking down the hallway in a high school and you meet someone who looks like a teacher—older, less colorful, unarmed. You ask, "What do you teach?" Or perhaps you are taking a break in the company lunch room and you overhear a group talking about their training classes. "Oh," you ask, "what do you teach?" The answers are predictable. In the school he or she will say, "I teach biology," or math, or English. In the training department they will say, "I teach software applications," or management skills, or forklift operation. And you will be terribly disappointed. You want them to say, "I teach kids!" or "I teach coworkers!"

This is the point. In education and training we go about, for the most part, teaching physics and OSHA compliance. *What* is on first, not *who*. Content experts become teachers and trainers, and then they teach content. Quite incidentally, in that process, *some people* learn *something*. They may even "meet the objectives," if there are any. But the learning is very, very far from optimized. If you think back on the handful of truly great teachers you have known, you may recall that they *cared*, or they *knew you*, or they made *it* (content) make sense to *you* (person).

Haven't We Met Somewhere?

So, I have to write this chapter based on some very general assumptions. If I knew you, I would write it differently and it would help you much, much more. For example, if I knew you as a college student in an instructional technology course, I'd interview lots of people like you. I would study your language, your values, your motivations. I would use pictures and diagrams and examples and questions that made sense to you. I would try to use a tone and pace that worked for you. I would try to acknowledge your fears or cynicism about learning, and even make you face these concerns. I might let you explore the content and come to your own conclusions, then dare you to make this content come alive in a personal project or simulation. *And* if I had multimedia technologies to help, I'd have a heyday with pictures and sounds and experiences that made sense to you.

Now, if I knew you to be a tired trainer in a hospital, I would write still differently. Maybe you want some very general ideas about "audience-centered" training design—a theoretical treatise about the why. Maybe you have inherited a ton of "traditional" instruction (i.e. boring, content-centered overhead transparencies) that you want to bring to life. You want a checklist or recipe that will help you to increase the value and interest of your training. Maybe you know all this stuff I'm talking about and just need a way to justify optimal learning to your boss. Or maybe, if you're lucky, your management has decided that training and education ought to become an integral part of organization strategy. You've been told to help increase profits and decrease costs, to make training accountable for real change in performance—to make it pay! *Good for you.* Now you have the motivation to optimize your impact. You will *want* to put who on first.

Here at Allen Communications, we have had our most important successes with multimedia instruction when we have taught people, not just content. Specifically, we and our clients have achieved real results (profits, savings, strategic positioning, quality, empowerment, etc.) when we hit the right audience with the right combination of methods and multimedia muscle. And we had to know the people before we could optimize their learning. It's very hard to do this, because everyone and their dogs will want you to focus on the content—especially the dogs. They will want you to cut the fluff and get to the meat of the subject. They will agonize over each step in a procedure, each word describing the system, each question about the schematic. But in their content-world they have forgotten that all dogs are hungry and *all learners are not*. So, *you* must put who on first.

So What's New About That?

But that's just good training, you complain. What's *new* here, and how does this apply to multimedia, anyway?

What's new is actually *doing* "good training," because we don't do it very often, and *how it applies* is the subject of the following paragraphs.

First, we will talk about the instructional development process, and where in that process the audience must be evaluated, acknowledged, loved, and taught. We'll even attempt to offer a checklist of sorts, including when and how to bring the learners back into learning. Then we'll offer three case studies that used this focus and process to achieve some remarkable results. My strong desire is that you, whoever you are, will be touched and taught. Then we will have bridged the "great irony" together.

An Instructional Design Process

So where can we reinsert the learner in learning? Let's look first at a rather standard and effective instructional development process. Now, don't get worried. This is not a soapbox sermon on any one particular instructional systems design (ISD) model. Nor will we argue the theoretical underpinnings of the various models. We will not debate the cognitive or social learning or behavioral doctrines, nor the "new" constructivist versus "old" structured approaches, nor the relative value of values and attitudes in learning.

Quite frankly, I would love to have these discussions with you some time. *Our* motivations and values as designers make a *big* difference in *their* learning as students! But we will not get into that now. Instead, take a look at Fig. 13.1, which shows the basic "systems" development model to which most of us subscribe.

But where do we focus on the learner? The picture of the process seen in Fig. 13.1 is too general, too far removed from actual development steps to help. We know that we must capture and understand the audience during the Analysis phase. But when and where? And how do we translate audience awareness into the remainder of the phases? Figure 13.2 represents a more specific model that works for interactive multimedia courseware development. It was adapted from my teachers, Walt Dick and Robert Gagné, with a touch of Mager and Merrill, and a lot of Allen thrown in. (See Dick and

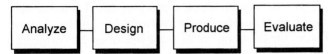

Figure 13.1   The systems development model.

Carey, 1990; Gagné, 1970; Mager, 1988; Merrill, et al., 1989.) Hopefully it is much like your approach. Note that not all critical steps, such as approvals, are included.

Is Fig. 13.2 similar to your process? Are you overwhelmed at the complexity, or underwhelmed by the simplicity? Or are you basically cynical about the whole "boxes and arrows" thing? We have found that this sort of instructional

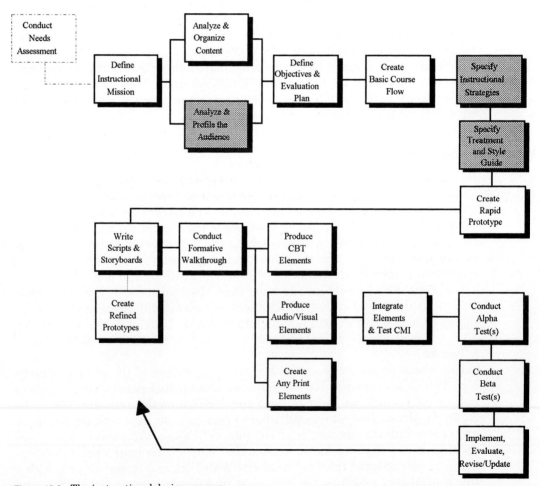

Figure 13.2   The instructional design process.

model works only when we work it, of course. It is important to note, however, that it is not a whimsical arrangement of steps. It is based on many decades of research and the results from many "real" applications. Specific checklists and tools are applied to each activity, and it works. If you are not following such a model, you can make great strides toward optimal learning simply by studying and adopting some such approach.

That said, the chief questions of this discussion now return: Where in all these activities can we focus to bring the audience to life? Which of these steps matters most, when it comes to final results?

Where and How Do We Put Who on First?

It has been our experience that *all* of the steps in our process make a difference to our instructional success. However, three of the major steps within the model seem to most influence our ability to create optimal learning, in conjunction with ongoing formative evaluation throughout the process. These include (1) the audience analysis itself, (2) the definition of strategies, and (3) the specification of a course treatment, including a style guide for "look and feel." (In order to make your reading interactive, look back at Fig. 3.12 and imagine that those three boxes are now colored differently and that they are flashing on and off. Cool, huh?!)

Of all the steps required to create great courseware, these three matter most. We have also found that these steps are least emphasized by most developers and trainers. For the most part, we have observed that a trainer will receive a mandate from the boss (the mission), collect and assess the content from subject matter experts (SMEs), organize it into "chunks" or modules, and then start writing a script, making transparencies, scheduling rooms, etc. After all, is there time for anything else—the dogs are after us, aren't they? So the trainer teaches content, and hopes the learning is caught, if not taught. No! There *is* time to do it right!

Analyze and profile the audience

During audience analysis, we try to find answers to the following kinds of questions. In our questionnaires and interviews, these are offered in a more random order, and "second questions" are often asked about a given area once someone is talking freely. Notice that we often combine additional content analysis with the audience analysis. Again, these are just sample items.

- In your opinion, what skills are most critical to success at your job?
- What is the most important attitude for someone in your job to have?
- What is most satisfying about the work you do?
- What do you find to be the most difficult aspect of your responsibilities?
- Why do some people "wash out" in your job area?
- What makes a real "star performer" in your area?

- In your mind, what is the most difficult part about working with _____ (specific skill, system, procedure to be taught)?
- In what area of _____ do you feel most certain about your skill and ability? Least certain?
- How did you learn _____? What was most helpful about this training? Least helpful?
- If you were to teach _____ to a friend, how would you do it?
- What motivates you to do a good job with _____?
- If you were "the boss," and could change anything about the way _____ is trained, what would you do?
- When you get stuck with _____, where do you go for help?
- Please *rank* the following activities in order of importance ("A" is most important, "B" next most important, etc.) on the left. Then *rate* their difficulty on the right ("5" is most difficult, "1" is least difficult).

Rank activity/task/issue	Difficulty	Comments
_____ Perform start-up procedure	5 4 3 2 1	
_____ Ask for the purchase order	5 4 3 2 1	
_____ Prepare the agenda	5 4 3 2 1	

Etc.

- What is your favorite sport or activity after work?
- What subject did you enjoy most in school?
- What is your favorite magazine and TV show?
- What music do you enjoy most?
- What do you do in your spare time (hobbies, interests, study, etc.)?
- How often do you think or read about something new to you (astronomy, geography, science, art)? What was the last thing that caught your attention?
- What else should we be asking about, so that we can make the new _____ training most effective?

As we gather audience data, we tend to follow this process:

1. Discuss the audience with our direct clients, management, and assigned SMEs.
2. Create questionnaires, and distribute to as many in the audience as is practical, or at least representative samples from known audience segments. Ensure anonymity, unless they choose to provide their names.

3. Gather and tabulate the data, then build follow-up interview questionnaires.

4. Conduct one-on-one interviews and focus groups, if possible.

5. Analyze the data and develop a short, concise Audience Profile, then gain client approval and acceptance of this description.

6. Encourage *everyone* on the design team to put this profile in front of them and to salute the audience daily. Focus on the profile in meetings. Challenge all subsequent decisions based on this profile.

As a result of all this effort, we become much more acquainted with our "whos," and if this understanding seeps into every crack of our courses, optimal results can begin to accrue. So, in addition to the omnipresence of the audience profile, how do you get that sort of transfer from analysis to courseware?

Define the instructional strategies

Walt Dick's book, *The Systematic Design of Instruction,* includes a fine chapter on the need to carefully, thoughtfully, creatively define instructional strategies in a course or course module (Dick and Carey, 1990). He starts with a basic outline of possible instructional events or strategies that have been shown to be most effective in most situations. They are modeled after Gagné's events of instruction (Gagné, 1970). He suggests that the designer consider the following options for each "chunk" of instruction. I am paraphrasing and adjusting Walt's list based on our experience.

Preinstructional activities
Gain learners' attention and build relevance/motivation.

Orient them as to what they should learn (objectives).

Verify that they know enough to start (prerequisites).

Get them comfortable with flow, options, grading.

Instructional activities
Present the key concepts and ideas.

Offer examples and nonexamples.

Provide practice with the concepts, and helpful feedback.

Guide students through integration of learning.

Focus on transfer of learning to the learner's job.

Postinstructional activities
Provide review as necessary/desired.

Require some sort of testing with feedback/scoring.

Provide remediation if necessary, and/or enrichment as desired.

All these events of learning are important. They may not all apply to every module or course, and they may not all be best used in this order every time. But the fact is that as you use these general strategies, your courseware will get better. How much better? That depends.

You see, even with the use of this tested outline, critical questions still arise. How will you gain the learners' attention? How will you present the key concepts? How will you help them to transfer learning to their job? *The answers are in the audience analysis.* Let's use an example.

Tulips, juvenile delinquents, and you

Suppose you offer your instructional design expertise to your community leaders on a voluntary basis. You want to contribute. You want to get involved. (I'm impressed!) They come back and tell you that they need a short course on planting tulips. The Beautification Committee has decided that tulips are the key to community success. Okay. You can do this!

You ask about the audience, of course, and they explain that there is quite a large group of "volunteers" from a local counseling clinic who know nothing about tulips, but who need to learn. They want every volunteer to be able to plant hundreds of bulbs quickly and correctly, so that none is wasted. (That's your "mission.") Volunteers are available at various odd hours for training, and they will need individualized instruction. The committee members strongly suggest computer-based training, and offer a solid rationale and the needed delivery systems. Good luck, they say, and you're off.

Here is the result of your discussions with your neighbor, a tulip expert. The lessons or modules break out rather nicely. You've got the content.

- Soil preparation (consistency, acidity, proximity to water, etc.)
- Bulb preparation (age, health signs, color combinations, etc.)
- Planting the bulb (depth, orientation, soil packing, etc.)
- Tools to use (spade, rake, trowel, ruler, etc.)

Then you go to the clinic to learn about the audience. You talk to management, conduct interviews, even use a questionnaire. You find *two* very *interesting* audiences.

Audience One

Juvenile delinquents on parole, ages 13–18
Hate-the-establishment adults in general
Love hard-rock music, *The Simpsons*
Court-ordered to do community service
Never gardened, but some love flowers
Live in jail at night

Audience Two

Older men (55–65), recently widowed

Getting counseling to overcome grief
Like classical music, *MacNeil-Lehrer*
Counseled to do service as therapy
Never gardened, but willing to learn
Live alone at home

You begin to write objectives based on the content outline and to build your evaluation plan. It becomes clear that both audiences need the same basic content. They will need to meet the same "performance objectives." That will make it easier, right? Wrong.

As you begin to select instructional strategies, you begin to see how the audience must drive your selections. Think about this for your "Planting the Bulb" module:

How would you...	For Audience One...	For Audience Two...
Motive, build relevance?	_____	_____
Present the key concepts?	_____	_____
Provide practice, exercises?	_____	_____
Guide integration?	_____	_____
Test and remediate?	_____	_____

Do you see how the audience must drive the specific strategies? Can you imagine someone trying to simply "teach tulips" to these two audiences? Can you picture the results? What would happen if you had not discovered the two different audience segments?

We have found that a table like the one above, with columns for each identifiable audience segment, is very helpful. As we select specific strategies, we force ourselves to design for the learner. Audience One may best relate to games and competition as the primary mode for presenting a key concept, and to testing and testimonials from credible peers for motivation. Audience Two may best relate to a self-help course where they discover what they need to know and then practice with simple, on-screen simulations.

When you really understand your audience and then drive your strategy definition based on that audience or set of audience segments, you take a long step toward optimal learning. Don't just teach tulips. Help troubled kids and mourning grandpas!

Specify the treatment and style guide

The third step in the design process that seems to be most critical to optimal learning, especially when the course will be delivered via computer, is what we call the *treatment*. That is, how will the course look and feel? Here are six examples of the issues most critical at this juncture that should be considered for each audience:

1. What is an appropriate general motif or overall look and feel (borders, icons, creative theme, cartoon character, tough guy)?
2. What will be the tone and pace of the instruction?
3. What colors and music are most appropriate for the customer?
4. What will the basic screen layout look like, and why?
5. What about reading level?
6. What about navigation conventions?

Did your treatment recommendations change, based on the audience? With these questions answered, we strongly recommend that someone on the project team (or from Quality Assurance) take the time to document all treatment decisions made and compile a binding style guide for all who work on the project. We like to make this an "on-line" style guide or a working prototype, so that everyone understands how the course will look and feel as early as possible. This approach also ensures consistency and eventually reduces costs, sometimes significantly.

And remember, remember: the treatment is taken from the audience analysis. In the case-study screen examples we'll be looking at next, you may be able to pick up on the way our designers adapted "look and feel" to each audience, even without the ability to discern color, animations, video, audio, etc.

Well, we have reviewed the three areas of the instructional design process that make the most difference to overall courseware results. I have tried to provide some checklists, some samples, and some examples that could help. In the next paragraphs, I'd like to share some real-world experiences in which audience-centered learning has made all the difference.

Three Case Studies

Union Pacific Railroad (see Fig. 13.3)

The problem. Deregulation and competition led to massive layoffs, restructuring and relocations, high-tech solutions in a low-tech environment, and overall poor performance. The reliability of their service was dangerously low. People inside the company were very unhappy, as were customers. Significant, traditional training efforts had failed to induce change.

Analysis. The content analysis suggested that the information and skills to be learned were not very complex. Why hadn't training worked? The audience analysis revealed that labor-management relations were poor, that relations

Figure 13.3 Union Pacific course.

among people in different job functions were weak or hostile, that few employees saw any big picture or much hope in the face of discouraging news. They had not changed because they did not want any more change. They were afraid and suspicious. We learned that they still valued the Union Pacific tradition (many third- and fourth-generation workers) and shield (logo), railroading in general, and country music. Deep down they wanted the railroad to make it, and they knew how to work.

Strategies. Create a short course that *all* employees would have to experience. It would openly address their real problems, attack issues honestly, acknowledge the company's cultural issues, challenge their thinking, persuade them to give learning and change a chance, and do it all in a surprising way. Here are just a few of the selected strategies:

Catch attention and motivate. Create a country-and-western music video that expresses anger, fear, and concern, but also hope and vision for the future.

Present key concepts. Create an interactive "argument" on-screen among employees and with management. Let learners participate so as to understand and to vent frustrations.

Provide practice and feedback. Show learners an employee error and have them discover how this mistake impacts all other employees in the organization. Show the "shield" breaking up, and have learners decide how to put it back together.

Provide enrichment. Allow learners to see an alternative ending of the music video, then take it home to share with families, change attitudes at home.

Treatment. Use Union Pacific colors, trains, and textures on the screen. Use extensive testimonials of real people to enhance credibility. Use simple navigation options to overcome fears of technology. Maintain simpler reading level, direct "voice," down-to-earth language. Create video and audio with very high production values to add credibility. Use UP shield throughout to capture tradition.

Outcomes. Over 120 hours of courseware have now been developed—all rolling out of the first "culture change" course. Over 10,000 people have been trained, and all have achieved 90 percent or better on posttests. UP has saved over 10,000 training days with the multimedia approach, plus related travel, per diem, time off the job, etc. They have enjoyed very high transfer of training to job performance, as evidenced by an increase in on-time deliveries of over 30 percent in areas where training has occurred. That represents a positive impact of millions in savings, and new opportunities. They believe training has given UP a significant strategic advantage over its competitors. The employees like the training and want more. It hit home. This series of courses was awarded the prestigious 1993 "Nebby" award for best interactive multimedia training in industry, as well as other awards.

U.S. Air Force maintenance continuation training program
(see Fig. 13.4)

The problem. F-16 and F-15 fighter planes are very complex and expensive, and extremely critical to our national defense. Those who maintain them are not highly educated, although a few are extremely expert in troubleshooting and fixing aircraft. Overall, of every three parts pulled off the aircraft, one was fully functional. This created a huge waste of costs in labor, parts, distribution, etc. (Please note that we have since found that most organizations have a similar "miss rate" in their maintenance areas.) The idea of the training was to improve troubleshooting skills and devise better cognitive strategies in order to reduce the number of parts pulled in error by 5 percent. The result would be a savings of $110 million over 5 years.

Analysis. Content analysis was performed through a relatively new technique we call "cognitive task analysis." We were able to capture the "mental maps" of the rare experts, their view of the various aircraft systems, as well as their "cognitive paths" through those systems, the thinking process they

Figure 13.4   U.S. Air Force maintenance training course.

use to troubleshoot. The audience analysis showed that the maintenance technicians were young, had little if any formal education beyond high school, enjoyed rock music, had limited knowledge of aircraft system intricacies, and had gained the habit of "swaptronics" in maintenance—i.e., continually replacing parts until the problem goes away. Unhappily, the "swaptronics" approach was reinforced by the technicians' immediate supervisors, who emphasized number of flights rather than quality maintenance. Finally, these technicians were patriotic and cared about their mission, and the experts were motivated primarily by pride.

Strategies

Establish relevance and motivate.   Create a rock-music video introduction and theme that emphasizes pride in country and job, demonstrates results of great performance, and uses credible peer experts to provide testimonials.

Present key concepts.   Use a Socratic "dialogue" approach to let learners show what they already know and to focus them on their gaps in knowledge. Build all instruction around problems to be solved. Use "tips from the experts" to present key ideas and skills.

Provide exercises and feedback. Use powerful, free-play simulations that allow technicians to think through many different problems. Demonstrate the impact of their decisions on time, cost, and mission readiness. Then show them how their thinking process compares to an expert's approach.

Provide remediation. Encourage technicians to experience the simulations over and over, until their thinking process has captured the power of the expert's approach.

Treatment. Use red-white-and-blue borders and icons based on aviation themes. Use a rock-music theme at all transition points and "under" key attitude messages. Use "expert" mentors to provide continuity and credibility. Design and use a limited number of screen layouts across all courses to enhance consistency and learner "comfort" with the instruction.

Outcomes. Over 220 hours of interactive instruction, delivered on-time and within budget. Hundreds of learners have been exposed to the instruction in pilot implementations. Attitude rankings by learners are very high. System knowledge improved by an average of about 35 percent among both experts and novices taking the courses. Ability to accurately troubleshoot aircraft breakdowns increased by nearly 80 percent across all courses, all audiences. Transfer of training to the flight line, and changes in overall performance, are currently being tracked. Initial indications are very positive. This series of courses was awarded the prestigious 1993 "Nebby" award for best interactive multimedia training in military/government, as well as other awards.

Alyeska berth operations center emergency training
(see Fig. 13.5)

The problem. While the chance of an emergency along the Alaskan Pipeline and at the docks (berth) in Valdez is remote, the potential impact of such an emergency is great—as shown by the *Exxon Valdez* oil spill in recent years. Yet the ability to train personnel in emergency preparedness is limited, since they cannot afford to shut down the pipeline for even a few minutes a year. The problem was how to create realistic, powerful simulations that would test technicians' abilities to quickly and properly respond to emergencies.

Analysis. Content analysis was performed through the same techniques previously described for the Air Force project, including "cognitive task analysis." We were able to capture the "mental maps" of system experts and the "best practices" procedures for dealing with emergencies. The audience analysis showed that these Alaskan technicians were rugged individualists who disliked "hype and fluff" and wanted to get their hands on their systems to test their abilities. They did not want lots of tutorials or "commercials" for management, or any other "frills." They simply wanted to have the knowl-

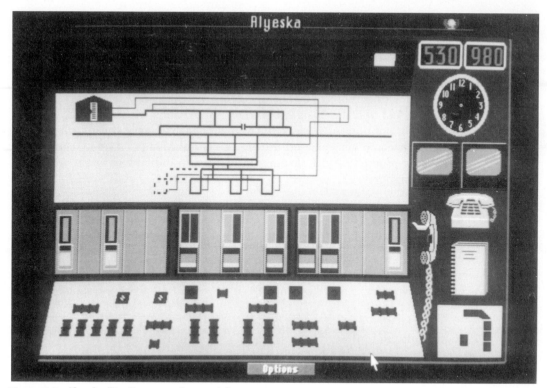

Figure 13.5 Alyeska Pipeline operations training course.

edge, confidence, and skill to deal with emergencies well. They were of all ages and backgrounds, with one common love: Alaska.

Strategies

Establish relevance and motivate. Put learners in a simulated emergency situation immediately and test their ability to respond, providing helpful feedback along the way. Use graphics, animations, sounds to recreate the tension of the environment.

Allow for practice. Use powerful, free-play simulations that allow technicians to think through many different problems. Demonstrate the impact of their decisions on time and cost. Then show them how their thinking process compares to an expert's approach.

Provide enrichment. Allow technicians to record their scores for the simulations and compare them to others'.

Treatment. Use cool Alaskan colors and images for borders, menus, and icons, including the "midnight sun," float planes, etc. Use lifelike graphics and animations to provide as realistic an environment as possible. Make the user interface as lifelike as possible by allowing learners to touch "real" buttons, read gauges, move in any direction, etc.

Outcomes.   One emergency training course is now installed along the pipeline and is in active use by the operators. This Berth Operations course is now in pilot-test and the design, based on simulations with remedial instruction based on simulation performance, has been well received by all technicians. They become very excited during the simulations and enjoy competing for time/cost productivity. Learner confidence in ability to handle emergencies is now higher.

In Closing, I'd Like to Thank You...

So, who are you, and what's in this for you? If you are still reading, you must be both disciplined and patient (or an insomniac?). In any case, thank you. I want this chapter to make a difference for you, and more importantly, for the learners in your care and keeping. To make optimal learning happen, we all have to grasp the broader vision. We have to care about real results in terms of people who change and perform better, faster, cheaper. Once again, that is very difficult, and all the tempest about us would have us focus elsewhere, it seems. In *Open Boat,* Stephen Crane wrote one of the best first lines ever to open a short story:

None of them knew the color of the sky.

He went on to immerse the reader in the message:

None of them knew the color of the sky.
Their eyes glanced level, and were fastened upon the waves that
swept toward them. These waves were of the hue of slate, save
for the tops, which were of foaming white,
and all of the men knew the colors of the sea.
The horizon narrowed and widened, and dipped and rose,
and at all times its edge was jagged with waves...
most wrongfully and barbarously abrupt and tall,
and each froth-top was a problem in small boat navigation.

Indeed, it is very hard for us to notice the sky when the storm rages around us. Navigation on the "sea" of training, especially multimedia training, is becoming increasingly difficult. Many would have you focus on bits and bytes, graphic resolutions and bandwidths, CD-I and DVI and MMCD and WHONOSWHAT. Others would lead you into the desert of content-contentedness. Amidst this tempest, the temptation—indeed, the *requirement*—is to focus at least some attention on the waves. However, real success—real *results*—demand that you pay *additional* attention to the sky. The color of the sky, the big picture, the *audience* will guide the boat and instill the needed courage into the sailors. The audience will help us to focus on what really counts, if we give them the chance. The rewards are real, and ultimately essential to our success both as individuals and as an "industry."

Thank you for listening, whoever you are. At least you now know *who* is on first!

Bibliography

Crane, Stephen, "The Open Boat," in *The "Secret Sharer" and Other Great Stories,* Abraham H. Lass and Norma L. Tasman, eds., New American Library, New York, pp. 217–218.

Dick, Walter and Lou Carey, *The Systematic Design of Instruction,* 3d ed, Harper Collins, New York, 1990.

Gagné, Robert M., *The Conditions of Learning,* 2d ed, Holt, Rinehart and Winston, New York, 1970.

Mager, Robert F., *Making Instruction Work,* David S. Lake Publishers, Belmont, CA, 1988.

Merrill, M. David, Zhongmin Li, and Mark K. Jones, "Second Generation Instructional Design," *Educational Technology,* September 1989.

14

CD-ROM and Its Impact on Education

Susan Kinnell

Pam Berger

Introduction

CD-ROM, which stands for compact disc–read only memory, is an optical technology used for the storage of and the gaining access to large amounts of information on a plastic 12-centimeter disc. This information can be read and subsequently used in a number of ways, but not altered on the disc in any way. (Although newer technological developments are under way for discs that can be erased and/or rewritten.)

The capacity for storage on a CD-ROM is impressive—over 650 Mbytes of data. That's the equivalent of 300,000 printed pages, one million library catalog cards, one hour of sound, or 15,000 graphic images. Because the discs are small and relatively indestructible, they have become very practical for use in schools.

This technology was first announced in 1983, a development of Philips and Sony. The first commercially available disc was BiblioFile, which was issued in 1985. Later in 1985, a group of industry leaders met at the High Sierra Casino and Hotel in Lake Tahoe, California, for the purpose of setting standards for the structural organization of files and data on a CD-ROM. This became known as the High Sierra standard, and subsequently it was amended slightly and formalized by the International Standards Organization as ISO 9660. Virtually every disc since that time has met those standards and is thus playable and usable on a variety of CD-ROM drives.

The first CD-ROM product for the school market was Grolier's Electronic Encyclopedia, which was announced in 1986 and became available along with Microsoft's Bookshelf in 1987.

In 1987, there were approximately 120 titles available for use on any type of CD-ROM drive. Fifty percent of these were indexing and abstract databases, priced in the $1000 to $3000 range. By 1989 there were more than 500 commercially available titles, and prices were beginning to come down to from $500 to $2000. Forty-five percent of the discs were source databases containing full-text, numeric data, or computer programs.

As of 1993 the number of available titles has grown to almost 4000, and the price range is from $20 to $3000. No longer are the majority of titles print-based; no longer are the choices limited to just a few resources specifically for schools. As the number of CD-ROM titles produced multiplies dramatically each year, the number of these available for schools increases proportionally. According to a recent survey by University Microfilm Inc., within the next two years 85 percent of school libraries are likely to be using CD-ROM, as compared with just 25 percent in 1987.

How CD-ROM Works

The disc

A standard CD-ROM is physically composed of three layers: a clear polycarbonate substrate layer, a metal layer, and an acrylic layer. Polycarbonate is used for strength and rigidity (it is the same material that's used for bullet-proofing). Aluminum is used for the metal layer, and a clear acrylic material is used for the top layer where the label and company information are printed.

The data on a disc are encoded and stored on a disc in the form of "pits" and "lands." Pits are depressions or hollows in the metal, and lands are perfectly flat areas. A laser beam reflects off the flat areas and is detected by the sensors in the drive. The light shining on the pits is deflected sideways, or defused so that it cannot be detected by the sensors. This pattern of nonreflective and reflective areas on the disc is interpreted by the drive circuitry as a pattern of 0's and 1's, and is thus translatable into machine language as binary code.

The focal plane of the laser is directly on the metal layer of the disc, so any scratches or marks on the polycarbonate should not interfere with the readings from the sensors. The pits and lands on a disc are on a single spiral track that is less than one one-hundredth the width of a human hair. If unwound, this track would be almost 4 miles long.

The disc, unlike a magnetic disk in a hard drive, spins at a varying rate of speed, called *constant linear velocity*. A magnetic disk, spinning at the same rate of speed (*constant angular velocity*), has tracks near the edge of the disk that are moving faster than tracks near the center. The sectors on these tracks must then be of bigger size to hold the same amount of data as the slower-moving sectors on the tracks at the center of the disk. The critical point is that the data must all pass the read head at the same speed. The sectors on an optical disc are all of equal size, which allows for many more sectors on any given disc. The tradeoff is less storage and more speed (of access and transfer) on a magnetic disk, and more storage and less speed on an optical disc.

The drive

Within the CD-ROM drive are various components and circuits:

- A small motor that spins the disc
- A laser that projects a beam of light onto the disc
- A detector that reads the reflected light from the disc
- A prism that deflects the reflected light onto a light-sensing diode
- A circuit that reads the voltages generated by the diode

When the disc is spinning in the drive, a detector is positioned to receive the reflected light from the laser beam. This detector moves to that part of the disc being read. The motor spins the disc at a varying rate of speed called constant linear velocity (as just noted), so that no matter which part of the disc is being read, it is spinning at exactly the same rate over the detector.

The reflected light from the lands (and the absence of reflected light from the pits) is deflected onto a light-sensing diode. Each pulse of reflected light generates a tiny electrical current in the diode, which is then passed on to the computer as a stream of 1's. These 1's are interspersed with 0's, which represent the places where no light was reflected.

Speed of access is one of the important criteria for a CD-ROM drive. When a CD-ROM disc is in the drive, the user searches for a piece of information on that disc by putting in a search query, by clicking on a button, or by typing in a word. There is a delay while the light on the drive goes on and the motor hums, and then finally the response to the query appears on the computer screen. How fast the drive finds the requested information and gets to its exact location on the disc is its *access time. Transfer time* is the amount of time it takes for that information to be transferred to the computer screen. The access time for today's new drives ranges between 200 and 380 milliseconds. Note that for this measure, the smaller number is better; that is, the fewer number of milliseconds it takes to access the data, the better. (Remember, CD-ROM drives are not fast by other standards in the computer world. A hard-disk drive accesses information in 15 to 50 milliseconds.)

Transfer time is measured differently on a CD-ROM drive than access time. Transfer time is measured by how many kilobytes of information are passed from the disc to the computer per second. This is called "kilobytes per second," or kbps. For many years the industry norm was 150 kbps, but in late 1992 and early 1993 there were many new drives introduced in the market that were rated at more than 300 kbps. Rumor has it that by mid-1994 there will be 600-kbps drives readily available, at similar prices to today's 300-kbps drives.

Remember that for transfer speed, the bigger number is better—more data gets passed from the disc to the computer faster. This is slow by other computer standards: the transfer rate of a hard drive is 600 to 2000 kbps.

The newer type of disc drives, called *double-speed, double-spin,* or "MultiSpin" (a NEC trademark), have the ability to transfer data from the disc to the computer at two different speeds. Audio data is sent at 150 kbytes per second (kbps), while video and graphics are transferred at 300 + kbps. This is a different measure of speed than the varying rate at which the disc is spinning in the drive, and should not be confused with that speed or the speed of access.

During the latter part of 1992, Eastman Kodak unveiled its new PhotoCD system. With this system, slide film is developed and the images placed on a compact disc called PhotoCD, using Kodak's proprietary process. A revolutionary aspect of this new process is its ability to store subsequent groups of images on the same disc. These discs, with multiple groups of images stored at various times, are called *multisession* discs. The images on the disc can then be viewed on a television monitor using a CD player, either Kodak's own player or any of the newer players or drives that are designated "PhotoCD-compatible." These drives are called *CD-ROM XA*—the XA stands for "eXtended Architecture." While all such CD-ROM drives will read a PhotoCD, some of them are rated for single-session compatibility and others for multi-session compatibility. The difference is that multisession CD-ROM drives can read those PhotoCDs to which more than one group of images has been added.

The single-session drives can only read a PhotoCD's first group of images. This has a lot of ramifications for long-term school use—school pictures, yearbooks, and the like.

The computer

Essentially CD-ROM provides the capability to access very large storage files, with the added benefit of being able to change the information in those large files by simply changing the disc in the drive. The kind of computer attached to the drive will determine to some extent the kind of CD-ROM usable in the drive, and how fast its information can be accessed. If the computer is a vintage 8088 machine (the old PC XT model), the fastest CD-ROM drive on the market will not function at its best levels. If the computer monitor is not a high-resolution monitor, preferably in color, a great deal of the visual excitement of CD-ROM will be lost. If there is no added sound board in the IBM-compatible type of machine, then the audio files on the CD-ROM will be silent. If there is a small amount of RAM (working, temporary storage in the computer), then the computer may not even be able to handle the CD-ROM at all.

There are some minimum requirements for running certain kinds of discs. Clearly if it is a text-based disc, an older and slower machine without sound and color will be able to handle it. However, if there are graphics, video sequences, audio files, or animation as well as text, then the computer behind the CD-ROM drive also has to have certain capabilities.

The Multimedia PC Marketing Council in Washington, D.C., established a level of minimum hardware requirements in an effort to standardize what people would need to be able to run a certain kind of multimedia disc. In May of 1993, they announced a second level of minimum requirements that extends the original list and also provides recommendations for maximum performance. Any CD-ROM that carries the label *MPC,* or now carries the label *MPC Level 2,* will run only on machines that meet those minimum requirements. The new MPC Level 2 minimum requirements are:

- A computer with 4-Mbyte RAM, 25 MHz, 486SX, and a 160-Mbyte hard drive

- A CD-ROM drive with 300-kbps sustained transfer rate, maximum average seek time 400 milliseconds, CD-ROM XA-ready, multisession-capable

- A sound board with 16-bit digital sound, 8-note synthesizer, and MIDI playback

- A video display with 640 × 480 resolution and 65,536 colors

- Ports for MIDI input/output, and a joystick.

The software

On the computer.   The next element to consider in connecting a CD-ROM drive to a computer is the software that enables that connection. If the drive were simply plugged into the computer's SCSI port (or, in some cases, to a serial port), the computer would have no internal instructions that would help it recognize the device or understand how to communicate with it. Those instructions come in the form of software, usually a single floppy disk, that is loaded in with the other operating system software.

If the machine attached to the drive is a Macintosh, then the process is simply one of copying four or five basic files onto the System folder. If the machine is IBM or IBM-compatible, then the enabling software is called *MSCDEX,* which stands for Microsoft Compact Disc Extensions. These are extension files for DOS, the internal disk-operating system. DOS can only recognize a file up to a certain size; most CD-ROM files are considerably larger than that. A statement is added to both the AUTOEXEC.BAT and the CONFIG.SYS files so that the computer will look for and recognize the presence of the CD-ROM drive when it is started up. There is also an application start-up file, which is simply a file that tells the computer how to start the CD-ROM application.

To search the disc.   The second kind of software is supplied with the disc to enable the user to search the disc or access the programs, files, or information on the disc. Sometimes this search software is accessed straight from the disc, and sometimes it is recommended that the software be copied from the disc to the hard drive. This approach lets the speed and power of the computer run the search software, so the CD-ROM drive only has to deal with accessing and transferring the information from the disc.

On the disc itself (dataware).   The information that is encoded on the actual disc has been called "dataware." Since this data takes many forms—text, illustrations and pictures, audio, video, and animation, for example—how it is physically placed on the disc can have some impact on the efficiency of the search software in finding the information on the disc. The capability to search the disc also takes many forms: single words may be searched; lists of topics or subject headings may be browsed; menus can be utilized; words can be located in relationship to other words or in their context; parts of words may be searched, with a whole variety of possibilities as a search result.

This whole process takes place when the disc is first created, or mastered. Databases of information, files of pictures or sounds, sequences of video or animation—whatever forms the data take are loaded into an authoring system. This system organizes the information according to the ISO standards, creates indexes of all the words, their relationships and contexts, filters out problems and misleading data, and arranges the final files, folders, directories, lists, pointers, flags and tags, and everything the authors can think of that will make the job of locating information on the disc easier for the user. In addition, error detection and correction routines are added to the file so that no mistakes will arise out of the disc's information.

Once the final version of the material has been settled and the master disc has been made, it is then replicated as many times as needed. Each disc is a perfect copy of the original file and contains the exact material as authored and indexed.

The network

One of the most exciting developments in the CD-ROM world is the enhanced ability to include CD-ROM on any given network. Although it is not yet feasible to network a fully multimedia disc (full-motion video is not yet networkable), networking of most CD-ROMs is both possible and desirable.

One of the main problems with a CD-ROM collection is the limited access to a particular product. For example, if the school library holds a 21-volume encyclopedia, it is possible for 21 different students to access that encyclopedia at the same time. (Not at all likely, since they would be looking for similar information a majority of times, but possible.) The same encyclopedia on a single CD-ROM would not provide as much access, therefore, as the print version. But by making that encyclopedia available on a network, with multiple workstations in various areas, many more students could access the same information. Since it is also likely that the research process will be speeded up on the CD-ROM, the number of students who can use the disc will be close to, if not equal to, the number of students using the print version.

Along with the computer, CD-ROM drive, and shared access software (such as MSCDEX provides), the requirements for networking CD-ROM fall into two categories, hardware and software. The hardware is a network interface card (NIC) that goes into every computer on the network. The kind of interface card will determine the kind of network, such as star, ring, tree, line, etc. These physical arrangements of computers linked to each other with cabling are called the *topology* or *architecture* of a network. The architecture also determines the speed of the data being transmitted between workstations.

The software required is a *network operating system (NOS)*. This works in conjunction with the computer's individual operating system to enable it to recognize the network and the individual protocols for sending and receiving data along the network. Also required is the *host* or *server* software, which enables it to store and regulate the sharing of files or programs by members of the network.

Each networking situation is different and depends on the number and location of the computers, as well as the age and capacity of those machines.

Management of CD-ROM in Schools and Libraries

CD-ROM is having a major impact on school and academic libraries. The depth and breath of its influence will come as a surprise to some people, especially those who are accustomed to the idea of research and information resources as being primarily print-based.

This relatively new technology is changing how business is carried out in school libraries and dramatically impacting library management and collection development, in addition to the instruction program and the curriculum of each school. Journal articles, conference presentations, and discussions with library media specialists all reveal not only ardent acceptance of CD-ROM, but a dawning awareness of some underlying problems and issues pertaining to CD-ROM's use and integration in schools.

Some of the issues that must be addressed by school library media centers fall into the following major categories:

1. Needs assessment and technology planning

2. Equipment decision making

3. Staff development and training issues

4. Collection development

5. Budgeting

Issues such as these are being explored at national conferences, such as the Databases in Schools Conference, professional literature such as *School Library Media Quarterly* and the *Information Searcher,* and even on the Internet in School Library Media and Network Communications listserve, "LM_NET." As these issues are addressed and resolved, the full impact of CD-ROM technology on student learning will be better realized.

Impact of CD-ROM on Students

The impact of CD-ROM technology on students is different from that on the administration, faculty, and staff. Students will be approaching CD-ROM as a source of information, as a tool for learning, as a reference or guide to other sources, and as a source of entertainment. Where they use the discs will depend on the school's facilities and arrangements. How they use the discs, and the results (both short- and long-term) they get, will depend on a number of other factors.

First of all, the success a student has in using a CD-ROM will depend in large measure on his or her familiarity with computers. Keyboarding, the use of function keys, understanding screen appearance, file management, and manual/visual dexterity are all part of the preliminary skills a student must have to succeed with CD-ROM.

Second, a student needs to understand the concepts of searching or using an electronic database, such as that found on a particular CD-ROM. Although students usually don't like to be instructed in the use of CD-ROM, preferring instead to explore by trial and error, it has been found that the very scope and size of the database causes it to elude the explorer. The depth of the subject material on the disc is not visually obvious to students, and they are therefore not aware of what they may or may not have missed in their research. In this case, practice does not make perfect. In fact, practice itself often is precluded because of the limited number of machines, sometimes the large number of students, and the limited time per student that is available for searching.

Therefore instruction of some kind is almost always necessary, and that brings up a whole variety of further issues: what kind of training (individual or group)? where and when? on individual CD-ROMs, or by sort/type of CD-ROM? and so on. Further, it has been shown that students at the secondary level who have received no skills training in searching electronic databases—training that will certainly be of great use to them in their college years—do not understand the complexities of such searches.

With regard to Bloom's Taxonomy, a scale of learning that ranges from simple identification through comparison and up to evaluation and synthesis, the CD-ROM search process ranks quite high. For students, there is no longer a feeling that simple identification and reiteration is enough; the challenge to find different sources, more material, and then evaluate those sources leads to a higher order of thinking skills and more active learning processes. There is an increase in student achievement with a corresponding decrease in student frustration, both of which will find favor with teachers, librarians, and parents.

The final issue is one that has wider scope than just using or not using CD-ROM. Today's generation of students is visually oriented, from lifelong exposure to television, movies, videos, video games, and the like. Attempting to teach low-motivated students with traditional print sources may prove difficult, and will meet with increasing resistance and frustration.

A Look at the Future

The future is bright for CD-ROM in schools. The incredible expansion in the number of available titles, the developments in hardware and networking, and the reliability of the medium itself mean that more and more schools will be turning to CD-ROM. The market really picked up speed when some kind of a breakeven point was reached—there were enough discs being published to make further hardware development feasible, and there were enough drives around to make publishing discs a profitable enterprise. Once that point had been reached, an enormous spurt of growth took place, with internal CD-ROM drives being included with new computers and with new discs being published every day and week. Developments in miniaturization along with increases in speed will bring machines that are easier to use and portable; chip and processor developments will continue to drive prices lower and make the technology more and more affordable. As this happens, more machines will be found in homes, and that will greatly encourage the use of CD-ROM in education.

With the accompanying proliferation of titles, teachers, librarians, and parents will be able to evaluate a wide number of discs, selecting only those that best meet their criteria. No longer will they be forced to buy the *only* disc on the market, but rather be enabled to buy the *best* disc.

As more and more schools turn to electronic resources—computers, disk-based materials, optical materials, and on-line resources—the result will be more and more students fluent in the use of computers to assist them in their studying, research, and schoolwork.

15

A Discussion of Standards

Jessica Keyes

The multimedia industry, like most other technology industries, doesn't lack standards. For the most part, readers should become familiar with the different standards and be able to differentiate between them. But unless you're a hardware or software vendor, it is not necessary to have an intimate knowledge of any of these standards. This chapter provides an overview of the standards that you'll run across as a multimedia developer.

This chapter is an introduction to the current standards-based terminology that the multimedia developer should have a passing knowledge of. After an explanatory introduction, the most noteworthy of standards are presented in an alphabetical glossary format.

Not all PCs are multimedia-enabled. What this means is that few of them have enough hard-disk capacity, the ability to reproduce sound, a CD-ROM drive, a super VGA graphics card or enough memory or speed to put it all together.

You'll soon discover a plethora of standards to consider. But why should multimedia be any different from any other technology? After all, proprietary standards is what sells hardware.

IBM calls their entry Ultimedia, but the rest of the world has labeled it *multimedia*. The Multimedia Marketing Council (MMC) has developed a specification for a PC that ensures quality playback of multimedia productions. Although it relies heavily on Microsoft's Windows as an operating system, (whereas IBM bases its standard on their very own OS/2 or DOS) Ultimedia and the Multimedia Marketing Council's MPC (multimedia PC) are so similar as to be nearly indistinguishable.

The MPC Level 3 Specification, announced in June 1995, provides for a much more powerful computer than the MPC Level 2 specification. Because the specification encompasses the entire spectrum of multimedia standards, it is presented here in its entirety.

MPC3 does not replace the MPC1 and MPC2 specification; rather, it defines an updated platform suitable for delivering enhanced multimedia functionality.

System Hardware: Minimum Requirements

Processor

- 75-MHz Pentium processor or other microprocessor capable of running x86 binaries at a comparable level.

RAM

- 8 MB required

Floppy drive

- 3½ inch, 1.44-MB floppy drive

Hard drive

- 540 MB minimum
- 15-ms access time
- 1.5 MB/sec sustained throughput

CD-ROM drive

- Sustained 600-KB/sec transfer rate
- Average access time of 250 ms (in 4× mode)
- No more than 40% of the CPU bandwidth may be consumed while maintaining a sustained transfer rate of 600 KB/sec and no more than 20% of the CPU bandwidth can be consumed while maintaining a transfer rate of 300 KB/sec. The CPU usage requirement should be achieved for read block sizes no less than 16 K and a lead-time of no more than is required to load the CD-ROM buffer with read block of data.
- Must be capable of reading Compact Disc Audio (Red Book) discs, as well as Compact Disc Mode 1 and Mode 2 (form 1 and form 2) formatted discs, including mixed mode and multisession media, as well as CD-ROM, CD-ROM XA, Photo CD, CD Recordable (part II), Video CD, and CD-I disks. Data must be transferred to the hostsystem in block sizes of 2048, 2336 and/or 2352 bytes, as appropriate for each CD format. In addition, the drive and included driver software must be compatible with Microsoft's MSCDEX version 2.2 or later (or equivalent), implement the extended audio APIs and be capable of reading Q channel information.

- CD-ROM drive with CD-DA (Red Book) outputs and volume control.
- CD-ROM drive must have on-board buffers and implement read-ahead buffering.
- Sequential access time: An application via the standard operating system access methods must have the ability to read sequential, error free, 16K blocks every 33.3 ms with each read taking no more than 13.3 ms.
- Background CPU utilization: The driver must not use CPU cycles, except in response to a host system request.

Audio

- 16-bit Digital-to-Analog Converter (DAC) with: linear PCM sampling; DMA- or FIFO-buffered transfer capability with interruption buffer empty; 44.1-, 22.05-, and 11.025-kHz sample rate mandatory; stereo channels; no more than 10% of the CPU bandwidth required to output 22.05 and 11.025 kHz; it is recommended that no more than 15% of the CPU bandwidth be required to output 44.1 kHz.
- 16-bit Analog-to-Digital Converter (ADC) with: Linear PCM sampling; 44.1-, 22.05-, and 11.025-kHz sample rate mandatory; DMA- or FIFO-buffered transfer capability with interrupt on bufferfull; microphone input.
- Wavetable capability required.
- CPU utilization for 16-bit stereo sound and wavetable cannot exceed 10%.
- CD-ROM drive with CD-DA (Red Book) outputs and volume control.
- Internal synthesizer capabilities with multi-voice, multi-timbral capacity, 6 simultaneous melody voices plus 2 simultaneous percussive voices.
- Internal mixing capabilities to combine input from three (recommended four) sources and present the output as a stereo, line-level audio signal at the back panel. The four sources are: CD Red Book, synthesizer, DAC (waveform), and (recommended but not required) an auxiliary input source. Each input must have at least a 3-bit volume control (8 steps) with a logarithmic taper. (4-bit or greater volume control is strongly recommended.) If all sources are sourced with –10 dB (consumer line level: 1 mW into 600 Ω = 0 dB) without attenuation, the mixer will not clip and will output between 0 dB and +3 dB. Individual audio source and master digital volume-control registers and extra line-level audio sources are highly recommended.

  Speakers: If external speakers are included in the system, the following are required:

- Must be at least a two-piece system.
- Frequency Response from 120 Hz to 17.5 kHz.
- Power rating must be measured and tested at a minimum of 3 W/channel at 100 Hz, 1 kHz and 10 kHz at 1% THD; 6 W RMS (3 W + 3 W) into 4 Ω, at 1% THD, at 1 kHz, with both channels driven.

- Sound pressure level must be measured at ½-meter on axis from speaker and should be capable of an SPL of 92 dB from 250 Hz to 7.5 kHz.
- Input connectors are as follows: 3.5-mm stereo jack, where tip is left channel, sleeve is right channel and body is ground or audio input using 3.5-mm stereo jack with industry standard channel orientation, supplied with at least a six foot cable to attach to computer sound source.
- Speaker connector must be mono type where tip is positive and body is ground or left speaker output 3.5-mm mono jack where tip is positive and case is negative. If stereo headphone output jack is included, it must mute the speaker when headphone is used.
- Noise ratio must be at least 65 dB.
- Input sensitivity requires no more than 300 mV for rated power output.
- Volume, treble, and bass controls included.
- Input impedance must be greater than 5000 Ω.
- In a three-piece system, the satellites shall have the same requirements.

  Subwoofer requirements:

- Frequency response must be at least 40 Hz to 250 Hz (± 3 dB).
- Power minimum is 15 W at 1% THD.
- Power ratings should be measured at 40 Hz and 100 Hz at 1% THD.
- Input sensitivity must be adjustable from 300 mV to 1 V for maximum output power.
- Both inputs must be mixed in the woofer circuitry.
- Input impedance must be greater than 1000 Ω.

Graphics performance

- Color space conversion and scaling capability are required.
- Direct access to frame buffer for video-enabled graphics subsystem required with a resolution of 352 × 240 at 30 fps (or 352 × 288 at 25 fps) at 15 bits/pixel, unscaled, without cropping.
- Test suite will test for acceptable graphics performance.

Video playback

- MPEG1 (hardware or software) with OM-1 compliance required.
- Direct access to frame buffer required with a resolution of 352 × 240 at 30 fps (or 352 × 288 at 25 fps) at 15 bits/pixel, unscaled, without cropping.
- All codecs—hardware and/or software—must support a synchronized audio/video stream with a resolution of 320 × 240, 15 bits/pixel, 30 frames/second, unscaled, without dropping a frame.
- Test suite will test for acceptable video playback performance.

User input

- Standard 101-key IBM-style keyboard, with standard DIN connector, or keyboard, which delivers identical functionality utilizing key-combinations.
- Two-button mouse with bus or serial connector, with at least one additional communication port remaining free.

I/O

- Standard 9-pin or 25-pin asynchronous serial port, programmable up to 57.6K baud, switchable interrupt channel.
- Standard 25-pin bi-directional parallel port with interrupt capability.
- 1 MIDI port with In, Out, and through, must have interrupt support for input and FIFO transfer.
- IBM-style analog or digital joystick port.

System software

- Multimedia PC system software must offer binary compatibility with Windows 3.11.
- System must offer binary compatibility with DOS version 6.0 or higher.

Minimum full-system configuration

A full Multimedia PC Level 3 system requires the following elements and components, all of which must meet the full-functional specifications outlined.

- CPU
- RAM
- Hard drive
- Floppy drive
- CD-ROM drive
- Audio
- Graphics performance
- Video playback
- User input
- I/O
- System software

The Components of Multimedia

Of course, the MPC3 specification means little if you have no way of "inputting" your multimedia element of choice into your application. This brief section covers the "multimedia objects" for which the MPC standard ensures the ability to seamlessly work on your hardware of choice.

Sound

In general, there are two types of sound files, WAV and MIDI files. WAV files capture the entire sound, which is the reason why these files take up so much space. Just 7 seconds of sound, recorded in stereo at 16-bits and sampled at 44 kHz takes well over one million bytes of disk storage. Fortunately, wave editing software has standardized compression options, which are a real necessity if the developer is to develop a multimedia application that uses a reasonable amount of disk storage.

Where wave files store the actual (digital version) sound, MIDI files store instructions for MIDI devices. Actually, MIDI is an acronym for *Musical Instrument Digital Interface*, which is an industry-standard connection for computer control of electronic musical instruments and devices. Perhaps the most popular is the synthesizer.

If you don't have a MIDI instrument then, depending on the software you have installed you can still take advantage of the power of MIDI.

Because Windows-based systems play either MIDI or Wave files, the inexpensive software and hardware that I've just described can really enhance your multimedia production making it look and "sound" a lot more professional than it really is.

Images

The multimedia developer has many options for the input of images into his or her production. There is a plethora of "drawing" packages on the market (e.g., CorelDraw, Designer, Freehand). All of these enable the graphic designer to create original designs and then save that design in a standard format, such as PCX (Paintbrush format), TIF (Tagged Image Format), EPS (Encapsulated Postscript), and as well as a half dozen other well-known standardized formats. Alternatively, the developer can buy ready-made "clip art" and even photographs from any number of multimedia (and desktop publishing) vendors, who will store the artwork in a standardized format.

For the most part, the PCX and TIF formats are the most prevalent standardized formats for "work-in-progress" designs, but are then translated into BMP (Windows Bitmaps) files for Windows productions and .GIF (CompuServe format, which is actually derived from a Unisys patent) for Internet imagery.

Video

Perhaps the multimedia element that gives developers the biggest "twinkle in the eye" is video. It's quite possible to add video to a multimedia production without ever having a digital video card. If you're creating in a Windows environment, video is stored as AVI (audio video interleave) files. Although the quality is far less than other digital delivery mechanisms, AVI does have a distinct advantage. That is, it permits the playback of video segments without a digital video adapter. In other words, AVI is a software-only solution. And because you can purchase literally thousands of minutes of video clips from dozens of multimedia vendors, you can easily add video to your production.

Of course, if you want to tailor video to your own specification you need some additional software to do this. And if you want to shoot your own videos, not only do you need a camcorder or VCR as an input source, you will need a video capture card as well.

Video is perhaps the most storage-intensive of all the multimedia elements. One minute, uncompressed, takes about 50 MB of hard disk. It doesn't take a mathematician to figure out that you'll quickly run out of storage space at this rate. Fortunately, most digital video software enables you to store the video clip you've created in a compressed (and standards-based) format—and it enables you to select the best compression method for your needs.

Animation

Simply put, animation is the process of creating, usually graphically, a series of frames and then having them display rapidly to get a sense of movement. In the world of multimedia (especially on a PC platform), multimedia and video overlap somewhat. It is quite possible to run an AVI (video) file that was created via animated means, rather than through a camera.

A plethora of software packages provide wonderful abilities to draw and animate objects. Sometimes even the authoring tool provides the ability to animate objects created within the context of the authoring package.

The Standards

So that the imagery, animation, audio, and video work flawlessly on your hardware platform of choice, the multimedia objects that compose these technologies must adhere to standards. The alphabetized glossary below describes the majority of multimedia standards in brief.

ART. Johnson-Grace of Newport Beach California licensed ART, a high-speed publishing technology, to Apple Computer in June of 1995. ART provides instant publishing for multimedia content delivered over regular phone lines. Full-color photos, graphics, and text can be transmitted using ART than with existing compression standards, such as GIF and JPEG. High-quality images compressed in the ART format play back in seconds, rather than in tens of seconds. This allows images to be blended with content, rather than being stored separately in download libraries. The technology uses a content-sensitive fuzzy logic engine to classify each component of a picture or graphic. This built-in intelligence enables the encoder to apply the best compression method automatically to any type of image so that the publisher has the ability to use one compression technology, rather than several—depending on the type of image being displayed. ART also reduces the perceived delay during an image download.

AVI (Audio Video Interleave). This particular technology was developed by Microsoft for its Video for Windows products. Although hardware is required for video capture, AVI requires no special hardware for playback.

CD.   As explained by Andrew Davidson of Philips Interactive Media of America to a CompuServe forum:

> In the beginning, there was CD-DA (Compact Disc-Digital Audio), or standard music CDs. CD-DA begat CD-ROM when people realized that you could store a whole bunch of computer data on a 12-cm optical disc (650 MB). CD-ROM drives are simply another kind of digital storage media for computers, albeit read-only. They are peripherals, just like hard disks and floppy drives. (Incidentally, the convention is that when referring to magnetic media, it is spelled "disk." Optical media like CDs, LaserDisc, and all the other formats I'm about to explain are spelled "disc.")

> *CD-I (Compact Disc-Interactive)* came next. This is a consumer electronics format that uses the optical disc in combination with a computer to provide a home entertainment system that delivers music, graphics, text, animation, and video in the living room. Unlike a CD-ROM drive, a CD-I player is a standalone system that requires no external computer. It plugs directly into a TV and stereo system and comes with a remote control to allow the user to interact with software programs sold on discs. It looks and feels much like a CD player, except that you get images as well as music out of it and you can actively control what happens. In fact, it is a CD-DA player and all of your standard music CDs will play on a CD-I player; there is just no video in that case.

> Next came *CD-ROM/XA (eXtended Architecture)*. Now we go back to computer peripherals—a CD-ROM drive, but with some of the compressed audio capabilities found in a CD-I player (called *ADPCM*). This allows interleaving of audio and other data so that an XA drive can play audio and display pictures (or other things) simultaneously. There is special hardware in an XA drive controller to handle the audio playback. This format came from a desire to inject some of the features of CD-I back into the professional market.

> Now, along comes the idea from Kodak for Photo CD—digital pictures on compact disc. They teamed up with Philips to develop the standard for Photo CD discs. At this point, a new problem enters the picture, if you'll pardon the expression. All of the disc formats mentioned so far are read-only; there is no way for anyone but the producer of one of these discs to store his/her own content on the disc—that is, to write to it. But there already existed a technology called *WORM (Write Once Read Many)*. This is an optical disc that can be written to, but exactly once. You can "burn" data on it, but once burned the data cannot be erased, although it can then be used like a CD-ROM disc and read forever. (Depending on your definition of forever, of course.)

> CD-ROM, CD-ROM/XA, and CD-I discs are normally "mastered," as opposed to burned. That means that one master copy is made and then hundreds, or thousands, or millions (if you're lucky enough to need that many) of replicates (or replicants, if you are a "Blade Runner" fan) are pressed from the master. This process is much cheaper than burning for quantities above a few dozen or so. Generally, disc pressing plants can handle all of these formats as the underlying technology is the same; the only difference is in the data and disc format.

> The reason that WORM technology was critical for Photo CD is obvious—the content of these discs is not determined by the manufacturer or publisher. For Photo CD, each disc will be different—a roll or few rolls of film per disc from a customer.

Kodak and Philips wanted Photo CD discs to be playable on both computer peripherals for desktop publishing uses *and* on a consumer device for home viewing. For the former, CD-ROM/XA was chosen as a carrier and for the latter CD-I, which was already designed as a consumer electronics device, and dedicated Photo CD players. This desire for a hybrid disc, or one with multi-platform compatibility, led to the development of the "CD-I Bridge" disc format. A *Bridge disc* is readable on both a CD-I player and a CD-ROM/XA drive.

This Bridge format is the reason there is so much confusion about CD-ROM drives for Photo CD. A drive that supports Photo CD must be a CD-ROM/XA drive that is also Bridge-compatible. (The technical description of Bridge discs calls for supporting certain kinds of sectors identified by "form" and "mode" bits, which is what you usually hear instead of the "Bridge" disc label.) That almost completes the picture, except for the concept of sessions.

Although a WORM disc can only be written to once, it is not necessary to write, or burn, the entire disc all at once. You can burn the disc initially with, for example, a few hundred megabytes of data, and then go back later and burn some more data onto it. Of course, each burn must be to a virgin part of the disc; once a spot on the disc is burned, it cannot be re-burned. Each burn operation is referred to as a *session*, and a drive or disc that supports this multiple burning operation is called *multisession*.

Originally, all WORMs were single session only. That is, you could not go back and add data to a WORM disc once it was burned, even if it was not full. For Photo CD, they wanted the consumer to be able to add more pictures to an existing disc as additional rolls of film were processed. So the extension of WORM technology to multisession was developed and adopted for the Bridge disc format. This required hardware changes to CD-ROM/XA drives and that is why there are a fair number of single-session XA drives on the market and multisession ones appearing more and more.

A single-session drive can read a multisession disc, but it can only read the contents of the first session that was burned. Incidentally, all Philips CD-I players are multisession, although all current CD-I discs have only a single session on them. (Generally, being mastered means a single session, although it is possible to master a multisession disc. I don't know of any software that currently supports this, however.)

CD-Audio   See Redbook audio.

CD-Bridge   Digital data can be written in any one of a number of logical formats, such as CD-Audio, ISO 9660, XA, CD-I. The CD-Bridge format conforms to both the CD-I and CD-ROM-XA specifications. This format assigns two separate disc label locations, allowing a CD-ROM-XA track to be played on a CD-I player. Kodak Photo CD discs are CD-Bridge discs, and thus can be played on CD-ROM-XA drives or on CD-I players.

CD-I.   The Green Book, as described by Lucy Lediaev, Manager of Developer Services for Philips Interactive Media of America:

> The "CD-I Full Functional Specification" (commonly known as the *Green Book*) is a comprehensive and detailed description of the standard for Compact Disc-Interactive hardware, operating systems and software. CD-I technology is licensed

by Philips and Sony Corporation, and the Green Book is published by the two companies to ensure world-wide adherence to a single standard for this licensed technology. The Green Book describes a "base-case" player that is the target for CD-I software developed all over the world. A base-case player contains the minimum set of functions that assures adherence to the CD-I standard. The Green Book also describes extensions to the base case, such as full screen, full-motion video (FMV).

In the United States, the Green Book is available to prospective CD-I developers from the CD-I Association of North America (301-444-6613). CD-I licensees receive the Green Book as part of the licensing process. For information on licensing CD-I technology or for more information regarding policies governing distribution and use of the Green Book, contact:

Bert Gall Coordination Office for Optical and Magnetic Media Systems Philips CEC
P.O. Box 80002, Bldg. SWA1
5600 JB Eindhoven
The Netherlands
Telephone +31 40 726409
Fax: +31 40 732113
CD-ROM (The Yellow Book—ISO 10149:1989)

CD-ROM XA   The major problem with first-generation CD-ROM technology is its inefficiency in dealing with multiple data types. With CD-ROM, different data types, such as graphics, text, and video need to reside in different files on the CD-ROM. The result is increased access time as the drive must seek data in multiple disk locations.

Standard CD-ROM is a two-step process. First graphics, video, and text files are loaded into RAM. Second, the information in RAM is sent to the display adapter while the drive accesses and plays back the audio file. Not only does this slow down the access time, but this process relies on large RAM buffers.

CD-ROM XA (*XA* represents extended architecture) is considered the next generation of CD-ROM technology because it solves the problems in the previous paragraph. XA uses a technology known as *interleaving*, which allows audio, video, graphics, and text to be combined in a single file. CD-ROM XA was developed by Sony, Philips, and Microsoft in 1989. Many others, such as Kodak, IBM, Toshiba, are following suit.

Each of the separate multimedia elements is divided into a number of smaller packets that are intermixed into a single interleaved file. Although data packets can be arranged in any way, the packets themselves are organized in repeating synchronized patterns. Each data packet is approximately 2.3KM and comprises $\frac{1}{75}$ of a second of playback time.

Reading information from the CD-ROM is a process known as *streaming*. Here, the packets are reassembled and output to the display adapter or speakers. Because all the data on a CD-ROM XA is synchronized, it appears as if all video and audio data is being played simultaneously.

To achieve this degree of precision, CD-ROM XA uses ADPCM (Adaptive Differential Pulse Code Modulation) compression. ADPCM enables a compression ratio of up to 16:1, depending on the sampling rate and audio level. The following listing shows what is possible.

	Sampling rate	Compression	Hours
B-Stereo	37.8 kHz	4:1	4+
B-Mono	37.8 kHz	8:1	9+
C-Stereo	18.9 kHz	8:1	9+
C-Mono	18.9 kHz	16:1	18+

Note: B audio is equivalent to FM sound; C is equivalent to AM CD-ROM XA can contain any data type including:

- 8- and 16-bit bitmaps and motion video
- Compression video such as JPEG, MPEG, and INDEO
- Text
- Binary executable code
- Data
- PCM and ADPCM audio

A single interleaved CD-ROM XA file that is pressed onto a disc as a continuous track is called a *stream*. Although the length of a stream can vary, the maximum length is the length of the CD-ROM itself—74 minutes. When playing back the CD-ROM from an XA drive, the data packets from the disc are split apart in real-time with the audio components being routed to a digital-to-audio converter and all the image data (video, graphics, and text) are routed to the display adapter. In essence, streaming ensures that each audio and video packet reaches its destination in a synchronized manner affording the user of the CD-ROM a seamless viewing and listening experience.

There are two other advantages as well. Because there is no waiting for files to preload, playback is immediate. And because it does not require a large RAM buffer nor a disk cache, use of CD-ROM XA requires less system resources.

CDTV   This is Commodore's entry into the home-based CD-ROM market. Its competitors are both CD-I and VIS.

COSE   A loosely affiliated grouping of Unix product vendors, including IM, HP, Sun, SCO, Novell, and USL, whose goal it is to develop a common desktop environment (CDE). Once CDE is in place, portable Unix-based multimedia will be possible.

The elements of this emerging standard are:

Based on Motif:

- A front panel based on Hewlett Packard VUE for storage of commonly used tools and icons.
- Windows management, object and folder management, and tools for basic administrative tasks such as interapplication communications and message passing.
- Personal productivity tools such as clock, notepad, text editor, and mail front end.

DVI (Digital Video Interactive) Hardware and software vendors (including IBM and Intel) got together and standardized on a hardware/software combination that yields very high compression ratios (up to 150:1) and smoother playback because it plays back full-color motion video at 30 frames per second. When it ties in with a mainframe computer, DVI playback approaches the quality of broadcast video.

DVI is a proprietary, programmable compression/decompression technology based on the Intel i750 chip set. This hardware consists of two VLSI (Very Large Scale Integrated) components to separate the image processing and display functions.

Two levels of compression/decompression are provided. Production Level Video (PLV) is a proprietary asymmetrical compression technique for encoding full-motion color video. It requires compression to be performed by Intel at its facilities or at licensed encoding facilities set up by Intel. Real Time Video (RTV) provides image quality that is comparable to frame-rate (motion) JPEG and uses a symmetrical, variable-rate compression. PLV and RTV both use variable compression rates. PLV and RTV both use variable compression rates.

Gold Sound Standard Council Founded in 1992 by a group of sound-card vendors (Ad-Lib Multimedia Inc., Cardinal Technologies, Inc., CPS, Focus Information Systems, Inc., and Yamaha Corp. of America),`this group's goal is to promote an open audio standard so that sound-card developers only need to write one set of drivers for DOS and one set for Windows. Even if this group is successful, the standard it creates will be competing against the popular de facto standards created by Creative Labs' Sound Blaster and Microsoft's Windows Sound System. The council can be reached via Yamaha, in San Jose, California at (800) 543-7457.

Green Book See CD-I.

High Sierra Standard Developed by a group of systems manufacturers and CD-ROM publishers at a 1984 meeting at the High Sierra Hotel in Lake Tahoe, this standard has been absorbed by the ISO 9660 standard.

HTML (Hypertext Markup Language) A superset of SGML. This is the standard for creating documents for Internet Mosaic usage. The HyperText Markup Language (HTML) is composed of a set of elements that define a document and guide its display. Users should be aware that HTML is an evolving language, and different World-Wide Web browsers might recognize slightly different sets of HTML elements. For general information about HTML, including plans for new versions, see http://www.w3.org/hypertext/WWW/MarkUp/MarkUp.html.

JPEG (Joint Photographic Experts Group) A compression standard for still images. JPEG compresses about 20:1 before the image is visibly degraded. JPEG also compresses rather slowly: about one to three seconds for a 1-MB image, depending on the computer.

JPEG uses a technique known as *lossy compression*. As its name implies, data is lost during the compression process, which is accomplished through an algorithmic process. JPEG breaks the image down into smaller, more manageable blocks, compresses the block, and then moves on to the next. This enables compression-on-the-fly and much higher compression rates (up to 20:1), compared to typical text compression ratios, which hover in the area of 3:1.

MPEG (Motion Picture Experts Group) A compression standard for video (motion) images. On August 28, 1995, the Frame Relay Forum and the ATM Forum ratified the new standard (the Frame Relay to ATM PVC Service Internetworking Implementation Agreement).

Presently, there are two MPEG standards—MPEG-1 and MPEG-2. A third, MPEG-4, is currently under development.

MPEG-1 is a small-picture mode of MPEG geared to a resolution of 352 by 240 pixels at 30 frames per second (U.S.), with full CD-quality audio. Originally optimized at slower transfer rates, for low-bandwidth applications, such as single-speed CD-ROM, MPEG-1 syntax can actually handle much larger picture sizes than 352 by 240 through interpolation or scaling, but MPEG-2 is more efficient.

Offering "main profile at main level," MPEG-2 is geared at a resolution of 720 by 480 pixels at 30 frames per second (U.S.), with full CD-quality audio. It's a picture size that allows full-screen playback on PCs or TVs. MPEG-2 can incorporate a range of compression ratios, which trade off economies of storage and transmission bandwidth, against picture quality. At compression ratios of 30:1 and smaller, MPEG-2 offers the perception of broadcast-quality TV. For greater economy, MPEG-2 supports up to 200:1 compression. MPEG-2 decoders, such as the IBM decoder chip, can also recognize and decode MPEG-1 bitstreams, enabling the IBM chip to support both compression standards.

Focusing on HDTV, MPEG-3 was dropped. It was discovered that with a little tweaking, MPEG-2 and MPEG-1 handle HDTV rates. In fact, it is now part of the MPEG-2 High-Level specification.

Currently in the application identification phase is MPEG-4. Its debut is currently scheduled for November 1998 or the official sanction of the proposed standard. Intended for very narrow bandwidths, MPEG-4 is exploring exciting ideas in frame reconstruction. MPEG-4 is considering speech and video synthesis, fractal geometry, computer visualization, and artificial intelligence to build accurate picture from minimal data.

MPEG-2 digital video compression/decompression, a set of standards designed to still be around 50 years from now, has shaken the world of multimedia information. The hope is that it will eventually deliver a true multimedia information highway to any and all would-be travelers much sooner than anyone expected.

Though more useful than analog, digital data takes up considerably more room. When analog NTSC video (U.S. television) is digitized at 30 frames per second, it hogs a billion bytes of storage every minute on screen—way beyond the entire storage of most desktop computers. What is the solution for this bandwidth dilemma: compression.

Video is often compressed via software codec (compression/decompression) routines, such as Intel's Indeo and others, often do the job, but these methods usually lose critical visual information: a compression ratio of 4:1 to 10:1 at 15 frames per second is inadequate for evolving uses. MPEG-1 brings up the frame rate to 30 frames per second, with high-quality compression at better than 6:1. But there is a drawback, it offers a resolution of only 352 by 240 and is ridden with enormously CPU-intensive, time-consuming encoding.

Delivering up to 200:1 compression ratio and offering full-screen video playback at 30 frames per second, MPEG-2 has greatly improved on its predecessor. MPEG-2 can deliver broadcast-quality video at compression ratios of 30:1 and better. Additionally, MPEG-2 decoder chips can be designed to be backward-compatible with MPEG-1, enabling them to support both standards.

Though presently quite difficult and costly, the new affordable MPEG-2 encoding chips should quickly make the process more affordable. Why compress video and audio? Simply put, uncompressed digital video carriers more information than required; far more information than our senses can process.

MPEG-2 deletes the unnecessary and systematically reduces the necessary to its bare, encoded essentials. Every byte of MPEG-2 can represent 200 bytes of raw video; thus MPEG-2 is an outstandingly efficient compression system.

This handy process can reduce bandwidth dramatically. It's instantly clear that a lot of the information on screen is spatially redundant. For example, if what is being broadcast on screen has a blue background, you can save a bunch of bandwidth by not identifying every pixel to a 32-bit hue depth and 24-bit chroma and luminance depth. All you would need is the capability to reduce it all to a certain blue and a certain brightness. This is basically what is done to produce an intra-coded or "I" frame. Smart I-frame construction can keep loss to a minimum through "adaptive quantization," an automatic process in which the MPEG encoder analyzes the input video bitstream and compresses it in an optimal way.

Also, if this blue background is not going to change in the next frame, all that pixel data doesn't have to be carried over. Just insert a code that enables the block to maintain the same color in the next frame. This mathematical process is entitled "2-D discrete cosine transform" and it tracks pixel changes and yields motion vectors, which predict where movement is most likely to appear in the next frame. This ability to look ahead and behind makes it possible to construct in-between frames very accurately.

In MPEG, the computer does this tweening. Analyzing movement directions in previous frames, it is able to construct predicted frames (P-frames)—estimating where things will be in the next frame. Bidirectionally predicted frames (B-frames) require the computer to calculate both ahead and behind to estimate movement. Taking up a minimum of bandwidth in transmission, P- and B- frames send, instead of pixel details, an operational description of frame content. Another bandwidth hog, is the vital audio track. MPEG-2 is designed to carry five channels of surround audio plus a sixth, very narrow channel, for subwoofer data. With our ever-increasing knowledge of perceptual psychology, we are able to divide the audio spectrum into bands, systematically removing the portions that are not vital for accurate for audio perception. Thus, the level of compression achieved without a noticeable drop in sound quality is on the level of eight to one.

These are very expensive compression techniques—desktop MPEG-2 systems costing in the tens of thousands of dollars. But things will soon be improved. IBM Microelectronics have been working on a new, hyper-dense 0.5-micron CMOS chip designs that will run cooler, be less power hungry and pack more wallop per cubic nanometer. They now have one chip to encode and one to decode MPEG-2 bitstreams. OEM will be able to purchase an IBM encoder chip for under $100 and IBM decoder chips for under $40 in volume.

Driven by a 32-bit, 50-MHz internal RISC processor, the IBM encoder chip performs real-time encoding of I-frames in MPEG-2 format. "It will process data in a way that will cooperate with the other components so that a full I-P-B encoder can be implemented," states Frank DeMara of IBM's Digital Video Products group.

The IBM decoder chip has its own wide-bus, special-purpose RISC processor at 40 MHz. This decoder chip, by scanning the coded bitstream for start codes, can handle both MPEG-1 and MPEG-2 bitstreams. The result—video output that bears a stronger resemblance to laserdisc video than regular television.

Advanced error trapping and concealment is responsible for this chip's amazing successes. The chip is capable of reconstructing and fixing a corrupted macroblock by looking at the data that is held in memory. Because the frame is corrected and patched in real time, the human eye will not detect anything out of the ordinary.

The most obvious application for IBM's real-time MPEG-2 encoding will be in video editing—thus, the average consumer might soon have the opportunities and the video professional.

MPEG-2 Video Encoder

- Dedicated real-time hardware for MPEG-2 I-frame compression.
- Built-in 50-MHz RISC processor for microcodeable flexibility.
- Acts as video I/O interface.
- Operates in real-time on input video data.
- Full compliance with MPEG-2 and MPEG-2 Main Profile and Mail Level, with extensions.
- Fully compliant compressed MPEG-2 video datastream.
- Scalable architecture for future I-P-B encoding.
- Field/frame encoding microcode selectable.
- 4:2:2 chroma format encoding in CCIR 601 resolution.
- Direct real-time encoding for YCbCr and RGB digital video sources.
- CCIR 601 to HHR (Half Horizontal Resolution) conversion and encoding.
- Color space conversion.
- 4:2:2 to 4:2:0 conversion.
- Automatic 3/2 pulldown inversion.
- S scene change detection.
- Micro-controllable features: adaptive quantization, motion compensation, and rate control.

- Programmable encoding parameter including: quantization matrices, scan pattern, and more.
- Direct interface to standard, inexpensive DRM.
- O.5u CMOS technology at 3.3 V.

MPEG-2 Video Decoder

- Dedicated real-time hardware for MPEG-2 decompression.
- Built-in 40-MHz RISC processor for microcodeable flexibility.
- Full compliance with MPEG-2 Main Profile at Main level.

Resolutions

- 720 by 480 at 30 fps
- 720 by 576 at 25 fps
  - ~ Sustained MPEG-2 compression rate at up to 15 MB/s (I-P-B frames).
  - ~ MPEG-2 pan-scan support.
  - ~ Automatic 3/2 pulldown for MPEG-2, variable 3/2 pulldown for MPEG-2.
- All video layers decoded on chip.
- Full on-screen display capability.
- Horizontal and vertical filtering for SIF to CCIR 601 expansion, plus 360, 480 and 540 to 720 upsample.
- Error concealment, including MPEG-2 concealment motion vectors.
- Interlaced display output at 60 fields/sec.
- 8-bit and 16-bit YCB Cr outputs.
- Direct interface to standard, inexpensive DRAM.
- Selectable host interface 8- or 16-bit host interface or serial-mode options.
- Support for chroma 4:2:2 input.
- Recognition of error start codes in video bitstream.
- 0.5u CMOS technology at 3.3 V.

For more information on MPEG, hyperlink over to the Moving Pictures experts Group Web Site in Italy at http://www.crs4.it/luigi/MPEG/mpegfag.html.

MPEG-2 MPEG-2 video is a developing International Standard, which will specify the coded bitstream for high-quality digital video. MPEG-2 Video builds on the success of the completed MPEG-1 Video Standard (ISO/IEC IS 11172-2) by additionally supporting interlaced video formats, increased image quality, and a number of other advanced features, including features to support HDTV. MPEG-2 Main Profile is a compatible extension of MPEG-1, meaning that an MPEG-2 Video decoder can decode MPEG-1 bitstreams. Also, like MPEG-1, MPEG-2 can support interoperability with the CCITT H.261 video telephony standard.

As a generic International Standard, MPEG-2 Video is being defined in terms of extensible Profiles, each of which will support the features needed by an important class of applications. Among the applications supported by the Main Profile will be digital video transmission—in the range of about 2 to 15 Mbit/s over cable, satellite, and other broadcast channels—enabling exciting new consumer video services. Another feature of the Main Profile is support for several picture aspect ratios, including 4:3, 16:9, and others.

The development of further profiles is already well underway. The collaboration between MPEG and the CCIR is bearing fruit with the definition of an hierarchical Profile, which extends the features of the Main Profile. This Profile is well-suited to applications such as terrestrial broadcasting, which may require multi-level coding. For example, this system could give the consumer the option of using either a small portable receiver to decode standard-definition TV, or a larger fixed receiver to decode HDTV from the same broadcast signal.

MPEG-2 Audio MPEG is developing the MPEG-2 Audio Standard for multi-channel audio coding, which will be compatible with the existing MPEG-1 Audio Standard (ISO/IEC IS 11172-3). MPEG-2 Audio coding will supply up to five full bandwidth channels (left, right, center, and two surround channels), plus an additional low-frequency enhancement channel, and/or up to seven commentary/multilingual channels. In Sydney, MPEG merged several proposals from the November 1992 London MPEG meeting into a unified specification. In its audio work, MPEG is collaborating with the CCIR to conduct subjective tests of the proposed multichannel system.

The MPEG-2 Audio Standard will also provide improved quality coding of mono and conventional stereo signals for bit-rates at or below 64 Kb/s, per channel.

MPEG-2 Systems The MPEG-2 Systems Standard will specify how to combine multiple audio, video, and private-data streams into a single multiplexed stream, allowing for the transmission, storage, access, and retrieval of the original streams, while maintaining accurate synchronization. MPEG-2 Systems will be targeted at a wider range of applications than the MPEG-1 Systems standard (ISO/IEC IS 11172- 1). As a generic standard, MPEG-2 Systems will support a wide range of broadcast, telecommunications, computing, and storage applications.

To provide support for these features, the MPEG-2 Systems standard will define two kinds of streams. The Program Stream provides for the creation of an audio-visual program, which could have multiple views and multichannel audio. It is similar to the Systems Stream of MPEG-1, with extensions for encoding program-specific information, such as multiple-language audio channels. The Transport Stream is new to MPEG-2. It multiplexes a number of programs, comprised of video, audio, and private data, for transmission and storage using a wide variety of media. The Transport Stream supports multi-program broadcast, storage of single programs on digital video tape, robust performance against channel errors, conditional access to programs, and the maintenance of synchronization over complex networks and through editing operations.

NISO *NISO* is a national standards-developing organization that develops and promotes voluntary standards for information science, libraries, and publishing practices. Of the many NISO standards the one of greatest interest for those in the multimedia community is NISO 9660, also known as *ISO 9660* or *ANSI 9660*. 9660 is the operative international standard for the placement of data on compact read-only optical disks (CD-ROM). It sets forth the volume and file structure for CD-ROM and specifies placement of files to ensure interoperability of CCD-ROM products. This is a 64-page standard and is priced at $48.00. It can be purchased through Transaction Publishers, Dept. NISO92, Rutgers University, New Brunswick, NJ 08903. From a practical perspective, you only need to purchase this volume if you are the makers of a CD-ROM drive. For the rest of us, just make sure that the CD-ROM drive that you purchase is 9660-compatible. If you absolutely must take a look at this standard, but don't want to spend the money, try an association library, such as the IEEE.

Other NISO standards in development include:

- ANSI/NISO Z39.72-199x. CD-ROM standard format for the submission of data for multimedia CD-ROM mastering.

- ANSI/NISO Z39-199x. CD-ROM standard interface retrieval protocol.

National Information Standards Organization
P.O. Box 1056
Bethesda, MD 20827
(301) 975-2814

NTSC (National Television Standards Committee) This is the video standard for North America. All signals, whether from a TV, VCR, laser-disc or camcorder, conform to this standard.

This standard, which has been in existence since 1952, decreed that a single frame of video consists of up to 525 horizontal scan lines drawn on the inside face of a phosphor-coated picture tube by a fast-moving electron beam every $\frac{1}{30}$ of a second, each taking $\frac{1}{60}$ of a second to draw.

Orange Book Standard which specifies the format for write-once and magneto-optical CD technologies (MO CD).

P*64 This is a video telephone conferencing standard from the International Telegraph and Telephone Consultative Committee (CCITT) for compression audio and motion video images. The standard incorporates multiplexing, demultiplexing, framing of data, transmission protocol, bandwidth congruence, and call setup and teardown. P*64 encodes real-time motion video and audio for transmission over copper or fiber-optic telephone lines at 30 frames per second, at a bandwidth between 40 Kb/s to 4 Mb/s.

PAL This is the European version of the NTSC standard. Unfortunately, NTSC and PAL are incompatible. However, much of the video software on the market enables you to output to either NTSC or PAL. PAL paints 625 lines at a frame rate of 25 per second, each field taking $\frac{1}{50}$ of a second to draw.

QuickTime This is the video codec written for the Macintosh. QuickTime video players are available to play QuickTime video on MPC platforms.

Redbook Audio (CD-Audio—The Red Book—CEI IEC 908) This international standard, ISO 10149, controls the creation of audio CDs. It's also known as the *Redbook Standard* because of the color of the standard's book jacket. Many CD-ROMs (and all MPC standard drives) allow the playing of audio CDs through the PC's CD-ROM drive.

The entire specification can be found in the International Electrotechnical Commission's "Compact Disk Digital Audio System 908; 1987." It covers such specifics as dimensions, optical parameters of the plastic, recording and play-back environment, signal measurement and fidelity, and the structure of the digital files that contain the music waveforms.

Digitally, Redbook audio is recorded as 16-bit words using a sampling frequency of 44.1 kHz and recorded in a 2-channel, linear format.

SECAM The Sequential Color and Memory video system is used in France, among other places. Although, like PAL, it is a 625-line, 50-Hz system, its base technology and broadcast method is different from PAL.

SGML (Standard Generalized Markup Language) Adopted as an ISO standard in 1986. This is a standard that allows organizations to structure and manage information in a cross-platform, application-independent manner. It tags documents as a series of data objects, rather than storing them as huge files.

Shared Frame Buffer Architecture (SFBA) Intel Corp. and ATI Technologies have joined forces to develop a new hardware architecture that combines graphics and video technology, reducing the cost of putting multimedia in a PC. SFBA is an open specification that enables makers of graphics chips and board makers to build a single card that combines graphics acceleration, video compression and decompression, and video-capture capabilities. SFBA supports system buses, including EISA (Extended Industry Standard Architecture), ISA, VESA-local bus, Micro Channel and Peripheral Component Interconnect.

Standard for Electronic Manuscript Preparation and Markup Version 2.0, introduced in August 1987, describes standard methods for authors and publishers to keyboard and mark up books, articles, and serials on a computer. The document contains explanatory information about the Association of American Publishers' (AAP) application of SGML, defines the application's formal syntax, and is, along with its appendices, the formal Electronic Manuscript Standard approved by the American National Standards Institute.

The standard is the result of the three-year Electronic Manuscript Project sponsored by the Association of American publishers and the Council on Library Resources, which drew on the expertise of over 60 publishing, bibliographic, and office industry groups around the world. The Electronic Manuscript Standard offers the first industry-wide application of SGML for the publishing industry.

A series of guidebooks is available for those interested: *The Author's Guide to Electronic Manuscript Preparation and Markup* explains how to prepare a manuscript with Electronic Manuscript Standard markup. *The Reference*

Manual on Electronic Manuscript Preparation and Markup condenses major concepts of the Standard into an easily-consulted guide with examples. For more information, contact EPSIG, c/o OCLC 6565 Frantz Road, Dublin, OH 43017. Or call (614) 764-6195.

VRML (Virtual Reality Modelling Language)   A description language that permits the modelling of three-dimensional worlds.

VIS   This is Tandy's competitive offering to CD-I. The device is physically similar to Photo-CD or CD-I, but is based on Microsoft Windows.

Yellow-Book   See CD-ROM.

XA   See CD-ROM XA.

ZV   Zoom Video, which was developed in collaboration by chip manufacturer Chips and Technologies Inc. and other third parties, is a proposed standard. It is a specification for designing a motherboard with a direct connection between the PCMCIA connector and frame buffer. Ultimately, ZV, or notebook-based video, will make it easier for mobile workers to use and cheaper for notebook makers to implement.

CD-ROM Standards for Unix

Andrew Young

Introduction

The Unix market, also known as the "open-systems" market, is driven by standards. Essentially and by definition, proprietary products are not "open," thus every major component of the Unix operating environment has in one form or another undergone a standardization process. Early adopters of the Unix operating system generally were universities and technical organizations whose primary interest was in pushing the envelope of whatever technology they could acquire. These users were price/performance buyers and did not exhibit a high level of brand loyalty. This was one of their primary reasons for selecting Unix systems; using Unix did not lock them into a permanent commitment to a vendor's proprietary products.

From very early on, many different computers ran very similar, though usually not identical, versions of Unix. While there has always been competition among vendors to deliver the most advanced Unix implementations, the market demanded reasonable interoperability among different Unix products. This led to a variety of efforts to bring workable standards to the industry. In the two decades since Unix was originally released, many components of the Unix environment have been standardized. The command structure and system interface both became standards through the POSIX committees of the IEEE, and subsequently were adopted by the International Standards Organization (ISO). Most of the programming on Unix systems has been done in the "C" language, which is commonly provided with the operating system since most of the operating system itself was written in "C." This language essentially became a de facto Unix industry standard at its inception, but it has also been formally standardized by the American National Standards Institute (ANSI).

Unix and Standards

The combination of these standards has offered Unix users an unprecedented level of code portability. Even in the early days, users wanted to, and in many cases actually could, port their software relatively easily to whatever were the newest and hottest platforms available in each new generation of Unix systems. Since these users generally did not discard their old machines, it quickly became important to connect these systems in extensive heterogeneous networks. Thus the next areas to undergo broad standardization were the physical and logical aspects of networking.

There are two primary types of standards in the computer industry: formal standards, developed and adopted by official standards bodies, and de facto standards, usually developed by one or more industry participants to solve a specific problem but made widely available to avoid the emergence of multiple conflicting solutions. Though there is a natural bias toward formal standards, in many ways it doesn't matter whether a standard is formal or de facto, as long as the industry as a whole supports the standard. The Unix market tends to adopt standards with its feet. In other words, one can usually identify the viable standards by looking at the various alternatives and identifying the one the crowd is flocking toward. In some cases this may mean that a formal standard will win out over another "technically superior" solution, but in such situations adequate, functional interoperability, enabling widespread support, is generally of primary importance.

CD-ROM Standards

One of the reasons CD-ROM (Compact Disc Read Only Memory) has become such a universal success is that the entire foundation of CD-ROM technology, from the physical structure of the disc to the logical organization of the information recorded thereon, has been standardized. Here the process began as proprietary, licensed, consumer audio technology, but the licensing terms were reasonable and the technology was so compelling that CD-DA (Compact Disc–Digital Audio) products became the biggest success in the history of consumer electronics. In the decade since the CD was invented, several variations on the basic technology have been released, of which CD-ROM is probably the best known. The fundamental specifications defining the successful variants generally have been codified as published international standards.

At the most fundamental level, the physical parameters and encoding of data on a compact disc are specified in a document known as "the IEC 908." This contains much of the information presented in the so-called Red Book, which specifies the physical size and structure of manufactured CD-DA discs, how digital audio data is to be physically recorded on the disc, how the individual data blocks are to be identified, the implementation of error-detection and -correction codes, and a variety of other details.

Layered on top of this specification is the ISO 10149, which encompasses the content of "the Yellow Book." This is the basis for CD-ROM technology. It details the extensions to the IEC 908 that support recording computer-readable digital data from a compact disc. This involves mechanisms for determining which of the recorded information is audio data and which computer data, and which of the available forms for recording this information are to be used. Further it specifies the use of an additional layer of error-detection and -correction encoding that increases the reliability of the medium from the relatively limited needs of digital audio to the high reliability required of computer storage.

Once raw computer data is able to be recorded on a high-capacity, random-access medium such as CD-ROM, one or more file systems usually will be designed to take advantage of this. Early work on CD-ROM file systems followed one of two main paths: adapting or porting file systems designed for other media to CD-ROM, or development of proprietary, CD-ROM-specific file systems.

Neither of these added significant flexibility to this new medium. File systems designed for other media were generally ill suited to the performance characteristics of CD-ROM drives. Proprietary file systems were not widely available and tended to be tuned to the applications, and sometimes hardware, provided by the developing vendor. The market floundered in the sea of incompatible solutions in which it was awash.

Soon a group of vendors decided they would all benefit from the adoption of a common file system standard specifically designed to perform well with the wide class of applications for which CD-ROM technology was expected to be used. Out of this effort the High Sierra format was born in 1986. Two years later a slightly modified version was adopted as the ISO 9660 standard. The ISO 9660 has become one of the major successes of the standardization process. More computers of different types from different manufacturers can read ISO 9660–format discs than any other disk or tape format, including floppy and hard-disk formats.

Standard Limitations

Yet the ISO 9660 has limitations which have raised concerns that vendors may choose to bend, break, or ignore the standard altogether in certain situations. Much of the concern is rooted in the "lowest-common-denominator" nature of the file system. In order to reach the widest possible range of target platforms, the file system places substantial restrictions on the character set acceptable for file and directory names, the depth of directory structures, and the range of file system features supported. While the ISO 9660 is well suited to DOS and VAX VMS systems, it leaves much to be desired when applied in the Unix and Macintosh environments.

Under the Unix operating system specifically, much early application of CD-ROM technology has been in the area of application and operating system software distribution. It is here that robust support for Unix file system features is most important. Many vendors found it difficult or impossible to create an acceptable model for distribution of their materials within a strict ISO

9660 structure, so a variety of non- or nearly ISO 9660 CD-ROM discs appeared, usually simply dumps of Unix file system (UFS) hard disk images onto CDs.

This trend caused concern for many in the traditionally standards-oriented Unix market. UFS, more a general set of file system design principles than an actual standard, does not provide any real interchange capability. UFS discs created on one system usually cannot be read on a system of a different type, sometimes even if they are from the same vendor. Further, UFS images dumped onto CD-ROMs generally were hit with substantial performance penalties compared to similar ISO 9660 discs, since UFS was designed to work well on fast hard disks.

The Rock Ridge Group

In 1990 a group of Unix and CD-ROM industry vendors formed the Rock Ridge Group to address this issue. Their goal was to develop a CD-ROM file system that would provide complete support for Unix/POSIX file systems and that could form the basis for a formal international standard. After considering a variety of possible routes to go down, the group settled on a draft proposal, submitted by this author, as the basis for their subsequent work. This proposal embedded the additional Unix file system information transparently within an ISO 9660 directory structure. This allowed a single disc, with a single physical directory structure, to have two logical appearances. In a compatible Unix environment, the disc would appear to be a complete Unix file system. To a system that understands only the basic ISO 9660, the disc would appear to be a normal ISO 9660 disc.

This approach supports the primary goal of the ISO 9660: universal information interchange. Since there is only one actual directory structure through which the data can be accessed, all the files are accessible from either view. The file names and even the directory structure may be different, but all the file contents are available. Further, to allay the concern of other, non-Unix vendors that use of the Rock Ridge Protocols may preclude simultaneous recording of other file system extensions, the proposal was split into two parts. The System Use Sharing Protocol (SUSP) defines a shareable, extensible, non-Unix-specific mechanism for recording additional information within the ISO 9660 directory record's System Use Area. The Rock Ridge Interchange Protocol (RRIP) uses the SUSP specifically to record the information required for a complete Unix/POSIX file system. Both of these proposals were released in the spring of 1991 with the support of more than a dozen major Unix and CD-ROM vendors.

When the SUSP was being constructed, features were added to allow coexistence with as many of the current uses of the System Use Area as we could find. When the fields that would be required for the RRIP were being defined, extra effort was made to make the encoding as flexible and non-system-specific as possible, to encourage the use of these fields in other non-Unix environments that also could benefit from extensions to the ISO 9660 such as

OS/2, Windows NT, the Macintosh, or the Amiga. This strategy has substantially reduced the number of possible conflicts with other industry interests and has nearly eliminated all resistance to support for the protocols.

The Rock Ridge Protocols currently have the status of a de facto industry standard. They constitute the only proposal that addresses the needs of the Unix market while remaining completely ISO 9660–compliant. Every major Unix industry vendor that is seriously concerned with CD-ROM support has implemented the Rock Ridge Protocols. Most of these vendors were themselves actively involved in the development of the protocols. Some are still involved as members of the IEEE Computer Society standards working group, chaired by this author, which is formalizing the proposals in preparation for their adoption as an official IEEE standard.

The Official UNIX Standard—XCDR

The only existing, official, Unix-specific CD-ROM standard is the XCDR, adopted by X/open, a Unix industry organization formed to promote open, standards-based computing. An ISO 9660 volume and directory structure provides fields for storing a wide variety of information about the disc that it describes, such as who published the disc, who prepared the data, multiple time stamps (creation, modification, effective and expiration dates), and whether the disc was designed to operate on a specific system or with a particular application. Much of this information is not directly accessible through a normal directory listing, which is all that most computer systems know how to provide.

The XCDR defines an application programming interface (API) for accessing all of the ISO 9660 volume and directory information. Support of this API would allow application or system programmers to conveniently utilize this information where this is awkward now, since each programmer must have sufficient knowledge of the ISO 9660 (and patience) to find and decode the data. The RRIP also proposes to extend this API to support the specific features it provides. Though the XCDR has been around for over two years, it has only recently begun to generate any significant interest from the Unix vendors. This interest is expected to grow as more diverse applications of CD-ROM technology are developed.

Standards on the Way

A variety of other CD-ROM-related standards efforts of interest to the Unix community are under way. Perhaps the most visible is the Frankfurt Format/ECMA 168/DIS 13490. This format provides an incrementally updatable file system to support the new generation of "Orange Book," CD-recordable (CD-R) drives. While the ISO 9660 and the Rock Ridge Protocols are widely being used with CD-R drives, they can be used only in a batch-write (disc-at-once) mode, in which the entire disc is written in one pass. This encompasses a large segment of the CD-R market, including the entire CD-

ROM publishing market, most batch backup situations, and virtually all custom data distribution applications, primarily because the vast majority of installed CD-ROM drives are not capable of reading incrementally written discs. Still, there are many applications for which incremental writing of information to CD-R would be useful. Owing to fundamental design decisions, the ISO 9660 cannot support this function, so another format is required and the Frankfurt/ECMA 168 serves this need well.

Whereas the High Sierra Group was composed almost exclusively of MS-DOS PC-oriented vendors, the developers of the Frankfurt proposal represented a much wider cross-section of the computer industry. Specifically, the Unix vendors were well represented, resulting in strong Unix/POSIX support within the Frankfurt proposal. Thankfully, this precludes the need to develop a Rock-Ridge-style extension to this proposal and assures that all vendors that implement Frankfurt/ECMA 168 drivers for Unix systems will provide full POSIX-style file system support immediately. Such products are expected to begin appearing in 1994, after the expected adoption of the Frankfurt/ECMA 168 as an ISO standard early that year.

There are other areas that beg for standardization. Several data-exchange (client-server search-and-retrieval) protocols are being promoted for standardization, but as of yet none has caught the attention of the market. Which, if any, of these will become either de facto or formal industry standards has yet to be determined.

There is a crying need for a baseline, full-text indexing standard. Currently few CD-ROM titles can be accessed under Unix without using DOS-emulation. An indexing standard would allow information vendors to sell their information on CD-ROM to anyone, and retrieval software, perhaps using enhanced proprietary index structures, only to those markets that the vendors believe justify their investment. On platforms not supported directly by the vendors, third-party software houses could develop retrieval software that could access many vendors' discs, or the users could develop their own retrieval software.

CD-ROM is the medium of choice for the distribution of multimedia applications, in part because of the level of standardization. This allows vendors to deliver multimedia products on a single disc to multiple platforms. Many of the standard formats used in the PC environment (TIFF, PCX, WAV) are becoming de facto standards under Unix as well, but the biggest barrier to Unix multimedia is actually having adequate support for multimedia delivery on a wide range of Unix platforms. Ironically, it is much more likely that one could establish a motion-video standard than an audio standard under Unix today, because a wider variety of Unix boxes support powerful color graphics processing than support even adequate audio output. Only recently have we seen a trend toward providing audio support on Unix workstations, yet no major vendor provides audio support standardly on its entire product line. Only when audio can essentially be assumed to be available on all desktop workstations from the major manufacturers will multimedia be able to show substantial growth in the Unix workstation market.

Clearly, support for CD-ROM under Unix has come a long way in the last few years, and this growth strongly parallels the development of appropriate standards. Before the ISO 9660 was introduced in 1988, there was no Unix CD-ROM market. While some progress was made in the interim, use of CD-ROM under Unix really started to grow only after the introduction of the Rock Ridge Protocols in 1991. Today CD-ROM is an accepted, often even required, component of the Unix workstation environment. If multimedia is ever to flourish in the Unix environment, it will be because adequate standards have been developed to support this function. To paraphrase Vince Lombardi, the legendary Green Bay Packers coach, under Unix "standards aren't everything, they're the only thing."

Legal Aspects of Multimedia Productions

Frederic M. Wilf

Abstract

The law protects works of art and expression, including multimedia works. Multimedia artists and producers (this chapter uses the term "artist") need to be aware of how the mechanisms of the law work so that the artist might get the maximum amount of protection for her work, while making sure that she does not trip over someone else's rights by mistake.

Why Multimedia is Different—from a Legal Perspective

The law responds to each new technological challenge by first studying it, and then, if appropriate, doing something about it. For example, the Copyright Office started accepting copyright registrations of computer programs as early as 1964, but it was not until 1980 that Congress amended the U.S. Copyright Act to explicitly protect computer programs.

Until the advent of multimedia, the Copyright Office and the users and owners of copyright-protected works had placed each type of work in its own pigeon hole. Photographs were registered in one way, and licensed by photographers and stock houses. Musical compositions were registered in another way, and licensed through ASCAP, BMI, and other organizations. The movie and television studios handled their own copyright registrations and licensing, with the help of the Harry Fox Agency and the distribution houses. However, multimedia blurs these distinctions.

A single multimedia work can contain:

- Text from an encyclopedia,

- Photographs from a magazine,

- Music composed by one person and performed by another,
- Sound recordings from a record album,
- Video from an old movie,

all of which has been altered and arranged to form a single integrated work. Indeed, the initials of the term "multimedia" are shared with an older, Yiddish word for a similar blending of many things into one: "Mish-Mash."

This sort of mish-mash makes for interesting legal issues. So far, the law deals with multimedia legal issues by reversing the mish-mash. The law looks at and analyzes each element that goes into a multimedia work as if the element were by itself. Eventually, the law will deal with the final result (the mish-mash), but until that happens, it is best to analyze the elements as they go into the work.

An element-by-element analysis might take a little more time to complete, but, as you will see, you do not need a lawyer to conduct this analysis. Much of this you can do yourself.

What This Chapter Covers

This chapter covers legal issues that multimedia artists should be aware of under United States law. For example, if an artist would like to digitize and incorporate a photograph from a recent magazine, and there is no copyright notice, can the artist do this?

Suppose an artist has completed a multimedia work on CD-ROM that consists of hypertext, video, and sound, as well as searching software. How can the artist protect the work, or at least have the right to sue anyone who pirates the work?

What if the artist wants to transmit a multimedia work across a local area network, wide area network, or across the global Internet? Do the answers to the questions change from one type of transmission to another?

There are fairly simple techniques to protect what the artist has created, as well as methods to enforce that protection. The other side of the coin is that the artist does not want to unwittingly infringe the rights of others, so a basic understanding of common legal problems can be helpful.

This chapter briefly covers copyright, privacy, and contract law as they apply to multimedia works.

What This Chapter Does Not Cover

This chapter discusses a number of legal issues that multimedia artists face, but it does not cover every legal issue. Nor does it say everything that needs to be said for each issue that it does cover.

This chapter discusses the law in the United States. Except for a few brief references, it does not cover international law or the law in any other country. More importantly, many issues in U.S. law (such as contract law) are a subject of state law, which means that the law will be different from one state to the next.

This chapter does not provide the "final word" on the state of the law. The law is a moving target because it continues to change. One example is the U.S. Copyright Act, which was completely rewritten in 1976. However, Congress has seen fit to amend the Copyright Act several times each year since then. All other areas of law covered in this chapter are also subject to constant change.

Finally, this chapter does not provide legal, accounting, or other professional advice. If legal advice or other expert assistance is required, the services of a competent professional should be retained.

Copyright Law

Copyright law is the primary means to protect multimedia works. Copyright law is designed to protect "expressions" of ideas, while making available to others the underlying ideas, facts, and information. Copyright law defines what is and is not protected, as well as the methods by which protection is enforced. This section covers the legal rights that make up a copyright.

Owning a copyright, as opposed to owning an object

When a person buys a book or a record, that person then owns the physical object: the book or record. Owning the book or record does not give the purchaser the right to copy the book or record, or make new versions of the book or record.

So, if you purchase a videotape of a 10-year-old movie, you can watch that movie and show it to your friends. However, you cannot copy scenes from the movie into your CD-ROM-based guide to cinema without the permission of the person or company that owns the copyright to the movie.

As for the videotape, you can also sell it to another person (so long as you don't keep any copies for yourself). In copyright law, this is called the *first sale doctrine*. Once the physical copy embodying the copyrighted work is sold, the purchaser can use or dispose of that copy any way she likes, so long as she does not make copies of all or part of the work.

Source of law

The United States Copyright Act is the sole copyright statute in the United States. This has been so since Congress pre-empted the field with the Copyright Act of 1976, which became effective on January 1, 1978.

No state is allowed to legislate in the area of copyright law, so there is no state copyright law. Nor is there a "common law" (judge-made) copyright law, so judges will not make up new rights or responsibilities, as they can in other areas of the law. Judges may interpret the U.S. Copyright Act, which means that a judge can create explanations and structures for resolving disputes where the Copyright Act is ambiguous, unclear or incomplete.

For those who have access to federal statutes, the Copyright Act can be found in Title 17 of the United States Code. When this chapter refers to a section number, it will be to a section number of Title 17. For example, the definitions of copyright terms are found in Section 101 of the Copyright Act.

Definitions of key copyright terms

Copyright law is whatever Congress says it is. The key to an understanding of copyright law is the terms that Congress uses in the Copyright Act. The definitions are important because a particular term will have one meaning in copyright law and a different meaning in a different area of the law. For example, the term *publication* in copyright law means dissemination to the general public; *publication* in libel law means any dissemination of libelous matter to any other person, in public or private.

The following are key terms defined in Section 101 of the Copyright Act.

Work. A *work* in the copyright lingo is any embodiment that contains expression that may be protected under the copyright law. Works include building designs, drawings, books or any kind of text, two-dimensional and three-dimensional art, computer programs, movies, etc. All of the things protected by copyright law and covered in this chapter are called *works*.

Audiovisual works. An *audiovisual work* is a series of related images and any accompanying sounds that are intended to be shown by the use of machines, such as projectors or electronic equipment, including computers and televisions. It does not matter whether the audiovisual work is embodied in tape, on film, or on floppy or CD-ROM disk. Most multimedia works are considered audiovisual works for copyright purposes.

Derivative work. A *derivative work* is a work that is based on one or more pre-existing works, regardless of the type of pre-existing work. The derivative work can be in any form in which a work may be recast, transformed, or adapted. Digitizing a photograph creates a derivative work (the digital version) of a pre-existing work (the film-based or analog photograph). A derivative work can constitute an original work of authorship that is separate and distinct from the pre-existing work. As noted, however, the copyright owner can control whether a person is allowed to make derivative works of the copyright owner's work.

One key issue involving derivative works is the point at which a derivative work is no longer considered derivative. For example, if you digitize a photograph, that creates a derivative work that can be recognized as a copy of the original. If you then alter the digitized version to the point where it is no longer recognizable in any way as a derivative of the original, then you have created a new work.

Think of it as melting down a bronze statue. If you melt it down partially, and part of the original is still recognizable (even a small part), then you have a derivative work. However, if the bronze is melted completely into a liquid and then poured into a new mold, an original work is created that no longer owes anything to the prior work, except for the raw material.

Thus, if you take a photograph on print film of the White House, that is an original work. If you digitize the print, you have created a derivative work. If you then use the digital version (the first derivative work) of the White House photograph to create new images, such as a Blue House, a Pink House, a Green House, a Fuchsia House, each of these variations would be a separate derivative work, owing to the original print-based work. However, if you so changed the digital version of the photograph that none of the original work is recognizable, then the newest version is no longer a derivative of the original work.

Fixed in a tangible medium of expression. The Copyright Act automatically protects all works including multimedia works as soon as they are written on paper, stored on a disk, or saved in some other medium. As an example, if one person talks to another person face-to-face, no copyrighted work is created. However, if one person records the conversation on audiotape or videotape, then a copyrighted work is created on tape.

Copyright exclusive rights. The Copyright Act grants five exclusive rights to a copyright owner, who may: (1) Copy or reproduce the work, (2) prepare derivative works, (3) distribute copies, (4) perform the work, and (5) display the work. Thus, the owner of the copyright can control who copies the work, who can make new versions of the work, who can distribute copies of the work by hard-copy mail or e-mail, who can perform the work on stage or screen, and who can display the work on the walls or monitors of an art gallery.

Author and owner. The *author* is the person who creates a work. The creator of the work is called an *author*—even though the creator might be creating a photograph, a videotape or a sound recording.

The *owner* is the owner of the copyright at any given time. Initially, the author and the owner are the same person because the author is the initial owner of the copyright. Then, the author might transfer the copyright to another person, who becomes the owner. Often, the terms *copyright owner* and *copyright holder* are used interchangeably.

License. A *license* is a contract by which the copyright owner allows another person to exercise any one or more of the five exclusive rights. An *exclusive license* means that only the licensee can exercise the licensed rights. A *nonexclusive license* means that the owner is free to allow people other than the licensee to exercise the licensed rights.

Assignment. An *assignment* is a document by which the copyright owner transfers all of the exclusive rights to another person, who then becomes the copyright owner.

Publication. *Publication* is the distribution of a work by sale, rent, or lending copies of the work. Generally speaking, any distribution of a copyrighted work to the general public is deemed a publication of the work, regardless of whether copies of the work are sold by mail order, door-to-door, or while standing on a street corner.

When copyright attaches

Copyright law automatically protects any copyrightable work that is "fixed in a tangible medium of expression." Another way to think of it is that copyright law protects any work that has some physical embodiment—even if it is only a series of magnetic blips on a tape or disk.

You do not have to register your copyright, although registration is recommended for most works that can be copied and which are worth more than the few dollars it costs to register the copyright with the Copyright Office (see copyright registration).

What copyright protects

At its most basic form, a copyright is a right to copy. The owner of the copyright can control who can have a copy and what can be done with it.

The copyright owner can allow one person to have five copies, another person to have three copies, and refuse to allow a third person to have any copies.

The copyright owner of a photograph can allow one person to make a copy of the photograph and incorporate it into a multimedia work, allow another person to use the same photograph for advertising purposes only, and license a third person for the sole purpose of distributing e-mail copies of the photograph to Internet addresses that begin with the letter "q."

The idea/expression dichotomy. Copyright law does not protect ideas, but only expressions of ideas. If there are many ways to express an idea, then copyright law will protect one expression from being copied or incorporated into another expression without the permission of the copyright owner. In copyright lingo, this separation of ideas and expressions is called the *idea/expression dichotomy*.

If there is only one way, or just a handful of ways to express an idea, then the Copyright Act may not be used to protect that idea, and other people may use any expression of that idea.

The problem with drawing a line between ideas and expressions is that the line is drawn at a different place for each work. Thus, for one computer program, the line might be drawn in one place, and in another computer, the line is drawn in a different place. Moreover, because most copyrightable works contain many elements and pieces, each element is separately evaluated for the purpose of drawing the line between idea and expression.

So, if a brochure contains photographs, text, and drawings, then each photograph, each paragraph of text, and each drawing constitute a separate element that must be evaluated to determine where the line is drawn between idea and expression. Is one photograph an unadorned picture of a man in a business suit? If so, then anyone can use the idea of photographing a man in a business suit, but this particular photograph cannot be copied or reproduced without the permission of the copyright owner.

Who is the copyright owner?

Under Section 201 of the Copyright Act, ownership of the copyright goes to the person or persons who created the work (the "authors" of the work).

Thereafter, the copyright owner may transfer ownership to another person, partnership, corporation, or other entity that can own property.

The exception to this general rule is "work for hire," which has two distinct and different definitions in Section 101 of the Copyright Act.

Work for hire in employment relationships. Under the first definition of *works made for hire*, an employer is deemed to be the author of all works created by an employee within the scope of his or her employment. It does not matter whether the work was created at the office or at the employee's home, and it does not matter whether the work was created when the employee was being paid, or was on a lunch break. As long as the type of work created falls within the broad boundaries of the tasks that the employee performs, then the employer automatically owns the copyright to that work. No written documents are necessary.

As an example, if a person who works as an accountant as an employee of a large accounting firm creates rock videos at night, then that accountant would personally own the copyright to the rock videos. Creating videos is not within the scope of employment of the accountant.

By contrast, if a person is an employee of a production firm to create rock videos by day, then her employer would own the copyright to any rock videos she creates at night.

Work for hire in independent contractor relationships. The first definition of "works made for hire" is limited to employment relationships. By contrast, the second definition of *works made for hire* is completely different in that it applies to independent contractors who create certain types of copyrightable works, and requires that each contributor sign a written document.

The second definition of works made for hire states that the copyright in specially ordered or commissioned works will be owned by one party, where all the parties expressly agree in a written document or documents signed by all of them that the work to be created is a work for hire.

This definition is limited to (1) contributions to collective works, (2) parts of a motion picture or audiovisual work, (3) translations, (4) supplementary works, (5) compilations, (6) instructional texts, (7) tests, (8) answers to tests, and (9) atlases. These nine classes of works may be thought of as "commissioned work for hire." This definition of work for hire does not apply to any other type of work. Many multimedia works can be "works made for hire" under the second definition if the work is an audiovisual work or instructional CD-ROM, and if the contributors agree in writing beforehand that the work is a work for hire.

Where work for hire does not attach. Work for hire does not apply to self-employed individuals who are creating copyrightable works by themselves. A person working alone (and not as an employee of anybody else or of any partnership or corporation) will own the copyright and will be called the *author* of the work.

Work for hire does not apply to independent contractors creating works that are not commissioned works for hire. So, a photographer who takes photographs of a product for an advertising campaign does not come under either definition of work for hire, and the photographer will own the copyright for each photograph. Photographs are not one of the nine types of commissioned work for hire in the Copyright Act—even though the photographer was commissioned by someone else.

Work for hire does not apply to independent contractors creating commissioned works for hire where there is no written agreement. If 10 people agree to contribute to the making of a film, but there is no written document signed by them, then the film is not a work for hire. Instead, all 10 people who contribute will be joint owners of the copyright in the film.

How to ensure that only one person or company owns the copyright. The Copyright Act defines who will own the copyright by default. However, the default may be changed at any time by use of a written document signed by the parties.

Regardless of whether either definition of "work for hire" applies to a type of work, you can always write and sign an agreement among those who contribute to a work that one person or company owns the copyright. Thus, the freelance photographer who takes photographs for an advertising campaign may assign her copyright to her client in writing. An employee and an employer may agree in writing that the employee will own the copyright to everything she creates, regardless of whether it is within the scope of her employment.

Copyright notice

Section 401 states that copyright notices are optional, but, if you are going to use them, then the notice should consist of three parts: (1) "Copyright," "Copr.," or "(C);" (2) if the work is "published," then include the year of first publication; and (3) the name of the copyright owner. Copyright notices are still strongly recommended, but are no longer required.

Under the Copyright Act, if the author places a copyright notice on a work, and later sues an infringer, the infringer cannot claim in court that she did not know the work was protected by the author's copyright. Prior to 1989, any work published without a copyright notice ran the risk of losing its copyright protection. This approach allowed artists to assume that any published work that did not bear a copyright notice was in the public domain, and thus available for re-use by everyone else. Now that the law has been changed, you must assume that all works are protected under copyright law, regardless of whether or not the work bears a copyright notice. The good news is that it is tougher to lose a copyright, but the bad news is that you must assume that everything is protected by copyright law, unless you are told otherwise.

Copyright registration

The first thing that you should know about copyright registration is that it is optional, but is recommended for many works. Section 408 will tell you that. The second thing that you should know about copyright registration is that you do not need a lawyer to do it for you. The Copyright Act does not say that, so I will. Registering a copyright is a fairly simple and painless process.

Congress uses a "carrot and stick" approach to copyright registration. The "carrot" is that if you file the copyright application early enough, you get additional rights should you need to go to court and sue an infringer. The "stick" is that you cannot file a copyright infringement lawsuit unless you have received the certificate of registration, or at least have filed the copyright application.

Why you should register your copyright early and often. Copyright registration is recommended for any work worth more than the filing fee (presently $20), and for any work that could be stolen or otherwise infringed. If the work is worth less than the filing fee, why bother? If the work cannot be stolen or infringed (which is not the case for most works), then there is no need to bother.

There are several reasons why early registration of copyrights is recommended. First, under Section 411, you need to have a certificate that shows the copyright is registered before you can sue anyone for infringement (although Congress has been debating removing this requirement). Because it normally takes several months to receive the certificate of registration, you would have to wait several months before suing an infringer, or you would have to pay an additional fee to get the certificate of registration back in a week. By filing early, you will already have the certificate of registration in hand in case you have to sue someone.

Second, in a copyright infringement suit, under Section 412, the copyright owner may get attorney's fees and additional types of damages if the copyright application was filed prior to the start of the infringement, or shortly after publication (i.e., within three months of the date of first publication). If the copyright is registered after the infringement begins, then the copyright owner cannot ask for attorney's fees or additional types of damages called *statutory damages* (see Damages and Remedies). Congress has been debating removing the filing of a copyright application as a prerequisite for attorney's fees and statutory damages, but Congress has not yet changed this part of the law.

How to get and file an application for copyright registration. You should not need a lawyer to file a copyright registration. Unlike federal trademark and patent applications, the process is simple.

To get applications for copyright registration, call the U.S. Copyright Office. If you call 202-707-3000, you might reach a live human being, who is very likely to be helpful. The people at the Copyright Office will tell you how to file your applications, but they will not give you a "legal opinion." If you call 202-707-9100, you will reach an answering machine that will take your order for forms and other information. It usually takes four to six weeks to get the forms. Once you have the forms, you can always make more forms for yourself by photocopying them onto a good-quality white bond paper. This will make the Copyright Office happy because they don't want to mail out any more forms than they have to. Examples of copyright application forms are found at the end of this chapter.

To register a copyright, you need to send the completed application (two sides of one piece of paper), a check for the filing fee (presently $20), and a copy or other specimen of the work. Different forms are used for different types of works, and the specimen will also be different from one type of work to another. The specimen of the work could be one video or audio tape, or it could be some other piece of the work that helps the Copyright Office to identify it.

Once you file the application, it often takes two or three months to receive the certificate of copyright registration. Neatness counts on the application because the Copyright Office will make a few marks on the application, and then photocopy the application onto a nicer piece of paper to create the certificate of copyright registration. If you can't easily read the application, neither will anyone else, least of all a judge who is trying to enforce the registration as shown on the certificate. If you later lose or misplace the certificate that you receive, you can always get another from the Copyright Office for a small fee.

Transfer of copyright

A copyright owner may transfer all or part of a copyright by a written document, or by bequeathing the copyright in a will like any other family heirloom. A copyright may not be transferred by an oral agreement, although the parties can make an oral agreement effective by following it up with a written document.

If the copyright is transferred by a written document, the person transferring the copyright needs to sign the document. The person receiving the copyright may sign the document, but it is not effective unless the person transferring the copyright signs the document.

A copyright is "divisible," which means that the owner of all five exclusive rights can transfer one of the five rights to one person, another of the rights to a second person, and the rest of the rights to a third person. This often makes it difficult to track down who owns which rights when the copyright has been parceled out among several owners.

Copyright term

Knowing the copyright term is useful because it allows you to plan how long you will have rights to your own work, as well as help you determine whether another person's copyright has expired.

Works created since 1978. Under Section 302, for all works created by individuals since 1978, the copyright is good for the life of the author, plus 50 years. If two or more individuals are the creators of a work, then the copyright expires 50 years after the last author dies.

Thus, if a particular work is created by an artist in 1997, and the artist dies in the year 2030, the copyright will be good until the year 2080.

For all anonymous works, pseudonymous works, and works made for hire, the copyright is good for 75 years from the date of first publication, or 100 years from the creation of the work, whichever occurs first.

Thus, for an audiovisual, work where all the contributors signed work for hire agreements, the copyright will last for 100 years from the date that it is created, or 75 years from the date that it is first made available to the public, whichever term is shorter. Another example is where an employee creates a multimedia work for her employer in 1995, but the work is not seen outside the employer's company and is never publicly distributed, in which case, the copyright will be good until the year 2095.

This assumes that the Copyright Act is not changed again in the interim; however, the Copyright Act will likely be changed on this issue. As this book went to press, it seemed likely that Congress would change the length of copyright protection for individuals from life-plus-50-years to life-plus-70-years. The term for anonymous works, pseudonymous works, and works made for hire, would be extended to 95 years from the date of first publication, or 120 years from the creation of the work, whichever occurs first.

Works created before 1978. During the period 1909 through 1977, the copyright on a published work was good for 28 years, and then had to be renewed (by filing a paper with the Copyright Office) for another 28 years. Unpublished works received unlimited protection. Just to complicate things, Congress wrote in Section 304 that the copyright in any work published prior to 1978, but still protected as of 1978, would be protected for up to 75 years. As you might expect, this led to confusion that made a lot of work for copyright attorneys. Unpublished works under prior law were protected so long as they were not published.

Thus, a personal diary written in the 1860s would be protected from copying forever under prior law, so long as the diary remained unpublished. However, under Section 303, all works not published by 1978 remain protected under the Copyright Act, but that protection would terminate no later than 2002 if the work remains unpublished, or no later than 2027, if the work is published between 1978 and 2002.

As a rule, you should assume that any work published before about 1922 is in the public domain (which means that anyone can use it), and that any work created (published or not) in or after 1922 is protected by the Copyright Act (until proven otherwise).

The real meaning of "public domain"

In the copyright context, the term *public domain* means that nobody owns or has a claim to a particular copyrightable work. Thus, anyone can use, copy, or make derivative works of a public domain work. Some people confuse *public domain* with *published work* or *publication*. A work that is publicly available or published is not necessarily in the public domain.

When a copyrightable work enters the public domain, it never leaves the public domain. However, anyone can take a public domain work, add new expression to it, and claim a copyright in the new work. However, the copyright in that circumstance covers only the new expression (the aspects that were added), so the original work will continue to be in the public domain for anyone else to use.

As an example, the stories of the Brothers Grimm are now in the public domain because they were published well before 1922. Anyone can copy the original stories, translate them into English, edit them, add new art work and video, and publish the result on CD-ROM. The Copyright law will protect the new art work, the video, the new translation (translations of human languages are considered derivative works), as well as the editing if the editing is more than trivial. If anyone does copy the CD- ROM or protected elements of the CD-ROM, then that person can be sued for copyright infringement. However, copyright law will not prevent anyone else from going back to the original stories, making their own translation, and publishing them with other art work in a different CD-ROM or across the Internet.

Infringement of copyrights

Once you have a copyright, you might need to sue a pirate. On the other hand, you might need to know what you face if someone accuses you of being a copyright pirate.

Filing a copyright infringement action. As noted, United States citizens cannot file a copyright infringement action unless they have received a certificate of copyright registration from the Copyright Office. Although Congress has debated removing this requirement, it was still in effect when this book went to press.

You should always have an experienced attorney represent you in court. Like the television commercials that show professional race car drivers on race tracks, you should not try litigating a copyright infringement case by yourself.

Your attorney will investigate the facts and make sure that your case can go forward. As part of this investigation, the attorney will likely need to speak with other people who know the facts and circumstances—especially if the infringer is someone that you know.

Once the attorney has investigated the case, she will file several documents with the court, including a "complaint" that documents your claims to the courts. Once the papers are filed, they must be served on the opposing party, who will then have the right to file motions to dismiss the case or file an "answer" that responds to each of the allegations and claims in the complaint.

Seeking a temporary restraining order "Ex Parte." If a person is infringing your copyright, then that person is likely to destroy any evidence of infringement as soon as she is sued. In that case, your attorney files an additional set of motion papers and asks to see the judge. Because your attorney will be seeing the judge without anyone representing the other side, this procedure is referred to as *ex parte*.

The judge will order a seizure of the evidence prior to trial if she is convinced that you have a very strong case and that seizure is the only way to preserve evidence prior to trial. If the judge does order seizure, then you will have to post a rather large bond to cover any damages that you might cause during the seizure—especially if it turns out that you were wrong and the defendant is not a pirate.

Pre-trial and trial. After the initial round of pleadings, and assuming that the case has not been dismissed by the court, the parties then begin a phase known as *discovery*. In discovery, each party has the opportunity to ask questions of the other party in writing or in person (while a court reporter takes down the person's answers to the questions). Each party can also demand access to all of the original materials that went into the copyrighted work, as well as all other documents and materials that might lead to information that is relevant to the case. Often, the parties will use the information gleaned during discovery to file a round of motions with the court asking the court to make a decision about the case prior to trial. Often, enough information is collected during discovery that a motion is filed to decide the case without a trial, or to limit the issues to be decided at trial.

If the case makes it to trial, then the defendant will have the right to a jury. Whether or not the defendant requests a jury, the parties will often take several days in court to present witnesses and enter exhibits. The judge will always decide strictly legal issues, such as whether a particular document will be allowed in as evidence. The jury (or the judge in the case of a non-jury trial) will apply the evidence and reach a decision.

Damages and remedies that a court might award. Under Section 504 of the Copyright Act, the copyright owner asks the judge to award either *actual damages* or *statutory damages*.

Actual damages are measured by taking the money lost by the copyright owner and adding to that the amount of money made by the infringer as a result of the infringement.

Statutory damages means that the judge picks a number in a range (presently $500 to $20,000) per work infringed and awards that amount as damages. Moreover, if the judge finds that the infringement was committed "willfully," then the judge picks a number from a larger range (presently $500 to $100,000) per work infringed. Statutory damages are usually chosen when the infringer has not lost much money as a result of the infringement, yet needs to teach the infringer a lesson by making the damage award much higher. Unfortunately, statutory damages are available to the copyright owner only when the copyright is registered prior to the beginning of the infringement, or shortly after the work is first published.

The judge can always assess court costs and order destruction of all infringing copies. The judge can also issue injunctions. Under Section 505, if the copyright was registered prior to the infringement, the judge has the option of making the infringer pay the attorney's fees and expenses of the copyright owner, which can total tens or hundreds of thousands of dollars.

Fair use of copyrighted works

Certain uses of a copyrighted work may not be prosecuted. One set of uses is called *fair use*, which is defined in Section 107 of the Copyright Act. Fair use is not a magic formula that instantly turns copying into a permitted use. Rather, it is a set of guidelines that balance the rights of the copyright owner with other rights and needs, including First Amendment concerns and the need to give students and teachers additional leeway for educational purposes.

Fair use is limited to a handful of certain types of uses, mostly related to teaching and criticism. Four factors are weighed to determine whether a particular circumstance is a fair use or an infringement.

In one case, several publishers sued a nationwide chain of copy shops located on college campuses. College professors assembled copies of articles from magazines and journals into a sort of textbook, and left the copies at the copy shop. The professors then told their students to go to the copy shop and pay for one copy of the hand-made textbook. When the publishers sued the copy shop, the copy shop claimed that it allowed to make copies as a fair use because the professors wanted the copies for teaching purposes. The courts sided with the publishers because the professors did not bother to ask permission from the copyright owners before copying the articles, and because the hand-made textbooks competed with textbooks sold by the publishers.

Types of uses recognized as fair uses. The making of copies without permission is excused as a fair use only when the purpose of the use is criticism, comment, news reporting, teaching (including multiple copies for classroom use), scholarship, or research.

The purposes are fairly narrowly constrained. So, teachers can invoke fair use when they make copies for their classroom, but publishers of classroom books cannot claim fair use because the book publishers are not directly teaching students.

First factor: purpose and character of the use. The first factor weighed is the purpose and character of the use, including whether such use is of a commercial nature or is for nonprofit educational purposes. Thus, if the person making the copies is doing so for a profit, that weighs against fair use. However, if the person is making copies for teaching at church, this factor will weigh in favor of fair use.

Second factor: nature of the copyrighted work. If the copyrighted work is one that generates large amounts of money, such as popular books, records, or movies, then any copying will be closely scrutinized. If the copyrighted work is not a money-maker, then fair use is easier to prove.

Third factor: amount used. It is an axiom of copyright law that an infringement occurs when even a small part of a work is copied—especially if the portion copied is of high quality or is important to the rest of the work. The third fair use factor recognizes that by weighing the amount and substantiality of the portion copied in relation to the copyrighted work as a whole. If one paragraph is copied from an 800-page book, then the portion is not substantial. However, if 20 seconds are sampled from a two-minute song, that is substantial—especially if the 20 seconds contains the chorus of the song.

Fourth factor: effect on the market. One of the primary purposes of the Copyright Act is to ensure that authors of copyrighted works are compensated. So, it is not surprising that the fourth factor of fair use is the effect of the copying on the potential market or value of the original, copyrighted work. If each copy made without permission replaces a copy that would have been sold, then that weighs against fair use. If the copies made do not affect the sales of the original, then this factor weighs in favor of fair use.

Application of fair use. Initially, the use of the copy should fit into one of the categories (criticism, comment, etc.). Then, all four of the factors are weighed together. Some factors can be more important than others. There is no mechanical application of "three-out-of-four factors wins."

For example, what happens when a publisher prepares and sells laser discs containing the copyrighted works of a recent playwright without the playwright's permission? The laser disc contains all of the text of all of the plays, plus full-motion video of one play that the publisher captured off a television re-broadcasting an old movie version of one of the plays. The laser discs are intended for classroom use at the price of $100 each. Is this a fair use?

First, you must consider the type of work. Teaching, scholarship, and research are all included as fair-use purposes, so the laser disc should be weighed under the four factors. The first factor cuts against a fair use. The publisher is making money in this venture—even though the purchasers might be nonprofit educational users. Second, the nature of the copyrighted work consists of highly profitable works (plays and movies, which are subject to video rental income and broadcast royalties)—even though the sales of texts of the play probably do not generate large amounts of income for the playwrights or other copyright owners (because the producer of the movie might own the copyright to that production).

The third factor also cuts against fair use because the laser disc contains the entire movie and the entire text of each play. Finally, the fourth factor also cuts against fair use because each laser disc sold replaces one copy of each play manuscript that could have been sold, as well as one copy of the movie that could have been sold. So, this is not a fair use, and the publisher should seek licenses from the playwright and the owner of the copyright in the movie.

International copyright law

The United States has signed a number of treaties over the years that grants protection of U.S. copyrights in other countries, and protects in the United States copyrighted works created in other countries. At this time, the number of countries that are not a party to a copyright treaty to which the U.S. also belongs is fairly small. Accordingly, you must assume that works created outside the U.S. are as well protected as works created inside the U.S. Similarly, works that are created in the U.S. are protected outside the U.S.

Most of the better-known copyright treaties use "national" treatment, which means that copyrighted works created in Germany are protected in the U.S. as if they had been created in the U.S. by U.S. citizens, and U.S. works are treated in Germany as if they had been created by German citizens in Germany. The details of the laws do change from one country to another, so caution is urged before marketing your products in any country that does not have a tradition of protecting copyrighted works.

Copyright collectives, stock houses, and agencies

You should consider what permissions you need for a work long before you begin production. You might find that a piece of music or a video clip is either unavailable for licensing, or is so expensive that it might as well be unavailable. License fees are negotiated based on the type of use, the market that you are selling to, the number of years that you intend to sell the work, and the geographic territory in which you are selling the work.

You can license the use of copyrighted works from others by using stock houses, copyright collectives, and other agencies. Each agency has the right to license the use of copyrighted works to others on the basis of a set scale of fees, or they have the power to negotiate fees with you on behalf of the copyright owner.

The agencies provide a large selection of works to choose from, which makes it easier to conduct one-stop shopping for licenses to use copyrighted works in your multimedia presentations. If your work needs only one or two permissions, for example, to use the music and lyrics of a few popular songs, which you are personally performing in your work, then you should contact the copyright owner or collective agency yourself and negotiate the transaction. By contrast, if you need permissions to use dozens of works, and you intend to sell your work commercially around the world, then you should consider hiring a permissions company to track down the permissions and negotiate on your behalf.

There are hundreds of agencies from which to choose. Several agencies have offices around the country. The names and principal addresses of several of the better-known agencies follow.

Permissions agents

Multimedia is at its best when different types of elements are juxtaposed. However, using pre-existing elements requires that you seek and obtain all necessary permissions. A permissions agent or company can do the work for you, and probably be more efficient, which helps your budget. One of the better-known permissions companies is:

BZ/Rights & Permissions, Inc.
125 W. 72nd St.
New York, NY 10023
(212) 580-0615

Text

Most text can be licensed directly from the author or the publisher. Terms are generally negotiable, although the license fees vary widely.

The Copyright Clearance Center was formed to help collect royalties on a variety of journals and other hard-copy publications, and more recently has started licensing online rights. The Center can be reached at:

Copyright Clearance Center
27 Congress St.
Salem, MA 01970
(508) 744-3350

Music

The licensing of music is broken down into several categories based on the type of music-related work, and the type of license sought.

Multimedia works might need (1) an original composition license if the final product includes covers of original compositions not previously recorded, (2) a mechanical license to cover a previously recorded song, and (3) a synchronization license, where music is combined with video.

Licensing of original compositions. Original compositions are the sheet music and lyrics written by composers and lyricists. Anyone who wants to record or perform an original composition should contact the appropriate rights organization for this purpose. Two of the best known are:

American Society of Composers, Authors, and Publishers (ASCAP)
One Lincoln Plaza
New York, NY 10023
(212) 621-6000

Broadcast Music, Inc. (BMI)
320 West 57th St.
New York, NY 10019
(800) 366-4264
(212) 586-2000

Mechanical and Synchronization Rights. Once a music record or CD is made available to the public for private home use, any song (original composition) on that record or CD can be recorded by another artist or group. This is required pursuant to Section 115 of the U.S. Copyright Act. The type of license is called a *mechanical license* (because records used to be considered "mechanical" reproductions) or a *compulsory license* (because the Copyright Act makes it difficult for the copyright owner to refuse permission). Mechanical licenses do not apply to music used for movies, television, or other visual images.

Synchronization licenses are licenses to use music in combination with visual images in movies, television, or home video. Synchronization licenses are negotiated on a case-by-case basis, and are not subject to compulsory license rates.

The agency best known for mechanical, synchronization, and related licenses is:

The Harry Fox Agency, Inc.
National Music Publishers' Association, Inc.
711 Third Ave.
New York, NY 10017
(212) 370-5330

Photography

Photography is often licensed through stock photography agencies, one of which can be found in virtually every city, and many large towns (check the phone book).

Almost all of the stock agencies are aware of digital uses, and many offer images in digital form in popular binary formats. License rates depend on the type of use and how many people are likely to see the photo or other image.

One agency on the cutting edge of digital uses of images is:

Media Photographers Copyright Agency
American Society of Media Photographers, Inc.
Washington Park, Ste. 502
14 Washington Rd.
Princeton Junction, NJ 08550-1033
(609) 799-8300

Movies and video

Several stock houses that handle still photography also license video stock. Movies and television video can be licensed directly from the copyright owners (usually the production firms) or their distributors.

You have to be careful about using movies and television because, like other audio-visual work, they incorporate the copyrighted works of others, including music and still photographs. The copyright owners of the movies might not have the right to license to you the background music or other pre-existing works incorporated into the movies. In those cases, ask the copyright owners for their licensing information so that you can get all of the permission that you need in writing.

Trademark Law

A *trademark* is anything that designates the source of goods or services, including words or terms, drawings, graphics, sounds, and even colors in some cases. In creating and selling your works, you must be careful not to infringe someone else's trademark by associating your work with the other person's trademark.

Trademark law is a matter of commerce. Trademark law is not concerned so much with originality as with the commercial impression created by the trademark owner. If you begin a training CD-ROM with a roaring lion above the phrase, "Ars Gratia Artis," then MGM's present owner might sue for infringement of their trademarks, which includes both the roaring lion and the Latin phrase.

Sources of trademark law

Unlike copyright law, there are several levels of trademark law in the United States. A *common law trademark* is one that accrues rights merely through use. If you adopt a distinctive term for your business and promote it, then you gain common law trademark rights on a "use it or lose it" basis. Your rights do not begin until you start using it, and are limited to the goods you sell or services you provide, in the geographic area in which you provide them, and last only so long as you continue to provide them. The price is reasonable, however, because there is no application and no filing fee.

Each of the states has adopted a trademark law. Any trademark registered with a state agency receives additional rights within that state, but those rights do not extend outside the state of registration. State trademark registrations are useful for marks used within only one state, and which are not worth the additional cost of filing a federal application for registration. Most states use simple application forms, and the filing fees tend to be between $50 and $150.

The third source of trademark law is Congress, which in 1988 substantially revised the federal Trademark Law (also known as the *Lanham Act* after Rep. Walter Lanham). A federal trademark registration provides the trademark owner with the right to sue any infringer in federal courts throughout the United States, and provides substantial remedies in favor of the trademark owner against infringers.

Unlike common law trademarks, where rights do not accrue without use, an application for a federal trademark registration can be filed without any use of the mark. Called an *intent to use (ITU)* application, the ITU application allows the trademark owner to gain a reservation on the trademark long before the goods are ready for market, but the registration does not issue unless and until the applicant files another document stating that the applicant has begun use of the mark on goods or in connection with services in some form of commerce that Congress can regulate, usually by selling goods from one state to another. Applications can also be filed on an "actual use" basis, which means that the goods or services have been sold across state lines, or between the U.S. and another country.

Federal trademark applications are more extensive than state applications, and the filing fee is, as this book went to press, $245 per class of goods and services. CD-ROMs are in one class of goods, and consulting services are in another class. Unlike copyright applications, trademark applications are difficult enough that you should consider retaining an attorney to file and prosecute the application.

Strength of a trademark

The more distinctive a trademark, the "stronger" it is. Trademarks are characterized by their strength. Stronger marks provide better protection and can be enforced against a wider range of other marks for different goods or services. Weaker marks can only be enforced against virtually the same mark for virtually the same goods or services. The spectrum of trademark strength follows.

Generic terms. A *generic term* or *design* is one that is used for a category of goods or services. A generic term cannot be protected as a trademark because it is needed for the purpose of classification. The term *multimedia* is generic.

Descriptive terms. A descriptive term or design is one that describes the goods or services, but is not generic for the goods or services. A descriptive term cannot be used as a trademark unless they gain a *secondary meaning*, which means that when people hear the term, they think of a particular source or set of goods, rather than all goods with that characteristic. The term *Windows* is descriptive of all software that uses windowing technology, but the term *Windows* has gained a secondary meaning, that of Microsoft's operating environment, *Microsoft Windows*.

Suggestive marks. A suggestive term or design suggests what the goods or services might be, but is not descriptive of them. The term *Microsoft* suggests microcomputer software, but the term does not describe the products of the Microsoft Corporation. Suggestive trademarks are protectable and make for good trademarks.

Arbitrary marks. An arbitrary term or design has a real meaning to most people, but the meaning is different from the goods or services it is associated with. The term *Apple* by Apple Computer Corp. is a good example of an arbitrary mark because most computers are not made of apples. Arbitrary terms and designs make for excellent trademarks.

Coined marks. A coined term is one that has no meaning, except that it is associated with the goods or services. The term *Borland* is a good example of a coined term as the term has no meaning outside of the fact that Borland International uses the term on its software. Coined marks are on the opposite side of the spectrum from generic terms.

Trademark notices

Any good that you sell or service you provide can bear a notice in the form of *TM* (*trademark*) or *SM* (*service mark*). It doesn't cost anything, but it puts the world on notice that you claim your trademark rights.

The circle-R character (®) is reserved for owners of current federal trademark registrations. It cannot be used by owners of state registrations (unless they also have a current federal registration). Similarly, filing a federal application is not sufficient to use the ™ symbol; a federal certificate of trademark registration must first issue.

Each of your works may also contain a notice that "[your trademark] is a trademark of [name of your company]." If you have a current federal registration, you can state that "[your trademark] is a registered trademark of [name of your company]."

If you are properly using the trademarks of another, then you should include a trademark notice. For example, if you prepare a training CD-ROM called *How to Use Microsoft Windows*, then you should include the trademark notice that "*Microsoft* and *Windows* are registered trademarks of Microsoft Corporation." You can use the approach for each trademark of which you are aware. Many works also bear a catch-all trademark notice; "[your trademark] is a [registered] trademark of [name of your company]. All other trademarks are trademarks or registered trademarks of their respective owners."

Likelihood of confusion

Trademark infringement is generally a matter of determining whether the consumers of the trademark owner are "likely to be confused" by a trademark used by another. In determining "likelihood of confusion," a court will consider how close the marks are in sound (because trademarks are often passed from person to person by word of mouth), how close the goods or services are, and whether the goods or services are provided in the same way or in the same "channels of commerce."

For example, the trademark *Excel* is a good one for both Hyundai and Microsoft. However, there is no likelihood of confusion because consumers will not mistake a Hyundai Excel car with a Microsoft Excel spreadsheet.

Privacy and Publicity Law

The rights of privacy and publicity are two sides of the same coin. The rights of privacy and publicity apply even if you photograph or record (video, audio, or both) a person out-of-doors in a public location, such as a park, town square, or walking down the street. The law deems that a person has the right to control how her image is used.

This is a growing area of law that is more closely related to trademark law. California and New York have passed statutes that protect privacy, and other states are likely to follow.

Don't make private people "public" without their permission

If the person is a private person, then she might prohibit the use of her image for your profit or gain. A private person has the right to remain private.

Celebrities have the right to control their publicity

If the person is a public person or celebrity, she may be able to prohibit your use of her image without proper compensation, primarily because she is deemed to have a property interest in her image. In other words, she can make money from her status as a celebrity, so you cannot use her status to help sell your product without her permission.

One good example of the right of publicity is the Bette Midler case. A car manufacturer wanted to run a series of commercials that featured Ms. Midler's singing. Ms. Midler decided not to participate, so the car manufacturer hired someone else who sang just like Bette Midler. Ms. Midler sued and won about $400,000 because people who listened to the commercials thought that she was singing in the commercial. Even though no image of Ms. Midler was used, her vocal style was sufficiently distinctive to serve as her trademark. Because everyone agreed that Ms. Midler's vocal style helped sell cars, Ms. Midler was held by the court to have the right to control when her voice and vocal style could be used to help sell cars.

Releases

There is no better way to ensure that you have all the rights that you need to use a person's image or other distinctive features than to get a *release*.

Professional photographers use releases all of the time. An example of one such release prepared by the American Society of Media Photographers is shown in the forms at the end of the chapter. However, you might need to consult an attorney to ensure that the release is enforceable under the law of the states in which you will use the release, and to make sure that the release covers every type of use that you contemplate.

When You Can Use the Works of Another Person

There are several ways in which you can use and incorporate the works of others into your own works. Ask yourself a few questions.

First, is the work in the public domain? As covered earlier, *public domain* means that nobody owns the copyright or other rights to the work. If you have access to an original Leonardo da Vinci painting or manuscript of a Mozart concerto, then make your own copies without fear of copyright violation.

Second, if the work is not in the public domain, can you get a license to use or copy the work? The saying goes that "it is easier to beg forgiveness afterwards than to ask for permission beforehand." However, for copyrighted works, permission is often easy to get and costs very little, and forgiveness is very expensive. At the very least, forgiveness (including legal fees, court costs, and damages) costs a great deal more than permission.

Third, will any original work that you copy be recognizable as a derivative work? As noted, a derivative work remains a derivative work only so long as any part of it is still recognizable as originating with its predecessor.

Fourth, does the work affect anyone else's privacy or publicity rights? If a person can be recognized by her looks, voice or other distinctive attributes, that person can request compensation. So long as you have appropriate releases from each individual, or if the person that you have licensed the work has the appropriate releases, then this will not be an issue.

Forms

The following are sample forms. Copyright Office Form PA for the performing arts (Fig. 17.1); Form TX for text, including literature, and most computer software (Fig. 17.2); Form VA for visual arts, including two- and three-dimensional art works; as well as a photographer's release form that can be adapted for use of a person's image in other types of works, including multimedia works (Figs. 17.3 and 17.4).

FORM TX

For a Literary Work
UNITED STATES COPYRIGHT OFFICE

REGISTRATION NUMBER

_____

TX _____ TXU _____

EFFECTIVE DATE OF REGISTRATION

_____

Month   Day   Year

DO NOT WRITE ABOVE THIS LINE. IF YOU NEED MORE SPACE, USE A SEPARATE CONTINUATION SHEET.

1

TITLE OF THIS WORK ▼

PREVIOUS OR ALTERNATIVE TITLES ▼

PUBLICATION AS A CONTRIBUTION If this work was published as a contribution to a periodical, serial, or collection, give information about the collective work in which the contribution appeared.   **Title of Collective Work ▼**

If published in a periodical or serial give: **Volume ▼**   **Number ▼**   **Issue Date ▼**   **On Pages ▼**

2

a

NAME OF AUTHOR ▼

DATES OF BIRTH AND DEATH
Year Born ▼   Year Died ▼

Was this contribution to the work a "work made for hire"?
☐ Yes
☐ No

AUTHOR'S NATIONALITY OR DOMICILE
Name of Country
OR { Citizen of ▶ _____
{ Domiciled in ▶ _____

WAS THIS AUTHOR'S CONTRIBUTION TO THE WORK
Anonymous?   ☐ Yes ☐ No
Pseudonymous? ☐ Yes ☐ No
If the answer to either of these questions is "Yes," see detailed instructions

NATURE OF AUTHORSHIP Briefly describe nature of the material created by this author in which copyright is claimed. ▼

NOTE

Under the law, the "author" of a "work made for hire" is generally the employer, not the employee (see instructions). For any part of this work that was "made for hire" check "Yes" in the space provided, give the employer (or other person for whom the work was prepared) as "Author" of that part, and leave the space for dates of birth and death blank.

b

NAME OF AUTHOR ▼

DATES OF BIRTH AND DEATH
Year Born ▼   Year Died ▼

Was this contribution to the work a "work made for hire"?
☐ Yes
☐ No

AUTHOR'S NATIONALITY OR DOMICILE
Name of country
OR { Citizen of ▶ _____
{ Domiciled in ▶ _____

WAS THIS AUTHOR'S CONTRIBUTION TO THE WORK
Anonymous?   ☐ Yes ☐ No
Pseudonymous? ☐ Yes ☐ No
If the answer to either of these questions is "Yes," see detailed instructions

NATURE OF AUTHORSHIP Briefly describe nature of the material created by this author in which copyright is claimed. ▼

c

NAME OF AUTHOR ▼

DATES OF BIRTH AND DEATH
Year Born ▼   Year Died ▼

Was this contribution to the work a "work made for hire"?
☐ Yes
☐ No

AUTHOR'S NATIONALITY OR DOMICILE
Name of Country
OR { Citizen of ▶ _____
{ Domiciled in ▶ _____

WAS THIS AUTHOR'S CONTRIBUTION TO THE WORK
Anonymous?   ☐ Yes ☐ No
Pseudonymous? ☐ Yes ☐ No
If the answer to either of these questions is "Yes," see detailed instructions

NATURE OF AUTHORSHIP Briefly describe nature of the material created by this author in which copyright is claimed. ▼

3

a

YEAR IN WHICH CREATION OF THIS WORK WAS COMPLETED This information must be given in all cases.
◀ Year

DATE AND NATION OF FIRST PUBLICATION OF THIS PARTICULAR WORK
Complete this information ONLY if this work has been published.
Month ▶ _____ Day ▶ _____ Year ▶ _____
◀ Nation

4

See instructions before completing this space

COPYRIGHT CLAIMANT(S) Name and address must be given even if the claimant is the same as the author given in space 2. ▼

TRANSFER If the claimant(s) named here in space 4 are different from the author(s) named in space 2, give a brief statement of how the claimant(s) obtained ownership of the copyright. ▼

DO NOT WRITE HERE OFFICE USE ONLY

APPLICATION RECEIVED

_____

ONE DEPOSIT RECEIVED

_____

TWO DEPOSITS RECEIVED

_____

REMITTANCE NUMBER AND DATE

_____

MORE ON BACK ▶ • Complete all applicable spaces (numbers 5-11) on the reverse side of this page.
• See detailed instructions.   • Sign the form at line 10.

DO NOT WRITE HERE

Page 1 of _____ pages

Figure 17.1a Form PA (front).

EXAMINED BY

CHECKED BY

☐ CORRESPONDENCE
Yes

FORM PA

FOR
COPYRIGHT
OFFICE
USE
ONLY

DO NOT WRITE ABOVE THIS LINE. IF YOU NEED MORE SPACE, USE A SEPARATE CONTINUATION SHEET.

PREVIOUS REGISTRATION Has registration for this work, or for an earlier version of this work, already been made in the Copyright Office?

☐ Yes ☐ No If your answer is "Yes," why is another registration being sought? (Check appropriate box) ▼

a. ☐ This is the first published edition of a work previously registered in unpublished form.

b. ☐ This is the first application submitted by this author as copyright claimant.

c. ☐ This is a changed version of the work, as shown by space 6 on this application.

If your answer is "Yes," give: **Previous Registration Number** ▼   **Year of Registration** ▼

5

DERIVATIVE WORK OR COMPILATION   Complete both space 6a & 6b for a derivative work; complete only 6b for a compilation.

a. Preexisting Material Identify any preexisting work or works that this work is based on or incorporates. ▼

b. Material Added to This Work Give a brief, general statement of the material that has been added to this work and in which copyright is claimed. ▼

6

See instructions
before completing
this space

DEPOSIT ACCOUNT If the registration fee is to be charged to a Deposit Account established in the Copyright Office, give name and number of Account.
Name ▼   **Account Number** ▼

7

CORRESPONDENCE Give name and address to which correspondence about this application should be sent.   Name/Address/Apt/City/State/Zip ▼

Area Code & Telephone Number ▶

Be sure to
give your
daytime phone
◀ number

CERTIFICATION*   I, the undersigned, hereby certify that I am the

Check only one ▼

☐ author

☐ other copyright claimant

☐ owner of exclusive right(s)

☐ authorized agent of _____
              Name of author or other copyright claimant, or owner of exclusive right(s) ▲

8

of the work identified in this application and that the statements made
by me in this application are correct to the best of my knowledge.

Typed or printed name and date ▼ If this application gives a date of publication in space 3, do not sign and submit it before that date.

_____ date ▶ _____

☞   Handwritten signature (X) ▼

**MAIL
CERTIFI-
CATE TO**

**Certificate
will be
mailed in
window
envelope**

Name ▼

Number Street Apartment Number ▼

City State ZIP ▼

9

YOU MUST:
• Complete all necessary spaces
• Sign your application in space 8

**SEND ALL 3 ELEMENTS
IN THE SAME PACKAGE:**
1. Application form
2. Nonrefundable $20 filing fee
   in check or money order
   payable to *Register of Copyrights*
3. Deposit material

MAIL TO:
Register of Copyrights
Library of Congress
Washington, D.C. 20559

Copyright fees are ad-
justed at 5-year inter-
vals, based on in-
creases or decreases in
the Consumer Price In-
dex. The next adjust-
ment is due in 1995.
Contact the Copyright
Office in January 1995
for the new fee sched-
ule.

▲ July 1992—100,000   ☆ U.S. GOVERNMENT PRINTING OFFICE: 1992—312-432/60,005

Figure 17.1b Form PA (back).

PA   PAU

EFFECTIVE DATE OF REGISTRATION

Month   Day   Year

DO NOT WRITE ABOVE THIS LINE. IF YOU NEED MORE SPACE, USE A SEPARATE CONTINUATION SHEET.

1

TITLE OF THIS WORK ▼

PREVIOUS OR ALTERNATIVE TITLES ▼

NATURE OF THIS WORK ▼ See instructions

2

a

NAME OF AUTHOR ▼

DATES OF BIRTH AND DEATH
Year Born ▼   Year Died ▼

Was this contribution to the work a "work made for hire"?	**AUTHOR'S NATIONALITY OR DOMICILE** Name of Country	**WAS THIS AUTHOR'S CONTRIBUTION TO THE WORK**	
☐ Yes	OR { Citizen of ▶	Anonymous? ☐ Yes ☐ No	If the answer to either of these questions is
☐ No	Domiciled in ▶	Pseudonymous? ☐ Yes ☐ No	"Yes," see detailed instructions

NATURE OF AUTHORSHIP Briefly describe nature of the material created by this author in which copyright is claimed. ▼

NOTE

Under the law, the "author" of a work made for hire" is generally the employer, not the employee (see instructions) For any part of this work that was "made for hire" check "Yes" in the space provided, give the employer (or other person for whom the work was prepared) as "Author" of that part, and leave the space for dates of birth and death blank

b

NAME OF AUTHOR ▼

DATES OF BIRTH AND DEATH
Year Born ▼   Year Died ▼

Was this contribution to the work a "work made for hire"?	**AUTHOR'S NATIONALITY OR DOMICILE** Name of Country	**WAS THIS AUTHOR'S CONTRIBUTION TO THE WORK**	
☐ Yes	OR { Citizen of ▶	Anonymous? ☐ Yes ☐ No	If the answer to either of these questions is
☐ No	Domiciled in ▶	Pseudonymous? ☐ Yes ☐ No	"Yes," see detailed instructions

NATURE OF AUTHORSHIP Briefly describe nature of the material created by this author in which copyright is claimed. ▼

c

NAME OF AUTHOR ▼

DATES OF BIRTH AND DEATH
Year Born ▼   Year Died ▼

Was this contribution to the work a "work made for hire"?	**AUTHOR'S NATIONALITY OR DOMICILE** Name of Country	**WAS THIS AUTHOR'S CONTRIBUTION TO THE WORK**	
☐ Yes	OR { Citizen of ▶	Anonymous? ☐ Yes ☐ No	If the answer to either of these questions is
☐ No	Domiciled in ▶	Pseudonymous? ☐ Yes ☐ No	"Yes," see detailed instructions

NATURE OF AUTHORSHIP Briefly describe nature of the material created by this author in which copyright is claimed. ▼

3

a

YEAR IN WHICH CREATION OF THIS WORK WAS COMPLETED This information must be given in all cases. ◀ Year

DATE AND NATION OF FIRST PUBLICATION OF THIS PARTICULAR WORK
Complete this information ONLY if this work has been published. Month ▶   Day ▶   Year ▶   ◀ Nation

4

See instructions before completing this space

COPYRIGHT CLAIMANT(S) Name and address must be given even if the claimant is the same as the author given in space 2. ▼

TRANSFER If the claimant(s) named here in space 4 are different from the author(s) named in space 2, give a brief statement of how the claimant(s) obtained ownership of the copyright. ▼

APPLICATION RECEIVED

ONE DEPOSIT RECEIVED

TWO DEPOSITS RECEIVED

REMITTANCE NUMBER AND DATE

DO NOT WRITE HERE OFFICE USE ONLY

MORE ON BACK ▶ • Complete all applicable spaces (numbers 5-9) on the reverse side of this page
• See detailed instructions   • Sign the form at line 8

DO NOT WRITE HERE

Page 1 of _____ pages

Figure 17.2a   Form TX (front).

EXAMINED BY	**FORM TX**
CHECKED BY	
☐ CORRESPONDENCE Yes	FOR COPYRIGHT OFFICE USE ONLY

DO NOT WRITE ABOVE THIS LINE. IF YOU NEED MORE SPACE, USE A SEPARATE CONTINUATION SHEET.

PREVIOUS REGISTRATION Has registration for this work, or for an earlier version of this work, already been made in the Copyright Office?

☐ **Yes** ☐ **No** If your answer is "Yes," why is another registration being sought? (Check appropriate box) ▼

a. ☐ This is the first published edition of a work previously registered in unpublished form.

b. ☐ This is the first application submitted by this author as copyright claimant.

c. ☐ This is a changed version of the work, as shown by space 6 on this application.

If your answer is "Yes," give: **Previous Registration Number** ▼   **Year of Registration** ▼

5

DERIVATIVE WORK OR COMPILATION   Complete both space 6a & 6b for a derivative work; complete only 6b for a compilation.

a. Preexisting Material   Identify any preexisting work or works that this work is based on or incorporates. ▼

b. Material Added to This Work   Give a brief, general statement of the material that has been added to this work and in which copyright is claimed. ▼

See instructions before completing this space

6

—space deleted—

7

REPRODUCTION FOR USE OF BLIND OR PHYSICALLY HANDICAPPED INDIVIDUALS   A signature on this form at space 10, and a check in one of the boxes here in space 8, constitutes a non-exclusive grant of permission to the Library of Congress to reproduce and distribute solely for the blind and physically handicapped and under the conditions and limitations prescribed by the regulations of the Copyright Office: (1) copies of the work identified in space 1 of this application in Braille (or similar tactile symbols); or (2) phonorecords embodying a fixation of a reading of that work; or (3) both.

    a ☐ Copies and Phonorecords   **b** ☐ Copies Only   **c** ☐ Phonorecords Only

See instructions

8

DEPOSIT ACCOUNT If the registration fee is to be charged to a Deposit Account established in the Copyright Office, give name and number of Account.
Name ▼   **Account Number** ▼

9

CORRESPONDENCE Give name and address to which correspondence about this application should be sent. Name/Address/Apt/City/State/Zip ▼

                    Area Code & Telephone Number ▶

Be sure to give your daytime phone ◀ number

CERTIFICATION* I, the undersigned, hereby certify that I am the

Check one ▶

☐ author
☐ other copyright claimant
☐ owner of exclusive right(s)
☐ authorized agent of _____

Name of author or other copyright claimant, or owner of exclusive right(s) ▲

of the work identified in this application and that the statements made by me in this application are correct to the best of my knowledge.

Typed or printed name and date ▼ If this application gives a date of publication in space 3, do not sign and submit it before that date.

                         date ▶

    ☞ **Handwritten signature (X)** ▼

10

| MAIL
CERTIFI-
CATE TO

**Certificate
will be
mailed in
window
envelope** | Name ▼

Number Street Apartment Number ▼

City State ZIP ▼ | **YOU MUST:**
• Complete all necessary spaces
• Sign your application in space 10
**SEND ALL 3 ELEMENTS
IN THE SAME PACKAGE:**
1. Application form
2. Nonrefundable $20 filing fee
in check or money order
payable to *Register of Copyrights*
3. Deposit material
MAIL TO:
Register of Copyrights
Library of Congress
Washington, D.C. 20559 | Copyright fees are adjusted at 5-year intervals, based on increases or decreases in the Consumer Price Index. The next adjustment is due in 1995. Contact the Copyright Office in January 1995 for the new fee schedule. |

11

* 17 U.S.C. § 506(e) Any person who knowingly makes a false representation of a material fact in the application for copyright registration provided for by section 409, or in any written statement filed in connection with the application, shall be fined not more than $2,500.

Figure 17.2b Form TX (back).

FORM VA
UNITED STATES COPYRIGHT OFFICE

REGISTRATION NUMBER

VA   VAU

EFFECTIVE DATE OF REGISTRATION

Month   Day   Year

DO NOT WRITE ABOVE THIS LINE. IF YOU NEED MORE SPACE, USE A SEPARATE CONTINUATION SHEET.

1

TITLE OF THIS WORK ▼   **NATURE OF THIS WORK ▼** See instructions

PREVIOUS OR ALTERNATIVE TITLES ▼

PUBLICATION AS A CONTRIBUTION If this work was published as a contribution to a periodical, serial, or collection, give information about the collective work in which the contribution appeared.   **Title of Collective Work ▼**

If published in a periodical or serial give: **Volume ▼**   **Number ▼**   **Issue Date ▼**   **On Pages ▼**

2

NAME OF AUTHOR ▼   **DATES OF BIRTH AND DEATH**
Year Born ▼   Year Died ▼

a

Was this contribution to the work a "work made for hire"?
☐ Yes
☐ No

AUTHOR'S NATIONALITY OR DOMICILE
Name of Country
OR { Citizen of ▶———————————
     Domiciled in ▶———————————

WAS THIS AUTHOR'S CONTRIBUTION TO THE WORK
Anonymous? ☐ Yes ☐ No
Pseudonymous? ☐ Yes ☐ No
If the answer to either of these questions is "Yes," see detailed instructions.

NOTE

Under the law, the "author" of a "work made for hire" is generally the employer, not the employee (see instructions). For any part of this work that was "made for hire" check "Yes" in the space provided, give the employer (or other person for whom the work was prepared) as "Author" of that part, and leave the space for dates of birth and death blank.

NATURE OF AUTHORSHIP Briefly describe nature of the material created by this author in which copyright is claimed. ▼

NAME OF AUTHOR ▼   **DATES OF BIRTH AND DEATH**
Year Born ▼   Year Died ▼

b

Was this contribution to the work a "work made for hire"?
☐ Yes
☐ No

AUTHOR'S NATIONALITY OR DOMICILE
Name of country
OR { Citizen of ▶———————————
     Domiciled in ▶———————————

WAS THIS AUTHOR'S CONTRIBUTION TO THE WORK
Anonymous? ☐ Yes ☐ No
Pseudonymous? ☐ Yes ☐ No
If the answer to either of these questions is "Yes," see detailed instructions.

NATURE OF AUTHORSHIP Briefly describe nature of the material created by this author in which copyright is claimed. ▼

NAME OF AUTHOR ▼   **DATES OF BIRTH AND DEATH**
Year Born ▼   Year Died ▼

c

Was this contribution to the work a "work made for hire"?
☐ Yes
☐ No

AUTHOR'S NATIONALITY OR DOMICILE
Name of Country
OR { Citizen of ▶———————————
     Domiciled in ▶———————————

WAS THIS AUTHOR'S CONTRIBUTION TO THE WORK
Anonymous? ☐ Yes ☐ No
Pseudonymous? ☐ Yes ☐ No
If the answer to either of these questions is "Yes," see detailed instructions.

NATURE OF AUTHORSHIP Briefly describe nature of the material created by this author in which copyright is claimed. ▼

3

YEAR IN WHICH CREATION OF THIS WORK WAS COMPLETED This information must be given in all cases.
◀ Year

DATE AND NATION OF FIRST PUBLICATION OF THIS PARTICULAR WORK
Complete this information ONLY if this work has been published. Month ▶ ——————— Day ▶ ——— Year ▶ ———————
◀ Nation

4

See instructions before completing this space.

COPYRIGHT CLAIMANT(S) Name and address must be given even if the claimant is the same as the author given in space 2.▼

TRANSFER If the claimant(s) named here in space 4 are different from the author(s) named in space 2, give a brief statement of how the claimant(s) obtained ownership of the copyright.▼

APPLICATION RECEIVED

ONE DEPOSIT RECEIVED

TWO DEPOSITS RECEIVED

REMITTANCE NUMBER AND DATE

DO NOT WRITE HERE OFFICE USE ONLY

MORE ON BACK ▶ • Complete all applicable spaces (numbers 5-9) on the reverse side of this page
• See detailed instructions.
• Sign the form at line 8.

DO NOT WRITE HERE

Page 1 of _____ pages

Figure 17.3a Form VA (front).

EXAMINED BY

FORM VA

CHECKED BY

☐ CORRESPONDENCE
Yes

☐ DEPOSIT ACCOUNT
FUNDS USED

FOR
COPYRIGHT
OFFICE
USE
ONLY

DO NOT WRITE ABOVE THIS LINE. IF YOU NEED MORE SPACE, USE A SEPARATE CONTINUATION SHEET.

PREVIOUS REGISTRATION Has registration for this work, or for an earlier version of this work, already been made in the Copyright Office?
☐ Yes ☐ No If your answer is "Yes," why is another registration being sought? (Check appropriate box) ▼

☐ This is the first published edition of a work previously registered in unpublished form.

☐ This is the first application submitted by this author as copyright claimant.

☐ This is a changed version of the work, as shown by space 6 on this application.

If your answer is "Yes," give: **Previous Registration Number ▼**   **Year of Registration ▼**

5

DERIVATIVE WORK OR COMPILATION Complete both space 6a & 6b for a derivative work; complete only 6b for a compilation.
a. **Preexisting Material** Identify any preexisting work or works that this work is based on or incorporates. ▼

b. **Material Added to This Work** Give a brief, general statement of the material that has been added to this work and in which copyright is claimed.▼

See instructions
before completing
this space.

6

DEPOSIT ACCOUNT If the registration fee is to be charged to a Deposit Account established in the Copyright Office, give name and number of Account.
Name ▼   **Account Number ▼**

7

CORRESPONDENCE Give name and address to which correspondence about this application should be sent.   Name/Address/Apt/City/State/Zip ▼

Be sure to
give your
daytime phone
◄ number

Area Code & Telephone Number ▶

CERTIFICATION*   I, the undersigned, hereby certify that I am the

Check only one ▼

☐ author

☐ other copyright claimant

☐ owner of exclusive right(s)

☐ authorized agent of _____
Name of author or other copyright claimant, or owner of exclusive right(s) ▲

8

of the work identified in this application and that the statements made
by me in this application are correct to the best of my knowledge.

Typed or printed name and date ▼ If this is a published work, this date must be the same as or later than the date of publication given in space 3.

_____ date ▶ _____

Handwritten signature (X) ▼

**MAIL
CERTIFI-
CATE TO**

Name ▼

Number/Street/Apartment Number ▼

City/State/ZIP ▼

**Certificate
will be
mailed in
window
envelope**

Have you:
• Completed all necessary
  spaces?
• Signed your application in space
  8?
• Enclosed check or money order
  for $10 payable to *Register of
  Copyrights?*
• Enclosed your deposit material
  with the application and fee?

MAIL TO: Register of Copyrights,
Library of Congress, Washington,
D.C. 20559.

9

☆U.S. GOVERNMENT PRINTING OFFICE: 1987—181—531 60.010

August 1987—100.000

Figure 17.3b Form VA (back).

SIMPLIFIED ADULT RELEASE

For valuable consideration received, I hereby grant to [Photographer] the absolute and irrevocable right and permission, in respect of the photographs that he/she had taken of me or in which I may be included with others, to copyright the same, in his/her own name or otherwise; to use, re-use, publish, and re-publish the same in whole or in part, individually or in conjunction with other photographs, and in conjunction with any printed matter, in any and all media now or hereafter known, and for any purpose whatsoever, for illustration, promotion, art, advertising and trade, or any other purpose whatsoever; and to use my name in connection therewith if he/she so chooses.

I hereby release and discharge [Photographer] from any and all claims and demands arising out of or in connection with the use of the photographs, including without limitation any and all claims for libel or invasion of privacy.

This authorization and release shall also inure to the benefit of the heirs, legal representatives, licensees, and assigns of [Photographer], as well as the person(s) for whom he/she took the photographs.

I am of full age and have the right to contract in my own name. I have read the foregoing and fully understand the contents thereof. This release shall be binding upon me and my heirs, legal representatives, and assigns.

Date: _____   _____

                                                        (Name)

_____   _____

          (Witness)   (Address)

Figure 17.4 Photographic release. (*Source: The American Society of Media Photographers, Inc. Copyright © 1986. All rights reserved. Reprinted with permission.*)

Authoring

Using Object-Oriented Tools for Faster, Easier Software Development

Glenn K. Morrissey

One of the key factors spurring multimedia market growth is new software tools. These new tools make multimedia software development faster, easier, and more effective. The best of these tools are event-driven and object-oriented. This chapter explores how these tools work, then describes how to use them for a range of specific types of multimedia applications.

Why the Multimedia Market is Expanding

The use of multimedia technology is exploding for a myriad of reasons:

- *It's effective.* Multimedia lets users communicate faster and still produces better retention of communicated information.

- *It's cost-effective.* Multimedia-enabled hardware is rushing to market, with prices for components from CD-ROM drives to audio and video boards lower than ever before.

- *It's a safe bet.* In 1992, Microsoft Corp. brought multimedia into the PC mainstream by including multimedia in its Windows operating system software. With a clear standard, buyers and sellers can participate in the multimedia market without worrying about betting on the wrong technology or specification.

- *It's compelling.* Users can't use multimedia without multimedia application software. And they won't use it if those applications aren't compelling. Happily, a new generation of affordable, easy-to-use software tools is spurring the rapid development of those vital applications.

The affordability and ease-of-use of these new-generation software development tools are producing two profound changes in the multimedia marketplace:

1. *An expansion in the base of software developers.* Until recently, applications were written by programming experts—the ones who understood the requisite programming languages. Today, applications can be written by "content" or subject-area experts, who need have little or no training in programming. That means the communication between the expert and the user is more direct, producing more useful software. Also, it means that more content experts can author titles, expanding the base of multimedia titles.

2. *A reduction in time- and cost-to-market.* For developers, new tools replace a considerable amount of time-consuming code-writing with a fast, easy graphical interface (much as Windows has replaced the text-based interface of MS-DOS for users). Much of the multimedia functionality that developers might otherwise have had to create for themselves is already built-in—and reusable. Applications under development can be tested without time-consuming recompiling. All of this cuts the time required for title development from years to months or less. And shorter time-to-market both expands the universe of available titles and reduces the prices that need to be charged for them.

Introducing Object-Oriented Tools

Several development tools now on the market provide varying levels of this new functionality. A key example is Multimedia ToolBook, a popular multimedia development tool for Microsoft Windows by Asymetrix Corp.

Multimedia ToolBook, introduced in 1991, was used to create many of the multimedia MPC titles, including Microsoft's Beethoven, Macmillan's Macmillan Dictionary for Children—Multimedia Edition, and Dr. T's Music Software's Composer Quest. Companies including Lotus and Turtle Beach use Multimedia ToolBook for their own MPC demos. And thousands of corporate developers, such as Andersen Consulting, Lockheed, and Intel, use it for in-house title development.

The tool is a software construction set that lets users build customized Windows multimedia applications. Exemplifying the features of new-generation tools, Multimedia ToolBook uses an intuitive graphical user interface; an object-oriented programming language called OpenScript; hypernavigation and linking among video, audio, animation, images, and text; and tools for editing and debugging applications.

How Multimedia ToolBook differs from traditional environments

Multimedia ToolBook differs from conventional development environments in several ways:

1. TookBook handles screen imaging automatically. Instead of writing code to display text and graphics, you create objects with Multimedia ToolBook's drawing tools. Objects persist between executions of your application, and Multimedia ToolBook handles all imaging for you.

2. Multimedia ToolBook objects are "smart." Because they come with built-in behaviors, you needn't program every action for your application, only those behaviors that are unique. A Multimedia ToolBook field knows how to display and scroll text. A Multimedia ToolBook player knows how to run a video clip, etc.

3. Multimedia ToolBook handles memory management. You no longer need to worry about writing to specific memory segments. Multimedia ToolBook, working with Windows, handles memory management for you.

How Multimedia ToolBook leverages multimedia functionality

Multimedia expands your development options. The challenge for tool providers is to offer new flexibility without adding complexity for developers. In Multimedia ToolBook, that's accomplished by building multimedia functionality into pre-scripted objects, called *widgets*, that make multimedia use a simple matter of cutting and pasting widgets, or their scripts, into the target application.

For example, a pre-built, VCR-like control panel can be pasted directly into an application to provide features (such as play, pause, stop, fast forward, and rewind) without writing any programming. Users can link to and control any standard Windows multimedia devices, including CD-ROMs, laserdisc players, animation software, waveform audio cards, overlay video boards, and MIDI sequencers.

Meanwhile, experienced developers can integrate customized multimedia functionality from whatever level they wish, using the C compiler language, Windows SDK, or other tools. And for developers who feel comfortable with a modest level of direct script-writing, Multimedia ToolBook permits this approach too, using clear, English-based commands. Where widgets offer greatest ease-of-use and C and similar tools offer the greatest power and customization, simple scripting brings together benefits of both approaches.

The following sections show the advantages of multimedia development using an object-oriented development tool, and how to leverage those advantages for development of specific applications.

Using an Event-Driven System

Unlike earlier tools, Multimedia ToolBook is an event-driven system. Understanding how that system works will enable you to leverage its advantages.

An *event* is any action the user takes in a window, such as pressing a key, clicking or dragging the mouse, or choosing a menu option. These events occur in random order—"at the whim of the mouse"—and the application must respond to them. An event-driven system can do this; traditional programming, with its linear code, can't.

Every event generates a message, which Multimedia ToolBook responds to. Programming a Multimedia ToolBook application, therefore, is essentially a matter of reacting to messages. Multimedia ToolBook generates idle messages at the Reader level when there is no other input. Even when the user is doing nothing, the application still receives messages. Reader level changes, unlike those created by the developer at the Author level, do not change the content of the title.

Input to a Multimedia ToolBook application comes in the form of keyboard events, mouse events, and menu events. Keywords in the OpenScript programming language correspond to the messages sent as a result of these events. Multimedia ToolBook has built-in responses to event-driven messages. For example, if a user clicks a menu command, Multimedia ToolBook's built-in response is to display the appropriate dialog box or carry out the action indicated by the command. Additional events come from system notification. For example, Multimedia ToolBook gives you an enterPage event every time that a new page is displayed and a leaveBook message is sent as the application closes down.

Sending messages

Although events occur "at the whim of the mouse," the messages triggered by events travel in a predictable direction. Messages are sent to objects in "books"—the metaphor for the Multimedia ToolBook application. Which object receives a given message depends on the message.

- Mouse event messages are sent to the object with the mouse pointer.
- Menu command messages are sent to the currently displayed page in the application.
- Keyboard event messages are sent to the object with the "focus," that is, the button, field, or record field, where the keystrokes will be typed.

Because Multimedia ToolBook is designed to be flexible, you aren't limited to its built-in messages. You can define your own, as needed for specific applications.

Handling messages

A message is sent; how will the Multimedia ToolBook application handle it? You program the response to an event-driven message in a *handler*. Handlers live in scripts. Any object can have a script. The handler receiving the message directs the response to the event. A handler does not have to live in the

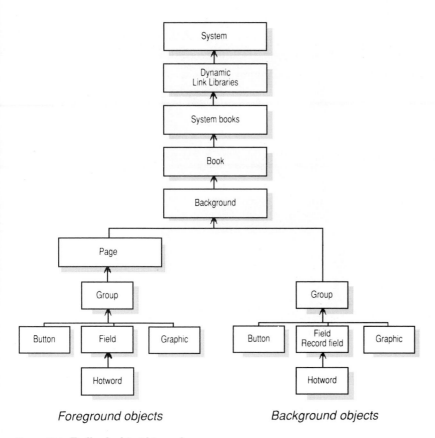

Figure 18.1 Toolbook object hierarchy.

script of the object that it handles. Messages are forwarded from object to object until a corresponding handler for the message is found. The direction in which a message is forwarded is based on the object hierarchy. Messages travel up the hierarchy in search of a handler (Fig. 18.1).

The place in the object hierarchy where a message enters is called the *target*. For example, a buttonClick message is sent upon releasing the left mouse button during a mouse click. The target of a buttonClick message is the object clicked. If no handler for the message resides in the object's script, the message is forwarded to the group script if the object belongs to a group; then, it is forwarded to the page. If none of the objects' scripts in the hierarchy contains a handler for a message, the message is forwarded to the Multimedia ToolBook system. At the system level, Multimedia ToolBook responds to a message with the default, or built-in, behavior. Because a Multimedia ToolBook application can rely on Multimedia ToolBook's built-in responses for much of its behavior, you can concentrate on writing handlers to add new or different behavior (Fig. 18.2).

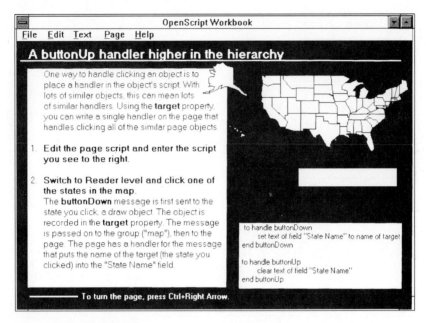

Figure 18.2 Toolbook handlers.

Writing handlers

Often, you'll place a handler in the script of the target object. However, placing handlers at different levels in the hierarchy permits greater flexibility in defining object behavior:

- *General behavior for multiple objects.* Placing a handler higher in the hierarchy defines general behavior for the objects below. The higher the handler, the greater its scope.

- *Exceptional behavior for an object.* Placing a handler lower in the hierarchy intercepts a message to block general behavior, whether defined by a handler in the application or by the Multimedia ToolBook system. For example, Multimedia ToolBook has built-in response for menu command messages; a handler could be placed especially to substitute a different response behavior.

- *"Staged" behavior for an object.* Including a forward statement in a handler forwards a message for more processing. A message can be forwarded up the hierarchy, directly to another object, or directly to the Multimedia ToolBook system. For example, a handler can use staged behavior by prompting a user for additional input, then forwarding a message conditionally, based on the user's response.

Developing Applications Using Object-Oriented Tools

You can use object-oriented development tools to create a range of multimedia applications, including:

- *On-line kiosks.* Stand-alone installations that provide user-directed information and more, such as accepting names and addresses to send additional information or products, and printing out maps (or other data) at the user's request.

- *Interactive training.* On-line tutorials and interactive education programs.

- *Hypermedia documents.* Encyclopedias and help systems with links so that readers can explore topics dynamically.

- *Databases.* Complete flat-file databases in Multimedia Toolbook, or front-ends to data from external sources.

Here's a closer look at using object-oriented tools to develop these applications.

Presentations and kiosks

In the era of music videos and video games, people are used to flashy visual input. On-line presentations and kiosks appeal to this visually sophisticated audience far more than traditional media (Fig. 18.3). The presenter controls the presentation with the mouse or keyboard, so it's easy to branch to corollary topics, include animation, or modify a screen during the presentation. In general, on-line presentations need even less programming than other types of object-oriented applications.

Kiosks provide even greater functionality. First, they operate without the need for a presenter; the user navigates through the information directly. Second, the kiosk can accept user information—such as names, addresses, and credit card data—to send additional information or products. Users can also receive hardcopies of requested information—such as ordering lists or maps—to take with them.

Figure 18-3 A multimedia kiosk.

As shown in Fig. 18.3, developers can create bullet lists that reveal themselves one bullet at a time. They can size the screen to hide the menu bar. And they can insert buttons with built-in functionality (e.g., "go to the next screen when clicked") that don't require any additional programming for use.

Scripts in kiosks. A self-running kiosk needs few controls beyond automated page turning. A scripted control structure flips through the pages at regular intervals. Using Multimedia ToolBook, you can provide this control via an idle handler. For example:

```
to handle idle
    send next
    pause 5 seconds
end
```

While idle messages are being received (i.e., while no user action is taking place), the application displays the next page. When the user presses a key, the keyDown message is sent and intercepted by a handler like this:

```
to handle keyDown
    request "Quit?" with "Yes" or "No"
    if it is "Yes"
        send exit
    end
end
```

If the user answers "yes" to the Request Dialog Box, the application quits.

Tips for effective kiosks. Here's a set of guidelines that you can use to develop effective kiosks:

1. You might wish to customize the interface for your kiosk. That's easy using a tool, such as Multimedia ToolBook. Hiding menu bars is as simple as inserting the instruction "hide menuBar at reader" in an enterBook handler. You can remove the title bar of your application by simply changing the visual property of the viewer.

2. Keep screens simple for better comprehension. For bullet lists, a maximum of five lines, with three to four words per line, is a good general rule.

3. If your kiosk is being made to a group, use colors, typefaces, and type sizes that can be seen by everyone. Sans serif type (e.g., Helvetica) is easier to read than serif type (e.g., Times). Subtle background colors (e.g., gray) are easier to view than are bold colors. Avoid dithered colors; they provide insufficient contrast.

4. Use a simple, consistent technique for smooth page navigation. Create a summary page that serves as a map for the user.

Interactive training

An object-oriented tool, such as Multimedia Toolbook and the CBT Edition of Multimedia ToolBook, is ideal for authoring interactive training applications because you can easily create screens with rich color graphics, place customized text where you want it and use animation to illustrate or capture a student's attention. You can create quizzes and store student responses, display hints, acknowledge correct answers, and track a student's progress from lesson to lesson.

Designing a workbook. Your interactive training application can be in the form of a "workbook" with different types of pages serving different functions.

- A table of contents page lists topics to be covered in the workbook. The background for these pages can include a script that places a check mark beside the topics that have been viewed by the student.

- Explanation pages present the concepts associated with a topic and introduce the exercises to follow.

- Exercise pages contain specific instructions and objects that the student can use to complete the exercise.

Tips for effective interactive training. In designing an interactive training application, consider these points:

- Keep the design simple so that students can spend time learning your content—not your format. Hide the menu bar or menu elements that are not needed for training. And use a few varied backgrounds that can be keyed to—and provide an intuitive clue to—the type of information being displayed.

- Establish user-defined properties to hold information about a student, such as the student's name, completed lessons, or quiz scores.

- Use the Request and Ask commands to display hints or prompt the student for information.

- Organize information in manageable portions. One concept per lesson is a good rule to follow.

- Provide clear, consistent navigation controls so that students will know where they are in an application and how to move around in it.

- Keep your design general and flexible so that it can be readily updated with additional lessons, as needed.

Hypermedia documents

Hypermedia documents use hotwords, buttons, and other linking devices to allow end-users to navigate through your information at their own direction and pace. Electronic textbooks, encyclopedias, kiosks, and point-of-purchase displays can all benefit from the linking tools in development products, such as Multimedia ToolBook. Those tools include navigational links and context-sensitive information.

Navigation links. Readers can browse topics by clicking buttons or hotwords linked to other pages in the book. When using these links, you should organize your document in a branching structure. Each main topic starts a new page in a linear progression; subtopics branch off the main path on their own pages.

The flexibility of open navigation through a book can also be a drawback, if the reader becomes—or just feels—lost. Control buttons on subtopic pages can let the reader decide whether to return to the main topic or go to a new one. Other icons and tools can restore even more user control. For example, a compass icon on each page can display an index to all book topics, showing their relationships and allowing readers to move to new topics of their choosing.

Another way to illustrate a book's structure is to use a contents page. Clicking a topic (a button with a buttonClick handler) can reveal subtopics (hidden grouped objects) under it. Readers can use the contents page to move directly to the desired part of the application.

The contents page from this "Multimedia Tour" title created with Multimedia ToolBook (Fig. 18.4) is a hypermedia document. It uses navigational links to let readers move directly to subjects of particular interest. Navigational buttons on this page appear in the same location throughout the book, making it easier for readers to navigate.

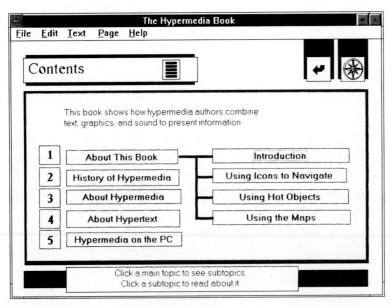

Figure 18.4 A table of contents structure.

Context-sensitive links. Context-sensitive links provide additional help to readers where and when they need it. The tasks they perform are based on where the reader is working. Using context-sensitive hotwords and buttons keeps pages uncluttered, yet provides quick access to additional information.

In Multimedia ToolBook's "Multimedia Tour," for example, a glossary page is made up entirely of context-sensitive hot buttons. Each button's script is a user-defined message that gets forwarded to a handler in the book's script. The handler displays a specific line of text in a request dialog box. Hotwords throughout the book bring up similar context-sensitive definitions by sending user-defined messages to the book. Both the glossary buttons and the hotwords use the request command to present the definitions.

By handling the buttonClick message in the book's script, consistent behavior is guaranteed for any hotword or button in the book. For example, in an on-line personnel manual, every mention of the word "overtime" could be a hotword that brings up a description of the overtime policy when clicked. To make script writing simple, you would set the name of the page to overtime. Now, the following handler in the book's script takes care of navigation for all overtime hotwords in the book:

```
to handle buttonClick
    if target contains "hotword"
        go to page (text of target)
    end
end buttonClick
```

The target is the overtime hotword, whose script is empty. When a reader clicks this hotword, the buttonClick message floats up the object hierarchy to the book in search of a handler. When the handler in the book script runs, Multimedia ToolBook goes to the page whose name is the same as the target's text.

Tips for designing hypermedia documents. Because information is so accessible in hypermedia documents, you need to take special care in organizing that information effectively. For example:

- Divide your information into discrete units of single concepts or ideas. Devote a new page to each. When you build links among the pages, the interrelation of ideas will appear more natural.

- Design your book around a relevant metaphor. For example, Macmillan New Media's *Macmillan Dictionary for Children—Multimedia Edition* uses a book metaphor. Asymetrix's *MediaBlitz!* uses a timeline metaphor. A metaphor gives the end-user an immediately recognizable context for your information.

- Use animation instead of text to explain actions that are better shown than described, such as how objects appear or act under different conditions or from different perspectives.

Database applications

A multimedia database can easily include video, photographic images, and audio, along with traditional text and graphics. Realtors, insurance adjusters, and museum curators are just three types of end-users who could benefit from maintaining multimedia databases.

Flat-file databases. Multimedia ToolBook can be used to create flat-file databases or front ends to external data sources. A flat-file database has a structure represented by a single, non-hierarchical set of fields, unlike a relational database, which can include multiple sets of fields with relationships established among them. Front ends give users an easy interface to large, complex, centralized databases.

A flat-file database written in Multimedia ToolBook can include graphics, buttons, and record fields to construct a simple screen useful for both data entry and browsing. Buttons and graphic controls on the background can contain scripts for creating, copying, and deleting pages and searching the database for character strings.

You can create a database quickly by importing an ASCII-delimited or ASCII fixed-field file into Multimedia ToolBook. Importing an ASCII file automatically creates a background with record fields to hold the data that you import.

A flat-file database in Multimedia Toolbook can include buttons and graphics that serve as controls for modifying records, searching, and navigation (Fig. 18.5).

Database front ends. When you need to maintain data in its original form, rather than importing it into the Multimedia ToolBook application, you'll want to use Multimedia ToolBook to create a front-end. This is useful, for

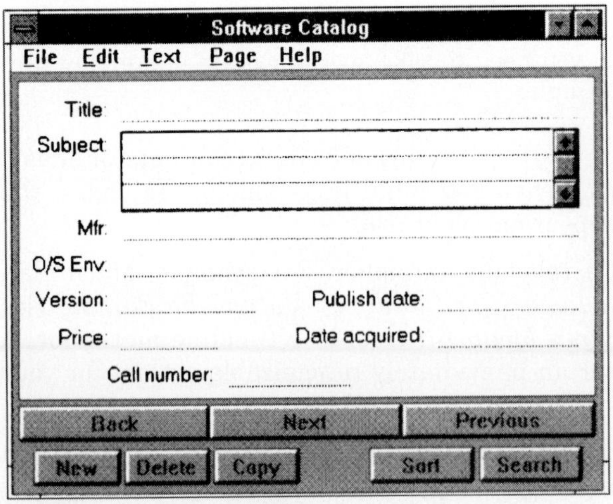

Figure 18.5. A flat-file database.

example, for data that needs to be accessed by other software. To access the data from Multimedia ToolBook, you can use Object Linking & Embedding (OLE), a Dynamic Link Library (DLL) or Dynamic Data Exchange (DDE).

A DLL is an external file, usually written in C, that defines functions a Multimedia ToolBook application can use. To use a DLL, you write statements in a script that link to the DLL and declare the functions you want. Then, you can use those functions in any handler in the book. Database access is just one example of what a DLL might do. DLLs can extend Multimedia ToolBook in other ways, such as driving multimedia devices or interacting with other programs.

DDE is a Windows communication protocol that makes it possible for two programs that support DDE to exchange data and issue commands to each other. DDE allows you to integrate applications to take advantage of the strengths of each. For example, Microsoft Excel is better than Multimedia ToolBook at number-crunching, but Multimedia ToolBook provides more flexible, exciting graphics for a better GUI. You might maintain data in Excel and access it from your Multimedia ToolBook application.

DDE in Multimedia ToolBook is built into a set of OpenScript commands you can use in scripts. To use DDE, you need a copy of the program with which you are exchanging data, and you need to know what DDE syntax that program expects.

Here's an example of using DDE in Multimedia ToolBook. It calls for the Multimedia ToolBook application to obtain updated information from an Excel database and display it in the Multimedia ToolBook front end:

```
—Update a summary field in the Multimedia ToolBook instance by
—requesting data from Excel
to handle buttonClick
    getRemote "Regional_Totals" application excel topic "region.xls"
    put It into text of field "summary"
end buttonClick
```

Here are additional ideas for database design:

- When you use record fields in a book, whether for a database, presentation, or other purposes, don't place objects over the record fields on the background. Overlapping background objects can have a significant impact on the speed of page flipping and scrolling.

- When you create a database front end with Multimedia ToolBook, you don't need to use record fields. The work of accessing and displaying data is done by the scripts that communicate with the external database so that you can use regular fields on the foreground of a page.

New Budgetary Considerations

Software development used to require a tremendous budget for programming work. With event-driven, object-oriented application development, that's no longer the case. Meanwhile, other parts of the multimedia development process (researching audio and video clips, negotiating and obtaining rights, producing original multimedia elements, converting from analog to digital, etc.) have become both time-consuming and expensive.

For example, using Multimedia ToolBook, the development staff at Dr. T's Music Software needed just two months to assemble Composer Quest, rather than the two years it might have taken with earlier tools. But recording musical selections, researching and writing biographies and history/art cross references, scanning photographs, etc. took many months longer.

Developers need to be aware of these new timeline and budgetary realities when they plan the development process. Developers also need to understand their options for obtaining multimedia elements. For an in-house application, non-professional video shot with a S-VHS or Hi-8 camera might be sufficient; certainly, it will be inexpensive. But for commercial applications or high-end corporate applications for use with clients, etc., developers might need professional-quality video that can cost up to several thousand dollars per minute of finished production. A flowchart, identifying all needed multimedia elements and explicit plans for their inclusion in the application, is a good idea.

Bibliography

ToolBook Ideas: An author's introduction to programming in ToolBook, Asymetrix Corporation, Bellevue, WA, 1989-91.

Using Multimedia ToolBook, Asymetrix Corporation Bellevue, Washington, 1989–91.

DLL Reference: A Guide to Using Dynamic Link Libraries, Asymetrix Corporation. Bellevue, WA, 1989–91.

Design Considerations
for Multimedia-Based
Executive Information Systems

.

Roger Karr

Executive Multimedia

Multimedia has been submerged in a wide range of definitions, ranging from "a PC that can play back an audio file" to "a sophisticated, high-powered workstation that can digitize, and with additional 'hooks,' analyze data in the form of video, audio, graphics, images, and text." When GUIs (graphical-user interfaces) were introduced in the early 1980s, few predicted how critical these interfaces would be to our ability to work more effectively, use tools more efficiently, and provide richer information in an easier-to-use and more understandable way. Today, there is not much future for software packages or application tools that are built *without* such interfaces.

Multimedia for executive-level applications is the "new" interface. It is no longer a considered a "toy box" technology that technocrats play in. The next step in the revolution of transforming raw data into information and information into knowledge is now considered to be the form in which this knowledge can be represented. It has been said that new forms of knowledge-representation will continue to revolutionize the way people use and deal with information.

With the click of a button, you can now receive a desktop video of your marketing vice president presenting a corporatewide strategy for introducing your new widget to the market. This revolutionizes the way information, and in its purest sense knowledge, is acquired, transformed, and communicated. Having knowledge of new product information, revenue projections, new management-team goals and deliverables, has translated into better-informed decision making and significantly improved corporate performance. And after all, improving the bottom line *is* the bottom line.

Focused work that improves the quality of interactions between top managers and at the same time upgrades the quality of the information and knowledge to be shared can do remarkable things for a corporation's level of global performance. The integration of multimedia technology into existing corporate legacy systems, databases, document management systems, and corporate communication systems has been shown to dramatically enhance the quality of both executive and line-management interaction. It does this by improving the quality of information—an absolute requirement in today's global marketplace.

Without getting much of a brain cramp, most people in the computer industry can define, in their own terms, what multimedia is. In the context of executive information applications, multimedia is *the ability to select any or all forms of data, manipulate them into meaningful information, and effectively integrate that information into a solution that solves a business problem and results in more efficient decision making.* Understanding the importance of integration is just as important as understanding how to choose the right medium or combination of media that will maximize technological advantage while transforming information into knowledge.

Multimedia applications for the executive

Perhaps the most obvious application of multimedia for the executive is in the area of corporate communications. Most executives, from senior managers right up to the CEO, have a need to communicate to all employees at all levels. As a general rule, a corporate communications session is developed and delivered once every quarter. Usually this is a big production (literally) and requires significant resources so as to coordinate a general assembly (or broadcast) and then reproduce and distribute it. More often than not, those who need to hear or see the session don't do so for a multitude of reasons:

- Companies typically are required to broadcast to multiple locations, but it may be that not all work sites have the satellite capability to receive the broadcast. Additionally, the costs for private broadcasts may be prohibitive.

- Videotape reproduction can be quite costly. Then too, the distributed videocassette often seems to get lost or to sit on a shelf in some person's office, collecting dust.

- The person receiving the videotape has the problem of trying to find the right time to play it, not to mention finding the answer to the age-old question, "Where do I get the TV and VCR?"

With a multimedia information kiosk positioned in a cafeteria, lobby, work bullpen, shop floor, or anywhere that "people take a break," people have immediate or "on-demand" access to the latest presidential address to employees, results and ramifications of the recent merger, shift in corporate strategies, incentive plans, etc. This communication vehicle, because of the richness of its multimedia interface, can also be entertaining even as it delivers vital information to the employees.

The results can be dramatic at all levels of the organization. One should never underestimate the value and importance of having a work force whose access to information is free and easy. The richness of information, when transformed into employee knowledge, can have a resounding effect on general work-force morale and on the whole concept of effective leadership. Take that transformation and apply it to your sales force, customer service division, Information Systems groups, and any other departments within the business and watch its effect on the bottom line. An effective organization is a well-informed organization.

Multimedia-enabled succession planning

Multimedia at the executive's desktop takes the shape of many specific applications. One such application would be succession planning for medium to large corporations. Succession planning has often been done the "good ole boy" way; what matters is who you know, what you know, and how well connected you are. The development of a multimedia-rich application that integrates corporate databases, corporate planning, and strategic planning processes can provide executives with the information they need when they need it. Avoiding the "good ole boy" approach enables more objective decision making.

Executive Information applications can use multimedia to break through the barriers that have long prevented management teams from getting the information they need to make well-informed decisions. Multimedia is the delivery mechanism to communicate messages in easy, efficient, and effective ways. In fact it is the new integration tool for giving a second life to existing corporate legacy systems, document management systems, and corporate personnel databases in which millions of dollars have been invested. Multimedia provides the ability to represent this wealth of information in one seamless, easy-to-use application.

A number of considerations are critical to the successful development and deployment of multivendor, multimedia applications for the executive's desktop. They vary in importance depending on the type of business opportunity/problem you are trying to achieve or solve. It is important to note that the operative word in this statement is *multivendor*. Until the market has been defined, most if not all successful multimedia applications will be multivendor solutions.

Configuring Worldwide Executive Multimedia Systems

The PC market is moving at such a rapid pace, it is hard to imagine any standard platform that can be used. Often the configuration of the desktop is driven by whether the application will reside in a distributed computing environment or as part of a single-user, stand-alone application. In the case of most multimedia applications designed for the executive desktop, many people have access to some of the same information, limited access to other levels of information. In these environments, distributed computing is the most efficient way to get information sorted and made available to whoever needs to use it.

In the context of succession planning, for example, information in all forms needs to be available: detailed performance data that allows effective analysis by the hiring executive; business segment performance; views on goals for both the individual and the corporation where he/she is employed; spreadsheet data to review budgeted versus actual spending; ROI calculations and overall budget performance. Using multimedia as the integration point, this data can be delivered in the form of text, graphs or bar charts, static images, audio, and audio combined with video. In most cases, during the succession planning process, the ability to collaborate with colleagues about the same information is crucial; therefore, allowing information and knowledge to be shared in a timely fashion is critical.

Broadcast-quality video

In this environment, networking is the key. Delivering near-broadcast-quality video over a 10-Mbyte network is a challenge. It also limits the number of clients or users that can be served at any given time. Distributing this information requires network servers that allow for the storage of large, data-driven files, files that have been stored digitally on a magnetic disk residing on a file server. In terms of configuration, the file server must have a sizable amount of storage. Specific size depends on how much video and audio will be used by the application, along with database and image type information. In general terms, a 1-minute video file that was digitized at 2 kbits per second will consume an average of 20 Mbytes of hard-disk storage. At this record rate, the video can be delivered to the desktop at 30 frames per second with excellent resolution.

The amount of storage required can vary significantly depending on the hardware and software used for digitization. Different compression algorithms—JPEG, MPEG, MPEG+, and now Fractal (none of which can be considered standard)—can drastically change the storage requirements. Careful consideration must be given to the hardware and software selected to handle the task in terms of audio and video digitization. For a network distributed solution, the "gotchas" would be in the form of network protocols being used, throughput of the network, and the configuration requirements of the file server.

Networking considerations

The type of network installed will determine the number of clients that can access the same file server. A 10-Mbyte network can safely handle an average of 6 clients at a data record rate of 1.5 kbits per second. Usable bandwidth on a 10-Mbyte network hovers around 7 or 8 Mbytes before significant throughput degradation is experienced. However, through the use of network repeaters the number of clients can be increased significantly at a relatively low cost.

A 100-Mbyte fiber-optic network can handle up to 80 clients from a single file server without experiencing any degradation in network performance. Splitting the network into several segments allows one to increase the number of clients per server almost twofold. These figures serve as examples of what different networks can support in the way of multimedia applications. It should also be noted that if video is not part of the equation, the storage requirements are significantly reduced.

Many considerations must be taken into account when identifying the number of clients on the network that can be served from one network server. When you are ready to head down the road of "state-of-the-art" multimedia solutions, be sure to have a dedicated network engineer develop your network topology. This person plays a critical role in the overall functional specification and design of the multimedia solution.

Depending on the size of the application and the types of data that need to be integrated into the solution, the configuration may include several file servers. For integration into a document management system, for example, a file server may be required to store the document images. This server may employ the use of optical storage devices that have the ability to store many terabytes of information on the file server. Another file server may be required as an audio and video server only.

The message here is that, in addition to acquiring the services of a network expert, it is also critical to the success and implementation of your solution that you have on-board an experienced application architect who understands the business opportunity or problem. With these two resources in place, the process of developing a high-level design can get under way.

The development of a high-level design is an iterative process, and it requires tight communication among the customer (in this case the executive), engineering, and delivery resources. With these components you now have a team that can design, develop, and deliver a high-powered multimedia solution for the executive(s). If you think that an army of engineers, architects, and project managers must be required to complete such work, note that Digital Equipment Corporation developed such an application with just a "few good [people]."

The PC configuration

In terms of desktop PC configurations, there are basically three areas that will significantly impact the performance of such applications. Again, it depends on whether they are distributed applications or stand-alone applications.

The first is the memory requirement for the desktop PC. In order to achieve the proper throughput on the desktop, a minimum of 12 Mbytes of memory should be configured. If the desktop is configured in a distributed environment, you may be able to get away with 8 Mbytes depending on other desktop applications you run locally. If the desktop is stand-alone, ideally 16 Mbytes should be configured into the desktop. As if to point up the fact that the personal computer industry is rapidly changing, Windows NT™ could transform the approach these applications take in a distributed computing environment.

The second consideration is disk storage. Again, in a distributed environment where you may require access to large amounts of storage on the server, disk storage does not play a critical role at the client level. Depending on whether you like to run your applications locally, aside from the multimedia application, a 160-Mbyte disk is more than sufficient. If the multimedia application resides locally on the desktop, local disk capacity is critical. This, however, depends on the types of data that have been integrated into the solution.

With video and audio files local and digitized at a 1.5-kbit record rate, 1 minute will consume roughly 20 Mbytes. Often this intense storage requirement scares people. However, if you consider the amount of information that can be communicated in a 1-minute video clip, the storage requirement suddenly becomes very reasonable. It also can be reduced significantly, depending on the required quality of the video. For example, if the record rate is 1.0 kbits and the video display requirement is 15 frames per second, that 1-minute segment now requires somewhere in the area of 5 to 7 Mbytes.

Executive-level multimedia applications have a tendency to need high-end video quality, especially if it is a corporate communications type of application. For these applications, disk storage requirements can range from 0.5 to 1 Gbyte. With this in mind, one of the major advantages to distributed computing is clear: investing in a well-configured file server can actually save in the area of client PC costs. In addition to the disk storage requirements for high-quality video, a good noninterlaced, multisync monitor should be part of the PC configuration.

The third desktop configuration consideration is the CODEC device used for compression/decompression. There are a number of these devices on the market. Many are hardware assisted and others are software playback only. Investing the time to learn about these many different devices is important.

Steps for Integrating Multimedia into the Executive Suite

Application content

Application content is perhaps the one area most critical to any executive information application, or multimedia application for that matter. In the case of executive multimedia applications, the content must be what the executive needs, not what you think the executive needs. In terms of a succession planning application or corporate communications application, the content must be current, professionally produced, and easily updated at a moment's notice.

When integrating a multimedia solution into existing corporate information systems, it is important to integrate only that data that enhances or enables the management team to make valued use of the application and, even more importantly, more effective decisions. For example, if the need is to integrate personnel profile records, pay attention only to the specific types (records) of information needed from the profile, not the entire profile. This will help you to manage the huge amount of data that needs to be changed or modified on a regular basis. Rather than use data just because it is there, use only that data that the application requires. This concept may spin off other work that needs to be done outside the application itself.

An example of this would be to execute database extractions outside of the multimedia application. When the extraction is complete, the manipulation of data may be done within or outside the application, depending on application dependencies. In layperson's terms, you should, when integrating large databases, do as much data manipulation/extraction as possible outside the application before importing to the executive information application. The "wins" here are (1) performance and (2) the advantage of distributed computing in another form.

Audio and video

In terms of video and audio content, make no mistake, this must be done professionally, particularly when the application is to be used by senior executive staff members. When you are using these data types in an executive succession application, it is absolutely critical that each person being viewed in video form has their best foot forward. Keep in mind that seeing a person presenting themselves on your desktop should be the same, in terms of quality, as seeing a person speak on television. There is an unspoken expectation that the video and audio segments seen on the desktop will be of equal or greater quality as those we all see daily on broadcast television.

To meet this expectation, most medium to large corporations and government agencies have a communications division that consists of a fully equipped production studio. Engage these folks early, for they have a wealth of knowledge and insight most application developers and architects do not have when designing a multimedia application that draws on the full array of data types including video and audio. This also leads to the advantage of having a human-interface engineer review the look and feel and flow of the application. (This is often a part-time job for experts in the field.)

Other content such as images, text, and graphics all need to be integrated, keeping one question in mind: Is the information useful and easy to understand, and does it flow well? From the end user's point of view, the ability to navigate easily from one data type to another is just as important as the actual content itself. "Popping" from an interactive spreadsheet session (say, a budget projection), to a business plan, to the divisional executive presenting the new fiscal-year strategy, is where a multimedia application really shows its stuff.

Business process considerations

Multimedia executive applications touch on a wide variety of traditional business processes, particularly in the succession planning procedure, where usually there are many processes that an executive board of directors goes through to select the next chief financial officer.

One must look at how these traditional processes are impacted. You may find that some are impacted very positively and others not so positively. An example of how a process was impacted by the development and deployment of an executive profiling application is one company's review of worldwide corporate performance. In this case, the board of directors wanted to get closer to the business. The first problem was the unfamiliarity of board members with the individuals responsible for particular business divisions, units, or segments. The challenge was to provide a tool that would not only introduce these individuals to senior management, but also deliver an electronic file folder for each individual containing information such as biographies, resumés, financial performance information, fiscal-year goals, personal performance data, personal development plans, etc.

In order to solve this seemingly intractable problem, processes were put in place to acquire this information in all forms. Standard formats were developed in terms of written reports, spreadsheet data, resumés, etc. Perhaps the most influential module of this application was the 10-minute video interview, in which the interviewees were asked specific questions about current corporate performance and what the corporation's strategy should be as it entered the twenty-first century. These very pointed and difficult questions were provided to the interviewer by the board of directors. The bottom line is that the board members now had the ability to learn, in a single day, about many divisions within the corporation, as opposed to the more traditional approach that could take up to 18 months.

This process required significant coordination by the individuals who set up the interview time with 30 senior executives worldwide. For those executives who were not in the corporate headquarters area, filming was done locally, while the actual interview was conducted via telephone. Significant savings were realized in terms of travel costs, and at the same time this process did not take the busy executive away from the business issues requiring his or her attention.

The other forms of data made it necessary to modify other processes. Most of the modifications were in the area of format and standards for reporting. Again, these were processes that were closely looked at prior to the actual commencement of work.

An example of the positive results accrued during this information-acquisition process: when an existing process for reporting was looked at to accommodate requirements for a multimedia succession planning application, it was determined that there were much better, more efficient ways to get this work done. Therefore the adoption of these practices became permanent. In addition the cost associated with putting together this application was far less than the cost (including executives' time) of getting 30 senior executives into the boardroom as candidates for not just one but many different positions.

Again, the processes that an executive information application uses are those that require significant attention. In today's business environment, companies are spending significant time and investing significant resources on process reengineering. Multimedia applications for executives can assist and become the "standard" way to deliver the results of this reengineering effort. Note as well that these types of applications can be of significant help in training executives in the results of such reengineering efforts.

Support

Finally, there is always the need for support. The term *support,* in the context of this chapter, refers to the need for a person, group, or division to maintain the application. This maintenance comes in many forms. A few to touch upon would be network maintenance, application maintenance and enhancements, application content, and updates. Unlike many point-of-information multimedia kiosk applications, where much of the content is static for a period of time, executive information applications require that the data be absolutely up-to-date on a moment's notice. Often an executive needs to update information or annotate certain documents and pass them on to a colleague. This can all be done with significant attention being paid to the design, maintenance, and support of the application.

It is critical that the system have the ability to update this information easily. The data may change monthly, weekly, and oftentimes daily. The ability to rid the application of old information and replace it with current information is critical to the success of the application. This task is often designed into the application in such a way that a nontechnical support person can update its content dynamically. Often executives want to have the option to update or purge information on their own. In such cases, having a knowledgeable support person in place when the executive gets himself/herself in trouble (lets face it, it happens) is vital. This support person must be fully trained in the use of the application, and he or she should also have immediate access to the development or engineering team. In many instances, support is provided by the same team that designed and developed the application.

Support also falls into the realm of those business processes we discussed earlier. These should be designed in a way that supports the use of the application and makes possible the automated update of information in a standard format. Make no mistake, these applications *are* highly sophisticated, but sometimes they require no more support than what the executive needs today, simply a better way to pull it all together. Often this provides a refocus and training opportunity for those who are the support staff for the executive office and the executives themselves.

Conclusion

We have only scratched the surface and looked at a very small sampling of how multimedia can be a significant competitive advantage for the management team of a company. We have discussed several ways in which such applications can produce significant cost savings in terms of succession planning and reengineered processes.

We have also discussed configuration considerations, the most important being those that impact network design, integration, and platform configuration.

Given the rate at which this technology is changing, perhaps the best advice I can give to you is to keep abreast of what tools (hardware and software) are hitting the marketplace and to learn how to turn them into a solution that will give executives a clear competitive advantage. But let's not forget that the application can also be a lot of fun to build and use!

Macintosh Multimedia Tools

Michael Kellner

The Elusive Paperless Office

With the advent of desktop computing and communication, the idea of a paperless office arose. Electronic documents, conveyed by wire to one's colleagues...a very compelling thought. Alas, the computer revolution has produced the biggest paper explosion ever.

Nonetheless, with new technologies, it is becoming increasingly difficult to portray certain types of information on paper. We are seeing an increased push toward the paperless office as it becomes necessary to keep the electronic document "on line" to fully receive much of this information.

How much of the information you see around you would you like to have at your fingertips, indexed and easily accessed? With current technology you can bring text, images, sound, and motion video into your desktop working environment.

This chapter will describe a variety of different hardware and software tools that you can use with your Macintosh to capture both dynamic and static information for use in your multimedia documents.

Types of information

There are two major types of information: *dynamic* and *static*. Dynamic information is composed of elements that change over time. For instance, video is composed of a sequence of pictures that change in time. Sound, stock quotes, and telemetry output also change over time.

Static information is data that does not convey its information based on time. For instance, one day's edition of a newspaper does not change over time. The information from that edition can be archived and obtained at any time. How the information is *interpreted* over time may change, but the data itself remains static. Other examples here include artwork, a company's quarterly results, and a photograph.

Computers traditionally have been good at handling static information. Recently desktop computers have been endowed with the ability to handle time-based information. Since there are so many types of dynamic information, it is necessary for a computer to have a solid architecture upon which to build the facilities that can manipulate dynamic data.

The Macintosh is designed for multimedia

Since its inception, the Macintosh has been able to handle various forms of static information easily and consistently. Graphics and text were manipulated in the same way throughout the entire environment. There were no graphics modes. Pictures could be copied and pasted in the same way as text.

The Macintosh was built around a solid architecture for static data processing. Being a well-designed architecture, it was easy for Apple to extend it seamlessly with new technologies such as true-color image manipulation. Extensions were made to the system without adversely affecting the current applications. In fact, extensions could be made to the system that added functionality to existing programs without changing or upgrading the applications.

In 1991, Apple released QuickTime—a set of technologies packaged as a Macintosh system extension. QuickTime was designed as an architecture for handling time-based data. Being an architecture, it defines in general terms how time-based data is to be handled. QuickTime is expandable, and as of this writing has been extended twice beyond the initial implementation to include new data types and digital image-compression schemes.

With the installation of QuickTime, all programs that used pictures, a standard Macintosh data-type, could now use compressed pictures automatically. New applications were written to take advantage of QuickTime's motion video capabilities, and upgrades to applications were released that allowed QuickTime movies to be inserted into electronic documents. A movie embedded within a document provides an opportunity to better explain a concept described within the document.

The benefits of multimedia documents are fewer if you are limited to one computer platform. If the electronic document you create cannot be shared with the audience you are trying to reach, you will either have to bring the computer and the audience together or convert the document to a paper representation of the data, losing much of the information contained therein.

QuickTime and the QuickTime movie files are becoming a de facto industry standard. There are currently versions of QuickTime that operate on the Macintosh, Microsoft Windows, and A/UX (Apple's UNIX) platforms that can use the same data files. QuickTime movie file support is even more widespread. Hundreds of Macintosh and Windows applications support creation and/or playback of movie files. Apple has also licensed some key compression technologies to Silicon Graphics Inc., so their machines can support the creation and playback of QuickTime movie files.

With the proliferation of media produced using QuickTime, and the increasing popularity of the QuickTime movie file format, it is only a matter of time before QuickTime tools are available on other platforms. The incorporation of the Kaleida joint venture between IBM and Apple, and the collaboration of Apple with key consumer products manufacturers, ensure that QuickTime will continue to be the premiere dynamic data technology.

Macintosh Multimedia Hardware Tools

Out of the box, the Macintosh comes with considerable multimedia capabilities built in. There are many additional multimedia tools available to you, to add to or extend those capabilities. But remember: *always* turn off your computer and all devices before connecting or disconnecting any device.

Scanners

A *scanner* is a device that converts an image on a piece of paper to a picture that the computer can manipulate. It is used to bring a picture or text into the computer so that you don't have to draw or type it in yourself. Used with OCR (optical character recognition) software, your computer can transcribe a text document into a file that you can save, modify, transmit, or otherwise manipulate.

Hardware.   There are many types of scanners, with various capabilities. *Flatbed scanners* are common, and operate somewhat like a photocopy machine. There is a glass surface upon which the document or book is placed. The scanner then passes a light and lens under the glass to make an image of what is on the glass. Some full-color scanners require three passes under the image.

Hand-held scanners require you to pass a small scanning device over the top of what you want to scan into the computer. They have a limit to the width that they can scan. If you can't cover the whole picture in one pass, you will have to connect the pieces together yourself, using a software tool such as PhotoShop. It can be difficult to align the scanned pieces so that the image looks coherent.

Slide scanners are used to scan 35-mm photographic slides. They produce high-quality, high-resolution images. However, slide scanners are of limited use. Not all the text or images you scan will be developed on 35-mm slides.

Software.   Most scanners come with DAs (desk accessories) or with applications that allow you to scan documents and save them as graphics files. Some come with software that allows you to scan from within your favorite drawing package (such as Photoshop). This makes scanning and manipulating images one step easier.

Connecting.   Most scanners that connect to the Macintosh do so through the SCSI port. Connect a SCSI cable and a SCSI terminator to the scanner. If there are no other SCSI devices such as external hard disks connected to your computer, connect the SCSI cable to your computer. If you have other devices, remove the terminator from the last device in the chain and connect the SCSI cable to the last device. Set the SCSI ID on the scanner to a number different than those of the other devices. Turn on all devices, then your computer. Install the scanner software provided with the scanner. For more information on SCSI, see the subsection SCSI Notes on p. 20.17 at the end of this chapter.

Video input

A computer with video input capabilities can be quite useful. Much as a scanner is used to bring pictures on paper into the computer, so video input and a video camera can be used to bring pictures of objects into the computer. For instance, using a scanner to get a picture of a building would require that you take a picture of the building, have it developed and printed, then scan it using a scanner. With a video camera, you can videotape the building from many angles, connect the camera to your computer, then use a frame-grabbing program to capture the picture (or pictures) that you want.

Instant pictures can be made by connecting the video camera to the computer and running it "live." This can be useful for making pictures of small, movable objects, people, or even, with proper lighting and setup, photographs. However, the quality of a video image is not nearly as good as an image obtained by using a scanner.

Used in conjunction with QuickTime, video digitizers can be used to "grab" sequences of video for storage and playback. These are known as *QuickTime movies.*

Hardware. If your Macintosh is not equipped for video input, you can get a video digitizing card. There is a plethora of these cards currently available. Many are combination display/video digitizing cards that can be used to add another monitor to your Macintosh, increasing your on-screen work area. Most digitizing cards have the capability to use S-Video as well as composite video input. S-Video is useful only if your video source (camera or videotape recorder) has it as well. Some cards offer hardware compression built in or as an upgrade option. Some cards combine audio and video input to offer a one-card solution to making digital movies.

Whichever digitizer you choose, make sure it is compatible with the model of your computer and offers the capabilities you need.

Software. Video digitizers come with system software that allow you to use their capabilities. These system extensions are known as *VDIGs (video DIGitizing components)* that allow QuickTime to use the card. With the VDIG, any program that uses QuickTime to grab movies will work with the digitizer. As well, many companies package software to grab pictures, make movies, and otherwise manipulate video images.

Connecting. With everything turned off, take the lid off your computer, find an empty slot, and push the card into it. Put the lid back onto your computer. If the board has display capabilities, connect the monitor cable to the card. This will result in faster video digitizing if you digitize to this display. Connect the appropriate cables to the card–S-Video cable, composite video cable, and/or audio cables. Turn on the computer and install the supplied software.

Hardware-assisted video compression

Hardware-assisted compression for video input takes the burden of compression off of your computer by processing the video with components designed specifically for this purpose. This allows you to make larger movies at a faster frame rate.

The frame rate is the number of different pictures per second that the movie displays. Standard television in the United States uses a standard known as NTSC, which runs at 29.97 frames per second. Movies run at 24 frames per second.

Hardware. Compression boards are designed either as a "daughter board" card, which plugs into an existing video input card, or as a separate card. Some video input cards, such as SuperMac's Digital Film, come with hardware-assisted compression built in. The MoviePak is an example of a daughter-board from RasterOps that plugs into a range of their existing video cards.

Software. Hardware compression cards come with system software that you put into your System Folder. QuickTime will notice that the card is installed and add it to the list of compression options available. When you create a movie using a movie recorder or an editing package, select the compressor that came with the hardware. Note, however, that if you create a movie with a hardware compressor, it is likely you will need the hardware to play back the movie. If the hardware compressor is a JPEG compressor (a standard type), you can play back the movie without the hardware but at a much lower speed than it was recorded at.

Video output

Video encoders give you the capability to record to videotape or display on a large screen everything that is displayed on your computer screen. This allows you to display presentations live to a large audience, or record to a videotape for archiving or viewing at a future time.

Hardware. Certain video input boards such as the Radius Video Vision have composite and S-Video output sockets that connect directly to a VCR or large-screen display. The Video Vision has a feature called *image convolution* that reduces the flicker of narrow horizontal lines at the expense of some image clarity.

Other video output solutions consist of external boxes that connect between your computer and your display. The box converts the computer's video signal to S-Video, composite video, or component video, all of which can be connect-ed to videotape recorders, large projection monitors, and television sets.

Software.   Combination cards such as VideoVision come with software that controls all features of the card, including video output. The external boxes require no software at all.

Connecting.   For the combination cards, connecting is as easy as plugging a cable into the output of the card and the input of the VCR or other video device. Other solutions have unique connection requirements. For example, the RasterOp's Video Expander II is an external box that connects to the video card in your computer. The box has output connectors for S-Video, com-posite video, and component RGB.

Consult the instructions included with your video converters to see exactly how they are to be connected.

(*Note:* You can try to videotape your computer screen with your video cam-era, but usually the results are less than satisfying. When you view the tape, a horizontal band appears on the computer display and slowly scrolls upward, only to reappear at the bottom. You may have noticed this on the local news or in poorly produced movies. Professional video cameras sometimes have a scan-rate adjustment that allows you to synchronize the camera and the dis-play to alleviate the problem. Other solutions include using a time-based con-verter to convert the scan rate of the computer to a rate suitable for the video recorder.)

Audio input

Audio digitizers are used to record sounds into your computer. If your Macintosh is equipped with an audio digitizer, you can send voice mail, annotate documents, or record sound effects for multimedia presentations. With QuickTime, an audio digitizer is used to record the audio portion of a movie.

Hardware.   Some Macintoshes have an audio digitizer built in. If yours doesn't, use an external box such as MacroMedia's MacRecorder to connect through the serial port to your machine. Some video-digitizing cards have an audio digitizer built in. There are also dedicated audio-digitizing cards, which provide professional-quality sound digitizing and manipulation.

Software.   System software included with audio digitizers allow them to be used in a standard way. With the software installed, all programs that use sound input operate similarly. For example, you can record a sound from with-in the "Sound" control panel no matter which audio digitizer you have. Just press the Add button and the recording controls will come up in a dialogue.

The audio digitizer you buy will come with software that allows you to record and manipulate sounds. QuickTime uses all digitizers in a common way and allows you to adjust the capabilities of the digitizer, such as the sampling rate and whether or not to use sound compression. For general multimedia presentations, a sampling rate of 22 kHz is fine.

[*Note:* The sampling rate can be defined as the number of times per second the computer records a segment of sound. Sound is vibrating air that moves your eardrum. The faster the vibrations, the higher the pitch of the sound. To record high-pitched sounds, the computer must check the digitizer many times per second. The sampling rate must be twice the frequency of the sound you are trying to record. Telephone voice quality requires a sampling rate of about 8 kHz (8000 times per second), whereas compact disc quality requires 44 kHz.]

Connecting. For built-in sound digitizers, there is a port on the back of the computer indicated by a microphone icon. This port takes a ⅛-inch mono minijack (see the Cables subsection on p. 20.11). Some external sound digitizers such as the MacRecorder use the same type of plug. Other digitizers use RCA plugs, which are common to most audio devices such as amplifiers and VCRs.

Adapters are available that convert RCA plugs to the ⅛-inch minijack. This allows you to connect your VCR or other audio source to your Macintosh's internal sound input port.

Audio output

All Macintoshes come with a built-in speaker that is adequate for nondemanding multimedia applications. To go beyond adequate, you can use the sound output port indicated by a speaker icon. Similar to the sound input port, this is a ⅛-inch minijack that may be capable of stereo output depending on the model of your Macintosh. An adapter can be used to connect this port to a videotape recorder or to external amplifier and speakers for playback to an audience.

Hardware. High-quality audio-digitizing cards and some combination video/audio-digitizing cards have output capabilities. These are either RCA-type jacks, which can be connected directly to VCRs or amplifiers, or ⅛-inch minijacks.

Software. Software included with some digitizing boards allow control of the sound output. For example, the VideoVision card has a control panel that allows you to adjust volume and mixing of its sound sources. The Macintosh "Sound" control panel allows you to choose between built-in audio output (which includes the sound output port) and external audio.

Connecting. Sound output connectors are either RCA-type stereo, or ⅛-inch stereo minijack. A minijack-to-stereo RCA adapter can be used for conversion of the two. From the RCA cables, you can connect to audio components such as amplifiers, mixers, equalizers, and recorders.

Graphics tablets

Graphics tablets are used instead of or in conjunction with a mouse, to draw and manipulate the cursor. For drawing pictures or painting, a graphics tablet is an easier and more accurate device to use than a mouse.

Hardware. A graphics tablet uses a pen or a puck to move the cursor on the screen. A *puck* is a hand-held device like a mouse with buttons and crosshairs that can be used to accurately trace images placed on the tablet. Some tablets can detect pressure sensitivity that is used, for instance, to draw a line thicker when the pen is pressed harder. Programmable buttons on the pen or puck can be set up to perform common tasks such as a double-click. Pens or pucks can be wireless or connected by a flexible cable to the tablet. The wireless pens are easier to manipulate but there is an increased risk of misplacement or loss.

Software. Graphics tablets come with system software that allow them to be used as a replacement for the mouse. A control panel is used to configure the tablet along the lines of pressure sensitivity, pen button function, and tablet orientation.

Connecting. Some graphics tablets such as the Wacom ArtZ use the Apple Desktop Bus (ADB) to connect to your Macintosh. This is the same port where the keyboard and mouse are connected. Connecting these tablets is as easy as finding a free ADB port on your computer or keyboard and plugging in the tablet's connector.

Other graphics tablets require an external interface box that connects between the tablet and the computer's serial port.

(*Note:* Since you can connect a number of devices to the ADB chain, connecting a digitizing tablet using ADB will leave a serial port free for something else, such as a MIDI interface or a modem.)

Light pens

Light pens are used to directly manipulate the cursor on the screen. A pen connected by a cable is used to move the cursor or to draw directly to the screen. The cursor is moved by putting the tip of the pen on the computer's screen. Mouse clicks are accomplished by either pressing a button on the side of the pen or pushing the pen to the screen.

While light pens give you a more direct manipulation of the cursor on the screen, it can sometimes be unwieldy to hold the pen to the screen. Also there are times when the pen obscures the item you are trying to manipulate.

Hardware. Light pens use the signals that the computer sends to the monitor to determine where the pen is located. An external box is connected between your computer and monitor, and another cable connects to your serial port to tell your computer where the pen is located.

Software. Like graphics tablets, system software is included that allows the Macintosh to use the pen as a cursor, instead of or in addition to the mouse. A control panel is used to calibrate the pen as well as to configure attributes such as which serial port shall be used.

Connecting. Using FTG Data System's PXL-780 light pen as an example: Connect the monitor cable from your computer to the pen interface box. Connect the box's monitor-out cable to your monitor. Plug the serial connector into an unused serial port. Plug the pen into the box and connect the power connector to the box. Install the supplied software. Use the software to configure the pen and to calibrate it with your computer and display.

Touch screens

Touch screens are used in stand-alone multimedia displays, interactive kiosks, and in schools. They come either as a complete monitor or as an overlay for an existing monitor. Similar to but not as accurate as light pens, they provide direct manipulation of the cursor on the screen. A person needs only a single finger to manipulate the cursor.

For kiosks, a touch screen is very useful. The user can manipulate the program directly from the screen, and all fragile hardware can be protected in an enclosure. Touch screens are good for specific applications that require the user to select an item from a group of items. They are not very good for use as an everyday alternative to a mouse. It can be difficult to perform double-clicks or to accurately press a small screen item such as a window's Close box.

Hardware. Touch screens come as a complete monitor, or as an overlay that attaches to an existing monitor. The control hardware typically is contained within an external interface box that connects between the screen and a serial port or an ADB port.

Software. Like light pens and graphics tablets, system software is included to allow the touch screen to be used as a replacement for or in addition to the mouse. A control panel is used to configure and calibrate the screen.

Connecting. Using the Elographics Acutouch monitor as an example: Connect the monitor as usual to your computer's display card. Connect the appropriate cable from the interface box to the interface connector at the back of the monitor. Attach the serial cable from the interface box to an unused serial port on your computer. Connect the power connector to the external box. Turn on the monitor, and apply power to the external box. Install the supplied software. Configure and calibrate the monitor.

MIDI

MIDI (musical instrument digital interface) is used to connect musical synthesizers and equipment to each other and to a computer. MIDI transmits control information, not sound, to the devices connected to it. By doing this, MIDI allows you to record the performance of a musician. The instruments, the key, or the tempo of the piece can be adjusted at any time. In order to use MIDI with your computer, you must have either a MIDI interface box or a MIDI sound module card.

To process digital audio, your computer must do much more work than MIDI. Liken MIDI to a conductor (the computer itself) directing an orchestra (MIDI devices). The conductor does not have to put forth the entire effort to produce the music.

MIDI songs require much less storage space than digitally recorded music. They typically require 25 Kbytes per minute to produce high-quality music, whereas comparable digital music requires over 10,000 kbytes per minute. However, talent is required to generate the compositions to be played. There are software packages of precomposed music to include in your presentation if you don't have the time or talent to produce it yourself.

Hardware.   A MIDI interface is a small box that connects to your computer through a serial port and has MIDI input and output ports. A MIDI sound module card is a whole synthesizer contained on a card that you plug into your computer. Audio-output cables connect the MIDI module to an external amplifier.

Software.   The preferred method of using MIDI with the Macintosh is with Apple's MIDI Manager software, which is bundled with most MIDI software packages. This software allows easy connection of different sources of MIDI information (e.g., music software) to destinations (e.g., MIDI keyboards or sound modules). Some MIDI software packages also have their own means of communicating with MIDI interfaces.

Connecting.   Using Apple's MIDI interface and a MIDI keyboard as an example: Connect the serial cable from the MIDI interface to your computer. Connect a MIDI cable from the output port of the interface box to the input port of your MIDI keyboard. Connect another MIDI cable from the input of the interface box to the output of the MIDI keyboard. Connect the power to the MIDI interface. Install the software and configure the MIDI Manager, specifying the appropriate serial port.

Storage

Hardware.   Multimedia can require massive amounts of data storage space, and digital video requires high data-access speeds. If you intend to work with digital video, you need as much disk space as possible. RAID (redundant arrays of inexpensive disks) are excellent for video acquisition, as they are faster than single drives and offer large capacities.

Removable media can be useful for long-term storage as well as data transfer. Since short (30-second) movies can occupy many megabytes of storage, floppy disks just won't do the trick. Syquest, Bernoullis, or magneto-optical drives are a good solution. Important factors to take into account are media cost and compatibility issues. If you do get a removable-media storage device to transfer presentations, make sure your destination computer also has the same type of removable-media device, or else you will have to tote your drive around (which defeats the purpose of removable media).

Cables

Behind most multimedia workstations is a rat's nest of cables. There are many different types of connectors and cables (see Fig. 20.1). In some cases the same type of plug and cable is used to make completely different connections.

(*Note:* Make sure that the two ends of a cable connect compatible components, otherwise you may damage your equipment.)

The following describes Fig. 20.1 in detail.

(A) Phono plug. Also known as *patch cords,* these are used for audio connections and are the same as those used for stereo components. These cables are

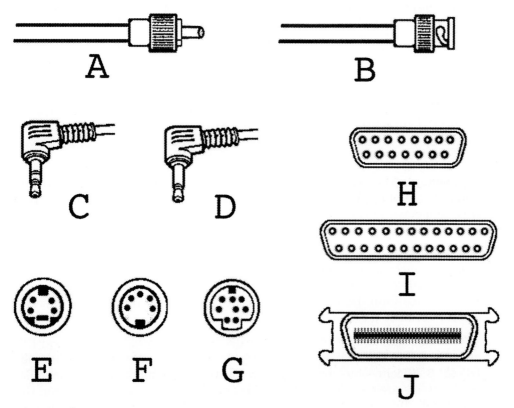

Figure 20.1 Connectors.

usually found as a pair (red plug—right channel; black or white plug—left channel). Some have a third plug for composite video (yellow). Some have only one cable (mono sound), while others have a mono sound channel and a composite video channel (yellow—video; white—audio).

(A) Composite video.   These are used to connect video sources to video inputs. They have the same phono plug as audio cables, but the cable itself is slightly different. They also are called *75-ohm video cables.*

(B) Component video/BNC connector.   Component video is used in high-end equipment and with some RGB monitors. The cable end is comprised of one or three BNC-type connectors. The quality of component video is higher than that of S-Video but is not as common. Some component video cables have a monitor plug (DB-13) at one end and three BNC-type connectors at the other. This cable is used to connect a video-display card to a component video monitor. This connector also is used to connect ethernet networks.

(C) ⅛-inch stereo minijack.   This connector comes in stereo and mono versions. Typically it is used to connect microphones and earphones. With an adaptor, it can be connected to phono-plugs as well.

(D) ⅛-inch mono minijack/Control-L.   This connector is found on microphones and monophonic earphones. It is also used in Control-L applications that control certain VCRs and video cameras for synchronization and automated control.

(E) S-Video/ADB connector.   S-Video is a video standard that provides better quality than composite video. The cable is the same as that used by the Macintosh's ADB (Apple Desktop Bus) devices such as the keyboard. In a pinch, an extra keyboard cable can be used in place of an S-Video cable. Make sure that the S-Video cable is connected only to S-Video sockets, and *never* connect an S-Video source to your keyboard socket.

(F) MIDI/5-pin DIN.   A MIDI connector is larger in size than the mini-DIN plug and S-Video plug. A MIDI cable is used for MIDI-in, MIDI-out, and MIDI-thru connections. This same connector occasionally is used for power connectors. Be careful not to connect a power connector to your MIDI ports.

(G) Serial RS-422/VISCA/8-pin mini-DIN.   The Macintosh serial port uses an 8-pin plug to connect to serial devices. Cables can have the mini-DIN plug on each end or a DB-25 on one end to connect to serial devices such as modems. A VISCA cable (mini-DIN 8 on each end of the cable) is the same as a serial cable and can be used interchangeably.

(H) Monitor cable/DB-13.   This cable is used to connect a video-display card to an RGB monitor. It has a DB-13 connector at the computer end and another DB-13, BNC connectors, or a custom connector at the monitor end. Some display systems use a connector that fits between the monitor connector and the monitor itself to allow the presenter or operator to see the display while projecting it to a large audience.

(I) Serial RS-232/DB-25/System SCSI connector. A DB-25 connector commonly is used as a port on modems and other serial devices. It also is used as the System SCSI connector on the Macintosh.

(J) SCSI (Small Computers Standard Interface). This cable can connect a variety of devices including scanners, hard disks, tape storage units, printers, and some high-end audio digitizers. There are three types of plugs for SCSI connections. The 50-pin connector is used to daisy-chain SCSI devices together. A DB-25 plug is used to connect the Macintosh to the SCSI chain and, sometimes, to connect SCSI devices together. The HDI-30 connector is used with the Macintosh PowerBooks to connect them to the SCSI chain.

Macintosh Multimedia Software Tools

Recorders/editors

In order to use the hardware tools to bring information into your computer, you need to have software that knows how to access the hardware.

Scanning software

Most scanners are supplied with the software used to access them. Many of these software packages are limited in their capabilities, and you will want to supplement their usage with additional, more specialized software. LightSource's Ofoto is a comprehensive image-acquisition tool. It provides image-manipulation tools such as color correction, rotation, and cropping. Ofoto is unique in that you can place a picture on the scanner's surface and press a single button. Ofoto will then scan the picture, rotate it so that it is straight, crop it, and adjust brightness and contrast to produce a usable picture without a lot of adjustments.

Adobe's Photoshop is a well-known image-processing package that has the capability to access a scanner directly. All that is required is a "plug-in module" that specifically works with Photoshop and your scanner. Other packages such as optical character recognition (OCR) software will also have a way to work directly with your scanner. ExperVisions's TypeReader OCR package has drivers for many popular scanners.

Movie recorders

With QuickTime and a video input card, you can use your Macintosh to capture movies for viewing and editing. Movie-recording software is used to control the video card so as to capture sequences of video and/or audio and save it to disk. Movie-recording software also allows you to set the compression methods to allow you to make the space-versus-quality compromise. Typically, better-quality images require greater storage space. Certain compressors do a better job of compressing than others but may produce lower-quality images. There are also compressors, such as SuperMac's Compact Video compressor, that produce a good-quality, highly compressed image at the expense of compression speed. With Compact Video, it is necessary to record the video with another compressor (or none at all) and compress after you're done recording.

With a QuickTime-compatible video card, any movie-recording software will work with your video card. Apple's Movie Recorder program is a basic video-capture program. It allows you to capture audio and video and set compression parameters. It also allows basic cut-and-paste of video segments.

Adobe's Premiere is a comprehensive video-capture and -editing package. Premiere not only works with QuickTime, it can produce an edit decision list (EDL) for use with professional video-editing equipment. You can use your Macintosh with Premiere to edit your video and use the EDL to produce the final cut. Premiere also allows you to add transitions to your video segments, such as fade-in/fade-out, zoom-in, and page-turn.

Tips on making good movies

1. *Experiment.*   Try the suggestions listed here, and try different things. The only way to find out how to make good movies is to try it under a variety of conditions. Some of the tips given here are surefire winners, while others depend on your particular computer setup and the subject of your video.

2. *Always use the best-quality equipment available.*   For example, if you have a VHS and a Hi-8 video camera, use the Hi-8, because the quality of Hi-8 is better than VHS. Likewise, if you have composite and S-Video output available on your playback video deck, use S-Video.

3. *Use hardware-assisted compression.*   Using hardware compression frees the Macintosh to perform other tasks such as digitizing audio and saving the video to disk. With hardware assistance, full-screen movies can be recorded at 30 frames per second.

4. *If you have more than one monitor connected, make sure the recording window is completely on the screen that is connected to your video digitizer.*   Most video digitizer cards that offer display capabilities will display digitized video to their own screen much faster than to another one.

5. *Don't pan the film—use a still background instead.*   Compression doesn't work well with moving backgrounds.

6. *Get lots of memory.*   With an abundance of memory you can record movies to RAM, which is faster than recording to disk. Note, however, that without huge amounts of memory (20 + megabytes), you will only be able to record small (size and length) movies before space runs out.

7. *Don't use virtual memory.*   Virtual memory uses your hard disk as extra memory. Since the hard disk is much slower than RAM, using VM to increase your memory space will not give you the speed increase that extra RAM will. VM will just slow the computer down and prevent it from making good movies.

8. *Don't use unnecessary system extensions.*   Many extensions force your computer to give them processing time at periodic intervals. The time that your computer gives to these extensions is that much less time it has to work on your movies.

9. *Use an appropriate compressor for the image contents.*   Compressors usually are developed for a particular image type. The compact video and video compressors are good for recorded video, whereas the animation and graphics compressors are good for computer-generated graphics. JPEG produces small, good-quality photo images but is too slow for motion video (unless it is sped up with hardware).

10. *Turn off automatic file compression software.*   QuickTime does the compression itself. Programs such as DiskDoubler or Stuffit SpaceSaver will try to compress files that have already been compressed.

11. *Turn off file sharing.*   File sharing takes a lot of effort on your computer's part. Turn it off when you are recording movies, and let the computer concentrate on making good movies.

Audio recorders

Most movie-recording software can be used for audio recording as well, by setting the option to not record video. This is a direct way of recording audio, but typically the output file is a movie file. Specialized audio-recording software such as MacroMedia's SoundEdit Pro has many effects that can be applied to recorded sounds. Reverberation effects, noise filtering, bending, and compression are a few of the effects available. SoundEdit Pro also can save the sound in formats other than the "Movie" format.

MIDI recorders

MIDI recorders (sequencers) are used to capture a musical performance from a MIDI-capable instrument, typically a MIDI keyboard. These recorders allow you to manipulate the notes that were recorded as well as the tempo and arrangement of the composition. They let you record one instrument, then record another while the first is being played back. In this way you can record a musical arrangement with multiple instruments entirely by yourself.

Titling software

Your Macintosh can be used to produce impressive titles both for digital video on your computer and for your videotape productions. Generic graphics packages such as MacDraw Pro will suffice for simple titles. Specific tools for manipulating text as graphics objects, such as Strata's Strata Type 3D, can produce intricate title screens using any font on your computer. They can also use graphics created by most paint or drawing programs. Strata Type creates three-dimensional objects and allows you to designate what the surface is made out of, such as gold or chrome. You can specify colored light sources and special effects, such as light coming through a window pane. Using tools such as Strata Type, you can produce results similar to the titles seen on broadcast television.

Media integration

Many multimedia packages are geared primarily to a specific type of media. For example, Adobe Premiere is an excellent digital video editing package, but it cannot manipulate MIDI data. To bring all of your multimedia information together, you will need a media integration package. Passport's Producer is a program that brings together slides (from presentation packages such as Persuasion), movies, pictures, sounds (such as speech), animations, MIDI, and music directly from compact discs. Producer allows you to arrange a presentation using time to specify when an item is supposed to display or play. For example you can produce a 30-second commercial with a montage of pictures and some music from a compact disc, then put spoken dialog in at the appropriate time.

With a video output device, you can use the Print-to-video feature to save the presentation onto a videotape.

Format conversion

A frustrating aspect of working with different computers and software packages is data incompatibility. Getting information from one program to another is much easier than getting it from one kind of computer to another. The Macintosh has many utilities to assist in format conversion.

To use data from an IBM PC–compatible computer, you can use Apple's PC Exchange software. With it, IBM PC–compatible disks look and act like Macintosh disks. Files on the disk can be viewed as icons and copied to and from Macintosh disks.

For conversion of data from IBM-compatible computers to the Macintosh, you can use Apple's Easy Open software in conjunction with translators from companies such as DataVis. These translators convert your data among the common formats found on each computer.

DeBabelizer from Equilibrium Technologies is a graphics-processing utility that has tremendous conversion capabilities. It can convert between 55 different graphics formats found on Macintosh, DOS/Windows, Amiga, Sun, X Windows, SGI, and other computers. DeBabelizer is scriptable, which means that you can tell the computer how to perform a graphics conversion once, then have it do the same thing for a number of files automatically. This is very useful when you have to use a large number of graphics files between different computers.

Cataloging

It is very easy to lose track of all of the information you have on your computer. With a media-cataloging program such as Imspace Systems' Kudo Image Browser, or Aldus's Fetch, you can keep track of all of your media files. Image

Browser has an interesting "riffle" feature that allows you to scan a large catalog of images quickly. With compatible software such as Quark Express, you also can drag and drop pictures from the database directly into your documents.

SCSI notes

1. Make sure your computer and all of the SCSI devices are turned off before you add or remove devices from the chain.

2. Devices on the SCSI chain are identified by the computer with SCSI IDs. Each ID must be unique and in the range of 0 to 6. If conflicting IDs are assigned to devices (e.g., if both a hard disk and a CD-ROM have an ID of 0), the computer will not operate properly or may not start at all. Turn off all devices, reset the IDs, and the computer will work properly.

3. If there is one internal hard disk, it usually will be set to ID 0. If there is more than one internal SCSI device, you can check their IDs by selecting their icons from the Finder and selecting "Get Info" from the Finder's file menu. If you reconfigure your devices often, it may be a good idea to label the device's front with the ID to save some confusion later. Alternatively, there are shareware tools available that allow you to scan and identify devices on the SCSI bus.

4. The terminator used for the Macintosh IIfx is different than the terminators used for all of the other Macintosh models. It is black, while the more common terminator is gray. Make sure you use a black terminator with the IIfx. You may not immediately notice a problem, but incorrect usage can result in data corruption.

5. Be aware that some SCSI devices are internally terminated. Check the documentation that accompanies the device to determine if this is the case. The internally terminated device needs to be at the end of the SCSI chain, and no external termination should be used. If you have any internally terminated devices in the middle of the SCSI chain, you must remove the internal termination before using.

6. Some advanced devices have self-determining termination; i.e., the device decides if it needs termination or not. See the documentation supplied with the device to determine if it has this feature.

7. If you've just been adding or removing SCSI devices or other cables behind your computer, make sure all the cables are securely connected. A partially connected SCSI cable or an unterminated SCSI chain is capable of causing data loss. If your computer starts to act strangely (spurious disk-read errors, incorrect icons, etc.), it's possible that your SCSI chain is incorrectly configured.

21

World Wide Web
Application Development

Mel Baiada

Since 1993, the Internet's World Wide Web has grown at a rate that is literally unprecedented. Although the Web's most common application is primarily the delivery of multimedia documents and information, a paradigm shift is currently underway. Leading-edge organizations are implementing some new and exciting uses for the Web. In particular, they are examining intriguing advantages of the Web as a platform for developing and deploying software applications.

To date, commercial use of the Web has been primarily as an Internet-related technology for organizations to communicate with outsiders. Although the most common current application is to respond to inquiries, other typical applications include: basic advertising; automation of fulfillment of requests for product literature; communication between suppliers and their customers; and search and retrieval of static corporate information.

This chapter covers one of the newly emerging uses of the Web, with a view to stimulating the thinking of managers responsible for developing and implementing software in their organizations. It also explains how organizations can use Web technology to disseminate information more easily, more efficiently, and more cost effectively. It is hoped that this chapter will stimulate readers into thinking about how they can leverage Web technology to give their organizations the competitive advantage they must have if they are to survive and prosper.

The Web as a Business Tool: Some Basics

The explosion of the Web within not only the technical community, but also upon the general awareness of the business world, has been astounding. Consider that within a timescale that can comfortably be measured in months, rather than years, it has shot up from an academic novelty to a pervasive medium for business communication. When developments pile on themselves this quickly, even the most technically savvy managers might find themselves with gaps in their knowledge. For this reason, it is useful to do a quick overview. (Users familiar with HTML, authoring tools, etc., might skip the next three sections if they desire.)

The World-Wide Web is a collection of computers attached to the Internet. Those computers (formally called *Web servers*) can be accessed from any other computer connected to the Internet. Web Sites differ from other computers attached to the 'Net (for example, those used mainly for electronic mail) in that they often contain highly colorful graphics, text, and/or audio files that a user can access via hypertext links. So, for example, a company might make its catalog of products available via its Web Home page, along with digitized pictures of the items; text descriptions and pricing information; and video clips of short product demos or testimonials. Someone viewing that information, need only "point and click" on an item of interest to get the information they desire. The source of that information could just as easily reside on the same computer as the home page, or come from another computer thousands of miles away.

Any Web pages can be highly interactive and often contains "links" to other Web sites, which might be of interest to those starting at one particular Home page. The Home page can be thought of as the initial place (scrollable screens) that the user sees when they first access a specific address on the Web. One of the reasons for the successful growth of the Web, is caused in part to the highly visual, creative, and interactive Home pages that companies are producing.

The Web was invented in the early 1990s at CERN, the world-renowned nuclear research facility headquartered in Switzerland. Researchers there wanted to have a way of making their research results—tabular data, audio commentaries, and animated graphics—available to research colleagues around the world.

Invention of HTML

The CERN researchers also invented a language used to set up a Web site. This language, Hypertext Markup Language (HTML), is a kind of shorthand language that lets users specify different forms of information at the home page. The person setting up the home page uses a different "tag" for different kinds of information and different display modes. For example, the tag H1 in front of text that says "Ourcompany's Home Page" causes "Ourcompany's Home Page" to be displayed as a Level 1 heading. A different tag specifies a file of digitized audio information, another one, a file of digitized video, and so on. HTML is very simple to learn, and most individuals can begin writing in HTML after a 30-minute lesson. HTML also supports various user interface objects called *elements*. Examples of elements are buttons and text fields.

Figure 64.1   Home page.

However, HTML did not flourish as a technology until a group of students at the National Center for Supercomputing Applications (NCSA) at the University of Illinois/Urbana created a piece of software called "Mosaic." Mosaic made it easier to:

1. Construct a graphical user interface

2. Display text and multimedia

3. Run on multiple computers and operating systems (e.g., PCs, Macs, UNIX, terminals)

4. Access ("browse") Web home pages

```
┌─────────────────────────────────────────────────────────────┐
│                    Netscape: View Source                     │
├─────────────────────────────────────────────────────────────┤
│    Title:  Bluestone, Inc.                                   │
│                                                              │
│  Location:  http://www.bluestone.com/                        │
│                                                              │
│  <!DOCTYPE HTML SYSTEM "html.dtd">                           │
│  <HTML>                                                      │
│  <HEAD>                                                      │
│  <TITLE>Bluestone, Inc.</TITLE>                             │
│  </HEAD>                                                     │
│                                                              │
│  <BODY>                                                      │
│                                                              │
│  <A HREF="/cgi-bin/std/imagemap/catalogs/welcomepage.map">  │
│  <IMG SRC="/catalogs/welcomepage.gif" ALT="Bluestone -      │
│  Transferring Advanced Development Technology" ISMAP></A>    │
│                                                              │
│  <HR>                                                        │
│  <P>                                                         │
│                                                              │
│  <IMG SRC="/gizmos/bignew.gif" ALT="New!" ALIGN="LEFT"      │
│  HSPACE=10>                                                  │
│  On September 11, 1995, Bluestone                           │
│  <A HREF="/press/1995-09-11_SaWeb.html">formally           │
│  announced</A> our newest                                   │
│                                                              │
│  Save...                                              OK     │
└─────────────────────────────────────────────────────────────┘
```

Figure 64.2 HTML from home page.

Vannevar Bush, a science advisor under President Roosevelt during the 1940s, is generally given credit as the original visionary who saw the importance of linking the various elements of information, (documents, photographs, notes, etc.) in an effort to automate and provide access to technical information. Ted Nelson is credited with originating the term Hypertext during the 1960s and has been a leader in the promotion of global access to information.

Design of the Web

Web technology was designed using client/server architecture. The *server* portion is the material (text, digitized audio, digitized video or graphics) residing on a computer somewhere so that it can be accessed by (serve) users. The material is retrieved by a piece of software called a *Web browser*, which then presents that material from the server so the user can view it, watch it, listen to it, or read it.

The browser (most commonly Netscape and Mosaic) is the software *client*. Web browsers have been written for every major windowing environment, including Windows, Motif, Presentation Manager, Macintosh, and even VT and IBM 3270 character-based terminals. This means that any Web Site properly designed can be browsed from both windowing and character-based systems, an incredibly important point to corporations having a mixture of cross-platform computers using different windowing systems.

Authoring tools

Authoring tools are another component in this system. These are specialized word processors and GUI editors, which convert or save documents with the appropriate HTML tags. The benefit of these tools are that they are simple to use. An end-user with no technical information systems background can use a popular word processor or authoring system to prototype a user interface, and then hand the results to the information systems professionals, who can then use a specialized software tool to add the database behavior and test the complete application.

Web popularity

Business users quickly saw the commercial possibilities of the Web, and began creating their own sites ("home pages") on the Web. Growth in the number of home pages has been phenomenal: the number of home pages rose from around 30 in early 1993 to more than 50,000 by mid-1995.

Another illustration of how popular the Web has become, can be seen by the growing number of newspaper ads, corporate letterheads, and television network news programs that now contain the addresses of Web home pages. Moreover, the *Wall Street Journal* has begun publishing an advertising section based on Web addresses. Taken together, these developments are a sure indicator of the utility and potential of the Web. The more utility the Web has, the more people will use it. This has significance for new uses of the Web.

So far, the Web has been used mainly for electronic publishing, with applications like communicating with the public, advertising, order-taking, etc. However, the natural history of all new technologies is that the more they are used, and the longer they are used, the more new uses are found for them. This is the case with the Web. One use, now in early stages of exploration, is to use the Web's capabilities as an avenue for developing and implementing intra-corporate applications.

Application Development in the Nineties: The Web as a Tool

In order to explore the Web's appropriateness for application development, it is useful to step back and look at the Web in terms of its attributes.

First, it is independent of any specific computer architecture, language, or operating system. As John Patrick, VP of Internet Business at IBM has said, "It is the GUI of the 90s."

Second, the Web is place-independent. It can be accessed from anywhere in the world, and attached computers can be located anywhere in the world.

Thus, a person using the Web doesn't need to know, or care, if the computer or home page is physically located across the hall or across the ocean. This also means that information can be distributed easily, quickly, and inexpensively over the Web.

Third, the Web is a multi-tiered computing architecture. The Graphical User Interface can be on one computer, the application on a second, and the database on a third. And it can mix multiple application and database servers providing flexibility through modularity.

Fourth, the structure of the Web means that information or applications on the Web can be changed incrementally, instead of all at once. On the Web, you can change any individual page as needs change, without affecting the other pages.

Together, these characteristics make the Web an extremely powerful facility. They are the same qualities needed for developing applications in the '90s, when organizations operating in multiple locations might find themselves using a widely differing assortment of computer architectures to access, exchange, or distribute information, which might be changing rapidly. Old-style application development—developing software in one place, for one central machine, using expensive talent—is now recognized as a dead issue. A key issue is, what will replace it?

Why the Web is a potential software development tool

First, the Web can shorten the process of application development by letting users compress the amount of time needed for developing the user interface. The user interface is a critical aspect of any application. A great user interface might not necessarily make an application particularly effective or useful, but a poor user interface will almost certainly doom an application. (Notice that software developers have set up usability labs specifically for the purpose of detailed study of the user interface, and spend heavily on them.)

The design and coding of user interfaces in applications can account for anywhere from 50 to 80% of the application development time. So, any tool that can reduce application development time will pay for itself in short order. The HTML language meets that requirement: it is simple, and a large base of consumer experience with it shows that HTML can be learned very quickly by non-technical personnel. (Indeed, HTML is much easier to learn, and to use, than development tools for software like Motif and Windows, which require at least some level of technical background to use.)

Additional properties make the Web very attractive as an environment for developing applications. For example, the Web is becoming a world standard for communications. It is accessible from virtually everywhere on the planet. The large number of naive or non-technical subscribers accessing it via some of the commercial on-line services is further testimony to its ease of use—practically anyone can become comfortable with it. In addition to use on a world-wide level, it is also being used more and more internally, as a means of intra-organizational communication, combining data and documents under one umbrella.

What characteristics will application developers need to prosper in the '90s?

Everyone in business is aware (often, all too painfully!) of how the pace of business keeps accelerating. Organizations must be nimble if they are to survive. Today, and more so in coming years, organizations will have to be able to respond very quickly to changes in the business/political environment, changes in customer demand, in the competition, and in internal needs.

In terms of their information systems, organizations will need certain characteristics to survive or flourish. They will certainly need the ability to:

1. Develop and deploy software quickly, in order to respond to shifts in customer demands, new products, new regulations, etc.

2. Create those applications with high reliability.

3. Create applications which are easily maintained, modified, or upgraded.

4. Develop robust applications, which can properly deal with user errors (e.g., in formulating queries) or other anomalies.

5. Integrate an organization's existing applications and databases with new applications.

6. Support an organization's current, operational applications, such as very large databases.

7. Implement these applications with appropriate levels of security.

Any tool that allows an organization to incorporate these characteristics into its application development efforts will be a long-term strategic asset.

Linkage between application development and the Web. The Web's characteristics make it an excellent environment in which to develop applications and to put them into production. For example, the client/server architecture of the Web is the same architecture that more and more organizations are using for their own applications. You can certainly look at the Web's components—http servers, graphical browsers, the HTML language—as mirroring the components used for more familiar application development tools, such as Windows, PCs, and middleware. This familiarity will shorten the learning curve for developers and application users.

Web application development technology. The key elements are a database that a user wishes to query or update; a program containing the code for accessing that database, a means of getting the query or update into that code (i.e., interfacing with it), and a facility for conveying the response to the user.

The program that reads or writes to the database is called a *Common Gateway Interface (CGI)*. The CGI is a conventional program. It might do some editing or checking of the input it receives (e.g., a reasonableness or range check), or edit a user's input to put it into the proper form, or do some other processing. On the output side, it will take the information it finds in the database and edit that—for example, expanding an indicator like "C1" into text that in essence says, "out of stock," so a user can better understand the returned answer.

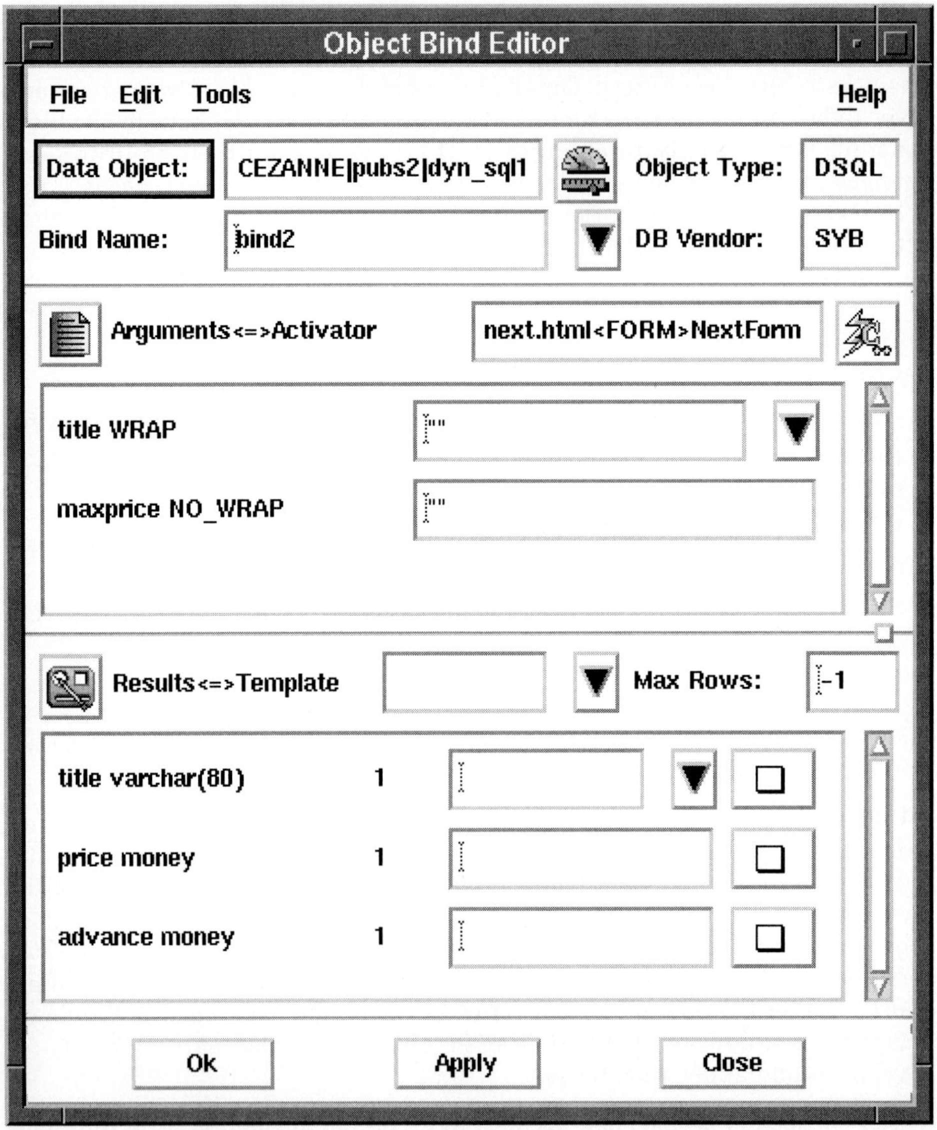

Figure 64.3 Bind editor.

The input to the CGI is called a *form*. A good analogy is any paper form or application blank an individual might complete. Output from the CGI, called an *HTML template*, is similar—a pre-defined format that holds specific fields. Defining all these elements might seem like additional complexity, but it actually simplifies the process and makes the application more robust.

Understandably, any tool specifically constructed to work seamlessly with these elements, would considerably reduce the amount of time needed to develop an application—to define it, test it, debug it, etc.—and to put it into production.

How and why HTML, CGI, and other Web elements are significant in terms of application development. HTML and other Web components have become a de facto industry standard for the Web. This adds to their ease of use, their value, and their universality. Developers write code to HTML standards, and HTML is the language that the most successful Web browsers use.

The Web is more than simply material being displayed (or available in audio form)—there is real processing going on! The real functionality comes from another standard, the CGI—the processing component.

Some Issues and Requirements for the '90s

The importance of standards

Hardware and software standards are a critical issue in information systems. Standards not only make the market for software, but without them, only a few hardy pioneers will commit corporate resources to a project. Standards are a way of insuring against sudden obsolescence of an organization's systems effort. Using a product that meets an established set of standards helps ensure the long-term viability of a project.

Examples of standards

Some familiar examples of standards are high-level languages, such as C, or C++; or the use of standard interfaces and links to other software, such as off-the-shelf APIs; or software that supports and uses standard networking tools and practices, such as TCP/IP, or which conforms to Web standards like HTML, http, shttp, and ssl. In general, standards-compliant software removes a source of anxiety for buyers and assures them that they are buying a product that will have high maintainability and usability.

Conformance to industry standards assures users that a piece of software is extensible, maintainable, and reliable. For example, such software can be easily integrated with software from other vendors. Similarly, software that conforms to standards allows buyers to upgrade individual components in their systems with high levels of confidence and minimal disruption.

A good tool for developing software on the Web should be able to use any HTML authoring tool or editor, access data in any major database, generate industry-standard C or C++ code, and integrate easily with other tools.

A tool example. Bluestone, Inc., has recently developed a tool that meets these standards, and that makes it possible to develop and deploy enterprise-wide applications on the Web in an easy, cost-effective manner.

The cross platform accessibility of Web technology is its most powerful feature. Individual companies have been expending costly resources for years trying to solve cross-platform problems while a solution has been quietly evolving. Sapphire/Web, is the first product to take full advantage of this evolution, allowing software developers to bind any HTML element to any of the following reusable objects:

1. *Any stored procedure in Oracle, Sybase or Informix.* Stored Procedures have become the de facto method of doing large client/server applications. The beauty of Sapphire/Web is that users can very easily bind HTML elements to any stored procedure.

   Stored procedures can be viewed as "business rules." They are popular for client/server applications for several reasons.

   First, it is SQL actually compiled into the database for increased performance. Second, they are reusable by many applications accessing the application. Third, they have referential integrity—meaning that if a database table is changed, then the database notifies the Database Administrator that there is a change that could affect the stored procedure. This is important in large projects, where there are many tables and stored procedures.

2. *Any Dynamic SQL (DSQL).* If you don't want to be locked into a database vendor's stored procedure method, you can use your own SQL code and store it in a Dynamic SQL repository. You bind your HTML elements to a Dynamic SQL the same way that you bind to a Stored Procedure.

3. *Any executable program.* Sapphire/Web also adds support for binding to any executable program. For example, a directory-listing command (ls in UNIX, dir in DOS/Windows/NT) can be bound to a hot list of directory names. The results would be a listing of subdirectories and files that could then be put into a resulting HTML template—perhaps in the form of a hot list again. This example shows an easy way to create an HTML file manager. However, in general practice, this puts a great deal of power behind HTML.

4. *Functions.* Legacy systems are typically written as a collection of functions. Sapphire/Web also includes easy binding between HTML documents and functions. This provides a simplified mechanism to put new HTML front-ends on existing applications. It also allows the developer to make use of the full power of their existing applications.

   It should also be noted that functions and executables can be distributed with Sapphire/Web, so they need not run on the Web Server, but can run on other application servers on the network.

5. *Any flat file.* Flat files can be used as a database. All that is needed is to tell Sapphire/Web the file name and the column location. An example of this feature is that with a Lotus spreadsheet that's been saved in an ASCII format, the user can add and subtract from the file from within the Web browser.

6. *Any CGI script.* The concept of reusable code applies to the Web programming as well. Sapphire/Web permits starting any CGI script and doing pre/post processing on the data. A CGI script is just another object to bind to.

How does Sapphire/Web facilitate application development on the Web? A hypothetical example. Here is an example of how Web technology could be used to develop and deploy an internal application. The application's requirement is to display the number of unused vacation days an employee has. Assume that the information itself is stored in Oracle as part of the Human Resources department's SAP application.

First, the HTML page would be laid out using any Web Authoring tool. The resulting file would be loaded into Bluestone's HTML Sapphire/Web software. Then, the Network object browser is used to view all the Oracle tables and the associated columns. After the developer finds the information he's looking for, he binds the HTML element in the form to the corresponding stored procedure that would pull the data from the database.

Then, the developer informs Sapphire of the type of pre-defined template he wishes to use to display the output. Finally, he would use the tool to compile and test the application.

Appendices

Web client/server application development tools

These tools are used by the professional developers to add behavior to forms after a basic HTML document has been designed with an authoring tool. These tools bind corporate databases, legacy systems or flat files to the front-end.

Authoring tools

Authoring tools are specialized word processors and editors that convert or save documents with the appropriate HTML tags. The benefit of these tools are that they are simple to use. A development team can let the end user use MS Word to prototype a user interface, then forward the HTML file back to the IS team. The application developer would then use Sapphire/Web or a tool like it to add the database behavior and test the complete application.

Web database APIs

For on-line commerce to become a reality, an application must be able to insert and delete information from the corporate database over a network. Tools, such as Sapphire/Web, allow a developer to do this, but APIs exist in the market that allow a developer to hand code this function. Hand coding is a time-consuming method, but some people prefer this method of development. A Web database API must be based on standards and available easily over the net for quick access and use.

Firewalls

For deployment of Web technology within a corporation, there is no need for a firewall. Whenever a company connects one of its computers to the Internet, experts strongly recommend that a firewall be used to protect sensitive company information. Without a firewall, all the files on a computer are vulnerable to hackers or others that might attempt to violate security.

Security

Many firms believe that before on-line commerce can really take off, all security issues must be solved. Security is evolving, and within a year, these issues are expected to be moot.

Web service firms

Service firms provide a valuable source of knowledge and experience. These firms can help you build your HomePage, install a firewall or even host your complete Website on the 'Net.

Text search engine firms

Data must be indexed and able to be accessed quickly if it is to become information, and be useful to others. Text search engines allow you to index and then find your data.

Hardware vendors

All major hardware vendors have Internet and Web Server offerings. Many have also gotten into the software and service game. See their HomePages for more information.

Internet access providers

Access providers provide the ability for your firm to connect a physical telecommunication line to the Internet. Once you have been connected via the access provider, they serve as a gateway routing all TCP/IP packets addressed to your site. The more advanced providers can provide additional services.

22

CD-I Developers' Source Guide

Lex van Sonderen

Lucy Lediaev

What Is Digital Video?

General features

Digital video (formerly called *full-motion video*) is an extension to the CD-I specification that adds the capability for playing moving natural pictures on the full screen with associated audio of compact-disc quality. Image quality is equal to or better than VHS. To play digital video, CD-I players need to be equipped with a digital video cartridge. Most base-case CD-I players have an extension slot for this cartridge. There will also be CD-I players with built-in digital video.

Technical features

Digital video uses the MPEG ISO 11172 standard for compression. Digital video is noninterlaced video and can have playback rates of 24, 25, or 30 pictures per second for film, PAL/SECAM, and NTSC source material, respectively. Regardless of the picture rate, digital video can be played back on NTSC and PAL/SECAM systems. Digital video performs temporal-frame-rate conversion without impact on picture size. Aspect-ratio distortion does occur, because PAL/SECAM and NTSC have different aspect ratios. A compatible aspect ratio is loosely defined as one that results in minimal distortion on both PAL/SECAM and NTSC systems.

The maximum picture size depends on the picture rate: 352×288 at 25 Hz or 352×240 at 30 Hz. Short and wide pictures (for example, 704×120) or high and narrow pictures can also be coded.

You can display only a subrectangle of the digital video image, and you can define the position of that rectangle on the CD-I display.

Digital video is displayed in the backdrop plane of CD-I. It is visible only where the two CD-I base-case planes are transparent.

Audio allows bit rates for mono speech of from 4 kbytes per second up to 56 kbytes per second, where 24 kbytes per second subjectively equals stereo CD-quality audio. Digital-video audio is mixed with CD-I base-case audio.

A typical full-screen video stream uses 146 kbytes per second. The size of a video stream is determined by the picture quality, the picture size, and the picture rate. One can have multiple video and audio streams, but only one of each can be active at a time. The maximum data stream is 170 kbytes per second.

Digital video allows for the following play modes: forward play; forward slow motion; freeze frame; forward and reverse scan/skip.

How do I make a title using digital video?

To play digital video, you will need an application program. There are three alternative ways of creating that application, depending on the level of inter-activity needed:

1. For simple linear roll-over titles, a production system will be available shortly.

2. OptImage MediaMogul can be extended with plug-ins for lightly interactive titles. Contact OptImage (address, etc., is on p. 22.5) for further information.

3. For more interactive titles, custom programming is necessary. To write custom programs, you will need a C-cross compiler and software libraries. The digital video specification is an extension to the Green Book (Chapter IX); the OptImage Balboa Run-Time System has been extended to take digital video into account.

Production of the needed MPEG data streams occurs in three steps: (1) audio encoding, (2) video encoding, and (3) multiplexing. Audio encoding can be done using software encoders that are sold by CD-I tool developers such as OptImage. Multiplexing is the process of combining the audio and video streams into one MPEG data stream.

Encoding MPEG video is a very computation-intensive task. As of yet there are no adequate desktop solutions that give adequate image quality within an acceptable conversion time. The following companies provide MPEG encoding services:

Leon Silverman
Laser Pacific Media Corporation
809 N. Cahuenga Blvd.
Hollywood, CA 90038
Phone: 1-213-462-6266
Fax: 1-213-960-2195

Bentley Nelson
Pacific Video Resources
2339 Third Street
San Francisco, CA 94107
Phone: 1-415-864-5679
Fax: 1-415-864-2059

Steven Blumenfeld
GTE ImagiTrek
2385 Camino Vida Roble, Ste 200A
Carlsbad, CA 92009
Phone: 1-619-431-8801
Fax: 1-619-431-8755

Klaus Beunk
Valkieser Multi Media
's-Gravelandseweg 80a
1217 EW Hilversum
The Netherlands
Phone: 31-35-23-48-58
Fax: 31-35-23-27-11

Launching CD-I

With the successful launch of CD-I in the United States, Philips is receiving an increasing number of calls from people who are interested in developing CD-I titles. Our goal is to encourage anyone to exploit this exciting new medium, and in the rest of this chapter we attempt to answer basic questions as well as to direct those who are new to CD-I to the many sources of CD-I development hardware, software, and information.

Where can I buy CD-I players and CD-I discs?

Consumers in the United States who want to know where they can buy CD-I discs and/or Philips CD-I players can call the toll-free number of the Philips Consumer Electronics Hotline: 1-800-845-7301.

Where and how can I sell my CD-I consumer titles and ideas?

Philips Interactive Media of America (PIMA). PIMA's primary focus is on the publication of high-quality CD-I titles for the home entertainment market. PIMA enters into a limited number of agreements with other organizations to coproduce home-entertainment and educational titles. Because of the large number of inquiries, we ask that prospective coproducers mail background information to Senior Vice President in charge of Product Development, Sarina Simon. She can be reached at 11111 Santa Monica Blvd., Suite 700, Los Angeles, CA 90025.

When sending your proposals to Ms. Simon, please describe the subject matter for the proposed title in two or three sentences. Because we cannot guarantee confidentiality in the handling of your proposal at this early stage of the proposal process, we advise you not to send a detailed outline or discussion of your ideas. But do provide detailed information on your company (brochures, company background, etc.), its personnel (resumés or biographies), and facilities. Because Ms. Simon receives a large number of proposals, it will be at least three weeks before you get a response. Upon approval of your proposal for further consideration, the next step is a business plan and a mutual confidentiality agreement.

If you are an independent producer seeking distribution of CD-I titles, contact Robert E. Schaulis, Vice President of International Product Management and Distribution, at 11111 Santa Monica Blvd., Suite 400, Los Angeles, CA 90025 (310-444-6627).

As part of PIMA's publishing activity, independent producers are encouraged to seek distribution agreements for their CD-I titles. PIMA establishes and maintains distribution channels in North America. PIMA can also arrange distribution through foreign channels. The procedure for obtaining a distribution agreement with PIMA is outlined in a document entitled *Guidelines for Distribution License Agreements,* which is available upon request from the International Product Management and Distribution office.

How can I make corporate or educational CD-I titles?

CD-I is not a proprietary system; therefore companies or individuals may develop their own CD-I titles. Suppliers of development systems can give assistance in finding complete solutions for CD-I development, and they often can provide courses for authoring and programming, as well as offer support.

Where can I buy CD-I development systems?

Philips Consumer Electronics (PCEC).   PCEC is the supplier of Philips hardware in the United States. This organization provides CD-I development players, and it is very active in the commercial and industrial markets. In addition, PCEC can assist developers in designing and putting together hardware systems. For further information, please contact your regional sales manager:

West coast: John Hill; phone 1-615-521-3101

Central: Jerry Huffman; phone 1-317-841-0224

East coast: John Elicker; phone 1-908-827-8648

Southern: Linda Olsen; phone 1-404-952-0064

OptImage.   OptImage, a Philips joint-venture company, is a major supplier of development systems for CD-I. It has a large catalog of hardware and software tools for CD-I designers and engineers. OptImage also organizes courses and workshops for CD-I authoring and programming. For further information, please contact

OptImage
Attn.: Pam Wilber
1501 50th Street
West Des Moines, IA 50625
Phone: 1-515-222-2073
Fax: 1-515-222-2080
Western region: Barry Horton (1-714-859-9162)

ISG. ISG is a supplier of development systems for CD-I. It has a catalog of hardware and software tools for CD-I developers. ISG specializes in Macintosh-based CD-I engineering systems. For further information please contact, in America,

Interactive Support Group
Attn.: Anne Badger
9420 Topanga Canyon Blvd., Suite 200
Chatsworth, CA 91311
Phone: 1-818-709-7387
Fax: 1-818-709-8160

In Europe:

Attn.: William Vablais
St John's Innovation Centre
Cambridge, United Kingdom, CB4 4WS
44-223-426114
44-223-420015

Script Systems. Script Systems is a supplier of development systems for CD-I. It has a catalog of hardware and software tools for CD-I developers. Script Systems specializes in MS-DOS-based CD-I authoring systems. For further information, please contact, on the East Coast,

Attn.: Jim Bertlesman
The Market Place, Building 5
Manlius, NY 13104
Phone: 1-315-682-8714
Fax: 1-315-682-4730

On the West Coast:

Attn.: Tom Bertlesman
214 Spring Grove Lane
San Rafael, CA 94901
Phone: 1-415-258-9768
Fax: 1-415-258-0673

In Europe:

Attn: Peter Theihzen
Phone: 31 5700 10655
Fax: 31 5700 10621

Where can I get information on CD-I outside of the United States and Canada?

You may contact, in Europe,

Philips Interactive Media Systems U.K.
Attn.: David Ward
Freeland House
Station Road
Dorking
Surrey RH4 1UL
United Kingdom
Phone: 44-306-875777
Fax: 44-306-875789

Philips IMS Authoring Systems
Attn.: Cees van Versendaal
P.O. Box 80002
5600 JB Eindhoven
The Netherlands
Phone: 31-40-736228
Fax: 31-40-734234

In Asia and Australia:

Philips East Asia
Attn.: Frank Pauli
35-1 Sagmiohno 7-chome
Sagamihara
Kanagawa 288
Japan
Phone: 81-427-410255
Fax: 81-427-495094

Philips East Asia
Attn.: Chris Hofland
28th Floor, Hopewell Centre
17 Kennedy Road, Wanchai
Hong Kong
Phone: 852-821-5340
Fax: 852-528-2259

Philips Australia
Attn.: G. Lee
Australia Centre
3 Figtree Drive
Homobush NSW 2140
Australia
Phone: 61-2-7428311
Fax: 61-2-7644060

What tools do I need to produce CD-I titles?

You can make CD-I titles by using an authoring system or by writing custom programming. Authoring is a method for creating an interactive presentation using user-friendly, high-level tools. An authoring system enables the producer to make interactive presentations by integrating thousands of images, hours of sound, partial-screen video clips, and on-screen buttons and controls.

An authoring system consists of a personal computer system (Macintosh or MS-DOS PC), a professional CD-I player, an emulator, and software packages. Usually the video or audio assets are created or captured on the personal computer and then combined on the professional CD-I player. At the present time, one cannot use popular personal-computing authoring packages (for example Macromind Director, ToolBook) to create CD-I presentations; thus, one of the several specific CD-I authoring packages that exist should be used.

For more complex presentations that require greater interactivity and faster execution, custom programming is necessary. Programming for CD-I can be done on a Macintosh, an MS-DOS PC, or a Sun, using a C-cross compiler and software libraries.

What system do I need for CD-I authoring?

The following are guidelines to some of the systems commonly used for CD-I authoring. No specific recommendation or price information is given here, because such information is best provided by the suppliers of the development systems. Before you make any decision as to which system to use, *consult your CD-I development system supplier first.*

Hardware.   Recommended equipment includes

High-end personal computer system

Macintosh II or Quadra, with at least 3 Nubus slots *or*

486-based MS-DOS-compatible PC, running MS-Windows, SCSI interface, and at least 3 empty slots

Lots of storage space

Minimal 2-Gbyte hard-disk space per production

8-mm Exabyte tape drive

Connections.   Recommended equipment includes

Ethernet cards + NFS software

Serial cables

SCSI cables

Professional CD-I player.   Recommended equipment includes

Philips CD-I 605

NTSC/RGB color monitor

Optionally: a low-end monitor to reflect end-user quality on the TV in the living room

Emulator, including software.   Recommended are

Philips CD-I emulator *or*

ISG emulator board for the Macintosh *or*

Script Systems emulator for PC-type systems

Capture and encoding hardware, including software.   We recommend

High-end audio-capture board

High-end video-capture board or scanner

Software.   There is a variety of software applicable to the task of producing a CD-I title.

Authoring

Media Mogul, for the Philips CD-I 605, *or*

Media Showcase, for the Philips CD-I 605, *or*

Designer Work Bench, for MS-DOS

Image and audio conversion

Audio-conversion utilities (ACUs)

Image-conversion utilities (ICUs)

Animation- and movie-conversion utilities

Image and audio conversion and asset management

Media Stockroom, runs on MS-DOS PC under MS-Windows

Audio- and image-editing applications

For example, for Macintosh: Adobe Photoshop, Studio 32, Macromind Director, DigiDesign SoundTools II

File transfer software

To transfer files from Mac or PC to CD-I: OptImage, ISG, or Script Systems

What system do I need for CD-I programming?

The following are guidelines to some of the systems commonly used for CD-I programming in the C programming language. No specific recommendation or price information is given here, because such information is best provided by the suppliers of the development systems. Before making any decision about the systems to use, *consult your CD-I development system supplier first.*

Hardware.   Recommended equipment includes

Computer

High-end personal computer system or workstation

Macintosh II or Quadra with at least 3 Nubus slots *or*

486-based MS-DOS-compatible PC running MS-Windows, SCSI interface, and at least 3 empty slots, *or*

Sun Sparc

Emulator

Philips CD-I emulator *or*

ISG Cassiopee board for the Macintosh *or*

ISG emulator board for the Macintosh *or*

Script Systems emulator board for the PC-type systems

Professional CD-I player

Philips CD-I 605 *or*

ISG Cassiopee board for the Macintosh

NTSC/RGB color monitor

Optionally: a low-end monitor to reflect end-user quality on TV in the living room

Connections

Ethernet cards + NFS software

Serial cables

SCSI cables

Capture and encoding hardware

High-end audio-capture board

High-end video-capture board or scanner

Software.   Recommended software includes

Programming

MPW on Macintosh, SunView on Sun

OS-9 Cross Compiler for Sun, Mac, or PC

OS-9 source-level debugger

ISG X-Link

GNU Cross-compiler on Sun or Mac

OptImage Balboa C Library

ISG C++ Library

Script Systems CD Vista C Library

Image and audio conversion

Audio-conversion utilities (ACUs)

Image-conversion utilities (ICUs)

Audio- and image-editing applications

For instance, for Macintosh: Adobe Photoshop, Studio 32, Macromind Director, DigiDesign SoundTools II

File transfer software

Software to transfer files from Mac or PC to CD-I: OptImage, ISG, or Script Systems

Disc building

OptImage Master/Green *or*

ISG CDL and BD

What is an emulator?

During the development stage of CD-I production, software is continuously tested and run. Because of the specific characteristics of the CD-I medium, the software cannot be run and tested with just a hard disk. In particular, the data delivery, the data rate, and the (slow) access time of the CD need to be taken into account. An emulator is an intelligent, computer-peripheral device with a high-capacity hard disk. During the development stage, a disc image is built onto the hard disk of the emulator. Then, when the emulator is switched to the emulation mode, it behaves in the same manner as a real CD player. The alternative would be to burn a CD-I disc for each test run, which is slower and more expensive.

Do I need a CD-recorder?

Usually, a CD-recorder is not required for development of CD-I titles. Typically an emulator is used, and only when the disc image is completely finished is it sent to a mastering house to be reproduced in compact-disc form. If one regularly needs to make a very small series of CDs (1–10), a CD-recorder can be useful.

What is "the Green Book"?

The *"Compact Disc–Interactive Full Functional Specification"* is better known as "the Green Book." The Green Book is the official standard for CD-I-compliant hardware and software. It is coauthored by Philips and Sony and is available only to official licensees of the Compact Disc–Interactive standard. To become a licensee, contact Philips, Sony, or the CD-I Association.

What are the technical specifications for a CD-I player?

A CD-I player plays all CD-I titles, CD digital audio (CD-DA), CD+Graphics, Photo CD, and CD-ROM-XA bridge discs.

Memory

2 banks of 512 kbytes RAM

8 kbytes nonvolatile RAM

650 Mbytes CD-ROM-XA

Audio

CD-DA: max. 72 minutes

ADPCM level A: max. 144 minutes, two channels, hi-fi quality

ADPCM level B: max. 288 minutes, two channels, normal quality

ADPCM level C: max. 576 minutes, two channels, speech quality

ADPCM audio can be played directly from disk, with negligible computer interaction, or can be loaded into memory to be played with precise timing.

Video

Resolution: 384×240 when displayed on NTSC, 384×280 when displayed on PAL

2 8-bit video planes

Background plane in 1 of 8 colors

16×16 hardware cursor in 1 of 8 colors

Video effects: transparency, mattes, color-keying, pixel-hold, mosaic

Programmable video processor to execute video commands on a field and line basis. Commands include: change CLUT; change coding method; change transparency factor; define video memory address, etc.

Each plane can have multiple image-coding methods (video modes) selectable on a per-line basis

Image-coding methods

CLUT4: 16 colors out of 16 million, double horizontal resolution (768 pixels)

CLUT7: 128 colors out of 16 million

DYUV: 16 million colors, for continuous-tone images

RL3: 8 colors out of 16 million, hardware run-length compression, double horizontal resolution (768 pixels)

RL7: 128 colors out of 16 million, hardware run-length compression. Note: DYUV and RL video modes do not allow direct access to the value of an individual pixel.

Two more video modes exist that are rarely used:

CLUT8: 256 colors out of 16 million; only possible in one plane, the other plane can only be DYUV; restricting compared to CLUT7.

RGB555: 32,768 colors, uses both planes, and requires twice as much data per screen; restricting and slow compared to the other video modes.

Processor

68K family, equivalent to 8-MHz 68000

Operating system

CD-RTOS: OS-9 with CD-I extensions. Lightweight, real-time, multitasking operating system

Notes

No responsibility will be taken by Philips or the authors for the information presented herein. For comments, additions, corrections, or if you have remaining questions, contact

Lex van Sonderen
Manager, Knowledge Transfer
Philips Interactive Media of America
11050 Santa Monica Blvd.
Los Angeles, CA 90025
Phone: 1-310-444-6689
Fax: 1-310-477-4953
Internet: lex@aimla.com
CompuServe: 71552,2204

23

Corporate Guide to Optical Publishing

Kurt Mueller

Introduction

In virtually every industry, leading corporations are looking at CD-ROM (Compact Disc, Read Only Memory) as a powerful business tool. For example:

- A leading computer manufacturer significantly improves the delivery of documentation, training materials, and maintenance releases by bundling a CD-ROM drive in its latest product line.

- A Baby Bell company publishes 300 telephone directories—covering every published listing in a six-state area on a single CD-ROM disc, with room to spare.

- A farm equipment supplier significantly improves its dealer communications by publishing its parts and price catalogs on CD-ROM.

- A major software company provides better technical support by distributing technical bulletins and help-desk information on CD-ROM, increasing the effectiveness of telephone support and distinguishing its products in the process.

- A U.S. government agency converts its 20,000-page loose-leaf Procedures manual to CD-ROM. Monthly distribution to field offices saves time and reduces staff requirements.

- A major oil company publishes product and competitive information on CD-ROM for use by sales representatives with portable CD-ROM readers.

Why have these organizations made major commitments to CD-ROM? Why has there been so much talk about CD-ROM lately, particularly when the technology has been available for over seven years? This chapter will attempt to answer these questions.

CD-ROM and Competitive Advantage

There are two reasons for the surge in popularity of CD-ROM. First, technological developments have substantially lowered the barriers to cost-effective use of CD-ROM. In the eighties, CD-ROM technology was still too expensive and applications too difficult to develop for many corporations. These conditions have changed dramatically. A technology that once was only potentially beneficial is now affordable, easy to use, and widely employed.

Second, CD-ROM has demonstrated clear benefits for business. More than 5000 CD-ROM titles are now in print for a broad range of applications, including over 3000 commercial products. One CD-ROM can hold the equivalent of 1500 floppy disks, 250,000 pages of text, or 12,000 scanned images, at an incremental media cost of only $2 per disc. This tremendous data-storage capacity and low cost have led many people to focus on the media cost savings alone.

Yet even greater benefits of the technology lie in the cost reduction and revenue generation it provides by delivering products and services more efficiently. CD-ROM technology is a powerful tool that can

- Improve sales performance
- Lower cost of sales
- Improve product and service quality
- Differentiate products in the marketplace
- Strengthen third-party distribution channels
- Dramatically improve customer service

For companies looking for a competitive edge, these are compelling benefits. Three areas are emerging as key competitive advantages for business in the nineties: knowledge, time, and information. CD-ROM can enhance improvement activities in these areas, and often serves as the core of a competitive solution.

The three areas of competitive advantage

1. Knowledge. With product lines expanding, boutique manufacturing operations, and increasing pressure to customize products, businesses today are faced with the challenge of having to provide a bewildering array of product possibilities and options. Retail, distributor, and support personnel are increasingly expected to attain more in-depth knowledge about a broader product line. Often, simply finding the correct information is difficult. CD-ROM can not only provide correct and current product information, it can assist in training personnel in the sale and use of products as well.

Newly emerging self-contained, portable CD-ROM and multimedia players are revolutionizing the sales process. Each salesperson can now carry an electronic reference that includes complete product catalogs, specifications, sample product applications, and sales and marketing promotions. Sales training time for complex products is reduced, a consistent and professionally prepared product presentation is delivered, and customer questions can be answered on the spot. The competitive advantage gained by organizations employing these technologies is substantial.

2. Time.   Decisions are being made in increasingly complex environments, where any delay can mean lost revenues and customers. Measured through the parameters of market presence or response, time is emerging as a key competitive advantage.

CD-ROM can assist in providing up-to-date information in a readily searchable format. Precious time isn't wasted searching for pertinent facts, and all appropriate details can be quickly assembled at once.

A major manufacturer of industrial heating and cooling systems identified a lower response time in the answering of product questions as a key competitive advantage. A target of one minute or less to respond to any customer question about any of the company's products established the overriding objective. Given that there were over 60 product catalogs dating back more than 50 years, a complete reengineering of the company's information systems was required. The reengineering included CD-ROM delivery of product information. Rather than using information technology simply as a productivity enhancement tool, it was identified as a way to reengineer the company's customer communications.

3. Information.   Corporate America today captures significantly more data than can be integrated for decision making. Distilling this data into a set of information useful for guiding the business requires both a business and technical perspective. The information challenge isn't about how much data can be captured, but about how to make the best decisions with the available data. CD-ROM is used to provide databases from which knowledge can be extracted by managers using sophisticated access software and "what-if" analysis.

CD-ROM Technology Today

A technology takes off

CD-ROM has been a fortuitous technological development. It emerged through the coincidental convergence of several developments: the appearance of CD audio in the mass-market entertainment industry; the proliferation and standardization of personal computers in business; the need for information providers of all types to find alternatives to distributing increasingly higher volumes of information on paper.

Over 3,000 Commercial CD-ROM Titles

Structured Data	Text
• Bibliographic Data	• Books
• Corporate Directories	• Government Regulations
• Credit Data	• Legal/Tax Information
• Financial Data	• Loose-leaf Publications
• Geographical Data	• Manuals
• Patent Information	• Medical Information
• People Directories	• Reference Collections
• Statistics	• Standards Information

Over 2,000 Corporate CD-ROM Applications

Structured Data	Text
• COM Replacement	• Audit Procedures
• Customer Data	• Contracts
• Forms Catalogs	• Engineering Standards
• Inventory	• Maintenance Releases
• Monthly Statements	• Policy Manuals
• Parts Catalogs	• Research
• Purchasing Data	• Technical Documentation
• Service Orders/Reports	• Training Manuals
• Spec Sheets	
• Transaction Histories	

Figure 23.1   CD-ROM titles today.

CD-ROM derives its low price and manufacturing availability from the consumer audio marketplace. CD audio is the most successful consumer electronics product in history, and it has created a stable worldwide standard and manufacturing base. The success of CD audio has fostered spinoff technologies such as CD-ROM.

CD-ROM is well on its way to becoming the medium of choice for electronic distribution. Today there are over 3000 commercial CD-ROM titles and in excess of 2000 corporate in-house titles.* Figure 23.1 illustrates representative subject areas.

Besides technological advantages, CD-ROM owes its success to three key advantages it provides to users: multimedia, multiplatform, and multiple language applications.

Multimedia.   The term *multimedia* refers to the delivering of text, data, graphics, audio, and video to end users. CD-ROM facilitates delivery of all of these information types in an integrated package. Information sets can be accompanied by audio and video clips describing significant areas. For example a service manual could contain, along with the written text and diagrams, a video or animation sequence showing a critical procedure. Multimedia will play an increasingly important role in the way information is distributed and

---

*Source: Infotech.

used in the nineties. Because multimedia presentations and interactive sessions require significant amounts of storage space for digitized images, sound, and video, CD-ROM is uniquely positioned to become the medium of choice for these new information formats.

Multiplatform. The term *multiplatform* refers to the use of one disc in different computer platforms. A formal CD-ROM standard, developed by an ad hoc industry group known as High Sierra, was approved by the International Standards Organization (ISO) in 1987. By laying out the CD-ROM files in ISO 9660 format, a publisher ensures that the CD-ROM will play on any standard CD drive attached to a computer with appropriate software. The ISO 9660 standard was developed to be operating-system-independent. If access software that provides for multiplatform support is employed, a correctly formatted CD-ROM disc can be used in any of a number of computer environments: PC, Macintosh, UNIX, and others. This has allowed CD-ROM producers to publish discs not just for the PC but for whatever workstation is on the end user's desk. CD-ROM can now replace paper, because it's accessible on every desktop.

Multiple languages. The term *multilingual* usually implies a user interface that contains operations, hints, and help-text in different user-selected languages. An initialization parameter determines the start-up language to be displayed, with an option for the user to change the operating language interactively. The content of the CD-ROM often is in only one language, although a number of emerging applications include multiple versions of the source content in different languages. Multilingual applications help to circumvent communication and training issues for international organizations.

The Software Challenge

A CD-ROM disc often contains 100 times more information than a typical personal-computer database, but the rate at which the CD-ROM drive can get to various locations on the disc is at least 10 times slower than a magnetic disk. The challenge for CD-ROM retrieval software is to gather a much greater volume of information quickly, despite an inherently slower hardware technology.

To create applications for CD-ROM, two kinds of software are required: software that helps the developer to build and prepare an application to be put onto the disc (known as *authoring software*), and software that allows the user to retrieve the information from the disc through his/her desktop computer (commonly referred to as *retrieval software*).

Because of CD-ROM's large capacity for data and its slow access speed, software originally designed for magnetic media is ineffective when applied to optical media. CD-ROM software must be optimized to minimize disc access. There are now several vendors offering software that has been optimized for optical media, and the best of these can equal or exceed magnetic media performance even while searching several hundred megabytes of data.

CD-ROM drives are increasingly attached to computers other than DOS-based PCs, such as Windows, Macintosh, and UNIX machines. The newest generation of CD-ROM development systems allows the development of discs on one platform that can then be accessed from a variety of hardware platforms and network environments. This new breed of software is often referred to as *multiplatform retrieval software.*

These next-generation systems increasingly will be required to prepare and deliver multimedia presentations in addition to data and text applications. The software challenges of the nineties will include not simply the delivery of multimedia but the integration of multimedia objects with corporate information collections, and the delivery of those integrated databases at exceedingly high performance levels on a variety of computer platforms.

CD-ROM advances—more for less

These software improvements are among the most important developments to change the immediate outlook for cost-effective use of CD-ROM. Five years ago, the creation of a single CD-ROM application through a service bureau cost from $50,000 to $100,000. For less money today, corporations can install a complete internal CD-ROM publishing capability, including both the software and the premastering hardware. Installations such as these are capable of turning out more than 50 applications per year.

Here are some other advances:

- The cost of mastering and replicating 100 discs has fallen from $5000 to $1500. Incremental discs can be purchased for less than $2 each.
- Capacity has increased from 550 Mbytes to 700 + Mbytes per disc.
- Stand-alone drive prices have fallen from $1500 to under $500. Half-height drives for IBM PCs are available for under $400. Volume purchases yield even lower prices.
- Recordable CD-ROM systems now available support complete in-house production of CD-ROMs for low-volume or security-sensitive applications. Blank media in low quantities start under $30, with cost savings for volume purchases.

Real Problems, Real Solutions

CD-ROM is solving real business problems today. Let's look at a few examples.

Problem.   Supporting a rapidly expanding product line cost-effectively.

Solution.   Take a cue from several computer manufacturers and improve the effectiveness of sales and service personnel by publishing broad-based and/or constantly changing product information on CD-ROM. This enables customers to help themselves when they might otherwise have called for support. Not only is the need for direct staff involvement reduced, but customer satisfaction is improved.

Problem.   Supporting a product in the dealer channel.

   Solution.   Leading companies, from farm-equipment suppliers to airlines, are taking advantage of this technology in the competitive dealer environment. Comprehensive catalogs for all products, including prices and specifications, are distributed on CD-ROM. This makes it easier for dealers to locate the right product.

Problem.   Selling products internationally without getting snarled in regulations and rising administrative costs.

   Solution.   Follow the lead of an international consumer products manufacturer operating in more than 50 countries. It has converted import/export databases to CD-ROM. The system reduces costly mistakes made by personnel, who must search among 50,000 products for shipping codes and regulations, and saves over $2 million per year.

Problem.   Improving sales training and efficiency.

   Solution.   Adopt the strategy of a leading oil company that puts product and competitive information on CD-ROM and equips field salespeople with portable CD-ROM systems. Salespeople use the systems to identify the correct product and point out competitive advantages.

Problem.   Increasing the productivity of professional staff.

   Solution.   Learn from a major drug company that scanned chemical-analysis reports to create a database of more than 100 years of research. Previously the information had been accessible only in paper files, and was therefore seldom used. The company has recovered the cost of the effort by eliminating the cost of duplicating previously performed tests.

   A summary of the potential benefits of CD-ROM information integration and distribution is shown in Fig. 23.2.

CD-ROM and other distribution technologies

Many years ago, the computer revolution promised the elimination of paper. We now know that the computer is the most voracious consumer of paper since the printing press. Paper has distinct advantages as an information distribution medium: it is completely portable, requires no additional hardware for access, and updates are simple (although incorporation of update pages can often be complex and time-consuming). Paper also has disadvantages: it's cumbersome, hard to search, and environmentally unfriendly.

   Virtually every large corporation and most small businesses are now producing, editing, and updating information electronically. The natural next

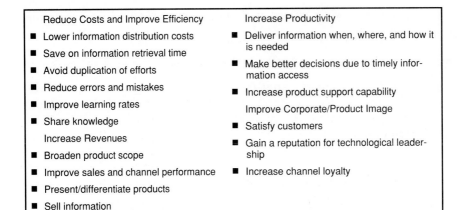

Reduce Costs and Improve Efficiency	Increase Productivity
■ Lower information distribution costs	■ Deliver information when, where, and how it is needed
■ Save on information retrieval time	■ Make better decisions due to timely information access
■ Avoid duplication of efforts	
■ Reduce errors and mistakes	■ Increase product support capability
■ Improve learning rates	Improve Corporate/Product Image
■ Share knowledge	■ Satisfy customers
Increase Revenues	■ Gain a reputation for technological leadership
■ Broaden product scope	
■ Improve sales and channel performance	■ Increase channel loyalty
■ Present/differentiate products	
■ Sell information	

Figure 23.2   The strategic benefits of CD-ROM.

step in this process is electronic distribution, and the benefits are not simply improved access and increased efficiency. For efficiency, cost, and environmental reasons, corporations and government agencies alike are embarking on significant efforts to reduce the amount of paper produced and distributed.

The general term *electronic distribution* embraces telecommunications and local-area networks; magnetic, floppy, and cartridge disks; computer output to microfiche; facsimile; and CD-ROM. Each is appropriate for different types of information and different distribution objectives. Telecommunications is best for smaller amounts of information that have a short life-span or must be updated frequently. The significant cost of creating and maintaining a telecommunications capability, and the inherent bandwidth limitations, reserve this alternative primarily for high-priority information.

Magnetic media is most appropriate for small databases requiring fairly frequent updates. Much of the information created by work groups on local-area networks will be stored magnetically. As this information accumulates, storage becomes increasingly unwieldy.

Computer-output microfiche and microfilm are used for high-frequency distribution to multiple locations, and for information archiving when search requirements are minimal. Although these are mature technologies, this technology isn't seeing wide use today due to dissatisfaction with both the media and the delivery system. Today there are fewer than one million microfilm readers, as compared to more than 100 million business and personal computers.

Facsimile is ideal for fast delivery of small amounts of paper-based information.

CD-ROM has broad areas of application, due to the following unique advantages:

- It features digital-based media capable of delivering text, data, graphics, sound, and/or video.

- It is compatible with personal computers and local-area networks.

- It can be shared over both local- and wide-area networks.

- Information can be exported to other computers and software programs.

- It offers very high capacity at a significantly lower cost than other distribution alternatives.

- It has a searching, sorting, and retrieval capability superior to paper, computer-output microfiche,* microfilm, and on-line.†

- The cost for volume distribution is low.

CD-ROM has certain limitations that make it inappropriate for some applications and not a viable substitute for traditional storage:

- It is read-only, with no ability to modify the data on disc. However there are some emerging technological approaches that will allow for the appending of data to an already existing data set on CD-ROM.

- A mastering step is required to create the master and replicas. Mastering costs $1500 and takes three days, with faster turnaround available for an extra charge. CD-recordable technology allows in-house mastering for low volumes of discs, but the blank disc is more expensive than mastered CD replicas.

- The slow speed and large capacity of optical discs require special software to provide application performance comparable to magnetic disk.

- The drive must be added to the typical desktop workstation at a cost of $400 to $800. Many of the latest generation of PCs now come with CD-ROM drive already installed.

CD-ROM's strengths make it most appropriate for applications with any of the following requirements (Fig. 23.3):

- Information distributed to multiple locations

- Mixed text, data, graphic, and/or audio/video information

- Large data volumes

- Fast access time

- Extensive searching, sorting, and retrieval

A Value Multiplier for Information Systems

Four current information-management technologies are emerging as high priorities for most organizations over the next decade: electronic publishing,

---

*Com fiche generally is searchable only on a single field. CD-ROM software permits every field to be indexed and searched in multiple ways.

†CD-ROM information retrieval is 3 to 5 times faster than on-line retrieval for large-volume databases.

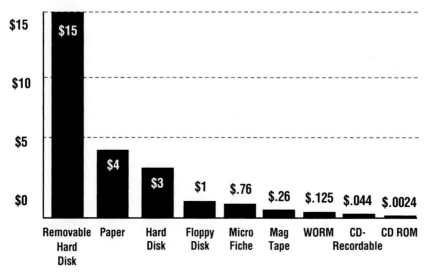

Figure 23.3 Cost per megabyte.

local-area networking, client-server architectures, and transaction processing. CD-ROM can broaden the application of these systems and enhance their value to the corporation.

Electronic publishing

To remain competitive, businesses that produce large volumes of paper-based information are moving to electronic publishing. Various types of information such as text, data, and graphics, can be combined electronically, saving substantial time in revising, reformatting, and producing a document. These advantages are great as far as they go, but usually they stop just short of distribution. Converting electronic information to a nonelectronic format when there are more than 25 million potential electronic readers on the desks of corporate America does not make sense for many applications. This is a large area for cost savings and productivity improvement.

Local-area networks and work-group computing

The CD-ROM standards were established with networks as an expected requirement. The ISO 9660 standard incorporates the basic hardware and media specifications required to make a CD-ROM network compatible. Once a network has been equipped with drives and appropriate software, virtually any CD-ROM disc—assuming it has the appropriate network license agreements and meets the ISO 9660 standard—can be shared on the local-area network. Each attached drive provides over 700 Mbytes of read-only information to the network nodes. By placing one or more CD-ROM drives on each local-area network or in each department, an organization provides ready

Service
- Documentation
- Maintenance Releases
- Service Call Reports
- Trouble Shooting Guides
- Maintenance Histories
- Parts Lists
- Inventory
- Warranty Listings

Marketing and Sales
- Catalogs
- Specification Sheets
- Parts Lists
- Prices
- Inventory
- Purchase History

Operations
- Inventory
- Parts Lists
- Stock Number Cross Reference
- Bill of Materials
- Order Data
- Engineering Standards
- Parts Where Used
- Facility and Equipment Registers

Procurement
- Inventory
- Bill of Materials
- Cumulative Order Data
- Vendor Cross Reference Data
- Index of Suppliers

Research and Development
- Research Reports
- Standards Information
- Bibliographic Databases

Figure 23.4 Work-group information requirements.

access to internal information and to externally purchased information relevant to that department or work group. Examples of typical work-group information requirements are shown in Fig. 23.4.

Downsizing and client-server architectures

Corporations and government agencies are rapidly replacing centrally located, monolithic information systems with distributed architectures. Driving forces include high maintenance on centrally located mainframe systems, long lead times on new application developments, and the increasing need for organizations to provide flexible and responsive information systems. Client-server architectures make possible a decentralized information enterprise, allowing local control and maintenance of information pertinent to the work group.

CD-ROM is often a vital component of downsizing efforts. While a new decision-support application for a centrally located information system may require lengthy lead time, extracting a copy of the information, committing it to CD-ROM, and using fourth-generation access tools for decision support is proving successful. This newly emerging use of CD-ROM is helping to accelerate many corporation's downsizing efforts.

Transaction-processing systems

Some of the best examples of information as a competitive tool are found in those industries that have been transformed by electronic transaction processing such as banking, brokerage, and travel. Other examples include the pharmaceutical and auto parts industries, and a variety of other retail businesses where transaction information is essential to the successful operation of the business.

The leaders in transaction processing are now taking the next step in strategic information delivery: CD-ROM. Purchasing activity in corporate and government organizations is converted to CD-ROM for trend analysis. Retailers in the auto, trucking, and appliance replacement-parts business are using CD-ROM to find the right part and make the sale.

Using CD-ROM systems to augment point-of-transaction information, improve customer service, and boost sales is widely applicable to other industries. The two technologies work in partnership: on-line transaction processing delivers accurate and time-sensitive information, while large volumes of related but less time-sensitive information are delivered on CD-ROM.

How CD-ROM Can Benefit Your Organization

Existing content

CD-ROM can have a significant impact on an organization's bottom line, but identifying where in an organization to start with CD-ROM applications can be difficult. Most organizations that see an immediate impact with CD-ROM base their initial applications on preexisting content. CD-ROM is used to improve and expand existing information sources. As these organizations integrate CD-ROM into their business systems, they introduce new content sources to further leverage the investment in CD-ROM development platforms and readers.

Information used and produced

To determine if optical information distribution is appropriate for an organization, it's appropriate to analyze the sources and uses of information. One recommended approach divides the organization's major activities between serving the customer and supporting infrastructure. Figure 23.5 illustrates a typical manufacturing company's primary and infrastructure activities. For each major activity, the information produced and the information used in performing critical functions is identified.

CD-ROM applications portfolio

After the information used and produced has been arranged according to priority, it can be organized into an applications portfolio for the organization. The applications portfolio identifies high-return activities by classifying information mission/activity-critical, management/support, and archival. CD-ROM will have the greatest impact on mission- and activity-critical information. Figure 23.6 illustrates the applications portfolio for an insurance firm.

Primary Activities	Operations	Marketing & Sales	Service	Customer
Information Used	Orders Engineering Standards Purchasing Information	Inventory Orders Parts Lists Design Specifications Market Information Sales Information Inventory	Training Parts Lists Customer Information Inventory	Documentation Maintenance Parts Catalogs

Information Produced	Parts Lists
	Inventory
	Ship to Lists
	Bill of Materials
	Parts Where Used
	Facility &
	  Equipment Registers
		Parts Catalogs
		Customer Database
		Prospect Database
		Purchase Histories
		Spec Sheets
		Pricing
		Contracts
			Service Call
			  Reports
			Trouble-
			  Shooting Guides
			Maintenance
			  History
			Training
			Service Orders
			Warranty
			  Listings
				Warranty
				  Information
				Product
				  Improvements
				Service Requests
				Customer
				  Information
				Orders

Infrastructure Activities	Research & Development	Purchasing	Human Resources	Financial & Admin.

Information Used	External Research
	Patent Information
	Standards Information
	Bibliographic Research
		Inventory
		Orders
		Bill of Materials
		Vendor Information
		Price Lists
		Product Information
			Government
			  Regulations
			Recruiting
			  Information
				Accounting
				  Standards
				Government
				  Regulations
				Accounting
				  Input
				Budget Input

Information Produced	Internal Research
	Engineering Standards
		On Order Reports
		Vendor Information
		Product Information
		Price Lists
			Training
			Manuals
			Personnel
			Records
				Policy &
				  Procedure
				General Audit
				  & Record
				  Retention
				Budget
				  Information
				Accounting
				  Information

Figure 23.5   Information used and produced.

This applications planning process results in a list of high-priority applications in which CD-ROM distribution yields substantial benefits. This application portfolio becomes the focal point in the technology acquisition process. Those applications that will serve as prototypes to test the technology warrant additional planning, so as to create a complete profile of the user, the information, and the anticipated benefits.

Value Multiplier	Agency Info	Marketing & Sales	Operations
Electronic Publishing		Renewal & Policy Changes	
Database Publishing		Policy Holders File	Claim Payment History
Product & Service Info	Rate Books	Rate Books	
Policy & Standards Info	Policy Manuals		Cumulative Policy Register
Customer & Transaction Info		Renewal & Policy Changes	Transaction Register

Activity Critical

Management Support

Archival

Figure 23.6   CD-ROM applications portfolio—insurance

Multimedia applications portfolio

The term *multimedia* typically implies adding new content through additional data types (such as audio and video) to existing applications. Adding multimedia is reasonable only when it provides significant productivity or communications improvement. Starting with existing content is recommended, as multimedia production costs can quickly accumulate. As with CD-ROM applications, those selected for development should be the high-value, activity-critical applications in an organization.

As with the CD-ROM applications portfolio, a portfolio of multimedia applications will pinpoint those areas in which applications development will have the greatest impact. Figure 23.7 illustrates a representative multimedia applications portfolio.

It's important to note that as of today multimedia delivery is in its infancy. Hardware, software, and data standards are just emerging. While traditional CD-ROM data types (data, text, and graphics) have arrived at platform-neutral standards, multimedia sources, such as audio and video, have not. Today a CD-ROM application with traditional content can be portable across

	Operations	Marketing & Sales	Service
Multimedia Publishing		Product Catalog with Sound or Video	Tech Doc. with Sound
Multimedia Database	Employee Databases		Parts Catalog with Sound
Multimedia Presentations	Management Presentations	Sales Presentations	
Multimedia Training	Personnel Training		Service Training
Multimedia Sales Systems		Multimedia Kiosks	

Figure 23.7   Multimedia applications portfolio.

numerous end-user computer platforms (assuming that appropriate multi-platform software has been employed). A multimedia application must be designed for a specific computer platform.

Selecting the Right CD-ROM Approach

Once CD-ROM has been identified as a viable technology given existing requirements, the next step is to determine the best approach to developing applications. This entails both a technical and business evaluation. As with most computer applications, software is the key component. Before considering the business options, it's important to understand the match of data type to software support.

Matching content with software

When evaluating CD-ROM application software, the type of information supported becomes critical. A brief explanation of the key information types—structured data, text, graphics, audio, and video—is provided next.

Structured data.   Structured data is the most prevalent data type on CD-ROM. Examples of structured data are information from computer databases, bibliographies, directories, catalogs, and numeric data (as illustrated in Fig. 23.1). Structured information may contain text fields, but unlike full text, structured data does not have to be exclusively in the form of sentences, paragraphs, and chapters. It can also be partially or entirely in phrases or fields. In a parts catalog, for example, the part name and description fields would use a classic keyword text retrieval. The part-number-, model-, year-, price-, and date-issued fields would utilize numeric- and date-range searching. Queries from all fields can be combined with boolean logic to find unique "and," "or," or "not" related sets of information. With structured data, an index file is created for each field, but developers may elect to index only fields of interest. Because the records are arranged in structured order, index searching with structured data is normally faster and returns less irrelevant information.

Text.   Text includes information derived from books, journals, reports, and documentation. Textual information often is structured by an outline for browsing purposes. Users can select chapters, sections, and headings as convenient access points, provided they know that the material of interest is located within that part of the text.

Keyword searches provide another way of accessing text. Users can find information when its location is not obvious, or when its occurrence is so frequent that looking through a book index becomes tedious or impractical. Key terms may be combined to find unique "and," "or," and "not" related documents. The leading text systems offer proximity searching (word A within 10 words of word B); truncation (entering a root word retrieves all variations);

and numeric-range searching. Phonetic searching and index browsing also are offered on some systems.

Many text-retrieval systems are enhancing search capabilities through the addition of hypertext. Hypertext describes different ways of linking related items to each other. In its simplest form, known as *sideways browsing,* the user selects a displayed word or phrase and with a single keystroke finds all documents that contain that word. More sophisticated systems search for related terms as well, or provide for item-linking created by the publisher or user.

Graphics.   Graphics includes pictures, charts, illustrations, and page images. These can exist as bitmapped images or structured graphics (vector). Graphics normally are associated with either structured data (such as a part catalog with part diagrams) or text (such as a maintenance manual with illustrations).

Some of the most common types of graphics found in CD-ROM products today are bitmapped page images. A scanner is used to capture an entire document page as a grid of black-and-white pixels. Text as well as drawings, pictures, and tables are represented as part of the same image. Captured this way, the text is not machine-readable and therefore not searchable. Only the whole page can be indexed and accessed. This approach is useful when the arrangement of the text on the page is complex and meaningful, when graphics appear with regularity, and when the user can find the desired page by means of a keyword or hierarchical index that points to the page image. The ability to integrate bitmapped images provides a general-purpose mechanism for incorporating a wide range of image types into optical applications. It is preferable to choose software with at least this capability. Vector graphics, prevalent in some technical-documentation applications, are supported by only a limited number of CD-ROM software products. Most CD-ROM software currently handles black-and-white, but some systems handle color. Color graphics are a key ingredient of multimedia applications.

Audio.   Audio includes voice, music, and sound clips. While the CD disc was originally developed for audio, the use of audio on CD-ROM is relatively new. Hardware and format standards are just now emerging, and often are computer-platform-specific. Developers who choose to add audio content to CD-ROM applications today must select from several emerging standards.

Video.   Video can range from animation sequences to full-screen, 30-frame-per-second display. Animation sequences usually are generated with a computer graphics package, while video is typically sampled from videotape or videodisc. Using CD-ROM for video is also new and immature. Hardware and media standards for rudimentary animation, much less video, are just emerging, and several standards are competing.

Many CD-ROM applications use graphics, audio, and video, and are developed with authoring software optimized for video, graphics, and sound, as opposed to data and text. Multimedia applications that also require sophisticated data- and text-searching must be merged with these multimedia "front-ends."

Because standards have not emerged for multimedia delivery, adding multimedia content to a CD-ROM title today typically limits the title to a specific computer platform. Some publishers elect to replicate the multimedia information on the CD-ROM, producing multimedia content specific to each target platform. This option requires substantial space on the disc for the multimedia objects.

Application development options

The business alternatives for developing CD-ROM applications range from complete in-house development to complete service-bureau contracting. Figure 23.8 illustrates some of the tradeoffs. However, the right approach for your organization also will depend on the software development path selected. A discussion of the four common development paths follows.

1. In-house software development. Writing customized CD-ROM software is the least popular option, because of the high development and maintenance costs. Keeping custom products updated in a rapidly changing multiplatform industry is also difficult. Many of the commercial publishers who opted to write their own software in the mid-eighties are now abandoning this approach and licensing software from vendors focused on multiplatform CD-ROM software development.

In those cases where the software developed in-house has been successful, the product typically was written for a single application of limited scope and duration. Unfortunately, when additional applications emerge, the original software frequently cannot be readily adapted or modified. Consequently the development process must begin all over again.

As a result, writing custom software is almost never cheaper than licensing. The cost of writing a simple program for CD-ROM access with documentation is a minimum of two person-years of senior programmer time. The best

	Services	In-House
Short Term Issues:	Prove Concept Overcome Data Prep Ensure Optimal Launch Learn from First Project	Data Availability Staff Availability Systems Availability Up Front $$ Availability
Long Term Issues:	Technology Infrastructure Keep Expense Variable Assignable Responsibility Insure Technical Response Avoid Up Front $$	Internalize Learning Curve Development Close to Users Lower Per Application Costs Increase Enhancement Control Avoid Priority Problems

Figure 23.8 Services or in-house development.

packages available today represent at least 10 times that much investment in programmer time, and their developers have greater resources to add features and enhancements.

2. Commercial software.   Over 20 commercial CD-ROM software products are available today for building databases and retrieving information from those databases. These packages range from simple and inexpensive text-only packages, to highly flexible "tool kits" for programmers, to multifunction authoring systems.

Organizations developing CD-ROM titles have several options. While the authoring software and retrieval engine must be acquired from the same vendor, there are various ways in which the user interface can be developed. Most (but not all) CD-ROM development systems provide a "standard" user interface. This interface is performance-tuned to the retrieval engine, and should permit substantial customizing without programming.

Some advanced systems allow development of custom user interfaces by writing software. Dividing the retrieval software into user-interface and retrieval-engine is a useful differentiation—it allows corporations that wish to develop highly customized user interfaces to capitalize on the advanced technology available in CD-ROM-based retrieval engines. This approach involves more time and personnel than a standard user interface, but results in a custom product tailored to the organization's needs. Figure 23.9 illustrates the tradeoffs involved in user-interface development.

User-interface development systems are emerging that attach to retrieval engines through linking mechanisms such as Dynamic Linked Libraries in Microsoft Windows. These allow CD-ROM developers to attach a third-party user interface to a CD-ROM retrieval engine, but generally require some programming. With the increasing popularity of client-server applications, development systems that support this architectural approach are expected to gain popularity in the future.

The PC software industry has produced several text-retrieval products not originally designed for CD-ROM. While many of these offer good-to-excellent

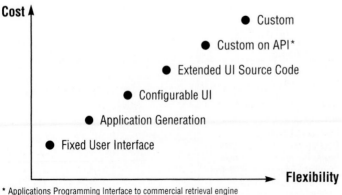

* Applications Programming Interface to commercial retrieval engine

Figure 23.9   Application development approaches.

Type of Search	CD-ROM Software	Typical Text Retrieval
Keyword	X	X
Wildcard - Trailing Truncation	X	X
Wildcard - Leading Truncation	X	
Wildcard - Within Word	X	
Multiple Wildcards Per Word	X	
Phonetic	X	
Line/Entry	X	
Numerical	X	X
Vector	X	
Date	X	
Binary	X	
Pop-Up Browse of Any Index	X	
Stopword Lists	Many	1
Cross Reference Search	X	
Adjacency - Word Level	X	Maybe*
Adjacency - Sentence Level	X	
Adjacency - Field Level	X	
Order Required	X	
Order Not Required	X	
Boolean and Wildcards	X	
Boolean and Adjacency	X	
Multiple Search Screens	X	
Encryption/Password Protection	X	
Graphics - Link to File	X	Maybe**
Graphics - Decompress & Display	X	
Graphics - Zoom, Size & Pan	X	

 * If there is any adjacency it is probably slow and limited. True adjacency
   requires complex indexing of the location of every word in the file. To avoid
   this, low-end software simply searches for all occurrences and then checks
   each occurrence to locate occurrences together. This is very slow, especially
   on optical media.
** Most PC software has no graphics display functions and simply allows a link
   to an external graphics file. Programs which display graphics often don't
   zoom and size images, making it difficult to read detail on most PC screens.

Figure 23.10   CD-ROM software vs. low-end text-management
software.

support for small collections of text stored on magnetic disk, they may be
inadequate for CD-ROM. Some of the most important differences between
mission-critical retrieval software and these low-end packages lie in the
range, flexibility, and sophistication of the searches that may be performed.
Without more powerful searching it's difficult to capture the needed information without being overwhelmed by unneeded material as well. Figure 23.10
illustrates some of the differences in the types of searching that may be performed with software designed for CD-ROM.

Applications vary according to the demand they place on the retrieval engine, and the engine's performance is only as good as the authoring software used to create the data structures. Thus before you purchase commercial software, it may be prudent to develop a product, and then have a service bureau evaluate the technology.

Service bureaus.   The early CD-ROM service bureaus became successful by creating CD-ROM products that provided them with a built-in opportunity for repeat business. In the beginning very little was known about making a good CD-ROM product, so publishers were captive customers, willing to pay high fees in order to avoid costly mistakes.

The biggest disadvantage of working with a traditional service bureau is the loss of control over the product. There is little flexibility to prototype or enhance a product quickly or easily. More importantly, the investment in a service bureau does not allow expertise in the technology to be leveraged within the corporation.

CD-ROM publishing platform.   A new type of company has emerged that is effectively a "hybrid" service bureau/software development company. This new generation of companies provides a transition strategy for organizations that would like to use CD-ROM but have not yet developed expertise in the technology. These new hybrids will both develop applications as well as license their CD-ROM development software in the form of a "publishing platform."

The hybrid service bureau/development company creates the first application by working closely with a company's technical staff. The technical staff learns how to create an application and can then bring the software platform in house for subsequent titles. A publisher can acquire a license to both the authoring software and the retrieval software it will distribute with the discs to its users.

The advantage of this approach is that control of the product development is in the hands of those most knowledgeable about the customer. In addition, software specifically designed for CD-ROM lowers the internal product-development costs and shortens the time required. CD-ROM expertise is developed internally, and as expertise increases, costs are reduced further.

The major disadvantage of the in-house publishing platform is the investment required for software, hardware, and support staff. These can be kept to a minimum in the early stages by creating a pilot application using the preferred publishing platform vendor as a service bureau. The vendor's product can later be brought in house so that the investment is not made until the software has proven successful and the applicability of the technology to the entire applications portfolio has been evaluated. While it may be required as a way of educating the vendor as to the data types and information-usage profile of your industry, the pilot program often is the optimal means of determining if the software is suitable. Staff can be added as needed, and the system brought in house when ready. This provides a smooth transition without inconveniencing existing customers.

Generally speaking, the more products, enhancements, and updates are planned, the more an in-house publishing platform makes sense. A publishing platform that can be leveraged across a wide variety of applications is the most cost-effective way to introduce CD-ROM technology into an organization.

Successful CD-ROM publishing in house

Assuming that potential applications justify in-house development, and that the publishing-platform approach is preferable, the next step is to select the appropriate hardware and software. First choose software that meets the applications portfolio requirements, then choose hardware that can support it.

The applications portfolio drives requirements for the software. It is from the combining of identified requirements for all applications that the ultimate needs for an authoring capability are derived. Figure 23.11 is an example. Most organizations will identify, at a minimum, a requirement to integrate text, data, and graphics. A vendor's retrieval software engine should be able to demonstrate its viability in commercial use. Concentrating on vendors that have published titles and have licensed software for in-house use will give you a short list of finalists to evaluate. A list of commercial CD-ROM products produced by using the vendors' retrieval engines is a good indicator of credibility. Seeing a demonstration of published CD-ROM applications is even better.

Other software considerations

Once software that meets the application requirements has been identified, several other factors should be considered before a decision is made.

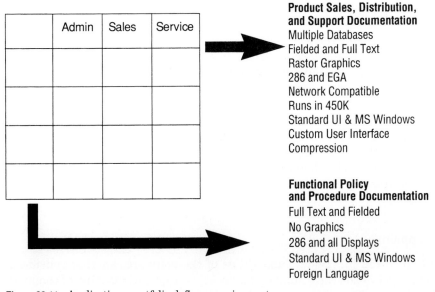

Product Sales, Distribution, and Support Documentation
Multiple Databases
Fielded and Full Text
Rastor Graphics
286 and EGA
Network Compatible
Runs in 450K
Standard UI & MS Windows
Custom User Interface
Compression

Functional Policy and Procedure Documentation
Full Text and Fielded
No Graphics
286 and all Displays
Standard UI & MS Windows
Foreign Language

	Admin	Sales	Service

Figure 23.11 Applications portfolio defines requirements.

Performance.   Users familiar with applications on personal computers have developed certain performance expectations, with most actions requiring not more than a few seconds. Actions that take longer must give the user some feedback that the action is in progress and, optionally, tell him or her how much is complete.

CD-ROM applications generally involve searching hundreds of megabytes, with drives that are much slower than magnetic drives. To solve this problem, the software must be optimized for both CD-ROM and the type of data. Vendors should be able to demonstrate that their product can handle applications with the number of records and megabytes of information that you require. CD-ROM-optimized software should meet user expectations for magnetic-based searching, even when searching hundreds of megabytes.

Multiplatform.   With appropriate software, the same CD-ROM disc can be used in any computer platform such as DOS, Windows, Macintosh, and UNIX. However, the development software must support this multiplatform authoring and provide retrieval software for each desired environment. Many commercial products are available for developing Windows or Macintosh applications only. They preclude using the CD-ROM in any other environment.

Limiting the application to a single platform may limit the number of benefits to be gained. This is especially true when replacing paper, because printing must continue until everyone's workstation is supported.

Information volume.   Many databases exceed the 700-Mbyte capacity of a CD-ROM disc today. Some of these applications may fit on a single disc, if compression is available in the authoring software. While standard compression schemes for text, structured data, and images can double effective disc capacity, multiple-disc sets are sometimes required. If multidisc applications are anticipated, be sure that the software selected will support this type of application.

The unique ability to place large amounts of multiple information types on a single disc places unusual demands on the CD-ROM software developer.

Normally, developers focus on a single area such as word processing, numerical databases, or graphics. The CD-ROM software developed must push the technological envelope in all three dimensions. Multiplatform and multimedia add additional dimensions. This multidimensional challenge must be met without sacrificing performance and ease of use on an inherently slower hardware technology. Given these challenges, choosing a software partner requires careful consideration of the capabilities of both the product and the vendor.

Application Development

In addition to the functional capabilities of the software, another consideration is the level of software support for creating applications. One of the main impediments to CD-ROM use has been the level of programming and the effort required to develop applications. For most organizations, only a few of the potential applications justify programming. The broad base of applications must be implemented by nonprogrammers. In evaluating CD-ROM authoring software, development capabilities that aid application-creation without coding should be considered.

Some advanced software authoring systems have front-end programs for reading and converting data from a variety of formats, including electronic publishing systems or on-line databases. These data-reading programs provide a broad funnel for capturing information. Photocomposition, database, and word processor formats can be supported by answering menu prompts, saving several person-weeks of conversion programming for each application. Publishers planning a CD-ROM product using a database that is already on line can usually format the database directly by using the authoring system.

Interface design and development determines how the end user will interact with the information. Query, display, print, export, and other capabilities are executed via the interface.

The most common model is a *fixed interface*. This option is popular with many text-only products, because the query options are limited. Products that integrate text, data, and graphics generally require a more sophisticated approach than is available in this model.

At the other end of the spectrum, the most flexible model is a "write-your-own" interface. The CD-ROM software consists of retrieval software and a set of calls to link the retrieval software to a custom-designed interface. This approach requires programming for every application. In addition, the programming investment is made prior to testing the match between the information and the retrieval software.

While clearly disadvantageous, many "tool-kit" products offer custom interface programming as the only option for publishers. While the capability to customize is essential to many applications, it should be viewed as an option, not a requirement, of the system.

The preferred approach borrows from the "application generator" techniques developed for DBMS access. The authoring software provides a model interface. Customizing is done by nonprogrammers through screen layout and painting, with the authoring software generating the code required in the background. Multiple user interfaces including search screens, data views, and print options are possible through switching and editing screens.

The more flexible this approach is, the less programming is required. Even when custom work is needed, the first complete application can be tested using the "standard" interface to ensure that the information and user requirements are met. The testing process also demonstrates the size of data and indexes, the amount of compression, the memory required, and performance if simulation capabilities are available. The test application can be used to obtain valuable feedback and to determine if the "standard" approach is in fact acceptable.

Testing and debugging of the application should be facilitated. System messages should be logged in a file for review. Indexes should be viewable, for instant access to all records containing an identified term. Reports on data size, index size, etc. should be available.

The software also should provide for application simulation prior to CD-ROM generation. Highly desirable are systems that simulate the slow CD-ROM access speed to give an indication of the actual performance of the finished product.

End-user application creation should include support for context-sensitive help screens, copyright notices, and an installation script generator to make end-user installation as foolproof as possible.

Foreign language version creation can be dramatically eased with proper support in the authoring system. Selection of the target language should provide automatic support for the appropriate keyboards, sorting sequences, character sets, and user-interface text files. Multiple language versions can be accessed by the user with a few keystrokes.

A robust authoring system contributes value in many ways. It increases the number of applications that can be produced, while improving the quality of each application. It increases learning throughout the organization and puts the technology in the hands of those people who best understand the user and the data. It saves time and money during development, and minimizes ongoing support and maintenance costs. Finally, it ensures that a majority of applications can be developed with a single system so that multiple systems need not be supported.

Staffing requirements

A single application engineer can develop and update a significant number of applications using a properly designed development system. The steps in the first table in Fig. 23.12 indicate the level of staffing required to develop a typical CD-ROM application using commercial authoring software. The second table indicates the level of staffing required as the application is updated. (*Note:* Use of a programmer's tool kit requires higher skill levels and generally more time.)

Given the time involved in indexing and developing a full application, the ideal approach is to prototype a complete application using a small subset of data. This ensures up-front that the data and software will work together.

Organizational requirements

For in-house CD-ROM publishing to be successful, there must be an organizational commitment to optical publishing. In some cases one division or group within an organization has taken the lead in successfully demonstrating the utility and cost-effectiveness of using CD-ROM for information delivery. In other organizations, a coordinated corporatewide effort has been launched simultaneously in many areas of the company.

Publishing corporate data on CD-ROM can be a high-profile activity. Getting discs into the hands of customers and distributors creates positive

Steps and Staffing Requirements for Application Development

Step	Skill Level	Time
Data Conversion and Filtering	Developer*	1 day plus
Database Definitions	Developer	1/2 day - 1 day
Screen Layout	Developer	1 - 2 days **
Indexing Specification	Developer	1/2 - 2 days
Indexing and Binding	None	10 Megabytes/hr.
Debugging and Texting	Developer	1 - 2 days
Help Screens	Skilled User	1/2 - 2 days
Install Program	Developer	1/2 - 1 day
Creation of Premaster Tape	Developer	1/2 - 1 day

* PC DBMS Developer
**Assumes screen painting interface design with no programming.

Steps and Staffing Requirements for Updates to Applications

Step	Skill Level	Time
Index and Bind	Skilled User	Set up, then machine time @ 10 Megabytes/Hr.
Quality Assurance	Skilled User	1 hour - 1 Day
Creation of Premaster Tape	Developer	1/2 - 1 day

Figure 23.12   Steps and staffing requirements for development.

exposure for the company. Internal information takes on a high profile when it appears on the same media as Mozart or Madonna.

Publishing partner

When you are making the commitment to optical publishing, make sure your technology partner is equally committed.

In a new and emerging industry, it is sometimes difficult to determine who the successful, long-term players will be. The credentials of the management team, the financial resources of the company, the reputation of the investors, and the company's track record become critical considerations. A history of software-development companies suggests that during the early stages of a new technology, having a focused product strategy is key to ultimate success. For example, most of the leading software products in the PC arena were originally developed by companies whose business was dedicated to one category, such as presentation graphics or word processing.

Finally, because of the high-profile nature of optical publishing, leading organizations have already taken the step and bet their reputation on the vendor they selected. The software developers most likely to be the long-term winners should already have a list of demanding yet satisfied customers.

Summary

In an age suffering from "information overload," an age "drowning in paper," CD-ROM technology is positioned to deliver substantial benefits. CD-ROM provides a means for solving certain information problems when applied to critical activities and undertaken with a clear sense of how information is used by the knowledge worker. CD-ROM fits naturally into corporate computing strategies and leverages major trends, including electronic publishing, work-group computing, and transaction processing.

Successful CD-ROM applications integrate knowledge about the information user, information content, and software/hardware technology. The ideal CD-ROM publisher is the group that best understands the user and information content. The publisher resides within the organization, and must control the software and hardware technology to effectively serve the user.

Technology solutions are available from companies that have focused their business on creating CD-ROM technology for in-house use. This focus is critical because of the challenges inherent in CD-ROM development, ranging from performance to multiple information types to indexing gigabytes of data on multiple discs.

Those organizations that have acquired the technology and delivered the applications are the greatest proponents of CD-ROM. Their experience suggests that CD-ROM will become a major competitive tool in the hands of information managers. Organizations that put this technology to creative use will reap substantial benefits.

Appendix A   Optical Publishing: An Industry Overview

Optical publishing is a term that describes the result as well as the process of distributing information on optical media. This is similar to the way in which the term *electronic publishing* refers to the distribution of information in digital form over telecommunication or broadcast systems, and *print publishing* refers to books, magazines, and reports on paper or microfiche. Estimates put print publishing at more than 90 percent of the publishing universe, with electronic at 10 percent. Optical publishing today represents about 5 percent of the electronic publishing share, or 0.5 percent overall.

The term *optical publishing* generally refers to information distributed on CD-ROM. Broadly speaking, it also can be used to refer to laser videodisc and interactive videodisc (used primarily for merchandising and training). The term *optical storage* (as opposed to optical *publishing*) refers to the use of write-once and erasable optical discs. The technologies are quite different, a critical distinction being that optical publishing embraces the idea of volume production and distribution.

The traditional publishing industry—book-publishing houses, magazine publishers, and educational textbook providers—increasingly is involved in optical publishing as the industry becomes more established. The publishers who took the initial risk to adopt the medium and get it established, however, are not household names with popular properties. They are publishers selling into library and technical markets with specialized information, new publishers with no prior publication history, and companies from the computer industry moving into publishing.

A majority of the first CD-ROM titles were transferred from the on-line publishing world, adapted from files already available by modem from remote host database services. Since then content has broadened to include numerous application areas, as indicated in Fig. 23.1. Most observers agree that this represents just the tip of the iceberg that is potential use of CD-ROM.

Libraries were among the first CD-ROM customers. The technology was a good fit for several reasons. A CD-ROM product has a known cost like a book or magazine subscription, and it can be budgeted and made accessible to all patrons without charging back variable on-line fees. Libraries are a known market that enable publishers to target those customers with particular needs and great purchasing power. Librarians also already had a great deal of experience with on-line searching. They were eager to learn about CD-ROM and to share their experiences with others in the field.

Corporations are the next major market for CD-ROM, and they have already significantly surpassed libraries in volume use. As was just pointed out about librarians, corporate users' broad familiarity with computers and on-line searching techniques puts them one step ahead of the game. Corporations are customers for reference products in resource centers; business, financial, and directory products at the departmental level; technical and scientific reference products at the research and engineering level; and desktop publishing and related products at the individual level. Corporations also are the leading producers of in-house titles for documentation, database distribution, corporate records, and other internal applications.

Computer software producers have become publishers and distributors. An increasing number are using CD-ROM to distribute software products, particularly when distribution on floppy disk is too unwieldy. In some products such as Lotus 1-2-3 and Apple Macintosh Hyper card, content becomes integrated with the application. Microsoft Corporation, the largest PC software producer, has made invaluable contributions to the optical publishing industry by means of numerous CD-ROM products, CD-ROM conferences, books about CD-ROM, and the MS-DOS extensions for CD-ROM.

Government is another major market. There are both commercial and in-house training applications in this market. Among the applications are documentation for military equipment, training programs, standards, and administrative information. Many government agencies are taking on a commercial publishing role with regard to government collections that are distributed to the Federal Depository Library network. They also have markets in the private sector such as patents, social, economic, agricultural and business data, and technical reports.

Other market sectors that today are primarily vertical and commercial include professions such as law, medicine, health, and education, as well as the emerging consumer market. CD-ROM has also been attractive to publishers and users in niche markets where very specialized information is used by a very specific group of customers.

Optical publishing is the subject of a major annual survey conducted by InfoTech,an international consulting and research firm specializing in optical-disc and information-technology markets. The most recent results (as of this writing) are published in the yearly *Optical Publishing Industry Assessment,* which is available from InfoTech, Woodstock, VT (802-257-1038). To create this report, InfoTech interviewed hundreds of publishers worldwide and applied a sophisticated methodology, drawing on over eight years of direct experience in the optical disc industry.

InfoTech established a tracking system in 1987, allowing it to measure the impressive growth in the industry from 1988 on. Titles in print have grown from fewer than 100 in 1986 to an estimated 5000 in 1992 (Fig. 23.13). The installed base of readers has grown from 9000 in 1986 to an estimated 4,000,000 in 1992 (Fig. 23.14). Total revenue, which includes titles and reader hardware for commercial and in-house applications, has increased from $31 million in 1986 to $3.9 billion worldwide in 1992 (Fig. 23.15).

InfoTech estimates that the commercial market shipped 3256 titles valued at nearly $2 billion in 1992, and it forecasts growth by 1995 to nearly 8000 titles valued at over $4 billion. Commercial revenue is calculated at retail prices and based on confidentially reported unit-sales data collected from over 80 percent of the publishers.

The in-house market is estimated to have released over 2000 titles in 1992, roughly 40 percent of all titles released. By 1995 the figure is forecast to be somewhere around 3500 titles. Titles published for in-house use are not directly counted, because of the great difficulty in identifying producers. They are

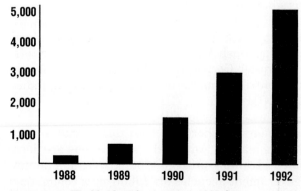

Figure 23.13 Worldwide titles in print. 1992 figures are estimates. (*Source: Infotech.*)

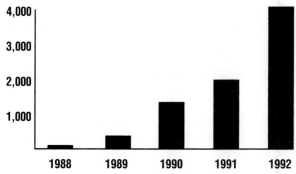

Figure 23.14   Worldwide installed base, in thousands of units. 1992 figures are estimates. (*Source: Infotech.*)

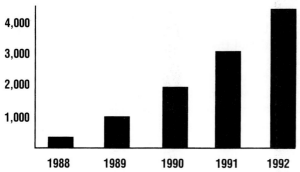

Figure 23.15   Worldwide revenues, in thousands of dollars. 1992 figures are estimates. (*Source: Infotech.*)

estimated by the vendors serving that sector with software, media, and hardware. Although the in-house data is not statistically valid, it is still a strong indicator of what the in-house sector represents to the optical publishing industry and is widely regarded as the best available estimation of output.

Appendix B   Estimating Costs

When you are considering CD-ROM, remember that costs must be viewed relative to alternative means of organizing, distributing, and retrieving information. Cost analysis is not complete without factoring in both performance and the competitive advantages that result from the availability of information on CD-ROM, such as ease of updating, accuracy of searching, ad hoc query capabilities, and inexpensive distribution.

Application development costs

Service bureau. The various steps of data preparation, indexing, interface creation, etc. require appropriate software and resources. This varies depending on the actual amount of data in the application, the complexity of the project, and the sophistication of the authoring software.

It is impossible to predict the cost of a CD-ROM application from a distance. For simple projects, a price of $10,000 to $40,000 would not be uncommon from a service bureau. This would include the use of its software, reading and "cleaning" the data, indexing, creating the user interface, pressing the discs, and licensing the retrieval software. Custom applications would cost more.

Publishing platform—software.   Software should be specifically designed for CD-ROM applications. It should be optimized to achieve maximum performance while minimizing the space requirements for the data and related indexes. Mature software specific to CD-ROM will offer substantial benefits, including sophisticated data-import capabilities, high-throughput indexing, and rich features and functionality in retrieving data from CD-ROM. Less sophisticated software sometimes costs more in the long run, because it requires more data conversion prior to indexing or more program development to add required features to the retrieval facilities. Worse still is the case where significant time is invested and the CD-ROM application is unacceptable because of slow performance.

Software specifically designed for the organization, indexing, and retrieval of information on CD-ROM can range from a few hundred dollars to $50,000. Cost differences lie in the type of information your application entails, the range of organization and indexing options available, the flexibility inherent in the software, and its performance.

Costs may also vary with the reliability and credibility of the vendor. Value is closely related to how complete the software is and how much custom development is required to create your CD-ROM application. A system that saves three person-months of programming per application is worth a significant premium over a programming tool kit.

Software for multimedia authoring also can range from a few hundred to thousands of dollars. The options and differences in costs here relate primarily to the types of information the authoring system supports.

Publishing platform—hardware.   Costs for the hardware for an in-house development capability vary. A minimum 486-based PC with extended memory is recommended if you are to achieve adequate index build performance. A price range of $2000 to $4000 is typical, not including disk drive, tape drive, or CD-recordable drive. Complete premastering systems range from $10,000 to $50,000 depending on features, memory, throughput, and vendor support. If you already have an installed 386 or 486 with sufficient magnetic-disk space, today a CD-recordable drive can be added for under $10,000.

A growing trend is indexing on high-performance UNIX-RISC-based machines. These machines offer substantial price/performance advantages if the throughput requirements warrant the higher processing speeds.

The major cost advantage of an in-house publishing platform is the ability to leverage the investment in software, hardware, and staffing across a number of applications. With as few as five applications, the fully loaded cost per CD-ROM disc falls below $20. In this report is a summary cost calculation for creating a complete application-development capability. Costs per PC, per disc, and per megabyte are included in this cost analysis.

If you are thinking about developing multimedia applications, the required components usually can be added to a publishing platform as needed. Depending on the type of multimedia (audio, video, etc.), various sound and video capture boards, videodisc players, cameras, and sound equipment may be necessary. Costs for these components vary greatly depending on quality, throughput, and features.

Staffing.   Personnel requirements for an individual project using an authoring system with no custom programming are summarized in Fig. 23.12. Projects that require custom interface development are more labor-intensive.

A single application engineer can develop and update a significant number of applications using a properly designed authoring system. Experience suggests that compared with a "tool kit," an authoring system increases application production 3 to 10 times.

Retrieval software costs

Retrieval software licenses are offered in one or more of the following ways.

CPU basis.   Useful primarily for internal applications, this pricing method is similar to PC software that is licensed for use on a particular machine forever. Regardless of how many CD-ROMs your organization creates, the cost for the retrieval software for that PC doesn't change. Charges for this "pay-once" CPU license vary with vendor and quantity. Pricing tends to parallel mass-market PC software: $250 to $500 per CPU for low volumes, and roughly half that for quantity purchases.

Per disc or per subscription.   For applications in which the publisher doesn't know or control the end user (e.g., discs distributed outside the organization), retrieval software is charged on a per-disc or per-subscription basis. Per-disc pricing usually is tied to volume-based plateaus and will vary from vendor to vendor. For a 200-disc volume, a price range of $25 to $50 per disc is typical. For a volume of 5000, a range of $10 to $20 per disc should be expected. (*Note:* It's important to ascertain how "volume plateaus" are computed by the software vendor. Ideally, all licenses can be grouped together, so that an organization can quickly reach and remain at the highest discount level.)

Annual subscription pricing, while somewhat higher, offers the option of updating the users' products without limitation during the year. At a 200-subscription volume, prices in the range of $75 to $100 should be expected. At 5000 subscriptions, the price per year should be $25 to $50.

Pricing outside these ranges usually indicates an organization that is underfunded and/or a new entrant to the market, complete with the associated risks. Software companies that have survived the ups and downs of an emerging industry and are providing quality products and services generally offer their products in the price ranges identified above. To survive in the PC software business, companies typically need to reach and sustain sales in the $10 million range in their third or fourth year. This can be illustrated by reviewing the few survivors in word processing, spreadsheets, or graphics from the early eighties. A good "going-concern" viability test is to divide the vendor's price into $10 million. That will give you the number of new customers they must attract each year.

Media costs—mastering the disc

If only a small number of replicas is required (less than 50, in today's economics), or if a prototype of the completed disc is desired, CD-recordable technology may be employed. Blank CD-recordable media today cost $30 in low quantities and less than $25 in high quantities, in addition to the costs for the CD-recordable drive.

Once a complete application exists, a premaster tape is created and sent to the pressing house. The first cost in this process is the setup charge (currently, $1000 to $2000). On the low end, five-day turnaround is typical. Higher prices can achieve one-day turnaround. The next cost is a disc charge, which is volume-related. Prices of $1.50 to $2.50 each are typical today. Because of the setup charge, companies normally produce the maximum number of discs likely to be required from each pressing.

In-house cost summary

The cost of bringing a complete CD-ROM application development capability in house is summarized below. Costs are broken into logical groups and summarized in the final section. Organizational overheads have not been included, as these will vary from case to case.

Initial investment.   These costs are one-time outlays for hardware and software that are assumed to have a useful life of 3 years (although actual life may be longer).

Hardware	
Premastering system (1 Gbyte plus tape drive)	$11,000
486 personal computer	4,000
Subtotal	15,000
Software	
Authoring system	30,000
Total initial investment	$45,000

Annual costs. These are average annual outlays for personnel, office space, and supplies. Experience suggests that these costs and manpower levels are sufficient to produce up to five different applications, with an average bimonthly update frequency. More applications or more frequent updates may require more resources.

Personnel	
Applications developer	$60,000
Office space	10,000
Supplies	5,000
Total annual costs	$75,000

Investment per workstation. These costs assume that 500 PCs in the organization are outfitted with CD-ROM drives and retrieval software. Higher volumes result in somewhat lower per-workstation costs, due to volume discounting. These investments also are assumed to have a useful life of 3 years.

CD-ROM drive with interface	$ 500
Retrieval software (perpetual)	200
Total investment per workstation	$ 700
Total workstation investment (500 PCs)	$350,000

Costs per CD-ROM application update. All steps in the application-development process, from acceptance of raw data on magnetic tape through generation of premaster tapes ready for the mastering/pressing facility, can be accomplished by the above personnel using the listed facilities. The premaster tapes are then forwarded to the mastering/pressing facility, where a setup charge is incurred for each master disc and a per-disc charge applied for the replication. Documentation can be prepared as a slip-insert to the CD-ROM jewel-case packaging.

Mastering (per application/master disc)	$ 1500
Replication (per CD-ROM disc)	2
Documentation (per CD-ROM disc)	1

Software maintenance cost. Software maintenance is assumed to run at 15 percent annually, the industry norm.

Cost summary. This section assumes that the organization is producing three CD-ROM applications: one updated quarterly, one monthly, and one every six months. The volumes are 200, 500, and 300 units respectively.

	Annual total	Annual per PC	Per disc	Per megabyte*
Initial investment				
(3-year life)†	$ 15,000	$ 30.00	$ 2.03	$ 0.01
Annual costs	75,000	150.00	10.14	0.03
Workstation costs				
(3-year life)‡	116,667	233.34	15.77	0.05
Application update costs§	49,200	98.40	6.65	0.02
Software maintenance¶	9,500	39.00	2.64	0.01
Totals	$275,367	550.74	37.23	0.12

*Assumes discs contain average 300 megabytes.
†45,000 / 3 = 15,000
‡350,000 / 3 = 116,667
§((4 + 12 + 2) * 1500) + ((200*4 + 500*12 + 300*2) * 3) = 49,200
¶(30,000 + 500*200) * 15% = 19,500

Multimedia Consulting

A New Frontier

Lewis Gruskin

Introduction

Innovative applications of multimedia technology are now spotlighted in almost every business magazine. A major steel company is using multimedia to train employees, reducing training time by 20 to 40 percent. Large retail firms are implementing multimedia kiosks to extend their retail outlets. IBM, Apple, and other firms are announcing powerful multimedia software development tools, in addition to personal computers with multimedia capabilities at less cost. It's clear that multimedia will have a significant impact on business—and soon.

To achieve these benefits, companies must add multimedia to their business operations effectively while avoiding the mistakes many companies made during the early days of the PC revolution. Then PCs were introduced haphazardly, often without management direction. This approach resulted in a disparate collection of computing devices that often used different operating systems, ran incompatible software, and worse, could not communicate with the corporate computers or with each other. As a result, PCs did not deliver the much-promised boosts in productivity and job enhancement, and corporate management missed out on many of the competitive advantages they could have gained by using this new information tool more effectively.

When examining the potential of multimedia, corporate management must address several major questions. How can multimedia help to solve critical business problems? How are multimedia solutions created, implemented, and supported? What new issues in application design must be considered? Above all, what is the best way to get started in this new field?

The Transformation of Business

The choices can be overwhelming, and the decisions crucial. Multimedia is much more than a recipe for jazzing up PCs with a mixture of speakers, video cards, and new software. It represents a new computing and business paradigm that affects the way people communicate, work, and learn. The multimedia synergy of incorporating voice, data, and video with computer power has the proven potential to become an integral part of corporate business processes and to radically change business operations—if it's introduced correctly.

Multimedia will transform a corporation's business activities in three areas. First, multimedia will provide interactive front-ends to existing applications to make them easier to use, a change that will affect every aspect of MIS operations. Second, multimedia will permit new MIS and business applications to be developed, such as sales automation, just-in-time training, and desktop conferencing, as companies learn to tap the power of interactive access to information in a variety of formats. Finally, the technology will serve as the cornerstone for new multimedia-based opportunities in much the same way that the potential of interactive TV is spawning new business ventures (see Fig. 24.1).

However, the full potential of multimedia to transform business can't be tapped just by using it to add impact to existing applications or to address individual or departmental problems. For maximum effectiveness, multimedia must be employed as a strategic information tool within a framework of long-term business requirements. Multimedia should be linked to other com-

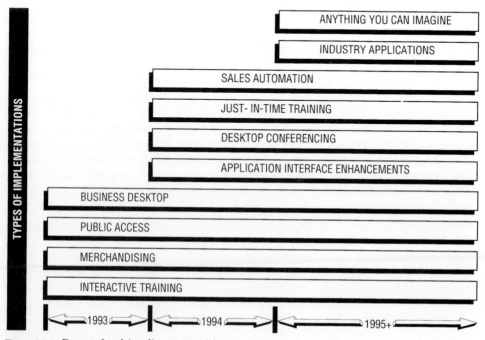

Figure 24.1   Range of multimedia opportunities.

puter resources and deployed with at least some understanding of how employees, customers, and vendors may react to the new technology.

The advantages of looking strategically at this new technology are clear. Think of the potential for individual and strategic advances if, from the very beginning, multimedia can be extended across a company's existing infrastructure of stand-alone and distributed computing. Imagine the strategic advantages of sharing information—whether in audio, video, image, or data format—throughout a distributed enterprise around the world. Consider the benefits of strengthening the links among employees, customers, and vendors through improved multimedia communication.

Yet achieving effective enterprisewide multimedia use is not easy, and the risks can be great. The technology involved in integrating data, text, and video is complex and confusing. Standards often differ. There are new categories of development tools to comprehend and presentation issues to be resolved, which can involve complex tradeoffs concerning storage, media file size, and bandwidth.

Multimedia also is a technological frontier whose landscape consists of numerous cutting-edge questions, ranging from, "Who owns the copyright for images used in multimedia presentations?" to "Which compression technologies should be adopted?" Find the right answers, and the payoffs will be greater profitability and productivity. Guess wrong, and money, time, and opportunity will be wasted (see Fig. 24.2).

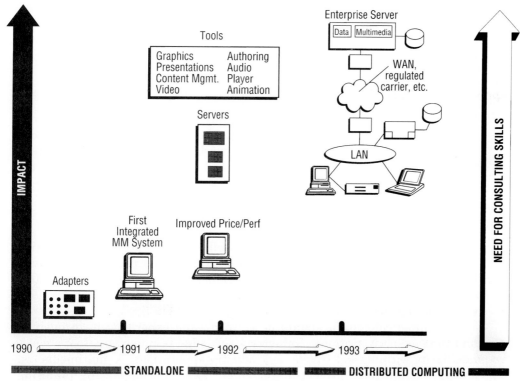

Figure 24.2   Customer needs.

Looking for Help

Faced with those high stakes, many companies are turning to consultants to guide them through the jungle of competing technologies, unexplored applications, design issues, and user acceptance. A consultant traditionally provides many benefits, especially when new technologies are involved or deadlines are tight. A consultant can offer an objective view of a problem in order to help speed a solution. A consultant also provides specialized expertise often unavailable in house. This expertise allows a consultant to know what can be done, how technologies can be applied, and what fundamental challenges must be met. Sometimes a consultant is brought in as an additional resource to ensure timely completion of projects.

Companies should be cautious, however, about the type of consultant they use when it comes to a technology with the impact and implications of multimedia. Such a complex technology involves new tools and skills such as authoring, media production, and large-object handling. During application design, multimedia also affects the analysis of the problem, the type of information gathered, and the implementation requirements. To complicate matters even further, multimedia can impact not only information systems but every area of the company's business, by the way in which it creates complex interrelationships among business practices, technology, human/machine interfaces, and media-based communications. To be effective in this field, a consultant must do more than copy what has been done before with other technologies. Rather, the consultant must be able to help a company mold the unique functionality of multimedia to create new strategic solutions for business problems.

Differences between Multimedia and Traditional Consulting

It's clear that if multimedia is to be introduced effectively, a new type of consulting must offer more than the traditional benefits provided by an MIS consultant. This new multimedia consulting works first to align the capabilities of the technology with the strategic goals and demands of the firm. Once this has been achieved, multimedia consulting can help the customer to define its requirements for specific situations.

Multimedia consulting for business applications requires more than just technical knowledge about multiple hardware platforms and operating systems, video compression, hardware and software compatibility, networking, and other complicated issues. It is a multidisciplined profession involving business analysis, goal-setting, benchmarking, programming, human factors, communications, and other skills, many of which require intensive and long-term training (see Fig. 24.3).

A qualified consultant should be trained—and experienced—in business and management systems. Industry knowledge is important too, such as familiarity with market trends and industry applications. A multimedia consultant should have project-management skills encompassing planning,

Figure 24.3 Strengths of the multimedia consultant.

tracking, risk management, and contracting. The consultant should understand how user expectations about interactive responses, nonlinear learning, video presentation skills, etc. are being transformed by today's communications industries, including television, movies, and advertising. Beyond business and media expertise, the consultant should possess strong personal skills, with the ability to lead, communicate, analyze, negotiate, and make decisions. The consultant should also have access to the multiple resources available from specialized consulting teams; the specialized teams can be part of the consultant's organization or associates of the firm.

Additionally, the international links of many businesses create a special need for cross-cultural sensitivities. As information in these businesses becomes distributed not only within the companies but across national borders, it becomes all the more imperative to use a consultant who understands the impact multimedia can have within different countries and cultures.

Extensive, diversified training and knowledge are only part of the arsenal of the multimedia consultant. Just as important is the consultant's perceptiveness about organizational and technological issues. The most knowledgeable and skilled consultant in the world will do little good unless he or she is sensitive to the client's concerns and focused on solving the client's business problems. After all, the central issue is not just introducing a new technology but rather solving business and operational problems, even if they don't necessarily involve multimedia.

When you review the capabilities of a multimedia consultant, it's also important that you distinguish between *consulting*—deciding what to do or how to do it—and *performing* or *executing* specific development tasks. The multimedia consultant concentrates on understanding the global business environment, the corporation's strategic goals, and the scope of the eventual implementation. After extensive client input, the consultant provides objectives, timetables, solution design, and performance standards. The consultant may lead prototype development so as to provide the "look and feel" of the multimedia solution and thereby gain client approval. However, once these parameters have been set, the project can be turned over to "perform teams" of people who are skilled in execution, such as graphic designers, script writers, video technicians, and interactive program authors. If appropriate, the multimedia consultant can play some of the "perform" roles, depending on the size and complexity of the project.

The benefit of using an experienced, qualified multimedia consultant will be new approaches and solutions to the age-old problems of increasing sales, improving productivity, and enhancing communications within and without your organization. Just as PCs should not be used merely to automate the old ways of doing business, so too the power of multimedia should not be frittered away by all those application "quick fixes" that often seem to be no further than an 800-number phone call away. Multimedia represents a historic opportunity to marry a high-potential technology with long-term business objectives. A multimedia consultant can help you to make the most of that opportunity.

A Multimedia Consulting Methodology

The effective multimedia consultant is skilled in the use of an organized, transferable consulting methodology. This methodology provides a consistent, measurable structure for planning, organizing, tracking, and executing business applications linked to the unique demands of multimedia. These unique demands—such as ownership and performance rights, physical-environment considerations, and media production coordination—have not yet been incorporated into traditional applications and are not part of most companies' processes and methodologies.

To guide a project effectively and consistently from understanding the business problem through formulating a concept to completing a multimedia solution, a tested, flexible methodology is needed. The IBM Multimedia Consulting Practice, a unit of the IBM Consulting Group, has developed a unique, client-centered methodology for planning and executing multimedia projects. This methodology is flexible enough to work either for corporatewide distributed business process solutions or for stand-alone training solutions.

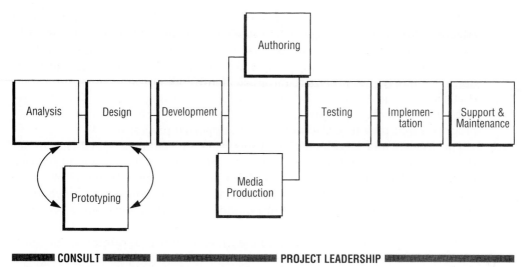

CONSULT **PROJECT LEADERSHIP**

Figure 24.4 Consulting methodology.

When used by an experienced multimedia consultant, the methodology employs repeatable processes (essential, as multimedia projects evolve from single-purpose solutions to corporatewide applications), reduces project risks, and maintains constant client participation.

The methodology is structured around nine phases (see Fig. 24.4) beginning with analysis and ending with confirmation of the client's short- and long-term arrangements for evaluation, support, and maintenance:

1. Analysis

2. Design

3. Development

4. Media production

5. Authoring

6. Testing

7. Implementation

8. Support

9. Maintenance

The first phase, Analysis, collects data about the business context for the intended application, analyzes related requirements from other areas of the company, proposes alternative solutions, assesses the impact of each solution, and presents recommendations. Prototyping may be used to clarify the client's requirements or expectations.

The Analysis phase receives special emphasis in the Multimedia Solution Methodology, because later media decisions will depend on the information initially gathered about users and processes. For example, to plan the most effective interactive strategy (or strategies), the consultant must have information about all potential users. If users include the client's customers, market research may be the only way to determine the characteristics of those users. Similarly, the project team must identify all of the business processes that will be affected by the project, including existing processes that the project will automate, new processes that the project will create, and manual processes that may feed the multimedia-supported processes.

The Design and Development phases work out detailed specifications for the application, including exact content, presentation flow, user interaction patterns, screen and media element descriptions, and programming interface requirements. Media element specifications, from master storyboards through scripts, detailed storyboards, and authoring requirements, are also completed during these phases.

During the Media Production phase, media and programming "perform teams" create the media elements and programs that are pulled together during the Authoring phase into the interactive application. End-user documentation, training materials, and other supporting components must also be completed on schedule.

The Testing phase verifies that all elements of the application work as intended. This phase can include acceptance-testing by the client and legal reviews of the completed application. Testing is followed by the Implementation phase, which brings the application into general use in the client's organization and "tunes" the application and related processes so as to get the most efficient performance during daily business routines. Implementation includes migration and production pilot activities, if appropriate for the project.

The final phases, Support and Maintenance, confirm that the client has appropriate long-range evaluation, support, and maintenance procedures in place for the application. Full ownership of the application, along with all required supporting materials, are then turned over to the client.

Special Features of the Multimedia Solution Methodology

The Multimedia Solution Methodology pays special attention to the unique requirements of multimedia work so that all major requirements are identified early in the project. For example, a client with seasonal business cycles may need to update the visual parts of an application every quarter. Traditional application development might consider this updating as a "maintenance" activity to be addressed late in the project. However, in a multimedia application, this updating can affect decisions about what kinds of visual elements should be used and how they should be stored. Consequently the multimedia methodology collects those requirements early, along with other business needs.

Similarly, the methodology organizes any specialized expertise that may be needed. For example, a distributed multimedia project may have need of someone knowledgeable about wide-area networking. In such a case, the IBM Multimedia Consulting Practice can recruit expertise from other IBM groups to design a solution. Other problems or activities may require the use of other skilled organizations. When a variety of skills is required on a project, the multimedia consultant can serve as "prime contractor." The structured topics, terminology, and tasks in the methodology help the multimedia consultant to coordinate the specialists and thereby meet the client's needs.

The methodology also distinguishes clearly between *consulting* and *perform* work. The consultant "consults" by helping the client to identify business requirements and potential solutions. The consultant can also help to work out (in the Design and Development phases) more detailed specifications for implementation. However, the closer the project gets to the "perform" work of creating storyboards, scripts, authoring structures, and media elements, the more the consultant functions as the client's representative, ensuring that designs and implementations meet the client's critical success factors and preestablished constraints, but not doing "hands-on" media work.

The Multimedia Solution Methodology emphasizes the crucial importance of keeping the client actively involved. More than in traditional application development, multimedia rework (such as reshooting a video segment or rerecording a voice-over) can be very expensive. To minimize these unnecessary costs, the consultant works to ensure that the client reviews and approves design, development, and media production activities at each stage to provide a solid foundation for the next round of project work. The methodology identifies major milestones and frequent checkpoints as a structure for involving the client.

Another special feature of the Multimedia Solution Methodology is that it provides a road map to define and transfer procedures and perspectives. The defined procedures establish a consistent baseline for measuring all outcomes. The processes also are transferable, so that the client's employees can leverage the consultant's knowledge and apply it to their own situation, using it to solve new problems. Transferability also allows a process to be used in multibranch or even multinational environments. Finally, if a process can be repeated, the risk from unexpected outcomes or even unexpected costs can be significantly reduced while encouraging a consistent implementation across the enterprise. This is much more than "not reinventing the wheel"; it is establishing a way to build wheel after wheel after wheel.

The benefits of these special features can be seen in several multimedia proposals in which the IBM Multimedia Consulting Practice became involved. A major telecommunications firm wanted to know whether multimedia was the best method for training and for improving retail sales. It also wanted to understand the best ways to ensure widespread acceptance of multimedia applications and to pinpoint the long-term costs and strategy of developing multimedia throughout the organization. IBM Multimedia Consulting suggested an approach that identified the company's business goals and objectives, multimedia's business value, the critical elements to be resolved with prototypes, and, finally, an approach for implementation. Then market research would determine potential market reaction to multimedia and would serve as the basis for a companywide implementation strategy.

In another instance, a major U.S. city expressed interest in placing service kiosks throughout the city. IBM Multimedia Consulting worked with a market research firm to plan how to determine both citizen acceptance of the kiosks and the most popular potential applications. The project also included a cost/benefit analysis to examine the costs of implementing different levels of kiosk networks and some potential revenue-generating options that could repay the city for its investment in the system. Finally, a conceptual model would be developed to define prototypes, outline steps to key milestones, and describe methods to validate success.

Criteria for Successful Consulting

The result of using a tested, structured methodology is much more than producing an isolated multimedia application for a specific set of users. The company also has a solution that is integrated with strategic goals and business processes. The application is built upon an analysis of the unique requirements of the eventual target audience, whether that is employees, customers, or prospects. The multimedia solution links the latest technologies to a thorough understanding of how developmental issues must change to accommodate new data types and user interface issues, learning requirements and presentation effectiveness. The outcome is consistent with the client's business goals, satisfying all the requirements that were identified at the beginning of the project.

Successful consulting also provides a basis for identifying other uses of the technology. This reuse leverages the investment the firm makes in the multimedia consultant as well as reduces the risk inherent in single applications. In essence a good multimedia consultant is a teacher, guiding the firm to new levels of understanding about larger goals and strategies as well as upcoming technologies. This education provides a valuable foundation for the firm's growth even as it provides employees with those new capabilities that result from the enhanced use of multimedia.

None of this is possible, however, unless the consultant can bring to bear all of the expertise needed for the project. The consultant's own technical understanding is just the beginning. He or she should also be able to draw on the resources of an organization to deliver the unique expertise that may be necessary for a specific multimedia project. This expertise can include skills in networking, user interfaces, and market research.

The successful multimedia consultant can apply these skills to specific design, authoring, and implementation work, but only after the scope of the project has been outlined within the context of larger business and organizational issues. While sophisticated tools are available to almost anybody to develop multimedia applications, it makes little business sense to generate applications based solely on the skills of a programmer and the demands of the moment. To embark upon individual multimedia projects without this larger vision of corporate requirements is like setting off on a journey without a road map.

Conclusion

Multimedia technology has advanced to the point where any company can easily buy or develop training, presentation, or retail applications. It's tempting for companies striving for every competitive advantage to jump into multimedia, especially when they read success stories about documented bottom-line savings.

But multimedia is so much more than the latest technology upgrades. If the power of multimedia is to provide maximum long-term benefits, multimedia must be closely integrated with larger business strategies as well as linked to immediate application needs. Those twin demands make it imperative that a multimedia consultant use a structured, consistent methodology to satisfy the client and to demonstrate a comprehensive approach to business application development. The payoffs will come in the form of tested solutions that make employees more productive and managers more effective, and that substantially improve communications in all parts of the enterprise.

25

A Virtual Poem:

Extending Classroom Reality?

David E. Hartman
Tim Brock

When we were asked to write a chapter on combining multimedia and virtual reality for the first edition of *The McGraw-Hill Multimedia Handbook*, we were faced with some unique challenges. First, while we both had some experience with and understanding of virtual reality, neither of us considered ourselves "experts." Second, although our college had provided us with some pretty good equipment, we had no virtual reality apparatus, such as gloves or head-mount displays. We were on the verge of saying, "Thanks, but no thanks," when the inspiration hit us: Why not accept our limitations and, better yet, turn them into parameters for a project that would demonstrate that useful virtual reality can be done without $20,000 worth of equipment (Fig. 25.1)?

It has been said that virtual reality is a solution in search of a problem. That certainly fit our dilemma. We needed to find a problem that could be solved using virtual reality. It went without saying that the project would have to be effective and affordable. It would have to be limited in scope, too, because we had only six weeks until our deadline! The result was "Petals," a virtual reality exploration of an Ezra Pound poem.

All the while "Petals" was in production, however, we couldn't escape the feeling that we were just scratching the surface. As we discovered what we could and could not do with the tools at our disposal, new ideas and applications began to suggest themselves: How about a means for students to explore some of the secondary critical material spawned by Pound's poem? What if students could add their voices to the critical chorus surrounding the poem? What about a link to a World-Wide Web page devoted to the poem and

25.2

Figure 25.1 A Virtual poem.

its author? What if we could find a way to let students create their own virtual-reality interpretations of the poem? As the possibilities solidified, so did our commitment to continue developing the project.

What follows is a week-by-week account of the project. During the first six weeks, we developed "Petals." The subsequent weeks were devoted to the remainder of the project.

Week 1

In this short week, we agreed to do the project, decided our project should involve a poem, picked the poem, decided to focus on a single word in the poem, researched that word's etymology, began searching for an appropriate metaphor to serve as our virtual "world," and decided to use Virtus Walkthrough as our virtual reality software.

The poem

The search was on for a suitable poem. It would have to be short because our time was limited. It would also have to be rich in imagery to succeed in a multimedia/virtual-reality environment. We settled on Ezra Pound's "In a Station of the Metro."

> *The apparition of these faces in the crowd;*
> *Petals on a wet, black bough.*

The images were evocative and starkly contrasting (Fig. 25.2). Better yet, nearly all of the words were, themselves, "virtual environments"—teeming with images, emotions, sensations, and associations.

One of these rich words, "faces," seemed to be the center around which the rest of the poem revolved. We realized that, by exploring the word "faces," we would, of necessity, also be exploring much of the rest of the poem. An etymological exploration confirmed our choice of the word "faces" as the focus for our virtual environment. We discovered that the words "appearance," "facade," and "shine" were tangled up in the translated Latin roots of "face." It thus was decided: We would go "inside" the word "faces."

The software

We decided to use Virtus Corporation's Walkthrough because of its intuitive interface, affordable price (less than $250), and relatively modest equipment and memory needs. Walkthrough and its companion "playback only" software, Voyager, were designed to allow the creation of virtual architectural spaces. An architect could, for example, create a home that prospective buyers could "enter," explore rooms, check for closet space, or even position furnishings. We could create a palace of poetry! And because Walkthrough uses a "through the window" virtual reality interface, we wouldn't need head-mount displays or any control devices more sophisticated than a mouse.

Week 2

During this week, we discovered some things Walkthrough couldn't do, saw Virtus come to the rescue, explored artists in our search for design ideas, and made some metaphoric decisions.

Virtual dilemma

Our "poetic palace" very nearly became a tumbling house of cards when we discovered that Walkthrough 1.1 did not have QuickTime or texture-mapping capabilities. In order for our project to be a true marriage of virtual reality and multimedia, QuickTime and texture-mapping were essential. Fortunately, Virtus Corp. was able to provide us with a texture-enhanced version of Walkthrough that was (at that time) in beta testing. The new beta version incorporated both QuickTime and texture mapping.

Looking for some help

For inspiration, like many before us, we turned to established visual artists, particularly Picasso, Escher, and Seurat. As we continued to gather material and ideas, we were drawn to Seurat's technique of pointillism, in which dots of primary colors are juxtaposed in such a way that, when viewed from a distance, they take on both form and hue. It is the distinct feature of pointillism, however, that when viewed up close, only the individual bits of color are distinguishable. Our approach to poetry was similar. We would "walk" up to the poem until we were so close that only individual bits of data were visible. The data of the poem, its "faceness" in this instance, could be explored fully before we "stepped back" to view the whole once again.

We were also intrigued by the recursive nature of much of Escher's work. One of the reasons that the poetic experience fails for many students is that they read poems only once, and at a literal level, at that. If students are to read poetry successfully, they must return to it repeatedly—from different angles and applying a variety of tools. We wanted the explorers of our project, like figures in one of Escher's "mobius" paintings, to somehow find themselves ending at the beginning, and thus encouraged to begin the journey again.

Finally, Picasso's "Guernica" helped us find expression. The elements of cubism and collage contained in "Guernica" gave us a sense of artistic direction while we were immersed in a world populated by rectangles and polygons.

On the road to a metaphor

We decided that, in the manner of the poem itself (which Pound reportedly cut to its present size from 30 lines), representation would take precedence over realism. Rather than try to create a realistic human face, for example, we would represent one by using a set of vertically stacked bars arranged to approximate the shape of the human face. These bars would serve as three-dimensional billboards onto which we would place QuickTime movies and

PICT files. And where there's a billboard, of course, there must be a road. We decided a road would be the most effective thread to tie our virtual layers together.

Week 3

During this week we produced our first "sketches" of the virtual environment, explored types of faces, began recording QuickTime movies from TV and live sources, and practiced placing QuickTime movies onto surfaces in the newly arrived Walkthrough Beta.

Storyboarding

In our impatience to get started, we found ourselves using the newly arrived Walkthrough Beta as a virtual storyboard. If one of us got an idea, we would quickly draw it on Walkthrough, which renders instantly, and try it out. Storyboarding in this manner is more recursive than linear. If we decided we liked something we had storyboarded, it was already there in the virtual environment, ready to be incorporated.

QuickTime

Using VideoSpigot hardware, we started collecting short movie clips of faces from television, focusing on various types. We knew we wanted to use facial parts for the first layer of "Petals;" however, we soon discovered that QuickTime movies cannot be cropped. Nothing on TV would give us that kind of close-up. We decided that we would have to use live models.

We practiced placing in our virtual environment some of the QuickTime clips we had picked up from television. We learned, not unexpectedly, that as the number of simultaneously running QuickTime clips increased, speed decreased. Even using the RAM disk on our Quadra 950, we found that using any more than three QuickTime movies at one time slowed movement in Walkthrough unacceptably. There was a silver lining in this cloud, however, as we discovered that Quicktime movies only exist on the "front" of a layer. In other words, once we traveled through or around a layer, the QuickTime movies on the front of it ceased to exist for all practical purposes. By positioning our layers carefully, we realized that we would be able to ensure that there would never be more than three QuickTime movies running at the same time.

Week 4

This week, we continued to pull QuickTime clips from television, edited some of the clips, videotaped models for facial close-ups, created text as texture, decided how text and QuickTime images would go together, applied textures to the first layer, and created a winding road for the virtual environment!

Facing our models

Using models from surrounding offices, we videotaped a selection of eyes, noses, and mouths. We taped all three with the audio turned off; then taped the mouths saying the Latin roots of the word "face." These clips were edited with Adobe Premiere.

Text as texture

Because Walkthrough Beta does not have text-generation capability, any text we wanted to use had to be created elsewhere and applied to our layer as a texture. Using Adobe PhotoShop, we created the text of the poem as well as the Latin root words for "face." For all of the text in "Petals," we used 20% gray Palatino reversed on black.

The first layer

We created five rectangular bars and stacked them ("floated them" might be a better term) with equal space separating each bar from the next. The middle bar was the longest, with bars getting successively shorter as they moved further (up or down) from the center. The road was made to pass between the bottom bar and the one above it.

It was time to add QuickTime. We found that we could "stretch" our square QuickTime format to fit the horizontal bars we had created, but the distortion was unacceptable. We already knew we could not crop QuickTime in Premiere, so we had to come up with another solution. We learned that we could "mask" QuickTime movies by covering unwanted portions with textures that were the same color as the background. Although the method was somewhat crude, it served its purpose well without slowing things down appreciably.

A QuickTime clip of a pair of eyes was stripped across the second bar from the top. A clip of a nose was then stripped across the next bar, and a mouth was stripped across the next one. All three had to be created larger than needed and then masked. Because the facial parts were taken from three different models, the effect was startling, yet oddly cohesive (Fig. 25.3). If examined long enough, they became working parts of a new, recognizable face!

A small strip of text containing a Latin root word and its English translation was textured at the bottom of each bar that contained a facial part. The words of the poem were textured onto a layer of widely spaced floating bricks, which were placed in front of the "face" layer. The effect was to make the QuickTime faces visible through the mesh of brickwork containing the poem.

The creation of the new layer and all of its bricks slowed things down quite a bit, adding a new problem: although QuickTime was active only in a 180° sweep, a complicated Walkthrough creation (such as our brick wall) was active as long as it appeared anywhere on the screen. It was time for some more creative engineering. Our solution this time was to create a wall that was the same color as the background, which effectively made the wall invisible. This wall extended roughly parallel to the road, blocking the brick layer

FACE: Front of the head.

Fa - (latin) appear, shine.

Facia - (latin) form, figure

Facere - (latin) to make.

Figure 25.3 Translating the words to imagery.

25.7

from view as travelers looped back around toward the starting point. The wall, which covered an area 10 times the size of the brick layer, slowed movement hardly at all! Evidently, having to recalculate large numbers of points really puts the brakes on Walkthrough—understandably enough. Our wall, massive as it was, still contained only eight points—one for each corner. In comparison, each BRICK in the brick wall contained eight points!

Week 5

During this week, we grabbed and edited QuickTime clips of crowds from television for use in the second layer, roughed out the concepts for layers two and three, videotaped models reciting the entire poem, scanned and edited slides of flowers for use in the third layer, created rooms to enclose layers two and three, and edited sounds.

Layer two

We weren't sure yet how we wanted Layer Two to look, but we knew we wanted to focus in on the first line of Pound's poem, "The apparition of these faces in the crowd." We began grabbing QuickTime clips of crowds from television, keeping the clips short to conserve memory. These were edited in Premiere. While we were in Premiere, we also created a composite movie of crowd clips and text.

Two models were videotaped reciting the poem. Eventually, one voice would be used for layer two and the other for layer three. As with the previous videotapings, extreme close-ups were used (Fig. 25.4).

Layer three

By now, we had the vague notion that we wanted layer three to actually be a room. In one of our earliest design sketches for "Petals," we had envisioned a room through which the viewer would move, viewing QuickTime movies, PICTs, and text on planes suspended at unusual angles. However, we discarded the idea as too confining and too reliant on an overworked paradigm. We returned to it now for layer three—with a major difference: The room would be a black one. The effect on the traveler would be as if he or she was suspended in the pure blackness of space.

While we were experimenting with layer three, we discovered that once we were inside a room, nothing outside of the room existed to slow us down. The room became a self-contained universe that existed in complete isolation from anything that lay outside its walls. The gain in speed was so significant that we decided to build a room around layer two as well.

We scanned slides of flowers taken with a macro lens using a Tamron Photovix Slide Scanner. The slides had either black or transparent backgrounds, which made them easy to edit out in PhotoShop. We wanted only the flowers themselves to appear—not their backgrounds.

Figure 25.4 Composite imagery.

Week 6

During this last, short, hectic week, we produced the third layer, produced the second layer, and tweaked, tweaked, tweaked. Then, we tested—and tweaked some more.

Three comes before two

Because we had some idea of how we wanted layer three to look, we produced it before layer two. Black panels were created and arranged inside our black room, making the panels, in effect, invisible. Onto these panels were placed QuickTime movies and PICTs of the flowers. Once placed, the flowers and movies appeared to float in space. The road, of course, continued through the room to keep travelers oriented. At the far end of the room, we placed a composite movie with a circular mask. The movie consisted of a time-lapse sequence of a flower opening and then fading into a pair of eyes. The road took the traveler directly through the flower/eyes.

Two sounds were edited and added to the final QuickTime sequence (that way, they'd be audible throughout the room). The first sound was of a model reciting the second line of the poem: "Petals on a wet, black bough." The second was of water running somewhere off in the distance. We used SoundEdit to add reverberation to the water sound (Fig. 25.5).

Finally, we decided that we wanted our journey into black space to be a surprise to the traveler. That posed a problem because a black room, from the outside, looks like a big black cube. Our solution? We created a room the same color as the background and just a tiny bit larger than the black room. We placed the black room inside the "invisible" room. A traveler standing outside the room would have no idea that it existed, but if that same traveler were to follow the road, he or she would suddenly be thrust into black space.

Last, But Not Last

For the second layer, we decided on a more literal billboard approach. We wanted our QuickTime and PICTs to appear as signs along a short stretch of the road. This was fairly easy to accomplish. We created panels that were the same color as the background, then textured QuickTime and PICTs of crowds onto them. Much of the time spent on layer two involved coming up with an effective arrangement of billboards.

At the very end of layer two, we placed a composite QuickTime clip of a road with faces along it. The movie was placed so that our road seemed to join the road in the QuickTime clip. The traveler was invited to literally go inside of the movie. We then moved layer three so that it was immediately on the other side of the QuickTime movie. That way, the traveler would go through the movie and be suddenly immersed in the blackness of layer three.

Figure 25.5 The road through the petals.

Tweaking, Tweaking, Tweaking

Once the layers had been completed, there were numerous small adjustments to be made. We played with the final position of the billboards in layer two, added a few textures, re-edited the water sound to push it further into the background, and re-edited one of our composite movies in layer two. One large adjustment was also made: We moved layer one so that it was closer to the end of layer three. That way, travelers would see layer one the moment they emerged from layer three. Finally, we changed the viewer perspective slightly, moving the viewer/traveler closer to the level of the road. This made the road easier to follow and enhanced the three-dimensional effect of some of the layers. The project was complete. Or so we thought.

The Road Goes on Forever

As often happens in the creative process, our project began to take on a life of its own. Other possibilities, other directions in which our work could grow became manifest. "Petals," originally conceived as a project unto itself, became a part of something larger and more ambitious. What form that something would assume was a major preoccupation during a two-month-long brainstorming session. Production then followed, off and on, over the next six months. The eight-month process is chronicled as follows:

Weeks 7 Through 11

During these weeks, we decided to add a module containing critical commentary on "In a Station of the Metro;" chose HyperCard to be the vehicle for that commentary; researched Pound, Imagism, Haiku and Renga; and toyed with the ideas of a virtual renga and an Ezra Pound World-Wide Web page.

Turning to poetry for direction

More than anything else, it was our exploration of poetry that gave us direction. For example, Pound's advocacy of "superposition"—the use of overlapping simultaneous images—seemed to us akin to collage. In our virtual poetry module, we attempted to create three-dimensional collages. To cite another example, our exploration of Haiku led us to *renga*, a Japanese form of collaborative poetry. We decided that we would attempt a renga-like approach to the critical commentary, encouraging students to add their commentary to the ongoing critical dialogue. As we learned more about Pound's poem and its rich Eastern heritage, ideas flew thick and fast. And although many trial balloons burst, some of them later floated back to life again in new forms.

The criticism

One important way to gain insight into a poem is to read the critical commentary that it has garnered. "In a Station of the Metro" has attracted its share of attention from scholars, and we wanted our users to experience at least some of that commentary. We also decided early on that we wanted our users to have the opportunity to participate in the critical dialogue. It was equally important that they have the necessary tools to continue researching on their own.

The vehicle

After some consideration, we settled on HyperCard as the vehicle for our critical module. Our familiarity with the application and its programming language made it an early favorite. In addition, HyperCard's ability to launch other applications would allow users to enter Walkthrough's virtual spaces and return in simple, if not entirely seamless, fashion. Finally, one of HyperCard's notorious weaknesses, its low-resolution graphics, suited our design needs. We had already decided to take a minimalist approach to designing the critical module for a couple of reasons. We didn't want to compete with the virtual environment, and we did not want to distract attention away from the main event, the critical material. Besides, subways are supposed to be gritty and grainy.

We established some criteria for our HyperCard stack. In addition to the critical material itself, we wanted students to be able to access and print bibliographic information. Because all good researchers must take notes, we knew that we must also provide a facility for note taking. And, of course, we wanted our users to be able to add their voices to the chorus of critical commentary.

The metaphor

We also decided that HyperCard should be the glue to hold the entire project together, no matter what shape it might finally assume. A front end of some sort would provide the necessary buttons for transit to and from our two modules, "Petals" and the criticism.

For our HyperCard "glue" to work, however, we knew we would need a strong visual metaphor. Fortunately, Pound's poem immediately suggested a powerful one: the subway. A subway suggests travel. It suggests submersion and return. It suggests labyrinths. All were effective metaphors for scholarly research. All encouraged movement and exploration. It was decided: Our users would enter a subway station and board a virtual A-train to their destinations.

Trial balloons

A few other ideas were tossed about and later discarded. One of them, however, found new life some weeks later in a different form. We had knocked about the idea of allowing students to actually create a haiku renga. As we originally conceived the idea, students would read a renga composed of haiku and then have the opportunity to add a haiku of their own to the work-in-progress. The collaborative poem would be part of a larger Haiku room that would highlight haiku's role in Pound's poetry. However, we discarded the Haiku room as potentially distracting, and the renga went on the shelf with it. But the ideas of a poetry room and an interactive poem were to resurface a few weeks later as key elements in our second virtual module, The Interactive Poem.

Weeks 12 and 13

Brainstorming continued. We defined our audience, and in doing so, settled on some objectives for our project.

The audience

For our project to be successful, we would have to consider our audience carefully. We decided that the target audience would be community college students in a freshman composition class. These students present a special challenge to literature instructors. Many of them have limited experience with poetry, and they have allowed themselves to be convinced that poetry is trivial on the one hand, and too complex to be understood by ordinary students on the other. Community college students also bring with them a wide range of reading and critical-thinking skills.

Reaching such an audience would be a juggling act. We wanted to entice our students to read and explore "In a Station of the Metro," but we did not want to trivialize Pound's poem or the act of reading poetry. And we most definitely did not want to interpret the poem for them. Somehow we had to encourage students to reach their own conclusions. Ultimately, we wanted our students to return to poetry as willing participants, to read and explore poetry for its own sake.

Weeks 14 Through 16

During this crucial period, the Interactive Poem idea began to take shape, the subway metaphor was more clearly defined, and HyperCard prototyping was begun.

The return of the Haiku Room

As brainstorming continued, we kept returning to the idea of a Haiku Room and its interactive possibilities. At the same time, we very much wanted to add a second virtual module using Walkthrough (Fig. 25.6). We discarded the notion of a virtual Haiku museum as being too static, too passive. We explored "Petals" a few times in search of inspiration. Wouldn't it be nice, we thought, if students could create their own virtual interpretations of Pound's poem? Bad idea. We had struggled mightily to produce "Petals" in six weeks; there was no way that students—lacking our experience with criticism, graphics, and design—could or should be expected to produce VR environments on their own. The idea, however, continued to nag us.

Figure 25.5 The road through the petals.

Compromising with textures

Refusing to give up on the idea of an interactive poem, we began to cast about for suitable compromises. We returned to Walkthrough and asked ourselves the following question: What was the most difficult aspect of creating a virtual environment? The answer came quickly. The most difficult part about building a virtual environment is creating the layout—placing and isolating the many polygons. Another problem, actually more tedious than difficult, was capturing and digitizing the images that would be used as textures. If students were to create their own virtual poems, we would have to help them overcome these hurdles.

Our solution lay in the way that Walkthrough handles textures. During layout, when a PICT or QuickTime movie is textured onto a polygon, Walkthrough creates a special link to the graphic file. Then, when the virtual environment is loaded, Walkthrough simply finds that file and textures it onto its designated polygon. For example, if a PICT with the file name "fish" is textured onto a polygon in a virtual space, the next time Walkthrough loads that virtual space, it will automatically look for and texture "fish" onto the appropriate polygon. Walkthrough doesn't care what "fish" is, however, as long as it finds a file named "fish," it will load it. If you were to take a PICT image of a cow and name it "fish," Walkthrough would load the cow PICT and texture it on the polygon to which the original file "fish" had been assigned. What this meant was that we could substitute images in a virtual environment merely by switching filenames. Students could be given a measure of control over the virtual environment after all.

We realized that the final model would involve quite a few tradeoffs. We would have to create a single layout and set of polygons. Students would be able to choose the image that would be layered onto a particular polygon, but not the location of the polygon. They would not be able to change the layout at all, in fact. Furthermore, because any substitute textures would have to exactly fit the polygons to which they were assigned, students would not be able to plug in any pictures they wanted. Instead, they would have to make their selections from an image bank. There would be a set of PICTs for Polygon A, another set for Polygon B, and so on. Students would simply choose one image from each set.

Digging the subway

In the meantime, we started prototyping subway environments in HyperCard. We wanted a clean, easy-to-use interface that clearly carried the subway message. Among the navigation metaphors we considered, were a subway station, a subway car, and a subway map. Eventually, all three navigation metaphors were incorporated.

Week 17

We developed a HyperCard front end and added a new dimension to the Interactive Poem.

The subway takes shape

Once we had agreed on the subway metaphor for our front end, pieces began to fall in place. Using photos found on the Internet and in magazines, Tim began to fashion the opening screen in HyperCard. Using HyperScan to scan in the photos, he was able to achieve a nicely textured, minimalist view of a subway station. This would be the embarkation point for an exploration of Pound's poem (Fig. 25.7).

We decided to use a subway car for the transition to the various stops along the way. The short subway ride also provided an excellent place to run our credits. For the subway car, Tim scanned in some personal photographs he had taken of the New York City Subway. Again, HyperScan coupled with HyperCard's low resolution produced an image that was both stark in its contrast yet apparition-like in its detail. By flipping cards in the HyperCard stack, Tim was able to make a series of ethereal images flicker by in the subway car's window. Disembodied faces, scenery, and even the Berlin Wall flash by during the 30-second ride, which ends with a squeal and swish of the brakes (Fig. 25.8).

As the ride ends, visitors are invited by a flashing sign to click on the window if they wish to enter "Petals." A small replica of an old New York subway map serves as the button that takes travelers to the criticism module (Fig. 25.9).

Figure 25.7 Interior of subway.

Figure 25.8   Interior of subway car.

Figure 25.9   Interactive map.

For the background of the criticism module, Tim used the same New York subway map, blown up to a much larger size. After the image was cleaned up to remove distracting detail, navigation buttons were added—even though we weren't entirely sure yet what they would link to.

World-salad surgery

A major hurdle in the conceptualization of the Interactive Poem was overcome when we began to examine the structure of "In a Station of the Metro." Dave broke the poem down into its grammatical components: "The apparition"—article, noun; "of these faces"—prepositional phrase; "in the crowd"—prepositional phrase, and so on. As we examined the parts, we were able to isolate seven distinct image groups, each represented by one of the following words: apparition, faces, crowd, petals, wet, black, bough. We knew we could easily find images to match each of those words, but we still weren't sure how we were going to turn them into an interactive virtual poem.

We decided to start by developing an image bank. In reality we would actually need seven separate image banks—one for each word on the list. A thesaurus came in handy as we searched for alternative images for each word. The synonyms often suggested new images that we could use. At some point, however, as we flipped through the thesaurus, the key to our interactive poem hit us. The solution was in the words themselves! For each word in the group, we would provide a list of synonyms. Users would first be shown the original word from the poem and then be asked to select a synonym from the accompanying list. What the user would not know is that each synonym would be assigned a corresponding image from the data bank. The image could then be textured onto the appropriate polygon in Walkthrough. Our virtual environment would contain seven polygons, and the synonym for "apparition" would be textured onto the first one, the synonym for "faces" on the next one, the synonym for "crowd" on the next, and so on. Once the substitution process had been finished, the user would be shown the "second-cousin" poem that he or she had created. Then, the user would be invited to view the virtual environment (Fig. 25.10) that he or she had unknowingly created!

Weeks 19 Through 22

HyperCard modules are clearly defined and navigation is clarified.

The criticism module gains focus

As brainstorming on the criticism module intensified, the scope broadened somewhat. We decided that the buttons on our subway map would link to (Fig. 25.11):

1. The "Petals" virtual poem

2. Critical commentary on "In a Station of the Metro"

3. A brief biography of Pound

4. An Ezra Pound World-Wide Web page

5. The Interactive Poem

Figure 25.10   Click here to see virtual poem.

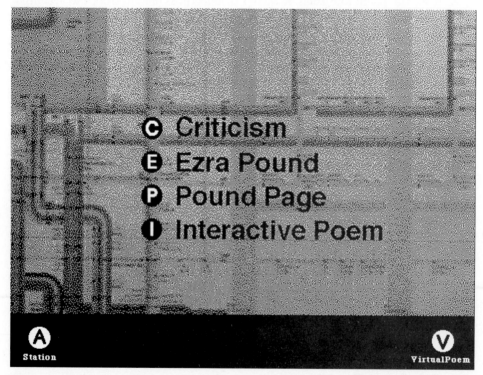

Figure 25.11   Interactive menu.

Keywords for critical commentary

We decided to use keywords as links, or threads, to the critical commentaries. Dave came up with a list of keywords that represented some of the important lines of critical insight into "In a Station of the Metro." These were ultimately reduced to "Haiku," "Imagism," "Rhythm," "Reduction," and "Context." Short critical discussions would be placed on HyperCard cards. The cards would also contain a hidden field containing all of the applicable keywords. Critical discussions could then be organized according to the keywords. Selecting the keyword "Compression," for example, might bring up a list of six discussion cards. Selecting the keyword "Imagism" might bring up another five. And a few of the entries might appear under both "Imagism" and "Compression." Each commentary card would also contain links to bibliographic material and a "notepad." Additional links would allow the user to read comments made by other students, and to add his or her own comments to the dialogue (Fig. 25.12).

Weeks 22 Through 30

These weeks were devoted to beta testing Walkthrough Pro 2.0 on our Quadra 950 and Power Mac 7100, and to researching the critical commentaries.

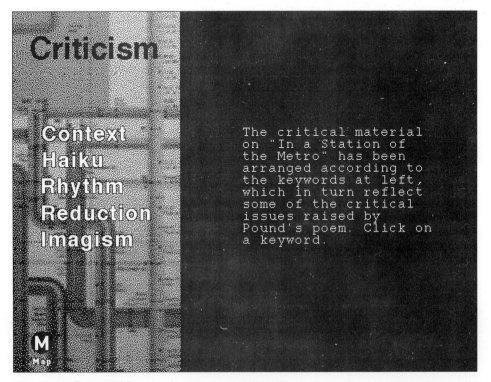

Figure 25.12 Poem criticism.

Compatibility problems

The arrival of Walkthrough Pro 2.0 was both anticipated and dreaded. The anticipation was for the speed increase promised by the native Power PC code. We expected our virtual environments to run much more smoothly with the upgrade, and they did. What we dreaded were the inevitable backward-compatibility problems that accompany any major software upgrade. All compatibility issues were eventually solved, however, and the project was able to get back on track.

Research

While Tim worked the kinks out of Walkthrough Pro, Dave continued researching Pound's poem, spending time on the Internet and at the University of South Florida Library. The Internet pickings were surprisingly slim.

At this time, Dave also began developing a World-Wide Web "Pound Page." The page consisted of a few Pound-related links, as well as links to other literary resources (Fig. 25.13).

Weeks 31 Through 33

The word substitution list was begun in earnest, and the first "roughs" were sketched for the virtual poem environment.

Working with words

We decided to limit ourselves to five synonyms for each original word. Five seems like a small number until it is multiplied by the seven different choices. For example, at five synonyms each, there are 125 possible combinations just for the words "wet, black" and "bough"!

At first, we took a literal approach in our search for synonyms. For "apparition," we came up with such words as "phantasm, spectre," and "spirit." For "crowd," we selected words such as "throng," "swarm," "flock," and "queue." As the selection process continued, however, our choices became less literal and the visual possibilities more diverse. For example, for "petals" we considered the words "fish," "butterflies," "clocks," "televisions," and "chairs." After all, Pound's simile worked with disparate images ("face" and "petals"); why couldn't ours?

Getting a rough idea

While the words were flowing thick and fast, Tim began sketching the layout for the Interactive Poem environment.

Based on our experience with "Petals," we had already decided that we wanted our layout to be circular, so the use would end at the beginning. We also wanted a road of some kind for our users to follow. To add variety and additional depth, we decided to use a series of stepping stones in the Interactive poem instead of a road. And finally, we wanted the background of

Figure 25.13 Welcome to the Pound page.

our environment to be black so that objects would appear to be floating in space.

Weeks 34 and 35

The first draft of the substitute word list was completed, some important design changes were incorporated into the interactive poem, and programming was begun on the filename-substitution routine.

Compromising words

As the first draft of the substitute word list took shape, we began to make some important design decisions. Some of the changes were made to reduce complexity, and others solved thorny problems. For example, the word "apparition" and its synonyms ("spectre," "spirit," "phantasm," et al.) are fairly abstract terms, which made it difficult to come up with effective corresponding images. We decided, therefore, to combine "apparition" and "face" into a single set of images—a series of ghostlike faces. In collage fashion, a QuickTime movie of crowds would be superimposed over the forehead of each apparition/face image. The QuickTime movie would not change—only the face image behind it (Fig. 25.14).

Another design decision revolved around the words "wet," "black," and "bough." To avoid clutter and complexity, Tim suggested that we use sounds, rather than images, to represent "wet." The "bough" images would continue to substitute, but would morph to substitute "petal" images and back again in a continuous loop (Fig. 25.15).

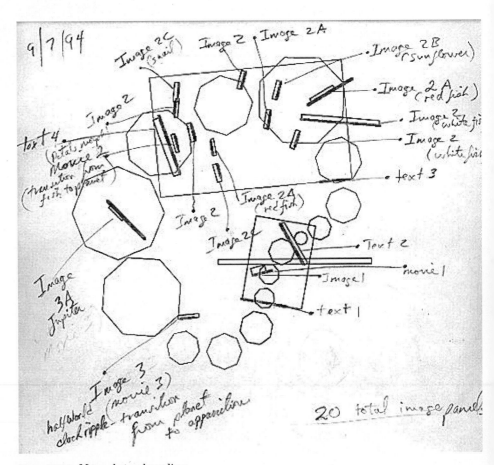

Figure 25.14 Manual storyboarding.

Figure 25.15 Interpreted poem line.

Switching filenames

We needed some additional programming muscle to write the routines that would substitute filenames in Walkthrough. A real pro—Larry Strickland, SPJC's coordinator of instructional computing—took on the task.

Week 36

During this extremely hectic week, we finalized the Interactive poem layout, began morphing, created text for the interactive poem, and began testing the filename substitution routines.

Locking in the layout

An important milestone was reached as we finished the layout of elements in the interactive poem environment, including polygons, textures, sounds and QuickTime movies. We also decided to include the words of the poems next to their corresponding images. To accomplish this, we arched the words over the path to evoke the image of a gateway. Each "gateway" would lead to a new set of images (Fig. 25.16).

Figure 25.16   Interpreted poem line.

Morphing madness

We had decided to use morphs in the interactive poem environment, both for their visual impact and for their kinship with Pound's notion of "superposition." The environment would contain only two morphs, but, unfortunately for Tim, it would require more than 50 morphs to account for all of the possible combinations! Gryphon's Morph program was used to create the morphs, which were then saved as QuickTime movies. The QuickTime movies could be substituted just like PICTs—by swapping filenames. Over 100 images, representing the word substitutes, were first scanned and then combined in the Morph program to create the 50+ QuickTime Morph movies.

When Tim wasn't morphing, he was creating the arched text for the interactive poem. He used Adobe Illustrator to generate the text and Photoshop to rasterize the images into PICT files so that they could be loaded as textures into Walkthrough Pro (Fig. 25.17).

Speaking of swapping filenames

While Tim was busy morphing, Larry completed an early version of his filename substitution routines. We tested them by swapping the names of the various "bough" substitution PICTs. The routines were a success, although we had to work out some filename conventions first.

Criticism modules nears completion

The prototype of the HyperCard criticism module was finally ready. Most of the content was in place and the links were functional. Dave added a running checklist that would keep track of where users had gone. The bibliographies had been completed, as had the "notepad." A preliminary version of the comments section had also been completed—although the look and functionality would undergo further changes (Fig. 25.18).

Week 37

Scanning images was the major activity this week; subway icons were created, and minor improvements were made to the subway interface.

The big scan

Much of Week 37 was devoted to scanning images to be used for all the additional word substitutes in the interactive poem. The images were brought into Adobe Photoshop using a UMAX scanner. They were edited and saved at screen resolution (72 dpi) as 320 by 240 PICT files, then imported into Walkthrough Pro as textures. Images came from a variety of sources, including magazines, television, and personal photographs. We even scanned a few objects—a glove, a sand dollar, and a sea horse (Fig. 25.19).

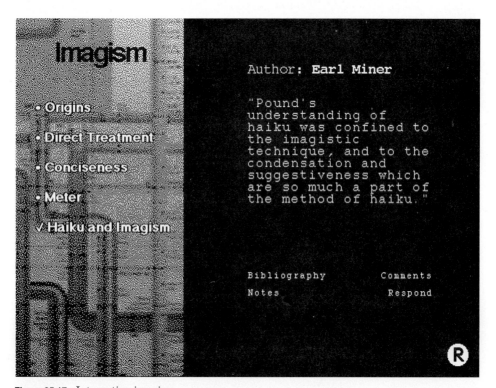

Figure 25.17 Intepreting imagism.

Figure 25.18   Intrepreted poem line.

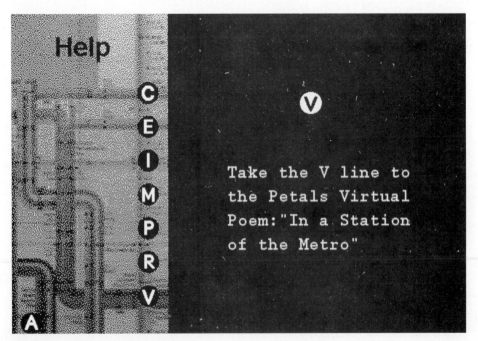

Figure 25.19   Subway metaphor.

Figure 25.20 Comments.

Improving the interface

We knew for some time that we would need a good set of icons to use when navigating the HyperCard front end. We settled on white letters reversed out of a round, black circle. The letter "R" would represent "Return," the letter "M" would represent "Map," the letter "V" the original Virtual (Petals) Poem, and so on. The white-on-black lettering was reminiscent of the signage used in the New York subway system (Fig. 25.20).

A number of minor improvements were made during this time. It took a while, but we finally came up with something that closely resembled the sound made by a subway car door as it opens. A number of icons were moved in the interests of consistency and ease of use. We scanned in a crinkled sheet of paper to use as the background for the "notepad" and commentary sections of the criticism module.

Week 38

Filename-substitution programming was finished, a Help section was created, final tweaking took place.

Final details

Larry finished programming the filename-substitution routine, and we began testing it with all of the various image combinations. The substitutions were working smoothly! Dave fixed a number of bugs in the HyperCard script and began final testing of the critical discussion cards and all of the links and buttons. The World-Wide Web "Pound Page" was tested on the Internet.

Where do we go from here?

Our project is at a crossroads of sorts. There is much more we would like to do. We'd like to add more content to the critical module. We also need to complete Ezra Pound's biography. We need to find more Pound-related resources on the Internet for the "Pound Page." And we would like to add more images to the interactive poem image bank. Perhaps we could even tackle another poem!

However, there are some important issues that we must settle first. The rapid expansion of the World-Wide Web, coupled with the development of the Virtual Reality Markup Language (VRML), opens a whole new set of possibilities. Virtual reality is now possible on the Web; HyperText always has been. By moving our project to the Web, we could increase access for our students, but would the tradeoff in performance be acceptable?

In the meantime, we are in the process of testing our project with students. Their insights and comments might give us some of the answers that we need.

Production Notes by Tim Brock

Using QuickTime in Virtus Walkthrough

For us, working with QuickTime in the Beta texture-enhanced version of Virtus Walkthrough was extremely straightforward and intuitive, provided enough memory was available.

In Virtus Walkthrough (WT), QuickTime (QT) movies are applied as textures with the WT surface editor. Once the specific plane of an object is selected, the surface editor allows users to place numerous (we found no real limit, except in terms of speed) textures or movies anywhere parallel to the selected plane. For example, textures or movies can be placed above or below the surface plane—without adhering to the actual dimensions of the surface. A movie or texture can also be assigned either transparent or opaque surface attributes.

Once the movie (including its audio) is applied, it can be viewed and interacted with instantly in the WT Walk View window. This immediate feedback is extremely helpful in testing the placement of the movies/textures in the virtual space. When viewed in the Walk View window, the movies continue to loop, as long as the steering (mouse) is engaged, and remain active within a 180° radius. Because the movies, like PICT files, are textures, their images are bitmapped and pixelate when viewed up close.

Overall, the extended capability of QuickTime in WT adds an exciting and easy-to-use multimedia function within the virtual space.

Hardware requirements

In order to effectively deal with numerous QT movies and textures in the WT project, a Quadra 950 with one megabyte (MB) of VRAM and 64 MB of DRAM was used. The only other computer hardware needed besides the standard keyboard, mouse and 17-inch monitor was a (formerly) SuperMac VideoSpigot board for QT image/sound capture. Other noncomputer hardware included the following input devices: Super VHS recorder (with 12" NTSC monitor), cable TV, VHS video camcorder, and slide scanner. For production and presentation, external speakers were useful, but not necessary.

System/software requirements

In order to produce a virtual reality product for the classroom, certain system requirements and various software programs were needed. System requirements included the QuickTime 1.5 or 1.6 extension and at least 40 MB of RAM— including the ability to create a RAM disk. The software used was (formerly) SuperMac ScreenPlay to grab QT movies, Adobe Premiere to edit QT, MacroMedia SoundEdit Pro for editing audio, Virtus Walkthrough to create virtual environments, and Adobe Photoshop for image processing of PICT files for textures.

TV input and other sources for virtual reality

The input sources used included television, video clips, slides, and text editors. The hardware used was a cable TV/Video hookup and Tamron slide scanner, both providing an NTSC signal (via RCA cable). These sources were plugged directly into the VideoSpigot board, which captured both digital video (QT) and video stills (PICTs). The stills were imported directly into WT to be used as textures, and the QT movies were almost always edited and compressed in a QT editing program. Text was generated in a paint program as a PICT file and also used for texture mapping in WT.

Creating QuickTime for virtual reality

To create QuickTime movies, several conditions were set to record both video and audio. First, a RAM disk was created (40 MB). To record sound, RCA cables from a video source were plugged into the external inputs of the Quadra 950. In software, (under sounds in the Control Panel), external audio was selected. To record video, the video source was connected with one RCA cable to the VideoSpigot board in the Quadra. With these conditions set, ScreenPlay (VideoSpigot Software) was used to record QuickTime to the RAM disk at 320 by 240 pixels (10 frames/sec.) including audio at 22 kHz, 8-bit mono.

Editing QuickTime for virtual reality

For this project, editing the QT movies for WT required reducing the movies to half the original size: from 320×240 to 160×120 pixels, and from 10 frames per second to 8 frames per second. If sound wasn't necessary, audio channels were cleared. Movies were kept as short as possible and edited to loop continuously. Adobe Premiere was the QT editor used, providing easy editing and quality compression.

QuickTime and sound design in virtual reality

When QuickTime was imported into WT, if audio was included in the movie, it became an integral part of the virtual space. In "Petals," the synchronized sound of the QT movies continued to loop with the video. This repetition was used as part of the design strategy. If the movies were too short, the audio would repeat often, which was not always desirable. To control this, portions of the audio would be edited out and the video channels extended. The portions of sound that were eliminated would then be placed in another movie that was looping at another rate. In various places, reverb was added to emphasize the content. This enhancing and overlapping of repeated sounds proved very effective in the total design.

Editing QuickTime audio for virtual reality

In order to edit sounds in QuickTime, the audio track of the QT movie was exported from Premiere as an AIFF file to MacroMedia's SoundEdit Pro and processed. SoundEdit Pro was used to amplify, reverse, extend, and add reverb to sounds. The sounds then were saved again as an AIFF file and imported back to Premiere to be either combined with another movie or be recombined with the original.

Through the windshield: navigation in the virtual classroom

In designing for classroom use, limitations were placed on navigation—not to hinder the student's ability to navigate, but for simplicity and to reduce confusion. In "Petals," the participant can move forward, backward, left, right, and the combinations thereof—but not up and down. In effect, participants are given a car, not an airplane.

Maximizing QuickTime in Walkthrough

In "Petals," nine QT movies and 26 textures were used. Because of the large number of movies and textures, three techniques were applied in order to maximize memory and speed in WT. First, all movies and textures were placed in RAM (a 40-MB RAM disk was created, allowing 20 MB of RAM free for the WT application).

Second, in WT, speed was increased considerably by selecting the unshaded rendering option. Unshaded rendering reduces program calculations by displaying objects without shading their various surfaces. For instance, a cube would have the same surface color on all six sides. This limitation, although providing speed for navigation, encouraged a creative use of textures, color and scale to suggest form and depth in the virtual space.

Third, "invisible" rooms (rooms created with the same color as the background) were made to surround two of the areas that contained QT movies (we found that three movies per room was the maximum to maintain navigation speed and adequate movie frame-rate). In WT, movies are not calculated if viewed beyond a 180° radius, or if blocked by a room or partition. This allows for more discreet placement of movies, reducing calculation to movies seen only by the navigator. In "Petals," these invisible rooms were assigned transparent openings so that the navigator could "see in," initiating the QT movies to play at the appropriate time.

VR applications for the classroom: maximum/minimum requirements

The total size of "Petals" is under 15 MB, including the application. For classroom use and presentation, the ideal configuration is to have a 15-MB RAM disk for the movies and textures and enough additional RAM to set the application to 20 MB.

However, with at least 12 MB of RAM, "Petals" can run from the internal hard disk of any PowerPC or 68040 machine. This configuration allows the WT application or Virtus player to be set at 8 MB of RAM, which is the absolute minimum to successfully run "Petals."

Animation, Video, and Sound

26

3D Animation

Bob Bennett

3D Then and Now

Few objects in the world are truly flat, and human beings are used to receiving their information in three dimensions. And yet much of human communication up to this point has been delivered on paper, the most familiar two-dimensional medium. Even the most complex three-dimensional structures are communicated in 2D drawings and blueprints that only professionals can decipher.

For centuries, designers have created 3D models out of wood, paper, or clay to help them communicate their concepts. But creating a 3D model in the real world is a tedious procedure that, once completed, can be modified only by means of even more work. As veteran builders of 3D models, architects, set designers, and design engineers were among the first to embrace the concept of computer-aided design. By generating their models on the computer they could enjoy many advantages.

For instance, they could attain viewpoints of the model unattainable with any physical model, regardless of size. They could travel "into" a computer-generated house to see it from the viewpoint of a prospective resident. They also could modify a computer-based model quickly and easily. Imagine being able to change the fabric or material of a chair from Naugahyde to canvas in a few moments using a computer. And even if you do go on to make changes in your original design, you can readily retain multiple versions of your model on the computer, without destroying the original.

The advantages of using the computer to generate models can be summed up in a single word: *control*. With the computer you have control over the shape and surface-appearance of objects without having to overcome the real-world constraints of physics. If you want to create a flower made out of concrete, your computer will happily oblige you. You can apply plaster, sculpt metal, or carve objects out of wood without having to learn each of these respective crafts.

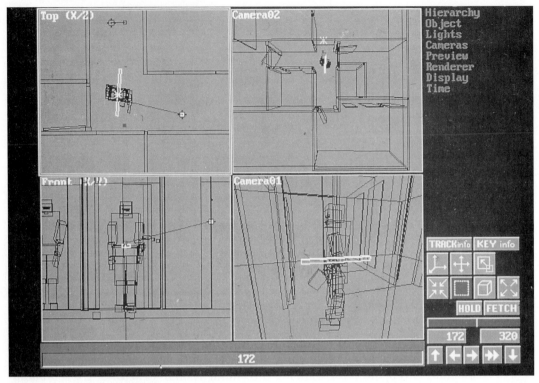

Figure 26.1 Courtroom animation.

This level of control also extends to the environment around your model. With your desktop computer you can place your design on a glass pedestal or in a field of wheat. Lighting can be adjusted so that the perfect tint and the ideal shadow is cast upon your scene. With this degree of control, your 3D model can deliver the specific message intended, without superfluous details. It is precisely this capability that makes 3D computer imagery so powerful as a courtroom tool. Only those details of a court case that are truly known need be presented. Unknown persons in a scene can have blank faces, while known bullet trajectories can be exhibited with precise accuracy in the same scene. Figures 26.1 and 26.2 demonstrate this. Both of these images, created by Alec Jason, are wireframe models rendered and animated for a murder trial.

If the advantages of using computers to do 3D modeling have been so great, why is it such a recent phenomenon? The answer lies in the price/performance curve of desktop computers. 3D modeling requires substantial processing power. Only in the past 3 years have desktop computers been fast enough even to create complex 3D models. Now the Macintosh, AMIGA, and IBM PC are all fast enough for 3D work. As personal computers (PCs) have become more powerful, computer software developers have rushed to supply software for these potential new customers. While CAD software is a common means for building 3D models, its purpose is primarily to support the design and

Figure 26.2 Courtroom animation.

manufacturing processes. When communication is the main goal, specialized 3D modeling software such as Swivel 3D from Macromedia is generally opted for. With a 3D modeling package, one can create 3D objects that are ready for the next stages of rendering and animation.

The Power of Animation

Often, people associate the word *animation* with "cartoons." Cartoons are great, but there is much more to animation than fun, animated characters. Animation has grown from being purely an entertainment medium to being one of the most powerful ways to get your point across. It has a universal appeal that transcends age and cultural boundaries. Delivered at 30 frames per second, it sends a concentrated message. Whether you are aiming to deliver complex visual information or simply to keep the viewer's attention, animation is truly a powerful medium.

Animation software on a desktop computer lets you exercise a tremendous amount of control over your final result. You can control form, color, lighting, and perspective using 3D animation software. You are not bound to physical laws of nature, and thus can create images that say exactly what you need to communicate.

Animation is, of course, a time-based, space-based medium. And as such it gives you control over the pace of your message. You can use animation to efficiently show in a few seconds a lengthy process (such as soil erosion) that takes months or years in the real world to occur. Conversely you can slow down an event that would normally be too fast to comprehend by making the animation take place over 5 to 10 seconds. You can show how things move over time—traffic, or a robot arm. You can vary the surface appearance of an object to show how a process such as rusting can alter an iron plate over time. Or, to really give your audience a feel for the space in which you have placed them, you can simply vary your viewpoint so as to travel through a 3D scene.

The Process

There are five basic steps to creating 3D animation that are common to most software packages, regardless of the computer platform you are using. You should

1. Create a 3D model.

2. Apply realistic materials.

3. Add lights and cameras.

4. Make it move.

5. Render.

Let's look at these steps in more detail.

Creating a 3D model

In a typical 3D modeler, there are numerous ways to construct a 3D model. First, objects can be generated from *primitives,* or simple 3D shapes such as cubes, spheres, cones, and cylinders. Many real-world items are in fact amalgamations of simple shapes such as these. For instance, a table often is comprised of four cylinders and a cube.

A second method involves creating 3D objects from 2D outlines. A profile of a wine glass can be "spun" 360° to form a solid 3D goblet. Similarly, a banana can be constructed by sending a circle along an arc, while its circumference is increased and decreased.

In addition, 3D models of common objects from cars to sharks are available in prebuilt form. Many of these models originally were created in CAD systems, and they are stored in standard Data Exchange Format (DXF) files. Some companies like Viewpoint Engineering now specialize in supplying 3D models to the multimedia developer. Often it is easier to purchase a model of the Statue of Liberty, for example, than to construct it anew yourself. Keep in mind that the suppliers of these models often use 3D digitizing equipment to speed the model-development process. In fact, many of these companies can

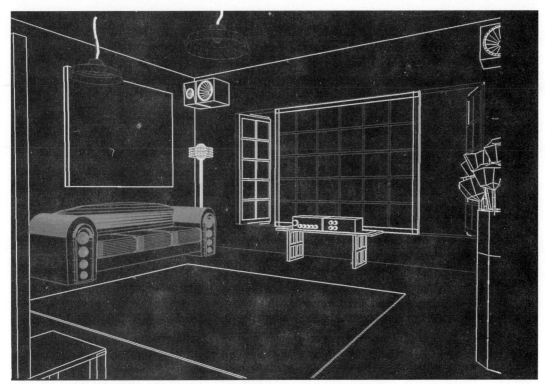

Figure 26.3   Autocad model.

even digitize real-world 3D items on demand if you can provide them with the physical object to be digitized. If you are obtaining 3D objects from a vendor, make sure they are in a format you can accept, as there are numerous 3D data formats utilized, one of which is shown in Fig. 26.3.

In the computer, most computer models ultimately are comprised of small triangles, or polygons. A small model may have less than a dozen objects, with less than 10,000 polygons total in the scene. A large model may have hundreds of thousands of polygons. Other methods of representing models rely on mathematical surfaces and store data in a more efficient manner than do individual polygons.

The best computer models are constructed with easy-to-understand names assigned to their components, simplifying the subsequent tasks of applying materials and animating them. Even better, some models are sold with all of their material appearances preapplied.

Applying realistic materials

Once geometry has been acquired or built, the next step in developing an animation is to apply material appearances to objects in the scene. Tabletops could be assigned a gray marble finish, chairs an oak-wood finish. Sometimes the goal is to make the scene look as believable as possible, a goal known as *photorealism*. Other times the goal is not so much to make the scene look real as to make it look fantastic or interesting. The ability to assign any material property to any object in the computer is one of the most powerful aspects of 3D animation. Often, computer software for 3D animation includes a built-in library of existing materials plus a "materials editor" for creating or modifying materials.

The most basic way to specify a material is to specify its color properties (e.g., how light will reflect off the object). Often these color properties are specified by using adjectives referring to three properties of light: diffuse, specular, and ambient. The *diffuse* component is the color of the object itself. For instance, you would want to assign a red color to the diffuse component to simulate a red plastic ball, as shown in Fig. 26.4.

The *specular* component is the shiny highlight on the surface of the object. If, for example, we wanted that same red ball to look as if it were made of glass, we might assign a small white specular highlight to the material (on a red surface, this will appear to be glass). By varying the size and color of the specular highlight we could also approximate the look of other common mate-

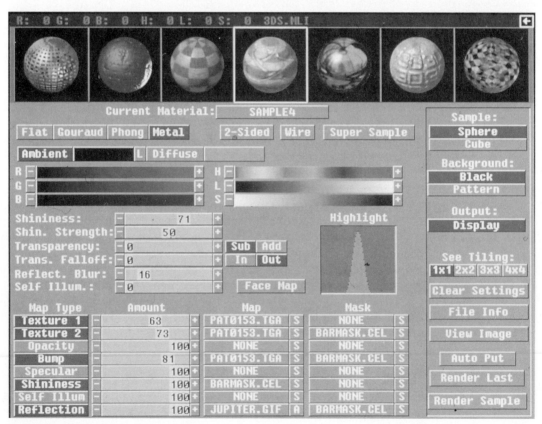

Figure 26.4   3D Studio's unique textures.

rials such as metal or rubber. The final color property, *ambience,* is the color of the surrounding light in the overall scene.

But color is only one basic way to create a realistic-looking material. Another way is through the use of texture maps. A simple use of a texture map is to apply a decal to an object, such as a red cross on the side of an ambulance. A texture map is simply a bitmap, that is, a raster file created in a paint program or perhaps scanned into the computer. If you wanted a certain carpet in your computer model, you could actually scan a sample of the carpet into the computer and apply it to the floor of an imaginary house. Any bitmap can be used as a texture map. Many computer artists believe that the skilled use of texture maps is one of the best ways of achieving believable results on a computer.

Texture mapping can be much more subtle than a pure decal such as the cross mentioned above. Textures can completely replace the base color of an object or be applied just as a percentage. For instance, if we were to add a marble texture to a yellow material and let it bleed through the yellow color, we could make the object look more complex—like a soup in need of stirring, perhaps. A texture map also can be applied to simulate a rough or pitted surface in a technique known as *bump-mapping.* Here the values in the texture map are used to simulate raised or depressed areas on a surface, so the resulting look is grainy, not smooth.

Texture maps also can be used to vary how transparent an object is, to make some portions shiny or dull, or to simulate the mirrored reflection of the surrounding scene in a surface, such as a wood tabletop. Textures need not be just still images, they can be a sequence of images. In this way you can simulate an event such as a burner on a stove getting bright red as it heats up, or make a television set in your scene appear to be tuned to a show.

One of the more advanced ways to create a material appearance is through a programmable procedure often called a *shader.* Let's say you want to have a brick appearance on a wall in your scene. You could either scan in a brick pattern and apply it as both a texture and bump map, or write a shader to simulate the look of real brick. Many common materials such as marble, wood, and brick can be approximated quite effectively through the use of computer algorithms. A "procedural" brick might have the additional advantage of appearing solid—that is, the brick material seems to pass all the way through the object. Procedural materials also generally lack the "seams" that classic texture-mapped materials sometimes exhibit. Finally, procedural materials tend to look good even when viewed from very close up, whereas a texture map can look highly pixelated (jagged) up close.

A wide variety of materials can be employed in a single scene. Objects in the background may not need very detailed materials to be assigned to them. An object that is the focus of attention may require a very detailed material that is applied with great care so as to avoid seams and other imperfections. A single scene may include hundreds of different materials. The materials used in a scene may actually occupy much more disk space than the geometry of the objects themselves!

Adding cameras and lights

When it comes to this part of computer modeling, the terminology may be quite familiar to you, particularly if you have some background in photography.

Just as in the real world, we must have light in order to see anything that has been rendered. There are different kinds of lights in most computer software programs, just as there are around you everyday. *Ambient* light is the basic level and color of light in the whole scene. If red ambient light is used to simulate the look of a sunset, any blue objects will tend to look purple.

Spotlights often are used to send a cone of light in a particular direction. You decide on the size of the cone and where the light should point. The spotlight usually can have its own color—or even a bitmap—assigned to it, much like a slide projector. A spotlight generally will be able to cast shadows behind objects it encounters. The softness of the resulting shadow usually is another parameter associated with the spotlight.

Keep in mind that spotlights have no shape or mass themselves, so you can place them in a scene without having to worry whether they will be seen. You also can place them in locations where no real light could ever go. Figure 26.5 shows a "blotchy" shadow map projecting through a carefully placed spotlight. This gives the impression of watery shadows cast on an ocean floor.

Most computer software packages of this type also include an automated camera. You can place one or more cameras in a scene and then look through them, with the resulting perspective corresponding to the characteristics of the "lens" you have specified.

There are no lens defects in a computer camera, which means you can create a wide-angle lens that could never be manufactured in the real world! You can put a camera in places where no real camera could ever go due to heat, water, lack of physical space, or other constraint.

The rendering process

Let's assume you have created a model and it has materials assigned to it. You can now easily move your camera to the desired position and "render" a single frame so as to get a nice picture. Rendering is the computationally intense part of the process, which means your computer may be tied up thinking for quite a while. It is sometimes said that rendering is "never fast enough."

There are several different levels of rendering, and these are sometimes referred to as *shading methods*. A common one is trading off rendering quality for rendering speed. The simplest and fastest shading method is *flat shading*. In fact, some computers can perform flat shading in hardware for instantaneous shading of small- to medium-sized models. But a flat-shaded rendering is not terribly impressive in appearance. Each polygon is assigned a single color, and the result is usually a faceted look that appears phony. Flat shading is useful during mode development and for producing motion tests prior to final rendering.

The next level of shading quality is *smooth* (often called *Gouraud*) *shading*. This type of rendering eliminates the faceted appearance of flat shading but

Figure 26.5 Automated camera.

takes a little longer to compute. Instead of each face getting a single color, a gradient of colors is assigned to each face to produce a smooth appearance. One level up from smooth shading is *Phong shading*. Phong shading looks even better than smooth shading, since it adds specular highlights to objects. While this takes longer to render, the presence of these highlights makes for a more convincing result. Imagine an excellent rendering of a billiard ball and you will have a good idea of what Phong rendering looks like. Figure 26.6 provides examples of various forms of rendering.

There are other kinds of shading methods, and rendering is still an area of very active research. *Radiosity* is a technique that makes it possible to simulate extremely realistic lighting of interior spaces. *Ray-tracing* is a very time-consuming technique that produces excellent results. With ray-tracing you get perfect reflections off shiny surfaces, and light is bent or refracted when it

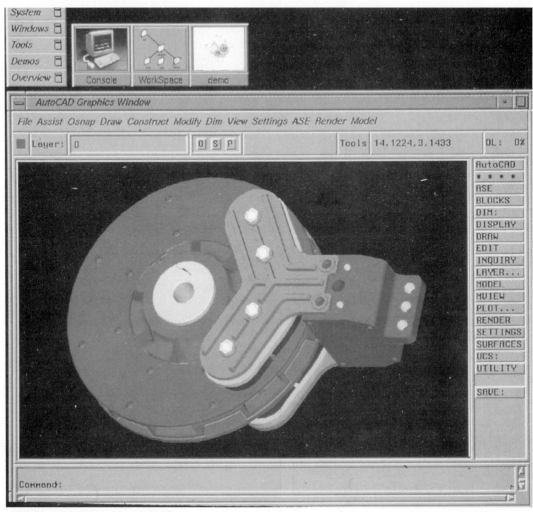

Figure 26.6 Various levels of rendering.

travels through an opaque or transparent object such as a wine glass. As mentioned earlier, you may not have the time to render using a technique such as ray-tracing, since it usually takes too long to be of practical value for creating on a desktop computer an animation of many frames.

Making it move

By now you should have some idea of how you will create, model, develop material properties for, and render out a single frame or picture. But how will you actually animate?

In the case of classic 2D animation, you traditionally would draw each frame of an animation, with each moving object drawn in a slightly different

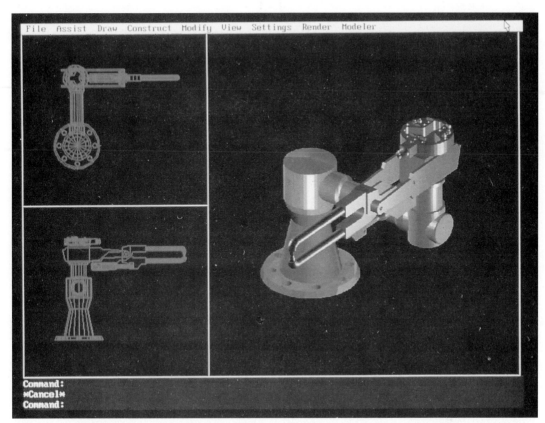

File Assist Draw Construct Modify View Settings Render Modeler

Command:
Cancel
Command:

Figure 26.6 (*Continued*)

position. Your point of view generally would be fixed, and objects would move in front of you. With 3D animation, the process is a bit different. You assign motion to objects on specific "keyframes" and move your camera on different frames to gain the best vantage point, and the software figures all of the "in-between" moves. This process is called *keyframe animation,* and it is the technique used to create most 3D animation today. Some 3D animation is produced in a slightly different manner, but before we get into that let's look at keyframing in more detail.

Keyframe animation can be defined as *the process of assigning motion to objects on specific numbered frames of an animation sequence and letting the computer interpolate the intervening motion.* If you position a ball up in the air on frame 30 and establish that as a keyframe, the computer will "move" the ball up smoothly from frame 0 to frame 30. Exactly how smoothly the ball begins and ends its journey is usually settable in the software. Sometimes you want an object at rest to move instantly (as in an explosion), while at other times you want it to move gradually (as when a boulder starts to roll down a slope). You have control over these "ease-in" and "ease-out" settings in

Figure 26.6   (*Continued*)

software products such as Autodesk 3D Studio. This is demonstrated in Fig. 26.7, where a path is created for a helicopter to follow in an animation.

Often it is useful to establish a hierarchy of objects when performing keyframe animation. In other words, you can establish links between objects so that they are affected by the characteristics of other objects in the scene. You may want to link a hand to an arm, so that if you move the arm, the hand moves with it. A walking person may have a very detailed set of hierarchies, so that, as the head turns, the eyes and nose also move, but the eyes can move independently of the head.

Just as you can keyframe objects to produce 3D animation, so too you can keyframe lights and cameras. You may want a spotlight to pan across a company logo for a Hollywood-type effect. Or you may want to assign a camera to follow a curving path as each frame is rendered. The possibilities are limitless.

Figure 26.6 (*Continued*)

Animation often boils down to a few basic types of movement. You can rotate an object around its local pivot point, or around some center point in the scene (such as a whirlpool). You can scale an object up or down, as when inflating or deflating a balloon. You can move an object from one location to another.

Some programs will allow you to "morph" objects from one shape into another. You could say by the keyframe on frame 120, "Morph the fish into a whale." This is a complex task for the software to accomplish, and restrictions may be placed on you such as requiring the number of points in the "begin" and "end" shapes to be identical. Often you can morph the material of the object, not just the shape. In this way you can make a leopard suddenly have the skin of a giraffe.

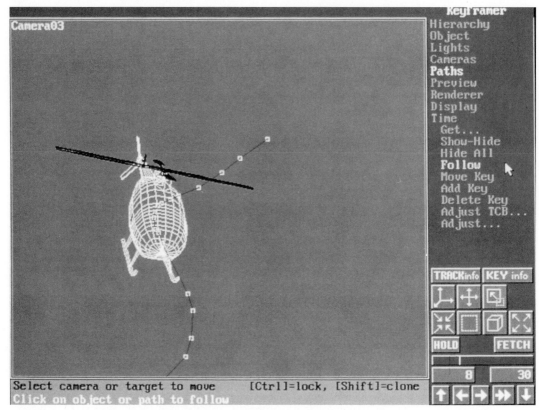

Figure 26.7 Helicopter path.

Generally, keyframing is done by using interactive graphics, where you visibly move objects in certain keyframes by means of a mouse or other pointing device. Sometimes a scripting language is used ("Move Ball 34,0,0 at Frame 30") to establish the animation sequence. Sometimes the process is even more automatic. Computer software is getting better and better at assisting the animator. In some cases the behavior of certain objects can be programmed. An explosion can be programmed to "shatter" an object in an animation—greatly simplifying the task of the animator. In professional animation software such as 3D Studio, airplanes can be automatically "banked" around turns, and balls can be set to bouncing without manually keyframing them up and down. Even effects such as waves and ripples can be automatically assigned using today's software. Expect tomorrow's software to increasingly take over the computation of common movements such as running and swimming.

In summary, the process of producing 3D animation can really be as simple or as complex as you choose to make it. One thing is certain: the personal computer technology necessary to produce 3D animation is now accessible, affordable, and understandable.

Technical Aspects of Multimedia Audio

Cliff Kondratiuk

Digital Audio Systems

Fast growth in the PC sound card market is today fostering fierce competition among the hardware vendors in the field. As a result, the marketing machines are throwing around statistics and buzzwords that imply their products offer the same audio quality as that to be found in a good home-stereo system. In order to wade through this mountain of claims and advertisements, it is important to have a basic understanding of how the perception of human hearing relates to digital audio systems. The important factors that determine the quality of a digitized waveform are the sample rate, the number of bits used to encode the signal, and the proper design of the analog input and output sections.

While the audio signal is in the digital domain, the two determining factors of quality are the sample rate and the number of bits used to encode the waveform. Through Nyquist's theorem, the sample rate defines the reproducible bandwidth of the encoded signal. Nyquist's theorem states that a digitally encoded signal may be used to record and reproduce frequencies from DC to one-half of the sample rate without introducing aliased noise components. With the bandwidth of human hearing accepted as being from 20 Hz to 20 kHz, this theorem shows that a sample rate of greater than 40 kHz is required to reproduce the audible range of frequencies. To satisfy this requirement, Philips and Sony chose the 44.1-kHz sample rate when designing the compact disc (CD). This same sample rate is now also used as the highest rate supported by the multimedia audio extensions found in Windows 3.1™. The other sample rates supported under Windows are 11.025 kHz and

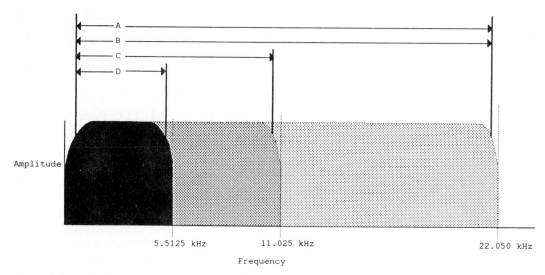

Figure 27.1 Bandwidths supported by Windows 3.1. A = 20 Hz to 20 kHz, bandwidth of human hearing; B = 20 Hz to 20 kHz, usable bandwidth of 44.1-kHz sample rate; C = 20 Hz to 10 kHz, usable bandwidth of 22.050-kHz sample rate; D = 20 Hz to 5 kHz, usable bandwidth of 11.025-kHz sample rate.

TABLE 27.1   Frequency Range of Common Sounds

Instrument/sound	Frequency range fundamental	Frequency of fourth overtone/harmonic
Grand piano	A_1 to C_8 27.01 Hz to 4.186 kHz	12.558 kHz
Flute	C3 to B6 261.63 Hz to 3.951 kHz	11.853 kHz
Electric guitar	E1 to E5 82.41 Hz to 1.328 kHz	3.984 kHz
Pipe organ	C2 to C10 32.7 Hz to 8.372 kHz	25.116 kHz
Trumpet	E2 to B flat 4 164.81 Hz to 932.33 Hz	2.797 kHz
Human speech	50 Hz to 800 Hz	2.4 kHz

22.050 kHz. Figure 27.1 shows the bandwidths that may be reproduced by these three sample rates.

These usable bandwidths show the highest frequency to be less than the theoretical maximum stated by Nyquist's theorem. In practical applications, frequencies equal to and greater than the Nyquist frequency must be significantly attenuated to avoid the introduction of aliasing noise. This attenuation is assumed to occur between the highest usable frequency and the Nyquist frequency.

In an attempt to correlate these frequencies to the real world, Table 27.1 lists the frequency ranges of some common sounds.

From this table we can see that, with the exception of the pipe organ, the largest fundamental frequency of these sounds is less than 5 kHz, implying that they could all be recorded without any loss at the low rate of 11.025 kHz. This would be the case if all of these sounds were comprised of only the fundamental sine wave, with no overtones or harmonics. Fortunately these sounds also include the harmonic overtones, which help to define the timbre of the instrument. This tonal quality, together with the rates of amplitude change, is how we differentiate between various musical instruments and other everyday sounds. To maintain the unique quality of these sounds, the frequency range chosen for digital sampling must also include these harmonics. The value of the fourth harmonic of the highest note or fundamental shows that higher sample rates are required to capture the frequency content of the entire instrument.

Percussion instruments such as snare drums, crash cymbals, etc. do not exhibit a frequency range as shown above. These types of instruments generally contain fast-attack transients that are made up of frequencies from the fundamental of the instrument up to 20 kHz in some cases. Thus, to properly record many percussion instruments, the 44.1-kHz sample rate would be required.

The second factor of audio quality is the number of bits used to encode the signal. This determines the available dynamic range and the signal-to-error ratio of the digital sample. Available dynamic range is defined as *the difference between the quietest or lowest-level signal and the loudest or highest-level signal that may be encoded.* In order to provide a more straightforward description, the following discussion will relate to the use of a linear PCM encoding technique.

In a digital system, an analog signal is encoded by assigning finite levels to the analog waveform at discrete periodic intervals. This introduces two distinct limitations on the encoding. The first limitation will be defined as *available dynamic range* and is related to the amplitude of the signal and the number of bits used to encode the sample. If a 16-bit word length is used, the system is capable of assigning one of 65535 distinct levels to the ideal analog waveform. If the analog signal is limited to a maximum voltage level of 1 V peak-to-peak, then the loudest signal that may be encoded is equal to 1 V and the quietest equal to $\frac{1}{65535}$ V. This yields an available dynamic range of approximately 96 dB.

A digital system's dynamic range and the perception of loudness in human hearing are often difficult to compare. The threshold of human hearing is measured as being 0 dB sound pressure level (SPL), which is equal to 10^{-12} watts/m^2 in acoustic power. A 16-bit recording is able to reproduce signal differences from 0 dB to approximately 96 dB. If the output of this recording were connected to a loudspeaker system capable of producing an output power of .0063 watts/m^2, or 96 dB (typical home-stereo loudspeakers can reproduce an acoustic SPL from 85 to 92 dB), Figure 27.2 would directly relate the dynamic range of the digital system to the human perception of loudness.

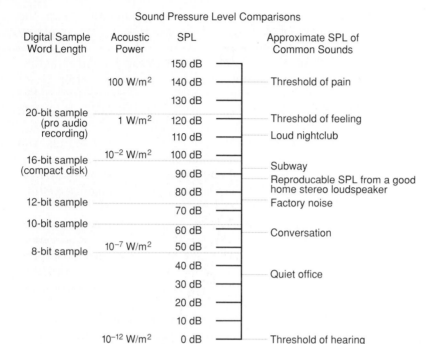

Figure 27.2   Comparison of digital to human perception of loudness.

The second limitation is the signal-to-error ratio, or digital signal-to-noise ratio of the encoding technique. When a finite digital level is assigned to the ideal analog signal, a measurable difference exists between the assigned level and the ideal signal amplitude. This difference is a form of distortion introduced by the digital encoding and is generally referred to as *quantization error*. As in the measurement of dynamic range, the amount of distortion is directly related to the number of bits used in the encoding. The power of this distortion is determined by the size of the individual steps in amplitude available to the digital sampler. An example of this error is shown in Fig. 27.3.

Like dynamic range, the signal-to-error ratio also is measured in decibels. It is calculated by taking the ratio of the maximum RMS signal value to the energy in the error signal across one sample interval. The results of this measurement yield a signal-to-error ratio for linear PCM encoding of $6.02n + 1.76$ dB, where n is the number of bits used.

For a 16-bit word length, this would yield a signal-to-error ratio of approximately 98 dB, which is about the same result obtained for the dynamic range. This holds true only for a linear PCM encoding technique. Other forms of digital encoding such as the μLaw/ALaw companding technique have signal-to-error ratios that are significantly lower than the reproducible dynamic range. μLaw/ALaw will be discussed later in the chapter.

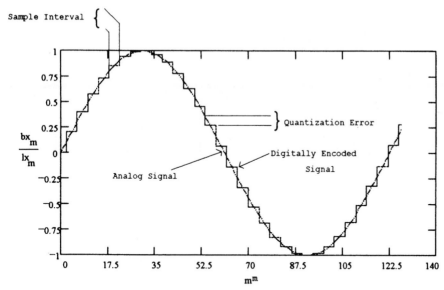

Figure 27.3   Distortion introduced by digital encoding.

The standard sample sizes offer the following ideal signal-to-error ratios:

Sample size	Signal-to-error ratio	Equivalent
8-bit	49.88 dB	Telephone
10-bit	61.92 dB	AM radio
12-bit	73.96 dB	Metal tape
16-bit	98.04 dB	Compact disc

These measurements show the ideal signal-to-quantization error for various encoding word sizes, and are the most often used to make dynamic-range or signal-to-noise ratio claims. There are additional noise components that may be present in a digital signal which are unrelated to the basic claim for dynamic range. The most unpleasant of these are a result of audible image frequencies and digital aliasing noise. Image frequencies are a component of digital systems that occur as a result of modeling a continuous time-analog signal with discrete time samples. Figure 27.4 shows the placement of these images in a digital sampling system.

When the sample rate, Fs, is 44.1 kHz, the Nyquist frequency, 0.5Fs, is set at 22.05 kHz. The images introduced from this sample rate will occur in between 22.05 kHz and 44.1 kHz, which is outside the accepted range of human hearing. Noise introduced from these image frequencies becomes a significant problem when the sample rate used for the signal is 22.05 or 11.025 kHz. These rates will create image frequencies well within the range of audible frequencies. To avoid a serious degradation in the output, these

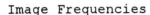

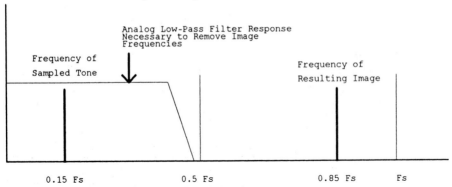

Figure 27.4 Placement of images in a digital sampling system.

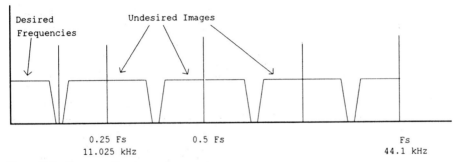

Figure 27.5 Oversampling image frequencies.

images must be removed by a steep rolloff-analog smoothing filter placed after the digital-to-analog converter. In order to accomplish this, a sound card would require an output filter with programmable cutoffs to match each of the supported sample rates.

Some digital systems have a set output sample rate matching the maximum supported rate of 44.1 kHz. To play samples designed for the lower rates, the system will interpolate, or oversample the data to the fixed output rate. This introduces more concerns with additional image frequencies created by the oversampling process. Figure 27.5 shows the additional images introduced when oversampling an 11.025-kHz signal to 44.1 kHz. Figure 27.6 shows the frequency spectrum of a 1-kHz tone sampled at 11.025 kHz and then oversampled to 44.1 kHz by merely repeating each sample four times.

The three additional peaks in Figure 27.6 are a result of failing to remove the images around the original 11.025-kHz sample rate after the signal was oversampled. In the digital domain, these frequencies must be removed through the execution of computation-intensive digital filter algorithms. Due to the processing power required, these algorithms must be performed on the sound card. Only digital signal processor (DSP)–based sound cards have the power available for this.

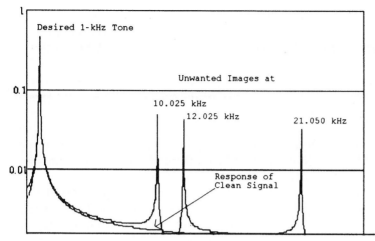

Figure 27.6 Frequency spectrum of noise.

Until now, our discussion of sound has been limited to the audio signal while it is still in the digital domain. Typically, the digital domain is where the lowest amount of noise is introduced into the signal. The high-speed digital signals found on the PC's ISA bus, and the lack of proper isolation between the analog and digital circuitry on the sound board, cause most of the signal degradation. Measurements of some popular sound cards show overall SNRs of less than 72 dB for 16-bit, 44.1-kHz sample recording and playback. The analog circuitry on some cards even picks up audible noise caused by data transfers from disk accesses and mouse movements. As a final determination of a given sound card's overall signal-to-noise ratio, the measurements taken from the output of the analog section should be used. To be of value, these measurements should be taken while there is a lot of activity on the ISA bus.

General MIDI

MIDI (Musical Instrument Digital Interface) was introduced by the MIDI Manufacturers Association (MMA) in 1983 as a standardized serial-communications protocol for controlling electronic music devices. This protocol allowed electronic synthesizers to communicate with each other, regardless of the manufacturer. MIDI takes the form of byte-wide instructions that have been standardized for assigning track and patch IDs, triggering notes, controllers, channel volumes, etc. on any MIDI-compatible synthesizer. Although this marked a breakthrough in the music industry, one component was missing from the original specification. While keyboard manufacturers supported the MIDI protocols, they still maintained control over the patch IDs in which the individual instrument sounds are located. Although the devices could communicate with one another, a given MIDI sequence was useful only for the equipment for which it was written. To use the program with different hardware setups, the user had to edit the patch locations in order to trigger the correct instrument sounds. This problem recently has been addressed with the General MIDI System–Level 1 specification introduced by the MMA in 1991.

The General MIDI (GM) mode of operation was added to the MIDI specification as a means of standardizing where each instrument sound can be addressed on a given sound device. This mode specifies where 128 specific melodic-instrument and 46 percussive-instrument sounds can be addressed on a General MIDI–compatible device (see Fig. 27.7). The introduction of this standard instrument-mapping allows application developers and composers to generate one MIDI file that can be played through any compatible sound device. In addition to supporting the standard instrument locations, General MIDI–compatible devices must be able to respond to each of 16 MIDI channels simultaneously, with different timbres on each channel. Compatibility also requires that the device have a minimum of 24 voices that are dynamically allocated for either pitched timbres or fixed percussion, or 16 dynamically allocated voices for pitched timbres and 8 dedicated voices for percussion. Higher-quality sound cards will offer up to 32 dynamically allocated voices. A detailed overview of the General MIDI specification is offered next.

The MIDI Manufacturers Association introduced the General MIDI System–Level 1 specification to allow MIDI data sequences to play on any MIDI synthesizer that complies with the specification. This was accomplished by defining minimum performance requirements for compatible synthesizers, sound modules, cards, or keyboards. As taken from the General MIDI System–Level 1 specification (1991), a PC sound card or module must have

Voices. A minimum of either 24 dynamically allocated voices, available simultaneously for both melodic and percussive sounds, or 16 dynamically allocated voices for melody plus 8 for percussion.

Channels

General MIDI support for all 16 MIDI channels
Variable number of voices on each channel (polyphony)
Different instrument sounds (timbres) on each channel
Key-based percussion on channel 10

Instruments

A minimum of 16 different timbres playing various instrument sounds
A minimum of 128 presets for instruments (MIDI program numbers)

Note on / note off

Middle C = midi key 60
All voices must respond to velocity
All voices dynamically allocated (note/drums reattack using free voices)

Controller changes

Controller 1—Modulation
Controller 7—Main Volume
Controller 10—Pan

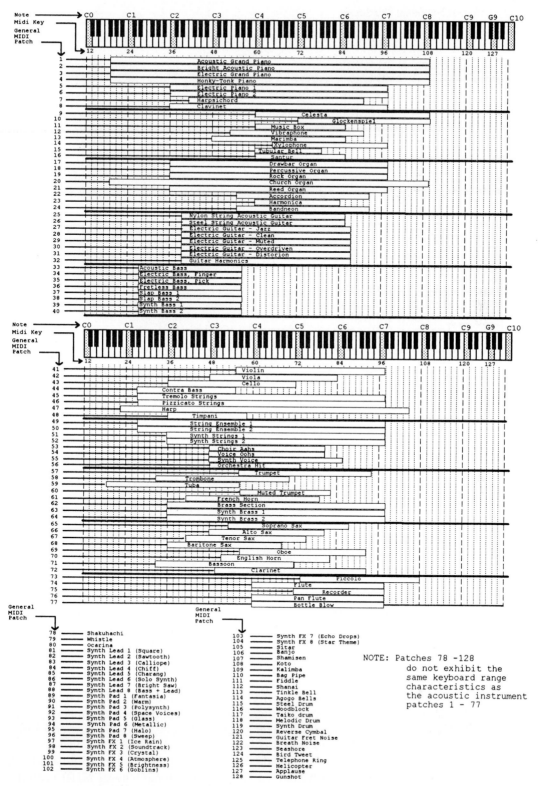

Figure 27.7 General MIDI synthesizer ranges.

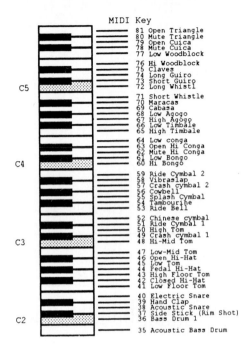

Figure 27.8 General MIDI percussion map.

Controller 11—Expression
Controller 64—Sustain
Controller 121—Reset all controllers
Controller 123—All notes off
Reg. Parameter 0—Pitch-bend sensitivity
Reg. Parameter 1—Fine-tuning
Reg. Parameter 2—Coarse-tuning

Channel messages

Channel Pressure (aftertouch)
Pitch bend—default ± 2 semitones
All channels respond to MIDI volume
Default powerup: pitch bend = 0; volume = 100; controllers normal

Within the GM specification, channel 10 is set aside as the MIDI channel used to trigger percussion timbres, as shown in Fig. 27.8. Channels 1–9 and 11–16 are used for any of the 128 melodic-instrument timbres.

It should be noted that this specification differs from the Microsoft implementation of MIDI. To allow for support of low-quality systems that are unable to meet the minimum voice and simultaneous-timbre requirements found in the General MIDI specification, Microsoft defined channels 1–10 for use by high-end music synthesizers and channels 11–16 for low-end music synthesizers. OPL2-based sound cards would be described as a low-end synthesizer and any GM-compatible device would be described as a high-end synthesizer. The concern with Microsoft's redefinition of General MIDI is that it essentially renders the upper MIDI channels useless to high-end synthesizers. A MIDI sequence authored to Microsoft's definition would use these channels for a simplified version of a song that could play on a low-end system. High-end synthesizers are not expected to respond to messages written to these upper channels, effectively reducing the usable number of MIDI channels from 16 to 10.

Basic Sound Card Features

With a growing number of sound cards available on the market, it is important to know what features are available and what is required for their intended use. The features described next include the minimum requirements that should be found on any sound card for use in a multimedia application. These may be thought of as the necessary functions, and they do not include any of the application-specific features such as voice recognition, effects processing, etc.

PCM playback and recording

The ability to play back and record PCM (pulse code modulation) files is considered a necessity for any useful audio device, given the large number of applications making use of digital audio. Among others these applications include voice annotation, speech recognition, speech synthesis, voice mail, sound clips for presentations/education, sound effects and speech for entertainment software. Although digital audio playback and recording is one of the base functions found on any sound card, the available formats, capabilities, and methods of implementation differ from card to card. These differences affect both the quality of the output and the number of applications able to make use of the card.

Digital audio formats

Useful sample rates for digital audio in multimedia applications range from approximately 8 kHz for telephone-quality voice to 44.1 kHz for high-fidelity music. For use with the widest range of applications, the card should be capable of supporting each of the following playback and recording formats:

- 8-/16-bit mono/stereo at 11.025 kHz, 22.05 kHz, and 44.1 kHz
- Adaptive delta pulse code modulation (ADPCM) 4:1 compression/decompression
- µLaw/A-Law 2:1 companding

The first entry is made up of the base formats supported directly through the multimedia extensions found in Windows 3.1. These offer a wide enough range of quality versus storage space for the majority of applications. Any sound card being considered for purchase should, at a minimum, be able to record and play back samples in any of these base formats These formats offer quality ranges from a level as low as telephone speech to levels approaching CD audio.

ADPCM is a lossy digitizing technique that allows the application or user to record and store samples at a 4:1 compression ratio. The samples are then decompressed as they are played back. The obvious benefit of using this type of compression technique is the reduction of the amount of hard-disk space required for storing samples. Given that a thirty-second sound clip recorded in 16-bit stereo at 44.1 kHz requires over 5 Mbytes of storage, this type of compression can become extremely useful. The downside of this type of algorithm is the signal degradation resulting from the processing. The encoding/decoding of the 16-bit signal results in an overall dynamic range of approximately 60 dB, as compared to 96 dB in the original 16-bit signal. This equates to a drop in dynamic range from close to CD-quality to approximately AM-radio-quality. The reproducible bandwidth is also slightly reduced to approximately 8 kHz for a 22.05-kHz sample rate, or 16 kHz for a 44.1-kHz sample rate. At this time, 2:1 ADPCM algorithms are not in wide use on PC sound cards. Although the compression ratio is lower, the dynamic range is reduced from the ideal 96 dB to only 90 dB.

There is a formidable compatibility problem with the ADPCM algorithms in use. Each vendor offering this encoding technique has effectively implemented a proprietary compression algorithm whose files could be properly decompressed only by the inverse algorithm. This sometimes results in sample files compressed using one manufacturer's method being useless for playback on any other make of sound card. To alleviate this, Microsoft has recently released their ADPCM algorithm for use by any sound card manufacturer or ISV. This should give applications developers the confidence to incorporate a standard compression technique without risk of limited support by hardware.

The µ-Law/A-Law companding technique is commonly used in telecommunications for a fairly-good-quality 2:1 compression of speech signals. The companding algorithms defined by the Compaq Business Audio specification are the same as those used in the telecommunications industry. This method uses a piece-wise linear logarithmic compression characteristic that results in a quantization noise power that is proportional to the signal power over a wide dynamic range. Essentially, this system gives the ability to encode soft or lower-volume signals with the same signal-to-noise ratio as louder signals. The end result is a relatively constant signal-to-noise ratio of approximately 40 dB, with a dynamic range approaching that of 12-bit linear PCM encoding. This method of encoding will find its primary application in voice mail and voice annotation. The reduction in signal-to-error ratio makes it a poor choice for encoding music signals.

Table 27.2 offers a view of the formats supported for recording and playing back digital samples. Where applicable, listed bandwidths set the upper range at a reasonable point to allow for proper attenuation before reaching the Nyquist frequency. Listed signal-to-error ratios for the linear PCM formats are calculated as an ideal bandlimited value. Signal-to-error ratios for the ADPCM formats are approximated, as they will depend on the actual

TABLE 27.2 Formats Supported for Recording/Playback of Digital Sample

Sample format	Linear PCM						ADPCM CD-I algorithm		μLaw/ALaw		
Sample rate	11.025 kHz		22.05		44.1 kHz		22.05 kHz	44.1 kHz	11.025 kHz	22.05 kHz	44.1 kHz
Bandwidth	20 Hz to 5 Hz		20 Hz to 10 kHz		20 Hz to 20 kHz		20 Hz to 8.5 kHz	20 Hz to 17 kHz	20 Hz to 5 kHz	20 Hz to 8.5 kHz	20 Hz to 17 kHz
Sample size	8	16	8	16	8	16	16 to 4	16 to 4	14 to 8	14 to 8	14 to 8
Ideal signal-to-error	48	96	48	96	48	96	60	60	38	38	38
Storage required(MEG)	0.63	1.26	1.26	2.52	2.52	5.05	0.631	1.262	0.63	1.262	2.52

algorithm used. Signal-to-error ratios for the μ-Law/A-Law companding format are based on ideal bandlimited signals for each sample rate. The storage space required is based on a 30-second, stereo sample file.

MIDI and Music Synthesis

Music synthesis and MIDI are closely related features on many sound cards. Different methods of designing the music synthesizer, General MIDI, and MPU-401 compatibility all lead to sound devices that have varying levels of performance and abilities. This section will first cover the basic methods of music synthesis being offered in today's market, and will then explain the different architectures and how they combine to become a General MIDI device.

Music synthesis

The quality of music synthesis found on sound cards available today ranges from the poor tinny sounds of two-operator frequency modulation (FM) to almost professional-quality sample-based synthesis. The intended use of the sound card will go a long way toward determining what type of synthesis method is suitable for the task. A descriptive rating of each of the methods currently in use will now be given.

Two-operator FM. Although two-operator FM offers relatively poor quality in terms of realistic musical instruments, this method enjoys the largest installed user base of any other form of music synthesis on the PC. At the time of introduction on the old Adlib and Soundblaster cards, the Yamaha YM3812 (OPL2) synthesis chip offered one of the only methods of generating musical-instrument sounds on a PC, and due to a lack of any real competition, soon became the standard still supported by most new applications. Even today many of the new "Soundblaster-Compatible" cards being introduced still make use of this outdated technology as their only method of synthesis. As newer technologies begin to take hold and their related price-points drop, it is hoped by many that two-operator FM synthesis will become a thing of the past.

The drawback of OPL2 is the inability of the simple two-operator FM algorithm to properly model the timbre of a real instrument. The results of the standard FM equation $x(t) = A\sin[(wct)+I\sin(wmt)]$ are generally waveforms made of a simple harmonic structure that lack any transients and inharmonic information. Synthesis of the unpitched sounds that define most percussion instruments is impossible to do realistically using this method, resulting in very poor sounds. Figure 27.9 shows the simplified waveform, amplitude envelope, and frequency spectrum that make up a piano sound as generated by the OPL2.

Figure 27.9*a* shows the relatively simple waveform created with the two-operator FM algorithm. The envelope for the sound is generated with a standard four-stage (attack/decay/sustain/release) ADSR, which results in a smooth shape that decays the fundamental at the same relative rate as the harmonics. This style of decay may be seen in the frequency spectrum of

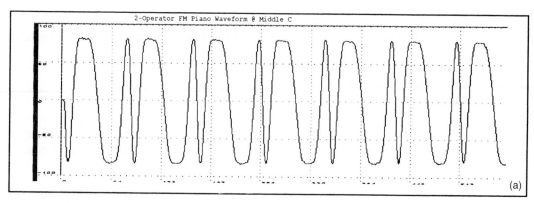

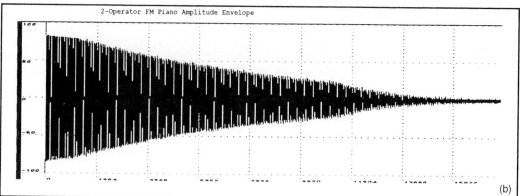

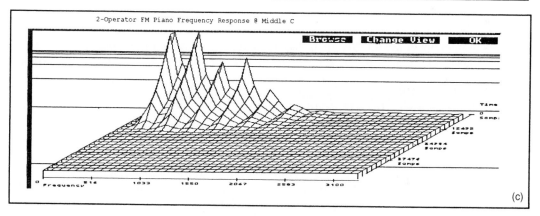

Figure 27.9 Waveform (*a*), amplitude (*b*), and frequency (*c*) of a piano sound.

Figure 27.9*c*. The frequency spectrum also shows that the resulting waveform does not contain any of the inharmonic data or transients that add to the coloring of a piano sound.

Apart from the poor quality of its music synthesis, the other problem with OPL2 is that it is able to generate only a very limited number of simultaneous voices. In what is referred to as the *melodic mode* of operation, this device is able to generate only nine simultaneous melodic instrument sounds. If a tenth note were to be struck while the other nine instruments were still decaying, one of those nine would be cut off to allow the new note to play.

The *percussive mode* of operation is somewhat more limiting. This mode sets the operators up for use as six melodic voices and five percussion voices. Within this, the percussion is limited to a kick drum, snare drum, tom-tom, hi-hat, and crash cymbal. Each of these percussion instruments also is assigned to a specific operator able to generate only that style of percussive sound, with any restriking of the instrument cutting off the previous sound.

The third mode of operation, referred to as the *additive mode,* is rarely used, as the instrument sounds generated by using the outputs of all 18 operators are usually of lower quality than those generated with the melodic mode. As all three modes of operation for the OPL2 fail to meet the minimum requirements laid out in the GM System–Level 1 specification, most General MIDI files would not be able to play properly. Many notes would cut out prematurely when new notes were triggered, resulting in a choppy-sounding sequence.

Sound cards that use the OPL2 can be viewed as a poor choice for anything but use as a game card for audio support in older games. MultiMedia presentations, newer entertainment software, and music composition require real-sounding instruments as well as compatibility with GM System–Level 1. The OPL2's shortfalls in these areas should take any sound card using two-operator FM out of the running as a serious multimedia product.

Four-operator FM.   The four-operator FM solution for music synthesis is considerably better than its two-operator predecessor. Although it was only recently introduced to the PC sound card market, the basic algorithms of the Yamaha YMF262 (OPL3) chipset have been in use for many years on consumer-level keyboards such as the DX100. The added complexity of the four-operator algorithm increases the quality of most of the melodic-instrument sounds. As an additional feature, the OPL3 is fully backwards-compatible with the OPL2 chipset, so that any older software written for the OPL2 will function properly on the OPL3.

When an instrument on the OPL3 is designed using the four-operator algorithm, the results usually are quite pleasing for many of the melodic-instrument sounds. Figures 27.10, 27.11, and 27.12 show the waveform, amplitude envelope, and frequency spectrum of a piano sound generated on the OPL3.

If the figures for the OPL3 are compared to those shown for the OPL2, it is readily noticeable that the waveform and frequency spectrum contain a great deal more harmonic information. This results in sound that is much closer to that of a real piano. There are however certain drawbacks with the OPL3. Sound cards using the OPL3 chipset generally claim to have a 20-voice synthesizer. What isn't widely known is that the number of available voices depends entirely on the mode of operation for which the chip is programmed. The first two modes of operation are for either 18 simultaneous melodic sounds or 15 melodic sounds with 5 percussive sounds.

When operating in one of these two modes, the chip is using two-operator

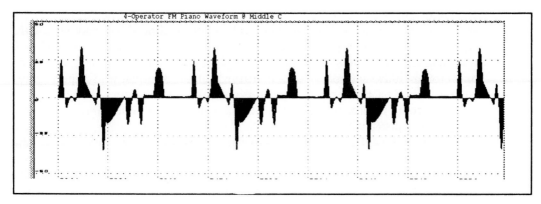

Figure 27.10   Wave of a piano sound—OPL3.

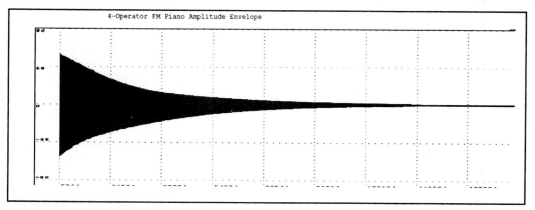

Figure 27.11   Amplitude of a piano sound—OPL3.

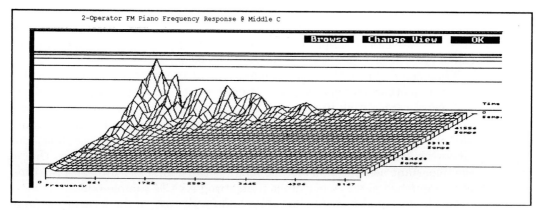

Figure 27.12   Frequency of a piano sound—OPL3.

FM algorithms for each of the voices. The richer-sounding four-operator instruments are not available. The end result is almost like having a card with two OPL2 chips on it. The other two modes of operation are either 6 four-operator melodic sounds plus 6 two-operator melodic sounds; or 6 four-operator melodic sounds, 3 two-operator melodic sounds, and 5 percussive sounds. The first four-operator mode is capable of producing only 12 simultaneous melodic voices, while the second can produce 9 simultaneous melodic voices and 5 percussive voices.

Although the OPL3 is able to offer more simultaneous voices than the OPL2, it still falls short of the minimum requirements for GM System–Level 1 compatibility. The only mode that approaches the required performance uses the lower-quality two-operator algorithm. In a similar manner to the OPL2, the OPL3 is unable to reproduce realistic percussion sounds and still has the limitation to the same 5 basic percussion instruments. This number of percussion sounds, as well as the specific assignment of sound to operator, greatly reduces the flexibility of the device. This structure doesn't allow for dynamic allocation of the base percussive instruments, as required for GM compatibility. To this is added the great difficulty in properly modeling unpitched timbres with the FM algorithms, resulting in the same poor-sounding percussion instruments found on the OPL2.

Although the OPL3 is able to offer much better-sounding melodic instruments than the OPL2, the limited number of four-operator voices generally results in many applications using the two-operator algorithms to generate more simultaneous sounds. Sound cards using the OPL3 may be viewed as a reasonably good choice for a multimedia device if the music-synthesis quality for melodic instruments can suffer a bit, and if there is no need for full GM System–Level 1 compatibility.

Wave-table lookup/sample-based.   The wave-table lookup method of synthesis is a relative newcomer to the PC sound card market. This method differs from the FM-based systems in that it uses looped samples of instruments to synthesize the musical notes. This method generally offers a higher quality of synthesis than the FM methods, due to the more complex harmonic information contained in the instrument samples. Figures 27.13, 27.14, and 27.15 show the waveform, amplitude envelope, and frequency spectrum of a piano sound generated with a wave-table/sample-based synthesizer.

When compared to the corresponding FM methods, it is readily noticeable that this method produces a more complex waveform, envelope, and frequency spectrum, resulting in a sound that is a great deal closer to that of a real piano. This complexity comes from modeling the instrument with two sampled waveforms, each having a complex, logarithmic 8-stage envelope that allows for more control of the output amplitudes as the note decays. One of the important benefits this method offers is the ability to synthesize the complex, unpitched percussion sounds from straight PCM sample tables.

This higher quality does come at an additional cost, in the form of the large amounts of ROM needed to store the library of wave-table loops and samples.

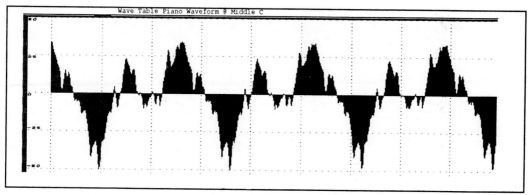

Figure 27.13 Synthesizer-based piano-sound waveform.

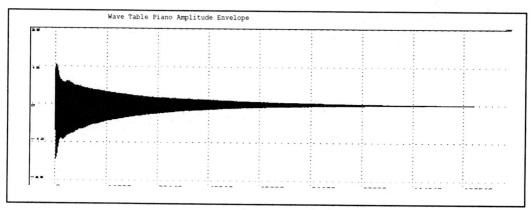

Figure 27.14 Synthesizer-based piano-sound amplitude.

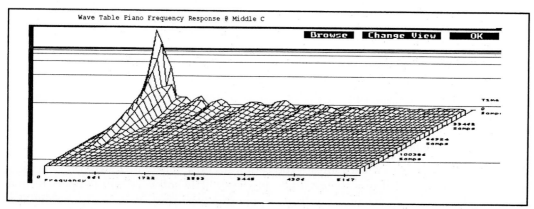

Figure 27.15 Synthesizer-based piano-sound frequency.

It is at this point that sound cards using a wave-table/sample-based synthesizer will begin to vary in both price and quality. The sound ROMs may be 8 or 16 bits wide, and vary in size from 0.5 to greater than 4 megs of stored samples. To approach professional quality, a system typically has to be made with 4 megs of 16-bit samples. Where professional quality isn't quite necessary, a 0.5-meg ROM is large enough to build instruments for the General MIDI map that are considerably better-sounding than either of the FM techniques. Another option found on some sound cards based on this style is the addition of RAM banks that allow the user to create custom instruments on the PC. This is especially beneficial for applications that require sound effects. The wave-table/sample-based sound cards on the market today offer GM System–Level 1 compatibility with a performance range of 24 to 32 dynamically allocated voices, depending on the synthesis chipset being used.

Although wave-table/sample-based synthesizers sound a great deal better than the FM solutions, the needs of the end user must still be the criterion used to determine which of the many sound cards using this method is best for the application. The best method of deciding is to set a purchase-price range and then audition the available cards that fall within that range.

MIDI and the sound card

To complete the GM System–Level 1 compatibility requirements, the sound card must offer some means of interpreting the stream of MIDI commands into the data required to set up and play the various instruments. This is accomplished through the use of a MIDI interpreter, which intercepts the MIDI messages and translates them into the format expected by the synthesizer. Depending on the design of the card, this interpreter will reside as part of an audio driver on the PC or be built into the hardware on the card through the use of a microcontroller. The method of implementation essentially comes down to a cost versus functionality issue.

The complexity of the interpreter would require the addition of a microcontroller and additional ROM or RAM to handle the translation of MIDI data. While this approach delivers a system able to work directly with more existing software packages, the additional associated costs typically make these devices the most expensive. The second approach is to build the interpreter into a PC-driver that talks directly to the synthesizer. Implementation of this approach generally results in a less expensive card, at the expense of a larger sound-driver existing on the PC. Neither approach has an effect on the quality of the synthesis.

Soundblaster compatibility

Whenever a new card enters the sound market, a catch-22 situation is created. No one will buy the card because very little software will support it, and the software developers will not support a card until it is in the hands of a large number of consumers. Although this has been alleviated somewhat through the development of the multimedia extensions under Windows 3.1, the most important support comes from the independent software vendors (ISVs), the companies that make the games. Because of this, it has become something of a necessity that new cards be backwards-compatible with a Rev. 1.5 Soundblaster card. This compatibility gives the card both instant support for existing applications as well as continued support from new titles, until the ISVs begin to support the new card in its native mode.

It should be noted that the need for this compatibility is starting to fade as newer software titles are switching to the use of audio APIs that allow software vendors to use one audio driver library that talks to secondary drivers supplied by the sound card manufacturers. The introduction of this philosophy allows these vendors to offer native-mode support of any sound card that supplies the secondary driver.

This feature is meant solely for use of the sound card with older entertainment software that was written with sound support for Yamaha's two-operator FM chip (OPL2) and the single 8-bit digital-audio channel found on the old Soundblaster cards. There are currently three methods being used for offering this compatibility; two work very well, and the other is a kluge that is prone to problems.

The first way to emulate Soundblaster is to design what is essentially a Soundblaster clone. This method will use either the Yamaha OPL2 or the backwards-compatible four-operator OPL3 chipset for the FM music synthesis, and a PCM channel that responds in the same way as on a Soundblaster card. Many sound cards on the market use this approach and are able to offer full compatibility with the older card. The net result is that all of these cards use the same tinny FM sound for both older and new applications, and are unable to offer the higher-quality wave-table and sample-based synthesis methods now appearing on the market.

The second way is to offer register (hardware) -level compatibility to make the card appear like a Soundblaster to the applications, but use a digital signal processor (DSP) to emulate the two-operator FM synthesis algorithms and handle the command interpretation. This method is then able to offer support to the older applications that were written for the Soundblaster, as well as to implement the higher-quality wave-table and sample-based synthesis methods for newer applications at no extra cost for additional hardware. The drawback to this approach is that the complexity of emulation may force the emulation to use a lower sample rate for the synthesis than what is used by the Yamaha OPLx chipsets. This causes a reduction in the reproducible bandwidth, resulting in a slightly duller sound.

The third method currently being used is the trickiest to implement and results in the least reliable form of emulation. This method uses a combination of a Terminate and Stay Resident (TSR) program on the PC, which intercepts the commands and data being written to the soundblaster, and a wavetable-based synthesizer. Many potential problems exist with this style of implementation.

Without getting into detail, the following drawbacks are found with this implementation. The lower memory used by the TSR is in some cases too large to allow the game to operate with full functionality. If there isn't enough lower memory available, the game either will not run or will run in some form of reduced functionality. Most software developers will drop or reduce the audio support first, to ensure that enough memory remains to let the rest of the game operate, rendering the TSR useless.

The second problem lies in the CPU overhead taken by the TSR. As some of the more complex games attempt to use all of the available processing power from the PC, the TSR's overhead may cause the game to slow down.

The third problem lies in converting FM parameters to a wave-table sound. The difficulty found in this conversion can result in the occasional wrong sound being played. This occurs most often when creating special effects from an FM operator.

The final potential problem is that the method of trapping the commands and data may not be supported by the hardware found in all machines. On the up side, the games that do work properly with this method will have a greatly improved soundtrack, as well as be able to offer at no increased cost the higher-quality wave-table and sample-based synthesis for newer applications.

The Digital Signal Processor Platform

As with so many high-technology purchases today, the consumer's underlying fear is of obsolescence. This concern is justified when it comes to purchasing a sound card for multimedia applications. Just within the last year (1993), four significant advances in audio-processing technology have arrived in the multimedia sound card market. These include speech recognition, speech synthesis, audio compression routines, and Qsound™ three-dimensional audio. Each of these technologies has one thing in common: each uses computation-intensive algorithms that require powerful microprocessors with special architectures to run in real time. To get an idea of the processing power required to implement these new features, look at this table, showing the percentage of utilization some of these algorithms require when they are executed on a 10-MIPS digital signal processor:

Algorithm	Percentage of 10-MIPS DSP
Speaker-independent speech recognition	33
ADPCM compression—mono, 22.05-kHz	32
ADPCM decompression—mono, 22.05-kHz	25
Qsound 3D audio—22.05-kHz	24

With the majority of sound cards being designed as closed systems that offer only the basic features, the only ways to introduce this new technology would be (1) with hardware changes and daughter boards, (2) by the purchase of a newer device, or (3) by relegating the processing overhead of new technology to the PC. The first two methods come at considerable expense to the consumer and shouldn't even be considered at this time. While the third approach doesn't require additional hardware, it is limited by the type of audio application and by the performance required to execute the algorithms in real time.

Algorithms such as speech recognition, speech synthesis, and ADPCM are able to function as a PC-based application. This is because these algorithms process the audio signal either after it has been recorded or prior to its being played back. In the case of speech synthesis, the application itself generates the digital signal. The only consideration for running these algorithms on the PC is the large processing overhead needed for real-time operation. The utilization table just given shows how large this overhead is. Other algorithms such as Qsound 3-D Audio and any type of reverb or chorusing effect require a much more integrated design that allows these functions to operate on both the PCM audio and music-synthesis signals. The only way to implement this would be to build these algorithms into the hardware. This could be done only on an open-ended system.

One of the newer entrants to the sound card market makes use of the open architecture required for implementing new technology while avoiding the expense of purchasing additional hardware and without taxing the limited resources of the PC. This architecture will use a multipurpose digital signal processor (DSP) as the main controller of all audio signals in the digital domain. The key feature of this system in the DSP is a dedicated microprocessor specifically designed to implement the computation-intensive algorithms that are the backbone of the new audio technology entering the multimedia market. The open architecture allows for new DSP applications to be developed and downloaded to the sound card. This allows the vendor to upgrade consumers with new developments at a very low cost, and without placing a heavy processing burden on the host PC.

Apart from the introduction of new technology, a sound card designed using the DSP platform gives the sound card the ability to perform functions that it is either not possible or practical to do on the PC. These functions may include the application of signal-conditioning algorithms on the digital audio stream, in the form of digital filtering to remove image frequencies and to avoid aliasing and noise-shaping algorithms and thereby mask the effects of signal manipulation in the digital domain. Other applications may take the form of real-time 3D audio, reverb, and chorusing algorithms, applied to the output of the music synthesizer on a voice-by-voice or MIDI-channel basis. These applications just can't be done on the PC, and can't be added to a closed-architecture system without additional dedicated hardware.

At this time, choosing a sound card that is based upon an open architecture and uses a digital signal processor is the wisest choice for the end user concerned about obsolescence. Even if upgrades to future technologies are not a primary concern, the additional processing taken on by the sound card frees up the PC to perform other functions.

Acknowledgment

I would like to thank Bill Arab for his patient editing and constructive criticism of this article—man, is he quick with a pen!

28

Bringing the Senses to Multimedia

Serge Timacheff

Adapting Machines to Humans

Narcissism runs rampant in the computer industry. We wallow egocentrically through technological developments and growth stages, believing we're the only ones who have experienced the process. This is a natural tendency, because it is shrouded by the technology itself—it's hard to believe that history is repeating itself when the products and inventions are so unique and different from anything ever created. In truth, however, many other industries, including the automobile, telephone, radio, and television industries, have experienced parallel stages of development, and taking a look at them can provide us with insights into our own efforts. Multimedia, in particular, takes advantage of a number of technological innovations and developments, and consequently it is more easily understood when its precedents have been seen from the perspectives of other industries.

Cars and computers

The IBM PC is barely more than 10 years old. It's easy to forget that, so prevalent is it in our lives. Yet that prevalence pales in comparison with the penetration of the automobile into everyday life. While millions of people do not know how to use a personal computer, an adult that does not know how to drive a car is not so much a rarity as an oddity. How did the car get to this point in our lives, and what does that have to do with the PC industry?

The beginning of any technology is characterized by the attempt to replace and better an existing process. The automobile was created as a replacement for the horse and buggy, and early cars looked very much like buggies. In fact they were capable of little more than buggies, and most people felt no compelling urge to buy one. The early computers, likewise, were simply replacements for typewriters and calculators, and held little promise of doing more than adding unnecessary complications to our lives.

Other manufacturers became interested in automobiles, which is when the design and form factors began to change. Although relatively few autos were being sold, the companies making them believed the market would grow if people could use them for tasks unsuited for horse-drawn vehicles. The only truly interested "users" were tinkerers who were willing to dedicate a great deal of effort to understanding the technology and dealing with the problems. And so it was for the early PC adopters. Essentially, the computer "nerd" and the car mechanic were of a piece—humans who had adapted to a machine.

Business became interested as auto designs and the roadways accommodated the needs of business. Cars became more reliable; roadways and car designs permitted transport of products; cars' speed and relatively low maintenance costs and issues (live animals were more difficult to maintain) made them more attractive. While autos were still not very easy to operate (they had many levers and parts, broke down frequently, required extensive maintenance and difficult-to-obtain parts, etc.), they began to service business in ways an animal-drawn vehicle could not. The official interest of business in this new technology served to legitimize it as a unique, accepted solution that bettered the previous method.

Similarly, businesses began to adopt PCs to do word processing, spreadsheets, and databases, which were essentially tasks that had been done by hand before but could be done faster and more accurately by a machine. As workable, reliable software became available, and compatible means of exchanging data, data entry and output, and other necessities became standardized, the PC quickly began to replace typewriters, calculators, manual methods, and other less sophisticated tools. As with autos, the interest of business in computers legitimized the PC as a unique tool for meeting basic needs.

When businesses began to order automobiles, and manufacturing became more automated and voluminous, prices dropped. At the same time people at home witnessed the advantage businesses and government derived from using vehicles for everything from mail and milk delivery to mass transit. With prices within reach of the family, "home users" became interested in automobiles because they allowed them to go places they couldn't reach before. Our national support and interest in large parks was largely tied to the ability of the average person to reach them recreationally. And the freedom of being able to drive to work independently without having to rely on mass transit was a new sport in itself.

While there was an early interest in "home computers," the home market didn't truly blossom until after computers had been firmly established in the workplace. The development of significant brands and choices of personal-productivity, recreational, educational, and home-office software helped to drive the interest in using computers at home. Furthermore, powerful laptop and notebook computers could be taken home from the office where family members could use them, or so that information could be transferred from one to the other.

With growth, however, come new problems. In the case of the auto, no matter how affordable, powerful, or reliable a car might be, it was of limited use if there were no roads to travel on, no standards of navigation, or no maps to guide people. Operational standards, as well, became an issue, so that a person would not have to go through a steep learning curve each time a new vehicle was purchased or driven.

Of course compatibility, network connectivity, standardization of hardware and software, and consistency of operation are issues that continue to plague the computer industry. In many cases users have found computers to be of limited use in circumstances where necessary hardware or software is unavailable, underpowered, or incompatible. For the average user, and for the new user in particular, these problems can be the greatest impediment and source of frustration in PC wrangling.

At the same time as it was tackling issues of navigation and accessibility, the auto industry was embarked on the exploration of another issue critical to technological product design, acceptance, and use: ergonomics. There are two halves of ergonomics, although only one is popularly recognized. When most people hear the word *ergonomics,* they think of what scientists call *physical ergonomics:* how a product is shaped to fit the body. This means making a seat that fits the average person but also adjusts for other sizes; developing a steering wheel that is at the right distance and with the proper (or adjustable) height, with controls accessible while driving, and so on.

Researchers commonly refer to another half of ergonomics, however, known as *cognitive ergonomics,* or in other words how a product is shaped to fit the *mind.* In the instance of an automobile, this would mean making a dashboard that includes symbols and gauges that can be easily read at a glance (before you career into a tree), and placing controls in logical locations. When you rent a car, it is cognitive ergonomics, made consistent, accessible, and universal, that permit you to easily read the controls and immediately drive away safely.

One good example of faulty cognitive ergonomics is the common kitchen stove. While the burners are positioned in a square, the knobs operating them are arranged in a line, thus requiring labeling (e.g., left rear, right front, etc.). The product has not been designed to logically fit the user's mind, even though the physical positioning of the knobs and burners may be perfect.

Physical ergonomics have been an important consideration in the computer industry for some time, including as they relate to such issues as radiation dangers from monitor emissions, proper office furniture and its positioning for the prevention of back pain and eye strain, and repetitive stress injuries like carpal tunnel syndrome. In software, having dark text on a light background, colors that are friendly to the eye, and even the ability to randomly access any point on the screen using a mouse (instead of cursor keys) make a difference physically. All of these factors continue to play a major role in the development of computers and computer-related hardware and software products.

Cognitive ergonomics play a role in both hardware and software, as well. Opportunities to make software more intuitive and accessible continue to abound, and products such as Microsoft Windows have increased personalization and customization capabilities dramatically. This makes for products far better tuned to the mind of the user. From a hardware perspective, the addition of a capability such as being able to attach a double-click to a single button on a multibutton mouse not only increases and simplifies usability, it also decreases repetitive motions and therefore has a physical benefit as well. As with the previous example of the stove, the logical placement of buttons, controls, disk drives, and the like can play a meaningful role in increasing cognitive connection between user and product.

While the auto industry presently has much more penetration into mainstream users than PCs, nevertheless the PC is on a similar track of development. Down that track will come additional opportunities as well as challenges. Today PCs are becoming even more like cars in that the market has become one of commodities, and it has become increasingly difficult to differentiate between products. Original, unique products are becoming more rare. Where is this track taking us, and what can we learn from the automobile?

There is still a long way to go before PCs are as common as cars. However, the recent and ongoing trend of systems toward the integration of sight, sound, and touch enhances the physical and cognitive-ergonomic attributes of the PC as well. By opening up the use of multiple senses, our access to multimedia is widened proportionally.

Adding Senses to Computers

If a person is hammering a nail into a board with a rock, the mentality of today's computer industry is to invent a complicated, overly "techie" device, hand it to the person, and expect him or her to somehow integrate the device into his/her set of tasks. Other industries that have been through the technological "gap," such as the auto industry, will observe the person with the rock, develop a tool—in this case, a hammer—give it to the person and say, "Try this; see if it does the job better."

We can no longer afford to throw technology at potential or actual computer users and expect them to integrate it with what they're doing. They just don't want to take the time. This simply will not work when it comes to the mass consumption of a technology—which is why the average person cannot program his or her own VCR. Perhaps the most fundamental and critical element of technological development is user perspective. While manufacturers realize that the general public is interested in their products, they should also realize that listening to the user is a critical part of the development process. Developers walk a fine line between leading with technological innovation and listening to what needs to be changed in existing technology.

Clearly, what users want from multimedia is integration, simplicity, and consistency. It's wonderful to be able to use sight, sound, touch, video, music, and everything else associated with multimedia, but if there is no easy way to use or learn to use these products together, once again people are frustrated. The industry seems always to stay one leap ahead of users, tantalizing and frustrating them with a glimpse of a higher, more exciting platform of technology just as they had managed to climb up to the previous one.

How can this be achieved? With the massive features sets and capabilities required of the average multimedia software package today, how can we possibly simplify product usage?

Consistency

Our first step in laying a path toward technological viability and user acceptance of multimedia applications and hardware must be to come up with consistency of interface in both hardware and software. If consistency is unachievable, then it must be replaced by simplicity. Microsoft Windows was a conceptual leap for the industry by offering the potential for a consistent interface among applications. Suddenly users were able to try out numerous applications without first reading the manual extensively, remembering large sets of commands, or wallowing through a tutorial.

Yet there is enough complexity and flexibility in the design of Windows applications that consistency can be lost, often with negative results. Very often this occurs when applications incorporate modules designed by separate groups or even separate companies. Corel Systems has been through this process in its development of CorelDraw 4.0, a popular Windows-based software package that integrates drawing, image-editing, animation, presentation graphics, charting, and other modules. Earlier versions of the program included modules that did not feature a consistent interface with the primary drawing module, and consequently these were used less, if at all. In some cases, such as with the Corel Photo-Paint image-editing module, the company actually went back and brought modules in house to develop from scratch so that they could be made consistent. This effort is paying off for the company in usability, reviews, and general success for the product overall.

The implementation of standards such as APIs (application program interfaces) to allow consistent access and interaction between various types of hardware and software also is as important as having common types of gasoline or consistently threaded gas-tank caps. The TWAIN standard, developed by Caere, Logitech, Aldus, Kodak, and Hewlett-Packard and supported by a multitude of hardware and software vendors, provides various Windows applications with direct support for digital scanners, cameras, and other imaging devices. Users are assured of a consistent interface and system for acquiring images with their hardware, no matter what application they are using (providing it is TWAIN-compliant). These types of standards make access to complex technology that much easier for the average user to gain.

Hardware consistency is important when it comes to products that incorporate significant hands-on control. Keyboards have faced this issue for some time; little explanation is necessary, other than to say that any new keyboard designs are faced with the challenge of keeping the keys in the same place while making significant other changes, such as making the board more ergonomic or incorporating a pointing device such as a trackball on-board. Another example is the DIP switches and jumpers on boards, which can be a nightmare to figure out when installing a new one into a computer; the answer here is to eliminate them completely and allow the user to make any changes through the software during installation.

There is an ongoing need to incorporate consistency in all applications, environments, and hardware. It is difficult to retrofit, and lack of foresight can be costly. It is in the design phase that the implementation of consistency must take place.

Touch, sound, and sight—the present and future of Senseware

By making a computer more "human," we adapt it to the user, instead of forcing the user to adapt to the machine. The way in which we give this more human character to a PC is by giving it human attributes—in particular, the basic senses of sight, sound, and touch. This general category of computing products and capabilities is broadly referred to as *Senseware,* a term coined by Logitech in 1992 as an umbrella definition of its diverse product line.

Unwittingly, the development of the graphical user interface (GUI) actually fits into the Senseware definition and largely facilitates the use of the senses in computing. Instead of remembering and typing commands, GUI users can visually navigate through programs and environments, can reach into the program using a mouse or other pointing device and "touch" things and move them around, and today can hear various things happen or can attach sounds or music to objects. Since a GUI is largely a standardized, consistent environment, users can wander and meander around relatively fearlessly and quite comfortably.

Scanners, digital cameras, and other imaging devices give computers a sense of sight; various types of pointing devices give it a sense of touch; and sound products give it hearing and speech. Various GUIs, as mentioned above, permit visual navigation using multiple senses.

The future of Senseware is not necessarily in the addition of smell and taste to the "sensorium." Rather it may be in the enhancement of the existing PC senses to make them more highly defined and sensitive.

Touch.   The incorporation of three-dimensional, interactive touch is a necessary and important step in the development of this computer sense, and will be of great use in multimedia. Today most users associate touch with being able to move and manipulate objects in a two-dimensional environment. In the near term, three-dimensional pointing devices will become widely popular and affordable. Today they are much more common in specific markets such as gaming, animation, robotics, and CAD. The mouse and trackball as we know them today will become antiques, as a variety of 3D devices emerge to accomplish all tasks necessary. This type of product will provide the same full range of three-dimensional motion (technically known as *six degrees of motion: x, y, z* axes combined with pitch, roll, and yaw) that your hand does.

Another very important development of pointing devices will be the incorporation of advanced interactivity. Almost all pointing devices today are limited to input only; however, to truly affect the sense of touch, the ability of the user to "feel" when inside the computer is necessary. Ultimately we'll be able to feel surfaces, textures, gradations, and the like with our pointing devices. Logitech has come up with a device, recently (1993) announced, which represents a primitive beginning of this new phase; the product, CyberMan, is a combination of a trackball and a mouse that includes full three-dimensional control along with a vibrator incorporated in the device. The device is called a "three-dimensional interactive controller," and is specifically designed for interactive role-playing games such as Castle Wolfenstein from ID Software. Every time the user is "zapped," the vibrator goes off. The 3D control allows the user to navigate easily through a full environment with one hand (joysticks, mice, trackballs, and other conventional pointing devices are all limited in their control of the 3D environment).

When these 3D pointing devices become more common in business and home use, we'll see some true enhancements to the way we compute. For example, in 3D it is much easier to store information; just as you stack information on your desk or in a filing cabinet, you can do the same on your PC. If you had a 3D "filing cabinet," you could use your 3D pointing device to rifle through the file "folders," read the label of each, pick one and pull it out, and open it. Users will find this a much more natural way of learning about accessing data than having to look for and call up files in a conventional text-based system, or even in text sections of a GUI.

In multimedia, pointing devices are critical to developing and controlling presentations, and as the multimedium grows, so will the need for more sophisticated devices and their capabilities. Three-dimensional, interactive control will become the standard, as will support for remote devices that allow a presentation to be controlled from a distance.

Sound. Almost more than any other medium, sound can add incredible depth, power, and variety to communication. The range and diversity of sound can be fully utilized with voice, sound effects, and music, but to do so the PC must be equipped to handle sound with a device that can acquire and output sound. Today, most PCs are limited to being able to record sounds, embed them and share them among applications using object-linking and -embedding techniques (OLE), and play them back via speakers or headphones. Unfortunately, sound on the IBM PC and compatibles is somewhat of a retrofit, since support for sound is not natively supported; this means that sound must be added as an aftermarket product.

The use of sound to control a computer will become increasingly popular, but it will not supersede pointing devices or other navigational GUI controls. Certainly, however, the use of sound to control PCs will have become commonplace well before computers are able to understand language or even to perform basic tasks such as taking dictation. This is true primarily because navigational control of software by a sound device is limited to the sound software having to recognize only a limited set of commands ("open," "close file," "search for," etc.). For a PC to take dictation is much more akin to OCR, with every word and sound in the language having to be recognized—which represents exponentially more detail and accuracy.

Sound is a critical element of multimedia, and will continue to play a leading role. Virtually every package supporting presentations or even graphics today includes support for sound, and as a result the hardware market supporting it is burgeoning, as is the software aftermarket of add-on products such as clip-sounds and music. Much like the revolution in clip-art and graphics that was ushered in by the explosion of the graphics market 5 years ago, sound is experiencing the same growth.

Sight.   While graphics are common in today's PCs, the ability to acquire them has not always been a simple or natural process. In the last few years, broader and more sophisticated support of scanners and other digital-imaging devices has made it easier for users to work with images; additionally, the various software applications supporting images can take advantage of the huge CD-ROM clip-art and clip-photo market. As mentioned earlier, standards such as TWAIN make it significantly easier to give a computer a sense of sight.

Multimedia images can be still- or motion-based, but in either case are indispensable elements on PCs today. Animation of graphic images (no matter what their source), and digital-graphic techniques such as morphing and warping, are now enhancing those images. The challenge is to make the integration of motion and still images an easy process for the average user, and to bring images and video up to the level of quality users have come to expect from home stereos, televisions, and cameras. The problem once again lies in the retrofit: the average IBM PC–compatible, no matter how powerful, simply was not designed to acquire, manage, and transmit the sheer volume of data required for sound and imaging today.

As we move on to future systems, the need for easy access to large information-storage areas and the ability to easily transfer that information among systems are critical issues for multimedia. Increasing the bandwidth of communication by increasing the sensory capabilities of the PC also increases the amount of information that must be processed and transmitted.

Conclusion

We know from research that the employment of multiple senses in the use and delivery of information is more effective, leads to better retention, and has greater impact. The ability of the system to incorporate these senses is a critical precedent to the use of multimedia. Without a Senseware-compatible system, multimedia is senseless.

Yet there are problems. Lack of consistency continues to plague users, an overabundance of often unnecessary features clutters the average application, and massive amounts of data crowd hard disks, as well as modem and network lines, as badly as Grand Central Station on a Monday morning.

A growing notion among manufacturers is that working interactively with users so as to understand their needs on physical, emotional, and cognitive levels is central to the development of successful products. Furthermore, companies are learning that strategic alliances can do more than just achieve saleable bundles—they can help companies to benefit from common experiences and can serve to develop more consistent standards in both hardware and software.

Before multimedia capabilities can be delivered to the masses, a number of key milestones will have to be passed. Other technologies have passed or are passing through similar curves of societal acceptance, and these provide a great deal of insight into our own plight in the computer industry.

The incorporation of the senses into computing is but one of these milestones. However, it will help computing to seem more natural to the uninitiated user, enhance existing applications, and be a necessary component of others. The computer equipped with senses is a computer equipped to communicate more effectively and efficiently with its user. It ceases to be an office machine and becomes an intellectual partner, a unique, creative tool suited and personalized to the unique and creative needs of its user.

Using Audio in Multimedia Applications

Potential Applications and Design Considerations

Mary F. Whiteside

J. Alan Whiteside

Types of Audio

Several different types of audio output—speech, music, and sound effects—can be incorporated into multimedia. To use each type effectively, multimedia developers need to learn more about how each of the types can be used to improve their programs.

Speech

Two types of speech are available for use by multimedia developers: *digitized* and *synthesized*. Digitized speech provides high-quality, natural speech, but requires significant disk-storage capacity. Synthesized speech, on the other hand, is not as storage-intensive, but may not sound as natural as human speech (Jones, 1989). Even with improved techniques for generating speech, it is not incorporated into multimedia programs as often as it could be. This may be due to a lack of understanding of how high-quality speech is produced, as well as to an undervaluing of the impact speech can have on computer-delivered instructional or informational programs. Speech is an important element of human communication and can be used effectively to transmit information. One advantage of using natural speech is the power of the human voice to persuade (Johnson, 1987). Another advantage is that speech can potentially eliminate the need to display large amounts of text on the screen (Dean and Whitlock, 1989).

Music

Like speech, music is an important component of human communication. Unlike speech, however, music usually does not carry the primary or instructional message of a multimedia program. Most often, music is used to set a tone or mood, provide connections or transitions, add interest or excitement, and evoke emotion. Music, especially when combined with speech and sound effects, can greatly enhance on-screen presentations of text and visuals. To make full use of its power, developers need to become more sensitive to the effective uses of music. Music should be considered as a powerful tool that can help to ensure the success of a multimedia program.

Sound effects

Sound effects are used to enhance or augment the presentation of information and instruction. Two types of sound effects are *natural* and *synthetic*. Natural sounds are the unadorned, commonplace sounds that occur around us. Synthetic sounds are those that are produced electronically or artificially. The sound effects produced for radio shows in the past elevated artificially produced sound effects to an art form.

In addition there are two general categories of sound effects: *ambient* and *special*. Ambient sounds are the background or "atmosphere" sounds that communicate the context of the scene or place to the listener. Special sounds, on the other hand, are uniquely identifiable sounds, such as the ring of a telephone or the slam of a door, that complement narration and/or visuals. Similar to the use of music, sound effects are an effective way of telling a story and communicating information.

Reasons to Use Audio

Audio can improve a multimedia presentation in many ways. However, *channel redundancy* and *motivation* are two reasons to use audio to ensure that the goals and objectives of the program are met. Since channel redundancy and motivation are principles that have emerged from research on human learning, they are particularly related to programs that have an instructional message. However, these principles also apply to informational presentations in which understanding and persuasion are important.

Channel redundancy

The research of Hsia (1977) shows that redundancy is the key to better communication. He defines redundancy as *the transmission of the same or closely related information to the receiver or learner through two sensory channels (usually the aural and visual channels)*. The capacity of the human information system is limited, and therefore information loss and error do occur. Redundancy is probably the key to minimizing these factors. Thus, presenting information via more than one communication channel increases the chances that the message will be attended to, understood, and remembered.

However, two conditions influence the effectiveness of using multiple channels:

1. Information presented in each modality must be congruent (similar and not contradictory).

2. Identical presentations of words in sound and text should be avoided.*

As an additional communication channel for multimedia, audio can improve a user's ability to understand and learn the information presented.

Increased motivation

The extent to which the instruction or information presented in a multimedia program will be received, understood, and remembered depends to a great extent on the user's motivation and interest. Motivation affects the amount of effort potential users will put into a program, and thus affects their commitment to accomplishing the goals or objectives of the program. A multimedia developer needs to be concerned about stimulating the users' motivation in all parts of a program, not just in the beginning. Audio can be an important tool for accomplishing this.

At the beginning of a program, the user's attention can be grabbed by inserting an interesting story delivered by a narrator or actor, or music can be used. In addition, using audio to vary the way different components or chunks of information are presented can stimulate curiosity and maintain the user's interest in the program.

Analogies or metaphors that are used to connect the program material to the processes, concepts, and skills familiar to the user will help to improve motivation (Keller and Burkman, 1993). Audio can be used to support these techniques. Music and sound effects can augment the use of metaphors, and narrative can be used to provide oral analogies and explanations.

Motivation also is improved by the use of anecdotes or vignettes related to the area of study or the information being presented (Keller and Burkman, 1993). Audio can be very effective in providing stories, interviews, or conversations that highlight the human or personal element. In fact, narrative speech can be used in a variety of motivating ways by relating the information to the user and making the presentation more personal. Music and sound effects also can increase motivation by adding realism and interest to visual presentations.

Audio also can provide an alternative learning mode and, therefore, attract learners who prefer to learn by listening. The use of multiple channels to present information does provide motivation for those learners who may have difficulty learning; they may find more success when learning from programs that use audio and visual modes. These users will be motivated by greater success or increased ease of learning.

---

*Hannafin and Hooper, 1993.

Motivation can be increased in a variety of ways by integrating audio. A skilled multimedia developer will capitalize on the use of audio to ensure that the goals of either an informational or instructional program are met.

Suggestions for Developing or Selecting Audio

Since the use of audio is new to many multimedia developers, few have had opportunities to learn how to integrate audio into informational or instructional programs. Very few published sources provide information about writing narration or selecting music and sound effects. However, general suggestions can be drawn from techniques applied in other media.

Developing speech

To produce high-quality recorded speech, a script should be written and professionally recorded. Digitized audio and small, high-quality microphones are now available, which means that recording can be accomplished without the use of sophisticated recording studios and expensive equipment. However, having a professional narrator with clear diction and the ability to correctly pronounce the technical words in the script is still a big plus.

To provide balance, both female and male narrators should be used. Nonprofessional narrators, such as subject-matter experts or corporate officers, may be used to provide credibility, and occasionally audience peers may be used to add interest to a program. However, when content needs to be explained or information needs to be delivered accurately, a professional should be used. Professional narrators usually can be relied upon to follow the specifications of the script and to deliver a professional-sounding audio track.

Overall, narration for multimedia programs should follow the general rules and conventions followed for other media, such as video, that integrate speech as part of the presentation of information or instruction. In general, to be effective, a narrator should

- Vary intonation to motivate, explain, provoke, exhort, or empathize
- Use a conversational tone
- Be amiable, candid, sincere, and straightforward
- Avoid sounding arrogant, pretentious, flippant, disrespectful, or sarcastic
- Avoid a lecturing tone
- Vary tone of voice to help viewers/listeners understand what is important

When you are recording narrative speech, be sure to eliminate background or ambient sound unless it is used to provide a realistic environment. On occasion, incorporating ambient sound can be effective, since it can be used to help establish a mood or to increase the feeling of reality.

Good writing techniques are essential to the development of successful multimedia programs. Thus, to integrate speech as an effective tool, developers must learn to write effective narration as a part of a program script. Very few of the many books and articles that explain how to develop computer-based or interactive videodisc-based programs include information about writing or using narration. However, general guidelines can be gathered from the techniques used for scriptwriting in other media. To develop narrative scripts for integrating speech, multimedia developers should

- Write the way people speak
- Use language the audience can understand
- Write as if the narrator were teaching or speaking with one person
- Write in a clear, straightforward manner
- Write in short sentences that can be spoken in a single breath
- Use second-person pronouns—*you* and *your*
- Use contractions and other simplified forms that are used in speech
- Emphasize clarity and simplicity
- Omit needless words
- Avoid slang
- Avoid the oral presentation of figures and statistics
- Use humor when appropriate
- Present information in small chunks
- Emphasize the objectives or goals of the program
- Interpret what the user or learner is seeing rather than simply describe it
- Make the visuals and narration go hand-in-hand; usually the visuals tell the story and the narration interprets, explains, or elaborates
- Adhere to time limits and length requirements
- Understand the capabilities and limitations of multimedia hardware and software, especially as related to the use of speech

Narration written for presentation in multimedia should be read aloud and then revised if it sounds awkward, stilted, or boring. Reading the narration aloud also allows the developer to check timing; timing is important, since the narrative often must be synchronized to the visuals being presented. As the narrator explains, elaborates, or focuses attention on visual images on the screen, visual effects such as changes in color, position, or size can be used to emphasize specific points.

Many writers suggest that narration is more human when it relates ideas to people. In other words, they say that we should develop topics in terms of people's problems, interests, and activities. To raise the level of user interest, quotes, conversations, and case studies could be included in audio scripts. Swain and Swain (1991, p. 60) write that "too often we let the element of life slip out" of written scripts. To improve the naturalness or personal tone of narratives, Langdon (1973) recommends that narration be produced in an audio format by recording oral explanations or discussions, then transcribing them without changing the natural style of the verbal information. The transcription can be used as the basis for a script that can be recorded using a professional narrator. Clarity and conciseness must not be sacrificed in the name of spontaneity and naturalness, however.

Selecting music

A wide variety of prerecorded music is available in digital format on compact discs from commercial music libraries. Many of the companies that market music for multimedia applications provide demonstration disks with samples of the types of music they offer. In addition, original music can be recorded and edited through a musical instrument digital interface (MIDI), which is a way to connect synthesizers, keyboards, and other musical instruments to computers.

Few articles or books have been published that provide detailed information or guidelines about the effective use of music in interactive programs. Some authors, especially those writing about producing video, do provide brief suggestions about the usefulness of music (Arwady and Gayeski, 1989; Cartwright, 1991; Van Nostrand, 1989). Van Nostrand (1989, p. 178) states that incorporating music begins with "identifying the function of music and making it an integral element of the script." Thus, the use of music needs to be considered as the program is being visualized and the script written. Generally, music can be used to

- Establish mood
- Set pace
- Signal a turn of events
- Indicate progress and activity
- Provide transitions and continuity
- Evoke emotion
- Accompany titles or introductory information
- Emphasize important points
- Support visual information
- Add interest, realism, and surprise

Since multimedia is designed to communicate with users, music should be selected that will become an integral part of a program's message by reaching people on an emotional level.

Music can have a wide variety of effects on listeners. Consider how music is used in movies and television commercials. It is not only "background," but also works in conjunction with the visual message to provide interest, excitement, tension, and realism. Nostrand (1989, p.178) suggests that scriptwriters "may need a wide range of musical-listing experiences to draw on: classical, pop, rock, folk, hillbilly, jazz, avant-garde, show tunes, blues, film scores, etc." Certainly, to use music effectively, developers need to become familiar with various styles of music, as well as gain an understanding of the effects of tempo, rhythm, activity, and style (Mullin, 1992).

Since music plays an important storytelling role, it should fit the pace and mood of the presentation and appeal to the audience's lifestyle, taste, and workplace position (Mullin, 1992). Burger (1992, p. 75) provides the following guidelines for choosing the right music:

- Make music an integral part from the start, rather than try to find music to "go with" the imagery later.

- Choose a music style that conveys the mood you wish to create.

- Convey personality through instrumentation.

- Use recurring themes as musical signatures to help the audience feel familiar with a character, place, or segment.

- Use tempo, dynamics, and pitch to establish energy levels.

- Use different styles of music and instrumentation to suggest time periods, cultures, locations, and a sense of place.

- Use musical genres to communicate to specific audiences; e.g., big band sounds for older audiences, or rap, metal, or pop for teenagers.

- Know when to hold them, when to fold them. Music should not compete with the narration or overwhelm the message of the program.

Listening to music in a variety of categories will help developers to gain an awareness of various types or styles of music and how they can be used to enhance multimedia. One way to do this is to review the demonstration disks provided by commercial music libraries. Since these companies use descriptive labels to categorize their music, developers can listen to selections in different categories and learn more about how different types of music can be used to establish different moods and pace. Sample categories include slow-tempo, medium-tempo, up-tempo, industrial, solo, specialty, and multimedia (Network Music, Inc., San Diego, CA).

The industrial category contains music that is called "highly motivational"; solo music features one or two instruments, and the specialty group is composed of Christmas, comedy, and other specialized styles. Interestingly, the multimedia category is described as "themes with recorded vocals" as well as "melodically similar instrumental elements" (Network Music, Inc., San Diego, CA). Another music library, Killer Tracks (Hollywood, CA) uses categories such as blues, comedy/animation, drama, fantasy, hi-tech, mellow, power/industrial, retail/institutional, warm/romantic.

Selecting sound effects

Natural, ambient sounds are an integral part of our daily lives. We use them to help us interpret and assess our surroundings. For example, "we listen to the thunk of a car door to find out if it has closed properly, to the gurgle of pouring liquid to know if a container is almost full, and to traffic noises to assess the danger of crossing a street" (Gaver, 1989, p. 70). In other words, sound provides us with valuable data that we process in a variety of ways. In multimedia applications, sound effects can be used with great benefit to inform users; affect their attitudes, emotions, and perceptions; and direct their focus of attention.

One researcher has noted that sound or nonspeech audio can provide different types of messages, including alarms or warnings and status or monitoring messages (Buxton, 1989). Alarms and warnings are signals that interrupt and alert a listener. These sounds, such as fire alarms and police sirens, normally are loud and easily identifiable. Status and monitoring messages are sounds that give us information about ongoing tasks. The click of the keys of a keyboard or the beep of the bar-code device at the supermarket are examples of these typically short sounds. Status and monitoring sounds fade rapidly from the listener's awareness and are significant only when they indicate a change; for example, when the sound does not occur.

In addition to these types of messages, Mountford and Gaver (1990) note that sound provides information about

- *Physical events.* We can identify whether a dropped glass bounced or shattered.
- *Invisible structures.* Tapping a wall helps us to locate where to hang a picture.
- *Dynamic change.* As we pour liquid into a glass, we can hear when it is full.
- *Abnormal structures.* We can tell when our car engine is malfunctioning by its sound.
- *Events in space.* We can hear someone approaching by the sound of footsteps.

Not only can sound effects provide specific information about an environment or setting, they also can be used to accomplish the following tasks:

- Create atmosphere
- Add realism
- Emphasize important points
- Indicate progress or activity
- Increase interest
- Establish mood
- Cue or prompt users
- Increase users' motivation

Recognizing the range of functions performed by nonspeech audio can help developers to identify ways that sound effects, both ambient and special, can be used to enhance understanding and learning in multimedia programs. Such recognition can be built by studying how sound effects are used in film and television productions, as well as in radio plays and commercials. Rather than being a cute afterthought, sound effects are a legitimate and substantive form of audio, and they should be integrated into the program script so as to enhance and lend credibility to the narrative, visuals, and music.

Three significant considerations should govern the use of sound effects:

1. They must be clear and easily identifiable.

2. They should not overwhelm the primary message.

3. They should be appropriate to the intended audience.

However, special sound effects often are difficult to record and, when recorded by amateurs, lack the required distinctiveness, subtlety, and appropriateness. Therefore, sound effects libraries usually are an excellent source of specialized sounds.

As with music libraries, sound effects are categorized by the type or use of the sound. For example, Sonic Boom (Anaheim, CA) lists pneumatics, buttons, switches; signals, levers, ratchets, gears; friction, stress, servo motors; small motors and mechanisms, electrical effects; compartments, doors, tape machines; and machines, motors, and engines. Background categories are labeled: interior work and manufacturing; packing, shipping, and conveyors; exterior work, labor, and industry; and constant-tone environments. Another company, Valentino (Elmsford, NY) provides more general categories: transportation, backgrounds, military, household, machinery, animals, and environmental. Companies that market sound-effect libraries provide an enormous selection of sounds on compact discs that have been professionally recorded using state-of-the-art equipment.

On the other hand, ambient sound usually is recorded as an integral part of a video production or as part of an audiotaped interview, conversation, or explanation. The background sounds are used to provide a realistic setting for the video or audio, and therefore slight imperfections add to the realism. Occasionally, however, background or ambient sounds are recorded alone so that they may be used as part of a still-media or textual presentation. As in the case of specialized sound effects, care should be taken that the ambient background does not overwhelm the narration or conversation and/or become annoying.

Current and Potential Applications of Audio in Multimedia Applications

Audio can be a powerful addition to many multimedia programs. Narration can be used to eliminate the need for long sections of on-screen text, increase understanding by using a second channel of communication, and provide interest through interviews and conversations with real-life people. Music can be used to establish a mood or to cue users about specific segments. Also, music adds a professional quality to a multimedia program. Sound effects can be used to add realism by integrating environmental or ambient sounds with narration or conversations, or by using special sound effects to augment visual and narrative information.

Speech

Since speech is one of the most common forms of human communication, it is a natural form of interaction, and one that can add an important dimension to a multimedia program. In some applications, speech is a necessity. For example, natural speech is required in programs designed to teach a foreign language or the pronunciation of new terminology. Spoken glossaries often are a valuable addition to programs where learners are faced with the task of acquiring a new vocabulary. Additionally, speech must be an integral part of programs designed for audiences with low literacy levels. Even for audiences without reading problems, the addition of the spoken word adds interest and increases learning by presenting the same message as the text.

Narration can be used to guide a learner through a task or procedure such as completing a form, assembling a piece of equipment, or setting up an experiment. Rowntree (1986, p. 246) refers to this as a "talk-through" technique. Even synthesized speech can provide guidance to a user. The "Postal Buddy" multimedia kiosk being field-tested by Electronic Data Systems (EDS) interacts with a potential customer through text, graphics, and the synthesized voice of an animated character (*The Dallas Morning News,* June 13, 1993, p. 11). In addition, the spoken word is effective in providing a general familiarization with technical and nontechnical content. However, if complex ideas or calculations are being presented, speech should be accompanied by succinct textual material and appropriate visuals.

The use of speech is particularly important when an audience member or learner is required to attend to more than one chunk of information at a time. For example, if learners must read detailed information that explains a chart, graph, or table, they are not able to study both the visual and the text explanation at the same time, especially if the two are on different screens. Using an audio explanation allows the learner to focus attention on the information or data displayed. Langdon (1973) suggests that additional learning effectiveness and efficiency can be expected when speech is used for tasks that require the user to attend to more than one chunk of content concurrently.

Speech also can be used in training or instructional experiences to provide discussions or interviews with practitioners or experts. For example, a multimedia program could provide audio segments of managers explaining how they dealt successfully with specific types of personnel issues. These segments would be accessed by the learners when they wanted additional information about the use of certain techniques or the solutions to difficult problems. Personal reactions, advice, interpretations, and commentaries can provide excellent background material related to the principle or issue being addressed. Also, conversations between patient and physician or salesperson and client could be effective in programs designed to teach questioning, listening, or interpersonal skills.

Speech, especially when coupled with environmental sounds, can also enhance simulations by adding an additional measure of realism to text and visuals. For example, an interactive patient-diagnosis simulation designed for medical students could be made more realistic by incorporating a patient's complaint as a narrative audio presentation with accompanying visuals and text.

Overall, speech can be a compelling element in a multimedia production. The persuasive qualities of the human (or even synthesized) voice should not be overlooked as a technique for improving the effectiveness of programs and maintaining the audience members' attention and motivation.

Music

The most obvious potential applications for the use of music in multimedia are those programs that deal with music as content. For example, a program such as *The Magic Flute* by Warner Audio Notes provides the complete opera by Mozart as well as on-screen commentary and annotation. Instructional programs about musicians and different types of music that include text, visuals, and music are useful applications of multimedia.

However, music can be a valuable addition to many other types of instructional and informational programs. Since music is an excellent way to "set the stage" or establish a mood, it could be used as a type of "advance organizer" to help viewers prepare for a change in the program (Arwady and Gayeski, 1989). For example, in a sales training program that provides a sample sales call, music could be used to indicate to the viewer/listener that something is going wrong with the salesperson's presentation to the customer. In addition, important points or ideas can be emphasized by the use of readily identifiable chords or a series of musical notes. In short, appropriately selected music can help to establish a feeling of expectation or excitement.

If the goal of a multimedia training program is to change attitudes, music can be an especially valuable tool. For example, in a program designed to increase the sensitivity of workers in long-term health-care facilities toward their elderly clients, appropriate music integrated with narration by patients and their families could provide a powerful new perspective for employees. In addition, Arwady and Gayeski (1989) suggest that somber music can be used to set a serious tone for training subjects such as safety instruction.

Musical signatures and custom jingles can also be used in multimedia programs. For example, a musical signature might be employed to tell the viewer when to use off-line materials such as workbooks or reference manuals (Arwady and Gayeski, 1989). This cueing function also can indicate to users when they are in a specific section of a program or when the program is accomplishing a specific function. A recognizable series of musical notes can be used to identify the practice session of each lesson or the end of an information segment. In a related cueing function, music can be used to provide a time for reflection or time to assimilate the information just presented. Custom jingles can be used by a company using multimedia to present a new product to its sales and service force (Arwady and Gayeski, 1989).

Overall, the use of music is an excellent way to add sparkle or glitz to a multimedia production. In other words, effective use of music can make a program come alive. For example, the appropriate use of music to set the pace and mood throughout various parts of a program will help the audience to relate and interact with the program, thus increasing the likelihood that the message will be understood and remembered. Additionally, music adds a professional, polished quality to a production, especially when it is used to tie program segments together in a cohesive unit.

Sound effects

Ambient sound often is included in video productions when the surrounding environment is being used as the setting. An example of one of the most effective uses of ambient sound is an interactive videodisc (IVD) program developed by Joseph Henderson, M.D. (Henderson, Pruett, Galper, and Copes, 1986). In this program, which is designed to teach specific procedures to physicians working under combat conditions, the noise and confusion of a field hospital, including the roar of the approaching and landing helicopters, are an integral part of the audio track. This sense of realism is continued even when the physician/user of the IVD program is branched to text menus and decision screens. Thus, as the physician is faced with making a decision based on information provided by a text screen, the audio track with the sounds of helicopters and field noise continues. This provides a realistic environment so that the physician feels at least some of the tension and pressure he or she would have to deal with in a real-life situation.

Ambient sounds can be used both to provide a sense of realism and to add interest to interviews, conversations, and explanations that are a part of multimedia training and informational programs. For example, an interview with a plant foreman could be audiotaped on location in the shop, so that when the interview is selected by users the information provided seems that much more true-to-life. Such "on-location recordings" can then be presented with digitized video, still media (such as photographs and graphics), or text screens. Explanations can be significantly enhanced by the addition of appropriate ambient sounds. Floyd (1991) reports that an overview of a manufacturing process, even though technically well produced, will be "fairly pedestrian" without the use of sound. However, with the addition of ambient sounds and a fast-paced music score, the same segment can be a powerful attention-grabber.

Simulations developed using either motion or still media can be made more realistic by the use of ambient sound. For example, a program designed to teach emergency medical technicians about specific procedures will simulate on-the-job conditions more closely if it contains street sounds recorded at an accident scene. For programs that do not incorporate speech or narration, the use of ambient sound can be an effective addition. Thus, a program about wild animals could present text, photographs, and illustrations about each animal, accompanied by an audio track of the animal's sounds in its natural environment.

Special sound effects or uniquely identifiable sounds can be used to add interest as well as to improve communication. Examples of the effective use of sound effects with still media are found in HyperCard stacks such as *Beyond Cyberpunk* (The Computer Lab, Louisa, VA) or *If Monks Had Macs* (BMUG, Berkeley, CA). In the *Beyond Cyberpunk* stack, the main menu is accompanied by a variety of appropriate cyberpunk sound effects; in *If Monks Had Macs,* the menu screen, which shows a monastery courtyard with a fountain, is accompanied by the sounds of a bird chirping and water flowing. Sound effects also are effective when used in conjunction with music and narration. Ringing telephones accompanied by up-tempo music can provide a secretarial training program with the right aura of a busy office. A troubleshooting program would be enhanced by simulating the sounds of equipment with various types of problems as they are examined and explained with visuals and narration.

Sound effects can be a powerful addition to the design of a multimedia program. We are familiar with sound effects as part of the interface of a personal computer. For example, a specific beep usually tells us when we have taken an incorrect action. When you are contemplating the use of sound effects as part of a multimedia program, keep in mind that the sounds should be appropriate, both in terms of the audience and the content. Also, sound effects should not distract or confuse the users. In most cases, since sound effects can add interest and realism, they are likely to increase user motivation to use and interact with the application.

Sound as part of the human-computer interface

Related to the use of sound in instructional and informational programs is research involving the use of audio as it relates to human-computer interface design. Specifically, Gaver (1989; Mountford and Gaver, 1990) has researched the use of auditory icons based on his work with an auditory interface called the SonicFinder, which provides auditory as well as graphical feedback. The SonicFinder extends the visual desktop of the Macintosh Finder by using information available from the existing interface to initiate the output of sounds sampled from recordings of everyday, sound-producing events (Gaver, 1989). In addition Blattner, Sumikawa, and Greenberg (1989) investigated the use of *earcons* or audio messages integrated into a human-computer interface to provide information and feedback to the user about computer objects, operation, or interaction. Simply defined, an earcon is *a brief succession of discrete pitches, usually no fewer than three and no more than six, structured to transmit specific pieces of information* (Blattner, Greenberg, Kamegai, 1992).

Based on investigations at the CommTech Lab at Michigan State University, several guidelines for the use of sound as feedback to users' actions have been suggested by Heeter and Gomes (1992):

- An auditory response should accompany every user-initiated command.

- Auditory responses should be diverse.

- Selected sounds should be meaningful, and related, if possible, to the function performed or the metaphor used.

- Within an application, sounds used for different functions should have a consistency or similarity that indicates relationship, not sameness.

- Each function should have a single, identifiable sound throughout an application.

Heeter and Gomes say that sounds may be short music clips, identifiable real-world sound effects, interesting noises, or speech, but that they must be short, unobtrusive, and distinctive. Investigations by these and other researchers will help multimedia developers to understand how sound can be more effectively incorporated into multimedia so as to meet a variety of purposes and goals.

Design Issues Related to the Use of Audio

If audio is to be fully integrated into an interactive multimedia program, a variety of design issues must be considered. Being aware of these issues early in the analysis and design process will help multimedia developers to avoid the pitfalls that ensnare those working with unfamiliar technology.

Clearly defined purpose

The reasons for using audio in a multimedia program need to be clearly defined from the beginning of the project. Each of the three types of sound—speech, music, and sound effects—can be a powerful addition to a multimedia program. However, developers need to analyze how each type of audio will help to impart the message or instruction to the users. Unless it is selected and integrated with care, audio can turn into a distracting or disorienting element in a program. Thus developers should use audio as a tool to explain, augment, or enrich the content or information being presented. For example, speech is effective when users are required to comprehend technical information, especially when it is presented in detailed graphs, tables, or schematics; ambient sound is effective for increasing realism in a training simulation; and music is effective for establishing a mood, setting the pace, or cueing the user. Audio that is not effectively used can interfere with the program's message.

Audio as an option

Determine early if audio will be included as an integral part of the program or if an option will be provided for users to turn it off. Developers need to analyze the audience, the delivery environment, and the goals of a multimedia experience before determining if audio will be optional. Audio often is made optional if it is used primarily to repeat on-screen text. This technique is used most often when the target audience contains a segment of low-literacy-level users. Even though repeating on-screen text as audio can be effective for low-literacy-level audiences, speech (as well as music and sound effects) can be used more effectively to supplement, enhance, and elaborate the information being presented on the screen.

Often, audio segments are designed to carry an important part of the message or instruction. Audio then becomes crucial to the effectiveness of the program. In such a case, the option to turn off the audio track should not be provided. However, developers should carefully examine the environment in which the program will be delivered. The need for user privacy, or the need to eliminate sound that could be distracting to other workers, are both important issues. Certain settings, such as offices in which workers are in close proximity to each other, may require that sound be optional or that the users wear headphones so that coworkers are not distracted or disturbed by the audio.

Also, if headphones are being considered, remember that they must provide high-quality sound and be as lightweight and comfortable as possible, especially if users will be wearing them for long periods of time. Some audiences may dislike wearing headphones, and this attitude could sabotage an otherwise effective program. A thorough investigation of the audience and the delivery setting, as well as the goals of a program, will help a developer to make the appropriate decision as to optional or integrated audio.

Branching

Many multimedia programs are nonlinear and designed to increase user interactivity through questions and choices the user can make. Since audio is linear, sound segments should be designed so that they can respond to the user's need to repeat the audio as well as the on-screen text and visuals. Thus, sound segments need to be designed to branch to different sections of content based on user responses. This may mean that several transitions need to be written, recorded, and integrated for each branching point.

In addition, care needs to be taken as the branches are programmed that users are provided with appropriate audio connections from each branch to the next viewing segment, as well as connections back to the previous instructional segment for review. When using audio, especially narrative, simply branching the user back to a specific segment of on-screen material may be disconcerting if the branch takes the user to the middle of an audio segment. Ensuring that audio is designed appropriately for all branching options is an important factor in the effective use of audio in nonlinear multimedia.

Aural versus visual processing

Even though listening can be as effective as reading for many purposes, transmitting information orally can be slow (Johnston, 1987). One reason for this may be that we can read or comprehend information faster than a person can speak (Fulford, 1993). Thus an important consideration in the use of speech to present information is whether normal speech will be too slow and cause users to lose interest.

One technique that has been investigated to alleviate this problem is the use of compressed speech (Fulford, 1993; Sticht, 1969). These studies found that increasing the speech rate from a normal rate of 175 words per minute (wpm) to approximately 260–275 wpm was effective. Fulford (1993) investigated the use of systematically designed text alone, text with normal speech, and text with compressed speech (262 wpm); she reports that the text with compressed speech was (1) as effective for mastery of objectives, (2) as efficient as text alone, and (3) more efficient than text supported by normal speech. Fulford (1993) suggests that systematically designed materials (those that are comprised only of "need-to-know" information, with little or no "nice-to-know" content) may have a high density of information and thus be "over-compressed" when speech compression is used. This is an important consideration if you are contemplating speech compression as a way of increasing the efficiency of speech delivery. Thus, incorporating carefully designed compressed speech with text and visuals can increase motivation and improve the effectiveness of a multimedia program.

Music selection

An issue related to the effective use of music concerns how the music selected for the multimedia application will affect the listener. A tune that has pleasant associations for a given developer could cause unpleasant reactions in the viewer/listener (Cartwright, 1986), in which case the music selection would interfere with the goals of the program. Cartwright suggests that indistinguishable tunes should be used whenever possible, since music should be used to call attention to the content of the program, not to elicit unrelated memories.

New skills

To use audio effectively, team members may need to acquire new skills, or new personnel may need to be hired. The use of audio requires skills that relate to writing narration, selecting and using music, using ambient sound, and identifying and integrating sound effects. For example, music selection requires an understanding of different types of music and their impacts, as well as a knowledge of how to mix techniques in order to achieve the appropriate blend when using music with narration and/or sound effects. Since audio is a tool that has not been widely used in the development of multimedia, many team members have not had the opportunity to learn how these new tools can be used to enhance a program.

Increased development time

Developing or selecting appropriate audio is a time-consuming task. For example, additional time will be required during the design and development processes to write the narrative script, locate a narrator, record the narration, and integrate the narration into the program. Additional time also will be required to develop appropriate transitions for all of the branches in the program. If the development team is considering the use of music, time is required both to determine when and how music should be incorporated into the presentation and to select, acquire, and then integrate the music into the appropriate parts of the program. Sound effects present similar time-intensive tasks: decision making as to how and where either ambient or special sound effects will be used, and then the selection, acquiring, and integration of the sound effects, or the recording of the required ambient sound. However, once developers have gained expertise in the use of audio and have built a library of music and sound effects, the time requirements should decrease. Most importantly, remember to weigh the increased development time (and associated costs) against the increased effectiveness of the multimedia program being developed.

Copyright

Copyright issues are complicated, particularly if the application is going to be sold to a client rather than used internally. The development organization should only use audio to which it holds the rights. This is especially true when using music and sound effects. Obtaining permission to use popular songs can be a long, complicated, and expensive process. Commercial-music and sound-effects libraries are excellent sources for obtaining the rights to use both types of audio in multimedia productions, and most libraries offer several different license or purchase options depending on the needs of the program (Mullin, 1992). Schneier (1992) provides several guidelines for ensuring that the material used in multimedia is legal; his guidelines suggest that developers should know what rights are being purchased, be persistent in tracking down permissions, and make sure that all relevant copyrights have been obtained.

Audio quality

The quality of the speech, music, and sound effects used is an important issue in multimedia applications. Audio needs to be clear, and free of distortion and extraneous noise. Therefore the audio must be professionally recorded and edited. Audio quality is especially important in the case of music. The internal capabilities of some computers are sufficient for speech and most sound effects, or for short music sequences. However, if music is to be a significant part of a program, an external speaker probably will be required.

An additional consideration related to quality is that the better the audio quality, the more disk or storage space it occupies. Thus the storage capacity of the delivery platform must be sufficient to contain the application at the audio quality-level chosen. A more technical discussion of the quality of audio recording may be found in Burger, 1993.

Response time

The response time required for an audio segment to play can sometimes be slow. Therefore, be sure to test segments that have been incorporated into the program and play them back on the delivery-system platform, to ensure that all types of audio will respond in a timely manner and without breaks or distortion.

General Guidelines

The following guidelines are presented as a way of summarizing our suggestions for using audio effectively in multimedia programs:

- To maximize the use of audio, analyze carefully the target audience, delivery environment, and content.
- Clearly define why and how audio will be used.
- Whenever possible, integrate audio into the whole program, and do it from the start of the project.
- Develop detailed scripts or storyboards.
- Allow learners to control audio, except when it carries the primary message.
- Make sound effects meaningful.
- Use the highest-quality audio possible, given the storage constraints of the delivery platform.
- Collaborate with others who have experience using different types of audio.
- Learn more about the use of sound, especially music.

References

Arwady, J. W. and Gayeski, D. M., *Using Video: Interactive and Linear Designs,* Educational Technology Publications, Englewood Cliffs, NJ, 1989.

Blattner, M. M., Sumikawa, D. A., and Greenberg, R. M., "Earcons and icons: Their structure and common design principles," *Human-Computer Interface,* 4, 11–44, 1989.

Blattner, M. M., Greenberg, R. M., and Kamegai, M., "Listening to turbulence: an example of scientific audiolizaton," in M. M. Blattner, and R. G. Dannenberg, eds., *Multimedia Interface Design,* pp. 87–107, ACM Press, New York.

Bove, T. and Rhodes, C., *Que's Macintosh Multimedia Handbook,* QUE, Carmel, IN, 1990.

"'Buddy' system automates postal services," *The Dallas Morning News,* June 13, 1993, p. 11H.

Burger, J., "In the mood: choosing the right music for a soundtrack," *NewMedia,* 2(11), 75, 1992.

Burger, J., "Sound thinking: audio in multimedia production," *NewMedia,* 3(7), 54–63, 1993.

Buxton, W., Introduction to this special issue on nonspeech audio, *Human-Computer Interaction,* 4, 1–9, 1989.

Cartwright, S. R., *Training With Video,* Knowledge Industry Publications, White Plains, NY, 1986.

Dean, C. and Whitlock, Q., *A Handbook of Computer-Based Training,* Kogan Page, New York, 1989.

Floyd, Steve, *The IBM Multimedia Handbook,* Brady Publishing, New York, 1991.

Fulford, Catherine, "Can learning be more efficient? Using compressed speech audio tapes to enhance systematically designed text," *Educational Technology,* 33(2), 51–59, 1993.

Gaver, W. W., "The SonicFinder: An interface that uses auditory icons," *Human-Computer Interface,* 4, 67–94, 1989.

Hannafin, M. J., and Hooper, S. R., "Learning principles," pp. 192–231 in Fleming, M., and Levie, W. H., eds., *Instructional Message Design: Principles from the Behavioral and Cognitive Sciences,* Educational Technology, Englewood Cliffs, NJ, 1993.

Heeter, C., and Gomes, P., "It's time for hypermedia to move to 'talking pictures,'" *Journal of Educational Multimedia and Hypermedia,* 1(2) 255–261, 1992.

Henderson, J. V., Pruett, R. K,. Galper, A. R., and Copes, W. S., "Interactive videodisc to teach combat trauma life support," *Journal of Medical Systems,* 10, 271–76, 1986.

Hsia, H. J., "Redundancy: Is it the lost key to better communication?" *Audio-Visual Communication Review,* 25(1), 63–85, 1977.

Johnston, J., *Electronic Learning from Audiotape to Videodisc,* Lawrence Erlbaum, Hillsdale, NJ, 1987.

Jones, M. K., *Human-Computer Interaction: A Design Guide,* Educational Technology Publications, Englewood Cliffs, NJ, 1989.

Keller, J., and Burkman, E., "Motivation Principles," pp. 3–53 in Fleming, M. and Levie, W. H., *Instructional Message Design: Principles from the Behavioral and Cognitive Sciences,* Educational Technology Publications, Englewood Cliffs, NJ, 1993.

Langdon, D. G., *Interactive Instructional Designs for Individual Learning,* Educational Technology Publications, Englewood Cliffs, NJ, 1973.

Mountford, S. J., and Gaver, W. W., "Talking and listening to computer," in Laurel, B., ed., *The Art of Human-Computer Interface Design,* Addison-Wesley, Reading MA, 1990.

Mullin, B., "Music libraries: the producer's friend," *Video Systems,* 33–42, September 1992.

Rowntree, D., *Teaching Through Self-Instruction,* Kogan Page, New York, 1986.

Schneier, B., "Practice safe multimedia: wear a copyright," *NewMedia,* 2 (12), 32–33, 1992.

Sticht, T. G., *Learning by Listening in Relation to Aptitude, Reading, and Rate-controlled Speech,* Human Resources Research Organization, Technical Report 69-23, 1969.

Swain, D. V., and Swain, J. R., *Scripting for the New AV Technologies,* 2d ed., Focal Press, Boston, 1991.

Van Nostrand, W. J., *The Scriptwriter's Handbook,* Knowledge Publications, White Plains, NY, 1989.

30

Digital Video a la Carte

Josh Hendrix

Alton Christensen

Introduction

It is now possible to use high-end personal computers and workstations to create broadcast-quality video off-line, without the use of an on-line suite. This is not the only way that a PC and video software can be integrated into the video postproduction process, and at the moment it is not the prevalent way. Nevertheless, low-cost computers and workstations are rapidly taking over many of the chores of postproduction, and in the process replacing traditional equipment that costs 100 times as much. The authors believe that within 3 to 5 years' time this scenario will have become almost commonplace.

This chapter is a guide to creating a broadcast-quality digital-video studio by choosing various products in an a la carte fashion. It contains information about the various pieces of hardware and software that can be combined together to create a custom studio that can have as much or more raw capability as much more expensive traditional video solutions. It answers the question, "What is the minimum set of equipment I need to produce video that is of high enough quality to be broadcast?"

One cautionary note should be sounded from the start. Due to the current speed of computing equipment, the digital studio described herein is by necessity a completely off-line environment. This is necessary because consumer-level computers and workstations currently are not fast enough to manipulate video in real time (30 frames per second), and consumer-level storage media also are not fast enough to retrieve it at that rate. Compensating for these factors does take time, and it has been said that the old adage "Time is money" is nowhere more true than in the broadcast business. If the nature of a project is such that time is the overriding critical factor (as in, "get it done yesterday"), then at this level of development the traditional editing suite should be used.

However, the advantages of a completely nonlinear editing environment, combined with the substantial cost savings over traditional solutions, can offset this time disadvantage for less time-critical projects. Furthermore, computing power and storage and retrieval speeds have been rapidly improving for several years at the consumer level. This trend shows no sign of slowing, which means that the time disadvantage will rapidly disappear. As less expensive, more capable equipment becomes available, one conclusion becomes clear: the future of video is digital.

It would be impossible to attempt to cover every single product within the scope of this chapter. By the time the ink dried on the pages of this book, the information would be obsolete. Instead, this guide talks in general terms about some of the types of products available. The goal is to give the reader a sense of what kinds of products are out there, and a vision of the minimal set of tools necessary to broadcast quality video on the desktop.

Let it also be noted, as a point of clarification, that in this chapter we will be referring to software and hardware that runs on a PC. We mean by that the generic term *personal computer*. Most people think of PCs as being IBMs or compatibles, or those machines that run the DOS or Windows operating system. However, most of the software and hardware available as of this writing, and thus in the authors' experience, operates on an Apple Macintosh®. We expect this to change as more software becomes available for Microsoft Windows™ and particularly when the PowerPC platforms emerge. However, the facts of our experience cannot help but color our perspectives, and the reader should take that into account.

Broadcast Quality

The term *broadcast quality,* as it is used in different contexts, generally has either a *subjective* or an *objective* connotation. It is important to distinguish between the two uses. Video technicians tend to use the term in its objective sense. Technically, whether a video image is of "broadcast quality" has nothing to do with the subjective impression of "image quality" that appears on-screen. Rather, a broadcast-quality image is one that conforms to Federal Communications Commission specification RS170-A, which all television broadcasters must comply with by law. The RS170-A specification addresses the synchronization and other physical characteristics of the video signal as it is transmitted. Broadcast quality in this sense of the term can be measured by a machine. This contrasts with the subjective use of the term, in which case its meaning is a matter of educated opinion.

In its subjective sense, *broadcast quality* refers to the subjective impression of image quality that a video clip leaves with the viewer. In other words, is the image "crisp" and "clean," devoid of artifacts? Are the colors true? Is the motion smooth? Have the "jaggies" been anti-aliased out? The answers to all of these questions will go to form the viewer's subjective impression of the quality of the image.

Among video producers, there are tacit standards of image quality that vary somewhat but are generally well agreed upon. At one time network television was widely thought of as a minimum standard for subjective broadcast quality. This has changed in the last few years, however, because the major networks and many cable stations have begun to broadcast, in the context of news shows and humorous home videos, some footage shot in the Hi-8 format. This has caused the definition of broadcast quality to become more a matter of content than of image quality. The skill with which the content is composed and shot is becoming the only clear line that can be drawn; there is no substitute for talent and experience when it comes to capturing content. In terms of image quality, however, video pros now tend to benchmark against the quality associated with different video-storage formats such as $\frac{3}{4}$-inch, Beta-SP, and D-1.

Both connotations of the term come into play when the characteristics of video software and hardware are being assessed. Various manufacturers of both claim that their products are of broadcast quality. When this claim is heard in reference to software designed for the composition of video clips it should be taken, unless specified otherwise, in the subjective sense. The software company is saying, "Our product helps you to create output that looks good enough to be broadcast on network television." This is a safe assumption, since most software is concerned with editing and creating effects, whereas special hardware usually is required to actually move video from computer to videotape.

The claims of hardware manufacturers require more thought. Hardware can affect both kinds of image quality, subjective and objective. Seen subjectively, broadcast-quality hardware must be able to store and display the digital image in a manner that does not notably degrade its visual quality. Seen objectively, broadcast-quality hardware that encodes a digital image for transfer to videotape must generate a video signal that conforms to the aforementioned FCC standards. Most hardware can pass the objective test, but one must carefully analyze and test all subjective claims.

Generating broadcast-quality video from a PC has less to do with the computer itself than it does with the output device and with the software that creates the video. It is the old computer principle of "garbage in, garbage out" in action. If the digitizing board is of poor quality, the resulting video will be no better. By the same token, if the output device for recording to tape is of poor quality, this will be reflected in the image that is recorded to tape. Thus if you want to do broadcast-quality work from a PC, it will be worth your while to spend the extra money for high-quality input and/or output devices. When it comes to other factors that affect the subjective quality of your video, tradeoffs can be made, but it is best not to compromise when it comes to input and output devices.

The Basic Video Creation Process

The process of creation, with respect to digital video at least, is once again evolving so as to embrace the new capabilities that advancing technology brings with it. The use of PCs as the sole video-creation engine is as yet so new that there are no commonly agreed-upon methods. Then too, PCs have a variety of still graphics and animation software already available, which means they often offer more capabilities than traditional methods of producing the same kinds of graphic elements in post. With so many new variables, and with software capabilities changing so rapidly, the process of evolution may never slow down again.

The following sections will depict a fairly common sequence of events that could take place in the creation of a video on a PC. Since the computer brings the creation process into the nonlinear age, none of these steps really has to follow in exact sequence except the last two, which can occur only when the video-editing process has ended. Assuming that the storyboarding process has been completed, the following steps can occur.

Gathering source material

This task should be familiar to video postproduction specialists, and thus requires little explanation. Production facilities and personnel may be employed to create new footage for editing and manipulation, or stock footage may be gathered. The effects of the nonlinear editing process may be felt even here, however, because it allows editors to play "what if" with the story line in an unprecedented manner. Thus additional footage may be shot at this stage, and more footage may be required later if the story line is allowed to evolve. The computer is itself capable of generating text, graphics, and even 2D and 3D animations. As such, these types of source material may not need to be *gathered* so much as they need to be *planned*.

Digitizing

Before any editing can take place, the source video must be converted into digital form by the computer and stored on disk. This process is known as *digitizing*, and involves special hardware. This is an important bottleneck in the process, not just in terms of time but also in terms of quality. An investment in high-quality digitizing boards is essential if broadcast-quality results are to be achieved.

Video input can come from many kinds of input devices, from consumer-quality VHS machines to traditional high-end tape equipment. However, the quality of the digital image is directly dependent on the quality of the medium from which it comes. While there are several methods of digitizing, they all depend on the quality of the source device. Thus the rental or purchase of a high-quality deck should be factored into the overall cost of equipment. Still frames to be included in the production can be created in the PC or brought in through a high-quality scanner.

The nonlinear video creation process

Once the visual raw materials have been digitized, the creation process can begin in earnest. Traditionally this process has been a linear one, due to the linear nature of the underlying technology. By facilitating a nonlinear editing process, however, the personal computer makes possible a great deal of freedom. The price of this freedom is that many more options are available, harder choices must be made, and creativity must sometimes be restrained as deadlines approach. The following steps may be engaged in almost any order within the limits of time, budget, and common sense.

Editing nonlinearly. The nonlinear editing process has many advantages. Most software products handle the editing process by facilitating the creation of an off-line, or a "model" of the final video, rather than by actually composing the video themselves on-line. This model contains information about how the video is to unfold over time. Various video clips are trimmed and then sequenced together with intervening transitions, wipes, and keys, and some programs have DVE-style layering for motion effects. Rather than manipulate the video files themselves, the model contains information about the files and pointers to them, much like a traditional off-line. Since the model is in the computer's memory, it can be continuously altered and updated with little time penalty. Also, multiple versions of the same project can be created from the same source, and stored for later evaluation.

Since video files are stored on disks for random access, cueing to a particular frame is almost instantaneous. Rearranging shot sequences and substituting one shot for another can be done with ease, letting the computer worry about the time codes. If special effects are being applied, their parameters can be tweaked repeatedly until the results are exactly as desired. Nonlinear editing enhances the creative capabilities of editors and producers by providing better tools and performing more of the "gruntwork" than did the traditional systems of the past.

Creating additional source. Since the computer is a general-purpose tool, it can be used for more than just the editing process. Static graphic elements can be assembled by means of professional-quality graphics programs, text can be generated, and 2D and 3D animations can be created. Changes to all of these production elements can be made right up to the last minute. It surprises some newcomers to the world of personal computers that the quality of output can be as good as or better than traditional postproduction tools.

Multiple storyboards. The computer allows the editor to create and store a model of the video project without creating the actual video. Since this model can also be duplicated, and the duplicate can be altered without altering the original, it is possible to create several different models of the same project. This means that the editor has the freedom to explore several different options (time permitting) and choose the best elements of each. Last-minute changes also are much more feasible.

Previews.   One disadvantage of the fact that the computer is assembling a model of the production and not the actual production itself is that on some systems it may not be possible to immediately see the results of one's work in full motion. To work around this, most editing software allows the user to preview a portion of the video by assembling a low-quality version of it. This version may be smaller in dimension, at lower quality, or play at a lower frame rate than the final video. However, previews generally are good enough to give the editor an accurate notion of what to expect in the final product and to aid in decision making when choices must be made.

The final render.   Once the creation process has ended, the resulting video model must be used to create an actual video. Simple editing such as cuts and transitions may not need to be explicitly rendered, but most complicated effects such as layering, compositing, and computationally intensive image-manipulation such as blurring do require it. During the rendering process the computer proceeds frame-by-frame through the model and performs all operations necessary to create a complete frame at the desired resolution and quality. This process can be very time-consuming, depending on the complexity of the model and the duration of the video. A business video with one or two layers, some graphic overlays, and transitions will take much less time to render than a music video with 20 or more layers composited together, multiple special effects, morphs, etc. There is no general rule of thumb for predicting how long a particular video will take to render; the best guide is experience.

   This stage constitutes one drawback to this type of editing process, due to its time requirements. However, since many compositing and special-effect computations are very processor-intensive, three sure ways to speed the rendering process are to (1) purchase a faster computer, (2) accelerate your current machine, or (3) take advantage of multiprocessor hardware and software to operate in parallel. Also, the final rendering step usually can be completed by the computer unattended. This means the machine can be left to render overnight when it would not otherwise be in use.

Recording to tape

The frames of the final production can be recorded to tape either in conjunction with the final rendering stage or after that stage is complete. To render and record at the same time, it is necessary to be able to record frame-by-frame to tape, because the computer usually will not be able to render the frame in under $\frac{1}{30}$ of a second. In this case, the frames may or may not be written to disk at the same time. Note that in order to save time using this method, the software involved must be able to cue the tape to record the next frame at the same time as the next frame is being rendered. Otherwise (i.e., if cueing and rendering happen sequentially), this process will be no faster than completely rendering the video before recording.

If the rendering stage is completed first, several options then exist for recording. In all cases, a device controller will be necessary to help the computer cue and otherwise control the recording deck. Recording frame-by-frame is the oldest and most widespread method, and generally produces the best-quality recordings. Newer devices exist that allow brief segments of the video to be sequentially recorded in real time from memory. A few seconds at a time of the video are loaded and played out to the recording device. Then the tape is recued while the next few seconds are loaded, and the process repeats itself. This hardware is a more expensive option, but it can pay for itself in recording time saved.

These five steps give you a general overview of the digital-video creation process on a personal computer or workstation. They are the context in which a system should be planned and put together. The following section describes the basic components of a digital-video studio.

The Basic Components

The fact that digital video has burst upon the scene may be attributed to several factors that have come together at the same time.

Fast machines

Central processing units, the brains of the computer, are getting faster and cheaper, and this trend will accelerate. It is commonly shared wisdom in the computer industry that processor speed doubles every 2 years, although it is now being debated whether that figure is closer to every 1.5 years. As computer hardware becomes commoditized, manufacturers have no choice but to fiercely compete on speed and price. This works to the benefit of the consumer. For digital-video manipulation, it is recommended that the fastest possible machine be bought that your budget will allow. Slower machines are just as capable of producing the same-quality output as the fastest machines available, but faster machines can accomplish much more in a given amount of time.

Speed claims by computer manufacturers are notoriously misleading, however. Currently, the best benchmark to use for comparison between different brands and platforms is the *specmark*. This set of tests measures the speed with which computers perform tasks most similar to those they are actually asked to perform in the real world. While not a perfect measurement, specmarks are more reliable than most other benchmarks such as MIPS (millions of instructions per second) and MFLOPS (millions of floating point operations per second). If your local retail outlet cannot supply these figures for the brands you are comparing, contacting the manufacturer should do the trick.

High-quality input/output devices

The quality level at which you can digitize and record video is the most important hardware consideration in a digital-video suite. If your input and/or output devices are not of broadcast quality, then the results won't be either. Broadcast quality comes at a high price, however, sometimes as high as or higher than the computer itself. But these costs will still be one to three orders of magnitude less than the cost of buying traditional video equipment.

If you do not need to record video for editing and manipulation, and you only need to create stills, cel animation, or animation in two or three dimensions, then you may only need to buy a high-quality output card. If you do need to record video, then you can buy devices that combine input and output or those that specialize in one or the other.

Add-in boards exist that can digitize long video clips directly to disk in real time (e.g., 30 fps), but generally these will not create broadcast-quality input. Different and more time-consuming methods are necessary. One method, digitizing from videotape frame-by-frame, is an older and a very common one. A newer method is to digitize to a RAM disk (a large bank of memory) in real time. There are advantages and disadvantages to each.

Digitizing frame-by-frame trades off time for quality. The highest quality is obtained at the expense of taking a longer time to digitize and store each frame. Frames usually are recorded as a series of separate numbered files that can be altered or reordered. Several components are needed to digitize in this manner.

First, a high-quality digitizing board must be installed. This type of add-in board is called a *frame grabber*. In order to automate the process of digitizing a large number of frames, an additional board must be purchased to control the storage device from which the video is taken. This "device control" board is connected to the video deck either via the computer's serial port or through a port on the board. Both of these boards come with software that allows unattended batch recording of multiple video frames to the hard disk. This recording does not take place in real time. Rather, it can take up to 30 seconds per frame to cue the tape to the appropriate frame, digitize the frame, and save it to disk.

Methods of recording in real time exist, with different tradeoffs. With one option known as recording to a "RAM disk," a sequence of frames can be digitized at broadcast quality in real time, but the frames are digitized into memory, not to disk. This is possible because the time it takes to store information in memory is a fraction of what it takes to store it on a disk.

To digitize in this manner, a digitizing board and a device controller are both needed. The memory may be in the computer or in a special device designed to hold large amounts of it. The memory is filled over and over again by subsequent groups of frames from the deck. After memory has been filled, the deck is paused and recued, and the frames can be saved to disk either uncompressed or compressed at a low compression ratio that does not affect the visual quality of the frame. In this case, the number of frames that can be digitized is limited by the amount of memory available. NTSC-size uncompressed video takes up about 1 Mbyte of space per frame, so 1 second of video takes up about 30 Mbytes of memory or disk space. Some computers can hold up to 128 Mbytes of memory, and RAM disk devices exist that can contain hundreds of megabytes. Obviously, there is an additional cost to each extra megabyte, but memory costs have dropped sharply in recent years, and for many of us the time saved will justify the expense.

The most desirable state of affairs would be to digitize directly to disk at broadcast quality, losslessly compressing the video so that the visual quality is unaffected. At the time of this writing (early 1994) there are no products on the market for PCs that can do this. Boards presently exist that can digitize directly to disk with compression, but the compression ratios necessary to achieve this must be high enough that the quality of the image is degraded below broadcast levels (the extent to which this is true is a hot topic of debate). The authors expect this to change quickly, however, so by the time you read this, products may exist in the marketplace that accomplish this feat.

Another broadcast-quality input option exists for video professionals and those who have access to postproduction facilities of some sort. It is of course possible to digitize video into an Abekas disk recorder or similar storage medium. One can then copy the video from the Abekas to a digital tape that can be read and written to by an Exabyte or similar tape drive. Some Exabyte drives, for instance, come with SCSI ports and thus can be attached to and used by a PC. Software is required to convert from the Abekas format to one that is PC-readable, and this is the time bottleneck here. However, the resulting video quality can be very high, and the costs can be lower in the short run than buying an expensive digitizing board and device controller and gaining access to a good deck.

The process of getting finished video out of the computer works almost exactly in reverse. Most digitizing boards also allow video to be recorded from the computer to tape. Batch recordings can be made one frame at a time, or recordings can be made in real time from memory, but the amount of memory limits the duration of video that can be recorded on a given pass. In either case, the device control board and software handle tape cueing and synchronization. Recording one frame at a time can take more than 30 seconds per frame. The average time per frame will be less for the RAM option, but this comes at greater hardware expense.

Note that the digital tape process also works in reverse for output. A video file is created by the computer software. This file is then converted to the Abekas or similar format (again, this step takes a significant amount of time) and recorded to some digital broadcast medium. As before, the long-term costs are those charged by the production facilities for conversion from Exabyte tape (for instance) to the Abekas or other storage medium.

When you are doing broadcast graphics on a PC platform, it is highly recommended that you purchase an NTSC monitor in addition to a standard computer monitor, attach it to your computer, and use it to view your work in progress before rendering your final output. You may be able to do this via your output board. There is a great difference between a computer monitor that is non-interlaced and flicker-free and a standard NTSC monitor that is interlaced. In general, the computer's graphics capabilities exceed those of the target output medium, videotape, since the computer monitor displays at a higher resolution and is capable of a wider range of saturations and luminances.

For example, thin lines that look fine on the computer monitor may beat or flicker on an NTSC monitor due to its lower resolution. Color saturation and luminance levels need to be watched so that they are "legal" for broadcast. Access to waveform or vector-scope monitors is a preferable but expensive option. Viewing your work before rendering it and recording to tape can help you to pinpoint and avoid these problems.

Time-based media storage formats

In order to store and retrieve massive amounts of time-based data such as digital video, special storage formats have been devised. File formats such as Apple's QuickTime™ and Microsoft's Video For Windows™ allow users to store and randomly access video and audio as well as other time-based information. The main advantage here is standardization of the storage format.

For instance, any QuickTime file generated by a video application can be read by any other QuickTime-compatible application. The same is true for Video For Windows–compatible applications. This eliminates time-consuming conversions between custom formats from different software developers, and frees programmers to concentrate on building better tools. Note, however, that conversion must take place between QuickTime files and Video For Windows files, and also that Apple supports QuickTime both on the Macintosh and on Windows™ platforms.

Other advantages include random access within the video file, and data compression. Random access eliminates the time-consuming process of cueing up that is necessary with a linear storage format such as videotape. Rather, any frame of the video can be instantaneously accessed at any time. This is necessary to support a nonlinear editing process.

Video compression is used to decrease the size of the video file, thus increasing the amount of video that can be stored on a given disk. Compression algorithms generally work by analyzing each frame and expressing the information contained therein more compactly. This is like writing & in place of *and* on a piece of paper. The ampersand takes less time to write and takes up less space, yet expresses the same information. An analogous process occurs in the compression of digital video.

Currently, digital-video compression is a two-edged sword. On the positive side, compressing digital video is necessary because (1) the storage requirements for digital video are enormous, and (2) compression increases the effective throughput of digital-video playback devices, which facilitates increased frame sizes and higher frame rates. On the negative side, some compression algorithms sacrifice the visual quality of the video in order to achieve smaller files.

A compression ratio is simply a ratio between the size in bytes of a frame before compression and its size after compression. The higher the compression ratio (i.e., the less space each frame takes up on disk), the greater the amount of information that has been removed. If the compression ratio is low enough, the visual quality will not be notably affected by the compression process. A rule of thumb is that compression ratios higher than 2:1 (considered a low ratio) probably will not affect visual quality. For more technical information on compression, see the appendix on p. 30.17.

High-capacity, high-sustained-throughput hard drives

Hard drives are a critical part of the digital-video studio. Time-based media in general, and video frames in particular, can have large storage requirements. Buying the right hard drive can make the difference between productivity and frustration. Depending on budget, a choice must be made between buying a hard drive and a disk array. Disk arrays store data more quickly by spreading the video data across multiple drives and writing it almost in parallel. They are correspondingly more expensive than a slower hard drive of the same capacity, but the performance increase is often worth the price.

There are four factors to consider when purchasing storage: sustained transfer rate, seek time, capacity, and price, in that order.

The *sustained transfer rate* is the average rate at which data can be written to or read from the disk, usually in megabytes per second. It has the highest priority, because all digital-video programs will spend an enormous amount of time just reading and writing frames to and from the disk. At the time of this writing, standard SCSI hard disks have transfer rates of about 1 to 2 Mbytes per second. More expensive, higher-throughput disk arrays can have transfer rates of 3 to 5 Mbytes per second. This is one piece of information that is harder to find than other attributes of a drive, so a call to the manufacturer may be necessary.

Seek time comes into play because, internally, a hard disk is structured somewhat like a record player. The disk is a platter than spins around at high speed, and the read-write head moves toward and away from the center of the disk and is able to reach almost any part of it. Seek time is the average time it takes for the read-write head to move from one area of the disk to another, and usually is measured in milliseconds. In general, seek times range between 7 and 15 milliseconds (0.007 and 0.015 seconds), and as technology advances these times decrease. Seek time is important because a disk drive, unlike a record on which all songs are stored sequentially in the record's groove, can break long files such as digital video into chunks that are located in physically separate areas of the disk.

For instance, a 2-minute-long video might be broken up into three separate chunks. To play this video, the disk head must move to the physical location of the first chunk and begin reading frames into the computer for display on-screen. When the head is done reading frames from the first chunk, it must move to the physical location of the next frame. This move must happen in a split-second, because a high (longer) seek time will cause a pause in the action while the drive head moves, whereas a low (fast) seek time will not cause a noticeable pause. Thus, seek time becomes important for digitization and playback of video in real time. The lower the seek time, the better.

Disk capacity is simply the amount of information a hard disk can hold. Due to the storage requirements of digital video, the typical digital-video studio requires at least one gigabyte of storage space. If digital archiving of original footage is desired, a tape-drive backup system can be a cost-effective solution. Prices per megabyte for 1-Gbyte-capacity-or-greater hard drives have recently fallen under $1.20 for external drives. Prices for disk arrays, which have the advantage of higher sustained transfer rates, have fallen below $2 per megabyte. The better the performance characteristics (sustained transfer rate, seek time, etc.), the higher the cost per megabyte. To put this in perspective, however, these prices are still fractions of the cost of the traditional equipment performing the same function in post houses today. See the appendix (p. 30.17) for more technical information about hard drives.

Broadcast-quality software

Software for personal computers and workstations now exists to create stills, edit video nonlinearly, create transitions, perform composites, render special effects, animate in two and three dimensions, and so on, and all at high enough quality for broadcast or transfer to film. No one package can do it all, however, so it is important to research the capabilities of different software from different vendors. The minimum feature-set necessary to ensure broadcast-quality output is comprised of 24-bit color manipulation, subpixel positioning, anti-aliasing, Alpha channel support, text generation that supports anti-aliasing of Postscript™ and TrueType™ fonts, field-rendering, and control of the output gamut. Special effects also are useful, but not essential. All of these features are now described.

24-bit color.   The most common representation of color in personal computers is familiar to video professionals as "component" video. Here, colors are composed of three channels: red, green, and blue. Each channel is represented by 8 bits (1 byte), for a total of 24 bits per pixel. Programs that generate 24-bit color output are essential to broadcast-quality work, because this color scheme can represent more than 16 million separate colors, more than the human eye can distinguish. Any program with less will not allow colors to be manipulated with sufficient subtlety. For a more technical explanation of this color scheme, see the appendix .

Subpixel positioning.   If your software has DVE-like features, subpixel positioning is essential for achieving smooth-looking motion of video layers and important for compositing. To achieve broadcast-quality motion, it is necessary to compensate for the computer's limited screen resolution. This is accomplished by creating the illusion that the number of screen pixels per inch is much greater than it actually is. Subpixel sampling is the frame-processing method that creates this illusion. The appendix contains more technical information about this process.

Anti-aliasing.   Anti-aliasing becomes important when the edges of any graphic object are diagonal to any degree, when rectangular shapes are rotated, or when smooth curves are desired, as with character generation. Like subpixel positioning, it is a method of compensating for the limited resolution of the screen. It accomplishes this by removing "jaggies" (stairsteps that appear as edges that contrast sharply with the surroundings), thereby smoothing diagonal lines and curves.

Without anti-aliasing, the edges of any object that is not perfectly vertical or horizontal will become jagged. If the resolution of the broadcast medium is lower than that of the computer, this effect will be exaggerated when the video is broadcast. This feature is so important that PC programs exist that do nothing else but anti-alias stills or animation sequences. If your chosen primary editing software does not support this feature, it is still possible to eliminate aliasing problems, but with a substantial time penalty.

Alpha channel support.   The Alpha channel contains transparency information for each pixel. Many video professionals are surprised to find that some PC-based graphics software, such as Photoshop™, is more capable of creating and handling Alpha channel information than, for instance, a Quantel Paintbox (the de facto standard broadcast paint system). To the video professional, this transparency information is a key signal that defines which parts of the video frame are transparent, which opaque, and which semitransparent.

The most common example of this may be seen on most newscasts. The character-generator used to overlay the type on the screen contains an Alpha channel. The layering device (a switcher) uses the Alpha channel to determine which parts of the overlay (the letters) will be opaque and which parts will be filled with the background image (a reporter standing in front of City Hall, for instance). This is similar but not the same as a chromakey, in which the key signal is generated from a chrominance value based on the incoming video.

There are a variety of standard uses for the Alpha channel. As mentioned above, overlaying text and graphics onto video is one such use. In addition to defining completely transparent and completely opaque areas, you also will want to use the Alpha channel to better blend graphic elements with the background in a subtle manner that mimics the appearance of a real object. This is done by making the edges of the object semitransparent, and it is essential for the creation of high-quality composites of any kind. Animation software, especially for three-dimensional animation, can benefit enormously from the including of an Alpha channel with each frame. This allows the compositing of 3D, computer-generated graphic animations into 2D backgrounds with ease, for example. Special effects that are aware of the Alpha channel can be used to warp images and their transparency information at the same time, allowing for greater realism in the effect.

There are, however, some drawbacks to using the Alpha channel. Storing transparency information for each frame of an animation means that storage requirements increase by 33 percent for each file containing an Alpha channel. Also, to obtain proper composites, several additional operations must be done to each pixel of the image when compositing, to take the transparency information into account. This increases rendering time by a fair amount. These drawbacks are small, however, compared to the benefits derived from using the Alpha channel.

Text generation.   The wide variety of high-quality fonts available for most PCs makes them a natural choice for text generation. Many video programs support both Postscript and TrueType, meaning that almost any typeface imaginable is available. Most software allows not just character-generation but on-the-fly editing late in the production process. Anti-aliasing is essential to the creation of clean-looking curves and edges, and text that has not been anti-aliased is generally considered to be not of broadcast quality. Text-keying usually is accomplished by means of Alpha channel manipulation. Special text effects include texturing, coloring, and stretching and warping.

Given all of these advantages, it is surprising to find that PC character-generation software generally has not reached the same level of professionalism that other kinds of software have. While most editing software facilitates basic titling, little attention has been paid to kerning issues and scrolling credits, two fundamental components of proper video typesetting. Until such tools become available, it may be necessary to use other programs that have kerning features, or to break credits down into manageable groups and convert the text to graphic elements separately and then import the resulting graphics into the video project.

Field rendering.   Since the final digital output must be recorded by analog-video equipment for broadcast, the analog format in which the video will be stored must be respected. NTSC video is recorded at 30 fps (frames per second), but each frame is made up of two fields of scan lines, meaning that the true recording rate is 60 fields per second. This avoids a staccato effect in the appearance of moving objects, because effectively the screen is changing 60 rather than 30 times per second.

Software must respect fields if it is to maintain broadcast quality. Since computer-generated animation files generally do not contain fields (unless the animation software specifically supports them), a way around this difficulty is to render the video at 60 fps, record to an output device, then play back at double speed. In this case the software generally will take twice as much time to produce an animation of a given duration (since it is creating twice as many frames), but the motion of objects will be much smoother when recorded to tape. Smarter software that respects fields will render at the same frame rate but store only the even or odd scan lines for a given frame, which will take about the same amount of time. It also is important to be sure that the recording software for both digitizing board and device controller are field-aware and can extract fields from a file that contains them.

Output gamut control.   It is important to note that many PC-video software programs will allow the use of colors that have higher saturation or luminance values than are legal for broadcast. To correct for this, prebroadcast processing may be necessary, and some programs have methods for altering "illegal colors" so as to conform to broadcast specifications. It is important to preview these alterations just in case, to compensate for any undesirable visual results. The best way is to preview on an NTSC monitor before rendering. It is possible to correct for this with traditional equipment after recording, but this increases time and expense requirements.

Visual effects.   The wide variety of visual effects available from microcomputer video applications amounts to a strong argument for going digital. Visual effects include standard transitions, DVE-style video motion control, layering and compositing, video image manipulation, keying, morphing, and too many more to mention. All these effects are not available in all programs, but they are all possible through various video applications on the PC. Indeed, it is possible to put together a suite of PC video tools that offers more video-manipulation capabilities than traditional video equipment costing upward of $500,000. Doing this at broadcast quality requires most of the software features mentioned in this section, however.

Tradeoffs

Trading old bottlenecks for new

The bottlenecks associated with traditional video-editing equipment are switcher capabilities, generation loss, and the limit to how many VTRs can be rolled at one time. All of these bottlenecks disappear when editing in a nonlinear environment on a PC. Switcher capabilities become moot, because the computer effectively becomes a switcher with infinite inputs. Since all video is stored on a random-access disk, any portion of any file can be accessed at any time. This also renders the number of virtual VTRs effectively infinite, since the physical limits to the number of files that can be made available are seldom encountered. Generation loss, which occurs when working around switcher input limits, also becomes unnecessary. The number of layers that can be composited together at one time is limited only by memory.

The *new* bottlenecks are speed and disk space. The speed of the editing process depends upon the speed of the computer's CPU, the speed of the disk drives, the speed with which video can be digitized and recorded, and the efficiency with which the software being used was written. Disk-space requirements will always be large, and disk-space management tasks become routine if backing up and keeping old digitized footage is required. Fortunately, the severity of both of these problems is continually diminishing as faster machines and peripherals and higher-capacity drives continually are introduced. Since the need for speed and disk space is not restricted to the video marketplace, increased competition in these areas greatly speeds improvements in existing products and spurs development of new technologies.

Quality versus time

Whether one is speaking of digitizing, rendering, or recording, there are explicit tradeoffs that can be made between image quality and time. It is possible to digitize video at real-time frame rates, but the quality of the quicker process and the necessity of compression for storage prevent this from resulting in broadcast-quality input. When rendering, subpixel positioning, anti-aliasing, Alpha channel manipulation, and special effects all can be performed at various quality levels or not at all. The lower the quality, the less time needed to perform the operation. Just as with digitization, it is not possible to play normal-size video at 30 fps without compressing to such a degree that loss of quality results. With all of the above operations, the speed of the computer will make a big difference, so it is best to get the fastest machine your budget will allow.

Quality versus expense

As previously mentioned, nowhere will the tradeoff between expense and quality be more apparent than with digitizing and recording hardware. With the rare exception you get what you pay for, and the price of broadcast-quality input and output can be greater than the cost of the computer itself. One way around this is to purchase a PC-compatible tape drive, with tapes that also can be read by a local postproduction facility. A tape drive of this type costs less than digitizing and recording hardware, but the post facility will charge a fee for transferring the video to a broadcast storage medium, so this may not be cost-effective in the long run.

Software with broadcast-quality features generally will cost more than software without them, but this is not always the case. Careful and thorough research into different software packages and their capabilities can result in the discovery of inexpensive software gems. They exist. Both computer magazines and now video magazines publish reviews of different software packages that can be highly informative. Once a list of potential candidates has been narrowed down, it is helpful to visit a local systems house or VAR (value-added reseller), where you can actually try the software and ask questions of salespeople intimately familiar with the program.

Conclusion

This has been an attempt to cover, in a generic fashion, the necessary tools for creating broadcast-quality video direct from the desktop. The capability to do this has really existed only for a short while, and the market is constantly changing as new products are introduced with more and better capabilities.

Today, however, it is indeed possible to use various combinations of software and hardware to achieve this end. The authors both share the firm opinion that the configuration described herein will bring the same revolutionary changes to video that desktop publishing brought to the publishing industry. This means that, while the need for high-end postproduction facilities will always exist, the personal computer will bring many of their technical capabilities out onto the desktop by virtue of its low price and high level of performance. Many more talented people will have the tools "all to themselves," because those tools will be affordable for individuals for the first time. Furthermore, as computers become ever cheaper, more and more developers will be lured into the arena of video production.

Appendix

More about compression

Many compression algorithms rely on the fact that there is much redundant information in an uncompressed frame. This can be removed in such a way that the human eye cannot perceive the difference. If enough information is removed, however, the eye *will* notice the difference as a loss of visual quality in the frame. There is thus an implicit tradeoff between visual quality and file size when compressing digital video.

Once digitized, one uncompressed frame of a standard NTSC-size video in true color (24 bits per pixel) takes up almost 1 Mbyte of disk space. At 30 frames per second, 1 second of uncompressed video takes about 30 Mbytes of storage. Although high-capacity storage devices are constantly falling in price, the costs for this much storage are still considerable.

Each compression algorithm is designed to be most effective for a certain type of video content. Ideally, different compression algorithms will be used for different types of video. Motion JPEG, for instance, is useful for "normal video" content, such as might be recorded by a news camera at the scene of a crime or a political rally. This type of video is considered "noisy," because the content is rich and varies greatly and, once digitized, the chance that any two adjacent pixels will be exactly the same color is rather low, but the chance that they will be similar is rather high. This contrasts with computer-generated animation, which is much less noisy, and in which the chances of any two adjacent pixels being exactly the same color is much greater, but the chance that any two adjacent pixels will also be very different is also greater (edges and boundaries are much sharper). The Motion JPEG algorithm will quickly begin to degrade the quality of computer-generated animations even at low compression ratios. Algorithms designed to compress animations well may actually increase the size of a "normal video" file. Thus, it is also important to match the appropriate compression method to the video content.

Hard drives

To understand why the sustained transfer rate is crucial, recall that 1 frame of uncompressed video takes up 1 Mbyte. It will take a drive with a transfer rate of 1 Mbyte per second about 1 second to retrieve 1 frame at sustained rates, whereas it will take a disk array between $\frac{1}{5}$ to $\frac{1}{3}$ of a second. Multiply this difference ($1 - \frac{1}{5} = \frac{4}{5}$ seconds per frame) by 30 frames and it will equal 24 seconds saved for each second of video rendered to a disk array, just in transfer time alone. Of course, since most video is compressed, the actual time savings will be smaller, but it will still be significant.

Where the video file is broken up into three separate chunks, frames 0:00:00 to 0:07:27 might be stored in one chunk near the center of the disk. Frames 0:07:28 to 0:43:12 might be stored in the second chunk halfway toward the disk's edge, and frames 0:43:13 to 1:59:29 might be stored in a large chunk along the disk's outer edge. To play a video, the head must read each frame sequentially. When the head is done reading frame 0:07:27, it must move to the physical location of the next frame. If the computer has been playing the video at 30 fps, this move must happen in a split-second in order to avoid a pause in the action as viewed on screen.

More specifically, $\frac{1}{30}$ of a second equals 0.0333 seconds. At 30 fps, 0.0333 seconds is the maximum time that the computer has to perform the following tasks: (1) move the disk head to the correct location, (2) read the frame into memory, (3) decompress the frame, and (4) copy the frame to the screen. The bulk of this time will be spent on steps 2 and 3, leaving very little time for steps 1 and 4. From this perspective, even 15 milliseconds seems rather sluggish with respect to the need to play 30 fps.

24-bit and 32-bit color

One bit is the smallest unit of information in a computer, representing two numbers, either 1 or 0. A byte is a group of 8 bits, each of which can be switched on or off. This means that a byte can represent $2^8 = 256$ numbers. If we start counting from 0, then the maximum number that 1 byte can represent is 255. Twenty-four-bit color means that a given color is specified by 24 bits, or 3 bytes, within the computer. It is common for each of these 3 bytes to represent the amount of red, green, or blue used to make up the color of 1 pixel. One byte specifies the amount of red, the next byte the amount of green, and the last byte the amount of blue used. Since each byte can hold 256 possible values, and since the value in each byte is independent of the values in the other two, the number of possible colors that can be represented in this way is 256^3 = more than 16 million colors, more than the human eye can distinguish, and more than enough for video.

The next most common step downward in terms of the number of possible colors a program can handle is by more than three orders of magnitude, to 16-bit color. In this representation, the amounts of red, green, and blue are specified by groups of 5 bits. Each group can represent $2^5 = 32$ numbers, and the three groups together can specify up to $32^3 = 32,768$ colors, or about 500 times fewer than 24-bit color can represent. The general consensus is that this is too few for broadcast quality.

In a 32-bit color scheme, the red, green, and blue channels for a pixel are represented by 1 byte each, and the Alpha channel is represented by an additional byte. Thus 32-bit color is really just 24-bit color with 1 byte of transparency information stored for each pixel as well. Since 1 byte can represent 256 possible values, there are 256 levels of transparency per pixel available in a 32-bit color scheme.

Subpixel sampling

To be sure that we understand why this technique is important, let's review the way in which visual elements are represented on the computer screen. To the computer programmer, the screen is a grid of square dots or *pixels* (for *picture elements*). Consumer-level monitors generally support up to 80 or so pixels per inch (or dots per inch, abbreviated dpi). This is the computer's *screen resolution*. The programmer has control over the color of each individual pixel, and exercises this control to create the graphical user interfaces that make using computers easier, as well as to display a frame of video on-screen for the user.

Similarly, one frame of video is stored as a grid of pixels, each of which can be manipulated. To display a stored frame of video on a computer screen, the programmer must somehow map the pixels from the video frame to the appropriate pixels in the computer screen. This "mapping" process sometimes can become complicated.

In the simplest case, suppose the computer screen has a resolution of 80 dpi and is 8 inches wide. If the video also was digitized at the same resolution, then to display a nonrotated video frame the programmer can use a one-to-one mapping, which means that each pixel from the video frame corresponds to 1 pixel on the computer screen. For convenience, let's assume that column numbers begin with 1 for the leftmost column and increase by 1 to the right, with the rightmost column being number 640 (80 dpi × 8 inches). Assume that row numbers begin at 1 for the first row and increase by 1 down-screen. Proceeding from the left column to the right, the program would then color the pixel in column 1, row 1 of the screen the same color (bright red, for instance) as the pixel in column 1, row 1 of the video frame. This would then be repeated for columns 2 through 640, then start over again with column 1, row 2. The process would end when all screen pixels had been colored the same as their video-frame counterparts.

Suppose now that the programmer wants the video image to move horizontally to the right over time, creating the "reveal-right" transition. To create this motion, the programmer would again copy the pixels from the video frame, but with an offset from column 1. The value of the offset is determined by the speed of the reveal. Thus for the second frame of video, the screen pixel in column 1, row 1 would be colored black (the background color as revealed), and the screen pixel in column 2 (1 plus the desired offset), row 1 would be colored bright red, the same as the video pixel in column 1, row 1. Similarly, the color of each screen pixel would be determined by the video pixel in the same row, but in a column determined by the desired offset.

Note, however, that this means that the on-screen image can move only in increments of $\frac{1}{80}$ of an inch, due to the resolution of the screen. The video moves a certain number of pixels to the right according to the offset, but only to distances that are multiples of the width of a pixel. Problems arise when the speed of the push creates offsets that should be some fraction of an inch that is not a multiple of $\frac{1}{80}$. This might happen with a very slow push, for example. In this case, rounding the offset to the nearest $\frac{1}{80}$ will not create smooth motion. Rather the motion will appear choppy, abruptly jumping one pixel to the right. This is one example of video output that most video professionals would consider to be below the subjective threshold of broadcast quality.

Subpixel sampling involves coloring screen pixels according to a weighted average that takes into account the true value of the unrounded offset. In the example above, the screen pixel in column 1, row 1 was colored black, while the pixel in column 2, row 1 was colored bright red. With subpixel sampling, the screen pixel at column 1, row 1 would be colored neither black nor red, but some color that reflected a weighted average of black and red, with the weights being set according to the offset.

Acknowledgment

The authors wish to state that this chapter was inspired by Thomas A. Ohanian's excellent book *Digital Nonlinear Editing* (Focal Press, 1993). This tome contains in-depth coverage of the past, present, and future of nonlinear film and video editing, as well as explanations of the underlying technology, and is highly recommended to those who wish to explore these issues more thoroughly. We just had to cover the little bit that he left out.

Real-World Applications
for MPEG Digital Video

Ray Harris

What Is MPEG?

MPEG stands for Moving Picture Experts Group, a joint committee of the International Organization for Standardization (ISO) and the International Electrotechnical Commission (IEC). MPEG is broken into two different specifications, MPEG I and MPEG II. MPEG I was designed for limited-bandwidth transmission such as a CD-ROM on a PC. MPEG II is used for the high-bandwidth transmission typically used in satellite-based broadcast television.

MPEG I was finalized in December of 1991, with the goal of a compression standard that would deliver 30-fps "movies" over a limited-bandwidth channel such as a CD-ROM. MPEG II is under development, and as of this writing (early 1994), only the video had been finalized. MPEG II is aimed at the broadcast television market and will most probably not be suitable for low-cost PC use. This chapter will concentrate on the MPEG I standard.

Reference frames and redundancy

In most movie scenes, the background remains relatively stable while action takes place. The background may move, but a great deal of the scene is redundant. MPEG starts its compression by creating a reference frame called an *I* or *Intra frame*. These I frames are placed every 10 to 15 frames. Each of the following frames is then transmitted as an annotation to the reference frame.

Inside an MPEG stream

The three types of pictures in an MPEG stream are

1. Intra (*I*)
2. Predicted (*P*)
3. Bidirectional interpolated (*B*).

Intra pictures provide entry points for random access, but only with moderate compression. Predicted pictures are encoded with reference to a past picture (Intra or previous Predicted), and in general will be used as a reference for future Predicted pictures. Bidirectional pictures provide the highest amount of compression but require both a past and a future reference for prediction. Bidirectional pictures never are used for references.

Finding the macro block (motion compensation).   The reference picture is divided into a grid of 16×16 pixel squares called *macro blocks*. Each subsequent picture is also divided into these same macro blocks. The computer then searches for an exact, or near exact, match between the reference-picture macro block and those in succeeding pictures. When a match is found, the computer transmits only the difference through what is called a *vector movement code*.

Tracking the changes (spatial redundancy).   After finding the changes in location of macro blocks, the MPEG algorithm will further reduce the data by describing the difference between corresponding macro blocks. This is accomplished through a math process call *discrete cosine transform* or *DCT*. This process divides the macro block into four subblocks, seeking out changes in color and brightness. The MPEG committee found that human perception is more sensitive to brightness changes than to color changes. Armed with this research, the MPEG committee specified the MPEG process so that the MPEG algorithm would devote most of its efforts to reducing color space rather than brightness.

Developing Markets for New Technology

The key to growing a market is to first have an industry standard that is (1) affordable and (2) easy to implement. At first release, MPEG met neither of those requirements. The algorithms required to execute the MPEG compression schemes were complex, and available only from a few firms in the first year after the standard was established. This limited the early acceptance of MPEG I and spawned numerous PC-based alternatives. These ranged from simple software products offering postage-stamp-sized video in a window, at a very low frame rate per second, all the way up to true high-quality video-compression hardware.

As the PC industry struggled to decide which alternative would replace the standard, the video industry wholeheartedly embraced MPEG I as being the true high-quality standard the committee had envisioned it would become. This schism between the PC and video industry explains why most PC-based users and analysts have failed to see the rapid growth of digital-video applications. The PC industry is now also looking to move more strongly toward the MPEG specification. This change in direction is due purely to a lowering of the price point at which MPEG may be delivered. While the first PC-based MPEG players were priced near $2000, the next generations are expected to come in well below the $1000 mark. The near future will bring us MPEG playback hardware for the PC priced under $500. These lower prices will spur the growth of MPEG and add a great deal of stability to the standardization of video compression on PC-based applications.

Early adopters

As is true with any new technology, there were the early adopters. These users are driven by technical needs and by a strong desire to establish themselves as leaders in their respective markets. In the case of digital video, the early adopters also saw a direct increase in functionality tied to a decrease in costs. These early adopters are now integrating MPEG digital video into a surprisingly diverse assortment of applications. These applications range from cable television to video kiosks, but all have one thing in common: the need for professional-quality visualization.

Early adopters of MPEG I saw the technology as a replacement for expensive videotape recorders and video laserdiscs. These video players have been heavily used in the video-kiosk, interactive-training, ad-insertion, and preview-channel markets. The advantages of digital playback are readily apparent when it is compared to the industry-standard videotape and laserdisc players. Its main advantages are delivery of video over a network and over phone lines, lower maintenance costs, and lower system costs. These are the keys to an understanding of the early and continued growth of MPEG I.

Applications

The applications for compressed digital video are enormous. Nearly every facet of our life will be touched by this new technology. Our videotape recorders, televisions, games, and shopping will all be enhanced by the addition of MPEG digital video. Given the global size of the digital-video market, it should come as no surprise that the silicon chip manufacturers all are looking at MPEG as the largest chip market ever to evolve. The following applications are just a sampling of actual uses of MPEG currently in development or being shipped.

Video kiosks

The kiosk market has evolved from a posted sign on an obelisk to a true multimedia application. Today's kiosk developers have a myriad of tools available. Touchscreens, software authoring packages, CD-ROM writers, and digital video all are enabling kiosks to impart a stronger, more interactive message than ever before.

The simple self-running tape in the grocery store's meat department has now become a tailored message on how to prepare one's food of choice. The video store that runs out of this week's top hits can offer an interactive kiosk that will help the potential customer to choose an alternative, complete with a 30-second movie trailer. In every case, the addition of interactive digital video to a kiosk increases a retailer's sales through the dissemination of usable information.

In the near future, walk-up bank tellers and auto dealerships will feature video kiosks with professional-quality digital video. These future kiosks will perform at even higher levels than today's advanced systems. The future will add complete interaction, transaction processing, and demographic processing for the developer. The video kiosk is a low-cost, highly effective tool for delivering an interactive, high-quality message that will soon encompass many aspects of our daily lives.

Cable TV advertisement insertion, and barker channels

Today's cable television is delivered from the satellite to head-end stations, and finally to the home. The head-end station is an unattended building that receives the incoming signal, mixes it with local content, and sends it out to the home. These head ends are filled with high-quality, fully automated, analog videotape recorders and laserdisc players. These analog-video devices are used to deliver local advertisements and previews of upcoming pay-per-view events.

MPEG professional-quality digital video is a perfect replacement for the high-maintenance analog devices found in the head-end station. The benefits of using digital video over analog are tremendous. Local advertisements that, with analog, previously required a physical delivery to every head end, can simply be downloaded electronically with a digital system.

This change in delivery of the ad spots represents a savings in terms of personnel and also benefits the customer via faster response times. Under the current analog-based system, the customer may have to wait 2 to 3 days for his or her advertisement to be copied and delivered to all of the pertinent head-end stations. With the new fully digital system, the customer's advertisement can be electronically transmitted to the head-end stations within hours of its creation. This increased flexibility will allow advertisers to adapt their message to timely changes in events. In addition, the digital-video system requires far less maintenance than the traditional analog players, with all of their moving parts.

Interactive training

The training and education market has long been a volume user of laserdisc players. These players deliver high-quality video content to students, corporate executives, and others. The two drawbacks of laserdisc players are (1) that they cannot be shared over a network and (2) that their level of interactivity is very low.

Replacing a laserdisc with MPEG digital video solves both the network and the interactivity problems. The content may easily be sent over standard networks in a "store-and-forward" mode, or interactively on a properly configured network. The addition of network capability opens up the access users have to the prepared content.

Interactive video is far more enticing than traditional closed-access systems. Digital video is a natural tool for the development of interactive training content. Touchscreens, pointing devices, and keyboards become the gateways to high-quality corporate training and educational media.

Arcade games and simulations

Arcade games and simulations are very similar in their construction and content. Both typically use computer-generated graphics or laserdisc video to create a simulation of a real-world experience. These applications require quick response from interactive media.

Digital video is the ideal solution to this application. The high-quality nature of MPEG, along with its minimal storage requirements, make it well suited both to arcade games and to simulations. Future arcade games will move from low-quality, computer-generated graphics to fully interactive graphics mixed with real video footage. The heightened sense of reality undoubtedly will create increased demand to play these new games, and subsequently increase revenue for the arcade owners.

Video on demand

Video on demand, or *VOD,* is a widely used term that has no specific meaning. In reality, any application that provides video at the request of a user is demonstrating a VOD capability. In the hospitality and home arenas, video on demand has come to be synonymous with certain applications such as movies. Given the nebulous nature of the term *VOD,* the potential areas of usage will be discussed individually.

Institutional video. Hotels and hospitals currently provide movies on a pay-per-view basis. These movies actually are played on a scheduled basis from videotape players located on the property of the institution. The drawbacks of such a physical solution are limited playing times and a limited selection of movies.

Switching to digital video with MPEG completely changes the scope of the service such institutions can provide. With properly networked MPEG videos, users can chose from dozens of movies and watch them at their own convenience. The benefits to the institutions are increased viewing and increased revenues from rentals.

Video dial tone. The phone companies are very aggressively going after their piece of the VOD market. Their vision is that we will all order, and receive, our movies through high-speed phone lines. Unlike the CATV infrastructure, which will have to be upgraded to provide sufficient bandwidth for VOD, the entire United States currently is wired to provide sufficient capabilities for the regional phone companies to enable this technology.

In essence, every home that wishes to have access to VOD through the phone lines will be required to have an MPEG decoder sitting on top of their television set and connected to their high-speed phone line. Users will interactively select the movies they wish to view, then sit back and enjoy. In the background a massive file-server will have been put into action, finding the requested movie and serving it up to the correct home. Virtually all of the regional phone companies are active in this area.

Cable TV. Interactive services and VOD are hot topics for the CATV industry. The drawback here is that given the current infrastructure, it is estimated that the cost to the CATV operators to upgrade their serviced homes to be VOD-ready will be around $11 billion. This figure is based on an estimate of there being a $200 set-top television decoder hooked to the cable system. Given the enormity of the investment, and the complexity of switching all of the head-end stations to large servers, this is expected to take several years to complete.

The first step for the CATV operators will be to use video compression on their satellite transmissions. This alone will enable the fabled 500-channel scenario. The next step will be to make the head ends capable of supplying an increased number of channels. The final step will be to install a TV decoder in every household. While many CATV operators are actively going forward with interactive CATV units, the prospect of widespread demand for VOD through the use of these interactive units appears to be at least a few years away.

Consumer applications

A number of consumer applications will utilize MPEG digital video to enhance the user's experience. These products include the Philips CD-I player with the FMV option, the JVC Video Karaoke, and the Interactive player from 3DO. The Philips CD-I and the 3DO will use MPEG to decode feature-length movies, add excitement to games, and possibly to act as a television decoder for cable broadcast. The JVC Karaoke represents the logical next extension to what has become an extremely popular pastime in the pubs and nightclubs of the world.

MPEG Is Transparent

In the coming few years, MPEG I and MPEG II will be used in numerous applications that affect our daily lives. The beauty of the MPEG algorithms is that most people will never know that the video they are watching has been switched from analog to digital. We, as users, will only know that we have been given a far greater number of choices in the movies we may watch, that our lives are touched by greater amounts of easily disseminated information, and that the world has become just a little bit smaller.

Introduction to Digital Video and Audio

Ken Morse

The Real World

Television was designed to reproduce natural images and sounds, and nature is basically analog. In nature, the brightness of an object can have any value, and the object can be shaded with minute graduation. Likewise, a natural object can take on any position that is consistent with the action of gravity, and it may be moved smoothly with microscopic precision. Real images and sounds thus are made up of intensity values and positions that can have any level—continuous functions in both space and time—that is analog.

The digital world of the personal computer can deal only with discrete levels, and it cannot process continuous values. Hence the video and audio signals must be converted into discrete values in time for manipulation by the computer. The following section introduces the principles of analog video as it is used in the television industry today.

Analog video

We've already established that most things in nature are analog. Real images and sounds are based on light intensity and sound-pressure values, which are continuous functions in space and time. Conversion of images or sounds to electrical signals is accomplished through the appropriate use of sensors, called *transducers*. Sensors for converting images and sounds to electronic signals are typically analog devices, with analog outputs. The world of television and sound recording is based on these devices. Video cameras and microphones (the sensors) are familiar objects to almost everyone, and their purpose generally is well understood. This section introduces the chief concepts associated with analog video, from its origin in a video camera to the thing itself. Right now, however, we will concentrate on how video cameras work.

Video cameras

Video cameras have become commonplace in today's society. Once found only in the domain of television studios, a modern video camera can now fit in the palm of the hand, due to advances in technology and integration.

The video camera converts an image in front of the camera into an electrical signal. Electrical signals are one-dimensional, i.e., they can have only one value at any instant in time. However, images are two-dimensional and have many values at all the different positions within the image. To convert the two-dimensional image into a one-dimensional electrical signal, the image is scanned in an orderly progressive manner called a *raster scan*. Scanning is achieved by rapidly moving a single sensing point over the image. The complete image must be scanned fast enough to capture the complete image before it changes too much. As the sensing point moves, the electrical output changes in response to the brightness or color of the image under the sensing point. This varying electrical signal from the sensor represents the image as a series of values spread out in time and is called the *video signal*.

Figure 32.1 shows a stationary monochrome image being scanned in raster fashion. The image scan begins at the upper left corner and progresses horizontally across the image, making a scanning line. At the same time, the scanning point is being moved down at a very much slower rate. When the right side of the image is reached, the scanning point returns to the left side.

Due to the slow vertical motion of the scanning point, it is now below the starting point of the first line. It then scans across again on the next line, snaps back to the left edge, and continues until the entire image has been scanned vertically by a series of lines. As each line is scanned, the electrical output from the scanning sensor represents the light intensity of the image at

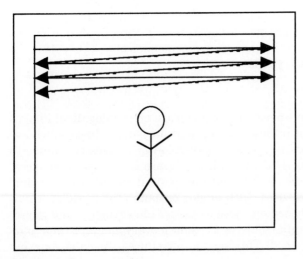

Figure 32.1 Raster scanning.

each position of the scanning point. During the snap-back time (known as the *horizontal blanking interval*) the sensor is turned off and a zero-output (or *blanking-level*) signal is sent out. The signal from a complete scan of the image is a sequence of line signals, separated by horizontal blanking intervals, called a *frame.*

Aspect ratio

An important parameter of the scanning process is the *aspect ratio.* This is the ratio of the length of a scanning line horizontally on the image to the distance covered vertically on the image by all the scanning lines. It also can be thought of as the width-to-height ratio of a frame. Aspect ratio for television was standardized very early on at 4:3. Other systems, most notably movies, use different aspect ratios that can be as high as 2:1.

Synchronization

If the video signal is used to modulate the brightness of the beam in a cathode-ray tube that is being scanned exactly the same way as the sensor, the original image will be reproduced. This is exactly what happens in a television set in the home or in a video monitor. The electrical signal(s) sent to the monitor must contain some additional information to ensure that the monitor's scanning will be synchronized with the sensor's scanning. This information is called *sync information* and consists of horizontal and vertical timing signals. It may be included with the video signal itself during the blanking intervals, or it may be sent on a separate cable (or cables) meant just for the sync information.

Horizontal resolution

As the scanning point moves across one line, the electrical signal output from the sensor changes continuously in response to the light level of the part of the image that the sensor sees. One measure of scanning performance is the horizontal resolution of the pickup system, which depends on the size of the scanning-sensitive point. To test the horizontal resolution performance of a system, which also measures the capability to reproduce horizontal fine detail, closely spaced vertical lines are placed in front of the camera. If the sensor area is smaller than the space between the vertical lines, the lines will be reproduced, but when the sensor is too large the lines will average out under the sensor and will not be seen in the output signal.

To achieve a realistic measure, the horizontal resolution must be related to other parameters in the image for consistency. In the television industry, horizontal resolution is measured by counting the number of black and white vertical lines that can be reproduced in a distance corresponding to the raster height. Thus a system that is said to have a horizontal resolution of 300 lines can reproduce 150 black and 150 white lines alternating across a horizontal distance corresponding to the height of the image.

Scanning a pattern of black and white lines results in a high-frequency electrical signal, and it is important that the circuits used for processing and transmitting these signals have adequate bandwidth. Broadcast television systems require a bandwidth of about 1 MHz for each 80 lines of horizontal resolution. Since the North American broadcast television system uses a bandwidth of 4.5 MHz, a theoretical limit to the horizontal resolution is 360 lines.

Vertical resolution

The second resolution parameter of interest is the vertical resolution, and this simply depends on the number of scanning lines used in one frame. The more lines there are, the higher the vertical resolution. Broadcast television systems use either 525 (North America) or 625 (Europe) lines per frame.

Not all of the vertical lines contain image information. A small number of lines in each frame are devoted to the vertical blanking interval. Both this and the horizontal blanking interval were originally intended to provide time for the scanning beam in cameras or monitors to retrace so as to start the next frame or the next line. In modern systems these intervals have many other uses, since they represent nonactive picture time during which different information can be transmitted along with the video signal. Video studios have used the vertical blanking to encode time-stamp information into the signal, and many television systems encode teletext or closed-caption information on these lines.

Frame rates for motion

If acceptable motion video is to be produced, many frames must be scanned each second to produce the effect of smooth motion. Standard broadcast video systems use frame rates of 25 or 30 frames per second (depending on the country). Although these frame rates are high enough to provide smooth motion, they are not high enough to prevent a video display from having flicker. The human eye can perceive flicker in a bright image that is refreshed at less than 50 times per second. However, to increase the frame rate to that range while preserving horizontal resolution would require a speeding up of all the scanning, both horizontal and vertical, and would therefore increase the system bandwidth. To avoid this difficulty, all television systems use *interlace*.

Interlace means that more than one vertical scan is used to reproduce a complete frame. Broadcast television uses 2:1 interlace—2 vertical scans for a complete frame. With 2:1 interlace, one vertical scan displays all the odd lines of a frame, then a second puts in all the even lines. At 30 frames per second (North America), the vertical rate is 60 scans per second. Since the eye does not readily see flickering objects that are small, the 30-per-second repetition rate of any one line is not seen as flicker, but rather the entire picture appears to be refreshed at 60-per-second. Other specialized systems have used higher interlace ratios, but the 2:1 broadcast standard is prevalent.

Color television systems

The color cameras just described were producing three output signals: red, green, and blue. This signal combination is called *RGB*. Most uses of video involve more than a single camera connected to a single monitor. The signal probably has to be recorded; we may wish to combine the outputs of several cameras together in different ways, and almost always we will want to have more than one viewing monitor. Therefore we usually will be concerned with a color-video system, containing much more than cameras. In RGB systems, all parts of the system are interconnected with three parallel video cables, one for each of the color channels.

However, because of the complexities involved in distributing three signals in exact synchronism and relationship, most color television systems do not handle RGB (except within cameras), but rather the camera signals are encoded into a composite format that may be distributed on a single cable. Such composite formats are used throughout television studios, for video recording, and for broadcasting. There are several different composite formats used in different countries around the world—NTSC, PAL, SECAM—and each will be discussed in the next section. Here we will concentrate on some of the conceptual aspects of composite color-video systems.

Composite color systems originally were developed for the broadcasting of color signals by a single television transmitter. However, it was soon found that the composite format is the best approach to use throughout the video system, so it is now conventional for the composite encoding to take place inside the camera box before any signals are brought out. Except for purposes such as certain video-manipulation processes, RGB signals do not exist in modern television plants.

All composite formats make use of the luminance/chrominance principle for their basic structure. This principle says that any color signal may be broken into two parts: *luminance,* which is a monochrome video signal that controls only the brightness (or luminance) of the image, and *chrominance,* which contains only the coloring information for the image. However, because a tristimulus color system requires three independent signals to achieve complete representation of all colors, the chrominance signal is actually two signals, called *color differences.*

Luminance plus chrominance is just one of the many possible combinations of three signals that could be used to transmit color information. They are obtained by a linear matrix transformation of the RGB signals created in the camera. The matrix transformation simply means that each of the luminance and chrominance signals is an additive (sometimes with negative coefficients) combination of the original RGB signals. In a linear transmission system, the number of possible matrix transformations that might be used is infinite; we just need to be sure that we use the correct inverse transformation when we recover RGB signals so as to display them on a color monitor. Psychovisual research (research into how images look to a human viewer) has shown that by carefully choosing an appropriate transformation, we can generate signals for transmission that will be affected by the limitations of transmission in ways that will not show (as much) in the reproduced picture.

In a composite system, the luminance and chrominance are combined by a scheme of *frequency-interleaving* in order to transmit them on a single channel. The luminance signal is transmitted as a normal monochrome signal on the cable or channel, and then the chrominance information is placed on a high-frequency subcarrier located near the top of the channel bandwidth. If this carrier frequency is correctly chosen, very little interference will occur between the two signals. This interleaving works because of two facts:

1. The luminance channel is not very sensitive to interfering signals that come in near the high end of the channel bandwidth. This is especially effective if the interfering signal has a frequency that is an odd multiple of twice the line-scanning rate in adjacent scanning lines, for visually the interference tends to cancel out. The selection of the right carrier frequency for the chrominance ensures this interlace condition.

2. The eye is much less sensitive to color edges than it is to luminance edges in the picture. This means that the bandwidth of the chrominance signals can be reduced without much visual loss of resolution. Bandwidth reductions of 2 to 4 are appropriate.

Thus, a composite system is able to transmit a color signal on a single channel that has the same bandwidth as each of the three RGB signals we started with. The transmission is not perfect, but it is good enough to be the basis of our worldwide television systems. This packing of the three RGB signals into the same bandwidth once used only for one (black-and-white) signal may seem like we are getting something for nothing, but that's not the case. What is really happening is that we are utilizing the spaces in the channel that are unused when transmitting only a single television signal, as we are also making compromises in the reproduction of the color information based on our knowledge of what the viewer can and cannot see in the final image.

Color video formats—NTSC

The NTSC color television system is the standard broadcasting system for North America, Japan, and a few other countries. NTSC stands for National Television Systems Committee, a standardizing body in the 1950s that chose a color television system for the United States. The NTSC system is a composite luminance/chrominance system, as just described. An important objective for the NTSC system was to be compatible with the monochrome color system, already in place with millions of receivers long before color television began. This objective was met by making the luminance signal of NTSC just the same as the previous monochrome standard, so that existing monochrome receivers see the luminance signal only, and the color signal present at the top of the bandwidth does not show up very much on monochrome sets.

In NTSC, the luminance signal is called the *Y signal,* and the two chrominance signals are *I* and *Q.* The color carrier frequency, which must be maintained very accurately, is 3.58 MHz. As already explained, the I and Q color difference signals have reduced bandwidths. While the luminance can utilize the full 4.5-MHz bandwidth of a television channel, the I bandwidth is only 1.5-MHz, and the Q signal is chosen so that it can get away with only 0.5-MHz bandwidth.

When the I and Q signals are modulated onto the color subcarrier of the NTSC system, they result in a color subcarrier frequency component, whose amplitude represents the saturation values of the image; the phase of the color subcarrier represents the hue values of the image. NTSC receivers usually have controls to adjust these two parameters in the decoding of the NTSC signal.

Figure 32.2 shows a single line of composite video, and illustrates the modulation of chrominance information on the luminance signal.

It should be pointed out that the NTSC system was designed to deliver satisfactory performance with the kinds of signals created by looking at real scenes. Today we also can generate video signals with computers, and problems can arise if a computer-generated signal does not follow the rules when it is expected to be passed through an NTSC system.

Color video formats—PAL

The PAL system, which originated in Europe, is also a luminance/chrominance system. It differs from NTSC primarily in the way in which the

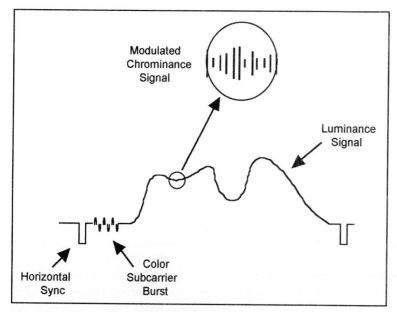

Figure 32.2 Baseband analog video.

chrominance signals are encoded. In PAL, the two chrominance signals have the same bandwidth (1.5 MHz) and hence a different set of chrominance components is used, called U and V instead of I and Q. In addition, PAL signals are more tolerant of certain distortions that can occur in transmission paths that affect the quality of the color reproduction.

Digital Video

A digital-video system is any system in which the information for images is represented as a series of digital bits. The most common digital-video system is the display portion of any personal computer. In a PC, the information for the video display is represented as a pattern of bits contained in the PC's memory. These bits are accessed by the display circuitry and manipulated to provide the computer displays that are so familiar. Two processes are examined in this section that form the backbone of digital-video systems. First the process for converting analog video into the digital domain is explained. This is followed by a description of the reverse process required to display the final image.

Sampling

Analog waveforms are continuous both in time and in value (amplitude). For an analog waveform to be converted into a digital signal, both of these dimensions must be changed into noncontinuous values. The amplitude is represented as a digital integer (with a specific number of bits) and time is represented as a series of these integer amplitude values taken at equal steps in time.

The process for converting amplitude into discrete values is called *quantizing,* and the process of converting time into discrete values is called *sampling.* These two processes together are referred to as *analog-to-digital conversion* (A/D), or sometimes *digitizing.* Since the continuous analog signal is converted into discrete steps by the A/D process, an approximation of the original signal is created. If care is taken in the choice of the correct numbers, A/D conversion can be carried out with sufficient precision that the approximation errors cannot be detected when reproduced by the digital system. The approximations of the initial conversion process may be the only approximations, since digital systems reproduce digital values exactly. Further approximations or errors may be introduced, but only if the designer introduces them.

Figure 32.3 illustrates the sampling process. For every clock pulse the instantaneous value of the analog waveform is read, thus yielding a series of sampled values. The sampling-clock frequency is referred to as the *sampling rate.*

Since the input analog signal is continuous, the value changes over time. The A/D conversion process takes a finite time to complete, hence the input analog signal must be held constant during the conversion process to avoid

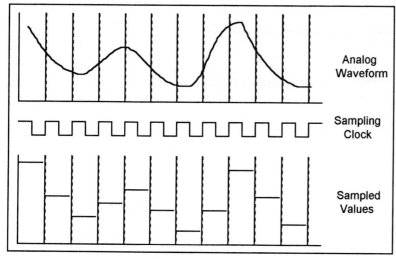

Figure 32.3 The sampling process.

conversion problems. This task is carried out by a sample-and-hold circuit. At this stage if the clock frequency is high enough, the samples will be a good representation of the analog waveform. However, it is important to note that at this stage the signal is discrete only in time, each sample is still analog, and each may have any value in a continuous range.

Quantization

Now all analog samples must be converted into digital values. This is achieved by quantizing them. Quantization establishes a series of equally spaced levels in amplitude, as shown in Fig. 32.4. In the figure there are 16 quantization levels, and the span between each two thresholds in amplitude is given a value from 0 to 15. Each sample is matched to the appropriate threshold level and assigned the corresponding numerical value. This value can then be represented digitally and coded. This simple digital-coding stream is called *pulse code modulation (PCM)*. Digital coding is not limited to a linear series of quantized values; it can replace the sampled and quantized values with any set of consistent numbers. Such non-integer coding is called *nonlinear quantization,* or more frequently *companding.*

Returning to the example of 16 quantized levels, the numbers for each level can be coded as digital values of 4 bits. Hence the quantization is at 4 bits per sample. To achieve an adequate representation of the analog signal, there must be a sufficient number of quantization levels. This digital signal may then be reconstructed by the reverse process of digital-to-analog conversion, which will be covered in a subsequent section.

From the previous discussion it is now clear that there must be a high enough sampling rate, and enough quantizing levels, to acceptably approxi-

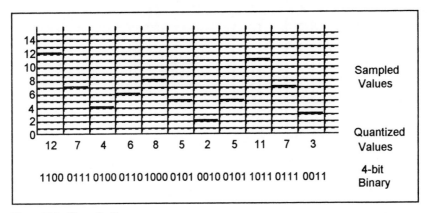

Figure 32.4 Quantization.

mate an analog signal. To better understand the effect of sampling rate, take a look at Fig. 32.5.

In this figure the analog signal to be converted is a high-frequency sine wave. In the first case the sine wave is sampled at a very high rate, so that 10 samples are generated for each cycle of the sine wave. In this first case, the samples represent the sine wave adequately. A sampling rate that is lower than the sine-wave frequency is used in the second case, with only one sample acquired for every two cycles of the sine wave. The output from this process in no way resembles the original signal. The third example illustrates a special case in which exactly two samples are taken per cycle of the sine wave.

At this rate, the frequency of the sine wave is present in the output but the waveform is square rather than sine. This special case illustrates the *Nyquist limit,* where the input sine wave is at the highest frequency that can be sampled with the sampling clock. The Nyquist theorem states that to reproduce a waveform that has a maximum frequency component F, the waveform must be sampled at $2 \times F$. Any attempt to digitize at a lower rate will result in an output that is incorrect for any high-frequency components in the input.

Care must be taken when sampling information above the Nyquist rate, since spurious output components are produced. This is known as *aliasing,* and most systems include an analog low-pass filter on the input before sampling, to remove any frequency components above half the sampling rate. Most modern designs will use a sampling rate higher than twice the input bandwidth, since analog filters cannot be designed to have an absolute cutoff (they cut off gradually with increasing frequency). With the introduction of competitively priced digital signal processors (DSPs), filtering can be carried out in the digital domain, where it is much easier to attain sharp cutoff characteristics.

The only limit on the quantizing process comes from the number of quantization levels used. It is very difficult to define how many levels should be

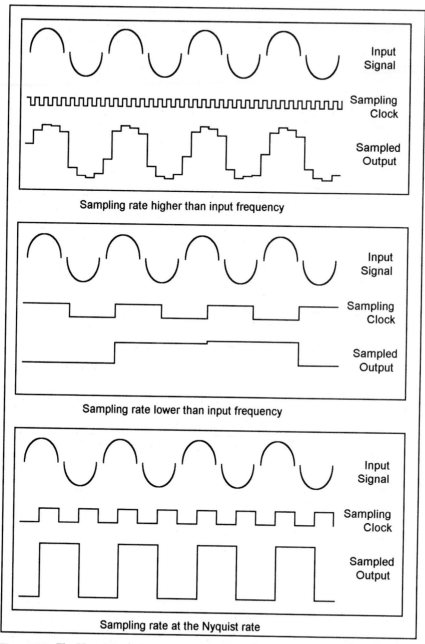

Sampling rate higher than input frequency

Sampling rate lower than input frequency

Sampling rate at the Nyquist rate

Figure 32.5 The Nyquist rate.

used in a particular case, but the amount of noise present in the input signal must be considered. There is no point in providing so many quantization levels that they reproduce signal variations that are less than the noise.

Video analog-to-digital conversion

When it comes to the actual analog-to-digital conversion process for a video signal, the first decision that must be made is what format the video should be digitized in. It will be seen that it is possible to digitize a composite video signal, but there are at least two associated problems:

1. By the very nature of the composite-encoding, artifacts are introduced that are not present in a non-encoded format such as RGB.

2. The resultant digital-video signal is difficult to manipulate in its composite form.

For both these reasons, most systems digitize a component scheme such as RGB or YUV.

The conversion of analog RGB to digital RGB is achieved by digitizing each of the R, G, and B signals using three parallel A/D converters. Video A/D chips normally contain all three converters and the associated sample-and-hold circuits in one chip. For systems where the original material already has been encoded into composite—e.g., videotape—an analog decoder converts the composite signal into RGB or YUV ready for digitizing.

A typical front-end conversion system is shown in Fig. 32.6. In this system composite, S-Video and RGB analog inputs are supported. The video decoder converts the NTSC- or PAL-encoded video into baseband RGB analog signals, which are then digitized by the analog-to-digital converter.

Pixels

The process of video A/D conversion described above converts the analog-video signal into a stream of digital numbers representing the original image. Each number represents adjacent points in the image that follow the same

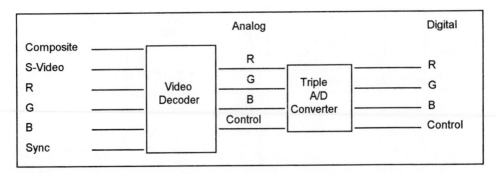

Figure 32.6   A simple video digitizer.

pattern as when the camera originally scanned the image. Each of these numbers represents a pixel, and when the image is reconstructed each pixel will be shown as a small rectangle filled with a color based upon the number. How realistic the resultant image looks is dependent on the number of pixels used and the color-encoding scheme used.

Every digital-video display can be viewed as a two-dimensional array of pixels. The sampling rate for digesting must be accurately related to the number of pixels required, and locked to the scanning frequencies of the input signal. Failure to do these two things will result in a digital image that has an incorrect aspect ratio.

Pixelation

The number of pixels in a digital image is analogous to the horizontal and vertical resolutions of an analog system, but the appearance to the eye of pixels is very different from that conveyed by the analog system. The analog signal is continuous, and as such provides smooth transitions horizontally as the image changes. In the vertical direction there is a step from one line to the next, which can provide some artifacts. A common artifact can be seen when watching sports coverage that includes boundary lines such as the markings on a basketball court. If the viewing camera shows the court from one of the court corners, the resultant diagonal lines appear to be stepped (also known as *the staircase effect*). This is because the video signal is not continuous in the vertical direction. Most systems today provide a form of filtering that helps to remove the staircase effect and blend lines together.

In an analog system with low resolution the picture will become fuzzy, but in a digital system an effect known as *pixelation* occurs. As the resolution decreases, each pixel represents a higher proportion of the entire picture, but it can provide only a single color to represent that area. With dwindling resolution, the resultant image starts to take on a blocky appearance. The human eye is very good at picking out edges, and as the resolution decreases the edges of each pixel become more obvious due to the increased color difference from one pixel to the next. If you are viewing low-resolution digital images, notice how they often look better when viewed with slightly closed eyes. This has the effect of blurring the edges of the pixels, and some low-resolution digital systems use a low-pass filter on the display output to create the same effect and reduce the pixelation.

How visible pixelation is depends on the distance from which the image is viewed. For example, for a typical 13-inch computer screen viewed from a normal desktop distance of 18 inches, 540 pixels vertically are required. Taking a 4:3 aspect ratio into account means that the desktop display should be at least 720×540 to avoid pixelation.

It already has been noted that there is no active picture information during the blanking periods. Digitizing the analog-video signal as has been described will also digitize the blanking intervals. This means that when you are

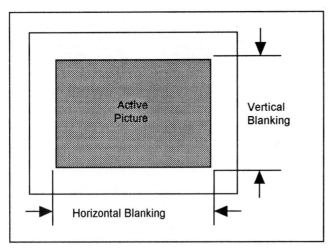

Figure 32.7 Removal of blanking intervals.

digesting video signals, the blanking-period data may be discarded and only the active image area is stored, as shown in Fig. 32.7.

Bits per pixel

By this stage there is a bitmap of pixels stored in memory, ready to be displayed. The realism of the image displayed is dependent on the number of possible colors, which in turn is determined by the number of bits per pixel. Different systems use different values, ranging from 1 to 32 bits per pixel. A 1-bit display system can display only two colors, usually black and white. Such a system has a place for computer graphics but cannot display a realistic image. (It also has a low memory requirement, which can be advantageous.)

What is required for realistic image display? It will be easiest to consider monochrome images first. We suggested earlier that a good signal-to-noise ratio for a video system is 46 dB, which generates a video signal with about 3 percent peak-to-peak noise. Using the earlier criteria for quantizing, set one level equal to the peak-to-peak noise. That will require 33 levels for the 46-dB system, with 3 percent noise. This could then be reproduced by digitizing with 5 bits (32 levels). However, images quantized at 5 bits do not look acceptable, due to a digital artifact known as *contouring*.

Contouring

The contouring effect occurs because all analog levels that fall between two thresholds of the quantizer are replaced with the same digital value, and thus will be reproduced at the output of the digital system with the same value also. Any part of the image that has a slowly changing analog level will be converted into stairsteps by the quantizing. The stairsteps will be clearly visible even when they are smaller than the random noise that was on the analog signal, because they are correlated with the image itself. (The analog noise was random and constantly changing—that is why 3 percent noise is not very visible.)

For noise patterns that are coherent, or correlated with the image, the visibility threshold is more like 0.5 percent. That is $\frac{1}{200}$ of the amplitude range, and would be achieved by quantizing with 8 bits per pixel (256 levels). For contouring to be invisible in monochrome or luminance signals, 8-bit-per-pixel quantizing is required.

Introducing color

It is now time to leave the realm of black-and-white monochrome images and return to the real world of color images. Processes similar to those in the monochrome case must be applied in the case of each of the three color components (RGB, YUV, etc.) if color images are to be reproduced digitally.

One common approach is to generate 24-bit RGB pixel values by using three A/D converters (8 bits for each of R, G, and B) in parallel. 24-bit RGB gives excellent reproduction, since the 24 bits are capable of generating more than 16 million colors. However, there are several problems with 24-bit systems. They are very expensive in terms of memory usage, storage, and the processing power required to manipulate the images.

Earlier reference was made to the process of digitizing the composite analog-video signal and handling that digitally. Eight bits per pixel is adequate, but the signal must be sampled at a rate of at least 3 times the color subcarrier frequency, which leads to an average size of around 420K for a 640 × 480 image. After one has considered the problems associated with manipulating the image in this format, it becomes clear that it is unsuitable for use in computer video systems. However, in the broadcast television industry the D2-standard digital-video recorders use this technique to overcome the analog limitations associated with multiple-generation recording.

Many systems use 16 bits per pixel as a compromise; 5 bits red, 6 bits green, 5 bits blue is a common split, since the human eye is most receptive to the green area of the spectrum. Sixteen bits gives over 65,000 colors, which works well with highly colored images and will exhibit contouring only in images that have subtle shadings of colors over large areas.

Techniques to reproduce good images with fewer bits than the above numbers are called *video-compression techniques*. There are a wide range of techniques available, and these will be described later. The introduction of video compression brings with it at least two additional concerns other than simply the image-quality compromises that may be necessary.

First, compression and decompression operations require some processing power that must be provided by the CPU unless additional hardware is provided. Second, it is very awkward to manipulate images when they are in compressed form. They must be decompressed, manipulated, and then recompressed, with all the inherent additional time and processing problems that go with this.

Color-mapping

The previous discussion of RGB24 and RGB16 described the mechanisms for displaying an image in which the pixel values directly represent the color values. There is another way of using a bitmap in memory to represent an image in which the pixel values do not directly represent the color sample values, but instead the pixel values are an index to a color lookup table (CLUT) that holds the actual color value.

This technique, called *color-mapping,* allows the number of colors represented by the pixel value to be a subset of a much larger set of colors (the *palette*) represented by the number of bits per pixel (bpp) in the color table. This subset of colors in the CLUT may be changed for each image displayed. For example the bitmap may be 8 bpp, but 24 bpp in the CLUT. This would be a system that can display 256 out of a palette of 16,777,216 colors, as illustrated in Fig. 32.8.

To display a realistic image with a CLUT system, the image must be processed by an algorithm that chooses the 256 colors that occur the most to create the CLUT. The pixels then are assigned the index value from the table

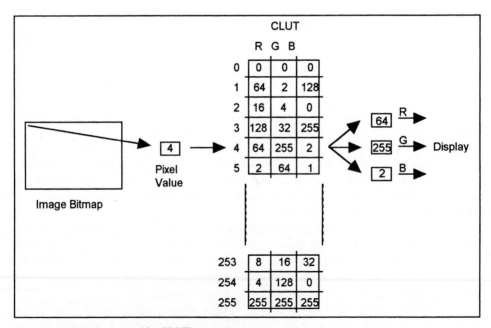

Figure 32.8   Color lookup table (CLUT) operation.

for the color closest to each pixel's actual color. Both the CLUT and the pixel values are then stored to save the image. When the image is later loaded for display, the CLUT data is loaded into the CLUT hardware and the pixels into the display memory. When the display hardware reads out the pixels to refresh the display, the pixel values will be converted to the color values by looking them up in the CLUT in real time.

By tailoring the color map to the image (which can take a lot of processing time), fairly realistic images can be constructed. One important exception is an image that contains skin tones, which may require too many of the CLUT colors to obtain the satisfactory smooth shading.

Color-mapping provides the simplest approach to compression to 8 bpp while still delivering an approximation to realism. The results depend on the number of colors in the image; images with few colors may look good, whereas elaborately colored images may suffer from severe contouring.

One final problem with color-mapping occurs when more than one image is to be displayed concurrently. In that case the palette will be split between the two images, and each will suffer a loss in quality unless there is a strong correlation between the colors in both. Either way, a large amount of processing power and time must be provided to calculate the optimum palette.

Overlay

In many digital-video systems there will be a need to allocate some of the bits in a pixel to purposes other than color values. For example, it may be desirable to define a region of the image where another image (maybe from an outside source) will be placed (or keyed) into the first image. With appropriate hardware responding to one bit in each pixel, this technique can provide a window of any shape on the screen where the video from an external VCR or other live source could be displayed.

For this to work correctly, there must be proper synchronization of the two signals (called *genlocking*). This technique can be extended to use 8 bits from each pixel to control a video mixer, which will allow a video dissolve between the computer's image and an external source. Twenty-four-bpp systems often are extended to 32 bits for such purposes. In most cases, the application of extra bits in this way will require additional special hardware, either inside the system or externally, to respond to the extra bit values and to carry out the desired process.

Analog-video generation

The final step toward displaying a digital image is the conversion process back to the analog realm used by video monitors. This is accomplished by using a D/A converter, which typically consists of a single chip containing three D/As, one for each of R, G, and B. The D/A converter simply contains some digital switches, which are controlled by the signal bits to deliver analog values equal to the value represented by each bit. These values are summed at the output to create an analog signal. Most computer systems use chips called *RAMDACs* that contain this function, and the color lookup tables required for color-mapping, in a single package.

As mentioned earlier, the visibility of pixelation can be somewhat reduced by including an analog filter on the output of a D/A converter. A filter with a bandwidth equal to the Nyquist limit for the pixel rate used will not change the resolution very much, but it will smooth some of the sharp transitions between adjacent pixels—only in the horizontal direction. Not all digital-video systems use these filters, however. Of course the results will be best when there are enough pixels that the eye will not see them anyway.

Video compression

The desirability of video compression should be clear to you from the discussion in the previous sections. Reducing the amount of data needed to reproduce images saves storage space, increases access speed, and is the only way to achieve digital motion video. Therefore, video compression is an important element in reaching a fully capable digital-video system.

A typical still image, 640 × 480 with 24 bits per pixel, consumes just under 1 Mbyte of storage. Obviously the storage of even a few images could pose a problem, and this is before the implications of digital motion video have been explored.

The example just given clearly illustrates how the digitization process results in a large number of bits for each image. However, the number of bits actually required to represent the information in an image may be substantially less because of *redundancy*. In general, three types of redundancy in digital images can be identified:

1. *Spatial redundancy,* due to the correlation between neighboring pixel values.
2. *Spectral redundancy,* due to the correlation between different color planes (e.g., in an RGB color image) or spectral bands
3. *Temporal redundancy,* due to the correlation between different frames in a sequence of images.

Compression schemes may exploit any or all of these aspects of redundancy. Another thing to keep in mind about displaying a digital-video image is that there is no need to display more than the viewer will be able to see. The human eye has poor spatial acuity for certain colors. Because of this characteristic of the viewer, you need not provide independent color values for every pixel—the color information can be transmitted at lower resolution. This principle is used successfully in NTSC and PAL color television, and it can be utilized in a digital-video compression system as well.

Image compression aims to reduce the number of bits needed to represent an image by removing these redundancies. There are many approaches to image compression, but they can be classed in two basic groups, *lossless* and *lossy.*

In lossless compression, the reconstructed image after compression is numerically identical to the original image on a pixel-by-pixel basis. Obviously, lossless compression is ideal, since no information is compromised. However, only a modest amount of compression is possible.

In lossy compression, the reconstructed image contains degradations relative to the original. As a result, much higher compression can be achieved than with lossless compression. In general, more compression is obtained at the expense of more distortion. It is important to note that these degradations may not be visually apparent.

Over the past few years, JPEG (the Joint Photographic Experts Group) has become the de facto standard for the compression of continuous-tone-color images. It is a discrete cosine transform-based algorithm that removes redundant image and color data.

JPEG can compress images at ratios of about 20:1, with no noticeable loss of quality. Compression ratios of up to 100 to 1 are possible, but the higher the ratio the greater the loss of detail and, sometimes, the more likely the appearance of artifacts.

Another advantage of JPEG is that it is a symmetrical compression algorithm. The same hardware or software can be used to compress and decompress an image. In addition, compression and decompression times are about the same. This does not hold true for most video-compression schemes, which are asymmetrical.

JPEG is also among the standards used for motion-video compression today. It can be used to compress video frames individually through a process called *intraframe coding*. This allows users to randomly access any individual frame within the compressed video, making it ideal for digital applications in which access to every frame is necessary, such as video preproduction. The downside of using intraframe encoding alone is that even at high compression ratios, a few seconds of 24-bit color video stored as motion JPEG takes up a lot of space.

The standards organizations that sponsor JPEG—the Consultative Committee in International Telegraphy and Telephony, and the International Standards Organization—have defined a compression standard called *MPEG* (Motion Pictures Experts Group) specifically to handle motion video. In addition to intraframe encoding for removing redundancies within individual frames, MPEG also employs interframe coding, which eliminates redundant information among frames. If the background of a video clip stays the same from frame to frame, for instance, MPEG will save the background once and store only the differences between those frames. MPEG supports compression ratios of up to 50 to 1, assuming the standard MPEG resolution of about 320 × 240 pixels for full-motion video. (MPEG-2 was proposed in 1992 for handling higher-resolution, broadcast-quality images.)

In addition to its interframe coding capabilities, MPEG differs from JPEG in its asymmetrical approach to compression, using more hardware and computer power to compress full-motion video and audio than to decompress it.

From Analog to Digital Audio

In contrast to digital video, digital audio has been available as a standard feature of personal computers since the introduction of the Apple Macintosh in 1984. On such systems it originally was used to generate system sound prompts and simple sound effects for entertainment titles. In the last few years there has been an explosion in the audio marketplace when it comes to personal computers. A wide variety of add-in audio adapters are available, providing a cost-effective audio solution.

The use of audio on personal computers has matured since the early days of beeps and squawks. Today's systems use audio to implement interactive help systems and to provide the soundtrack to digital-video movies as well as musical scores.

This section will describe the processes involved in bringing audio into the digital domain, as well as provide an overview of the compression techniques available and an introduction to synthesized audio.

Digital audio

A common initial first impression is that digital audio is much simpler compared to digital video, since the bandwidth of audio is hundreds of times less than that for video. This, unfortunately, is not the case. Although digital audio requires many of the same considerations as digital video, there is one aspect that is very different. With video it is possible to impose a structure of lines and frames. With audio this is impossible—audio is a continuous signal with no blanking intervals or other structural features that could make the signal easier to handle.

In addition, there's no equivalent to a still frame in audio. When the processor gets behind in manipulating video, it can always display a still frame while it catches up. If this is not held for too long, the viewer will not notice. With audio it is impossible to stop without causing a loss of information and of synchronization. Hence, audio has its own problems that easily compensate for its lower bandwidth.

Although audio most often is associated with accompanying video, there are many applications that involve audio only. Sound effects in modern computer games, help systems, and musical scores are but a few examples.

Analog audio

Natural sounds are analog. Sounds cause very small pressure variations in the air, which can be picked up by various pressure-to-electrical transducers. The most common of these made specifically for sound pickup is the microphone. It is designed to model the frequency-range and the pressure-value characteristics of the human ear. The output of the microphone is an analog electrical signal that closely matches the pressure variations in the air around the microphone.

The audio industry is a mature one, and a full range of equipment is available for storing, processing, and reproducing analog-video signals. The equipment suppliers serve the three main markets: broadcast, professional, and consumer. Traditionally, audio production has taken place in the analog domain, using microphones and tape recorders. The music industry utilizes some of the most complex audio production facilities available. These can be found in most major cities around the world and they allow audio from many sources to be equalized, effects to be inserted, and the sources to be mixed into the tracks that will be used by the final application. Typically an audio production house will work with many parallel tracks on magnetic tape—24-track machines using 2-inch-wide tapes are common.

There is an emerging trend in audio production and postproduction to move to digital equipment. This trend started in the broadcast market and has moved down through the professional market into the consumer market. The driving force toward an all-digital process was the release of the compact disc medium to the consumer in 1983. Now, a decade later, the CD is king, and many record companies are discontinuing vinyl record production altogether. Studios and production houses have fully digital recording suites and mixing systems that allow recordings to be digital throughout the entire recording, production, and transmission cycle. Digital audio tape (DAT) was released several years ago and embraced by recording studios but not by the consumer market, which was skeptical of yet another potential standard. The last year has seen the release of the digital compact cassette (DCC) and the minidisc (MD), both of which attempt to address the consumer requirement for digital-audio recording. Time will tell whether either of these formats is accepted.

Audio analog-to-digital conversion

To process audio in the personal-computer environment, the analog-audio signal must be converted to digital using an A/D converter. (Alternatively, if the audio is already on a digital medium, such as DAT, only a simple format conversion is required.)

As with video, the A/D process consists of sampling and quantizing, but at much lower frequencies than those attributed to video. In audio systems the maximum bandwidth is 20 kHz, hence sampling rates need to be between 40 and 50 kHz. These rates are slow compared to video, but they are slightly offset by the need to have lower quantization and hence more bits per sample. In the earlier discussion of video sampling, a signal-to-noise ratio of 46 dB was considered good. An audio signal of the same quality is not acceptable, and signal-to-noise ratios of greater than 70 dB must be attained if the noise is not to be heard during normal listening. When the additional requirements of production are taken into consideration, the standard for audio digitizing becomes 16 bits per sample, giving a signal-to-noise ratio of 96 dB.

Audio compression

The standard quantizing method for 16-bit digital audio is *linear pulse code modulation* (PCM), with each quantization step having equal size. It is this format that was adopted and used on audio compact discs. If samples have less than 16 bits per sample, several other quantizing methods may be used. A form of PCM known as *companding* (or *nonlinear PCM*) is best used when 12 or 14 bits per sample are available. In this approach the quantization steps at low signals are smaller than the steps at high signal levels.

Higher levels of compression can be achieved by the use of *differential pulse code modulation (DPCM)*. This time only the differences between adjacent samples are coded by the quantizer, rather than the samples themselves.

This approach rests on the assumption that most of the time the difference between samples will not be as large as the samples themselves, and therefore fewer bits can be used for coding. This works well if adjacent samples are of similar amplitude, but if the signal contains a lot of frequency components that are near the Nyquist limit, the adjacent samples will be very different. The DPCM system will be unable to keep up and will cause severe distortion of the high-frequency sections of the audio.

An adaptive system was introduced to solve the problems inherent in DPCM. This system, called *ADPCM,* applies a scale factor to the difference bits that can dynamically change, depending on the signal level or high-frequency content of the audio signal. Hence when the signal is small, the difference bits control small steps of amplitude, and when the signal is high they control much larger increments. Since an ADPCM playback system must know the scale factor, it is contained within the stream of difference bits that the decoder processes. There are many ADPCM implementations, the most popular of them based on a CCITT standard that uses ADPCM at 4 bits per sample and is commonly referred to as *ADPCM4*. The quality of the reproduction can be increased simply by increasing the sampling rate, but with the inevitable increase in bandwidth. Distortion may be heard when a large amount of adaptation is required by a sound that changes too fast for the system.

The MPEG specification includes a section devoted to digital-audio compression to accompany digital video. These compression schemes are highly computationally intensive and make use of the audio-masking characteristics of the human ear. Even when such techniques are used, compression ratios are limited to a factor of 6:1, which is enforced by the lack of structure in an audio signal and the resultant low possibilities for any redundancy.

Synthesized audio

The rapid advances in electronics and computing have also enabled a new breed of musical instruments: electronic synthesizers. Synthesizers have come a long way since the early analog-sound-generator-equipped Moogs. Synthesizers have made the transition to the digital world, and modern examples can be used to recreate almost any sound imaginable. Yamaha introduced a synthesis method known as *frequency modulation (FM) synthesis* with their early DX line of synthesizers, which revolutionized the marketplace. FM synthesis works by generating a sound by modulating a series of sinewaves together. By careful selection of the frequencies, and modulation, a wide variety of sounds can be achieved. Since then many other techniques have been introduced, as equipment manufacturers have battled to produce the most natural-sounding systems.

Until recently, the controller and the sound generator had been part of the same piece of equipment. Today, however, the controller and the sound generator have been separated, and there are digital sound generators that can be controlled by any kind of player interface. For example, controllers are available that play like guitars or violins even though the sound generation is electronic.

How is this flexibility achieved? They key ingredient is MIDI, the Musical Instrument Digital Interface, a communications specification that enables the exchange of musical information among electronic musical instruments, computers, and peripheral audio equipment. When combined with music-synthesis capability, MIDI allows a personal computer to become the control center of a musical production system. Although initially used by musicians to perform music, MIDI is now an integral part of the audio-generation technology for multimedia productions.

MIDI augments the use of waveform audio in multimedia. Waveform audio normally is used to reproduce speech and many nonmusical sounds but, as stated previously, requires a large amount of memory to faithfully reproduce music. MIDI represents music using far less storage and allows greater editing flexibility, but does require a music synthesizer to generate the actual music. MIDI describes music in terms of high-level command sequences, for example "Play Middle C on the French horn loudly for one second." This is encoded into 6 bytes, 3 bytes to start the sound and 3 to terminate it. Compare this to CD-quality PCM data at 176 kbps for the same "information."

Because MIDI is a symbolic representation of music, not the audio waveform data itself, the quality of the sound is related primarily to the quality of the music synthesizer, not the MIDI data. Most synthesizers produce stereo sound, and some can very convincingly reproduce acoustic musical instruments. Speech and sound effects, recorded as specific musical sounds, are limited by the synthesizer's memory.

MIDI messages can be stored on a computer as MIDI files. Playing back MIDI files on a suitably equipped system reproduces the recorded performance exactly. In addition to allowing you to simply play the file back, the performance may be edited, instruments changed, the tempo or the musical key modified—all by simple modifications to the MIDI data.

The amount of data required to store a performance is many orders less than that required to sample the performance in the traditional methods described previously. Hence MIDI is an alternative mechanism that augments the use of waveform audio in multimedia titles. With the number of MIDI-enabled systems growing, and given the rate of development for music, it is expected that every personal computer soon will have a built-in capability for realistic audio.

Conclusions

This chapter has introduced the principles of digital audio and video. Both are rapidly extending the capabilities of personal computers to present information in new and exciting ways. The large bandwidth requirement of digital video has accelerated the research effort with regard to video compression. Large reductions in the bandwidth requirement may be accomplished by removing redundant information in the video sequences. Such reductions are possible only because of the inherent structured nature of video (lines and frames). Audio, however, does not exhibit a structured nature, which consequently limits the amount of compression achievable. High-quality compression schemes attempt to model the acoustics of the human ear to determine which components might be redundant within the audio signal.

Broadcasting is moving into the digital realm with the introduction of digital broadcast radio and with the first field trials of interactive televisions based on standard video-compression schemes such as MPEG. Such systems enable applications such as "video-on-demand," bringing the age of consumer-driven television that much closer.

33

Understanding PC Video

Claude Leglise

Enhancing Business Communications

Imagine trying to explain to someone how to tie a shoe—using only written or spoken words. Even if you use pictures and diagrams, it's still awkward and time-consuming to "talk" someone through this everyday procedure. People are likely to respond with "Just show me!", because they catch on far more quickly when they can *see* how something is done rather than read or listen to instructions. Likewise, many types of business information cannot be conveyed effectively with words and images alone. This information requires a much richer mode of communication, one that not only includes visual elements to enhance the spoken word but also captures movement and visual expression as well.

The personal computer (PC) has enhanced business communications dramatically in the last decade, allowing people to communicate information with text, data, and graphics. The next logical step is the addition of motion video to PCs. PC video integrates visual elements with the spoken word and motion, bringing a rich new data-type to PC communications. It combines the impact of video with the PC's ability to manage, access, and present data.

Off-the-shelf hardware and software that support PC video are available today. New technologies are making PC video not only affordable but also easy to install and use. As a result, we are beginning to see exciting business applications that use video to enhance the effectiveness of business communications. This chapter will take a close look at PC video and its applications, and explain how easy it is to add video to your PC.

PC Video Applications

The PC is rapidly becoming the platform for communicating and distributing information. People already are using PCs to send and receive documents, faxes, and e-mail messages over LANs and across phone lines. Video is a natural and powerful extension to PC-based communications and information distribution.

Given the ready availability of PC-video software, and the ease of incorporating and using video, you can get started right away enhancing your business communications. In fact, products such as Microsoft's Video for Windows, with Intel's Indeo video technology, allow you to play back video clips that have been incorporated into existing applications such as word processors, spreadsheets, databases, and presentation graphics. It's as easy as pasting in a graph or a drawing. And with the addition of video-capture hardware, you can record video right at your desktop. Think of the possibilities...!

Business presentations

PC-based business presentations are rapidly increasing in popularity because they look good, are easy to create, are highly portable, and can be played on just about any PC, including portables and laptops. Over one hundred million PCs have been installed to date, so you can show your presentation in almost any business office without scheduling a conference room or setting up additional equipment. Or you can hook up a flat-panel projector to your PC and project your presentations using an overhead projector.

With PC video, you can add a whole new dimension to your business presentations. Imagine the impact of a sales presentation that includes "live" customer testimonials, or electronic product brochures that include video product demonstrations. PC video offers other benefits as well. For example, you can quickly create a marketing clip on a new product without the expense of producing a full-blown video. Sales and marketing are not the only areas in which you can use PC video. You can also add impact to staff presentations, announcements, and many other corporate communications.

Education and training

Because of the rich and portable nature of video communication—not to mention its cost-effectiveness—videotaped training programs are heavily used in business. Video adds impact to training programs and holds an audience's attention. In addition, a 1991 study by Inteco Corp. shows that video presentations increase audience retention of information by up to 38 percent.

However, videotaped training programs have their limitations. Because videotape is sequential, sequences cannot be randomly accessed; videotape cannot be integrated with computer-based training; and people typically cannot view videotapes at their desks. PC video overcomes the limitations of videotape. It combines the benefits of computer-based training with the impact of a video presentation.

Video on the PC is convenient, and even more portable than videotape—it can be run on just about any i486-based PC. And it's easy to combine video with text, graphics, and other data types so as to optimize communication. You can use PC video for many training and education purposes: employee orientation, human-resource updates, sales training, product training, electronic employee newsletters, safety courses, and many others. For example, service and maintenance manuals can be enhanced to include video clips of certain operations, such as installing an oil filter in a car.

Video databases

Video databases combine the power of video with the ability of computers to manage, access, and present data. Imagine going into a real estate office, entering into a PC your requirements for a new home, then viewing video clips of houses that meet your specifications and budget. Real estate is only one of many areas that can be enhanced with video databases. Physicians in remote locations can take advantage of a video database containing medical procedures; and video can be added to insurance claims databases.

General-purpose video communications and information distribution

Just as e-mail has revolutionized communications, so too will PC video eventually revolutionize e-mail. Video e-mail is particularly effective at facilitating cooperative projects in which several coworkers need to share information. For example doctors can share patient records, engineers design approaches, and insurance adjusters claim information. Video e-mail also can be used to distribute information—such as service bulletins and product updates—quickly and effectively.

Next-generation applications

In addition to enhancing existing applications such as presentations, PC video opens the door to new applications that simply were not possible before. One exciting example is desktop videoconferencing, in which users may not only see the other party, but also send, annotate, and share documents in real time. As a result of these applications the PC will become an even more powerful business tool, one that allows interactive business communications combining text, graphics, voice, and video.

Minimum System Requirements

What hardware and software you'll need to run PC video will depend on whether you plan to record video at your desktop or simply play back video clips recorded by others.

Requirements for playing video

Your PC may already be capable of video playback. All you need is an Intel 486 microprocessor-based personal computer running the Windows operating

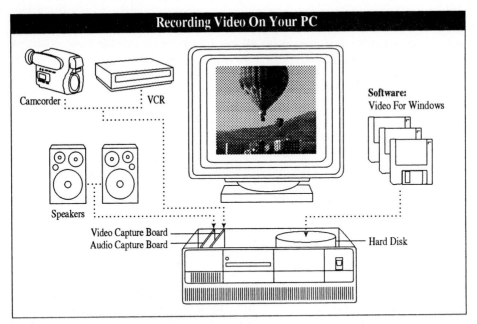

Figure 33.1 Components needed for recording video.

system. The PC should have a i486SX/25-MHz CPU or higher, a hard-disk drive, and a 256-color VGA board or greater. You'll also need a PC audio board and speakers or headphones, which are readily available and easy to install.

With this setup you can play back video titles that have been recorded elsewhere and supplied to you on diskette, CD-ROM, or via a network. This means that tens of millions of i486 microprocessor-based PCs are potential video-playback units. As you can see, playing back video to your PC is easy, and doesn't require a lot of expensive equipment.

Requirements for recording video on a PC

If you also wish to *record* video on your PC, you'll need a few additional components, as shown in Fig. 33.1:

- A video-digitizing (or capture) board, to convert the analog-video signals to digital information

- A hard disk with a minimum of 30 Mbytes of free hard-disk space, or more

- A source of video input such as a video camera, VCR, or laserdisc player, which you connect to the video-capture board

- Video software (such as Video for Windows) that includes video-capture, compression, playback, and basic video-editing utilities

You cannot play back video at a higher quality than was captured, so you should give particular attention to the quality of video recording.

By recording at the highest level of quality possible, you ensure that you will achieve the highest-quality playback when you need it. Video image quality depends primarily on three factors: viewing-window size, video "frame rate," and color-presentation capability. What it is important to note is that quality depends on a combination of these three factors. Therefore remember, when you are evaluating video software and hardware, that it is important to look at all three quality factors.

In addition, the level of video quality that you enjoy is directly related to your PC hardware configuration, in particular to the PC microprocessor, the graphics board, and the speed of the hard disk. We'll discuss the relationship among hardware and video capture and playback quality later. But first let's look more closely at the three factors that jointly create video quality.

Viewing-window size

Viewing-window dimensions are expressed in pixels—for example, 320 × 240 or 160 × 120 pixels. Note by way of reference that a standard VGA screen is 640 × 480 pixels, which means that a 320 × 240 video-playback window takes up about one-fourth of a VGA screen. Standard PC video-window playback sizes, as shown in Fig. 33.2, are 160 × 120 ($\frac{1}{16}$ screen) and 320 × 240 ($\frac{1}{4}$ screen).

Video frame rate

The *video frame rate* specifies the number of frames per second (fps) of video images displayed on the screen (see Fig. 33.3). The higher the frame rate, the more fluid the motion appears. The highest-quality, or best-quality, frame rate available is 30 fps, which appears to the human eye as completely fluid motion. Lower frame rates (below 10) still appear as motion, but are noticeably "jerky."

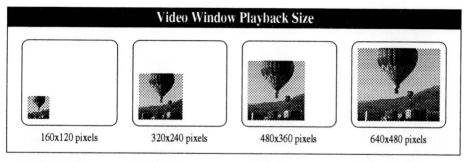

Figure 33.2 Video-window playback size, expressed in pixels.

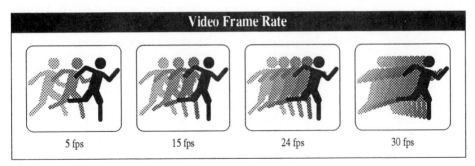

Figure 33.3   Frame rates range from 0 (still) to 30 fps.

For reference, 0 fps is a still frame (no motion); 24 fps is the frame rate used in motion pictures; 30 fps is used in television; 10 to 15 fps is the rate that most people find acceptable for fluid motion.

Color presentation capability

Color presentation capability depends on the color depth and the spatial color resolution. The term *color depth* refers to the number of different colors available. The more colors, the higher the quality and the truer the representation. Color depth on PCs ranges from a VGA palette of 4 bits (16 colors) up to 24-bit true color with 16.7 million hues. You'll need at least a 256-color VGA card, or higher, for video. The term *color resolution* refers to the spatial "graininess" or "blockiness" of the color. The highest quality results when every pixel is assigned its own color.

Blockiness results when the same color is assigned to all four pixels in a 2×2 area or larger. Many compression algorithms reduce file sizes by grouping pixels into color blocks. To help reduce the graininess during playback, interpolation or dithering techniques are employed to smooth out the color over the blocked-out areas.

Recording Video on Your PC

Recording video on your PC is a simple process. You can capture live action using a video camera, or you can capture existing video clips from a VCR or laserdisc player. Video cameras, VCRs, and laserdiscs communicate video information to a television set using a standard analog-video format such as NTSC (North America and Japan), PAL (Western Europe), or SECAM (France and Eastern Europe).

The video-capture board in your PC converts this analog-video signal into digital information, and records it on a hard-disk file. The file format depends on the video-recording hardware and software used. Raw uncompressed digitized video files are quite large. For example, 1 minute of video can range from 35 to 50 Mbytes on your hard disk, depending on preset capture parameters. So it's necessary to compress—or shrink—raw video files to a size that is more manageable on a PC.

Compression

Video-compression techniques take advantage of the fact that, as you move from one frame of video to the next, much of the "information" remains the same. Compression routines look at each frame and identify and save only the changes from frame to frame—for example, changes caused by motion. Additionally, compression routines "eliminate the redundancy" within each frame. If, for example, an area of the screen is made up of a group of pixels all the same color, the compression software stores color information about the area as a whole rather than storing separate color information for each pixel.

These compression techniques dramatically reduce video file sizes. For example, video software that incorporates Indeo video can compress a 50-Mbyte raw video file to about 9 Mbytes. Indeo video, Intel's advanced video compression/decompression software technology, is a key component of Microsoft's Video for Windows and Apple's QuickTime products. IBM also has endorsed Indeo technology and plans to incorporate it into its operating environments. This will allow users to interchange video files freely between Windows, Macintosh, and OS/2 platforms.

One-step versus two-step capture and compression

There are two basic video-capture techniques: one-step capture and compression and two-step capture and compression. Older video-capture boards use a two-step process. Capture and compression are two separate steps because video input comes into the PC faster than the compression routine can process it. In the first step, you capture the video and store the raw digitized video information on a hard-disk file. In the second step, you compress this file off-line (see Fig. 33.4).

This two-step process requires disk space to hold not only the uncompressed video file but also the compressed file (for a total of 45 to 60 Mbytes for 1 minute of video). In addition, the off-line software-compression step takes a lot of extra time: as much as 15 to 30 minutes for every minute of video. During that time the PC is completely dedicated to compression, and cannot be used for other work. Fortunately, newer compression technologies use a combination of software and hardware to compress video much more quickly. For example, The Intel Smart Video Recorder digitizes, compresses, and stores the video data all in one easy step (see Fig. 33.5).

This is accomplished by incorporating Indeo technology and Intel's i750 video processor into The Intel Smart Video Recorder board. Real-time, single-step capture and compression offers important advantages. It minimizes the cost of PC video, because it uses far less hard-disk space (9 Mbytes of hard disk for 1 minute of video in a 160×120 window, versus 45 to 60 Mbytes). This often eliminates the need to add large and fast hard-disk capacity to

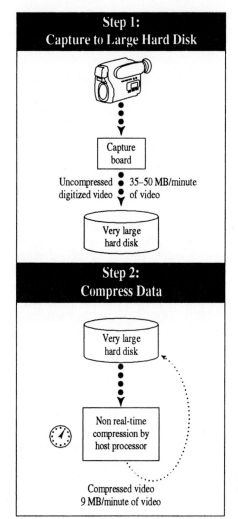

Figure 33.4 Two-step capture and compression.

your PC. It also offers convenience and time savings, because there is no lengthy compression process involved.

Video-capture quality

Single-step capture and compression has an important advantage, in that the video quality is not as sensitive to the hardware configuration as it is when two-step capture and compression is used.

With two-step capture and compression, video quality is directly related to your PC hardware configuration: the more powerful the microprocessor and the faster the hard disk, the higher the quality. With two-step capture and compression, all uncompressed video data must be transferred directly to the hard disk. In many configurations, the speed of the microprocessor and hard disk cannot keep pace with the large volume of incoming data. The system

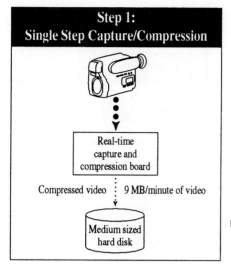

Figure 33.5   Single-step video.

becomes overloaded and begins to "drop" frames. So you may not be able to achieve the full frame rate (quality) that is specified for the video-capture board.

For example, a two-step video-capture board rated at 30 fps may in reality capture far fewer fps on less powerful hardware configurations.

One-step capture and compression, on the other hand, compresses video data before it is transferred to the hard disk. As a result the amount of data that the hard disk must handle is dramatically reduced—by a factor of up to 6 to 1. Thus very few frames, if any, are "dropped" during capture. A single-step video-capture board rated at 30 fps will deliver 30 fps even on less powerful system configurations.

Distributing Your Video

You can distribute your compressed video files just as you would any other file type—either on diskette or over a network. People who have Video for Windows can play your video clip without any additional software. If you are planning to distribute your video clip to people who don't have Video for Windows, you will need to attach a copy of video-player software (also called a *runtime player*) to the compressed file. Video-player software is included with Video for Windows and with the Intel Smart Video Recorder.

Playing video files on your PC

You can receive video files for playback on diskette or through a network. You can view these files even if you don't have any specialized video-playback hardware on your PC. If you have video-playback software such as Video for Windows, you can take advantage of its simulated push-button controls, which look much like those on a VCR or cassette player.

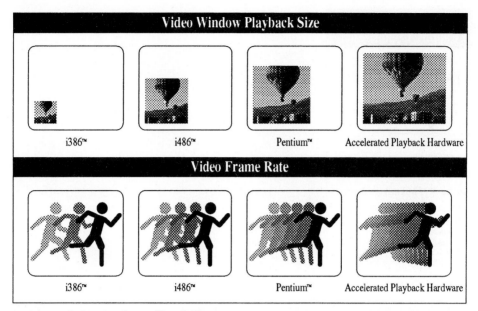

Figure 33.6 Increasing the quality of video.

Playback quality depends on hardware

As you move up in processing power, such as from an i386 to an i486 to a Pentium microprocessor, you can take advantage of larger playback window sizes and faster frame rates, enhancing playback quality. The result is a larger viewing area and more fluid motion, as shown in Fig. 33.6. The table below shows how different hardware configurations affect video-window playback size and video frame rates.

Depending on the hardware configuration, you may need to make tradeoffs between window size and frame rate to optimize video quality for particular purposes. For example if the most important thing to convey is motion, then you would opt for a smaller window playback size to get a faster frame rate. If however you are more interested in visual details, you would trade off frame rate for a larger window playback size. The following table shows typical window sizes and frame-rate tradeoffs for popular hardware configurations. The numbers shown depend on the specific hardware configuration, and may vary based on such factors as disk-drive speed, available RAM, and the VGA card installed.

Playback Performance Tradeoffs

System	180×120	320×240
486SX/25	15 fps	4 fps
486DX/33	20 fps	5 fps
486DC2/66	30 fps	8 fps

All systems based on 8 Mbytes RAM; 11.8-millisecond hard-disk speed; VGA card with 512-kbyte memory and 256 colors.

Smart video software

Because of the variety of hardware configurations available, a wide range of playback qualities are possible. As a result, video software should be "smart" enough to determine what hardware is available and optimize playback quality for that hardware automatically—without requiring you to change the software or the video clip file.

This intelligence is sometimes referred to as *scalability*. During playback, Indeo video's scalable technology automatically determines what hardware is available and optimizes playback quality for that configuration. When recording Indeo video files, the Intel Smart Video Recorder's one-step capability ensures that frames are never lost. As a result, more powerful PCs are able to tap into this stored video data during playback, delivering progressively faster frame rates. Therefore, as computer users upgrade their systems with faster Intel microprocessors, they benefit from the security of knowing that video recorded on The Intel Smart Video Recorder will "upgrade" along with them.

Scalability protects your investment, because video recorded today will play faster on tomorrow's machines. This is not the case for video clips captured on two-step boards, which often lose frames. These lost frames never can be recovered and played back, no matter how fast your upgraded CPU. Without scalability, video quality will be the same on the faster CPU as it was on the older one.

Video Trends

Recent advances such as Intel's Indeo video technology bring PC video to the business user. PC video is affordable and easy to install and use.

As a result, you immediately can begin to use video to enhance your business communications: presentations, educational and training programs, video communications and information distribution, and even video databases.

PC hardware

Today's microprocessors have the horsepower necessary to handle the demands of high-quality video. The next generation of microprocessors, such as Intel's Pentium microprocessor, will be even better equipped for running video-based applications. And your investment in video is protected, because Indeo video software technology is scalable. That means the video you capture today will run on tomorrow's hardware to the full extent of the quality of the video capture. In addition, storage capacities are increasing and costs are plummeting. Disk drives of 200 to 300 Mbytes are now standard on many PCs.

Video hardware

Intel offers a variety of video boards to simplify video capture and to enhance playback quality by using Indeo video technology and the i750 video processor. Intel recording boards offer all the advantages of one-step capture and compression, which result in significant disk-space savings, time savings, and higher recorded frame rates.

Operating system software

Microsoft, IBM, and Apple have all committed to supporting video in their operating system software. Video for Windows and QuickTime, which incorporate Intel's Indeo video technology, are available today from Microsoft and Apple. IBM has announced its plans to incorporate Indeo video into OS/2.

Video tools and utilities

A number of video-capture, editing, and playback tools and utilities are already available for working with video on your PC. Many of these programs have been integrated with operating environments such as Video for Windows.

Video clip art

Clip-art suppliers are beginning to market "video clip art," offering you a wide selection of prerecorded video that you can incorporate into your business documents. Video for Windows includes one of these video-clip libraries on CD-ROM.

Applications

Existing standards such as Object Linking and Embedding (OLE) make it easy to include video in the Windows operating environment. Over 150 existing business applications support OLE, including word processors, spreadsheets, databases, and business presentations. This paves the way for the integration of video into compound documents without the need for specialized software. OLE ensures that you can easily incorporate video into existing files, even if these were created before PC video capabilities were available.

Distribution

Distribution infrastructures such as LANs and the telephone network are already in place and can support limited digital-video transmission, such as low-volume store-and-forward. As video-compression techniques advance and network bandwidths widen, we'll be able to increase the volume of store-and-forward video transmission so that large-scale video e-mail becomes a reality. Advancements in digital communications technology such as the Integrated Services Digital Network (ISDN) are making it possible to send video beyond the local-area network.

Ultimately we'll be able to handle the transmission of full-motion video in real time, enabling videoconferencing and other exciting new video applications. As we have seen, many PC video capabilities already are available. And they are only the beginning. New advancements are occurring every day, at all levels of information technology. The next generation of PC hardware will include more powerful microprocessors, larger disk drives, and faster graphics subsystems, resulting in even better PC-video quality. In addition, higher compression rates will enhance our ability to send and receive video via the telephone or local-area networks. As new technology becomes available, prices will continue to drop, making PC video even more affordable.

Conclusion

PC video is here today, and it's here to stay. It's affordable, it's easy to use, and it opens the door to numerous applications that can dramatically enhance business communications. New technologies such as Indeo video make playback easy and affordable—often without any additional hardware.

In addition Indeo technology, in conjunction with The Intel Smart Video Recorder, permits single-step capture and compression, making the process fast and efficient so that you can create your own video clips right at your desktop. Through the continuing development of more powerful microprocessors such as the Pentium microprocessor, Intel is paving the way for more sophisticated video applications that will allow PC video to fulfill its true potential.

34

System Support for Integrated Desktop Videoconferencing

Amy Pearl

Introduction

In the last 15 years, the ability of computers to capture, store, and manipulate information has been augmented by an ability to transmit that information to other computers. As computers become increasingly connected by means of various networks, they increasingly are being used as communication tools. Much of that communication comes in the form of forwarded and stored data such as electronic mail and bulletin boards (*Byte,* 1985). These tools support asynchronous communication between people, allowing communication to occur even if the recipient is absent. However, such tools have not replaced the need for interactive, or synchronous, communication, even in computers. For example, for as long as computers have supported multiple users, people have found simple text-based interactive "talk" programs useful. Our research at SunSoft is focused on the new possibilities for interactive collaboration between remotely located workers who use networked workstations. One of the early prototypes we developed is a digital, integrated videoconference application called *videoconf.*

Videoconferencing is a technology that has been emerging over the past 30 years, motivated by a recognition of how much of our face-to-face communication is visual, or nonverbal. For example, there have been efforts to augment telephones to include the transmission of visual images. Recently the Computer-Supported Cooperative Work (CSCW) community has been exploring the use of computer-controlled analog audio and video transmission to support group work (Root, 1988; Olson and Bly, 1991; Vin et al., 1991). Recent advances in media-compression technology, along with shrinking component size and cost, are making digital video feasible. Unlike analog video, digital video can take advantage of the growing number of digital communication networks, including phone (e.g., ISDN) and institutional networks (e.g., LANs and WANs). It is also possible for programs to manipulate digital video, the effects of which are just now being explored (Liebhold and Hoffert, 1991). An example of this is the morphing of video images.

At Sun Microsystems Laboratories Inc. (SMLI) and SunSoft, our conferencing and collaboration project explores issues in computer-assisted collaboration for geographically distributed small groups. Videoconf is part of a set of workstation tools built for use studies. (For reports on related use studies see Tang and Isaacs, 1993, and Isaacs and Tang, 1993.)

The videoconference application was built on the Advanced Multimedia Platform (AMP) (Calnan 1991), also developed at SMLI. AMP was designed to provide system support to network multimedia applications. AMP defined multimedia as *the combination of standard data types* (*text, graphics, images, etc.*) *with data types that have timeliness constraints (or time-critical data).* It provided applications with support for managing the resources required for multimedia, including hardware devices. AMP used a video board to capture, digitize, compress, and display video in windows on the workstation. Our goals for developing the videoconference application were to (1) determine the feasibility of integrating digital audio/video conferencing into a standard networked UNIX desktop workstation, (2) exercise the AMP multimedia platform, and (3) evaluate how much system support AMP was providing for the development of collaborative applications.

Through our early videoconferencing prototype, we learned about the requirements for integrating videoconferencing into a networked workstation. After describing the system support that applications require in order to name, protect, share, and optimize the resources needed for videoconferencing, this chapter will describe our application architecture in light of past CSCW literature. Finally, it will describe features we expect to see prototyped, and the further system capabilities required to support them. This includes an important addition to the class of time-critical data: general-user actions in multiuser applications.

Requirements

Most of the difficulty in a videoconference application is in handling aspects of the network: finding conferees and the necessary resources (such as video cameras and video displays), providing access control and security, sharing resources, and sharing network bandwidth fairly.

Resource naming

One of the first problems a distributed environment must address is how applications locate and reference services or resources. For videoconferencing, there are three things we need to be able to find and reference: people, devices, and conferences.

Figure 34.1 Identifying people prior to initiating a conference.

When users start a conference, they think in terms of the people to whom they want to talk or the name of the meeting they want to join. Applications need system support if they are to map the names of people ("Connect Amy's camera to John's and Dave's video displays") and conferences ("Add me to the SMLI staff meeting") to the resources and attributes associated with them. AMP associated multimedia resources, such as video and audio devices, with machine names, and provided references to those devices. In order to allow users to refer to people or conferences by name, an application needs to map those names to the relevant machines.

Videoconf provided a phonelike invocation model, in which users needed to know the name of each person with whom they wished to confer (Fig. 34.1). However, users found videoconf's phone-call model very limiting. Individual applications can provide their own mapping of people and conference names to the appropriate machines, but this support should be provided by a collaboration platform.

Users want the ability to join a conference in progress (in which case they usually are referred to as *late joiners*). For example, if two people are conferencing and a third contacts one of them, they may want to add the caller to the existing conference. Users of videoconf were unable to do this for two technical reasons: AMP provided no support for finding a conference, and AMP references to devices could not be shared between applications. Truly general-purpose platforms for multimedia and collaboration should provide support for these capabilities. At a lower level, this means that the underlying network protocol must support the adding and deleting of connections dynamically.

Security

Once there are network-connected cameras and microphones on individuals' desks, with software allowing remote access of these resources, it becomes possible to eavesdrop on conferences and to monitor individuals. There are two areas of security, security *of access* and security *of transmitted data,* and two reasons for providing security mechanisms at the platform level:

1. Security is a service that many multimedia applications require, especially those that provide group support, and it shouldn't have to be replicated by each of them.

2. It is critical that these mechanisms be robust, and that users of these systems be able to trust that they are secure. This requires that security implementation be embedded at a level out of reach of the end user.

Security: access

At a minimum, users want to know if someone wants or attempts to view or listen to them. They may also want to restrict access to their local multimedia resources in various ways. This is an issue of concern in any distributed multimedia environment that has multimedia devices located on desktops that can be accessed remotely. Because security was not a focus of our research, AMP provided minimal security. Whenever a video camera is initially accessed on a machine, AMP audibly notifies the user on that machine and prints a status message in the console window (the global workstation status window). This mechanism does nothing to restrict access, relying as it does on users' awareness to mediate security.

Videoconf provided additional security by imposing a more restrictive access policy, symmetry of functionality ("If I can see/hear you, you can see/hear me") (Borning and Travers, 1991). While this meets the requirement of having a simple model and is simple to implement, it is not a very scalable, flexible, or practical model.

In our experience with a system that provides very little security control, we saw that much of access control can be socially mediated. This may in part be true because our target users are those who work closely together. We plan to prototype communication applications with a less restrictive policy than symmetry of functionality. For example, many more of our workstations are equipped with audio than with video. We would like to be able to impose symmetry on audioconferencing only, and allow video to be used, if available. In such a case, either the access policy may be socially mediated or the application may impose a policy of symmetry of security ("I am unable to see you unless I have permission to see you and you have permission to see me"). This would require that the system include the concept of user-access permissions for each resource.

In the example of symmetry of permissions, the access control was on the basis of each resource. It can be useful for conferences to have permissions. In the example of locating and finding a conference ("Add me to the staff meeting"), the policy may be that conferences that have a privacy attribute have a more restrictive admission procedure. In such a case, users may have to contact and obtain permission from a conference leader first, or no one may be allowed to join who is not already on the membership list.

Security: data

Users who transmit sensitive video data may want to prevent some people from monitoring it. Digital video opens up a wide array of data-protection possibilities.

For example, both analog and digital images can be altered, but it may be easier, through techniques such as *checksums,* to determine the authenticity of a digital image than to authenticate an image on paper. We can protect digital images through powerful digital encryption techniques such as DES. However, while we must be concerned with issues of individual privacy when there are new ways to invade it, we also should consider just how private many of our current communication transmission mechanisms are. Conventional paper mail can be compromised in many ways. Electronic mail is often notoriously lax in its security. Telephone communication over lines can be tapped, and wireless communications are even more vulnerable. Many of our uses of communication and media rely on socially agreed-upon security mechanisms, not technical ones.

No security system is invulnerable; therefore the most important design goal is that the security model be well understood by programmers and end users. The security requirements of collaborative applications vary widely. When applications are geared toward sharing big collections of information among large, loosely connected groups of people, the security requirements are likely to be much greater than for the sharing of targeted collections of data among a closely connected work group. Security mechanisms should be flexible and sophisticated, so as to accommodate a wide range of needs.

Shared resources

Once applications have located their resources and the system has verified that they may access them, multiple clients may potentially share the same resources. Sharing resources is not unique to collaborative applications, but it is inherently part of them. There are many ways in which resources may be shared, and there are different requirements for each. Some resources are shared by partitioning them, so that users are protected from each other. For example, our digital-video board supports up to four independent video displays. Other resources are shared outright, and the actions of one user may affect others. For example, a user may pause in the transmission of his or her video camera for privacy during a conference; all display clients of that camera are then effectively halted.

Our videoconference application required three kinds of sharing:

1. Multiple receivers must share the data from a source.

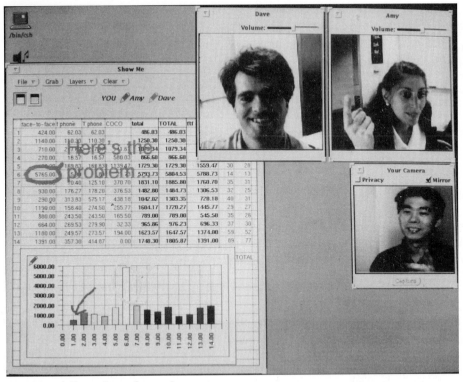

Figure 34.2   A three-site conference in progress.

2. A display of multiple video images shares a single frame buffer.

3. Multiple users share control of video streams.

Let's look at each of these more closely.

1. *Transmitting each video camera output to multiple users' displays.* Each conferee's camera must transmit its data to a display on each conferee's machine. The displays share the camera data stream either by getting their own copy of the stream or by monitoring a single broadcast stream (see the discussion of optimization of video data transmission). AMP handled these connections and the choice of transmission.

2. *Displaying video streams from multiple cameras on each user's workstation.* The video board on each conferee's workstation must display the multiple streams it receives (Fig. 34.2). Again, this was handled by AMP, since the need for multiple video displays on a user's workstation is not limited to collaborative applications.

3. *Allowing multiple users to share control of each video stream.* In our videoconference application, each of the users receiving the video data was able to control its behavior by pausing or resuming it. This could affect the view of others receiving that stream. AMP provided no mechanisms to negoti-

ate sharing control of resources. As a result, that capability was provided only in a very limited way by videoconf. Those resources may be shared by multiple applications that have no knowledge of each other. Any platform that manages shared resources must provide applications with the ability to negotiate control of those resources. Because the AMP platform did not do so, videoconf does not provide users with the ability to manipulate many shared video characteristics such as frame rate and image resolution.

Users of a desktop videoconferencing program really don't share data in the same sense as users of a multiuser editor do. The data that videoconference users share is really only the multiplexing of the video sources to all the relevant displays. Unlike a shared editor, a videoconference does not contain persistent data that is manipulated in different ways by the various users who receive it.

Performance characteristics

Digital videoconferencing has very specific performance requirements. This is because of the need for interactivity, the need for multiple video displays on each workstation, and the large volume of data in a digital-video stream. People perceive audio delay when it lasts longer than 200 milliseconds. Our video board allowed conferencing between up to five people at a time. Like several existing digital-video standards, the compression scheme AMP used generated over 1 Mbit per second for each video data stream at full-motion-video rates.

Prior to the development of our prototype system, we at Sun conducted a study of dedicated videoconference rooms between the east and west coasts of the United States (Tang and Isaacs, 1993). The vendor-supplied systems enforced audio and video synchronization. Users found that the significant transmission delay (over 500 milliseconds) interfered with natural verbal communication. Users frequently switched over to using the telephone for an audio channel, because the absence of delay made conversation more natural and productive, even though the audio and video were then out of sync.

Our multimedia platform originally was designed to support media stream synchronization, achieved in part by liberal use of buffering, which introduces delay. Our videoconference-room study showed that this approach is at odds with the needs of low-latency conferencing. The platform was redesigned to take this into consideration. Because a multimedia platform hides details such as buffer size from applications, its design must carefully take into account the requirements of all multimedia applications. The importance of low audio delay may also mean that some audio data should be treated at a higher priority than other time-critical data.

The volume of data is an important consideration when it comes to both data storage and transmission. Generally, the higher the quality of compression technique used, the more computation required to achieve the results. For single-user multimedia applications, it makes sense to use whatever computational resources are available for decompression of that user's data streams. In conferencing, however, we want to display multiple streams at once. In addition, the number of streams is variable. This means that, unless the system can dynamically scale the complexity of the decode algorithm appropriately, it is desirable to use a less computationally intensive decode algorithm, even at the cost of lower quality or higher data rate. The AMP platform provided a very simple algorithm with a relatively low compression ratio (about four times). It also required relatively little computation. Our system had usable results with this algorithm, and as better compression techniques become available, either image quality will improve or the data rate will get lower, or both.

The goals for integrating video into a desktop collaboration environment must include sensitivity to the use of the shared network resources. A single desktop-video data stream often will have multiple destinations. Examples are three-way conferencing and broadcasting a lecture. In a bus-based network like Ethernet, there are three ways to have multiple destinations receive the data: through point-to-point addressing, broadcast, and multicast.

Point-to-point addressing requires sending each of the destinations a copy of the data. Replicating video data for each destination adds significant load to the shared network bandwidth.

A *broadcast* mechanism sends a single stream of the data out on the network, and all machines on that network receive it. Broadcast has two disadvantages; first, by convention, broadcast messages are limited to a local network in order to prevent wide-area-network overload; second, every machine on the network receives the video data, whether it is interested in it or not. This puts significant extra load on processors not even involved with the conference.

Multicast, or *group addressing,* sends a single stream out on the network, but only machines with users interested in the data can receive it (Deering, 1990). AMP used multicast connections when possible, minimizing applications' impact on the network. While multicast transport is not explicitly a requirement of interactive video, network performance optimization is.

Application Architecture

There are two general approaches to designing multiuser applications: a *centralized* approach, in which a single copy of the application is run on one machine, and is explicitly or implicitly connected to user-interface code on each participant's machine; and a *distributed* approach, in which each user interacts with a separate copy of the application, and some mechanism is used to keep all copies of the application synchronized. The advantages and disadvantages of both schemes have been well documented in the case of applications employing text and graphics (Lantz, 1986). In applications that make heavy use of audio, video, or high-resolution still images, performance considerations often will dictate that at least the media-intensive parts of the application should be distributed.

In our case, one of the most useful functions provided by AMP was the management of distributed multimedia. Applications used AMP to allocate resources and to hook them up in the desired way. This took care of distributing the flow of media. We then had to decide whether to make the videoconference application itself centralized or decentralized.

Beyond having AMP and the network window system allocate and connect resources, the application's primary function is to mediate user requests to pause, resume, and exit. Because of the CSCW literature and the fact that we were building a conferencing application, we expected that it would be preferable to write videoconf as a distributed application. However, because the application was a prototype, it was expedient to write it as a centralized application. It was much simpler to write that way, because all the communication was within one process. Much to our surprise, as we sought to establish which functionalities were not provided by our centralized implementation, we found that the only one was reliability. Reliability in the face of machine failure, though a classic advantage of distributed architectures, is not a major issue when it comes to the small-group collaboration addressed by our application.

It is worth noting that, while the sophistication of distributed computer systems is increasing, the number of applications taking explicit advantage of this new sophistication is not (Rodden and Blair, 1991). Our experience with AMP has been that the environment finally is becoming rich enough to make distributed functionality easier. This is good news for those working on collaborative applications.

Future Work

Extending the platform for conferencing support

The application-specific data that is exchanged in a multiuser collaborative application is also time-critical, and is subject to exactly the same synchronization problems as the audio and video. Consider the example of an application that employs audioconferencing and provides a shared telepointer. A user who says "Look at the picture I'm pointing to" wants some assurance that collaborators on remote machines are receiving the utterance and the pointer update at approximately the same time. This suggests that the services required of multimedia by CSCW environments are not simply audio- and videoconferencing. Application-specific data also must be delivered in the same timely manner as the media.

Like most general-purpose computer operating systems and networks, ours do not currently recognize data as having time-critical requirements. In an effort to minimize its impact on other network traffic and other processes on the workstation, such as other current multimedia efforts, AMP made three assumptions about the time-critical characteristics of multimedia:

1. Data is sampled at regular intervals.
2. Individual data samples decay quickly (if one arrives late, it rapidly loses relevance).

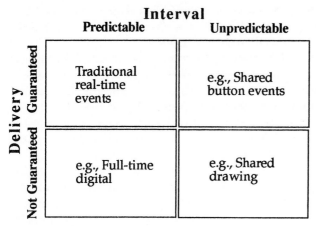

Figure 34.3   Characterizing time-critical data.

3. Synchronizing multiple streams of data (e.g., audio and video) is a priority.

These assumptions drive the design and implementation of multimedia toolkit support. However, these assumptions are not true for all time-critical domains.

In Fig. 34.3, time-critical data samples have been characterized on two axes: how regularly it is sampled, and its need for guaranteed delivery. The top-left quadrant contains traditional real-time events. These kinds of events, for example on a factory floor, occur at predictable intervals, and the servicing of these must be guaranteed. Samples from a videocompression algorithm that captured and transmitted a complete data sample 30 times every second would be in the "predictable interval, nonguaranteed" quadrant. That data requires regular sampling and delivery within the sampling interval, and each sample is independent of the others. Data samples that don't correctly and completely arrive before the next interval may be discarded; they will be replaced by later samples with more current information. Some compression algorithms send full base frames at less frequent intervals, supplemented with frames containing just the difference information in the intervening intervals. Because the base frames require reliable delivery and the difference frames do not, such algorithms are a hybrid on the full/incremental update axis. AMP supported exactly this class of events.

Events in multiuser applications occur at unpredictable intervals. These events need to be shared in a timely manner, and some require guaranteed delivery while others do not. In general, keyboard events and mouse events (such as mouse-up, mouse-down) must be reliably delivered, even if some delay is involved (top-right quadrant). Events generated by drawing continuously using a mouse or stylus do not require guaranteed delivery. Delivering fewer events results only in a coarser representation, not an inaccurate one. These are the kinds of data generated by shared drawing. A platform for collaboration must support this class of time-critical events.

Once we have a platform that supports a wider range of collaborative applications, we can expand our concept of a conference on the workstation beyond that of a videoconference. A conference can be an object that contains a set of applications, including a videoconference application. That set can be dynamic, and actions in the different applications could now be synchronized, or be subject to shared attributes. Interesting future directions for conferencing include exploring richer models of conference naming, characterizing, and browsing; other models of security; and shared user control of parameters during a conference, such as security attributes, recording function, video frame rate, and image size and resolution.

Summary

One of our goals was to determine if it was feasible to develop a videoconferencing prototype on a standard UNIX workstation. The software platform on which we built the application provided many of the services required for conferencing, and it was relatively easy to build a simple videoconference application for up to five conferees, running on a standard network.

While our distributed multimedia platform provided much of the system support needed to accomplish our goals, additional requirements are needed for a collaboration platform. For example both platforms need to provide applications with the ability to name network entities, such as people and devices. Additionally, a collaboration platform needs to provide the ability to reference conferences, or sessions. Both platforms need to be able to associate attributes with their entities, e.g., access permissions and whether the data need to be secure. Collaborative applications also need to have elements of a conference, such as the people and applications required, be part of its attributes. Both a multimedia and collaboration platform need to provide the resources for multiple displays on each workstation, but a collaborative platform must also provide the ability to deliver a source, such as the data from a camera, to multiple destinations. Both multimedia and collaborative applications require platform support to be "good network citizens." Both can benefit from data compression, but collaborative applications also require intelligent connection management.

A collaborative platform needs to provide some services not required by strictly multimedia applications. It must provide applications with support for negotiating the sharing of control of shared devices. Collaborative applications may have strict timeliness requirements for some data streams such as interactive audio. A collaborative platform also should be able to support the application-specific data of multiuser applications in a time-critical manner, just like video and audio.

Acknowledgments

First and foremost, I must acknowledge the contributions of my two COCO project collaborators, David Gedye and John Tang. Their insights and contributions were and are innumerable, and always invaluable. I also am grateful for the contributions, both in thought and practice, of our colleagues on the AMP team, led by Greg McLaughlin. In addition I thank Roger Calnan, Trevor Morris, Alan Ruberg, Rab Hagy, and Brian Raymor for guidance and comments on this paper.

References

Borning, A., and M. Travers, "Two Approaches to Casual Interaction Over Computer and Video Networks," SIGCHI 1991 Proceedings, pp. 13–19.

Byte magazine, December 1985 issue on Computer Conferencing, vol. 10, no. 13.

Calnan, Roger S., "The Advanced Multimedia Platforms Project," 2nd International Workshop on Network and Operating System Support for Digital Audio and Video.

Casner, S., K. Seo, W. Edmond, and C. Topolcic, "N-Way Conferencing with Packet Video," Technical Report ISI/RS-90-252, USC/Information Sciences Institute, Marina del Rey, CA, 1990.

Deering, Stephen E., and David R. Cheriton, "Multicast Routing in Datagram Internets and Extended LANs," *ACM Transactions of Computer Systems,* vol. 8, no. 2, May 1990, pp. 85–110.

Isaacs, Ellen, A., and John C. Tang, "What Video Can and Can't Do for Collaboration: A Case Study," Proceedings of the ACM Multimedia '93 Conference, August 1993, Anaheim, CA, in press.

Lantz, K. A., "An Experiment in Integrated Multimedia Conferencing," Proceedings of the ACM Conference on Computer-Supported Cooperative Work, ACM, NY, NY, 1986, pp. 267–275.

Liebhold, Michael, and Eric M. Hoffert, "Toward an Open Environment for Digital Video," *Communications of the ACM,* vol. 34, no. 4, April 1991, pp. 103–112.

Olson, Margrethe H., and Sara A. Bly, "The Portland Experience: A Report on a Distributed Research Group," *International Journal of Man-Machine Systems,* vol. 34, no. 2, February 1991, pp. 211–228. Reprinted: *Computer-Supported Cooperative Work and Groupware,* Saul Greenberg, ed., Academic Press, London, 1991, pp. 81–98.

Rodden, Tom, and Gordon Blair, "CSCW and Distributed Systems: The Problem of Control," Proceedings of the Second European Conference on Computer-Supported Cooperative Work–ECSCW '91, Kluwer Academic Publishers, Bannon Robinson and Schmidt, eds., 1991, pp. 49–64.

Root, Robert W., "Design of a Multi-Media Vehicle for Social Browsing," Proceedings of the Conference on Computer-Supported Cooperative Work, Portland, OR, September 1988, pp. 25–38.

Tang, John C., and Ellen A. Isaacs, "Why Do Users Like Video? Studies of Multimedia-Supported Collaboration," *Computer Supported Cooperative Work: An International Journal,* in press. Also available as Technical Report TR-92-5 from Sun Microsystems Laboratories, Inc.

Vin, Harrick M., Polle T. Zellweger, Daniel C. Swinehart, and P. Venkat Rangan, "Multimedia Conferencing in the Etherphone Environment," *IEEE Computer,* vol. 24, no. 10, October 1991, pp. 69–79.

35

Voice-Recognition and Voice-Response Systems

Mike McGonagle

In the movie *Star Trek IV: The Return Home,* Chief Engineer Scott sits down in front of a twentieth-century computer and prepares to communicate with it. He addresses it: "Computer." Once more, with feeling, when it doesn't respond: "Com*pu*ter!" Dr. McCoy hands him the mouse and Scotty turns it over in his hand and speaks into it: "Hello, computer!" At this point his host says, "Just use the keyboard," to which Scotty dryly replies, "The keyboard. How quaint."

While this scenario is humorous in its comparison of current versus futuristic computer usage, it is typical of almost all literary and movie references to computer interfaces in the future. Users will be able to talk normally to computers, and they will not only understand but respond verbally as well. Predicting the distant future is a difficult and often frustrating activity. Better just to ask, how close are we to this vision today? Can we build a system today that would satisfy Chief Engineer Scott?

Introduction

This chapter will discuss the technologies that enable computers to understand spoken language and to respond in kind: voice recognition and voice response, respectively. Already there are many examples of this technology in use, mostly in "consumer" sorts of applications such as banking, telephone dialing, VCR control, etc. As the quality of these systems has improved, they also have been applied to providing handicapped people with access to computers, and to educational areas such as foreign language training. Since the focus of this chapter is on multimedia, we will touch on such applications only briefly in our discussion of technology.

Principally we will discuss voice recognition and response as general interface options in building multimedia systems, as input/output mechanisms to be used in conjunction with or instead of keyboards, mice, touchscreens, graphic displays, sound files, etc. This is a logical extension for many multimedia systems, since this technology is supported by many of the commercially available sound cards. The main focus of the technology examples and applications dealt with in this chapter will be on the PC, but this technology is equally available on MacIntosh, UNIX, and many other platforms. Although the chapter will mention and discuss several voice-recognition and -response products, it does not intend to be a comprehensive product comparison. Products are mentioned in order to illustrate various features, and the inclusion or exclusion of a specific product or company should not be construed to be either an endorsement or rejection of them. A list of the companies mentioned in this chapter, with addresses and phone numbers, is included at the end of the chapter, to assist anyone interested in investigating this technology in more detail.

The vision inherent in voice recognition and response is one of computer systems that are able to fully understand normal spoken language for command and data input, and that are able to formulate responses in the same way, speaking in a natural-sounding (i.e., nonmechanical) voice. This is a natural extension in the development of human-computer interfaces. Humans communicate principally via spoken language, with writing being used primarily when the communication is not going to be immediate and interactive. As our use of computers has evolved from batch-oriented processing to real-time, interactive computation, the interest in building voice-oriented computer interfaces has naturally increased.

Man's interest in "talking automata" dates from ancient times, when statues were made to speak via hidden voice tubes. This fascination continued down through the Middle Ages, and through the early decades of this century. For an interesting discussion of these historical efforts, I would refer readers to Chapter 2 of Gordon Pelton's book *Voice Processing* (see the References at the end of the chapter). Since the advent of computers in the middle of this century, the focus of these efforts to create speaking and hearing automata has been shifted to the computer.

There has been academic and research interest in speech generation and recognition for several decades, and there have even been commercial products in these areas for much longer than most people realize. Actually, over the last several years there has been a minor explosion of products in these areas. This explosion has been fueled in part by the availability of general sound-processing boards, such as the Sound Blaster from Creative Labs and the ProAudio Spectrum 16 from Media Vision, which have tremendously increased the number of workstations able to produce quality sound. Once quality sound was available, it was a natural step to go beyond playing music and sound snippets to processing speech input and output.

Users want speech processing, and vendors see it as a way to make their sound-board products more desirable in the business world. There are now several software-only products available that provide speech synthesis or voice recognition via any number of the most popular sound boards. While most of the high-end systems still come with their own specialized hardware, many of these vendors also offer a lower-end version of their product that works with industry-standard sound boards. This trend can be expected to continue, providing users with increasingly robust and affordable products.

A brief analysis of human-to-human spoken interaction will point out some of the serious challenges to accomplishing voice recognition and response.

In conversation, our voices rise and fall to give emphasis, pose questions, etc. This characteristic is called *prosody*. The prosodic features of what we say often convey more information than the actual words themselves. Anyone who has ever repeatedly said "Come here" to a stubborn dog has had first-hand exposure to this effect. Although the dog may recognize the wave forms that compose the phrase "Come here," it is the tone of the speaker's voice and which word receives the emphasis that tell the obstinate animal whether it is in trouble or not. Some words even change their meaning under different pronunciations. *Permit* is a noun with the emphasis placed on the first syllable, but a verb when the emphasis is shifted to the second syllable. Anyone who has ever had to read a passage aloud has probably experienced the embarrassment of misemphasizing a word or phrase, thereby completely changing the meaning of a sentence or rendering it as gibberish. Properly dealing with these prosodic features is critical to the production of human-sounding computer speech.

In listening, we often use our visual sense as well as our auditory one. This is especially important in determining who is actually being addressed. So too, the computer has difficulty detecting that you have turned your back to it and are speaking to someone in the doorway to your office, not still giving it commands. (In a scene from *Star Trek: The Next Generation,* Worf turns away from the computer console and says to Data, "You mean it's alive?", to which the computer answers: "Insufficient data to support that conclusion." Worf then turns and says acidly to the computer: "I wasn't talking to you!" Apparently this problem has not been solved even in the twenty-third century!) In listening, we also determine the meaning of words and phrases by the context in which they are used. For example, a person can easily tell whether a speaker said "I'd like *to*" or "I'd like *two*" based on the context of the conversation.

The correction of misunderstandings, whether between humans or between a human and a computer, is also an important component of any spoken interface mechanism. People normally do not understand 100 percent of what is said to them. To compensate for this, they take a guess at what was meant based on the context in which something was said. For example, the phrases "wreck a nice beach" and "recognize speech" are similar-sounding, but obviously differentiable based on the context in which they appear. In face-to-face communication, we can interrupt the speaker to ask him or her to repeat, or to clarify, what was said. This poses problems when building a human-to-computer interface, partially because of the difficulty in modeling both the interaction and the context awareness, and partially because of the loss in accuracy that may occur when comparing voice input with normal keyboard and mouse interaction. While a voice-driven system has great appeal due to its natural and intuitive feel, if it means that our work becomes more error-prone, it will not be used.

It is these interface-oriented challenges that are in many cases more difficult to overcome than the mechanics of word or phrase recognition and synthesis. Therefore, the primary focus of current systems is on those applications in which the interface can be sufficiently well defined so as to limit these problems, rather than on the free-form communications depicted in the science-fiction literature. But even working within these limitations, voice recognition and response have tremendous potential today, as interface options, to build effective and user-friendly systems.

Technology Overview

Voice recognition

Before beginning our discussion of applications, a brief review of the technology and the terms used is in order. This will allow us to more accurately categorize and compare products, and to look at how they fit into different application areas.

In the voice-recognition area, products typically are categorized as utilizing either *continuous* or *discrete* recognition, as being able to handle either a small or large vocabulary, and as either *speaker-dependent* or *speaker-independent*. Normal human speech is continuous, with an unlimited vocabulary, and speaker-independent, but in many applications none of these characteristics is required.

In products that utilize discrete recognition, the speaker must pause briefly between words or phrases, the delay normally in the range of a few milliseconds. This type of system usually can recognize as single entities either individual words or short phrases. In products that utilize continuous recognition, the speaker can talk normally without pausing between words/phrases, and the system is able to pick out the words that were spoken from this continuous stream. In a voice-dictation system, this would mean that all of the words were recognized and processed, whereas in a voice-command system only the *command* words would be picked out of a continuous stream of speech, all other words being ignored. Because of the difficulty inherent in continuous human speech in detecting word boundaries, discrete word systems are much easier to implement and generally more accurate. On the other hand since this is not a natural speaking style, they can be awkward to use in those situations (e.g., dictation) where a continuous mode of speech normally is used.

Vocabulary size in voice-recognition systems is generally categorized as small or large, with the former being under 1000 words/phrases and the latter above it. This delineation is important not only because of the obvious difference in the number of words recognized, but also because it requires changes in the way the system is set up. Several commercially available systems manage several vocabularies, organized in a tree-structured fashion. When a command is recognized that starts or returns to a different application, the voice-recognition software replaces the current vocabulary with one for that specific application. This mechanism allows each individual vocabulary to be limited in size, while still supporting a large number of diverse applications. Vocabulary size can be an important consideration, since processing time, as well as the resources required for recognition, can grow in a nonlinear fashion as vocabulary size increases. In addition the *confusability* level of the system, i.e., the amount of difficulty the recognition mechanism has in differentiating similar words, also goes up rapidly as vocabulary size grows.

The difference between speaker-dependent and speaker-independent systems is fairly self-explanatory. In the former case, the system needs to be trained to recognize each user's individual voice patterns, while the latter type of system contains a general voice model that is meant to allow any user to be understood. Given all of the differences in accent, pitch, inflection, etc., speaker independence is a difficult challenge, and most of the commercially available systems are speaker-dependent. While most provide a generic voice template that users can attempt to utilize, they normally provide much better recognition rates if users take the time to train them for their individual speech patterns.

The type of training these speaker-dependent systems require varies according to the specific system and vocabulary size. Most small-vocabulary systems require the user to repeat each word a number of times. This information then is used to create both a model of the word, and a *variability factor*. This last element helps the recognition engine to take into account changes in pronunciation, since each utterance of a word will differ slightly.

As an example of this, Fig. 35.1 shows the waveform generated by three repetitions of the word *multimedia,* each said in succession. As you can see, they are similar but not identical. In order for a voice-recognition system to work consistently, each of these waveforms must come to be recognized as the word *multimedia.*

Large-vocabulary systems, by their very nature, usually require a different training mechanism. Repeating several thousand words several times each would be both time-consuming and of dubious value, given the effect of overuse on the user's voice. It also would not reflect the way in which many large-vocabulary systems perform the recognition task, since they often base their recognition on elements smaller than a word such as syllables or phonemes.

Phonemes are the smallest distinguishable sounds in a dialect of a language. Each phoneme actually represents a family of sounds, since the actual pronunciation of a specific phoneme varies according to the surrounding phonemes, an effect called *coarticulation.* A specific instance of a phoneme as

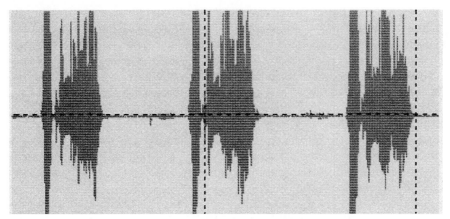

Figure 35.1 Waveform of three repetitions of the word *multimedia.*

spoken is called an *allophone*. Phonemes are important, since there are far fewer of them than there are words in a given language. Only around 40 phonemes are required to speak in the English language, which is comprised of over 40,000 words. For a more thorough discussion and analysis of the mechanics of speech production, I would refer the reader to either Gordon Pelton's, *Voice Processing* or Chris Rowden's *Speech Processing* (see References section at end of chapter).

The training of systems that base their recognition on phonemes, or similar entities, typically involves the repetition of a series of words, phrases, and/or sentences that allows the recognition system to build a voice model for these subword units. Undertraining of any speaker-dependent system can lead to very unsatisfactory results, so care should be taken that training is thorough. Retraining of the system also may be required occasionally, due either to changes in the user's voice caused perhaps by a cold or hay fever, or to a change in equipment, such as a different microphone.

It also is important to use a normal voice when training the system. Many people, when they think of "voice training," think of teaching a young child to speak. In the latter case most people will speak slowly and clearly, using careful enunciation, and may even speak in a louder-than-normal tone. This is precisely the wrong approach to training a voice-recognition system, for the system needs to be able to recognize the user's normal, everyday speaking voice. Training in an artificially "careful" voice may actually reduce the accuracy of the system.

A fairly recent development is the introduction of *speaker-adaptive* systems. A speaker-adaptive system is constantly updating its word models based on the actual speaking patterns employed during use. This can allow an operator to start using the system sooner, since it can shorten the formal training time required, and it also helps to build word models that represent true speech patterns. It can be difficult to get people to relax and speak naturally during training, as just mentioned, which often means that the system is being trained to listen to a different voice than that which will be employed during actual usage. The current feeling in the industry is that a speaker-adaptive system, built on top of a basic speaker-independent model, offers better recognition accuracy than the strictly speaker-dependent system.

Voice response

In the voice-response arena, systems are divided into *synthesized* versus *digitized* (or *recorded*) voice systems. In the latter case, words and/or phrases are spoken, recorded, indexed, and saved. These speech fragments then are pieced together by the application to form the spoken response. Chris Rowden, in his book *Speech Processing,* refers to this technology as *copy synthesis,* so as to differentiate it from the capture and playback of complete, unfragmented, digitized voice messages, as in voice-annotation systems. Although the vocabulary that can be handled is limited by the storage requirements of the recorded speech segments, the quality of the speech usually is very high, since it is actual recorded human speech. Extending the vocabulary of a digitized voice system can be a problem if the same person is not available to record the new phrases. Mixing fragments recorded by different speakers may be obvious and therefore distracting to the users.

For the most part this chapter will deal with the other option, synthesized speech, since it seems to have much more applicability to the building of multimedia interfaces. In general, synthesized-speech systems allow a much larger vocabulary, unlimited in some applications, but their quality is limited by the quality of the synthesis hardware/software. At the low end, the voice produced is very mechanical-sounding, but higher-end systems provide much more control over both the quality and the characteristics (i.e., sex, pitch, tone) of the voice.

All of these systems either have rules for pronunciation that they use to determine how a given word should sound, or are table-based, in which case each word is looked up in a pronunciation dictionary. Many current systems are hybrids, using a combination of rules in conjunction with a basic pronunciation dictionary. The quality of a speech-synthesis system is directly related to the robustness of these rules, and in order to account for English's many exceptions to the rules most speech-synthesis systems allow the user to define entries in an *exception dictionary.* The pronunciation for a given word is placed in this dictionary, usually specified phonetically, and the system will look there first when attempting to pronounce a word. The system may provide a basic set of exception words, but it will be up to the user to load any special technical words or, especially, peoples' names, since this latter group frequently require foreign rules of pronunciation.

In order for a text-to-speech synthesis system to be well accepted, it must provide the following:

- *Correct pronunciation.* Because of the importance of speech in our lives, people tend to be very critical of a speech-synthesis system that consistently mispronounces words. Mispronunciations also can prove distracting, drawing the listener's attention away from the content of the message and actually lowering the effectiveness of the system. Rowden describes the problems in this area as "related to the irregular correspondence of the written form of the language, the orthography, to the sounds of the spoken form, the phonology." While he is speaking of British, as opposed to American, English, the statement holds true for both. He cites an example of this by comparing the written representation, versus the spoken pronunciation, of the syllable *cam* in the following four words:

1. cam

2. came

3. Cambridge

4. cameo

- *Intelligent interpretation of content.*   In a free-form text-to-speech system, it is critical that the speech-synthesis system be able to correctly handle nonword items such as abbreviations, numbers, symbols, etc. The speech engine also needs to be able to differentiate the end of an abbreviation from the end of a sentence. Rowden cites five sentences as an example of how various elements such as these should be handled. They are:

1. Kiteflying is such fun, I'd do it all day!

2. Mr. Smith lives in St. George St.

3. 121,040,011 is a large number, $65,000 is a 'city salary,' 508-229-4980 is a 'phone number.'

4. World War II broke out on 3/9/39; will NATO prevent another one?

5. I arrived at 8:00 and stayed till 3:30.

To get an idea of how one commercial system handles these, take a look at how Monologue for Windows (a description of this product will come later) read each of these sentences. Monologue is a very low-end system, but did a fairly good job on these sentences. The results were these:

1. *Kiteflying* was pronounced more like *kitfling,* but Rowden anticipated that that word would be a problem. Inserting a space, i.e., making it *kite flying,* or placing it in the exception dictionary handled the problem.

2. This sentence was pronounced almost perfectly. *Mr.* was expanded to *mister,* the first St. became *saint* and the second became *street.* But the system hesitated at each period, treating them as an end-of-sentence marker.

3. The phone number was interpreted as an arithmetic string (i.e., five hundred eight minus two hundred twenty-nine...) but the other num-

bers were handled correctly, including the inclusion of the word *dollars* in the appropriate place.

4. II was not read as a roman numeral and so was spelled (i.e., /ay/ /ay/), but the rest of the sentence was handled correctly. 3/9/39 became March ninth, nineteen hundred thirty-nine, and NATO was correctly pronounced.

5. The system didn't recognize 8:00 or 3:30 as being in time format, so it read each component of them separately (i.e., eight zero zero, and three thirty).

Of the 15 items identified in Rowden's analysis as points of interest in this test suite, Monologue handled 9 correctly without having to resort to adding items to the dictionary or respelling items.

■ *Correct prosody.* Since this information is not inherent in the text but usually is supplied by the reader based on knowledge of the material or application of common knowledge rules (e.g., how to properly change inflection to convey a question), speech-synthesis systems often can sound flat and monotone. Since a flat, monotone voice is a cultural trigger to the listener that the information is boring, the listener can be tuned out simply by the presentation.

■ *Nonmonotone presentation.* This is different from prosody, which has accepted rules for inflection. This category relates more to the voice control that an experienced speaker uses, varying speed and loudness not to convey information but to keep the audience listening. These characteristics generally are referred to as *delivery,* especially when applied to actors.

The above criteria are most important for a free-form text-to-speech system. In the case of a system that needs only a limited vocabulary, the application can do things, such as spell words phonetically, that will make up for shortcomings in the underlying speech engine.

Application Overview

Voice response

In the voice-response area, applications can be roughly divided into two areas: *computer reading,* and *interactive voice response (IVR).* The latter generally is associated with interactive telephone-response systems, but the same type of applications can just as easily be built around an interactive computer interface as the phone.

Computer reading. This area encompasses a number of different actual and potential applications, ranging from reading free-form text, as would be found in a memo or a mail message, to proofreading applications that deal with a more limited vocabulary, as might be found in a typical spreadsheet. To date,

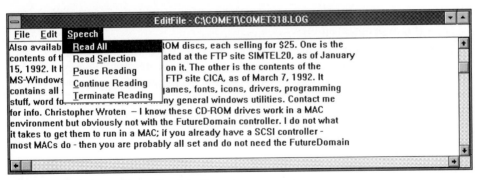

Figure 35.2   Sample speaking-editor interface.

free-form text-to-speech reading applications have most commonly been found in systems built for handicapped users. The main reason for this is that the current technology has difficulty producing a pleasant, non-machine-sounding voice. The technology therefore is suitable for providing access for people who could not use the system otherwise, but a visual interface is preferable when at all possible.

Reading a passage aloud does have its uses, since often it is easier to pick out grammatical problems by hearing them than by looking at them. Spelling errors also can become obvious when the speech-synthesis system pronounces the misspelled word. As an example of this type of application, let's look at a speaking text editor that I've built as a test system for working with text-to-speech technology. The basic interface is shown in Figure 35.2, illustrating the speech options that are available.

In building this application I used ProVoice for Windows from First Byte, described more fully later in the chapter. This product, which provides a programmatic interface for performing text-to-speech conversion, allowed computer reading to be easily added on top of the normal editing functions. The total code was approximately 100 lines, on top of that already in place for the base application. The editor code uses functions provided by ProVoice to first parse the text sentence by sentence. Each sentence then is converted to a phonetic string, which is passed to the speech engine to be said. An even simpler interface could be constructed that would just pass the entire block of text and have it spoken as a single step. However by breaking it out the way I have, I provide the ability to interrupt the computer after each sentence. Otherwise the user would have to wait until the entire block of text had been completely spoken, which clearly could become annoying if it was a large section of text. This points up an important consideration when purchasing or building a text-to-speech system: How easy is it to interrupt when it is speaking?

The same type of functionality illustrated in this simple example can be added to many other products, even without "programming," by using inter-process communications mechanisms such as DDE under Microsoft Windows, or Sun Solaris's ToolTalk on Sun Sparcstations. Some third-party applications provide powerful macro-writing capabilities, which potentially could also be used to extend the applications you are using today and allow them to perform text-to-speech conversion. Some products, such as Microsoft's Window Sound System and First Byte's Monologue for Windows, provide this type of proofreading capability, for spreadsheets, as part of the product. When using this feature, the current cell or selected range is read directly from the spreadsheet. This can be a great aid in checking a row or column of numbers to ensure that they were entered correctly, since it allows the user to validate the data in an "eyes-free" mode rather than continually shift from the monitor to a sheet of numbers.

Interactive voice response.   The area of interactive voice response holds a great deal of potential for building interactive, multimedia-oriented interfaces. On the one hand there are an increasing number of small devices, ranging from laptops to personal digital assistants (PDAs) coming into everyday use. Screen real estate is a valuable commodity with these devices, and therefore IVR offers you the ability to convey important information without having to display it. Even on desktop systems with full-size monitors, our visual senses often are inundated. This problem becomes especially acute when dealing with graphic-intensive applications such as CAD/CAM, or drawing applications. Many of these applications require that attention be focused on the spot where you are currently drawing, even as they provide coordinate information at the bottom of the display.

Anyone who has had the experience of trying to accurately position an object while shifting his or her eyes back and forth between two areas can appreciate the benefit of having the coordinate information provided orally. Adding speech synthesis to applications in this manner can greatly increase their usability, and can be done easily by utilizing existing text-to-speech technology. Concerns about mispronunciation and monotone delivery are greatly reduced for this type of limited application.

A related but unique potential area for speech synthesis is in providing warning and alert messages. The current range of computer beeps and bells is becoming greatly overworked as a means of gaining a user's attention. As a user, I can't tell if my workstation beeped to say that my file transfer has been completed or that I received a mail message, or to alert me that a network node has failed. If I'm concentrating on some other task, I may not want to be interrupted in the first case, but may in the last two. A solution that would have the computer announce which event has occurred has been proposed by several people, even to the point of giving the voice different characteristics for different events. Today's workstations assume that they already have the user's undivided attention, but as the ways in which we use computers change, this assumption increasingly will become less valid. Our computers will need to learn to get our attention, just as that visitor standing in your office doorway does.

Voice recognition.   In the voice-recognition area, applications may be divided into two categories: *voice command* and *voice dictation*. Voice-command systems allow a user to run the computer via voice, either in conjunction with or as a replacement for the keyboard and/or mouse. The entire system can be operated by voice command, customized voice-driven applications can be built, or both options can be supported. Voice-dictation systems basically are voice-driven typewriters. There are systems currently in use in areas such as medical-report dictation, and by handicapped people unable to use the keyboard and/or mouse. The differentiation between these two types of systems is important not only because of the variance in usage, but more so because of the distinctions in the criteria for selecting an appropriate system. The two types of systems, at least as we are dealing with them here, can further be defined by the following characteristics:

- *Vocabulary size.* In a voice-command system, this can run from the handful of commands needed to operate a highly specialized application to the several hundred commands needed to operate Microsoft Windows as defined in the Microsoft Sound System. This means that a small-vocabulary system can be used, and is in fact more desirable due to reduced processing time, confusability concerns, and resource requirements. A voice-dictation system, on the other hand, generally will require a large-vocabulary system if it is to be useful. This may range from moderate size, for a restricted-use voice-dictation system such as medical diagnosis, to unlimited size, for a "voice typewriter" style of application.

- *Continuous versus discrete word/phrase recognition.* In a voice-command system, the user generally is issuing short, specific commands, with a pause at the end of each. This means that a discrete word/phrase system can be used and it will still feel natural. The restriction of having to pause between words in a voice-dictation system could lead to reduced productivity, as the users were forced to adjust their working style to the limitations of the tool. Therefore continuous recognition would seem to be far preferable in voice-dictation systems. There is a certain amount of debate on this point since, as Biermann et al (1985) hypothesize, "Users seem to be able to learn to speak machine-recognizable discrete speech more easily than they are able to speak machine-recognizable connected speech."

- *Speaker dependence/independence.* In voice-command applications such as telephone dialing, speaker independence is mandatory, but in the types of multimedia interface developments being addressed here, most voice-command systems will have a well-defined set of users. Using a speaker-dependent system is therefore desirable because of its higher accuracy rate, since voice-command systems must operate in a near error-free mode, as opposed to voice dictation, where the minimum goal is to perform better than a human typist. In the voice-dictation area, the issue is more how a speaker-dependent system can adequately be trained, given the assumption of a large vocabulary.

Now let's look at these areas of voice command and voice dictation separately.

Voice command. Accuracy is of paramount importance in building a general, voice-driven user interface. As was mentioned earlier, any significant increase in the error rate of the work produced will often lead to the new interface being scrapped in favor of the more reliable keyboard and/or mouse approach. There are several types of errors that can occur in a voice-command system:

- *Failure to recognize a spoken command.* In this situation, the system does not believe that what was said matches any of its known commands. While this may just mean that the command must be repeated, it can quickly lead to frustration. The natural tendency is to repeat the command with increased emphasis, which may make it that much less likely that the command will be recognized. This is another example of a fundamental difference between conversing with people and talking to a computer.

- *Misrecognition of a spoken command.* In this case the operator issues one command but the system mistakenly takes it for another (i.e., the user says, "Page down," and the system hears "Page up") This mistake, often a result of poor training, can range from the slightly annoying to the catastrophic, depending on what action the computer carries out. Since a voice interface is inherently less accurate than keyboard/mouse input, care should be taken to ensure that there are confirmation dialogues associated with "dangerous" actions such as file deletion.

- *Recognition of a spoken command when none was given.* This error may occur because someone else said something that the computer picked up and interpreted, or may be caused by the operator answering the phone or turning to talk to someone, without remembering that the computer is desperately attempting to interpret what they are saying as valid commands. As with the previous point, this mistake can range from the slightly annoying to the disastrous. To handle circumstances such as these, most systems have a simple mechanism that turns off recognition. The challenge to you, the operator, is to remember to use them!

Training, or retraining, can go a long way toward the reducing of these errors. The equipment being used, especially the microphone, also can be an important factor in this. Quality noise-canceling and/or unidirectional microphones are those that most voice-recognition system suppliers recommend. In my own work, I have gotten the best results with a relatively inexpensive headset microphone. It picks up very little outside noise, and the fact that it is a constant distance from my mouth helps to reduce the variability in my voice. The speed of the underlying system also can be a factor, at least with some voice-recognition packages. I have experienced a difference in accuracy of more than 10 percent when moving from a 386/33 to an equivalent 486/33 machine, given the greater accuracy of the faster machine.

Many voice-command systems operate by issuing a series of keystrokes that correspond to the command that was detected. Examples of such systems are the Microsoft Sound System, Media Vision's ExecuVoice, and Command Corporation's IN3 product. This is a very direct and intuitive way of adding voice command on top of an existing interface, such as Microsoft Windows. Since this type of installation is becoming so popular, let's take a moment to ask some of the questions you will want to ask when you are evaluating products.

How easy is it to turn off recognition if I need to converse with someone else? Some systems have a command-bar button that allows the recognition state to be toggled on or off via a mouse click. Some also support turning recognition off and on via voice command. This does not actually turn voice recognition off, but rather limits the valid recognizable vocabulary to a single phrase, which will turn full recognition back on. This is a very convenient feature, although care must be taken not to turn it on inadvertently when speaking on the phone or to another person.

How are commands executed? Some current systems have "macro" commands, such as EXEC, that allow a program to be started without having to go through the "FILE, RUN..." sequence, while others require that each command be converted into a specific series of keystrokes. This latter approach can be bothersome if the system handles these keystrokes as if they actually had been typed at the keyboard, since some people may find the flickering menus distracting.

How well is the system able to handle background noise? This may be only a minor consideration in a typical office environment, but it can be critical to the usability of a system intended for a factory, sawmill, etc. In general, if a system is going to be deployed in one of these noisy environments, a higher-end system, such as that produced by Verbex, will be needed.

Does the voice-recognition system interfere with the operation of other parts of the system? Some of the lower-end products, at least in the Microsoft Windows environment, do not allow sounds to be played while the voice-recognition software is active. This is an unacceptable situation, since it forces the user to choose between having the system listen or speak.

How responsive is the system? This can be a function of either the basic workstation configuration or the voice recognition software, or a combination of the two. When you are deciding on a system, both of these factors will need to be taken into consideration, and tests run that use the actual target configuration. The ease of use of a voice-command interface will mean little to you if it is appreciably slower than your current keyboard-and-mouse usage.

How easy is it to add commands, and to train the vocabulary? Most systems seem to have a simple, easy-to-use training mechanism. However, with some, if the word model becomes "corrupt," as it may if the user mistakenly says the wrong word during training, the only remedy is to delete and reload the command. This is due to the fact that the existing word-pronunciation model, based on a different word, is so different from the correct one that the system cannot reconcile the two, thereby causing it to reject new attempts to retrain the command with the correct word.

In terms of adding new commands, most systems make it easy for an individual user to perform this function. In a corporate environment, however, vocabulary definition may be performed centrally and then distributed to the individual workstations. Most of the low-end systems do not support this concept very well, but some of the higher-end ones do allow a vocabulary to be defined and trained as independent tasks.

Putting Together a Voice-Command System

In this section we will describe the six steps you should take to build a voice-command system. As a real-world example of the application of each of these steps, I will be citing a multimedia technology demonstration system built for the Computer Corporation of America (CCA). This system was intended to demonstrate the integration of CCA's client-server tools with state-of-the-art personal computer technology, including voice recognition. The system was set up as a travel-planning aid, displaying a series of maps and, ultimately, detailed information about specific locales. The user could issue voice commands to navigate through the maps and the detailed information windows.

The six steps are as follows:

1. *Decide whether the system will support multimode input (i.e., keyboard, mouse, touchscreen, pen, etc.), or whether it will be a voice-only system.* This will determine what options are available to correct those errors that arise from misrecognition.

In our example system, the decision was made to support keyboard, mouse, and touchscreen input, as well as voice recognition. This was done so as to have an adequate mechanism to handle voice-command errors and to allow users who had not trained the speaker-dependent system to access the application.

2. *Define the vocabulary for the application.* If possible, this should be set up in a hierarchical fashion, since many products will support this type of structure. What this means is that certain commands are valid only after other commands (see Fig. 35.3 for an example of a hierarchical vocabulary structure, taken from the Microsoft Sound System's Voice Pilot). This allows the total vocabulary to be divided into a series of subvocabularies, only one of which is valid at any point in time. Therefore the voice-recognition software can limit its search for the correct word or phrase at each point, improving accuracy and response time. The initial vocabulary for the example system was around 45 words/phrases and is shown in Fig. 35.4. Because of its small size, it originally was set up without any structure, but the need to use the same phrase to perform different actions based on the application context eventually dictated a hierarchical structure.

3. *Choose the hardware/software products that will be used to support the voice-recognition aspects of the application.* This decision will be based on factors such as vocabulary size, speaker dependence/independence, operat-

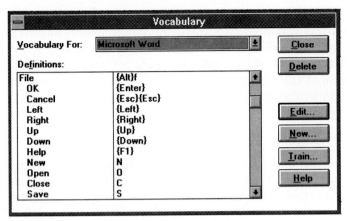

Figure 35.3   Hierarchical structure of a vocabulary.

Amsterdam	Exit	New York	San Diego	Yes
Back	Good Bye	Next	San Francisco	
Baja	Help	Next Window	Size	
Boston	Maximize	No	Switch To	
Cabo	Menu Bar	OK	Tab	
Cabo San Luca	Mexico	Page Down	U.S.	
Cancel	Minimize	Page Up	UK	
Caribbean	Move	Paris	United States	
England	Nashville	Previous	utah	
Enter	national parks	Previous Window	Window	
Europe	new orleans	Restore	wyoming	

Figure 35.4   Sample application vocabulary.

ing-environment characteristics, etc. A discussion of several commercial products for voice command will be presented later, in order to compare their features.

The example system had a small vocabulary and was intended to be used in a controlled, relatively quiet environment. It also was intended to have a limited number of predetermined users, so a speaker-dependent implementation was preferable. Since the system also required a general sound-support capability, the Microsoft Windows Sound System was selected. It contains a sound card as well as voice-command software, and allowed our custom vocabulary to be created and supported. It was also, at the time, one of the only inexpensive options available, although of late this has changed dramatically.

4. *Select a microphone to use with the system.*   If you are to make the right choice, you will need to take into account the operating environment of the system (i.e., hands-free operations, background noise, etc.), and also to ensure that the microphone chosen does not introduce recognition errors into the system by inconsistent operation, picking up background noise, etc.

Since the example system supported keyboard, mouse, and touchscreen input as well as voice, a hand-held microphone was deemed unreasonable. Testing showed that accuracy was better with a microphone that attached to the user (i.e., lapel or headset) than with a stationary type. Fashion concerns dictated the use of the lapel microphone.

5. *Assuming that a speaker-dependent system is being used, remember that it must be trained by the user community.* Initially there were two users for our example system, and in order to ensure the highest possible accuracy, separate profiles were created for both the lapel and headset microphones, giving a total of four "users." Training of each profile took only 5 to 10 minutes.

6. *Put the finishing touches on the miscellaneous aspects of the system.* In our example system, this mainly involved selecting the proper PC configuration to use. Testing yielded much better results using a 486-based system over a 386, so the former was chosen.

As we ran the example system cited here, the voice-command software performed very well. Recognition was in the 90 percent range, which was good although not perfect, and the system's responsiveness was excellent, working by voice as fast as with any of the other input modes. The one problem occurred when one of the operators was suffering nasal congestion due to a bout of hay fever. This required that we retrain the system in order to compensate for the change in voice characteristics, after which the system once again performed excellently.

This experience points up an important issue that real-world voice-recognition systems need to handle, since an individual's voice can change due to colds, allergies, etc. and also can have different tonal qualities at different times of day. The volume level of an individual's speech also changes in response to different situations. This problem is especially pronounced in voice-recognition systems when it becomes necessary to repeat commands.

It is only natural to add extra emphasis when repeating a command, but with most systems this reduces the chances of successful recognition. Retraining our small-vocabulary example system was easy, but a large-vocabulary system should help you to avoid retraining by having greater flexibility to handle changes in an individual's voice.

Thus far our discussion of voice-command systems has focused on interfaces that convert a recognized word into a series of keystrokes, and in fact this is how most of these systems operate. There may be situations in which a program calls for direct access to the commands spoken, as when there is no keyboard and/or display involved. Examples of this include mail sorting, manufacturing control systems, and financial trading, where a direct programmatic interface is desired of the kind supplied by Verbex Voice Systems, IBM, and Dragon Systems. In a custom application development effort, using a direct programmatic interface may make for a more intuitive, voice-oriented interface, as opposed to attempting to overlay voice commands on top of a morass of existing menus, buttons, and dialogue boxes.

Voice dictation

When people think of voice-recognition systems, most commonly they think of voice dictation, in which the computer is able to transcribe everything that is said to it. Although systems of that kind (those produced by Dragon Systems, for example) have been available for a few years, they have not been widely implemented. This is partly because of cost (these systems are expensive) and partly because of the interface (they are speaker-dependent, discrete word systems). This requires an investment in training the system, and an adjustment to speaking style in order to utilize the system. To date these systems have been most popular among handicapped users, where they are necessary in order to access the computer. Many of these folks are very happy with their voice-dictation systems and report that they have adjusted their speaking style without any problem, but most computer people have been reluctant to give up their keyboards.

This reluctance may begin to erode over the next few years, as advances in continuous-speech recognition, coupled with a continuing drop in the cost of technology, make voice dictation both more affordable and more usable. IBM's recent announcement of their Interactive Speech Server Series gives a good indication of the technological side of this trend, if not the economic. This system can accept dictation at a rate of 70 words per minute, which is much faster than most users can type, although slower than a skilled typist.

There are really two types of voice-dictation systems that can be envisioned, differentiated by where the user's attention is focused. In the classic voice-activated-typewriter case, the user is focused on the computer as well as on the material being input. This means that error correction can be immediate, and that the system can prompt the user for information in the case of an unrecognized or ambiguously recognized word. In the other case the user's attention is directed elsewhere, and he or she is basically "thinking out loud" so that the computer can capture those thoughts. An example of this type of system is the radiological dictation system that IBM markets in Italy. This application allows a radiologist to dictate a report while examining an X-ray film, and clearly it is important that the system not distract the user in the middle of dictating to ask for clarification. Errors, if they occur, would more appropriately be flagged and dealt with later, when possible. In both cases the recognition system may need to handle long pauses and unintended noise that the speaker may make while formulating his/her next thought.

These problems will crop up most frequently when the user's focus is on the creation of material, not the dictation of a document.

The challenges facing a voice-recognition system increase rapidly as the vocabulary size goes up, and as the system attempts to process continuous rather than discrete speech. This explains why there are relatively few voice-dictation systems in use, especially when compared to the burgeoning voice-command area. But as the technology continues to improve, this area will receive more and more attention.

Commercial Applications

Commercial applications are not the focus of this chapter, but it is appropriate to discuss them briefly, if for no other reason than that most people's first exposure to voice-recognition and voice-response systems will be in this arena. One of the common threads that runs through almost all of these applications is that they are telephone-oriented. This comes as no surprise, since what the telephone does well is to handle voice, both as input and output. It is not, however, a very good data-entry tool when having to use the keypad, as anyone who has ever had to type a long name into a voice-mail system can attest. As more and more services from banking to computer dating are developed around telephone access, the need to improve the overall user interface becomes increasingly important.

One of the first steps in telephone applications was the introduction of interactive voice response (IVR), which was in fact the technology that got this whole industry off the ground. Using IVR technology, systems could be built that provided the user with instructions at each step of the process, not to mention the information that was the eventual goal of the entire exercise. Most of these systems were and still are built using digitized voice technology. This is appropriate in telephone management applications, since the vocabulary generally is limited and the quality of the voice is of paramount concern. Some telephone applications, such as interactive catalogs, use synthesized speech because of the size and variability of the vocabulary that they must handle.

The next step, currently (1994) in full swing, is to add limited voice recognition to these systems. This is being done to improve the interface of some systems by limiting the amount of number-punching required, and also to provide access to these services from the 39 percent of homes and offices equipped with non-touchtone phones. Since these services are accessible by large numbers of people, speaker independence is required, but the fact that only a limited vocabulary is needed simplifies the problem greatly. Continuous-speech processing also is a requirement, since the general population will not adapt easily to a discrete-word speaking style. These systems can further be improved by the incorporation of word-spotting algorithms. Word-spotting allows the system to pick out or spot words within a continuous stream of speech, so that the system could pick out the account number if the user says, "Let's see...I think it's here. Okay. 81364."

Current product offerings of voice recognition in the commercial area already cover a wide range of applications. Customers accessing telephone-based services can now say their zip code, account number, etc. rather than punch it on the telephone's keypad. As another example, some cellular phone companies are offering a service that allows customers to place phone calls by voice command, to anywhere in the world, by saying the name of the person to be called. This is done by first dialing a central number that gives the customer access to the voice-recognition portion of the system. Field-testing of some of these systems has yielded accuracy rates of as high as 97 percent.

Another application of voice-recognition technology in the commercial area is in voice control. Examples of this include car phones that can make calls in a hands-free mode, by voice command, and the VCR voice controller. This latter device allows users to control their TVs and/or VCRs by speaking commands into a control unit, thereby simplifying the user interface greatly. As voice-recognition technology improves, expect to see more applications of this type. Providing nontechnical users with a simple, voice-driven interface to what is otherwise an intimidating and nonintuitive system will be an extremely well-received initiative.

There are many other examples of commercial or specialized uses of voice recognition and response, ranging from voice-alert systems that can dial a phone number and call for help to the voice-driven navigation system on an America's Cup yacht. We will not go into them here, but it should be noted that as computers steadily infiltrate our lives more and more, the technologies that they bring with them, such as voice recognition and response, also will play an ever-increasing role in our everyday lives.

Product Breakout

This section briefly will describe several products in both the voice-recognition and voice-response areas. This is done to give the reader some sense of the different features and characteristics to be found in commercial product offerings, not to compare or recommend them. For further and more current information, the reader should contact these companies directly.

Voice-response systems—digitized-speech systems

A great number of companies offer products in this area, but since most of them are focused on telephone management systems and are not targeted at general multimedia usage, I won't list them here. Still, there are some interesting developments in this market segment that are worth mentioning. The first is the joint interest shown by multimedia developers and telephone-management application-builders in editing digitized sound files. Right now the sound-file-editing companies seem to be focusing on one segment of the industry or the other, but undoubtedly this will change over time, thereby bringing more robust multimedia-editing packages to the market.

Another interesting development in digitized speech is the Smooth Talker product from Parity Software. This is a digitized voice system with a twist. It stores alternate pronunciations of words in its vocabulary, which allows different inflections to be used when using the same word in different contexts. For example, Smooth Talker would pronounce the word *two* differently in the phrases "ninety-two," and "two hundred and one."

Microsoft Corporation.   The Microsoft Windows Sound System Proofreader is the one product that it seemed appropriate to talk about in this section. Offered as part of the Microsoft Windows Sound System product, this component can be used to read to the user sections of a Microsoft Excel and/or Lotus 1-2-3 for Windows spreadsheet. It comes with digitized speech fragments to handle the type of data normally found in a spreadsheet, i.e., numeric data in different formats. It can be extended to recognize items, such as text strings, and play back a user-recorded speech fragment when one is encountered.

As with most digitized-speech systems, the quality of the voice is very good. The inclusion of user-recorded speech fragments can be somewhat distracting, since they utilize a different voice than the surrounding items, and even the digitized voice can sound somewhat mechanical and choppy due to the small fragments that are being strung together. For example, the entry "$1,086.49" would consist of the fragments

(one)(thousand)(eighty)(six)(dollars)

(and)(forty)(nine)(cents).

Despite this, the overall effect of this system is quite good.

Synthesized speech systems

Digital Equipment Corporation.   Digital Equipment Corporation produces DECTalk, a very flexible and high-quality speech-synthesis system. DECTalk is positioned more as a telephone management tool, but it also has the capability to be used as a general voice-response system. The DECTalk product gives the user control over a variety of the elements of the speech produced, such as

Male, female, or child's voice

Speaking rate (from 120 to 350 words per minute)

Baseline pitch

Pitch range

Breathiness

Smoothness

Head size

Forte

Laryngealization

Pauses

The ability to control all of these elements, along with the completeness of the rules used, allow a pleasant voice to be produced, although one readily identified as produced by a machine. The text to be spoken is passed to the DECTalk unit, which can be configured either as a separate, external box connected via a serial communications link or as a board within the PC. The external option makes DECTalk very flexible, in terms of its ability to be connected to a wide variety of systems.

First Byte.   First Byte produces Monologue for Windows, a very inexpensive (street price of less than $100) speech-synthesis system. There also is a version of Monologue that runs under DOS. Monologue for Windows, as well as ProVoice discussed next, works on any multimedia personal computer

(MPC)–compliant sound card. (It also can be used via the standard PC speaker, but on most PCs the quality of the voice produced in this manner is so poor that it is not a viable option.) The voice is mechanical, but clear and understandable, and the price will allow many users to get their first taste of voice response without having to spend an arm and a leg. The Windows product, Monologue for Windows, supports three different interfaces. Text can be copied to the Windows Clipboard, and Monologue can then be told to speak it. On a more automated note, a DDE interface also is supported that allows macros and/or programs to directly pass text to be spoken to the speech engine, without user intervention. Monologue also supports an Excel mode, which allows spreadsheets to be proofread, similar to the ProofReader feature of the Windows Sound System.

First Byte also produces a "sister" product to Monologue, called ProVoice for Windows. This product provides an application-programming interface (API) for performing text-to-speech conversion directly under program control. When it comes to building custom applications, this mechanism is far preferable to any of those offered in the Monologue product. The API is robust enough to cover functions for dictionary lookups, conversion of text to phonetic strings, and actually speaking a string, and even for coordinating an animated character's mouth with the actual words being spoken.

Voice-recognition systems—voice-command systems

Command Corp.   Command Corp. offers the IN^3 (pronounced *in-cube*) voice-command system. This originally was offered on Sun Sparcstations, and is now available for Microsoft Windows as well. On the PC, IN3 can run on any MPC-compliant sound board. IN3 utilizes continuous-recognition and word-spotting technology, so it is able to pick commands out of a string of continuous speech. It comes with a standard command vocabulary for its target environment and can be extended with additional, user-supplied commands. The company has taken a somewhat unique approach to spreading the word on their product. In addition to the normal marketing channels, there is a "demo" version of IN3, available on several bulletin board services such as Compuserve, that allows potential users to try the system out, in a limited but useful fashion.

Microsoft.   The Windows Sound System, Microsoft's business-oriented sound board, comes with Voice Pilot, a Windows voice-command system. This system is based on technology licensed from Dragon Systems (to be discussed in a moment), and works only with the Windows Sound System board. It comes with an extensive set of vocabularies for operating Windows and many of the more popular Windows applications. It also is extendable, so that a user can create new voice commands within an existing vocabulary and/or create new vocabularies for custom applications.

Verbex Voice Systems.   Verbex offers a product called Listen for Windows in a number of configurations; it runs on Verbex's own Speech Commander DSP (digital signal processing) sound-processing card. Listen for Windows can handle continuous speech in a speaker-dependent mode, and is oriented toward the development of custom voice-aware applications rather than the overlaying of a voice-to-keystroke mechanism on top of existing applications. The software is priced based on the size of the vocabulary it can handle, while the Speech Commander hardware comes in several configurations, including a plug-in PC board, an external desktop unit for non-PC hardware platforms (i.e., UNIX, VAX, etc.), and a portable unit that works with laptop and notebook computers. Verbex also allows the vocabulary to be defined, in a text file, independent of the voice-processing system. This text file is passed through a conversion utility to build the preliminary binary vocabulary, which then is ready to be loaded onto the board and used.

Covox. Covox has been supplying consumer-oriented voice-recognition systems for the PC longer than anyone else. Their traditional product offering uses Covox's own Sound Master family of hardware, and runs under DOS. Recently they have extended their product line with Voice Blaster, a voice-command facility that operates under either DOS or Windows on most MPC-compliant sound boards. Both of these systems are speaker-dependent, discrete-word systems, and both handle a small vocabulary. As with several other products in the Windows voice-command area, the total vocabulary can be organized into several smaller "subvocabularies," only one of which is active at any one point in time. It should be noted that, in order to operate, the Voice Blaster product requires a "dongle," a hardware security device that attaches to the printer port. This device does not interfere with normal printer output but should be tested with other printer-port-attached devices, such as tape or CD drives.

Media Vision. Media Vision recently has begun to offer a voice-command package with their ProAudio Spectrum line of sound cards. This package, named ExecuVoice, is based on technology licensed from Dragon Systems and will work with any MPC-compliant sound board. It comes with a predefined vocabulary, but currently is not extendable. This means that it probably is adequate for running Microsoft Windows and most popular applications, but is not adaptable to custom applications.

Voice-dictation systems

One note to be made before discussing Dragon Systems' and IBM's offerings is that, while their larger vocabulary systems clearly are targeted to the voice-dictation market, they both also offer configurations that are usable as voice-command systems. All of their products are discussed under this single heading for simplicity, but they also should be considered when evaluating voice-command systems.

Dragon Systems. In many ways, this company is the leader in the voice-recognition area. This claim can be made based on the length of time they have been installing systems, and on the number of companies that have licensed their technology for inclusion in their own products. These include

- *IBM.* IBM VoiceType Control for Windows and IBM VoiceType 2 are based on Dragon's similar products.

- *Microsoft.* The Windows Sound System's Voice Pilot is based on technology licensed from Dragon.

- *Media Vision.* ExecuVoice also is based on technology licensed from Dragon.

- *Articulate Systems.* Voice Navigator II, a Macintosh voice-command system, is based on Dragon's speech-recognition technology.

In addition to all of this, Dragon also markets its own line of voice-recognition systems. Three examples are: DragonDictate-30K, DragonWriter-1000, and Dragon Talk-To Plus. All three use discrete word recognition and are speaker-dependent, although the DragonWriter-1000 is better described as speaker-adaptive. The DragonDictate-30K is a large-vocabulary system intended to be used in general, free-form, voice-dictation applications. DragonWriter-1000 can access a 1000-word active dictionary and is more focused on voice-command, or constrained voice-dictation applications. This product also has an API available, for use in developing customized voice-aware applications. Both of these products require that Dragon's speech-recognition board be present. The last product, Dragon Talk-To Plus, is a small-vocabulary system, supporting a 64-word active vocabulary at any point in time. It is aimed at voice-command applications and supports third-party audio boards.

IBM. IBM offers a number of different products in the voice-recognition area, a couple of which were mentioned a moment ago. This section will describe two products based on IBM-developed technology. The first is the IBM Speech Server Series. This recently announced offering from IBM runs on OS/2-based personal computers; RS/6000 machines running the AIX operating system (IBM's version of UNIX); or on a combination of the above in a client-server mode. This system supports a large vocabulary (20,000 words, plus 2000 user-added words), is speaker-dependent, and operates in discrete-word mode. In addition to extending existing applications to accept dictated speech, the system also provides an API that can be used in the development of customized voice-aware applications.

The other product is the IBM Continuous Speech Series. This is a small-vocabulary system, although that calls for some explanation. The system will support a 20,000-word vocabulary, total, but this is organized into twenty 1000-word vocabularies, only one of which can be active at any point in time. The system is speaker-independent, and accepts continuous speech. Because of the small active vocabulary compared to the Speech Server Series product, this product is focused not on general dictation usage but more on voice-command or constrained-dictation applications such as medical reports. As with the previous product, it also provides an API for users who wish to develop customized voice-aware applications.

Both systems require that a special IBM audio-capture and playback card be installed.

Summary

With any emerging technology there are champions and critics, and the situation is no different in the voice-recognition and -response area. I hope this chapter has helped you to see that this technology is here to stay, as evidenced by the large number of diverse applications available today. In the report *Voice Recognition and Response Markets,* Market Intelligence projects that the advanced-voice-processing-technology equipment market (in the United States) will triple from $700 million in 1991 to $2.5 billion in 1998, growing at a 20 percent compound annual rate. This same report predicts that voice-recognition systems will grow from 9 percent of this market in 1992 to 11 percent in 1998. During this same time frame, voice synthesizers will expand from 10 to 13 percent. In support of these projections are the number of voice-recognition and -response products on the market, many of which have been discussed, and the introduction of related products such as Wen Technology Corp.'s 486 Super-Note-Voice notebook computer, which comes complete with voice-recognition and speech-synthesis capabilities.

John Oberteuffer, president of Voice Information Systems, has predicted the obsolescence of the keyboard by the early 2000s. While he may be right, the focus of this chapter has been on the much nearer term, to illustrate how this technology can be applied *today.* As has been discussed, total voice dictation and response is not quite ready to replace the keyboard and monitor in all instances, but voice command, as another axis of control along with the keyboard and mouse, is certainly available, and in many cases both technologies can make users much more productive today.

In applying this technology, care must be taken when selecting not only the hardware and software to be used but also the target application. Today's operating systems and applications are mouse- and keyboard-oriented, and some may be more amenable to a voice-centric approach than others. This is obviously less of a problem when building custom applications, where the voice-command integration can be incorporated right from the start.

In applying speech synthesis, care must be taken to tailor the application to both the linguistic and acoustical abilities of the user, and to take account of the complexity of the material being presented. As the material's technical and/or linguistic complexity increases, the need for the speech-synthesis system to be acoustically correct in its pronunciation also increases. The interface may also need to change, since most people, when faced with a difficult passage in a book or technical journal, will go back and reread it several times, if necessary, until they understand what is being said. A computer-based reading program should be able to support this mode of operation.

The length of the text being read by a speech-synthesis system is also a concern, because while there are no empirical studies to support this, it seems intuitively obvious that comprehension on the part of the listener will decrease as the length of a monotone passage increases.

Voice recognition and response is a hot topic in the world of academic and industrial research and development. Over the next several years you can expect to see advances in many different areas, such as

- The introduction of operating systems and applications that were developed from the beginning to be voice-oriented. A shift away from the current menu-navigation-oriented systems to a more direct-command type of interface will make the integration of voice recognition much more seamless than it is today.

- The application of technology, such as wave-guide, to the problem of speech synthesis. Wave-guide technology, which produces sound based on a computer model of the physical instrument being mimicked, holds out great promise in terms of allowing more natural voices to be produced. This is only part of the challenge of producing human-sounding speech, but overcoming it will represent progress.

- The development of speech *understanding,* not just *recognition,* in computers. The difference between these is that recognition deals with the problem of having the computer determine which words were said, while understanding addresses the issue of what the speaker actually *means.* Clearly, human conversation deals with speech understanding, voice recognition simply being a necessary but insufficient condition for arriving at this understanding.

- The ability of the computer to determine when it is being spoken to. Simple methods, such as microphone arrays, may hold out short-term hope of dealing with this problem, while research in the area of visual speech analysis may bear fruit in the future.

This research eventually should lead to the development of voice-oriented systems, such as those depicted in the science fiction movies and literature. But users do not have to wait for that day. Voice-recognition and -response systems are robust enough to be used today, and early adopters of this technology can begin to reap the productivity gains right away.

Vendor List

Articulate Systems
600 W. Cummings Park, Ste. 4500
Woburn, MA 01801
800-443-7077
Voice Navigator voice-command
  system
Apple Macintosh

Command Corporation
3675 Crestwood Parkway
Duluth, GA 30136
404-925-7950
IN³ voice-command system
Sun Sparcstations
PCs

Covox
675 Conger St.
Eugene, OR 97402
503-342-1271
Voice command systems
PCs

Digital Equipment Corporation
146 Main St.
Maynard, MA 01754-2571
508-493-5111
DECTalk speech synthesis
All platforms

Dragon Systems
320 Nevada St.
Newton, MA 02160
617-965-5200
Voice dictation/command
PCs

First Byte
3100 S. Harbor Blvd., #150
Santa Ana, CA 92704
714-432-1740
Speech-synthesis products
PCs

IBM
White Plains, NY
800-772-2227
Voice dictation/command
PS/2
RS/6000

Media Vision
3185 Laurelview Court
Fremont, CA 94538
510-770-8600
ExecuVoice voice-command
  system
PCs

Microsoft
Redmond, WA 98052-6399
800-227-4679
Windows Sound System
PCs

Parity Software
25 Stillman St., Ste. 106
San Francisco, CA 94107
415-931-8221
Smooth Talker digitized-voice
  system

Verbex Voice Systems
1090 King George's Post Road
Building #107
Edison, NJ 08837-3701
800-275-8729
Voice-command systems
All platforms

Wen Technology Corp.
11 Clearbrook Road
Elmsford, NY 1052
800-377-4936
Voice-oriented laptop computer

Bibliography

Acero, Alejandro, *Acoustical and Environmental Robustness in Automatic Speech Recognition,* Kluwer Academic Publishers, Boston, 1993.

Bailly, G. and Benoit, C., *Talking Machines: Theories, Models, and Designs,* Elsevier Science Publishers, Amsterdam, 1992.

Biermann, A. W., Rodman, R. D., Rubin, D. C., and Heidlage, J. F. *Natural Language with Discrete Speech as a Mode for Human-to-Machine Communication,* Communications of the ACM, vol. 28, 628–636.

Blattner, Meera M. and Dannenburg, Roger B., *Multimedia Interface Design,* ACM Press, New York.

EDGE, Work-Group Computing Report, vol. 4, no. 149, March 29,1993.

Haber, Lynn, "Searching for the Speech-Recognition Holy Grail," MIDRANGE Systems, vol. 5, no. 11, June 9, 1992.

Laface, Pietro and De Mori, Renato, eds., *Speech Recognition and Understanding,* Springer-Verlag, Berlin, 1990.

Linggard, R., *Electronic Synthesis of Speech,* Cambridge University Press, Cambridge, 1985.

Markowitz, Judith, "The power of speech," *AI Expert,* January 1993.

Market Intelligence Research Corporation, voice-recognition, -response, and -synthesis markets.

Pelton, Gordon E., *Voice Processing,* McGraw-Hill, New York, 1993.

Rowden, Chris, *Speech Processing,* McGraw-Hill, UK, 1992.

Tucker, Tracey, "Voice for the masses: voice mail extends its reach," *Teleconnect,* April 1993.

36

MIDI Means Music!

Rob Wallace

The General MIDI Specification, and How to Use a MIDI File

MIDI is an acronym for musical instrument digital interface, which enables keyboard samplers/synthesizers, sequencers, sound cards, and computers to be connected. MIDI hardware and the MIDI data format are defined in such a way that devices, cabling, and data flow all are spelled out for uniform compatibility.

A Copy of the Level 1 Specification documents for General MIDI is available at a cost of $5 from the International MIDI Association, 5316 West 57th Street, Los Angeles, CA 90056.

Recently, the uniform implementation of instrument patches has been defined. A *patch* is a program number assigned to a musical instrument within 16 families of instruments with 8 groups each (see Fig. 36.1).

General MIDI also includes a "percussion key map" (see Fig. 36.2).

The MIDI file format (MFF)

"Opening.mid" could be the name of the file that contains all the MIDI data that will make the sound card in the system running your program play your opening music when the program is evoked.

Please understand that "opening.mid" *does not* contain *any digital sounds* whatsoever. A MFF file contains only a stream of data that instructs a MIDI device to perform functions as specified within the data stream. The .mid file tells the sound card to play patch #1, the Grand Piano, on channel 1 at a certain volume and velocity within the left/right pan position using a particular pitch bend, if any, with or without sustain, and—most important of all—which notes to play, when, and at what tempo. A richly orchestrated 1-minute .mid file will contain only 5 to 35 kbytes! The same music digitized at 22 kHz in a .wav file played through a 16-bit sound card in stereo would be more than 10 Mbytes in size!

Program number	Instrument	Program number	Instrument
(1–8 PIANO)		36	Fretless Bass
1	Acoustic Grand	37	Slap Bass 1
2	Bright Acoustic	38	Slap Bass 2
3	Electric Grand	39	Synth Bass 1
4	Honky-Tonk	40	Synth Bass 2
5	Electric Piano 1	(41–48 STRINGS)	
6	Electric Piano 2	41	Violin
7	Harpsichord	42	Viola
8	Clav	43	Cello
(9–16 CHROMATIC PERCUSSION)		44	Contrabass
9	Celesta	45	Tremolo Strings
10	Glockenspiel	46	Pizzicato Strings
11	Music Box	47	Orchestral Strings
12	Vibraphone	48	Timpani
13	Marimba	(49–56 ENSEMBLE)	
14	Xylophone	49	String Ensemble 1
15	Tubular Bells	50	String Ensemble 2
16	Dulcimer	51	SynthStrings 1
(17–24 ORGAN)		52	SynthStrings 2
17	Drawbar Organ	53	Choir Aahs
18	Percussive Organ	54	Voice Oohs
19	Rock Organ	55	Synth Voice
20	Church Organ	56	Orchestra Hit
21	Reed Organ	(57–64 BRASS)	
22	Accordion	57	Trumpet
23	Harmonica	58	Trombone
24	Tango Accordion	59	Tuba
(25–32 GUITAR)		60	Muted Trumpet
25	Acoustic Guitar (nylon)	61	French Horn
26	Acoustic Guitar (steel)	62	Brass Section
27	Electric Guitar (jazz)	63	SynthBrass 1
28	Electric Guitar (clean)	64	SynthBrass 2
29	Electric Guitar (muted)	(65–72 REED)	
30	Overdriven Guitar	65	Soprano Sax
31	Distortion Guitar	66	Alto Sax
32	Guitar Harmonics	67	Tenor Sax
(33–40 BASS)		68	Baritone Sax
33	Acoustic Bass	69	Oboe
34	Electric Bass (finger)	70	English Horn
35	Electric Bass (pick)	71	Bassoon

Figure 36.1   Uniform implementation of instrument patches.

Program number	Instrument	Program number	Instrument
72	Clarinet	100	FX 4 (atmosphere)
(73–80 PIPE)		101	FX 5 (brightness)
73	Piccolo	102	FX 6 (goblins)
74	Flute	103	FX 7 (echoes)
75	Recorder	104	FX 8 (sci-fi)
76	Pan Flute		
77	Blown Bottle	(105–112 ETHNIC)	
78	Skakuhachi	105	Sitar
79	Whistle	106	Banjo
80	Ocarina	107	Shamisen
		108	Koto
(81–88 SYNTH LEAD)		109	Kalimba
81	Lead 1 (square)	110	Bagpipe
82	Lead 2 (sawtooth)	111	Fiddle
83	Lead 3 (calliope)	112	Shanai
84	Lead 4 (chiff)		
85	Lead 5 (charang)	(113–120 PERCUSSIVE)	
86	Lead 6 (voice)	113	Tinkle Bell
87	Lead 7 (fifths)	114	Agogo
88	Lead 8 (bass + lead)	115	Steel Drums
		116	Woodblock
(89–96 SYNTH PAD)		117	Taiko Drum
89	Pad 1 (new age)	118	Melodic Tom
90	Pad 2 (warm)	119	Synth Drum
91	Pad 3 (polysynth)	120	Reverse Cymbal
92	Pad 4 (choir)		
93	Pad 5 (bowed)	(121–128 SOUND EFFECTS)	
94	Pad 6 (metallic)	121	Guitar Fret Noise
95	Pad 7 (halo)	122	Breath Noise
96	Pad 8 (sweep)	123	Seashore
		124	Bird Tweet
(97–104 SYNTH EFFECTS)		125	Telephone Ring
97	FX 1 (rain)	126	Helicopter
98	FX 2 (soundtrack)	127	Applause
99	FX 3 (crystal)	128	Gunshot

Figure 36.1 (*Continued*)

The MFF is assembled, usually in real time, by the computer musician playing a MIDI-able keyboard controller through a MIDI interface card sitting in a slot that sends the data to the CPU, which routes the data to the sequencer software in the system. The file data captures the performance exactly, and can be played back through another MIDI device.

When I write a .mid file I "echo" the data in real time to my General MIDI sampler, so that when I play a note I hear it in real time while it is being cap-

Key No.		Key No.	
35	Acoustic Bass Drum	59	Ride Cymbal 2
36	Bass Drum 1	60	Hi Bongo
37	Side Stick	61	Low Bongo
38	Acoustic Snare	62	Mute Hi Conga
39	Hand Clap	63	Open Hi conga
40	Electric Snare	64	Low Conga
41	Low Floor Tom	65	High Timbale
42	Closed Hi-Hat	66	Low Timbale
43	High Floor Tom	67	High Agogo
44	Pedal Hi-Hat	68	Low Agogo
45	Low Tom	69	Cabasa
46	Open Hi-Hat	70	Maracas
47	Low-Mid Tom	71	Short Whistle
48	Hi-Mid Tom	72	Long Whistle
49	Crash Cymbal 1	73	Short Guiro
50	High Tom	74	Long Guiro
51	Ride Cymbal 1	75	Claves
52	Chinese Cymbal	76	Hi Wood Block
53	Ride Bell	77	Low Wood Block
54	Tambourine	78	Mute Cuica
55	Splash Cymbal	79	Open Cuica
56	Cowbell	80	Mute Triangle
57	Crash Cymbal 2	81	Open Triangle
58	Vibraslap		

Figure 36.2   Percussion key map.

tured as data. The file is constantly edited and new tracks are added, then balanced, until the final version has been completed.

The sequencer I use is very much like a word processor, with a full battery of editing and authoring tools.

Making the music for your project

Before your composer gets to work, you should be able to tell him or her what kind of music you need in your project, and where. Write down your ideas. Be as descriptive as possible about the mood and even the type of instruments you want to hear. Use examples of existing music to draw parallels with what you want. Write down the styles or artists that evoke the mood or feel you need. A good composer can better produce for you when you can communicate your concept clearly and specifically.

On the other hand if your trust level is high, and your experience with the composer is such that you can give him or her free creative reign over your project, then you may just end up with something better than anything your mind could have conjured up! Producers I have worked for tend to balance their direction by drawing on both of these two styles.

Tweaking your music

Some elements of a MIDI file are relatively easy and simple to change, some are not. As the producer, you can alter these musical elements to fit your vision. If, however, the basic music isn't right, none of the following suggestions is likely to help.

Changing patches is simple. If you want to hear instruments from the list shown in Fig. 36.1 playing certain parts such as the melody, bass line, or percussion, tell the composer, "I want to hear a trumpet or some sort of brass instrument playing the melody." Or, "There isn't a punchy enough rhythm feel; bring up the percussion and add some bongos, congas, or something."

Tempo is easy to fix. Tell your composer to speed it up or slow it down a few bpm (beats per minute). Find out at what bpm your song currently is, for a reference point. A ballad usually is 60 bpm, a rock ballad 90 bpm; a typical universal tempo falls between 100 and 120 bpm, and a typical hard rocker is 150 to 200 bpm. It is amazing how shifting tempo can alter the character of a piece.

MIDI hardware—which soundcard?

I will not endorse a particular manufacturer here, although there are many people who will be glad to tell you which one is best. First you need to ask yourself what quality and what type of sound you want for your project, and decide how dependent your project is on music.

There are two types of sound reproduction, *FM synthesis* and *wave-table synthesis.*

FM synthesis.   Not that long ago, all you heard from a computer was a beep or series of beeps, perhaps at different frequencies, through the PC speaker.

You heard only one at a time (monophonic). Then along came the Adlib™ sound card, and shortly thereafter Creative Labs' Sound Blaster, and polyphonic music began to flow from your computer.

The heart of the technology is the Yamaha OPL chip and its various incarnations through the OPL3. The OPL chip produces sound by FM synthesis, FM meaning frequency modulation of an operator(s) that can produce a variety of waves: sine, sawtooth etc. By changing elements of the waveform such as attack, delay, and frequency multiplier(s), different timbres are produced, from clarinets and flutes to the wacky arcade beeps, boops, and sci-fi-like sweeping sounds associated with computer games and arcade games.

FM synthesis has its limitations. In some applications, such as Windows™, you can play only 9 or 11 notes at once. By definition, you can hear only synthetic instrument tones. FM cards can't begin to sound like a real piano and many other instruments.

FM cards are severely limited when it comes to producing the percussion sounds familiar to us on other media. FM percussion sound is essentially variations on white noise, and leaves much to be desired when contrasted with traditional percussion.

As the technology progresses, we will see FM synthesis slip farther and farther into the background.

Wave-table synthesis.   More and more sound cards are appearing that use wave-table synthesis to produce outstanding musical sounds. When you hear a grand piano or timpani on one of these devices, it sounds very close to the real thing—mostly because it *is* the real thing captured in a "sampled" form in ROM. This sample contains digital recordings of the actual instrument, mapped in such a way as to faithfully reproduce the acoustic range of the instrument.

Leading manufacturers of wave-table synthesis devices often have proprietary techniques of reproducing instrument sounds. Among the leading MIDI sound card devices in this category are The Roland Sound Canvas family, SC-55, SCC-1, SC-7, and TAP 10; Creative Labs' Wave Blaster; Turtle Beach's Multi Sound; the Aria chipset family of cards; Gravis's Ultrasound; and The Ensoniq Soundscape. This listing is by no means complete, and new devices are coming on-line rapidly.

When you are choosing among these, base your decision on which device sounds best to your ear. If you don't trust your "ear" for music, get some recommendations from your composer and your hardware advisers.

Supporting diverse sound cards?

If your project requires that your MIDI file or digital waveform files must play on more than one type of card, then you need to use the AIL drivers from Miles Design for your MIDI data, and the digital drivers available from The Audio Solutions' DigPak toolkit.

For AIL, you may leave a message for John Miles on the following BBS: 512-454-9990. To get information on DigPak, leave a message for John Ratcliff or the Sysop at 314-939-0200. If you e-mail me on Compuserve, I will provide you with their compuserve addresses. I can be reached at 71042,1410. AIL and DigPak have been used successfully by entertainment and educational software developers on hundreds of products.

The MIDI interface

To deal with MIDI data, you must have a MIDI interface within your system. Some sound card manufacturers build a MIDI interface into their cards, but you may need to use a stand-alone interface card. In any case, the interface is a hardware requirement not unlike a controller card for your drives or the card for your CD-ROM.

MIDI Music Is a Powerful Tool

Luckily for you as a producer, the hardware and software now exists that allows you to integrate MIDI files into your project that can play devices astounding in their depth and musical quality. You also can play digital voice and sound effects on top of this music, and create a true multimedia mix of sound. Even though the ability to do this is recent, the tools are stable enough that you can maintain control of this power and develop it for a reasonable cost within a reasonable time line.

You are limited only by your imagination and that of your computer musician/composer. Today the PC has even more powerful abilities to deliver sound than film, TV, and radio, because ours is an interactive environment by nature. There are ways to have the music change the mood instantly to fit what the user is doing within the program.

Interactive musical scores are here, now. And they sound fantastic!

Glossary of Terms Found in the MIDI Domain*

Accent   Stress given to a musical tone.

Accidentals   In music these are sharps, flats, or naturals not indicated in the key signature. MIDI software programs tend to represent accidentals as sharps (e.g., F-sharp rather than G-flat).

Access   In computing, the verb is encountered more often than the noun. *Synonymous phrase:* "to communicate with." *Illustration:* A sequencer that lets one directly access hardware.

Aftertouch   The change in pressure on a key after the initial attack. Determines vibrato and other characteristics.

Algorithm   A step-by-step procedure for problem solving.

Apple Macintosh   Apple computers were among the earliest to offer MIDI-computing capacity. Others now in the field include IBM-compatible PCs, Atari, and Amiga.

Articulation   The percentage of a note's duration that actually plays. This could represent the difference between a staccato and a legato effect.

Attack   When the musical note begins. *Antonym: release.*

Audio   Sound, or its transmission and reproduction.

Auto accompaniment   Sometimes called *orchestration* or *auto chord,* all the terms refer to the rhythmic styles that sound when a fingered or one-finger mode is selected. Auto accompaniment usually comprises a drum pattern, a bass line, and other enhancing sounds such as a piano arpeggio or a strummed guitar.

Bar   A synonym for *measure:* musical time, a grouping of beats.

---

*Reprinted by permission of Eugene A. Confrey, Ph.D.

Beat   Literally, a single stroke or pulsation. Tempo is expressed in beats per minute (bpm). The beat value affects the metronome. *See also* Tempo.

Buffer   A temporary storage area in memory.

Bulk dump   Denotes a series of system-exclusive messages. Sometimes this involves transferring a mass of data, such as several choruses of a song that have been stored in memory, from the keyboard to the sequencer or vice versa. Settings at both ends must be coordinated. A keyboard "bulk-dumps" to a sequencer as a system-exclusive message (Syex). Conversely, a keyboard can receive such data as a system-exclusive message.

Cancel   An often-misunderstood command. It does not mean delete (e.g., the file) or "send it to the moon." Usually it means, quite simply, "turn off the display now on the screen."

Channel   In ordinary language, a channel is a path for passing data. In MIDI, channels are used to separate different sections of a song that are going to play together. Each channel is assigned to a single instrument in any particular instant of time. One channel usually is reserved for a percussion voice. To *channelize* means to move to another channel.

Choking   What happens when the sequencer receives too much continuous data. *Result:* Tempos slow down and speed up randomly.

Chord   Three or more tones—preferably harmonious—sounded simultaneously.

Classical music   A broad umbrella term, usually contrasted with jazz, folk, rock, pop. The "classical" tradition is best illustrated by examples: symphony, opera, chamber music. *See also* Jazz; Rock.

Clef   It's that sign at the beginning of a staff—the one that determines pitch.

Clock   A clock is used to synchronize two devices. In MIDI, the term *clock* is used to denote a single time source, which everything plays along with. MIDI clocks actually are special messages sent 24 times (normally) per beat, and used to synchronize two sequencers or a sequencer and a drum machine. Usually the sequencer's clock is the important one. Other clock sources rarely are used, and, typically, only when doing a final recording.

Codes   In MIDI, as in general computing, the term *code* refers to program instruction. One type is a *source code* (human-readable). Another is a *machine code* (executable).

Compose-arrange   Two activities that can be facilitated by MIDI-computing. The composer creates music, the arranger enhances it—by scoring for other voices or instruments.

Compression   In MIDI-computing, the phrase *compression and expansion* refers to the process of changing the range of a song. Compression makes the loud parts softer, the soft parts louder.

Continuous data   Controllers, pitch bend, aftertouch...

Controller   Most often, the term refers to the instrument: keyboard, guitar, drums, etc. (as in *master controller*). A second meaning, in sequencing, refers to a setting, a parameter, as in "Controller 7 = Volume." In this sense, a controller is a MIDI event.

Controller change   This event will be displayed in the Event List editor. It refers to a change in the synthesizer setting. There are 128 controllers. *Example:* the loudness of notes. *See also* Program change.

Count in   A command in a sequencer that plays a metronome for several measures until you are ready to record.

Crescendo   A gradual increase in volume. Antonym: *decrescendo.*

Cut-and-paste   In word processing, this function means moving text from one place in a document to another. In MIDI, one can copy a section of a musical passage and paste it elsewhere.

Damper   The damper pedal on an acoustical piano functions to stop the vibration of a piano string. (In contrast, the sustain pedal holds or prolongs the note.) Unfortunately, sustain pedals on electronic pianos often are called *damper* pedals, thus blurring the distinction. *See also* Sustain.

Data bytes   These follow the status byte in a MIDI message; e.g., what note has been struck, how hard. *See also* Status byte.

Default setting   In MIDI, as in general computing, this is a choice made by the program (when the user does not specify an alternative).

Design; Program   Two distinct functions. The *designer* of a sequencing piece of software, for example, conceives and plans the product and all its functions. The *programmer* addresses the issues of programming languages, data structures, how data is stored and manipulated, etc.

Digital   In MIDI, the phrase *digital recording* is contrasted with *analog recording.* Long-playing phonograph records are analog recordings. That is, they capture information in a continuously variable form, a fluctuating waveform. Telephone lines work on the same principle. Digital, in contrast, involves binary numbers, 1's and 0's. MIDI-computing represents digital encoding.

DLL   A file extension standing for "dynamic link libraries." A DLL is part of an application's executable files, and often it is used to link the application to the hardware.

Downbeat   The maestro's downward stroke, indicating the first beat of a measure. In contrast, the upbeat is unaccented.

Dubbing   Making a new recording of sound already recorded. Sometimes used to describe the process of mixing sounds from several sources into one recording.

Duration   The length of time (number of beats) of a note or chord.

Dynamics   Variation in the intensity of musical notes.

Edit   Editing, in MIDI, involves altering, deleting, revising the musical passages that have been captured in a digital recording and are now displayed on the monitor screen. This display will offer two options. In the first, the notes are listed by track and number, by event (such as "Note on"), by the specific note G4, the beat, the channel, etc. The second option for editing is to use a musical notation display. Here the notes are arrayed in clefs, (1) like a piano roll (the piano-roll display sometimes is referred to as *graphic notation*) or (2) in conventional musical notation. Editing options include changes in notes, measures, transpose, volume.

Enable; disable   Antonyms, meaning *to turn on* or *to turn off*. Synthesizers and sequencers have many controls requiring such action (such as MIDI THRU).

Engraver-quality   A complimentary descriptive term, referring to a professional-looking job of printing music.

Entry-level   An adjective used to describe beginners (those trying to learn MIDI, for instance). They may be devoid of experience in computer engineering or in electronic music.

Envelope   The changes of a tone; e.g., attack, sustain, decay, release.

Error messages   The message says "Something's wrong!" In MIDI, you could be told that "memory is full," that you've committed a "track error," or made a "protect error" (attempted to write to a protected disk).

Event   In ordinary language an occurrence, a happening. In MIDI, the signal that is transmitted, such as note on, note off, program change, control change. *See also* Program change, Control change.

Event-chasing   Scans data in a sequence before the start-point of the recording. Looks for patch changes, for example.

Event list   An alphanumeric display of all MIDI events on a single track. *Examples:* notes, time signature, tempo, program changes, control changes.

Faders   Controls for changing effects gradually, such as decreasing loudness.

Field   Traditional computing defines this as a location in a record. *Examples:* name, address, zip code, etc. *Illustrative fields in MIDI:* Song title, track name, instrument, channel.

File types   A MIDI File Type 0 is a single (multiple-channel) track. A MIDI File Type 1 contains one or more simultaneous tracks.

Filter   The noun and the verb, in MIDI, are used primarily in connection with events (note on, program change, tempo change) and with channel changes. Each event is either filtered (deleted), transformed, or passed through.

Fingered mode   Provides automatic rhythm, bass, and orchestral accompaniment. The bass and orchestral accompaniment reflect the notes in the chord of the left hand. *See also* Auto accompaniment.

FSK   Frequency-shift keying. Modulation involving two different frequencies.

Ganged   When tracks are "ganged," they will move simultaneously. *Analogy:* A variable capacitor in an early radio receiver.

Gate time   The length of a produced sound (e.g., legato, staccato).

General MIDI mode   A convention specifying how a sequence (song) should be constructed, so that it will play on a variety of hardware.

Glide   This effect plays the sound of a semitone below the pitch, then slides up to normal pitch.

Global editing   Affecting an entire file or program. Transpose is illustrative. The contrasting function is *local editing,* such as changing one event.

GUI   Graphical user interface. A display that permits a user to select commands, menu items, by pointing at an icon (with a mouse) and clicking.

Hardware sequencer Sequencing can be performed by software programs or by hardware. Hardware sequencers also work with synthesizers, controllers, sound modules to create and edit songs. A hardware sequencer is—as the name implies—hardware, containing a single-purpose program, one designed to provide sequencing.

Humanize A term used to refer to the introduction of random irregularities in note-timing and velocities, in order to reduce the mechanical character of a performance. *See also* Quantization.

Implementation chart Look for the MIDI Implementation Chart in the manual of your master controller (e.g., the keyboard). This will tell you what is transmitted (or recognized) for the various functions such as note number, velocity (pressure on a key), aftertouch (change in pressure), pitch bender, control change, program change, system-exclusive message, etc.

Import To bring data from one program into another. *Antonym: export,* meaning to transfer to another program. (Some sequencer manuals use the term *export* to mean convert and save—as a MIDI file—preparatory to transferring elsewhere.)

Initialization *Initial* means first. To initialize is to set a program to a starting position, to prepare the program for use.

Instrumentation The selection of instruments in a MIDI arrangement.

Intros and fills The jazz man's vamp—a couple of measures repeated before a solo.

Inverse video The reversal of light and dark on a screen character. *Example:* an indication of whether Automatic Rewind is on (enabled) or off (disabled).

Jazz Another umbrella term, often (erroneously) defined in terms of volume and tempo. Its basic ingredient is improvisation, accomplished melodically, harmonically, or by rhythm changes. *See also* Rock.

Keyboard A reminder: In MIDI-computing, one has to remember which one is involved in a documentation reference, the computer's or the controller's.

Key signature Musical notation shows this in terms of sharps and flats after the clef. Software sequencers sometimes show a song key as "F major/D minor" and indicate the number of sharps or flats. B-flat major/G minor has two flats, for example. *See also* Accidentals.

Looping Used to repeat a section of a recording.

Marker Something used to record a position. MIDI markers identify, for example, musical cues. They work like tab stops on a word processor.

Mapping The process of identifying patches and keys, so that sound files can be played properly. A *key map* will translate values for MIDI messages, so that the correct keys will be played. A *patch map* functions to identify the correct patches (sounds, instruments).

MCI Media control interface. Standard used primarily by Windows, for all media interfaces.

Measure delete This command removes specified measures (e.g., measures 4, 5, and 6). *See also* Measure erase.

Measure erase The contents of specified measures are erased, but the length of the song is unchanged. *See also* Measure delete.

Media Player   Microsoft's term for the Windows application that will control the playing of sound cards, CD-ROM drives, and videodisc players. It also will play MIDI sequencer files.

Melody   One of the three basic elements of music (the other two being harmony and rhythm). Melody is a succession of tones—hopefully pleasing.

Merge   To combine or blend into one. *Example:* merging two tracks.

Messages   The net effect of MIDI-computing is sound: melodies, harmonies, rhythms. But the MIDI message (the MIDI event) itself is not a sound. Transmitted are digital commands—about 1000 events per second.

Meta events   In ordinary language, the prefix *meta* often means *above* or *beyond*. In computing, a *meta*character conveys information about other characters. In MIDI, a meta event would be illustrated by such things as track name, patch name, tempo, time signature, etc. Meta events are contrasted with *data streams*.

Meter   The basic pattern of note values, e.g. beats per measure. *See also* Time signature.

Metronome   A device that marks time by producing a repeated tick. The older type, a triangular box with a vibrating arm, was succeeded by an electrical unit. In MIDI, the ticks are computer-generated.

MIDI   A protocol. The musical instrument digital interface comprises a MIDI card and cables connecting the computer to an electronic instrument, such as a keyboard. The MIDI card (a printed circuit board) normally is mounted in an expandable slot inside the computer. Keyboard synthesizers also can communicate with other synthesizers by means of a MIDI connection.

MIDIEX file   Created by saving the current contents of the buffer. MIDIEX is a standard format containing raw MIDI data without a header (a line identifying the program).

MIDI Mapper   Microsoft's utility program, which can help you to remap patch, channel, etc. during playback.

MIDI pitch wheel switch   Determines whether continuous controller information (e.g., note on, key pressure, control change, program change) will be recorded.

MIDI sound generator   For authentic reproduction of acoustical instruments. It uses samples—instrument sounds stored as digitized audio. This actually is another term for *synthesizer*—converting MIDI events into real audio sound.

MIDI Thru   One of three ports (connections): MIDI In, MIDI Out, and MIDI Thru. MIDI In receives information from other equipment. MIDI Out sends information to other equipment. MIDI Thru duplicates the information, and sends it to other equipment. By means of the latter, a synthesizer can echo messages to other synthesizers.

Modulation   In music, one usually thinks of modulating as passing from one key to another, by means of intermediate chords. In MIDI, modulation usually means applying a vibrato effect to a sound.

MPU-401–compatible   The reference is to a standard interface. (It derives from Roland's initial design.) *Important:* MS-DOS MIDI software often supports this user base, but not always.

Multitimbral   In sequencing, a multitimbral sound module can play several parts on different channels simultaneously. A multitimbral device is one that is prepared to sound like more than one instrument at a time.

Multitrack recording   Normally, one records on a single track ("normal-mode" recording). Multitrack recording is feasible, however. *Example:* from a guitar, with each string on a different channel.

Multivoice mode   A setting on a multitimbral tone generator (such as a keyboard) for receiving multiple MIDI channels, each channel having a different voice (instrument).

Musical score   Most often, the written copy of a musical composition. Compose in MIDI, print the notation, and voilà!—there it is.

Mute   A sequencer command to turn off specified tracks. *Reason:* so you can listen exclusively to one track. *See also* Solo.

Noise   That disturbance of a signal that can occur if your MIDI cables are too long— exceeding 15 meters in length, for example.

Normal mode   When a (controller) keyboard has this setting (as contrasted with *split,* or *fingered* modes), the sounds, from the lowest note to the highest, are all of one voice. In this mode, the resemblance is to an acoustical instrument. *See also* Split mode, Fingered mode.

Octave notation   MIDI software and electronic keyboards use notations such as F4 to represent the specific note F located in the fourth octave of an acoustical piano.

Open command   Loads an existing disk file.

Pads   (Sometimes *multipads*). On keyboards, where you store percussive sounds.

Pan   To *pan* is to move the sound between full left and full right in a stereo sound field. It resembles the "balance" function of a stereo receiver-amplifier.

Parameter   A tough word to define. In mathematics, it's a variable or an arbitrary constant. In MIDI, it's a value assigned at the beginning of an operation. *Examples:* pitch bend, sustain, voice number, volume, reverb.

Patch   In some early keyboard synthesizers, one selected "instruments" to play (e.g., vibraphone, clarinet.) Later the term *voice* emerged, in part because some of the sounds went beyond instruments (police whistles, human voices, etc.). In contemporary MIDI-computing the word *patch* is prominent, one reason being that a single keyboard setting, such as 99, may encompass a large range of percussive sounds. In any event, to a sequencer, the patch setting will determine the nature of the sounds.

Patch layout   A potential source of trouble for MIDI users. Manufacturers of synthesizers have not standardized the correspondence between patches and numbers. The celesta patch number might be 24 on a Roland keyboard, 09 on a Yamaha. Microsoft's MIDI Mapper is designed to help rectify this situation. *See also* MIDI Mapper.

Pattern recording   Establishing a pattern, e.g. a bass drum beat, then embellishing it.

PCM   Pulse code modulation—a process of digital recording.

Percussion   A percussive instrument is sounded by striking or shaking it. *Examples:* Bass drum, snare, bongo, cymbal, high-hat. By extension the term also encompasses so-called "background sounds" such as wind chimes, thunder, voices.

Piano-roll editor   A common notation used for editing by many sequencers. The notes of each track are shown as horizontal bars, the vertical position representing pitch, the horizontal length representing duration of the note (or chord). *See also* Edit; Event list editor.

Pitch   The property of a musical tone—determined by frequency.

Pitch bend wheel   A wheel on the keyboard that allows notes to be bent up or down. *Example:* a sliding trombone sound. "Pitch bend" is a MIDI message.

Platforms   Computer hardware. Some MIDI software will run on one platform (e.g., IBM PCs) but not on another (e.g., Macintosh).

Player   In the realm of MIDI-computing the sequencer is still the virtuoso, but MIDI players are prominent too. They play the sound files. They compile play lists of songs and sometimes group them into albums.

Play list   A list of tunes to be performed in succession. The sequence is preprogrammed.

Polyphony   From the Greek, meaning "variety of tones." In MIDI the question is, "How many notes can be played simultaneously?" Maximum polyphony cannot be exceeded.

Port   A location in the hardware from which data is passed in and out. In setting up MIDI one must make port assignments, so that channels can be correctly addressed.

Port address and interrupt settings   *Addresses* are locations within the computer. These addresses are used by devices (such as a MIDI keyboard) to communicate with the software. An *interrupt setting* signals when the device is ready to send or receive data. Addresses and interrupts must be unique for each device.

PPQN   Pulses per quarter-note. A measurement of time resolution.

Program change   Like controller change, this event will be displayed in the event list editor. An illustrative program change would be the introduction of a new voice (instrument). *See also* Controller change.

Pulse   The tick of a computer clock is sometimes referred to as a *pulse. Example:* one clock pulse defined as $\frac{1}{240}$ of a quarter-note.

Punch recording   A feature that allows automatic on-off recording at specified points.

Quantization   To *quantize* is to force all notes played to fall on the nearest beat specified. It shifts events (like note-on) to an exact rhythmic position.

Radio button   A small circle in a menu display. When it is pressed (clicked), it activates an option.

Real time   In MIDI there are two types of recording procedures, *real-time* and *step-time*. The former resembles traditional recording—as with a tape recorder. Step-time recording really is sequential: note-by-note, chord-by-chord.

Record   In the world of sound, to register something reproducible on a disk, such as a phonograph record, or on magnetic tape. Traditional recording captures the amplitude (height) and frequency (number) of wave forms. MIDI-computing does not really "record." It encodes messages, digitally—by means of numbers. Because of established usage, however, the words *record* and *recording* often appear in MIDI-computing, along with *play, rewind, fast forward,* and so on. In MIDI-computing, these words really are metaphors. A typical sequencer will "record" all of the MIDI events received, along with the time they were received.

Reset   Keyboards, like computers, sometimes "lock up." To restore normal operation, the *system reset* is used. There is another meaning of *reset* in MIDI software: to return to the first measure.

Rest   In music, a rhythmic silence. *Examples:* a two-beat rest, a quarter-note rest.

Ritard As a verb, to gradually slacken tempo (sometimes used at the ending of a song). *Antonym of the noun:* accelerando.

Rock Like "jazz," a broad umbrella term. Rock is a form of popular music, usually played on electronically amplified instruments, with a heavily accented beat.

Sampling Emulating the sound of an acoustical instrument by digitizing (converting to digital sound) the waveforms produced by the instrument.

Save as... If no file name has yet been assigned, this is the command to use. If your MIDI file already has been christened, and you have edited it, the appropriate command is Save.

Select Do you want to edit (insert, delete, copy, cut)? You must first "select," i.e. highlight, block.

Serial Appearing in succession, one at a time. For instance, MIDI messages, as displayed in an Event List.

Sequencer So called because such a program arranges melodic and harmonic patterns in successive positions. Strictly speaking, one should define a sequencer as something that stores note-on and note-off events in memory, then plays them back.

Sequencer memory It is in RAM (random-access memory). It is measured in the number of events that can be accommodated.

Slider An input device to increase or decrease volume. Also refers to an on-screen image (such as a button control) that one can move with a mouse.

Snap-to-grid A grid consists of two sets of lines that crisscross. A snap-to-grid feature facilitates step-entry of notes.

SMPTE Usually indicates a standardized time code developed by the Society of Motion Picture and Television Engineers. The time code is used in the MIDI world as a way of synchronizing MIDI to external events.

Solo If you want to listen exclusively to one track, you can mute all other tracks. *Alternative:* Select a track to "solo" (a feature that some sequencing programs offer). *See also* Mute.

Song clear To erase the contents of all tracks. *See also* Track clear.

Sound device Any device is part of the system's hardware. (*Examples:* a printer, mouse, modem, etc.) A sound device could be, for instance, a MIDI synthesizer, a CD-ROM drive, a videodisc player.

Sound driver Device drivers are software that control communication between devices (a mouse, printer, modem) and the computer. A sound driver controls the sound card or the sound device, such as a MIDI-compatible synthesizer. The sound driver must be correctly configured for your computer.

Sound module The component in a device (such as a keyboard) that produces the sound (e.g., a violin melody, a drum rhythm). This is another term for MIDI sound generator.

Sound recorder A Microsoft Windows accessory that can play, record, and edit sound files in the WAVE (non-MIDI) format.

Speed; pitch Perhaps the most important benefit gained from using a sequencer is that tempo can be changed without affecting pitch. Thus a difficult passage can be recorded slowly, then played at a faster tempo—with no change in pitch.

Split mode Divides a keyboard into two sections, each of which can play a different instrument. *Example:* From the split-point (say, C#3), the left hand can be producing the sounds of an organ, while the right hand plays a flute melody line. *See also* Normal mode.

Split-point In a split mode, the location on a keyboard where one voice (instrument) is differentiated from another. G2, for example, might be set to allow one voice (say, choir) in the left hand, another voice (say, violin) in the right hand. *See also* Normal mode.

Standard MIDI file Identified by its extension (.MID; sometimes .MFF or .SMF), this is a file that can store MIDI messages, such as songs. The data in a MIDI file can be played, manipulated, edited. A MIDI file comprises actions performed on an instrument (keys pressed, how hard). There is a standard MIDI file format. A principal advantage of a MIDI file: It uses comparatively little disk space, but more importantly it is standard across platforms and sequencers.

Status byte In a MIDI message, this announces what kind of message is being sent, e.g. "note-on." *See also* Data bytes.

Staves Plural of staff—those horizontal lines and spaces.

Stomp boxes Floor pedals for enhancing tones, used principally by guitarists.

Sustain To sustain is to hold a note (or a chord). The musical tones fade out gradually. *See also* Damper.

Synchronize To make synchronous or simultaneous. *Example:* to synchronize a drum pattern to play with melodies and chords on a synthesizer. MIDI synchronization is a coordinating function—involving a sync signal.

Syncopation Changing a regular metrical accent, e.g. by coming in early or late on a beat. It is a form of rhythmic improvisation. *See also* Jazz.

Synthesizer (Often shortened to Synth.) A device driven by a microprocessor that contains a programmable chip. *Examples of instruments that can control synthesizers:* Guitar, keyboard, wind, string, drum controllers. The keyboard itself does not produce musical sound. A synthesizer circuit, built into the keyboard, accomplishes this function. Originally a synthesizer was so called because it synthesized acoustic instruments. Nowadays the term refers to the sound-generating circuitry of any MIDI gear. Another term is *sound module.*

Sysex Short for a system-exclusive message. *Illustrative data:* voices, drum patterns.

Tempo In music, the rate of speed (such as allegretto). Electronic keyboards provide controls to set or change tempo. A quarter-note setting may range from 40 to 240 beats per minute. Software sequencers also set and change tempo. *Examples of tempo settings:* Viennese waltz—190 bpm; disco-rock—104 bpm; swing—166 bpm. Sequencers display the exact beat (e.g., beat number 29) of the music being recorded or played. *See also* Beat.

Time base The number of clock ticks per beat. *Illustrative range:* 120–768.

Time signature In traditional musical notations, this is expressed as a fractional sign, such as ¾. The denominator indicates the unit for the beat; the numerator shows the number of notes per measure. *See also* Meter.

Tone generator   Essentially, a synthesizer without a keyboard.

Touch response   A feature of some electronic keyboards, enabling one to control loudness according to how hard the keys are pressed.

Track   In MIDI, the term *track* designates a location where one records or plays back a musical message—usually a portion of the total arrangement. To illustrate, one might record an oboe melody line on Track 2, then record a bowed bass line on Track 3. When played, the sounds can be simultaneous. Most MIDI software now accommodates 64 tracks of music, enough for a rich orchestral sound. *Important:* Tracks are purely for convenience; channels are required. *See also* Channel.

Track clear   To erase the contents of a specific track. *See also* Song clear.

Track merge   To merge the contents of two tracks and store in a third track.

Track names   Names such as "melody line," "bass line," "left hand," etc. are assigned to tracks to help determine the instrumentation of a sequence.

Transcription   The word has been used extensively in music. *Example:* arranging for some instrument or voice other than the original. In MIDI, a common usage refers to converting a MIDI file into musical notation for printing. This is accomplished by means of notation software.

Transpose   To perform a musical composition in a different key. Both synthesizers and sequencers can carry out this function.

Tuning   440 hertz is the normal tuning value. However, the pitch of a synthesizer can be altered—raised or lowered. Changes in the tune value are expressed as plus or minus signs.

Tuplet   A *triplet* always designated three notes over two beats. The word *tuplet* is a generic term—in fancy language, "non-integral duration values." Think of quintuplets (5) or sextuplets (6). (Notes, not offspring from a single birth.)

Undo   This command could be a lifesaver. It reverses your last mistake, such as inadvertently recording or inserting MIDI data. "REDO" undoes an "UNDO."

User-friendly   A popular "buzzword" in computing. *Synonym: intuitive.* It means "directly comprehended." For many users, a method of pointing at icons and clicking is more "user-friendly" than entering many keystrokes to select menu items, like commands. Intuitive programs are more quickly grasped by the "computer-naive" (another buzzword).

Velocity   Velocity is the MIDI way of determining how hard a note has been pressed on the keyboard controller.

Waveform   A representation of a wave's amplitude over time.

Zoom   To magnify the image on a monitor screen; especially useful when editing notes in Standard MIDI files.

References

Books

Eiche, Jon F., *What's MIDI?,* Hal Leonard Publishing Corp., 1990.
Microsoft Press, *Dictionary of Computer Terms,* 1991.
Starr, Greg R., *What's a Sequencer?,* Hal Leonard Publishing Corp., 1990.

Articles

Petzold, Charles, "An introduction to the Musical Instrument Digital Interface," *PC* magazine, March 17, 1992.

Kendall, Robert, "MIDI goes mainstream," *PC* magazine, March 31, 1992.

Wilkinson, Scott, "Sequencing made easy," Parts 1 and 2, *Electronic Musician,* March and April 1992.

Petzold, Charles, "MCI, MIDI, and the nature of time," *PC* magazine, September 29, 1992. (A more advanced discussion.)

Multimedia and Video Editing

Marco Pinter

The Need for Multimedia-Based Editing

The computer age has resulted in revolutionary advances in many fields, cutting costs and labor by factors of 10 or even 100. A case in point is the publishing industry. Prior to the widespread use of computers, producing a simple newsletter with some different typefaces and a few photographs required equipment costing several hundred thousand dollars and many hours of specialized labor. Since the advent of desktop publishing in the 1980s, an amateur with a $5000 system can produce in a short amount of time the same newsletter of essentially the same quality.

The 1990s are seeing a similar revolution occurring in the video industry. In the early days of videotape, the editing process consisted of physically splicing tape segments under a microscope, using equipment costing several hundred thousand dollars. Over the years the process has been simplified somewhat, and today a low-end videotape-editing suite can be assembled for under $10,000.

These systems, however, have a number of problems. Most importantly, they are completely *linear*. A linear editing solution means that the user needs to constantly seek from one portion of a tape to another in order to view various segments, which is very time-consuming. Nonlinear solutions are available, such as systems that incorporate a number of videodisc machines, but these generally cost at least $100,000. Then too, performing even the simplest video effects, such as wipes and dissolves, calls for additional equipment starting at $30,000.

Clearly, there has to be a better way. Many industries, from training to education to public relations, use video constantly, and simply cannot afford such expensive systems. Desktop video has provided the answer. Today, for

$1000 to $5000, one can purchase hardware and software capable of nonlinear editing with special effects. True, a more expensive solution is required if one wishes to preserve the original picture quality, just as one needs more equipment than a simple desktop publishing suite to print at a high resolution. However, these advances are coming rapidly, and probably will have been incorporated into low-cost solutions by the year 2001.

The advent of the multimedia age also has affected desktop video in other ways. With the release of QuickTime on the Macintosh, and Video For Windows on the IBM, most personal computers now are capable of motion-video playback. This has created a large market for computer-based video programs in the areas of entertainment and education. The developers of these programs, as well as interested consumers, now need video-editing solutions for their multimedia video. Unlike users in the videotape realm, these people are using the computer as their medium, not just as a tool. They need to repeatedly update and reedit their video, and see it instantly in their applications. To these users, desktop video-editing programs are critical, an integral part of their authoring workstations.

Current desktop-video-editing needs can thus be classed in two major categories, which we will focus on in turn:

1. *Computer as Tool* encompasses those users whose goal is to edit videotape, and who use the computer as a tool to accomplish this task more efficiently and effectively.

2. *Computer as Medium* describes the exploding market of multimedia users who are editing digital video on the computer, with the goal of incorporating the video into their interactive programs.

Desktop Video Editing—Computer as Tool

Analog editing systems

Before we can discuss the revolution in desktop editing, we first must look at analog systems. This will provide us with a clearer vision of the advantages of using the computer as an editing tool.

Simple analog systems consist of the following, at a minimum:

1 playback VCR (or camcorder)

1 recording VCR

Picture/sound monitor (i.e., television)

Controller

The *controller* is a hardware device that interfaces with VCRs and controls the following functions: play, rewind, fast forward, pause, step, and seek. The seek function causes a VCR to cue up at a particular frame. Editing technology identifies individual frames by a *time-code* stamp, which gives every frame of video a distinct number. (Time-code standards are described in the subsection Formats, Time Codes, and Standards on the next page.)

One factor that separates low-end from high-end editing systems is the *frame accuracy* of the edit control. Medium- to high-end systems usually are 100 percent frame-accurate, which means they can play back and record from an exact frame with no margin of error. Low-end and consumer-grade systems typically have lower frame accuracy. Generally this is due to the quality of the playback/record decks. Fully frame-accurate VCR decks start at $3000 and can go up to $100,000. Cheaper, non-frame-accurate systems usually specify the margin of error in terms of frame offset, i.e., ± 5 frames. For normal scene-editing, a few frames of error, which amount to less than a tenth of a second, are unnoticeable. However for montage-style edits, as in many music videos, frame accuracy is critical.

The edit suite that has been listed is a bare-minimum configuration. It does not allow for any transitions between scenes. Transitions are used to change between scenes in a smooth, visually appealing way. Typical transitions include

Wipes.   Scene B wipes across Scene A.

Dissolve.   Scene B fades into Scene A.

Iris.   Scene B appears as a small circle on Scene A, and enlarges until it fills the screen.

Transitions use a process known as *A/B roll,* which means that two source decks are playing simultaneously and the image from deck B must be merged with that of deck A. This process requires the following setup (see Fig. 37.1):

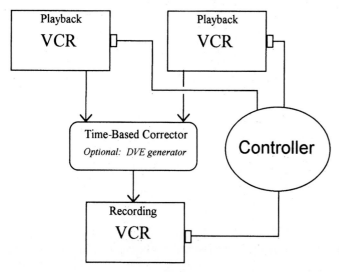

Figure 37.1 What's needed for an A/B roll.

2 playback VCRs

1 recording VCR

Picture/sound monitor (i.e., television)

Controller

Time-based corrector/digital video effects (DVE) generator

The time-based corrector (TBC) allows for synchronization of the signals from the two playback decks. Without a TBC, the final video image would be unstable. The digital video effects unit, typically combined with a TBC, performs the actual transitions. This DVE unit often also includes functions for color correction (i.e., tint and contrast), as well as overlay of titles and graphics.

Overlays of this kind are accomplished through a process known as *keying,* in which one image (i.e., titles or graphics) is set on a black background. The DVE unit allows video to pass through any black area, leaving colored areas on top. In the example shown in Fig. 37.1, the key color is black. Keying also can be used to mix two video signals, for instance a weatherman keyed on top of a satellite map. In these cases the weatherman is filmed in front of a blue background, and blue becomes the key color.

The functionality described in the previous paragraphs is typical of analog editing systems. These kinds of systems can cost from $40,000 to $300,000. This price point limits these systems to video production houses and large corporate clients. Others have had to settle for hybrid solutions. For instance, many people edit a "rough cut" on a low-end system, then rent time at a production house to perform their final edit. This usually runs them at least $250 per hour, and clearly is inconvenient as well. These factors have been the major reason behind the drive toward desktop editing solutions.

Formats, time codes, and standards

If you are entering into video editing, whether analog or digital, you will need to understand different formats and standards, in order to ensure compatibility of tapes, cameras, and equipment. Here we provide a summary of these issues.

Video signal standards.   It is by means of the video signal that images are electronically stored and transmitted. Unfortunately, there is no international standard for this. Therefore an American VCR cannot be hooked up to a German television and a French VCR cannot be attached to an American television. Some signals also differ with regard to the number of images per second that appear. The standards are as follows:

NTSC (USA, Japan): 30 frames per second

PAL (most of Europe): 25 frames per second

SECAM (France): 25 frames per second

Video signal formats. Distinct from the issue of signal *standards* is that of signal *formats*. Signal formats include

Composite

Y/C (luminance/chroma)

RGB (red/green/blue)

The most common format is *composite*. The video signal that comes out of your VCR or into your television is composite. High-end video equipment also supports Y/C and RGB formats. The Y/C format splits the video signal into its brightness and color components and stores these separately. The RGB format splits the video into three signals, one each for red, green, and blue. These component formats provide higher-quality video signals.

Tape formats. Most people are familiar with differing videotape formats. For instance your VCR requires a VHS tape, while your camcorder may use an 8-millimeter tape. Tape formats include the following:

VHS ($\frac{1}{2}$-inch): Consumer video

8-mm: Consumer camcorders

Super-VHS: Midrange video

Hi-8: Midrange video

Betacam: High-end video

U-Matic ($\frac{3}{4}$-inch): High-end video

D1/D2: High-end video

Type B (1-inch): Broadcast video

Type C (1-inch): Broadcast video

Typically, within a certain standard (i.e., NTSC), one can connect decks using different formats. However some decks, e.g., Super-VHS, can use component signals (Y/C), while other decks, e.g., VHS, can function only with a composite signal.

Time code. As already discussed, time code is used to number individual frames of video. The international standard is called *SMPTE time code*. This format can be encoded on a tape in two ways: *longitudinal* (*LTC*), and *vertical interval* (*VITC*). Also, broadcast video often is recorded using *drop-frame* time code, which means that every few minutes a frame value is skipped. Most users, however, use standard, non-drop-frame time code.

Edit decision lists (EDLs). Video producers typically like to keep track of the choices they have made during an edit session, so that they can return to a project later without having to start from scratch. Most editing systems store this information in an *edit decision list (EDL)*. There are several formats for displaying and storing the EDL information. Common formats include CMX/ASCII and Grass Valley. EDLs also can be saved during a "rough cut" and brought to a production house for a fast final edit. In this scenario, the rough cut is called *off-line editing* and the production level session is called *on-line editing*.

Linear/nonlinear.   *Linear* editing is the norm in the analog world. The user scans back and forth through the tape, and locates all desired scenes. Then the controller sends commands to the decks, which assemble the scenes in order. This method is very time-consuming for the user, who spends long periods of time rewinding and seeking through the tape.

Nonlinear editing is the superior solution. Essentially, this technique provides a way to store many individual sequences separately, so that any sequence may be viewed or modified immediately. In the analog world, these systems are extremely expensive, because they involve storing to laserdiscs or large numbers of tape decks. However, as we will see, digital video provides a much more efficient solution.

Moving to the digital desktop

In the previous sections we have demonstrated the need for a cost-effective, computer-based solution to video editing. The role of the computer in editing works at many levels, and we will be examining each of these in turn.

First, we have seen that there is a need for a more efficient method of basic editing. Since production houses typically charge $150 to $500 per hour for off-line editing, the average user needs something more affordable. Many of these users have turned to computer-based controllers to perform their editing.

On another level, most people quickly become dissatisfied with the general analog editing process. It involves watching scenes many times and recording a scene with obscure time-code numbers. This is a tedious and nonintuitive process. At the next level of computer editing, the computer digitizes one or more still images from a video sequence and uses these *thumbnails* to represent each scene.

These solutions, however, still require the user to wait as decks are rewinding and seeking. The final solution, then, is purely digital. The computer digitally records all motion-video sequences and stores them on the hard drive. Some people use these solutions to perform their rough cut as efficiently as possible. Others, however, take computer-based editing to its highest level by using the computer to convert the finished digital-video sequence back to tape.

The computer as control device

Using a computer to control video decks is not a new idea—it's been done for over 20 years now. The earliest CMX systems used computer control, but at that time these solutions cost several hundred thousand dollars.

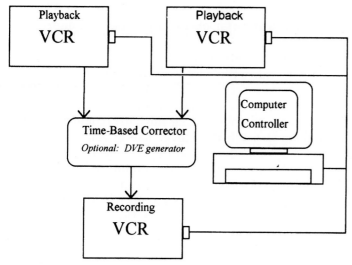

Figure 37.2 Computer-controlled editing suite.

The typical computer-controlled editing suite has the following components (see Fig. 37.2):

2 playback VCRs

1 recording VCR

Picture/sound monitor (i.e., television)

Computer controller

Time-based corrector/digital-video effects (DVE) generator

In all of these systems the computer acts as the control device, sending messages to playback and recording decks. In some systems with digital overlay boards, the computer also acts as the monitor, passing through video and audio on the screen.

The interface with computer control typically is done through mouse control. VCR controls appears as buttons on the screen, which can be clicked on. The computer then sends messages to the VCRs by means of a *control language*. Consumer-based control languages include Control-L/LANC and ViSCA control. The ViSCA control language works specifically with the Sony V-Deck and V-Box.

Frame accuracy is achieved through the use of time code. In addition to the professional SMPTE time code, desktop editing solutions often use rewritable consumer (RC) time code. Computer-based solutions also sometimes make use of a control network to access several decks. Popular networks include V-LAN by Videomedia Inc., and the ARTI system (Advanced Remote Technologies Inc.).

A popular computer-control program for PCs is Gold Disk's Video Director. This program uses Control-L and infrared to control standard camcorders and VCRs. It does not provide frame-accurate control, but at under $200 the program is very affordable. Video Director also will provide computer monitoring if a digitizing board is present.

Perhaps one of the most popular editing systems of all time is the Video Toaster by Newtek. This system takes the first step toward digital video and can be thought of as a "digitally enhanced" analog A/B-roll system. The Video Toaster is a hardware/software combination that works with the Commodore Amiga computer. The system can control multiple video decks and provides a wide variety of special effects through the clever use of computer video. However, the Video Toaster is *not* a nonlinear editing system. Transitions are accomplished by means of a "pseudo A/B roll" paradigm, in which a still image from deck B is captured and then merged with motion video that is passing through from deck A. A number of other systems also use the pseudo A/B roll method, such as Studio Master Pro from the AT&T Graphics Software Lab.

Nonlinear digital editing

The step to fully digital video editing is a long one, and has many ramifications. First, digital video has very high storage needs, requiring huge amounts of disk space. Depending on the video-compression method used, digital video can require from 9 to 30 Mbytes per minute. Therefore an adequate nonlinear system will use multiple gigabytes of storage. Currently, magnetic storage costs about $2000 per gigabyte. Another solution is optical storage, which is gaining popularity and rapidly decreasing in price.

Digital editing has two main uses. The first is as a tool, for making a rough cut or work print, with EDL output used for subsequent on-line editing. The second use is the pure digital solution, and involves outputting the completed digital movie directly to tape. The advantage of the latter method is that computer software can provide almost infinite flexibility when it comes to creating transitions and special effects, which would cost a fortune if produced with a hardware DVE generator.

Unfortunately, digital video has disadvantages when printing to tape. Digital artifacts appear, such as pixelation, contouring, and aliasing. While artifacts also exist in the analog world (smearing, streaking, and color-fringing), the general public is very tolerant of these, as they have been a part of our lives through television for decades. By contrast, since digital artifacts are a recent phenomenon, most people are intolerant of them. As a result many producers are hesitant to print from digital format to tape, unless the digital video is stored with a very high resolution and color depth.

A nonlinear desktop editing system consists of the following (see Fig. 37.3):

1 playback VCR

1 recording VCR

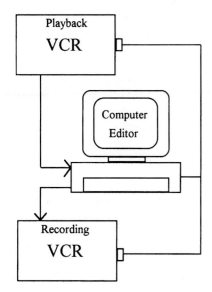

Figure 37.3 Nonlinear desktop editing system.

Computer

Note that the computer has taken on the roles of controller, player, recorder, and DVE generator.

One popular nonlinear editing system on the PC is D/Vision by TouchVision, Inc. This system uses DVI technology to digitize, compress, and play back video. It provides a number of transitions and effects, as well as overlays and titling. Systems such as D/Vision typically range from $4000 to $15,000, depending on configuration and options.

Platforms and systems

Often one's first decision when exploring desktop video is what type of computer to buy: PC, Macintosh, or something else? For the most part the host computer is relatively unimportant, as long as it is compatible with the editing system that best fits one's needs. Because of the widespread use of the PC, there is more software for that environment than its competitors. However, some very good packages exist for all platforms.

One platform that does offer some specific advantages is the Amiga. The Amiga features coprocessors for audio, graphics, and animation. Also the Amiga's video-signal-timing is compatible with NTSC, which makes it ideal for systems like the Video Toaster. However the Amiga also has some graphics limitations, and outside the video-editing world the Amiga has a fairly small market share.

A number of editing systems exist on the various platforms, other than those already mentioned in this section. Of note are Sundance 2.0 by the

Sundance Technology Group, Video F/X by Digital F/X, and the Avid Media Composer. The Avid system is quite popular but is somewhat higher-end, and ranges from $30,000 to $70,000.

The use of the computer as a tool for editing videotape has grown rapidly in the past few years. The software and hardware systems are rapidly evolving and coming down in price as competition increases. However, with the advent of low-cost multimedia hardware, another parallel market for editing is beginning to explode. This will be explored in the next section.

Computer as Medium

The previous pages have described the evolution of desktop systems for editing videotape. These systems are used by a variety of professionals, ranging from broadcast-television producers to advertisers to small production shops, with uses ranging from movies and commercials to wedding videos. Certainly the market for videotape will be there for years to come.

However, recent technological advances have brought about the evolution of a new market for video. This market focuses not on videotape but on the digital motion video used by computers. Applications are widespread, and range from interactive training programs for industry to multimedia encyclopedias and entertainment programs for consumers. The video content of these applications also needs to be edited. This has brought on a new set of tools designed specifically for this purpose, adding new features that would be impractical in a tape-editing system.

If you are going to effectively use and edit digital video, you must first explore the issues of formats and compatibility. With the knowledge that exploration brings you, you will be able to produce and edit quality digital videos that can be ported to multiple platforms.

Digital video as a medium

We've already explored the relative advantages and disadvantages of digital versus analog video. For various reasons, the quality of most digital video on a computer appears inferior to that of television. Compounding this problem is the fact that computer users typically are less than 2 feet from the computer screen, whereas the TV set is viewed from a much greater distance.

Digital-video quality is primarily affected by three issues:

1. *Data rate.*   How many bytes per second are used by the file
2. *Compression degree.*   How much the video frames are compressed (more compression produces lower-quality images)
3. *Use of interframes.*   How often there are "key" frames

Item number three requires additional explanation. Most video-compression methods, e.g., MPEG and DVI, use what is known as *interframe* or *delta-*

frame compression. This means, for instance, that only 1 in 15 frames is stored as a true image and all other frames store only the *difference* from the last frame, which is essentially any movement that has occurred. The 1-in-15 true-image frames are called *key frames.* This type of compression affects performance, because video sequences with large amounts of movement, such as pans, may appear jittery. Some compression methods, e.g., JPEG, do not use interframe compression, but this lowers the effectiveness of the total compression.

It would be easy to ignore these issues and work with uncompressed video that had no limits on data rate. As we shall soon see, this is impossible, because there is a limited amount of space to work with and many storage units, such as CD-ROM, can retrieve only a certain amount of data per second. To illustrate this, let us look at a hypothetical scenario.

We will say that an uncompressed image requires 100 units to store, and that the data rate we are using allows for 300 units per second, or an average of 10 units per individual frame. We therefore need a 10:1 compression ratio.

Let us now say that our compressor gives us 5:1 compression on still frames, and results in acceptable quality. If we also use interframe compression we can cut the data rate in half, resulting in 10:1 compression. However, this will limit motion. Yet if we do not use interframe compression, we will need to push our compressor to 10:1 for each image, which results in lower quality. In the end there is no clear answer, and one simply must find the best solution for each situation.

This example is an oversimplification, but it does well represent the thought process involved in producing multimedia video. Other factors affecting data rate include the following three:

1. *Frame size.* Video at 640 × 480 pixels looks excellent, but takes 16 times the data of video at 160 × 120.

2. *Frame rate.* Producing video at 10 frames per second will result in 3 times less data, but also will make motion look stuttered.

3. *Color depth.* Decreasing the number of colors available to video can save significant space, but may also cause the video to appear "cartoonish."

The first two issues, *frame size* and *frame rate,* are straightforward. The third, *color depth,* is an important one that must be well understood. The technical term for this is *bit depth,* and refers to the number of bits per pixel used for color. The best-quality images are 24-bit, where each pixel can be any of 16 million colors. This level of quality typically is used only for photographic and broadcast-quality imagery. A popular midrange format is 16-bit, in which each pixel can be any of 65,000 colors. This still produces good-quality video, when used with a VGA monitor that can support that many simultaneous colors. However the most common format is 8-bit, where there are only 256 colors to choose from. This format is used because it requires less data, and because currently most computer monitors can support only 256 simultaneous colors. The 256 colors used must be chosen carefully, and are placed in a *palette* or *CLUT* (*color lookup table*). If one chooses 256 shades of gray, the resulting video will be high-quality black-and-white. However since using color is much more popular, most editing programs allow one to *optimize* the best palette for a video once it is complete. It is possible to optimize different palettes for different sections of a movie, but on most computers this produces an awkward and unpleasant flash on the screen called a *palette change*.

There also is another type of color depth used, called *color subsampling*. Popular subsampled formats include 9-bit, 4-1-1, and 4-2-2. Basically, these formats store more brightness information than color information, because humans are perceptually less aware of changes in color than changes in brightness. These formats result in high-quality images at a reduced data rate. Usually, however, one does not need to worry about this, because most 16- and 24-bit compression algorithms do color subsampling internally.

Digital-video formats

A digital-video format essentially is a specification for the storage of interleaved video and audio data. There is an important distinction between *format* and *compression*. Some digital-video formats, e.g., Video For Windows, can support multiple compression algorithms within the same format.

The primary video format on Apple computers is QuickTime. On the PC, the most popular format is Video For Windows (established by Microsoft). There also is a QuickTime for Windows format, which is identical to the Apple QuickTime format. This allows those files to be played on both the PC and Macintosh. Also, around the time this was written, Microsoft announced drivers for playing Video For Windows on the Macintosh. In addition, as one might expect, there are conversion programs that allow one to go back and forth between each format.

Other formats exist for specialized uses. One popular format for training and marketing applications is the AVS format, used only with Intel-hardware-supported compression methods. This format exists on the PC, in DOS, Windows, and OS/2.

Compression options

Compression of video data is an absolute necessity if such data is to be used in computer applications. One frame of video data, at 512×480 resolution and 24-bit color depth, requires 737,280 bytes of data. At the same time digital video often is distributed on CD-ROM, which has a maximum data throughput of 150,000 bytes per second. Since usually there are 30 frames of video per second, this makes a requirement of 147:1 compression (737,280 $\times$ 30 = 22 million = 150,000 $\times$ 147). This level of compression is not easy to obtain, and over the years a number of compression algorithms have appeared to perform this task.

Compression can be accomplished either in hardware, during the capture/digitization process, or later in software. Generally the choice depends on the cost of the capture hardware.

Low-end capture boards, such as Video Blaster, run from $250 to $350. They capture motion video as a series of uncompressed images, in a very large file. Later one can filter this file through an editor and compress the video in software to a more manageable size. On the PC, files typically are compressed with the Microsoft Video Compressor, the Indeo algorithm (by Intel), the RLE algorithm, or the Cinepak codec. While inefficient, boards such as Video Blaster are an excellent value for the money, and have helped to put digital video into the hands of many consumers.

It should be noted that RLE (run-length encoded) compression does not provide a high compression ratio, but it is lossless, which means the compressed image has 100 percent of the quality of the original. RLE is best used for animation, as well as with video having only small areas of motion.

Midrange boards generally include real-time compression with capture. These boards, ranging from $400 to $600, include the Video Spigot (using Supermac compression), Intel's Smart Video Recorder (using Indeo compression), and MediaVision's Pro-Movie Studio (using Microsoft Video Compression).

High-end hardware, starting at $1500, also includes hardware-assisted playback. This means that special hardware decompresses the video very fast and can play it back full-screen, giving the highest video quality. Unfortunately this limits distribution, because only users with the special decompression hardware can play the video.

One very popular high-end board is ActionMedia II, made by both Intel and IBM. The ActionMedia board supports Intel's DVI and Indeo compression algorithms. Also, VideoLogic sells the MediaSpace board, which provides motion-JPEG compression and decompression.

Other higher-quality proprietary compression algorithms exist that require you to send your video to special sites. Intel's PLV (production-level video) is one such algorithm, and costs approximately $200 per video-minute to compress, at sites such as Horizons Technology in San Diego, CA. One drawback, however, is that, once compressed, these videos cannot be manipulated, and editing is limited to very simple cut-and-paste operations.

Digitizing issues

Anyone editing and producing computer-based video needs to be aware of capture and digitizing issues if they are to get the best-quality product. First, one should capture video with the highest-quality video deck. Using consumer-grade VCRs brings the problems of both analog and digital artifacts into the final product, and thus should be avoided.

The analog-video format generally is unimportant in the digital realm, but one needs to make sure that the output format of the deck, e.g., Y/C or RGB, is compatible with the input formats of the capture board.

Finally, if at all possible one should use a time-based corrector. TBCs synchronize and stabilize the video picture, making for a much better digital image when captured.

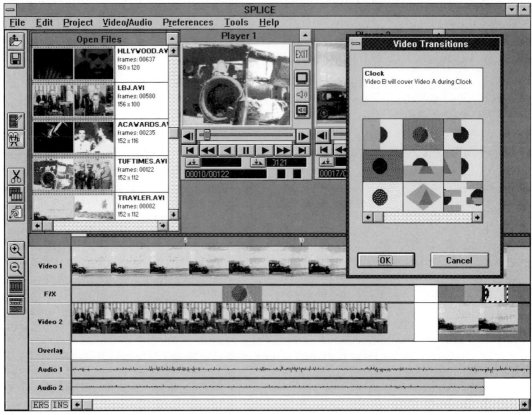

Figure 37.4 SPLICE editing software.

Editing software—Macintosh

The most popular editing software for digital video on the Macintosh is Adobe Premiere. This program allows for a number of interesting transitions and special effects, and is very flexible. Also popular is DiVA VideoShop, which allows easy incorporation of edited clips into applications.

Editing software: PC

Several digital-video editing programs exist in the PC environment, most under Windows. One popular program is SPLICE (see Fig. 37.4). SPLICE is compatible with the following formats: Video For Windows, QuickTime, and AVS, and can convert between any two of these formats. SPLICE has an intuitive time-line-based interface, and a number of special effects and video filters. The product also ships with a CD-ROM of sample video clips, which can be used in editing. In addition many other effects and filters are available as add-ons to the SPLICE product.

Also available is ATI's MediaMerge, which includes support for Video For Windows and QuickTime. MediaMerge incorporates an audio editor and several layers of video overlay.

Finally, there also are a number of programs for postproduction video effects. One popular consumer program is Morph by Gryphon Software. This program allows one to add morphing effects to Video For Windows sequences.

Editing and the Authoring Process

Video production and editing is an integral part of the interactive video authoring process. Many have tried to separate them and have ended up reshooting and reediting large amounts of material later, when it was discovered that important sequences were missing from the program. The process should be carefully planned and organized. A description of the five key steps follows.

1. *Make a flowchart.*   Always make a detailed flowchart of any sections of the program that will incorporate video or audio. Be sure that *all* branches are accounted for, so there will be nothing missing as the program is being authored. Such deficiencies can cause large delays in programming.

2. *Write a script/storyboard.*   Write a detailed script for every scene. Accompany all changes in action with a storyboard, which sketches out the scene that is to be shot. Note that with interactive video, similar events often are repeated with different outcomes. Working from a careful script will help you to avoid unnecessary shooting of certain pieces and keep costs down.

3. *Review and digitize.*   All raw footage should be reviewed. If your digitizing is to be done externally (as with PLV video), you will need to make a precise chart of the time code to be used, making sure that you choose only important clips. This should be done carefully, since recompressing extra segments later will bring on big delays in development. Also, unnecessary digitization can cost over $200 per minute.

For in-house digitizing, you will simply need to digitize those general sections of the tape that are needed. Precise cutting can be done by the video-editing program.

4. *Synchronize video and audio.*   Individual clips now can be loaded into the editing program. Many interactive video productions incorporate narration that was recorded separately. Editing programs such as SPLICE allow one to visually lay out video and audio on a time line, to allow for precise synchronization. Often you also will want to add background music or external sounds, e.g., an alarm ringing. Most editing programs have a second audio track used for mixing. You will want to make sure your program has relative volume control and audio fading, to allow for the best-quality soundtrack.

5. *Match images and audio.*   Most interactive programs have long segments of audio that are interspersed with still images. Before authoring, it is very important that you lay out a chart listing audio files, image files, and appropriate frame numbers for insertions. Time-line-based editing programs

are very helpful in this process, for they allow the user to slowly step through audio files and locate exact frames corresponding to specific words on the soundtrack.

Desktop Editing Tips

A number of "rules" exist for video editing, rules that establish meanings for various types of cuts and transitions. They were established a century ago during the production of the first black-and-white films. Though we are not conscious of them as viewers, we expect these rules to be followed and we understand the "language" that is presented through them. For instance, in a static scene, we expect the action to be *balanced* in the center two-thirds of the screen. If the action is off-center, we get a sense of motion or urgency. Ignoring these rules can confuse the viewer, whereas following them helps you to take advantage of subliminal cues that were not present in the original footage.

Continuity of action is critical. If at all possible, make sure the video is shot from multiple vantage points, for additional flexibility in editing. Cutting from a medium shot to a closeup is common, and can suggest emotion. Never cut between two shots of the same scene at the same distance. This is known as a *jump cut,* and is very distracting to the viewer.

Edited scenes should follow the action. If you have a training sequence of someone operating machinery, cut to a closeup of the hands, giving a sense of the importance of a particular action. At the same time, always keep in mind the *pace* of your movie. A rapid number of cuts in sequence, as in music videos, suggests excitement. Relaxed subject matter should be edited at a slower pace.

Transitions between scenes can be enhanced by means of *transparent editing*. Programs such as SPLICE allow one to manipulate video and audio tracks separately, so that audio from the first scene can lead into the second, or vice versa. For instance, in the first scene two characters may be talking about where they are going. When cutting to the second scene, continue the audio of the conversation from the first for an extra two or three seconds. This produces a smoother, more meaningful transition.

Many editing programs offer a variety of interesting special effects and transitions. One must fight the urge to overuse these. Effects sometimes can distract from the action of a scene. If possible, use them only when they complement the action. For instance, when cutting from a scene of a character thinking of his/her friend to a scene of the friend, you might use an *iris effect,* originating from the head of the character and opening to fill the screen. Used in this way, effects can enhance a movie considerably.

Consumer Distribution

When it comes to applications that will be mass-distributed to a consumer market, several issues should be kept in mind during the editing process.

First, remember that most consumers have low-end machines that probably will play back video more slowly and less smoothly. As a result, you may want to add more flash and excitement to the video to compensate. Image-warping and video-morphing are popular techniques. Keep in mind, however, that a fast, flashy transition may be skipped over entirely by the video driver on a slow machine.

When putting together a program, you also should be careful as to the palettes used. Since digital video usually is no more than 320 × 240, often it is framed on a background screen. If the background screen is made up of more than 20 colors, and if palettes are not carefully chosen, video play will cause unsightly palette changes unacceptable to the consumer. The SPLICE program allows the user to incorporate a base palette of background colors when optimizing palettes for a new movie. This allows several movies to play on the same background without altering the visible palette.

As discussed previously, data rate for video is a key issue, as most programs are delivered on CD-ROM. Also, CD-ROMs can hold only 70 minutes of video. Some applications require more, which calls for a further limiting of frame size and frame rates. Some developers have turned to a new compression technique (developed by Iterated Systems) called *fractal compression*. This provides higher-quality video at lower data rates.

Most developers are very interested in cross-platform compatibility. We've discussed various video formats and the platforms on which they run. The most important issue, however, is the type of compression used, since you can always convert between video formats.

Finally, performance is always an important issue when delivering to consumers. Compounding this is the fact that, as of this writing, the Video For Windows drivers do not guarantee video and audio synchronization. This means that on a slow machine, video can look like a badly dubbed foreign film, with the mouth moving out of sync with the voice. Unfortunately there is no good solution for this, other than to limit the amount of closeup speech.

Future Directions

The 1990s are witnessing a rapid evolution of editing technologies. Costs have dropped dramatically, and will continue to do so.

Increasingly faster computers also will affect editing systems. The need for hardware-accelerated video playback may dwindle, as CPUs and VGA boards grow both in power and speed. Also, as more consumers are able to play smooth-motion videos on their PCs, the market for digital-video tools and applications will burgeon dramatically.

Adding Full-Motion Video to Multimedia Presentations

Bruce A. Rady

Introduction

Software capture/edit tools provide all the functions of conventional video-editing systems but offer many additional benefits. These tools store your video and audio files digitally on computer disk, using advanced video-compression techniques.

Well-featured capture/edit tools will have the capabilities described in this chapter.

The *disk storage method* means that these tools can provide virtually instant access to any scene or frame in any random order you choose. The need to wait for videotape to cue is completely eliminated.

Given the digital storage of video and audio, and the random access to any frame or scene, the more sophisticated capture/edit tools now available provide the user with "nonlinear" editing capabilities (see Figs. 38.1, 38.2, 38.3, and 38.4). Nonlinear editing allows you to place a new scene or shot in between existing ones without having to copy any of the subsequent scenes. This saves considerable time.

Since nonlinear editing is much faster and you can see the results instantaneously, it's easier to experiment with different edits. Nonlinear editing also makes it possible to "undo" edits, even to save different versions of a program. And because the editing is done without copying tape, video (and audio) quality are maintained regardless of the number of edits.

Overview of the Creation Process

An introduction to software capture/edit tool capabilities

The new breed of software capture/edit tools have everything you need to help you create edited digital "movie" files that can be played in other multi-

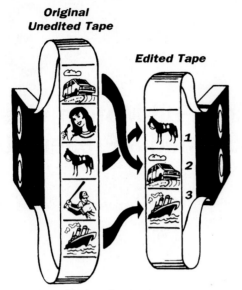

Figure 38.1 Linear editing means copying.

Figure 38.2 Nonlinear editing means disk-skipping.

media programs. They allow you to "capture" original material from virtually any video or audio source, and provide you with easy-to-use yet powerful editing capabilities.

These tools also allow you to export video programs to Microsoft Video for Windows (AVI) files, or Apple's Quicktime (MOV). Video for Windows allows you to play motion video and audio on a PC without any compression hardware at all. This means that the audience for your multimedia program can be any PC running Windows 3.1. To hear audio, an audio card and speakers are required.

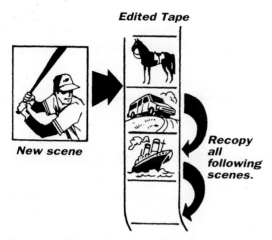

Figure 38.3   Linear changes are difficult.

Figure 38.4   Nonlinear changes are easy.

The better capture/edit tools are ideal for Video for Windows, because they allow you to capture and edit at the highest digital-video quality and then export your program to a variety of formats with differing qualities/data rates. The same video program then can be sent to a very wide audience, from Video for Windows customers at the low end to videotape users at the high end. This flexibility to maximize the audience for your multimedia products is an important consideration.

Additional software tools allow you to add "interactivity" to the edited video you create with capture/edit tools. IBM's Ultimedia Tool Series, for example, offers a variety of compatible products to give you a complete "suite" of functions to develop exciting, rich, interactive multimedia. Many of these tools have versions both for the occasional user and the frequent "professional" user.

The balance of this chapter will show you how to create full-motion, interactive multimedia programs using capture/edit tools.

The multimedia development process

Developing a multimedia program consists of seven basic steps (see Fig. 38.5).

1. *Script and plan.*   Creating a good multimedia program should start with a good script and plan. Determine exactly what you are trying to accomplish with your program, who your target audience is, and what messages you are trying to convey to them. Then write a complete script and plan out such things as the type of video/audio segments you will need, where animation, graphics, or text would be effective, the type of music you want, a flowchart of any interactive branching, etc. A "shot list" of the camera positions you want is also an important part of the script. Even if you are using the most flexible capture/edit tools, a good script is likely to save a large amount of time and money that otherwise would be wasted.

2. *Shoot the video/audio.*   Using your shot list, shoot your video. Also, record any narration or extra audio you need. While you're shooting video, get some "on-location" sound effects such as keyboard typing, machine sounds, ambience, and other audio unique to your story. These are very easy to edit in and they will greatly add to the realism of your program.

3. *Create graphics/animation/titles.*   Using an animation, paint, or graphics package, create the graphic, animation, and textual elements you desire. Depending on which capture/edit tool you use, these elements can be stored in a Targa, PCX, or other file format and then directly imported. Or you can create them in almost any format and convert them using utilities such as HiJack. The Ultimedia Tool Series includes a number of tools that perform these functions.

4. *Capture video/audio.*   Capture the video and audio you shot during Step 2. *Capture* means digitize the audio and video onto your computer's hard-disk drive. Also you can capture "wild" audio such as music from CDs, audio tapes, sound effects, direct microphone narration (use your camcorder's mike if nothing else), audio-only portions from your videotape, etc.

5. *Edit motion video/audio.*   Using your capture/edit tool's edit function, create your edited movie or sequence. If the tool offers nonlinear editing capabilities, you easily can change your sequence at will and even capture more video/audio/graphics after you've edited a rough version of your story. Using a nonlinear editor, the process becomes "iterative" and allows you to change your script quickly if you're not happy with the results. When you're done, you can output an edited digital-video file in formats such as Microsoft's Video for Windows (AVI) or Apple's Quicktime (MOV).

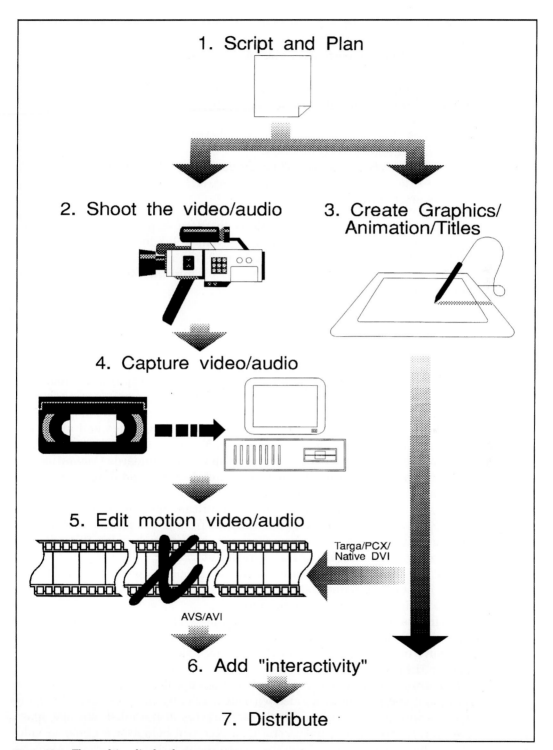

Figure 38.5   The multimedia development process.

6. *Create the "interactive" portion.*   Using a multimedia-based presentation or authoring program, add the "interactive" aspects of your program: icons, branching, hypermedia, etc. Include digital-video windows in which you play the edited motion-video files you created using the capture/edit tool. Bring in animation, graphics, and titles from Step 3 directly, if you so desire. Again, you have a number of choices of presentation and authoring tools available to you from the IBM Tool Series. Many of these also include a run-time "player" version that you can use to distribute your interactive program to your target audience's computers.

7. *Distribute the program.*   This can be done via CD-ROM if you are publishing a title, on a network for video e-mail, or kept on a laptop for a sales or business presentation.

Of course, there are many variations on these steps. For example, if you simply wanted a motion-video file to play in a window under Windows or OS/2's Media Player, you could skip Step 6 and exclude any "interactivity" from your program. In that case, just call up into the Media Player the file you created using the capture/edit tool.

Capturing Video and Audio

Defining *capture*

Steps 4 and 5 described above are performed using the capture/edit tool. Step 4 actually consists of two steps, *capture,* a required step, and *logging footage,* an optional step.

Capture is the process of digitizing and compressing video and audio into your computer and storing it on hard disk. You can capture from any NTSC video source (NTSC stands for National Television Standards Committee and is the standard TV format in both the United States and Japan) such as a VCR, camcorder, etc.

You also can capture audio—either simultaneously with, or separately from, video. For example, you can capture from a CD player or audiotape recorder without any video. You then can easily synchronize this with the video any way you like, using the capture/edit tool.

Once the video or audio source has been properly connected, you simply play it into the computer and the system captures it in "real" time—that is, 1 minute of video takes 1 minute to capture.

During capture, the video will be compressed using hardware such as Intel's i750B chip on the ActionMedia II board. Compression is a method used to remove unneeded data from the incoming video and make it take up less space in the computer.

This crucial step makes high-quality motion video on a PC possible. For example if you just digitize video without using any compression, 30 seconds of video will require approximately 600 Mbytes of hard-disk storage space. However, that same amount of storage space will hold over an hour of video when it has been compressed by the ActionMedia board.

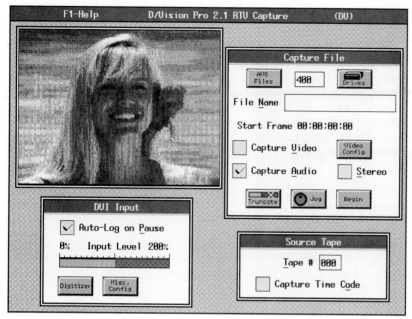

Figure 38.6 Capture screen.

The end result of capture is an AVS file (audio/video subsystem file) in which both the digitized video and audio are stored. This file can be converted into a variety of formats including a Microsoft Video for Windows (AVI) file, either before or after editing.

A sample capture session

This subsection will "walk you through" 12 steps that will show you how to capture material using one capture/edit tool, D/Vision. This particular tool allows you to capture in real time at a variety of picture resolutions/data rates. It also gives you the option of "marking" a still frame image as a reference for a video segment. During editing, this reference still frame is displayed as a "thumbnail" for fast retrieval of the video segment.

1. Figure 38.6 shows the "Capture Screen" in D/Vision. The image from your video source is shown in a video window on the upper left. The "DVI Input" window is on the lower left, and the "Capture File" window is on the upper right.

2. Load a tape into your VCR. If you are going to capture to a new file, select the "Video Config" icon in the Capture File window. Figure 38.7 appears, allowing you to select from four different resolutions. Each of these has a different data rate, as indicated by the number in the parentheses:

- SupeRTV (1000 kbytes/second)
- High-res (1000 kbytes/second)

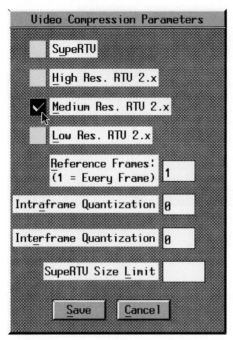

Figure 38.7   Video configuration screen.

- Medium-res (300 kbytes/second)
- Low-res (150 kbytes/second)

The higher the data rate, the better the picture quality, but also the more hard-disk space required per second of video running time. Data rate versus picture quality is discussed later, in the section Outputting a Digital Video File. Once a resolution setting has been chosen for an AVS file, it cannot be changed later (however, you can intercut between different resolutions during edit). In Figure 38.7, the selected resolution has a checkmark next to it.

3. If you are capturing footage to an existing file, choose the "AVS Files" icon in the Capture File window and the "Select AVS File" screen will appear (see Fig. 38.8). The new video you are about to capture will then be appended onto the end of the selected file.

4. Select the name of the file you wish to use.

5. Move your VCR to the start of the footage you want to capture, and put it in pause. Then click on the "Digitizer Control" icon in the DVI Input window. The Digitizer Control's pop-up window appears.

6. Adjust the Digitizer Control to obtain the picture you want (see Fig. 38.9). You may also want to play a segment of the tape and adjust the

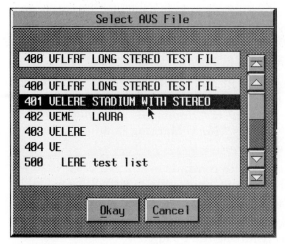

Figure 38.8 Select AVS File screen.

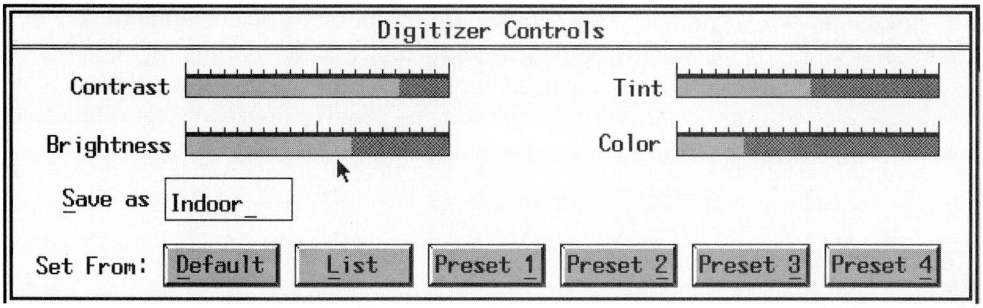

Figure 38.9 Digitizer controls.

Digitizer Control. Then move back to the start of the section you want to capture. The upper-four "slider" icons are similar to the controls that exist on a TV set, a professional video monitor, or a time-base corrector. These controls are

Contrast.   How much difference there is between the light and dark areas in your picture. The contrast and brightness of your image are related, since once an overall brightness level has been fixed, the picture can be made to look darker or lighter by contrast adjustment.

Brightness.   How dark or light the overall picture is.

Tint.   The actual colors in the image. This control makes flesh tones look natural, or colors appear realistic.

Color.   The "saturation" of color in the picture. This does not change the actual color but only how "strong" it is.

To operate the slider controls in this example, you would use the computer's mouse to click within any control.

7. Put your VCR into "Play" and let it come up to speed. Then hit the "Begin" icon to start capturing to disk.

8. If you wish to "mark" a reference still frame, hit the "Enter" key where a new shot begins (i.e., where the scene content significantly changes). This allows the use of a "Source Catalog" of "thumbnail" still images for fast retrieval during the editing process. (*Note:* Marking is an optional step. You can capture—and even edit—your material without it.)

9. Repeat Step 8 as long as you want to continue capturing. Each time you see the content change, hit Enter, and a new still image will be stored for display in the Source Catalog.

10. When you have reached the end of the portion of the tape you want to capture, pause RTV Capture by hitting the F3 key.

11. You can easily add more to the end of any file by going back to Step 3.

12. "Logging footage" is an optional step in which you enter information such as shot descriptions or scene and take numbers, for each segment of video and audio. A well-featured capture/edit tool will let you log footage as you capture it, eliminating the need for a separate logging step. These tools also may have a cataloging function, to greatly speed up searches performed during editing.

Editing Audio and Video

Introduction to editing

When capture is complete, your next step is to edit the audio and video. Editing is done using the AVS files created during the capture process.

Using D/Vision as an example, Fig. 38.10 shows the unedited source files being displayed in one video window (on the left) and an edited "movie" sequence in another video window (on the right). This is the D/Vision Edit Screen.

This Edit Screen simulates two videotape recorders. The window on the left "plays" the source video and audio, the window on the right "plays back" your recorded edited program. The controls under the windows act just like the controls of a VCR. They are

1. *Play.*   Lets you view the video (and hear the audio) at the normal speed of 30 frames per second.

2. *Jog.*   Lets you use a computer input device, such as a trackball, to look at the video footage at variable speeds, from frame-by-frame jog to 50 times normal speed, forward or reverse.

3. *Seek.*   Allows you to locate specific frames in the footage.

Figure 38.10   Edit screen.

4. *Rec. (record).*   Available only on the right-hand "Record" window, this control instantly "records" material from the source into your edited program.

Figure 38.11 shows how you can access video material quickly via a "Source Catalog," which presents a visual catalog of the digitized source material.

Each of these still images is from a different shot that has been captured, so you can easily and quickly see all of your editing options. Just select the shot you want, and it's instantly loaded into the source window.

Next you play or jog the video or audio segment to "record" a shot on the record window. Select which portion of which shot you want first, then second, then third, etc., until you have assembled an entire edited "movie" or "sequence." Figure 38.12 is an example of how an edited sequence might appear on what is called a "Time Line" on the Edit Screen.

There is a block for each of four elements: overlay (graphics), video, audio channel 1, and audio channel 2. Wherever the blocks are vertically connected, the video and audio are "sync"—that is, the audio originally was recorded with the video. In the example shown in Fig. 38.12, all the audio is sync for each shot in the Time Line. A vertical line called the "Time Line Cursor" tells you where your recorded program is "cued to."

The more sophisticated "nonlinear" editing tools can play back the sequence without assembling an edited digital-video file. They display a simulation of the edited movie that is so real it cannot be distinguished from an actual edited file.

Figure 38.11   Source catalog screen.

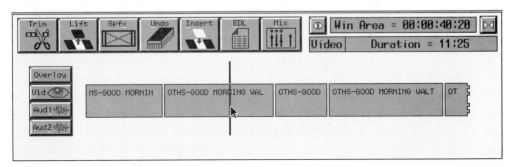

Figure 38.12   Time line #1.

Here is how the "nonlinear" simulation is accomplished. The address of each segment chosen is called an "event" and is stored in an edit decision list (EDL). Capture/edit tools using this method will use the EDL to direct the PC's hard disk to skip around during the simulation, picking up only the video and audio segments you want. The software is so fast that the "playback" is completely seamless, with no pauses or glitches at edit points. Not only is the video "nonlinear" but so are up to six audio tracks and a graphics overlay "track." Regardless of where the video, graphics, and audio are stored—on the same disk or on different disks—the simulation is seamless and plays at a true 30 frames per second.

Nonlinear capture/edit tools with this simulation capability provide you with tremendous flexibility when it comes to making creative choices. They allow you to add, remove, or rearrange material anywhere in the edited sequence, and instantly see the results. You can edit in "wild" sound on two or more separate audio tracks completely independent from the video. You can even make many different edited versions from the same source material, and recall them one after the other to decide which is the best.

All this is done without copying or rerecording any material. The differently edited versions are simply different EDLs, directing the disk to pick up video/audio/graphical elements in a different sequence.

Furthermore, nonlinear tools allow you to "undo" multiple previous edits, or create special video effects such as dissolves and wipes. During all of this editing and reediting the tools continuously—and transparently—update the EDL with the latest changes.

Software capture/edit tools also can provide powerful multitrack audio mixing capabilities, with CD-quality digital audio (44.1 kHz, 16-bit sampling).

Editing video only or audio only

The editing described thus far has used both video and the original audio that goes with it. But it is also useful to be able to edit audio or video separately and independently. For example, you may wish to edit in a narrator, or the audio of interviewers, over the video of their subject. Or you may want to edit silent video over a piece of music.

To accomplish these kinds of edits, the software capture/edit tool must treat audio and video as two completely independent entities. This means that at any point in the edited sequence the video can come from any frame in the source material, regardless of where the audio comes from and vice versa.

Moreover, if two or more channels of audio are fully independent of each other, you have increased creative flexibility. You can then combine three elements that come from different parts of the same disk or from entirely different disks—still with seamless playback.

Figure 38.13 shows how a Time Line can give you an intuitive visual display of the relationship between your video and audio elements. It visually indicates when the video and audio elements are in sync by connecting them vertically.

The "Mode" icons (see Fig. 38.14) at the left of the Time Line determine which of the elements—graphics overlay, video, or one of the several audio channels—are affected in any editing operation. One or any combination of these may be selected to determine which element will be affected by editing.

To record audio only or video only and have the new material overwrite (replace) existing material, you "insert" the new material by selecting the Insert icon and one or more Mode icons. You may select any combination of these icons. The mode(s) selected will determine which elements from the source footage get recorded. The recording of any element will be made at the location of the Time Line cursor. Since this example assumes Insert editing, no change will occur in the positions of the video and audio events following the new shot you're recording.

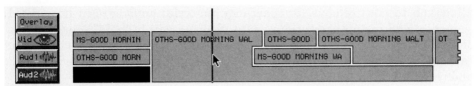

Figure 38.13   Time line #2.

Figure 38.14   Mode icons.

Figure 38.15   Time line—video-only editing.

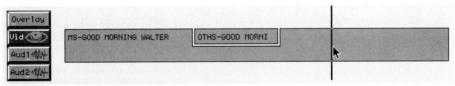

Figure 38.16   Time line—after-video recording.

Figure 38.15 is an example showing the recording of a video-only insert shot. The shaded region on the Time Line will be replaced by the new shot, and the total length of the video will stay the same. When the recording has been completed, the Time Line will appear as in Fig. 38.16.

You will see the "over the shoulder" (OTSH—GOOD MORNING) while still hearing the "medium shot" (MS—GOOD MORNING, WALTER). It is also possible to turn Insert off and then record new footage that "pushes" everything else down in the sequence.

Creative audio editing and mixing

Creative audio editing is one of the most powerful dimensions to motion pictures. A well-featured software capture/edit tool will give you the same flexibility for handling audio that it gives you for video.

With this degree of capability, you can mix and edit multiple audio tracks in sync with, or completely independently from, your video. You can fade down music and fade up a narrator's voice, or cross-fade from one piece of music to another. A particular word or phrase can be made louder or quieter, edited out, or even rearranged. These capabilities easily let you fine-tune your audio and make your finished program a polished, professional presentation. Up to six overlapping audio channels can be edited and mixed while editing audio.

In addition, by creatively using the editing functions, you can add many different types of sounds into an edited program. A virtually unlimited number of audio channels can be "layered" together, six at a time, by editing the output of one sequence into another.

The audio profile

The audio levels at any point in the sequence and on any channel can be changed dynamically. One way to represent this is to use a series of lines and points known as the *audio profile*. A typical audio profile is shown in the Aud 1 and Aud 2 elements of the Time Line in Fig. 38.17 (see the white lines and dots).

The audio profile shows you the volume setting at each point in your edited sequence. You have complete control to change the audio profile at any point, as often as you like—up to once every three frames. All the changes you make are memorized by the system and played back when you choose "Play" or "Jog" under the Record Window. This is like having an automated mixing studio right in your computer.

The black horizontal line running through the middle of each audio channel represents the "normal" volume level for each channel. This is the level at which the audio originally was captured, and represents no attenuation or boost (i.e., it is "flat" audio). This is 0-dB "line level" if your incoming audio was 0 dB. Whenever the audio profile is "flat," the Profile line covers the "flat" line. In the example shown in Fig. 38.17, Aud 1 in the event "THE YEAR WAS..." is flat audio.

When the audio volume is boosted above normal, the Profile is above the flat line; when the volume is lower than normal, the Profile is below the flat line. By setting the two channel's audio profiles, you can vary the relative levels and create mixed audio tracks.

The audio profile actually consists of a series of points connected by lines. These are called *mix points* and they represent the points in time at which you have made changes in the audio levels.

Figure 38.17 Audio profile.

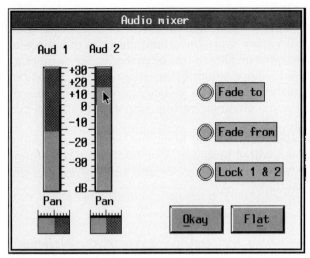

Figure 38.18   Audio-mixer window.

The "Audio Mixer" window

When you insert or adjust a mix point, the "Audio Mixer" window appears, as shown in Fig. 38.18.

This is the main control panel used for setting or changing a mix point. It contains the following functions.

1. The vertical "Faders" labeled "Aud 1" and "Aud 2" on the left are used to adjust the volume. Volume can be adjusted from approximately − 40 dB to + 30 dB, as indicated by the scale between the Faders. The lower, light area on each Fader is the actual volume setting; the higher it is, the higher the volume. Using an input device such as a trackball, you can point and click inside the Fader to the level you want.

2. The "Pan" bars underneath each Fader adjust the left and right balance for each channel.

3. The "Fade to" icon determines whether or not the audio profile into a mix point will fade (up or down) from the previous mix point. If it does not fade, it will step to a new level at the point.

4. "Fade from" determines whether or not the audio profile will fade (up or down) from the current mix point to the next one. If it doesn't fade, it will step to a new level at the mix point.

5. "Lock 1 & 2" locks the levels on both channels together, so that a change made to one channel automatically changes the other as well.

6. "Flat" automatically resets both Volume and Pan controls to normal (0-dB) levels.

It is important to turn on the Mode icons on the Time Line for the channel(s) you want to adjust before clicking on the Mix icon. This determines which channel is active in the Audio Mixer window. If a channel is not active, its fader is "ghosted" and cannot be adjusted.

Creating special video effects

Until now we have discussed only "straight cuts" between events. Using a "Special Effects" ("Spfx") function, you can change a straight cut into a special-effect transition such as a dissolve or wipe. The following four categories of special effects are very useful:

1. *Dissolve.*   The end of one scene is superimposed over the beginning of another.

2. *Wipe.*   The picture will show a portion of the end of one scene, along with a portion the beginning of the next. Many different types of wipe patterns are available. For examples, see Fig. 38.19.

3. *Fade.*   The start of a scene fades up from black (fade in) or the end of the scene fades out to black (fade out).

4. *Freeze-frame.*   The video at any point in an event can be still-framed for as long as you want.

All of these effects can be programmed for various lengths of time. It is also possible to combine a freeze-frame with any of the other three categories of effects (e.g., wiping out of a freeze-frame into a motion event). In addition, you can convert any special effect back to a straight cut at any time.

The more powerful capture/edit tools create freeze-frames instantly, and build dissolve, wipe, and fade effects in nearly "real time"; that is, a 1-second dissolve takes only about 3 to 4 seconds to build. It is created as a separate file on the disk, and you can play it back as a part of the sequence. You can even jog slowly through the effect at that point in the sequence.

In addition to these effects, graphics and overlays can have special effects. You can fade into a title or fade out a logo. Some capture/edit tools even let you animate the overlay layer in real time for rolling credits, flying logos, etc.

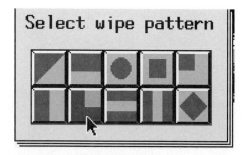

Figure 38.19   Select wipe pattern.

Another category of special effect is sophisticated multisource digital-video effects. These include split screens, dual/quad splits, "pan-and-scan" types of effects, compositing of video layers in a montage, etc. These also include slow- and fast-motion effects, including reverse motion. Since all the video is stored digitally, the number of possible effects is virtually limitless. However, many of these types of effects must be "rendered" to the disk and then edited in as "Source" material, because they are too complex to create in real time during editing.

All special effects are accurately included in your edited digital file during exporting to Video for Windows.

Graphics

In addition to editing video and audio, sophisticated capture/edit tools let you edit graphics simply as another element. Targa, PCX, and other graphics file formats can be imported into the edit tool and edited along with the video and audio. Graphics can either be "keyed" (i.e., overlaid on the video) or put up as still images with audio running under them. It is even possible to import a series of graphics files as an animation sequence and edit that into the video, or key it over the video.

Outputting an Edited Digital-Video File

Once you have completed your editing and have the final version of your program, you will create a real, edited, digital-video file. This is called *outputting,* and includes the steps of *assembling* an actual file and then *exporting* it to the desired resolution and file type.

The exporting utility of your capture/edit tool should let you adjust many parameters in the digital video. For example, you may be able to convert high resolution to low resolution, or introduce "frame-differencing" to reduce the data rates.

Assembling and exporting a digital-video file

An *Assemble* function automatically and frame-accurately recreates all video edits, audio edits, audio mixing levels, qraphics, overlays, animations, and special video effects that you have edited.

The assembled file then can be exported into a variety of formats, including

- Microsoft's Video for Windows (i.e., AVI) file format
- Apple's Quicktime (i.e., MOV) format
- Intel/IBM's DVI file format
- WAV file formats for audio-only files

These edited digital-video files can be played in any authoring or player packages that support, for example, Video for Windows. In fact, using Object

Linking and Embedding (OLE), you can play a Video for Windows file on any computer with Windows 3.1—even if it does not contain Video for Windows. (You will, however, need a sound card and speakers to hear the audio.)

This means that you can send a video clip embedded in WordPerfect, MS-Word, or Excel documents, and the recipients can play them instantly when they view the document, even if they don't have any special software or hardware installed (other than Windows 3.1 and a sound card and speakers).

A digital-video file may be stored on any hard disk, CD-ROM, rewritable optical disk, or other medium having adequate space and data-throughput capability. Also, the file can be networked, allowing motion video/audio to be sent over standard digital networks.

Data rate versus picture quality

A fundamental issue in digital video is the data rate of the video file. Digital video requires that the user make a tradeoff between data rate and picture quality. The higher the data rate, the better the picture quality. However, higher data rates also mean that the files take up more space on the disk and require faster computer platforms to play them back. For example, a digital file that plays well on a fast hard disk may freeze periodically or not play at all on a CD-ROM. For a file to play back without interruption, the data rate of the player platform *must exceed* that of the digital-video file.

It is extremely important to determine the data rate of the target platform on which your digital-video file will play. The disk is a major factor affecting data rate. A fast SCSI hard disk can sustain 500 kbytes per second or more, while most CD-ROMs may be limited to approximately 150 kbytes per second.

Other factors affecting data rates include CPU type and speed, disk controller, operating system overhead, wait states/CMOS setup, etc. Many disk manufacturer's specifications give burst data rates or rates of the controller and not of the disk itself, so often it is very difficult to determine the ongoing, sustainable data rate of a particular platform.

It is *strongly* recommended that you prototype sample digital files on your slowest target player platform, using exactly the same configuration and operating system your audience will use for your final product!

Because of the picture-quality/data-rate tradeoff, some capture/edit tools allow you to easily adjust and experiment with different picture-quality/data-rate tradeoffs in your exported file. To see how this is done, look at Fig. 38.20.

During the outputting procedure, this "Select Export File Type" window appears. By choosing one of the following top five checkboxes, you can select a type of file and a level of picture resolution for your exported file.

1. *High-res AVS.* This provides a standard Intel DVI file with the best-looking video quality, but it requires the most disk space and the highest data rate (approximately 600 kbytes per second). If the target player system has a fast, unfragmented SCSI disk, and your operating system has been configured for fast video playback, this is your best option.

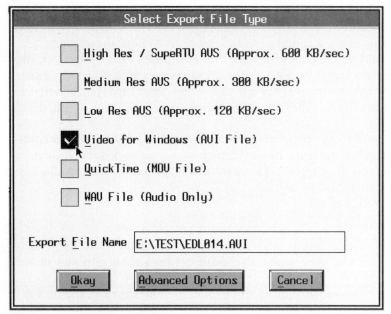

Figure 38.20 Select export file type.

2. *Medium-res AVS.* This provides a standard Intel DVI file at medium picture quality and half the data rate of "high-res" (approximately 300 kbytes per second). If the target player system has an unfragmented IDE or fast MFM disk, this is a good choice. You may also have to configure your operating system with larger buffers/files and other adjustments to allow fast video playback.

3. *Low-res AVS.* This provides a standard Intel DVI file at low picture quality and data rate (120 kbytes per second). If your target system will use a CD-ROM or slow hard disk, or your operating system cannot be configured for fast video playback, this is your best option.

4. *Video for Windows (AVI file).* This provides a direct output to Microsoft's Video for Windows file using Intel's Indeo algorithm video file and "WAV" audio file formats. This is not an AVS file, and its data rate is low enough to allow playback of files from slow hard disks and CD-ROMs in most systems.

5. *Quicktime (MOV File).* This provides a direct output to Apple's Quicktime file. It is used on the Mac platform, and its data rate is low enough to allow playback of files from slow hard disks and CD-ROMs in most systems.

A sixth option, WAV, is for audio only. All six options actually are simplified presettings of many parameters that can be adjusted using the "Advanced Options" icon at the bottom of the "Select Export File Type" window. The Advanced Options allow you to "tweek" the quality of the video and audio to bring it in line with the target-player platform you are using.

Note that it is not possible to increase the resolution of the exported file beyond what was used during capture. However, you can *decrease* it. Therefore, be sure to capture the video at or above the highest resolution you will want to export.

Conclusion

Software capture/edit tools make the production of video programs much easier and faster than it is when you are using conventional videotape-editing methods. They also tend to offer you greater creative freedom, since making edits does not require the recording or copying of material. This encourages that creative experimentation so often needed to tell a compelling, interesting story.

Because the programs created with these tools can be viewed on many platforms—including PCs without special video hardware—the potential audience for your program includes almost anyone with a PC.

Advanced Topics

Communications for Multimedia

Glenn Becker

Vince Walisko

Introduction

In order to facilitate later discussions about protocols and standards, we first will briefly review the seven communications protocol layers as described by the International Standards Organization/Open Systems Interconnect (ISO/OSI), as shown in Fig. 39.1.

The *application* layer defines the task being performed from the user's perspective. Examples include e-mail, computer conferencing, and computer-based training.

The *presentation* layer handles any conversions required to prepare files for presentation to the user, including controls of the desktop PC to play an audio file or display an image file. The *session* layer includes access control and addressing of the information being delivered. Access control can be

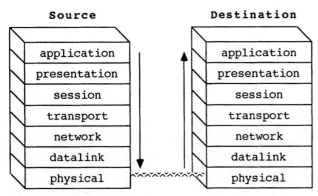

Figure 39.1 ISO protocol layers.

implemented by password or by keys built into the application software. Addressing is an important feature when it comes to delivering information to the appropriate place and not using up excess communications capacity and storage for files.

The *transport* layer is responsible for end-to-end file delivery. This layer includes protocols for detecting and correcting errors that occur during file transfer. The *network* layer is responsible for delivering packets of information that will be assembled into files in the transport layer. Routers operate at the network level to determine which *path* can be used to access the destination computer. Routers also can offer congestion control, which should improve overall system performance. CCITT X.25 is one common example of a network layer protocol.

The *data-link* layer defines the frames of data traveling through a network, as well as correction and retransmission schemes. The frame format may include CRC checks and error-correction codes, which allow the link to appear virtually error-free to the user. LAN protocols (Ethernet and Token Ring) and passive bridges are implementations of data-link protocols.

The *physical* layer defines how unstructured binary digits (bits) travel over the physical media between machines. Physical-layer protocols define pin configurations for cables and voltage levels. Examples include EIA RS-232-C, RS-449, and CCITT V.24.

Standardized protocols have allowed many communications systems vendors to respond to the demand for network interoperability. By building a protocol convertor from RS-422 to V.35 (both physical-layer protocols), two otherwise incompatible systems can be connected. Protocol converters also can be built at the data-link and the network layers. Network interoperability has been a hot topic of late, since it allows users on one network to connect to a different one without having to replace one of the networks.

In this chapter we will concentrate on the physical media available for high-speed communication. For this reason most of the discussion will involve only the physical and the data-link layers.

Determining requirements

When you are sizing a project, remember that some basic parameters define the goals and ultimately drive the solution. All of the following questions are insultingly simple, yet once they have been answered you should have your network solution.

What is the required daily data volume through the network? Determine the volume of data that you expect to flow through the network on a daily basis. The goal here is to be conservative but not too conservative, because "bandwidth is money." An important part of this calculation must include the data-link and network layer protocols that may be used. Some protocols, such as packet-switching protocols or forward error correction, can add significant overhead to your data volume.

How fast must the data arrive at the intended destination?   The delay from the moment a unit of data is submitted to a network for delivery to that when it arrives at the destination is referred to as *latency*. Latency at the transport layer is how long the network takes to deliver a file. If your application requires the timely delivery of data such as news, stock market information, or an address from the company chairman, then latency must be reduced by increasing bandwidth and/or compression, or decreasing overhead. Multimedia applications that depend on real-time delivery of digital audio and video have very strict throughput requirements.

How much of the data received by each destination actually is used by that site? This question does not directly relate to the network but addresses the storage-capacity requirements and the location of the data storage. For some applications it is more efficient to store the data at a central hub and then distribute it over a network on demand. Other applications require local storage of the data at each destination. In most cases data that is used regularly is stored locally for quick retrieval, whereas infrequently used data is stored centrally and transmitted only on demand.

What percentage of the total data goes to many as opposed to only a few destinations?   The answer to this question will determine whether the communications network should be point-to-point or point-to-multipoint (broadcast). If information needs to be sent to several hundred sites or more, and if more than half of the information is required by all sites, then a satellite broadcast solution usually is best. If the number of destinations or the amount of data common to all sites is low, then point-to-point transmission usually is best.

Is the data transmission bursty and irregular, or is it steady throughout the day? Steady data transmission calls for full-time access to a data path. In some cases bursty data transmission is best served by networks that offer part-time usage fees or dial up access on an "as-needed" basis. If you are sending data more than 20 to 30 percent of the day, then full-time access generally is warranted. If you are sending data less than 20 percent of the time, then a part-time communications path may be more cost-effective. Many existing networks offer part-time access at reduced rates for overnight traffic, if your application lends itself to such a schedule.

Are the destination sites friendly or hostile?   One of the most important issues to address when designing a new network is the environment of the communications equipment at the remote sites. If this remote equipment is located in a friendly environment, where technical assistance is available and children with ice cream cones are not allowed, then installing equipment that requires regular maintenance is not a problem. If it is to be located in a hostile environment, however, the installed equipment must require little or no on-site maintenance and must be packaged in such a way as to discourage tampering and intrusive ice cream cones.

Is the data flow one-way or two-way?   This question is fundamental, since most communications paths are by nature either one-way or two-way. In many applications with two-way data flow, the data volumes are not symmetrical (far more data is flowing one way than the other). For such applications, two separate paths sometimes are the best solution. Consider as an example networks that broadcast many megabytes of data over satellite each day, then retrieve small data transactions from the remote sites via dial-up phone lines.

Can you piggyback on an existing network that has excess capacity?   Sometimes this question alone will determine which network your application will use. Often it's hard to beat free or very inexpensive access to an existing data path. Data transmission in the VBI (discussed later) of a video signal does not change the cost of sending the video signal. Remember, however, that additional equipment still is required to insert data into the VBI and retrieve it again.

What level of security do we need?   Requirements for data security may determine whether you use public data networks or private ones. If security is important, current encryption technology offers sufficient protection for the vast majority of applications.

How geographically dispersed are the remote sites?   Terrestrial communication links generally charge by distance, whereas satellite links are indifferent to distances within the "footprint" of a single satellite. The axiom of network implementation is "keep it simple." The fewer things there are to break, the better. Networks cost money to install, and more money to operate. The correct network solution must be a winner in both of those areas.

Current Technology Options

Most of the current technology and standards for communications existed before the advent of desktop multimedia. Yet some of these technologies, such as the CD-ROM, are much more successful now due to multimedia.

Point-to-point delivery

CD-ROM.   A great deal of the multimedia being delivered today is being delivered on CD-ROM. CD-ROMs have proven themselves to be a successful way to distribute multimedia reference materials such as encyclopedias, atlases, historical information, and computer-based training (see Fig. 39.2).

A single CD-ROM can hold up to 660 Mbytes of digitized audio, images, text, video, and program information. CD-ROMs can be copied in large quantities for less than $2 each. The cost-versus-data-capacity ratio for CD-ROMs makes them very attractive to publishers of reference materials, since they are much less expensive to produce than books.

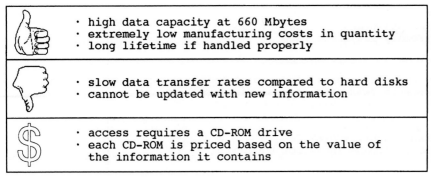

- high data capacity at 660 Mbytes
- extremely low manufacturing costs in quantity
- long lifetime if handled properly

- slow data transfer rates compared to hard disks
- cannot be updated with new information

- access requires a CD-ROM drive
- each CD-ROM is priced based on the value of the information it contains

Figure 39.2 CD-ROM.

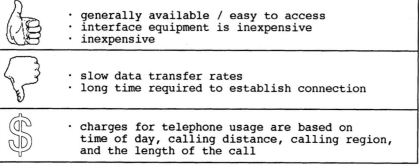

- generally available / easy to access
- interface equipment is inexpensive
- inexpensive

- slow data transfer rates
- long time required to establish connection

- charges for telephone usage are based on time of day, calling distance, calling region, and the length of the call

Figure 39.3 Dial-up analog telephone service.

Unlike hard disks, CD-ROMs cannot be updated with new information. For this reason they work well for archiving reference materials but not for applications that require frequent updates.

One limitation CD-ROMs have imposed on multimedia applications is a data-transfer rate of 150 Kbps (kilobytes per second). This data-transfer rate originated as the "Red Book" specification. However, applications started to use high-resolution color images and full-motion video. These new demands prompted CD-ROM manufacturers to start to build CD-ROM players that operate at two and four times the original data rate.

Dial-up analog telephone service.   Using modems to send and receive data over basic dial-up telephone lines is now commonplace in both the office and the home (see Fig. 39.3). Typical baud (bits per second) rates range from 1200 to 9600 and even 14,400.

While the available data rates do not offer much capacity for the delivery of large quantities of multimedia, dial-up service represents an inexpensive path for the sending of data updates and the retrieval of status information from remote sites.

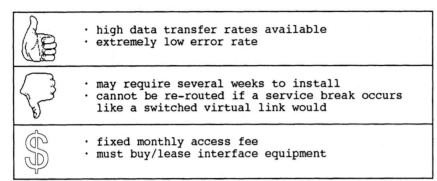

· high data transfer rates available
· extremely low error rate

· may require several weeks to install
· cannot be re-routed if a service break occurs
  like a switched virtual link would

· fixed monthly access fee
· must buy/lease interface equipment

Figure 39.4   Leased-line telephone service.

TABLE 39.1   Major Grades of Leased Lines

Service	Number of voice channels	Baud rate in Mbps
T-1 or DS-1	24	1.544
T-2 or DS-2	96	6.312
T-3 or DS-3	672	44.736
T-4 or DS-4	4032	274.176

New technologies will help to keep dial-up telephone service in the multimedia ballpark. Two such technologies are CCITT V.fast and videophones. The CCITT standard V.fast will offer data-transfer rates of 28,800 baud (or 28.8 kbps) over voice-grade lines.

Videophone standards, such as M-VTS which synchronizes video and audio, will make it possible for multimedia presentations to be sent directly to your telephone.

Leased-line telephone service.   Dedicated high-capacity data lines may be leased from telephone-service providers. Table 39.1 shows the major grades of service and their associated data rates. T-# services typically are for short distances of 200 miles or less. DS-# services support longer distances by using the main communications paths built by the phone companies for interstate-call routing (see Fig. 39.4).

Fractional T-1 services are extremely popular for point-to-point communications and also to transfer data from a source to a satellite uplink facility. Fractional T-1 services generally are sold in increments of 56 kbps.

Some packet-switching network vendors have services that create permanent virtual circuits using the frame-relay protocol. These permanent virtual circuits are the main competition for fractional T-1.

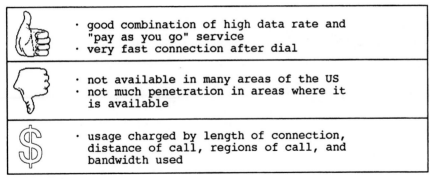

👍	• good combination of high data rate and "pay as you go" service • very fast connection after dial
👎	• not available in many areas of the US • not much penetration in areas where it is available
💲	• usage charged by length of connection, distance of call, regions of call, and bandwidth used

Figure 39.5   ISDN.

Integrated services digital network (ISDN).   Currently, the infrastructure of our telephone system uses digital circuits for call-transmission and number-switching. ISDN is the underlying technology that supports such features as automatic caller identification. Only the "last mile" to your home or desktop is analog. As the ISDN continues to roll out, digital service will be available directly from your telephone.

ISDN offers basic-rate service (BRI) and primary-rate service (PRI). Basic-rate service includes two 64-kbps B channels and one 16-kbps D channel. The B channels are used for data transfer, either 64-kbps two-way transmission or 128-kbps one-way. The D channel is used for switching and flow-control information. Primary-rate service consists of 23 64-kbps B channels and 1 64-kbps D channel. If you combine all of these numbers you will see that primary-rate service actually is a T-1 circuit. PRI commonly is used for LAN-bridging, since it offers far more throughput than analog dial-up service.

Broadcast delivery via ISDN has been discussed by some as possibly being desirable for multimedia applications, but no current implementation is available (see Fig. 39.5).

Point-to-multipoint delivery

In cases where large volumes of information need to be delivered to many locations, the techniques employed are quite different from those used for point-to-point delivery. The differences are analogous to those between a letter and a newspaper. Just as it is more efficient to put a general advertisement in a newspaper than to do direct-mail advertising to everyone, so too it is more efficient to do a data broadcast over satellite than repeated point-to-point transfers to a large number of remote sites.

The basic law of satellite communications is that the more money you spend on the ground the less will have to be spent in space, and vice versa. Costs on the ground include the terminal equipment, which includes the antenna, a low-noise-block down converter (LNB). Costs in space are determined by how much of the available spectrum your signal will consume. For

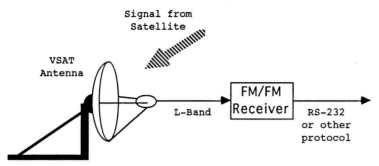

Figure 39.6   Satellite communications.

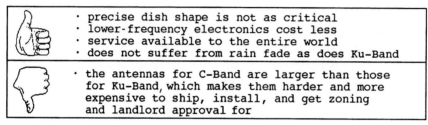

- precise dish shape is not as critical
- lower-frequency electronics cost less
- service available to the entire world
- does not suffer from rain fade as does Ku-Band

- the antennas for C-Band are larger than those for Ku-Band, which makes them harder and more expensive to ship, install, and get zoning and landlord approval for

Figure 39.7   C-Band.

large numbers of users, spending less on each terminal and more on the space segment (which is divided by all the users in figuring a per-site cost) is more cost-effective. However, a large space segment is expensive, and many receivers are required to justify the expense (see Fig. 39.6).

The satellite section is broken up into the commonly used frequencies C-Band and Ku-Band, and then different modulation and control techniques for one-way and two-way communications. Any given system can work with a combination of these alternatives (for example, one-way C-Band).

Operating frequencies

C-Band.   C-Band was the first frequency band used for commercial satellite communications on a large scale (see Fig. 39.7). C-Band employs uplink frequencies from 5.925 to 6.425 GHz, and downlink frequencies from 3.7 to 4.2 GHz. C-Band antennas range in size from 2 to 3 meters.

Ku-Band.   Ku-Band has come into widespread use just in the last 10 to 15 years (see Fig. 39.8). Ku-Band uplinks from 14.0 to 14.5 GHz, while it downlinks from 11.7 to 12.2 GHz. Ku-Band antennas range in size from 0.5 to 2 meters.

Modulation techniques

Spread spectrum.   Spread spectrum simulates natural noise by pseudo-randomly jumping the carrier frequency around. This allows for very good signal

- antennas are small (2 meters or less) for easier shipping and installation

- antenna must be precisely manufactured
- Ku-Band frequencies are attenuated by rain, snow, and water vapor (rain fade)

Figure 39.8 Ku-Band.

- extremely small antennas
- impervious to interference
- coding scheme makes encryption inherent

- extremely large amount of space segment required in comparison to other techniques
- receiver does not lock into signal instantly

- $500–1,000 per receive site for installation
- monthly space segment costs

Figure 39.9 Spread spectrum.

- requires relatively little satellite power for the bandwidth
- low cost receivers

- data must be delivered to a common hub to be combined with other data for aggregate uplink
- changing data rate requires changing hardware

- $400–900 for receive site equipment
- monthly fee for space segment

Figure 39.10 FM/FM.

discrimination in low carrier-to-noise-ratio situations. When other technologies were more expensive, it was a good approach to distribution to large universes of users (tens of thousands). See Fig. 39.9.

Frequency modulated on frequency modulated (FM/FM). The trade names for FM/FM are "FM on FM" or FM Squared. FM/FM is a series of frequency-division-multiplexed phase-modulated signals that are then collectively phase-modulated. This allows the rf high-frequency components of the satellite receiver to handle a large signal, and only after demodulation to lower frequencies are the smaller signals discriminated (see Fig. 39.10).

	• inexpensive receiver equipment • the data rate can be changed by software
	• data must be delivered to a common hub to be combined with other data for aggregate uplink • overhead is added to aggregate for timing and signaling
	• $600–1,000 for receive site equipment • monthly fee for space segment

Figure 39.11   TDMA SCPC.

	• requires relatively little satellite power for the bandwidth • low cost receivers
	• data must be delivered to a common hub to be combined with video for uplink • changing data rate requires changing hardware
	• $400–900 for receive site equipment • monthly fee for space segment

Figure 39.12   FM above video.

Time division multiple-access, single channel per carrier (TDMA SCPC).   The trade name for TDMA SCPC is FM Cubed. Like FM/FM, TDMA SCPC is a method of aggregating together a number of digital data signals. In this case the multiplexing is a matter of time division rather than frequency. The result is the same, in that the receiver can look at a big signal that is easier and less expensive to discriminate (Fig. 39.11).

FM above video.   Same as FM/FM, except that in this case data is frequency-division-multiplexed with video and other subcarriers. This is a popular method for companies that already have video transmission capabilities, since the data travels along with the video for free (Fig. 39.12).

Single channel per carrier (SCPC).   SCPC is a technique that can be used for point-to-point or point-to-multipoint transmission. A single data signal modulates a single rf carrier, which is relayed by a satellite (Fig. 39.13).

Flow control for two-way VSAT networks

Two-way VSAT (very-small-aperture terminal) networks are based on a single hub site that controls the access of a large number of remote VSAT sites

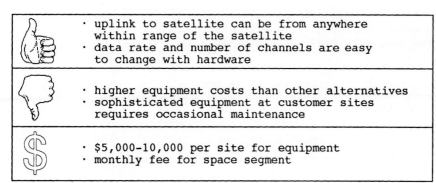

Figure 39.13 Single channel per carrier.

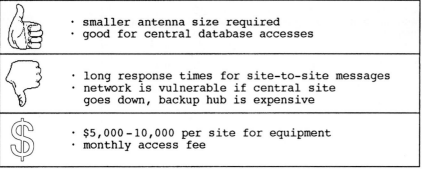

Figure 39.14 Star network.

via channels in the space segment. The channels support data messages from a remote site to the hub, the hub to a remote site, and in some cases remote site to remote site. Various protocols are used to determine which site can "talk" at any given time and for how long.

Star network.   The star network is the most common type of control protocol, one in which the sites and the hub can "talk to each other." If a message is addressed from one site to another, it must go through the hub on the way (Fig. 39.14).

Mesh network.   A mesh network allows all sites to "talk" to all other sites directly (Fig. 39.15).

Access to the Home Market

Telephone

The most common channel of digital data communications into the home today is over voice-grade telephone lines. The current population of personal computer users is accustomed to using modems to access bulletin-board ser-

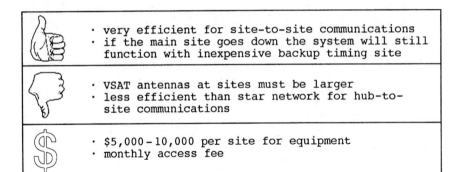

Figure 39.15   Mesh network.

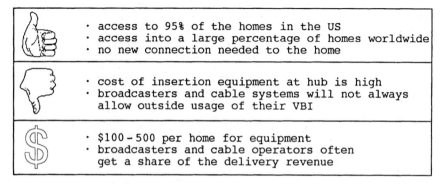

Figure 39.16   Vertical blanking vertical.

vices and to send files between computers. The low data rates available on dial-up voice-grade lines make this communications method inefficient for most multimedia applications.

Vertical blanking interval (VBI)

The vertical blanking interval is a period in a TV signal during which the raster beam travels from the bottom of the screen back up to the top of the screen. Inserting data in the VBI is a way of putting data in the unused space on a television signal, between the end of one frame and the beginning of the next. A decoder box can be attached to the TV antenna or cable. Current technology limits data throughput to 9600 baud per VBI line. Most commercially available VBI equipment handles only one VBI line. Some new systems support two lines and offer throughput of 19,200 baud (Fig. 39.16).

TV Cable used for digital data delivery

This is an approach to using existing Cable TV channels to deliver data into the home. A decoder is connected to the cable just as a TV would be. Tests of this technology are beginning to appear across the United States. Services

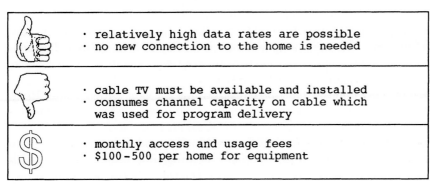

Figure 39.17 TV cable for digital-data delivery.

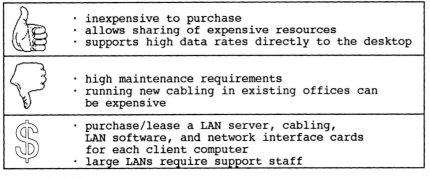

Figure 39.18 LANs.

that allow subscribers to connect to their cable, such as a LAN or a one-way data receiver, soon will be available (Fig. 39.17).

Access to the Desktop Market

All of the communications options available to the home also are available to the office, with the exception of TV cable. Cable has not penetrated office buildings to the same extent as it has the home market.

Local-area networks (LANs)

LANs have become commonplace in most office environments (Fig. 39.18). They offer data-transfer rates of from 4 to 16 Mbps. LANs allow many desktop users to share expensive resources such as large storage devices and laser printers.

The most common data-link protocol for LANs is Ethernet. Virtually all Ethernet implementations run at 10 Mbps. A new version called Fast Ethernet, which runs at 100 Mbps, soon will be available. On an Ethernet LAN, each system is responsible for controlling its dialogue with the LAN. If a computer needs to send information over the LAN, it checks the LAN for data traffic. If there is no current data flow, it will try to send its information. If two or more systems start to send at the same time, a collision occurs and each sending computer must stop sending and retry at a later time. The control protocol that manages the interface to the LAN is called Carrier Sense Multiple Access/Collision Detection (CSMA/CD).

The second most popular data-link protocol for LANs is called Token Ring. Token Ring avoids the collision problem by having one system, and one system only, act as the *active monitor* (*AM*). A token is passed around the network until it arrives at a system with something to send; this system starts to send and continues to send until the token-holding time limit is up, at which time the token is passed on. The system with the token is the active monitor.

The bandwidth requirements imposed on current LANs by multimedia applications often cause performance problems. Current protocols were not designed to deliver the sustained data throughput required for driving real-time digital-audio and -video presentations. New schemes for handling multimedia applications are in the works for both Ethernet and Token Ring.

Fiber distributed data interface (FDDI)

FDDI, which offers transfer speeds of 100 Mbps, is used primarily to interconnect LANs in a metropolitan area network (MAN) or a wide area network (WAN). Copper distributed data interface (CDDI) uses the same standards as FDDI to deliver 100-Mbps traffic over copper wiring, but only for short distances (within an office). See Fig. 39.19.

Switched multimegabit data service (SMDS)

SMDS is supplied by the phone companies and gives users with bursty high-bandwidth requirements access to DS-1 (1.544-Mbps) through DS-3 (45-Mbps) levels of service.

SMDS offers dynamic bandwidth allocation, which is ideal for delivering large multimedia files. SMDS, however, is not good for delivery of real-time data. Since the data is packetized and switched through routers, it may not

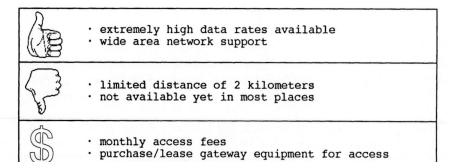

👍	• extremely high data rates available • wide area network support
👎	• limited distance of 2 kilometers • not available yet in most places
💲	• monthly access fees • purchase/lease gateway equipment for access

Figure 39.19   FDDI.

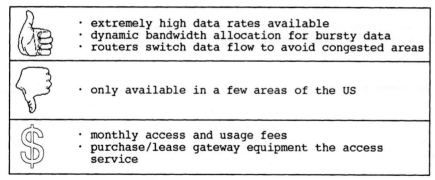

👍	· extremely high data rates available · dynamic bandwidth allocation for bursty data · routers switch data flow to avoid congested areas
👎	· only available in a few areas of the US
💲	· monthly access and usage fees · purchase/lease gateway equipment the access service

Figure 39.20 Switched multimegabit data service.

arrive in the same order it was sent, and there may be delays between the delivery of consecutive packets (Fig. 39.20).

Emerging Technology

Channel-modulated video delivered over existing LAN wiring

One innovative approach to delivering video over existing LAN wiring is to channel-modulate the video onto the LAN cable, just as the many channels of TV come into your home on a single cable. To leave room for FDDI bandwidth, most of these channel-modulation schemes use the frequency space from 300 to 450 MHz. Frequencies below 300 MHz are reserved for normal LAN and FDDI traffic, while frequencies above 450 MHz suffer severe attenuation.

Modulating video onto a LAN requires special equipment that can take a baseband video source and channel-modulate it onto the LAN, and then a demodulator to convert the video back to baseband at each desktop.

The pricing of this equipment follows the usual model for such systems, with the modulator costing several thousand dollars and the demodulator at each desktop costing only a couple of hundred dollars.

Ka-Band frequency over satellite

Ka-Band is a higher-frequency band than Ku-Band or C-Band. Ku-Band uplinks from 27.5 to 31.0 GHz, and downlinks from 17.7 to 21.2 GHz. Today the Ka-Band spectrum is largely unused, but as applications for broadcasting more digital data arise, this space will be called into use.

Ka-Band offers the advantage of having very small receiver antennas (around half a meter in diameter), but it suffers more severely than Ku-Band from rain fade.

High-definition television (HDTV)

Now that the standards are converging to make it possible for HDTV to be entirely digital, the possibility of inserting more data in the video and audio signal exists. Current HDTV plans call for delivery via tagged digital data packets. Each packet's tag describes the data contained in the packet. This tagging scheme allows some amount of data to travel along with the packets of digital video and audio.

Asynchronous transfer mode (ATM)

In the communications world, ATM is the hottest thing since sliced bread. The infrastructure for ATM is only beginning to be built, but soon it will be competing with FDDI and other WAN interconnection networks. At first ATM will be a bit more expensive than networks already in place, but it does offer some useful advantages.

ATM packets will be of fixed size, which makes for fast hardware switching. These fast switches will compare favorably with X.25 and frame-relay switches. ATM also offers scalable "on-demand" bandwidth for bursty data-delivery applications.

Initial ATM usage will be through X.25 or frame-relay interfaces that emulate existing communications links and LAN interconnections for compatibility.

Conclusions

When designing any network, it is important that you size the requirements early in the process. This information will focus your attention on those technologies that can do the job. You also must unit-test the transmission of your data over the prospective network, so as to get real statistics on things such as error rates, overhead, and net data throughput. Problems are inevitable in any integration project. The key to success is to find the problems early, before they can become "showstoppers."

But above all else: "Keep it simple"!

Glossary of Acronyms and Abbreviations

ATM   Asynchronous transfer mode

C/No   Carrier-to-noise ratio; a measure of signal strength

CCIR   International Radio Consulting Committee (wireless and spectrum usage)

CCITT   International Telegraph and Telephone Consulting Committee

CDDI   Copper distributed-data interface

CSMA/CD   Carrier Sense Multiple Access/Collision Detection

Ethernet   IEEE 802.3 (uses CSMA/CD)

FDDI   Fiber distributed-data interface

FM/FM   Frequency-modulated, multiplexed, and frequency-modulated again

GHz   Gigahertz (billion cycles per second)

IEC   International Electrotechnical Committee

ISO   International Standards Organization

ISDN   Integrated Services Digital Network

ITV   International Telecommunications Union (a treaty organization of the United Nations consisting of the CCITT and CCIR)

kbps   kilobits per second (data rate)

Mbps   Megabits per second (data rate)

MHz   Megahertz (million cycles per second)

OSI   Open systems interconnection

PAD   Packet assembler/disassembler

SCPC   Single channel per carrier satellite modulation scheme

SNA   Systems Network Architecture; IBM proprietary standard for communications and network interoperability

SNMP   Simple Network Management Protocol, from Internet; also SNMP2, which has many new features including security

10BaseT   Twisted pair LAN

10Base2   Thin-wire LAN

10Base5   Thick-wire LAN

TVRO   Television-receive-only satellite terminal

TCP/IP   Transmission Control Protocol and the Internet Protocol

Token Ring   IEEE 802.5 LAN communications protocol

VSAT   Very-small-aperture terminal (satellite antenna)

X.25   A standard DTE PAD to DCE PAD protocol

40

Distributed Multimedia Requirements

Les Dunaway

Requirements

If we are to understand the requirements for implementation of multimedia applications, we must first focus on the objects that make up the application. In one sense multimedia is "just computing." That is, data objects are created, manipulated, distributed, stored, displayed, and destroyed. Additionally, these data objects have behaviors and relationships that change with use.

In another sense, multimedia is "a new computing paradigm." That is, the data objects are very complex and very large, have many complex, dynamic relationships, and require special hardware and software for creation, manipulation, distribution, storage, and display. While creation, manipulation, distribution, storage, and display are the actions seen by the end user, the system functions that enable them make up a different list—a list containing some of the same words, just to enhance confusion.

Storage

The requirements for storage of multimedia objects differ from those of conventional data processing in two ways: size and complexity. Some primitive systems are unable to deal with BLOBs (Binary Large OBjects); that is, they exhibit sensitivity to certain sequences of bits, often interpreting them as control sequences. When this behavior is encountered, one must decide whether to eliminate the primitive system (good idea!) or forgo the value of multimedia (bad idea!).

Size

Multimedia objects tend to be quite large. The smallest is quite manageable: an icon, about 1000 bytes. Audio and video files are at the other extreme, running to a storage-capacity-limited number of giga or terabytes. An uncompressed motion-video stream amounts to width × height × colors × frames-per-second bits per second; for example, a clip intended for display on a VGA monitor with only 256 colors is 640*480*8*30 or 73,728,000 bits per second or 9,216,000 bytes per second. Going to 16 bits for color, generally considered the minimum number acceptable, gives a storage requirement of 18.4 Mbytes for each second of video.

Audio is digitized by sampling. Sampling must be done at some multiple of the highest frequency to be reproduced. For audio the calculation is samples/second × size of sample × channels. For "CD quality" the numbers are 44,000 × 16 × 2, or 176 kbytes per second. It's easy to see why the compression algorithm is critical to space management. There's an alphabet soup of them: MPEG, JPEG, P*64, PLV, RTV, FIF. Each of these has its tradeoffs of speed, space, cost, and quality. That's a discussion that could fill a book, and it would be out of date before the ink was dry. For our purposes here, lets just say that the state of the art is such that compressed motion video with sound needs about 150 kbytes of storage for each second of the clip.

Complexity

The second issue within that of storage is complexity. The storage subsystem must deal with a level of complexity that is both high and ever-changing. A video clip is an example. While a video clip can be treated as a BLOB, many applications require that it be treated as a time-sequenced set of pictures (frames) with two or more associated time-sequenced samples of sound. Further, depending upon the compression algorithm, there may be relationships between frames. For example, with RTV or PLV a full frame is compressed and then a series of frames contain only the changed pixels (bits) from their predecessor. So now we have two kinds of frames, *reference* (*full*) and *difference*. A sequence of difference frames has meaning only in sequence, following the associated reference frame. Also, playing of a section of a clip must begin at a reference frame, so an index to reference frames is needed.

Another contributor to complexity is the need to change or replace the soundtrack. Now we must deal with synchronization.

The other aspect of complexity is that of the relationships between objects. A multimedia production is made up of clips, stills, graphics, animations, text, etc. in a defined order, with defined paths between certain objects. The same set of objects may be part of any number of productions. The same production will change, over time and with use. The storage subsystem of a multimedia system must support complex and changing relationships.

Distribution

The requirements for distribution of multimedia objects are those of traditional data-processing objects plus some new ones. The reasons for distribution have been *moving* and *sharing:* moving data to the point of use, and sharing of data or resources. With multimedia there's a new reason for distribution: *interaction*. A geographically dispersed group of people can interact, via a distributed multimedia system, with a multimedia object. For example, a floor plan can be displayed on several screens. Each participant can "mark" it with a "crayon"; each of the others can see the marks and the "owner" of the plan can decide which marks become permanent.

Management

The requirements for management of multimedia objects in a multimedia application are similar to the requirements in a conventional system.

The objects are large, numerous, and complex. Therefore while the actions needed are familiar, the tools and procedures must accommodate these new characteristics.

The users of multimedia systems often are less computer-literate than those of traditional systems. Further, they are less amenable to training—they don't know computers, and they don't want to learn! That's one value of multimedia systems: users don't have to become "computer jocks." A basic law of human nature applies here: the less a person understands about a system, the more he/she expects of it ("Hey, if I can't understand it, it must be able to do anything I want!"). This leads to new requirements in the management of the system's objects. They must be available, they must be reliable, and they must behave as expected.

Access

Access has two aspects: control of who can access the database, and helping them to find what they need. Access control must be both unobtrusive and effective. It must allow the user to gain access to the database in an easy and reasonable manner. Interestingly, these are the requirements for *navigation* as well.

Storage

As we look at storage in more detail, it will be useful to consider the different functions in a distributed database and to consider the storage needs of each of these. The three major functional component types in a distributed application are the network server, the LAN server, and the workstation, as shown in Fig. 40.1.

Clearly, in a small enterprise, the network server and the LAN server can be one and the same. Even in a large enterprise, the topology may not include a network server, as shown in Fig. 40.2.

Network server

The network server is a "server server"; that is, it provides services to machines that are, in turn, servers to workstations. A network server can

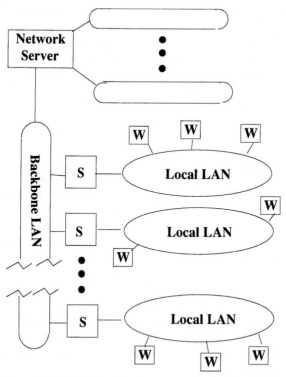

Figure 40.1   Major functional components of a distributed database.

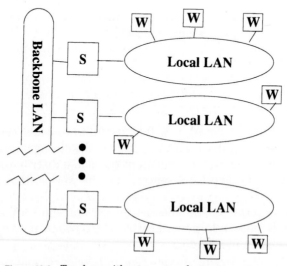

Figure 40.2   Topology without a network server.

range from a 386 up to a mainframe. The storage requirements for this class of machine range from very large to huge.

There are two kinds of storage that may be provided by a network server: *raw* and *application*. Raw storage is simply disk space made available to the client—sometimes this is called "virtual disk," since applications on the client see it as just another disk. It is used and "owned" by the client application. The server has no knowledge of the content.

Application storage is access to files belonging to applications, and it is seen by the server as files. This is sometimes necessary, but it is always dangerous. It creates logical dependencies throughout a network that are unknown to the owner of the application. Any change can bring down all of the dependent applications. A much better approach is message passing or transaction access of the data.

LAN server

The LAN server is what we think of as a server. It is on a LAN with workstations, to which it provides services: disk space, processing, communications, etc. The storage requirements for a LAN server will vary, depending on the applications it supports and on whether it has a network server "above." Storage on a LAN server must be big enough and fast enough to support the local application needs plus the workspace requirements of downloaded temporary objects. Careful analysis and management of this space is necessary; analysis, to ensure an adequate minimum, and management, to ensure that temporary objects are temporary.

Workstation

Storage on a multimedia workstation can range from zero (a "diskless" workstation) to many gigabytes. Most multimedia applications can be supported across the LAN—given a reasonable number of workstations per server, and a reasonable-capacity LAN. However, some multimedia applications have data rates greater than those available on the LAN. These must run in a download or a store-and-forward mode; that is, the objects must be copied onto the workstation's disk and displayed from there.

Distribution

Distribution is the movement of objects across a network. Objects are moved for purposes of transport, sharing, and interaction. Each of these will be illustrated by the light of the following multimedia application situation, a common one.

An enterprise has a corporatewide multimedia application. A group at one location is responsible for the creation of new and the maintenance of existing objects: clips, graphics, stills, etc. Groups at other locations must incorporate these objects into presentations: courses, product descriptions, reference documents, etc.

Transport

An object is created by the services group and then is sent to the end user. Simple, right? Well, not really. The services group probably cataloged the object based on a work request. The end user will catalog it based on the family of presentations into which it will be incorporated. So, somehow, the work request must be related to the finished object and to the project that caused its generation, and that relationship must be used to relate the new object to the project. The transport functions must support the transport of these relationships, as well as the object itself.

Sharing

Sharing is "virtual transport." The object is made available at another location but is not moved. We can also say that a copy is sent. However, proper sharing ensures that the identity of the original is always maintained. In terms of our example, sharing occurs when the services group wants to show work in progress to the end user, for comments or approval. A copy of the object is moved to the end user(s). It is reviewed, annotated, and returned. The original is the updated version, based on the reviews and annotations. The "old original" and the copy may be retained as a record, in which case they become part of the descriptors of the "new original."

Interaction

Interaction is the new requirement brought to the table by multimedia. If we take the review example above and make it real-time, we have interaction. The services group schedules an interactive conference. A copy of the object is displayed on each participant's workstation. Each person can annotate or even edit his/her copy. These changes can be viewed by all the others. The owner of the object then can choose which changes will become part of the new object.

Management

Management of basic multimedia objects resembles the management of a library. Management of the more complex objects resembles the management of an assembly process. In the first case, we are concerned with managing a storehouse where new objects are added and old objects are examined and copied but never (or seldom) deleted or changed. In the second case, we are concerned with managing the creation of new assemblies from the objects in the storehouse. In addition to these two types of multimedia object management, there is a third. This comes into play when multimedia objects are used in a controlled environment, one where the results of their use can be measured or inferred. In this environment there must be a feedback of results, which leads to the creation of new presentations and new objects. This has been called "training management," since it was born from the use of multimedia in training applications. The name is now a misnomer, as many applications can be monitored for effect and value.

Content management

Every multimedia object database has two logical parts: components, and assemblies. The components are stills, clips, sounds, graphics, and text. These must be managed to allow their location and retrieval so that they can be used in the creation of assemblies. It is important to note that when a multimedia component is made part of an assembly, it does not necessarily lose its identity. The same physical component may be part of any number of assemblies at the same time. If the database system requires that an object be copied into an assembly, there is an unlimited market for new disk files. Also, if the database system has such requirements, it probably is defective in other respects as well.

The assemblies are the instances of the use of the components. These can be called *presentations* or *books* or *experiences* or *games* or *courses* or...Whatever they are called, they must be managed. They must be managed in order to be located and used and, indeed, to become components in yet greater assemblies.

Training management

Training or *effect* or *value* management (the terms are synonymous) is simply a feedback loop that generates change and addition requests to the processes that create both components and assemblies. In general, the change requests are directed to the process that creates assemblies, and that process may generate requests to the process that creates components. Management of multimedia objects requires facilities for cataloging, indexing, retrieving, checkout/-in, export, and import.

Access

Access is the point of all this. Most of the rest exists simply to support access to the objects in the library. There are three parts: cataloging/indexing, access support, and access control.

Cataloging/indexing

Cataloging is the process whereby the incoming objects are entered into the "card catalog." Using the familiar book library as an example, each book is cataloged and indexed by subject, author, ISBN number, Dewey decimal number, etc. The details of the catalog/index will vary with the intended use of the multimedia database (library). However, the architecture must support storage of the objects with a basic index, additional standard indices, and an unlimited ability to create new (permanent and temporary) indices "on the fly." This requirement is one of the main reasons why relational databases are not suitable for such applications. The root of this requirement is in the way libraries are used. First, no one can predict how users will want to access the library. Second, the users must be able to make a list of their "finds" as they work.

Access control

Access control is driven by the user profile: the library card. Each user of the library is identified and authorized by the library card. In a traditional library, building the user profile is an ad hoc process—the librarian decides if a given user should be allowed to see or check out a given book. In a distributed multimedia library, that function requires the user profile.

Access support

Access support also depends upon the user profile. However, rather than preventing a user from accessing any particular object, it assists the user in accessing all those for which he/she is authorized and masks the fact that he/she is not authorized for all. This last is important, because people tend to react negatively to being denied access. If the system is able to help them achieve their objective without mentioning that certain objects are off-limits, they have a better image of the library and of themselves.

Access support can take many forms. It is, generically, a personalization of the library that lets each user work in the way that is best for him/her. An obvious example is an audio output of the catalog for a blind person looking for Braille or recorded materials. Another is the differences in the interfaces presented to a child of six, a teenager, a teacher, and a businessperson. Further, as a given user may play different roles, the user can be given the ability to select from a set of interfaces.

Conceptual Design

This section sketches the major subsystems of a distributed multimedia application. The system described could support a wide range of applications: product design/development, product support, training, marketing, and others.

Figure 40.3 shows the major subsystems of a distributed multimedia application. This diagram makes the assumption that the remote sites are not connected with "multimedia-capable" communications links: backbone LAN, T1 point-to-point, etc. Therefore, the distribution manager maintains databases at each remote site containing the objects required for that site. In a backboned system, the central site library could support all of the remote sites. This would cut down on complexity (having a distribution manager), but it also would decrease robustness by making all users dependent upon one server.

Creation subsystem. This provides the user interface and functions used in the creation of multimedia objects. This subsystem is made up of three major components: user interface, drawing/paint tool(s), and the window/control tool(s).

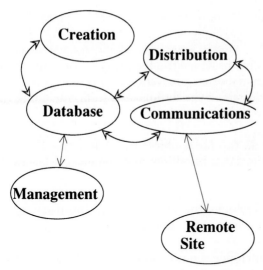

Figure 40.3 Major subsystems of a distributed multimedia application.

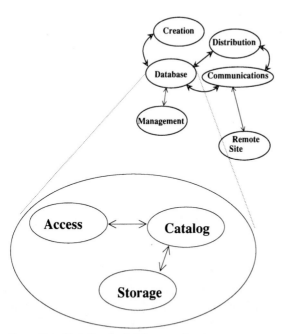

Figure 40.4 Details of a database system.

Distribution subsystem. This provides the user interface and functions used in the distribution of multimedia objects to the remote-site servers.

Database subsystem. This is detailed in Fig. 40.4.

Communications subsystem.   This provides the capability to connect to the remote-site servers.

Management subsystem.   This provides the facilities for managing the central library and, through the distribution subsystem, the remote-site libraries.

Figure 40.4 shows the details of the database system, including the access, catalog, and storage subsystems.

Storage subsystem.   This is the basic object database: the physical storage capabilities, recovery, transaction handling, and the object classes that make up the particular database.

Catalog subsystem.   This includes the librarian-user interface and the functions needed to support cataloging and indexing.

Access subsystem.   This includes the user interface and the functions needed to support access control, access support, and searching.

Networks for Multimedia and Collaborative Computing

Mike Evans

Why Collaborative Computing?

The multimedia applications developed in the early 1990s are only a small part of what can be achieved once a communication infrastructure supporting multimedia has been installed. As a result of the lack of such a communications infrastructure, multimedia applications thus far have not been sufficient to attract the mainstream user: the business user. Business users primarily are interested in communicating with other people, whether in the local office area, another part of the company, other companies, or in their homes.

While multimedia communication can be personal between two people, it is more likely that several people will be involved in the communication. Examples of group communication, or collaborative computing, include the sharing of work in progress such as a spreadsheet, chart, document, or photograph, so that all the members of the team can see and modify it.

Such collaborative applications can save businesses both time and money; are more effective, because the emotions of each person are visible to the entire team over both voice and video; and are more successful in team- and consensus-building and thereby in producing more effective results.

Business users prefer to have access to this type of communication directly from their own offices, and they want it to be available without the need for additional hardware on the desktop. If a desktop PC already is present, then users will be more comfortable using it rather than a combination of it and a telephone. Or, if a PC is not wanted on the desk, then the telephone can be upgraded to provide the capabilities required for collaborative computing.

Passing Limitations

Before collaborative multimedia computing can become ubiquitous, a new multimedia-capable communications infrastructure is needed that can connect multimedia traffic from people in their local office area to people in other locations. This traffic can be real-time video and audio, and it can be data that is either synchronized or interactive with the video and audio traffic. The infrastructure must be inexpensive; it must be low-latency, to minimize irritating delays end-to-end; and it must allow full duplex traffic in both directions. A number of people in different locations should be able to access the infrastructure's services. Finally, the process of communication must appear as seamless as today's telephone call.

While desktop machines are capable of performing the functions involved in assembling multimedia communications, a number of new factors are emerging to surmount the technical and price hurdles involved in building a multimedia communications infrastructure.

Video and audio components

Video cameras have dropped rapidly in price. Video-capture cards are available that will capture video from a camera in full color at 30 frames per second at SVGA quality. Most monitors now have SVGA screens with full color. In other words, from the video perspective, many of the components required for collaborative computing are now available at a reasonable cost.

Video compression/decompression is becoming increasingly cost-effective. Without video compression, most collaborative multimedia communications applications would not be possible.

Data rates (bandwidths) of 200 Mbits per second are required to provide uncompressed full-motion video at 30 frames per second for a single VGA screen in full color. Video compression can reduce this bandwidth requirement to about 1.5 Mbits per second, a rate that is compatible with both compact disks and with Ethernet local-area-network data rates. If the data is to be sent over the public network, the user can select smaller windows on the screen for collaborative applications, or the video-compression scheme can compress data even further.

Audio features already are being introduced on all multimedia PCs. Audio takes a small amount of bandwidth relative to video. Audio suitable for collaborative computing could use two 16-bit stereo channels, for a data rate of 256 kbits per second. This can be compressed by a factor of three if required. Voice can be compressed much more, down to data rates less than 10 kbits per second, although voice data rates are more typically compressed to 32 kbits per second. In many local area network-based multimedia applications, audio compression isn't necessary.

LANs and Collaborative Multimedia Computing

Most business desktop PCs are now connected to a local-area network (LAN). LANs allow users to access files, e-mail, and other applications that are shared with other users in the same office. The most popular LAN today is Ethernet, with most new installations moving to 10BASE-T Ethernet. All versions of Ethernet transfer packets at a fixed data rate of 10 Mbits per second, as specified in the IEEE 802.3 standard.

With a maximum data rate of 10 Mbits per second, files the size of a megabyte take a few seconds to transfer. This transfer occurs in a number of bursts of data comprising many packets, whenever network traffic allows. Normal Ethernet, as with most standard networks including Token Ring and the first generation of FDDI (Fiber Distributed Data Interface), requires messages to wait until their is time available on the network. This type of packet transfer is unsuitable for the transfer of real-time audio and video information. Video traffic must appear smooth, and audio must be undistorted.

As multimedia applications—which require good-quality video and audio— become more widespread, the capabilities of older packet-based LANs are coming under scrutiny.

Packet LANs and delays

Figure 41.1 shows the many applications that will need to use future LANs. Obviously, present-day applications still will need to be supported, such as accessing normal data files (probably from a file server) or new packet-based applications such as writing to printers over the LAN.

But LANs will need to support any multimedia PC for new multimedia applications. The simplest application is video playback of movies, where video files may be stored in a video server and the file transferred across the LAN to one or more PCs. Taking this example one stage further, the video

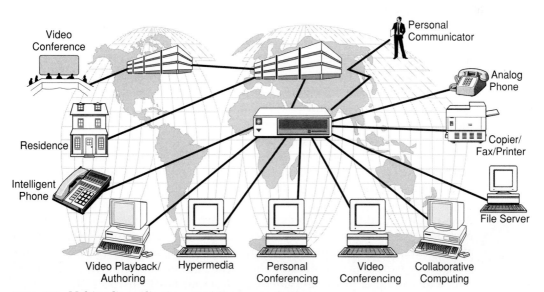

Figure 41.1 Multimedia applications requiring communications.

files may require interactivity, where the user can select any part of the video quickly, fast-forward or reverse, or zoom in, or freeze a frame.

Training is an example of an application that would require interactivity. An associated application is video authoring, where the user must be able to retrieve previously stored video files from the server and modify them locally, then transfer them back over the LAN to the server. These types of applications may function with existing LANs, but new applications including personal conferencing and collaborative videoconferencing have far more stringent requirements than can be supported over packet-based LANs.

Personal conferencing is two or more people talking to each other using video cameras attached to their PCs, with microphones and speakers for voice or audio. The camera can be moved to focus on any object. This kind of application is very demanding for a number of reasons: the video and audio need to be synchronized; the information being transferred is full duplex; and interactivity requires that there be minimal delays end-to-end in both directions. This kind of capability could be satisfied with an ISDN link, but the quality or window size would have to be sacrificed due to the limited bandwidth of basic-rate ISDN—128 kbits per second. The logical alternative is to use the LAN already attached to the PC, because of its higher data rate. Even so, picture quality deteriorates as more people join in the conversation, because the typical LAN was not designed for continuous traffic over long periods of time. And as more people become involved in the conference and more demands are put on the LAN, the more frustrating using the conference becomes.

Connection path using packet LANs

Figure 41.2 shows a typical connection path for a videoconference between two multimedia PCs in different locations. The path might be through Ethernet, connected through a bridge or router to a backbone such as FDDI, and then through a router to a private or public network. There is likely to be a similar setup on the other end of the connection.

If the conference is intracompany, then there may be a T-1 link between the different company locations.

But a substantial amount of videoconferencing will take place between people in different companies. Intercompany connections will need to be made over the public network, usually using the X.25 protocol. X.25 is a protocol for conveying packet traffic between LANs at different locations. X.25 typically runs at 56 kbits per second over digital networks, or even lower over analog phone lines. Some X.25 links run over ISDN (Integrated Services Digital Network).

The problem with the protocols seen in Fig. 41.2 between the two multimedia PCs is that the delays experienced are all unpredictable—even inside each PC. Packet-based networks offer only limited control of timing. Each step has its own maximum and minimum timing parameters. Thus the first frame may experience minimal delays, the second maximal, the third minimal. For example, after the video-compression block in the right-hand PC has output the first frame into main memory, the PC then waits for the

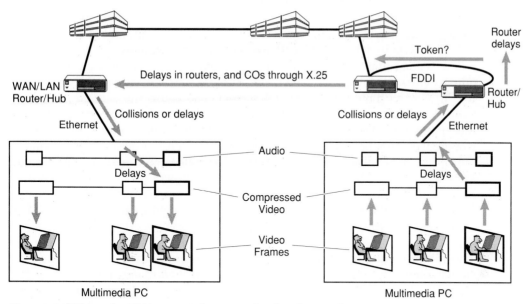

Figure 41.2   Video and audio transported over a packet-based network.

Ethernet controller to add a header and then transmit the composite header and compressed video in packet format. During a two-way conference, the same Ethernet controller also is receiving incoming packets of compressed video from the other PC at random times, making the delays inside the PC even more unpredictable. The wait may be short for the first frame, if the Ethernet controller does not face delays or collisions on the Ethernet link to the hub.

At the hub, now carrying the video, there is a bridge or router to FDDI. This router may not be busy, so delays through it are minimal. Then, on the FDDI ring, the FDDI frame may instantly catch the token as it is going around the ring, so the frame can instantly be transferred to the X.25 router. Minimal delays occur in the router to the X.25 link. The packet then is sent over X.25 from the customer premises across the central offices or public exchanges of the telephone companies, and again delays may be minimal over the wide area. Likewise, the delays may be minimal back into and through the LAN at the other end. The next compressed video frame may experience maximal delays all along its route, from inside the PC through the network to the other PC. The next compressed video frame may again experience short delays all the way along. The effect of varying delays is jittery video and distorted audio, as Fig. 41.2 shows.

Solutions for Collaborative Computing: A New Idiom

There are solutions that can help to minimize the problems of jittery video and distorted audio associated with packet-based LANs.

The first solution is to speed up the whole path. This may be possible with some of the components, by using the fastest PCs or routers, but there are no guarantees as to delays if the call goes outside the company.

The second approach is to install buffer memory into the PCs, to smooth out the variable delays. Obviously, all the PCs participating in the conference would need to have the additional memory, so again there is no guarantee that the person at the other end has installed buffer memory. Even *with* buffer memory, the maximum size of the buffer has to be larger than the worst-case delay between video frames. Such a solution will result in smooth video, but depending on the frame rate the video could arrive a full second after it was sent. While this is tolerable for one-way video such as lectures and presentations, most users find such delays intolerable for conferencing. Delays of a third of a second are considered the longest that users in a video-conference will tolerate.

A better solution that eliminates delays and jitter is a new idiom for LANs. The idiom (common in telephony, but almost unheard-of in data LANs), called *isochronous connectivity,* is to set up an end-to-end link between the two PCs at the beginning of the call, then send the video and audio down the now-established pipe in totally synchronized fashion in both directions simultaneously. Such a protocol results in minimum and maximum delays that are known, and that are much smaller than those a packet-based approach would yield. These delays are small enough that a buffer memory is not required, and the user will see smooth video, as shown in Fig. 41.3.

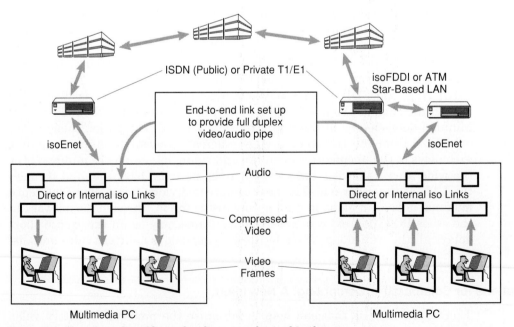

Figure 41.3   Smooth-quality video and audio over end-to-end isochronous.

Isochronous services

There are many ways to explain isochronous services. The word *isochronous* is derived from the Greek: *iso* for *equal*, and *chronos* for *time*. But this definition hardly helps us to understand what isochronous services are.

A simple way to view the isochronous is to define it as *time-stamped data*. Isochronous services are defined by the worldwide standard 8-kHz clock used for telephone communications. In other words, an isochronous network must be able to synchronize and remain synchronized to an 8-kHz clock. The minimum number of bits per clock is 8, so isochronous data comes in multiples of 64 kbits per second.

The synchronization of isochronous services is extremely important, especially for conversations. Any delay beyond a few hundred milliseconds is sensed by the ear, and such a delay in communication is uncomfortable, at best.

An isochronous multimedia call

Setting up an end-to-end link between two PCs at the beginning of a video or other multimedia call is known as *call setup*. The user originating the call places the call in a manner similar to today's telephone call, but through a PC. Typically the originating caller requests a certain bandwidth and the destination address. The bandwidth requirement is sent indirectly by requesting a particular screen video size and picture quality. The destination address is indirectly selected from a lookup table that links people to their phone number. This information is interpreted at each hub along the way and sent to the next hub on the path. At the far end, the receiving PC either accepts the call or does not. If the call is accepted, the message comes back to the originating PC and the two-way link is established.

This type of call setup cannot be accomplished with packet-based LANs. Call setup is part of the new isochronous LAN idiom that is a symbiosis of the best of both data and telephony solutions.

Fortunately, products supporting the new idiom became available in early 1994. Packet-based Ethernet is enhanced with isochronous Ethernet (isoENET), and FDDI with either the FDDI-II (also called isoFDDI) or the asynchronous-transfer-mode (ATM) LAN protocol. ISDN is used in the public network between customer premises. The new isochronous LANs can connect to either basic-rate ISDN (BRI), or primary-rate ISDN (PRI).

Isochronous Ethernet

Isochronous Ethernet (isoENET™), developed by the National Semiconductor Corporation of Santa Clara, California, is a LAN standard that provides a combination of the packet-type services presently used for data LANs and the isochronous services required for collaborative multimedia computing.

Isochronous Ethernet, because it maintains packet services for normal Ethernet, is evolutionary, and allows people to build on the installed networks they already are using—it is estimated that in 1994 10BASE-T installations total 20 million. While maintaining packet-based services, it adds isochronous services for multimedia communications. National's isoENET proposal was unanimously accepted by the IEEE 802.9 standards committee in March 1993 as a working document.

An isoENET LAN offers 10-Mbit-per-second Ethernet data services, but adds an additional 96 64-kbit-per-second "B" channels for a total of 6.144 Mbits-per-second bandwidth for isochronous communications, plus a "D" channel for signaling and call setup. Each of these three paths—data, the B channels, and the D channel—is separate, both at the node (or PC) and at the hub. They are combined only on the 10BASE-T wiring, as shown in Fig. 41.4.

10BASE-T is hub-oriented and is wired, like normal office phone wiring, in a star configuration. 10BASE-T wiring uses two voice-grade unshielded twisted-pair wires of up to 100 meters in length from the desktop to the hub.

Isochronous Ethernet can use the same wiring as 10BASE-T, because it uses the same frequencies on the cable as does Ethernet. Ethernet appears as 10 Mbits per second to the user, but isoENET bandwidth is encoded with clock information that allows synchronization.

While all Ethernets use Manchester encoding, which doubles the data rate to deliver a maximum data rate of 20 Mbits per second on the wire, isoENET uses a more efficient coding scheme called *4B/5B*. This coding scheme yields a maximum data rate of 20.4 Mbits per second. This data rate is so close to the Ethernet standard that no wiring changes are required to meet FCC emission requirements. This is an important feature to MIS manager, because no rewiring is required to install isoENET if 10BASE-T is already in place.

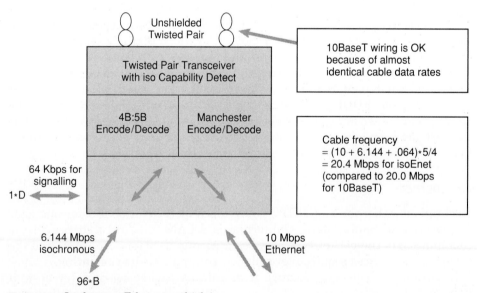

Figure 41.4 Isochronous Ethernet multiplexer.

Users who want to add isoENET will add an isoENET hub in the same wiring closet that already contains the LAN (and PBX) wiring. Users who do not wish to add isochronous services can still connect to the isoENET hub, and their Ethernet connections will operate normally. Any combination of isoENET and Ethernet PCs can be connected to the isoENET hub, allowing users to upgrade as they require isochronous services.

Isochronous Ethernet data rates

The isochronous data rate used in isoENET was chosen for three reasons. First, to keep the total data speed traveling over the installed wires as close to 10BASE-T's data rate as possible. Second, because 6.144 Mbits per second is the lowest common denominator of North American and international telecommunication data rates. It is four times the T-1 data rate, 1.544 Mbits per second exclusive of the 8-kHz framing, and three times the E1 data rate of 2.048 Mbits per second. Third, because it is quite adequate for all SVGA- or VGA-based multimedia applications that incorporate video-compression technology. Most applications using video compression require less bandwidth.

Call setup

The 6.144-Mbit-per-second data rate also is useful because it maps easily onto the standards of the public network, particularly on ISDN. ISDN uses a number of Bearer or "B" channels for information, and a "D" channel for signaling. The call setup to make the end-to-end link is done over the D channels, using the internationally accepted Q.931 call setup procedure, which includes the number of B channels required and the telephone address of the person on the receiving end. The message is passed by the PBX or some other hub to the local central office, and by each central office along the way to the person receiving the call. If the call is accepted, the signaling information is then sent back along the same path to the call originator. Basic-rate ISDN (BRI) allows the use of two B channels, while primary-rate ISDN (PRI) allows the use of from 1 to 23 B channels in North America and up to 30 B channels elsewhere.

Signaling down the D link in isoENET is very compatible with ISDN, making the translation between isoENET and ISDN quick and easy. This translation can be used when connecting either from an isoENET environment to the wide area or from an isoENET PC to an ISDN link in the same customer premises.

Once a call has been set up from one PC to another through the wide area, the video and audio are mapped into the same repeated B channels every 125 microseconds (8 kHz) for each segment along the way. This guarantees minimal delay across the wide-area network and also guarantees that the video and audio are synchronous with each other as well as with any data sent in the same manner. The data pipe is also full-duplex, ensuring that video and audio going in the opposite direction are guaranteed to have minimal delay. These features make the isoENET/ISDN connection ideal for conferencing and collaborative computing.

Additional benefits

Isochronous Ethernet, aside from being able to set up isochronous data pipes, offers other technical benefits that make it attractive as a multimedia communications network.

First, isochronous data is processed directly. In other words, the video and audio information can totally bypass the PC bus and memory, significantly reducing delays inside the PC.

Second, the iso paths in an isoENET hub connect separately into a circuit switch, by taking advantage of isoENET's switching protocol. This means not only that isoENET is a switching protocol, but that hubs can be designed so that the switch can be nonblocking, meaning that any PC on the link has isoENET's full 6.144-Mbit-per-second data rate dedicated to the link in both directions, independent of any other link. Thus each link can have its own 96 B channels. For example, in a 16-port hub designed with a nonblocking switch, the hub will have an aggregate bandwidth of almost 200 Mbits per second. The more ports, the higher the aggregate isochronous bandwidth, not counting the normal packet Ethernet (which also can be switched on a per-port basis).

The switching circuit in the hub allows any B channel on any link to be connected to any other B channel on any other link. These links don't even have to be within a particular LAN; the linking structure also can link from one hub to another, or to a PBX, or to an ISDN link—in other words, to any other isochronous link, including FDDI-II and isochronous ATM.

All of these features are ideal for conferencing and collaborative computing. They also significantly boost the quality and performance of other multimedia applications including one-way video playback, hypermedia, and video authoring. Therefore the applications shown in Fig. 41.1 could all utilize isoENET, as illustrated in Fig. 41.5. Any PC connected to isoENET can perform any of the different functions at different times, just as PCs do now.

Isochronous Ethernet offers smooth-quality synchronized video and audio for video playback, and it is highly interactive to any number of users on the LAN, each accessing his/her own dedicated video streams provided from a server. Video mail provided from a server can be downloaded smoothly. In video authoring, taking video shots normally requires a lot of bandwidth and local storage, but using video compression and isoENET allows the movie to be prepared at the PC, compressed, and instantly transferred directly to a server over isoENET without occupying much local storage or processor bandwidth. Similarly, for editing video, there is no need to store any video locally on the PC—it can instantly be retrieved using isoENET, then decompressed and displayed on the PC. Users can sift through video and audio hypermedia information, with optional associated data information, very interactively using B channels in both directions. The hypermedia information can be outside the user's premises and the quality and performance will still be good. For video-conferencing and collaborative computing, isoENET allows any number of users to talk to each other, including users outside the customer premises.

Isochronous Ethernet also allows any of the multimedia applications to take place at the same time on different PCs, as well as allowing normal LAN

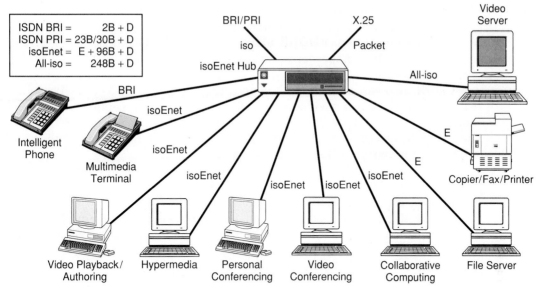

ISDN BRI =   2B + D
ISDN PRI = 23B/30B + D
  isoEnet = E + 96B + D
  All-iso =   248B + D

Figure 41.5 Isochronous Ethernet in a multimedia cluster.

traffic to take place independently. Iso. Ethernet costs only a little more than Ethernet, both in the PC and in the hub. This makes isoENET a powerful yet evolutionary protocol.

FDDI-II

FDDI-II is an upward-compatible second generation of fiber distributed-data interface (FDDI). Both are ANSI X3T9.5 standards. FDDI-II, or isoFDDI, adds isochronous capabilities to existing FDDI in the form of a circuit-switched service. FDDI-II, similar to isoENET, can handle both packet and isochronous data. The only difference is that in isoENET the isochronous channels are added as additional bandwidth to basic Ethernet, whereas in FDDI, isochronous channels come out of FDDI's basic 100-Mbit-per-second bandwidth budget.

FDDI-II can operate either in Basic or in Hybrid mode. In Basic mode, the ring operates like an FDDI ring with packet service only. In Hybrid mode, the ring becomes a time-division-multiplexed-(TDM-) based switching matrix, which divides the bandwidth into 16 wideband channels (WBCs) of 6.144 Mbits per second each. Each WBC, as in isoENET, can be divided into 96 B channels.

Uses for FDDI-II in collaborative computing

FDDI-II may be used as a local network where multimedia traffic is very intense.

Because its isochronous services are divided into B-channels, FDDI-II serves as an excellent backbone for isoENET's isochronous services. If FDDI-II is used in Hybrid mode, then the isochronous channels of isoENET can be directly mapped into the isochronous channels of FDDI-II, while Ethernet packet traffic can be bridged or routed to FDDI-II.

In this configuration, FDDI-II alone serves as the backbone for isoENET hubs, and links both Ethernet packet and iso traffic across all the hubs in the customer premises.

FDDI-II also can serve as a link to a file server for packet traffic using FDDI frames, and as a video server for traffic such as compressed stored movies for video playback applications using isochronous frames. FDDI-II's iso channels also can link through ISDN's primary-rate interface to either the PBX or to the central office for outside calls.

And as with isoENET, the division of isochronous capabilities into B channels or 6.144-Mbit-per-second wideband channels simplifies connection of isochronous communications to the public network.

FDDI-II also can be used purely for isochronous traffic, keeping Ethernet packet traffic separate and allowing the packet traffic to be repeated or bridged between hubs. In this configuration, a great deal more isochronous bandwidth is available for those users who require it.

Asynchronous transfer mode (ATM)

Beginning in 1992, a number of LAN and switch developers have worked in a standards body called the ATM Forum to adapt the CCITT (Consultative Committee on International Telephone and Telegraph) broadband ISDN specification into an ATM LAN architecture.

ATM is a switch-based architecture that utilizes fixed-size cells with a payload of 48 bytes. The protocol is designed to give each connection as much bandwidth as it requires without having to contend with traffic on a shared medium.

Like isoENET and the Hybrid Mode of FDDI-II, it is a connection-oriented technology. Virtual circuits (data pipes) are established between communicating stations before data transfer begins. This enables ATM to be another viable backbone for isoENET.

The ATM Forum has defined four different physical layers for ATM. Three of these four layers specify synchronization to an 8-kHz clock to create isochronous ATM services.

Figure 41.6 shows clusters of isoENET-based PCs, each hooked to ATM by a fiber spoke with a data rate of 155 Mbits per second dedicated to each cluster. All of the spokes are connected to a central ATM switch hub, which could be a future PBX that handles telephone calls as well as isochronous data transfers. The central hub initially will connect to the wide area through an ISDN primary-rate interface, and by the year 2000 probably through an ATM-based broadband ISDN (B-ISDN). Video links can be set up from an isoENET-based PC through the ATM backbone.

Once an ATM switch has been installed, users who need more isochronous bandwidth than 6 Mbits per second can migrate to an ATM link that may be twisted-pair copper wiring if the link is less than 100 meters long. There are likely to be two bandwidth options available for these 100-meter links, 25

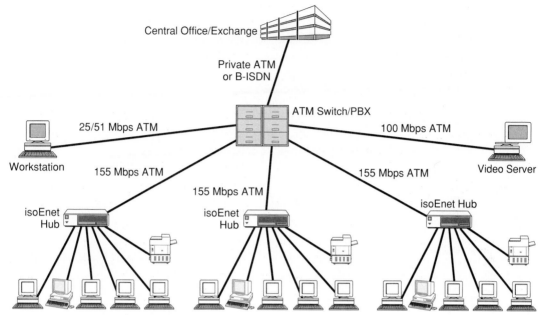

Figure 41.6 Multimedia-based LAN.

Mbits per second and 52 Mbits per second. It is unlikely that the majority of users will require more dedicated bandwidth to the desktop until the end of this century. Video-compression ratios will continue to increase, so as users demand HDTV-level video quality, there should be no volume desktop requirement for bandwidths greater than 52 Mbits per second for quite some time.

Getting from Here to There

Isochronous services became available early in 1994 within a single office or company campus, allowing local collaborative computing. Getting a multimedia call off-campus, however, will require ISDN services.

ISDN is an ideal connection medium. Isochronous multimedia calls can be directly transferred over either primary-rate interface (designed for business users) or basic-rate interface (designed for home and small-company users). It is estimated that by the end of 1994 over 65 million users in North America may have the capability of a BRI connection. This does not mean that they will *have* the connection, only that if they then request it, it will be physically possible to deliver it. It also does not mean that if a connection is requested it will be made; that will depend on the regional Bell operating company in North America or on other countries' PTTs.

Nonetheless, as businesses begin to experience first-hand the productivity enhancement that collaborative computing makes possible within their own establishments, increasing pressure will be placed on telephone carriers to widen the installed base of ISDN.

42

Networking Multimedia on Standard Data Networks

Prem Uppaluru

Overview

The availability of cost-effective add-in hardware and software for integrating compressed digital video and audio into desktop computers, coupled with the introduction of video-networking products, is making networked multimedia applications possible for the first time. These trends are driving the development of new solutions for users sharing business-video information over networks, in applications that require the capturing, storing, retrieving, and playing of frequently updated video clips. Examples include

- Integrating business video into networked applications, such as on-line information services, video databases, and on-line help systems

- Delivering networked multimedia courseware to school classrooms from a central file server

- Updating point-of-information and point-of-transaction kiosks with new products or services from remote locations

- Delivering just-in-time training in shop-floor applications over the network, providing shared access to video data, and enabling rapid content updates in response to changing information

Digital video represents a new data type for computers and networks, requiring the management of real-time, high-bandwidth, continuous flows of data. The capture, storage, distribution, access, and presentation of digital video requires specialized system software capable of managing real-time continuous data streams within a network computing environment.

Networking Video: Technical Challenges

Industry leaders, including Apple, IBM, Intel, and Microsoft, currently offer *stand-alone* digital-video products integrated into personal computers. These products consist of digital-video compression/decompression and capture/presentation hardware, as well as digital-video management-system software. All of these products depend on the interleaved storage representation of audio and video for the support of audio/video synchronization, and support networking of digital video by accessing video data through a file redirector. However, seeing as today's packet-based networks are not designed for motion video, performance over the network is limited by several fundamental technical challenges:

- *Real-time data over non-real-time networks.*   Computer data networks are designed for asynchronous transmission of data, but digital video and audio are inherently synchronous, real-time data types. Network delays that have little impact on text or graphical operations can cause audio and video data streams to lose synchronization and even to drop out critical information.

- *High data rates, limited network bandwidth.*   Full-motion compressed digital video requires relatively high data rates to transmit and display as digital information. Depending on the compression algorithm and the compression ratio used, a single video and audio data stream can range from several hundred kilobits per second to several megabits per second. In a standard 10-Mbits-per-second Ethernet or 10BaseT network, where only 6 to 7 Mbits per second is available for data transfers, the capacity to support motion-video data rates is limited—especially when typical applications require the network to support video playback from several clients at the same time.

- *Unpredictable availability of network bandwidth.*   As network usage and traffic varies, so does available bandwidth. When available bandwidth decreases below the minimum data rate required by a digital-video stream during playback, video and audio quality deteriorate sharply. Making video a practical data type in networked applications requires that video and audio be resilient to network bandwidth variations.

Solving the Network Problem with Scalable Video

The key to solving this networking dilemma is support for scalable video—the capability to dynamically adapt video data rate to available network bandwidth, allowing motion video with synchronized audio to be sustained even under heavy load conditions.

The goal is to incorporate client-server session-management protocols and stream-transport protocols that support independent handling of audio and video over networks, and rate control techniques for digital video that prioritize audio over video and support adaptive load-balancing in standard local-area networks.

Audio/video stream separation

A main feature of scalability is the separation of audio and video into two distinct streams early after retrieval from storage. The software retrieves a file, parses the information according to the specified file format, and dynamically separates the audio and video information into its internal representation. The separation and independent handling of audio and video streams, coupled with the human perceptual tolerance for variation in quality and frame rate in the presentation of video, allow *dynamic* scaling of video and audio over the network.

Typically, people perceive motion when video presentation rates exceed 15 frames per second. Moreover, instantaneous smooth variations in video presentation rates are practically unnoticeable. However, human aural perception is quite intolerant of variations in the presentation quality or rate. Typically, humans perceive noise when presentation rates are not adhered to, and clicks when brief periods of silence are injected into audio streams. Scalable video takes advantage of these inherent human perceptual constraints and prioritizes audio transmission and delivery over video. This prioritization of audio over video extends over the entire data flow of audio and video streams, starting from their retrieval from storage containers and ending up with their presentation.

By prioritizing the retrieval, transmission, decompression, and presentation of audio over video within a network computing environment, and by relying on their resynchronization before presentation, scalable video optimally can utilize the available computing, compression, and network resources while maintaining an acceptable presentation of audio and video.

Adaptive load-balancing

Server software must manage the flow of video and audio data to requesting clients, and monitor the rate of delivery to the client. As the delivery rate slows under network load condition, impacting video and audio quality, the server smoothly slows the rate at which it sends data, allowing the client to "catch up" with the data stream without causing irritating breaks in video and audio quality. When the data bottleneck clears, the server responds by increasing the data rate on the video stream, resulting in improved video quality at the client's end.

The system administrator must be able to configure the maximum number of users allowable at one time, as well as the maximum data rate available to each client on the network. This allows the administrator a large degree of control over how much of the total network bandwidth will be consumed by video and audio data streams.

To avoid situations where data cannot make it to the client in time for synchronized playback, video and audio must be processed in a "read-ahead" manner, preparing the data for quick transmission across the network. It also applies adaptive rate-control algorithms that selectively drop video data when it is clear the entire data stream cannot be transmitted.

Configuring Networks for Multimedia

The number of users who can simultaneously play video segments over the network is based on many factors, including the speed of the server's CPU, network card, and fixed disk, as well as the network topology. Multiple Ethernet or Token Ring segments may be connected to a single file server to increase the number of video users per server.

The following lists define optimal system requirements for the network, server, and clients to ensure acceptable video/audio playback quality on clients. The requirements are based on the assumption that approximately 6 multimedia clients playing stored files back at 1.2 Mbits per second (Mbps) can be supported per Ethernet network segment. Therefore, if users are playing back at rates lower than 1.2 Mbps, more clients can be supported.

Network requirements

For 5 users: One Ethernet segment on one or more repeaters, or one token ring

For 10 users: Two Ethernet segments on two or more repeaters, or one token ring

For 25 users: Four Ethernet segments on four or more repeaters, or three token rings

Server requirements

Software

NetWare Version 3.11 or 4.0.

Hardware

For 5 users. You can install Fluent's FluentLinks®, a NetWare®-loadable module (NLM), on your standard network server and support five audio/video clients with no hardware changes. However, for optimal performance, the recommended configuration for a server PC supporting five users on one Ethernet segment or Token Ring is

- 386 EISA or MCA personal computer with a 33-MHz processor
- 8 Mbytes of RAM

- One 16-bit Ethernet network card
- One hard drive with 12 milliseconds (ms) or less access time and 2 Mbytes per second or greater transfer rate
- One 16-bit disk controller
- Hard-disk storage (10 Mbytes per minute of stored audio/video)

For 10 users.   The recommended configuration for a server PC supporting 10 users distributed evenly on two Ethernet segments or one Token Ring is

- 486 EISA or MCA personal computer with a 33-MHz processor
- 12 Mbytes of RAM
- Two 32-bit Ethernet adapters or one 32-bit Token Ring adapter
- Two hard drives with 12 milliseconds (ms) or less access time and 3 Mbytes per second or greater transfer rate
- One 32-bit disk controller
- Hard-disk storage (10 Mbytes per minute of stored audio/video)

For 25 users.   The recommended configuration for a server PC supporting 25 users distributed evenly on four Ethernet segments or three Token Rings is

- 486 EISA or MCA personal computer with a 50- or 66-MHz processor
- 16 Mbytes of RAM
- Four 32-bit Ethernet adapters or three 32-bit Token Ring adapters
- Four hard drives with 11-milliseconds (ms) or less access time and 4 to 5 Mbytes per second or greater transfer rate
- Two 32-bit disk controller
- Hard-disk storage (10 Mbytes per minute of stored audio/video)

Performance considerations

The performance is affected by three basic factors.

1. *The effective bandwidth of the network segment.* For example, the effective bandwidth per Ethernet segment is 6 to 8 Mbits per second (Mbps), while the effective bandwidth per Token Ring is 14 Mbps.
2. *The presence of bridges or routers between the server and clients.* Performance on a specific client may be reduced if there are bridges or routers on the network segment between the server and the client.
3. *The rate at which clients are playing back files.* For example, if each client is playing back a file at 1.2 Mbps, then the configuration described can support 5 to 6 clients on a single Ethernet segment or 10 to 12 clients

on a Token Ring. If however each client is using software video decompression to play back the same files, 10 to 12 clients per Ethernet segment or 20 to 24 clients on a Token Ring can be supported, since the data rate is much less.

A Sample Configuration

At NetWorld '93, Fluent demonstrated a 24-client video network consisting of a 486-based server with NetWare 3.11, FluentLinks 1.0, and four Ethernet segments of six computers each. The first part of the demonstration showed that this configuration, without FluentLinks software, supported 3 to 4 video playback sessions before video and audio quality degraded severely. In the second part of the demonstration the FluentLinks NLM was loaded, and all 24 client PCs retrieved and played video clips with imperceptible degradation in video and audio quality.

At Brainshare '93, Fluent and Novell demonstrated a 96-node network supported by a 486-based server, including 24 video clients and 72 clients running a variety of popular spreadsheet and word-processing applications. The Brainshare configuration consisted of the following:

File-server.   486/50 DX2 EISA server, with 2 Gbytes of storage and four 32-bit Token Ring cards

Network Operating System.   NetWare 4.0

Video-networking software.   FluentLinks 1.0 NetWare Loadable Module

Network topology.   4 Token Rings of 6 video-enabled personal computers each, plus 1 Token Ring of 72 nonvideo clients, all connected through a Token Ring concentrator

Video-enabled personal computers.   486/33 or higher models running DOS 5.0 and Windows 3.1, with 8 MBytes of RAM, VGA adapter and display, 16-bit Token Ring card, speakers, and motion JPEG cardset supporting motion-video compression and decompression.

Video data.   Video clips were compressed in ISO JPEG format to an average data rate of 2 Mbps, and stored in a single volume. During playback over the network, the actual data rate fluctuated in response to available network bandwidth, resulting in actual streaming data rates of 1.5 to 2 Mbps, and displayed video frames rates of from 20 to 30 fps.

The following list shows expected performance per segment for various network topologies, based on transmission of video streams recorded at a resolution of 320×240 pixels and a data rate of 1.5 Mbps:

Ethernet.   10-Mbits-per-second bandwidth available, generally 6 to 7 Mbits per second usable for data; application performance per network segment: 4 to 12 users at 12 to 30 frames per second.

Token Ring.   16-Mbits-per-second bandwidth available, 13 to 14 Mbits per second usable. Estimated application performance per network segment: 8 to 20 users at 12 to 30 frames per second.

FDDI.   100-Mbits-per-second bandwidth available, 80 to 100 Mbits per second usable. Estimated application performance per network segment: 40 to 100 users at 12 to 30 frames per second.

Now desktop computer users can integrate time-important, full-motion video into applications over businesswide networks, instead of distributing CD-ROMs or videodiscs. The key benefits of scalable video are shared storage, efficient video distribution and access, and compatibility with existing NetWare installations.

Building a Standard for Cross-Platform Delivery

John Colligan

Joseph Dunn

Joseph Fantuzzi

Donna Hefner

Introduction

The rapidly changing multimedia industry is challenging developers to consider many issues when they are producing interactive multimedia titles. Among these is choosing the best platform—or platforms—to deliver multimedia productions.

While no single hardware leader has captured the multimedia market, two distinct types of systems have emerged: personal computer and consumer platforms, as shown in Fig. 43.1. Today, standards do exist on the personal computer side—Macintosh and Windows. This is not true for consumer platforms, and it is likely that no leader will appear anytime soon.

Macromedia believes that standard platforms cannot be imposed on an emerging market, but rather must develop from it. Because of this, authoring software must support a variety of platforms, allowing multimedia developers to do the same. This chapter will explore the delivery options today's developers encounter, offer tips to make cross-platform delivery easier, and illustrate the kinds of cross-platform projects developers are creating now.

Creating a Standard for Multimedia Software

Like producers in Hollywood, multimedia developers want their productions to play on screens everywhere. But the multimedia industry does not

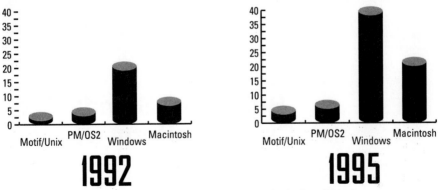

Figure 43.1   Number of Macs and PCs to double by 1995 (units in millions).

have one "big-screen" standard as the movie industry does. Rather, the market is comprised of several little screens, each incompatible with the next.

Industry analysts predict that by the turn of the century, multimedia will be a multibillion-dollar industry. As hardware manufacturers scramble to get a piece of the market with their new multimedia machines (and new platforms), multimedia developers are looking for the best way to leverage their time and resources so as to produce titles for a broad audience without reworking productions for each machine. Macromedia makes this easy by providing standard multimedia software to ensure that productions are played on screens everywhere.

Designing cross-platform applications is becoming increasingly popular, because it allows developers to leverage their resources to turn a profit. Off-the-shelf software packages such as Authorware Professional and Macromedia Director are helping to simplify the conversion process to the most popular systems, thereby opening new markets to developers in a timely and affordable manner.

Creating Cross-Platform Applications

More than 1000 multimedia titles are available today and 3000 others are under development, according to GISTICS, Inc., a market research firm based in Larkspur, California. By conservative estimates, more than 5000 multimedia titles will be on the market by 1995. Authors of these titles want them to play on multiple platforms without requiring significant additional time and resources.

Designing an application for multiple platforms, however, can be quite a challenge. Even the most highly compatible file formats cannot account for all

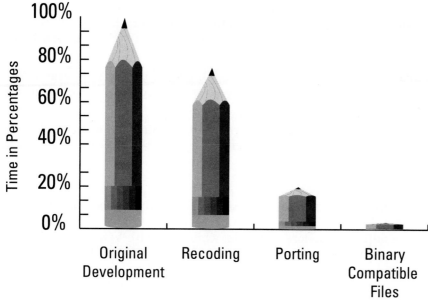

Figure 43.2   Binary-compatible files enable cross-platform development.

the differences among systems, such as individual machine performance, screen size and resolution, use of color, use of fonts, and sound support. Because of these differences, a developer sometimes needs to create similar but separate versions of a production for it to run smoothly on different machines.

Developing cross-platform applications does become easier with experience, as authors become familiar with each system and adjust their techniques to work around the differences. Some cross-platform applications, such as Macromedia's Director Player for Windows and Authorware Professional, are packaged with in-depth design guidelines so as to simplify the transition between platforms.

Working with differences in machine performance

When creating multimedia projects, developers must assume that their customers have the appropriate hardware to play back the productions. However, even with sufficient hardware, machine performance varies widely from machine to machine.

The amount of memory available on a particular machine affects how fast a multimedia production will run. Although a machine with low memory may have the capacity to play a particular production, that application may run more slowly than desired. To optimize performance, use general memory-management techniques:

- When creating a large production, use scripting to control and optimize performance. For example, unload data from memory if it is not needed, and design load time at places where the CPU is idle and the user will not notice (while they're reading or looking at a still).

- Use memory-intensive effects, such as bitmapped images and large internal sounds, wisely. Consider cutting large bitmaps into pieces or using external sound, if necessary.

- Be sure to test the production on a range of machines, so as to check both highest- and lowest-level performance.

Ensuring good color

Colors can be difficult to manage in cross-platform projects, because different platforms use different palette-mapping systems. A color Macintosh, for example, has millions of colors available, while PCs with VGA Graphics offer only 16 colors, and PCs with Super VGA graphics offer millions of colors. When converting a Macintosh file to Windows, all colors are mapped to their nearest equivalents. Several authoring techniques help to guarantee the truest possible colors:

- Make sure you use color palettes that can be recognized by the destination platform. For example, consider working with a standard VGA palette while authoring on the Macintosh, and creating cross-platform productions for the PC, if you will be delivering to 16-color computers.

- Optimize color quality by saving the original images in high resolution and applying an 8-bit diffusion dither to the images in Adobe's PhotoShop. For highest quality, use a product such as Equilibrium's DeBabilizer to dither the original images to a customized palette that works well with a variety of images in your production.

- When crossing from a computer-based RGB display to a consumer-based NTSC display, do not rely on the use of color to communicate information, because palettes may vary considerably. Programs such as Macromedia Director allow use of a custom NTSC palette to help keep colors true on television screens.

Working with different monitors

Many multimedia presentations keep the same pixel resolution when converted to other platforms. Because the pixel resolution may differ from platform to platform, movies can fill the screen or window differently on each. Here are some rules for good design:

- Use the "TV-safe" area of the screen—720 × 486 pixels or less—when creating for consumer platforms. This keeps you from unintentionally cropping the picture or text in your productions on different-sized screens.

- To avoid unintentionally cropping a production when it plays on different computer screens, create it in 640 × 480 pixels, the size of a Macintosh 13-inch display and the typical PC-system display.

- Many Macintosh customers own 12-inch monitors, 512 × 384 pixels. When designing productions for these screens, place a color, texture, or PICT image in the background, for playback on larger screens.

- When designing for consumer platforms, keep text to a minimum, and at least 18 points in size. Also, consider using shadows behind the text to help it stand out. The resolution of a NTSC television screen is much lower than that of a computer monitor, making copy hard to read.

- Avoid single-pixel horizontal lines, graphics, and animations when delivering to NTSC displays. Because these displays use an interlaced signal, single-pixel images may result in flickering.

Mapping fonts

If a project includes text in fields, or requires the user to enter text, developers may incur font problems (specifically size and shape issues) when crossing platforms. The Macintosh and Windows environments, for example, create visually different text, even when created from the same font and size information. Therefore, when working with text, keep in mind the following techniques:

- For text in boxes, center the text, leaving open space on each side so as to avoid possible word-wrap.

- For the closest possible mapping of text, use a standard font such as Times, which usually is available on different platforms. Also consider TrueType and Adobe Type Manager fonts, which provide standard fonts for Macintosh and Windows. These fonts still vary in size on each platform. (See Fig. 43.3.)

- Avoid high-level ASCII characters, as well as outline and shadow styles; these are not commonly supported on multiple platforms.

- To guarantee that text will look identical on both platforms, convert it into bitmaps before converting the file. Be aware, however, that bitmapped text uses much more memory than standard fonts, and cannot be edited.

Using sound

Although every Macintosh provides at least 8-bit audio, only PCs that meet the MPC standard are guaranteed to have this capability. In fact, many Windows-equipped PCs have no digital audio capabilities at all, and require an additional sound card with an appropriate driver to play sounds. When creating sound files in cross-platform productions, keep in mind the following:

- Many sound cards do not support all of the commonly used sampling rates on the Macintosh. Use 11-kHz and 22-kHz 8-bit audio for best results and compatibility.

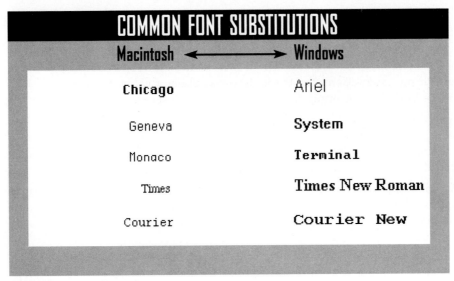

Figure 43.3 Font substitutions.

- Make sure that sound files and any linked external sounds are in an appropriate format for the destination platform. Common Macintosh sound file formats include AIFF, SND, and SoundEdit. Common Windows sound file formats include PCM, WAV, and MIDI.

- Consider using Red Book CD audio by including it on the multimedia CD-ROM. That way, you can play the audio directly from the CD-ROM drive as the production is running from the hard drive. This saves memory, and frees the CPU for better performance.

Designing different user interfaces

One of the most basic (but often overlooked) rules of thumb for cross-platform delivery is to be sure a title's content is *appropriate* for a specific platform. While new software is making it easier to leverage development work across platforms, the dynamics of *how* a user interacts with these platforms are quite different. In general, you would do well to follow these guidelines:

- Be sure to design the interface consistent with the published guidelines of the destination platform.

- Use a computer-based platform if the program requires a lot of text, or use of a keyboard. Most consumer players do not have a keyboard and use a low-resolution NTSC television screen, making text difficult to read.

- When creating productions for both computer- and consumer-based platforms, make each interface element large enough to touch with a finger, enabling it to be run on platforms that use a touchscreen display.

Multimedia's Future Direction

As the multimedia industry continues to unfold, developers will have more and more delivery options for their productions. Macromedia expects multimedia authoring and production to continue to be enhanced on the leading computer platforms: Macintosh and Windows-based PCs.

Eventually, after a hard-fought battle among contenders, multimedia delivery platforms will solidify into two or three major consumer platforms in addition to Macintosh and Windows. This means that even as the market stabilizes, a single delivery platform may not be a viable business option for multimedia-title developers.

Macromedia is committed to helping developers leverage their work across platforms by supporting the leaders as they emerge. From Macintosh and Windows to ScriptX-compatible computers, 3DO, and other leading consumer players, Macromedia's multimedia software will provide a standard that ensures that productions play back on screens everywhere.

Developer Examples

Crossing platforms for peanuts

When Image Smith released *Yearn 2 Learn—Peanuts,* the program captured the imagination not only of children but of the multimedia industry worldwide.

Peanuts targets children aged 3 to 10 years by using the well-known Charles Schulz characters of Snoopy, Woodstock, Charlie Brown, and the gang* to teach math, geography, and reading in a fun, interactive way. The program automatically adjusts the level of difficulty to the child's skill level, allowing the title to interest all the children in a family and to continue to challenge them as they grow older.

Peanuts has been extremely well received, and the Macintosh version exceeded sales projections by 150 percent in its first 3 months on the market. *Yearn 2 Learn—Peanuts* was released for Windows in June 1993.

While the Macintosh version was developed in 8 months by a full-time team of four, one dedicated person converted the program to Windows in just 45 days. The alternative was complete recoding, which would have taken approximately six months. The Player gave Image Smith a head start in capturing the Windows market.

Image Smith's success with *Yearn 2 Learn—Peanuts* is just the beginning of a series of Yearn 2 Learn titles that set a high standard for interactivity, playability, and educational value. (See Fig. 43.4.)

Multimedia fosters multilingualism

The Central Intelligence Agency's (CIA) Federal Language Training Laboratory and Analysis Corporation of Washington, D.C., made headlines

---

*Peanuts characters copyright © 1992, United Features Syndicate, Inc.

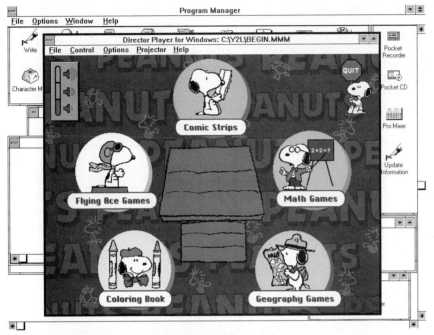

Figure 43.4   Sample of multimedia system.

around the world when they announced their intention to commercialize state-of-the-art multimedia language courses developed for CIA employees.

The courses, developed with Authorware Professional, combine full-motion, full-screen video with native-speakers' voices, text, graphics, animation, and audio record and playback. "Interactive multimedia is the ideal medium for language learning," explains George Conrad of Analysas Corporation. "The visual and auditory reinforcement helps motivate students, enabling instructors to be more efficient by making optimal use of class time."

The first course, called Exito, covers Spanish, and it has proven itself to be effective in teaching basic Spanish to CIA officers in just 10 days, assuming 4 to 5 hours of study a day. Courses in Russian, French, and Arabic also are under development. The programs focus on everyday situations such as arriving at the airport, meeting people, asking for directions, and ordering a meal.

"Our goal for the language courses is to bring this national treasure back to the public," Conrad explains. "And to reach the broadest audience, we decided to deliver the program to both Macintosh- and Windows-based computers." Analysas uses schools and universities to test-market and enhance the courses, which are delivered on five double-sided videodiscs and one CD-ROM. Eventually they hope to market simplified versions of the CIA language courses worldwide.

"There is an incredible groundswell of interest in language learning," Conrad says. "Perhaps this will be the start of bringing multilingualism to mainstream America."

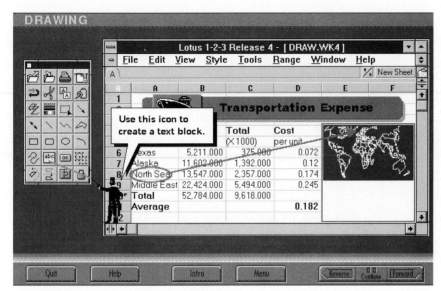

Figure 43.5   Multimedia training example.

Gaining an edge with interactive introductions

Lotus Development Corporation understands multimedia's "edge" when it comes to effectively conveying new information. Recently the company developed the 1-2-3 Release 4 for Windows Guided Tour, using text, graphics, and animation to show the new features of 1-2-3 Release 4 for Windows. (See Fig. 43.5.)

The tour ships with every copy of 1-2-3 Release 4 for Windows and has received rave reviews. It opens with an animated introduction, which leads into an interactive tour of 1-2-3 Release 4 for Windows. The program includes high-impact graphics and interactivity, to keep the user engaged throughout the program.

Created exclusively for the Windows platform, the guided tour initially was designed on the Macintosh, then converted to Windows.

Making the Move to Distributed Multimedia Computing

Peter B. Blakeney

Introduction

Multimedia is poised to deliver fundamental improvements in how we train our work force, make our buying decisions, and communicate with one another. As a cavalcade of multimedia capabilities proliferates on the desktop, it will likely become the most popular human interface for our personal computers, extending the once-revolutionary graphical user interface (GUI). Many predict that by the year 2000 every computer will be equipped to handle multimedia applications. The resultant impact on how we do business is destined to be profound.

Multimedia combines the interactivity of a computer with a natural user interface (NUI) that includes audio, still images, animation, full-motion video, and voice recognition. Over the past decade, multimedia has proven its worth as a uniquely powerful set of technologies when used to support applications such as training, business presentations, and marketing kiosks. Most of these applications have been stand-alone, due to the limitations of the communications technologies needed to manage and transport multimedia information. While stand-alone applications may be valuable, they don't necessarily optimize the competitiveness of an organization. Therefore, for multimedia to reach its full potential, it must move beyond the limits of stand-alone technology and be integrated into the existing information-system infrastructure.

Today's organizations generate traditional information consisting of text, numbers, and graphs more productively than ever before; store and retrieve that information more efficiently through the use of databases; and share that information more effectively through the use of electronic mail, facsimile transmissions, and telephone communications. These same organizations are increasingly aware that their applications will become that much more valuable with the addition of multimedia content. They will expect just as much flexibility and transportability in their distributed multimedia networks as they now enjoy in their traditional data networks.

Most industry observers agree that even though there is a substantial and accelerating use of multimedia in industry today, it will be 1995 or 1996 before multimedia gains the widespread acceptance that it is expected to. Adoption most likely will come in stages. According to Dr. John M. McQuillan, president of McQuillan Consulting, "High-resolution graphics, photographs, drawing, and the like, will generally be the first multimedia objects that users will incorporate into an application. Audio (spoken words or music) will come second, followed by full-motion video and, finally, animation."

Note that the proliferation of multimedia also will depend on advances in related technologies. These include end-user platforms; specialized devices that capture, record, and play back video and audio; public telecommunications systems; and enabling software development tools. Corporate networks will have to adapt to multimedia applications, especially in terms of bandwidth and delay-sensitive delivery. Over time, standards will be established and interoperability achieved, and this will propel distributed multimedia into the mainstream.

This chapter will focus on the following topics:

- Distributed multimedia applications
- Enabling enterprisewide distributed multimedia computing
- Multimedia server solutions
- Multimedia standards

Distributed Multimedia Applications

Networked multimedia information systems will inevitably improve productivity, through more effective internal and external communications. Consider the possibilities. Companies can communicate product information to customers in the format and location that those customers prefer. In advertising, creative designers can share ideas for video commercials with colleagues and customers through audio/video-enhanced electronic mail and multimedia documents. Medical professionals can collaborate by sharing diagnostic images or videotaped procedures across the world, using multimedia-enabled distributed systems. In educational settings, multimedia's power of interactive visualization is already augmenting traditional lectures and laboratories through multimedia navigational tools, and enhancing the process with self-paced instruction and distance learning. There are strategic applications across all industries in which multimedia can improve competi-

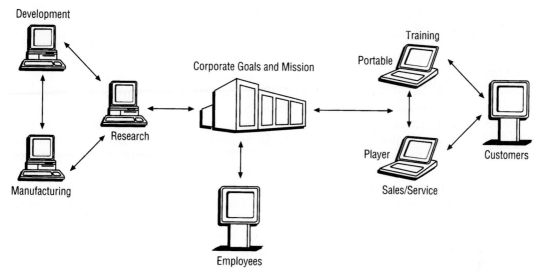

Figure 44.1 Business functions impacted by multimedia.

tiveness through the increased efficiency, effectiveness, and quality of communications.

To envision the magnitude of the impact and benefits of distributed multimedia on traditional business practices, consider the following scenarios (see Fig. 44.1).

Research and development

In the development of a complex product, engineers work independently to design segments of the product and then transfer the design to development engineers for integration. They continuously change and update the design and manufacturing process throughout the life of the product. The design consists of drawings, images, text, and prototypes, and the process includes meetings and conversations, both within and across product segments. With multimedia-enabled networked systems, researchers can send voice-annotated notes with images or video clips of prototypes. Developers can videoconference across multiple manufacturing sites in order to ensure integrated product development. This multimedia collaboration solution reduces the R&D cycle and improves quality.

Manufacturing

The R&D collaboration just described reaches into manufacturing as well. When a manufacturing problem arises, a plant-floor worker can communicate from a workstation to a development engineer to show a defective part via a videoconference. The engineer can actually see the defective part and make his or her recommendations instantly. The worker might also reference, right from the workstation, training videos, or a central video database of solutions to common problems. Training and video information on demand enables workers to solve problems quickly and to learn new techniques on the job.

Sales and service

A high-priced, complex product often requires a specialized sales force and extensive customer support. Often the sales cycle is long and expensive. A manufacturer can shorten the sales cycle by equipping the sales force with multimedia presentation and training systems, and by providing information/transaction kiosks in stores and sales offices. A multimedia presentation system and kiosk adds to the sales effort videotaped testimonials, product demonstrations, competitive comparisons, and interactivity. Customers can request more information from a technical database and provide valuable feedback to the company. They can dial up and videoconference with an expert at the company's headquarters. Because multimedia gives the critical information to the customer at the right place and at the right time, businesses can increase service and at the same time enhance the company image.

Training

It's not always possible, practical, or affordable to provide training the moment that it is needed, especially when training needs to be delivered to individuals at multiple remote locations. With networked multimedia technology, office workers can receive "just-in-time" training without leaving their desks. A widely dispersed class can view a lesson on PCs and interact with an instructor who is also at a PC, via fax, audio channel, or two-way video. This phenomenon, known as *distance learning,* saves on travel costs and increases productivity by allowing office workers to gain immediate access to materials rather than wait for scheduled classes. In this way multimedia protects investments in skilled personnel and helps corporations to maintain their competitive edge.

Corporate communications

Communicating company goals and vision to employees and customers is often difficult. The CEO cannot easily make frequent visits to every manufacturing and sales site. And often the corporate message gets modified as it is disseminated through the layers of an organization. Companies now show videotaped speeches, but multimedia technology can enhance the delivery process. Rather than view a two-hour videotaped speech, an employee can access an interactive application that includes clips of the speech filed by topic, plus related information such as a response form. In such a case the one-way message becomes a two-way interactive communication.

Each of the previous applications extends multimedia from being a stand-alone application to being a networked, strategic solution for fundamental business operations.

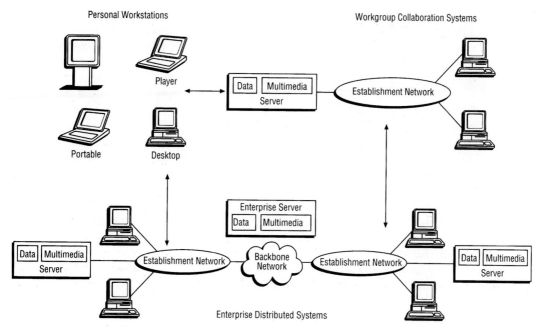

Figure 44.2 Multimedia systems solutions.

Enabling Enterprisewide Distributed Multimedia Computing

In a stand-alone environment, multimedia content, such as audio and video, is produced and captured at the viewer's desktop. In a networked multimedia environment, the audio and video may be distributed in real time from a videoserver, located in the same city or across the continent. That same videoserver may be sending the same audio and video content to multiple individuals distributed across a wide geographic area. Alternatively, many individuals may be collaborating and involved in an audio/video conference. The resulting audio and video datastreams are distributed among the work-stations used by the individuals participating in the conference.

To enable enterprisewide distributed multimedia computing, existing strategic system platforms need to be enhanced to support multimedia applications. These enhancements will result in an open distributed system enabled for multimedia, as seen in Fig. 44.2.

Distributed computing framework

Due to the large size of multimedia objects (their transmission as continuous streams of data when played or captured), and the need to control and synchronize them, key elements of distributed computing must be enhanced to support work-group collaboration and enterprise-distributed systems. In order to map the development of distributed multimedia computing solutions, we will use a "distributed computing framework" to describe those key elements of distributed computing that will be enhanced to support multimedia. This framework is targeted for heterogeneous computing, thus ensuring interoperability, data exchange, and common user access (CUA) across many dissimilar systems, with selected and emerging international de facto standards as a foundation.

An important objective of open distributed systems is to make a network of heterogeneous systems appear as a single-user system. All computing resources and services that a user is authorized to access, local and remote, appear as local resources and services. The Interactive Multimedia Association (IMA), a consortium of leading companies in the information industry, published a "Multimedia Services Request For Technology" in December 1992. The objective of this RFT is to achieve distributed multimedia services across heterogeneous systems. IBM, along with its Common Operating System Environment (COSE) partners, will be submitting to the IMA a specification for achieving distributed multimedia services, in hopes of establishing a standard.

Many facilities are required to implement location transparent, distributed computing, including application development tools, presentation management facilities, data management facilities (which use the services of interprocess communications), directory services, networking, and subnetworking. These facilities process a service request using the client-server computing model, in which one entity provides a service for another. In addition, they use relevant international and de facto standards to ensure interoperability across multivendor systems. Figure 44.3 represents a system framework that outlines the generic facilities needed to support both collaborative and client-server computing.

Two characteristics unique to multimedia will drive extensions to existing systems: object size, and datastreams. Multimedia data objects, such as digital video or high-quality digital audio, require large storage facilities. Most systems are designed to handle kilobyte data objects, not the gigabyte objects employed for a full-length movie of VHS quality. Storing many such data objects may require terabytes. Thus the automated storage management facilities that catalog, back up, migrate, relocate, and archive files must be upgraded to handle large multimedia data objects. As the number of multimedia objects increases, users have a greater need to classify, abstract, and index the objects—functions best controlled by a data management facility. Therefore, existing data management facilities must be enhanced to manipulate and deliver multimedia objects.

Multimedia data objects are unique not only in size but also in nature. Objects, such as audio and video, are time-based, continuous datastreams of information that must be delivered at a constant rate with minimal delay between source and target in order to preserve human perception. For example, digital audio from a compact disc results in two continuous datastreams, each flowing at about 706 kbps (a total of about 1.4 Mbps). Compressed VHS-quality digital video played off a CD-ROM results in a composite datastream

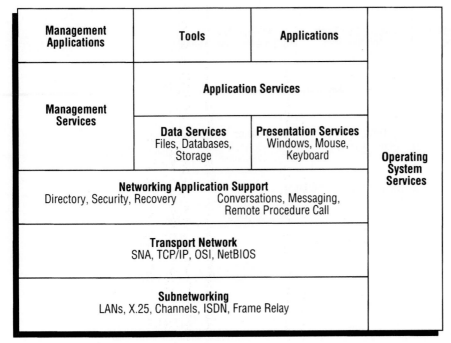

Management Applications	Tools	Applications	
Management Services	**Application Services**		Operating System Services
	Data Services Files, Databases, Storage	**Presentation Services** Windows, Mouse, Keyboard	
Networking Application Support Directory, Security, Recovery Conversations, Messaging, Remote Procedure Call			
Transport Network SNA, TCP/IP, OSI, NetBIOS			
Subnetworking LANs, X.25, Channels, ISDN, Frame Relay			

Figure 44.3 Distributed computing framework.

flowing at 1.2 Mbps. To manage datastreams, the lower four layers of the distributed computing framework require continuous datastream handling capabilities to provide real-time control and synchronization of the audio and video datastreams that together form the movie clip.

The objective of this chapter is to describe the requirements for integrating multimedia extensions into the existing facilities of distributed computing. The following sections examine each affected layer of the distributed computing framework, together with the extensions required for each layer to support enterprisewide multimedia.

Multimedia enhancements to the distributed systems framework

The goals of distributed multimedia computing are two: open computing, and the integration of multimedia extensions into strategic platforms. Figure 44.4 shows all of the multimedia extensions that will be discussed in the context of a distributed computing framework.

Application tools and services

Supporting multimedia requires new application tools, such as those provided through the Ultimedia Tools Series (UTS), an interoperable family of application development tools from IBM and independent software vendors. Most UTS tools fall into one of five categories:

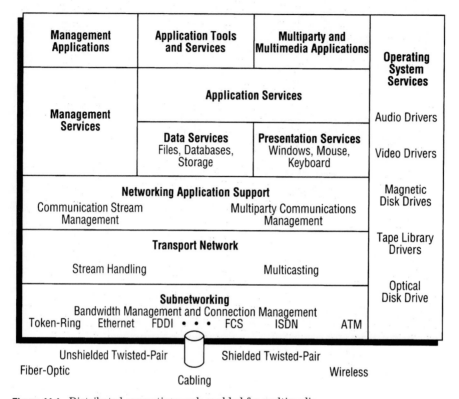

Figure 44.4 Distributed computing work enabled for multimedia.

1. *Authoring tools,* which integrate text, sound, graphics, and video into a multimedia production

2. *Graphics tools,* which enable the user to create still graphics, images, and special effects—or edit digitized photographic images

3. *Animation tools,* which add motion to graphics and text

4. *Audio tools,* which capture and edit or modify sound

5. *Video tools,* which capture and/or edit digital motion video

In addition to application tools, new application services are needed, including extensions to the following:

- Common user access services
- Object management facilities
- Data conversion services

Common user access services. CUA extensions will provide standardized graphical screens for interacting with multimedia applications, including icons representing virtual volume-control buttons, virtual slide bars, and other graphical data objects. When CUA services are standardized across multimedia applications, programmers can learn consistent methods for interacting with multimedia content, such as touching a media icon with a mouse or touchscreen.

Object management facilities. As multimedia applications are employed by an organization over time, an inventory of multimedia data objects will grow across various systems on the network. The interrelationships among the data objects will become more complex, and many types of data objects will proliferate. In addition, multimedia data objects will be stored as files, as entries in databases, in byte spaces, or stored on different types of storage devices such as a VCR tape. As a result, object management can become very complicated.

A distributed object management facility will be needed to simplify the access to multimedia data objects by means of application programs and multimedia tools. This facility will provide a uniform programming interface to applications.

Data conversion services. Currently, there are multiple data formats for each type of digital medium. Data interchange among multimedia tools, as well as application programs, can be difficult to achieve. There is now a concerted effort in the information industry to define a unique data format for each type of digital medium. Once the standards for representing digital images, video, audio, and animation have been accepted and supported, data conversion services will be needed to convert old data formats to new data formats (and perhaps vice versa). IBM currently is making multimedia conversion services available through Multimedia Presentation Manager/2 (MMPM/2), an extension of IBM's OS/2. The Resource Interchange File Format (RIFF) implemented by MMPM/2 and Microsoft Windows is an example of the generic data structure, or *wrapper,* that will be used to standardize multimedia data formats and thereby allow data interchange among systems.

Presentation services

In distributed multimedia computing, client systems perform the important role of presenting multimedia and datastreams to the user. The primary client platforms are the PS/2 and Value Point personal computer families. IBM has enhanced the multimedia capability of these platforms by extending the presentation-services component of OS/2 2.1 with MMPM/2. MMPM/2 provides a common programming interface to control both multimedia devices and the datastreams that flow from those devices.

Data services

The role of data management in developing multimedia applications will grow, as more multimedia information is stored digitally and as applications evolve toward distributed client-server implementation. Data management includes three major components:

1. File systems
2. Database management systems
3. System managed storage

   The ability of these three components to support multimedia data is critical to the success of distributed multimedia computing. Multimedia content (video recording, animation sequence, etc.) typically is both time-consuming and expensive to produce, and frequently represents a valuable corporate asset. Data-management technologies become key to protecting these assets and to maximizing their use, just as they have done for more traditional information assets, by sharing, saving, cataloging, archiving, and recovering multimedia content.

File systems.   Existing file systems provide the basic ability to "store-and-forward" blocks of media data files, and they can be used to develop a number of client-server multimedia applications, such as distributing a video training course to an employee's workstation or updating video content for use by a kiosk application. Because of the time-based, stream-oriented nature of multimedia data, file systems themselves cannot effectively deliver such data to multiple users in real time, unless the number of users on the network is severely restricted. In order to accommodate the time-based nature of multimedia data, additional client, server, and communications components must be developed.

Database management systems.   As the numbers of stored multimedia data objects increase, they are likely to become more important to an enterprise business. Efficient data services will be required to organize, manage, search, and deliver these objects to one or more users. These capabilities, provided by Database Management Systems (DBMSs) for more "traditional" data, are equally important to application developers and end users dealing with multimedia data.

   DBMSs simplify and facilitate application development and operational procedures by providing functions that support

- Data definition, organization, storage, and navigation
- Search and retrieval
- Consistent user/application interface
- Data security, integrity, recovery
- Concurrency control for access from multiple users
- Distributed data, client-server application topologies
- Specific view of data to each application, without physical data redundancy
- Consistency of all data related to the same object

Utilizing databases will allow multimedia application developers to focus on addressing unique application requirements, rather than on solving data-management problems.

System managed storage.   Multimedia has a significant impact on storage requirements, due to the size of media objects. As a reference point, consider that a 500-page textbook requires 1 Mbyte of storage. Ten fax-quality images require 640 Kbytes, whereas 10 color or detailed images could require as much as 75 Mbytes. Five minutes of uncompressed voice-quality audio requires 2.4 Mbytes of storage, and 52.8 Mbytes of storage are required for premium-quality audio (compact disc, digital audio, CD-DA).

Digitized video requires the greatest storage capacity of all data forms. Without compression techniques, practical storage of digital video is impossible. For example, animation-quality video requires 147 Mbytes per minute for a one-quarter screen size video. But with today's compression techniques, this same animation-quality video can be compressed to 1.44 Mbytes (3.5-inch diskette). A two-hour, television-quality video can be compressed to about 2 Gbytes of storage.

Early multimedia applications introduced analog storage devices—such as audiotape recorders, VCRs, and laserdisc players—as workstation peripherals. These peripherals typically have been single-function, and positioned in a stand-alone environment. However, effective use of multimedia content requires shared access across the enterprise, and that shared access requires in turn networked storage systems.

Distributed multimedia applications demand storage devices and libraries that include both analog and digital devices. These applications will benefit from the flexibility of digital media storage, including not only traditional hard disks but also such optical devices as CD-ROM players, write-once, read-many (WORM) rewritable optical drives, and optical "jukebox" libraries.

As support for various types of multimedia storage devices develops, the scope of the storage hierarchy needs to be extended. High-quality digitized images, audio, and video data stored on these devices will require automated data management to store, retrieve, back up, archive, restore, relocate, protect, and control access to data. The data files will be independent of the storage device. System managed storage now offers these facilities.

Networking application support, transport network, and subnetworking

The networking application support, transport network, and subnetworking layers of the distributed computing framework together form the "arteries" of distributed systems. The networking application support layer consists of components supporting program-to-program (or interprocess) communications, directory services, and such systems services as security, transaction management, and recovery management. The transport network includes the support for Systems Network Architecture/Advanced Peer-to-Peer

Networking (SNA/APPN), Transmission Control Protocol/Internet Protocol (TCP/IP), Network Basic I/O System (NetBIOS), and Open Systems Interconnect (OSI). The subnetworking layer includes the physical network support and network attachment.

In a multimedia-enabled network, the networking application support component expands to include both simplex (one-way) datastream communications and multiparty communications. For conferencing to become ubiquitous, standards will have to be developed that encompass a programming interface, communications protocols, and control mechanisms.

A common function of distributed multimedia computing is the delivery of audio/video datastreams from server platforms to clients in response to a media control "play" request or a request to videoconference. The videoconference datastreams have to be delivered in real time, with minimal delay, to ensure intelligible communication. The "play" request is serviced transparently; the application or user need not know whether a network was used or not.

Accomplishing this transparently can be done by means of existing transport networking facilities, coupled with careful network configuration design. However, to ensure a very robust quality of service, a new capability, network datastream handling, will be required in the transport network layer, plus extended subnetworking services that include bandwidth management and new physical network interfaces.

There exists a need for client-server video applications that efficiently utilize local-area networks (LANs) while maintaining an acceptable level of service. This can be accomplished by a digital videoserver that uses a scalable digital-video compression algorithm to adaptively control video datastream parameters such as frame rate, based on feedback about transport network performance. The client system receiving the video datastream decompresses it and presents the video at a quality commensurate to what could be handled by the network without seriously degrading every other network user.

While some applications require the real-time video transmission facilitated by scalable video, others require only conventional store-and-forward transmission of multimedia data objects. For example, multimedia objects will need to be uploaded and downloaded between clients and servers, or accessed while under the control of a distributed file management system. There is, therefore, a requirement to provide extensions to networking protocols as appropriate, so as to support the store-and-forward transmission of the large objects that accompany multimedia.

Multimedia requires changes in the subnetworking layer of the framework—the physical transmission network. There are three primary types of high-speed physical networking technologies under active development and applicable to multimedia:

1. Local area networking
2. Fiber-optic channel switching
3. Fast packet switching

Local area networking.   LANs and their supporting interconnect products were designed to meet the needs of high-speed data networking applications where the data-packet traffic is sent in bursts. Integrating multimedia into distributed computing requires that LAN technology be enhanced to support the transmission of unpredictable, continuous datastreams of data packets. However, any enhancement must attempt to protect the customers' existing investment in LANs, such as Ethernet and Token Ring.

Ethernet is intrinsically limited, by its access protocol and transmission speed, to supporting fewer VHS-quality digital-video datastreams than a 16-Mbps Token Ring LAN, which can support approximately 10 video datastreams.

IBM, along with its business partners, is evaluating an isochronous-transmission enhancement to Ethernet LAN products. Isochronous communication delivers a signal at a specified rate and time interval, making it desirable for delivery of continuous data such as voice and full-motion video. This enhancement requires an intelligent wiring hub that employs a time division multiplexing scheme to deliver both 10-Mbps Ethernet service and wideband circuit-switched service to a personal workstation over the same physical network interface (in this case, unshielded twisted-pair copper cable).

Token Ring LAN technology incorporates unexploited access control mechanism capability (in the form of priority scheduling for frame transmissions) that can support multimedia applications by giving isochronous traffic higher priority than asynchronous data traffic. Assigning a high priority to the frames that make up the multimedia datastream will ensure that they are among the first to pass across the LAN. The development of Token Ring adapters and the necessary network control software for managing priority assignments will allow voice, video, and data packets to flow over Token Ring LANs.

Along with evaluating how best to enhance Ethernet and Token Ring LANs to support multimedia, IBM is evaluating an alternative approach to delivering high-speed multimedia communications to the desktop. This alternative is based on the observation that limiting the number of attached systems can ensure multimedia support on the LAN. Optimizing this approach requires an intelligent wiring hub capable of a high-performance bridge that, in turn, supports many LANs, each incorporating one or only a few attached systems. This approach will provide the maximum LAN data transmission rate to each system, and confine all LAN changes to the intelligent wiring hub.

Fiber-optic channel switching.   Fiber-optic channel switching (FCS) originally emerged as a solution for the high-speed connection needs of high-performance computer applications. Fiber channels transmit in the 120 Mbps to 1 Gbps range over a distance of several kilometers, and typically are used to connect either engineering and scientific workstations to "supercomputers" or host computers to such high-performance storage systems as disk arrays. Electronic channel switches dynamically set up and take down fiber channel connections in microseconds. A connection usually lasts for milliseconds (enough time to transmit a burst of several megabits of data), but can stay set up indefinitely if needed. IBM sees the requirement for making FCS one of the LAN options available to client-server multimedia applications implemented on the high end of its personal workstations and ES/9000 system platform.

Fast packet switching.   The transmission capacity demands (bits-per-second) of digital voice, data, compressed image, and compressed video are extremely varied. Controlling the performance of a multimedia network can be achieved by accepting only fixed-length packets (cells) into the network for transmission. This approach has led the telecommunications industry to explore asynchronous transfer mode (ATM), aka *cell relay,* in which a 53-byte cell, consisting of 5 bytes of header and 48 bytes of data, is presented to the network for transmission.

The design of the header assumes that the intelligence exists in the network to interpret it. The header specifies routing and network control information. It allows related multimedia connections to be set up as virtual channels that make up a multimedia conversation. These channels are grouped together into a virtual path so that they may be routed and controlled by the network and synchronized at the end points. In addition, the header allows the transmitter at the origin to indicate which cells are candidates to be discarded by the network when there is a problem.

The success of ATM will depend on the practicality of migrating existing LANs to the ATM platform. According to ATM Forum member Rob Hamilton, such a migration may proceed as follows:

> At the wiring-hub level, Ethernet and eventually Token Ring networks will be increasingly segmented into smaller networks capable of correspondingly higher performance. Backbone networks, such as fiber distributed data interface (FDDI), will continue to collapse to a centralized multiport bridge/router, improving throughput and performance.
>
> The next phase introduces local LAN hubs with ATM hub-switching capabilities, while retaining the bulk of the original LAN equipment investment. This phase retains the functional advantage of the collapsed backbone, while attaining improved throughput and performance with high-speed switching. Underlying this migration will be the transition from a FDDI ring architecture to ATM switching hubs as the core premises technology. Finally, with the ATM backbone switching and ATM on the desktop, end-to-end ATM will support voice, data, text, graphics/imaging, and video on the desktop over a point-to-point network with premises-based cell switching.

Two new developments suggest that cells and packets will be parallel technologies for the rest of the decade. One is the increase in Ethernet speed to 100 Mbps, and the other is the practice of leaving the 10-Mbps Ethernet channel alone but adding an isochronous channel above it to support multimedia applications. Ultimately, though, ATM switches will likely be the best solution for providing LANs with the stable, dedicated links that super-high-bandwidth multimedia applications will require in the future.

Broadband Integrated Services Digital Network (BISDN) is another emerging force in distributed multimedia computing, representing the telephone companies' initiative in exploiting ATM. According to Steve Crowl, Director of Broadband Service Development for Sprint,

> The term "BISDN" describes tomorrow's all-purpose, all-digital network, which will accommodate diverse user requirements by providing a wide range of service mixes, including the following:
>
> ■ *Synchronous services,* such as voice and video
> ■ *Connectionless data services,* for LAN interconnection
> ■ *Connection-oriented services,* for packet-switched data, such as X.25
> ■ Variable-bit-rate services, such as video, where only changes in scene are transmitted

Networking cabling infrastructure

Another aspect of protecting a customer's investments in a networking infrastructure is determining how existing cabling systems may be used to deliver multimedia networking services. Today, VHS-quality digital video requires about a 1.2-Mbps transmission rate. Motion Picture Experts Group (MPEG) MPEG-II compressed broadcast digital video will require 4 to 8 Mbps; advanced digital TV will require 30 to 130 Mbps. On this basis, it will not be necessary to use fiber-optic cable to deliver video to the desktop. Copper cabling system installation is viable for most multimedia applications.

Impressive digital signal processing (DSP) advances have recently occurred that make it possible to achieve high-speed digital transmission over unshielded twisted-pair (UTP) cable. In fact, UTP cable may be used to deliver digital video to the desktop.

IBM is investigating how to achieve reliable transmission in the range of 25 to 45 Mbps over typical UTP cable lengths (e.g., 100 meters) found in the office and factory. If successful, UTP cable would be usable for most networked digital multimedia applications. Alternatively, shielded twisted-pair (STP) cabling, which provides a bandwidth of 500 MHz, offers excellent flexibility for broadband transmissions. Using frequency-multiplexing techniques, different types of transmission services may be delivered simultaneously over STP cabling, including LAN services and CATV.

Systems management

As intelligent multimedia equipment (digital VCRs, audio/video storage libraries, digital cameras, etc.) proliferates across distributed systems, centralized management will become very important. Networked kiosk applications already have identified the need for centralized systems management to control the distribution of multimedia content to the kiosks and to perform problem determination. Multimedia-based training and education applications will become networked, allowing courses to be taken on demand or delivered "just-in-time." It is essential that system/network management products meet the system management requirements of distributed multimedia applications.

Multimedia Server Solutions

Sharing multimedia content in a distributed computing environment poses unique challenges to the capabilities of traditional servers. New multimedia server solutions are now emerging that optimize the server's support for sharing multimedia data.

To facilitate shared access to data, multimedia servers need to control very large volumes of continuous datastreams, the media devices that store those datastreams, and the networks and communications that distribute the datastreams to and from the users in real time. Multimedia servers also have to control and manage the request-admission process, so that each data request is accepted only if the server can guarantee that the request can be satisfied without adverse impact on the execution of other requests.

Because multimedia data can be represented and stored in either analog or digital form, multimedia servers should be able to manage both data forms. Analog servers control the devices that store the data, such as laserdiscs or TV tuners. Digital servers control the data itself, retrieving it from the files or databases.

Digital servers offer a number of advantages to organizations, including the ability to incrementally add, delete, or edit stored multimedia content on an ongoing basis, often through the use of digital video editing techniques. Digital servers also allow multiple clients to have concurrent interactive access to the same media devices.

For many interactive multimedia applications, digital multimedia servers also will require digital communication of multimedia content between the server and the clients. However, for some applications, it also might be desirable to use digital servers in tandem with analog distribution, in order to exploit the 70-channel available bandwidth on existing twisted-pair Token Ring cable using F-Coupler technology. In this scenario, the data must be decompressed and converted to analog form prior to distribution. During distribution, F-Couplers merge analog TV signals and digital LAN data onto the same network cabling (see Fig. 44.5).

Synchronization and management of multiple audio and video datastreams is a challenging task even in a stand-alone environment, where a single system encompasses the datastream handlers, the data they operate on, file devices, and the playback devices. In a distributed multimedia configuration, a server owns the stored data and file devices that are remote from the clients. Client systems and their respective playback devices must connect to the server via a network, introducing the potential for delays and interruptions in the continuous delivery of datastreams for playback.

Further complicating delivery, the server and its data concurrently support more than one client on the network. Several clients can make simultaneous requests for the same or a different datastream, located on the same or a dif-

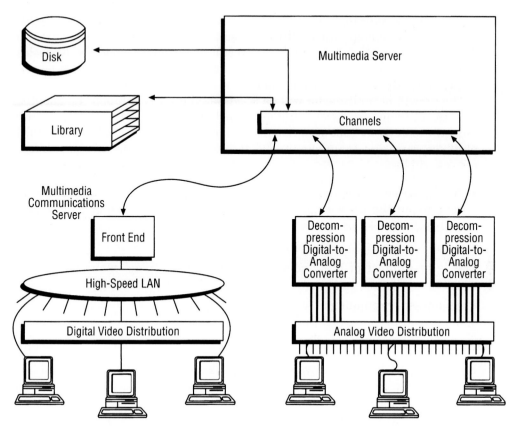

Figure 44.5   Multimedia server for analog and digital distribution.

ferent storage device—thus increasing the potential for server resource contention and datastream interruption.

Therefore, in addition to developing the isochronous network support capabilities, one must evaluate the development of other components that will ensure the end-to-end isochronous delivery of multimedia datastreams between server and multiple clients. These include the sync/stream management, buffer management, request admission management, file management, and communications management components.

Multimedia Standards

Standards are one of the critical success factors in the widespread acceptance and growth of multimedia applications and products. A significant inhibitor to growth has been the "alphabet soup" of multimedia data formats, vendor-proclaimed and industry-developed multimedia standards that continue to proliferate and even to compete against each other. At the same time, widely accepted international standards to guide developers in creating applications are lacking. The result is incompatibility and complexity in data exchange among multivendor platforms. The lack of widely accepted standards also has resulted in system-specific multimedia tools, and authoring systems that produce applications that "play" only on specific platforms. This leads to obsolescence as technology evolves. Application developers and information owners need standards that can accommodate new technology as it emerges.

The growth of multimedia will be accelerated greatly through the adoption of such unifying standards. Organizations such as the IMA are driving the industry to develop a set of common standards specifying data formats, multiplatform scripting language, and distributed multimedia services. Likely results will be

- An increased willingness to invest in the production of digital multimedia content, in the knowledge that applications developed using that content will be "playable" on future systems
- A rapidly expanding set of multimedia applications
- A large number of PCs and workstations able to "play" many varieties of content
- Businesses expanding at significant growth rates

Conclusion

Enabling open distributed systems with multimedia is a challenging goal that spans many core technologies and includes many evolving technologies from information systems, telecommunications, and consumer electronics. Over the next few years, users can look forward to a plethora of networked multimedia application solutions that incorporate international standards, and associated system integration services that span multimedia workgroup systems, enhanced desktop conferencing, and networked kiosks. As developing technologies become easier and less expensive to implement, the impact of distributed multimedia computing will be felt all over the world. What a great way to enter the twenty-first century!

Essential Network Capabilities: Multimedia Readiness

Christine Hemrick
Paulina Knibbe

Multimedia applications are fast becoming an essential part of business productivity tools. A wave of new business multimedia applications, such as desktop conferencing, collaborative computing, and video kiosks are being developed and deployed. In addition to increasing productivity, networked multimedia applications provide benefits, such as reducing the need for travel, providing timely information, enhancing customer support, and providing faster and more effective learning. Just as client/server computing has revolutionized the way businesses use information technology (IT) for the last 10 years, networked multimedia applications are beginning to change the way that businesses use networks.

Business multimedia applications represented a $1.5 billion market in 1993, $3.0 billion in 1994, and even more dramatic growth is forecast for the next two years. This fast-growing market is attracting significant investment, resulting in key advancements of associated technologies. Technology breakthroughs have increased the quality of multimedia applications and have dramatically lowered the cost of their implementation.

Lowering the cost barriers of multimedia applications, combined with increasing usefulness and ease of installation, has a two-fold effect on enterprise networks. On one side, businesses are planning to use more and more multimedia applications organization-wide. On the other side, individual users and workgroups are installing multimedia applications, creating a "bottom-up" effect. More than 80 percent of the personal computers sold during

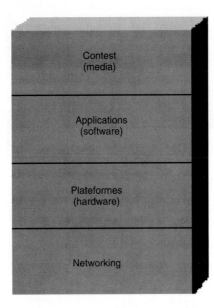

Figure 45.1 Multimedia industry structure.

1995 will be multimedia-capable. Most of these computers can be quickly and easily enhanced to support videoconferencing with a color video camera for just a few hundred dollars. These types of enhancements are allowing individual users and workgroups—the same dynamic responsible for igniting the local-area network (LAN) explosion a decade ago—to benefit from networked multimedia applications and to drive their increased deployment.

The changing expectations of enterprise networks require network designers and managers to be aware of multimedia technologies and to effectively plan for them.

The Multimedia Industry

The multimedia industry consists of four segments (Fig. 45.1).

- The first segment consists of the multimedia content providers, such as the news industry, the television industry and the entertainment industry. There has also been a recent explosion of companies producing multimedia CD-ROMs. These multimedia content providers are interested in using networks as a vehicle for delivering their content to a larger set of consumers.

- The second segment constitutes the multimedia application developers. Applications include distance learning, desktop videoconferencing, workgroup collaboration, multimedia kiosks, entertainment, and imaging.

- The third segment consists of the multimedia platform builders. Silicon Graphics, Sun, Intel, Apple, and other hardware vendors are announcing or delivering multimedia-capable computers. Initially, multimedia-ready computers will use primarily local content (accessing multimedia CDs, for example). However, there is a growing demand for access to multimedia applications across a network. Users expect application performance over a network will be comparable to the performance of a local application.

- The fourth multimedia industry segment is the network infrastructure. Two very different networking environments poised to use multimedia applications: today's business networks and the emerging public networks. Networking of multimedia will likely accelerate initially in businesses over the private networking infrastructure. However, in the next 12 to 18 months, there will also emerge a large demand for multimedia applications across public networks such as the Internet for home, education, business, and entertainment.

Network View of Multimedia Applications

From the point of view of a network, multimedia applications can be described along two dimensions (as shown in the following list), based on the number of participants and the delay sensitivity of the application.

- Data Streams
- Point-to-Point
- Multimedia notes
- kiosks
- Financial broadcasts
- Live broadcast
- Real-Time Interactive
- Multimedia mail
- Distance learning
- Multipoint LAN TV
- Desktop conferencing

The simplest type of application involves adding a multimedia data object to a traditional data object (multimedia e-mail or multimedia notes, for example). This type of application uses existing point-to-point networking technology and is not interactive in real time.

A second application category involves sending multimedia data objects to multiple hosts, such as with LAN TV or other forms of broadcasting. This category needs to go to multiple locations, but does not tend to require much real-time interaction. A third category is point-to-point applications that could be real-time interactive. Many vertical industries are planning multimedia kiosks, for example. Some real-life examples include:

- The financial industry using multimedia kiosks in banks to provide detailed information about financial services.

- The retail industry placing kiosks in stores to help customers locate merchandise and find out additional information about merchandise—virtual storefronts.

- The entertainment industry displaying kiosks as points of sale and as advertising for scheduled entertainment events, such as the theater, concerts, plays, etc.

- The entertainment industry is also leveraging multimedia kiosks to allow multiperson video games to occur over networks.

A fourth category is applications offering both multipoint and real-time interactive capabilities. The primary example of this category of traffic is desktop videoconferencing. Desktop videoconferencing requires real-time interactive communication among groups of individuals who may not be at the same location.

Networked Multimedia Requirements

Most organizations can implement multimedia applications today on their existing data networks without expensive and disruptive upgrades. Leading internetworking vendors have analyzed the characteristics of many leading multimedia applications and have participated aggressively in developing and standardizing of technologies that satisfy network multimedia requirements.

Three primary requirements for networked multimedia applications have emerged:

- Scalable bandwidth
- Consistent quality of service
- Efficient Multipoint communication

Optimizing current bandwidth

Although it is often assumed multimedia demands enormous bandwidth, multimedia applications actually have a wide range of bandwidth requirements. Thanks to continual improvements in coding and compression technologies, multimedia applications are becoming increasingly efficient—well within the range of most corporate internetworks. Figure 45.2 shows the bandwidth requirements of different classes of applications compared with bandwidth per user.

The cost of providing higher bandwidth where needed is still a concern for network managers. The bandwidth costs include two parts: equipment cost on LANs for bandwidth to the desktop, and operational cost on WANs for bandwidths outside workgroups. In a WAN environment, high costs of operation are in the way of faster adoption of multimedia applications and 60 to 80 percent of these operating costs are connection charges. Leading internetworking vendors offer both hardware and software together as solutions to minimize capital costs that are associated with LAN bandwidth and to minimize operational costs associated with WAN connection charges.

Upgrade LAN bandwidth as needed

Today's networking vendors offer a wide range of means to provide the required bandwidth optimally. Workgroup switches enable network managers to provide higher bandwidth to desktops by reconfiguring the network without rewiring or replacing network interface cards (NICs) at every desktop.

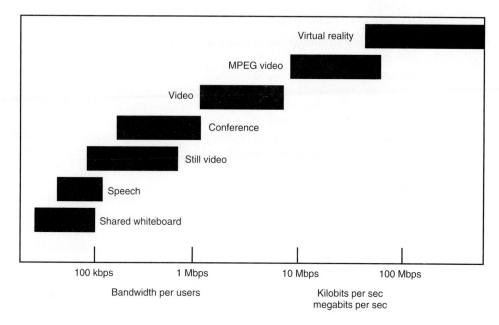

Figure 45.2 Most multimedia applications are accessible by today's users.

Using LAN segmentation and micro-segmentation, and LAN switches enable network managers to provide individual users with bandwidths of 1 megabit per second (Mbps), 10 Mbps, and 100 Mbps. Savings are realized through upgrading only as needs grow without investing in very high-bandwidth networks up front; when equipment is upgraded or changed, the change takes place only in the wiring closet without recabling or making changes on every desktop.

Three different multimedia environments frequently require more bandwidth. Individual desktops running multimedia applications often share a LAN segment with many other users. The most cost-effective way to add bandwidth for these users is to microsegment the LAN by putting fewer users on each segment.

This technique is very cost-effective. LANs can be segmented gradually as applications usage patterns require. Most multimedia applications today will run very well in these environments.

The second environment that will need more bandwidth because of multimedia applications is the workgroup or campus backbone. Today's backbones frequently use FDDI. FDDI provides 100 Mbps and is used today for high-speed servers and as a backbone. Early adopters are beginning to add ATM switching as a mechanism for increasing the amount of bandwidth available in these places.

The third environment requiring more bandwidth is the wide-area network (WAN). Bandwidth in the WAN is typically expensive and is often a recurring cost. Because of this factor, WAN bandwidth needs to be managed carefully.

Minimize WAN operational costs

The major challenge in supplying sufficient bandwidth for multimedia today concerns the enterprise WAN, where monthly line charges comprise the vast majority of a network's operational costs. Technologies addressing WAN cost savings include dial-on-demand routing and bandwidth-on-demand features, such as policy-based routing, which optimizes operational costs. For example, using policy-based routing in an Integrated Services Digital Network (ISDN) WAN configuration, extra B channels can be activated as a multimedia application is launched, leaving the already established link for non-multimedia data traffic intact. This feature eliminates the need for a costly, constant large bandwidth connection.

Network vendors provide a wide range of products for networks of all sizes to meet user solutions for workgroup to campus-wide to WAN networks. These products, providing superior functionality, interoperability, and cost savings, enable scalability from a workgroup to an enterprise internetwork. In a workgroup environment, internetworking leaders support intelligent switching with workgroup switches and, for users with specialized needs, Copper Distributed Data Interface (CDDI) and Asynchronous Transfer Mode (ATM) switching. High-speed servers might require other techniques, such as CDDI, 100-Mbps Ethernet, or, possibly, 25-Mbps ATM. CDDI and 100-Mbps Ethernet are available now and provide a dedicated 100 Mbps.

In a campus-wide environment, vendors support Fiber Distributed Data Interface (FDDI) and ATM connectivity. Mid-range to high-end routers support FDDI and ATM interfaces, switches provide workgroup ATM connectivity, and advanced switches provide enterprise ATM connectivity.

In a WAN environment, a select few internetworking vendors support a comprehensive set of technologies, including dedicated lines, Frame Relay, X.25, Switched Multimegabit Data Service (SMDS), ATM, and ISDN. This unique capability helps users integrate large, complex networks, providing a complete solution. In addition to saving network upgrade costs and operational costs, internetworking technology guarantees quality of service and efficient multipoint communications, ultimately providing networks with enhanced multimedia capabilities.

Guaranteed Consistent Service

With the addition of audio and video to enterprise networks, providing service quality and consistency grows in importance compared with network traffic consisting of data only. Multimedia applications are non-elastic in nature, meaning that the traffic they produce must be delivered on a certain schedule or it becomes useless. Quality of Service (QoS) is critical in a networked multimedia environment; this refers to parameters, such as bandwidth, latency, delay, and variance in delay (jitter) that characterize traffic flow. When a network provides variable latency for different packets, it introduces jitter. Jitter is particularly bad for audio streams because it can cause audible pops and clicks that are often disruptive to communications.

Latency

Real-time, interactive applications such as desktop conferencing are sensitive to accumulated delay (latency). For example, telephone networks are engineered to provide less than 400-ms round-trip latency. Multimedia networks that support desktop audio/video conferencing also need to be engineered with a latency budget less than 400 ms round-trip.

The round-trip latency budget is consumed by the sending computer, the network, and the receiving computer. As a rule, the sending computer will take a few ms to send a packet. The network contributes to latency in several ways, including propagation delay, transmission delay, store-and-forward delay, and processing delay.

- Propagation delay is the length of time it takes information to travel the distance of the line. This is essentially controlled by the speed of light and is independent of the networking technology used. It takes approximately 20 ms to send information between San Francisco and New York.

- Transmission delay is the length of time it takes to put a packet on the media. Transmission delay is determined by the speed of the media and the size of the packet.

- Store-and-forward delay is the length of time it takes for an internetworking device (such as a switch, bridge, or router) to receive a packet before it can send it. Most internetworking devices receive a packet before sending it out on another interface. The amount of delay that is introduced depends on the size of the packet and the speed of the media.

- Processing delay consists of steps, such as looking up a route and changing a header. When a packet comes in, the networking device (bridge, router, or switch) needs to decide which interface it should be sent out on. In some cases, the packet also needs to be manipulated (by changing the data link layer encapsulation, changing the hop count, etc.).

There is a great deal of difference in the amount of processing delay introduced by different networking vendors. Scott Bradner of Harvard University periodically conducts latency tests on submitted network equipment. For example, in August 1994, Bradner's tests showed the leading internetworking vendor's device had less than 50 ms of delay for 64-byte IP packets.

Voice communication requires low latency in order to maintain audio quality. Data networks carrying voice traffic will need to be engineered similarly to low-latency telephone networks. Network providers are meeting these QoS challenges with new technology and standards-based solutions. These advances include queuing algorithms designed to safely partition bandwidth to prevent one type of application from interfering with another, as well as methods for reducing latency and minimizing jitter for multimedia traffic.

Networking vendor solutions should provide quality of service, priority output queuing, custom output queuing, weighted fair queuing and the Resource Reservation Protocol (RSVP).

Priority output queuing

Priority output queuing enables network administrators to classify traffic into different priorities and provide the available bandwidth to the queues in the order of their priority. The highest priority queue gets as much bandwidth as it needs before lower priority queues get serviced.

Custom output queuing

Custom output queuing enables a network administrator to define a virtual bandwidth reservation scheme. Different queues are confirmed to correspond to different traffic types, where each queue has access to a predefined amount of bandwidth.

Weighted fair queuing

Weighted fair queuing allocates bandwidth "fairly" among multiple sessions of traffic. A low-bandwidth application not using its proportional "fair share" of a link receives priority handling over bandwidth-intensive applications that try to consume more than their "fair" portion. This is analogous to super-stores servicing customers with only a few items through express lanes and other customers through regular lanes. The resulting interactive traffic consisting of small packets will generally be handled with low-latency accompanied by "consistent" delays for all sessions.

RSVP (Resource Reservation Protocol)

RSVP, as mentioned earlier, allows applications to specify particular service requirements to the network, enabling the network to reserve end-to-end quality of service, such as bandwidth and latency. This capability gives corporations a proactive approach for avoiding network "over subscription" because of unexpected traffic load. RSVP is currently an Internet Engineering Task Force (IETF) draft that has been publicly demonstrated by several internetworking, application, and middleware vendors.

Efficient Multipoint Communications

The most important multimedia applications—including videoconferencing, remote training, and interactive workgroup collaboration—generally involve communication between three or more points. As a result, effective multimedia applications require efficient multipoint communications.

Multipoint access can be provided in the following three ways:

- *By using unicast mechanisms.* A separate copy of the data is delivered to each recipient. This approach wastes bandwidth and cannot accommodate large numbers of recipients.

- *By using broadcast mechanisms.* A data packet is broadcast and forwarded to all portions of the network—even if only a few of the destinations are intended recipients. This is another bandwidth-wasteful approach.

- *By using multicast mechanisms.* A single multicast packet addressed to all intended recipients is sent, and the network replicates the packet only as needed at the last possible fork. This technique provides efficient communication and requires intelligent networking devices that are capable of dynamically building efficient paths to all destinations.

Protocol Independent Multicast (PIM) provides efficient multicast routing for IP networks. PIM is a second-generation IP multicast protocol that was developed to provide efficient operation in a variety of configurations ranging from a few senders and a few receivers to many senders and many receivers. Unlike other multicast routing protocols, PIM augments, rather than replaces, the IP unicast routing protocol already in place within a network. It provides a smooth and incremental evolution to multicast functionality.

Many host and application vendors support the ability to send and receive IP Multicast packets. These vendors include Sun, Silicon Graphics, Cisco Systems, Hewlett-Packard, Microsoft, and FTP Software.

The first major networking vendor to develop PIM was Cisco Systems, Inc., which implemented PIM in 1994. PIM is on the IETF standards track and is currently being used on several networks including Mbone, the experimental multicast backbone running on the public Internet. Leading multimedia application vendors are depending on PIM to provide multipoint access for their applications.

Networking vendors are also starting to support efficient multicast on AppleTalk networks with Simple Multicast Routing Protocol (SMRP) through a licensing agreement with Apple Computers. SMRP enables multiple users to conference with each other using Apple's Quick Time Conferencing (QTC) software. QTC is planned for system bundling with all PowerPC-based computers from Apple.

Experience Multimedia Today

Multimedia applications signal an exciting new phase of business communication, one fostering faster training, increased productivity, and enhanced collaboration. Businesses can realize immediate value from such widely used applications as multimedia e-mail, desktop videoconferencing, distance learning, and collaborative computing. Multimedia applications can be added to most organizations' existing network infrastructures without major changes or upgrades.

Users need to look to leading internetworking vendors to develop comprehensive networking technology for scalable bandwidth, consistent quality of service, and the efficient multipoint communication necessary to support networked multimedia. Remember, multimedia architectures grow with the needs of the organization, from a local-area network, to a campus-wide network, to a wide-area network, providing investment protection for many years to come. Multimedia networking applications, such as video-conferencing, distance learning, kiosks, multimedia books, multimedia mail, and simulations can add significant value to today's businesses. Adding these applications to the existing data network is a cost-effective way to obtain these benefits.

46

Virtual Reality in a Nutshell

Richard V. Kelly, Jr.

Forms of Virtual Reality

Most of virtual reality's essentials can be described in threes. There are three general forms of VR, for example. There are also three kinds of VR application, three levels of necessary VR software, and three general types of VR hardware peripherals.

The most common form of virtual reality, called *through-the-window VR,* is already well known to the general public through its widespread use in arcade games and motion-based seat theaters. Through-the-window VR allows a participant to look into a virtual world from a seat in the real world. The "window" the user looks through may be as small as a home-computer monitor, or as large as a two-story movie screen. Motion-based seat theaters, the most common manifestation of through-the-window VR, allow for no true interactivity. The user is simply flown through a 2D-film-based world, usually at high speed on a bumpy ride, without being given any chance to change the itinerary or to interact with objects in the world. Through-the-window arcade games, however, usually are based on computer-generated images, not film, and thus are often more effective, usually allowing both 3D effects and some interactivity.

In a through-the-window theater experience, the participant views scenes on the screen while the seat lurches and shudders in response to the images portrayed: roller-coasters, swan-dives off buildings, and cliff-edge dune-buggy rides. The images are almost always "real" images (that is, photographed with a motion-picture camera) rather than "virtual" images (created in software). And any participant who looks away from the screen during the experience "falls out of" the world and back into the reality of the theater. But the sensations of speed and rapid movement while looking at that world can be convincing.

Immersive VR, on the other hand, is done with a head-mounted display and emphasizes interactivity with a virtual (software-derived, not filmed) 3D environment. The head-mount allows the participant to enter and become immersed in the virtual world. The principal differences between immersive and other forms of VR include the fact that the user in an immersive system can turn around, look behind, and see something in the virtual world—swimming fish, exploding volcanoes, angry wasps, or the back door—not just the back of a theater seat. An immersive virtual world is genuinely three-dimensional and inclusive.

Usually, immersive worlds also are *interactive:* the participant decides where to travel. This freedom may even extend to traveling outside the models built by the VR world-developer, even allowing the user to fly up through the ceiling or into the walls. And immersive worlds often are manipulable; that is, the objects in the virtual world can be "collided" with and can respond with a behavior as a result of the collision. A virtual dog can, for example, after being contacted in the virtual world, back up, or disappear, or fetch a bone, or attack the user.

The head-mounted display actually has two components to it that make possible the effect of immersion. One is the display itself, typically LCDs mounted in front of collimating lenses that straighten out the light rays from the LCDs, making them appear to emanate from optical infinity rather than 4 inches from the eyes. The other element is a tracking device that records the movements of the user and sends the coordinates it collects to the computer. Those coordinates tell the software rendering the images onto the LCDs where the user is looking. Without a tracker, the user's viewpoint would not change as the head's coordinates changed, and the effect of immersion would not be cogent.

The third type of VR, *second-person VR,* uses a camera to capture the image of the participant and insert it into the virtual world. Users then watch their own images on a television or movie screen interacting with objects in the virtual world. One popular game in second-person VR features virtual hockey rinks with virtual nets and skaters, and pucks that are deflected by a real keyed-in goalie.

In most second-person systems, the insertion of the participant into the virtual world is done via chroma-keying. This sometimes creates highlights around the participant, or image-resolution differences between the participant and the background (similar to what TV viewers see when they watch the meteorologist stand in front of weather maps on the local evening news). And it often takes a minute of practice to correlate one's own body movements with what is happening on the screen. But in time the user easily gets the hang of interacting with objects and scenes in the virtual world.

A combination of second-person and immersive VR yields a hybrid type known as a *cave.* In a cave, the participant walks into a room and is surrounded by a virtual environment. The environment may be displayed on multi-TV walls or on rear-screen projections. The user can interact with the projected objects because a camera, or an optical or magnetic tracker, captures the user's coordinates and sends them to the system, notifying the computer where the user is in the world and thereby triggering responses from the virtual inhabitants, who are displayed on the walls, floor, and ceiling.

Of these three main forms of VR, the one people most often think of as "real VR" is immersive. But *virtual reality*'s definition has been stretched as widely as *multimedia*'s has, and it is likely to be stretched farther as marketers begin to call everything from 3D video games to network visualization systems "virtual reality."

VR Application Types

There are three general types of VR application, each with its own benefits, limitations, and uses. They are *perambulation, synthetic experience,* and *realization/reification.*

Perambulation involves walking or flying through some form of model. This may take the form of rolling through the CAD rendering of a hospital in a virtual wheelchair, checking for architectural barriers to access. Or it may involve meandering down a human esophagus at the end of a virtual endoscope, looking for lesions or ulcers in the stomach. In a perambulation, the user is mostly interested in observing aspects of the virtual world and in discovering something about that world. Interactivity generally is limited. Interactivity may focus on moving objects around in virtual space (repositioning furniture in a virtual house), or removing objects from the scene (excising tumors from a duodenum). But for the most part, perambulation applications center on observation rather than manipulation of the virtual world.

Synthetic experience, on the other hand, involves the training of muscle memory. Synthetic-experience applications, such as virtual surgery or power plant-control-room operation, allow participants to safely and cheaply practice skills that are dangerous or expensive to develop in the real world. In synthetic experience, the most important aspect of the virtual world is not its appearance but its ability to allow direct interaction between a user and objects in the virtual world. A participant in such a world learns how to perform actions, usually with the hands, by practicing them (not just observing them), in the same way as a pianist learns to play a new composition.

The actions performed in a synthetic-experience world often are those that may someday mean life or death to the participant, but that occur so rarely in real life that they can't often be practiced ahead of time. Firefighters, for example, can learn to direct water onto those areas of a virtual chemical fire that will yield them the greatest fire-reduction the fastest. Police officers can learn to defuse virtual bombs. Plant workers can practice adjusting the level of flow through pipes in a virtual refinery. The goal of such VR systems is to allow participants to practice certain critical actions over and over until they become second nature, in the hope that their instinctive reactions will then serve them well when those reactions are needed in the real world.

The third type of application, *realization/reification,* allows users to see and to graphically manipulate profuse context-dependent data. *Reification* means making a thing out of an idea, and *realization,* an extension of scientific visualization and visual languages, refers to the representation of complex data in a graphical fashion. Such a representation, unlike most scientific visualizations or visual language icons, usually is both three-dimensional and interactive.

The chief uses of realization are in industries that process prodigious quantities of data in real time. These include network industries such as telecommunications, utilities, and financial services. The benefit that realization/reification offers is the presentation of directly manipulable data, i.e., something one step beyond ordinary graphical displays.

In a traditional spreadsheet, for example, what-if analysis can be done by changing a single number in the spreadsheet and watching the other columns of numbers change in response. An ordinary graphical presentation of this data allows the user to see those changes occur on a bar chart or scatter graph. VR, however, allows not only the graphical presentation of the results but graphical manipulation of the data; that is, not just graphical *output,* but graphical *input.*

A realization system allows the user to reach out into a seascape of livefeed data that the user sees as waves moving across the screen in real time. The user can view, say, Spot FX data (foreign currencies) as they emerge from a Reuters feed, and can perform what-if analysis interactively with the live data. By reaching out with a wand or glove, the user can press down on Japanese yen prices to see the system reveal the concomitant increase in wave heights for the British pound and Swiss franc, or push profits from sales of a minor currency, such as the Swedish krone, across the screen into purchases of a major one, such as the French franc, seeing the resulting predicted effect on the whole portfolio.

The engine behind such a system is the same as that behind any network predictive system: part expert system rulebase, part inductive algorithm, part neural net. What VR adds is the ability to reach out and touch data directly, and to see the results of those actions immediately displayed in the data-seascape virtual world.

VR Software and Graphics

In order to run any of these VR applications, three pieces of software are necessary: device drivers, world model builders, and navigation tools.

Device drivers connect the unique devices needed to navigate in and interact with virtual worlds to the code that renders the images. They allow the user to communicate with the virtual world.

Typical devices include everything from optical coordinate sensors that track the movements and head orientations of a participant, to spaceballs that allow unlimited flight through virtual worlds, to the motion-based seats that respond to the user's movement in virtual space, to soundboards that add a sonic component to virtual worlds. All of these devices capture signals from the participants and send them to the virtual world, or take signals from objects in the virtual world and send them to the user. And it is the device drivers that process and route those signals.

World-development kits, the next level up in the VR software hierarchy, allow the builder to construct stationary models to later be flown through, manipulated, or animated. Most standard CAD packages can act as development environments. CAD world-development kits generally allow creation of objects in wireframe. These objects then are imported into the navigation engine, where they can be filled, animated, imbued with lifelike behavior, positioned, and lighted. World development is the construction of the stationary model to be traveled through and also the dynamic objects that act in virtual space. But another piece of software is needed to allow the user to travel in that virtual space.

The *navigation/rendering engine* (not to be confused with the hardware "rendering engine," the graphics board that provides the processing power to draw the images on the screen) is a software tool used to navigate through, manipulate, and enliven the images created by the world-development software. Navigation engines are the real workhorses of VR, the software components that make VR a possibility. Some are object-based, some C++–based, some provide their own scripting language. Some even provide easy iconic graphical environments for object construction, making them combined world-development kits and navigation engines. Others focus on navigation and rendering processing power alone.

When building a virtual world, a VR world designer has three levels of graphics with which to construct a new reality. The largest-scale level is the *geometry primitive.* Common geometries are spheres, cones, and cubes. These can be variously shaded, lighted, colored, positioned, and animated to provide a world that conveys the impression of being filled with recognizable objects.

The more detailed level below geometries is the *polygon.* Think of polygons as the faces of the cube or the sides of the pyramid. Onto these polygons can be mapped textures (scanned images such as photographs, zebra stripes, or brick patterns) that add to the photorealism of the final world.

At the lowest and most processing-intensive level are *voxels,* three-dimensional pixels. This is the level at which medical imaging is done. Because the amount of detail it can convey is huge—and, consequently, its CPU demands prodigious—voxel-level work in VR is, at least so far, not readily attainable. But as this is nothing more than a performance limitation, not requiring any fundamental breakthrough in the technology, only more horsepower, it is likely to dissolve as a limitation over the next several years.

Peripherals

Peripheral devices also fall into three categories: audio/visual, tracking, and navigation/manipulation.

The visual side of VR encompasses everything from the movie screens at theme parks, to the standard VGA monitors that most developers use to build and test their worlds, to the head-mounted displays that occlude the peripheral vision of users and make them feel that they are inside the virtual world.

On the audio side, there are ordinary MIDI boards that release sampled sounds when buttons are pressed or virtual objects contacted. But there are also audio boards that allow for "spacialization" of sound (giving the impression that a sound is coming from a given direction and altitude). They may even allow particular sound parameters to be tied directly to objects in the virtual world, such as airplanes whose engine roars doppler-shift as they approach the listener. And because touch is still a difficult sensation to emulate in VR, many developers substitute sound cues for tactile ones. This *sonic feedback collision announcement* allows users to hear a sound cue when they have touched an object, rather than actually feel it.

Tracking devices, another major group of VR peripherals, are used to send the coordinates of the participant's head, hands, or body to the renderer, so that the computer will know where the user is looking. Trackers generally work within "6 degrees of freedom"; that is, they handle movement in X,Y,Z space (position) and roll, pitch, and yaw (orientation). (*Roll:* turn your chin to the left and the top of your head to the right. *Pitch:* lift your chin up, and dip the back of your head back. *Yaw:* turn your head to the right or left. In all three instances your body stays in the same X,Y,Z position, but your orientation changes.) Trackers come in optical, sonic, inertial, direct physical, and magnetic varieties.

Navigation/manipulation devices, the last major peripheral component of a VR system, include everything from gloves for picking up objects in the virtual world, to globes for sailing through them, to foot pedals, joysticks, wands, and gyroscopic flying mice. The more advanced work in this area is now being done in the use of biological signals as inputs to the virtual world. Biofeedback signals such as EEGs, EKGs, galvanic skin response, and myography (muscle tension) are now being used as inputs that manipulate objects, viewpoints, or actions in the virtual world. This work may eventually lead to direct linkage between human bodily processes—even thoughts—and actions in the virtual world.

The Range of VR Applications

Not unexpectedly, the most rapid development of VR applications is now occurring in the entertainment field. Within a couple of years, VR entertainment in arcades and homes will be ubiquitous. Most arcade VR games, because they are relatively expensive and are time-fee-based, are testosterone-driven and involve little or no learning. The user simply dons a headmount or sits in a motion-based gondola and the experience begins, usually involving shooting opponents of some kind. Home-based VR tends to be far more involved and complex, because home players spend far longer inside their games and prepay a lump sum for the experience rather than a by-the-minute fee. Thus home games tend to be far richer, more learning-driven environments. However, they too tend to concentrate merely on thwarting villains.

In the field of medicine, the Holy Grail is the virtual cadaver. Attempts to develop a virtual living body are being made via four different approaches. *Film-based endoscopy* allows a user to travel down a virtual esophagus, cobbled together from several thousand photographs of real throats. *MRI-based systems* construct whole body sections, organ by organ, from scan data. *Microtome reconstructions* embed a real cadaver in wax, slice it, digitize the 2D slices, and arrange them into a 3D image in the computer. And *software-based organ development* builds models of living organs from scratch, out of polygons and voxels.

My own work in this field has centered around animating virtual organs and organ systems using the principles of Artificial Life, a technology for modeling extremely complex living processes. This method combines 3D cellular automata, neural nets, genetic algorithms, and production rules together with VR as the display mechanism, in order to portray processes such as tumor development or immune function, or to reveal approaches to gene therapy using engineered viruses as the mechanisms for site-directed mutagenesis (employing hand-changed viruses to insert their cargoes into malfunctioning cells).

In the network industries (telecom, utilities, financial services, and medical infomatics), VR work is concentrating on developing new metaphors for dealing with data: expressing relationships between vast amounts of related data; allowing users to interact directly with graphically displayed data; and representing data in three dimensions so as to elicit "intuitive understanding" of prodigious quantities of data.

The work in these fields includes the exploration of novel metaphors for the displaying of profuse data: everything from Christmas trees the color and shape of whose bulbs represent types of problems in a network, to hydraulic models that show energy-transmission lines as pipes and reveal capacity by the diameter of the pipe and usage by the height of the water in the pipe, to rolling, wavy seascapes of continuous livefeed data that can be processed and speculated against by pushing and pulling as if the data were interactive taffy.

In architecture, most VR work has focused on edifice-prototyping and -testing. Edifices range from rooms in a private residence, to hospitals, to vast chemical-plant facilities. This approach allows the user to construct the virtual building first, then test it for compliance with various regulations or for the comfort and well-being of future denizens.

Our work in this arena has concentrated on linking the construction of the virtual building to a spreadsheet, so that design considerations can be visualized and their financial outcomes viewed simultaneously. Viewers can then make changes to the building in real time, to satisfy design-versus-finance constraints. They can then view the building to see whether it looks the way they want it to look, and study the resulting spreadsheet created by the system to see if costs are in line with budget. We've also built in comments on the environmental impacts of design decisions, allowing a client to view the effects building decisions will have on the environment as well as on the purse and on the eyes.

The area of VR development currently undergoing the greatest amount of corporate and industrial exploration is the field of skill-based training. VR's unique benefit over film and ordinary 2D graphics is that it allows users to interact with its objects. This has allowed VR developers to construct worlds in which users can practice those skills they must use in the real world.

Synthetic experience investigations in my lab, for example, involve telephone-line-worker training, switching-station training, and process control diagnosis training in large plants. This has led to an interest in "living history" and "wraparound" educational applications that allow a user to become immersed in an historical environment (the Wild West, a slave auction, traveling steerage across the Atlantic to America, under the bodhi tree with the Buddha, in Thomas Edison's lab, at a summer gathering of the nations of the Iroquois confederacy, on the battlefield at Gettysburg, in Timbuktu at the height of the Kushite empire). And beyond these real-world applications lies the ability to practice viewing and working in environments that human beings have not yet experienced (a colony on the surface of the moon, en route to Mars, a journey to the center of the earth, and worlds that exist only in the imagination).

The Real World Is Messy

In all of the commercial areas beyond entertainment, VR developers have discovered that pure VR applications seem to be relatively few. As a result, most commercial work in the field now involves either coordination with or direct integration to other technologies. Behavioral animation (the insertion of life-like behavior into creatures in the virtual world), for example, may require half a dozen technologies and techniques outside of VR. In such a working environment, VR becomes one technology among many. And it is likely that, in time, as VR entertainment develops, these same concerns will become important to game-builders as well, as they broaden their scope from just 3D graphics in a helmet to genuine artificially enlivened universes.

The future of virtual reality points in that direction, to the commingling of other technologies with VR. For example as optic fiber replaces copper, and bandwidth limitations recede, long-distance networked VR is becoming a reality. As CPU processing power increases, detailed voxel-level images are being experimented with. As GUI designers begin to work in three dimensions, desktop metaphors gradually will be replaced by "landscape" and "interactive data-taffy" interfaces. As Artificial Life begins to play its role behind the scenes in behaviorally animating virtual objects, virtual worlds will begin to take on the richness and complexity of the real world. And as all of these advancements accelerate, it will become possible for participants in virtual experiences to feel for the first time that they are *natives* in the virtual world, not just tourists.

47

The Design of a Multimedia Adapter

Ken Morse

Introduction

In the mid-to-late 1970s the dominant user interface was based on a keyboard, a black-and-white text display, and a complicated command line. A few machines had simple graphics capabilities, but it wouldn't be until the release of the Apple Macintosh in 1984 that bitmapped graphics became a standard feature. With this shift toward graphics, user interfaces shifted away from the command line to mouse-driven windows and icons.

Audio has taken even longer to become accepted, but in the last several years developers have incorporated it into mainstream applications such as desktop presentations, in addition to entertainment titles.

Since the introduction of the Macintosh nearly a decade ago, the basic graphical user interface (GUI) has been only modestly improved. Color graphics displays now are commonplace, but generally with a small number of colors. New graphics adapters are being introduced that accelerate graphics performance by providing an on-card graphics processor to relieve the present burden on the host CPU.

During those 10 years since the introduction of the Macintosh, there have been some staggering technological advances: VLSI densities have increased 16-fold, enabling more complex designs to be implemented; VLSI speeds have increased eight-fold, providing a leap in processing power; networks are pervasive, and high-capacity optical-storage mediums such as CD-ROM are available at low cost.

These four major advances in basic computer technology, coupled with equally major advances in digital-video compression algorithms and video-processor architecture, have transformed the monochrome graphics display subsystem of 9 years ago into today's rich and highly dynamic video subsystem. Displays can now feature full-screen, full-motion video, high-resolution video stills, video special effects, 3D real-time synthetic video, and very fast, true color graphics—all of which form the heart of a modern multimedia system.

This chapter will examine the requirements for a multimedia subsystem and use an actual adapter by way of illustration. Multimedia is not limited to personal computers and will, over time, be available in a wide variety of products, from information booths to intelligent televisions to hand-held personal assistants. However, most designs will be very similar to those now found on personal computers; the difference will be that the degree of specialization and integration will be greater in these new applications.

Multimedia Subsystems

What is multimedia? This is a common question, but rarely does one hear the same answer. Ask one person and she will say it is the combination of graphics and text, ask another and he will add audio to the list, ask a third and he will introduce video, and so on.

My definition of a multimedia system is one that is *capable of presenting a predefined or interactive experience in a compelling and intuitive manner.* Using this somewhat simple definition, a simple graph chart could be considered a multimedia datatype. It conveys information in an intuitive manner, even if it doesn't provide compelling experience.

This section will try to provide some insights into those issues that must be addressed by a multimedia adapter designer, such as functionality, cost, and integration. The data types of still images, motion video, and audio also will be discussed, with the emphasis being on their effect on a multimedia adapter's design.

Graphics

An obvious requirement for any multimedia system is graphics support. As mentioned earlier, the dominant interface until the late seventies was built around a monochrome text display. With the introduction of the Macintosh, bitmapped graphics started to appear as a standard feature. IBM introduced the enhanced graphics adapter (EGA) in 1985, which provided color displays at resolutions of up to 640 × 400. At this resolution, however, the number of colors on-screen was limited to 16—useful for presentations and simple line art, but not much more.

The emergence and growth of graphical user interfaces (GUIs) prompted the rush to market of new graphics adapters that provided higher resolution. The base requirement for GUIs was 640 × 480, a resolution provided by VGA graphics systems. However, users of window-based GUIs quickly found themselves in need of more room on their "desktop" displays, and new adapters, termed SVGAs, appeared, pushing the resolution up to 800 × 600.

Just as GUIs were pushing the resolution up, desktop publishing was creating a need for higher color depth. Desktop publishing applications, which ran under the GUI environment, coupled with the introduction of affordable laser printers, created an explosion in document manipulation and generation. The availability of flatbed scanners allowed real images to be read into the computer and composed with text and graphics to form professional documents. Graphics adapters of the time were able to show acceptable gray-scale images using 256 gray scales, but users were demanding higher-quality color displays.

Current graphics adapters provide resolutions of up to 1280×1024, with 1024×768 the most commonly used mode (display monitors that support 1280×1024 tend to be expensive). At these resolutions the adapters support over 65,000 colors on-screen simultaneously by using 16 bits per pixel. Each pixel specifies the color in red-green-blue (RGB) color space, with common bit allocations of RGB:565 and RGB:664. For high-end publishing applications, 24-bit RGB is used, which provides over 16 million colors for true-color representation.

One important area that has to be addressed, given the increased resolution and color depth, is performance. A GUI requires a large amount of graphical image manipulation; for example, windows may be picked up and placed in other areas of the screen. This involves moving all the pixel data in memory representing that window to a new location in memory.

Moving from an 8-bit color display to a 24-bit display increases the data bandwidth by a factor of 3, and will cause performance to degrade by a factor of 3. This problem has been addressed by the advent of graphics accelerators, which remove some of the burden from the CPU. These accelerators implement graphics primitives for such tasks as line-drawing, polygon-filling, and area moves (bit-blitting), and can speed up graphics performance to a rate 50 times that achievable by a CPU-managed display. The CPU merely requests the accelerator to carry out the required operation, which then is executed in parallel to the CPU task.

Another area in graphics that is rapidly advancing is the use of three-dimensional objects to add realism to presentations. The talk of "virtual reality" and "virtual worlds" that can be explored from the comfort of your own armchair is everywhere in the press. Much research is being carried out in this area, and technology slowly is catching up with theory. The aim is to display on a computer screen or head goggles a believable world, one realistic enough to fool the brain. This requires a great deal of processing power to produce the real-time, realistic shading and light reflections of the natural world. High-end graphics workstations, from companies such as Silicon Graphics, are able to provide this realism. Now the challenge is to bring this technology to the wider marketplace.

Still image support

Still images form an important part of any multimedia title by introducing realism. With the explosion of desktop publishing, images were one of the first of the multimedia data types to be added to personal computers. Initially these images were simply stored as the raw pixel values. However, given the increasing resolutions and color depths involved, their sizes became too large to be efficiently manipulated and they consumed too much memory: a 1024 × 768 image, stored as RGB24, consumes over 2 Mbytes of memory. The solution was to use compression techniques to exploit the redundancy in the image and encode the image to save both memory and storage space. In theory there is no time constraint on the compression of the image, since this is carried out only once. However, the decoding of the image must be carried out as quickly as possible, so that the least amount of delay is passed on to the user. Software-only solutions tend to be based on a run-length encoding mechanism that is easily decoded to give acceptable performance but at the cost of compression. Other more exotic schemes exist that provide much better compression but at the cost of a longer decode time.

Most compression schemes are *lossy,* meaning that they lose some image data during the compression process. The amount of data lost depends on the complexity of the original image and the compression ratio selected. The higher the compression ratio, the more data lost. Which compression ratio you choose will depend primarily on four things:

1. Image type
2. The desired resolution, which in turn depends on the context in which the image will be used
3. The amount of storage space available
4. The processing capabilities of the storage and playback devices

Over the past few years, JPEG (Joint Photographic Experts Group) has gained wide acceptance as a standard for compression of continuous-tone-color images. The algorithm is based on a combination of the Discrete Cosine Transform, quantizing, and arithmetic encoding that removes redundant image and color data.

Studies of human perception have proven that when viewing color images, for instance, the eye more readily notices changes in brightness (*luminance*) than changes in color (*chrominance*); JPEG takes advantage of that fact and, during compression, eliminates more chrominance than luminance information. JPEG can compress images at ratios of about 20:1, with no noticeable loss of quality. Compression ratios of up to 100:1 are possible, but the higher the ratio the greater the loss of detail and, sometimes, the more likely the appearance of artifacts.

Another advantage of JPEG is that it is a symmetrical compression algorithm. The same hardware or software can be used to compress and decompress an image. In addition, compression and decompression times are about the same. This does not hold true for most video-compression schemes, which are asymmetrical.

Until recently, the mechanism for translating photographic images into computer-readable form was through a flat-bed scanner. Either the photograph or a negative was scanned, providing a digital image that could then be manipulated and displayed on the computer. In 1992, Kodak introduced the

Photo-CD system, which makes the translation from photographic image to digital image much smoother. Photographs may be taken using a standard camera, and the film then taken to a developing agency. The negative is developed using standard processing techniques, but then is scanned at three different resolutions into three digital images. These images then are compressed and written to a CD-ROM. Up to 100 photographs may be stored on the CD-ROM in each of the three resolutions, using a proprietary compression scheme. It is too early to judge the success of Photo CD in the consumer market—after all, it took 5 years for audio CDs to become an accepted consumer medium. However, it certainly *is* being embraced by the multimedia development community, which now has a simple way of importing high-quality photographic images into their systems.

We see then, from our discussion up to now, that the requirement for still images is to provide a large color-depth, at an acceptable resolution, so as to support photorealistic images and to provide support for image-compression and fast decompression, and thereby to save valuable storage space.

Motion video support

If a single picture is worth a thousand words, then motion video can tell a complete story. Motion video support comes in two flavors: live, and recorded. Live motion video, or *passthrough* video, is used when the video material is stored on media such as laserdisc or VCR tape. In this case, the laserdisc player or VCR is connected to the multimedia system and its output mixed with the computer-generated text and images. This is very popular for interactive educational and training titles whose playback devices are controlled by the computer—normally by means of a serial connection. The advantage of this system is that the picture quality is excellent, since no compression is involved. Unfortunately the additional cost, and system requirements, limit its application to niche markets.

The solution is to provide a mechanism that can store previously recorded material on the computer system and replay it on demand.

Much research has been directed toward the area of digital-video compression, and with the rapid increase in VLSI capabilities, computer-based digital motion video has become a reality. The need for compression becomes obvious when the data rates are considered. For example, a 320×240 image in an RGB16 color space requires 152 kbytes of memory. To attain full-motion digital video, the clip must be played at 30 frames per second, giving rise to a data rate of over 4.5 Mbytes per second. These kinds of data rates cannot be handled by current PC designs, and therefore compression techniques must be employed.

Most video-compression schemes attempt to reduce the data rate to that provided by CD-ROMs, 150 kbytes per second. The CD-ROM has become accepted as the medium for multimedia titles, since its large storage capacity (over 600 Mbytes) is required to contain typical multimedia titles. The 150-kilobytes-per-second requirement means that each compressed frame in a 30-frames-per-second sequence must average 5 kbytes—quite a difference from the 152 kbytes occupied by the original 320 × 240 RGB16 image.

Several image-resolution standards are being adopted, such as 160 × 120 and 320 × 240. The algorithms in use require additional hardware if they are to provide optimal results, but with the increase in microprocessor performance it is now possible to decode digital motion video on systems such as Intel 486s and Motorola 68040s using the CPU alone. The drawback is that most of the CPU bandwidth must be allocated to the task of decompressing and displaying the video—80 percent of the CPU cycles is a typical figure.

JPEG is also among the standards used for motion video compression today. It can be used to compress each video frame independently of other frames. This is referred to as the process of *intraframe coding*. This allows users to randomly access any individual frame within the compressed video, making it ideal for digital applications (such as video preproduction) in which access to every frame is necessary. The downside of using intraframe encoding alone is that even under high compression ratios, a few seconds of 24-bit color video stored as motion JPEG takes up a lot of space.

The standards organizations that sponsor JPEG—the Consultative Committee of International Telegraph and Telephone, and the International Standards Organization—have defined a compression standard called *MPEG* (Motion Pictures Experts Group) specifically to handle motion video. In addition to intraframe encoding for removing redundancies within individual frames, MPEG also employs *interframe coding,* which eliminates redundant information among frames. If the background of a video clip stays the same from frame to frame, for instance, MPEG will save the background once and store only the differences between those frames. MPEG supports compression ratios of up to 50:1, assuming the standard MPEG resolution of about 320 × 240 pixels for full-motion video. (MPEG-2 was proposed in 1992 for handling higher-resolution, broadcast-quality images).

In addition to its interframe-coding capabilities, MPEG differs from JPEG in its asymmetrical approach to compression—using more hardware and computer power to compress full-motion video and audio than to decompress it.

From this discussion it is clear that a multimedia system that supports motion video must have the ability to support high, sustained, data-transfer rates as well as provide real-time decompression capabilities for playback.

Audio

A system with digital motion video is not much use without an accompanying audio soundtrack. Digital audio has been available as an option for PCs for several years, and is now in its third generation. The first set of 8-bit audio adapters has been superseded by 16-bit stereo audio adapters that also provide MIDI capabilities and simple FM synthesis.

PCM audio is the most prevalent form of audio found on personal computers today, but it carries a high bandwidth and storage requirement due to its uncompressed nature. Digital audio has a lower bandwidth than raw digital video but is harder to compress, since the human ear is very unforgiving.

Simple compression is achieved by reducing either the sampling rate or the number of bits per sample. Unfortunately, the effect of both of these options is very noticeable, and more complicated compression schemes are available, such as ADPCM, that provide acceptable quality with a lesser number of bits per sample.

In addition, the MPEG audio group has defined several audio-encoding schemes to accompany MPEG video. These schemes employ subband encoding to achieve compression. The audio signal is split into a series of frequency bands and then analyzed. The analysis is based on the human ear's *masking* characteristic: at an instantaneous point in time, the ear may "mask out" some frequencies close to a high-amplitude frequency component. For example if there is a strong frequency component at 6 kHz, the ear may be unable to resolve a frequency component at 6.2 kHz. Hence the data that represents the 6.2 kHz signal is redundant, and may be removed to achieve better compression. Yet even when utilizing the most complex audio-encoding schemes, the compression achieved is only a factor of 6:1.

New sound systems based on *surround sound* are being introduced that contain up to six audio channels. These systems work by adjusting the balance and delay of the audio channels between the front, back, and side speakers. Since there is a known relationship between these additional surround signals, audio-compression schemes for surround sound can achieve overall higher compression than 6:1.

The other important thing to remember about audio is that it is real-time, and therefore cannot be interrupted without the listener being aware of it. Hence, although the bandwidth is lower, the audio delivery and decode tasks must have a high priority within the system if it is to guarantee that audio data will be delivered on time.

Up to now our discussion of audio has addressed only the integration of "real-world" sounds, but there is a second category of audio: *synthesized sound*. Synthesized sound first arrived in the 1960s on Moog synthesizers, which used analog techniques to generate the sounds. With the amazing technological advances of the last 30 years, synthesized sound has made the transition into the digital domain.

MIDI, the Musical Instrument Digital Interface, is a communications specification that enables the exchange of musical information among electronic musical instruments, computers, and peripheral audio equipment. When combined with music synthesis capability, MIDI allows a personal computer to become the control center of a musical production system. Although initially used by musicians to perform music, MIDI is now an integral part of the audio-generation technology for multimedia productions.

MIDI augments the use of waveform audio in multimedia. Waveform audio normally is used to reproduce speech and many nonmusical sounds, but it requires a great deal of memory if it is to faithfully reproduce music. MIDI represents music using far less storage space, and it allows greater editing flexibility, but it does require a music synthesizer to generate the actual music. MIDI describes music in terms of high-level command sequences; for example, "Play middle C on the French horn loudly for 1 second." This command is encoded into 6 bytes—3 bytes to start the sound, and 3 bytes to terminate it. Compare this to CD-quality PCM data at 176 kilobytes per second for the same "information."

Because MIDI is a symbolic representation of music, not the audio waveform data itself, the quality of the sound is related primarily to the quality of the music synthesizer, not the MIDI data. Most synthesizers produce stereo sound, and some can very convincingly reproduce acoustic musical instruments. Speech and sound effects, recorded as specific musical sounds, are limited by the synthesizer's memory.

Programmability

The algorithms of video and audio compression are advancing rapidly, given the release of optimized performance implementations for existing algorithms and the results of research into new compression techniques. The multimedia market is very young and, as is typical with emerging markets, there are no fully adopted standards in place. (JPEG has a foothold in the still-image fraternity, and MPEG is starting to make inroads into the motion video marketplace, but already there are a wide variety of specialized algorithms in use.) Keeping this in mind, it would be foolish to tie a particular multimedia subsystem to one particular algorithm or system.

Programmability is the key to a longer lifespan, since it enables the same subsystem to support a wide variety of algorithms and implementations. However, there is an associated price to be paid that goes along with providing a programmable solution. Programmability tends to have a twofold impact on the system. First, it increases the cost of the system, since the programmable unit must provide general-purpose facilities to support the wide variety of algorithms and implementations. Second, it tends to reduce system performance. Because it caters to a wide variety of algorithms, it is often the case that no single algorithm executes to the maximum—we are in the area of "jack of all trades and master of none." In the consumer marketplace there is a different outlook regarding programmability, as will be described later.

Data Delivery

It has been shown in previous sections that a multimedia system will utilize a high-data bandwidth. Graphics, audio, and video data, in both compressed and decompressed forms, must be supported by the adapter, while avoiding bottlenecks in data transfer and delivery since audio and video are real-time quantities. The original PC bus—known as the ISA bus—was designed over 10 years ago, and is not suitable for high-bandwidth transfers. Hence designs must attempt to minimize the amount of data transferred across this bus. This can be achieved by ensuring that only compressed data flows over this bus. However, the multimedia adapter must be able to support local transfers of high-bandwidth uncompressed data. Hence a high-performance bus usually is implemented on the adapter, to meet those data delivery requirements.

System Integration

Given time, many of the multimedia components such as digital audio and video will be folded into the motherboard design and become standard features on all new systems. In the short term, however, multimedia adapters must take the form of an add-in card, just like any other system add-on. This raises system-integration issues that the adapter-designer must address. For example, how is the digital motion video, provided by the adapter, to be combined with the existing graphics generated by the base machine? Perhaps the multimedia adapter should provide its own graphics system, thus making the base graphics redundant.

Software support

All the hardware features in the world are useless if the software supplied cannot access them. The effort required for software development should never be underestimated, for it is at least as much as for hardware development. A typical software model is the *layered* approach. At the bottom layer is the hardware-specific code that communicates with the adapter and provides low-level services. Above this are the support modules, which abstract away the hardware dependencies and provide an adapter-independent application programming interface (API) for the programmer. The layered approach, and the use of hardware abstraction, make it possible for easier code migration to support follow-on hardware implementations.

Until recently, multimedia had been overlooked by operating-systems designers, but in the last two years multimedia extensions have been added to operating systems such as Microsoft's Windows and IBM's OS/2. These extensions provide a high-level set of common commands that can be used across different operating systems. For example, the commands provided in the Media Control Interface (MCI) layer in Microsoft Windows are identical (apart from a few variants) to those provided in the MCI layer of OS/2's Multimedia Presentation Manager (MMPM/2). This commonality has greatly helped developers, who now can port their titles across platforms more easily. With this in mind, any software provided with an adapter should integrate with the multimedia software extensions provided by the host operating system if it is to be fully utilized by application developers.

Networking

Another area that has seen rapid growth in the past decade is networking. Classical networks consisted of dumb terminals served by a small minicomputer or mainframe. This configuration placed large burdens on the central computer, which was responsible for executing all the programs required by the users. With the rapid growth in microprocessor power over the last few years, this network model is changing. Terminals have been replaced by personal computers, and the central computer—the server—is often just a high-performance personal computer with a large on-line storage capability. This evolution has moved more processing power onto the terminal, allowing high-performance applications such as multimedia to be run locally. For example, consider a Token Ring network that has a 16-Mbit bandwidth. Such a network, with multimedia-equipped terminals, can easily support up to 10 digital motion video sessions (each at 150 kilobytes per second) to provide an interactive training facility.

The widespread use of networks is opening the door to *group-working,* which allows all users to share documents and communicate through the network, a simple example being electronic mail. Adding the exchange of digital video and audio over the network opens up the possibility of videoconferencing. A camera mounted on one user's machine can capture his/her image, send it over the network, and display it on a remote machine. Likewise the image of the user at the remote machine can be sent and displayed on the original machine.

Systems are being introduced for videoconferencing that use existing telephone lines and new digital (ISDN) systems to transmit the video and audio signals. Of course compression plays a large part in squeezing the large amounts of video and audio data into the relatively low-bandwidth transmission lines. Systems are not limited to the exchange of video and audio data; computer data such as drawings or charts can be transmitted, enabling real-time data exchange and presentation.

The logical extension of networking in the office is to the home. Already phone lines and video cable systems have been installed in homes, and these can form the backbone of an interactive network. Work is under way by both the phone and cable companies to run trial systems, offering such services as video-on-demand and interactive television.

A multimedia adapter that supports digital motion video could be used in conjunction with a network interface to provide the basis for such systems. *Latency* is the most critical area that must be addressed in network delivery; for example, if the latency of the compress-transmit-receive-decompress loop in a videoconferencing application is high, it will cause communication difficulties between the two parties of much the same kind as the delays experienced on transatlantic telephone conversations.

Capture and compression

Thus far our discussion has been driven by playback concerns; how images and audio are replayed on users' machines. However there is also a market for importing real-world data into personal computers, i.e., *capture.* A capture system must encompass an array of multimedia data types; for example, a still image from a camera, a motion video sequence from a VCR, an audio track from a recital.

Such features are required primarily by multimedia title developers, and hence should not be included as part of the standard adapter but rather offered as an extension, thus reducing the cost for those users who require only playback capabilities.

A capture subsystem should allow standard devices (microphones, cassette recorders, cameras, VCRs, laserdisc players) to be connected, thus allowing as wide a range of source material as possible to be imported. We have already seen how the high data-storage requirements of audio and video require the original data to be compressed. This compression can be carried out at the time of capture, or as a subsequent process. For data types with extremely high data rates, such as motion video, compression often is carried out in tandem with the video capture and is termed a symmetrical capture-and-compression process.

An example of a case in which such a symmetrical process is required is the previous one of videoconferencing. The video sequences must be kept to a low bandwidth to match the transmission lines over which they are sent, and additionally the system must exhibit a low latency—buffering of the video and audio data must be kept to a minimum.

Cost

Finally, there's no such thing as a free lunch! A price tag is attached to the implementation of all the aforementioned functionality, and cost plays an important part in the design process. At the end of the day the product will sell only if the customer is willing to buy at the selling price. Thus the design process tends to be a balancing act between functionality and cost. Tradeoffs constantly are made until the best product for the money has been achieved in the designers' eyes. An example of such a tradeoff is the point raised earlier, regarding the programmability of the multimedia adapter. Some implementations may address fixed functions in a high-volume marketplace, in which case a programmable solution is less desirable than a cost-effective one.

ActionMedia II—A Practical Design

Now that we have some understanding of the requirements of a multimedia adapter, the description of an actual implementation can be presented. The adapter I have chosen is called ActionMedia II and is the result of a joint development by Intel and IBM, based on digital-video interactive (DVI) technology. The DVI technology was originally conceived in 1984 and has undergone a steady evolution, culminating in the release of ActionMedia II in 1992. Both Intel and IBM wanted to provide a system that was affordable and that had the following attributes:

- Integration to existing graphics system
- Programmable audio- and video-compression algorithms
- High-quality audio with compression
- Photorealistic still images, with compression

- Playback of video (decompression and display)
- Real-time capture and compression of video
- Passthrough of live analog-video and analog-audio material (e.g., laserdisc)
- Extendible software architecture

The following sections will provide an overview of the design, and indicate how each of the objectives listed above was achieved. As you will see, ActionMedia II is by no means an ideal solution.

Introduction

DVI is not new. The David Sarnoff Research Center in Princeton, New Jersey, started work on DVI in 1984, when the laboratory was the central research facility for RCA. The Digital Products Research Group carried the project through the years when General Electric acquired RCA to bring it to the point of demonstration in early 1987, when it was first shown publicly on March 1 at the Second Microsoft CD-ROM Conference in Seattle. In October 1988, GE sold the DVI technology to Intel, who then brought the technology to market later that year.

The first DVI product was available as a 7-adapter set that provided reasonable-quality digital motion video output, but with an attached high price tag of $10,000 to $15,000. By 1989 IBM was looking for a partner with which to enter the desktop-video marketplace, and a joint-development agreement was entered with Intel. The first fruit of this alliance was the ActionMedia 750 (named after the 82750 chipset on-board), which reduced the 7-adapter design down to 2 adapters. This increased integration brought a new lower price and better performance, since processor power had risen due to interim advances in VLSI technology.

ActionMedia II is the latest in the line of DVI technology and takes the integration a step farther by making further use of VLSI integration techniques to reduce the design to a single adapter for playback, which retails for $1000, and a daughter card for capture, priced at $500.

The following sections detail the ActionMedia II technical design, with explanations offered, when appropriate, as to why a particular design choice was taken.

System overview

ActionMedia II consists of a single ISA or Micro Channel (IBM PS/2) adapter, based on the i750 video-processor architecture, with an optional daughter card to provide capture capability. The motivating force behind the design of the i750 video-processor architecture was the desire to integrate all the processing functions required for multimedia into a single programmable chip set. This involved the design and development of basic video and logic building blocks that would find application over a broad range of algorithms. While a hardwired implementation may at first appear to offer better performance for a particular algorithm, a programmable approach ultimately is

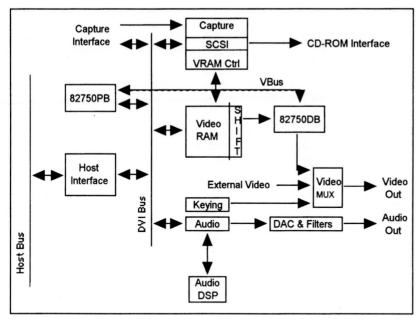

Figure 47.1 ActionMedia II subsystem.

superior, since it can be reprogrammed to track the evolution of an algorithm or standard, and at the same time support each of the diverse algorithms required in a full multimedia system.

The ActionMedia II display subsystem is shown in Fig. 47.1. Its engine is the 82750PB pixel processor (PB) and the 82750DB display processor (DB). Separate from the host processor, PB is responsible for most of the classical data-processing and control functions in the subsystem. The pixel processor compresses and decompresses image data from memory, generates fast graphics and special effects, and acts as the master arbiter for subsystem memory and interdevice transactions.

The display processor performs real-time display functions, including data-format transactions, color translation, and pixel-value interpolation. It also provides outputs that support image-capture and video-synchronization. The DB generates all the timing signals required to drive display devices, including digital and analog RGB or YUV pixel outputs. An 8-bit digital word-of-alpha channel is provided so as to obtain a fractional mix of DB outputs, with another video source to achieve video effects such as titling and graphic overlays.

DVI technology performs its operations in YUV color space. Each YUV component is represented as a series of 8-bit samples. In this color system the luminance, or brightness, information (as given by the Y information), is separated from the chrominance, or color, information (as given by the U and V components).

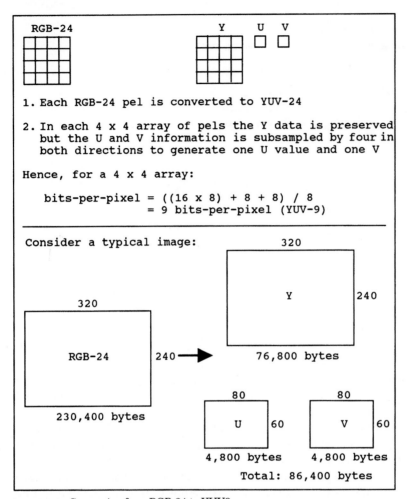

1. Each RGB-24 pel is converted to YUV-24

2. In each 4 x 4 array of pels the Y data is preserved but the U and V information is subsampled by four in both directions to generate one U value and one V

Hence, for a 4 x 4 array:

```
bits-per-pixel = ((16 x 8) + 8 + 8) / 8
               = 9 bits-per-pixel (YUV-9)
```

Consider a typical image:

Figure 47.2   Conversion from RGB-24 to YUV9.

Working in this domain allows various psychovisual effects to be exploited. Most notably, color information need not be stored at the same resolution as the luminance data. For this reason, color information is stored at one-half or one-quarter the luminance density in each dimension, without significant loss of image quality. Since luminance and chrominance information are stored at different resolutions, they are placed in different bitmaps. An example of how an RGB-24 image is converted into YUV-9 is shown in Fig. 47.2.

The 82750PB pixel processor

The 82750PB was designed as a cost-effective, real-time video-and-graphics processor for multimedia applications. Its architecture, with fully static, 25-MHz, single-cycle instruction execution, supports real-time, full-screen encoding and decoding of digital motion video at 30 frames per second. The PB can

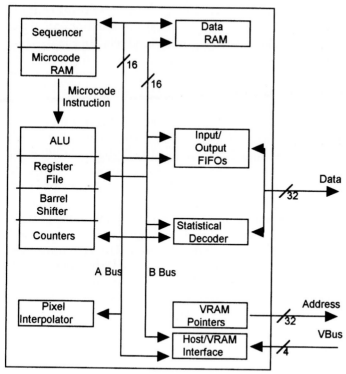

Figure 47.3   82750PB pixel processor.

simultaneously perform a wide range of video effects, including scaling motion video into windows, texture-mapping video onto surfaces, and many screen-transition effects.

The PB architecture was designed to be simple, efficient, and highly parallel. Figure 47.3 is a simplified diagram of the 82750PB.

A 32-bit linear, byte-addressable, external address bus and 32-bit data bus are used to communicate with external memory and external devices. Internal data paths are either 16 or 32 bits wide and designed to allow the simultaneous processing of two or more 8-bit pixels. Functional blocks are connected to one another using one or more of these buses, and the PB can transfer data simultaneously over any one of them during any given cycle.

A 16-bit ALU, augmented by a 16-bit barrel shifter, is used to perform most arithmetic, logical, and control operations. The ALU supports 32 types of operations specific to processing video data, such as operations on dual "side-by-side" 8-bit pixel values. The ALU and barrel shifter (as well as most other functional blocks) communicate with a multiport 16-word × 16-bit register file and a 512-word × 16-bit data RAM. The RAM can be accessed from two 16-bit buses via four independent pointers. These "C-style" pointers can be auto incremented and decremented, as well as take part in general-purpose ALU operations.

The PB also contains two specialized, semi-independent structures that are optimized for image-processing tasks. First, the pixel interpolator calculates fractional spatial movement of pixels, scales groups of pixels, and is used for various filtering operations. Second, the statistical decoder decompresses video data in real time. It is a specialized input FIFO that reads variable-length serial-bit sequences from memory and decodes them into fixed-length, 16-bit values.

As mentioned earlier, multimedia operations process large amounts of data. Because of the large quantities of memory data that must continually pass through the pixel processor, four independent FIFO channels allow PB to efficiently read, process, and write data. Each FIFO packs and unpacks data words and bytes, buffers data, and initiates transfers to and from the memory array.

Two FIFO channels are dedicated to supplying continuous streams of input from memory, these containing compressed and uncompressed images as well as the microcode routines required to operate on them. The remaining two FIFOs are output channels used to store the intermediate pixel values required during the construction of complete displayable images.

Instructions are stored and executed from a pipelined 512-word $\times$ 48-bit static cache, and can be executed in a single clock cycle. A microprogramma-ble cache control algorithm is used to guarantee maximum cache "hit" efficiency, and can be tailored for different types of system- and device-level operations.

By coordinating the operation of the 82750 assembler with dual-word cache accesses and appropriate PB instruction control fields, zero-delay branches can be performed without conscious programmer intervention. The ability to perform any logical operation and then to effectively perform a simultaneous two-way branch based on the results of that operation yields a significant performance increase over typical microprogrammed processors.

The 48-bit PB instruction word is divided into a total of 11 different control fields, designed to allow highly parallel operations. For example, ALU operations on pixels fetched from memory can be performed simultaneously with iteration counter updates while the pixel interpolator is operating on pixels decoded by the statistical decoder—and then branch—all within a single clock cycle.

The pixel interpolator

As long as the only objective of video data compression is the faithful repro-duction of the source image, decompression itself is relatively straightfor-ward. But if any additional transformations are required (the image is to be enlarged or reduced, scrolled, rotated, or intentionally distorted), a simple correspondence no longer exists between the original stored pixels and those destined for the display.

Simple attempts to adjust the image often produce undesirable artifacts known as *aliasing effects*. Anti-aliasing algorithms exist that eliminate those artifacts at the expense of processing cycles. Given that high cost, they are not appropriate for use in real-time systems.

An example: When the size of an image is reduced, the space between each stored pixel exceeds the space between those to be displayed. This means that each displayed pixel falls somewhere between two rows and two columns of pixels in the original image. In principle, the color and intensity of each displayed pixel can be derived by averaging the values of the four stored pixels that surround it, weighted according to how far the displayed pixel is from the rows and columns to the top, bottom, left, and right. By programming the pixel interpolator with these boundary values, the weighted average pixel values can be generated.

The pixel interpolator is designed to operate in several different modes. Most common is a *pipelined sequential* mode that allows interpolated pixels to be generated at a maximum rate of one pixel every other clock cycle. Additional modes optimized for interpolation over random pixel "quads" and different horizontal and vertical weights are included.

The statistical decoder

The statistical decoder is a specialized input channel that reads encoded bit streams containing variable-length symbols and decodes each symbol into fixed-length values. In image compression, certain values occur more frequently than others. One means of compressing such data is to use fewer bits to encode the more frequently occurring values and more bits to encode less frequently occurring ones. This type of encoding scheme is called *statistical* (or *Huffman*) *encoding,* because it depends on the frequency of occurrence of any particular value that is to be encoded.

The statistical decoder receives long series of variable-length symbols from memory as a sequence of 32-bit data words. Each symbol encodes both its length and value, and ignores the natural boundaries between memory words or bytes. The decoder must concatenate these variable-length sequences, examine the initial bit patterns, extract the substrings, and then realign the remaining data and repeat the process for the next symbol.

Each of the above operations is performed automatically for a variety of codes (code books) and coding conventions. To use the decoder, a starting address and code book are loaded. Thereafter, programs may simply read an indefinite series of expanded symbols in parallel with other operations.

Input and output FIFOs

The PB contains two input and two output FIFO channels that are used to read and write pixel and program data to external memory. Each FIFO has its own 32-bit address pointer that can be programmed to sequentially increment or decrement through 8- or 16-bit data types. Each FIFO double-buffers 32-bit data words so as to allow more efficient program execution and to allow hardware memory controllers to take advantage of the sequential nature of FIFO memory accesses to optimize main memory accesses.

Microprogram performance

The 82750PB typically is 5 to 10 times faster than a conventional micro-processor at the same clock speed (even faster for operations such as image-decompression and -manipulation, which take advantage of the special hardware assists provided). There are two reasons for its efficiency: single-cycle instruction execution, and the inherent parallelism of the dual-bus, multifield instruction. Single-cycle execution means that instructions execute faster, and parallelism means that fewer instructions are required to complete the task.

PB does not have a hardware multiplier, but algorithms involving multiplication often can be implemented efficiently, using combinations of the two shifters available (single-bit parallel shifter, and multibit barrel shifter). For example, the JPEG image-compression algorithm is very multiply-intensive. However, PB can decompress a 512×480 JPEG encoded image in less than 1 second—about an order of magnitude faster than typical 25-MHz processors (including those with a hardware multiply capability). This is but one illustration of the power and flexibility of programming PB at the microcode level.

The PB is not limited to digital-video manipulation. For example, a PB implementation of the ADPCM audio algorithm can decode an audio stream using between 5 and 10 percent of the available PB cycles. This flexibility permits the design of low-cost multimedia systems in which a single PB provides both the video and audio processing. However, in the ActionMedia II design, a dedicated audio processor was employed.

The 82750DB display processor

The 82750DB incorporates all of the digital and analog processing elements necessary to form the basis of a low-cost display subsystem. By programming internal control registers, video timing can be modified to accommodate a wide variety of scanning frequencies and display characteristics. A large selection of bits-per-pixel, pixels-per-line, and pixel heights is available, allowing designers a wide latitude when selecting display resolution, frame rates, and memory requirements.

The display is programmable on a line-by-line basis, enabling the on-screen mixing of graphics modes. To support this feature, the CLUT also may be loaded on a line-by-line basis. A luminance interpolator is provided to assist horizontal scaling by a factor of 2:1. DB provides support for an 8-bit alpha channel, allowing the weighted mix of DB outputs and an external source enabling smooth fades and transitions. Both analog and digital RGB outputs are provided, enabling connection to a video monitor or a digital liquid crystal display (LCD).

Perhaps the two most important real-time operations carried out by DB are *chrominance interpolation* and *YUV-to-RGB conversion*.

The chrominance interpolator

The task of the chrominance interpolator is to expand the subsampled color information up to the corresponding luminance resolution.

During programmed blanking time, subsampled chrominance data is read from bitmaps into color-information line-storage RAMs within DB. The interpolator determines when new chrominance information is needed, based on the current display position of the raster.

During active display time, when subsampled color video is being shown, DB performs a bilinear interpolation so as to expand color information to the resolution currently being displayed. To accomplish this, the chrominance interpolator expands compressed color data in both vertical and horizontal directions by a ratio of 2:1 or 4:1 in each direction.

After interpolation, DB can mix chrominance and luminance on a pixel-by-pixel basis. This ability to mix video and graphics on the same screen at any position, with any size, and with any aspect ratio, is one of the distinctive features of the i750 architecture.

YUV to RGB conversion

The YUV-to-RGB color space conversion matrix is compatible with the CCIR 601 standard. The conversion is done fairly late in the processing cycle, after things such as color lookup table operations and chrominance interpolation have been completed.

For source data that is coded in RGB format, or for systems that draw only in RGB color space, the programmer can choose to bypass this function.

The color-space conversion is accomplished by performing a matrix manipulation on the YUV pixels. Since the coefficients all are constants, the multiplications may be done with lookup ROMs and adders. Saturation circuitry is included, to ensure that any arbitrary YUV pixel converts to an RGB value that is within the allowed ranges.

Compositing

Since ActionMedia was designed to complement the existing graphics subsystem of the personal computer rather than replace it, a mechanism was required to mix the system graphics output with that provided by ActionMedia.

It is easiest to think of this scenario as two independent graphics subsystems that must be merged. The two systems may be displaying different resolutions and color depths, but a way must be found to combine their outputs.

Initially, since both systems are running independently, a way must be found to "lock" the two outputs together, before functions such as overlay can be considered. This is achieved by synchronizing the vertical and horizontal sync signals of ActionMedia with those provided by the system graphics—a function known as *genlocking*. Genlocking is achieved by the DB in conjunction with two phase locked loops, and this configuration can synchronize to a range of system graphics modes including 640 × 480 and 1024 × 768.

Chroma-keying

Now that the two signals are synchronized, their outputs must be combined to form one signal to drive the display monitor. Consider the combination of

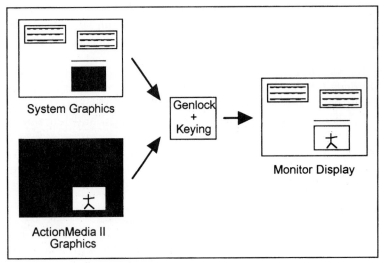

Figure 47.4   Combining system graphics and ActionMedia output.

images shown in Fig. 47.4. The system graphics display consists of several windows, including one that the programmer has identified as containing an image provided by ActionMedia II. Hence a mechanism is required that will identify which of the system graphics or ActionMedia graphics outputs are displayed at each point on the screen.

There are two accepted techniques for providing this mixing capability: *chroma-keying,* and *bit-mask manipulation.* The latter is achieved by providing a separate bitmap that has one bit corresponding to each pel in the display. This bit determines which of the system graphics or multimedia graphics are displayed. This technique has several disadvantages. First, the bit-mask bitmap requires valuable memory space, and second, the bit-mask can be difficult to manipulate and impose an extra overhead on the host CPU.

Chroma-keying uses a simpler approach, one that reduces the need for interaction from the host CPU and has no memory requirement.

Chroma-keying uses one of the system graphics colors to specify which of the two outputs is to be displayed for each pel position. Any area painted in this keying color is replaced by the contents of the multimedia adapter at the corresponding position. For example, black is used as the keying color in Fig. 47.4. The client area of the window that will contain the image from the multimedia adapter is painted black, and the keying circuitry then replaces any black in the system graphics by means of the multimedia adapters' output. Note that the remaining pels in the multimedia adapter display also are painted black. This ensures that any black pels in windows out of the programmer's control will still be black.

Two forms of chroma-keying exist, digital and analog, both exhibiting specific advantages and disadvantages.

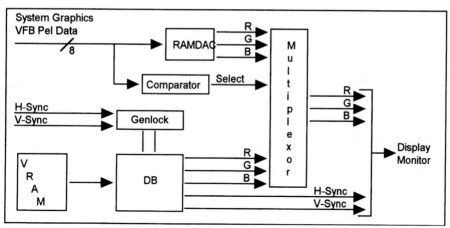

Figure 47.5 Digital keying.

Digital keying makes use of the video feature bus (VFB) provided by the system graphics adapter in personal computers. For IBM-compatible PCs, this consists of 8-bit pel data and the associated synchronization signals. Hence the digital keying system is limited to operating in modes of 256 colors or less.

A second limitation is imposed by the bandwidth of the VFB, which limits the transmission of pel data to display resolutions up to 640 × 480. Higher resolutions cannot be digitally keyed using the existing VFB implementations. Figure 47.5 illustrates the digital keying circuitry used by ActionMedia II. The 8-bit system-graphics data is compared with the chroma-keying color, and the result used to control a multiplexor that selects which of the two graphic streams is to be sent to the display monitor. Since the incoming data is palletized, ActionMedia II must include a CLUT to convert to the actual RGB values, which are then sent to the multiplexer. For correct color-tracking, any manipulation of the system CLUT must be trapped, and the corresponding changes made to the CLUT on ActionMedia II.

To provide chroma-keying at higher resolutions, analog keying, which has no immediate bandwidth restrictions, must be used, as shown in Fig. 47.6. The operation is similar to that for digital keying but with one restriction: the keying color is fixed and is black. Since the comparator must operate in the analog domain, complete with noise, only black (which corresponds to zero-level output on each of R, G, and B) can reliably be detected. (In practice, a black threshold level is defined, and any output below the threshold is keyed.)

Most of the limitations imposed by keying will be solved in the future by using a single unifying frame buffer for both system graphics and multimedia images. This requires all the display content to have the same color depth and format, for example RGB-24. The use of a single frame buffer will reduce overall system cost, since it will remove the redundancy of providing two display systems (as found in current designs such as ActionMedia II). Many

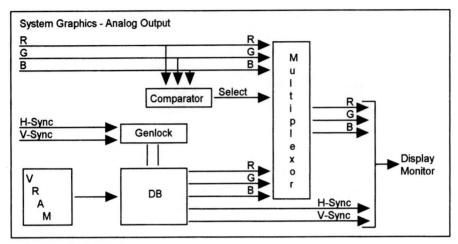

Figure 47.6   Analog keying.

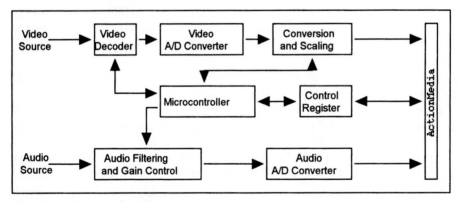

Figure 47.7   Capture subsystem.

companies working in the field of graphics accelerators are now starting to include multimedia as part of their requirements, and it is only a matter of time before such systems become available.

Capture subsystem

The capture subsystem is provided as a daughter card that can be attached to ActionMedia II and provides three basic capabilities:

1. Digitization of still images
2. Digitization of motion video
3. Digitization of audio

The block diagram for the capture subsystem is shown in Fig. 47.7. The basic process for digitizing still and motion images is the same, and is as follows. A video signal with either PAL or NTSC timings may be connected to the capture subsystem using any of composite, S-VHS, or RGB connections. This signal enters the video decoder which, under the control of the microcontroller, decodes the video signal into three analog signals, R, G, and B. These signals then are digitized by the A/D converter, and provide a 24-bit RGB input to the video formatting chip.

The video formatter provides two basic tasks, *color conversion,* and *image scaling.* Incoming 24-bit RGB data may be converted to YUV or passed directly through, as in the case of high-resolution stills capture. However, for motion video, the data is converted to YUV-9 format, which greatly reduces the data bandwidth at a slight loss in quality.

Images with resolutions of up to 768×576 may be captured, but for motion video the image is scaled down to more manageable sizes such as 256×240 or 160×120.

The audio circuitry supports a single stereo input with three gain settings: *microphone, line-level,* and *CD-level.* This signal is filtered and then digitized using a stereo A/D converter and sent to the ActionMedia II as a serial digital bitstream. All operations are under the control of the capture subsystem microcontroller, which communicates with the host and the pixel processor through the control register. This local management enables more of the host CPU's and pixel processors' cycles to be used for multimedia processing.

Audio subsystem

ActionMedia II includes an audio subsystem that provides the necessary audio functionality to complement digital video. It was not designed as a general-purpose audio subsystem, hence features such as 16-bit audio and MIDI are not present.

A digital signal processor (DSP), which forms the heart of the system, relieves the burden on the PB and the host CPU. In addition the DSP is another example of a programmable element, allowing the migration over time to different audio algorithms by simply downloading new DSP object code.

Currently, 8-bit PCM and ADPCM4 algorithms are supported in both mono and stereo at a range of sampling rates up to 44.1 kHz (the sampling rate of CD-DA). The DSP contains on-chip instruction and data memory, and reads and stores audio samples in the system VRAM.

Software Support

The ActionMedia II software environment is provided by the *audio/video kernel (AVK),* which was jointly designed by Intel and IBM. The objectives for AVK were that it would be portable to multiple platforms and operating environments, support windowing environments, be able to expand as the power of available hardware grew, and minimize reliance on the host CPU. The architecture was able to avoid dependence on the host for processing by relying instead on the high-performance i750 multimedia processors.

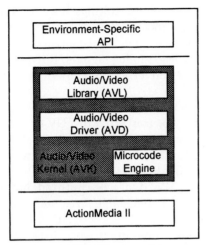

Figure 47.8   AVK software model.

The AVK system architecture is built in layers, as shown in Fig. 47.8. The lowest layer is called the *microcode engine,* because it includes a set of microcode tasks for the 82750PB processor; for example, a routine called DoMotion manages decompression tasks and buffers, and another routine called CopyScale copies and scales video images in real time into the display buffer.

The next layer is the *audio/video driver,* which encapsulates the details of the ActionMedia II hardware. The AVD interface provides functions for accessing the multimedia board's local video RAM, setting display formats for the 82750DB, and loading microcode functions from VRAM into the 82750PB's on-chip instruction memory. This last function is key to AVK's ability to accommodate new features and algorithms. The AVD also provides the interface for the audio subsystem and the video-capture card.

The third layer is the *audio/video library (AVL),* which supports the specialized data types needed for the manipulation of video and audio. These data types are generalized into *streams* that are then collected together into *groups.* A group is a collection of streams that need to be controlled synchronously with functions (such as play, stop, or pause) that operate on the groups. The AVL implements these functions in addition to the read and write data functions, for capture-and-display data-buffers. This layer also provides control over the attributes of these data types; for example, as functions for adjusting the volume of an audio stream or the tint of a video stream. This layer is essentially platform-independent, and so can easily be ported to other hardware and operating environments.

The AVL includes a set of functions that manage VRAM, format bitmaps, and generate and manage command lists. A *command list* is a set of microcode functions and their parameters. These lists can be built in memory and then scheduled for execution by the 82750PB as a group. Command lists can be active for a single image or for a video stream. If a list is active for a video stream, it will be executed on every frame until it has been replaced or canceled.

There's one more layer that is needed to link the architecture to an operating environment. It's an environment-specific *application programming interface (API)* that performs two critical functions for AVK. It reads and writes data into the host file system, and integrates AVK into the host windowing environment. Because these functions need to be optimized to a specific environment, they are defined as being outside the AVK architecture so as to maintain its portability.

Two examples of an API that can be implemented on top of AVK are the Media Control Interface, as defined for Windows 3.1, and Apple's QuickTime. Because AVK was designed to be independent of both the API and media formats, it will easily port to emerging standards. AVK presently is available under the Windows 3.1 and OS/2 operating systems. It is also architecturally independent of specific compression and decompression algorithms, and will easily accommodate new algorithms as they are developed.

The AVK interface was developed by identifying and abstracting a number of objects, with their associated behaviors and attributes. These objects and their relationships are shown in Fig. 47.9.

The *connector* object can be thought of as a mixer that accepts data flow, optionally manipulates the data, and sends the data to a destination. Connectors allow rectangular regions, referred to as *boxes,* to be defined for the source and destination bitmaps. Boxes can be resized and relocated in real time so as to provide good system responsiveness in windowing applications.

AVK implements a three-layered buffered data structure that provides for simultaneous execution of multiple tasks; for example, compressed data is input from a storage device by an input task, which then loads it into a compressed data buffer. A decode task then decompresses the data and loads it into a decompressed bitmap buffer. Individual bitmaps are then processed by a copy/scale task and sent to the display buffer, where a display task sends them to the screen, as shown in Fig. 47.10.

Task scheduling in AVK requires real-time response, a capability not provided by most operating systems found in desktop computers (OS/2 being an exception). The solution for AVK was to depend on the 82750PB to schedule all real-time tasks. Thus, on ActionMedia II boards, the video-processor chip also schedules audio operations. The video processor schedules tasks through the microcode engine. For example, while video streams are being processed, the DoMotion task continuously loops between the master command-list processing task and the buffer/stream processing task. For playback, the buffer/stream processing task looks for a frame of compressed data to be available, and for a free bitmap into which the data can be decompressed. When these conditions both have been met, the buffer/stream processing task calls the appropriate decompression algorithm.

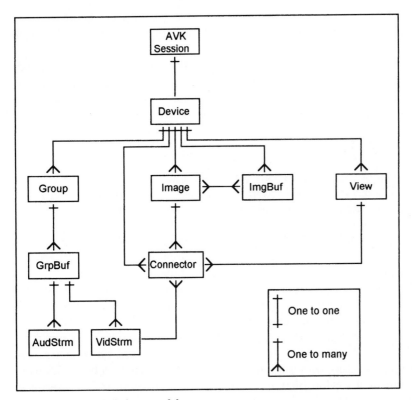

Figure 47.9   The AVK object model.

AVK supports two types of video algorithms that execute on the PB, *production-level video (PLV)* and *real-time video (RTV)*. PLV provides the highest achievable image quality but is very asymmetrical. PLV material is compressed off-line, without the time constraints of sending them to a display, and therefore does not need to be performed in real time. However, the PB can decompress images processed by PLV in real time.

On the other hand, RTV is a symmetrical process that PB can compress in real time. RTV supports resolutions up to 256×240 but is normally implemented at lower resolutions, resulting in data bandwidths that match that provided by a CD-ROM (150 kbytes per second). The image quality provided by RTV is lower than PLV's—a result of the real-time constraints placed on the RTV algorithm.

Both compression techniques use interframe encoding, which stores information only on pixels that change between frames. A frame for which all the pixels are defined is called an *intraframe,* and serves as an access point into the video data stream. By removing the constraints of real-time compression, PLV can employ a technique known as *motion estimation.* This time-consuming technique matches areas in the image that have moved from the previous frame, and encodes only the vector corresponding to the movement.

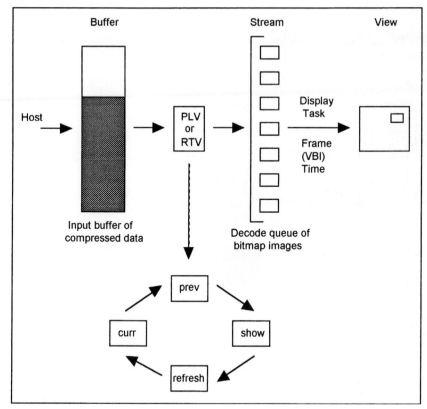

Figure 47.10 Video-decompression tasks.

Figure 47.11 illustrates the processes involved in RTV capture and compression. The digitized odd field from the attached video source is stored in VRAM until it is required by the display task, which then copies and scales it into the view.

The same display task takes the even field and places the bitmap in the encode queue, ready for compression. When the RTV task finds a bitmap in the encode queue, it will compress the frame—using the previous entry in the encode queue to determine whether an inter- or intraframe will be generated. Finally, the compressed frame is placed in the output buffer for collection by the host.

Still-image support is provided for images up to 512×480 in both YUV-9 and YUV-16 format. (This limit is based on the available memory on the ActionMedia II: 2 Mbytes.) These images may be compressed and decompressed using proprietary algorithms, in addition to an implementation of the JPEG standard for compressing and decompressing 9-bit images.

AVK's data flow and object organization have deliberately been designed to allow future enhancements. When processor power and I/O bandwidth increase in future systems, AVK's architecture will permit the number of

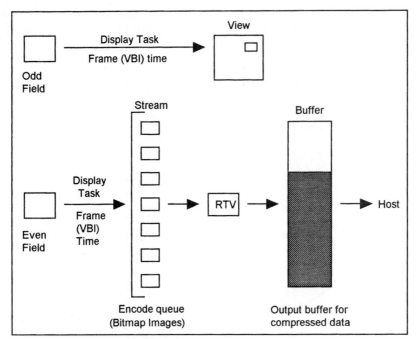

Figure 47.11   RTV compression tasks.

streams processed simultaneously to increase. By allowing the host to program its microcode engine, AVK can accommodate custom microcode for video effects and new image compression/decompression algorithms without requiring changes to the basic structure of the software.

This extendability was recently shown with the introduction of Microsoft's Video for Windows system extension. Video for Windows (VFW) provides an MCI-compliant interface for controlling digital video playback and record, and enables high-end processor-based systems (such as Intel 486's) to play back digital video without any additional hardware. This requires that the frame sizes be based on square pixel aspect ratios for optimal performance. (For example, on a 640 × 480 screen, valid square pixel frame sizes are 160 × 120 and 320 × 240.) Before the release of VFW, AVK operated on rectangular pixels with frames sizes such as 128 × 120 and 256 × 240. To support VFW, new microcode was written for RTV to support square pixel resolutions, and a new environment-specific layer was written to interface AVK to the VFW MCI layer. Figure 47.12 illustrates the basic components of the VFW system and the corresponding mapping of AVK and ActionMedia II to the new environment.

Conclusions

The requirements for a multimedia subsystem have been presented, and an actual implementation described. Multimedia encompasses a wide range of

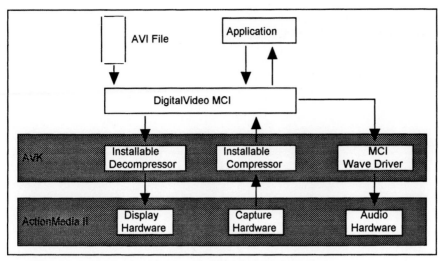

Figure 47.12   ActionMedia II implementation for Video for Windows.

data types, and even with the VLSI integration capabilities available today it is impossible to provide a full-function multimedia system on a single adapter. ActionMedia II addresses the areas of digital motion video and still images, and provides the audio capabilities to complement them. However, audio facilities such as 16-bit samples and MIDI are not provided.

The rapid technological increases of the last decade have made digital movies available on today's desktop systems. One can only guess what advances the coming years will bring.

Networking Video Applications

James Long

Barbara Baker

Introduction

Desktop video is an emerging technology that over time will come in many flavors. More and more applications in areas such as training and education are moving from the classroom to the desktop, using digital video as one of the communication tools. Today, applications using digital video have become part of familiar office-productivity software, such as spreadsheets and presentation applications. New ways of managing these desktop video applications are on the horizon. And it has become clear that many of these applications are more effective when networked and used by widely distributed work groups, not just individual users.

In this chapter we'll take a look at a few applications for networked video, their characteristics, and the requirements for and challenges of adding video to a network. We will examine the problems associated with handling video in today's networking environment, and we'll look at strategies for coping with these problems. We will provide strategies for improving servers, networks, and client computers so as to make video networking convenient, reliable, and relatively inexpensive. We'll start with a look at how applications use video today, and how they will be using it in just a few years.

Video Applications—Today

Training applications are a natural place to integrate digital video with the desktop computer. As an innovative training method, "performance support systems" are being developed by large businesses and other institutions, and these are revolutionizing the way employees learn their jobs and perform their tasks. Instead of large amounts of up-front classroom training, performance support systems provide training on demand at the desktop. These systems call for servers that can deliver powerful audiovisual information to the desktop, so that training can truly be integrated with employees' daily workload. Training costs come down while retention increases significantly, since students learn new information in context rather than in classrooms.

Many major productivity software applications, such as those for word processors and spreadsheets, have made VHS videotape training available today. And third-party trainers are moving to desktop video courses. In addition, developers of productivity applications are taking the next step: linking digital video directly to their software's on-line help resources. For example, you can purchase a CD-ROM version of Works with multimedia on-line help and reference, and on-line tutorials for Microsoft Word, which incorporate full-motion digital video.

In the education market, most major suppliers of educational software systems are marketing or developing "integrated learning systems" that consist of student applications and teacher management systems. With an integrated learning system, teachers become better resource managers, assigning students to courseware according to their abilities and needs. Almost without exception, the developers of integrated learning systems perceive networked video as being a vital tool in the classroom, marshaling engaging and meaningful educational resources. As Marshall McLuhan said, "Anyone who sees a difference between education and entertainment doesn't know the first thing about either one."

Businesses can use networked video presentation systems to instantly send corporate resources to the desktops of all employees. Information, which for example might consist of sales videos or employee data, may be viewed on the spot (for review of important company information) or captured to create customized sales presentations. By putting the video on a server, businesses allow many people to access the resources without forcing them to travel to an audiovisual facility or to buy a VCR/television—or an editing suite!—to use the information.

Video Applications—Tomorrow

In the very near future, networked video documentation systems will allow institutions of all kinds to maintain multiuser audiovisual databases. Advertising agencies, for example, who may have hundreds of hours of video used in a random, on-demand fashion, can use this type of system. Today these agencies use hundreds of VCR tapes that must be located, copied, and then delivered to account executives or clients. A video database would allow easier and quicker access to this information. Other potential users include health-care institutions, which have extensive audiovisual records; travel agencies, which show videos about vacation destinations; and public utilities, which need to maintain records of power-generation facilities and equipment.

For example, several state highway departments have still-video databases of every mile of their highways, allowing employees to instantly view any stretch of road.

Video teleconferencing is gradually coming to the desktop as well. In this area, businesses can own cost-effective conferencing services so as to support worldwide communication needs and thereby increase productivity. Another live-video application is distance learning, in which the teacher is not located in the same place as the students. This flavor of videoconferencing allows the teacher and students to interact almost as if they were in the same room.

Characteristics of Video Applications

As pointed out in the previous sections, there are many good rationales for distributing video to users at their desktops. The characteristics of the video "service" required for these applications drive the type of computer system needed to support them, as follows:

- Video file services
- Video object services
- Stream management services

Video file services

The simplest level of video application—video file services—requires store-and-play or basic file service for video. A video file service gives one the capability to store video and to retrieve it for viewing. The material generally is static, and some access delay may be tolerable. A system offering this service is much like today's data-network file servers. A good example of this level of complexity is simple playback of training or on-line help videos.

Video object services

The next step in networked video sophistication consists of video object services, which make an application highly interactive with video information by supporting quickly changing video and audio "object" relationships. As an example, a video and audio "database" can be used to combine objects to produce a new video stream, to edit the video, or to instantly add video and audio to another document type. This requires fast access to the video objects and the ability to change their relationships to one another. Users will want to access many objects at the same time. For example, an advertising agency would require this level of video service to combine many video clips and thereby provide a quick look at a "rough cut" of a new ad concept. This is a good example of a system that needs more than just store-and-play function.

Stream management services

The third category, stream management services, is required when many users simultaneously need access to live video. Desktop video teleferencing and distance learning fall into this category of video applications. Video stream management service often involves live video transmission—from a variety of sources—to many simultaneous users, and management of the video streams on the network. Users may even require different data rates. Or users, for example, may need to record a teleconference for later viewing. For these applications, users may be sharing *codec pools*—expensive devices that compress and decompress the video—so that the video service can be provided to more desktops.

Requirements for Adding Video Services

The demand for networked digital audiovisual systems will grow exponentially over the next few years, as businesses, government, and other institutions increasingly turn to digital networks. Networks will be used to distribute audiovisual information for education, presentation, and reference applications. Networked digital-video systems will allow many people to simultaneously view audiovisual information from a server, while retaining their current network functions. Applications that work on the network today should remain untouched when video is added.

From the point of view of users, therefore, video must be added to the network invisibly. Users should be able to access video files from a variety of client computers (e.g., IBM compatibles, Macintosh computers, UNIX workstations), and from a variety of applications. To avoid the need for duplication of large video files, one copy of a digital-video file should serve as many kinds of computers as possible. In addition video must be incorporated into existing applications, such as video annotation in a word-processing document or spreadsheet. Digital video used in applications comes in a variety of compression schemes, depending on the application. Networks and servers need to handle the many different compression and file formats (e.g., Indeo, Video 1, motion JPEG, PLV, MPEG, Cinepak, P*64, True Motion, and other standards as they develop).

In order to promote the widespread installation and use of digital audiovisual applications, the client network connection should be standard and low-cost. That means the use of existing network connections on the client, rather than special or additional network connections, to provide video services. By centralizing video service resources at the server, you reduce the total cost for institutions that have many video application users, particularly when you are adding additional desktop users.

Problems and Challenges of Adding Video to Networks

Networking has become a critical technology for almost all segments of the computer market, particularly in business and education. Large and small businesses and institutions have come to depend on network servers—dedicated-purpose computers—for a variety of reasons. Today's local area network (LAN) environments were designed to handle the data and file sharing needs of typical office-productivity applications, which deal mainly with text and simple graphics files. Managing and transmitting digital video data poses two major challenges: dealing with large sizes, and handling the time-dependent demands of video datatypes. Both are particularly difficult when you are sharing the information on networks and servers.

The large file sizes associated with digital audiovisual information pose an obvious need for large disk drives or multiple-disk systems and high data transmission speeds. Even compressed video, such as Intel's Production Level Video (PLV), requires a continuous 1-to-2-Mbps transmission speed, and 0.5 to 1 Gbytes of storage for 1 hour. A less obvious problem results from the nature of audiovisual information itself, which is fundamentally different from the kind of data that typically travels across a LAN (i.e., word-processing, database, or spreadsheet data).

Digital audiovisual information takes the form of a stream of data that must arrive on time. In other words, typical LANs work with bursty requests for data. File systems and most server communication buses are designed to handle this bursty traffic. They are, however, inefficient when it comes to handling the simultaneous, continuous, large block data transfers that are needed for streaming audiovisual data. It is also extremely difficult to manage random, bursty data and streaming data applications with the same microprocessor.

Streaming audiovisual data also conflicts with the way that LANs and multitasking operating systems allocate resources via "democratic" schemes, in which applications take turns. When the network, bus, or other resource is busy, the system slows down. No data takes priority over any other data. To a typical network, bits are bits, regardless of the type of information represented. The inefficiency of democratic resource-sharing schemes is compounded by the overhead needed to allow applications to take turns and for the detection and correction of errors. These functions are important for the typical software application, but not as important for audiovisual media. The human eye can overlook one incorrect pixel in a television image, but an incorrect number in your bank balance would not be tolerated!

Audiovisual information, which is based on time, isn't useful if it slows down and speeds up according to network traffic flow. Even if the hardware and software can cope with slowdowns, the video would play back in slow motion—not acceptable! Therefore, managing data flow is key to all multimedia computing, especially in networks.

Video demands a kind of "Federal Express" attitude toward data: it "absolutely, positively" has to arrive at the client computer on time. If bandwidth isn't available for a highly reliable connection (to assure that the video information arrives on time), one of two things must happen: the server must tell the requesting application that the data temporarily isn't available, or the server must somehow reduce the amount of data (by dropping video frames, image size, resolution, etc.) to a level that the network can support reliably. Having the ability to change the video information so as to meet the bandwidth needs is known as *scalable video*.

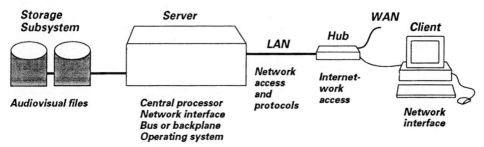

Figure 48.1   Network bottlenecks.

The important network function for audiovisual media isn't fair allocation of resources or error-checking; it is making sure that data flows at the proper rate between the server and client, or between client and client, and guaranteeing that data arrives on time.

Digital Bottlenecks for Video

Audiovisual data on a network hits a series of bottlenecks. This isn't surprising, since personal computers and networks weren't designed to handle this kind of data. Along the digital path, which connects the disk drive on a server to a client computer, these bottlenecks limit the video-stream speed or interrupt the video. The bottlenecks occur in disk drives, system buses, processors, networks, and the various interfaces and buffers that are found between the parts of the system. The problem areas are highlighted in Fig. 48.1.

Let's look at a typical setting for networked digital video: a training room with 30 PLV stations and a video server. Mission-critical training requires that users instantly view video when it is requested. In this example, high-resolution PLV requires a rate of about 1.5 Mbps per video stream. Therefore each desktop must continuously handle 1.5 Mbps, while the video server must handle an aggregate of 30 streams—45 Mbps—simultaneously.

A system such as this will run into many problems if it uses ordinary client server hardware and software. Referring to the bottlenecks diagram (Fig. 48.1), note that the storage subsystem will have to handle 30 simultaneous users—even if they were to request the same 60-second video clip 2 seconds apart. The server will have to handle the same 45 Mbps throughput internally. The network will have to handle 45 Mbps from the server and 1.5 Mbps per desktop, reliably. Finally, the client network interface will have to receive the video and still allow concurrent access to other networked applications (e.g., e-mail, text, databases, etc.). Unfortunately, a normal networked file server system could not accomplish this.

Solution Strategies

One way to deal with the bottlenecks confronting networked multimedia data is to throw away all the software and hardware that cause the streams of data to "bump" into one another, and replace it with new software and hardware that keep each stream running at the proper rate. This works, but it means you've thrown away something of great value to almost all computer users: the network software that allows us to use our servers for many other purposes.

Four strategies offer a range of solutions for dealing with the bottlenecks:

1. Do nothing.
2. "Turbocharge" the bottleneck areas.
3. Replace the bottlenecks with higher-performance devices.
4. Install a parallel system in order to circumvent the bottlenecks.

Let's look at these four alternatives to see how well they handle both the bottlenecks and the general requirements for adding video to the network.

Do nothing

Leave the system alone, and make sure that the data stream never exceeds the limits of the bottlenecks. This is practical for client desktop computers, which never have to deal with more data than they can decode and play. By avoiding the need for client hardware changes, you save costs, since clients far outnumber other network components. But doing nothing to standard networks and servers limits the number of users and the expected performance of the video services, since existing networks and servers have trouble handling video for multiple clients simultaneously.

"Turbocharge" bottleneck areas

Improve the offending hardware and/or software so that it can handle more data. Like adding a turbocharger to an engine, these improvements don't replace all the existing hardware—they just make it faster. This improves the general performance of the server and network, but it may not address the different processing requirements for video and traditional data applications, such as the critical time-dependent nature of the audiovisual data.

Replace bottleneck devices

Replace the server and network hardware altogether, with faster hardware and larger storage capacity. For example, one way to increase a network's raw capacity is to replace copper wiring with optical fiber and interfaces that can easily carry 10 times more data. Unfortunately this is expensive and doesn't necessarily solve the resource-sharing and time-dependent needs for video. By replacing the server with a higher-performance computer that has more storage, you may increase the horsepower of the server, but you still don't address the differences between video and other application datatypes.

Install a parallel system

Install a system dedicated for video. This is all right if it means the addition of a separate server for video, but no one wants a separate physical network or a separate video computer. By establishing a parallel software world for video while sharing the same network and client hardware, you can allow the system to optimally handle both types of information. But remember, when you are using a parallel approach, to be sure that video and nonvideo information can be easily integrated within the same application.

As you can see, no single strategy gives the best solution to breaking through the bottlenecks and meeting the requirements for adding video to the network. A better approach would be to take the best of each choice and change the network so that it can cost-effectively handle data applications and video service. How can this be accomplished? Let's return to our training-room example and look at the client, the network, and the server to show how video can be added to the network.

Handling Video Needs at the Client

Since client computers typically need only one or two streams for video, bandwidth is not a problem. The data rate for a video stream is about 1.5 Mbps—slower than the amount of data that comes from a typical hard disk. Therefore no special networking hardware is necessary at client computers. This data rate supports Intel's Indeo and PLV compression technologies, and the in-development MPEG (Moving Pictures Experts Group) standard. It's also within the capacity of a typical Ethernet network, which is about 10 Mbps—leaving plenty of capacity for other data or higher-bandwidth video technologies, such as MPEG II.

So far we've been talking about a single client. But what happens when we have *30* clients? In a typical network, all of the 1.5-Mbps streams share the same cables, quickly overwhelming a typical Ethernet network. Although upgrading to an expensive fiber-optic network (e.g., FDDI) will considerably increase the capacity, it is still a shared resource and therefore has trouble dealing with the time-dependent needs of video. A better solution can be found in a star network, such as 10BaseT Ethernet, with dedicated lines to each client computer. This network configuration already is the most popular, and as we'll see, can be turbocharged to support the video-capacity needs without expensive fiber.

Handling Video Needs over the Network

Star networks satisfy video requirements

The need to exchange digital data among a variety of peripherals and computers with varying operating systems (e.g., Video for Windows, QuickTime, UNIX) and applications has resulted in complex networks. Network hardware includes wires, such as the simple twisted-pair wires that also are used for telephone networks, and more exotic wiring such as coaxial cable or optical fibers. Networks can be arranged in several physical structures, or *topologies*. In the past the most common kinds of networks have used *bus* and *ring*

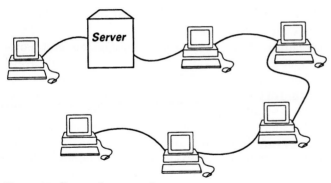

Figure 48.2 Bus or ring network.

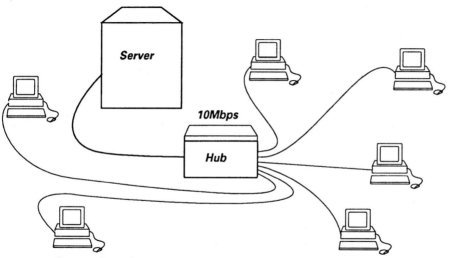

Figure 48.3 Star topology (shared networks).

topologies. To create a bus or ring network, a wire snakes from one computer to the next (Fig. 48.2). Each computer on the network broadcasts data that's monitored by all computers on the network; however, only the intended recipient "pays attention" to the incoming data. To draw an analogy, a server on a bus or ring network is like a radio station that broadcasts a signal. While it is transmitting to one client, no one else can communicate with it.

Today, computer users increasingly are turning to star-topology networks based on inexpensive twisted-pair phone wire and a line for each client computer (Fig. 48.3). These networks are popular because they use inexpensive telephone-style wire and are installed in the same way as a typical phone system. Moves, adds, and changes are simplified because, as with a telephone network, each client has its own cable, unlike the "snaked" cable of a bus network, which has to be rerouted for new clients, moves, and changes. For these reasons, networking experts see star networks or "structured wiring" as the favored way to go in the 1990s and beyond. These networks also offer the best topology for serving the bandwidth needs of video.

To create a star topology, "hubs" have become increasingly common hardware features on LANs. One of the most popular hub devices is the 10BaseT type of hub for Ethernet networks. 10BaseT Ethernet already represents about 70 percent of new Ethernet installations. Another popular network, IBM's Token Ring, has used a star topology since its introduction.

Although today's 10BaseT Ethernet and Token Ring networks are wired as stars with hubs, they still operate like a bus or ring. This means that all desktops connected to the hub still share a limited amount of bandwidth (10 to 16 Mbps). This is not enough bandwidth to support typical applications, such as our example of the training room, which needs 45 Mbps. The shared nature of bus or ring networks also makes it difficult to guarantee the dedicated bandwidth required for smooth and reliable video delivery.

One solution would replace Ethernet with 100-Mbps FDDI. Not only is this very expensive, it is still a shared medium that presents problems in terms of the real-time needs of video. A better solution is to "turbocharge" the Ethernet hub so as to dedicate 10 Mbps per desktop, or several desktops, in effect giving users their own Ethernet networks (Fig. 48.4).

Although this solution increases the hub cost, it doesn't require replacement of the wire or client hardware, so the total cost is reasonable. Note also that a 10-Mbps bandwidth meets each user's video and data needs. What's more, since the "turbocharged" network gives users dedicated connections, video's real-time demands can be handled reliably. Such turbocharged or switched Ethernet hubs already are available from network vendors. This approach also works with Token Ring networks.

Star topologies with "turbocharged" 10BaseT hubs (Fig. 48.4) can handle the large amount of data required by video, giving each user enough bandwidth. However, this solution does not solve the second problem having to do with the time-dependent characteristics of video over the network, which we'll discuss in the next section.

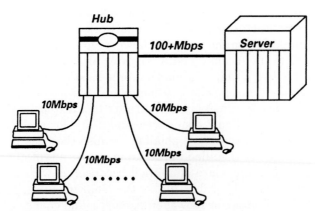

Figure 48.4 "Turbocharged" switched hub network.

Network protocols for video

Networked computers communicate via *protocols,* which are standard signals that govern the exchange of data. The computers send each other requests such as "I would like this data," "Begin sending," "Stop sending," or "Send that again, it arrived with an error." These protocols are arranged in layers, so that various parts of the computer—the hardware, the operating system, and the applications, for example—can talk to one another without needing to know special information about one another. The two main purposes of the protocols are (1) to ensure that the data arrives without errors, and (2) to ensure that the "traffic cop" functions are carried out, regulating the data flow.

In today's typical network protocols, the emphasis is on data integrity through error-control protocols. Flow control and timeliness of delivery are secondary. For the reasons we've explained, these priorities need to be reversed for audiovisual data.

One way to handle audiovisual data streams more effectively, as just noted, is to replace the existing networking protocols with special new ones. But if you throw out all the old protocols, you lose compatibility with other software. If you modify existing ones, you lose the specialty performance required for each type of data. Ideally, the network protocols for audiovisual data should peacefully coexist with the standard network software. In such an environment, applications would call for data from the server in a normal manner. The network, perceiving that audiovisual data had been requested, would use a special video protocol to make sure there was a highly reliable connection for an uninterrupted stream of data. For nonaudiovisual data, normal protocols would be used. With this "parallel-protocol" approach, audiovisual data becomes available to an application concurrently with other information on the same network.

The combination of "turbocharged" Ethernet and parallel software protocols addresses the client and network bandwidth requirements for our training-room example. The last area to address is that of the server.

Handling Video Needs at the Server

Since video characteristics differ from other data applications, we might expect that the file server requirements would be different. Dedicated servers can eliminate the compromises that ordinary servers make between short, "bursty" data and large streams of data, optimizing performance for the latter. When dealing with audiovisual data, the server architecture should bypass "democratic" contention schemes, substituting more of a real-time system that assures reliable data flow.

Storage subsystems need to be managed in such a way that many users can access audiovisual data files at the same time. That means optimizing the storage subsystem for many simultaneous accesses to large, continuous data files. Alternatives, such as analog laserdisc jukeboxes, allow access to large quantities of video but have problems with access delays when multiple users play different segments of video. Arrays of Winchester disk drives offer a cost-effective method for storing large quantities of video data, and can be configured to support our training example of a 30-user group.

If audiovisual data is to be incorporated into existing applications, the video data should look like ordinary data to any application. To an SQL database application it should look like SQL, to a Lotus spreadsheet it should look like spreadsheet data. To the operating system, it should look like another part of the file structure. Ideally, this should be accomplished with only one copy of the data and yet support a range of computer platforms and operating systems!

Finally, a video networking solution should be able to handle any type of video application, including desktop teleconferencing. That means the server should be able to manage data streams just as a telephone switch handles audio traffic.

We've briefly described how a server optimized for video can efficiently break video network bottlenecks. To create such a server, you could either enhance an existing server or add an "application-specific" video server to the network. Enhancing an existing server will likely result in many compromises, and have a negative impact on its ability to handle nonvideo data. A video server, on the other hand, can bypass the compromises and operate in parallel with the data file server.

Multimedia Solutions in Today's Environment

In summary, the solution for networked multimedia doesn't have to be an expensive fiber-optic network or a parallel video network. Today's star networks can do the job at reasonable cost, without special client networking hardware. A switched 10BaseT hub, or segmented Ethernet users, allow us to serve the video clients within the existing network environment. Using those parallel video-specific network protocols that coexist with today's standard networking protocols, we can maintain compatibility with current applications and deliver reliable video services on the same network. And finally, a dedicated video server can handle the processing and storage management needs of audiovisual media *and* provide superior video support, without compromising the current networked applications.

Requirements for Pervasive Multiparty Desktop Video Collaboration

Les Wilson

Defining Multimedia Communication

This author prefers to define multimedia communication as *that which enhances or transcends our current electronic communication qualities.* Without this enhanced content in the communication channel, adoption of multiparty videoconferencing may be limited, while people continue to modify a fax or e-mail image over the telephone as they do today.

Terms that accurately reflect what should happen on the desktop include *multiparty videoconferencing, teleconferencing,* and *collaboration.* Collaboration between people occurs today when two people exchange a fax and then pick up the phone to discuss the diagram on the fax. Taking the next step to enhance content in collaborative communication, the fax-like features, voice, and video of today's collaboration are integrated into a superset that we call *desktop video collaboration.*

Multiparty—more than two people collaborating—videoconferencing is generally used for consensus building, decision making, or training. The two-party conversation commonly is the execution discussion that precedes and follows a consensus meeting. This chapter will focus on multiparty videoconferencing activity. About 60 percent of the new installations of room conferencing systems support multiparty conferences, and that percentage is growing. Desktop video collaboration systems may see a similar growth.

Market Acceptance Factors

Most workplaces can support the cost of videoconferencing and document sharing at the desktop, when the additional cost is less than one-half the cost of a personal computer or workstation. The average PC price is about $2000, meaning that for desktop video collaboration facilities to become pervasive at the desktop, they will have to cost $1000.

Just as many companies still have doubts about the value of and the productivity to be gained from computers, so too a similar doubt will slow the acceptance of desktop video collaboration.

As the desktop video collaboration application develops, users and MIS managers will decide how and when to adopt video at the desktop. The decision will be based on need, bias, cost, and corporate environmental factors. Likewise users, not the manufacturers, will decide which compression methods become standard.

There is some speculation that the "Nintendo generation," also sometimes called the "MTV crowd," will demand video simply because they are exposed to far more hours of video per day than was the previous generation of young people. The next-generation work force really understands interactive video, thanks to Nintendo's successful sales—currently estimated to be at about 90 million units.

Defining quality

People are beginning to debate the value of seeing a person during a video conversation. Some say that *not* seeing the other person makes it easier to say what they are thinking, while others believe that seeing one's conversational partner is part of the total message.

While clear savings result when people avoid travel costs by using video-conferencing equipment, the question remains: "Was the quality of communication acceptable, and a reasonable substitute for travel or for just using a phone?" Acceptable performance is based on image quality, audio quality, and ease of data sharing. Different users will have different priorities. For some the priority may be data sharing/application sharing; for others, audio quality; and for others video quality. Good performance can mean faster results, better understanding of the message, more productive meetings, and lower costs. Travel costs are a key saving, but the most important resource we save is *time*—people really can be in two places at once.

The quality of the images used in the conversation are critical to the value of desktop video collaboration. At 7 to 10 frames per second or slower, voice and video appear to lose lip synchronization. This confuses people and usually is not acceptable. Delays in the channel greater than 300 milliseconds are noticeable.

Quality of communication also is dependent on the ability to effectively share the images that are typically part of the workgroup communication; thus data should be shared and possibly annotated by others during the conversation.

Electronic chalkboards offer several methods whereby the people in the conversation can share data. Some exchange file descriptions compatible to particular applications such as Excel. Others relay data by generating a bitmap of the application file, thereby allowing those at the other end to use a simple viewer to see a representation and to interact. Typical interactions may include reviewing a printed document and marking changes, or looking for a problem in a section of C source code. The bitmap method saves the cost of installing Excel and other applications on every remote station. In theory, a call can be "bootstrapped" by sending the chalkboard utility and file of interest through to each participant when the call is initiated.

Although video is used, it is only one part of the communication channel. Video sometimes is seen as the emotional channel, or truth channel. Body language influences the quality of the other data presented. During a sale or negotiation, body language may convey half the message. At other times video merely conveys data, such as the demonstration of a procedure, and body language does not have to be scrutinized in order to verify the quality of the data. Video can convey a procedure or technique much faster and with greater memory retention than can a written or verbal description.

As a matter of procedure, a conversation may start with a very important component called the *video handshake,* which is a visual greeting such as a nod or a hello. The video handshake is personal and helps to establish the relationship. During the conversation, data or documents may be more important, and finally at the close of the meeting video again is important, as the next meeting is arranged and good-byes are said. Perhaps negotiation meetings will continue to use video throughout, while engineering meetings will tend to proceed in the beginning-and-end manner just described.

Market size

Let's assume that by 1995 technology can deliver quality video communication. At least some small portion of the 100 million installed personal computers and workstations now can be enhanced with the new technology. But what is really critical is reaching the last 100 meters to the desktop. Both PBX equipment vendors and LAN vendors are working on ways to reach desktops from a central hub or switch, but as of now videoconference equipment vendors are not capable of bringing their solutions that last 100 meters to the desktop, so this issue is bigger than any one company. Several forums have been established to arrive at standard methods of crossing the 100 meters and to deal with many other issues including compression and the user-interface and applications areas. The desktop is viewed as a market opportunity many times larger than the videoconference room market.

Today about 20 million desktops are estimated to have 10BASE-T Ethernet local area networks, and these can easily be upgraded to isoENET to provide desktop video collaboration.

Factors Affecting Acceptance of Desktop Video Collaboration

Video collaboration needs have changed with end-user experience. As users are exposed to room conferencing, they find new ways to leverage the communication offered by it. This section lists yesterday's reasons justifying room conferencing and those used to justify purchases today. The last item, future plans, is significant, in that most companies with experience have a need to communicate with their customers and vendors so as to further improve corporate performance.

Yesterday's justifications for room conferencing:

- Improved communication
- Made possible distance learning
- Improved productivity
- Reduced travel costs
- Allowed more frequent worker meetings
- Facilitated company mergers
- Connected geographically dispersed offices
- Decreased time to market

Today's justifications:

- Speeds decision making
- Allows key management to conduct extensive multipoint meetings, ad hoc meetings, megameetings
- Connects to partners, leading to market wins
- Makes possible remote interviews
- Decreases cost of focus groups
- Allows traveling execs to stay in touch as they travel
- Makes possible internal research
- Aids in the development of custom applications
- Facilitates the work of product development teams

Future plans:

- Implement links to customers and suppliers
- Direct-link to government agencies to speed drug approval
- Etc.

Here are some of the key changes in companies and competitive environments that are driving the use of video collaboration:

- Business focus is becoming more global.
- Organizations are redesigning for competitiveness.
- Global workgroup teams are being empowered.
- There is an increasing focus on knowledge-worker productivity.

- Knowledge workers are becoming people-centric rather than building-centric.
- Environmental issues are emerging.
- The possible imposition of an energy tax.
- A gridlock tax encourages telecommuters.
- The desire to control pollution.
- Organizations are becoming learning organizations.
- The "video generation" is entering the work force.
- The demand for higher social content in media requires the addition of video.

Telecommuters

An important part of the enterprise and workgroup collaboration environment is the home. Recent U.S. estimates place 34 million offices in the home. Some home offices are used by telecommuters who work at home and also in a commercial office. Desktop video collaboration will integrate home-based workers into the work force more closely, allowing them to participate in planning and ad hoc meetings. When desktop video collaboration facilities successfully connect the workplace with the employee at home, the company, the worker, and the environment all are winners.

The company can reduce the need for travel and conference rooms. Meetings can occur without waiting for a room to become available. Other employees can join a meeting as passive observers in a read-only mode, allowing them to learn from the meeting without slowing it down. Today passive observers are excluded from meetings simply because the room is too small or out of a desire to avoid overloading meeting dynamics.

Telecommuters generally spend a portion or even most of their work time at home. By reducing the number of days per week they spend in the office, workers enjoy the benefits of saved travel time as well as reduced car expenses. Just 2 days at home per week saves the average worker in California about 2 hours of travel and 60 miles of wear on the car. Due to increasing housing costs and suburban sprawl, typical commute times today are more like 40 minutes one way, or even a two-hour-and-forty-minute round trip over 120 miles of road. Everyone benefits when there are fewer drivers on the road. Potentially, road repairs and expansion of lanes are reduced. Having fewer cars on the road also helps to improve air quality. Everyone gets to work faster!

What's in it for workers? They can purchase larger houses further from work. Auto insurance companies may lower their insurance premiums, since fewer miles are driven. Workers spend less time stressed-out on the freeway and more time with family and friends.

Seeing as the public, the environment, companies, and workers all benefit from telecommuting in a multiparty framework, perhaps all of them will share the cost of purchasing equipment to make this future possible.

Here are some of these telecommuting employee benefits:

- There is easy contact with distant time zones.
- Less travel time each week means more personal time.
- People can live in their area of choice, purchase lower-cost homes with more land, greater natural beauty, and better schools.
- People will pay less for car insurance, gas, repairs.
- Sick people may recover at home, working without spreading colds and flu.

From an employer's perspective, telecommuting

- Supports dispersed work groups
- Decreases costs of office space, energy use
- Is an alternative to relocation
- Supports restructuring of the company
- Attracts employees from all over
- Reduces labor costs
- Increases productivity

Yet if telecommuting is to work, many issues must be watched closely:

- Worker must create an office at home.
- Employers must trust workers.
- Employees must be self-motivated.
- Telecommuters may work weird hours.
- Employees must be judged by their *output,* not by their mere *presence.*
- Workers still need social interaction with coworkers—*possible,* through video!
- Employers must avoid treating telecommuters as second-class citizens because they are not always "on campus."
- Telecommuting studies have measured productivity jumps of 15 to 45 percent, but could not determine if the selected individuals represented the norm.

Specific applications

Multiparty communication serves meetings when three or more people or channels are involved. Sometimes a channel may be a feed from a database during the conversation. A typical example is training or education. Although training can be interactive with a database on a CD-ROM, the human teacher still is difficult to replace; thus, multiparty videoconferencing supports virtual classrooms. Here teachers interactively share their knowledge and skills across a group of people during the learning process. Corporate "distance learning" can train people in field offices far from corporate headquarters.

Multiparty video communication will be of tremendous benefit to medical workers. A doctor, for example, may request more than one video surgical procedure from a remote computerized database, so as to compare them and decide which procedure will be best for a particular patient. The doctor may decide to use portions of both procedures during the operation, reviewing them right in the operating room. In such a case, video quality will be very important.

Video quality is less important than interactivity in the multiperson games played by means of videoconference technology. Imagine flying your fighter jet against others you have never met. While entertainment is not a driving need in the workplace, we all do spend quite a few dollars for home entertainment. Perhaps telecommuting and entertainment will justify the consumer purchase of videoconferencing capability at home.

In any case, there are a number of issues that should be resolved to improve the application of video collaboration. The following list summarizes a few items collected in conversation, regarding how to improve what we do today, based on experience with today's videoconference rooms and existing desktop conferencing systems.

- Conference room collaboration tools are largely unused because they are not integrated with workers' desktops and PCs.

- One cannot tell the true color of garments and fabrics.

- Multipoint connections are expensive—$100,000 per multipoint control unit (MCU).

- The CCITT international H series videoconferencing standard does not yet support all areas, and leaves some issues open; therefore, minor incompatibilities result.

- All local exchange carriers (LECs) and international exchange carriers (IECs) do not yet support ISDN-1.

- Desks and offices are smaller overseas, so equipment should be smaller.

- U.S. users use white boards, whereas other cultures do not.

- Some markets have cultural barriers to accepting videoconferencing. One such barrier is a dislike of direct facial viewing, which strikes some as threatening. Video mail, however, is acceptable in these cultures.

- A limited number of circuits are available for international calls.

- The tools often are not integrated with fax.

- Some dislike the need to schedule use of the room.

- Company culture sometimes limits access or application.

- The special table shape, to meet the constraints imposed by a single camera, limits the interactions of those in the room.

- Users need training to use equipment.

- No installation proceeds without problems.

- The question arises: "Should MCU be on-premises or at-carrier?" The issue is one of encryption and security.

All of these issues must be resolved in desktop video collaboration applications.

Relevant Standards and Proprietary Solutions

Many different standards are in development for various aspects of multimedia videoconferencing, as are a host of proprietary solutions. These approaches may be roughly divided into those standards that try to encompass the entire videoconferencing realm and those standards and approaches that relate to key portions of that realm, such as compression and local area network standards to allow videoconferencing at the desktop.

A "megastandard" that tries to encompass all of videoconferencing from the wide area network (WAN) to the desktop has been in development by the telephony industry's standards-making body, the CCITT (Consultative Committee for International Telegraph and Telephone). While elements of this standard, described in a moment, may be suited for desktop videoconferencing, much of the standard would result in equipment that is costly and that lacks the performance benefits of other solutions for desktop applications.

Resulting collaborative desktop video solutions are likely to incorporate parts of the international standard, as well as local area network standards and proprietary solutions.

Telephony-oriented videoconferencing standards

In December 1990, CCITT completed major portions of its international videoconferencing standard. This H.320 standard series will influence, as did modem standards before it, how telecommunications companies support multiparty collaborative video. The completed portions cover two-way video between two parties. The multiparty standard was projected to have been completed by this year.

The H series of standards were defined principally by telecom-related assumptions. The bandwidth performance assumptions targeted the smallest common bandwidth, which is two 64-kbits-per-second bearer or B-channels (128 kbits per second) of ISDN (Integrated Services Digital Network, also defined by CCITT) up to the T1 connection (1.5 Mbits per second in the

Name	Description	Status as of 1993
H.261	Video coding (compression)	Adopted, 1990
H.221	Framing information	Adopted, 1990
H.230	Control and indication signals	Adopted, 1990
H.320	Overall requirements for ISDN systems	Adopted, 1990
G.711	64 kilobit per second audio coding	Adopted, 1984
G.722	48/56/64 kilobit per second audio coding	Adopted, 1986
G.728	16 kilobit per second audio coding	Adopted, 1992
H.223	Encryption	in development
H.231/H.243	Multipoint conferencing	in development

Figure 49.1 CCITT standards applicable to desktop video collaboration.

United States, 2.0 Mbits per second E-1 in Europe). Although not restricting the use of local area network (LAN) connectivity, the CCITT standards do not take advantage of the higher bandwidth offered by the LAN to the desktop. The H.320/H.261 standard is also called *P*64*. The various CCITT videoconferencing standards are listed in Fig. 49.1.

Some analysts predict that by 1994 about 50 percent of telephone and other switched channels in the United States will have ISDN capacity. Pacific Bell committed to complete ISDN service capacity by 1997. In contrast, today, only a few thousand ISDN-capable connections exist in the United States.

The wide area network (WAN) capacity of Switched 56 kbits per second (SW/56, a more available digital standard in the United States) and ISDN (a worldwide standard) is important to connecting the workplace and the home with high-quality images and faster file-sharing. Today's primarily analog telephone connections (plain old telephone service, POTS) strain the idea of workgroup collaboration and productivity because their single 14.4-kbit-per-second channel greatly reduces the quality of communication. In addition, analog phones are not compatible with workplace PBX systems and are therefore not likely to become widespread in the commercial office or video-conferencing telecommuter's home. ISDN's basic-rate interface (BRI) and SW/56 are much more robust technologies for desktop video collaboration than POTS for telecommuters working at home.

Audio/video control interface

Areas in which the videoconferencing standards are weak are multiparty conferences and user interface.

Microsoft and Apple each developed a video/audio control interface, known as AVI™ and QuickTime™ respectively. Both are targeted at reading data from mass storage devices such as CD-ROM.

Videoconferencing with multiple streams of video and audio to the LAN and WAN may be more than current versions of AVI and QuickTime can support.

LAN standards

The CCITT's H.320, which is primarily a wide area network standard, specifies an ISDN-like connection for videoconferencing applications.

Isochronous Ethernet, a local area network technology developed by the National Semiconductor Corporation, supports this standard by delivering 96 B-channels (6.144 Mbits per second) to the desktop. Isochronous Ethernet (isoENET) equipment will be available this year. It is a superset form of switched-circuit Ethernet that brings videoconferencing the last 100 meters to the desktop with good cost/performance. The IEEE 802.9 committee, which is responsible for integrated services standards that support multimedia communication within the LAN, has adopted isoENET and is considering the adoption of its call setup procedures in the 802.9 standard. This is a step toward affordable desktop interoperability with the LAN and WAN for worldwide desktop video collaboration links.

Meanwhile, the American National Standards Institute (ANSI) X3T9.5 committee has completed work on the physical components of a second-generation fiber distributed data interface (FDDI) 100 Mbit-per-second LAN, FDDI-II, or isoFDDI, which also supports isochronous services and B-channel interfaces and will begin to be deployed this year, primarily for backbone applications.

Also working on those isochronous services that will be required if LANs are not only to connect to the WAN but also support collaborative desktop video is the ATM Forum, which is developing even higher-speed solutions than either isoENET or isoFDDI.

Another networking solution that is frequently mentioned for high-speed applications is 100-Mbit-per-second Ethernet. This is based on Ethernet's packet protocol. As a result, delays from packet collisions make this solution less than ideal for videoconferencing applications, where tolerance for delay is minimal. Additionally, users must consider the delays that accumulate over the entire Ethernet network. Bandwidth alone is not the measure of whether or not a network is suited for desktop video collaboration.

System Design of Multiparty Communication

Digital signal processors, LAN, WAN, display, and audio and video compression/decompression (CODEC) technologies are critical to video communication systems. Software also plays an important role.

H.320/H.261 hardware

Elements of H.320 are likely to be required as lowest-common-denominator defaults in desktop video collaboration systems. The costly hardware to implement these defaults, such as the H.261 CODEC, are likely to be placed at the LAN-to-WAN interface as a shared resource rather than burden the local area network at each desktop with their cost.

Single-channel H.261 CODEC integrated circuits are extremely complex, therefore more costly than most circuits found in a typical PC. If for example a system is designed for six locations or parties in a conversation, there are five channels of audio and video to decode and one channel, that of the sender, to encode per station. Given the $150–$400 range of cost for H.261 integrated circuits per channel, a multiparty system based on H.261 hardware CODECs may be too expensive for desktop systems. In addition there are other circuits required at the desktop; video analog-to-digital and digital-to-analog converters, an audio CODEC, video-in-a-window circuits, and LAN interface. These circuits fill multiple PC-AT boards quickly and raise system cost substantially.

Multichannel video transmission

In the example just cited, the system supported six channels of video and audio. Six seems like a reasonable number, since meeting dynamics tend to bog down with larger groups. In addition, some people can join the group conversation from a telephone. Several channels or streams of H.261 video per desktop represent quite an investment. The H.231/H.243 section of the CCITT standards defines an MCU (multipoint control unit) that acts like a small PBX. This unit combines multiple streams of video and audio so that each user in a conference can see the other parties. Today the MCU cost is about $90,000 for a unit that can service two conversations of four parties or four conversations of two parties. The MCU cost and the additional cost of $7000 per desktop restricts multipoint videoconferencing using the H.320 specifications to special conference rooms and perhaps a few select desktops.

In contrast, an isoENET system does not need a separate MCU to create multiparty conversations, due to the high bandwidth and switch capacity of the isoENET hub. The typical isoENET hub can switch 100 to 300 Mbits per second of isochronous B-channel bandwidth, contrasted to a maximum of 2 Mbits per second per channel for H.320, thus offering much higher performance at dramatically lower cost than H.320-style systems, which also require costly MCUs. Figure 49.2 shows an example of isoENET providing multiple streams of data to each desktop, and Fig. 49.3 shows an isoENET LAN.

Multichannel audio transmission

In the isoENET LAN, with 96 B-channels per desktop, one B-channel can support voice-grade audio without compression. In addition isoENET users may access high-bandwidth information, including hi-fidelity stereo audio, which may require from three to six B-channels. By contrast, the CCITT's G.711 standard limits users' access to one B-channel for audio. If a WAN's basic-rate interface (BRI) is installed, then communication is restricted to two B-channels, about one and a half used for video and a half for audio, and CCITT's G.728 standard defines a method of audio compression with a 4:1

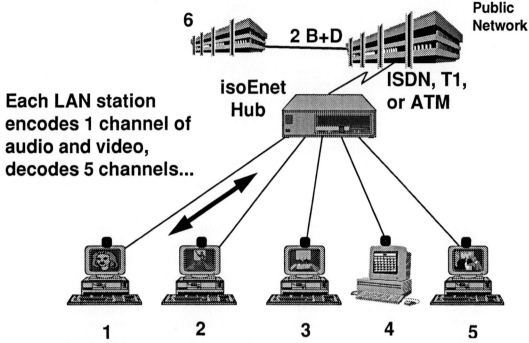

Figure 49.2 Multiparty channel requirements.

compression ratio to fit into a 16-kbit-per-second bandwidth. Facilitating G.728 compression requires a more costly floating-point digital signal processor than does the G.711 standard.

Audio streams must be combined so that each receiver hears all senders. This combination can occur in the isoENET hub or in a node resource that conforms to the CCITT's G.114 specified delays for audio and video. Less than 150 milliseconds is considered ideal, although less than 400 milliseconds is acceptable for one-way delays.

The standard CCITT H.231/H.243 approach mixes the audio streams in the MCU. The MCU is dialed through to become part of the calling network. The typical MCU has ISDN- or SW/56-compatible ports.

The traditional MCU approach is less flexible and more expensive than using a switched isoENET hub to perform the switching, mixing, duplication, and routing of the audio and video streams. Isochronous Ethernet hubs allow each desktop to receive audio in separate streams. Separate audio streams may be used with Surroundsound-like techniques to help listeners know who is talking while they are focusing on a document.

User interface

The user interface must be a work of simplicity if it is really to improve productivity. Workgroup video collaboration must be as easy as dialing a phone.

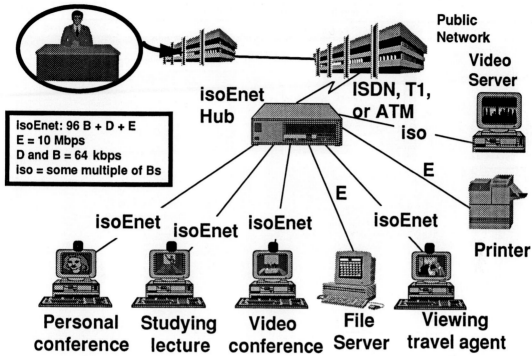

Figure 49.3 isoENET Hub.

Get rid of the current LAN, which must be baby-sat and managed, and is still down twice a week. We are talking about critical real-time communications, not deferred transmission of an e-mail that gets there when the server reboots tomorrow. This system must be available for use without a call to system administration or the need for a degree in computer science.

The user display portion of the interface shows the other parties in the conversation. If voice-only members are present, an icon blinks when they talk. Users may be assigned a name or a picture during call setup. During the conversation the user should have the freedom to place the speaker windows anywhere on the screen or even behind the screen, while the screen area is shared for applications or chalkboard windows. As a person speaks, his or her image is given priority and exposed, if needed, onto the screen, while dormant speakers may be flipped to the background. With this technique six or more participants' images can share the screen with data images. Figure 49.4 illustrates a four-party conversation.

Yet to be created is the phone book that will keep all the numbers users may wish to call. Today each application has its own phone book, and users type in, once for each application, the numbers for their modem program, their fax card, and their videoconferencing equipment. One hopes that in the future a standard will create one phone-book file for all applications.

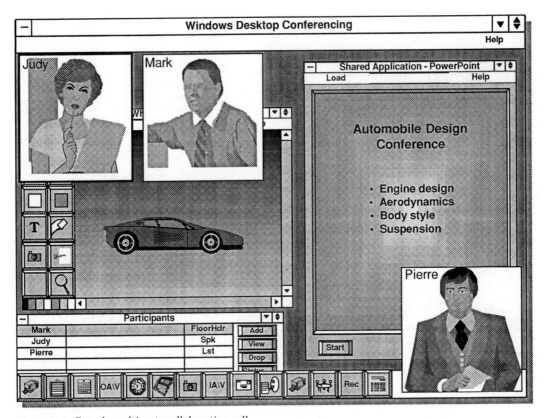

Figure 49.4   Sample multiparty collaboration call.

Possible video collaboration product characteristics

The following list shows features that may be present on a desktop video collaboration product somewhere in the 1994–95 time frame. The list defines a product that could plug into a PC. The Macintosh product would be similar.

Total price (per user, plus shared MCU features): less than $2500 per station, toward the end of 1995

Multiparty conferencing over both LAN and WAN

CCITT H.320 interoperability with other WAN locations, without restrict-
. ing LAN usage to H.320 limitations

Shared white board

Shared file view and annotation

Up to 6 live video windows on-screen at 15 to 30 frames per second

Up to 6 additional audio-only channels (for telephone connections)

Basic phone service

Scheduler/caller functionality

Snapshot of camera view, screen, or contents of window

Image exchange/viewer

Print images or data during conference

Clipboard—a personal note pad

Outgoing audio/video controls

Incoming audio/video controls

High-speed file exchange—up to the maximum network speed

Conference-control—speaker-management—color-coding for the floor-holder and speaker

Recorder

16-bit color VGA, SVGA, 800 × 600 or better

Six real-time windows up to 640 × 480 pixels each, overlapped—can be a combination of player, conferees, and images

Selection of visible conferees' images or icons

Hue, saturation, and brightness controls

Set frames per second (for transmission)

Monitoring user's image (self-video)

Moveable windows of variable size, variable quality

Camera and scanner inputs

Robust LAN connection—backward-compatible

Windows accelerator: BitBLT, clipping, line drawing, font acceleration

Multimedia PC (MPC)–standard compatible—Windows 3.1+:

   16-bit stereo audio

   Audio mixer

   CD-ROM interface

   Synthesizer sound for presentations and games

   Optional midi and game ports

Full duplex speakerphone with echo cancelation

Fax—G3-, G4-compatible access through LAN–WAN bridge

Video capture, edit, play; limited authoring

Windows graphical user interface (GUI)

Unification of teleconference facilities with existing office automation facilities, i.e. voice mail, e-mail, fax, printing, collaboration tools, etc.

Voice recognition

Encryption

Video and audio quality-server-access across LAN and WAN

Video mail support

Voice mail—answering machine

E-mail X.400

Call screening

Powerful antivirus protection

Secure access to dialer so that unauthorized people are unable to use the caller's resources

Time and billing

Remote control and access

Seamless LAN and WAN integration

The LAN and WAN connection should be transparent to the user. The LAN should simply represent the last 100 meters of connection to the office desktop. The isoENET LAN, due to its isochronous ISDN-like timing and signaling protocol, is easy to interface to the WAN. The H series protocols easily map, with some enhancements, to the isoENET LAN, thus making it easy to set up a call or tear down a call to anywhere in the world that supports digital services.

Local calls reside in the isoENET/isoFDDI/isoATM campus environment, while an out-of-campus call passes through the hub/PBX into the WAN. A typical electronic meeting could have four callers in different buildings of the campus, with a fifth caller coming in through a WAN connection. Each user in the LAN can see all others in the conversation, but the WAN-based call can be limited to two B-channels of ISDN and cannot reproduce simultaneous high-quality images of all parties in the conversation. If affordable, additional B-channels or primary-rate interface service supports multiparty viewing to WAN locations. The WAN-based user may be a telecommuter with access to either SW/56 or basic-rate interface ISDN (2B + D). To see others during the conversation, the WAN-based user can have a voice-activated switch to select who is displayed.

Interoperability

Interoperability is a primary concern for users who purchase desktop video collaboration technologies in the expectation of fulfilling tomorrow's requirement for connection to vendors, customers, and telecommuters. Initially, new methods of compression will be introduced and used. Nonstandard methods offer lower cost or better image qualities. If H.320/H.261 standards are adopted by many users, the cost of standard systems may drop and become competitive with other methods. Still, the ideal is interoperability, and generally the use of standards delivers connectivity.

Interoperability can be achieved by means of proprietary or other de facto compression methodologies and today's standard method (H.261), working in the same environment, as long as the connection can be made to look compatible.

Theoretically, by using portions of the H series, with enhancements, and adopting a new experimental National Semiconductor software or hardware video-compression method, the cost per network is significantly reduced. Initial cost estimates for a multiparty network using National compression and isoENET are one-third the cost of a similarly equipped H.320/H.261 network. In addition, isoENET and National's multiparty compression maintains compatibility at the WAN interface and thus provides worldwide interoperability.

Compression

Compression will be essential for desktop video collaboration. It is a way of dealing with low bandwidth and expensive storage or transport costs. Video and audio compression use different methods, due to the difference in information type and the difference in the way we perceive audio and video data.

Video compression

Video compression typically reduces the data by discarding those things less important to our perception of the image.

The human eye is insensitive to random high-frequency visual information. It is, however, very sensitive to nonrandom high-frequency image content such as the edges of objects. Our eyes are less sensitive to color than to intensity changes, so color information may be formatted with lower resolution than intensity information, therefore affecting compression. Our vision also is more sensitive to noise in simple flat areas of an image where not much is happening. Consideration of these human factors is important when dealing with compression algorithms if we are to deliver what is perceived as high-quality video.

There are many applications for video compression, each with its different cost or performance requirements. Here's a sample list of applications:

Video conversation

Collaborative computing

White board

Multiple-person games through networks

Training

Education

Entertainment

Enhanced PC- or Mac-based games

Interactive video manuals

Video mail

Customer service

Security cameras

Many of these applications require hundreds of megabytes of low-cost storage. CD-ROM with about 650 Mbytes of storage can store images, video, and sound. Compression stores 72 minutes of movies on one platter.

Two good examples of CD-ROM storage are the following.

- *The San Diego Zoo Presents the Animals.* Features 60 minutes of video clips; more than 200 exotic mammals, birds, and reptiles; more than 1000 color photographs and descriptions; 2500 pages of habitat descriptions, articles, and scientific data
- *The Software Toolworks World Atlas.* Features motion video of the world's greatest cities; visits more than 200 countries; 1000 location photographs; currency conversion values; country and city maps; creates and combines maps, charts, and graphs

These two examples show typical uses for JPEG or still-image compression and MPEG, and other full-motion video-compression methods.

Although the general belief is that standards cut costs or widen the availability of solutions, compression used over LANs may exist with several popular de facto standards. Software compression has a niche where cost is a primary concern. Today new algorithms are developed every few months that are better than the standard H.261 or MPEG methods for some applications. The ever-increasing performance of CPUs and digital-signal-processing technologies may lead to new compression software sent to users on a floppy diskette or through the LAN with the compressed data.

In collaborative desktop videoconferencing, compression is likely to be found in two forms: software, and hardware. Software compression is ideal for one or two channels, but hardware compression accelerators will be required to support multiparty conferences.

Within the areas of data compression there are both proprietary and standards-based compression methodologies embedded in both software-compression and hardware-compression technologies.

Standards-committee types of image compression

Four major compression standards already have been specified for image compression: JPEG, MPEG 1, MPEG 2, and those embodied in the CCITT's H.320 series for teleconferencing with video content.

JPEG is a group of methods for picture compression. The standard supports lossless compression of about 4:1 for high-quality storage, or lossy methods where compression of 15:1 is quite useful. Further compression notably degrades image quality. JPEG is used to send pictures electronically through a network, or to decrease storage requirements for a database. Some motor vehicle departments use JPEG to store drivers'-license photographs on computers.

MPEG 1 is a generic coding standard for compression of moving pictures and associated audio for storage devices (i.e., CD-ROM, DAT, disk drives, etc.) and telecommunications channels such as primary-rate ISDN in the WAN and various LANs.

MPEG removes redundancies in a manner similar to JPEG for video compression, in addition to using several prediction modes (forward, backward, bidirectional) entailing motion estimation/compensation techniques. CD-quality audio is achieved using either 64 or 128 or 192 kbits per second, and a systems transport mechanism is specified for proper synchronization and presentation. The intended MPEG application is for decode only (i.e., entertainment-quality playback), as MPEG 1 only specifies a bit-stream syntax for a decoder. MPEG 1 yields very long delays in multiparty or two-way exchanges, and therefore is not suited to real-time videoconferencing.

MPEG 2 is an extension of MPEG 1 with the intended application of distribution-quality video compression for cable television, satellite digital television broadcasting, home television theater, HDTV, etc. MPEG 2 also is a generic coding standard, since the complexity and bit rates vary between 4 Mbits per second for television programming up to 30 Mbits per second for HDTV. Technically, MPEG 2's primary differences from MPEG 1 lie in the ability of prediction modes (i.e., field/frame) to better handle odd/even fields so as to attain higher-quality video and multichannel audio modes for Surround sound, a low-frequency channel, and multilingual audio channels.

The CCITT's H.320 standard, Narrow-Band Visual Telephone Systems and Terminal Equipment, has rapidly emerged as the future standard for interoperability between videoconferencing systems. It provides for compatibility among various CODEC vendors in terms of compression, transmission, interchange, and display of audio and video. It answers the growing need for interoperability, similar to facsimile and modem technologies. Future videoconferencing systems will support the H.320 standard, at least as a default fallback, and many organizations are performing interoperability tests with H.320 standards.

Aside from interoperability testing of various implementations of H.320, a second barrier to interoperability for pervasive desktop video collaboration is the wide area network itself. Either ISDN or SW/56 is a requirement for reaching beyond the corporate campus to remote locations.

AT&T and Northern Telecom are major ISDN switch-providers in the United States. Originally they implemented ISDN differently, creating a networking barrier to interoperability. Bellcore, however, introduced National

ISDN1 (NI-1), which has been universally adopted by ISDN providers in the United States and will soon break down the WAN interoperability barrier.

Another networking barrier is the Inverse Multiplexer (I-Mux), which links a CODEC to a switched network. This function is responsible for dividing a compressed signal from the CODEC into multiple 56- or 64-kbit-per-second signals for transmission and resynchronizing at the receiver so as to provide a transparent WAN connection to multiple end stations. Since a standard was not available before the product was needed, proprietary schemes were used. Today, however, a common protocol has been adopted by a group of 32 I-Mux manufacturers calling themselves BONDING (Bandwidth-on-demand Interoperability Group), after they saw the acceptance of H.320.

Another obstacle to interoperability over the WAN has to do with providing gateways among different networks. AT&T, MCI, and Sprint already have discussed how to tackle this problem, and gateways should be available soon.

Software compression

End users increasingly are aware of desktop video application opportunities. Video capture boards have entered the market and received an enthusiastic response from early adopters. As of now, captured video is restricted to local disk storage, and is not readily distributed. These boards use simple compression methods to compress "on the fly" at ratios of about 15:1 for storage to the disk. This restricts the application of video to enhancing presentations or video book forms.

With the increased availability of Ethernet embedded in PCs and isoENET products, users will demand the ability to channel video to other viewers in the local campus or network. Such channeling will open up new applications in education, training, and communication. These applications will be based on systems that have the following modules: a capture device (i.e., video camera or CCD lens); audio-capture analog-to-digital converter; video and audio compression/decompression (CODEC); transport and display. Today PC vendors add multimedia capabilities to their products to differentiate them and to add value. Several PCs in development carry most of the modules just mentioned.

PC processors are performing at higher levels, and some vendors include a digital-signal-processing chip on the PC mother board. This increased capacity may support compression of video and audio in software without additional board or chip resources, allowing users to use multimedia PCs for authoring, playback, and communication.

National's experimental compression method is unique in several ways that are important to the end user. The compression relies on a technique that uses 100 times less computation than the complex mathematical methods used in standards such as H.261. Since the compression scheme requires less computation power, the algorithm can run on the host PC without add-in cards.

Additionally the algorithm supports chalkboard collaboration, because it preserves the edges of text, or lines captured from the screen, or other scanned documents. The NSC method of compression supports easy scaling of size and aspect ratio, so that the end user can position the appropriate viewing resource on the screen. National's experimental compression method may be available in software versions. Additionally, it has been designed for real-time multiparty desktop videoconferencing, and therefore yields much lower delays than do other standards for high-quality desktop video collaboration. Reduced delays at the end-user desktop compensate for possible delays in other parts of the system.

Software compression trends

Several vendors have software decoders, but few provide real-time encoding of video and audio in software. Given increasing CPU power, real-time encoding is now practical in some methods. Low-cost software can ship with the PC as part of the operating system package. In this situation there is no need to be compatible to H.261 or MPEG standards, because software CODECs can be stored on the CD-ROM or transmitted to the receiver during call setup, so no extra hardware is needed. Today all software CODECs are proprietary, and the software decoder market is still open to de facto standards.

Internet is experimenting with video over public switched and LAN networks. This is exposing thousands of users to LAN-based video mail. As a part of this experiment, Internet supplies a package called PictureWindow™ videoconferencing software, for Sun SPARC stations that connect to Internet.

The value to the desktop customer of software CODECs and compression/decompression algorithms is that some level of videoconference capability is realized at a low investment. This method of software videoconferencing can support midrange to high-end PCs and new integrated circuits that contain some standard multimedia features, thus adding additional new features almost at the same investment level. Environments that have 10BASE-T Ethernet or isoENET maintain a low-end entry point by using this software to establish simple point-to-point video capability.

Today there are few solutions for software videoconferencing. The H.320 method of video compression requires 1.5 to 3 Giga operations per second, thus requiring dedicated digital signal processing hardware.

Several vendors today offer proprietary software decoding at about 15 frames per second. For faster decoding and better image quality, a board is added. In the future new compression methods, increases in CPU performance, or very low-cost silicon may change the competitive environment.

Sample CODEC products

Software compression will soon become a standard feature in all PCs shipped. Hardware upgrades will provide better performance and features. Analysts estimate that by mid-1993 about 1 million copies of Apple's QuickTime had shipped, and about 50,000 copies of Video For Windows. Both environments and their software CODECs continually are being improved. The following list provides a sampling of the vendors now supplying software CODECs for Macs, PCs, and workstations:

Apple. Has some real-time decoders for the QuickTime environment in Operating System version seven, but the compression ratio is low, and encoding is not performed in real time.

Digital Equipment Corporation. Digital's Alpha CPUs are reported to decode H.261 video (a resolution of 360 × 240 pixels) at 28 frames per second. H.261 is an asymmetrical standard, so compression is much more difficult than decompression.

Intel. Has delivered a software CODEC called Indeo, packaged in the Video for Windows sold by Microsoft. Indeo cannot do real-time encoding without a special digital signal processor circuit that increases system cost. Software-only decoder performance is 15 frames per second, with 320 × 240 pixel resolution operating on an i386 33-MHz platform and 24 frames per second on an i486 33-MHz platform.

Iterated Systems. Has a real-time decoder at 30 frames per second using a fractal-based method. This method yields good scaling and high quality. Fractals are very hard to code in real time, even with hardware digital-signal-processing. Microsoft's Encarda CD-ROM encyclopedia uses this method to store pictures.

Media Vision. Offers 15-frames-per-second, 160 × 120 pixel software decompression. Compression is too slow for videoconferencing, but fine for CD-ROM storage. Media Vision licensed its method to Microsoft, so it is included in Video for Windows.

Microsoft. Has some real-time decoders for the AVI environment in Windows, but the compression ratio is low and does not provide real-time encoding.

National Semiconductor Corporation. Has developed an experimental compression algorithm that targets two-way, real-time communication, as well as storage on CD-ROM. This technology is capable of two-way communication using software alone, or supports multiple channels when using hardware acceleration. The algorithm has a low delay and preserves the quality of text in an image, thus achieving good quality and compression tradeoffs.

Sun. New SunVideo™ technology includes a software compression method called CELL that can do two-way compression and decompression when running on Sun 10 workstations.

SuperMac Technology. CompactVideo can display 15 frames per second in a 320 × 240 pixel window, or 30 frames per second in a 160 × 120 pixel window. The CompactVideo CODEC is licensed to Apple in version 1.5, and later versions of QuickTime. The CODEC is called Cinepak. While real-time compression in software is not practical, the decompression quality is considered quite good.

Xing. Has demonstrated an MPEG-like video decoder in software that uses a digital signal processor for audio decompression. The Xing product decodes in real time.

Meanwhile a host of companies, ranging from AT&T to Zoran, are offering or have announced video-compression integrated circuits that doubtless will find their way into add-in boards and perhaps into main system boards as well. Although hardware compression is more costly than software compression—adding perhaps $500 to the price of the end-user product—it is likely to be required in some multiparty desktop video collaboration applications. It is conceivable that hardware compression could reside on a local area network hub, so that hardware compression costs were spread among several users.

Conclusions

Desktop video collaboration represents new challenges, standards, and opportunities that will serve to improve and advance the quality of remote communication worldwide. Reliability and ease of use are critical to the acceptance of a new communication paradigm. The technical challenges of multiple streams of full-duplex video and audio are clearly supported by new LAN technologies such as isoENET, isoFDDI, and isoATM, and lower-complexity, lower-cost compression methods other than H.261. Interoperability between compression methods must be established so as to spur market growth in campus environments as well as in pervasive applications. As local area network technology prepares to interface with wide area network standards, local and international exchange carriers will have to deploy ISDN in the wide area network before telecommuters, customers, and vendors are able to participate in worldwide desktop video collaboration.

50

New Metaphors
for Communications:
What the Web Makes Possible

Jeffrey V. Nickerson
Wing F. Wong

The Web is a new medium for communication (Fig. 50.1). When a new medium arises, it can only be described through metaphors that give a sense of what is possible. Radio was perceived in terms of theater, television in terms of radio. The Web is sometimes seen as an encompassing medium because text, images, music, and movies can all work within its structure. But eventually the Web will reveal its own special characteristics. In the meantime, it can be described through the following set of metaphors:

Metaphor 1: The Playing Field (If You Build It, They Will Come)

Architects have long understood that building shared, open spaces, such as playing fields or parks help create a sense of community. Architects of Internet technologies have come to a similar understanding: designing standard ways of communicating on top of shared electronic networks can create dynamic communities.

The Internet is a wide-spread, rapidly growing telecommunications infrastructure. A standard set of protocols, naming conventions, and services sit on top of these physical connections. The World-Wide Web (WWW) depends on both the physical network infrastructure and the standards. The Web is

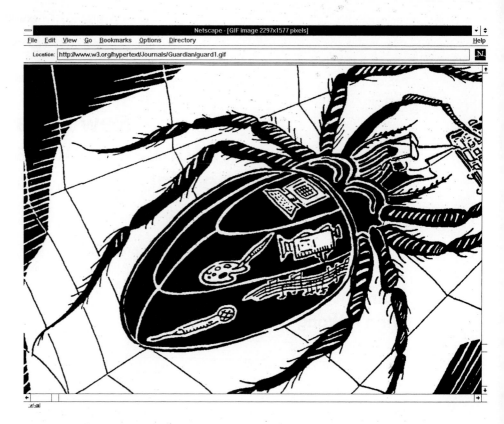

Figure 50.1 Joe Levy's depiction of the WWW, snagged by a Web browser. The original comes from a Guardian article, Nov. 1993.

comprised of standards, the most important being the Hypertext Markup Language (HTML). A graphic user interface application, known as a *browser*, displays data formatted in HTML. Although the Web was first thought of as a means to disseminate information, the utility of the browsers has made them the preferred interface to all of the Internet services.

The Web began in March 1989, when Tim Berners-Lee of CERN (a collective of European high-energy physics researchers) proposed it as a means of transporting research and ideas effectively throughout the organization. The successful sharing of information sparked today's exponential growth of the Web. In hindsight, the Web's explosion was a result of a series of smart decisions that started more than 25 years ago with the advent of the Internet (Fig. 50.2).

Over time, the Internet community grew to include more commercial subscribers, intent on using the Internet to reach out to the general public to promote products and services. Simultaneously, more members of the general public plugged into the Internet as potential consumers of these products and services. This growth has been catalyzed by a number of rapidly progressing technologies:

- In the past 12 to 18 months, the continued drop in desktop computer prices has put multimedia workstations into the homes of many families throughout the United States.

- The availability of 28.8-Kbps modems at very affordable prices provided individuals with the necessary telecommunications hardware.

- The commercial availability of TCP/IP protocol suites for the desktop gave individuals access to the necessary software.

- The reductions in the price of access costs from Internet service providers extended the fringe of the Internet to any home with a computer, a modem, and TCP/IP software.

Metaphor 2: The TV Set

It is inevitable that our thinking about the Web will be influenced by implicit comparisons to television. The surfing of channels on cable seems analogous to the surfing of pages on the Web. It is a short jump from the remote control to the mouse. World events reach television and the Web about the same time. So, in some ways the metaphor works. But when we consider the display of real-time video, the technical characteristics of television and the Web are very different.

The Internet can function as a television broadcast medium through the use of the MBone. The MBone allows recording, playback, and multicast transmission of conferences over the Internet backbone. It requires 128 Kbps for video transmission and 64 Kbps for audio. Even this amount of bandwidth does not come close to television. The image is a quarter of the screen size and the frame rate is at most 5 frames per second (fps), in contrast to television's 30 fps. If it takes 200 Kbps to transmit a quarter-size video at 5 fps, how much bandwidth is required to transmit TV video? Assuming a 640-x-480 display, with each pixel represented by 3 bytes, 27 Mbps are required.

Timeline

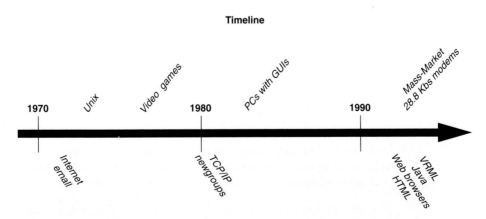

Figure 50.2 The Web timeline.

Table 50.1

Play Time/Image Size	640×480	320×240	160×120
1 Second	27 MB	6.75 MB	1.68 MB
1 Minute	1.6 GB	400 MB	100 MB
1 Hour	97 GB	24 GB	6 GB

Table 50.2

Compression/Play Time	1 Second	1 Minute	1 Hour
1:1	27 MB	1.6 GB	97 GB
3:1 (compress)	9 MB	540 MB	32 GB
25:1 (JPEG)	1.1 MB	65 MB	3.9 GB
100:1 (MPEG)	270 KB	16 MB	970 MB

Table 50.1 shows the approximate amount video data tabulated, based on the length of the videos with corresponding image sizes.

The Internet backbone is made up of a series of different-sized pipes. T3s and T1s supply 45 Mbps and 1.5 Mbps respectively. In many locations around the world, the pipes are much smaller. As can be seen from Table 50.1, uncompressed video files are just too large to be transmitted across the Internet and are too large to be handled by most Web servers today. Clearly, video data has to be compressed to be practical. By using various compression algorithms, the sizes of the video data can be reduced (Table 50.2).

Transmitting MPEG compressed video requires about the same bandwidth as today's 2× CD-ROM, 300 Kbps. From the table it is evident that 1 second of playback requires 270 KB. If you assume that home users have dial-up modems receiving at 28.8 Kbps, it will take approximately 75 seconds to receive a 1-second playback of video. A 10-second video will take 12.5 minutes to download. The much greater bandwidth required in order to achieve real-time (30 fps) video playback brings up a few important observations:

- Even at MPEG compression ratios, real time transmission of video clips at 30 frames per second requires at least 1.5 MB of bandwidth.

- Any attempt to use video clips in multimedia Web pages would require the image size of the video to be scaled down to 160 × 120 and the frames per second reduced to below 10.

- ISDN (2B + D channels) connectivity providing 128-Kbps bandwidth will be necessary to provide minimal live video; that is, video-conference quality with a small number of pixels and a low frame rate (Fig. 50.3).

The Web differs in many ways from television. The Web is mainly interactive, whereas television is pre-programmed. Television is generally broadcast-based, moving data in one direction. The Web is inherently interactive. It is clear, for now, that treating the Web as a form of television will, on the one hand, create disappointment because of bandwidth issues, and on the other hand, miss some of the positive aspects of the Web that other metaphors suggest.

Metaphor 3: Instant Publishing

The motivating force behind the creation of the World-Wide Web was the desire on the part of scientists to publish instantly. Many ideas take years to reach a journal. The web short-cuts the publishing process; a completed document can be read by an entire community days after completion (Fig. 50.4).

Instant publishing works for corporations also. News about a new product, or a problem with a product, can be published instantly without the marketing expense of direct mail or print advertising. Technical support departments for software and hardware vendors are often required to produce numerous manuals, updates, bulletins, and bug reports. Much of this was accomplished through paper. Recently, some firms have converted these manuals to CD-ROMs. CD-ROMs are invented to store GB of data and programs geared specifically for multimedia applications, and are less expensive to produce than paper, but still require distribution. Now, through the use of the Web, technical support manuals, fixes, can be organized on a vendor's Web server. Users can connect to the server whenever they have a technical problem. Manuals can now include images and simple animation as part of the instruction in resolving the problem (Fig. 50.5).

Metaphor 4: The Mall

The interactive nature of the Web makes it possible to make purchases, through the use of credit cards or some other form of electronic currency. And some companies have already done this. It is possible to buy books, CDs, and a range of other products by visiting a Web page and entering a credit card number.

Yet, the differences between real and electronic malls create problems. Since consumers are not presenting information in person, the possibility of fraud is greater. As a result, service providers are attempting to create secure

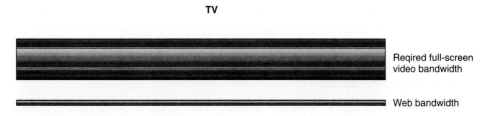

TV

Reqired full-screen video bandwidth

Web bandwidth

Figure 50.3 Bandwidth required for video is large.

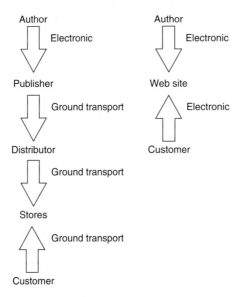

Instant publishing

Author

Electronic

Publisher

Ground transport

Distributor

Ground transport

Stores

Ground transport

Customer

Tpyical publishing flow

Author

Electronic

Web site

Electronic

Customer

Web publishing flow

Figure 50.4 Publishing flows.

transactions using encryption technology. We believe that these efforts will eventually succeed, creating a safe electronic marketplace (Fig. 50.6).

Electronic versions of stores create interesting possibilities. Physical comparison shopping takes time and effort, and for this reason, individuals sometimes hire professional shoppers to function as their agents, scouting stores and finally buying products on their behalf. In the electronic world, this type of activity can be performed much less expensively through the use of software agents. These agents are capable of moving around the Web looking for desired products, performing price comparisons, and initiating purchases for the lowest price.

Certain kinds of products and services demand handling or in-person viewing, and these products will probably not be sold successfully through the Internet. On the other hand, new products created solely for Web purchases might arise; information and entertainment might be packaged into small, network-transmittable packages for instant consumption. It is possible, in the electronic world, to solicit very specific requests from consumers and create made-to-order products in a way that is not possible when products need to be distributed through retail outlets.

Metaphor 5: Hyperspace

Hyperspace is a mathematical term for space of many dimensions (Fig. 50.7). The term *hypertext* was created to suggest text that can move in many inde-

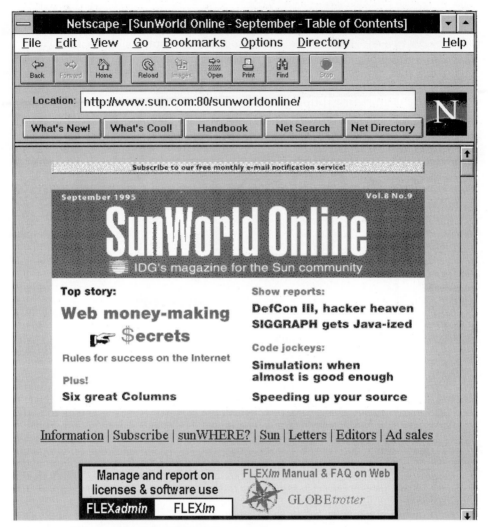

Figure 50.5 Web example of SunWorld online magazine.

pendent directions, freed from the one-dimensional sequence of words on the page.

The mechanism for achieving this multi-dimensionality is the hyperlink. In practical terms, it is the word or image that, when clicked on, brings the viewer to another page. The power of this link is the power of association—it is possible to link a footnote to the source text, to link the mention of a product to an order entry screen, and to link an idea to a related idea (Fig. 50.8).

From the viewing side, it means that you can move from page to page, across machines, following our interest. At any instant, there are a number of different directions that we can move. You can surf over a multi-dimensional ocean of pages.

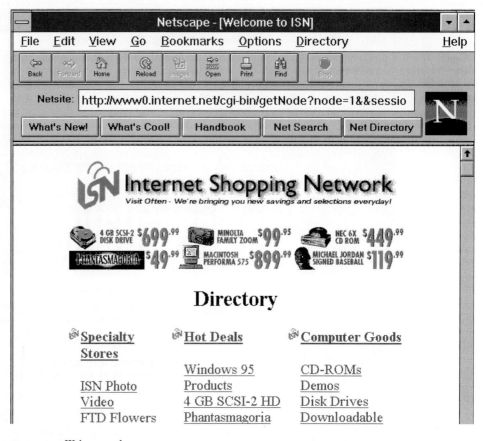

Figure 50.6 Web example.

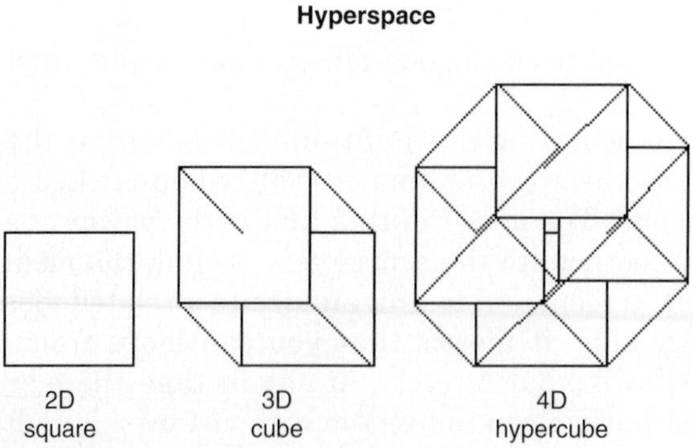

Hyperspace

2D	3D	4D
square	cube	hypercube

Figure 50.7 Visualizing hyperspace.

html

```
Netscape <A
HREF="/newsref/pr/newsrelease45.html">
   announced</A> that
```

Netscape announced that

Figure 50.8 HTML example.

Using the Metaphors to Browse and Buy

The Web can be looked upon as a collection of constantly changing pages of documents, images, sound, and video clips. The interconnectivity among these pages present an environment worthy of browsing, searching, and shopping. As consumers of information and products, we have established skills in scanning newspapers, in reading catalogs, in window-shopping. These skills easily translate over into the electronic world of the Web.

Searching, on the other hand, is more specific and more structured. A search often starts with a set of key words, and can be refined using Boolean logic. The search engines available on the Web today provide both subject area and keyword searches on the vast amount of multimedia information.

The techniques and strategies that help in both browsing and searching on the Web:

1. *Learn how to use a Web browser.* This requires investing time moving around the net and becoming familiarized with the key directories of registered Web sites. The use of electronic bookmarks in Web browsers help you to quickly revisit sites that have the right information. Helper applications that display Postscript files, play sound, and show movies can be installed to enhance the multimedia experience. An informal training session with a well-versed colleague is the best jump-start into hyperspace (Fig. 50.9).

2. *Practice using search engines, such as Lycos.* When you can move around the Internet with ease, the engines provide the best way of quickly getting you into the heart of the territory you wish to discover. Start with company names—yours and your competitors. Branch out into subject matter key words, and master Boolean searches. Lycos (www.lycos.cmu.edu) indexes millions of Web pages, so even the most obscure queries normally come back with results (Fig. 50.10).

3. *Find news groups of interest and subscribe.* Finding relevant Usenet newsgroups, mailing lists, or special groups within your service provider can give you a running commentary on a particular field. Also, doing so will draw you into electronic communities, in which you begin to recognize and interact with others with similar interests.

4. *Learn how to use intelligent agents.* Internet providers are beginning to make available ways to perform net searches on an ongoing basis by making use of agent technology. It is possible to create ongoing searches for any reference to a particular company, a new product, or to a prominent individual.

Using the Metaphors to Market and Sell

When individuals and companies decide to create Web pages, the metaphor they draw from is instant publishing. Some providers of information do nothing more than transform the normally static text and graphics images from paper to HTML. The individuals and companies that are most successful are those who understand the medium through the metaphors we have described. The nature of hyperspace, the sense of community, the reality of network bandwidth, the possibilities of electronic commerce—all of these concepts come into play when building Web pages (Fig. 50.11).

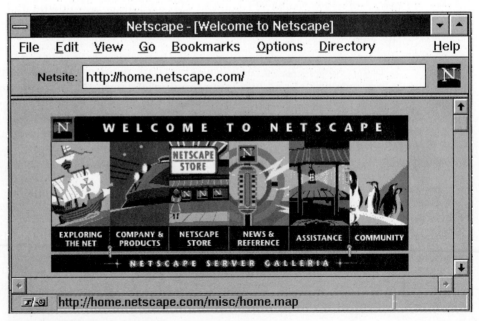

Figure 50.9   Netscape home page.

Figure 50.10   Lycos WEB searcher.

We detail the series of steps necessary to successfully build and deploy Web pages. In our experience, these projects are most successful when modeled on the methods that are used in building software applications.

In such projects, there are often two cycles. The first cycle deals with the overall conceptualizing and scoping of the project. The second is a repeated loop of designing, implementing, and testing (Fig. 50.12).

[Welcome]
[Hot Topics] [Services] [HR/Recruiting] [Offices]
[Library] [Industries] [International] [Feedback]

Other Coopers & Lybrand Web Sites

- Coopers & Lybrand (Australia)
- Coopers & Lybrand (UK)

Please send questions or comments to webmaster@colybrand.com

©Copyright 1995 Coopers & Lybrand L.L.P. *All rights reserved.*
Last updated on: 7 September 1995

Figure 50.11   Coopers & Lybrand home page.

Lifecycle

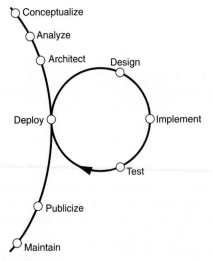

Figure 50.12   Web development cycle.

1. *Conceptualize.* Before anything else, a company needs to answer the following questions: What purpose will the page serve? Who is the intended audience? Is there a tie-in to actual transactions? The purpose of page might be to inform, or might be to sell products and services. The concept needs to be clear before proceeding.

2. *Analyze and architect.* Creating a web server involves time and money. A hardware platform might be purchased, or time might be rented. Telecommunication lines might need to be priced. The initial design and construction phases need to be planned and priced. In order to do this, the volume and the complexity of the information to be placed on the Web server have to be determined. In addition, performance goals need to be set. The amount of information, the anticipated number of users, and the performance goals will determine the hardware platform and bandwidth requirements.

   A corporation typically has two options for getting on the Web. It can rent a space from one of the many Internet and Web space providers for a monthly fee, based on size or the usage of the homepage. Alternatively, it can maintain its own Web server with connection to the Internet provided by any of the Internet server providers.If the decision is to buy a Web server, then the hardware needs to be sized. The CPU, disk I/O, network adapters, memory, and network bandwidth all need to be carefully chosen.

   The best estimating and sizing is done by those who have done it before. For this reason, companies building pages for the first time often solicit advise from experienced technology consultants.

3. *Design.* The design stage focuses on the style and form of the information to be presented to the viewer. How many graphics, sound or video clips should be included and how should they best be put together? If these multimedia objects are large, they might take minutes to download.

   Besides the content of the home-page, the styles in which these messages are delivered to the viewers are equally important. Without proper design, Web pages can distract, confuse, or overwhelm the users with inconsistent styles, banners, or voluminous amount of flashy graphics. Soliciting the help of graphic design and multimedia professionals is usually warranted at this stage of the project.

   For systems that involve electronic commerce, interfaces to external systems need to be designed. Standards, such as the Common Gateway Interface (CGI), might need to be adapted to simplify these interfaces. Security aspects of the financial transactions need to be considered. Backup and recovery, error handling, and maintenance need to be considered and designed for.

4. *Implement.* Once the content, the style, and the form of the information have been planned out, the realization of the concepts and design through HTML are left. The layout of the home-page can be done manually by writing HTML code or by using commercially available WWW authoring tools.

5. *Test.* From the publishing metaphor, it is clear that pages need to be proofread. Because a Web site involves a number of software products, the entire installation needs to be integration tested to ensure that all the software and hardware components work together. Because users might use different browsers, testing from different types of client configurations needs to be performed. All performance goals need to be verified to ensure that, with the intended numbers of users, the response time will be acceptable.

   One of the most common annoyances of surfing the Web is following a link to a non-existent site. If a Web page has many links to pages on other remote Web servers, these links have to be checked on an ongoing basis.

6. *Deploy.* The deployment of a new Web server typically takes on an iterative approach. An initial design and implementation of a home-page will be made available on the net to "field test" and solicit feedback from the intended viewers. Viewers are either asked to answer a handful of questions or are given an e-mail form to elaborate on their comments or thoughts. Web servers provide the ability to track the number of times pages were accessed and the links followed in viewing the pages. Well-designed pages contain a mechanism to solicit feedback from the viewers. The comments and suggested improvement can then be used to redesign the Web page.

   The iterative approach starts when the home-page is first put on the Internet and will continue throughout the existence of the home-page on the Internet. This will ensure that the content and form of the Web page will reflect not only what the viewers are looking for, but will frequently present a new look to viewers on the net.

7. *Publicize.* Putting a lot of effort in designing, implementing, and deploying the Web page will only ensure that viewers who found the Web page will stay longer or will revisit the Web page in the future. How should a Web page be promoted so that the targeted viewers will visit the page and the past visitors will revisit periodically? Numerous options are worth pursuing:

   - Register the home-page with a registry, such as Yahoo, or search engine, such as Lycos. The description will serve as the search keys to locate the home-page.

   - There are many well-known or well-established home-pages that are heavily trafficked. Depending on the content and the targeted viewers of the home-page, it often pays to establish a hyperlink from these pages.

   - Including URL (Universal Record Locator) in conventional paper-based advertising is another powerful way to transition to the more dynamic marketing vehicle of the Web (Fig. 50.13).

8. *Maintain.* Web pages go into maintenance once they are deployed. At the same time, a new design and implementation cycle begins so that new release of the page can be deployed.

Hyperspace

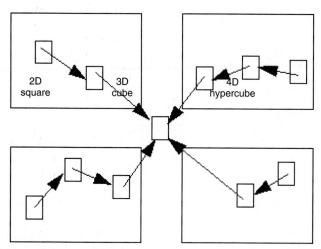

Figure 50.13   Web networks.

The Web Microcosm

The Web is a universally accessed shared space. But Web technologies can be used to set up a microcosm of the web within a company. All employees can use their Web browsers to connect to a departmental or corporate server. Those outside the company are denied access. For the employee, it means that the world of information is available at many different levels. For the company, it means that in-house publishing can be substantially reduced (Fig. 50.14).

A researcher can use a single browser to access concentric sets of data, ranging from the personal to the universal. Some companies notice that the Web seems to work well for searching through unstructured data. By using associations, users can rapidly find what they are looking for without having to master structured methods of creating queries. So, these companies are storing information in HTML formats, and allowing users to browse this internal data in the same way they would browse external corporate data. In many cases, no applications need to be built. The only requirement is that current in-house documents are converted into HTML formats and hyperlinks are established among these documents to address the interrelationship of corporate and external data.

The types of information companies convert to HTML include project plans, employee handbooks, directories, travel topics, technology trends, and industry trends. It is possible to create ways of viewing particular types of information—to look at competitive territory in new ways, to integrate with geographic information systems, to view marketing scenarios. Instead of building customized vertical applications, Web browsers can be used. Browsers can run on a variety of different platforms, and can provide a standard interface for an information architecture.

Microcosm

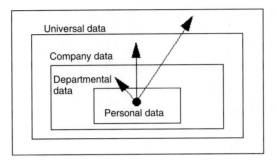

Figure 50.14 Microcosm.

The Future: From Pages to Spaces

The terminology of the Web is still rooted in the publishing metaphor. We speak of Web pages, of bookmarks, of text markup languages. The alternate metaphor is that of three-dimensional space. We can represent the real world, and create simulations of real spaces. For example, it is possible to create virtual rooms, where we interact with people who are geographically dispersed. The more bandwidth available, the more convincing these spaces can be, incorporating video conferencing and computer-generated images to smooth over distance.

A standard called *VRML (Virtual Reality Modeling Language)*, has been proposed to encourage the synthesis of virtual reality and the Web. If we enrich our interface to the Web with 3D goggles and datagloves, then new kinds of physical participation become possible. By floating data in space as physical objects, then allowing the manipulation of these physical objects, we can create a new kind of information landscape. By recording physical sensations and letting others try them out, we can come close to sharing experience. The Web already has community. The Web already is multi-dimensional. By adding technology that gives us a kinesthetic sense of presence, we will enhance what is already a very powerful new medium for communication.

Bibliography

Birkerts, Steven, *The Gutenberg Elegies: The Fate of Reading in an Electronic Age*, Boston: Faber and Faber, 1994.

Booch, Grady, *Object-Oriented Analysis and Design*, 2nd Edition, New York: Benjamin/Cummings, 1994.

Braun, Mike, "Multimedia—Life After Point-Click-and-Watch," *The Red Herring*, July 1995, 48–52.

Dieberger, Andreas and Bolter, Jay D. On the Design of Hyper "Spaces," *Communications of the ACM*, August 1995, 98.

Gelernter, David, *Mirror Worlds*, New York: Oxford University Press, 1991.

Hypermedia and Literary Studies, Delany, Paul and George P. Landow, (ed), Cambridge, MA: MIT Press, 1991.

Kelly, Kevin, *Out of Control*, Reading, MA: Addison Wesley, 1994.

Lynch, Patrick J., *Yale C/AIM WWW Style Manual*, Yale Center for Advanced Instructional Media, 1995. *Metaphor and Thought, 2nd Edition*, Andrew Ortony (ed.), Cambridge: Cambridge University Press, 1993.

Nadin, Mihai, *Mind: Anticipation and Chaos*, Stuttgart: Belser Press, 1991.

Nelson, Ted, *Literary Machines*, Sausalito, CA: Mindful Press, 1987.

Rowe, Lawrence A., Berkeley Video-on-Demand Server presentation—Berkeley Plateau Multimedia Project, 1994.

Rowe, Lawrence A., Video Compression presentation to Usenix 1994.

Silberman, Steve, "Real Virtuality," *Netguide*, October 1995, 57–60

Sterne, Jim, "Missing the Point, Network World's Capitalizing on the Internet," *Network World*, September 1995, 25.

51

SPJC Multimedia Case Study: Training the X-Generation Cop

Mike O'Berry

Tim Brock

Julie Capsambelis

Larry Strickland

Gary Robbins

Bill Tonnies

Why Not Train the Next Generation of Police Using Multimedia and Virtual Reality?

In a field where "experience is the best teacher," these new tools combine both cognitive and experiential learning into a single package. With the traditional, current teaching methods primarily consisting of oral tradition and multiple choice tests leading to a final state exam, new cadets have been finding themselves still learning, sometimes literally, in a "trial by fire" mode once they were on the job. For this reason, St. Petersburg Junior College proposed a multimedia-based approach to the State of Florida and found itself with a $350,000 grant and one year to produce.

Here are a few of the reasons why we chose to use multimedia to train future cops:

1. Next-generation students are more "media motivated" to learn.

2. Scoring on state exams has traditionally been low—some cadets consistently aren't passing certain parts of the exam.

3. Actual patrol techniques are becoming more "high tech" in nature and will require more "technology literate" users.

4. As the next-generation criminal becomes more technology literate, next-generation cops need the technical preparedness to meet the initial challenges of patrol and officer survival.

5. Interactive multimedia enhance learning by offering an increased level of realism that can't be achieved by traditional instructor-led classroom methods. Multimedia also offers a much wider variety of instructional methods. Cadets can actually gain experience from interactive video scenarios, by experiencing patrol simulations firsthand. Information learned in the classroom can be used on the street, and cadets can learn quickly from their mistakes without being exposed to the hazards of learning on the job.

Motivated by this challenge, the SPJC Criminal Justice Institute and the SPJC Office of Instructional Computing combined forces, and an "In-House" multimedia design team was formed. Less than a year later, the first phase of the project "BEAT," (Basic Enforcement Academy Training), was completed. The following narrative offers a look at this "Multimedia Project Notebook" from the unique perspective of each member of the design team.

Multimedia Project Notebook: A Project Coordinator's Perspective

Mike O'Berry

I can't believe that I've been producing an interactive multimedia project for almost a year. I still go into shock when I consider the changes in technology in the past two years, QuickTime VR was the latest in a series of mind-blowing leaps in multimedia technology. Still, I firmly believe that each change is another contribution to the vast inventory of tools available for multimedia development and production. As project coordinator, tracking these changes has become a big part of developing the BEAT courseware presented in this chapter. Having been involved in computer graphics for more than a decade, I've found that researching these changes has evolved into an ongoing process, and BEAT is the direct result of this type of on-the-fly research and development.

What is a BEAT?

First, what is BEAT? *BEAT (Basic Enforcement Academy Training)* is the title of the interactive multimedia courseware being developed for the Center of Emphasis grant that was awarded by the State of Florida to the Criminal Justice Institute at St. Petersburg Junior College. This innovative project is designed to use interactive technology as a training tool for law enforcement academies. The final courseware will be delivered using multimedia computers equipped with 16-bit audio and dual-speed CD-ROM drives.

Sophisticated animations, digital video, and digital stereo audio are being used to illustrate basic patrol concepts to cadets. Virtual reality software eventually will be linked to the instructional material to provide real-time interaction with a virtual 3D environment.

The BEAT multimedia courseware uses a patrol car metaphor to involve students in learning activities that present a series of state-approved objectives. Specifically, BEAT allows students to use computers to learn patrol objectives and interact with patrol-related scenarios. The courseware consists of three parts: an interactive set of objectives, a real-world scenario, and a testing module. The scenario includes related objective information and a variety of branching options that allow the cadet to experience life on the streets. As students complete each set of activities, they are able to review the objective information using a unique set of navigational controls, an interactive glossary, and an electronic notebook.

Practice exercises prepare them for the more involved real-world scenarios. After completing all of the objectives and scenarios, cadets complete a multiple choice test, which is automatically scored and saved on a network server for retrieval by the instructor (Fig. 51.1).

Figure 51.1   Through the windshield.

Project planning

Successful planning and execution of interactive projects often depends on the ability to follow the rapidly changing path of multimedia technology. Everything from the authoring software to the hardware used in delivering the final product must be considered, and anticipating the important changes is critical to the overall strategic planning needed in a large project. Decisions made up front have to be lived with for a very long time. Careful planning and a few hours each month reading the latest trade rags will help make you sleep better after a long day of project coordination. In a recent discussion with a friend who heads a local multimedia company, I reviewed the latest releases in graphics and authoring software. We both agreed that keeping up with current changes in technology is one of the most important steps in project planning.

The project was originally presented to me by Tim Brock, St. Petersburg Junior College's Computer Graphic Specialist, who ended up as the art director for BEAT. I was really surprised when he told me there might be an opportunity to head up a multimedia project for the college. At that point, I was using Adobe Premiere, and had some experience with Macromedia Director, but my background was really high-end color prepress and postscript imaging. BEAT seemed to be the chance I was looking for to really expand my knowledge of multimedia development. It also offered me an opportunity to produce a finished project that could incorporate many of the ideas Tim and I had originally talked about.

Our first official act was to attend a training session in New York City on Macromedia Director. This was literally the first thing I did as project coordinator. The Monday I started, Tim and I flew to New York for training. During the training, we discussed many of the ideas that are included in the final version of BEAT. It amazes me that some of the very elements Tim created in the beginning of the project are still a functioning part of the interface design. Based on what we learned in New York, we made some hard decisions about the look and feel of BEAT. We both started researching multimedia projects that were similar to what we wanted to do, starting with Broderbund's *Myst* CD-ROM game. We still exchange CD-ROMs and Director files downloaded from the World Wide Web, which is a great place to look for ideas. Tim has been great about establishing a visual approach to interface design. Many of our ideas were story-boarded right in Director. It soon became our method of choice for presenting ideas and resolving interface design issues. Without this "just in time" approach, many of our best ideas would probably not have been created.

Multimedia toolbox

For producing the multimedia content, we purchased several different Power Macintosh computers, two 7100s, and two 8100s. The project coordinator has a PowerMac 7100/66 with 24 MB of RAM. This machine was configured for light production work, development, administrative tasks, and e-mail capabilities. The project secretary has a similarly equipped Mac 7100/66 with similar software.

The real workhorses are the two Power Mac 8100 workstations. The programmer's machine, a Power Mac 8100/80, has 65 MB of RAM and a 500-MB hard drive. The software on the machine is configured to support basic multimedia development, Macromedia Director, and Adobe Photoshop. (In hindsight, it would have been smart to include Adobe Premiere for QuickTime editing.) This workstation is connected to the College network via ethernet, and has a set of Yamaha stereo speakers attached to it. We also have a Umax flatbed color scanner connected to it. The majority of the programming for BEAT was produced on this machine. Although very capable, it could use a much larger hard drive—at least two gigabytes.

Our most powerful workstation for digital video production is a Power Mac 8100/110. This monster has 80 MB of RAM and a two-GB internal drive. The heart of this beast is a Data Translation's Media 100 Digital Video System, attached to a pair of Micronet 4-GB drives. The combined drives provide 8 GB of storage for video projects. Although this system represents more power than is currently needed for 320 × 240 QuickTime, it allows us to produce full-screen, full-motion video using nonlinear editing. Our philosophy has been to buy systems that can support future advances in video compression technology. The workstation also has a full inventory of multimedia authoring software, including Macromedia Director, Adobe Premiere, Adobe Photoshop, Macromedia Sound Edit 16, and Strata Studio Pro 3D modeling software.

Student workstations

Because the needs of the college always come first, we selected Compaq Deskpro Multimedia computers for the classroom. These 66-MHz machines are very fast and the price was much less than for equivalent computers. Although many of us prefer Macintosh systems for multimedia, our Corporate Training Division, which will share the use of the classroom, offers more Windows classes than Mac classes. In addition, we were told that many of the training centers eventually using the final BEAT product also had Windows-based machines. The final decision to purchase the Windows PC machine was based on more than just the brand of computer we liked. The bottom line—price, performance, and compatibility—became the basis for our decision.

The student workstations have performed flawlessly during the evaluation phase of the project. The BEAT courseware runs very quickly, and the platform is quite stable. One thing we didn't want was a hardware problem while we were testing the courseware.

Before we bought the 28 classroom machines, we ordered one for evaluation. Because we already had created the interface and had a few sample modules linked to it, we were able to really put the evaluation unit through its paces. This is probably a good idea if you're going to buy specific hardware for your final project, or if you know the type of machine your work will be used on. I have to thank the technical coordinator of the project, Larry Strickland, for that bit of system wisdom.

The development team

As project coordinator, I reviewed the positions and people involved in the project. We needed a street-smart, computer-oriented, subject matter expert; an instructional designer with lots of courage; a technical guru with excellent cross-platform/C++ programming skills; a Lingo programmer who could tolerate our many changes; and, of course, a computer graphics genius. Sounds like the cast for a remake of The Wizard of Oz, doesn't it? Well, it's this truly talented team that you'll meet in the rest of the chapter. I can't say enough about the BEAT team. Each person has contributed hard work and great ideas to create a very unique, interactive, multimedia courseware product for police cadet training.

A Technical Coordinator's Perspective

Larry Strickland

Choosing the right programming tool

One of the first considerations in any project is to choose the right tool for the job. This is not unique to multimedia projects. Such saws as, "When all you have is a hammer, the whole world looks like a nail," are rampant in the language. Computer projects, though, often have such disparate pieces that the "tool" might not be the single hammer mentioned.

The BEAT project was no exception to this. We spent a considerable amount of time looking for the right tool for the job. It wasn't until sometime into the project that we realized there were several jobs to be done.

We needed to be able to produce state of the art multimedia presentations, do Computer-Assisted Instruction (CAI), gather, and report data—all in a cross-platform compatible manner. No one tool we examined could do everything we wanted.

Why Macromedia Director?

After examining a number of tools on the market, we finally decided that Macromedia Director would be the best choice for most, but not all, of our needs. It combined the ability to do high-end multimedia presentations with most of the primitives necessary for CAI work.

The weak areas, though, were the database operations necessary for effective CAI and the ability to interface with other applications directly in a cross-platform independent way.

Enter X-objects. The final reason for our selection of Macromedia Director was the ability to create and use X-objects. An *X-object* is an external program, normally written in C or C++, which can then interface with the operating system in whatever way is desired. X-object messages (functions) can return integer, floating point and string values. Messages can also directly set and read Director global variables, an ability that would be very useful later in the project.

X-objects were available on both the Macintosh and Windows platform. As a result, we could hide cross-platform problems behind a standardized interface. In addition, we would be able to use X-objects to interface with database programs and other applications. Again, this could hide cross-platform problems.

What really happened

Because of time restrictions, we were not able to fully implement our desires. Creating and using the X-objects was also more difficult than originally planned. Finally, C++ problems, most likely with name mangling, caused some difficulties.

We were eventually able to overcome most of the difficulties. We ended up writing two programs in the Windows environment. The first, a native Windows 3.1 application, was written in C++. It allows a manager to create new student accounts and to modify where data is stored (for both local and network applications). It also has features to allow "correction" of information that was entered incorrectly or changed during the time a student was in class.

The second application written was a DLL. This was the actual X-object, called *BEAT*, that formed the user database interface with our Macromedia files. This X-object allows a Macromedia program to extract and/or modify student demographic information and student test and quiz information. The demographic information is kept in a (slightly) encrypted form. The test and quiz information is kept both globally and on a per-student basis. These information files have been constructed in such a way as to be easily imported into database and spreadsheet programs, including Lotus 1-2-3, Excel, Access, and FileMaker Pro.

Remaining tasks

The current X-object and management programs are written only for the Windows platform, as that was our first platform for delivery of the BEAT project. We also intend to port these programs to the Macintosh environment as soon as they have proved themselves in the delivery of the material.

We also hope to extend our X-object, or create a new X-object, to give more precise control over external applications. In particular, it is our hope to include some Virtual Reality as part of the BEAT project in the upcoming year, assuming we have additional funding.

Conclusion

Although no one tool can satisfy all your needs, the ability of Macromedia Director to interface with the operating system and other applications through X-objects goes a long way toward removing the restrictions that have previously existed in these areas.

You do need a good programming team to accomplish this, though. Scripting in Director is not the same as programming in C or C++. Lingo is an excellent language, but it does need the supplements that C or C++ can provide to make it a total package.

A Content Expert's Perspective

Sgt. Gary Robbins

I have been a police officer with the City of St. Petersburg, Florida (St. Petersburg Police Department or SPPD) for many years. St. Petersburg has a population of approximately 250,000 residents, as well as many visitors and tourists. The SPPD has slightly more than 500 sworn officers, and a total payroll of 700-plus employees. In addition to my patrol duties, I also have been an adjunct instructor for the SPJC Criminal Justice Institute since 1986, for generalized instruction (Report Writing, Patrol Procedures, Officer Safety) as well as high-liability instruction (Defensive Tactics, Firearms, and Driving).

A majority of my law enforcement experience has been as a Field Training Officer, whose responsibility is to teach new police officers how to take the fundamental knowledge that they acquired in the academy and apply it "on the street in real-life situations." One of my attributes is my tactical experience in "SWAT" situations as a team member and leader for more than 10 years. All of this experience and knowledge is given to the recruits and new police officers whom I train. My current position at the SPPD is that of sergeant in the Field Training Unit, and team leader for the SWAT team.

When I had first met with the designer, coordinator, and programmer (development team) for a new concept in instruction—multimedia—I must say I was excited about the idea. I have some computer background/knowledge and had been employing multimedia in a home environment for about a year. The development team sat in class during my lectures to basic recruits at SPJC's Criminal Justice Institute (CJI) and solicited input for ideas and suggestions for teaching the patrol block of instruction.

During my years of teaching at the CJI, I found that a major void in academic training was the lack of practical scenarios or situations that give the recruits constructive feedback on their knowledge and actions based upon the specific scenario or situation. Throughout my work with the development team, I've found that multimedia can fill that void and create a positive learning environment for recruits. My first course of action was to find out what limitations multimedia had. To my astonishment, I found that every suggestion or idea I presented to the development team could be accommodated. Some modifications had to be made, but the working relationship between me and the development team was very open and creative.

I also found that some focus had to be placed on educating the development team in the fundamental aspects of law enforcement from the patrol officer's perspective. Some ride-along time was set up to accomplish this training, which centered on patrol techniques and officer safety tactics that are considered general principles of police work.

My particular task, as it applied to this program, was to structure scenarios that:

- Were realistic to "today's officers." Otherwise, the recruits would dismiss the training within the first few minutes.

- Could be applied to any police department or jurisdiction because the Police Academy instruction had to be "generalized" to meet the needs of all of the departments that utilize it.

- Would directly address the guidelines and objectives of the course curriculum.

In developing the scenarios, I also had to consider how they were going to be videotaped. A meeting was set with the development team to discuss a "routine" traffic stop. A question arose as to how we were going to portray the officer during the scenario (i.e., through the eyes of the camera or a second person). We decided that through the use of multiple cameras (or taping), both of these perspectives could be taped and assembled by the programmer.

Another task I examined was how to choose actors in the scenarios. We discussed professional actors versus police officers, and came up with the same obstacle the development team originally had. If we used professional actors, we would have to teach them how to respond and take actions as an officer would. Given the position I have in the department and the amount of time I've spent working with several officers and detectives throughout the Tampa Bay area, I hand-selected officers who would be excellent role players in the scenarios.

A few ideas were brought up, and after the Development Team went "on patrol," we all were unanimous with the decision that a "routine" traffic stop truly encompassed several learning factors in a minimal amount of time. The scenarios from the basic or routine traffic stop could easily lead into more complex and challenging situations.

We started to story-board a scenario and had a general idea of the objectives we wished to accomplish, but nothing was finalized until we brought all the role players together and walked through the scenario. I used two under-cover detectives as role players. This produced a circumstance that required consideration: If undercover officers are used, they must know that they will be seen by sworn as well as non-sworn students. The officers must be aware of the exposure of themselves, as well as any vehicles being used, so as not to jeopardize their safety or any active investigation that they might be involved in. We found that the role players who were picked added an authentic and realistic portrayal of the type of violator(s) that an officer would face during a vehicle stop (Fig. 51.2).

As we began developing realistic scenarios on videotape, I noticed that multimedia began to have an enormous advantage over traditional classroom instruction. Multimedia offers individualized instruction to the student, as opposed to group or classroom instruction. With the use of multimedia, applicable scenarios can be used to reinforce classroom presentations. This gives the recruits a chance to develop their skills and knowledge as they progress through the courseware. It also gives them a chance to see how their knowledge and abilities compare with those of the other students.

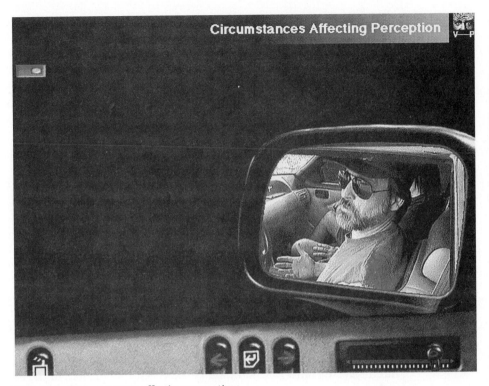

Figure 51.2 Circumstances affecting perception.

The scenarios I planned were developed with the concept of the Field Training Officer training his or her recruit. A "four-step method" of instruction is utilized that instructs the student on a task, shows the student how to acceptably perform the task, allows the student to execute the task with coaching, and evaluates the student once he or she has achieved an acceptable level of performance on the other three steps. We used some "branching" scenarios to provide the latitude of discretion that officers have available to them. We even built some remedial training plans into the program, which are meant to bring the student up to an acceptable standard of performance in a deficient area.

What's in store for the future? Once the basic foundation is perfected, nothing is out of reach. I can see the development of networked scenarios where several students participate in various role-playing activities during the same scenarios (e.g., primary officer, back-up officer, supervisor, detective, technician, et al). We also can set up advanced exercises for building searches or SWAT training, as well as scenarios for promotional examination assessment centers. With the use of multimedia and the working relationship that the Development Team and I have, the possibilities are endless.

A Designer's Perspective

Tim Brock

As the BEAT art director, I faced two challenges: First, the initial phase of the project had to be done in less than a year; second, our design production staff was made up of only two persons: the project coordinator and me. Although the project coordinator had excellent production skills in electronic imaging and we had the necessary tools from the college to do the initial phase, we found ourselves having to perform nine jobs—and in a very short time. The jobs: Screen Layout Design, Interface Design, Authoring/ Programming, Sound Design, Video Production, 3D Animation, Digital Video Production, Compression, and CD-ROM Production.

What follows is my step-by-step account of the project from a designer's perspective, which covers all the design skills that were required to do the first phase of the project.

Defining the scope of the project

For me, as a designer, the most difficult part of any project is getting started. Getting a handle on a project of this size required an initial "stab" at a plan—both short term and long term.

In collaboration with the Technical Coordinator of the project, Larry Strickland, the plan took shape as a 10-page document, including a vision statement, project overview, content overview and timeline, as well as a proposed budget and a brief listing of equipment needed. This document indicated the specific curriculum to be covered and the techniques to be used to deliver the instruction, including the projected production and testing schedule.

My first job was to help decide on appropriate content from the available curriculum that would fit our time frame and available technology. After discussions with content experts, it became clear that the Patrol section of the curriculum would be appropriate. The Visual Perception course was the logical starting point because of its visually rich content, and more importantly, it was the foundation course to the Patrol section. By choosing the appropriate content, the general parameters of the project became clear and the hardware and software tools also became easier to identify.

The College already had the necessary hardware and software to get started, and that helped to determine early on that the Mac would be our primary development station. Our starting platform was a Quadra 950 with 64 MB of RAM. It had a 400-MB internal drive and an external 2-GB Raven Micronet high-speed array that also connected to a CD-ROM Writer (JVC Personal Archiver). Other peripherals included a Radius VideoVision Studio Digital Video Card, two Apple monitors (17" and 13"), an NEC CD-ROM 4× player, UMAX 600-dpi color scanner, and one Panasonic NTSC monitor.

The software we chose was Macromedia Director. However, before we could begin, both the new project coordinator, Mike O'Berry, and I felt we needed more training. To learn some of the tricks and to save time, we both took one week of Macromedia training in New York City—both in Director and Lingo (Director's programming language). This brief time offered an excellent return on investment because we both quickly became comfortable with the software and were able to "hit the ground running" as soon as we returned.

Finding a metaphor

By the end of our NYC training, and armed with a good sense of what Director could do, Mike and I agreed that the patrol car was a potential metaphor for the project. Because we were starting with the Patrol section of the curriculum, the patrol car could offer a visually rich environment, providing many "gadgets" for effects-based learning for both multimedia and computer-based training (CBT). We also felt that the source material would be relatively easy to obtain. Fortunately, these things turned out to be true.

Some of our initial research led us to two CD-ROMs, Broderbund's *Myst* and Isaac Asimov's *The Ultimate Robot*. After reviewing these titles, we had a better idea of what we wanted. We liked the intuitive, "VR-like" navigation of *Myst* and the disciplined interface of *The Ultimate Robot*, so we decided to combine them in the BEAT project.

Next, we began talking with our content specialists, primarily Gary Robbins, a sergeant with the St. Petersburg Police Department. According to Robbins, the patrol car is the cop's "on the road office." From it, the officer receives briefings, radio dispatch, information on wants and warrants, makes radio calls, and files reports. The patrol car could offer a realistic metaphor for the project, as well as numerous "dashboard" interface capabilities.

With this input from our content specialists and our own research, we accepted the patrol car metaphor and made the following list of criteria for the interface:

- A suspension of disbelief should be maintained through a consistent and relatively realistic patrol car interior environment.

- There should be some trainee involvement with radio dispatches, wants and warrants, and calling another officer.

- It should provide an experiential approach to learning, possibly through a scenario-based PDA-type "quizzer."

- The CBT or "Briefing" section should provide drill and practice, as well as state-exam-based testing within the patrol car metaphor.

- The "Briefing" should have a glossary, note-taking capability, and student tracking functions.

Creating the concept: community sketching in director

The initial challenge was to produce a short concept piece. Our goal was to take a small microcosm of the project and carry it through each step of the production process and then present it on the final delivery system, which was a Pentium 586 PC.

First, I began scanning pictures of car interiors, car door latches, radios, and other potential interface controls. I took two front views of the dashboard and combined them in Director, using a pan transition to create a believable, virtual car interior. The radio control was adapted to display video. The air-conditioning control was converted to a PDA-(Personal Digital Assistant)-kind-of-quizzer. In a very short time, two-dimensional pictures were used to create a believable 3D interior view of the dash (Fig. 51.3).

Generic QuickTime movies were imported into Director to provide "place holders" for future scenario movies. They were placed in the "adapted" radio controller to create the look and feel of a radio/video dispatch center (Fig. 51.4).

At the same time, across town at another site using a Mac 7100 Power PC, Mike was developing CBT drill and practice "sketches" in Director. He was gathering material, through the Internet, using generic visual perception content. This included text, images, and sounds to be put into a simple multiple-choice question/answer format. This became a model for our CBT drill and practice section.

Figure 51.3 The speedometer.

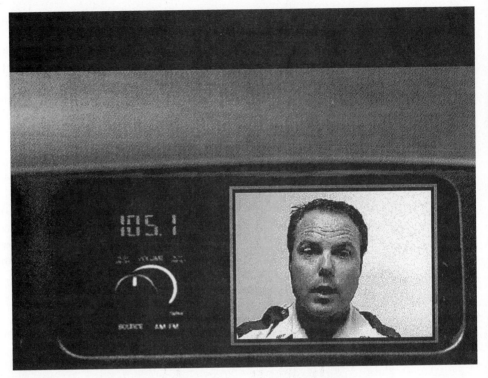

Figure 51.4   Onboard computer.

At another SPJC site, Technical Coordinator Larry Strickland was configuring a PC platform (with Macromedia Director for Windows) on the college network. This was to be our final student delivery machine.

Through the College LAN, within one week, Mike and I were able to combine our "sketches," using Director's flexible design that seamlessly allows for one movie to call another, then return back to its initial position in the original movie. I also "flattened" the QuickTime movies and reduced their data rate (more about that later) for PC and CD-ROM playback. With Larry's help, we were able to run our finished concept on the PC with minor adjustments, just in time for the final presentation. In less than a week, we were able to demonstrate the look and feel of the concept, including both experiential multimedia-based and informational CBT-based learning environments within a believable patrol car metaphor on the final delivery system. Fortunately, the administrators of the grant were pleased and our concept "checked off." We were on our way!

Developing a dummy

When we presented the concept piece as a microcosm of the entire project, we established, what the production procedure would be for the entire project. As designers, it was necessary for us to perform many functions (the nine jobs mentioned before) on a very small scale in order to gain acceptance for a direction. In addition, we were very fortunate to be able to actually use portions of the concept piece for the prototype or "dummy," as well as for the final production version. As someone has said, we created a process, not a prototype—because we never really threw our prototype away.

Once our concept was approved, we immediately began to experiment with some of the functional specifics of the project, creating a dummy. The following account briefly describes the process, as well as some of the software and hardware used to produce the dummy.

Although the term "dummy" implies very little content, our aim was to include some content while emphasizing its functionality.

The cast

Macromedia Director uses a movie metaphor that includes a stage, potential cast members and the programming tools to make a script for a story. We had the basic story line from the Patrol curriculum and the content specialist. Director itself was the story board. The first thing we needed was the cast. I began gathering the cast by scanning more images of car interiors, using sources from magazines, brochures, and actual patrol car video footage. To scan the images, I used Adobe Photoshop and a UMAX 600-dpi color scanner. To videotape the patrol car, I used a Panasonic S-VHS ×12 Zoom camcorder. To digitize the video, I used the VideoVision Studio digital video board, using both Adobe Premiere (QuickTime editing) and Adobe Photoshop (image processing) to prepare QuickTime digital video and individual pict image files.

Once scanned, the image (pict) files were touched up and edited in Photoshop. Images from car gadgets, police car radios, patrol belt items (such as walkie talkies, guns, car telephones, flashlights, etc.) were transformed and "tweaked" in Photoshop. Rear view mirrors were tilted and expanded, becoming interface "visualizers" for animation. Interior dash air-conditioning devices were redesigned into personal digital assistants, capable of displaying QuickTime movies, images, and text. Car door latches were turned into navigational buttons. To create a custom button cast member, for example, I cropped part of an image of an original air-conditioning control button and placed the text, "Start Your Patrol Beat," in light yellow and saved it. To create the pressed version of that button, I replaced the yellow text with red text and darkened the entire image 25 percent, then saved it as the "pressed" version of the button. Later, these two image files were loaded into Director as cast members. They then were scripted to alternate at the touch of the "mouse," simulating a "pressable" button (Fig. 51.5).

With the help of the content specialist, Gary Robbins, we began shooting fictitious scenarios of a traffic stop that he had scripted, which eventually included "plainclothes" cops, fast black cars, guns, and fake radio dispatching. We videotaped most of the scenarios in first person, with multiple "branching" options. This video footage was used to create QuickTime movie cast members. I chose to digitize the QuickTime movies at 320 by 240, (30 frames per second), rather than 640 by 480, in order to conserve space. Later, we compressed these movies to Cinepak. I reduced their frame rate to 15 and

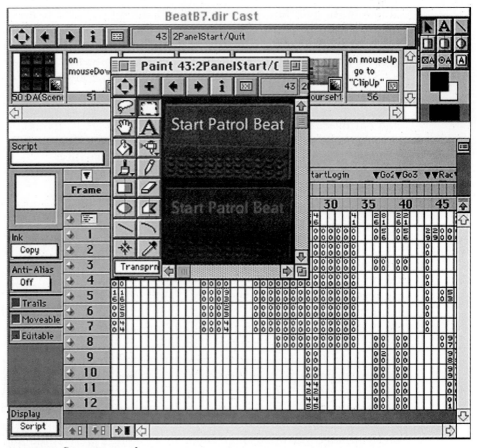

Figure 51.5 Computer panel.

their data rate to 280 KB per second (for CD-ROM playback) using the Apple "Convert To Movie" program. I also "flattened" these movies (to single fork) so that they would run on a PC using QuickTime for Windows.

I also created a cast of AIFF (Amiga Image File Format) sound files from the scenario videos. Using VideoVision Studio and Adobe Premiere, I captured and edited isolated sounds to be used in QuickTime movies. I also edited sounds to be used as "stand alone" cast members in Director. These sounds included miscellaneous effects (i.e., Walkie Talkie static, radio burps), as well as radio dispatch and other interior car sounds. Other sound sources included CD sound effects libraries, background sound track CDs, and recordings from everyday life, such as keyboard clicks and phone beeps. All these sounds were "captured" in Premiere, "sweetened" in Macromedia's SoundEdit 16 program, then imported into Director as AIFF files.

Another cast element was animation. We created animation cast members in several ways. First, we needed a transition from the Scenario-based car interior scene to the CBT-based rear-view mirror/car door scene. Instead of using a transition in Director, we chose to use sequential PICT files. These numbered PICT files were generated from full-screen, full-motion video (QuickTime) captures. They then were converted to sequential PICTs in Premiere at eight frames/PICTs per second. We also created sequential PICTs from QuickTime movies created by Gryphon's Morph Program. These were used as an emorphic transition between two different views of the rear view mirror. Third, we used Strata Studio Pro to generate traditional 3D computer animation. This technique was used for the opening BEAT logo (designed by Mike) that previewed before running the BEAT application (Fig. 51.6).

Each of these animation techniques could be "cast" into Director as either sequential PICTs or as QuickTime movies.

In addition, other cast members had to be created inside the Director program, such as text fields and scripts.

With all the cast prepared and assembled, we were ready to import them into Director and begin sequencing their actions.

The stage

After "importing" all these cast members into Director, I began "dragging" the specific cast members onto "the stage." This automatically put them into a specific channel in "the score" for one frame. Director uses a score sheet that has 48 channels, two audio tracks, a transition track, a timing track and a script

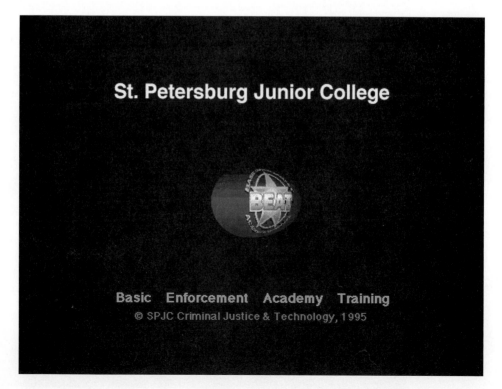

Figure 51.6 Start screen.

track. Once on the stage, each cast member can be designated to appear or disappear at a specific time. This means in theory that 48 cast members can be doing different things on stage while two audio tracks are playing. All these activities can be intricately timed and programmed to lead to other events. In reality, the speed and memory of the computer being used limit these choices.

First, I placed a 2D image of a car dashboard as a background image on the stage (in the first channel of the score). This became the foundation or backdrop for the other cast members, which were gradually "layered" on top. The higher the channel number, the "more forward" the cast member appeared in relation to the other cast members. For example, 2D images representing navigational buttons were placed "on top" of the interior dashboard image. This caused them to appear "embedded" into the surface of the dash. I continued to build up the imagery on the dash, adding other 2D image cast members, gradually filling more channels in the score. This gradual layering of 2D images helped to create a believable patrol car interior (Fig. 51.7) "on stage."

The second step was to decide how long the cast would appear on stage and then program their function. As these 2D image cast-member functions were defined, other cast members, such as QuickTime movies, sound, text, and animation could be added.

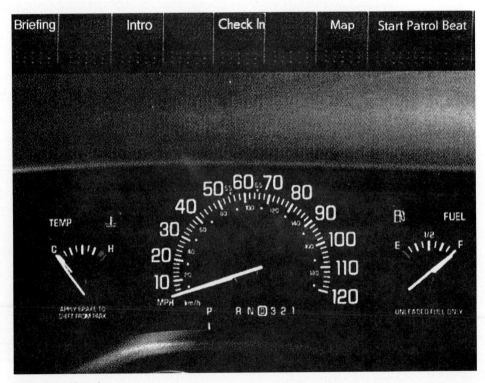

Figure 51.7 Menu bar.

Figure 51.8   Security.

Creating the interface

The interface function of the dummy began to take shape as we chose a "behind-the-wheel" viewpoint of the patrol car interior. This behind-the-wheel viewpoint became the "home base" for navigation. As mentioned, a row of buttons (embedded into the upper dash) provided navigation to the various learning modules of the patrol car. The function of these buttons is briefly described:

The check-in button. When the "Check-In" button is pressed, immediately a click sound is heard and an animation of a descending clipboard is initiated. This (image of a) clipboard has several text fields that allow the cadet to enter his or her name, password, etc. Once the cadet has entered this information, the clipboard cast member exits "upper center stage." After checking in (Fig. 51.8), the cadet can then begin his "Briefing."

The briefing button. The Briefing button initiates the CBT, drill, and practice module. When the Briefing button is pressed, a full-frame PICT animation, with sound, occurs. This provides a transition to the car door/rear-view mirror Briefing module. The sequential PICT animation is a close-up view of a key turning in the ignition slot on the post of the steering wheel. (This quick-action animation can transition to just about any part of the patrol car metaphor

Figure 51.9 Onboard computer.

without affecting the "suspension of disbelief".) The rear-view mirror then "morphs" into a close-up view of the mirror, which instantly displays a QuickTime movie of a "talking head" (field training officer) introducing the CBT and the Patrol curriculum objectives. The entire transition is a sequential PICT file animation leading to the rear-view mirror metaphor, which contains/displays the QuickTime movie. From there, the cadet can progress through the CBT material at his or her own pace, using buttons located in the door/rear-view mirror metaphor (Fig. 51.9).

The start-your-beat button. To start your beat, this button begins a panning motion (a transition found in Director), revealing the right side of the interior dash. Here, the cadet can use a simulated pushbutton phone mechanism to activate an adjacent text display screen (Fig. 51.10). The scenario pushbutton options are based on extracted functions of the radio—the basic information center of the patrol car. There are nine push buttons. Six of these represent different scenario options for the cadet to "experience." Scenarios include Traffic Stops, K-9 Patrol, and Pedestrian Arrest. The remaining three buttons provide a return function, course map help, and further navigation through the courseware (Fig. 51.11).

The scenarios

When the cadet selects a scenario, a PDA (Personal Digital Assistant) kind of quizzer ascends from bottom middle stage. This quizzer is a PICT cast member adapted from a car-interior AC device and is divided into two sections. The top section displays QuickTime scenario movies. The bottom half displays the text, the observation button and the task list. Once the quizzer is up, immediately a scenario video begins to play, putting the cadet in a position to make observations and take action from the task list. Both observations and actions result in scenario branching consequences. For the dummy, we focused primarily on the Traffic Stop. We had video footage from the script that Gary Robbins developed and we needed to implement only a small portion of that for the dummy (Fig. 51.12).

For example, in our Traffic Stop scenario, the cadet experiences the violation (through the quizzer video window)—a Ford Mustang running a stop sign. If he misses the violation, the video continues, but eventually stops. The field training officer appears in the video window of the quizzer and prompts the cadet to start again and to watch more carefully. The action eventually leads to the pullover, and the occupant is asked for his driver's license. At this point in the video, the driver begins to open the glove box. If the cadet fails to observe this action, the video branches and the driver immediately pulls a revolver from the glove compartment and fires into the face of the cadet—and

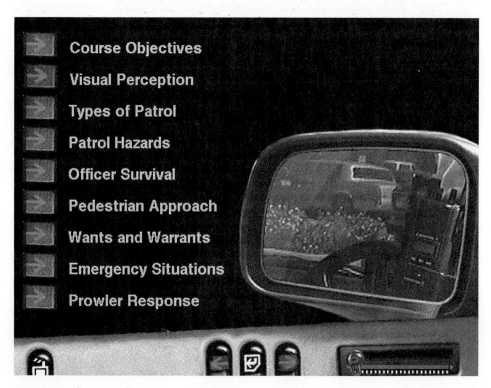

Figure 51.10   Course outline.

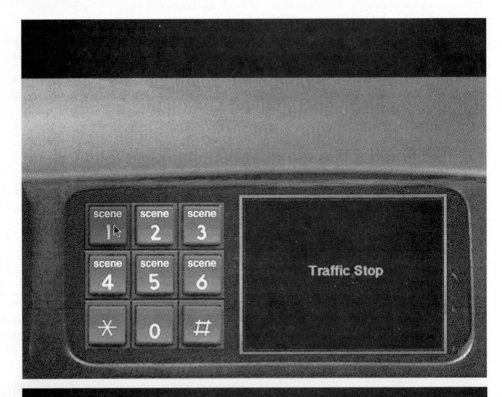

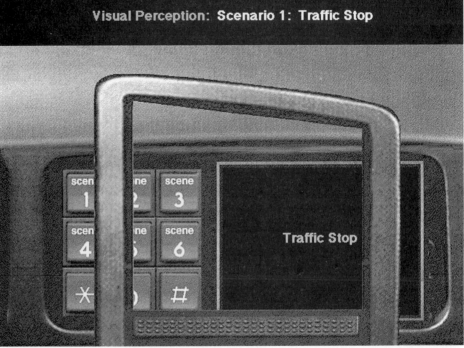

Figure 51.11 Traffic stop simulation.

Figure 51.12 Make observation task.

the screen then goes red. The onscreen mentor (Field Training Officer) then appears in the quizzer video window and advises the cadet to always watch the driver's hands. The recruit then is prompted to either start again or return for more "Briefing."

Videotaping scenarios

To prototype the scenario section, we decided to quickly improvise a quick shoot of the Traffic stop. Gary Robbins offered himself in uniform, Mike was a willing talent, and I was the eye behind the camera. Mike volunteered his Ford Mustang, sunglasses, and an attitude. Gary provided the "on-the-job " expertise, his patrol car, radio, and gun. I took the college Panasonic S-VHS camcorder and played shadow to Gary. Within one hour, we had "improvised" a traffic stop with three branching options centered around the glove box. Gary performed the initial pullover, with his shadow (me) following uncomfortably close behind—in semi-first person. Gary approached Mike according to patrol standard and asked him for his driver's license and registration. Here, we staged three outcomes that branched from Mike's hand reaching for the glove box. First, the normal outcome showed Mike handing over the requested items. Second, Mike is shown opening the glove box, revealing the hand gun as Gary states, "Sir, don't touch that gun." The camera then zooms in. Third,

Mike is shown opening the glove box and immediately pulling out the gun to shoot Gary. The (empty) gun is quickly aimed into the lens of the camera.

With this "sketch" video footage, I was able to return to my office, digitize the video clips (at Super-VHS quality), using the VideoVision Studio, and create QuickTime (QT) Cast members for Director. Within several sittings, I was able to implement the QT clips into the Scenario PDA quizzer to illustrate the functionality of the dummy.

With the necessary "cast" on "stage," a functional interface providing transitions to other interior "scenes" of the patrol car, and some basic CBT and scenario content, the beat dummy or "Alpha" was complete. The project was presented at a CJI Conference in Tampa and we "checked off" once more—and again, just in time!

Transitioning to production

Once our concept and prototype were accepted, we immediately went into production. A larger "in-house" team began to form, which included an instructional designer from the college, Julie Capsambelis. Julie began to work with Mike organizing the flow of content going into the BEAT CBT module. We also hired a programmer, Bill Tonnies, who was contracted from a local interactive media training company (Sealund and Associates). Bill, under Mike's coordination, began to quickly "flesh out" the CBT shell on one of the new PowerMac 8100s that had just arrived. This helped to establish a central computer platform for the "Production" or "Beta" version of the project. Larry Strickland, in addition to setting up the Beat Windows NT server (which served as our community bin for sharing resources), began to program X-objects for Director. These X-objects were designed so that student records could be input and output from the "Check In" module of the program. Other outside help was contracted from another local company, REGGAE, Inc. This interactive multimedia group provided considerable graphics support by producing "tons" of CBT visuals and animations. They also produced the CBT test module. Mike as a good coordinator, was starting to "stoke the fire."

Working with Mike in production was great. Because he also was a designer, we seemed to speak the same "visual" language. As a coordinator, he was very supportive of my art direction initiatives. He was also very receptive to new, "visually oriented" interface ideas. This synergy, I believe, really helped to lead to the eventual success of the project.

In production, my role began to shift from being a "jack of all trades" multimedia designer to that of full-time art director. I still functioned as a designer, but my focus was more on refining the interface. From that perspective, I began to oversee the "look and feel" of the entire project, offering art direction to help maintain a consistent visual format, based on the patrol car metaphor.

This was not to be done in a vacuum. The expanded team dynamic called for more communication, as we were beginning to affect the production version from at least four different perspectives: programming, instructional design, graphics/animation and interface design. Mike was a good catalyst for keeping us all producing at maximum potential.

Redefining the beat interface

With this growth in productivity, interface standards needed to be set for both sound and visuals. With the arrival of more content, the first challenge was balancing the need for screen real estate while still maintaining an uncluttered and consistent "suspension of disbelief."

To maintain the consistency of the interface, we decided to (1) stay within our current metaphor and not introduce other metaphors, and (2) limit color, typefaces, sounds, and other visual distracters to keep proper focus on the content.

Staying within the metaphor. We found the refinements of the interface in the patrol car environment itself. For the CBT interface, the walkie talkie, the car door, and the rear view mirror were the primary inspiration for refinement.

The walkie talkie (WT) key pad was expanded for courseware navigation. Bill quickly programmed rollover capabilities into the WT keypad buttons to show the function in the LED display just above the WT keypad. The keypad buttons provided navigation to the curriculum objectives, the Patrol Beat scenario section, Checkout, the Testing module, Glossary, and Help. Audio was used from a sound effects library CD for the "TouchTone" quality of sound—found in most TouchTone phones. We always tried to preserve a sense of reality through sound and movement when "re-purposing" these devices to maintain a suspension of disbelief. The WT was "summoned" by clicking on a custom button "layered" onto the left side of the car door. When the button was pressed, the WT popped up (a 5 to 10 frame animation) from the bottom stage left. Buttons were also included on the WT to "send it back down" and to control volume. All these additional buttons were "carved out" of the existing controls on the original WT image and then redesigned for their particular function (Fig. 51.13).

The upper section of the car door was used to frame the lower portion of the CBT Briefing screen. Gadgets from the car door, such as electric window controls, were customized for "paging" forward and backward. Another air-conditioning slider device was customized to provide quick "scans" of the CBT courseware. A return button (located between the "paging" buttons) would allow for return to the original location after scanning. All these functions were integrated into the car door to help create a believable environment for interactivity.

The rear-view mirror (RVM) was slightly enlarged to quarter-screen size and was placed in the lower right portion of the screen or stage, just above the car door. The RVM was used to "visualize" the courseware content, becoming a CBT "viewer" for images, animation, and text. The courseware objectives were displayed, as bulleted text in the left portion of the screen. Images and animation would dissolve or pass by in the rear-view mirror. These images and animations in the RVM served to illustrate the adjacent text (Fig. 51.14).

The only problem with this version of the RVM was the size and angle. Because of the need to show QuickTime movies direct to stage in Director (primarily for the Windows version), the mirror had to be further enlarged

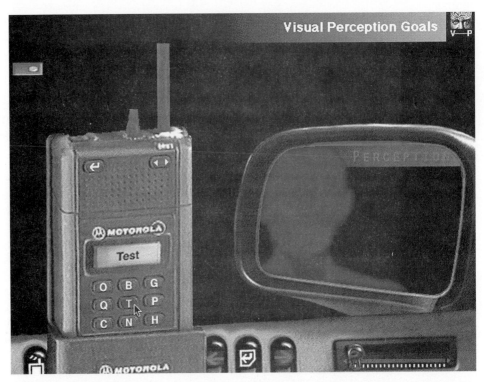

Figure 51.13 Perception screen.

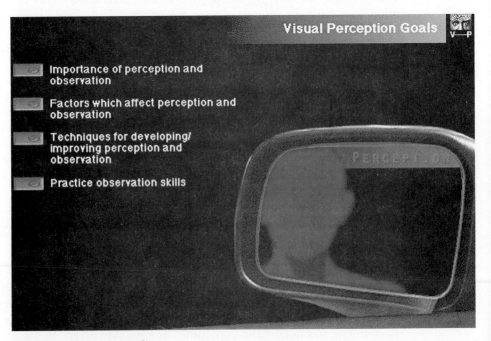

Figure 51.14 Perception outline

and tilted to a "straight-on view" or rectangular format. This change to the RVM took too much screen real estate, making it impossible to display adjacent bulleted text. To get around this, I chose to have two different versions of the RVM. The smaller RVM was fine for most generic CBT functions, but when we needed to show a QuickTime movie, we morphed (as described before) to the larger RVM version, including zooming sound effects. (This technique actually proved very effective in grabbing the imagination of the cadet, giving a signal that something important was about to happen.) When the QT movie was over, the RVM would morph back down to the original size and angle. (This same technique, of zooming into the larger RVM, was used to access the glossary information.)

Interface production notes. All the interface images were edited in Adobe Photoshop and imported as cast members into Director. I would then make final adjustments in Director. (It's always a good idea to do final touch-up in Director—especially with silhouette images on a white background. Artifacts usually remain associated with an image "on stage" when the "background transparent" function is used in Director.) As the interface designer, I would send a new Director movie with the new interface "cast" to the BEAT Server through the College network. From there, Bill would copy the Director file to the Mac 8100 (the programming production machine), open the file, and copy/paste the new cast members into the CBT Beta. After "pasting" the new cast members into the Beta, he would begin to program their function.

This production process worked great from a design perspective, as well as from a programming perspective. As a designer, it was important for me to get involved with the authoring and programming for two reasons. Initially, it really helped to have programming skills to present early prototypes for "check off." It also helped for demonstrating new prototypes to the development team, including the programmer. Second, being "clued in" on how things are scripted helps when working with a programmer in production. This goes both ways. For example, I could prepare all of the graphic elements for the walkie-talkie and anticipate exactly what Bill would need for programming, without interrupting him. On the other side, Bill could send me some basic Lingo "code" for developing a scenario concept. I could then "run with it" in demonstrating a prototype to the development team. Overall, as a designer, I know that it helps to understand authoring limitations and possibilities, which in turn helps to make the programmer's job easier. It was great to work with someone as competent as Bill, and his expertise and energy helped to make my job much easier.

Final production details

By establishing a production process in creating a dummy, the final production was an echo of that same process on a much larger scale. The various cast members of the dummy were "place holders" for the final cast.

Scenario module. In the Scenario module, for example, the old Traffic Stop (TS) QuickTime movies of Mike and Gary were updated with new versions that showed plain clothes detectives in an undercover black Mustang. Old "place holder" QT movies were replaced with real mentors giving recruits feedback on specific branching consequences in the TS scenario. Temporary radio sounds and effects were replaced with final audio "recorded on location." The cast members were different, but the process for creating them was the same.

Some unexpected surprises occurred, however, that affected our production schedule. This is just one example of how the scenario section content began to "grow" in size and complexity. We had planned to include fake radio dispatching after the final TS videos were shot. The content expert, Gary Robbins, was instrumental in setting up this condition. Sometimes, because of emergencies, he had to cancel meetings and it became necessary to work around his schedule. Gary and I were up one night until 3 A.M. at the St. Petersburg Police Station creating these fictitious radio calls and station dispatches. These radio calls were then edited into the final Traffic Stop videos, just in time for final implementation.

CBT module. For the CBT module, I continued to meet with Mike and Julie to discuss the relationship of new content to the CBT interface. I also began working closely with Bill to make screen layout adjustments. We were able to quickly adjust the text, color, and sound to match our interface standards. With all this new content coming in, my job as an art director was to maintain a consistent "look and feel." These were some of the issues that surfaced during production on the CBT Briefing module.

Bullets. In the CBT Dummy, we originally used images of "bullet shells" for the text indicators. It was a fun approach at first. The "bullets" would blink until pressed. When pressed, they would "shoot," sending the slug horizontally across the screen with the new text trailing behind. (We digitized audio of guns firing, etc., and each bullet had a different "gun shot" sound when pressed.) Initially, this was entertaining and seemed to be motivating for moving through the course material, but as we began to "live" with the interface, it became more and more annoying. We went back to our list of interface standards and decided that the bullet idea, although part of the patrol experience, went beyond the patrol car metaphor, and that it drew more attention to itself than to the content. We went back to a more generic text indicator, which was more consistent with the patrol car metaphor (Fig. 51.15).

Layout. Another issue was screen layout. This included the organization of text on the CBT screen, choice of typeface, and color. As different modules of the CBT began to be developed, the text would sometimes appear in "nonstandard" places. One CBT screen would have text appearing slightly higher, another slightly lower. Some screens would have text centered, others flush left. We again went back to our interface standards list and chose to establish

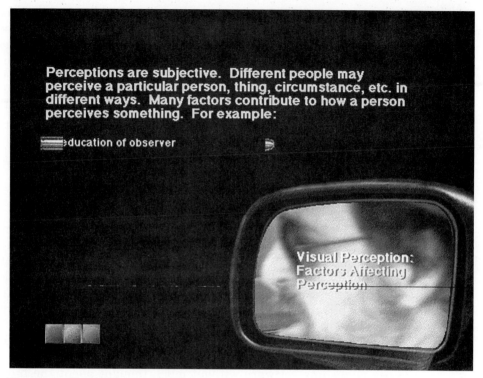

Figure 51.15 Perceptions are subjective.

a simple grid for the placement of text. We also decided on a standard layout for the title header and created a small icon representing the specific material being covered, such as Visual Perception, Patrol Hazards, or Types of Patrol.

We chose a sans serif typeface for simplicity and because it followed the patrol car metaphor. The color was limited to two or three standard choices based on colors used within the metaphor. One example of the need for layout consistency occurred when REGGAE, Inc. brought in the Test module. The programmer had done a magnificent job on the module, but in the process, because of screen real estate issues, the car door had been shifted down and the rear-view mirror had slightly shrunk. The text was much smaller and different colors were used. With a little tweaking, we were able to use the same size car door and RVM, and arrange the text according to the previous set standards. As a result, the interface didn't "jump around" or distract from the content. These adjustments all helped to preserve the "suspension of disbelief."

CD-ROM testing

While focusing on all these details, it was easy to lose sight of the big PICTure. The final step, just as with the first concept piece, was to use the college network to put all the various Director movies or modules together on one computer. All of the pieces eventually came back to my computer to be placed on an external hard drive specifically "partitioned" for CD-ROM recording. The hard drive volume was partitioned at 625 MB and easily contained all the various Director files, projectors, QuickTime movies, and audio files needed for the BEAT project. After adjusting the way we wanted to organize the resources on the CD and tweaking the directory paths in Director—after all that, everything worked, right? Not exactly. We had some connectivity bugs to work out, but we were certainly "in the ball park." With another week of CD-ROM testing, we were finished with the BEAT Beta and the first phase of the project was complete—just in time.

An Instructional Designer's Perspective

Julie Capsambelis

Multi what? Okay, I had actually heard of multimedia, but had no experience with it. I have been an instructional designer, developer, and sometimes trainer for a dozen years or so. I have developed instructional programs in a variety of formats—nonautomated self-instructional materials, classroom delivery materials, linear video, and an early version of interactive video. So, what's the problem? Surely I could apply what I know to any type of instructional program. That proved true—to a point.

I have always been the type who really doesn't care why boats float or planes fly. I just expect them to. I have felt the same way about computers. I use publishing software without much thought about the programming or hardware involved. I just expect it to work, and work quickly, at the touch of a key or the click of a mouse. This approach does not lend itself well to a technical multimedia project. Although the same instructional "rules" apply, I had to make some adjustments. The overall lesson I learned was that I had to find a balance between the "old school" instructional design approach and the capabilities and limits of our new technology.

When I received my first call to come to a meeting for this project, the project coordinator and technical folks had already done a significant amount of work on the first module. They had some nerve not involving the instructional designer early on! How could they have survived to this point in the project—even with a comprehensive list of objectives from the State of Florida and access to subject matter experts—without me? I soon learned there would not have been much for me to do until they determined what software and hardware would be used, and then went on to exterminate several different species of technical bugs.

This project was being managed on a "just in time" basis. Now it was time to explore the course content from an instructional-design point of view. I was given a demonstration of what I would call a prototype module segment on computer. It was cool. I couldn't believe how talented my new techno friends were! Immediately, I had a million ideas for my part of the project. Armed with the list of objectives and content outline, I went away to do some work on my own.

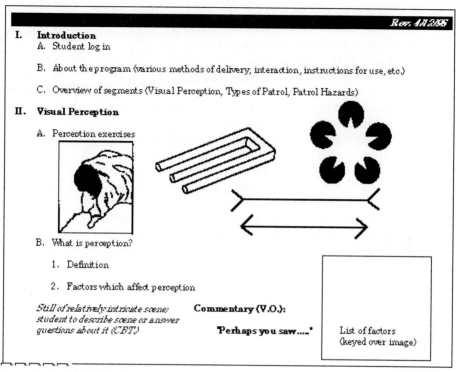

Figure 51.16 Protoyping.

Back in my office, I started to visualize the objectives coming to life on the computer screen. I developed what I called a content-and-delivery strategy outline for the objectives of our first module. I included illustrations and expanded descriptions that made it more like a story board than a content outline (Fig. 51.16).

While I was working on this, the project coordinator was having the objectives and content information from the state entered into our module, primarily in CBT format. This gave me a great base from which to work when our team got back together. I submitted my suggestions and the artists and technical persons made counter suggestions. We had several sessions like this that were really high energy and fun for me. Where the system could handle it, my suggestions were accepted and even improved upon—and where it couldn't, we agreed on alternative approaches. We ended up with a "first draft" module that contained a combination of CBT, QuickTime movies, animated segments, and still pictures, and illustrations.

Although I'd like to think I'm full of good ideas for all facets of a project, my most significant contribution on this project was probably on the CBT segments. The project coordinator provided me with hard copies of each screen in our first draft module. I used the hard copies to make my edits. I adopted a format in which I wrote the audio portion (primarily transitions, explanations, and feedback) and the text portion, and suggested any visual enhancements, such as illustrations for each screen. I found that I was removing much of the text content that had been "dumped" onto each screen. Full sentences that introduced the various content chunks were delivered as audio only. The text on each screen was pared down to single definitions or bulleted points. This increased the "white space" and helped the user focus on main points (Fig. 51.17 and 51.18).

Our CBT programming guy used these edited hard copies to make the changes to the module (Fig. 51.19 and 51.20).

The final version of our first module includes a course map, an introduction to the module, text, audio, video, animation, other visual enhancements, a notebook, a glossary, and a test.

As we begin development of our second module, we are using the "lessons learned" from the first module. I have learned a great deal, and although I still don't really know all the details about what makes this boat float, I feel a bit smarter about multimedia than I was prior to this project.

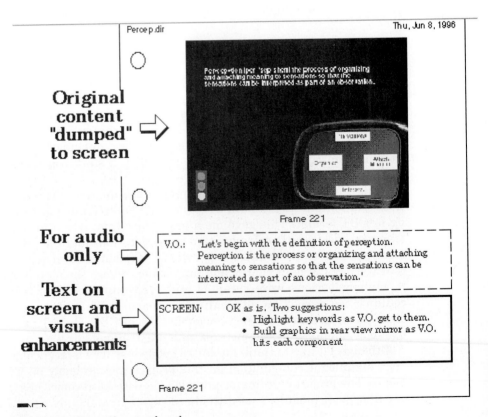

Figure 51.17 Perception storyboard.

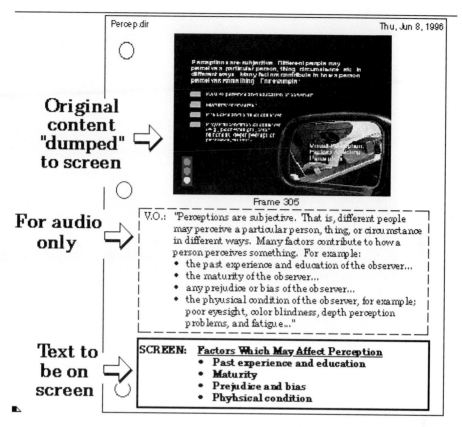

Original content "dumped" to screen

For audio only

Text to be on screen

Figure 51.18   Perception storyboard.

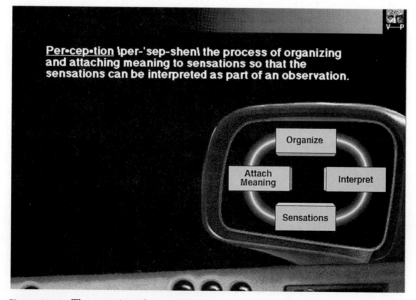

Figure 51.19   The meaning of perception.

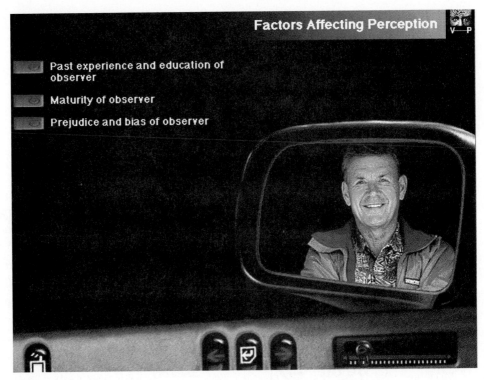

Figure 51.20 Perception factors.

A Lingo Programmer's Perspective

Bill Tonnies

As an outside contractor on the project, I was not entirely certain of what my role on the project was to be (or the roles of the other members of the team, for that matter). I even had doubts that we would be able to produce a cohesive product. One advantage of the situation was that I would be working onsite, which allowed rapid feedback on my work and continuous interaction with other members of the team.

A preliminary design had been established for the project's user interface, but the interface still had to be implemented. When it came time to actually start full-bore development on the project, the BEAT team found itself lacking the manpower that could be dedicated to the undertaking. The team contracted with Sealund & Associates, a local training and consulting firm, to supply someone with the necessary Director and Lingo background.

The first milestone I was to undertake was to get the Visual Perception module into a state so that it could be presented at a law enforcement multimedia conference. In keeping with the automobile motif established for the learning environment, we chose to use a traffic light metaphor. The student could click on the red, yellow, and green buttons to move backward through the course, access a control panel or move to the next screen in the course, respectively.

To present the content, which consisted of lists of bulleted items, we used a graphic of an actual bullet as the "bullet" on the screen. To further add interest to this concept, the on-screen bullets would flash and emit randomized gunshot sounds when clicked (Fig. 51.21).

With these enhancements, my participation in the first phase of the project was complete.

One-and-a-half months later, I was called in again to work on finalizing the interface for Visual Perception. In the interim, the team had being doing some major revamping of the interface. The traffic light navigation tool was replaced with buttons located on the inside of the car door, which serves as the frame through which the student views the training. Also, the gunshot sounds accompanying the bullets were replaced with a more subdued click. (The gunshot sounds were humorous at first, but quickly became tiresome.)

The greatest surprise awaiting me was that the team wanted to include some new interface elements. The first was a walkie-talkie that the student could summon at any point throughout the training. The walkie-talkie would serve as the control panel from which the user could exit the course, access a glossary, access a notebook in which to take notes and change the volume level of the audio in the course, among other things.

The inclusion of the walkie-talkie forced me to analyze my use of the script channels provided by Director. I decided that channels 1 through 24 would be

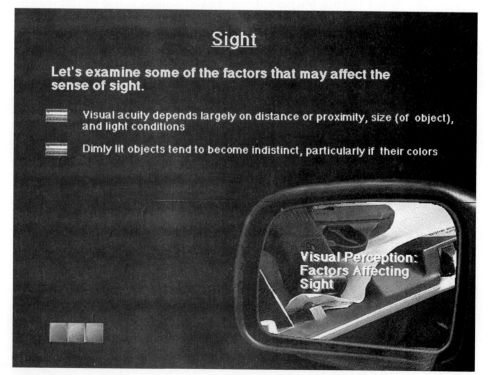

Figure 51.21 Sight task.

used for cast members involved in presenting the content. Channels 25 through 48 would be reserved for cast members used to implement the interface. This allowed me to change channels 1 through 24 into puppet sprites when the walkie-talkie was summoned, thus leaving the content in the background.

The other addition to the user interface was a slider knob the student could use to quickly move through the course. When the student drags the slider to a new location along its path, the training proceeds from that point. Also, as the student proceeds through the course, the slider moves along its path.

This presented a much greater challenge. First, I had to come up with a logical way for the slider to move through the course. I settled on building a list of marker names, representing the module objectives, which would be referenced as the slider moved. Fortunately, Lingo does not exit the script it is executing when it encounters a go to (at least within the same movie). This allowed my script to continuously query the mouse's position and continue going to different frames as the student moved the slider. The correct list element was selected by determining the ratio of the sliders distance from the beginning of the path to the length of the entire path and multiplying by the number of list elements and adding one. A portion of the slider logic is illustrated in Fig. 51.22.

With the ability to arbitrarily jump to different locations in the course, we decided we needed a way for the student to return to his or her previous location in the course. We had an extra button in the interface that could be allocated to this purpose. Once again, I used a list to implement a stack that could hold a predefined number of previous locations (we chose three). When the student moved the slider, the previous location in the course was pushed onto the stack. When the student pressed the return button, the topmost location on the stack was "popped off," then accessed.

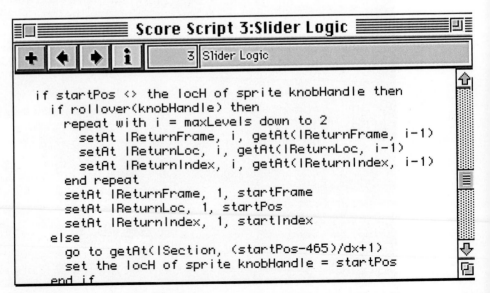

```
if startPos <> the locH of sprite knobHandle then
    if rollover(knobHandle) then
        repeat with i = maxLevels down to 2
            setAt lReturnFrame, i, getAt(lReturnFrame, i-1)
            setAt lReturnLoc, i, getAt(lReturnLoc, i-1)
            setAt lReturnIndex, i, getAt(lReturnIndex, i-1)
        end repeat
        setAt lReturnFrame, 1, startFrame
        setAt lReturnLoc, 1, startPos
        setAt lReturnIndex, 1, startIndex
    else
        go to getAt(lSection, (startPos-465)/dx+1)
        set the locH of sprite knobHandle = startPos
    end if
```

Figure 51.22   Score script for slider logic.

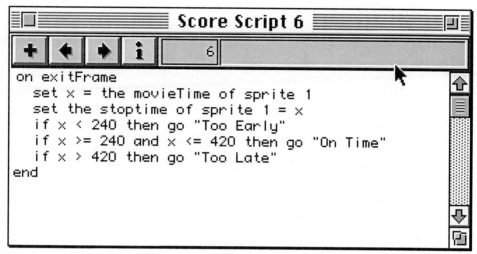

```
Score Script 6
6
on exitFrame
    set x = the movieTime of sprite 1
    set the stoptime of sprite 1 = x
    if x < 240 then go "Too Early"
    if x >= 240 and x <= 420 then go "On Time"
    if x > 420 then go "Too Late"
end
```

Figure 51.23 Sample code.

To allow the slider to move automatically as the course progressed, I used an "on enterFrame" movie script that found the ratio of the difference between the current frame number and the previous objective markers frame number, and the difference between the next objective markers frame number and the previous objective markers frame number. This would locate the knob in the proper location on its path.

Using an "on enterFrame" movie script necessitated using an "on enterFrame" script in the script channels associated with the walkie-talkie and notebook functions. This script simply performed a "dontPassEvent," which stopped the slider's position from being updated. This was important because the walkie-talkie and notebook logic was after the last frame of content and the slider would have been positioned to an invalid location.

Another interesting facet that had to be integrated into the project was the video scenarios in which the student is presented with a QuickTime video. The student is required to make appropriate observations and "call in" via clicking on a button on the screen when the appropriate observation is made. This would be perhaps the greatest indicator of the effectiveness of the training up to this point.

For the scenarios to be effective, it was necessary to devise a way in which a "window of opportunity" could be imposed on when the student could "call in." The training would branch based on whether the student called in before, during, or after this window. Fortunately, Director provides facilities for controlling and monitoring QuickTime videos and the process became fairly straightforward.

The instructors would determine at which point during the video the significant event occurs and how long after the event occurs a valid "call in" can occur. These times could be converted to ticks (1/60 of a second) and compared to the value returned by the movieTime property. An example of this function is illustrated in Fig. 51.23.

In the example, the first statement stores the current movie time in a variable. This is done (rather than use the movieTime in each subsequent step) because the movie continues to run after the student "calls in" and the "window of opportunity" might expire during the execution of the script. The next statement stops the movie at the point when the student "called in." Finally, the last three statements compare the student's "call-in time" with the parameters established for this scenario. In this case, the student is viewing a car running a stop sign. The car passes the stop sign at four seconds into the movie (240 ticks). If the student waits longer than three seconds (180 ticks, or a total of 420 ticks into the movie), then the car will have gotten away.

Other enhancements made to the interface involved heavy use of rollovers. For example, when the walkie-talkie is summoned, as the student moves the mouse over each button, the button's function is displayed on the walkie-talkie's LCD panel.

Additionally, all buttons were made to darken when clicked. For this, I created a "pressButton" handler located in a movie script. The handler takes up to four parameters: the sprite channel containing the sprite to modify, the cast numbers of the darkened and normal sprite, and an optional sound to be used in place of the standard click used throughout the course. The handler monitors the rollover status of the sprite so that if the student moves the mouse away from the sprite, the sprite returns to normal.

At this stage, all the interface logic is in place and all that remains is some final tweaking of the locations of visual elements on the screen. We are also considering replacing the bullet "bullet" with something more innocuous.

The project is still undergoing some final tweaking in the audio and incorporation of graphics and animations being provided by another vendor. The training will shortly undergo testing before being presented to the cadets.

I have found this project to be a rewarding experience altogether. Although I was an outside contractor, I was never treated like one—and at times didn't act too much like one either. Working on site allowed a seamless integration of my work with other team members' input and we (hopefully) were able to produce a successful and effective training program.

Final Notes from the Coordinator

Nothing is ever as easy as it looks. From the beginning of the project, both Tim and I knew that there were many interface issues to resolve. Each part of the project needed to be developed, then refined to make a seamless package. As coordinator, it was my job to attempt to convert existing objectives into a multimedia package that utilized as many of the capabilities of the system as possible. Although we had many of the people needed to do this here at SPJC, we also used several outside consultants during critical periods. The main advantage of this approach is that we were able to double our efforts during these periods. This combined effort allowed us to meet several important deadlines.

In the beginning, I knew that most of the work would be occurring at the end of the project. BEAT started as a fairly simple idea, but changed into something much more complex as we began production. Several good ideas for interface design and navigation controls were conceived at the end of the project. Although multimedia projects should always be planned thoroughly from the beginning, be prepared for the workload to increase as the project moves toward completion. Little changes frequently have much more impact on production deadlines than can be imagined, and as the project grows, changes become increasingly complex. (Screen shot of module with radio.)

During the evolution of the project, the team developed the concepts needed to present the objectives now being taught traditionally. The subject areas were Visual Perception, Types of Patrol, and Patrol Hazards. We also analyzed the methods that would be used to represent each objective. After some consideration, I decided to call on several other designers and programmers I knew locally, to provide some consulting on the overall design and production of the objective modules.

With a little help from our friends

The first multimedia consultant I contacted was a friend of mine, Roger Green, who owns his own company, REGGAE Inc. Roger's background in electronic imaging includes some very serious use of Photoshop, Premiere, and Director, as well as a couple dozen other imaging programs. His associates, Jerry White of Great White Graphics and Bill Villers of WSV Consulting, rounded out his team. Jerry is an excellent illustrator and has been working with Roger on several Director projects. Bill is a cross-platform expert and runs his own integration company.

Once we started working on BEAT, I brought them a draft copy of the project and asked for some ideas of how we might animate the objectives. At the same time, I asked Bill if he would work on a testing module similar to the one he had demonstrated in the networking project. Roger and Bill suggested we also use Jerry White for the illustrations that would be used to animate the objectives. Because they were already working together on an interactive catalog project, it made sense to use all three of them on this project. The lesson here is, spend a little time getting to know the local consultants. You never know how they can help you until you talk to them about your project needs.

The end result was an excellent blending of skills. I was also able to dramatically increase my productivity by using outside consultants. Because I knew Roger really well, I was confident that we could keep things on track with Jerry and Bill. To get them started, we copied a complete set of interface elements onto a Syquest disk and transferred them to Roger and Bill's system. In the end, everything came together perfectly. Each of the consultants knew what the other was doing. They provided us with a master shared cast file containing all the PICTs needed to create the animations in Director. Bill Toonies, our Lingo programmer, positioned the animations in the final Director movies, based on samples created by Roger. What can I say? You get lucky every once in a while. Things worked out right on deadline. I found out later that all three consultants burned a ton of midnight oil to get things done. Even now, I still call them just to say thanks for doing a great job. Remember, you can never say thank you too much! (Fig. 51.24).

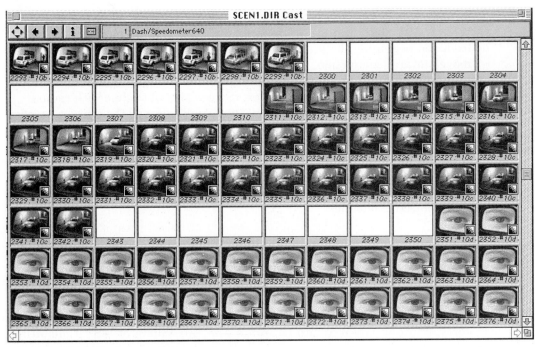

Figure 51.24 Dash/speedometer clips.

Finally, Bill was able to produce an excellent testing module that included some very original programming. Tim worked with Bill to fine-tune the layout for the screens and Bill made the final adjustments. The test module was created on a separate Director movie. Our idea was to be able to place it at the end of each of the objectives as a drill and practice section.

Our use of outside consultants ended up being a lifesaver. As the deadline for our final test came closer and closer, I was able to use the consultants to increase our productivity. I think we could have accomplished much of what was needed without them, but we would have not been able to incorporate any of the interface design improvements that we needed. At one point during production, we had four consultants—with Tim and I—all working on final revisions. This expanded team approach allowed us to put in a considerable amount of extra time on the project. We added and refined content, while making the necessary adjustments to the interface design. The lesson to be learned here is that the workload will increase as the project evolves. Always have a contingency plan for increasing production to meet critical deadlines. I knew that we would need additional help, and had planned from the beginning to use consultants to increase productivity. By adding more consultants, I was able to make all the necessary interface changes, and still keep the project on schedule.

Project testing

Testing is quite possibly one of the most overlooked phases of multimedia development. Early testing of each version of the BEAT interface design led to a variety of important changes. The size and position of text, interface controls, and scripting of interface functions are all critical revisions made to BEAT during testing. Much of the testing was done by Tim Brock and I, using an ongoing test-and-revise approach. Each week we would meet and go over the schedule for the following week. This became a regular process of combining Tim's interface designs with concepts for delivering the course objectives. As each version of BEAT was completed, other team members were then asked to review the work and provide feedback.

Cross-platform testing became a major goal later in the project. We set up a test machine based on the same system being used in the classroom. This test machine was connected to the network and files were regularly sent to it for cross-platform evaluation. In the end, this became a standardized method of producing the final test version. We started each phase on the Macintosh, then passed the files to the Compaq test machine running Windows. For the most part, things went smoothly. However, we found some variations in QuickTime for Windows vs. QuickTime for the Mac and made a few changes in the scripting to compensate. Additionally, we found that certain typeface revisions needed to be made because of the difference in operating system fonts.

Another important revision, which was the result of cross-platform testing, was the extensive use of animations. The animations were created from a series of PICT images made from video frame grabs, instead of QuickTime movies. Ongoing testing revealed that the PICT images played much faster than the equivalent QuickTime movie. Technical considerations like this can have a tremendous impact on the final quality of your multimedia project. The bottom line is, test every element, script, animation, or movie on the platform that will be used to deliver the final project. It's going to take more work than you think to finalize things, so allow some extra time at the end for testing (Fig. 51.25).

Student testing

Because our project was designed to teach specific patrol objectives, we needed a testing module to be used at the end of the objective section of the courseware. This testing module was produced by one of our consultants, Bill Villers. He provided us with a complete Director file that presented the student with 50 questions. Tim designed the interface controls and gave Bill several PICT images to place his test module in. Bill then produced a prototype and brought it by for evaluation. Tim and Bill finalized the design and it was linked to the existing BEAT courseware.

Figure 51.25   Video clips.

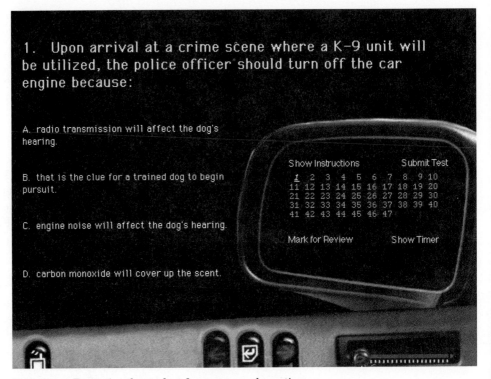

Figure 51.26 Prompting the student for unanswered questions.

Once the computerized test was completed by the cadet, the scores were sent to an X-object that saved them on the network server. The testing module also included a timer because the test was to be completed in an hour. The test questions could be viewed randomly and could be marked before they were answered. As answers were chosen, the color of the question number changed to indicate that an answer had been selected. Finally, the student was prompted if he or she had not answered all the questions before the test was submitted (Fig. 51.26).

Our final testing phase used the completed BEAT courseware and the testing module. The academy class was split into two groups. Half of the cadets attended the traditional class and the other half used the BEAT courseware, in the new multimedia lab. The class was scheduled for the normal five hours. At the end of each class, the student took the 50-question test. The students using the BEAT courseware finished in about four hours and the test results were very close to the traditional class. The cadets using BEAT actually scored a little higher than the students in the other class and they covered the material much faster. The overall comments about the courseware were very good. Suggestions were made by the cadets, and everyone enjoyed the opportunity to participate in the test.

A word to the wise

Don't try this at home, kids! Well, at least make sure someone experienced with multimedia is there to supervise. Things can get really ugly in a hurry. It pays to have someone onboard with a ton of experience. For our team, it was Larry Strickland. I can't even count the times Larry stepped in to provide some concise thinking and excellent direction at the beginning of this project. Larry helped out every time something really bad was going to happen. His configuration of the Windows NT network server was just one of the things he accomplished with little effort. Larry also suggested that we test everything under a beta copy of Windows '95 to make sure BEAT would work on machines running the newest version of Windows, when it was released. I hated to admit it, but Larry was right again. One more thing to remember— always plan ahead. It pays to have a few experts around to help in the initial planning of a project. You never know, Windows '96 might be released next year. Just kidding! Oh, I almost forgot: Thanks, Larry!

In this section, I thought it would be good to tell you about some of the bad things that can happen. Until now everything that has been said has been pretty rosy. As we all know, things can go wrong, and frequently do—usually, at absolutely the last moment. For example, we are still replacing logic boards in one of our most important machines, the Power Macintosh that houses our Media 100 video digitizing system. We were fortunate because the College provided us with a Radius VideoVision Studio system that we were able to use as a backup to meet project deadlines. The system that keeps going down is Tim's production machine.

We were lucky a second time too; our consultants bailed us out by digitizing about a hundred images from video for us. I'm sure we'll pay them back somehow. Maybe the system will be up tomorrow. I think there's still an Apple technician working on the problem right now. Their service is really great. Thank goodness it's still under warranty.

Thankfully, nothing else really bad has happened. We all have had a few late nights trying to get ready for presentations and testing. Just remember, more is better! More people, more consultants, more memory—especially more time. I recently talked to Roger Green, who is one of the consultants. He told me that he was burning the second CD-ROM archive disk, for a total of 1.2 GB. This is just to store his original files for the animations he created for the Visual Perception objectives. The shared cast file he provided us has grown to about 50 MB. Be sure that you consider the size of your project, including all support files. These things sometimes get swept under the carpet. *Be sure to get a large hard drive, or two!* Just remember, more is also more!

Oh yeah, about the time thing. It always takes more time to do it over than to do it right in the first place. I know, I know—it's an easy thing to say when you're in a meeting, and a whole different story when it's midnight and your presentation is due at 9 o'clock the next morning. OK, just remember this. It takes time to do it right! Sure, you might already know this, but it does bear repeating once in a while.

Closing Thoughts from the Project Coordinator

I still have difficulty explaining to my friends what I do for a living. Multimedia Development isn't a very common job title. I'm still trying to define what multimedia really is. BEAT is a concrete example of what we had in mind when we started the project. Interactive multimedia training is a proven concept. I think the fact that we had created something unique finally began to sink in after our final test. We went from a "pie-in-the-sky" concept, started less than a year ago, to a beta version of actual courseware being used to teach an academy class. BEAT has become a reality. Oh, I'm sure we'll make some minor changes before all's said and done, but it's a really solid package now. I also think we all believe that BEAT thoroughly demonstrates the capabilities of using multimedia for computer-based training. By programming dynamic links between animations, video, and sound, we have created an instructional environment that presents information on a whole new level.

The X-generation cadet will be able to learn a variety of skills from multimedia courseware, and access even more information from the Internet. This dynamic relationship between student and subject matter will evolve into a very powerful new medium delivered by very fast multimedia computers. I recently read an on-line article that showed a chart of Power PC chips being developed. A 600-MHz chip was slated for 1997. I nearly fell out of the chair, 600 MHz; that bears repeating! I can't even imagine a computer that fast. With those kinds of speeds just around the corner, I don't think full-screen, full-motion video is going to be a problem. Oh, that leads us to future storage methods. One of the new devices I saw specs on was a 6× CD-ROM drive that can store more than 3 GB of information. One article said that multilayer CD-ROMs can hold more than 5 GB of information. We should begin seeing these for sale sometime in the next two years.

Video conferencing over the Internet will also contribute to this miraculous evolution of technology. Alliances between companies such as Netscape, Macromedia, and Adobe will create an entirely new delivery method. Three-dimensional multimedia front-ends, with real-time links to Internet resources are just around the corner. The virtual classroom of tomorrow will be truly something to see. BEAT is just the tip of the instructional iceberg. On-line multimedia interactive technology is just beneath the surface of this vastly changing technological sea. Just be ready to catch the next wave of the future, it's going to be a big one.

Digital Editing:
The Key to Digital Production

Alan Briggs

Fact:

- Broadcast-standard television programs can be made using domestic video-cameras and a domestic PC.

- Current television production budgets can be cut by 75% using a domestic PC.

- Television production schedules can be cut by 50% using a current PC.

- Every day, more cable-TV stations come on line. Next year, these will be even further multiplied by the advent of digital television. They need more programs. These programs can be made on current domestic computers.

- PC-produced programs look and sound no different than filmed or taped programs.

- Fortunes are waiting to be made by anyone willing to be first in this area. This single fact alone will mean that, whatever the "old-timers" and "established professionals" might feel, a great many newcomers will soon jump onto this bandwagon, just for the sake of the money. No experience required, just some time to get to grips with a computer! Professionals: ignore this at your peril!

When it comes right down to it, there's an awful lot of kit out there that claims to be the right thing for you if you want to use your computer to record video and edit it into something watchable.

The first thing I can honestly suggest is that before you actually part with your money, phone the manufacturer, and ask them to tell you where you can see a working demonstration. If they can't show you it in action, don't buy it.

Simple. It's your money. If you want to throw it around, do so. If you want value for your money, take a look at what you're about to buy. And remember: if they won't let you see it in operation, ask yourself "Why?"

Now, let's look at what you actually want to do. You want to find out how to use a computer to turn out some kind of video productions that might enable you to make money, or at least will look fairly convincing when you play them back to your friends.

Digital Standards

Let's define the standards we're talking about. If your ambition is to come up with a piece of work that you might actually be able to sell on a professional level, then the standards we're looking at begin with an on-screen image that is at least in the 800-×-600 region. British TV is 768 × 576; in the US, it is slightly less. Anything else isn't real, won't sell, and will just waste your investment—unless this is just an expensive hobby for you. You have to be looking at kit that will give you full-motion video of 25 and/or 30 frames a second as well as 768 × 576. A lot of pretty boxes out there have big, bright letters claiming full-motion video, but they only have very tiny letters confessing that you'll only fill a quarter of a TV screen with their end result. And that isn't real, won't sell, and will just waste your money.

And if you're still limited to 256 colors, then it'll look like crap on video, unless you give up and settle for "arty, grainy black'n'white." And that isn't real, won't sell, and will still waste your money. 16-bit stereo sound is not necessary, but it's certainly preferable.

And now, here's a *major* issue, before you go any further: PC, Mac, or Amiga? Or something else, like a Silicon Graphics system? I started my exploration of this subject on a PC, because that was what I had at home, and this all grew out of a hobby that I was interested in.

But that was just my choice: if you've already got a computer, then your choice is also pretty much made for you. If you haven't, maybe you're already working for a video company, and they want to move over into computers as an expansion of the business, or maybe you're about to start your own business. Then, you have to decide what platform you will use.

All existing professionals will tell you the same thing: "Silicon Graphics are the BEST for this kind of business, but they are FRIGHTENINGLY expensive!"

Nowadays, they're only partly correct: today's PCs and Macs can do pretty much anything that a Silicon Graphics can do, but they might just take a little longer. And Silicon Graphics are DEFINITELY much more expensive. They're in a "Niche" position in the business; although they have brought prices down, their kit still works out way more expensive! They'll scream otherwise, but by the time you buy all the bits and pieces—especially the software, you won't get a lot of change out of £50,000 ($75,000) per workstation.

In reputation terms, the Mac has been progressing steadily in this area for some time, but because they're mainly used by companies, rather than individuals, their pricing is reflected in this: they cost more, though their dealers will do all they can to convince you otherwise.

However, two of the very best pieces of kit are available for the Mac, and only slowly coming to terms with the fact that the PC would be a vehicle for greater profits, if they entered this side of the marketplace.

The PC, however, being a personal computer, tends to be owned by individuals instead of companies. Individuals don't have the ability to throw money around the way some companies do, they don't have the access to company borrowing facilities, and they don't have the same level of income. PC manufacturers realized this a long time ago, and most of the digital production equipment for the PC is priced accordingly.

And then there was the dear old Amiga...From a dazzlingly good product, a huge market-share was established. Then the company got big and began to fall apart.

Loads of peripheral companies created wonderful kit, at "pocket money" prices for the Amiga, but Amiga blew it: they wound up running the company so far downhill that they couldn't even manage to save it by buying the company out from within. Now, they're just a name, owned by a big German PC company, and never really likely to recover.

Nonetheless, those peripheral companies, like Newtek, are moving over to the PC, and soon all those Amiga goodies will be available again. But I bet the prices won't be as low...

If you're entering the business "virgin," it doesn't really matter which computer you buy: you can do all that you need to do on any platform.

If super-speed is the issue, and money doesn't matter to you, and you want a "big guy" image, buy Silicon Graphics. If super-speed is the issue, and you don't have that much money, then buy several computers, and network them up to speed up the work. It's still cheaper than Silicon Graphics. But if price is the issue, then go for the PC: all the top-end Mac kit will be PC-available by the time this is published, and so will the equally good, but low-priced Amiga stuff.

So, you've done your research, and you know what you've got to spend. If you're already in the computer business, no problem! Just go out and do it. But for the newcomer to computers, it's got to be scary! What if computers are tough to learn? What if the software just threatens to fuzz up your brain? What if... ?

Hardware

It's easy! It's a breeze! But it can be agonizingly S-L-O-W-! (Not the learning: but the amount of time taken by the software to do even the most basic effects.) Now this depends largely on your machine, and its configuration. More RAM helps, for sure, and anything less than a 486 DX-2 66 MHz with a SCSI-drive will send you into fountains of frustration when it comes to running a preview, or saving a file. This is not essentially because the software isn't up to it, it's because you're asking the whole system to do so much.

Try this in your own machine—just load up a picture: any picture that has a screen size of 800 × 600, in 24-bit color. See how long that single frame takes to load up. Now think of a PAL video sequence, 15 seconds long, (375 frames), and another sequence 10 seconds, (250 frames), with a simple cross-fade transition between the two that lasts for 3 seconds (75 frames). You are asking your computer to deal with 550 "normal" frames, and 75 frames that have to be "processed" for the cross-fade.

However, I am led to believe (I haven't tried it yet!) that the speed issue can be resolved satisfactorily by the Truevision Targa 2000 board, which claims to accelerate the main functions in video editing by as much as 700%!

Leaving aside speed, which is really down to the performance of the host system, the major considerations for a video editing system have to be:

- Can it do everything that a tape editing system can do? If so,
- Can it do them cheaper?

The answer is a definite "yes!" to both, and there is an extra bonus: A tape system is essentially copying a section of video from one tape onto another. Like it or not, copying always introduces an amount of degradation.

Computerized video editing doesn't degrade in quality. You are in the realms of digital video now, so the degradation of picture quality is a thing of the past (once you've got your system set up properly, I have to add!).

So what is a "properly set-up system" then? PC or Mac, it needs the fastest processor, as much RAM as you can afford, and the biggest, fastest disk-drive that you can lay your hands on. And a big monitor helps too, because you are editing, not just linking strings of still frames. That means that you're selecting "takes" for the way that they fit together, for the way the whole sequence will "flow" once you're done. And that means that you want to be able to see detail in every frame.

You must set-up your computer to give you the very best monitoring capabilities when you play back video. If you're linking clips of video together, you must be able to see them play back in the most natural way, as close to finished video quality as you can get it. If that means buying a faster hard disk, buy it. If that means buying a faster graphics card, buy it. You cannot judge your edit if you are watching a halting, jerky movement, with those infuriating vertical rolls dribbling down the screen!

The system must have satisfactory sound on board, and it must output to a VCR, which in turn displays on a monitor of its own, with good-quality sound monitoring, as well. Use an old hi-fi from a car-boot sale if you have to! Don't rely on the speakers in a TV!

And, because digitized audio-video files take up a ton of space, you need to worry about disk-space, or file-compression. Decisions, decisions...

Fact

- Large hard disks are expensive.
- Compression causes image degradation.

So, you've got to decide. But until you do decide, keep as much video as possible on tape, and only digitize what you need, as and when you need it, and do all you can to avoid compression! Or at least, stay away from high compression-ratios! Try not to exceed a ratio of 3 to 1, and you're safe. Then, when you're through editing a sequence, free up more disk space by exporting the finished clip to fresh video tape.

Editing Software

The editing software: Adobe or U-Lead. That's the choice. All the others don't come near these two. Adobe is more expensive, and I see no reason to spend money unnecessarily. When I've tried to communicate with these two companies with requests for information, or advice on what a professional editor (as opposed to a computer-person) wants to see in edit software, Adobe never replies, but U-Lead does. Make of that whatever you wish . . .

Both are easy to use, both are overloaded with features that you'll probably never use, and both come with manuals that nobody ever seems to read. But the truth is that a computer-based editing suite is far more than just that: it is also a special effects suite, and a full post-production facility. It can even be a time machine...

Imagine: you're watching through the day's shoot. You need a right-hand view of the leading man turning to face the bad guys, to match their left-hand response. Take 2 was by far the best, but for some reason, the lighting was just a little bit too dim. Creative use of the filter effects can boost the brightness, tweak the color, and adjust the contrast just enough to compensate for what was wrong—without touching a camera or paying an actor or crew. You've, in effect, gone back and re-shot the unusable scene and set different light levels! Either of the two editing software systems let you set the key colors, and use the plug-ins of an image editor, so you can matte out a background, and superimpose the remaining foreground action on top of another sequence. (I know, I'm simplifying things, but the manuals have all the fiddly details, so there's no point in me repeating the manual. Just to try and sound knowledgeable!)

You can put anything behind your foreground. If your foreground happens to be an actor, talking to camera, you could "place" him in front of a background clip of a Hawaiian Island sequence, or move him to Hong Kong, or the Tower of London. I know you can do that with a conventional tape system, but with a computer, you can take a 3-D modeling software, and build the interior of a spacecraft, or a Martian landscape. In conventional production terms, you're incurring design costs, construction and painting, props, and studio hire as well, and they all take up time.

The computer lets you build "Virtual" sets and locations, they only take a few days, and only cost you the price of the software (which is a one-off cost). You might also need a design artist, if you can't do it for yourself. So, digital editing is the doorway to digital production.

Audio

The most you're going to get on the fanciest tape system will be four tracks, unless you spend a ton of money, buy a whole sound studio, and spend more money synchronizing this to your video studio. Digital systems now offer you hundreds of channels of audio to work on, and all the effects processing you can think of. Again, this is all digital, so the nasty things, like tape hiss, go trailing off into history. Another financial outlay discounted!

Software Packages

But now this editing software is starting to get really clever...You can set motion paths, and create 3D effects, and create morphs that will impress the fussiest Movie-Fans! All with one package!

Digital video editing was only the start. As this software begins to compete, and tries to tackle all the tricks and effects that movie and video professionals need, they might have gone astray slightly to begin with, by packing in a lot of things that software developers thought we picture professionals need. But now the developers are listening to the users. A lot of the unnecessary stuff, like some of the over-fancy wipes and fades (sorry, transitions, because I'm speaking computer-ese) will be tucked away in separate menus, and the most frequently used will be speeded up so that they no longer need things like a Video Explorer card or a Targa 2000 to artificially beef up the software performance.

So What Does This Really Mean?

A new generation of movie makers, and video producers, is what this technology means. People will understand how to create their own virtual locations, in photorealistic 3D; and will understand how to plan their shots in relation to their virtual sets, in relation to the editing they're already seeing in their mind's eye, which links with the music they're already anticipating. These people will be planning an entire production in the virtual dimension.

The images that they will create on-screen will start, not on bits of paper, or in their head, but in the computer. There they will remain, where they can be improved, perfected, or amended, until the finished result is ready to come out to tape or film.

And they *will* come out to film! A year ago, resolutions of 4000 × 4000 were considered huge, but now the software that builds the sets and locations will go up to 8000 × 8000, above what's needed for Cinemascope.

Beginning now, a new breed of "Auteur" movie/videomaker is evolving. People who "see" their entire production in this virtual dimension will now be able to execute their vision, single-handed, if that's their wish.

Picture this: how many homes have computers? How many of those homes also have camcorders? Most of them, I'd be willing to bet. Already, video editing software is being given away with video grabbers that will digitize video at

TV resolution and TV color depth, and play the finished product back onto video at TV speed, and for less than $500. If people have access to something like this, they will grab it. They are doing it now, and not everybody realizes it.

Some manufacturers see the marketplace as being the professional user, and they pitch their product and their price accordingly. Some manufacturers see the marketplace as being mainly the hobbyist, the enthusiastic amateur, and they make their pitch accordingly. But that same amateur still wants TV resolution, TV motion, TV color, and he's getting it. For pocket-money prices.

He's getting it, and he's using it. He might not have access to the finances to obtain the expensive 3D software, so instead, he steals somebody else's locations, or uses footage lifted from tourist board promo videos, or TV nature shows, or just goes out and films Main Street on his camcorder, and puts all the bits together. When it's so easy to do, and so cheap to get hold of the equipment, why not?

So, where do all these new "home movie" videos end up? Right now, a lot of them get sent to me because I've been talking about this in Europe for some time. They also end up on the Internet, where everybody can see them, share them, criticize them, and swap ideas.

Production companies will spring up on the Internet, with producers, directors, crew, cast, all miles apart, countries apart—never even meeting. Others will quietly watch, observe, and learn.

Some of these videos are already good enough to be shown to audiences. And business being what it is, somebody will find a way to bring these productions to an audience, and the new Movies will begin to circulate, on video, CD, and on the Internet. Broadcast TV will have to follow in time...

Some of these videos end up as demos, for so-called "real movies." Sony Pictures began doing this in 1993. Rock musicians do it all the time, using the same computers that they use to record their music.

Here in England, TV is about to go digital, and we're currently expecting something like another 50 TV channels to come on line, in the next year or so.

Digital video editing will instigate the supply of new programs that all of these channels must have. Digital video production is simply a logical and easy extension of what these simple-to-use editing packages can already do. And 50 channels broadcasting 24 hours a day...that's a lot of production. Either existing production houses are going to have to rush to keep up, or new companies will jump in ahead of them.

The software companies are gearing up for this now: they know that their software is the heart of this change, and they know that their software has to get faster, and easier to use. They know that demand will dictate their product. The best companies will respond to this, and the companies who feel that they know best what the market wants from them will get a nasty surprise!

Right now in England, a Pentium PC with 16 MB of RAM, a Movie-Machine video grabber, ordinary Soundblaster soundcard, and U-Lead's Media-Studio will cost less than £2000.

That system will let you digitize video at TV resolution, at 25 frames a second, in 24-bit color, in stereo. The output from programs produced and edited on this system, when exported to a Hi-8 VCR, (hire it in: you only need it when you've finished your piece of work!) and Sony's new Metal tape, will be accepted for broadcast by the BBC, and their quality standards and requirements are internationally respected.

So, a "one-horse" setup that costs less than $3500 will get you into the world of TV production. The quality of production, however, is a matter of the production skills of the individual. Because you can afford it doesn't mean that you can do it!

Acknowledge the fact that this kind of work might be the most creatively satisfying work on the planet, but it involves a financial risk. You might well be in a position to develop your writing skills into a script, then visualize your imaginings in the storyboard.

You might well assume the roles of producer, director, camera operator, lighting designer, sound engineer, music writer, musician, editor, video-box artist, and copywriter. There's still no guarantee that the rest of the world will enjoy viewing your work as much as you enjoyed creating it.

Always, the control factor will and must remain production skills. The key to these skills is no longer a degree from an art college or university turning out "Qualified Film and Video Producers." The key to this now rests in little boxes in software stores, boxes like Media-Studio and Premiere. Boxes bought by the most unlikely people, maybe kids on their school holidays, or unemployed people with time to teach themselves the new skills.

And the most important thing to appreciate about this software is that they are easy, and quick to learn. You can be performing basic editing tasks inside a day! The defining factor will lie now in the speed with which people learn to utilize their knowledge of what the software can do, and to combine this with their vision of what they want to do. Intuitive software will "connect" with artistic intuition far faster than any degree course of studies.

Program buyers don't give a damn about who makes the program: they only care about whether it is of a good enough quality to broadcast, and whether the program content is good enough to attract their attention.

Mighty changes are coming...

Interactive 3D Graphics

John Sievel

Introduction

Imagine a world in which the melting points of objects can be changed at will, allowing objects that are normally solid to become pliable. Imagine being able to manipulate objects made of metal as if they were made of clay. What about being able to live in a tree with termites? All of these are possible, now that fast 3D graphics are available.

This chapter assumes that you have some familiarity with the concepts and jargon of 3D graphics.

Definition of 3D Graphics

All 3D applications share some common characteristics. In all cases, a model of the world is maintained, and all objects in the world are defined in terms of three coordinates, usually labeled X, Y, and Z. Because computer output devices are currently usually capable of displaying two dimensions only, the three dimensions of each world coordinate are mapped to the two dimensions of the output device, be it a monitor or sheet of paper. The software that performs the mapping from three to two dimensions is the rendering engine, and the process is referred to as *rendering*.

Examples of 3D Applications

3D applications can be classified by their level of interactivity. The level of interactivity is determined by how much control the user of the application has over the world. The following application categories are presented in order of interactivity, with the least interactive first.

Computer-aided design (CAD)

CAD had perhaps the first use of 3D graphics. Historically, the 3D world, which might consist of a machine part or building, for example, is rendered as a wire-frame, where each object edge in the 3D world is mapped to a line in two dimensions. More recently, objects have been rendered in exquisite detail, with surface characteristics, such as color, reflectivity, and texture rendered beautifully.

Usually, this type of application is minimally interactive, and a single view of the world is rendered from a specific viewing point. Sometimes, the user can change the light-source locations and characteristics. Typically, the user must resort to working with a series of 2D views of the world in order to change objects in the world.

Visualization, walk-throughs, and virtual reality

In visualization, walk-throughs, and virtual reality, the rendering engine is so fast that an illusion of moving through the world is maintained. Typically, an input device, such as a mouse or joystick, is used to change the user's current position. The world might be specified in true 3D, or, more recently, as a series of 2D photographs taken from various angles. The user usually cannot change the world itself, only navigate through it.

Games, simulation

The most interactive type of applications are those which allow the user to modify most of the characteristics of the world. New objects can be created, and existing ones destroyed. The shape and surface characteristics of objects can be changed interactively. Forces in the world that act on objects, gravity for example, can be controlled. Most of the rest of the chapter will focus on this type of application, since it is probably the most challenging.

An Interactive 3D Application, Working Model 3D

Working Model 3D, developed by Knowledge Revolution of San Mateo, CA, is a motion-simulation application. Objects can be created, and forces acting on them can be specified. Objects can be connected by springs, for example. Once the world and objects in it are defined, a simulation can be run, in which the objects interact according to the physical laws specified. The following sections describe the application in detail.

Object creation

When Working Model 3D is launched, a new, untitled document is created. A window which contains a set of X, Y, and Z axis and a grid of blue lines in the X-Y plane is displayed. Adjacent to the window is another window, which contains the tool palette, as shown in Fig. 53.1.

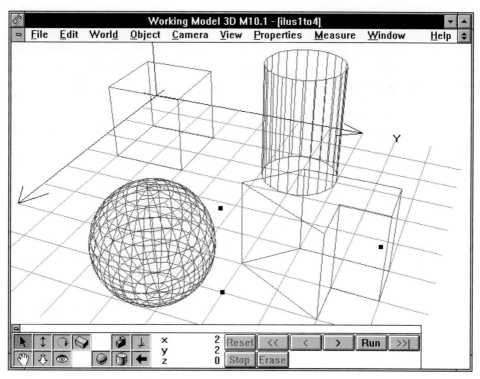

Figure 53.1 Step 1 of making a 3D model.

Objects are created by using the buttons in the tool palette. For example, to create a box, the user first clicks on the button that contains a small box. The cursor changes to a cross-hair. The user then positions the cross-hair at what will be one corner of the box on the grid, and holds the mouse button down. Now the mouse is moved to where the opposite corner of the box will be. As the mouse is moved, a rectangle is displayed, which shows the size of the box in the plane of the grid. The extent of the box in X, Y, and Z coordinates is updated live in the tool palette window. When the proper size is obtained, the user releases the mouse button, and the profile in the plane of the grid is determined. Now, as the user moves the mouse, the depth of the box changes, and is displayed. When the proper depth is obtained, a single mouse click freezes the box, and completes its generation. In a similar way, spheres and cylinders are created by first hitting the button in the tool palette for each of these primitives. Besides these objects, there is a way to extrude a rather arbitrarily shaped solid. First, click on the button with the staircase-like icon, which causes the curser to change to the cross-hairs, as before. Now, a single mouse click defines a boundary point on the plane of the grid. As many points can be generated as needed. When the mouse button is pressed over the original starting point, the outline is frozen, and further mouse movement defines the depth of the object, which is extruded from the outline given. Figure 53.1 shows a box, cylinder, sphere, and extruded object.

Views into the world

Objects can be rendered in four basic ways, as determined by the View menu. Figure 53.1 shows wire-frame mode, in which each edge of an object is displayed as a line of the same color as the object. Hidden-line mode, shown in Fig. 53.2, is similar, except that edges or portions of edges that would not be visible are not displayed. This mode provides much more depth information, and resolves ambiguities of depth. For example, the box in Fig. 53.1 could be going into or coming out of the paper if the grid were not displayed. Figure 53.3 shows full shaded mode, which provides the most information about object surfaces. Notice the shiny highlights on the sphere and cylinder, which help to give these objects reality. Fig. 53.4 shows full-shaded anti-aliased mode. This is similar to full-shaded mode, except that the edges of objects are blurred to remove the staircasing that results from the discrete pixels of a digital display. This is particularly noticeable on the top edge of the box in Fig. 53.3, which is not visible in Fig. 53.4.

Besides the rendering modes, the View menu has an option to change the type of projection. The default projection, which is shown in Figs. 53.1 through 53.4, is 3D perspective. In this mode, objects further away from the camera are smaller than those that are closer. The alternative projection, shown in Fig. 53.5, is isometric. In this mode, the size of objects are independent of their distance from the camera. This mode can be useful when it is important to compare object sizes, but it does so at the expense of an important depth cue. The Camera menu allows one to move the camera to one of several predetermined positions, such as front, back etch, and to define a home position. Finally, the Window menu allows one to go to a four-panel layout, which has simultaneous 2D windows for front, top, and left views, as well as a perspective 3D window. Also, three tools in the palette can be used to change the user's view.

The most dramatic is the eye tool. When it is activated and the mouse button is held down anywhere in the 3D window, the camera will be moved from side to side and up and down as the mouse is moved in these directions. Figure 53.6 shows the same objects viewed from a different camera location using the eye tool. The second tool that can modify a view is the zoom tool, which looks like the fat arrow coming out of the screen in the tool palette. When this tool is activated and the mouse is moved up and down after being clicked in the 3D window, the lens of the camera is zoomed in and out, for a wider or more narrow view. This is very useful for closeups, as shown in Fig. 53.7. The final tool for image manipulation is the hand tool. This tool allows you to pan the camera, as if the camera was moved to the left, right, up, or down.

Object manipulation

Working Model 3D relies on direct manipulation to work with objects. The user can reach into the 3D world to touch and move objects, as opposed to working with 2D views of the world.

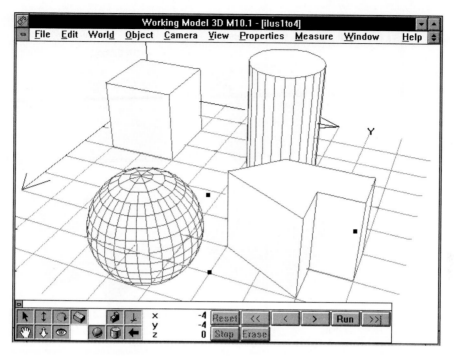

Figure 53.2 Step 2 of making a 3D model.

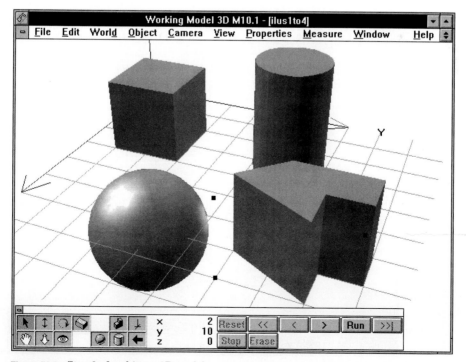

Figure 53.3 Step 3 of making a 3D model.

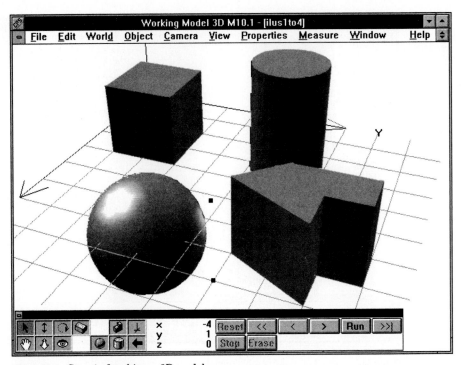

Figure 53.4 Step 4 of making a 3D model.

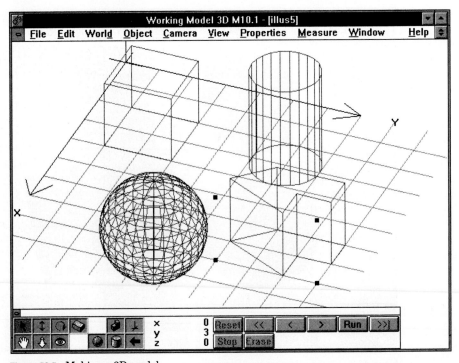

Figure 53.5 Making a 3D model.

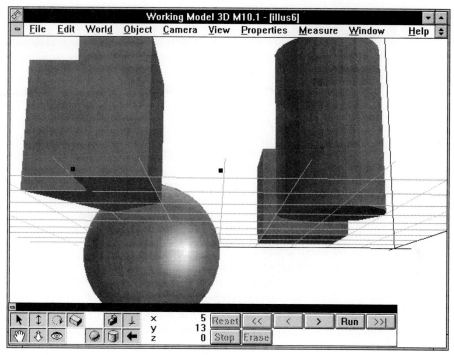

Figure 53.6 3D model.

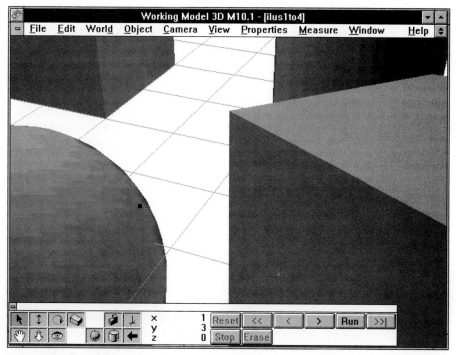

Figure 53.7 3D model.

Prior to manipulating an object, it must be selected. To do this, the button with the diagonal arrow is pressed using the mouse. Now, when the curser is in front of any surface of an object and the mouse button is pressed, the object is selected. This is indicated by the display of small black squares, which surround the selected object's profile. Additional objects can be selected by holding down the shift key while clicking the mouse in front of them.

Alternatively, a range of objects can be selected by pressing the mouse button when the curser is not in front of any object, and dragging the mouse to another location not in front of any object. Any objects within the rectangle are all selected. To de-select all selected objects, press the mouse when the cursor is not in front of any objects. Once an object or objects have been selected, two tools are available to move it or them. When the arrow tool button is active and the mouse button is held down in front of selected objects, the objects can be dragged with the mouse anywhere in the plane of the grid, usually X-Y. The tool button containing the vertical line with arrows at each end can be used to move objects perpendicular to the grid plane, usually Z. To do this, the tool is activated by clicking it, and pressing the mouse button when the curser is in front of a selected object. Vertical mouse movements now will drag the object perpendicular to the grid plane. Objects can penetrate the grid plane, as shown in Fig. 53.3.

Besides these tools, which change an object's position, the rotate tool can change an object's orientation. The rotate tool looks like a dotted circle with an arrow indicating direction. With this tool activated and the mouse moved around the object's center, the object rotates about an axis coming out of the screen. If only a single object is to be moved or reoriented using either of these three tools, it will automatically be selected when the mouse is held down in front of the object so that it can immediately be moved in one quick motion.

Simulation

Now that a world has been built, it is time to see how Working Model 3D can be used to observe how objects would interact if the world actually existed. To illustrate this, you could create a simple world consisting of a coin and a slab. The slab will be anchored to the earth by a revolving joint, which will allow it to spin. The coin will be dropped onto the slab, causing it to spin and the coin to bounce off. The constraint tool, which looks like three perpendicular lines in the tool palette, is used to anchor the slab to the ground.

When the tool is active, the curser displays as a small circle. Pressing the mouse button while the curser is in front of any surface of an object causes a small square to be displayed. This square shows the orientation of that surface. When the mouse button is released, the connection point will be applied to the object at that point. The properties menu can then be used to define the type of the constraint; in this case, it is a revolute joint. Figure 53.8 shows the coin, slab, and constraint in the wire-frame mode. There are many possible types of constraints, such as hinges, slots, and even things like springs, which can connect constraints on two objects. The properties menu is also

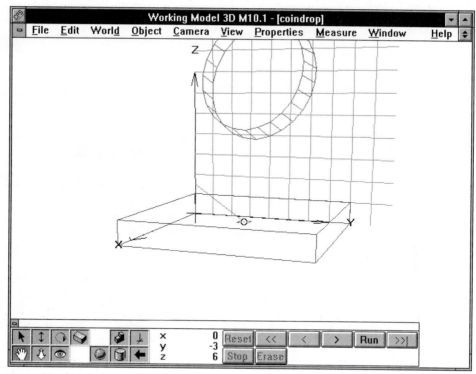

Figure 53.8 Coindrop.

used to define many other physical properties of a selected object, such as mass, friction, etc. that define how they interact and look. The Gravity item of the World menu allows one to select gravity going straight down, and to define its value.

Once all of the object properties have been set, a simulation can be run. The buttons to the right of the tool palette control simulations, which can be started, stopped, advanced by a single frame, and rewound to the beginning or end. The Measure menu can be used to display physical properties in real time. Figure 53.9 shows the coin after bouncing off the slab. The position display clearly shows when the coin contacted the slab. Also notice that the slab has rotated. All of the features of Working Model 3D can now be used to iterate on a design by changing objects in the world and their properties, and rerunning the simulation in a very interactive way.

Rendering Engine Requirements

Now that we have an overview of what a typical interactive 3D application looks like, it is time to explore how the 3D rendering engine meets these requirements. Flash render, by Gnomon Inc., is the rendering engine used by Working Model 3D. Although rendering engines are available in many flavors and capabilities, the features that are helpful in supporting interactive 3D

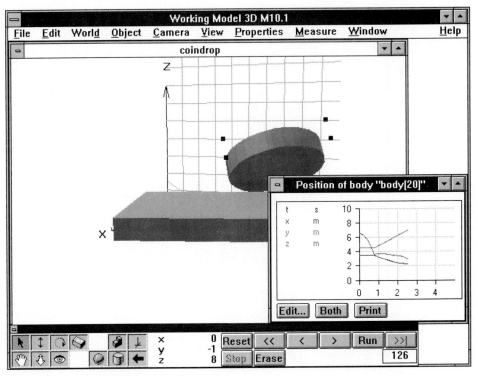

Figure 53.9 Graphing the model.

graphics are the focus. These are covered in order of importance for an application like Working Model 3D.

Speed and memory

The requirement of very fast rendering cannot be overemphasized. In a CAD application, rendering speed is nice, but not essential. For virtual reality and interactive applications, speed is essential. In an interactive application, the user input depends on quick availability of the 3D image. If it lags, the user feedback will be delayed. The result will be a frustrating user experience. For example, when an object is to be moved away from the camera, the user moves the mouse down. If she does not see the object move, she will overcompensate by moving the mouse more than the amount required. When the image is finally rendered, it will be too far away. The user will then have to compensate by moving the mouse in the opposite direction. The rendering engine must be fast enough to provide sufficiently real feedback. A factor of 1 to 2 times in rendering speed can make the difference between a smooth, efficient user interface that is a pleasure to use, and one that's jerky and frustrating. In evaluating rendering engine speed, it is important to not rely solely on published benchmarks, but instead to evaluate the renderer with a world that is of comparable complexity to that which the application will handle. Rendering speed versus complexity vary tremendously. Some rendering engines do very well with worlds of a few hundred polygons, some do best with thousands, and some have a fairly flat performance curve. Also, the size, in pixels, of the rendered image can affect speed tremendously. A renderer that does well producing a 256-x-256 pixel image might run at 1/4 speed for a window that is 512-x-512 pixels. The desired image size should be considered when selecting a rendering engine.

Another parameter to look at is memory usage. The most obvious measure of this is the amount of RAM that will be necessary to render a world of the required complexity. Weather this memory is allocated in your applications space or system space, the computer must have enough RAM to comfortably support it. How well does the renderer work with virtual memory, if this is a factor with a given machine? Also, how large is the rendering engine itself? A library that implements the features you need in 100 KB is likely to be more concise, and probably faster and more reliable than a library that consumes 2 MB to implement the same features. A fast, tight application needs a fast, tight renderer. More is not necessarily better.

Application program interface (API)

The calls that the application code makes to interact with the rendering engine must also be considered. First, calls must be available to map coordinates back and forth between the output pixels and the 3D world. This is essential because the user input will be in the output image. The application needs to know where this point is in the 3D world. Also, the application will need to know which object and which polygon within the object were touched. The engine must provide this info quickly. The API must be easy to use within the framework that the application is to be written in. For example, FlashRender returns a pointer whenever a world, object in a world, camera, or light are created. This pointer is later used to access the entity. This scheme can easily be integrated into an object-oriented framework, for example. Any number of worlds, cameras, lights, etc. can co-exist. Another variable to consider is the size of the API. Is the sheer number of calls intimidating? Is it necessary to master a large number of calls to implement even the simplest interface? Do the calls add value by providing features that are useful within the context of the application? Again, more is not necessarily better.

Primitives, types of rendering

The number and kind of primitives the rendering engine supports should be considered. It is useful if the engine supports the primitives that will be available to the user, such as boxes, cylinders, and spheres. Usually, 3D vectors are also important. Do they need to penetrate other objects? How does the renderer represent things like spheres and cylinders internally? Are these primitives decomposed into a fixed number of polygons? FlashRender, for example, varies the model complexity, depending on the size of the rendered primitive. This prevents wasting time rendering polygons that would be very small. If your application is to handle large surfaces, such as landscapes, for example, it is useful to have a primitive type devoted to this representation. Some engines use triangle grids, and FlashRender uses crystalline objects to model this situation. Some rendering engines support more complex primitives. The performance of these should be carefully considered. Although easy to use, they might be quite expensive from a time standpoint.

The types of rendering that the application requires should be supported by the engine. For example, Working Model 3D requires wire frame, hidden line, full shaded, and anti-aliased modes because each presents different tradeoffs between speed and depth and structure information. The anti-aliased mode can be particularly useful for low-resolution devices, such as LCD stereo glasses. For this to be practical, the anti-aliased mode must be fast.

The engine should be capable of easily switching among the rendering types that will be used. For example, Working Model 3D has an option in the View menu, which automatically switches to wire frame mode while editing objects, then back to the requested mode when the object extent is determined. This allows the speed-information tradeoff to be made automatically.

Shading

The shading capabilities of the rendering engine determine the realism of the rendered image. The engine should support the number and kind of light sources which the application requires. Types of lights usually supported are ambient, distant, and sometimes spotlights. For example, Working Model 3D uses one ambient light and two distant lights—one to illuminate the front and one for the back. The most common type of shading is Gourard, where the light is interpolated across the surface. Though Gourard shading accurately displays surfaces that have a fairly dull surface finish, such as plastic, it does not do well with shiny objects. For this, Phong shading, where the surface normal is interpolated across the surface, does much better. The resulting highlights add sparkle to the scene, and can dramatically help to define orientations as objects or light sources are moved.

The following shading affects are nice, but might not be important for your application. They all can require a significant amount of time, so it should be possible to turn them off if they are not needed.

Texture mapping can provide realism, but often at the expense of speed. Depth blurring, where more distant edges are blurred, can add realism to applications that seek to simulate atmospheric effects. Translucency and transparency can be nice for engineering work. Cast shadows can add a lot of realism, but usually require plenty of time.

Solid vs. surface renderer

A solid renderer can handle object intersections, and a surface rendered requires that the intersections be pre-computed and defined by surfaces. A solid renderer can simplify programming by eliminating the task of actually computing intersections, but it usually does so at the expense of speed. On the other hand, a surface renderer is often faster, and often the object intersections can be pre-computed once, and need not be handled on every frame. Also, surface modelers inherently obey the rules of the real world—two objects can never occupy the same space.

Platform availability

These days, most applications development is cross-platform, in order to spread the development cost out among the largest number of copies. Therefore, the rendering engine should run on multiple platforms, and use the same API on each. This makes the 3D portion of the application identical across platforms. Another factor to consider is support for RISC architectures. RISC is very well suited to rendering because this task is so computing bound. Applications running on RISC platforms have a performance edge over CISC. Ideally, the renderer will run on CISC also. Any rendering engine that is fast enough to run on CISC will simply run faster on RISC. Those that do not run on CISC probably will run more slowly on RISC also.

Hardware acceleration

There is no question that, over time, most 3D rendering will be done by hardware. A plethora of hardware solutions of various kinds is now becoming available on all types of platforms.

Although hardware promises huge speed increases, be cautious while evaluating the claims. For example, rendering rates of hundreds of thousands of polygons per second are sometimes claimed, but what does this really mean? Usually the polygons are composed of 25 pixels, and the polygon edges need a particular configuration to achieve this rate. The actual environment might require larger polygons and less optimal organization. Another factor to consider with a hardware solution is how much work must the host CPU do to keep the hardware running? This can significantly reduce performance. For all of these reasons, sometimes hardware solutions deliver actual performance that is only marginally better than that attainable by a fast software renderer. Finally, hardware solutions are often quite rigid because they are "cast in silicon." For example, most accelerators perform Gourard shading, which can produce output that lacks the sparkle of Phong shading. Software shaders, on the other hand, can be easily updated to allow for a myriad of shading affects, including procedural shaders, which are programmable.

The Future

Now it's time to leave current reality behind, and look ahead to the not-too-distant future. The following section contains some possible new uses of interactive 3D graphics, and the applications that implement them.

Changing physical laws

One of the more interesting uses of interactive 3D graphics is that it can free us from reality. For example, Working Model 3D allows one to change gravity and friction to create worlds that could previously only be imagined. Now we can actually spin a penny on a frictionless table, and watch the surprising results. Finally, we are free from the "gravity of reality."

Collaborative software

Increasingly, teams of people, often physically distant from each other, need to combine forces to create a new car, building, etc. Or perhaps multiple people want to interact with each other by sharing the same virtual environment. This could be a rich educational experience, or also just fun. These functions can be accomplished fairly easily with existing rendering engines and communications capabilities. Each user can have a copy of the virtual world, and only changes in the world need to be computed among users. Often, this information is very compact and would require a relatively low bandwidth to transmit. For example, the location, orientation, and size of an object can be represented by a 4×4 transformation matrix, which is fairly inexpensive to transmit.

New object modification tools

Wouldn't it be nice to squash and poke objects into shape with a magic wand? What about a force field whose shape was programmable? The distances from the wand to each vertex would determine the force amount and direction exerted. The likelihood of moving a particular vertex could be controlled by a surface tension variable, for example. In this strange world, objects would cease to exist as only solid, liquid, and gas, as the boundaries blurred. The possibilities are endless, and require only moving vertices using whatever mathematical law you can imagine.

New devices

Finally, it is interesting to take a quick look at some of the more unusual input devices that are now available, and to speculate about how they might be used. One example is the RingMouse, by Kantek. It is a 3D mouse that can be worn on a finger. The device uses infrared and ultrasonic energy to determine a position in three coordinates. With this inexpensive device, it would not be necessary to use two separate tools to position an object in space, as is now required in Working Model 3D. Instead, when the wearer virtually "touched" an object, or was close enough to it, the object could then be dragged to the new location with one clean motion.

Perhaps it won't be necessary to even lift a finger. Envision using eye-tracking technology, similar to what is already available to output eye angles of what someone is looking at. It could then be dragged to a new location by simply looking at where it is to go. The implications of this for handicapped people could be enormous. Perhaps the most exotic input device that is just around the corner is mind control. Devices will shortly be available to allow physiological measures taken from the skin to control a computer. This technology seems destined to be used to control the strange, ephemeral virtual world with nothing more tangible than thought.

Multimedia Groupware: Using Multimedia Conferencing Tools on the Internet/MBone

Dr. Schahram Dustdar

This chapter is about the use of multimedia groupware on the Internet's MBone. The *Multicast Backbone (MBone)* is a virtual network and is layered on top of portions of the Internet. This virtual network is called the MBone and connects more than 10,000 users on some 1000 networks in over 20 countries. The MBone is composed of islands that can directly support IP multicast, such as multicast LANs like Ethernet, linked by virtual point-to-point links called *tunnels*. The multicast-routers are connected through tunnels, where multicast packets encapsulated within normal IP packets are being forwarded. A multicast-router can be a production router or a workstation-class machine configured for the routing of multicast packets. Each tunnel is associated with a metric and a threshold parameter. The metric counts for routing decisions, a numerical larger value denotes a more-expensive path (e.g., a backup tunnel should have a higher metric than the primary path). The threshold is used for scoping of packets, each router compares the packets time to live (TTL) against the tunnels threshold and forwards the packet only if the TTL exceeds the threshold setting. Additionally every multicast router decrements the TTL by 1[3].

The MBone became so important because it meets the growing need for real-time human communication through computer networks. Because many people are depending on their workstation computers for daily office work, it was natural to implement the MBone tools for multimedia communication support on a packet-switched network, such as the Internet. This process began with the transmission of live audio from a meeting of the Internet Engineering Task Force (IETF) in March 1992. Some 30 researchers participated remotely from Australia, Sweden, the UK, and the US, both listening and interactively participating in the conference by asking questions. Steve Deering developed IP multicasting in 1988, but it was not widely deployed because of insufficient demand. The IETF meeting transmissions provided the demand for multicast to support wide-area distribution of this event, plus a ready audience for the freely available software. This boosted the development of the MBone. Figure 54.1 provides an overview of major MBone routers and links on the Internet.

Because of the nature of videoconferencing and audioconferencing events, the need for distributing data to a group of participants, called *multicasting*, arises. Multicasting of packets differs from *unicasting*, where datagrams are delivered from one sender to one receiver, and *broadcasting*, where datagrams travel from one sender to all receivers, in a way that datagrams are only delivered to members in a so-called "multicast group." To manage dynamically changing multicast groups and individual memberships within these groups, the Internet Group Management Protocol (IGMP), which fits into the existing suite of Internet Protocols, has been suggested and implemented. Multicast is not only the native form of delivery in group communication, it also makes efficient use of the network resources. As for a number

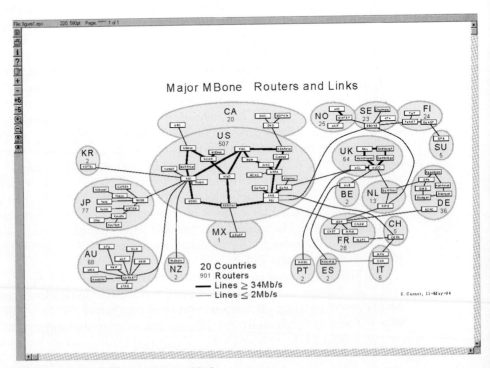

Figure 54.1   Major MBone routers and links.

of n receivers, it is not necessary to send n copies of each packet, only one copy of each packet is multicasted and only duplicated at branches along the routing path. The members of one multicast group are allowed to be located anywhere on the Internet. Packets are sent to a multicast group (i.e., audio packets in a conference, are routed to each group member regardless where he is located geographically). The routing of multicast packets is not yet implemented in most of the router boxes; therefore, a virtual network connecting multicast-routers was set up.

Multimedia Groupware

The first paper on the use of multimedia groupware on the MBone was written by Macedonia and Brutzman. In this paper, the authors show that using desktop multimedia conferencing for collaborative work on wide area networks, such as the Internet, is possible. In the past, researchers have often discussed the failure of video to support interpersonal communication. This chapter provides a summary of conclusions others have reached about computer-supported communication tools. Further, we review the design, hardware and software requirements as well as organizational issues in desktop multimedia conferencing systems on the MBone. We draw on our experiences from multiple multimedia conferences on the MBone.

As Johansen shows, group work is a natural way of doing business. Early groupware systems and electronic meeting systems lacked the ability of manipulating multiple media types, such as audio, video, and textual information in one integrated multimedia system. The merging of workstation technology and real-time computer conferencing has had a significant impact on CSCW and group decision making and lead to the term "desktop conferencing." Research on early multimedia conferencing systems, such as that developed at AT&T Bell Laboratories, Bellcore, or NEC had as their aim the provision of the facilities found at face-to-face meetings with remote groups. It is generally accepted that computer-supported decision making and communication results in many changes in communication patterns, greater task orientation and shorter meetings. Regarding the video component, Ishii, Kobayashi, and Grudin point out the importance of gaze awareness, the ability to monitor the direction of someone's gaze and thus the focus of the attention. Similar results were found by Heatch, Luff, Mantei, et al.

Technical Requirements

Preparation and realization of desktop multimedia conferencing has two aspects, the technical setup procedure and organizational issues, which will be discussed in the following sections. The requirements for highly integrated desktop multimedia conferencing on a packet-switched network, i.e., the IP (Internet Protocol) based Internet, can be divided into three categories: Support for packetized data transport and routing of data packets by the network software, support of encoding audio and video streams and reassembling of audio and video packets into continuous audiovisual output. This should be accomplished by specialized hardware or software codecs (coder/decoders). The control and application software should be integrated into the graphical user interface (i.e., the widespread X-Window system).

Network and transfer protocol requirements

This chapter concentrates on the usage of multimedia groupware in packet switched networks. In a packet switched network, transmission lines are not reserved in advance, the data is sent in small portions, called *datagrams*, from the sender to the receiver or to a group of receivers. On the path from the sender to the receivers, the packets are forwarded by special machines, called *routers*. The packet switching approach is sometimes called *connection-less* or *state-less delivery service*, in contrast to the *connection-oriented circuit switching method*, where lines are reserved for the connections. The Internet is a large packet-switched network, but it is widely believed that real-time traffic requires a connection-oriented network service. Recent research and experiences revealed that packet switching, compared to circuit switching techniques, is not less efficient in meeting real-time scheduling and delivery constraints. The weaknesses of packet-switched networks, namely the variation in the delay of each packet, usually called *jitter*, and packet loss because of occasional packet dropping by routers can be diminished by buffering of incoming packets and the usage of loss-tolerant coding methods. Network jitter results in variation of packet interarrival times and out-of-sequence packet delivery. The audio replay at the receiver (without taking into account jitter) will at least be hardly understandable. Network jitter is removed by buffering the incoming data packets at the receiver and replaying the signal with some delay. The chosen coding method for audio and video data must be able to reconstruct the data with minimal distortion, despite of the packet loss.

Desktop machine requirements

The real-time processing of video and audio data requires adequate processing power, which is offered by workstation-class machines. On most workstations, Unix-derived operating systems are in use, so research activities have focused on these machines. The necessary operating system kernel extensions have been implemented into the most common operating systems, like Solaris, Irix, and Nextstep. Most workstations are equipped with audio capabilities (e.g., a built-in speaker or line-out plug, a built-in microphone, or line-in plug and device-driver software).

For video captures, a frame-grabber board and a video camera is required. The viewing of the video sequence requires a graphics display. Audio encoding and decoding is usually done in software. Video encoding can be done in hardware or software, and decoding is usually done in software. Hardware encoding boards are expensive, so encoding on powerful workstations is often done in software. Common coding techniques are Pulse Code Modulation (PCM) for audio, which results in a bit rate of 64 kbit/sec for 8-bit resolution audio sampled at 8 kHz.

The packet overhead, resulting from the address and control information inserted into the packets, raises the bit rate to 75 kbit/sec if the Real-Time Transport Protocol (RTP) is used. The RTP adds timing and sequencing information into the packets, which is used to reduce distortion caused by network jitter and packet loss. For video coding, a commonly used value for the data rate is 128 kbit/sec. To reduce the impact on the network you are free to choose a lower rate (i.e., 66 kbit/sec has been used in the described conference). These extremely low rates are achieved through data-compression techniques. The methods of video compression implemented in the video tools we used are based on frame prediction, motion estimation, and transform coding techniques. One disadvantage of such a low bandwidth allocation is the low frame rate required in the order of magnitude of two frames/sec, which depends on the motion in the picture. A quick changing image sequence results in unpredictable frames, and thus a reduced data rate (because frames have to be coded without prediction). Fortunately, in a conference session, quick scene changes seldom occur, the small movements of the conference participants can be effectively coded using motion estimation. In motion estimation, a displacement vector related to a block of pixels in the previous frame is coded, rather than the image content itself.

Organizational Context

Conferencing events on the Internet/MBone can be divided into two categories: open conferences where everybody can join in, and conferences for closed groups. Open conferences are usually announced a few weeks ahead by sending an electronic mail to the appropriate mailing lists. Before the conference actually starts, an announcement in the session directory (sd), an X-Window application program, is made. The sd entry is flooded, according to the conference scope, over the Internet and contains the conference name, a short description, multicast group addresses, coding format, scope, and extent of the conference.

Figure 54.2 shows an example of an open multimedia session. In this figure, three windows are open. On the left bottom side, the sd window shows the currently available MBone sessions. By clicking on one session, the associated audio-, video- or whiteboard tools will be activated. In this case, the audio tool (vat) and the video tool (nv) were activated for transmission of the NASA space shuttle mission to the desktop workstation. Because, in this example, the MBone tools are used for transmitting an event with no interaction from remote participants, there is no whiteboard available. The conference can be any combination of audio-, video-, and whiteboard sessions.

An alternative to sessions announcement by sending an e-mail to a list is to use the World-Wide Web (WWW) forms. The WWW approach is more clear and collision detection (e.g., two conferences at the same time with overlapping scope, can be done automatically). Some WWW Servers provide a "video-on demand" service of recorded MBone conferences.

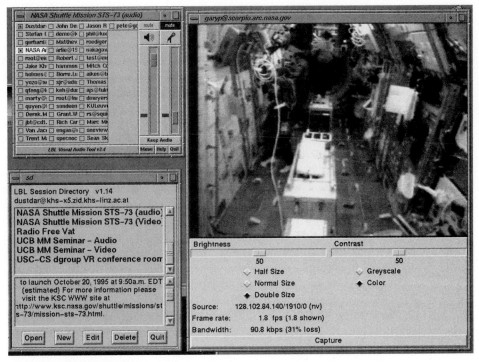

Figure 54.2 NASA example.

Beyond the announcement, the training of the conference participants and preparation of the desktop multimedia conferencing facilities is essential. Specifically, the conference participants have to know to use the tools (i.e., how to mute the microphone in the audio tool vat, how to resize windows in one of the video tools (such as nv or vic), or how to load postscript slides into the whiteboard wb). Figure 54.3 shows an example of a vic session on the MBone, which can be quite complex.

Additionally, the surroundings of each participant has to be adjusted (i.e., avoid background noise by locating the microphone, speakers, and camera close to the human interactor and providing natural lighting conditions). Finally, one important aspect is to remind the conference participants to be disciplined (i.e., not to speak concurrently).

During the conference, one participant should act as moderator: setting the conference schedule, serving the speaking requests, and troubleshooting. The troubleshooting, in fact, is the responsibility of the technical staff. If the conference is transmitted to an audience using overhead projection, as it is quite often, additional staff is necessary. Speaking requests from the audience must be coordinated by this person. Before one starts a conference on the MBone, the tunnel between the two sites and (if possible) an alternate route (tunnel) (in case the main tunnel breaks down during the conference) should be configured.

In our multimedia conferencing sessions, one of the first reactions of conference participants was the idea that they would be able to reduce travel.

Johansen questioned the assumption that conferencing would reduce travel. Very often it was the subjective feeling of conference participants that they saved a lot of time and hence travel costs; they did not necessarily calculate the real costs and compare. They did not regard desktop multimedia conferences on the MBone as a substitute to face-to-face meetings. The participants wanted to use the system for their convenience to be able to hold meetings more frequently than they were able to hold face-to-face meetings.

The system administrators in MBone-based multimedia conferences should limit the video bandwidth and keep the rest for audio and shared whiteboarding, which is more important than full-motion, 25 or 30 frames per second "talking heads." The reason for bandwidth limitation for video is that you should keep bandwidth for audio and shared data, such as whiteboard contents (text, postscript, or pictures).

Implications for Future Research

To summarize, it is very important to train the prospective users of desktop multimedia conferencing systems on the MBone, regarding the usage of soft-

Figure 54.3 Audio example.

ware and to give guidelines of usage of the conferencing tools. In some situations, it was not obvious to the participants that if two participants talked at the same time, some audio packets would get lost. The second proposition is that prospective users of desktop multimedia conferencing systems should have a clear idea of what quality they can expect. Particularly you can witness a high degree of user expectation regarding video quality. The video quality needs to have a minimum frame refresh rate of 15 frames per second to give the impression of real full-motion video. This refresh rate can only be achieved in high-bandwidth networks. The conference participants needed some "private-time" during decision-making processes to discuss issues amongst themselves, without the feeling of being "broadcasted." Hence, we propose the implementation of the functionality to direct video and audio streams to certain users within a multicast group and to implement features in software that show the remote participant that the local site has switched to mute and is not able to receive audio or video. This would help users to have a feeling of privacy and enhance security. Regarding security and privacy, one major problem on the MBone is that it is only possible to configure multimedia conferences reaching the site of the organization, a region or the world, but it is not possible to configure a multimedia conference as a closed conference.

Everyone within the scope of the TTL-value is able to receive and send packets. There is no anonymity, although conference participants can see through the e-mail address, who joins a conference. This restricts the use of multimedia conferencing on the MBone. Interested organizations who have full Internet access can use the MBone for their internal multimedia conferences between distributed sites, but they will not be private.

Research on desktop multimedia conferencing and its application in decision-making processes is interlinked with other information processing, communication and coordination activities. Desktop multimedia conferencing is not a substitute for face-to-face meetings, but enables and sometimes forces people to change decision-making processes and communication patterns. Daft and Lengel's theory of information richness states that face-to-face meetings have the highest degree of media richness. We argue that desktop multimedia conferencing enables decision-making processes and communication processes on a new dimension.

The question is not if desktop multimedia conferencing is about to substitute for face-to-face meetings, but which "new qualities" or "opportunity enhancements" it can offer. Experiences on the usage of multimedia conferencing on the MBone shows that desktop multimedia conferencing enables decision-making processes that have no equivalent in face-to-face meetings. Further research needs to be undertaken regarding design and implementation issues of desktop multimedia conferencing systems for decision-making processes using the MBone. I am convinced that this research area needs interdisciplinary efforts because multimedia groupware itself is an interdisciplinary field. We can expect new impulses to the emerging field of multimedia systems and propose joint research of the research communities of computer science, communication research, organization design, human-computer interaction and information systems. As Ishii, Kobayashi, and Arita state, we are interacting not with computers, but through computers.

References

S. R. Ahuja, J. R. Ensor, and S. E. Lucco, "A comparison of application-sharing mechanisms in real-time desktop conferencing systems," *Proceedings of COIS,* 1990. 238–248.

A. A. Angehrn and T. Jelassi, "DSS research and practice in perspective," *Decision Support Systems,* 12:267–275.

S. Casner, "Frequently Asked Questions on the Multicast Backbone" University of Southern California, Information Sciences Institute, http://www.research.att.com/mbone-faq.html, 1995.

C. Chin, C. W. Holsapple, and A. B. Whinston, *Computer support in distributed decision environments for supporting decisions processes,* Amsterdam: Elsevier, 1991. 335–356.

D. D. Clark, S. Shenker, and L. Zhang, "Supporting real-time applications in an integrated services packet network: architecture and mechanism," *Proceedings of the ACM SIGCOMM '92 Conference,* September 1992. 14–26.

R. L. Daft and R. H. Lengel, "Information richness: a new approach to managerial information processing and organization design," *Research in organizational behavior,* Greenwhich, CT: JAI Press, 1984. 6:191–234.

S. Deering, "Request for Comment 1112," *Host Extensions for IP Multicasting,* Network Working Group, Stanford University, August 1989.

C. Egido, "Teleconferencing as a technology to support cooperative work: its possibilities and Limitations, *Intellectual teamwork: social and technological foundations of cooperative work,* Erlbaum, Hillsdale, 1990. 351–372.

R. Frederick, "nv - X11 videoconferencing tool," *Unix Manual Page,* Palo Alto, CA: Xerox.

W. Gaver, T. Moran, A. MacLean, L. Lovstrand, P. Dourish, K. Carter and W. Buxton, "Realizing video environment: EuroPARC's RAVE system," *Proceedings of CHI '92,* Conference on Human Factors in Computing Systems, 1992. 27–35.

R. C. Harkness and P. G. Burke, "Estimating teleconferencing travel substitution potential in large business organizations," *The teleconference resource book: a guide to applications and planning,* Amsterdam: Elsevier, 1984. 256–264.

M. Hatcher, "A video conferencing system for the United States Army: Group decision making in a geographically distributed environment," *Decision Support Systems,* 8:181–190.

C. Heath and P. Luff, "Disembodied conduct: communication through video in a multi-media office environment," *Proceedings of CHI '91,* Conference on Human Factors in Computing Systems, 1991. 99–103.

R. Huber, "First Experiences with MBone, Test Report for the Austrian Ministry of Science and Research," Department of Computer Science and System Analysis, Austria: University Salzburg, November 1994.

H. Ishii, M. Kobayashi, and K. Arita, "Iterative design of seamless collaboration media," *Communications of the ACM,* 37, 8, 83–97.

H. Ishii, M. Kobayashi, and J. Grudin, "Integration of inter-personal space and shared workspace: clearboard design and experiments," *Proceedings of CSCW '92,* Conference on Computer Supported Cooperative work, 1992. 33–42.

V. Jacobson, "Multimedia Conferencing on the Internet," *ACM SIGCOMM '94 Conference Tutorial,* London, August 1994.

V. Jacobson, *Unix Manual Page,* Lawrence Berkeley Laboratory, University of California.

V. Jacobson, S. McCanne, "vat - X11-based audio teleconferencing tool," *Unix Manual Page,* Lawrence Berkeley Laboratory, University of California.

V. Jacobson, S. McCanne, "Using the LBL Network Whiteboard," Lawrence Berkeley Laboratory, University of California.

R. Johansen, *Teleconferencing and beyond: communications in the office of the future,* New York: McGraw-Hill, 1984.

R. Johansen, *Groupware: computer support for business teams,* New York: The Free Press, 1988.

R. Johansen and C. Bullen, "Thinking ahead: what to expect from teleconferencing," *Computer-supported cooperative work: a book of readings,* San Mateo, California: Morgan Kaufmann, 1988. 185–198.

A. Klemets, "The design and implementation of a media on demand system for WWW," *Proceedings of the First International Conference on the World-Wide Web,* Geneva, May 1994.

M. R. Macedonia and D.P. Brutzman, "MBone provides audio and video across the Internet," *IEEE Computer* 27, 4, 1994. 30–36.

M. M. Mantei, R. M. Baecker, A. J. Sellen, W. A. S. Buxton and T. Milligan, 1991, "Experiences in the use of media space," *Proceedings of CHI '91, Conference on Human Factors in Computing Systems.* 203–208.

S. McCanne, V. Jacobson, *sd - Session Directory,* Lawrence Berkeley Laboratory, University of California.

A. Niemiec, "CMITS: Communication and Craft," *The teleconference resource book: a guide to applications and planning,* Amsterdam: Elsevier, 1984. 109–115.

T. Rodden, "Technological support for cooperation," *CSCW in practice: an introduction and case studies,* New York: Springer, 1993. 1–22

R. W. Root, "Design of a multi-media vehicle for social browsing," *Proceedings of CSCW,* 1988, 25–38.

L. A. Rowe, "Video Compression: What to do when everything is changing?" *Invited Talk Usenix 1994 Conference,* 1994.

H. Schulzrinne, S. Casner, R. Frederick, and V. Jacobson, "RTP: A Transport Protocol for Real-Time Applications, Internet-Draft," Internet Engineering Task Force, Audio-Video Transport Work Group, July 1994.

K. Watabe, S. Sakata, K. Maeno, K. Fukuoka, and T. Ohmori, Distributed multi-party desktop conferencing system: MERMAID, *Proceedings of CSCW,* 1990. 27–38.

55

Speech Recognition

Eric Nahm
Deborah Slater

Although speech recognition has been around for more than 20 years, its potential has barely been tapped by the mass market. While other technological advances in the computer industry have made a tremendous impact on the average PC user, the ability to speak to one's PC has not yet caught on.

The Sleeper on the Information Highway

While many computer technologies have come a long way, speech recognition is just now beginning to catch up as a useful tool for the mass business and home PC markets. This is the only technology whose market expectations have been set by Hollywood! The average PC user still has the "Star Trek" mindset: simply start talking into the air, like to another human being. Someday, this will be the reality, but with only a little compromise; most users can get many of the same benefits of interacting with their computers or microprocessor-controlled devices by voice now.

Today, you can type a letter and perform all the editing functions by voice, leaving your hands on the keyboard. You can enter numbers into a spreadsheet, leaving your hands free to handle the source documents from which the numbers are being copied (Quicken). You can dictate a letter, provided that you have the patience to do so with today's word-at-a-time systems. You can switch between applications and you can navigate through Windows, replacing a series of mouse clicks with simple verbal commands. So why isn't everyone using speech recognition software?

One answer lies in the trend syndrome. Technologies become trends, based on such powerful factors as the accessibility of the technology, the amount of marketing hype by manufacturers and the media coverage of these technologies. Recent "mindshare" winners include multimedia in the early '90s and the Internet in 1995. Although many technologies are available today, it takes large marketing budgets to initiate a trend. This leads to consumer awareness, which creates demand, which creates media interest, which leads to increased consumer awareness...Many advanced, very useful technologies are in the wings, waiting for their moment in the sun. Some of these will emerge later this decade, some will linger on the sidelines, and many won't make it in the marketplace. Many people believe speech recognition is on the next wave. Let's examine why they are likely to be proven correct.

Technology Advances Make Quality Speech Recognition Available Now

If everyone sounded alike, speech recognition would be easy. But people don't sound alike. The diversity in human voice patterns is as awe inspiring as the diversity in human appearance. In early generations of speech-recognition systems, each user trained the system to understand his or her own unique voice. But who likes to train to use any consumer device? Is a VCR so hard to use, or are we just too busy (or lazy) to read the manual and follow the instructions? So, the technology has to adapt to the way that consumers want to use it.

It has to understand almost everyone's voice, without training. This is called *speaker independence*. It requires much more computing power than earlier systems, but with the consumer acceptance of the Intel 486 and Pentium systems, processing power is no longer an issue.

Several years ago, you had to train the system to learn your voice pattern (speaker dependent) for thousands of words. This process was tedious and time-consuming. Today's more advanced systems provide speaker independence (built-in voice files representative of the native language), often with an option to train words or phrases on the fly (as needed) to achieve very high accuracy.

Continuous Speech Recognition vs. Word Recognition

Early systems recognized words, but people don't speak in single words. Newer systems recognize phrases spoken naturally, the way people speak. True, even this technology has some rules to follow, but so does a keyboard or mouse. In human interaction, we signal each other via pauses, punctuation, and volume fluctuation. We have trouble understanding people who speak in monotone, with no inflection or pauses. So does the computer. But following the rules of natural speech, which observes common "signaling" techniques that we learn early in our lives, the computer—with today's continuous speech-recognition systems—does a respectable job. Like with humans, these systems only understand words they know, but the human mind is still far more sophisticated in combining known words into new phrases and being able to imply meaning.

Today's continuous speech recognition systems can understand known phrases with high accuracy, and future generations of technology will incorporate neural networks to "learn" new phrases comprised of known words. But let's not overlook the facts of human verbal interaction. How often does someone ask that a phone number or name be repeated because it wasn't understood the first time?

Consumers also have the right to be inconsistent. They commonly accept their keying errors; they accept the limitations of the mouse and similar pointing devices for Windows, such as not double clicking fast enough, or clicking at the wrong time and getting an unintended result. But let the speech-recognition system not accurately understand what they said and watch out!

Companies that try to change consumer expectations usually fail; those that respect and adapt to these expectations have a better chance of having their products accepted in the marketplace. So, speech recognition must achieve accuracy, which is consistently high (98–99+%). Although this is not a trivial challenge, a number of products claim to have achieved this, and this chapter was written using such a system, Listen for Windows, by Verbex Voice Systems.

The Office is Not a Quiet Place

Have you ever tried having a telephone conversation with the TV on, or when a group of people standing nearby are having a conversation? The office, including the ever-more-common home office is a noisy place, with fax machines, copiers, printers, phones ringing, and background conversations. If speech recognition is to be a generally useful computing technology, it has to function effectively, in spite of all these distractions. That means both correctly interpreting commands and ignoring noise not intended for the PC. I recall a conversation with a retired gentleman in Florida who had seen our continuous speech product in a computer retail store, and called to ask how it was different from the speech recognition program he had gotten as a part of a computer sound system he had purchased. His primary complaint was that whenever he turned on the dishwasher while he was using the computer in the next room, the system constantly reacted with unintended actions, which caused the disabling of the program.

Effective noise filtering, an integral part of advanced speech recognition programs, solves this problem. Continuous speech-recognition systems, in general, are far more tolerant of noise than word-at-a-time systems.

Getting Started—The Basics

Given the complexity of installing new devices into a Windows environment, I wouldn't blame you for being a little skeptical. After all, we are talking about a PC, not the dashboard of the Enterprise.

Actually, it's quite simple. All you need is a Sound Blaster-compatible sound card and a microphone of average quality. The handheld microphones that look like Karaoke microphones are usually at the low end of speech signal capture, but many speech recognition systems are available with high-quality noise-canceling microphones. Don't underestimate the importance of the microphone—it functions as the primary input device to your speech-recognition software. As in most applications, garbage in...garbage out.

For example, Listen for Windows from Verbex Voice Systems offers a variety of microphones (Fig. 55.1). A headset microphone provides the best quality in nonquiet environments because the range of the microphone element is 1" to 2".

These are easily adjustable, lightweight, and won't mess your hair. The boom can be moved away from your mouth to make talking on the phone easier, for example, and a good speech recognizer, with out-of-vocabulary rejection, will not pick up unintended data or commands, in most cases.

For quiet offices, a desktop- or monitor-mounted microphone will do just as well. These provide a range of 12" to 18" for the user, and they usually incorporate some background noise cancellation.

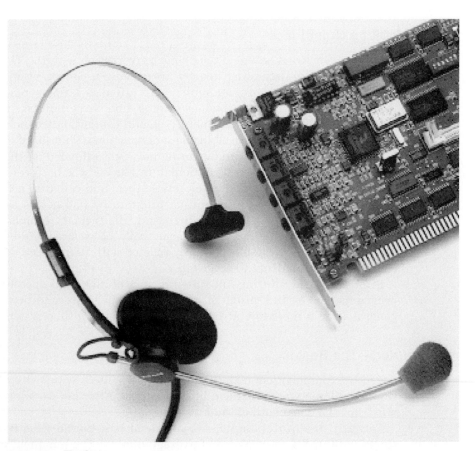

Figure 55.1 Headset.

Many notebook PCs with built-in sound capabilities incorporate average-quality microphones into the system enclosure. These might prove adequate for speech recognition, depending on the quality of the element and its placement in respect to other system components. Placement on or above the keyboard means that you will have to lower your head to talk to the system, and placement over or on the side of the screen will more easily pick up your voice while you are looking at the screen. Most of these systems have either an external stereo jack, connected to the audio chip or a PCMCIA slot, to accommodate a sound card, into which a headset or desktop microphone can be plugged. For use in a noisy airplane, for example, a headset microphone will provide maximum performance and privacy.

Once the software is installed, either by the PC manufacturer or the user, and the microphone is connected, the user can easily start talking to the system with minimal training. Listen for Windows, for example, comes with a 5-minute tutorial that walks you through the speech-recognition system features.

Among the features users value most is the ability to customize the commands or to create new commands easily. This enables users to personalize the system to their most comfortable work style, which has the benefit of making the commands easy to remember. Also, everyone uses the same programs differently, so the ability to match the speech commands to your style provides a level of custom integration not available in most Windows programs. After speaker independence, this capability is the feature early users asked for most often.

Adding Speech to Your Applications

Many speech-recognition products come with a set of commands for the top-selling applications—word processors, spread sheets, and the like. Listen for Windows, for example, comes with more than 16,000 built-in commands. But what about adding speech to your applications? Is it hard? Does it require a redesign? No way!

The most typical interface between advanced speech recognition and the application is a simple one—keystrokes. The speech recognition acts as an alternative to the keyboard (or mouse). The algorithm that interprets speech, after a successful recognition "event" sends the equivalent keystrokes to the application, and the applications reacts as if it received keyboard input. So, adding speech recognition to an application is really quite simple.

Where this becomes a tremendous advantage is in complex applications, where a function involves multiple steps to perform by keyboard or mouse. A single voice command can represent dozens of keystrokes, making applications easier to learn and use. For example, an order-entry screen might be populated by saying "Order 4 dozen of item 6124358 in blue," rather than tabbing between fields and entering each field individually. Such "power commands" are the reason that speech recognition is becoming a favorite add-on for software developers looking to differentiate their products.

For system integrators building applications on Lotus Notes, the process of layer-by-layer application entry and exit can cause problems if users don't follow established procedures carefully. Switching between functions by voice eliminates the potential problems by hiding the steps in the command, and letting the user focus on the job function, not how the application works. For those of us who've "menu surfed" to find the function we are looking for, this approach is particularly appealing.

Once familiar with how a speech-recognition system's toolkit works, a user can "speech enable" a typical application in one or two days of development. Demos or prototypes can frequently be done in two to three hours. For developers, speech recognition is a low-cost, high-payback way to show users and MIS departments that they truly understand how the application and user interact!

New Applications Drive Consumer Interest

Dictation systems

Today's dictation systems are attracting a lot of attention. Although they can provide some utility for people who don't like to or are unable to use a keyboard, they have some serious limitations. Because a word sounds different in context with other words, these systems require that you speak one word at a time. Each word is recognized as it is spoken, and errors or homonyms are handled during document creation, word by word. This can be cumbersome, and might be difficult to use for people used to dictating to a recording device for subsequent transcription by a secretary. In an article in *The Wall Street Journal* (Aug. 17, 1995), discrete word recognition was postulated as being a voice-abusive process, and comparisons were drawn to the impact of keyboarding and mouse usage as contributing to repetitive stress injuries. Nonetheless, dictation systems are an example of a creative and important use of speech-recognition technology by consumers. Although their sales are relatively small today, it can be expected to grow as their usability improves with time.

Telephony uses

Consumers are likely to have their first experience with speech recognition when using their telephone. These are intentionally limited applications, designed to make using telephones easier, in particular, cellular car phones. Phone companies are using these simple applications, typically voice dialing plus a few command words (operator, collect, yes, no) as a market test of the technology, and a way to learn how to integrate speech recognition into their network infrastructure. This makes perfect sense because the customer already is speaking into a microphone built into the telephone.

Expect these systems to be deployed in more complex telephony applications during the next few years, as over-the-phone speech recognition technologies become more advanced. You will see phone service providers offering speech recognition to more easily access advanced functions (billable services), and to address the safety issues involved in using mobile phones while driving.

Personal digital assistants

These devices are gaining marketshare, as consumers demand access to their phone directories and calendars wherever they are. Early devices tried to use handwriting recognition, but this technology has proven to be elusive. The physical attributes of these devices make use of a keyboard difficult, both to enter data and retrieve it.

Although the old adage that a person can never be too slim or too rich is politically incorrect today, it is accepted that a PDA can never be too small or lightweight. Speech recognition is the only reasonable solution to this problem. And it is not even a certainty that PDAs will be carried with you, given the cost, battery requirements, and difficulty of maintaining duplicate databases on the PDA and the home or office PC. Why not let your PC act as a "virtual PDA," calling it from any phone and asking for the information you want? For example, "What is Debbie Slater's fax number" or "What is on my calendar for Friday September 8 at 10:00 a.m.?"

Improved Application Interface for PC Programs

As PC use becomes ever more pervasive in the home and office, the user interface becomes increasingly important. Windows, and the thousands of applications for Windows, are inherently complex because of the myriad of choices available. Clearly, Windows is a major improvement over DOS, but many features require multiple, repetitive steps. This problem is most evident in more complex applications, such as computer-aided design, graphical drawing programs, and the new workflow management systems.

Speech recognition replaces the mouse and keyboard as the primary application interface, and enables the user to hide multiple steps under a single spoken command, such as "open monthly sales forecast" or "select color cyan." Although Windows'95 aims to simplify this by reducing some of the earlier processes, in some ways it adds even more complexity. As consumers start to use on-line services, such as the Internet, or sophisticated multimedia encyclopedias on CD-ROMs, the need to easily find information will become a compelling application for speech recognition.

Home Automation

The ability to control the home environment is an idea whose time is coming later this decade. Already, small companies and Universities are experimenting with systems that offer the disabled a means to better control their lives. A student at Radford College has automated a dormitory room for handicapped students; a major supplier of hospital beds has provided a bed that enables patients who can't use their hands to dial the phone, use the TV, adjust the bed, and call for a nurse. Many small companies are developing PC-based integrated home control systems.

What all these systems have in common is the user interface; speech recognition is the only practical method. And how about accessing the 500 channels of entertainment and information on the "information superhighway?" Would you rather spend 15 minutes navigating menus to find out what's available, or simply speak into a handheld device to find out what movies are on? An early trial of interactive TV in Orlando, Florida is incorporating speech recognition as a key component. And don't be surprised to see simple versions of speech-recognition systems embedded into microwave ovens, washers, VCRs, and other appliances in the future. Not only does it simplify use, but it also costs less to manufacture than knobs and keypads.

Ergonomically Correct

With the widespread use of computer products, particularly the mouse, wrist injuries have increased dramatically. Known more commonly as repetitive stress injuries (RSI), conditions such as Carpal Tunnel Syndrome (CTS) are rising at an alarming rate. Many CTS patients are forced to go on disability, and might not be able to return to the workplace, depending on the extent of the injury. Some injuries are so extensive that surgery is required, and doctors are now recommending post-surgery patients eliminate their use of the computer entirely. Ergonomic products designed to ease the pain or minimize wrist motion have proven successful, but are not a total solution.

Use of speech recognition by RSI sufferers is on the increase, and has proven successful. Mission Critical Technologies, a computer software company in Concord, MA, has integrated Verbex's Listen for Windows in their program AdFAX, which seamlessly combines voice, keyboard, and mouse. The program is targeted at newspaper advertising departments, and is currently being used at *The Washington Post*. According to Mission Critical, the implementation of AdFAX has increased worker productivity to 90%, and has brought back many employees from the disabled list.

Implementation of speech recognition as an alternative input device for RSI sufferers will undoubtedly increase with the new ergonomics proposal from the Occupational Safety and Health Administration. The standard focuses on what experts call "cumulative trauma disorders" that cause neck, shoulder, arm, and back pain, including Carpal Tunnel Syndrome. If passed, the proposal would require that all companies make adjustments in the workplace to reduce repetitive stress injuries (The Newark, N.J. *Star-Ledger*, November 1, 1994). Although larger employers might be able to cope with the requirements, smaller companies might find it financially impossible to implement what is considered necessary to make the workplace ergonomically correct. Speech recognition is likely to be a low-cost and highly viable solution for small and large employers alike.

In fact, the U.S. Dept. of Agriculture has established what is referred to as a *target center*, focused on computer-based technologies to assist government employees with disabilities. Under the leadership of Ophelia Falls, this department has established a showcase of computer technologies from America's leading companies, and this center serves as a resource to numerous other Federal Agencies. Speech recognition is among the key technologies being shown and used here, and demonstrates the emerging acceptance of this technology as a workplace ergonomic device.

Your Voice as a Third Hand—How Industry Uses Speech Recognition

Speech recognition has also proven a viable technology used in conjunction with automatic identification technologies, such as bar coding. Workers and management alike have discovered that efficiency and accuracy has improved when using voice in tasks involving data collection, package and mail sorting, or inspection applications. For example, LXE, a manufacturer of handheld industrial terminals, is incorporating speech recognition into their family of products (*Auto ID News*, May 1995). By combining voice, bar code, and wireless data transmission capabilities, the system allows users to keep both hands free for their work, while capturing information and sending it to a computer for processing. The U.S. Post Office uses voice sorting systems from Verbex Voice Systems extensively throughout the mail sorting process, as a supplement to automated sorting equipment, as do many of the leading private package handlers. Major automobile manufacturers use speech-recognition devices for inspection (Nissan, Honda, Ford) and for gathering test data during vehicle road testing (GM Proving Grounds).

Speech recognition as a hands-free alternative is now in high demand in many manufacturing, distribution, financial, and medical applications.

The Coming of Age

In the future, speech recognition will be a standard feature on your PC, just as a mouse is today. Some forward-thinking companies are already shipping multimedia systems, components, software, and games with various speech-recognition technologies. The indications of general market acceptance are all around us. Speech-recognition companies are springing up all over, challenging the current leaders. Microsoft announced a "standard" that should help software developers integrate speech recognition from various suppliers. New consumer devices are emerging with voice control, from VCRs to telephones. But consumer expectations will remain high.

These are exciting times for speech recognition—it is finally arriving. Once speech recognition is accepted as a standard for the PC, it will then be ready to make the transition to consumer appliances of all kinds. Emerging technologies, such as DSPs and more powerful microprocessor chips, will help this transition, making it possible for speech recognition to become the primary user interface to any device with an embedded chip.

Home automation, vehicle navigation, even automatic teller machines, will all be controlled by voice, and you'll be able to interact with movies and other entertainment media as though you were in the studio. Looks like Hollywood was right all along!

56

Game Play, Story Sense, and Interface Design

Steven Bussard

New interactive products combine skills currently used by the software, game, and film businesses. In each of these industries, the best creative minds have a special sensibility that helps them create great products. In software, it is called *interface design*. In games, it is *game play*. In the film business, they call it *story sense*.

What are these three special skills? How are they related? How are they different? Can they be combined?

Introduction

Corporations are spending billions of dollars to explore the new worlds of interactive services. Entertainment will be one of the most lucrative businesses in the new media.

Successful interactive entertainment products will require core competencies from three existing businesses: games, storytelling (films, drama, novels), and computer software. Each product must appeal to customers as a game, a story, and good piece of software. A weakness in any one of these three areas will weaken the product as a whole.

When building games, stories, or software, there is an understandable tendency to focus on the mechanics. What's the budget? Where will we make it? How long will it take?

Although these issues are important to the creators of a product, they mean little to the customer. Customers want to know what the product will do for them and what the experience of using it will be like.

Take a classic example, from one of America's biggest corporations, Proctor and Gamble. In 1878, Harley Proctor realized that if his company carved a small line down the middle of its laundry-size bar of soap, customers could break it into two toilet-sized bars.

In another example, a refractory batch of soap went out to customers which had been "incorrectly" mixed with too much air. A customer wrote back requesting more of the floating soap. Proctor and Gamble astutely realized that to that customer, the production "mistake" was actually a benefit. The company began adding more air to Ivory soap, so customers could more easily find it in their bathtubs. It was the same soap in both cases, but it was easier to use. Currently, the best games, stories, and software are made by people with skills in three areas:

Games	game play
Stories	story sense
Software	interface design

A great game designer knows when the game play is flawless. A great development executive, producer, or writer knows when a story feels right. And a great software designer knows when the user interface is correct.

People with a knack for any one of these skills are already valuable today. People with a feel for all three will be priceless tomorrow. These three sensitivities combine science with art. They determine how a product feels to customers, and they make or break products.

This chapter is a brief exploration of the nature of these three issues of game play, story sense, and interface design.

Stories

A story is an obstacle course, in which the relationships between characters change as they struggle to overcome roadblocks in their paths.

Example

John and Mary sit on the sofa.
Is that a story? No, we have characters, but nothing happens.

John and Mary go to the store.

Now we have characters, and they are doing something, but it's not very interesting.

John and Mary go to the store.
A fierce tornado sweeps down the street.
It misses them.
John and Mary go home.

We have characters and something exciting happens, but it does not involve our characters.

John and Mary go to the store.
A fierce tornado sweeps down the street.
It picks them up and carries them into the next county.
John and Mary get on a bus and go back home.

This is better. Something happens, and it involves our characters. In addition, the characters have to take action to overcome an obstacle. But the obstacle (getting back home) is too easily overcome. In addition, the relationship between our characters does not change. Consider this next scenario...

John goes to the store to buy butter.
Mary goes to the store to buy milk.
They have never met before.
They wait outside the store for the store to open.
A fierce tornado sweeps down the street.
It picks up John, Mary, and a cow, dumping them into a swamp.
Dazed and shaken, John and Mary find themselves thrown together in the wilderness.
Using their wits and courage, they struggle against many obstacles, bringing the cow with them.
At first, they argue constantly.
By the time he's saved her life and she's saved his life a few times, they are in love.
John, Mary, and the cow get back home.
John and Mary get married and start a dairy.

This is now a story. We have characters, obstacles, relationships, and a resolution.

Story sense

The great producer or development executive has a finely developed sense of story. Although there are no guarantees of box office success, these producers and studio executives can repeatedly pull a good story out of a pile of chaff. They can also tell when no amount of rewriting will fix a fatally flawed story.

Games

A game is a contest between you and something else. You can play a game against another person, a group of people, a machine, or even yourself. Games are defined by their rules.

Throw a ball in the air.

That might be entertaining for a while, but it's not much of a game.

Throw a ball into the air.
Pick up a jack before the ball hits the ground.

Now we have a very simple game. But it has only one level of play. It would soon become boring.

Throw a ball into the air.
Pick up a jack before the ball hits the ground.
Throw the ball in the air again.
Try to pick up two jacks before the ball hits the ground.
Keep throwing the ball in the air and picking up one more jack than the last time.
When you fail, let the other player try to pick up more jacks than you were able to.

Now we have a game with virtually unlimited levels of play. It also has a social aspect because each person tries to outperform the other.

Game play

A good game designer has a well-tuned feel for game play. Does the game offer a satisfying balance between obstacle and achievement, repetition and surprise, skill and knowledge? Does it contain the elements that will keep people playing it for hours at a time?

Software programs

A program is a set of instructions to a computer. Like a cake recipe, these instructions must be precise and complete.

Suppose John and Mary have a robot, and they want it to get them some milk. They issue the following instruction:

Go to the store and buy milk.

To a computer, the above instruction would be too vague. A program needs the precision shown in the following set of instructions:

Walk to the closest Ralph's supermarket.
Get a shopping cart.
Go to the dairy section.
Place three quarts of Altadena skim milk into the cart.
Go to the checkout counter.
Find out the total grocery bill.
Write a check for that amount, plus $50.
Leave the grocery cart at the front door of the supermarket.
Bring home the milk and the $50.

Interface Design

The best software not only works reliably, it also is a pleasure to use. The great software designer understands how people use software. The software is designed to be easy to learn and easy to use. The interface design of a piece of software can make it or break it. Though people have formulated rules for interface design, it remains a subjective skill. Like story sense and game design, only so much can be taught: the best designers just have a knack for it.

How do Stories, Programs, and Games Compare?

Interactivity

Stories are usually determined in advance by the writer. The writer works hard to carefully construct the best balance of elements to give his audience a satisfying story experience. Printed or filmed stories are then played over and over the same way.

Although programs and games are designed in advance, they retain a key aspect that is missing from stories: the actions of the user or player affect the nature of the experience. Most stories we read or see are presented exactly as they were written.

Games and programs behave differently. The game player takes an action and is greeted by a response. A software user presses the mouse, and something happens on the screen. The nature of the experience is determined by the user/player. This responsiveness is the interactivity that is so talked about today.

Interactivity is a quality missing from modern storytelling. Whether it should be added, and if so, how, is a key design issue for the next decade.

Rising tension

Games and stories usually have an increasing feeling of tension over time. The characters in a story must overcome more and more challenging obstacles. The game player must reach new and more difficult skill levels. Programs generally do not have this aspect. They sit patiently, waiting for the user to finish a report or complete a spreadsheet.

Character

Stories rely on interesting characters. The characters are what make the audience want to follow the story. Because the audience cannot get directly in on the action, it must enjoy watching the involvement of the characters in the action. If those characters are not interesting, the audience does not really care what happens.

Most games have limited characters. The King and Queen in chess do not reveal character. They are simply embodiments of a few rules of movement. In games among people, the aspects of character are often a combination of the game and the player. In football, quarterbacks get to do special things, yet the difference between one quarterback and another also reflects their personal character.

In computer games, because the player is going up against a machine, an effort is sometimes made to endow objects in the game with character. Currently, these objects offer only minimal character traits. Sonic the Hedgehog or Mario are pretty thin in the character department.

One of the challenges for game designers will be to give more character traits to the elements in computer games. Adding this aspect from storytelling will make games more involving. Software programs have their own type of character, represented by their look and feel. Some people love WordPerfect, and others swear by Word for Windows. Both programs do basically the same things, but how they do it is different. Some software even offers built-in characters, called *guides* or *wizards*. These pseudo-characters give the user help and information.

Can Games, Programs, and Stories be Combined?

The new information technologies make it possible for stories, programs, and games to be more like each other. What impact will this have?

In the program area, it can be argued that the Graphical User Interface (Windows, Macintosh, etc.) has already added a more playful and game-like feel to spreadsheets and word processors. To the extent that we are more entertained while writing budgets or reports, we also are more attentive and productive.

Some programs will begin to include story-like aspects, leading their users down a path of obstacles to overcome. Examples of such types of programs would be software that helps users write business plans, resumes, wills, and so forth.

The most creative mixture, however, will come from combining games and stories. This combination will produce a new type of entertainment. For now, let's call it a *story-game*.

If we combine the nature of story and game, we have an experience that offers these characteristics:

1. Obstacles to overcome (games and stories)

2. Rising sense of tension (stories)

3. Increasing skill levels (games)

4. Interesting characters and relationships (stories)

5. Dynamic response to audience (games)

6. Sense of resolution (stories)

How can this be done? Many people in Hollywood feel plot possibilities would quickly become overwhelming. Many people in the computer game universe see film as a "static" medium, one that ties them down to prerecorded outcomes.

The solution lies in adapting some of the key principles of games and stories.

Principle: Action flows from character.

Good writers take great care to develop their characters. Once the characters are developed, they take on a life of their own. Writers often say they are merely the conveyer of the character's natural wishes and responses. This underlying nature of good writing is similar to the algorithmic thinking described by Chris Crawford in his article in the February, 1994 issue of *Interactive*.

Entertainment Design

Thomas and Johnston quote a Disney animator in their book *Disney Animation*. The animator is responding to changes in the storyline for *The Fox and the Hound*.

> All right! Now you feel that the story comes out of the personalities—it is not a plot you are trying to push the characters into—it doesn't even feel like a story! It's just something that happens when you get these personalities working against each other!"

Good characters, a well-defined universe of behavioral rules, and imaginative writers can propel a set of characters through many storylines. Consider the longevity of Sherlock Holmes, James Bond, Punch and Judy, *M*A*S*H**, and *The Mary Tyler Moore Show*.

As long as writers are true to the nature of their characters and the rules of their story universe, an initial situation and set of characters can develop into many different stories.

> *Proposition: If characters and situations are defined with enough completeness, and if the rules of storytelling are correctly implemented, a computer program can respond to the audience's input with differing, yet quite believable, story pieces.*

This approach will create stories that propel themselves, responding to input from the player. Instead of just playing with chess pieces or moving sprites, the player is interacting with full-blown characters and situations.

> *Principle: Filmed images can be intercut to create quite different meanings.*

Film editors and directors know that much of a film is "written" in the editing room. The way that film segments are put together determines how an audience perceives the action. Leave out the close-up of the witness's nervous hands, and his testimony might seem credible.

> *Proposition: As the access time for retrieving film segments from the source medium decreases, it will be possible to construct whole new storylines by rearranging building blocks of visual actions.*

This concept is partially realized by the interactive movies being developed for specially equipped theaters. The film is recut on the spot, presenting a different experience each time.

> *Principle: Media experiences are built up in layers.*

As any filmmaker knows, the film gets more powerful as it adds in music, sound effects, and special visual effects. Each layer increases the viewer's suspension of disbelief. Add a music cue, for example, and a seemingly innocuous line of dialogue takes on a sinister tone.

> *Proposition: By separating and recombining media elements, new experiences can be presented to the user.*

For example, a film scene in a car chase could be shot with the stoplights in intersections turned off. The computer could then map in a color for the stoplights, depending on what would be interesting to see in the game.

In some situations, the player would be confronted with a red light, in others, a green light. The computer would know which light the viewer was seeing and react to the viewer's responses appropriately.

Principle: A good interface is based on a clear metaphor.

The GUI interface is often referred to as "point and click." This phrase sums up the underlying metaphor of the interface design. The user points to little objects on the screen and clicks (or double-clicks). The system responds.

Proposition: The metaphor of the interface should complement the metaphor of the game's universe.

Because the player interacts through the interface, their experience is shaped by it. Their interaction should be enhanced by the interface, and the style of the interface should match the style of the game. Anyone who has driven a Cadillac, Shelby Mustang, and Triumph Spitfire knows how the interface can influence an experience.

Another case in point would be the interfaces for Myst and Doom. These games are at the top of the charts today, yet they paint much different universes. The slow, but smooth, response of Myst fits the nature of that game. The twitchy, fast interface for Doom matches that game's universe as well.

Conclusion

By combining stories, programs, and games, we will enrich both our work and our play, making play more fun and work more productive.

Recent and future advances in information technologies open exciting ways to enrich age-old human experiences. Miguel de Cervantes made great advances in written storytelling in 1605, when he wrote *Don Quixote*. D. W. Griffith advanced the art of filmed storytelling in 1915 with *Birth of a Nation*. Perhaps 1997 will be remembered as the beginning of a new type of storytelling.

References

Apple Computer, *Macintosh Human Interface Guidelines*, Reading, MA: Addison-Wesley, 1992.

Common User Access Advanced Interface Design Guide, IBM, 1989.

Crawford, Chris, "How to Think: Algorithmic Thinking, Interactive Entertainment Design," February 1994.

CyberArts, Edited by Linda Jacobson, San Francisco: Miller Freeman, Inc., 1992.

"Document Design: A Review of the Relevant Research," Edited by Daniel B. Felker, American Institutes for Research, Washington, 1980.

"Film Craft in User Interface Design," Siggraph 93 Course Notes 61, Chuck Clanton and Emilie Young, 1993.

Flesch, Rudolf, *How to Make Sense*, New York: Gramercy Publishing Company, 1954.

Flesch, Rudolf, *The Art of Clear Thinking*, New York: Harper & Brothers Publishers, 1951.

Guidelines for Document Designers, Edited by Daniel B. Felker, Washington: American Institutes for Research, 1981.

Heckel, Paul, *The Elements of Friendly Software Design*, Warner Software, 1982.

Laurel, Brenda, *The Art of Human-Computer Interface Design*, Reading, MA: Addison-Wesley Publishing Company, 1990.

Norman, Donald A., *The Design of Everyday Things*, New York: Doubleday Currency, 1988.

Price, Jonathan, *How to Write a Computer Manual*, Menlo Park: The Benjamin/Cummings Publishing Company, 1984.

Root, Wells, *Writing the Script*, New York: Holt, Rinehart, and Winston, 1979.

Scott, DeWitt H., *Secrets of Successful Writing*, Reference Software, 1989.

Thomas, Frank and Johnston, Ollie, *Disney Animation: The Illusion of Life*, New York: Abbeville Press, 1981.

Tufte, Edward R., *Envisioning Information*, Cheshire: Graphics Press, 1990.

Williams, Robin, *The Non-Designer's Design Book*, Berkeley: Peachpit Press, 1994.

57

Multimedia for Technical Documentation

Jay Murray

Multimedia can be a tremendous aid in technical documentation. Whether we're going to create reference materials, quick memory aids, or detailed online tutorials, an intelligent use of full color graphics, sound, and animation can make the difference between material that sits orphaned on the bookshelf and material that actually gets used (Fig. 57.1).

Pictures are worth more than words, but 10 seconds of animation can speak volumes (Fig. 57.2). Sound and video, together, can carry an emotional quality that all humans respond to, and that print and paper rarely achieve.

Everything is a tradeoff, though. Ten seconds of animation is a demand that documenters should not take lightly, for not everyone is prepared to meet it. By demands I mean, for one thing, the need for some pretty advanced hardware by today's standards: A fast graphics controller; 2 MB of free disk space; data transfer rates that outpace many CD-ROM devices that still ship today in large numbers.

Even more significant is the greatest demand of all that for trained and talented authors who know how to use multimedia effectively and efficiently. This demand is much harder to meet than any hardware standards.

There are landmines everywhere in this landscape. I know because I've stepped on most of them myself. Here are a few of the ones I've mapped out so far.

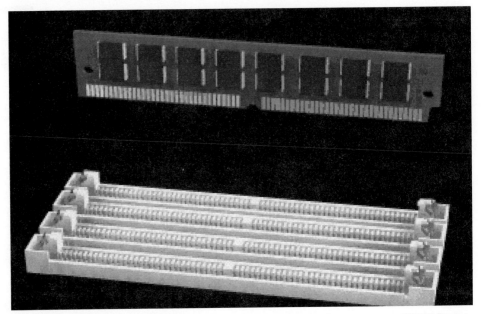

Figure 57.1   Frame one of a thirty frame FLC animation showing how a memory SIMM fits into its socket.

Figure 57.2   A screen from one of Gateway 2000's Online Guide series.

Planning is Everything

There are good reasons and bad reasons for doing just about anything (bor-rowing money and getting married spring to mind). Using multimedia for technical documents is no different. Before you embark on this venture, creat-ing your full-color, animated users guide with soundtrack, you'll do yourself a huge favor if you ask yourself a few questions first. You might save yourself some heartbreak.

Why am I putting it on-line?

Before we go any farther, let's stop to acknowledge an important point: paper documents have served us extremely well from Gutenburg's day until the dawn of the twenty-first century. Books have had a cultural significance that's probably unrivaled in the modern age, and they are still the standard form of prolonged, anonymous communication in the industrialized world. Bookstores still outnumber software outlets by a wide margin, and we all turn to books instinctively for detailed study, for reasoned analysis, and for understanding of complex and abstruse subjects. Heck, I'm a professional in electronic documents, and I spend more time reading from paper than I do from a computer screen, probably by a factor of 10!

This primacy of paper and print will be with us for the foreseeable future. Electronic documents are oddballs, the exceptions, and they are likely to become our troublesome foster children whenever we try to replace paper with them. Documents should go electronic and replace paper if, and only if, there is some advantage to doing it that way.

Having said all that, I now go on to say that there are instances where it does make sense to take documentation off paper and put it on a computer screen. One case is when a computerized document adds value to the product. Software applications are probably the purest example of this. If you need to prod your memory for one of those Pagemaker key combinations (I still do, after years with the program), it's much easier to find it in the Windows Help utility than it is to look it up in the manual. Assuming you can find the manual, of course.

Online documents enhance the value of some products; you learn the com-puter (or software) by using it. Also, they're harder to lose than a manual.

When the technology enhances communication

Some rather simple procedures can be devilishly difficult to describe verbally. Here's a sample from a manual I wrote a couple of years ago:

> You'll have to tilt the modules about 45 degrees as you insert them. Pushing them erect inside the slots should make them snap into place. Note that the little tabs on the ends of the mounting brackets fit through the holes in the ends of the SIMMs.

Did you get all that? Did you even read all that?
I seriously doubt it.

A 30-frame FLC animation, requiring about 6 seconds to run from beginning to end, shows how to insert a SIMM in its slot. In fact, after viewing the animation, virtually anyone can (1) perform this operation correctly on the very first try and, (2) be sure that it was done correctly.

This is a wonderful example of the strengths of animation. All the important details: *right-side up, slotted end this way, tilt it like this, the pins go here, etc.* are easy to demonstrate, and even easier to absorb, visually. Humans are visual creatures. Words just get in the way.

Sound is invaluable in instructional titles for language studies, music, bird calls, and a host of other things you can think up as easily as I can. If you have a multimedia PC with a microphone and a sound card, you can hear yourself speaking a foreign language and compare your accent with that of a native speaker. Nothing a paper document can do comes close to this.

When timeliness is everything

Electronic documents can be updated quickly and distributed electronically. Businesses can use them for catalogs, rate sheets, phone lists, errata, late-breaking changes, etc. As long as everyone concerned has the viewing hardware and knows how to use it, the information flows at a rate paper can't compete with.

When storage is everything

It's more efficient to give everyone on a network access to the Oxford English Dictionary than to give everyone a paper copy. This can hold true for parts lists, maps, etc.

Bad reasons for multimedia

It's been my experience that the usage of bad reasons for multimedia documents seems to outpace the use of good ones. Also, the people who champion multimedia for these absurd reasons seem to do so chiefly for other people and rarely, if at all, to use it themselves. My advice: be wary of the pharmacists who shun their own concoctions.

These are the specious, superficial, or in some other way inadequate reasons I've heard for using multimedia:

Because multimedia is cool. No, it's not.

Okay, it's cool for those of us who know and appreciate the ingenuity and sheer diligence it took to get that media into a format that we can see on a computer. We're hoping to sell this stuff someday to the public at large, though, and not just to each other in the computer industry.

I remember the first time I saw *Encarta*, Microsoft's groundbreaking encyclopedia on CD-ROM. It had sound. It had video clips, all playing right there on my computer screen. It had style. It had panache. I was dumbstruck.

Then, I showed *Encarta* to my wife. She yawned. It's like TV, she said, only not as good. I was dumbstruck. Again. But she was right. If the content isn't insightful, original, or engaging in some other way, then the novelty of computer animation and sound aren't enough to keep anyone interested. It's just primetime, network TV.

And we already have enough of that. We're saving (pick one) trees/time/money. No, were not.

That Print button just means that the reader, rather than the publisher, is paying for paper and printing. Creating electronic media demands specialized skills, expensive equipment, and time. Doing it well demands quite a lot of at least one of these.

Is paper dead? The question is absurd. It's still true that the greatest works of art in the English language were written with a quill pen. Here's an interesting experiment you can perform for yourself: get one of those novels on CD. I don't know, *Deerslayer*. *Don Quixote*. *Cat's Cradle*. Now, get someone to read it onscreen. Tell them they can sit right there at your computer and read as long as they want. You'll wait.

You won't have to wait for long. Chances are, you won't even need to find a chair in the time it takes your reader to remember some important errand he was going to run, excuse himself, and flee the scene. The reason: extended reading on a computer screen is stultifying. Try it yourself if you still don't believe it.

The lesson here is that paper still reigns supreme for many, many uses, with extended reading at the top of the list. There are no plans for an on-line version of this book, for example.

Just because we can. Not a good enough reason. Not even close. Define your task and your audience. The style and structure of your document will vary according to the readers you expect to see it. As every seasoned technical writer knows, it's just about impossible to fully satisfy both novices and experts with a single document. Let's consider each of these briefly.

Novices. Most people in the general population have still never used a personal computer. Those of us in the PC industry often forget that this is true, and that it will still be true for years to come. A lot of our documentation, therefore, needs to be written for these first-time users. What is truly surprising is how few of us have given much thought to the reading habits of this huge segment of our readership.

Novices don't read a technical manual the way experts do. Novices scan tables of contents and chapter headings, looking for something that catches their interest. They look over illustrations and read the captions and callouts. They browse and backtrack. They use a computer document not to search for a specific detail (they probably don't know what to look for), but for general familiarization. They're grazers, looking for a comfortable place. When they find it, they'll settle down and stay a while. But they're always ready to leave. They are intimidated, even hostile, when our manuals refer casually to concepts they're not familiar with.

Experts. Experts are different. They are probably looking for a specific detail (Do I need a BIOS update to install an EIDE hard drive?), or the answer to a problem (Why do I need a new video driver for AutoCAD?). They are probably rushed, frustrated, and in a foul temper—even before they've picked up your manual, and they will become very impatient, very quickly unless they can find the answer that they need. They hate to backtrack!

Detailed, progressive explanations are wasted on these people. Interestingly enough, it's been my experience that the novice who finds text that was written for the expert and, conversely, the expert, finding text that was intended for the novice, both of these people become equally animated at that moment. It's a striking transformation and all the more startling for the well-meaning tech writer because he's the object of all the animosity. The novice (or expert) will declare, indignant, that he's not an expert (or novice), and resents being taken for one. He then goes on to speculate on the rationality, qualifications, motives, and finally the genealogy of the idiot who writes this tripe.

This is not an easy crowd to please.

Your goals

What all this means to you is that you must decide at the outset which of these mutually antagonistic tribes you're targeting. This will tell you, basically, what it is that you're designing: an introductory tutorial, a list of troubleshooting tips, or a comprehensive reference.

Introductory tutorials. This, in my opinion, is where multimedia rules. Graphical content, well designed, puts the reader at ease while it lends a professional and pleasing air.

More importantly, it has communicative power that can leave text miles behind. You can illustrate the difference between a serial port and a parallel port in such a way that no one with any wits about him, having seen your illustration, is likely to mistake the two. To educate a novice to the same level with text, you're going to have to count the pins, covering "male" and "female" connectors, and point out the wide side and the narrow side of the connector. And much more.

A few words on the subject of humor: Don't shun it, but don't use it carelessly either. Most readers appreciate a break from the solemn tone of the run-of-the-mill technical manual. This is tricky ground for the unwary, though; there are insecure and ultra-sensitive readers who will feel diminished by the need to sit through your tutorial, and they will imagine that you're making fun of their inadequacy. Others, serious and hardworking types, will interpret a lighthearted tone as frivolous and irrelevant. When in doubt, it's probably best to stay serious.

Avoid verbal irony, meaning, the use of some wry expression (you're really going to love this little tidbit) in the intent to communicate the precise opposite. Until we in computerized media devise some on-line equivalent to a wink and a nudge, some viewers won't get it. The same is probably true of hyperbole, (I've said this at least 60 million times) and inside jokes (fill in your favorite Bill Gates witticism here). When in doubt, understate.

Conceptual understanding. This is dangerous ground for multimedia documents. Insight and comprehension do not come equally to all readers. For some of us, they never come at all. For others, they come slowly, imperfectly, and in stages after careful and selective review, contemplation, and repetition. Some of us need to see the same point explained from a number of different viewpoints.

All of this prolonged study suits the printed page, which lies there before you until you turn it. You can't effectively vary the playback speed of sound and video, and replaying them is clumsy.

All this is especially true for material that is abstract or conceptual. You can discuss the future, democracy, or electromagnetism, verbally, but I have no idea how you could do it graphically. This sort of work is the province of print, and will remain so for a while longer, I suspect.

Putting It On-Line

Assuming, now, that you're putting your documentation on-line for one of the right reasons, and you're pretty sure of both your audience and your goals, then you're ready to get started. Your next step is planning your presentation. You've got a lot of decisions to make: how much sound and animation to use, photorealistic or artistic graphics, color depth, navigation from menus, hot graphics or hypertext, and all sorts of other issues.

Remember that, to be truly useful, on-line documents have to be planned and developed for onscreen presentation, not paper documents converted for onscreen reading. The media are as different as novels and movies, and converting from one to the other is likely to be as difficult as adapting, for example, *The Brothers Karamozov* for the screen.

Here are a few of the rules I've tripped over in the past couple of years: Minimize pop and sizzle. Rule #1 is, content rules! Rule #2 is that you should always endeavor not to forget Rule #1. Earlier I mentioned my *Encarta* example. The point is that the subject matter itself must be well organized and then presented with imagination and pace, or you'll lose your audience. Kids, especially, will be bored very quickly by a presentation that relies on snappy effects or up-to-date music.

If you're a writer, the good news here is that you are still needed. Your skills as a communicator and a reformulator of information are needed just as badly in this environment as they were in the reign or paper and print. The bad news is that an astonishing number of producers have yet to realize this. Witness the massive barrage of oddly organized, confusing, and quite simply awful multimedia titles that line the shelves at software outlets.

In short: Don't create more primetime TV. Aim higher!

Go graphical whenever you can. Graphical instruction is almost always more effective than verbal instruction, whenever you can use it. Sometimes, of course, you can't; I recently spent a few days grappling with Dr. Steven Hawking's mind-bending *A Brief History of Time*. There is instructional material in this book that utterly defies any sort of illustration that I can imagine. If you can illustrate concepts like *relativity, uncertainty, and infinity*, please call me. I want to be your disciple.

Graphics inevitably invoke hardware issues. Consider the delivery platform's likely combinations of video cards and monitors and then write to the lowest common denominator. 640 by 480-pixel, 256-color VGA is a good choice, although this opens the Pandora's box of palette issues. You're going to need to worry about synchronizing your system palette with your presentation palette; otherwise, your viewers will witness the much-dreaded palette-flash between screens. The old SDK utilities PalEdit and BitEdit are your best survival tools in this wilderness.

Another thing: drop-shadows and gradient fills are staples of computer artists everywhere today, and they're all gorgeous on the 24-bit displays most of us use as our authoring platforms. Dithered down to the 256 colors most of our viewers are using, though, they look more like the ring around a bathtub. Disgusting.

Animation and sound

These are the grand luxuries. They can elevate your instructional or technical title to giddying heights. But all those FLC, FLI, AVI, and WAV files have one thing in common: they are all huge. A 30-frame FLC plays in about five seconds and needs about half a megabyte of storage space. There are compression methods to help you with these issues (and they do help), but you're still going to have to make some hard choices because those multimedia data files are, I repeat, *huge*.

Also, the display hardware issues that I mentioned, concerning graphics, are magnified tenfold when you want to play animation. Older systems, without local bus graphics, are likely to slow to a crawl, stop, or crash when you try to play a video. Consider your delivery platform.

A good trick you can get a lot of mileage out of is faking animation. By this, I mean any of several techniques, such as sprite animation (a static image fragment, simply moving about the screen) and fades between still images. As a matter of fact, if you're careful, you can often achieve most of the benefits of full animation by simply fading from one fixed image to another—at a fraction of the storage and display requirements.

Of course, you can't fake sound. But you can be economical with it. A single click, whistle, per-chonka sound probably occupies less than 20 KB of storage space, no matter how many times you play it. With a little creativity, you can fill your viewers' ears with recycled sounds, assuming, of course, that you really want to do that.

Find a designer

Find a professional designer to create your interface if you possibly can. No matter how painful and costly this is, it's probably worth it. The professional look this gives your title creates much more than visual appeal; it creates credibility. If you still have to go it alone and design your own interface, just resign yourself to the fact that everyone who sees it will know this immediately. (*Nice car you got there, buddy—build it yourself, did you?*)

Try to keep the following in mind: Design around unifying elements. Keep your standard navigation elements in the same spot from screen to screen. The Continue button should appear in one and only one spot on the screen, every time your reader sees it. Don't overlook the use of colors as navigational keys. Warm colors advance and cool colors recede.

Invisible "hot" spots that trigger explanatory pop-ups are interactive and fun, but some readers don't know enough to go looking for them. If you put them in a resizeable window, someone is going to resize them right off the display and never know they're there. Figuring out some way to mark them without cluttering up your screen is tricky, but worth the effort.

Organization matters

Online authoring gives you far less control over the reader's topic sequence than paper documents do, so you can't develop complex subjects as thoroughly as you can on paper. Also, your reader is likely to be looking for a solution to a present problem; he won't take time for background study and analysis. Your best solution is often to assume that the reader is fundamentally competent, but give him plenty of hypertext links to whatever background you think he might need.

Readers have a tendency to get lost in hypertext documents, too, so leave lots of milestones so that they will always know where they are in the overall title. Escape hatches, like a *Return to Contents* button, are just as important so that the befuddled reader can always get back to a place he knows. Even then, many readers will hesitate to click on "hot" words because they're not confident that they can find a way back to where they are now.

Keep your sentences and your topics short. Making your reader scroll down the screen for page after page of unrelenting text is just about the best way I know to lose his interest.

The development team

The last words of advice I have are for people who are inclined, as I am, to go it alone and do it all yourself. Generally speaking, my advice is, Don't do it unless you're willing to pay the price, which is a form of schizophrenia.

I'm serious. You'll write the script first and do your graphics next. Some of the problems you encounter creating graphics will convince you to rewrite your script. You'll go around this circle until your deadline begins to loom and you have to start programming. Then, you'll begin a new dance: something that's harder to program than you expected it to be will make you wonder whether you should rewrite, or reillustrate. Or both. Sometimes you shouldn't. Sometimes you should. It's hard to be sure.

Development teams go through the same process, of course, complicated by other issues, such as competing egos and different communication styles. But with a team you get the final ingredient that seems to make all the difference: fresh viewpoints. Three or four bright and involved people, confronted with a spectrum of dynamic problems, will outperform you, the dedicated individual, by an order of magnitude. Every time. I've experienced it and it's an eye-opener.

Conclusion

I hope that some of my recorded experiences as a multimedia hardware documenter help you in the event that you get the urge to do this sort of work. It's a lot of fun, and it can be rewarding.

Chapter

58

The Vision is First

Rob Morris

The single most important element of a multimedia project is in you. This element cannot be bought, or quantified. It is both personal and powerful. It makes all the challenges of the technology worthwhile. It comes first. Without it, projects fall flat. It is your Vision; the idea behind the details; the point of it all. How this Vision is realized is the subject of most of this book. The Vision itself and its role in the project are the subject of this chapter.

The Vision itself is the compelling experience you want to impart. It is not just the goal; it is the journey; it is the world around the goal. The Vision has to be woven into the project in such a way that the user becomes immersed in it and accepts it as natural and believable. The Vision will carry the user along—even if the content is weak in spots because the user enjoys traveling in your new world. Using a multimedia application can be like taking a vacation into your project.

The Vision is best if it comes from the heart, but others think that true motivation comes from the purse. It does not really matter as long as you are true to it throughout the project. The Vision becomes the anvil that is used to shape all the pieces into a single compelling whole. When the Vision is lost, the project turns into a muddle.

The reason that the Vision is so critical is the nature of Multimedia itself. Multimedia is a uniquely personal form of communication. Movies are big and bold, with interstellar travel, romantic encounters, and heart-stopping chase scenes. Television is intimate, with all the close-ups, dirty secrets, and familiar faces. Both of these forms require little from the audience. All they have to do is sit there and not disturb their neighbors. Multimedia is fundamentally different. Multimedia is personal. The interactive nature of multimedia is not a gimmick. It changes the location of control, and puts it into the users' hands. Once the control is released to the user, he becomes personally active in the world you have created. He uses what he knows from his own real life to interact with the world you have built from your Vision.

From the user's perspective, he is using his mind to explore, win, or use your world. In a real sense, he is exploring your mind. Can your Vision stand up to that? Some projects are better suited for a different medium, and there is no shame in that. For example, Mozart's music is fine just the way it is. Passive appreciation for a work of art is satisfying. People bring their own perspective to the work and understand it according to their own points of view. The work itself stands apart from the audience, and great art does so for centuries. It evokes feelings basic to the human animal and spirit. By retaining control, the traditional artist is able to use time-tested techniques to realize his Vision. Currently, there are very few time-tested techniques for success in multimedia.

Multimedia, however is a medium that requires you to be aware and sensitive to the mind of the user. Because you must create an "intuitive user interface," you must think about how the user will fit into your world. How he will find his way, and get your point? Your Vision has to envelop him; it has to be real and consistent. More than that, it has to keep his interest and satisfy him.

When you are sure that your Vision is best suited to be realized as a Multimedia experience, the next step is to use the power of the medium to realize your Vision.

Design

The biggest factor in delivering your Vision to your users is control. As a rule people do not like surrendering control. Oddly enough, this includes multimedia designers, too. When people use computers, they already feel subject to arbitrary rules dictated by software developers. Rules they do not really understand, based on assumptions about which they are not familiar. Because most people do not think like software engineers, they find using software to be annoying. This annoyance comes from the difference between the way people think on their own, and the ways they have to think to work with software.

For this reason, your Vision must be the basis for the project. Your Vision has to extend far enough that the user shares it, and finds the experience natural and satisfying. Because multimedia is so personal, people must not feel trapped. If they do, they will walk away.

People will share your Vision if they are allowed to, and if they are invited in through reward and discovery. When people enter a multimedia project, they start with a sense of hope and curiosity. They know that they are entering a new world of your design. They decide quickly if they enjoy it or not. Those first few mouse clicks are the true test of your Vision. Do your users feel welcome and respected when they first enter? Do they feel comfortable and rewarded for their time and effort in your world? This might sound like basic good manners, but as a designer, you have to give people a warm welcome and invite them in for more. Your users will discover your Vision one mouse click at a time. As your world surrounds them and they get more deeply into it, they are willing to accept new rules for that world, but they do not want to be trapped or tricked.

Keep the personal nature of human/machine interaction in mind. People forget they are using a machine and they act as if they are dealing with a personality. This is a real feeling and it is based on the fact that someone's intelligence is at work inside the machine. Dealing with that intelligence is what most people think of as using a computer.

Interaction

The way users interact with your project forms the basis of their experience. The ideal is the creation of a natural simple interface that seems to disappear as the user becomes more immersed in the project. In the real world, there are a lot of poor attempts at this. The reason for most of these failed attempts is the assumption that the user knows what the designer thinks he knows. Worse yet, the designer tries to force choices on the user, thus tricking and trapping him with a technological snare. If the designers really implemented in their Vision and trusted the users to enjoy it, these snares would be unnecessary. Give users a choice and a motivation for taking it and they will. Force the same information on them and they will turn you off. Every opportunity for the user to click the mouse, is also an opportunity for the user to turn off the project. The data, graphics, or victories might be there, but if it is a pain to get there, people would rather not bother. Using computers is not an end in itself for most people. Rather, computers bring some unique capacity to the job at hand. You can use that unique capacity to realize your Vision, and make the project work.

If the technology does not improve the process, why use it? For example, if you have a multimedia database and you make people go through 15 steps to find the information, you will not have happy users, or any users after a while. If your game is hard to use, there is always a board game in the closet.

The role of the Vision in determining interaction is not mysterious, as you might think. Use common sense. Think in terms of the real world. If you were going to pick up an apple, you would stretch out your hand and pick it up. You would be surprised how many multimedia designers would turn this into a multi-step process like:

1. Find object menu

2. Select fruit

3. Select apple from fruit submenu

4. Select action menu

5. Select pick up

6. Select combine

7. Combine pick up with apple

This might seem like an exaggeration, but it does indicate the problem. The multi-step process is the result of a design that does not reflect a well-executed Vision. Who would have made a fruit submenu in the first place? The designer who stuck fruit into the project somewhere in the middle of making it, that's who. It was tacked on and not integrated into the project as part of the whole. Instead of coming up with a natural way of picking up the apple, the designer has segmented his world into arbitrary types: objects and actions. It might be easier to add new types that way, but this kind of segmentation drives users nuts. How are they supposed to know that you think that way? Have you ever looked up "movies" in the Yellow Pages? It is under "theater." How about "exterminators," they are under "pests." Get the point?

People think differently, but if your Vision is convincing, the difference between the way you think, and the way your users think can be minimized. It might never disappear.

What is the solution? In this case, think of the hand. The hand is the human interface to reality. The hand picks up the orange. Instead of chopping the hand's role into actions, try to operate the hand more naturally. The software knows what the hand is working on. The software can narrow the possible hand actions according to circumstance. When the hand is over the orange, it can move away or pick up, for example. The idea is to remove the computer from view and use it as an intelligent interpreter. This way, the system helps to reinforce the Vision. The user is not operating the computer to get to the story, but rather the computer is providing assistance to the user. This lets the user interact with the material as naturally as possible.

Appearance

The next key element is appearance. I asked a 10-year old computer fan what she liked about multimedia and her response was "Cool graphics and movies." Later that day, I found her playing a game with blocky four-color graphics, so this was not a policy statement. It was her idea of the medium.

When you implement your Vision, appearance is very important. Appearance includes interface, graphic treatment, artwork, sound, font selection, 3D animations (if any), digital movies, menus, dialog boxes, and so on. It also includes what happens between things: fade to black, wipes, palette shifts, sound fades, etc. All these elements should work together. They have to reflect the underlying Vision, and each part adds a little more to the creation of a new world in the mind of your user. The watch words are consistency and continuity. You are creating a new world for your users. You are asking them to come along with you. You have to take the same care with the last image that you made with the first. It does not matter if your project is used to sell carpet, save souls, or is simply for fun and games. The care you take with the appearance reflects on the content. Ask yourself: Would you buy an idea from this interface? Think of it as packaging, but it is more than a container. Think of it as staging in theater, as atmosphere in a restaurant, or as environment and you are more on the right track. When consistency and continuity are lost, the world you create loses validity. You want people to pay attention to your project, but they will scrutinize it. So, don't suddenly change the font, drop the audio level, or change the background color without a reason. Let the Vision drive the project, but keep an eye out for detail.

Interface

I have been designing multimedia applications and tools since 1986. One clear point is: one tool cannot possibly do everything. As you work with a tool for a while, you start to think of your project in terms of what the tool can do, not the other way around. This is a fatal error. Create your Vision with no thought of how it will be done. When the design is complete, then figure out what tools to use. If you are always working around your tool, maybe you have the wrong tool.

Looking at new tools is a time-consuming task, but when you find the right tools, you might well get new ideas about your project. Be open to the power of this—even if the search is long. Suppose, for example, that you want to make a simulation for an educational project. In addition, the financial people in our company actually have the model in the form of an Excel spreadsheet. Their model is totally data driven and predictive. Too bad you can't include that spreadsheet into your educational model. Instead you have to rebuild parts of it within the authoring system. This time-consuming, tedious, and error-prone task could be omitted if the author had just found the right system. There are systems that allow you to include this kind of data, but you have to find them, For example, Ozone allows authors to add different data types in cases like this.

Authoring systems are designed primarily for "nonprogrammers" who want to develop multimedia projects. The authoring software does this by handling the implementation details. The author tells the system what to do, and when to do it. These commands are typically held in a file called a *script file*. When the project is running the "run time" (or playback) software reads the script and does what the script says to do.

We knew that we had to build a system that was easy to use right out of the box, so we looked at what the authors were using now. To us, the whole charm of Windows is the common user interface. This reduces learning time and lets people get up and going as soon as possible. People do not like to spend a lot of time learning, so we wanted to give them familiar territory in which to work.

We studied the users' reaction to a number of the most popular authoring system interfaces. However, instead of choosing one, we decided to use four. Four different interfaces would make our system easy for experienced users to migrate to and would make our system acceptable to new users because it would have an interface that would meet their expectations. The multiple view approach also would let authors use the strengths of all without being penalized by the limitations of each.

The multiple perspectives would make it more natural to work a wide variety of projects. Use the Time Line when you want a timed show. Use the flowchart when you need to build the logic. Use the spreadsheet view for fast editing.

These four interfaces would be views onto the same script. Each one might be used to create and edit a project without the others, but changes in one would be reflected in the others. This way, the script, which is central to multimedia creation, would always be central in our system.

- A *full script-based system.* The people who liked this kind of interface were the power users, and people who were not worried about writing computer programs. People liked this for reasons of control, and because they could see and read the details of the script. This direct and detailed control over the project seemed to us to be a good reason to have this interface. This interface also allowed designers to have the use of text editor features to speed development.

- A *flow-chart interface.* Designers, who wanted to see the logic of the interactive program represented graphically, liked this interface. This interface let them run the project while looking at the flowchart; in this way, they could watch the logic execute as the blocks turned on and off. This seemed to be a valuable way to seeing an interactive project, and we thought that if we could add data flow as well it would be even more useful (Fig. 58.1).

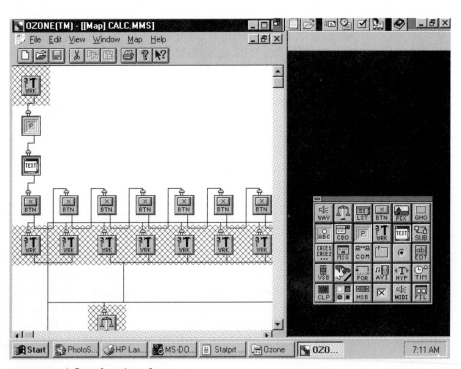

Figure 58.1   A flow-chart interface.

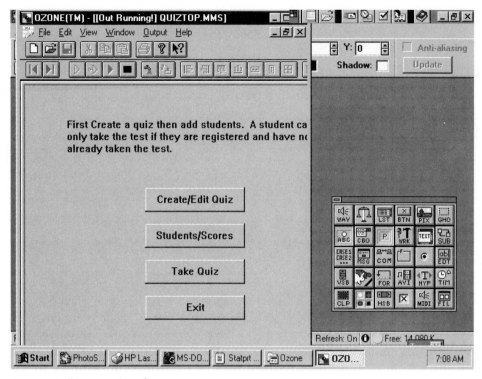

Figure 58.2   An output interface.

- *A time-line interface.* This construct seems to have become very popular among multimedia developers. Users add media elements to a multi-line time line with this interface. Each kind of element has its own line, and many elements of that type can be added to the line. The position of the element signifies the start time, and the length of the elements signifies the running time for that media piece. By arranging media elements on these lines, like beads on an abacus, the relative position of the media elements in time is determined.

- *An output interface.* This interface is the good old WYSIWYG interface found in the desktop publishing world, and the graphic arts tools. It is now moving into development tools like Appstudio, Visual Basic, Powersoft, and more. This interface is necessary for creating screens, and multimedia is all about making screens (Fig. 58.2).

- *A frame-based interface.* This approach borrows from the movies and assigns frames to the events that happen on the screen. Often there are key frames, where a significant new element is introduced, followed by change frames where that element does something. The fans of this interface most often come from the film and television arts and this is a natural extension of what they are used to. We decided that a frame-based interface was basically a time-sliced view of the time line. In other words, each frame acts as a slice at a time mark in a time line.

Don't Forget Fantasy

One of the wonderful things about multimedia is that it is not necessary to stay within the confines of reality. You do have to keep your Vision in tact. Discovering magical connections, revealing silly animations, and hearing rich music are part of satisfying multimedia experiences. Adding to reality encourages users to proceed. Small visual pleasures are devoured like mind candy. The user enjoys worlds with the details filled out. This encourages exploration and discovery, and keeps them in your world.

What Messages Does Your Design Communicate?

Is this project all business, fun and games, reference, sales, or what? You decide when you first create your Vision. A graphic artist, perhaps you, can make an environment that evokes the right feeling for the project. Is that enough? It would be if your project were a film or TV show. However, because you choose multimedia, design decisions also include that happens when the user clicks. The more work you do for the user, the happier he will be. Try to anticipate the user's needs, according to where he is in the project.

Naturally, you might be wrong, so you have to let him have access to all the information he might need, but a little help rounds out the Vision for the user. If you can guess what he needs, he will feel well-taken care of in your world. For example: you have made an automotive disk and the user is looking at pictures of cars. Then, he goes down a few logical layers to look at images of mufflers. Next, he goes into a data base to find out about muffler hanger part numbers. Now, you should start the data base in the muffler section instead of at the top. Starting at the top of the data base forces him to spend time taking the steps to find mufflers again. From his perspective, he was already looking at mufflers, and you are just wasting his time. Looking out for your users, giving a little boost along the way, anticipating his needs at every step does a lot in realizing your Vision for the user. He feels that you are working with him; that is why he is using your project to start with.

Help Systems

Many people hate computers because the computer makes them feel stupid. The longer I work with computers, the more stupid they make me feel, too. This happens because I try things. If the things I try don't work, and I know they should, and I can't figure out the magic word to make it go...This is not fun.

For example: I went to install a new hard drive. This usually takes 20 minutes or so. In this case, it took 5 days of trying everything...and I mean everything. I was on all the help lines for hours. No one could help. In desperation, I started making changes to my system that seemed totally unrelated to the hard drive. When I set the video ROM BIOS shadowing to Enabled, suddenly everything worked. Huh? No wonder people hate these things. Do not do this to your users. Don't trap them in situations with only one way out. Give them hints, help, and if they ask, tell them outright. Provide an openness to the system that gives the user plenty of options. If help is needed, make it pleasant to work with. Don't punish users for not thinking like you. If they thought like you, they would be competitors wouldn't they?

Implementation

Your original Vision plays an important role when it comes to actually making the project a reality. If you want everyone to see the project, you have to use tools that create an output that is playable on everyone's equipment. If your Vision compels you to make an arcade game, then it has to work within that kind of system. If your Vision is to build the ultimate trade show display, then your hardware environment is within your control. You might have a kiosk plugged into the Internet with real-time videoconferencing. Just be sure that all of this snappy technology does not get in the way of your Vision. Be sure that the gizmos do not run the show, but rather add important elements to realizing the Vision. The Vision is the thing to protect and project. The implementation is just the how. Don't confuse how with why. The Vision answers the why question.

Delivery

The Vision is the genesis of the project. It is what compelled you to make it, and it is what will bring others to it. When you do deliver the project to the client or distribution network, you have to place this Vision firmly in the mind of your audience before they see the work. They have to know how to think about it before they can start thinking about it. Failure to do this can ruin the best implementation of the best project. The power of your vision can only work if people are looking in the right place to see it. When your ideas are very creative, people need help in seeing your Vision. This is called *positioning* and it will make or break your project.

Vision drives the project. It brings in the user. It makes the market. Nothing is more critical to the success of your work.

59

Creating Electronic Publications

Kevin Daniel

Electronic publishing (e-publishing) represents the first major new field in the publishing media since movies and television allowed literature to be broadcast in dramatic form. Books, magazines, poetry, and even more mundane items, such as brochures and training materials, are beginning to appear in electronic versions (e-pubs). Computers have made paper-based publishing easier, but electronic publishing allows materials to be presented in ways impossible to duplicate in printed text.

Producing an electronic publication involves converting text, illustrations, and other materials into a stand-alone computer program that readers can view on their systems. In the past, this has required expensive technical expertise to achieve, but tools are now available that allow even novices to easily and quickly produce quality e-pub applications, without resorting to programming languages or complicated scripting. On-line services and the Internet also now provide a framework for promoting and distributing e-pubs at much lower cost than for printed media. And the big publishing houses, attracted by the low cost of paperless publishing, are actively courting authors of materials that can be converted to electronic formats.

If you can print it on paper, you can probably produce an effective electronic version of your work at very low cost—particularly for short-run projects. But the real excitement in producing an e-pub comes with giving your readers new ways to interact with and explore your materials. Providing them with controls to allow them to seamlessly jump between topics and related subjects gives readers the opportunity to approach the publication from individual angles (Fig. 59.1). And as an author, you are freed from the linear structure

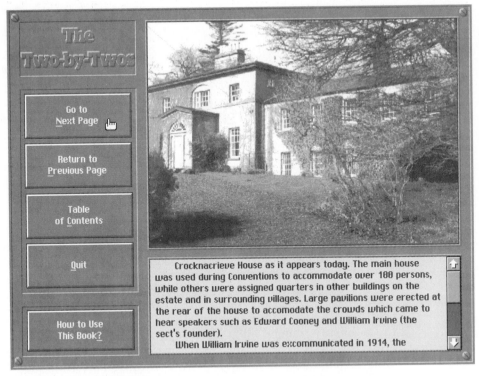

Figure 59.1 Menu and display.

imposed by printed media. For the first time, you are able to provide natural connections between several parallel lines of material.

Preparing Materials

What you'll need

At its most basic, publishing your work over the wire requires only an authoring tool geared to e-publishing, and a computer on which to run it. To illustrate your publication, you might also want to add a paint-type graphics program. If you have photographs, you can either have these scanned by a local typesetting service bureau, or purchase scanning equipment. Adding audio or animation elements to your publication might also require that you have a sound-editing application (often included with the computer's audio card) and/or animation software. Because of the need to keep your publication small, however, you will want to limit the use of sound and animations—and you might want to forgo these entirely until you are more comfortable producing e-pubs. In order to make your electronic publication available to the world, you will also need access to a modem with connections to the Internet or to an on-line service.

Choosing an authoring tool

First, consider whether your publication will be read on-line, or whether your readers will download the publication for reading at their convenience. This will determine what kind of authoring software you will use. If your readers must read your publication while connected on-line, then you will probably want to invest in an HTML (hypertext markup language) editor. Unfortunately, HTML is an emerging format and not all browsers will be able to view everything you are capable of inserting into a publication. HTML also is limited in the range of artistic control you have over the look of the publication. Most Web publications have a dull sameness to their appearance. Graphics, animation, and other large files are also excruciatingly slow to display over standard phone lines.

Many authors find it much more attractive to author publications using an electronic publishing application, and to allow readers to download the publication from an Internet site or on-line service to read at leisure, while not connected. This method also can save the reader connect-time charges. NeoBook Professional is one such authoring tool and allows you to compile text, graphics, animations, and sound files into a single, compact, self-running file. NeoBook (Fig. 59.2) has the added advantage of being able to be run under

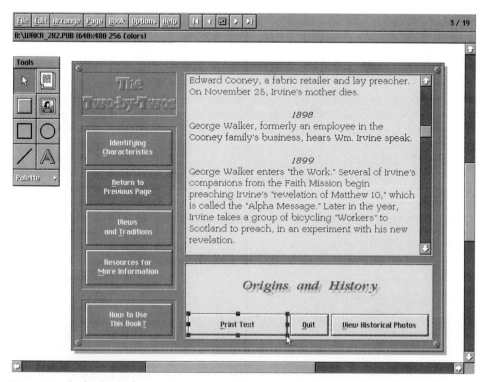

Figure 59.2 Authoring tools.

plain DOS—allowing publications to be run on older PCs—as well as under Windows 3.x, Windows 95, or OS/2. You will retain best control over how your publication is presented by selecting an authoring tool that lets you include text, graphics, and sound effects, while allowing easy to use screen page design features. You should also aim for an authoring tool that produces a publication that can be read on a wide array of popular computer hardware, while keeping the size of the publication small enough to fit on one or two diskettes, at most.

Selecting subjects

Subjects that are best for electronic publishing are those that are enhanced by liberal use of graphics, color, and/or use interactivity to give readers new ways to explore the subject. It might be cost-effective to present long stretches of text in an electronic format, but it might be easier (and more convenient for the reader) to actually read this type of material in printed form. In an electronic publication, however, interactive controls might be used to direct the flow between pages, subjects, and chapters in ways that are impossible to duplicate in print. It is easier to design an electronic publication around subjects that can be divided into chunks of information that can be related to other chunks. For instance, a biography of Catherine the Great, could include buttons that allow readers to jump to sections on economic conditions, international politics, or social developments during the period covered by the page being viewed—or a catalog description might include buttons that bring up a picture of the item, installation instructions for the item, quantity pricing, etc.

Selecting Illustrations

Because graphics greatly affect the speed and size of your final publication, take great care when selecting pictures. Illustrations should be used to add emphasis to important points, and to give visual interest and consistency to your pages. Because pictures lose definition when displayed on the computer screen, choose those that are clear, with good contrast. Use color images that fit well with the other colors used in your publication.

Considerations for the Internet and On-Line Services

Page and writing style

One of the advantages of publishing electronically is the ability to include color illustrations at little or no additional cost. Backgrounds can be splashy illustrations or soothingly conservative. Don't overwhelm your reader with a confusing abundance of disparate visual elements. Try to settle on a stylistic theme that can be carried over the entire publication. Instead of clumping multiple images or blocks of text on a single page, try limiting each screen to a single block of text and one or two small illustrations. Unlike printed pages, using more electronic pages adds little to the publication's size or cost—and can greatly enhance clarity and ease of reading. If your publication is text-intensive, you might also wish to experiment with larger fonts and muted backgrounds to reduce eyestrain.

Another feature unique to electronic publishing is its ability to include interactive controls—used to turn pages, pop up related images, topics, etc. For the convenience of your readers, design your screens so that most controls are positioned in the same spot from screen to screen.

Writing style and subject segmentation

Because most computer screens display less information than a printed page, it will be easier for your reader to deal with short blocks of text. As you write, build in pauses where the text can be pushed onto a new screen. Scroll bars may be used to tab down through lengthier blocks of text, but be careful of allowing yourself to ramble too long without allowing the reader to take a visual "breather" by switching to a new page or screen. Reader attention span in electronic media is limited, and clicking through a seemingly endless column of text while staring at a bright screen is too much for many readers. Just because you can fit 20,000 words into a single scrolling text field, doesn't mean that this is an effective use of the electronic medium. When you use a scrolling text field, try arranging each field to contain less than 50 lines and continue your narrative on the next screen page (Fig. 59.3).

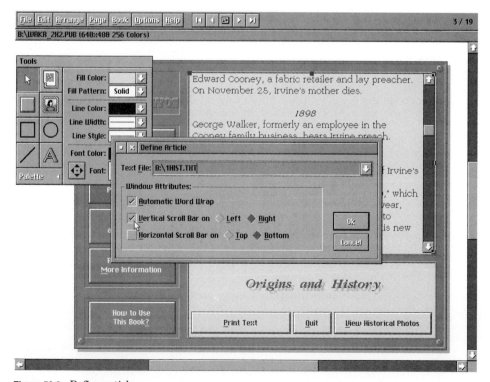

Figure 59.3 Define article.

As you write, build in pauses where the text can be pushed onto a new screen, or at least to another scrolling text field. Often, you'll want to place a new graphic to illustrate the progression of the subject matter when creating a new screen/page. Wherever possible, provide interactive controls to allow readers to jump to screens containing related material. Remember that these controls should allow your readers to explore the material in their own ways.

Publication size restrictions

Try to keep the size of your publications small. On the Internet, the smaller the publication's size, the more attractive it will be to those trying to download it onto their systems. File transfers can be agonizingly slow—even on faster modems. Some users might be charged for the time it takes to retrieve your publication, and those charges mount up quickly. A 1-Mb file will be a reasonable size for most Internet users. But even a file half that size can take about 15 minutes to download using a 14.4K modem. The amount of text generally has the smallest effect on the publication's total size, but overuse of graphics, fonts, images, animations, and sound files can greatly bloat the size of your project. Look at your publication's size from the user's perspective. Most people will not want to spend more than a few minutes downloading an electronic brochure, but the same people might spend an hour to retrieve an electronic novel or magazine they've heard praised elsewhere. Keep the size appropriate to the material.

Auxiliary files

You might wish to include a few files to describe your publication, to tell how to install it, and to list any restrictions on using or distributing the publication. These files should be written in the ASCII text format so that they can be easily read using any word processor or editor.

Packaging the publication's files

Once your project is finished, you will need to use a utility to place all the files comprising your publication into one compressed package, which will be easier for readers to locate and download. One of the most popular file compression utilities is PKZIP from PKWare, Inc. PKZIP can turn multiple files into a single file, and it does an excellent job of reducing the size of a publication. Although most Internet users will have a utility that enables them to "unpack" a compressed file, PKZIP also includes a utility (ZIP2EXE), which enables you to allow the compressed file to "unpack" itself; this can be a real convenience to less-experienced readers.

Integrating Graphics, Animation, or Audio

Graphic palettes and resolution

Computer images are divided into individual dots (called *pixels*) each of which is assigned a color. The number of individual colors used is contained in a "color palette." The fewer colors in an image's palette, the smaller the size of the image file. You can drastically cut down on image size by using a paint program to reduce the number of colors (or shades of gray) to a bare minimum (to do this, simply substitute colors that appear infrequently in the illustration with similar shades). Nor, in most cases, should graphics fill the entire screen. Use a paint program to "scale" images to a size that will fit on the display without obscuring interactive controls or text fields. Many paint programs also include a "crop" feature that allows you to reduce the size of an image by cutting out only a piece of an image.

Reuse of graphic, animation, or audio elements

Because image files can be very large, the use of too many illustrations can bloat your publication to an unattractive size for readers to download over the Internet. You can keep your publication smaller, while maximizing its graphical impact, by reusing the same image throughout the publication. Some small images can be "tiled" repeatedly over the same page for backgrounds, at a fraction of the disk-space required by a single large image. Animations and sound files also eat up a lot of space. Here too, keeping the animations small, the sound clips short, and repeating the same files elsewhere in the publication, can reduce your publication's size.

Hardware considerations

You should keep in mind that many of your readers might be using computers that do not have the capability to display higher resolution images. Standard VGA allows a maximum of 16 colors to be displayed, and other boards allow 256 or even 16-million colors to appear simultaneously. You should be sure to preview your publication in 16-color resolution to make sure that your publication is clear to users with standard VGA systems. Remember, the fewer colors used in your images, the smaller the resulting publication.

Also remember that not all readers will be running the latest model computers. Do not rely solely on sound files to present vital information, unless you are certain that all of your readers will be using systems equipped with audio cards. Some animations and other special effects might bog down older computers and computers with limited memory or other hardware resources. And avoid authoring packages that produce output for only high-end systems. The fewer requirements your electronic publication makes of your reader's computer, the larger your audience.

Putting It All Together

Page layout

Some authoring systems, such as NeoBook, allow you to set up a "master page," which contains the buttons and graphic elements (Fig. 59.4) that appear on all or most pages. Not only does this save you time in placing controls on each new page added, but it keeps lines, buttons, and other elements at the same position on each page. This prevents a flickering effect, caused by slight misalignments, when turning between screen/pages. If your authoring system supports it, begin by selecting colors, backgrounds, and other elements for the master page. Otherwise, create your basic layout and copy it to each page of your publication. Visualize where you will place text and images on the pages, and settle on a basic color scheme that works with the illustrations you will use.

Fonts and other graphic elements

Limiting yourself to two or three fonts will unify your publication, and will usually save disk space and speed up your publication. Other graphic elements, such as rules and frames, should be used to provide interest and draw the eye to important topics. Rules and other graphic elements usually con-

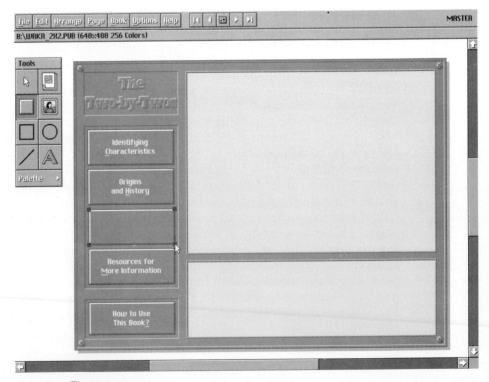

Figure 59.4 First screen.

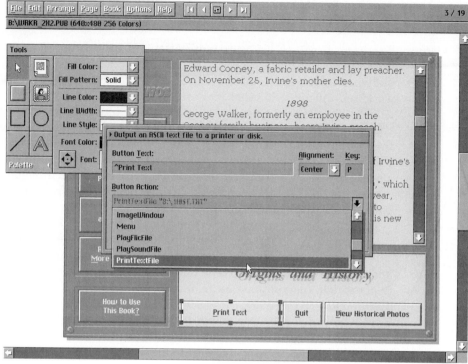

Figure 59.5   Outputting a file.

sume much less disk space than imported illustrations. Background and font colors can also be used to spice up your pages, without adding much to your publication's size.

Interactive controls

Try to keep control buttons, which readers will use to page through your e-pub, in the same location on each screen/page. At a minimum, you will want to include a control to turn to the next page, a control to return to the previous page and a control to exit the publication. You might also want to include "Table of Contents" controls (Fig. 59.5) to allow users to jump to other sections of your work. A Help button is also useful for jumping to instructions on how to use the publication. Other buttons can be used to jump to pages containing related topics or to pop-up windows that contain related illustrations. Some authoring packages even support controls that allow readers to jump to another computer program that performs a task or views an operation, without leaving the publication.

Completing the Publication

Submitting your work

The easiest way to get your publication onto the Internet is to upload your file to major on-line services, such as CompuServe and AOL. With the wide audience addressed by these services, interested browsers might find your work and upload it to other sites on the Internet. You can also "surf" the net, looking for sites that deal with information touching on your subject. Once you've identified a compatible site, then e-mail the administrator to ask if they would allow you to upload your publication. Some authors of electronic publications advertise their work over the Internet by allowing readers to download just a portion of a publication. If readers are intrigued, or find the publication useful, they can order the full publication from the author. These partial publications are known as "teasers."

Other authors, looking for commissions, place full-blown publications on the Internet. And electronic magazines or other frequently updated periodicals are made available for download in order to attract regular subscribers and advertisers. It is important that all these types of publications must contain explicit instructions as to who to contact and how to pay for further materials.

So, whether you are considering adapting an existing work to electronic format or beginning a new project, adhering to a few simple concepts will keep your publication exciting and easy to market:

1. Keep your e-pub as small as possible, to make it attractive and inexpensive for readers to access;

2. Use control buttons to give readers alternative ways to interact with your publication;

3. Make use of color, graphics and other multimedia elements, using these efficiently to avoid slowing your program and bloating its size;

4. Give each publication a basic overall style and color scheme;

5. Try to address audiences that might not be running the latest and fastest computer systems;

6. Take advantage of free additional pages by breaking your text into easy to digest chunks of information that might be continued on another screen page; and

7. Don't confuse your readers by placing controls in awkward or inconsistent positions. But above all, be creative. As a pioneer in developing electronic publications, you should feel free to invent fresh ways for readers to approach material, unrestricted by what is considered acceptable in other publishing media.

60

Fitting Promotional Interactive Media on a Floppy

Kirk Mahoney, Ph.D.

Although it is true that many advertisers have switched to CD-ROMs or the World-Wide Web (WWW) to promote electronically their products and services, some well-known companies use promotional floppies very effectively today.

These diskettes fall into at least four categories:

1. Software demos

2. Telecommunication applications

3. Test-drives

4. Catalogs

Software demos are available from companies, such as Claris Corporation. This company has a reputation for developing software applications that fit on a single diskette, so it's no surprise that its demos do, too.

Telecommunication applications are given away in the hundreds of thousands, if not millions, by companies such as America On-Line and CompuServe, who stuff diskettes into magazines and mailboxes. Strictly speaking, you might not call these promotional diskettes. But, although the applications that are given away are true working tools, they only work with the promoting company's on-line service. And, each application, through the look and feel of its interface, acts as a constant promotion of the on-line service.

Perhaps the best-known test-drive diskettes have come from Buick Motor Cars. Year after year, Buick has mailed promotional diskettes to customers who have bought or are likely to buy a Buick. Recipients of these diskettes enjoy not only the interactive nature of the access to the automotive information, but also the digital golf game, which makes a great tie-in to an on-line service. Each application, through the look and feel of its interface, acts as a constant promotion of the on-line service.

And, even if you place promotional software on a CD-ROM or on your Web site, but want to make it easy for one customer to share the promo with other customers, it makes sense to limit the size of the promo so that it fits on a high-density diskette.

When to Use Interactive Media on Diskettes as a Promotion

You should consider using diskettes to promote your product or service when you need any or all of the following, listed in no particular order:

1. Highly random access and linking
2. Easy capturing of data
3. Calculation
4. Time-based response
5. Attention
6. Inexpensive updating at a low distribution rate

Let's look at each of these situations.

1. This means that the recipient of your software—the user—will have lots of questions or interests that require accessing several different portions of the content. Perhaps an index in a brochure or book would not work as well because it would require the user to spend too much time with the index. In contrast, mouse-clickable connections between one portion of the content and another could provide the user with highly random access and linking.

2. This refers to recording how the user proceeded through the promotion—how long at each screen and the sequence of screens—an impossible or prohibitively expensive task with other forms of promotion.

   This also refers to such features as radio buttons, check boxes, and text-entry fields for the user to modify in response to a survey or to place a catalog order, the results of which are returned by modem or diskette to you.

   This can be superior to asking the user to use a number-2 pencil to color numbered bubbles corresponding to his or her answers to a multi-part, several-question survey. A software-based survey requires little manual dexterity, can prevent the respondent from answering the same question in two different ways, and can require that the user give some answer to every question. A customer-administered paper-based survey can do none of this, and a telemarketing survey would cost more, except for a relatively small sample-size.

Similarly, a software-based order form:

- can ask the user to confirm an unusual order (e.g., several shirts at one size, plus one shirt at a different size)

- can prevent the user from requesting a feature that is not available for a selected product (such as an unavailable color)

- can suggest additional items that are complementary but quite valuable to the order (such as strapping tape to seal the cardboard shipping boxes being ordered).

3. Calculation gets at the heart of what computers do best. A typical application is computing the subtotal, sales tax, shipping fee, and total. An example of a less typical, but just as valuable application would be calculating the number of rolls of strapping tape to seal the number of cardboard shipping boxes being ordered. A human telemarketer could do this, too, but at a greater expense.

4. Computers are more than just calculators; they all have clocks. Time-based response refers to the ability of computer software to respond to the user based on the season of year, the part of the season, the week of the month, the day of the week, or the hour of the day. Even the best-trained sales personnel cannot have the consistency of time-based responsiveness that is possible with promotional software.

5. Attention refers to capturing the customer's attention, a key component of successful promotion. Promotions that use interactive media are still a novelty, so they capture your customers' attention as well as, if not better than, most other approaches that you might consider for the same cost.

6. If you have duplicated diskettes that contain an obsolete promotion, you can bring them up-to-date just for the cost of duplication of the new master diskette. Even if you have obsolete duplicates, you need not buy new diskettes, assuming that you ensured that the diskette labels contain nothing that could become obsolete that fast. Plus, with diskettes, you can choose to update a relatively few copies with the latest promotional interactive media, at a per-unit duplication cost that is relatively close to what you would get with a high-volume order.

In contrast, if you have any paper-based promotional materials, such as brochures, and they become obsolete, you cannot re-use the paper medium; you must buy new paper and ink—the major part of the duplication cost. And, the typical minimum number of printed duplicates that you would need to order is much greater than the minimum number of duplicates that a diskette duplicator would require. If you have a promotion that changes often, this over-ordering syndrome inherent with print materials can waste a lot of your promotional budget.

What to fit on a floppy

You really can put almost any kind of data and code on a floppy diskette, but it cannot hold everything—at least, not a lot of everything!

Among the choices to consider are:

- Animation and interactivity code
- Audio
- Graphics
- Photos
- Text
- Video

We will look at each of these choices in some detail, with each followed by a bottom-line comment that summarizes the details.

Animation and interactivity code

The computer code that directs an animation or that handles interactivity is typically among the most efficient of the components of an interactive-media application.

"Code" here refers to the script, the flowchart, or the list of commands that you create to control the animation or interactivity.

No matter what form the code takes, the authoring tool condenses it to a set of instructions that the microprocessor understands or to a set of instructions that the tool's playback engine understands.

For example, if a graphic is in one screen location at one time-point and is at a different location at another time-point and follows a straight line between the two locations between the two time-points, then the authoring tool needs to record only a few bytes of information for its playback engine, such as:

- A linear-move instruction for the playback engine
- Which graphic is being moved
- The graphic's reference point or hot spot
- The initial location of the graphic's reference point on screen
- The final location of the reference point on screen

- The time at which the graphic is in its initial location
- The time at which the graphic is in its final location

Typically, only one or two bytes would be needed to identify an instruction to a playback engine. Only two bytes are needed to identify one of 65,536 graphics; only one byte is needed to identify one of a set of 256 graphics. Defining the graphic's reference point or hot spot requires four bytes (or less, with good design of the authoring tool). Defining the initial and final locations of that hot spot on screen would require four bytes each. Defining the starting or ending time—even down to a fraction of a second to account for the individual video-refresh frames—would require no more than eight bytes each, and this relatively high number is necessary only when storing a time-point in character-string format.

So, at its worst (highest), the above example requires 2 + 2 + 4 + 4 + 4 + 8 + 8 = 32 bytes to instruct a playback engine to move linearly a specific graphic from one screen location to another over a duration specified by starting and ending times. (This sentence uses thirty-two bytes.)

Our imaginary authoring tool could record 10,000 of these fairly inefficient instructions to a high-density diskette and still leave over three-fourths of the diskette free for graphics and a playback engine. Granted, it might not make for a very effective promotion, but you should be able to see from this example that animation code, compared to the other components of a promotional application, places a relatively low burden on storage space.

Interactivity code can be even more efficient—especially if the playback engine contains sets of computer instructions that can be called with a one- or two-byte command.

For example, suppose that you have a button on the screen that inverts its colors while clicked. In a script, you might tell the authoring tool:

- which graphic is to act as the button
- that you want an invert effect while the button is clicked
- the screen (or word or line, in the case of hypertext) to which to jump after releasing the mouse over the button

This example would need only 2 + 1 + 2 = 5 bytes, given up to 65,536 graphics, up to 256 effects, and up to 65,536 screens. Thus, putting 100,000 hypertext links into an application would consume only about one-third of a high-density diskette!

Of course, this is a simple example, but it illustrates an important point: interactivity code can be more efficient than animation code and yet have just as profound an effect on the power of the final application.

Bottom line: animation and interactivity code provides the biggest bang for the byte.

Audio: How AM Radios Can Seem Better Than Compact Discs

If you're expecting much CD-quality audio to fit on a promotional diskette, you're in for a surprise. Let's take a look at the math. We need three numbers to calculate how many bytes are needed in one second on an audio CD.

The standard frequency range of human hearing is 20 to 20,000 Hz (a Hz or Hertz is one cycle per second). When audio is put into digital form, engineers refer to this as sampling.

For a digital recording to reproduce accurately all frequencies in an audio source, it must have been created by sampling the source at twice—or greater than twice—its highest frequency. This is described mathematically by something called the *sampling theorem* or *Nyquist theorem*.

If a source is sampled at less than twice its highest frequency, then "aliasing" occurs. You often see this in a movie western, in which the stagecoach wheels seem to rotate backward as the stage coach moves forward. The frequency at which one spoke of the wheel rotates into the position formerly occupied by the spoke rotationally ahead of it is so high that the motion-picture camera, which records the scene through its lens at just 24 frames per second, "undersamples" the rotating wheel.

You also see aliasing as banding in photocopies of some images. Every photocopier has a resolution (for example, in a fraction of a millimeter) below which what is being photocopied blurs together. In other words, the photocopier is not capable of reproducing accurately any image data beyond a particular frequency; it will alias everything at frequencies higher than that.

Undersampled audio is audio that has been sampled at less than twice the highest source frequency. Undersampled audio, which is difficult to describe, also contains aliases.

Knowing that the range of human hearing—at least, early in life—goes up to 20 kHz, the engineers who developed the technology for audio CDs decided to choose a sampling frequency that is at least twice this. Audio CDs are produced with a sampling frequency of 44.1 kHz.

This means that audio-CD data changes 44,100 times per second. This is the first number that we need to calculate how many bytes are needed in one second on an audio CD.

The second number that we need is easier to explain. Dynamic range is another feature of audio recordings. *Dynamic range* refers to the number of discrete steps, or levels, in the volume of the recording.

The dynamic range of digital recordings is given in bits. Every bit represents one of two discrete values. An 8-bit audio card is one that can play back audio over 8 bits of dynamic range.

That is, an 8-bit audio card can reproduce audio over $2 \times 2 \times 2 \times 2 \times 2 \times 2 \times 2 \times 2$ volume levels. This is the same as 2-to-the-8th-power, or 256, volume levels. You could think of this as having an audio amplifier with a volume knob that has 256 discrete settings.

Audio CDs are produced with a dynamic range of 16 bits. This is the same as 2-to-the-16th, or 65,536, volume levels.

A 16-bit dynamic range puts more distance between signal and noise in a sampling than does an 8-bit dynamic range. So, if your audio source has much noise in it or has many low-volume portions, you might want to sample it at 16 bits instead of at 8 bits.

One byte is 8 bits long. Another way to describe the dynamic range of audio CDs, then, is to say that it is 2 bytes.

Because every one of the 44,100 samples in a one-second period on an audio CD can have its own volume level, this means that every sample needs 2 bytes of space. This the second number that we need for our calculation.

The third number that we need is the easiest to explain. Audio CDs are recorded in stereo. That is, there are two separate channels of sampled audio in every recording. This is the third number that we need for our calculation.

Putting these three numbers together, how many bytes are required by one second of CD-quality audio? $44,100 \times 2 \times 2$ bytes, or 176,400 bytes, or 176.4 KB.

A high-density diskette can hold only 1400 KB. This implies that you can put 7.9 seconds of CD-quality audio (uncompressed) on a diskette, with no room for photos, animation, or anything else!

What can you do to put longer audio than this on a promotional diskette? Any one of the following choices will double the duration.

- Choose monaural instead of stereo sound.

- Choose 8-bit instead of 16-bit dynamic range.

- Choose 22.05-kHz instead of 44.1-kHz sampling frequency.

Making two of these choices will quadruple the duration. Making all three choices will increase the duration by a factor of eight.

Another way to look at this is that monaural, 8-bit, 22.05-kHz audio only needs 22,050 bytes per second (Table 60.1).

How does mono/8-bit/22-KB sound? Well, it sounds something like the audio from an AM radio: only one speaker; no super-fine resolution of the volume or gain; medium-fidelity. (Most AM radio stations broadcast audio at a wider (better) dynamic range than that of 8-bit audio, which is just 48 decibels.)

Before committing to a particular combination of these choices for the audio on your diskette, you should test several combinations with your source material. If you have an audio editing program, you can do this yourself. Or, you could ask your software developer to create some test samples for you to compare.

For example, the frequencies in human speech typically do not go above 5 kHz. So, if you are digitizing speech, 22.05-kHz sampling should be more than adequate. (Remember the sampling theorem?)

On the other hand, if you plan to include on your diskette lots of high-frequency sounds, such as from violin strings, then you may want to use 44.1-kHz sampling. Otherwise, if you sample at only 22 KB, then those strings might sound more like cat gut!

Table 60.1

Length of 300 kB of Digital Audio

Monaural	8-bit	22.05 kHz	13.61 sec
		44.10 kHz	6.80 sec
	16-bit	22.05 kHz	6.80 sec
		44.10 kHz	3.40 sec
Stereo	8-bit	22.05 kHz	6.80 sec
		44.10 kHz	3.40 sec
	16-bit	22.05 kHz	3.40 sec
		44.10 kHz	1.70 sec

Will your users have stereo speakers, or will they be satisfied with monaural sound? Some laptops have stereo speakers, but they are so close together that the stereo effect is lost. By choosing monaural over stereo sound, you will free up several kilobytes for more audio or for other components in your promotional software.

And, would 16-bit dynamic range be overkill? Many PCs play back only 8-bit audio, which means that they effectively ignore half of the dynamic-range data in 16-bit audio! As with mono-vs.-stereo, you probably could make the more memory-efficient choice without the user noticing the difference, unless there was a lot of noise in the audio source, or unless you need to play back many quiet passages.

A couple of other methods to fit more audio on a diskette deserve your consideration, but at this writing neither enjoys widespread support. One is the Interactive Multimedia Association's audio-compression standard, which can compress stereo, 16-bit, 44.1-kHz audio into ¼ of the space needed when uncompressed. As more audio editing and playback tools support the IMA standard, you might want to consider using it.

The other is MIDI audio. MIDI uses simple, compact commands to play an on-board set of sounds, such as synthesized or sampled notes from musical instruments. When you are certain that the sound system in your user's computer supports MIDI playback, MIDI is ideal for most music.

Bottom line: AM-radio-quality audio could actually be superior to CD-quality audio, depending on your needs.

Graphics: When One (Bit) Can Be Enough

Many graphics are composed only of lines and dots. For example, most clip art, such as most of the DigitArt series from Image Club, is just black-and-white.

Although you might want to use complicated, multi-colored graphics in some situations, many situations demand only relatively simple color schemes. Relying on color alone to carry a message (e.g., to indicate small cities vs. large cities on a political map) can produce unreliable results with users who suffer color-blindness of some kind.

So, you usually should use color as a supplementary visual cue in your graphics. One company known well for encouraging strong graphic design and proper use of color is Apple Computer, Inc. Apple, in its book *Human Interface Guidelines*, encourages developers to design icons in black-and-white first, then to add color to them.

This approach leads to icons that carry a message with or without color. The same can be said for other kinds of graphics. Macromedia Director is one tool for development of interactive media that simplifies the addition of color to black-and-white (one-bit) graphics.

Director lets you set the foreground color and the background color of any one-bit graphic on the screen (called a *sprite* when on the screen). For example, you could leave the foreground color black and set the background color within the sprite to something other than white—for example, to grab attention or to reinforce the message of the sprite.

Suppose that your sprite acts as a button that moves or depresses when selected. You could temporarily change the foreground color, for example, while the object is selected, to give a supplementary indication that the object is selected. Even if not black, if the foreground color were distinctly darker than the background color, your one-bit graphic could still carry its black-and-white message. All of these examples demonstrate that you need not use 8-bit, 16-bit, or 24-bit graphics to convey a message; "one bit can be enough."

Bottom line: One-bit graphics are a great way to maximize your use of space on a diskette without necessarily meaning that they always or ever appear black and white.

Photos: Drop Some Colors, Save Some Space

Many photos contain a lot of information that is visually redundant. That is, because of limitations in color-phosphor technology and in human perception of color, you can have two adjacent pixels with two different red-green-blue color combinations and not be able to see the difference.

The JPEG (Joint Photographic Experts Group) approach to image compression, which can achieve a 20:1 or higher compression ratio, takes advantage of this.

However, even if your authoring or playback software does not support images in the JPEG format, you still often can modify your images so that they need less space.

If your images are 24-bit-deep, but the playback display system only supports 8-bit-deep images, then two thirds of the diskette space needed by your images is going to waste. Plus, the way that an 8-bit system displays a 24-bit image might not be to your liking.

The obvious solution is to scale all of your 16- and 24-bit (true-color) images (such as what you would pull from a Photo CD) down to 8-bit depth, which is endorsed by advertising agencies that use or produce interactive media, including members of the Coalition for Advertising-Supported Interactive Entertainment (CASIE).

When you decrease an image's color resolution to 8 bits, each pixel in the image can have only one of 256 total possible colors. Most tool-makers refer to this range as a palette or color look-up table (CLUT).

You have several choices when you convert a 16- or 24-bit image to 256 colors. One is to convert the image to the system palette—a CLUT that the operating-system maker has defined as its standard set of colors for the desktop. This means that you can display a system-palette image against the system desktop without causing any shift in the colors of the desktop.

A second choice is to convert a high-bit-depth image to a CLUT that is optimized for that image. Optimization involves selecting the most frequently used colors in the original image. Many conversion tools account for the lack of visible distinction between two similar colors by assigning pixels of either color in the original image to just one color in the 256-color image.

This second choice of image conversion produces the best-looking 256-color images, although it restricts how these images are presented.

A third choice is to convert a high-bit-depth image to a CLUT that is optimized for a set of images. The conversion tool examines all of the original images and computes a single CLUT—often called a super-palette—that is reasonably sub-optimal for conversion of all the images. DeBabelizer is an example of a Macintosh tool that can create a super-palette.

Which of these three choices should you make?

- Choose the system-palette approach when your promotional software does not cover the entire desktop and your users would be bothered by a shift in desktop colors.

- Choose the optimized-per-image approach when each image will appear with no other image on-screen.

- Choose the super-palette approach when two or more images must appear together on a screen.

No matter which choice you make, it usually works best to dither colors during conversion. For example, you should select dithering in the dialog that appears when you switch the image mode from RGB (24-bit color) to 8-bit indexed color in Photoshop.

If you look closely at a dithered image, you will see pixels of one color (for example, a dark blue) scattered among pixels of another color (for example, a turquoise) in the boundary between two solid areas (one of dark blue, the other of turquoise). The visual effect at a distance is a relatively smooth blending between the two colors.

Dithering makes it possible to represent a gradient originally made of several colors (e.g., from red to yellow) with just two colors (red and yellow, in this example) and frees the rest of the CLUT for colors needed by pixels elsewhere in the image.

Dithering is especially useful when you need to convert a high-bit-depth image to use the 16-color (4-bit) palette found on older video systems on the Windows platform. Some very successful promotions have been produced with dithered, 16-color images. Notice that the dithering in 4-bit images can be very obvious and crude, if the original images were not selected or preprocessed carefully.

As mentioned, the previously described second choice of image conversion restricts how images are presented. If you choose to optimize the CLUT individually for each image, then you will see color-flashing as you move from one screen to the next in your promotional software unless you do one or both of the following:

1. Design the software to fade to black between two screens that have two images with different CLUTs. Black should be in the same position in the two CLUTs, or this does not work. (The Macintosh prevents you from specifying the color of the final position in a CLUT; it's always black.)

2. Reserve a portion of each CLUT (e.g., the final 16 colors) prior to converting the high-bit-depth images to self-optimized, 256-color images. Place the same sequence of colors needed for your interface (buttons, frame, etc.) in each of those custom CLUTs, and design your interface to use only those reserved colors.

Notice that each CLUT consumes space on the diskette, especially if you will be using images with several different, custom CLUTs. For example, if each of the 256 positions in a CLUT refers to a 24-bit color, then the CLUT needs $3 \times 256 = 768$ bytes. If you have several small images (for example, 27 × 27 pixels, or smaller), this suggests that you should create them all to use the same CLUT, or you might find that the CLUTs themselves consume more space than the images!

Bottom line: With a little bit of care you can cut space demand by as much as two thirds without much loss in fidelity, when you convert high-bit-depth photos to 256-color mode.

Text: Bitmapped vs. Character-Coded

There are two ways to store text in your software: bitmapped or character-coded.

Bitmapped text begins in character-coded form. The developer uses a graphics tool to convert it to a picture, often called a *bitmap*.

If each pixel can show only one of two colors—black or white—then every pixel can be represented by a single bit (the source of the name bitmap).

Suppose that a character on the screen is five pixels wide by seven pixels tall. (We will ignore the needed space around it.) Then that black-on-white (or white-on-black) character is represented by $5 \times 7 = 35$ bits. This is equivalent to more than four bytes for one character.

In contrast, ASCII is a character-coding scheme that represents each character by just seven bits. This seven-bit scheme lets one represent a total of 128 (2 to the 7th power) different characters.

Several of the lower-numbered ASCII characters, such as TAB and LF (line-feed) and CR (carriage return) are non-printable. But, ASCII does represent all of the uppercase and lowercase letters in the English alphabet, all of the numerals, and all of the other characters seen on a typical American keyboard.

For data-management simplicity, many operating systems use 8 bits (one byte) to represent each character. (In contrast, a lot of text that flows through the Internet and computer bulletin-board systems does so in 7-bit form, with the 8th bit used as a check bit to ensure data integrity.)

So, to represent a particular string of text with every character formatted in the same way (same font, same color, same style, same size, and so on) would require only the length of the string times one byte, plus one or a few bytes for formatting information.

Continuing with our previous example, this would contrast with, for example, the length of the string times nine bytes, and the text could only be in black or white.

With such a heavy storage penalty (more than 4:1 in the example) for bitmapped vs. character-coded text, why would you want to store text in your software as pictures, rather than as character strings? Answering this question requires that we look more closely at character coding and fonts.

Makers of operating systems, as well as the International Standards Organization (ISO), have extended the ASCII scheme to eight bits, which allows for a total of 256 (2 to the 8th power) different characters.

By taking advantage of all eight bits in a byte, these extended character sets can represent such characters as the British pound sign, the German sz ligature, the Icelandic thorn, the French cedilla, and the Spanish inverted question mark.

Unfortunately, these 8-bit character sets are not supersets of one another. Instead, the character code for a special character in one set refers to a different character in another set.

Even the ISO-Latin-1 character set, something of a standard among one-byte character sets, has some deficiencies. For example, it lacks the TM (trademark) symbol, whereas one can enter this superscript symbol directly on a Macintosh (by holding down the option key and entering 2 on the main keyboard) or with Windows (by holding down the alt key and entering 0153 on the numeric keypad).

Some makers of tools for interactive media have recognized the variability among character sets and offered ways to hide this variability from the developer. For example, Macromedia provides with Director for Macintosh a file that translates the extended character codes to and from Windows; it provides a similar file with Director for Windows to translate extended character codes to and from the Macintosh operating system.

However, translation files are not the complete solution. Some fonts do not contain all of the extended characters that you might want. (We are using the word font here in a broad, generic sense, although there are specific distinctions between typefaces, font families, and fonts.) For example, one font might show for a given character code a small "a" with an acute accent over it; another font might show an "ff" ligature for that character code.

This variability in character-set compliance among fonts means that giving your users their own choice of font to apply to your text could result in their seeing some strange characters in place of what you saw with your choice of font on your computer.

A milder form of incompatibility occurs in style support. Your choice of font might support normal, bold, italic, and underline, whereas the font that your user chooses might support only normal and italic. If you were to ask that user to click on the underlined word in a paragraph, he or she might not be able to find the word!

Another challenge that faces the user of character-coded text is this: a given font might vary slightly, but perceptibly across platforms—even if the font is from the same maker! The kerning might vary, the height or width might vary, and the shape of an individual character might vary.

The result might be mildly annoying to disastrous. Certain characters might not look quite right at various sizes. All of your work to make words wrap at specific places might be for naught on a different platform. Or, perhaps the worst, text might run beyond the edge of the screen.

Suppose that you have found a font that looks good on both platforms, supports all of the characters that you use in your text, and has cross-platform variability that you can manage or that you are willing to accept.

Continuing this scenario, suppose that you want to include this font with your software. You still might opt for bitmapped text, if:

- The font cannot be licensed from its maker for inclusion with your software

- The font can be licensed from its maker, but the license costs too much in an up-front fee or in royalties

- You do not have a friendly method of putting the font on the user's system and then managing it after it is there

- You do not want to upset users who do not like software that adds fonts to their computers' hard diskettes

- You own the font, but do not want it released to the public

So, for all of the space-saving efficiency of character-coded vs. bitmapped text, you might decide that you are willing to use the extra space for bitmapped text, instead of tackling all of the challenges inherent in character-coded text.

On the other hand, if you really need the space-saving efficiency of character-coded text, then you might want to use it in the following situation:

- Where you don't care about where word-wrapping occurs
- Where you use the ASCII (7-bit) character set only (e.g., where you are willing to live with straight-quote and double-quote marks, instead of left- and right-hand "curly" quotes and double-quotes)
- Where character height and line spacing is not critical
- Where character width and kerning is not critical (e.g., with a monospaced font)
- Where you use only a normal style, or where you are not concerned with specific support of non-normal styles
- Where you are using a "system" font (i.e., one that comes with the operating system), or where the font that the system substitutes for the requested font is acceptable
- Where text aliasing is acceptable, or where on-the-fly anti-aliasing of text is available

This last requirement is one reason that many developers convert all of their text to pictures. As described in the section on audio, aliasing occurs when a source is not sampled at a frequency that is high enough to prevent misrepresentation of the source.

An aliased character is one that shows "jaggies" or "stair-stepping." You see jaggies on the diagonal edges of characters. This occurs when the size of the character is small enough relative to the pixel resolution of the computer monitor (typically, 72 pixels per inch) that the monitor must represent a relatively large portion of the character with a single pixel.

Graphics tools, such as Adobe Photoshop, have the ability to anti-alias text as it is imported (e.g., from Adobe Illustrator) or typed into a picture. Photoshop accomplishes this anti-aliasing for black text on a white background by filling pixels adjacent to a stair-step with a gradation of increasingly lighter gray pixels. Photoshop takes a similar approach with a character of any color against a background of any other color by placing near the stair-step pixels that have a color interpolated between the character and background colors, and by filling any pixel that contains both a piece of the character and a portion of the background with a mixture of the two colors.

This means that a picture that contains anti-aliased text is, by necessity, greater than one-bit deep. Many developers anti-alias their text into 8-bit images, although you could anti-alias your text into a 4-bit image, with some care and the willingness to accept cruder anti-aliasing or a more limited range of text and background colors (Fig. 60.1).

So, with anti-aliasing, the memory stakes between character-coded and bitmapped text are even higher. Returning to our initial example, a single 5×7-pixel character would be represented by only one byte in a character-coded scheme, ignoring the formatting byte(s). That same character would consume 35 bytes, if anti-aliased in an 8-bit picture (vs. 4+ bytes in a 1-bit picture).

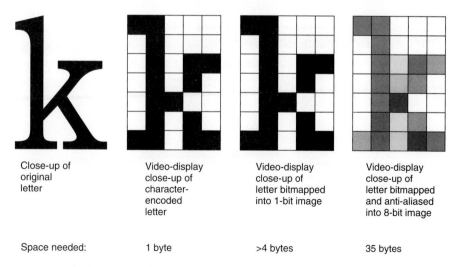

| Close-up of original letter | Video-display close-up of character-encoded letter | Video-display close-up of letter bitmapped into 1-bit image | Video-display close-up of letter bitmapped and anti-aliased into 8-bit image |

| Space needed: | 1 byte | >4 bytes | 35 bytes |

Figure 60.1   Anti-aliasing and space required.

You might decide to forego anti-aliasing of your text, if these memory stakes are too high. Two situations where text aliasing is acceptable are:

- When the font size is so large that the stair-stepping is minor relative to the size of a character

- When the font has been designed specifically for high legibility on-screen—even at relatively small sizes

Bottom line: Use ASCII-character-coded text with system-standard fonts. Bitmap any text that uses a non-standard font or non-ASCII character or for which you care about jaggies, unless your software makes heavy use of that text and you have the license and desire to distribute that font.

Video: A Valuable, But Short, Small Contributor

One still, 640 × 480 (full-screen), 8-bit, uncompressed image uses 307,200 bytes. Full-motion video runs at 30 frames per second (fps). These numbers mean that one second of a silent, full-screen, full-motion, 256-color digital video needs 9.216 MB without compression. A 24-bit (full-color) version needs 27.648 MB.

Digital video codecs (compression/decompression algorithms) for the QuickTime and AVI file formats take advantage of interframe and/or intraframe redundancies to achieve a compression ratio typically somewhere in the neighborhood of 20:1 at this writing for software-based decompression. Hardware-based codecs can achieve higher ratios, but need special decompression hardware in the user's computer, which you might not have the luxury of requiring for a promotional diskette (Table 60.2).

Table 60.2

Length of 1 MB of Digital Video*			
	8-bit	160x120	1.74 sec
		640x480	0.11 sec
Not Compressed			
	24-bit	160x120	0.58 sec
		640x480	<0.04 sec
	8-bit	160x120	34.72 sec
		640x480	2.17 sec
Compressed 20:1			
	24-bit	160x120	11.57 sec
		640x480	0.72 sec

*30 frames (single fields) per second; no audio

This means that you might be able to put three seconds of 20:1-compressed, full-screen, 256-color video on one diskette, with essentially no room for anything else. If the digital video's dimensions were 320 × 240 pixels, this would increase to twelve seconds. At a postage-stamp-size 160 × 120 pixels, this would increase to 48 seconds. Dropping the frame rate of such a postage-stamp-size video to a choppy 15 fps would increase this to 96 seconds.

Putting any other content on the diskette, including audio to accompany the video, as well as some sort of playback application, could cut drastically into the video.

Although you can include digital video on a diskette, you should consider using it judiciously. In some situations, it does not make sense to digitize video for a promotional diskette. Listed are three such situations, each of which is followed in parentheses by a space-saving alternative:

- Digitizing the title sequence of a movie (vs. bitmapped or character-coded text)
- Digitizing a talking head (vs. a still photo plus audio)
- Digitizing an animation (vs. a software-based animation)

With each of the alternatives, you would save space on the diskette and obtain superior image quality.

Some situations for which it does make sense to digitize video for a promotional diskette are:

- Historical footage
- Video of people in action
- Time-lapse or slow-motion cinematography

Another valuable application of digital-video file formats is for giving the user control of the viewing direction, rather than for presenting a linear sequence of images in time. An example of this is QuickTime VR, which allows the user to use a mouse to look out from a center point in any direction around a complete circle. All of the imagery is static, but seamlessly joined around 360 degrees.

Depending on the pixel dimensions and the number of photos used to construct the 360-degree data, such a digital video could easily fit on a promotional diskette.

The challenge with digital video, which now is quite easy to produce with tools such as Adobe Premiere, is to use it for what it does best or for what only it can do, so you still have room on the diskette for the rest of your promotion.

Bottom line: Digital video, used for its best or unique features, can play a valuable role on a promotional diskette, provided that you do not expect full-screen, full-motion, full-color video—at least not with the codec technology available at this writing.

How to Develop for Several Platforms Simultaneously: Planning Ahead

Although there are several operating systems for personal computers and workstations, Macintosh and Windows dominate the market today.

Several tools for interactive-media development support playback on either OS. If you look closer, however, you will see that there is much variability among computers that run one or the other OS.

For example, some older Windows and Macintosh computers can display only 256 colors, whereas newer ones come with built-in support for 16- or 24-bit color. Some Macintosh computers and Windows-PC sound cards support 8-bit audio, whereas others support built-in playback of 16-bit audio.

With either of these features—color depth or audio dynamic range—it's obvious that you need to author for the simpler technology (8-bit color and 8-bit audio), unless you know for certain that your promotional diskette will fall only into the hands of users with better hardware.

Even then, you might still decide to author your promotion for the simpler technology to take advantage of the space savings and to avoid the work of creating and distributing several different versions.

One variable that many first-time authors of interactive media overlook is screen dimensions. This is especially true for software to be played on a Macintosh.

The 640- × 480-pixel screen is fairly standard for most Windows-compatible and Macintosh computers, although many people run computers at higher pixel dimensions, such as 800 × 600 pixels on a 15" monitor, or 1024 × 768 pixels on a 17" monitor.

So, if you design for a 640 × 480-pixel screen, it should be okay, right? Well, not exactly. The built-in video on some Macintosh computers is 512 × 384 pixels at 256 colors. And, Apple has sold many Macintosh PowerBook (portable) computers that display 256 colors or several gray levels on a built-in screen that is 640 pixels across, but only 400 pixels tall.

What can you do about this? Here are two options.

1. Author for 640 × 480 pixels only.
2. Author for 512 × 384 pixels, 640 × 400 pixels, and 640 × 480 pixels.

Option 1 makes sense when you are 100% certain that your audience has, or can obtain access to, a computer with 640 × 480-pixel support. Otherwise, option 2 makes sense.

How could you implement option 2 without three times the work and without creating three different applications? Many video-game makers, wanting to sell to those whose computers display only 512 × 384 pixels, have taken the approach of centering a 512- × 384-pixel stage against a black background (which, of course, is hidden, if the screen displays only 512 × 384 pixels). See Fig. 60.3.

Another approach, which Engaging Media used when it created 365 Marketing Ideas, is to use what the motion-picture industry calls a *letter box*.

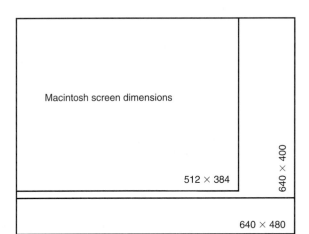

Figure 60.2 Macintosh screen dimensions.

Figure 60.3 Video game approach.

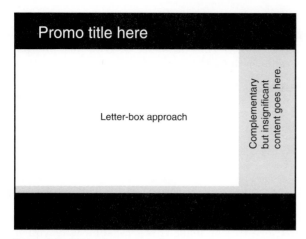

Figure 60.4 Letter box approach.

This approach puts an 80-pixel-high black strip at the top of the screen and another such strip at the bottom. No content appears beneath the 384th row, and a reversed title appears against the top strip, but not beyond the 512th-pixel column of that top strip (Fig. 60.4).

The user of a 640- × 480-pixel display sees a letter-box-style application. Complementary, decorative, but insignificant content appears between the strips in the 513th- through 640th-pixel columns.

The user of a 640- × 400-pixel display sees an application with a reversed title along the top 80 pixels. This user also sees the insignificant, but complementary, content beneath this strip in columns 513 through 640 (the rightmost 20% of the screen).

The user of a 512- × 384-pixel display sees an 80-pixel-tall reversed title and a 512- × 304-pixel area of significant content.

Although the video-game and letter-box approaches are fairly straightforward to implement, they do sacrifice much of the usable space of a 640- × 400-pixel display or of a 640- × 480-pixel display.

So, you might want to implement a more sophisticated approach—dynamically adjust your application's layout at playback. This approach also allows you to make full use of the "real estate" of displays larger than 640 × 480 pixels, too.

Some authoring tools allow you to query the computer to learn the display dimensions. Or, you can query the user for the dimensions by displaying a test pattern and asking what he or she sees.

The catch is that you must write a program that dynamically builds each screen. Or, you must embed a set of screens for each set of pixel dimensions within your software and then include an instruction that uses the set of screens that is appropriate for the user's display.

Which variation makes more financial sense depends on how many promotions you expect to create that will need to support multiple screen dimensions. However, the big advantage to this size-on-the-fly approach is that you need not duplicate or triplicate your resources; your application will draw from the same internal or external database of graphics, photos, etc., no matter what the screen dimensions are.

No matter which approach you take, with some planning and a little extra work, you can avoid getting a call from a customer who asks, "Why don't I see any buttons when I run your promo on my Mac IISi?", or from an account exec who asks, "Why is the text clipped along the bottom of the screen on my PowerBook?"

Why You Should Use Installer Software: It's More Than Just for Appearance

You could ask your user to drag and drop your promo from its diskette to the hard diskette, but there are at least three reasons why you might need or want, instead, to distribute your promo with a mouse-clickable installer.

One reason has to do with the fact that the first impression that a customer gets from your diskette-based promotional interactive media is during installation.

Most installer builders, such as DragInstall (for Macintosh) and Wise (for Windows), let you add splash screens, help files, and music to the installation. Good use of this packaging can entertain the recipient of your promo, distract him or her from the time and hard-diskette space needed to install it, and set the proper mood for use of the installed promo.

Another reason has to do with size. Most installers compress your application, read-me files, and other resources by as much as 50% or more.

For example, 365 Marketing Ideas, mentioned earlier, requires 2 MB of space on a hard diskette. However, the Macintosh-version installer, which was built with DragInstall, uses less than 890 KB of a high-density diskette and leaves over 500 KB free. The Windows-version installer, which was built with Wise, leaves over 200 KB free on a high-density diskette. (The Windows version of the playback engine for this product is over 300 KB larger than the Macintosh version of the playback engine.)

A third reason has to do with proper set-up. Installer builders, such as Wise and DragInstall, let you define tests and actions to ensure proper set-up.

For example, if your promo needs 256-color support, you can include a test for this at the start of installation. Installer builders also let you test for the proper system extensions, install support files, and delete an old copy of your promo from your customer's hard diskette.

Also, you might build into the installation the automatic opening of a read-me file or the automatic launching of the promo. Some installer builders, such as Wise, even allow you to include an uninstaller of your promo.

For all of these reasons, it makes a lot of sense to distribute your promo with an installer. By using an installer, you will be able to put more content into your promo, to ensure proper installation, and to make a great first impression.

Where To Go For More Info: Resources

If you are not yet surfing the Web on the Internet, you are missing out on easy access to a lot of great resources for creating promotional floppies. By using a browser such as Mosaic, Navigator, or Netcruiser, and entering any of the following "http" lines into the browser, you can jump to a company's Web site in a matter of seconds.

At most Web sites, you will find these kinds of resources:

- Product announcements
- Press releases
- Freebies and contests
- In-depth product documentation
- Catalogs and order forms
- Annual reports

Listed are some tools mentioned earlier, along with an electronic resource or two to learn more about each. AOL indicates America On-Line; BBS indicates a bulletin-board system run by the tool's maker; CIS indicates CompuServe Information Service; WWW indicates a Web site.

Director   An Authoring Tool for Macintosh and Windows
WWW: http://www.macromedia.com

DigitArt   Clip Art for Macintosh and Windows
WWW: http://www.adobe.com/imageclub

DragInstall   An Installer Builder for Macintosh
AOL: SAUERS
CIS: 70731,2326

Premiere   A Video Tool for Macintosh and Windows
WWW: http://www.adobe.com

QuickTime VR   3D Video for Macintosh and Windows
WWW: http://www.apple.com

Wise   An Installer Builder for Windows
AOL: GLBSInc
BBS: 810-363-6418
CIS: 75111,606

The "http" lines listed are called *Uniform Resource Locators (URLs)*. After the "http://" portion, which tells your browser to use the HyperText Transfer Protocol, nearly all URLs are prefixed by www. Commercial sites are suffixed with .com, whereas educational sites are suffixed with .edu, and sites more directly affiliated with the Internet itself are suffixed with .net.

Even if you do not see here the Web address for a company that you wish to contact, you might be able to jump to that company's site by following this convention for prefixes and suffixes. For example, if the company were named ABCD, you could try entering the following URL into your browser:

http://www.abcd.com

If a search for this URL were to fail, then you could search for the company's site with a site dedicated to helping you find other sites. Perhaps the site best known for helping Web users find other sites is Yahoo! (Yet Another Hierarchically Officious Organizer), at http://www.yahoo.com.

Special Offer From Engaging Media:

40% Discount on 365 Marketing Ideas

Engaging Media, of which author Kirk Mahoney is president, creates commercial software for personal development, as well as specialized software, in English or Spanish, that engages customers to buy from its clients.

365 Marketing Ideas is the first commercial interactive-media application available under the Engaging Media label. Aimed at owners of small businesses who want to improve their marketing, this product also uses many of the techniques that Mahoney describes in his chapter.

U.S. residents can obtain a copy of this application for 40% off the $24.95 list price by sending the enclosed coupon to:

Engaging Media
6102 Winsome Lane #5
Houston, TX 77057

along with an indication of the target operating system (Macintosh or Windows) and a check or money order for $14.95 + $1.00 handling + $1.23 sales tax for Texas residents.

365 Marketing Ideas comes on one 3.5", high-density diskette. The software requires 2 MB free hard-diskette space, 256-color support, 8 MB RAM, and Macintosh System 7.0 or higher, or Windows 3.1 or higher. 8-bit sound support is optional, but recommended.

Organizing the
Interactive Company

Steven Bussard

America's communications and publishing corporations are investing billions of dollars in interactive education and entertainment.

The following businesses are among those investing:

- Video game companies
- Computer software companies
- Movie studios
- Book publishers
- Magazine publishers
- Newspaper publishers
- Telephone systems
- Network broadcasters
- Cable systems

Each of these businesses brings its own ideas about how to develop and distribute its product or service. Each business has something to offer, but none of the existing organizational models will work by itself.

When the New York *Times* is distributed over telephone lines, for example, how should this business be organized? As a newspaper publisher, a phone company, or a cable TV service?

The business of making interactive entertainment demands a new type of organization, one that can handle new technologies and produce new products. At the top of these organizations must be a new type of executive, one who understands both the entertainment industry and the computer industry.

These executives must build the right organization. The organization must be lean so that it can respond quickly to the marketplace. It must have depth, so it can manage large projects over long periods of time.

This chapter proposes an organization for an interactive company. Like all business models, this initial plan will be refined by the fire of experience. This model roughs out a foundation for the future.

What is the Product?

Interactive entertainment is software that provides users with enjoyable experiences that respond to their input. Early forms of interactive entertainment included computer games, such as Pong or PacMan. Those early computer games pale in comparison to what is now possible. Today's interactive entertainment ranges from CD-ROM games to location-based virtual reality experiences.

The ages of customers for interactive products range from three to 93. Users can be technically sophisticated or naive. As more and more people buy preassembled multimedia computers, they will become less tolerant of technical requirements, such as knowing IRQ (interrupt request) settings or how to install a new video driver.

As more CD-ROM products hit the marketplace, potential customers will demand products that offer something they have not seen before. Competition for shelf space will increase, and brand loyalty might become important. If the example of King's Quest is followed, authors like Roberta Williams might become popular, just as film directors like Spielberg or Lucas are recognized by the public.

Software products have features and an interface. Being able to save the current state of a game is a feature. Whether the player does this with an icon, key sequence, or voice command is part of the interface. The situation is similar to movies, which combine stories with production values.

The best product has features its users need, combined with an interface that they can easily use. Both are needed for success. In addition to its features and interface, interactive products must work as software. They require troubleshooting support. The producing company provides this support with a technical hot line, error messages, on-line Help screens, an appendix in the user manual, or all of the above.

How Does The Product Get Made?

In some businesses, projects are short and simple. In retail sales, medical care, or the service industries, for example, projects might involve many small transactions with customers, patients, or clients.

In other businesses, projects are complicated, but of short duration. They involve many people, but do not take long to complete. The evening news, a rock concert, a baseball game—these events require many people working together for a limited time.

Some businesses have long-range projects that require only a small number of people. The farmer, the sculptor, the scientist—they undertake projects that take months or even years, but they do not need large numbers of people to perform the tasks.

Interactive products usually require a team of people, with differing skills. The products are complicated, and they might require six months or more to complete. Each product relies heavily on rapidly changing technology, both for its creation and dissemination.

Interactive entertainment projects have three important features:

- Each project requires the efforts of many people over a long period of time.

- Each project is different from the previous one and is in effect a new venture.

- The manufacturing part of the business is much simpler than the creation and production of the product. (Stamping 1000 CD-ROMs is much easier than making 1000 cars.)

Of these businesses, two industries are most relevant: motion pictures and traditional software. The following material draws upon lessons learned from both industries.

In order to create the appropriate structure for making and selling interactive products, it is important to understand the process involved.

Interactive products pass through six specific stages. During each stage, one aspect is more active than the others. For example, during the development phase, the Development people are quite active on a project, while the Support people are only slightly involved.

The list below shows the six stages of a project.

1. *Development.* This stage produces a design that answers the question: What is the product? The design describes the behavior and appearance of the product in enough detail that other people can build it. In movie terms, the design is a script. In software, it is a functional specification.

2. *Production.* This stage implements the design, creating the product itself. In movie terms, this is all the work that turns a script into a final cut. In software it is the work that produces the final build of working software.

3. *Testing.* This stage pokes and prods at the product, making sure that it meets the design requirements and that it does so robustly. The company must test the product to be sure that it has no bugs. It must also work on a wide range of computing systems. In addition, it must be tested with its potential customers, to be sure that it does what they want. Although limited in movie projects, this stage is critical in software projects.

4. *Marketing.* Once the company finishes a product, it presents it to the marketplace. This stage uses the tools of advertisement, promotion, publicity, and product packaging to generate an audience for the product.

   In movies, this step is critical and very expensive, mostly because it relies on television. For business software, the costs are smaller; reviews and magazine ads can carry the message. Interactive entertainment marketing costs fall somewhere in the middle.

5. *Manufacturing/Distribution.* During this stage, the company takes the product to market, generating cash flow. In both the movie and software business, this step is pretty straightforward.

6. *Support.* This stage is virtually non-existent for films; it is critical for software products. Each customer of an interactive product must get the product to run on his or her particular computer system. Hardware and software consistency issues arise: Why don't I get any sound? In addition, users have questions about how the product is supposed to operate: How do I get to the wizard's castle?

With an understanding of how interactive products are made, we can tackle the challenging question of how an interactive company should be organized.

Organize By Product or Job Type?

In businesses with large projects that require many people, the question arises: Should the company be organized by project or by job function? In the project-oriented approach, teams of people work together on one project, under the supervision of a project leader. A film shoot works like this, under the supervision of a director.

In the job-function organization, all workers with similar jobs are collected into a single group, which reports to a manager of that job type. A movie studio's Publicity Department works like this, providing services for all the films released by the studio.

Software companies have periodically restructured themselves from project-oriented systems to job-function systems. These reorganizations are disruptive. The companies go through them, however, because neither the project-oriented nor the job-function system seem to work well.

The job-function structure

The job-function system (Fig. 61.1) promotes cross-project communication—programmers on a word-processing project mingle with database programmers. In addition, those people who are a minority on a project, such as the lone documentation writer, have the support of a Documentation Manager. It is easier to institute standards, such as a documentation style manual, when all the writers report to the same person.

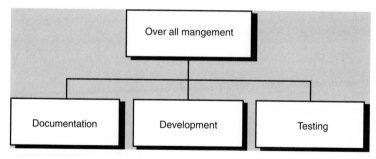

Figure 61.1   A job-oriented structure.

This approach has disadvantages. Dividing the staff by job type tends to reinforce an us-and-them mentality. Writers might say, "If only the programmers would finish on time." Programmers might complain, "How can we do our job when those writers keep interrupting us?"

A second problem with this approach is that people's attention scatters across a range of projects: they lose focus. In addition, a project's schedule often becomes less important than keeping the employee "busy." Critical tasks sit in employees' in-boxes, while they work on other, less critical jobs (Fig. 61.2).

The project-oriented structure

Under a project system, teams of people work on a common project. They do different jobs, but they focus on a shared goal. Sharing that goal cements the workers into a team. The documentation writer, for example, is involved from the beginning. He or she earns the respect of the programmers, as well as an understanding of the programmers' problems and challenges. The team shares the project schedule; it pulls together to accomplish necessary tasks.

The project-oriented structure also has disadvantages. The us-and-them mentality in this structure encourages interproject competition. Although interproject competition can be healthy, a strong manager must keep it within bounds. It is unacceptable for project teams to sabotage each other in a fight over limited resources or bonuses.

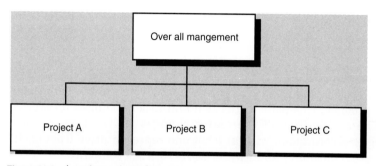

Figure 61.2   A project-oriented structure.

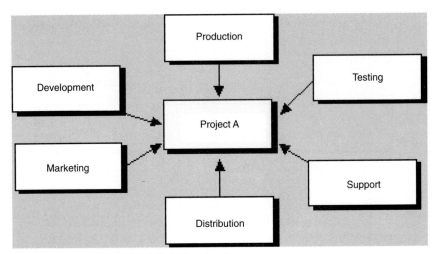

Figure 61.3   Resource pools supporting a project.

When project orientation is too rigid, the organization as a whole loses valuable wisdom from each project. Anything as complicated as business software or interactive entertainment is a learning experience each time. The lessons learned from one project need to be shared with the next.

A Combined Structure

This chapter proposes a structure for an interactive entertainment company that combines job orientation and project orientation.

Resource pools

Each of the six stages needed to build interactive products is represented by a resource pool. A resource pool provides the people, software, and hardware needed to do one step in making the product. Each resource pool is managed by a resource coordinator. This person uses the company's resources efficiently to meet the overall company goals. For example, the production resource coordinator decides who gets to use the sound stage on Friday.

Project teams

Resource pools provide people and equipment to individual project teams (Fig. 61.3). Each product has its own team, devoted to the successful completion of the product. This team works as a unit to set and meet its project goals.

The composition of the teams changes, as the project moves through its stages. A core team, with at least one representative from each resource pool, ensures continuity and awareness across the company.

Representatives from the future stages prepare their unit for the project. They raise red flags when they see potential problems. Representatives from completed stages provide oversight and make sure that the project stays on target.

A few hypothetical examples illustrate this concept:

1. The Marketing representative starts thinking about the campaign with plenty of lead time.

2. During initial design, the representative from Testing points out that allowing user-definable menus in the product will increase the eventual testing costs.

3. During production, the Development representative modifies aspects of the design that are unclear or incomplete.

This combined approach has two advantages for overall management:

1. The project orientation gives each product its own budget, schedule, and accountability. Overall management can turn to one person for a status report on any project.

2. The job-function aspect lets top management give resource control to the people who understand the day-to-day issues. Overall management can talk to one person to assess how each resource supports the company's projects.

The next section presents a detailed description of what each of these steps involves.

What does development do?

The Development department is a small team of people that concentrates on three goals:

1. Seek out people and ideas to create great products for the company.

2. Use these people and ideas to create complete and viable product designs.

3. Provide guidance to other departments as the product moves through its life cycle of production, testing, marketing, distribution, and support.

Skills needed for development. The people in the Development department are like development executives at motion picture studios. They are the architects, designers, and editors. They also serve as the interactive division's front-end, greeting people eager to hawk their wares.

In the film model, successful development executives come from many different backgrounds. They have been trained as talent agents, book agents, attorneys, writers, theatrical producers, or book editors. Although some might have directed or produced a student film, most have never made a feature film. Production skills are not needed for Development jobs.

The people on this team enjoy developing stories and characters. They have an eye for talent and a nose for great concepts. They are professional and gracious, able to turn down supplicants without giving offense. They are the Max Perkins and Irving Thalbergs of the world.

Although production experience is valuable in these people, it is not required. They do not need to know how to program in C++, how to create a 3D image, or how to press a CD-ROM disc. They might learn these things over time, and they certainly need to understand the limitations of their medium. Their required skills, however, are in design and visualization, not execution.

The interactive division's eyes and ears. The people in Development are knowledgeable about the competition's products and products in other media. They know which films are coming out of their studio and the others. They scrutinize the studio's coverage of plays and novels. They keep abreast of developments in the cartridge business, comic books, etc.

These people nurture relationships with those writers, producers, programmers, and designers who show promise of being able to deliver terrific interactive products. The members of this team establish relationships with agents and attorneys who can clue them into significant people or events in the marketplace.

In addition to seeking out people and projects, Development handles those people who approach the company with ideas. They know how to take pitches and sort through the good and bad ideas thrown over the transom.

Shaping and reshaping. Once the company accepts a project, Development takes charge and shapes it into a firm design. In traditional movie terms, the final design is a script, along with decisions about producer, director, and principal casting. For interactive products, the design is more complex. It requires a script, an interactivity map, and an interface design.

Oversight. Once a project goes into production, Development's involvement drops, as it turns its attention toward new projects. The department is always available, however, to work with other departments to alter and improve the product's design and presentation.

What does production do?

Production is where "the tire meets the road." This department turns the scripts and flow charts from Development into actual lines of code, images, and sounds. While Development wrestles with story, characters, and game play, Production battles against time, money, and technological gremlins.

Production takes Development's detailed design and figures out the best way to turn it into a real product. Budgets and schedules are generated here. If an outside company handles the actual production work, Production monitors it. If the production work is carried on in-house, this department needs technical savvy, equipment, and development tools.

What does testing do?

The Testing group is responsible for several types of testing:

1. *Initial user testing.* Tests are conducted with potential customers to determine if a product's design makes sense. Because the product does not yet exist, this testing is done with a clear understanding that it is largely hypothetical.

2. *Unit testing.* As Production finishes each piece of the project, Testing compares it to the design, to be sure that it performs as specified.

3. *Integration testing.* The pieces of a product must work together, and integration testing makes sure that they do. Often problems crop up at this stage—even though each piece worked fine by itself.

4. *Regression testing.* As the product takes shape, it must be continually retested to be sure that today's fix does not pull apart last week's code.

5. *Final user testing.* Once the product is functioning pretty well, Testing brings in potential customers to try it. Ideas that looked good to the designers might turn out to be problems for ordinary users. In addition, users might have requests for special features the designers never thought of.

6. *Compatibility testing.* Testing must ensure the product works on a wide range of customer equipment. With the variety of sound cards, CD-ROM drives, and video cards thrown together in customers' machines, this testing helps avoid later problems for Support.

What does marketing do?

The people in the Marketing Department introduce the product to the marketplace, creating an audience of satisfied customers. They are aware of the trends and the competition. They know how to use the media to reach potential customers. They know the company's product mix and how to build its customer base.

Although the Marketing department should not design products, it does provide guidelines about product areas worth pursuing. It tells Development when the competition has saturated a genre or product type, and it identifies trending new areas.

What does manufacturing/distribution do?

The Manufacturing/Distribution department handles the duplication of the product and its transportation to the customers. This includes printing the manuals, boxes, CD-ROMs, and other materials. Outside suppliers can do much of this work.

What does support do?

The Support department is crucial to a software company. For people coming from the film or television business, customer support will be a new concept.

Interactive products differ from books, newspapers, magazines, CD audio, and television. Although there might be great sophistication in the development of material for these traditional media, the viewing experience is relatively simple. Television networks do not get phone calls from viewers about how to change channels.

Interactive publishers do get calls. Calls about how their software is supposed to work with printers, sound cards, and computers. Calls from users who do not understand how to work the software. Calls about bugs in the code that show up after the product ships.

Support works closely with Testing, so they are both aware of problems in the field. In addition, Support feeds the knowledge it gains back into the development loop, so the next products can avoid the problems of the current ones. Support is also a valuable source of suggestions from customers about how to improve the company's products.

Support is an ongoing task, and the company must calculate its cost realistically. Because it is a recurring expense, customer support is part of the overhead of software publishing.

With each new product, support costs rise. Companies must ensure that support costs do not bleed away profits. Careful design and thorough testing help lower the eventual costs of support because a well-designed and robust product generates fewer support calls.

Overall management

The key to this approach is a strong management with several goals:

1. Ensure fair competition among the projects.
2. Obtain and allocate resources for the good of the organization.
3. Provide mechanisms and motivation for the teams to share their hard-won lessons.
4. Help each team develop challenging, but reasonable, goals and schedules.
5. Buffer the teams from outside interference.
6. Scout outside the organization for useful resources and ideas that the company should acquire.

One of the most difficult aspects of developing interactive products will be allocating the proper time and resources to accomplish the job.

People from a movie background might not appreciate the amount of work needed to make and test software. People from a software background might not appreciate the time needed to make filmed or animated entertainment. Preproduction and script development might take longer than they expect.

Overall management must work inside corporations that were formed for purposes other than interactive entertainment. This will require diplomacy, strength, and an understanding of the challenges of both software development and film development.

The interactive entertainment business is exciting, its future full of surprises. This new business demands a new type of executive, one who combines technical skill, artistic sensitivity, and business acumen. These executives must operate within an effective organization.

This chapter has proposed a structure for that organization.

62

A Primer on Quality and Productivity for Multimedia Producers

Jessica Keyes

In Tracy Kidder's book *Soul of a New Machine*, he details the riveting story of a project conducted at breakneck speed, and under incredible pressure. Driven by pure adrenaline, the team members soon became obsessed with trying to achieve the impossible. For more than a year, they gave up their nights and weekends—in the end, logging nearly 100 hours a week each! Somewhere buried in the midst of Kidder's prose we find that at the end of this project the entire staff quit. Not just one or two of them, but every single one!

The Information Systems (IS) field is ripe with stories such as this one. Software development projects are usually complex and often mission critical. As a result, the pressure on staff to produce is great. Sometimes, as in the Kidder example, even with success comes failure.

Because multimedia and Internet development are closely aligned with traditional software development, the metaphors and mores of this more highly developed field really do apply. This chapter covers productivity and quality in general terms. It is hoped the multimedia and Internet developer will take heed.

Successful software development projects (i.e., get the product done on time—and not lose staff members) have something in common. Each of these projects, in some way, shape, or form, followed one or more principles of quality and productivity. This chapter focuses on "expert" advice that can be used to achieve this ideal.

Productivity is extremely important to Hewlett-Packard because HP relies on new product development to maintain its competitive strength. HP introduces an average of one new product every business day. 70% of HP's engineers are involved in software development. Half of all R&D projects are exclusively devoted to software development.

This significant investment in software development prompted HP's president to issue a challenge to achieve a 10-fold improvement in software quality within 5 years. He also asked that new product development time be reduced by 50%.

An early outgrowth of this response was a process assessment program called *Software Quality and Productivity Analysis (SQPA)*, according to SQPA team member Barbara Zimmer[1]. A few words about the company's general organization and history will help put this information in context.

HP's corporate structure is built on many different divisions or operations that operate more or less autonomously. These separate entities are organized into various groups based on product types. At the top levels of the hierarchy are product group sectors and, finally, corporate management.

At the entity level, a division or operation will normally include manufacturing, marketing, and administrative functions, as well as a research and development laboratory.

The lab manager, who reports directly to the division manager, will have responsibility for several section managers, who in turn oversee project managers. The labs vary greatly in size, ranging from 50 to 150.

The roots of the current software quality and productivity effort are in the Corporate Software Quality Council, which grew out of a task force that was initiated in 1983. The council set some software development guidelines involving the use of Total Quality Control methods.

SQPA's original charter was based on the need to leverage HP's software development efforts in response to the evolution from a total technological approach to software development to one that includes consideration of quality and productivity with special emphasis on culture, change agents, methodologies, and human factors.

SQPA's major objective is to develop and implement a software engineering review process and a software management decision support system. Its tactic is to assess the state of each HP lab and draw comparisons with other HP labs and the rest of the industry. It focuses on eight key areas that impact software development:

- Methodologies
- Staff variables
- Project management and control
- Programming environment
- Tools
- Defect prevention and removal
- Physical environment
- Measurement

After measuring variables in each of these categories, the program identifies strengths and weaknesses, pinpoints areas for improvement, makes recommendations and provides follow-up measures to show progress over time. In the process, a quantitative and qualitative baseline of key factors impacting software development is established.

The SQPA methodology is based on a set of standardized questions that have been checked for validity and reliability. The questionnaire has continued to evolve, reflecting HP cultural anomalies, changes in technology and HP management priorities, and incorporating what has been learned through SQPA team experience.

The SQPA process begins with a request from a lab, and a subsequent scheduling and information exchange. After the request, the lab will generally be asked for demographic data, organization charts, and product descriptions. The formal interviews with lab and section managers, a representative sample of project managers, productivity and quality managers (if appropriate), and a representative sample of engineers take place next, usually over 2 days, depending upon the size of the lab. One engineer from the SQPA team conducts each 1- to 2-hour interview using the questionnaires from the preceding paragraphs.

After the interviews, the SQPA team does an analysis, including a statistical comparison with HP and industry data and a narrative summary of key findings. This is presented within a day or two to the R&D manager and anyone else that he or she invites. The two-hour presentation consists of a description of strengths, constraints and weaknesses, graphs that compare the lab with HP and the industry in the eight key measurement areas, and recommendations for improvement. It is important that this immediate feedback session be interactive to clarify any misinformation or misperceptions and prepare managers for the written report to follow.

Over the next 3 to 4 weeks, the SQPA team confers on quantitative and verbal responses and consults with experts as appropriate to diagnose or prescribe specific activities. The final results are summarized in a formal written report containing graphs, text and statistics and is sent to the R&D manager. The level of detail in the report can provide sufficient information on which to base specific improvement strategies. Finally, the database containing all the HP data collected to date is updated to allow for HP-wide trend analysis.

The last step in the SQPA process is follow-up analysis to measure and report changes and improvements, a step which normally occurs 12 to 18 months later.

The Search for Quality

Although quality and productivity are foremost on the minds of management, few understand as well as HP how to correlate the tenets of quality to the process of information systems.

Total Quality Management (TQM) was actually born as a result of a loss of competitive edge to countries such as Japan. In fact, the father of TQM, W. E. Deming, finding no forum for his radical new ideas on quality in the

United States, found eager listeners in Japan. Today, Deming's ideas on quality are considered the basis for all work on quality in this country, as well as Japan.

Deming's studies were only the start of a flood of research in the field. For example, Y. K. Shetty, a professor of management at Utah State University's College of Business and the coeditor of *The Quest for Competitiveness* (Quorum Books, 1991), suggests that even though most corporate executives believe that quality and productivity are the most critical issues facing American business, many do not know how to achieve it. Particularly in the area of IS.

Essentially, IS quality can be defined as *software that exhibits the absence of flaws and the presence of value*. At the current time, over 70% of the software development budget is spent on "maintenance." The art of detecting bugs and errors of omission or commission, as well as an accurate interpretation and implementation of user requirements, is still an aspiration, seemingly just beyond the reach of many software engineering departments.

According to Tom DeMarco, author of *Software Systems Development* published by Yourdon Press, in 1984, 15% of all software projects with more than 100,000 lines of code failed to deliver value. And in 1989, according to Capers Jones[2], of all software projects with over 64,000 lines of code, 25% failed to deliver anything; 60% were significantly over budget and behind schedule and only 1% finished on time, on budget, and met user requirements.

Because early TQM programs were largely manufacturing-oriented, Information System (IS) researchers, academicians, and consulting firms were required to interpret and extrapolate TQM tenets and create quality paradigms that could be used to significant advantage. As a result, there is no single TQM methodology in use today that has garnered wholesale industry acceptance. All of these methodologies, however, are based on TQM tenets and all, if used properly, will provide organizations with a clear path toward better quality in their systems.

Be warned though, one size does not fit all. In a report by Ernst & Young[3], the notion was challenged that quality programs were universally beneficial for all organizations. Based on a study of 584 firms in North America, Japan, and Germany, the report noted that Total Quality Management practices are not generic. What works for some organizations might be detrimental to the performance of others.

Instituting a quality program requires a careful study of techniques available, as well as applicable to the organization in question. Although IS/Analyzer can't tailor a specific quality program for each of our readers, we can offer a bird's eye view of "tried and true" quality techniques.

The Components of Productivity and Quality

Productivity is indelibly linked to the concepts of quality, although sometimes achieving both becomes something of a catch-22 situation.

Most systems folks would agree with the notion that the more code a programmer churns out, the more productive he or she is. However, introducing quality to the mix might, in fact, reduce the amount of code a programmer can produce in a day. But so too would system complexity. That is, a real-time missile launch system, for example, demonstrates a much higher level of complexity than a batch Accounts Payable system. Therefore, the number of lines of code produced daily in the missile system would more than likely be lower than in the A/P system. Does that make the programming staff working on the missile system less productive?

Productivity is truly a quantitative term. It's insufficient to claim a percentage increase in productivity without having an appropriate method of measuring that increase.

It's also insufficient to measure productivity without taking into account the many factors affecting productivity, such as system complexity and addition of quality monitoring. Other, more subtle, factors affect productivity, but unfortunately receive little attention and pack a big punch.

The factors affecting software engineering productivity and quality fall into three broad categories: methodology, measurement and non-technical factors, or "peopleware."

Although many organizations tackle each of these independently, in fact, they are indelibly intertwined. Where methodology provides the "road-map," the organization will use in developing its systems, metrics provide the gauge used to measure mileage. Finally, peopleware ensures that everybody arrives on-time, well-rested and in good spirits. Ultimately, in the productivity game, the whole is indeed greater than the sum of its parts.

A Choice of Methodologies

It probably comes as no surprise that the majority of software development shops are using no discernible methodology. Those that do dabble are, for the most part, divided into two camps: those that practice "safe computing" or the tried and true structured techniques and those that carry the information engineering banner. Then, there are the explorers who have ventured forth into the unchartered territory of object-oriented methodologies.

Structured methodology is really a series of competing methodologies, all of which have their devotees. Notable among these variations are Gane-Sarson, DeMarco-Yourdon, and the Warnier-Orr (or LBMS) approach.

Structured methodology is probably the most widely used of all methodologies, it's also the most misunderstood because it has long since been pronounced "dead." Interestingly, it continues to thrive and even evolve. Where the '70s version of structured methodology provided only Data Flow Diagramming (DFD) as a tool, today's version has evolved to deal effectively with real-time systems by adding control flows and control processes to the DFD, as well as adding an entirely new modeling tool—the state transition diagram.

But as Ed Yourdon[4] admits, even the best methodologies don't guarantee the technical success of most systems development projects and technical success can't save a project from the larger issues of corporate politics in these whirligig days of mergers and downsizings.

Information Engineering (IE) was born out of the desire to accommodate software development to this rapid-fire pace of change. In 1981, James Martin and Clive Finkelstein, published their now seminal work in the area. "Information Engineering"[5] paved the way for a whole new way of thinking about software development.

Long since gone their separate ways, Martin and Finkelstein are now the forebears of two separate IE movements. The first variant uses the existing functions of an organization as the starting point; data needed by the functions are then defined. In this DP variant, business knowledge is incorporated from users often by interview; but significantly there is subjective interpretation of the users' input by DP personnel. This is sometimes referred to as *Application Information Engineering* or *DP-driven Information Engineering*. It is supported by many of the Information Engineering software products on the market today.

The second variant starts with the strategic plans set by management at all levels of an organization. From these plans are defined the data, and later the functions, needed to support those plans. This approach is more user-driven than the DP variant and is referred to as *Enterprise Information Engineering* or *Business-Driven Information Engineering*. It is defined, according to Clive Finkelstein[6], as follows:

> Information Engineering is an integrated set of techniques, based on corporate strategic planning, which results in the analysis, design and development of systems that support those plans exactly. Information Engineering is applied by managers and users with no knowledge of computers, but instead with an expert knowledge of their business—in conjunction with expert systems which provide rapid feedback to management for refinement of the strategic plans.

But of all the methodologies on technologists' plates today, the object-oriented variety seems to garner the most interest—if the least use. OO methodologies are still quite new, and many do not address all the concerns of the IS analyst. Especially in the area of productivity and quality.

When Margaret Hamilton[7] was director of software development for NASA's Apollo and SkyLab projects at MIT during the late '60s and early '70s, she began an empirical analysis of the massive amounts of information generated by these critical missions. As a result of this analysis, Hamilton, a recipient of the Augusta Ada Lovelace award for Excellence in Computing, spearheaded an extensive effort to minimize software errors in future critical software projects. The result was the embryo of a theory of systems engineering and software development that, if used correctly, could be a way to eliminate the majority of errors in a system before it is implemented. Twenty years and much research later, this embryonic theory has fully matured and is known as *Development Before the Fact*.

Development Before the Fact is a paradigm that fosters productivity and reliability. According to Hamilton, we fix most systems after the system has been implemented. This, in fact, is the reason that our maintenance budgets often exceed our development budgets. Development Before the Fact is a way to be sure that errors are eliminated before the system is delivered.

Preventative development under the Development Before the Fact scenario requires that systems, whether they be in the area of simulation, missile systems, mission planning, integrated computer-aided manufacturing, battlefield management systems, communications, or even world-wide banking funds transfer, be created, building-block fashion, on a foundation of reusability and integration.

Development Before the Fact enables developers to create blocks of error-free code that can be continually reused. The best part of it is that these error-free blocks can be integrated to create new and increasingly more complex systems. Unfortunately, today's object-oriented paradigm concerns itself with the reusable components only. But what about the mechanisms that integrate these blocks of code? The Development Before the Fact paradigm is a software methodology that ensures that these mechanisms, or the infrastructure of the system under construction, is reliable and error-free as well.

McDonnell Douglas

Creating a robust design environment is not easy under any circumstances. But when the company is McDonnell Douglas and the target is commercial, as well as military avionic systems, the task is particularly complex.

But this was the task that Ed Lanigan[8], then Electronics Unit Chief at McDonnell Douglas, choose to undertake. Lanigan wanted a set of methodologies and tools that would allow McDonnell Douglas to smoothly evolve all the avionic systems from the customer requirement to the delivery of the product. With that goal in mind, the team at McDonnell Douglas set out to find a way to allow the marriage of technology with the philosophy of reliability and traceability.

What initially attracted McDonnell Douglas to the Development Before the Fact approach, according to Lanigan, was that its approach was very similar to the one that electronic engineers use. That is, you develop low-level reliable components, then build your reliable systems based on those component structures.

What also attracted Lanigan was that the Development Before the Fact methodology was rooted firmly on an object-oriented infrastructure. But, according to Lanigan, Development Before the Fact goes several steps further.

Lanigan contends that the design approach from the onset needs to be object-oriented in nature and here, Development Before the Fact, is way ahead of the pack. With this methodology, according to Lanigan, the architects of the system can talk the same language as the detail designers.

Lanigan was dealing with a host of complexities in attempting to build a general design environment that would ultimately be shared by all departments within McDonnell Douglas. Capturing the requirements for a task of this magnitude required a methodology that exhibited a high level of quality and productivity. According to Lanigan, Development Before the Fact is the only modern methodology that fits that bill.

Deloitte and Touche's Misuses of Methodology

It probably comes as no surprise but you can misuse as well as use any methodology. Ken Horner[9] is a partner in the Management Consulting practice of Deloitte and Touche. From his experience, as well as an informal survey of over 50 of his customers, all of whom have used one or more methodologies at some point, there seems to be several common benefits and problems. At least five, common denominator methodology "misuses" are identifiable:

1. *Religious fanaticism.* This is the situation, where an organization holds to the theory that there can be nothing else, but the methodology—a "methodology-centric" view of the world, if you'll permit the use. Such rigidity is seldom useful or productive. It might also be a symptom of other poor management practices.

2. *Bureaucracy.* Here the methodology gets wrapped up in a less-than-effective organization, which adds yet another layer of protection and excuse as to why no products are produced. Using a methodology in an organization that might already have top-down communications problems and multiple management layers between the programmers and the management will not help. It will just cause people to push more paper.

3. *The end in itself.* Very similar to misuse #2 is the failure resulting from the total focus on the process of developing systems and not on the end results. Personnel are indoctrinated into the process and become wedded to the idea that step 16 must come after 15 and before 17, and that every last step must be completed and documented—even when it is obvious that performing the activities in a step will add no value to the result or that what they are doing has no real business benefit.

4. *Using the wrong one.* This is rare but is sometimes seen. The few cases Horner has seen personally seem to arise because a methodology in place has failed to keep up with the times. For example, having no methods that focus on JAD or on structured testing or, trivially, a customer's methodology, which still requires the use of a paper screen layout form when screen painters and prototyping provide far faster and more effective user interaction. A methodology incorporating no guidance in data modeling would be of little help in implementing a system using a modern relational database system.

5. *Lack of organizational penetration.* The most common problem is still lack of consistent use, starting with lack of commitment by management. Project leaders who get trained and start off by trying to conform will tend to fall by the wayside if not encouraged and coached to do better.

Rating methodologies

Ultimately, the IS analyst must choose between a wide variety of methodologies. One size does not fit all. Choosing the best one for your organization is a lengthy and tedious process. Sam Holcman[10], a vice president at CASE vendor KnowledgeWare, has devised a series of questions that will start you off on the right foot in your search for the right methodology.

1. Does the methodology identify the steps necessary to produce each deliverable of systems development/evolution?

2. Does the methodology house and deliver the details necessary for developing/evolving systems?

3. Does the methodology simplify the systems development/evolution process?

4. Does the methodology encourage and provide the means to implement a standard approach to systems development?

5. Can any aspect of the methodology be customized to meet specific standards and practices of the using organization?

6. Can changes to the methodology be verified as correct?

7. Does the methodology support current techniques and technology or is it based on dated practices?

8. Does the methodology cover all aspects of systems activities?

9. Can the methodology be realistically followed by the systems organization or does it present overwhelming details?

10. Can cohesive pieces of the methodology be extracted for use on focused projects?

11. Is the methodology driven by the production of deliverables?

12. Is the methodology organized in terms of discrete methods that are linked by the deliverables they produce?

13. Does the methodology provide techniques that describe how to conduct its methods?

14. Can the methodology embody the standards and practices of the using organization?

15. Does the methodology identify the roles (types of job functions) that are involved in each method?

16. Does the methodology identify the support tools appropriate for the execution of each method?

17. Does the methodology allow for predefined paths that accomplish specific objectives?

18. Is the methodology expressed using formal models whose structural integrity can be automatically verified?

19. Can the methodology be expediently searched to retrieve methodology information?

20. Can select pieces of the methodology be published as project handbooks?

21. Can the methodology be ported to external software (tools)?

22. Is the methodology supported by a complete line of educational services?

23. Are services available to integrate the methodology with the standards, practices, and conventions of the using organization?

24. Is the vendor capable of demonstrating any aspect of the methodology on a real project?

25. Are services available to customize the methodology to incorporate the using organization's experiences?

26. Are services available to guide an effective roll-out of the methodology?

Measurement programs

When an organization institutes a long-term productivity and quality improvement plan, one of the first tasks they usually undertake is to put a measurement program into place. Although, according to research performed by the author[11], less than 10% of software-producing organizations worldwide have any kind of ongoing measurement program, more and more organizations are realizing that measurement is an inexorable part of the productivity/quality equation.

In answer to the question, "why should an organization measure?" there are two proverbs that truly characterize the state of software engineering today: "If you don't know where you are going, any road will do," and, "If you don't know where you are, a map won't help!"

Dr. Howard Rubin[12] is a Full Professor and former Chair of the Department of Computer Science at Hunter College, and CEO of Howard Rubin Associates. Through his experience and research, Dr. Rubin has collected data on more than 13,000 software projects as a basis for analyzing software productivity and quality trends. Dr. Rubin recommends that the first step that an organization should take in putting a measurement program in place is to assess "measurement readiness." He offers these eight questions as a quick assessment:

1. How intense is the organization's desire to improve its performance?
   (0) No Desire (5) Intense

2. Is the organization willing to invest time and money to improve systems performance with measurement?
   (0) no (5) Funds and people are allocated

3. What is the current level of the systems skills inventory in regard to being able to use metrics?
   (0) None (5) Already in wide effective use

4. To what extent are measurement concepts known and understood by the systems staff?
   (0) No staff have been exposed (5) 100% trained

5. Is the systems culture adverse to using measurements at the organizational and individual level?
   (0) 100% against (5) Anxious to implement

6. To what extent is a support structure in place to foster measurement practices and perform metrics technology transfer?
   (0) None (5) In place

7. Are tools and repositories for acquiring and analyzing metrics data in place?
   (0) No (5) Full suite available

8. Does the systems organization understand its role in the business processes?
   (0) No (5) Yes, the business processes are documented and tracked through metrics

If the answers to all of these questions is at the low end of the scale, the organization's measurement readiness is quite low. Radical change, according to Rubin, will be needed to get things going. A good starting point is to contact professional societies so that experiences in measurement can be shared and exchanged. Good contacts can be made through the IEEE Computer Society and the Quality Assurance Institute[13].

There are as many metric systems as there are firms using them. The following list contains those that are most frequently encountered:

- Lines of code
- Pages of documentation
- Number and size of tests
- Function count
- Variable count
- Number of modules
- Depth of nesting
- Count of changes required
- Count of discovered defects
- Count of changed lines of code
- Time to design, code, test
- Defect discovery rate by phase of development
- Cost to develop
- Number of external interfaces
- Number of tools used and why
- Reusability percentage
- Variance of schedule
- Staff years experience with team
- Staff years experience with language

- Software years experience with software tools
- MIPs per person
- Support to development personnel ratio
- Nonproject to project time ratio

Most organizations that measure still use a simple source-lines-of-code (SLOC) metric. Even with this metric, however, there is room for variation. In their 1986 book, *Software Engineering Metrics and Models*, published by the Benjamin/Cummings Publishing Company, authors Conte, Dunsmore, and Shen proposed this definition of SLOC: "A line of code is any line of program text that is not a comment or blank line, regardless of the number of statements or fragments of statements on that line. This specifically includes all lines containing program headers, declarations and executable and nonexecutable statements."

The SLOC metric is often further redefined into distinguishing the number of noncomment source lines of code (NCSLOC) from the lines of code containing comment statements (CSLOC).

Along with SLOC measurements, the weekly time sheet provides other gross statistics often used for productivity measurement. The total number of labor hours expended, divided by the total number of NCSLOC, provides an overall statistic that can be used to compare productivity from project to project.

One problem with the SLOC measurement is that it does not take into account the complexity of the code being developed or maintained. Lines of code and man-months hide some very important things. For example, the SLOC measurement for a name and address file update program might be 600 lines of code per day.

On the other hand, the output for software that tracks satellites might be in the range of 40 to 50 lines of code per day. To look at this output on a purely gross statistical level, one would conclude that the name-and-address project was more productive and efficient than the satellite project. This conclusion would be wrong.

So, starting from this base, two researchers at the Massachusetts Institute of Technology's Center for Information Systems Research in Cambridge, Mass., examined this complexity issue. Chris F. Kemerer and Geoffrey K. Gill[14] studied the software development projects undertaken by an aerospace defense contracting firm.

The Kemerer and Gill team began their research by reviewing the original measure for complexity as developed by Thomas McCabe. McCabe, now president of McCabe & Associates, a Columbia, MD, consulting group, wrote the article, "A Complexity Measure" in *IEEE Transactions on Software Engineering* in 1976. McCabe proposed that a valid measurement of complexity would be the number of possible paths in a software module. In 1978, W. J. Hansen in his article, "Measurement of Program Complexity by the Pair (Cyclomatic Number, Operator Count)" in *ACM SIGPLAN Notices*, March, interpreted McCabe's mathematical formula into four simple rules that would produce a numerical measure of complexity (i.e., the higher the number, the more complex):

- Add 1 for every IF, Case or other alternate execution construct.

- Add 1 for every iterative DO, DOWHILE or other repetitive construct.

- Add 2 less than the number of logical alternatives in a Case.

- Add 1 for each AND or OR in an IF statement.

The results of the Kemerer and Gill study showed that increased software complexity leads to reduced productivity. They recommend the use of more experienced staff and a reduction of the complexity of the individual software module. To reduce complexity, they suggest the establishment of a complexity measure that could be in use as the code is written, and adherence to this preset standard.

The goal of these studies is to transfer the generally accepted processes of measurement from the manufacturing arena to the software arena. The problem with the software industry is that we think everything we're doing is new.

In 1983, A. J. Albrecht, with IBM at that time, first proposed the function-point concept in a paper for *IEEE Transactions on Software Engineering* called "Software Function, Source Lines of Code and Development Effort Prediction: A Software Science Validation." This metric is a combination of metrics that assesses the functionality of the development process.

Most people are using function points because it is the only metric that comes close to matching the economic definition of productivity, which is costs or services produced per unit of labor and expense. Of 400 companies studied by Capers Jones, the national average was calculated to be five function points per person-month; IS groups averaged eight function points per person-month.

These numbers can dramatically increase with productivity tool usage (i.e., CASE) to the degree that it is possible to achieve 65 function points per person-month with a full Case environment and reusable code. This metric will decrease when the development environment is new, but will regain momentum when familiarity with the toolset increases.

Jerrold M. Grochow[15], a vice president of American Management Systems, Inc. (AMS), Arlington, Virginia was an early believer in the function-point concept. With over 2200 systems professionals and supporting 28 product lines, AMS needed a metric system that worked. The company has been measuring productivity for over 10 years. The firm found that its traditional metrics of lines of code and work-months was hiding some very important information: Not all work-months are created equal.

There are experienced people and not so experienced people, expensive people and not so expensive people, according to Grochow. If the company could find a way of optimizing this mix, then it would find increased productivity. To this end, AMS needed a measure that would foster economic productivity. Function points filled the bill.

Function points, however, are one of the most difficult of metric systems to successfully implement. IS analysts seriously interested in this measurement system are urged to contact the International Function Point Users' Group for more complete information[16].

The IEEE Standard Dictionary of Measures

Organizations will find that the road to measurement success is littered with potholes. There is no such thing as a perfect metric, function points notwithstanding. The best approach might be to use a variety of metrics.

The IEEE is no doubt familiar to most IS analysts. But what most don't know is that the IEEE has painstakingly gathered together some of the most robust of metrics and published them as the *Standard of measures to produce reliable software*[17].

The IEEE standards were written with the objective to provide the software community with defined measures, currently used as indicators of reliability—and hence productivity and quality. What follows is a subset of the IEEE standard, which we found to be the most easily adaptable by the general IS community.

Fault density

This measure can be used to predict remaining faults by comparison with expected fault density, determine if sufficient testing has been completed, and establish standard fault densities for comparison and prediction.

$$F_d = \frac{F}{K_{SLOC}}$$

Where:

F = Total number of unique faults in a given interval, resulting in failures of a specified severity level

K_{SLOC} = Number of source lines of executable code and nonexecutable data declarations in thousands

Cumulative failure profile

This graphical method is used to predict reliability, estimate additional testing time to reach an acceptable reliable system, and identify modules and subsystems that require additional testing. A plot is drawn of cumulative failures versus a suitable time base.

Fault-days number

This measure represents the number of days that faults spend in the system from their creation to their removal. For each fault detected and removed, during any phase, the number of days from its creation to its removal is determined (fault-days). The fault-days are then summed for all faults detected and removed, to get the fault-days number at system level, including all faults detected and removed up to the delivery date. In those cases where the creation date of the fault is not known, the fault is assumed to have been created at the middle of the phase in which it was introduced.

Functional or modular test coverage

This measure is used to quantify a software test coverage index for a software delivery. From the system's functional requirements, a cross-reference listing of associated modules must first be created.

$$Functional\ (modular)\ test\ coverage\ index = \frac{F_E}{F_T}$$

Where:

F_E = number of the software functional (modular) requirements for which all test cases have been satisfactorily completed

F_T = total number of software functional (modular) requirements

Requirements traceability

This measure aids in identifying requirements that are either missing from, or in addition to, the original requirements.

$$T_M = \frac{R_1}{R_2} \times 100\%$$

Where:

R_1 = number of requirements met by the architecture

R_2 = number of original requirements

Software maturity matrix

This measure is used to quantify the readiness of a software product. Changes from previous baselines to the current baselines are an indication of the current product stability.

$$S_{MI} = \frac{M_T - (F_a + F_c + F_{del})}{M_T}$$

Where:

S_{MI} = Maturity index

M_T = Number of software functions (modules) in the current delivery

F_a = Number of software functions (modules) in the current delivery that are additions to the previous delivery

F_c = Number of software functions (modules) in the current delivery that include internal changes from a previous delivery

F_{del} = number of software functions (modules) in the previous delivery that are deleted in the current delivery

The Software Maturity Index can be estimated as:

$$S_{MI} = \frac{M_T - F_c}{M_T}$$

Number of conflicting requirements

This measure is used to determine the reliability of a software system resulting from the software architecture under consideration, as represented by a specification based on the entity-relationship-attributed model. What is required is a list of the systems inputs, its outputs and a list of the functions performed by each program. The mappings from the software architecture to the requirements are identified. Mappings from the same specification item to more than one differing requirement are examined for requirements inconsistency. Additionally, mappings from more than one spec item to a single requirement are examined for spec inconsistency.

Cyclomatic complexity

This measure is used to determine the structured complexity of a coded module. The use of this measure is designed to limit the complexity of the module, thereby promoting understandability of the module.

$$C = E - N + 1$$

Where:
C = complexity
N = number of nodes (sequential groups of program statements)
E = number of edges (program flows between nodes)

Test coverage

This is a measure of the completeness of the testing process from both a developer and user perspective. The measure relates directly to the development, integration, and operational test stages of product development.

$$T_C(\%) = \frac{implemented\ capabilities}{required\ capabilities} \times \frac{program\ primitives\ tested}{total\ program\ primitives} \times 100\%$$

Where:

▪ Program functional primitives are either modules, segments, statements, branches or paths

▪ Data functional primitives are classes of data

▪ Requirement primitives are test cases or functional capabilities

Data or information flow complexity

This is a structural complexity or procedural complexity measure that can be used to evaluate: the information flow structure of large-scale systems, the procedure and module information flow structure, the complexity of the interconnections between modules, and the degree of simplicity of relationships between subsystems; and to correlate total observed failures and software reliability with data complexity.

$$weighted\ IFC = length \times (fanin \times fanout)^2$$

Where:

IFC = Information flow complexity

$fanin$ = Local flows into a procedure + number of data structures from which the procedure retrieves data

$fanout$ = Local flows from a procedure + number of data structures that the procedure updates

$Length$ = number of source statements in a procedure (excluding comments)

The flow of information between modules and/or subsystems needs to be determined either through the use of automated techniques or charting mechanisms. A local flow from module A to B exists if one of the following occurs:

1. A calls B

2. B calls A and A returns a value to B that is passed by B

3. Both A and B are called by another module that passes a value from A to B.

Mean time to failure

This measure is the basic parameter required by most software reliability models. Detailed record keeping of failure occurrences that accurately track time (calendar or execution) at which the faults manifest themselves is essential.

SEI's Process Maturity Framework

The Systems Engineering Institute (SEI) at Carnegie-Mellon is the bulwark of engineering productivity research. In their studies of thousands of firms, they've discovered some common characteristics that can be used to measure how progressive a firm is in terms of its maturity in the quest for productivity and quality.

SEI has developed a five-level framework that can be used to assess the quality of the software development process in an organization. It is disheartening to note that SEI has determined that over 86% of companies assessed fall in Stage 1, and only 1% of firms achieve Stage 5.

Level one (initial) is characterized by a software engineering department that does things in an "ad hoc" way. There is little formalization (i.e., no measurement system in place, inconsistent or non-use of methodology) and tools are informally applied to the process. To move to the next level of "process maturity" requires the organization to initiate rigorous project management, management review, and quality assurance.

A level two (repeatable) organization has achieved a stable process with a repeatable level of statistical control. Firms in this category can improve (i.e., get to the next level) by establishing a formal process group or committee charged with establishing a software development process architecture and ultimately introducing software engineering methods and technologies.

Level three (defined) organizations have achieved a foundation for major and continuing progress. The key actions for these organizations to progress to the next step are to establish a basic set of process managements to identify quality and cost parameters; establish a process database and then gather and maintain process data. Process data, when used in conjunction with metrics, can be used to assess the relative quality of each product.

Level four organizations, of which there are few according to SEI's Watts Humphrey, are characterized by substantial quality improvements and implementations of comprehensive process measurement systems. Although level four is a much vaulted stage—even these organizations can improve. To do so, they must support automatic gathering of process data and then use that data to analyze and modify the process. Only then do these organizations have any chance at reaching the much sought after level five of process maturity—optimized.

Nontechnical Factors in Promoting Productivity

Quality and productivity are obviously tightly linked; the approaches used to address these issues—metrics, methodology and tools—must be interconnected. Yourdon suggests that simply throwing technology or methodology at the problem is not enough. Information Systems (IS) departments must also use peopleware solutions.

For example, one way to improve development is to hire better developers. Rather than spend lots of money trying to bring in a new methodology, why not just bring in better people? According to Yourdon, there is a 25:1 differential between the best and the worst people, and a 4:1 differential between the best and the worst teams, maybe the best way to improve productivity and quality is just to improve hiring practices.

If you take a random group of 100 people and put them in a room with a complex programming exercise, one of them will finish 25 times faster than the others. Another peopleware improvement to productivity is to help managers improve their skills, as well as to foster a teamwork approach among developers. Peopleware solutions boost productivity and quality more than any tools or techniques. This might very well be the surest path to productivity.

Given the enormous variance in the productivity of programmers, there is a large opportunity for improvement. According to statistical measures by Barry Boehm[18], when the experience of a programmer increases from one month to three years (36-fold increase), productivity is improved by only 34%. This appears to show that experience seems to have no effect on software project costs. In another study by Boehm, it was shown that the difference in productivity between a programmer who uses no tools at all and one who uses the most up-to-date, powerful tools available, on the most powerful machines, is no larger than 50%.

Motivating programmers

Studies have also shown that programmers have a motivation pattern, which is different from that of their managers and from workers in other industries. This difference might well explain why some well-intentioned software managers fail to motivate their programmers. Motivation factors that affect productivity include:

- *Recognition.* The reaction of the organization to the programmer's performance. Indifference leads to a drop in motivation which leads to a decline in productivity.

- *Achievement.* The satisfaction that the programmer gets from doing a challenging task. This implies that the organization must keep supplying the programmer with challenging tasks to maintain motivation.

- *The work.* The nature of the tasks that must be executed is a powerful tool to motivate a programmer.

- *Responsibility.* This is derived from basic management theory. That is, if you want something to happen, make someone specifically responsible for it.

- *Advancement.* A programmer who feels that he or she has the possibility of career advancement in the organization is more motivated than one who does not.

- *Salary.* A programmer who feels that he or she is being paid adequately, and who anticipates that salary increases will continue on par with performance, will be more motivated than one who does not.

- *Possibility for growth.* This factor measures the possibilities for professional growth within a programmer's company.

Interpersonal relationships

- *Status.* This measures the importance of the worker in his or her company, such as participation at meetings, participation in decision making, ceremonial functions, usage of restricted services and privileges of the corporation.

- *Interpersonal relations with superiors.* This is controllable to the extent that the manager has latitude in assigning group leaders.

- *Interpersonal relations with peers.* Because teamwork is a key ingredient for the success of any group effort, the manager should take care in dividing staff into working groups.

- *Technical supervision.* This measures the willingness of the programmer's supervisor to help the programmer solve technical problems, orient efforts and make choices.

- *Company policy and administration.* This factor measures how clearly the command structure of the company is defined, how rational it is and how easy it is to determine who each worker reports to.

- *Working conditions.* This factor represents working conditions in the traditional sense, such as office space, light.

- *Factors in personal life.* Given that the programmer's personal life influences motivation and job performance, the manager can assign key positions or tasks to those that have the best conditions.

- *Job security.* This factor is very important.

Management factors

Peopleware is really a two-edged sword. The employee (i.e., programmer) is not solely responsible for productivity. The actions of the manager are a big part of the equation as well. Poor management produces a host of woes including:

- Unrealistic project plans are caused by poor Planning/scheduling/estimation skills. Staff can lose motivation because of the inability of management to manage a creative staff.

- A lack of teamwork can develop due to inability to build and manage effective teams. There can be poor project execution because of inadequate organization, delegation, and monitoring.

- Technical problems can develop because of lack of management understanding of disciplines, such as quality assurance, configuration management. The danger of maintaining an inadequately trained staff because of a short-sighted, rather than a long-term perspective.

There are some possible solutions to poor management problems. Some organizations have had much success with the definition of dual career paths for technical and managerial staff. Training managers to be good managers is just as important as training programmers to be good programmers. Some organizations make an active practice out of mentoring and supervision of staff by senior managers. Finally, increasing delegation of responsibility and matching authority is a definite step in the right direction.

The quality imperative

Quality is as much of a mindset as anything else. Utah State's Professor Y. K. Shetty[19] found some characteristics that quality-oriented organizations have in common. She refers to these as the Seven Principles of Quality.

- *Principle 1.* Quality improvement requires the firm commitment of top management. All top management, including the CEO, must be personally committed to quality. The keyword here is personally. Many CEOs pay only lip service to this particular edict. Therefore, top management must be consistent and reflect its commitment through the company's philosophy, goals, policies, priorities, and executive behavior. Steps that management can take to accomplish this end include: establish and communicate a clear vision of corporate philosophy, principles, and objectives relevant to product and service quality; channel resources toward these objectives and define roles and responsibilities in this endeavor; invest time to learn about quality issues and monitor the progress of any initiatives; encourage communication between management and employees, among departments, and among various units of the firm and customers; and be a good role model in communication and action.

- *Principle 2.* Quality is a strategic issue. It must be a part of a company's goals and strategies and be consistent with and reinforce a company's other strategic objectives. It must also be integrated into budgets and plans and be a corporate mission with planned goals and strategies. Finally, quality should be at the heart of every action.

- *Principle 3.* Employees are the key to consistent quality.
   The organization must have a people-oriented philosophy. Poorly managed people convey their disdain for quality and service when they work. It is important to pay special attention to employee recruitment, selection and socialization and to reinforce the socialization and quality process with continuous training and education. It is also a good idea to incorporate quality into performance appraisal and reward systems, and to encourage employee participation and involvement.
   Effective communication throughout the department, between departments, and throughout the organization is required to reinforce the deep commitment of management and creates an awareness and understanding of the role of quality and customer service.

- *Principle 4.* Quality standards and measurements must be customer-driven. It can be measured by: formal customer surveys, focus groups, customer complaints, quality audits, testing panels, statistical quality controls, and interaction with customers.

- *Principle 5.* Many programs and techniques can be used to improve quality, such as: statistical quality control, quality circles, suggestion systems, quality-of-work-life projects, and competitive benchmarking.

- *Principle 6.* All company activities have potential for improving product quality; therefore teamwork is vital. Quality improvement requires close cooperation between managers and employees and among departments. Total quality management involves preventing errors at the point where work is performed and ultimately every employee and department is responsible for quality.

- *Principle 7.* Quality is a never-ending process. Quality must be planned. Quality must be organized. Quality must be monitored. Quality must be continuously revitalized.

Motorola's Six Sigma Defect-Reduction Technique

In 1987, Motorola took some of these principles to heart and set in motion a five-year quality improvement program. The term *Six Sigma* is one used by statisticians and engineers to describe a state of zero defects. The result of this program has produced productivity gains of 40%, as well as winning Motorola the Malcolm Baldridge National Quality award in 1988.

Benefits to Motorola included increased productivity by 40%, reduced backlog from years to months, increased customer service levels, shifted IS time from correcting mistakes to value-added work, more motivated staff, and Motorola saved $1.5 billion in reduced costs.

Six Sigma Defect Reduction is easily reproducible by IS analysts:

1. Identify your product. Determine what service or product you are producing. IS must align what they do with what the customers want.

2. Identify customer requirements. IS must determine what the customer perceives as a defect-free product or service. The unit of work that the user is dealing with must be considered. An example is in a general ledger system in which the user worries about defects per journal voucher and not defects per thousand lines of code.

3. Diagnose the frequency and source of errors. Four categories of metrics were established to target defect reduction: new software development, service delivery, cycle time, and customer satisfaction, which is composed of a detailed service metric with the intent of validating the first three metrics.

4. Define a process for doing the task. Motorola refers to this process as *mapping*, but this is closely aligned to the reengineering process. The process involves using personal computer-based tools to determine flow-through of processes and answering the following questions: Which processes can be eliminated? Which processes can be simplified?

5. Mistake-proof the process. By stream-lining a process and eliminating any unnecessary steps, it is possible to make the process mistake proof. By using metrics, a process-control mechanism is put into place so that problems can be addressed before it affects output.

6. Put permanent control measures in place. Once Six Sigma is reached, this level must be maintained. At this step, the Six Sigma metrics are set-up to be used to continuously monitor the process. Monthly quality review meetings are held where each person gets up and discusses their metric, its trend, diagnosis of source cause of errors, action plan to correct.

Coopers & Lybrand SQM Strategy

Bill Smillie is a partner in Coopers & Lybrand's Washington, DC Federal Systems Consulting practice and Partner-in-charge of the firm's Software Quality Management Practice. According to Smillie[20], Coopers & Lybrand have taken appropriate elements of Total Quality (TQM) and successfully applied them to software delivery organizations. It has developed a specific four-phase methodology, dubbed *Software Quality Management (SQM)*, which provides a framework for managing continuous improvement for software delivery.

1. *Assessment.* The purpose of the Assessment phase is to evaluate the organization's current environment and determine how well the organization meets or is likely to meet its customers' software quality requirements. In any Assessment phase, a measurement system must first be designed as a tool and to establish a quality baseline.

    During Assessment, it is important to understand the activities involved in the software development process, as well as the organizational roles and responsibilities. The measurements currently being used by the organization must also be identified and assessed. Whenever possible, existing measures should be used as part of the quality assessment to promote familiarity and acceptance.

2. *Planning.* The analysis of the data collected during the Assessment provides the foundation for the quality improvement plan. The Assessment defines the organization's quality profile and identifies opportunities for improvement. The objectives of the Planning phase are to establish strategic and tactical direction, as well as consensus and commitment for improvements identified in the Assessment. A Process Improvement Plan is the final outcome of this strategic planning effort.

    The organization's vision of what quality software means and where it expects to be must be agreed upon early in the Planning effort. Most organizations find that there are several areas where improvement efforts can be focused, however, trying to do too much at once is not a good idea. Priorities should be assigned to targets based on the following criteria:

    - Criticality
    - Cost
    - Resources
    - Timing
    - Risks
    - Opportunity for near-term success

The projects that are selected as top priorities will require further discussion and decisions regarding the manner in which the improvements are to be implemented. The result will be a prioritized statement of quality objectives, the process improvements to be achieved and the measurements that will demonstrate success. In addition, each quality-improvement project should have:

- A mission statement that includes improvement goals
- Schedules and resource and cost estimates for each project

- An organization structure responsible for quality management
- Measurement procedures to validate the meeting of goals

3. *Implementation.* Introducing measurement systems and the concept of continuous improvement will require far-reaching changes to an organization. During the Implementation phase, these changes begin to occur. Implementing the quality improvement plan means incorporating the measurement and improvement efforts into the organizational culture and discovering which behavioral changes need to occur. This effort, therefore, requires a corresponding change in the reward structure. A reward system should motivate the staff to change development procedures in a way that is consistent with the goals of the improvements efforts.

   Once a new reward system is in place, Implementation should turn to those short-term projects that were identified in the Planning phase. These might include:

   - Project tracking techniques and tools
   - Formalizing reviews and walkthroughs
   - Implementing Joint Application Design (JAD) sessions
   - Applying new approaches to testing

4. *Institutionalization.* Institutionalization requires that the lessons learned during Implementation be captured and transformed into organizational assets to form the basis of a continuous improvement culture. As a first step, the experiences gained in near-term improvement projects should be analyzed, packaged, and communicated to everyone in the organization. Successes must be validated and publicized. The experience is packaged into self-contained units including approach, results, techniques, tools, manuals, and training, to transform the knowledge gained into the organization's culture.

The basic techniques for institutionalizing continuous quality improvement include:

- Analyzing the results of short-term projects and comparing the results with the targets defined in Planning;
- Synthesizing the experience into lessons learned, domain expertise, rules and models;
- Packaging the experience as products that can be delivered to the organization.

References

1. Barbara Zimmer is part of HP's Corporate Engineering Department, which is located at 1801 Page Mill Rd., Bldg. 18D, Palo Alto, CA 94304. Her phone number is (415) 857-4894.

2. Capers Jones can be contacted at Software Productivity Research. One New England Executive Park Drive, Burlington, MA 01803. His telephone number is (617) 273-0140.
3. More information about the Ernst & Young Quality Studies can be obtained from Paul Kikta, National Performance Improvement Office. Paul is located in Ernst & Young's Cleveland, OH office and can be reached at (216) 861-5000 extension 5128.
4. Ed Yourdon is the author of a multitude of books including *Structured Design* published in 1979 by Yourdon Press/Prentice-Hall.
5. The seminal work referred to here is *Information Engineering* written by James Martin and Clive Finkelstein and published by the Savant Institute in 1981. The Savant Institute is located in Carnforth, Lancs, the United Kingdom.
6. Clive Finkelstein is the founder of Information Engineering Systems Corp. Because he is located in Australia, interested readers can contact the president of the firm, Glen Hughlette, for more information on Information Engineering. He is located at IESC, 201 N. Union St., 5th Fl., Alexandria, VA 22314. (703) 739-2242.
7. Margaret Hamilton is president of Hamilton Technologies, Inc., which is located at 17 Inman St., Cambridge, MA 02139. Her phone number is (617) 492-0058.
8. Ed Lanigan has since departed McDonnell Douglas and is now president of The Lanigan Group, which is located in St. Louis. He can be reached at (314) 725-0980.
9. Ken Horner can be reached through DRT Systems, which is a joint venture between Deloitte & Touche and a Japanese firm. DRT Systems is located at 1633 Broadway, New York, NY 10019. His telephone is (212) 492-3600.
10. Sam Holcman is a Vice President at KnowlegeWare, which is located at 39555 Orchard Hill Pl., Ste. 450, Novi, MI 48375. His phone number is (313) 348-1420 extension 6072.
11. Jessica Keyes is president of Techinsider, which is a high-technology consultancy. Techinsider is located at 200 W. 79 St., Ste. 8H, New York City, NY, 10024. Her phone is (212) 362-0559.
12. Howard Rubin is president of Howard Rubin Associates located at Winterbottom Lane, Pound Ridge, NY 10576. He can be reached at (914) 764-4931.
13. The IEEE Computer Society is located at 1730 Massachusetts Ave., NW, Washington, DC 20036. Their phone is (202) 371-0101. The Quality Assurance Institute is located at 7575 Phillips Blvd. #35, Orlando, FL 32819. Their phone number is (407) 363-1111.
14. Information about this study can be obtained through Professor Chris Kemerer who is located at the Sloan School at MIT, Cambridge, 02139. His phone number is (617) 253-2971.
15. Jerry Grochow can be reached at his offices at AMS. The address is 4050 Legato Road, Fairfax, VA 22033. His phone number is (703) 841-6498.
16. IFPUG is located in the Blendonview Office Park, 50008-28 Pine Creek Dr., Westerville, OH 43081-4899. Their phone number is (614) 895-7130.
17. This section references the IEEE Standard of Measures to Produce Reliable Software. Standard 982.1-1988. More information can be obtained from the IEEE Service Center, 445 Hoes Ln., Piscataway, NJ 08854. Their phone number is (908) 981-0060.
18. Barry Boehm is a giant in this area. Readers interested in more on this subject should read Boehm's book, Software Engineering Economics which was published in 1981 by Prentice-Hall.
19. Y. K. Shetty can be reached at Utah State University's College of Business. Her phone number is (801) 750-2369.
20. Bill Smillie works out of several Coopers & Lybrand offices. His phone number is (410) 323-2468.

The Internet

63

Multimedia Impact on Web Pages

Valerie Taylor
Chris Ammen

Communication on the Internet can take many forms. For most of us, the communications model that applies to Web sites is that of publishing. You make information available. Your audience will seek out your Web pages and access the information. Attracting and holding reader interest is critical. Unlike traditional print publishing, the Web supports multimedia and hypertext links within the text-based page framework.

For the purposes of this discussion, the Internet and the World Wide Web are the same. Actually, the Web is a subset of the Internet. Mosaic was the first Web browser that was easy to use. Finally, the Internet was accessible by the rest of us. Mosaic supported multimedia and was distributed free. Others soon followed. The best-known and most frequently used browser is the Windows version of Netscape Navigator, but there are many other browsers on the market, and more special-purposes browsers are in development.

The Internet and the Worldwide Web are expanding at a rate of 50% or so a month. This explosive growth is having a profound affect on everything associated with the Web.

Web Site Design

Web site design is key to putting together a coherent, informative, memorable Web presence. The Web is becoming more crowded. Standing out and attracting attention is becoming increasingly important. Once the user finds your site, the real process of document distribution begins. As users navigate through your pages, they are finding information (or not) and developing an image of your company, as well as your products and services. This might be your only chance to get your message across to a potential customer. It must be memorable as well as productive. Your message must be clear, concise, and complete. Adding appropriate multimedia can make it memorable.

There is a general misconception about multimedia and Web sites that has hindered the development of really useful Internet-distributed information. Multimedia is not just text and graphics, as the press would have you believe. Multimedia includes video, audio, and animations. Furthermore, the bandwidth exists today to allow the inclusion of all multimedia object-types on Web pages.

New technologies are being developed for business, education, consumer product marketing, scientific research, and art. These new developments are constantly changing the playing field for anyone planning to use the Internet for business, education, or recreation.

Internet Communications 101

In textbook terms, there are three basic forms of communication. These apply whether communicating in person or via electronic media, such as the Internet. Each form is characterized by the number of participants and the direction or directions of information flow.

- *Dialog.* A dialog takes place between two parties. The communication flows in both directions. E-mail is a good example of this form of communication. Web pages are rarely sufficiently interactive or responsive enough to be considered a true dialog.

- *Discussion.* A discussion involves more than two participants. Electronic bulletin boards, newsgroups, etc. are good examples of many-to-many communication. Specialized software is available to provide chat-like discussions on the Web.

- *Delivery.* Most Web sites fall into the category of delivery-type communications. The communication is one way. The Web page contains the information accessible by any and all who seek it out. However, unlike broadcast, this delivery is passive. It just sits there until someone requests the information be downloaded.

Unlike selling magazines or sending out catalogs and brochures by the thousands, aggressive potential customer contact is considered a breach of netiquette. On the other hand, you aren't at the mercy of a distribution channel or the U.S. Post Office to reach these people either. It is important to design your Web presence with this in mind.

Multimedia is important. It makes your message attractive and memorable. It might get you written up in the trade press or in *The Wall Street Journal.* If nothing else, your customers and prospective clients will benefit from an engaging multi-sensory presentation of your information and that is the primary objective.

Web browsers can handle some types of multimedia directly, like in-line GIF files. For other media types, browsers rely on Helper applications. Today, there are some technical limitations to multimedia inclusion and playback, but there is a lot of development effort and resources being focused on providing solutions. The appeal of multimedia on the Internet has generated tremendous public interest and raised expectations for global communications and information exchange.

Text

Web pages are inherently text-based as defined by the HTML language use to construct Web pages. *HTML* stands for *Hyper Text Markup Language*. Some of the earliest browsers only support text and hyperlinks. It is easy to put together an interesting and informative set of text-only pages. The display of text is entirely dependent on the display capabilities of the browsers and user settings of selectable parameters. This is good news and bad news. The HTML files are small—usually a few kilobytes each. However, a page that looks great on your computer might not be what the user sees. The text will all be there, but the formatting can look completely different.

There are many different audiences for your Web pages. Try to accommodate a broad range of connectivity and interests—the techie, the consumer, the power user. Unlike print or broadcast, you are rarely limited in the amount of content that you can provide on the Web. Users appreciate having access to detail product specifications, frequently asked questions, back issues of newsletters, etc. So long as the navigation through the site is well laid out, the more information you provide, the better.

Graphics

Graphics are the easiest and most visible additions to any Web page. A splash of color, a dramatic image or an identifiable logo can be added as an in-line graphic in GIF format. Virtually all browsers have the ability to display GIF format images. JPEG format images are also displayable by some browsers. Large JPEG images can be displayed as separate pages using helper applications.

Images and graphics files can be very large if color and resolution are important. A 640-×-480 24-bit color image is about 1 MB uncompressed. Illustrations and photographs can be much larger. A large format photo like those taken from a satellite can be 60 MB.

Interactivity

Hyperlinks are the most exciting feature of the World Wide Web. The ability to electronically reference other pages located anywhere on the planet is a great concept. Users like to be involved and control how they navigate through information.

Hyperlinks are particularly useful for compiling lists of references to related information and Web sites owned and maintained by someone else—other authors, documentation sources, resources, program files—whatever. Be sure to validate links periodically—especially links to outside sources. Pages are frequently changed, moved or renamed without warning and without forwarding addresses.

Additional interactivity is achieved through Common Gateway Interface (CGI) scripts or programs that can be linked to Web pages. Forms are one common way to encourage user communication. CGI scripts or programs attached to Web pages also can be used to access databases, customize Web pages in reply and a host of other applications. Forms are also used to promote interactivity through survey questionnaires, registration forms, and structured feedback requests.

Rich Text

Layout, fonts, graphic placement, and image detail can be as important as the text content. Newspapers, magazines, and forms rely on exact layout to convey image, present material and comply with information input requirements. These rich text documents can be created and distributed on the Web. Until the HTML standard is revised and browsers updated to include style and enhanced layout information, other proprietary formats are available.

Adobe Acrobat has become the rich document standard. Each Acrobat page file contains explicit formatting information to display the exact layout and fonts of the original document. Some examples of each are found in the Web versions of *The New York Times*, Amherst College humor magazine, and the Federal government forms archive. The Acrobat file might be much larger than an HTML version of the same text and graphics, but these might be a reasonable trade-off if layout is important.

The *Acrobat Reader* is available free from the Adobe site. Acrobat documents will always display exactly as created regardless of the platform used for display. Netscape has committed to including .PDF format display in future releases of Navigator. Proposed changes to the HTML standard to include style information provide some similar capabilities.

Multimedia

We live in an information-rich society. Via the Internet, the audience is global. Multimedia allows you to influence a broader audience with more information in more formats. Using multiple appropriate media types adds interest, reduces customer support costs, improves sales productivity, and provides another opportunity for product and service information distribution.

Adding multimedia elements to Web site design and implementation requires planning. Video, sound, and animation files are usually large and require a lot of data to be transferred to the user. Compression techniques help to reduce file sizes significantly, but compared with text, all these media formats require large numbers of bits for even short clips.

Multimedia files provide impact to a Web page. Used sparingly and appropriately, multimedia can add considerable impact to Web pages. Unlike gratuitous in-line pictures and wallpaper, the user decides to access these files. All links to files should include file size, playtime, and a description of the content to help the user determine if they really want to download this file.

Streaming vs. Download Then Play

For reasons of protocol limitations, file size and modem speed, it has not been possible to play audio, video, and animations in real-time. The files are downloaded to the user's computer. Once the entire file has been transferred, most browsers can then launch a helper application to play the file that is now sitting on the user's computer or hard drive. This arrangement has several serious limitations—transfer time, lack of browsing/preview capability, and copyright issues.

Several technology developments address these problems. The most important is streaming playback. Early implementations are now available that allow the user to play (hear or view) the multimedia content as the file is being transferred from the host site. Most streaming implementations allow the user to determine which part of a file to transfer/play, eliminating the need to download an entire file before playing any of it. The user can start at the beginning or in the middle. The transfer time is approximately the same as the playtime so that there is no long delay between starting the transfer and playing.

With streaming players, copyright holders are more confident that their rights are not being violated. The user never gets a complete copy of the material. Most streaming players are reusing the same disk space as they play the material, overwriting the previously played portion of the file. With the "download-then-play" helpers, the entire file must be downloaded (at least temporarily) onto the user's hard drive before the player program is launched. Adequate free hard drive space must be available to hold the entire downloaded file.

Streaming players are in the works. Xing and others are coming out with streaming video players. VocalTec and RealAudio have distributed hundreds of thousands of streaming audio players. It is only a matter of time until users and content owners will decide which transfer method to use.

Audio and Sound

Audio, sound, music, narration can all add impact to a Web site experience. There is less standardization in sound file formats than in other areas of multimedia. The AU sound format is the most portable and can be used on all platforms. However, most Windows sound files are in WAV format. Macintosh sound files are usually in AIF format. These sound files are downloaded then played.

RealAudio and VocalTec are two of the early entrants into the streaming or browsing audio player software arena. Each have proprietary audio formatting and compression software for the host server. The client or user player software is available free from Web sites using these technologies and from the vendors.

Audio is good bang for the byte-buck. Hearing a voice or music or sound provides more information than text alone. The file size and bandwidth for audio is a fraction of what is required for even primitive video. Audio-only can be just as effective as talking head video.

Audio can be used in conjunction with a graphic image. For example, a client wanted to include a complex satellite image on a page. In order to see the detail, the image must be displayed on the full screen. However, that covered the description of the image. Adding an audio file describing the image that could be played while the image was on screen resolved the problem.

Video

Video is the most powerful of all media objects. Now you can add video to your repertoire of cool Web stuff. However, video files can be huge. For MPEG-1 and QuickTime/Cinepak video, files are about 10 MB per minute.

Apple Computer's QuickTime is currently the most widely used video format on the Internet. Software-only players are available for download from the Apple site. QuickTime can be played by the broadest range of users. Download times and video playback quality can be altered to meet a broad range of requirements. Quarter-screen or smaller images and low frames rates (2 to 15 frames per second) work best. *See* Digital Video for more information about technical capabilities and trade-offs.

The Motion Picture Expert's Group standard—MPEG-1, is also being viewed as an important video format for use on the Internet. VHS or better playback is possible—full screen, 30 frames per second, with CD-quality audio. The compression algorithms are sophisticated and require lots of computing power or hardware-assistance for playback.

Much of the MPEG-1 video currently on the Internet is of poor quality. Really good MPEG encoding is being done for specialized commercial multimedia CD-ROM titles and Video CDs and has yet to migrate to the Web in quantity. As MPEG hardware becomes more widely available, MPEG will emerge as the Internet standard. For those applications where broadcast quality is required, MPEG-2 can deliver, but the data files are huge (more than six times larger than MPEG-1).

Novell is using video to promote their NEST technology. Video clips of Novell CEO, Robert Frankenberg demonstrating the technology have helped promote the concepts to employees, resellers, and clients around the world. The video clips dramatically show the simplicity of the user interface, which is extremely complex when described in text only.

Joint venture: Silicon Valley, an organization that brings together businesses and local government to promote the region, has effectively used digital video on their Web site. Landmarks, local industry luminaries, working environments, high tech know how and quality of life are all featured in the video clips.

The video has prompted many inquiries from outside the United States, as well as from businesses considering relocation to the San Francisco Bay area.

WWW and digital video

The storage and distribution of digital video files over the Internet is an important addition to any Web site. In this video-rich world, video plays a key role in selling products and services, communicating complex information, bridging cultural gaps, educating young and old, and informing and entertaining us. Video also represents the most challenges in terms of digitization, compression, storage, and Internet distribution. Audio and animation files are closely related to video files in size and complexity.

We are not talking about feature length movies yet. Traditional business-to-business communication often includes a video tape or a slide presentation. Many applications can be effective with small, lower resolution video using new or existing video (and audio) to enhance text-based Web pages. The intended audience and message is key to determining which format is appropriate (Fig. 63.1).

This chart illustrates some interesting choices being made by Web surfers. The vertical bars represent individual videos. The height of the bar indicates the size of the video file—the taller the bar, the bigger the video file. The videos are arranged from most frequently downloaded on the left to least frequently downloaded on the right. The shaded area behind the bars shows the number of downloads for the video. The left half of the chart is pretty clear. Small videos are downloaded more often than large video files.

However, the right half suggests that size is not as important as some other factors. Other influencing factors include video content and location in the

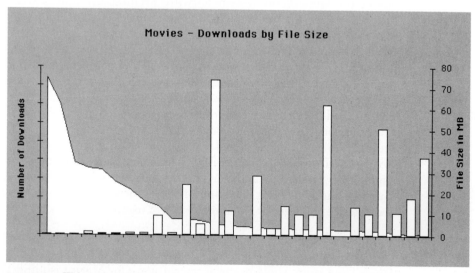

Figure 63.1 Web surfing choices.

list of videos available. If users want the information, they are prepared to download relatively large files (some of these files are more 30 MB).

The connection and bandwidth capabilities of Web users vary tremendously. The Web might be universally accessible, but not all access is equal. Users with 14.4 modem wait two hours to download a 1-minute video clip. The same file can be downloaded via a T1 link in just over 1 minute. What is intolerable to some users is just fine for others. From some remote region of the country or world, just having access to information can be well worth the wait—however long that might be. This broad spectrum of users can be accommodated by offering choices of file size and format.

Video guidelines

Here are some guidelines for using video on Web pages. Many of these suggestions apply to any multimedia files. These are not intended to represent a definitive work on digitized video. These are intended to get you thinking about some of the issues associated with digitizing video.

Although there are other video and audio formats, MPEG and QuickTime are emerging as the best choices. QuickTime is an Apple extension for Macintosh and Windows to integrate time-based data into applications. MPEG (Moving Pictures Experts Group) is a family of ISO (the International Standards Organization) standards for digital video (sequences of images in time) and audio compression that define a compressed bit stream, which implicitly defines a decompressor.

QuickTime is a software architecture that supports the inclusion of many different compression/decompression schemes to play specific file formats. MPEG files can be played by QuickTime software with the appropriate decompressor. Cinepak video compression is SuperMac's software video codec technology under the QuickTime system-software architecture and is widely supported. Currently, most references to QuickTime really refer to QuickTime with SuperMac's Cinepak or some other widely distributed compression algorithm, such as Apple video, animation, or JPEG. MPEG usually refers to files that conform to the MPEG-1 standard. Both MPEG and Cinepak video-compression technology use interframe compression to achieve high compression rates.

We encourage you to provide video in both QuickTime and MPEG-1 formats. Specialized video-compression/decompression (codec) hardware is still relatively expensive so offering software-only playback is advisable. In general, QuickTime files can be played with software on most computers being used to access the Internet today. MPEG-1 plays back at better quality but requires a high-end computer or additional hardware to assist in the decoding process. By choosing both QuickTime and MPEG-1 for your video presentation, you can reach and empower the broadest range of users.

QuickTime

QuickTime is an Apple proprietary software for Macintosh and Windows that enables the integration of time-based data into applications. Time-based data types contain data that can be stored and retrieved as values over time. Examples include sound, video (MPEG, Cinepak), animation, data produced by scientific instruments, financial results, music information (MIDI), and other similar data types.

There are different compression algorithms for specific content types—JPEG for still pictures, video, animation, playback from CD-ROM (Cinepak), Intel's Indeo, and others. The resulting file sizes can vary widely, depending on the source video, image size, audio and video quality parameters chosen, and the compression method selection.

The compression and playback characteristics can be varied by the encoding software. The average compression ratio is 20:1, compared to original source material. The exact compression ratio depends on the complexity of the video content and the quality desired in the video playback. The data rate for a ¼-screen video with audio can be 10 MB/minute. That is as large as an MPEG file, but the QuickTime file is more universally playable today. A 30-second video that is a series of still images with narration could be as small as 1 MB. The file of the same video produced with another compression method might be as large as 5 MB. If the content of the video is very complex and has a large number of changes between frames, then more space will be required to store the needed information. The more complex the content, the more space it requires, and the lower the compression ratio. There are lots of choices, depending on the desired results and necessary trade-offs.

Cinepak video compression is SuperMac's software video codec technology that has been adopted by Apple, Microsoft, 3DO, Sega, Atari, Creative Labs, and Cirrus Logic. Cinepak video-compression technology allows authors and publishers to create one version of their video products for the entire Internet. Cinepak video-compression technology uses 320 × 240 pixels (¼ screen) of video displayed from 12 to 30 frames per second. The technology is scalable and takes advantage of whatever power the system can provide.

Professional QuickTime encoding services are available as well. Several software developers are introducing products and services to enhance the quality and playback of QuickTime video. Very good results can be achieved by these professionals using sophisticated software tools.

Windows and DOS don't recognize the resource forks in Macintosh files. To run Macintosh movies on Windows platforms, files must be "flattened" by appending the resource fork to the end of the data fork and removing the old resource fork. Utilities are available to do this.

Players applications for most platforms are available from the Apple Computer World Wide Web site.

MPEG-1

MPEG (Moving Pictures Experts Group) meet under ISO (the International Standards Organization) to generate standards for digital video (sequences of images in time) and audio compression. In particular, they define a compressed bit stream, which implicitly defines a decompressor. The compression algorithms are up to the individual manufacturers, and that is where proprietary advantage is obtained within the scope of a publicly available international standard. There is actually a family of MPEG standards. MPEG-1 is the more compressed version. MPEG-2 delivers much better quality, but the files are at least five times larger. For most Internet users, the sacrifice of quality for a smaller file size is acceptable.

MPEG-1 is the best bang for the digital video buck. The various hardware and software decoding systems offer MPEG video and audio decompression with output to standard VGA and audio cards as decoded video, audio or system streams. Reasonable frame rates of 30 frames-per-second (fps—full motion) can easily be achieved on these systems. The compact video stream plays back full frame 640- × -480 pixels with CD-quality audio. The resulting file size is approximately 10 MB/minute.

MPEG-1 is designed for data rates from 1 to 5 MB per second or 125 to 625 KB per second. Image size, although variable under the specification, is usually set to 320 × 240 at 30 fields/second or SIF resolution. Most MPEG players display a full-screen presentation by line-doubling the data to 640 × 480 pixels. Within MPEG, there are variations, specifically VideoCD and CD-I. The MPEG hardware manufacturers all support VideoCD, which specifies image size, data rate, and audio formats. Data rates that are higher or lower than specified in the VideoCD standard will not play back consistently on all systems.

High-quality MPEG-1 encoded files compare well with VHS tape when played back. For business-to-business presentations, videographers, and video production companies, MPEG-1 is the best choice in Internet video file formats. MPEG encoding is still relatively expensive. Recreational MPEG encoding systems start at $4000. High-end cinematic-quality MPEG encoding suites with sophisticated pre-filtering software can cost hundreds of thousands of dollars. Highly skilled compressionists can do scene-by-scene encoding optimization, which delivers superior results over the less-expensive systems.

Decoding is processing intensive. Although it can be done with a fast computer and software alone, the addition of a hardware assist is desirable. 20 to 30 MPEG decoding boards, priced from $300, are available for Windows machines. Macintosh MPEG hardware decoders are available as well. Xing's XingMPEG Player and Duplexx's Net Toob software can play MPEG-1 without additional hardware on Pentium-class PCs. Most high-end Unix workstations also play MPEG-1 video.

For Internet use, compression is essential to reduce the amount of data transferred. Cinepak, MPEG, and JPEG are good choices.

The color depth has a direct impact on file size. For QuickTime and Apple's video compression, using 256 colors or even 4 or 16 grays can significantly reduce the file size. However, some compressors, such as Cinepak and MPEG, only work with millions of colors. If you are trying to save file size by reducing colors, be sure to choose a compression method that works with a reduced color palette.

Audio compatibility is a significant problem for software codecs, such as QuickTime/Cinepak, and software MPEG players because they rely on the audio subsystem in the computer to decode the audio. Many multimedia systems cannot handle CD-quality audio (44 kHz/16-bit audio) and the video's audio track is lost. This does not apply to MPEG hardware decoders. MPEG hardware decoders are well standardized, so compatibility is not a problem.

Use video sparingly. A 20- to 30-second clip to add a personal note or to introduce a guest speaker or a corporate officer, can be very effective. A 30-second demonstration of a complex procedure—like installing a printer toner cartridge—is more effective than pages of diagrams and text explanation.

Use video to do what video does best—show motion, demonstrate complex concepts visually, add sound and music. Remember, someone has to download this video before they play it. Be sure it is worth their while. Users do not want to wait for a 5-MB file to download just to see a corporate logo fly about the screen.

Reusing existing video for inclusion into a Web page works and is a good way to test the water. Editing and clip selection are critical. Rely on the text to provide the linear framework. Use video to add interest. Make every second count.

Animation

Macromedia's Director is used for most multimedia CD-ROM titles, as well as for interactive presentations, training, and kiosk applications. A Web version of the Director player is being developed and will add a new level of interactivity to Web page design.

Sun Microsystems has announced Hot Java, a multimedia authoring system with object-oriented applications that run on the user desktop, an authoring language, and additional server functionality to support these new concepts. Several sample uses are already available—interactive animation and dynamic stock quotation updating.

Creativity

Web page design is an evolving art form. Regular surfing is the best way to stay current on new capabilities and find exciting new ways to use the technology. New Web-related technology is being introduced daily that can significantly enhance your Web site experience.

Your look can also make you stand out from the competition. Although it is important to have a consistent look to your site, variations on the theme are important to distinguish between the pages—especially if there are large numbers of pages. A family of brightly colored graphics based on a theme or a logo style can help to present a consistent image across a large number of Web pages in a site.

To be noticed, you might have to resort to promotional gimmicks, contests or give-away programs. Advertising on other frequently accessed sites can also generate traffic for your site.

Helper Applications

Most browsers recognize file types other than just HTML text and GIF format graphic files. When the URL points to one of these other files, the browser downloads the file and launches the appropriate application program for the file. These are known as *Helpers* or *Helper applications*.

For most multimedia types, one or more Helper applications are available. Some helpers are programs that a user might already have—Powerpoint, Word, QuickTime, MoviePlayer, Windows Media Player. Others can be downloaded from various Internet sites—for example, Adobe Acrobat, VMPEG, Sparkle. Others can be purchased from computer vendors and retailers—MPEG decoding boards and associated application software. Once the software is installed, helper applications in the Preferences options in the browser can be launched automatically.

Most browsers have additional configuration options available. To maximize file transfers, increase the size of buffers and cache settings in the Network and Cache options menu. This allows your computer to gather bigger chunks of the file during download.

Bandwidth

The bandwidth issue is raised in every multimedia on the Internet discussion. So here is our perspective. If bandwidth is an issue for users now, it won't be for long—unless users choose to stick with their 9600-baud modems.

Dramatic changes have occurred in the growth of bandwidth and traffic on the Internet since 1991. As the interest and demand goes up, so does the bandwidth.

Statistics of video file transfers from sites all over the world show that the server speed directly impacts the transfer time. Transfer delays over the net are never more than 5 to 10 milliseconds in hundreds of samples. The bandwidth is there if both the sender and receiver are capable of reasonable transfer speeds.

If the receiver only has a 9600-baud modem, server speed has little effect. For business-to-business information distribution, server speed is critical. Today, there are tens of thousands of T1 lines installed and the number is growing by 400 to 500 per month. Frame relay and partial T1 lines are being installed in even larger numbers. These users can download files in the time it takes to play them. Waiting one minute for the download to view a one-minute video is considered acceptable. Streaming video playback is possible at this file transfer rate.

Homes and businesses everywhere are getting connected with ISDN lines. Although ISDN is not fast enough for full-motion, full-screen video on-demand, it is adequate for most demonstrations, conferencing, and learning applications.

Telephone companies and cable providers have the connectivity to the users home and office. With changing regulations, both groups see delivery of data from the Internet to desk and set-tops as important to their long-term growth (or even survival).

On-Line Publishing

So what is happening in on-line publishing? Generally speaking, the quality of published information is improving. The level of professionalism in Web page design is evident everywhere. Major corporations are producing Web sites with great graphics, interesting audio and video, and sophisticated interactivity. For example, Silicon Graphics has great graphics. Oracle is demonstrating how customized Web pages can be produced from a database of information to fit the requirements of a single user on demand. Sun Microsystems and its clients have developed a number of Hot Java applications.

The quantity of information is growing. Sites are expanding. Having a Home Page is a start. However, many sites now have hundreds of interconnecting pages describing the company, products and services and offering online technical support through frequently asked questions—FAQs for most customer problems. Apple, HP, and Sun all maintain large complex sites.

Commercial distribution of information is beginning to take off. Some of the early adopters are financial and stock quotation services, specialized industry specific newsletters, software retailers, and a wine merchant (Virtual Vineyard). Some are offering information as a one-time charge. Others are using the subscription model—pay one price for multiple issues of a magazine. The entertainment industry is keenly aware of the potential of the Internet as a new outlet for its products and services and distribution channel for its content.

Because there is so much information, it is often difficult and time-consuming to sift through all the apparently related information to find the reliable sources of information. Editorial and Review Services are beginning to make their mark. Although they do not create the information, they review it and summarize and/or identify the best sources. Users are willing to pay to have this culling done. The time savings can be well worth the money.

Two of the most active Internet sites provide free service to users. Yahoo categorizes site listings. Info Seek offers extensive search and retrieval capabilities. Both services now charge for advertising on their popular sites. Charging for advertising appears to be the most successful way to make money for providing Internet content and navigation-related services.

Summary

The advent of the World Wide Web technology has enabled millions of content owners and users to provide and retrieve information. As the Web matures, more multimedia objects will be added to text and graphics-based messages. People all over the world will be able to promote products and services, educate themselves and others, and forge new relationships with the power of video, audio, and animation.

Sure, communication in text and pictures works. It has for centuries. When more senses and communication styles can be integrated, the process improves. You might not be able to read all the words in a foreign language text, but you hear the enthusiasm in the voice and see the smiles and fine gestures in the video. Multimedia can add impact to any Internet message. Try it. You'll see and hear the difference!

64

Internet Access via Cable Television: High-Speed Access to Multimedia on the Worldwide Web

Lynn Jones

Cybersurfers are catching the Internet wave in record numbers. The World Wide Web is growing exponentially with new video, audio, and text being added daily. The information available on the Web is staggering, but getting to all this multimedia with a standard dial-up telephone modem just isn't fast enough. Enter cable television. Cable isn't just for television anymore. Cable data networks are now springing up around the world, providing fast, affordable, convenient access to the Internet.

How do you separate the hype from the hypertext? For that matter, what is hypertext? This chapter will answer these questions and more, providing a framework within which to understand how such a network is implemented. It will give you a crash course on the Internet and cable TV networks and show how the information highway is being created today with the Internet and cable TV.

Introduction

Internet over cable TV will receive more general press (Information Superhighway) attention than any other carrier-based activity in 1995 and become the most important tool for work-at-home since the advent of the PC, modem and facsimile terminal.

Dr. Jerome Lucas, *TeleStrategies Insight Newsletter*, January 1995

The commercialization of the Internet has opened the door for access to the largest information network in the world. The Internet connects an estimated 40,000 networks, 6,600,000 hosts, and over 30,000,000 users in more than 154 countries around the world. In early 1994, it was estimated that on the average, a new computer was added to the Internet every 30 seconds. The growth of the Internet continues to be exponential.

Homes, businesses, schools, and institutions can access the Internet at speeds unmatched in price/performance by any other medium by using the ubiquitous, existing infrastructure that the cable TV industry has in place today in the US, Canada, and many countries around the world. Users can get high-speed access at a much lower cost—a key criteria for Internet users.

Rapid access to and provision of pictures, sound, video, audio, and integrated text and graphics are all made possible by accessing Internet sites on the World Wide Web, using a Web browser program from a personal computer connected to the Internet via cable television. By using standard channels, one forward and one reverse, on an existing entertainment cable system, cable operators can offer businesses, telecommuters, doctors, teachers, students, and consumers access to the state-of-the-art capabilities available on the information highway today.

This chapter covers creating such networks using an Ethernet to cable TV bridge, brouter, or personal modem at each business, hospital, school, or home, coupled with a translator in the cable TV headend and a backbone router to the Internet at one location on the network. Each user on the network has access to the Internet, as well as shared 10-Mbps access to each other. With the addition of data networking capability to traditional entertainment, the value of the cable connection is increased by orders of magnitude.

The key is the ability to use cable to provide a fully distributed network, rather than using expensive point-to-point leased lines for direct connection to the Internet, or slow dial-up lines for indirect connection through on-line services.

The goals of this chapter are to explain the network technology, components, and architecture, and the methodology that will provide the reader with a foundation on which to implement such a network. Case studies of actual networks are used to illustrate possible configurations.

The convergence of the cable and data communications industries provides enormous opportunities, but carries with it the challenges of learning about new technologies. This chapter is intended to serve as a starting point, assuming that you have little or no knowledge of data communications, the Internet, or cable television.

A Brief History of the Internet

The evolution of cable TV data networks can be seen to parallel the development and growth of the Internet. Both have the roots of their technology growing largely out of military applications with initial use and promotion of the technology by the education and research community, followed by adoption in the commercial marketplace, and finally reaching widespread use in the home.

A brief history of the Internet helps to understand why it is organized the way it is, and how cable networks connect to it.

In the mid-1970s, the Defense Advanced Research Project Agency (DARPA) funded research to develop a set of networking standards or protocols, that specify how computers would communicate over an internet, as well as a series of conventions for interconnecting networks and routing traffic. The result was TCP/IP (Transmission Control Protocol/Internet Protocol). During the late 1970s, DARPA also funded research into packet switched networking and implemented a network called the *ARPAnet*.

TCP/IP became the only effective way to communicate between computers from different manufacturers. It appealed to schools, institutions, and businesses, who did not want to be tied to one vendor's equipment, and who wanted to protect their investment in existing equipment.

In the early 1980s, Ethernet local area networks (LANs) proliferated. Ethernet, developed by Metcalfe and Boggs in 1976, used a coaxial cable network, in which all stations monitor the cable (the ether) during their own transmission, terminating transmission immediately if a collision is detected. This created a new demand: rather than connecting to a single large time-sharing computer per site, organizations wanted to connect the ARPAnet to their entire local network. This would allow all the computers on that LAN to access ARPAnet facilities.

In 1986, the National Science Foundation founded NSFNET to connect its networks centered around its six supercomputers into a network backbone that ties into the ARPANET.

This network arrangement was enormously successful, and the Internet was born. With success came the need to upgrade computer resources and leased line speeds, which continues today.

Management of the Internet

The Internet has evolved from a loose federation of networks, to a network with a character all its own. There is no central management, but rather a group of organizations who steer its activities. These groups include the Internet Architecture Board (IAB), the Internet Society (ISOC), and the Internet Engineering Task Force (IETF).

Another unique aspect of the Internet is that, as it is not owned by any one party, it is also not paid for or funded by any one organization. NSF, which subsidized its development, has phased out its $11,500,000 subsidy. Privatization of the Internet remains a hot topic. Many third-party Internet access providers have sprung up to offer Internet access to businesses and individuals.

The Commercialization of the Internet

Those who stand to gain most from the commercialization of the Internet are small businesses, K-12 schools, home workers, and recreational users. Corporations, research institutions, and universities have been using the Internet for many years. Big business has also been using private wide-area networks (WANs) for years as well. (WANs being essentially company-owned internets.) Prior to the commercialization of the Internet, small businesses, schools, and individuals could not afford the high price of private WANs, and were not allowed access to the Internet. Commercialization opens the door for access to resources previously only available to large organizations. It also opens up a whole new range of possibilities. Virtual corporations and electronic shopping malls are not only possible, but possible on an international level. Internet marketing and advertising will change the way products are promoted.

The commercialization of the Internet will forever change the future of both small business and worldwide commerce. It will also forever change what the Internet is.

Who Are the Users?

Users of the Internet include companies, universities, colleges, K-12 schools, research groups, and individual users.

The majority of universities and research facilities have Internet access. Many companies also have access. There is now a major initiative to connect K-12 schools. Individual users are largely an untapped market, because (until recently) acquiring Internet access required specialized knowledge of UNIX and TCP/IP.

The popular press is rife with articles on the wealth of information available on the Internet, as well as on the need for a national, as well as global, Information Highway. This has sparked a feeding frenzy of interest in connecting up to the Internet. To people today, the Internet is the Information Highway.

What Are the Applications?

Applications on the Internet started out with simple text-based applications, such as electronic mail. Today's applications are highly visual—containing color pictures, sound, graphics, video, and other data-intensive information formats. The increase in such applications drives the need for the "big pipes" that cable TV can provide.

Electronic mail

The most commonly used application on the Internet is electronic mail (e-mail). Each user has a unique address and can be reached by anyone else with e-mail access to the Internet.

Electronic mail is a low-bandwidth, text-based application. It is a store and forward service, meaning that it does not require communicating users to have an end-to-end communications path set up at the time the message is sent. The message is forwarded and stored on subsequent computers until it reaches the recipient.

Traditional low-bandwidth, store and forward applications, such as e-mail, do not necessarily require the high-bandwidth capabilities of a cable TV network.

The World Wide Web

The World Wide Web (Web) is the newest and most often talked about application on the Internet today. The World Wide Web provides easily accessible, organized access to the huge amount of data available on the Internet. The Web uses hypertext, in which displayed information contains highlighted words that can be "expanded" with the click of a mouse, providing links to other information or files. These links can be to text, pictures, video clips, audio clips, graphics, etc.

The Web is a client-server based application. Information databases are stored on computers called *Web servers*. In order to access the Web, a user's computer needs a piece of software installed called a *client*, or in hypertext terminology, a *browser*.

Multimedia, client-server based applications, such as the Web, are the future of the Internet, and fuel the need for cable TV speeds. It is becoming commonplace for small businesses, schools, and municipalities to have their own Web servers. This trend necessitates high-speed symmetrical access, meaning that access speed is the same in either direction, which cable TV is in a unique position to provide.

Wide Area Information Servers (WAIS)

WAIS provides a means to search indexed material using a string of text supplied by the requester. It allows the user to easily look for information, regardless of where it is located on the Internet. WAIS is one of many such search tools, which instead of browsing randomly, allows a user to locate specific information.

Gopher

Gopher allows a user to tunnel through the Internet and access information without having to know its address. Using gopher is like having a library card catalog to access information, rather than having to search for it randomly.

News

News allows users to access information on a variety of topics or special interests, and is analogous to a discussion group or bulletin board.

File Transfer Protocol (FTP)

The File Transfer Protocol (FTP) is a client-server based application used for copying files from one computer to another over the Internet. FTP sets up a real-time connection between the two computers while the copying is taking place.

Telnet

Telnet is another client-server application that allows a user to log in to another computer on the Internet. It can allow users to access databases, public information, and library card catalogs.

Summary

One of the primary lamentations of Internet users is the inability to get high-speed access to applications, such as the World Wide Web from their desktop (particularly from home), where a dial-up line might be the only available option. A dial-up line might be fine for e-mail, but it is totally unsuitable for applications, such as the Web. The time it takes to download an image is just too long for the average user to endure. Symmetrical access is also key, as small companies, schools, and home-based businesses set up their own Web servers.

The Case for Internet Access Via Cable TV

...sometimes it makes sense to back out of the driveway at 900 miles per hour.

Vint Cerf, author of *TCP/IP/Internet Designer*

Communications mirrors society and changes the way that it interacts. Both data networks and cable television evolved to bring information to people in physically distant locations. People and networks have become more decentralized. An outgrowth of the ability to communicate over wide distances has fueled the growth of virtual companies, telecommuting, distance learning, and other phenomena. Key to these models is that the people using networks can be either producers or consumers of information, or prosumers. This societal model, coupled with the need to access the data-intensive applications used in these activities, requires high-speed symmetrical network access.

Key to the commercial growth is the ability to provide users in remote locations, at small companies, and at home with the same high-speed access to information both on community networks and on the Internet that they are used to having in the workplace.

As Vint Cerf, one of the founding fathers of the Internet, points out:

"The information superhighway model, with low-speed access to a high-speed backbone, is flawed. My experience with data networking is that sometimes it makes sense to back out of the driveway at 900 miles per hour. We need to support both low-speed and high-speed access. For that reason, narrowband, 128-Kbps integrated services digital network connections are not bad, but developments like cable TV-provided 10-Mbps Ethernet links are even more interesting."

Standard telephony lines simply do not have the capacity to bring the same bandwidth to the home as cable TV.

Cable TV Network Architecture

Cable television was initially designed in 1948 to enable people in remote or mountainous locations to receive over-the-air television signals. Originally known as *Community Antenna Television (CATV)*, it consisted of an antenna constructed on a mountain top, or other high point, which received the TV signal, and a distribution network that carried the signal to customers' homes.

How Does Cable Television Work?

Television signals are electromagnetic impulses. In broadcast television, they travel through the airwaves. In cable television, the antenna picks up signals from the airwaves, satellites, or microwave transmitters, and sends them to a central site called the *headend*. The headend consists of equipment that receives the radio-frequency (RF) signals and transmits them out over the distribution network. The term *headend* is used to refer both to the building where the equipment is located, as well as the equipment itself.

The cable TV distribution network consists of coaxial cable and/or fiber optic cable, amplifiers, and other components. The original cable systems used coaxial cable, or coax, which is economic, tolerant of many environmental conditions, and provides good shielding from electromagnetic (EMI) and radio frequency (RFI) interference. These systems provided one-way distribution of analog video signals from the headend out to homes. These broadband networks are analog mediums that use both active and passive components. Active components require power, and passive components do not. Amplifiers are used in the cable system to boost signals levels when they get too weak, or attenuate, over a certain distance. As cable systems evolved, they began incorporating fiberoptic cable, which carries signals as pulses of light conducted over strands of glass. Fiberoptic cable offers very fast throughput, is immune to electrical interference, and can carry signals over long distances without the need for amplifiers.

The traditional structure of a cable television system used a tree and branch topology, whereby a large trunk cable carries signals from the headend to smaller feeder cables in local neighborhoods.

Amplifiers are used to boost the signal as needed. Cable service is brought into the subscriber's home via a smaller drop cable, which is then connected to the TV.

The network cable is divided into 6-MHz channels. Existing cable networks are usually 400- to 500-MHz systems that can carry 50 to 60 channels. Cable systems can be either sub-split, mid-split, or high-split, which refers to the split between the number of forward and return channels. Typical entertainment channels only use forward channels, or channels that are outbound from the headend to the subscriber community. Two-way interactive services, such as data communications, also require the use of a return channel, or a channel that is inbound from the subscriber community to the headend. Most cable systems are sub-split (5 to 30 MHz inbound, 54 MHz and above outbound), but they can also be mid-split (5 to 108 MHz inbound, 162 MHz and above outbound), or high-split (5 to 174 MHz inbound, 234 MHz and above outbound).

Return channels are therefore an especially precious commodity to cable operators. Cable plants can also be single or dual, with most entertainment networks being single plants, as described. Dual plants have two physical cables, one for transmitting and one for receiving. Some cities have Institutional Networks (INETs) built specifically for business or institutional use, which are most often dual plants. Many universities also have dual plants. In a single plant, the translation from transmit to receive frequencies occurs at the headend, and requires a piece of equipment called a *frequency translator*. Dual plants do not require such translators.

The hybrid fiber coax network

Over the last few years, cable operators have been gearing up to offer interactive data, telephony, video-on-demand, and other services in addition to traditional entertainment. To meet the needs of such services, cable TV networks have been evolving into a hybrid combination of coaxial and fiberoptic cable, referred to as a *hybrid fiber coax (HFC)* architecture. This architecture uses a digital fiber backbone and a distributed star, tree and branch topology, as opposed to the totally analog tree and branch system. (*See* Fig. 64.1). One advantage of this approach is increased network bandwidth with improved reliability because of fewer amplifiers and other active components. This approach also lets cable operators use a build-as-you-go approach, capitalizing on their existing coax infrastructure and building fiber further out into the system as more bandwidth is needed. The newer HFC systems are 750-MHz networks that can carry up to 110 channels.

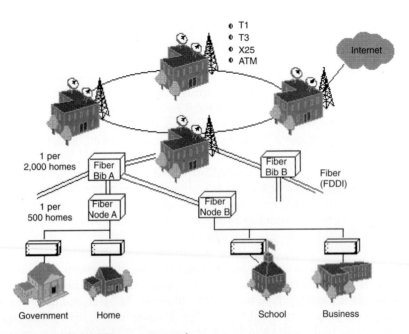

Figure 64.1 Hybrid fiber coax network.

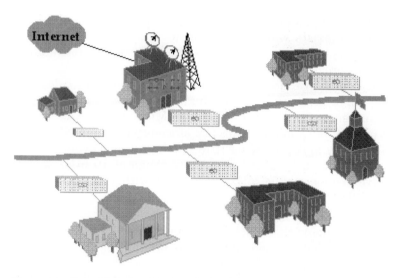

Figure 64.2 Community Internet access via cable TV.

How Does Internet Access Via Cable TV Work?

Data networks use devices (such as repeaters, bridges, and routers) to extend, as well as segment, local area networks.

A repeater, whether in a LAN or in a cable TV network, connects two segments of network cable. It retimes, regenerates, and forwards a digital signal. Repeaters, however, can only extend a high-speed LAN a few thousand yards.

Bridges are used to connect two networks that use the same network signaling and the same media access-control protocol, such as Ethernet. Routers are used to connect two different types of networks—in this case, to route IP datagrams (Fig. 64.2).

Internet backbone

Routers are also used to connect LANs to WANs, and make up the Internet backbone. A backbone is a central network to which other networks are connected.

It is important to remember that in the same way that a Local Area Network is a network of computers, the Internet is essentially a network of networks, consisting of thousands of computer networks interconnected by routers. It is also important to make a distinction between an Internet backbone router and a router on the community Ethernet network, or on the customer LAN, as illustrated in later scenarios.

Cable TV networking protocols

UniLINK. An example of a protocol in use today for extending a LAN by cable TV is UniLINK, developed by LANcity Corporation. It provides two-way, symmetrical and asymmetrical data transmission at a signaling rate of 10 Mbps, and it extends Ethernet beyond its distance limitation of 2.2 miles out to 200 miles. It coexists with entertainment and other services on a commercial cable TV network, which provides the same data rates and services that an Ethernet provides.

The cable data modem is specifically designed for cable TV networks. It uses a bi-directional single- or dual-cable plant to provide symmetrical data transmission at a signaling rate of 10 Mbps. It uses Quadrature Phase Shift Keying (QPSK) and has a spectral efficiency of 1.67 bits/Hz. The data modem is frequency agile, allowing it to operate in any available standard 6-MHz channel, over a transmit frequency range of 10 MHz to 174 MHz and a receive frequency of 54 MHz to 550 MHz, with a bit error rate (BER) of 25 dB C/N: <1 in 109.

802.14. Realizing that a standard communication protocol is needed for cable TV-based broadband communications networking, the IEEE 802.14 working group was formed.

The 802.14 protocol will define multiple physical layer protocols, a MAC layer protocol, cable topologies supported, and other criteria. The goal is to define standards that will allow the interoperability of equipment from many different vendors and which will handle many diverse multimedia applications. Some of the criteria that are being considered, for example, are the real-time needs of digitized video and voice, where transmission delays are a prime concern. Compatibility with Asynchronous Transfer Mode (ATM) is also a goal.

Hosts, nodes, gateways, and routers.   Internet backbone routers were originally called *gateways*. Gateways were developed to deal with the fact that for internetworking to work, computers communicating across multiple types of networks needed a way to talk with each other, as well as to talk to the intermediary networks in between to pass packets. What was needed was an end-to-end protocol.

An assumption was made in protocol design that the networks themselves could not be modified in order to internetwork them. Therefore, the gateways had to handle such things as differing maximum packet lengths and error characteristics among networks. The gateway would know about the end-to-end protocol used by hosts (end-user computers) communicating across multiple networks.

Other terms that might be encountered include nodes, or packet switch nodes (PSNs), which were also originally called *interface message processors (IMPs)*. These terms all refer to packet switches in the Internet backbone. An important distinction is that the term node, when talking about the Internet, means something entirely different than it does when talking about an Ethernet. A node in Internet terminology means a router; a node in Ethernet terminology is the end-user computer, or the Internet's equivalent of a host.

Cable Internet brouters

A cable Internet brouter is a combination bridge/router designed to work over commercial cable TV channels, and has a form-factor similar to a standard set-top box.

Using a cable Internet brouter, all packets that are destined for users on the Metropolitan Area Network (MAN), or the community network, are transparently bridged using the IEEE 802.1D Spanning Tree protocol. In other words, packets destined for the community network are handled by the bridge portion of the brouter.

Routing tables, which determine where to send packets that are destined outside the community network, or somewhere out on the Internet, are maintained using a routing protocol called *RIP1*. RIP1 is an interior gateway protocol used to execute distributed routing and reachability algorithms with other routers.

For packets going out to destinations across the Internet, or IP packets, the cable Internet brouter conforms to specific Internet protocols including the Internet protocol (IP), Internet Control Message Protocol (ICMP) and others when required. This ensures that other computers in the network receiving the data packets will be able to process and route them to their destination (i.e., that they "speak the same language").

The brouter interfaces between an Ethernet LAN and the cable-TV network and performs required functions, such as encapsulation and decapsulation of the data (i.e., putting the data in an envelope with an address on it, and taking it out of the envelope), sending and receiving datagrams, performing IP destination address translation, and network flow control and error handling. All of this is transparent to the user, but internally, a complex system of data transmission, traffic control, and error handling ensures that data reaches its destination intact, and in a timely manner.

The brouter receives and forwards Internet datagrams, providing buffer management, congestion control, and fairness. This activity allows data waiting to be sent to be stored in holding areas, or buffers, and ensures that each user "gets a turn" to transmit or receive data when the network is being heavily used, or is "congested," the equivalent of a system of on-ramps and traffic lights to control traffic during rush hour.

The brouter also chooses a next hop destination for each IP datagram. This means that the network chooses which computer to send the data to next. Each computer in the chain from sender to receiver is called a *hop*. Internally, the network keeps track of the best routes for data at any given time, dependent on various conditions in the network. For example, it might have detected that a certain computer is not operational. Even though taking this route might be the fewest "hops," and hence the natural first choice to send the data to, it will choose an alternative route.

For non-IP packets, the Internet brouter uses the Spanning Tree algorithm and automatically learns the locations of devices by listening to network traffic, forwarding packets only when necessary. Packets that are not forwarded are filtered.

Cable TV modems

Cable TV modems enable individual users to telecommute to corporate offices, access training programs and courseware for distance learning, access the Internet, and many other high-speed, media-intensive applications (Fig. 64.3).

One example of a cable modem, manufactured by LANcity Corporation, uses the aforementioned UniLINK protocol to provide access. The modem operates at 10 Mbps upstream and downstream and can operate in either a symmetrical or asymmetrical mode, depending on the requirements of the application. The modems are designed to work in business or home environments. An important factor of the modem is its frequency agility, which allows it to work in any sub-split, two-way cable plant in the frequency range of 54 to 550 MHz and a transmit range of 5 to 42 MHz. This flexibility is important to cable operators who do not want to move entertainment channels, a nuisance to both the operator and the subscriber community, in order to offer new data services. The cable modem plugs in to the cable network using a standard "F" connector, the same type of connector that is used to connect a television. A splitter is used to split the incoming cable in two—one for the TV and one for the PC. The same type of splitter is used when connecting two TVs to one incoming cable. The PC must run Ethernet to use this type of cable modem.

The cable modem gets its operational parameters from a reference node, which resides in the headend. The cable modem scans to determine operational receive frequencies and automatically listens for transmit frequency. In order to join a cable TV data network, the cable modem must receive permission from an authorized network utility server.

The network utility server provides centralized configuration and support for the cable data network and provides assignments for cable modem parameters, IP addresses, and network parameters. It also ensures network

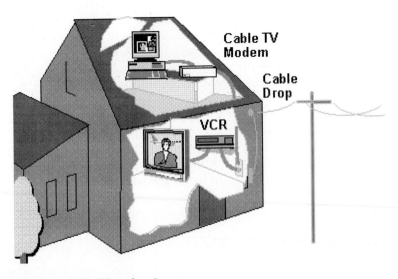

Figure 64.3 Cable TC modem.8

access authorization and the security of parameter transfer. Only the network operator, through the network utility server, can control transmit and receive frequencies. All parameter assignments are authorized by a digital signature.

Cable data network management

Largely caused by the decentralized nature of the Internet, there is no central network management. Each IP network is responsible for managing itself. Out of necessity, evolved a common technology used to manage the individual components of the Internet, which, like many other protocols originated for the Internet became adopted as the standard for non-Internet networks as well.

This management framework is called *Simple Network Management Protocol (SNMP)*. SNMP evolved from the Simple Gateway Monitoring Protocol (SGMP), which was designed for monitoring IP gateways in wide area networks.

SNMP is the defacto standard for network management today. By using SNMP network management, cable Internet brouters, bridges, and modems are fully integrated with the network management of all the other IP networks on the Internet.

SNMP allows the collection of network statistics from widely diverse network components by defining the minimum amount of information that each IP device should provide, via a structure called the *MIB (Management Information Base)*. An SNMP agent is the software that interfaces between the MIB and the network management station (NMS) and processes all of the MIB and management requests and responses to a device. It uses the SNMP protocol to package the request and responses.

In a cable bridge, Internet brouter, or modem, the implementation of an SNMP agent supports MIB II objects (an extended MIB to cover different types of network devices) and includes proprietary extensions to the MIB for management of cable TV objects. Also included are the UDP and IP protocols required to exchange SNMP packets with a network management station.

These network management capabilities offer cable operators an added benefit by providing additional information for troubleshooting the physical cable plant, thus improving reliability of the entertainment network as well.

Cable data network security

Once one computer is connected to another, some security risk exists, no matter how slight. It is often said that the most secure network is no network at all. The more connections there are, the greater the risk, and the greater the potential that the network can be broken into by a hacker.

Security can have many different definitions, but basically includes the areas of data integrity, user authentication, and privacy.

According to Al Hoover, vice president of information and application services at ANS, there are three questions you want to ask :

- What are you protecting?
- Why are you protecting it?
- What are you protecting it from?

The most common security risk in a computer network is also the easiest to overlook: password security.

The first level of security planning is also the toughest: ensuring that users do not pick passwords that are easy to guess, such as the names of family members. Password generation programs are sometimes used to inhibit this. Hackers will sometimes use stolen password lists in what is referred to as a *dictionary attack*. Another possibility is that the hacker has a password capture program, whereby when a legitimate user logs in, his or her password is "captured" and reused by the hacker. Training users on password security is a key factor in creating a secure network.

For a community-wide Ethernet network connected to the Internet, security is addressed on several different levels.

Closed user groups

From the community side of the network, security can be provided via a system of closed user groups, as implemented in the UniLINK protocol. Using this system, users are assigned to one or more user groups. Ethernet data from one bridge or brouter can only be read by another bridge or brouter if it is a member of the same user group. This system allows multiple users to share the same RF channel, but operate as if they are on different networks—essentially creating multiple logical networks on one physical network. Schools could be on one logical network; hospitals, medical centers, and doctors' homes on another, and a business and its telecommuting employees on a third.

Filtering, authentications, and scrambling

Security is also provided in a community Ethernet network via features, such as IP address filtering, traffic type filtering, broadcast and route filtering. In addition, built-in security measures are on different networks—essentially creating multiple logical networks on one physical network. Schools could be on one logical network; hospitals, medical centers, and doctors' homes on another, and a business and its telecommuting employees on a third.

Application-layer gateway

Another security option is an application-layer gateway. With an application-layer gateway, the user is not directly connected to the Internet, although to the user it appears as if he is. The gateway actually executes the user commands. The gateway can also examine the source and destination address and commands entered. A user accessing the Internet must pass an authentication process to gain access through the gateway. The gateway can also be set up to prohibit a user from using certain commands that could pose a security risk to the organization.

Tunneling

One risk to firewall security is the practice of tunneling. Tunneling can have positive uses, or can be used to circumvent security. *Tunneling* refers to the practice of encapsulating a message from one protocol in another, and using the facilities of the second protocol to traverse some number of network hops. At the destination point, the encapsulation is stripped off, and the original message is reinjected into the network. In a sense, the packet burrows under the intervening network nodes, and never actually sees them. There are many uses for such a facility, such as encrypting links and supporting mobile hosts.

Regulatory issues

The legal and regulatory environment in the cable and telco world, coupled with the growth of data networks like the Internet, has created the need for major reform in telecommunications policy in the US, Canada, and countries around the world. The regulatory environment is politically complex, and the need to relax existing cable and telco regulations in order to build a global information infrastructure is recognized.

The Internet, on the other hand, is currently unregulated. This is in keeping with the fact that common carriers are considered natural monopolies, and therefore are regulated, but services provided over common carriers are not. This regulatory policy is not consistently administered, however, because services provided over telco lines are regulated. This has caused some public interest groups to call for similar regulatory requirements for the Internet.

The issue of universal access is also integrally tied to the debate over regulation of the Internet. The concern is that the Internet not create a society of "haves" and "have nots" on the global information infrastructure. The current thinking is that a certain level of "basic service" should be available to all citizens for a modest fee. But the debate rages on as to what defines "basic service" and how to subsidize such universal access.

Given the high "public good" quotient that such networks bring to municipalities, schools, and the general citizenry, in addition to businesses and for-profit enterprises, it is unlikely that government regulatory agencies will regress into imposing a strictly regulated environment that would hinder the growth of the national information infrastructure.

Comparison of Internet access options

The term *Internet access* is often used as if there is only one type of access available. In fact, Internet access runs the gamut from low-speed dialup access to high-speed dedicated network access. Some of the primary alternatives follow.

Dedicated access. Dedicated access is appropriate for institutions and businesses who want to be hooked up to the Internet. For dedicated access, the user needs: a dedicated leased line (56 Kbps or faster), a router. This kind of connection in the US costs at least $2000 initially, with monthly fees starting at $1500 per month to much higher charges as the line speed increases. Dedicated access allows all computers, and all users on a Local Area Network (LAN) to connect to the Internet through the router. It allows users access to the full functionality of the Internet. Because of the cost of a dedicated connection, this is not a practical option for home users.

SLIP and PPP. A less-expensive option is to use standard phone lines and high-speed modems, and connect to the Internet using the Serial Line Internet Protocol (SLIP) or Point to Point Protocol (PPP). For dial-up access, the user needs SLIP or PPP software a high-speed modem (V.32 or higher).

With SLIP and PPP, the user has full access to Internet resources, but saves on the high connection costs of a dedicated leased line. With these options, the user is actually "on the Net," as opposed to accessing it through another system. They are suited to connecting an individual or home user to a larger LAN, which has dedicated access to the Internet. This solution is not appropriate to connect a network of any size to the Internet because of the line speeds.

The connection to the Internet is provided by a national or regional access provider. A provider like PSI or UUNET charges about $250 per month for unlimited SLIP or PPP service; alternately, there might be a lower monthly charge, with an additional hourly fee. Service providers might supply 800 numbers or local access numbers in major urban areas to minimize telephone costs.

Dial-up access. The low-end option for Internet access is a simple dial-up connection to a computer that has dedicated access. For dial-up access, the user needs a terminal emulation package and a modem.

In this case, the user is not really "on the Net." The advantages are that it is cheap and easy to set up. The disadvantages are that the user might not be able to access all Internet services, and is dependent on the service provider for services and disk space.

The user might also have to pay the phone charges, if 800 numbers or local access numbers are not provided.

The cost of service is typically $20 to $40 per month, (possibly with some additional per-hour access fee). The cheapest rates apply if you contract for off-peak service only (i.e., nights and weekends).

Cable TV Internet access. The advantage to the user of accessing the Internet via cable TV is that he does not need his own leased line in order to get high-speed 10-Mbps access to the Internet. In the past, these speeds, because they required a dedicated leased line, were out of reach for all but large corporations. By connecting businesses, institutions, municipal offices, and home users into a community wide network over cable TV, performance can be improved by three orders of magnitude while cost is reduced.

Comparative Internet access scenarios

This section depicts several typical Internet access scenarios and compares and contrasts them with Internet access via cable TV.

Telco models. One typical method for corporate connectivity uses a router and Data Service Unit (DSU) to tie directly into an Internet Service Provider's network. A methodology called frame relay can also be used for this purpose. Figure 64.4 shows a typical scenario for connecting corporate users to the Internet. In this scenario, the remote or home users can log on via modem and dial-up line.

Typically, corporate users access the Internet via leased lines. The company buys one or more leased circuits that connect one or more routers at the customer premise to a router at the Internet service provider's site. Available line speeds range from 56 Kbps to 45 Mbps (T3). The Internet service provider might supply the router at the customer site.

Pricing for such services vary. One Internet service provider, Uunet's Alternet, has pricing which begins at $795 per month for a local 56-Kb link, T1 starts at $1250 per month. One key point is that the customer, and not the Internet service provider, is responsible for procuring the leased lines.

Another option that might be used by small companies, who do not need the high band-width that leased lines provide, is frame relay. PSI and Sprint,

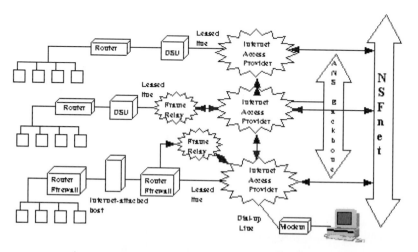

Source: Data Communications - April 1994

Figure 64.4   Corporate connectivity to the Internet.

for example, offer frame relay services. In this scenario, users need a router with a frame relay interface and leased line to the Internet Service Provider's point of presence (POP). In this case, unlike leased lines, customers only pay for the bandwidth that they actually use.

PSI's Interframe includes a router and frame relay DSU installed at the customer site. Committed information rates (CIRs)—the maximum average speed of the connection—range from 56 Kb to a T3, depending on management and equipment. Sprint offers a zero-CIR service (no maximum average speed) that allows for bursts of traffic at up to T1 for a flat rate of $400 per month.

The cable TV models. There are multiple alternatives for the configuration of cable TV networks, which offer Internet routing.

Figure 64.5 shows multiple IP networks on a cable network connecting to the Internet using Internet brouters. In this scenario, there are multiple IP Networks on each cable network. This is a practical scenario for a community, which includes multiple IP addresses that requires IP routing with cable TV connectivity. In this scenario, each site could have its own IP network, and each would have an Internet brouter. Each site would have its own IP address space, and its own IP administration. The security firewall would be at the brouter at each site. This scenario would allow for increased security, ease of management and administration, expansion (the ability to add more sites/IP networks), plus freedom and ease of communication.

A second scenario is having a single IP network on each cable network (Fig. 64.6). In this configuration, the entire cable TV network using the bridges will be a single IP network. In this scenario, all sites would share the same address space, and would have common IP administration. The security firewall would be at the single router entry point, and there would be no IP firewalls between sites.

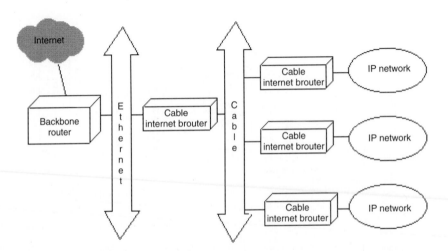

Figure 64.5 Multiple IP networks on a cable network.

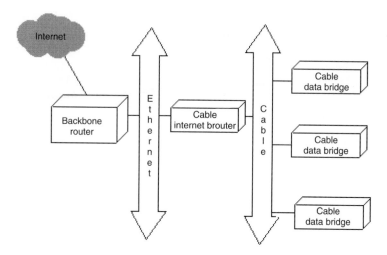

Figure 64.6   Single IP network on each cable network.

This implementation might not be practical for a city with multiple businesses and institutions using the same network, and would require coordinated management of IP addressing for all of the users.

Ultimately, in a third scenario, multiple cable TV networks could be connected together as an IP network over a WAN, via a long-distance carrier such as MCI or AT&T, or a Competitive Access Provider (CAP), such as Teleport. In this scenario, the cable TV networks could either be bridged or routed.

Case Studies

Electronic Commerce Network (ECnet)

Phoenix, Arizona

ECnet was one of the first data networks set up over cable television. The network was developed as a collaboration between Times Mirror Cable Television, Digital Equipment Corporation, and Arizona State University. ECnet connects together manufacturing companies in the Phoenix area for the purposes of concurrent Computer Aided Design (CAD), video conferencing, electronic whiteboarding, and access to the Internet. Companies using the network include McDonnell Douglas, Tempe Precision Aircraft, and Modern Instruments.

The backbone of the ECnet network is a 100-Mbps FDDI (Fiber Distributed Data Interface) fiber ring, which connects four headends. Connected to each headend is a community Ethernet network, comprised of one to three companies. Each company site itself houses its own LAN, which can be comprised of hundreds of users. Bridges are used to connect the LAN sites to the community network.

The physical media in the network include dedicated fiber in the backbone, shared AM fiber for the headend trunks, and coax. The fiber ring is supporting distances as great as 36 miles between headends, and the longest fiber/coax headend trunk extends over 15 miles to a customer site. The network operates downstream at 336 to 342 MHz, and upstream at channel T8 (11.75 MHz to 17.75 MHz).

Access to the Internet is provided by Arizona State University. Security is provided, which includes 24-hour/7-day monitoring, file encryption, protocol monitoring, automated alerts, and lockouts.

Hawaii Public Schools

The Hawaii public school district includes 360 schools located on six islands. This unique geography has perhaps contributed to the Hawaii Department of Education being on the leading edge of networking technology.

Oceanic Cable, a Time-Warner subsidiary, Digital Equipment Corporation, and Convergence Systems, Inc., a Digital reseller, have collaborated on the Hawaiian school network.

The Hawaiian schools original network consisted of a T3 (45 Mbps) microwave backbone, 28 T1 (1.5 Mbps) leased lines, which didn't meet the needs of the school system. "Leased lines are expensive and they don't really provide us with the bandwidth we need for the applications we'd like to run on the network. We needed a high-bandwidth, high-speed network. With the telephone company, that would have meant a T1 line for every school, which would have been very expensive," said Kyunghak J. Kim, director of network support services for the state of Hawaii's department of education.

Hawaiian schools are using the Internet for collaborative learning with schools on the mainland, accessing images from weather services, maps, and information from libraries and universities. "The main thing ChannelWorks has provided students is the ability to effectively communicate with other students in other parts of the country and the world, and the capability to access resources available in other places," comments Kim. The ChannelWorks solution has sped up Internet access considerably at Hawaii's schools: sending a message from the University of Hawaii to the mainland and back can now be completed in seven or eight seconds, which is 100 times faster than what was possible on phone lines.

How to Set Up a Community Ethernet-to-Internet Network

Setting up a community Ethernet-to-Internet network involves a cooperative effort between the community, the cable operator, and often an Internet service provider. Although the idea for starting such a network might come from individuals or institutions in the community, the cable operator actually creates the network and the business of offering Internet service to the community. It is important that the community and the cable operator work together to understand each others needs, motivations, and constraints. Setting up a cable television network for Internet access involves both business and technical issues for a cable operator. To begin, a business case must be completed to show the cost of network implementation, the projected market, and the economic return for offering data and Internet access services in a community. The scope, schedule, and budget for the network must be defined. A project team, project manager, installation team, and site contact for each site must be identified, and a project plan prepared.

Network planning and design

The next step is the network design and network map. The design must include network layout, site locations, amplifiers, channel assignments, network components, leased lines, etc.

The basic requirements to set up a community Ethernet to Internet network are: one forward and one reverse channel, one bridge or brouter per site, one translator at the headend (not required for a dual system), diplexors (either sub-, mid-, or high-split), an Internet point-of-presence (i.e., access to a backbone router on the Internet) either via one of the user sites on the network, or via the headend.

Several decisions need to be made during the network planning phase, including:

1. Which sites will be in the same Closed User Groups?
2. Which sites will be on the same IP network?
3. What are the security and firewall requirements, and where should firewalls be located?
4. Where will the connection to the Internet be located? Will it be in the headend or at a user site?
5. If the Internet connection will be at the headend, who will install and manage the connection?
6. Who will procure, assign, and manage the IP addresses?
7. Who will secure the leased line connection to the Internet Service Provider? What line speed is required? How much will it cost? How will it be paid for?
8. Who will manage the data network?
9. Who will supply help desk support? What is the problem reporting procedure? What are the service hours? What are the problem escalation procedures?
10. What is the monthly service charge? What are the billing procedures? The services of an Internet consultant or Internet Service Provider might be used during the network planning and installation phase of the project to help answer these questions and devise the network plan.

As early as possible in the project planning, a certification of the cable plant should be done. The certification of the cable plant is an important first step. A detailed checklist is used to ensure that all requirements are met so that the network will function properly.

The first requirement for the network is that one forward and one return channel must be allocated for the network. The transmit frequency range is 10 to 174 MHz. The receive frequency range is 54 to 550 MHz. As early as possible in the project planning, a certification of the cable plant should be done. The certification of the cable plant is an important first step. A detailed checklist is used to ensure that all requirements are met so that the network will function properly.

Management

Network management might be supplied by the cable operator or a third party. As a network grows in size, so does the need for network management. The plans for network management should be put in place during the planning and design phase.

Conclusion

The capacity of the Internet will continue to grow, as will the user systems connecting to it. Multimedia and client-server based applications, such as digital libraries, telecollaboration, concurrent engineering, and visualization will proliferate. Multicasting, taking video or audio material, digitizing it, and sending it over the Internet, will benefit greatly from cable. Videoconferencing over the Internet to the home PC or to the desktop will become possible. Cable TV can make high-speed access to the multimedia Internet of tomorrow a reality today.

65

Evaluating and Implementing a Web Site into Your Integrated Marketing Program

Jeffrey P. Geibel

With the rapid growth of the Internet and easy access to home pages and other on-line services, more and more companies will begin to evaluate and utilize Web pages or forums as part of their marketing communication effort. Not all of these efforts will be successful, and as measurement and accountability increase, non-effective Web sites will become even more apparent. (By *non-effective*, I mean sites that cannot be found to contribute to sales or revenue, or to help identify purchasers.) For the Web page designer, a good understanding of how your page can support the company's marketing effort can go a long way to having that page viewed as a marketing asset, and you, of course, viewed as an electronic Picasso.

The purpose of this chapter is not to make you into a marketing maven. Rather, it is to explain how marketing impacts the use of a Web site, and what both visitors and the company can expect to get from that site. By understanding these principles, you are in a better position to integrate the web site into the overall marketing effort, to make a case for your Web site and perhaps even get some of those scarce budget dollars allocated to supporting the home page.

The Role of Technology

The primary use of technology in marketing is for rapid communication and data manipulation. Technology is not, and cannot, be used as a substitute for human interaction. However, it can, and often is used to help buyers and other interested parties to obtain the information they need quickly. This, in conjunction with low cost, helps to ensure that when they do contact the selling organization, the buyer is informed, conversant, hopefully qualified to buy, and in general, a much better sales prospect. If your Web site serves these purposes, it is a valuable asset to the marketing effort.

An important aspect to remember is that the impact on the sales prospect is largest early-on in the marketing (or awareness) cycle. The more that the prospect knows about you and your products, the less that an interactive technology medium will be able to answer their questions. In the overall context of marketing, it is important to remember that the Web site will have its most value in the Marketing Funnel, which leads to the Sales Cycle, and in Stage I of the Sales Cycle (see Figs. 65.1 and 65.2).

When the prospect is in the marketing funnel and early phases of the sales cycle, "raw" interactive information helps to attract them to you and evaluate what you have to offer. However, the value to seller and buyer diminishes once they enter to Sales Cycle (see Fig. 65.2), and the further into the sales cycle, the less use it has (see Fig. 65.3). At that point, the sales interaction has to be a human contact, unless you are selling a commodity, where price is the only distinction. If you have to convince a buyer to purchase from you, as opposed to another vendor—only a human salesperson can perform that task. The optimal changeover point from technology to the human interface is something that you should carefully evaluate so that you get optimal use from both your technology and human resources.

The Marketing Funnel

The Marketing Funnel (see Fig. 65.1) are those activities that precede the sales cycle. Because the actual intent and buying schedule of the information recipients in the marketing funnel is unknown, the need is for low-cost

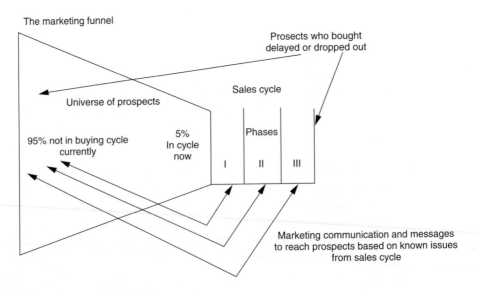

Figure 65.1 The marketing funnel.

Alignment of buying & selling phases

Phase I	Phase II	Phase III

Buyer

Need definition	Evaluate alternatives	Take action
Do I need to change? What do I need? How much does it cost?	Is there a solution? Which ones meets my needs? Can I afford it?	Should I do it? What are the consequences? Is it the right price?

Seller

Need development	Proof	Close the sale
Define their needs with our product bias. Quality buying process	Demonstrate how product meets defined needs. Help cost justify.	Why us? Why now?

Figure 65.2   Alignment of buying and selling phases.

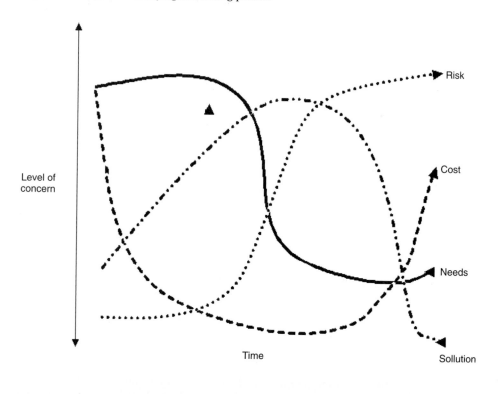

Figure 65.3   Shifting buyer concerns.

communication, with the ability of the seller to control the content, and the potential buyer to access it when they desire. Hence, the Internet and other on-line services are ideal for this phase of the marketing cycle.

Some commonly accepted statistics for the Marketing Funnel are worth remembering: Only 5% of the entire prospect universe in your marketing funnel are in buying mode at any given point in time. The key question is: Which 5%? Hopefully, if your Web site or forum is properly integrated into the marketing effort, they will be attracted (or directed) to it, and there will be an easy mechanism for them to contact your company and identify themselves. The related question concerning this audience is: How do you reach the other 95%? Remember, the operative word is not that they are not buying, it is not now. Also, remember that there is constant churning of prospects and buyers as the members of this prospect universe are making decisions and either entering or leaving the prospect universe.

The Sales Cycle

The sales cycle consists of those activities that occur once the buyer enters into the buying phase, and you have to sell to them (Figs. 65.2 and 65.3). Selling is nothing more than the efforts involved in bringing about a transaction. The buyer has certain concerns and agendas, and the seller is most successful when they put themselves in alignment with these agendas. Some points are important to remember: The #1 reason the sale is lost, research has found, is when the seller is out of alignment with the buyer. (See Fig. 65.2 for both issues and alignment of seller/buyer actions.)

Conversely, the #1 reason for buyer resistance has been found to be when the seller applies pressure to the buyer. The beauty of an Internet Web page or on-line forum is that the potential buyer is under no pressure—they can leave at any time. The downside is that you, the seller, have no control. In most cases, you don't even know their identity. If your Web page is in alignment with their issues, they will identify themselves to you so you can begin the sales process.

Sales and Marketing Principles Don't Change

Much of what has been written about the Internet would have you to believe that there will be wholesale changes in the way that business is conducted. In some ways, that is correct (much the same way that the fax and cellular phones changed business), but in many ways, it is misleading. The sales and marketing principles that arise from basic human behavior are not going to change.

For example, people still buy from people, not a machine or electronic interface, unless they have already made their choice and your Web page is nothing more than an electronic vending machine. In the part of marketing where you can have the most influence, such as getting your message to the decision maker early-on, and making a case for your products or services, there still must be a human interface. The tricky part about designing a Web page is where to require the viewer to make that transition. You don't want to force it too early, on the other hand, you don't want to frustrate the prospect by making it occur too late, or making it difficult in any phase of viewing the Web page.

A key factor to remember is that prospects proceed at their own pace—not yours or at the pace you want them to have. However, you want to know the nominal sales cycle for a prospect so that you can both structure and integrate the Web page into this sales cycle. Many of the factors in the sales cycle are beyond your control, so the best marketing role of the Web page is to reinforce and integrate with other elements of the marketing program.

A caveat to remember in designing a Web page to integrate with the marketing effort is that the purpose of marketing is to create and support the sales environment. If this is overlooked, it is very easy to design an Internet presence that has entertainment value, and little else. If you are not in the entertainment business, that is not very good use of your Web presence.

Where Technology Fits

In developing a Web site that has an integrated role in the marketing program, it is important to remember the role that technology, and specifically, the Web site, plays. It is a sales and marketing tool, but it is only one of many tools. There is a tendency to look at an Internet presence as a be-all, end-all. As a stand-alone, it has limited value and appeal. It must be integrated into your marketing program for maximum effectiveness. The real value of an Internet presence is that it permits an interested party to access you at any time, from any place and to the extent they desire, both in content and duration. Generally, they will have been directed to your site by some other element of your marketing program. Because of this, your Web site should reference all other elements of your marketing program, preferably graphically. This gives them a starting point to explore your site, then you establish the threads that lead them where you want them to go. One caveat here: Someone has to think through the entire process. That is, put themselves in the shoes of an interested party, and try to access the Web site to get the information they would want, based on as much as is known about prospect perspectives. If they hit a wall, or if the design of the site frustrates them (lack of content, no contact point at your company if they want personal attention, etc.), then it needs more work.

What Technology Can Do

Because the essence of marketing is communication, and one of the strongest uses of technology is communication, where it serves to provide cost-effective presence in marketing funnel. That is, it enables you to reach those suspects and prospects in the marketing funnel with your marketing message, at a cost that allows you to establish and maintain a presence. Technology also helps you in other ways because it shortens your response time to the prospect (and if used properly, serve to qualify them as well). Technology can also serve to reduce the cost of sales call, providing much of the necessary information in advance and enabling the salesperson to concentrate their time on valuable customization of your offerings to the prospect's needs. Lastly, technology also helps you to evaluate sales and marketing effectiveness—providing feedback and tracking of your sales and marketing programs so that you can allocate your budget in the most effective manner.

What Technology Can't Do

As importantly as understanding what technology can do for your marketing program, it is equally important to understand what technology can't do. Technology is not the magic bullet that many seek after: that gimmick, technique, or method that will eliminate the need to sell. This has been mentioned as one of the reasons that the Internet appeals to so many technology people—they have traditionally never been very good at selling, and often resented turning over their technology or products to the marketing or sales folks for commercial success. With the Internet, they think that they have the ultimate solution, technology that will sell their technology to other users, without the need for sales intervention. Not so. Dream on. No matter how good the technology is, there are many necessary tasks that it cannot do: It can't completely qualify the prospect—only a salesperson can do that. There are simply too many nuances prior to the close. It can't make a sales call—evaluating needs, responding, guiding the discussion, answering objections, and most importantly, it can't close the sale. In a nutshell, one of the limitations of technology, especially in a human interaction mode (which is certainly a good description of marketing and communications), is that it can't deal with fuzzy logic—that often illogical behavior or actions that only another human can deal with. Technology such as the Internet can help you, but it is not a solution in and of itself.

Your Sales and Marketing System

When developing Web site, bear in mind that you want your site to be able to respond to a range of interest and intent. Everything from a qualified buyer to those who are merely curious. The topics in the Web site should mirror the issues of the sales cycle: the prospect will gather information, evaluate options, and make a decision. Your site should have information available, help them to frame their options, and then steer them to contacts in your company as they get close to making a decision. Cross-link your marketing programs so that they refer to the Web site, and the Web site in turn refers to them. For example, if you advertise, include your Web address. In the Web site, have an icon that is a graphical image of your advertisement, so that someone who was drawn to the site will immediately recognize it, and use it as a starting point. Then, hypertext link the key themes in your advertisement to other topics at your Web site. This process should be repeated for your direct mail program, public relations, etc.

Each step between the various parts of your marketing program should require some kind of prospect qualification. There are many ways to do this in a subtle, unobtrusive manner. For example, by having a prospect answer some questions, you can determine what issues interest them. If your hypertext links offer several clear and distinct options—the links that are hit tell you something about the viewer's interests.

If your Web site is supporting your marketing, sooner or later you want to provide human contact. List corporate contacts and roles, and be sure to present the option that the viewer can contact your company whenever they want to. As obvious as this seems, many advertising and marketing programs make it a mystery when the prospect wants to contact the company to begin the buying process.

Last, remember to track and evaluate all contacts with your Internet or other on-line site. Several commercial services are available that will track the number of hits, volume by time of day, duration of the visit, areas viewed, files downloaded, and just about anything you want to know. Because it is a given that you want to constantly change the topics and layout of the site, this kind of information is very useful in evaluating changes and improvements to your site.

Online: Reaching Suspects on the Internet and Other Services

From the principles discussed so far, you can see how online services can be a cost-effective presence in the marketing funnel, reaching out to both suspects and prospects in addition to providing resources for current customers. Few marketing tools are that flexible with that range of reach across the marketing spectrum, and offer the marketing potential of on-line services. However, when evaluating the amount of resources to be targeted to suspects in the marketing spectrum, bear in mind that many users of on-line services appear to be tire kickers—that is, their purchasing intent and ability remain unproven. In fact, they often will not visit a site that requires them to identify themselves. Unidentified visitors have little value to your marketing program because you have no way to reach them as individuals.

For that reason, most of your marketing planning for on-line services should concern itself with evaluating the influence of an on-line presence on your prospects (meaning those who are an identifiable sales lead) and current customers decision-making. Query them about their on-line usage levels, and what they look for. "Surf" your competitors and vendors on-line to see what they offer and how they offer it. Don't be surprised if you find that the best use of your on-line presence may be customer support and technical forums. For example, a number of savvy prospects now surf the user forum message threads to identify the types of user complaints and problems that you are having with your installed base—and you really can't hide this kind of information short of shutting down your forums.

Summary: Some Tips for Using On-Line Technology

For marketers who are planning to utilize on-line services and design Web pages as part of their marketing effort, it is critical to the success of the effort to have a plan for the on-line effort, to determine its place in your marketing program, and to integrate it with all other marketing communications. Your other marketing communications should both reference your Web site on-line presence, and in turn be referenced by the Web site.

In building your on-line presence, survey your current sales prospects and customers—because they will be the major user groups of your site. Don't forget to build in hit analysis and market research capabilities—this will often be a valuable benefit of your on-line effort, providing you with real-time, early on information about your markets and prospects. In addition to on-line measurement, remember to track suspect, prospect, and sales conversion rates—you want to know where your customers are coming from, and how they get the information to make crucial buying decisions—preferably in your favor. Lastly, watch out for the "MarketingHype.com" syndrome—the unchecked enthusiasm and claims for the Internet and other on-line services, which, upon scrutiny, have no basis in fact. Remember, the marketing wave of the future doesn't pay today's bills.

Checklist for developing an integrated online or Web site:

- *Know the key issues in your sales cycle.* If the Web site or forum is supposed to support the rest of the marketing effort, then it should be supporting the key issues in the sales cycle (Fig. 65.2). If you know what your prospect is looking for when they search for information, evaluate their options and then make a decision, you will be in a better position to design the site to reinforce the desired behavior.

- *Review the rest of your marketing program and communications.* Your online presence should fit in with the rest of your marketing, and be a complement to it, not a stand-alone. Review each component of your marketing and marketing communications, and ask yourself: How could an on-line presence enhance this? What value could be added? For example, something as simple as adding the on-line address in the troubleshooting section of the user's documentation or Read Me file: pointing the user to a resource, where they can get their questions answered, files downloaded, etc. Complementing your advertising is one place where your online presence can stand out—because it is often the case that advertising creates almost as many questions as it answers—and on-line, the reader can explore the issues in depth, to the extent of their interest.

- *Find out how many of your prospects (and customers) have online access.* Your current customers and prospects are probably going to be the first, and remain the largest, user group of your on-line presence. It makes sense to determine the extent that they access on-line services, and which services they use. This on-line census should be repeated every year, to determine usage trends of your site, and to monitor the popularity of the various on-line providers.

- *Review the online sites or forums for: your competitors, your strategic partners (vendors, etc.) and several that are top rated.* Your on-line site should be created in the context that it will be used: in comparison to your competitors (for prospects or customers who are doing comparison shopping), your strategic partners (vendors, etc.). Also check the other sites that are top-rated. Beware attempting to duplicate a top-rated site—like restaurant reviews, they are often subjective, and based on factors that have little bearing on their marketing purpose, such as the sexiness of the graphics. This is one area that bears careful watching. On-line designers are sometimes so enamored of this new media that their designs actually hinder the communications effectiveness of the site, and frustrate the visitor. Remember, you really want a site that is sales supporting more than award winning.

- *Ask yourself: What can my site provide that my other communications vehicles cannot provide?* As part of complimenting your marketing effort, your on-line site should not attempt to duplicate a print ad or video commercial, but take advantage of its on-line interactive uniqueness. Give this some thought, and design it in from the start.

- *Design your site or forum with both your customers and prospects in mind.* As mentioned before, your customers and sales prospects will probably be the heaviest users of your site. Their needs are different than those of a casual surfer. If you design your site for the surfer—then your customers and prospects probably won't visit it very often. Conversely, if it is designed solely for customers—it will be over the head of the casual visitor. Probably the standard 80/20 rule is a good place to start: design 80% of the site for customers and prospects, and 20% for visitors or surfers—and make sure you have site road signs for each group.

- *Incorporate measurement.* There are currently several on-line measurement services for forums and Web sites. Typically, they consist of software that resides on the server, and uploads activity counts to the service bureau, which in turn generates a report to you. Have one of these services monitor your site, and keep tabs on the activity at and within the site. See how this changes when you redesign or modify the site. This type of measurement is one of the best real-time market research measurements you can get.

- *Put someone in charge of the effort.* Like a lot of activities, your site will take on a life of its own if there is no one in charge. You would be surprised at the number of on-line experts you have if no one person has to establish goals, set priorities, and meet a schedule. Generally, this should be someone who reports to the top marketing executive.

- *Make your executives and staff visit it and critique it—especially user's forums.* It never fails to amaze me the number of executives at technology firms who don't even use their company's software, or are technologically illiterate. If you want your site delegated to the back waters, just make sure that the executives and staff never visit it. The best way to avoid that outcome is to arrange an in-house demo when the site first comes on-line (and there is a lot of excitement). Set up an on-line briefing room and walk everyone though the site. Once they see it and how to access it, it's not so intimidating. Also, provide access to some one-on-one coaching to your executives to should them how to access the site from their desktop or laptop computer. A little coaching and nurturing here can get you some early, and important, on-line fans.

Chapter

66

Nomadicity in the NII

Cross-Industry Working Team

This chapter advances the goal of making information services and applications ubiquitous and flexibly available to people on the move. It provides a vision to guide the evolution of underlying technologies, shape new uses, and accelerate the on-going revolution in information technology applications. The chapter is the product of XIWT's Nomadicity Working Team, led by Leonard Kleinrock, Chairman of the Department of Computer Science at UCLA and a member of the XIWT Science Council.

According to Kleinrock, Nomadic computing and communications will dramatically change the way people access information—and a paradigm shift in thinking about applications of the technologies involved. It exploits the advanced technologies of wireless, the Internet, global-positioning systems, portable and distributed computing to provide anytime, anywhere access. It is beginning to happen, but it makes everything much harder for the vendors.

Nomadicity, in this chapter, means that people can easily access services, other people, and content while they are on the move, at intermediate stops, and at arbitrary destinations.

Realizing this capability and integrating it into the rapid evolution of the NII presents a daunting set of technical challenges to meet requirements, such as interoperability, security, and flexibility.

The underlying mechanisms of nomadic computing and communications must support traditionally understood requirements of mobility, portability, and wireless communications, such as data transport, user authentication, and privacy. There will also be new requirements.

Among the most challenging are:

1. supporting the multiple roles desired by a user and dealing with varying sets of technologies, services and data

2. configuring data to maintain critical content characteristics across the varying media the nomad encounters or commands as he or she moves about.

The underlying technologies for these requirements are often quite distinct, but must work together seamlessly and reliably to create the broad benefits of tomorrow's NII. XIWT will refine the concepts and technical challenges identified in the White Paper through additional study and experimentation.

Introduction

The dictionary defines a nomad as a person who constantly moves from place to place, a wanderer. Today's nomad might move from her normal workplace to a temporary one—a remote office, a hotel room, an airplane. He might also move from one role to another; focusing at one moment on his business, at another on his children's schooling. Nomads and nomadicity have particular relevance for the National Information Infrastructure (NII). If the NII is to provide ubiquitous access to communications and computing services, nomadicity must form part of its foundation. By ubiquitous, we mean that access to communications and computing services via the NII will be at least as common as today's telephone. Moreover, the NII will facilitate connectivity through a wide range of electronic devices, including portable, mobile, and wireless computing and communications.

By nomadicity, we mean the ability of people to move easily from place to place, retaining access to a rich set of services while they're moving, at intermediate stops, and at their destination.

A person is a nomad vis-a-vis the NII if she moves as little as from one desk to an adjoining one or as far away as across the continent.

Incorporating nomadicity into the NII's basic structure will cause a paradigm shift. The mechanisms for supporting portability, mobility, and wireless computing and communications are often quite distinct.

Nomadicity requires that these mechanisms be presented in a manner that preserves their desired functionality, while coordinating them and making them more manageable.

This chapter defines concepts, examines possible applications, explores technical considerations, and takes steps toward a vision of nomadicity.

Several assumptions underlie this discussion:

1. Some degree of nomadicity is characteristic of modern life.

2. Everyone wants to carry on with their lives independent of current location.

3. Communications and computing capabilities will be available almost everywhere.

4. Individual needs for information and communications services will vary from place to place and from time to time.

5. Available information and communications services also will vary greatly from place to place and from time to time.

6. Many of these services will not interoperate.

7. Preferences will vary from user to user and from time to time.

Underpinnings of Nomadicity

Some things are designed with nomadicity as their central focus. Hand-held cellular phones are one notable example, the newspaper *USA Today* is another. Some things are evenly balanced between catering to the nomad and serving other needs: The electronic appointment book and the automated teller machine (ATM) fall into this category. Some things are not nomadic. The stand-alone desktop personal computer is such a device.

The central characteristic of nomadicity is support of the nomad. This section explores some of the defining motivations, challenges, and concepts of nomadicity.

What Motivates Nomadicity?

In the past, people traveled because they had no choice. If they wanted to transact business or converse with friends, they had to meet in person. However, transportation costs made certain meetings and activities prohibitive. A long series of technological developments—including the pony express, railroads, automobiles, and the telephone—have aimed at lowering the costs associated with transaction and conversation. Computer-mediated communications are just the most recent development in that progression. Even so, people still travel and still meet in person. This section explores some of the reasons why.

- *Increased productivity.* In many situations, the expenses associated with hiring, integrating, and developing staff account for much of the total cost entailed in deploying a given organizational capability. Thus, if an organization needs hands-on contact at a location, it is increasingly more effective to provide the capability with a centrally located person who travels, rather than with a person in-place at the site. Customer service is an obvious example.

  If service can be provided without an on-site engineer, costs are lowered. The more expensive the engineer, the more pressure to have one person serve many customers.

- *The personal touch.* Another motivator is the social requirement for personal contact. The salesperson goes to the customer, shakes hands, and looks at the facilities. Workers in different groups travel to the staff meetings of their colleagues to establish rapport. Friends get together for dinner. In all these situations, the requirement for movement is rooted in the desire to meet, take the measure of, and enjoy the company of others.

- *Personal environment.* The many parts of our lives—our family life, business life, personal social life, business social life, etc.—each frequently involves a different physical location. People move between these places as they move between the different aspects of their lives. They go to their children's school to meet with the teacher, they go to the country club to have a round of golf with a new prospect. Doing the appropriate thing in the appropriate place is key to the way many people organize their lives.

- *Interactivity.* Much of the communication in intense human interactions is nonverbal and therefore requires face-to-face contact. There are certain situations where the give and take goes beyond words. The personnel evaluation meeting in business, the town meeting in government, and the family meeting to decide on a vacation destination are all common examples of the need for interactivity.

- *Setting.* For various reasons, people frequently carry out business in locations other than in their own office. Some of these locations are preferable to others: A winter meeting in Florida probably will be better attended than one in Nova Scotia. On the other hand, people sometimes simply find themselves in the midst of a chance encounter with a business transaction opportunity.

Challenges Presented by Nomadicity

Nomadicity, and the motivations underlying it, create a series of high-level requirements, or challenges, for NII communications.

These requirements, which both motivate individuals to be nomadic and define ideals for technologically mediated human communication, are:

1. Greater productivity for mobile individuals
2. Personal contact
3. Individuals partitioning their lives
4. The full range of human communication modalities
5. Personal location preference

This section describes the NII requirements implied by nomadicity.

- *Location independence.* Today, we communicate with individuals in terms of the location of their communications instruments; for instance, the nearest telephone or fax machine. If, as the NII develops, it takes over the worries related to finding the individuals with whom we wish to communicate, transparently directing our communications to the appropriate device at the appropriate location, it will create an environment in which people are communicating with other people, not with the devices they use. People will be calling their mother, not their parents' kitchen. People will be writing to their business associates, not sending faxes to the XYZ company fax machine.

A significant challenge for the NII is to make the process of establishing communications with a nomad largely transparent to both the nomad and her correspondent, regardless of which one initiates the exchange. The NII must therefore supply an ubiquitous and reliable implementation of location independence that places no special burdens on the nomad.

With location independence, an individual can do what he wants to do where he wants to do it. It is the character of the nomad that he needs to do his job, irrespective of location. Consequently, anything that supports nomadicity must be useful in as broad a range of locations as possible.

- *Device independence.* Being a nomad means not always accessing the NII from the same place or through the same device. So, communication with the nomad might be through a device—for example, a borrowed telephone or a portable phone—that has quite different capabilities than the one he commonly uses when at home. Thus, the NII must support device independence: It must be able to match people to devices with different capabilities, at different locations, through different access paths, and under different access conditions.

- *Widespread access.* Because an essential component of nomadicity is that individuals remain as connected as they desire from wherever they desire, the communications devices and channels on which connectivity depends must allow for widespread access.

- *Security.* Nomadicity imposes special security requirements, particularly with regard to identification, certification, and billing. Because the device is not the person, technology can hide the identities of the communicating parties. Ensuring that the individual at the other end of the communications channel is whom she says she is, is critical to establishing effective access. Similarly, when the individual is in motion, switching between devices and locations, many other security issues are exacerbated.

- *Adaptability to new technologies.* The prevalence of cellular phones has conditioned the public to expect totally tetherless access in the near future. And the rapid development of wireless transmission technology, as evidenced by low-orbital satellite systems with global span and digital systems with throughput capability measured in megabits and gigabits, has forced reconsideration of the choice between wired and wireless systems. The rapid pace of technological change challenges the NII to adapt continuously to new technologies. System components supporting nomadicity are likely to be among those changing most rapidly.

- *Friendly interface.* Public acceptance of new technology is largely based on the extent to which this technology is familiar and consistent with other technologies—that is, similar to models users already know. So, the success of the cellular phone, for example, is partly due to the fact that the image the system presents to a user is consistent regardless of location, and the fact that the technology is quite familiar because it is almost the same as that of the wired telephone. The complex interface devices and services that will probably characterize the NII make realization of this friendly interface somewhat difficult. Nomadicity adds further complexity with its requirements for specialized devices and more complex connections.

- *Partitioning.* Movement between individual social contexts will impose special requirements on the NII. In other words, a given person might use the same device (or set of devices) for accessing the NII in various separate personal environments— business, family, etc. Users will want to keep those environments separate: They will not want business calls intruding on a family weekend. The communications environment must be partitioned so that the user can filter and manage incoming communications.

    One method for partitioning would be to provide each user with several NII identifiers (the equivalent of telephone numbers). These identifiers would partition that user's communications space into different environments—for instance, home, office, family, and leisure. Another way might be to create a richer connection dialog—one that takes the environments of the communicating parties more fully into account.

Concepts that define nomadicity

This section examines some concepts that will help you to understand and respond to the requirements posed by nomadicity.

Context. Every environment has several alternative contexts. These contexts are based on people's various perceptions and expectations of that environment. So, for instance, most people perceive a shopping mall as a central location for buying a wide range of goods: This is the normal—or overt—context of a mall. But a police officer's dominant context, or primary focus, for a mall might be as a crime scene. For a teenage couple, the dominant context might be as a place for a romantic rendezvous.

People are aware of alternative contexts, but generally focus on the context most significant to them. However, one context might override another. Having a romantic interlude at a crime scene might seem the wrong thing to do. Also, the time of day or history might change the normal context of a location. After nightfall, the normal context for a warehouse could change from *place to do shipping* to *dangerous place to be avoided*. Thus, all contexts are group-social phenomena which affect an individual's ability to pursue his own activities.

When a person enters a given environment, she might wish to focus on a context not well-supported by that place. It could be difficult to balance a checkbook in the dentist's office or to order heating oil while stuck in rush-hour traffic. Nomadicity can be thought of as providing the ability to maintain an individual's chosen context regardless of the normal context of the environment presently occupied. In this way, context speaks directly to motivations arising from increased productivity, individual environment, and setting. It also addresses the requirements of location independence and partitioning of the communications environment[1].

It is possible for people at different locations to share a context. This results in a distributed context. The video conference is a first step toward modern system support of distributed contexts.

The combination of a shared computer link and a simultaneous telephone connection is another such step. Distributed contexts that persist over time without continuous participant interaction form the basis for virtual communities. The traditional mail system provides basic support for virtual communities, as does the traditional telephone system. These aspects of context speak to the nomadic motivations of maintaining a personal touch, greater interactivity, and an individual environment in communications.

The characteristics of contexts that interact most strongly with the nomad are:

1. The communications and information access mechanisms present
2. The type of interaction those mechanisms must support—immediate, delayed, or both
3. The physical relationship between the participants the mechanisms support—co-located, separated, or both
4. The requirements for participant authentication and privacy

Degree of proximity. Not only do nomads carry on their lives in many locations, but they also move between the locations. One important class of contexts, then, involves physical motion. Further, these contexts fall into two categories: vehicles and personal movement. The difference between these two categories can be explained by degree of proximity.

For example, vehicles maintain consistent contexts for an individual because the proximity of things relative to the individual and each other is maintained within them. Support of nomadicity in this situation means keeping everything functioning in the same way—even though the vehicle is in motion. Cellular telephones do this reasonably well in automobiles. Radio stations do this within range of the transmitter.

Things are nearby if a person does not have to change location significantly to use them. Things are co-located if a person does not have to change location at all to use them. The phone on the desk is co-located with the personal computer on the desk. The fax in the next room is nearby.

Proximity movement and context. Context might, from the user's point of view, move with her. The interplay of movement and context exposes another dimension of nomadicity, the moving context. There are two types of moving contexts:

- *A group of individuals moving together.* Examples of this type are two people walking down the street or a military squad in the field. In these cases, the combined communications mechanisms carried by the group create a context that is made up of nearby, moving components. The burden of support for nomadicity in this situation is to maintain the local context while the group moves.

- *A distributed context with individually moving participants.* In this case, the requirement is for establishing the context of the virtual community for all the participants in their various locations.

User device independence. A computer network or telephone system does not recognize the existence of human beings per se; it instead recognizes the devices they use. These devices are presumed to be controlled by a particular person at a particular time, and authentication techniques work to ensure that the association between user and device is maintained.

When nomadicity is involved, these assumptions present special problems. Each location might contain many communications devices: telephones, fax machines, networked computers, television sets, etc. It is reasonable for all of the individuals in the locations sharing a context to want access to all the communications devices available. They do not want to be dependent on only those devices they can carry around with them. Thus, the dynamic association of devices and individuals is central to nomadicity.

The issues are as much social as technological. The awkwardness of having to ask someone to use the telephone on his desk is often more of a limitation than is getting an outside line. If there is a device that is inherently single user in a location, how does it get associated with a particular user? Who decides?

Elements of a Nomadicity Model

This section presents the elements of a model of nomadicity that takes into account:

1. The motivations for nomadicity
2. Some high-level requirements derived from those motivations
3. Various concepts that help organize our thinking about nomadicity.

Development of this model will help in understanding, discussing, and responding to the issues posed by nomadicity.

Locations

Locations are defined relative to individuals. Everything in proximity, everything that is co-located or nearby, is in the same location.

Location coordinators

Location coordinators keep track of the individuals, devices, and communications system capabilities at a given location as they change. They implement the concept of proximity, allowing assumptions to be made about which individuals are at a location and what capabilities are available to them.

A location coordinator knows the characteristics and addresses of all the devices at a location. It is responsible for identifying the individuals and mobile devices that enter and leave the location.

In an office example, a location coordinator would know the phone number of the office phone, the TCP/IP address of the personal computer in the office, and the phone number of the fax machine around the corner. It would know the physical relationship of the phone, fax machine, and personal computer; and it would know the capabilities of the devices. And, if an individual made it known that he was co-located with any of the devices, the location coordinator would be able to infer that the other devices could be at his disposal as well.

Destinations of communications

At the far end of the pipe are destinations of communications. Clearly, there is overlap between this and other elements of the model.

The most common example of a communications destination is another person, but it could as easily be something standing in for a person, such as an answering machine. A person getting messages from her own answering machine is asking her stand-in to pass the message along. Other stand-in communications destinations include the bank computer at the other end of the line from the ATM, the voice response system at the power company, and the computerized information service at the stockbroker.

It is possible for both the communications destination and origin to be non-human. The automated system at the bank that validates a check for the check authentication system computer is an example.

People who move

Because people are nomads, the NII must—in delivering communications and information services to individuals—take into account that people move both in space and through the various aspects of their lives.

Access devices

The many access devices with which a user directly interacts are the things that communicate. These devices are the portals between the user's physical world and the electronic world of the NII.

Telephones, fax machines, computers, television sets, ATMs, and pagers are examples of things that communicate.

Access devices can move. Some are designed to; some move only rarely. A pager is designed to move; the office printer moves only when it is relocated.

Some access devices move with people, and some are only in occasional proximity to them. The cellular phone will often move with the individual; the office fax machine will only be near the person when he is in the office. No device (even implanted heart monitors) can be guaranteed to be in one-to-one correspondence with an individual.

Devices are either tethered—that is, in a fixed location because of physical attachment to a communications channel—or untethered. In either case, a location must be defined for the device if it is to be integrated into a context. Current networks provide only inexact location information. A device like a large printer, which moves infrequently, can have its location stored in a static database.

But an active cellular phone, without triangulation, can be located no more exactly than within a cell capture area. Under any circumstances, the underlying systems of the NII must be supplemented by mechanisms to associate physical location and electronic location.

Untethered devices carried by individuals and associated with them can be an effective way for associating individuals with places—provided, of course, that authentication appropriate to the context is supported. A smart card that only responds to a challenge/response sequence when a particular person has her right thumb on its sensor provides reasonable validation of a person's location and identity.

Services

In our model, services are the individuals or things with which a person communicates. One might exchange information with these services or get them to act on one's behalf. When communication is with another person, the service might be the individual and will be mediated—that is, facilitated and/or limited—by the device(s) available to the individual.

In a broad sense, there are at least three types of services:

1. Those in support of the communications system (e.g., routing, link-level service)
2. Those that might serve both the communications system and end users (e.g., encryption, location brokerage)
3. Those that serve only the end user (e.g., electronic banking).

The communications system

Everything between the representatives of the communicating parties forms a communications system, which provides connectivity between devices and services. The NII will provide many different communications paths. Within it, users will be able to choose among these alternatives, based on their cost, performance, coverage area, and other characteristics.

Nomadicity adds the dimension of dynamic movement within communications systems and among systems available at a particular location if a user's needs change. To facilitate that capability, the various systems will need mechanisms for managing quality of service, communication of service capabilities, and coordinated inter-enterprise interaction. At a higher level, the alternatives will have to be communicated to the user in some manner so that he can choose among them.

Under some circumstances, the definition of the communications system is thought to be complicated because elements considered to be internal to the system are made available to end users. Examples are the billing, directory, configuration management, and maintenance subsystems, which, although used primarily by the communications system provider to keep the system running, can be of value to its customers as well.

We believe the definition of communications systems can ignore this distinction. If an internal system component is unavailable to the user, it is still part of the communications system. If it is packaged so the user can get at it through the system provider, it is a service as well. And, if the same service is provided by someone other than the communications system provider, it is a service, but not part of the communications system at all.

Context. A context, as part of the model, is made up of at least one location, the devices at the location(s), the individuals at the location(s), and the activities those individuals wish to pursue. A person's integration with the other elements of the context are characterized by psychological factors (social expectations, setting, requirements for security, etc.) and physical factors (level of interactivity, level of proximity, etc.). Nomadicity requires that the user's dominant context be maintained as the user environment changes.

Aliases. An alias is an abstraction of an electronic entity that represents the user in the electronic world while managing communications with her in the real world. Rudimentary present-day examples of aliases are the answering machine and the electronic mail (e-mail) system. These stand in for the individual when he is not available.

As they have evolved, both of these systems have started to differentiate themselves, offering user configurability and additional functions.

For example, the answering system might notify a pager of an incoming call. This is a form of media translation and abstraction. The medium through which the message is delivered is changed, and the message is abstracted to its simplest form: notification that it occurred. In the case of computer-controlled answering machine-modem-fax machine combinations, a person can receive a message via e-mail and have it faxed to her current location. The fax number is specified via a call to the answering machine.

Thus, while not well-integrated at this time, many of the elements of an alias exist within current electronic environments: maintenance of status information regarding the individual, acting as a contact point for the individual, translation and abstraction of information for the individual, delivery of information to the individual on demand, and support for the individual's ability to control access.

Notice that a person might have several aliases representing various aspects of his life and interests. Similarly, an alias could be formed to represent the aspects and interests of entities other than individuals. Groups, departments, or temporary associations might be actualized with an alias.

Nomadicity and Traditional Systems Issues

This section covers those concerns that every computer system must address and which nomadicity brings into sharp relief. This chapter ties the motivations and high-level requirements associated with nomadicity to these traditional concerns. It also addresses the relationship between traditional system concerns and nomadicity's concerns for location and context.

Security

Security is broadly divided into authentication and privacy. Authentication means certification that the parties in an exchange are whom they represent themselves to be and that the message received is the same as the message sent. Privacy means limiting information about an exchange to the intended parties.

Security requirements in computer systems are often met by a mix of administrative controls, cryptography, and physical security measures. In current systems, these mechanisms are usually organized into administrative domains associated with organizations and constrained by geographic areas. Universities on their campuses and businesses at particular sites are examples of security domains.

People can access their systems from beyond their normal work locations, generally through connections that terminate at the system they normally use—for example, by dialing in via a modem.

In this situation, the remote-access device and communications path almost certainly fall outside the security domain maintained by their organization. Consequently, one impact of device and location independence on security systems is that secure communications paths and devices cannot be assumed. While moving, intermediary devices (e.g., cell sites) change. Thus, a second impact of nomadicity on security is that motion independence must be taken into account.

The dynamic nature of communications paths and the lack of physical security inherent in nomadicity affect the most basic security issues. How do you ensure that a person is whom he says? How can you be sure that previous conversations have not been monitored and passwords compromised? How can you guard against the unsecured parts of the communications systems being compromised? When a person deals with multiple security domains, how do you maintain security without making her personal management issues excruciatingly complex?

This last case is illustrated by the multiple password problem, an aspect of the requirement for a friendly interface. A person might have voice mail at work, an answering machine at home, a bank card, a telephone card, and an office computer—all of which have different personal identification numbers (PINs) and passwords for access. Some of these devices have different remote and local access protocols; often, a person cannot access his computer away from the office in the same way that he accesses it at his desk.

There are solutions to these individual issues, including smart cards, end-to-end encryption, and voice prints. But these technologies are not widely deployed or uniformly accepted. Neither are they static: New technologies continue to emerge. The NII will have to adapt to these new technologies if nomadicity security requirements are to be satisfied.

The new technology issue can also be viewed as another dimension of device independence. Security systems must be flexible enough to accommodate not only new technologies, but simultaneous use of differing, current technologies.

Technological considerations are not the only aspects of nomadicity that interact with security. Calling home to ask if anyone needs something from the grocery store clearly requires a different level of security than transferring money for the house payment. At work, the special project has different security requirements than an expense report.

These are examples of the association of context and security. Further, when a context contains individuals from different (and perhaps competing) organizations, maintenance of the distributed context must take into account the varying security requirements of the participants. If individuals form virtual communities, those communities might become the basis of security domains.

Distribution and synchronization

User requirements for location, motion, and device independence affect decisions regarding distribution and synchronization. If a person always wants his phone book with him, how and how often does he reconcile that phone book with backup copies or with a corporate phone book which might have updated numbers? If the person wants to access phone numbers stored on a personal digital assistant (PDA) while at his desk, how will the storage on the device be integrated with the fax system in the desktop computer? If the person buys a new PDA from a different manufacturer, how will the new device fit in? These examples show how decisions regarding distribution and synchronization are affected by user preference, dynamic environments, and technological change when nomadicity becomes a design consideration. Traditional designs—where most elements are under the developer's control—will fail for nomads.

If a person is at home balancing her checkbook and wants to look up a phone number, should her phone book look in her private phone numbers first? If she is at the office working on the XYZ account, should it first look up numbers associated with that account? Moving between contexts could affect data access decisions. When the person is in a distributed conference, should the system first display information on the other participants and their organizations?

The interaction between distributed contexts and information access must be addressed by any system supporting nomadicity. It is a small step to see that virtual communities might provide an organizing principle for data and data distribution decisions. With knowledge of the likely locations of context or community members, costs might be minimized through relocation of data or processing. If the participants are moving, the various impacts of moving contexts will change distribution and resynchronization decisions.

Nomadic individuals are likely to draw on a variety of communications, computation, and information systems simultaneously. This creates the potential for parallel content in those systems. A common example is a phone number in a written personal phone book, programmed into a phone book on a personal computer, in memory on a cellular phone, and in a PDA. When the number changes, how do they all get updated? Intersystem synchronization issues exacerbate intrasystem issues, such as temporary disconnection, update latency, failed transactions, and cancellation of updates. Both inter- and intrasystem synchronization requirements must be addressed.

Location

Nomadicity has uncoupled individuals from places. With that uncoupling, the implicit binding of access capabilities to individuals has been broken. I'll send him a fax; now has new dimensions of uncertainty. Where is he? How close is he to a fax machine?

What is its number? Does it need a special header for guests? Could a computer just print the message near him? When has the individual left the location?

Device independence interacts with the increasing use of mobile devices to complicate the notion of location even further. The variety and capability of devices individuals carry are increasing.

Mechanisms are needed to define a location dynamically and to connect the user. As technology advances, the ability to adapt to new technologies must be built into any such location management system.

There are multiple communications paths into many locations (video cable, computer networks, telephone lines, broadcast media, etc.).

These paths might terminate in a variety of devices (television sets, telephones, fax machines, pagers, cellular phones, computers, building control systems, etc.). They might also present varied and changing quality of service. As nomads and their devices move in and out of locations, a significant challenge is the dynamic coordination of communications channels and static devices with individuals.

Beyond these technical challenges, there are personal and social issues. The demand for friendly user interfaces motivates removing the burden of managing all this complexity from the user. Resources must be allocated fairly when multiple individuals are present.

These issues cannot be addressed from the perspective of a single industry. A better cellular telephone interface will not by itself ease the burden of receiving a fax while in an airplane. Mechanisms that bridge different systems for the nomad are required. Such solutions must take into account that parallel systems will always exist. No one will use all of them, but all of them will be used by someone. The connections between systems must provide useful coordination while having enough flexibility to allow variation and change.

Context

For the nomad, any place he hangs his hat is home, office, or entertainment area. Any system that supports the nomad must help him maintain these various contexts. Such support for context maintenance must include:

1. Identification of the context on which the individual wants to focus

2. Maintenance of the state of the activities and information associated with the context

3. Knowledge of the preferences the individual has for interaction with the context

4. Application of those preferences to the location from which the context is being accessed

5. Simultaneous management of multiple contexts

Context identification can be either specified—I want to balance my checkbook now—or implicit—I've just placed a call to the Smith Industries' account manager. In any case, there must be support for reestablishing the state of the context. This might be complicated by the context's level of autonomy. Some contexts will be active even when the nomad is not in contact with them. An ongoing electronic meeting is an example. In that case, reestablishing the state of the context might involve some means of summarizing the portion of the meeting that the nomad was unable to attend.

For less autonomous contexts (e.g., periodic payment of a credit card bill), the charges would be posted to the account throughout the month and the individual would only examine them periodically. Reestablishing context in that case would be relatively simple. Another consideration regarding context identification is that different people will choose to define more complex contexts. The person who does her books at the end of the month will have a context of checking, savings, bills, and credit cards—all of which need to be organized in such a way that she can see the state of her finances. Supporting automated systems will therefore have to take into account varying levels of specification, autonomy, complexity, and the interactions among them.

This context scope is an example of individual preferences. People can be expected to have preferences for every aspect of their interactions with computer and communications systems. Those preferences will include the permissible demotions they will allow in different locations. An example of a permissible demotion is having an e-mail message read over the telephone. Graphic information is lost, but the message is conveyed. A further demotion might be having just the message's key words—drawn from a list of filtering key words, such as call as soon as possible—read over the phone. Other preferences might include what contexts could be established from what locations and what level of security would be involved. Perhaps an individual would only allow purchases of up to $50 to be authorized via phone, but would allow up to $300 to be authorized from an ATM.

These are examples of applying preferences to the communications channels and devices available at different locations. They illustrate the interaction between context, preferences, and location.

Finally, individuals certainly will want to maintain some interaction with several contexts simultaneously. The priority call that has to get through is one example. Any person who keeps several things going at once will have a requirement for maintaining multiple contexts.

Although we expect that integrating the notion of context into traditional computer, communications, and information systems is necessary to support nomadicity in the NII, we also believe that integration will require significant alteration in system design. NII developers that use context as an organizing principle in their designs will probably have an advantage when addressing nomadic needs.

Operating environments

Although the issues covered thus far have been couched in application-level terms, support for them must lie at least in part in the operating systems and networks on which the applications run.

One concern in this regard is application visibility. Some classes of application might not need to be "aware" of the changing distributed environments in which they operate. System-level adaptations can maintain connectivity on the application's behalf.

Early examples of this kind of support are operating systems supporting process migration and the X Window System. Process migration (ideally) is transparent to the application.

X allows users to decide where an application displays its output. In both these examples, conservative applications do not need to be modified in order to operate in dynamically changing environments. In other situations, the applications must be aware of and support distribution and synchronization. The phone book in the earlier example is one such application; most graphically demanding applications (e.g., window systems, imaging applications, design, etc.) are another.

Location services are just one example of system-level activities affected by nomadicity. The division of labor in the realm of security between computer system, communications network, and applications is another. So, there could be end-to-end security where only the devices carried by nomads were trusted. At the other extreme, internal computing and communications systems could take responsibility for all security.

The architectural boundaries within the NII are not yet fully defined. As the builders of the NII work out new industry and organizational boundaries, their activities will interact with technological considerations to establish the NII's architecture. A central challenge is to establish architectural boundaries that ensure interactivity between components of the emerging (and continually changing) system, while not limiting participation in it. With respect to nomadicity, architects and developers must additionally account for its central concepts—movement within physical space, social space, and channels of communication—when defining the new systems.

Applications

Arguably, operating environments (operating systems, network operating systems, middle-ware, etc.) are moving to support the distributed system capabilities, which the NII requires. Applications software, however, is adapting more slowly—and, in some cases, only incrementally.

Many applications are designed to take into account only minimal distribution issues. They depend on reliable local capabilities, and, if they take remote capabilities into account at all, they characterize them as either being fully available or fully unavailable. Issues of changing bandwidth, latency, or reliability are almost never considered.

Nomadicity complicates software requirements even further. Today's nomad might spread her computing and communications activities over many different devices and access many remote services. The applications she draws on need to adapt to her various environments. When she is working from a portable computer, her applications must be sensitive to the requirement for alternative communications paths and the computing capabilities of her machine. Thus, a mechanism must be developed for applications to sense and adapt to changing environments and user preferences.

Clearly, the distribution of function between applications and operating environments is not yet defined. Just as there will undoubtedly be many different capability sets within the NII's system components, some applications will deal with nomadicity issues internally and others will draw on services. The challenge in software is similar to the system component challenge: ensuring interoperability without restricting the potential for innovation.

We cannot hope, in this chapter, to explore all the systems issues associated with nomadicity. But notice that for each application-level requirement outlined here, there is a set of system-level capabilities that underlies it.

Summary

Nomadicity—the ability to move easily from place to place and retain access to a rich set of information and communications services while moving, at intermediate stops, and at the destination—is a new paradigm for information processing and communications.

Its basic characteristics include location independence, device independence, motion independence, widespread access, and ease of use. In order to design systems that will meet nomadicity requirements, we need to address these characteristics, as well as privacy and security—issues that are exacerbated in a nomadic environment.

Developing a model of nomadicity will help in designing systems that meet the requirements posed by nomadicity. Elements in this model include locations, communications destinations, the nomadic user, access devices, services, the communications system, and context. Another key model element is the location coordinator—an entity that keeps track of the individuals, devices, and communications system capabilities at a given location as they change. Location coordinators know the characteristics and addresses of all the devices at a location and are responsible for identifying the individuals and mobile devices that enter and leave the location. A final element is the alias, which is the electronic entity that represents the user in the electronic world while managing communications with him in the real world.

Simply stated, in this model, the location coordinators provide information to a user's alias about where she is and what capabilities are at the location. The alias then opens connections to her and establishes the desired contexts as completely as possible using available resources. On the service side, the alias is a reliable point of contact for services and other aliases. Issues of security, quality of service, and location are minimized for services with which the alias interacts. Knowing the user's capabilities, preferences, and requirements, communications between the alias and the user are better coordinated than if the exchanges were handled by each service individually.

Potential and actual nomadic applications are plentiful, as illustrated by the numerous examples cited in the appendix to this chapter. Moreover, it is obvious that virtually all of us are already heavily engaged in such applications. The need for nomadicity in the NII is clear; it now remains for us to develop the principles, concepts, technology, and infrastructure to support it.

Examples of Nomadicity

There are many practical examples of nomadicity in the NII[2]. Several are presented in this section to illustrate the opportunities available to business and government to enhance the value of the NII by addressing nomadicity concerns.

The portable office

Both individuals and organizations are trying to squeeze the most out of available resources. The portable office will let people coordinate their business activities from anywhere. Today, the portable office represents both the least and most successful of the application areas covered in this appendix. It is the most successful in that large numbers of people have already created some kind of portable office for themselves. By 1996, for example, laptop and notebook computers will account for one-quarter of all new computers sold in the United States[3]. On the other hand, the frustration faced by those who do establish portable offices points up the lack of infrastructure in place to support them.

The portable office is not just the 9-to-5, work-for-pay environment, but any place where a person assembles the tools necessary to carry out his work. For example:

1. *Education.* Students as well as teachers maintain offices in a strict, although unconventional, sense. They travel between home and school, and work in both places. They are nomadic, and the NII must let students and teachers do their work regardless of location.

2. *Manufacturing.* The manufacturing process has many stages, including product planning, design, forecasting, production, delivery, and service. Increasingly, these activities are geographically disbursed and centrally coordinated. One disadvantage of this coordination, however, is the inevitable need for a certain amount of travel. Productivity would be enhanced if the information infrastructure that supports the process took people's mobility into account.

Financial trading

For the financial trader, time is of the essence, and information is the staff of life. She might participate in transactions from anywhere—whether on the floor of the stock exchange or while traveling to and from customer sites. The trader requires not only information, such as client names, account balances, and price quotes, but interactive communications for customer contact and transaction initiation.

Crisis management

In a crisis, people have to get on site fast, understand what's going on, and take effective action quickly. That means rapid installation of equipment, rapid access to information, and rapid prioritization and analysis. The situation at the site can be critically affected by access to information and communication with individuals at remote locations. By its very nature, a crisis management team is nomadic. The infrastructure that supports it must take that into account.

Several application areas where the NII must deal with the nomadic aspect of crisis management are:

1. *The mobile clinic.* In emergencies, such as train wrecks, earthquakes, or industrial accidents, mobile emergency rooms are deployed. If the NII supports remote consultation and analysis and automated patient records, these services will have to be available in these dynamically deployed environments.

2. *The firefighter.* While the fire trucks are on the road, the dispatcher is relaying information to them, telling them where the fire is, what material the building is made from, if injuries have been reported. Once on site, the firefighters discover new problems and need new information. How close is

the gas line to the building? What is the layout of the 23rd floor? Coordinating the team involves keeping track of both human and physical resources. If the command center can't get at the floorplan stored in the city's computer, a significant value of the NII will not be realized.

Personal services

Personal services support an individual's activities outside the work context. These are generally leisure and family or home maintenance activities. The NII will make possible a broad range of innovative personal services.

Currently, personal services for most people are supported by various communications media—the television, telephone, and post office. The NII must accommodate these delivery mechanisms, support new ones, and be able to deliver content (movies, shopping, banking, person-to-person communications, etc.) over combinations of them. The ability to switch messages between them will become increasingly important.

Nomadicity has implications for all personal service applications. The NII will have to support multimedia conversations when the participants are not only separated, but on the move, as well as delivering an individual's favorite television program when he is away on a trip.

These are not the only personal activities for which the NII will need to take nomadicity into account. Consider computer application sharing, computer conferencing, games, gambling, video messaging, voice messaging, e-mail, paging, information-on-demand, video-on-demand, home shopping, and voice communications.

People will want access to all of these services from different places, with different delivery capabilities, and with different preferences.

Distributed management

Although we have focused on individuals as nomads, the NII cannot ignore the potential of devices as nomads. Distributed measurement involves the sensing, collection, analysis, and dissemination of data originating in remote locations. An NII that supports distributed measurement will allow small—possibly portable, possibly mobile—sensors to be integrated into the fabric of everyday life. Collected data can be transmitted to processing sites. At those sites, the data can be analyzed, stored, and acted upon either by individuals or automatic programs. Given a supporting infrastructure, important data can be collected with lower cost, higher integrity, greater longevity, and greater value than if each data collection system had to have specially designed communications mechanisms.

Ready examples of distributed measurement applications that would improve the quality and efficiency of people's lives follow:

1. *Health care.* Distributed patient monitoring systems allow doctors to evaluate patients' conditions without costly office visits or hospitalization. Remote recording of vital signs enables a physician to monitor the

progress of a recovering patient carefully—even though that patient has already left the hospital.

2. *Environmental monitoring.* Sensors floating in rivers, sending back information on water quality, flow rate, and location, would allow for dynamic tracking of changing conditions. The ability to deploy sensors rapidly to remote locations would allow for quick response in dangerous situations.

References

1. Notice that this ability to superimpose a favored context on the current normal context has been a cornerstone of value added for some time. The travel industry has been especially sensitive to it: Hotels that are just like home or that provide an office on the road; exemplify this idea.

2. The examples in this appendix are based on information in EDUCOM, IR for the NII: Technical Challenges C.10, Portability, Mobility and Ubiquity; Washington, DC: 1994, pp. 77–80.

3. *IPC Week* (June 27, 1994) reports that, in 1996, of all personal computers shipped in the United States—excluding servers and home use—77.1 percent will be desktop and 22.9 percent will be portable. *Computer Retail Week* (June 20, 1994) reports that 28.6 percent of all personal computers shipped in 1996 will be portable versus 71.4 percent for deskbound machines and servers. The latter article also gives the annual growth rate for portable sales through 1998 as 15.7 percent versus 3.8 percent for desktop sales.

Konstantin Guericke

What is VRML?

The World Wide Web is based on networking protocols, such as HTTP (Hypertext Transfer Protocol), and on a number of formats that describe how text, images, sound, and video are represented across the different types of computers that are connected to the Internet. The most common format today is HTML (Hypertext Markup Language), which allows text and graphics to be displayed together using a two-dimensional page metaphor. The latest trend among HTML browsers, such as Netscape Navigator or Internet Explorer, is to include HTML authoring capabilities because many people previously content to just browse the Web are becoming interested in publishing their own home page.

VRML (pronounced "vermal") stands for *Virtual Reality Modeling Language* and is to 3D what HTML is to 2D. Although HTML specifies how two-dimensional documents are represented, VRML describes how three-dimensional environments can be explored and created on the World Wide Web. Because 2D is really just a subset of 3D, any two-dimensional object can be easily represented in a three-dimensional environment. Tim Berners-Lee, the "father" of the Web, reasons in Mark Pesce's book *VRML: Browsing and Building in Cyberspace* that VRML is the future of the Web because it is more natural for us to be immersed in a three-dimensional space than to click our way through hyperlinked 2D pages.

Using VRML not only adds sizzle to your Web site, but leverages that each of your visitors has spent their entire life navigating in three dimensions. We make sense of the world by quickly analyzing factors, such as the speed of approaching objects (e.g., a car), the location of light sources and the texture of surfaces. Because many of these processes happen subconsciously, a clever designer can guide visitors through spaces and focus their attention without forcing them to make explicit choices. Similar to the real world, the visitor maintains a first-person perspective and completely controls how close to move toward an object and from what angle to view it.

What Does VRML Do?

VRML doesn't really do anything. It is simply a scene description language that standardizes how three-dimensional environments are represented on the Web. Unlike programming languages, such as C++, VRML does not have to be compiled and run. Rather, VRML files get grammatically analyzed (parsed) and then displayed. Because this is a much faster process, the creation of VRML files is much simpler than programming. It also allows for more interactivity and facilitates incremental improvements.

Here is how VRML works from the user's perspective. First, you have to obtain a tool that "speaks" VRML. There are freely downloadable versions of products, such as Caligari Fountain, Intervista WorldView, Paper Software's WebFX, and TGS WebSpace. Some allow just for browsing in 3D, and others allow for various levels of 3D creation and VRML authoring. Because most people browse before they build, we focus on browsing here and cover the creation of VRML worlds later on.

A VRML file is loaded the same way as accessing an HTML file: either by clicking on a link or typing a URL and hitting return. Based on the speed of your connection and the size of the file, the loading time can be as little as a few seconds or as much as a couple of minutes. Well-structured VRML files will allow your VRML browser to load the file in pieces, which lets you explore right away while the browser fetches more detailed objects and those that are not currently in your view.

As you navigate through the scene, you will notice that some objects are linked. If you click on them, you will jump either to another VRML world or to another media type, such as HTML. Although this gets you to other places quickly, it leads to the same problem as "jumping" from link to link in HTML: you jump from a document on one topic on a server in one place to another document on a different topic in a completely different place. This is what Mark Pesce, co-creator of VRML, describes as (by way of Gertrude Stein) "there is no there there." Contrast this with navigating through a 3D environment. Because you see everything that is in between your origin and your destination, you will experience a sense of continuity, which not only helps you find your way back, but also reassures viscerally that you know how you got to your destination.

For example, when you walk through a town, you look around and build a mental map of the place. If someone tells you that you have to turn right at the next intersection, you can visualize this and get to where you want to go. There is a sense of continuity, and you can see how quickly you progress toward your goal. Sometimes you get lost, but this is part of the experience—often that is how you discover new places or meet new people. Typing a URL and watching the byte counter as the destination loads onto the screen just isn't the same.

Although this is not intimidating to experts, the majority of people will only get on-line if it works like the real world. Abstract URLs are difficult to remember, and jumping from one text fragment to another is not something that people encounter on a daily basis. However, once the Web allows you to use your spatial perception and conforms to the way you work (rather than forcing us to adopt the way computers work), the Web will become just another place you go to accomplish chores, chat with friends, or learn new skills.

How Does VRML Compare to HTML?

VRML allows for much richer interaction than HTML. When viewing two-dimensional home pages, your options are basically limited to jumping from page to page and looking at images from a fixed, pre-determined perspective. When visiting VRML worlds, however, you can freely choose the perspective from which to view the world. In addition, you can navigate unencumbered through 3D environments, the contents of which are only limited by the imaginations of their creator.

VRML spaces are inexpensive to build, can be bigger than the earth, and the objects in it can (and often do) defy the laws of gravity. As you walk or fly through such worlds, you can pick up objects and inspect them from all sides; if your VRML application includes authoring capabilities, you can even create and modify 3D objects. Don't like the color of your house? Just re-paint it with a few clicks of the mouse! Thus, VRML allows 2D home pages to expand into 3D home worlds. Traditional commercial Web sites can draw in new users by adding three-dimensional environments that are fun to explore and by providing a natural way to navigate through the information available on the site. Ultimately, you will be able to collaborate with other users in context-rich and visually descriptive 3D environments, rather than typing away at the command prompt in a text-based chat room. How do VRML files get displayed as graphical 3D environments?

What Bandwidth is Needed for VRML?

Experienced Web site administrators must consider the bandwidth required to make enhancements to their site enjoyable to their visitors. Many early Web enthusiasts, who relied on high-resolution images, sound, and video to spice up their site, found out the hard way that these additions made their site slow or inaccessible to the millions of people who connect to the Internet via a regular 14.4K modem. However, because most HTML browsers have added support for incremental loading of images, many Web administrators overhauled the images on their site to be loadable in chunks. This has made even graphics-intensive Web sites much more accessible to the average modem user. When images are loaded progressively, you can start reading text and clicking on links before the images have fully arrived.

Although VRML files are usually more compact than video files and often even smaller than high-resolution images, the better VRML tools will allow you to access and save 3D spaces in chunks. Through a technique called *in-lining*, you can break up large VRML scenes into smaller files that can be loaded incrementally. This works even better than in 2D. Although an HTML browser has no idea what image or what part of an image you are most interested in, a VRML browser "knows" where you are and which direction you are facing. Because you have a first-perspective view in VRML, you just need look in the direction of where you want to go and your VRML browser will give highest priority to loading the objects that are in your view. The remaining objects are loaded in the background or as you change your point of view. Of course, because most of us don't use head-mounted displays yet, *looking* means moving your mouse as to display the part of the scene you want to explore.

Most VRML files are actually surprisingly small and might not even require in-lining. Images, sound, and video files are large because they store every piece of information that appears on your screen, bit by bit. Because this approach would get very unwieldy in three dimensions, VRML files contain only the salient coordinates of each object with instructions to the 3D browser on how to connect the coordinates and display the surfaces. The 3D browser then generates the three-dimensional environment from this information. Therefore, the real bottleneck for large-scale VRML environments is the speed of your CPU and, to a lesser extent, the bandwidth of your Internet connection.

To deal with slower CPU's, VRML includes a feature that has been used successfully by game developers for years: levels of detail. Through levels of detail, your browser can take some shortcuts and display an approximation of an object before calculating it in detail. Because you have a first-person perspective in VRML, the browser "knows" what you are looking at. For example, if you are still quite far away from an object, the browser can just display the approximation, which is the same object with a lower level of detail. As you move closer to this object, the VRML browser dynamically displays higher resolution versions of the same object. By the time you get close enough to the object to pick it up, you will see the object in all its glorious detail. If the creator of the world chose the right switching points, you won't even notice the transitions because far-away objects are so small that you can't perceive the more detailed features anyway.

Through levels of detail you can use a lower polygon version of an object whenever you won't really notice the difference between it and the original because the object is in the background or you move through a scene very quickly. This technique helps your CPU maintain decent frame rates by lowering the number of polygons that have to be rendered in real time. Although moving closer toward an object will increase the number of polygons for that particular object, the total number of polygons that have to rendered in the scene might actually go down because other objects might move out of your view and no longer need to be displayed. Using levels of detail, the experienced designer can keep the total polygon count in your view fairly constant, thus allowing your browser to maintain a decent frame rate as you move through the environment. You might wonder how this affects loading times because the browser will have to have to download several versions of every objects that contains levels of detail. This is where in-lining comes in. One of the key features of VRML is that you can combine levels of detail and in-lining, which means that you can display a scene with little delay and only load more detailed versions of an object as you move closer toward it. Thus, levels of detail and in-lining are two crucial features of VRML that, when used together, make it possible to build very large worlds.

For What Web Sites is VRML Appropriate?

In the long run, the answer is simple. Every site that is set up to engage visitors and keep them coming back will eventually be three-dimensional. Except for cases where the content is highly symbolic and where the potential visitors are well-trained to access information through command-line interfaces, there is a role for 3D in virtually every Web site. Even if the content of your site is primarily symbolic, you can use 3D to help less symbolically inclined visitors to visualize your data. For example, a mathematician who just published a major paper could use VRML to let people visually explore the dynamics of a symbolic system. Through trial and error, visitors could gain an understanding of the matter without needing to comprehend the exact equations that drive the simulation.

In the short and medium term, you will have to consider your audience, the goals of your site and the nature of your content more carefully. For example, if you run an entertainment site, your audience will probably expect you to stay on the cutting edge of interactivity and to spice up your site with new technologies like VRML and Java.

However, you still need to consider the bandwidth and equipment of your visitors, so you don't end up with a gorgeous VRML world that is painfully slow to navigate through and will never be visited again. VRML is an obvious choice if you are trying to reach a very broad audience because 3D is something that is familiar to everyone. Even children who have not yet learned to read are often quite capable not only of navigating through 3D environments, but also of manipulating simple building blocks to create interesting play environments.

The creations of kids are often surprising as their creative expression tends to flow without self-censorship. More recently, the real-world 3D experience of millions of children around the globe has been supplemented by countless hours of playing with their Nintendos and learning to navigate through three-dimensional spaces.

The lack of a language barrier in VRML is another factor that would make your site more attractive to a general audience. Although most Europeans and Japanese who currently use the Internet have some command of the English language, they tend to appreciate content that is not culturally biased (unless they are actively seeking out American culture). Because VRML architecture tends to go beyond the mere replication of reality and sometimes borders on the grotesque, it tends to be equally accessible or inaccessible to people of varying cultural backgrounds.

When you use spaces to communicate, you appeal to fairly fundamental cause and effect relationships. Whereas people from other cultures might have difficulties with American humor or some of the more fiercely fought moral debates, a well-designed space is understood across cultures. When visitors from China enter Notre Dame Cathedral, they instinctively know that this is a sacred space and they behave accordingly. Without having to read anything, they are drawn toward the altar and lift their eyes up to the heavens above. Although they might not agree with the spirit that is expressed in this space, they certainly leave the space with a sense of what Notre Dame is all about.

The caveat about using VRML is that you need to create a lot of content from scratch and that you might need to hire expertise that you don't have in-house. Not every Photoshop wizard makes a good 3D modeler. Designing a space requires visualization skills that even experienced page layout artists might lack. Many accomplished architects might not make the transition either because the virtual medium offers opportunities and challenges quite different from those of the physical world.

You will also have to spend more time on selecting the right tool. Although anybody can build a simple home world with tools, such as Caligari Fountain or ParaGraph's Home Space Builder, a commercial implementation requires industrial-strength modeling tools. Although the modeling features are important, you must also consider usability.

Tools that sport a traditional two-dimensional interface might be easy to learn, but are often neither easy nor fast to use. The best tools have been developed over many years and incorporate suggestions from thousands of users on how to work more productively in 3D. Although text editors, such as vi, were sufficient to convey the most complex ideas via HTML, you will need to invest in good 3D creation and VRML authoring tools to design worlds that go beyond simple spheres and cubes. Although it is theoretically possible to type a VRML file that describes the geometry and all the surface attributes of a complex construction, this really doesn't work in practice. Text is adequate for symbolic reasoning, but it's a poor visualizer. We can easily conjure up the image of a complex object, but to convey all of its details is simply impossible.

What Tools are Available for Browsing and Building VRML Worlds?

Most tools today fall in one of the following categories: VRML browsers, VRML authoring packages or 3D creation tools. Because the whole market is still very young, the tools not only vary by features, but also by navigation paradigms and object manipulation methods. In addition, the tools differ considerably in terms of ease of learning, ease of use, reliability, price and system requirements. Although VRML is new, 3D creation tools have been around for a long time. Although many CAD packages allow for 3D design, the preferred tools for game designers and multimedia producers have been modeling and animation packages, such as Softimage, 3D Studio, Strata Studio and Caligari trueSpace. Although VRML currently does not support animation, it is very likely that it will do so in the future, so it's wise to purchase a 3D creation tool from a vendor who will be able to add functionality as VRML evolves into a language for describing interactive multi-participant environments.

Some 3D creation tools already allow models to be saved in VRML, but others require you to purchase or download separate translation utilities that convert from the vendor's internal format to VRML. Direct VRML output is preferable to converters because something always gets lost during a translation. It's a good idea to make sure that the tool you are considering not only writes VRML files, but can also import them. In addition, you should be aware of what elements get lost when you save a scene in VRML, rather than in the vendor's format or else you find yourself with completely washed-out scenes because your tool supports light attenuation, but VRML doesn't. Because there are various levels of VRML support, you should also check to what extent VRML is supported. For example, most modeling packages cannot write out VRML primitives.

Although most 3D creation tools are developed by established vendors, many VRML browsers are written by companies that were started after the first VRML spec was drafted in late 1994. Most of these companies have a networking, rather than 3D graphics background, but they were able to beat larger competitors to the market because they recognized the importance of VRML early on.

Some browsers (e.g., WebSpace) rely on HTML browsers to fetch VRML scenes, but others (e.g., WorldView and Fountain) have built-in networking support and only need to communicate with HTML browsers when coming across an HTML document. Although most VRML browsers rely on DDE to communicate with HTML browsers, WebF/X integrates seamlessly with HTML browsers, such as Qmosaic and Netscape Navigator. Caligari Fountain is the only VRML browser that also includes 3D creation tools and VRML authoring.

Virtus Walkthrough, WebSpace Author, Home Space Builder, and Caligari Fountain are the most popular authoring tools. Although all of them allow you to add hyperlinks, only WebSpace Author and Caligari Fountain support in-lining and levels of detail. WebSpace Author runs on SGI machines and includes some sophisticated polygon-reduction technology. However, unlike Caligari Fountain, it does not include any 3D creation tools. Caligari Fountain runs on Windows 3.1 and Windows 95 and is freely downloadable for non-commercial use.

How Do I Find the Tool That is Right for Me?

Because products differ so widely, you need to evaluate which features are essential and which ones would be merely nice to have. For example, if you already have certain 3D models in-house that you want to use, you need to be sure that your VRML authoring tool can import those objects. In particular, you should be sure that your tool imports VRML objects or else you will not be able to take advantage of all the objects that you can grab off various VRML sites on the Web.

Even if you generally rely on pre-built models, chances are that you will want to create a few objects of your own or merely modify some of the ones that you found on the Web. If you already have a modeling tool and your artist knows how to use it, you probably don't need to purchase another. However, you should keep in mind that many traditional 3D modelers were built with photorealistic output in mind and might be overly complicated or lack features essential for interactive 3D graphics. Although most modelers still force you to work in wireframe mode, the latest breed of tools allows you to manipulate texture-mapped objects in real time. Before spending a lot of money on a high-end tool, you should evaluate if traditional modeling features, such as lathing and extrusions are sufficient, or if you will need advanced functions, such as organic deformations and 3D Booleans. Deformations can add sizzle to your environment, but they also increase file size and place a heavy burden on your visitors because a higher polygon count will mean reduced interactivity as their computers need to render your environments in real time.

Although you should keep the average configuration of your target audience in mind, you also need to check which tools run on your authoring platform of choice and how much memory they require. For example, if you have an SGI, you have access to some of the best modeling tools in the industry. However, you will pay a high price for your software, and the selection of VRML authoring tools will be much more limited than on the PC. Pricing for Macintoshes is more in line with those for the PC, but software selection is much more limited. Most VRML browsers don't even work on the Mac yet.

Currently, the best selection of tools is on the PC, and stiff competition will continue to keep prices both for software and hardware lower than on other platforms. However, some tools might require you to purchase more RAM, or you might have to deal with incompatibilities and crashes. Because most of your users will explore your VRML worlds with Windows browsers, you should have a very good reason if you choose not to use the PC as your primary development platform.

Rather than settling on one VRML tool, you might consider purchasing several and using each of them for the tasks for which they are best suited. In this case, you need to be sure that the tools interoperate well and that there are no unexpected surprises when transferring scenes from one tool to the next.

If you have existing 2D assets, you should make sure that your VRML tool can leverage these assets. If you want to use 2D illustrations, you should be sure that you can import at least PostScript files. You can convert most image maps to JPEG format, but it is a good idea to check out what bitmap formats are supported by both your VRML authoring and browsing tools. Compatibility problems are minimized, of course, by choosing an integrated tool that can do it all. However, unless you want to optimize your VRML site for a particular browser, you still need to check on how your scenes look in the most common browsers.

Because VRML is hot, you will encounter many packages that claim to do VRML authoring. However, please keep in mind that VRML is an ASCII format and any text editor can technically claim to be a VRML authoring tool.

However, unless you enjoy working directly with the straight ASCII file, you should make sure that you can create levels of detail and in-line objects without having to do any editing by hand. If modeling is not your strongest suit, you should select a tool that includes polygon reduction so that you don't have to model levels of detail separately.

Although you need strong 3D creation tools to generate the objects and spaces you want, the material editing capabilities determine how those 3D objects and spaces will look. To keep maximum flexibility, look for tools that let you assign material attributes not only for entire objects, but also on a per-face basis. For example, you might want to use one texture map for someone's pants and another for his belt. Because texture maps increase the amount of data that has to be transferred, you should look for advanced paint tools, such as vertex painting.

Vertex painting allows you to create multi-color gradients across surfaces and often eliminates the need for texture maps. When evaluating VRML tools, you should pay close attention to options for reducing file size. By stripping out normals, ASCII formatting and default values, a good VRML tool can reduce file sizes by as much as 50%. Files can be reduced even further by collapsing hierarchies, reducing precision, using VRML primitives and saving only one instance of an object that appears in various places. If you use GZIP after having trimmed the VRML file to the bone, you might end up with files that are only 5% of its original size. This will dramatically speed up loading times for your users, and it will allow you to serve more users without adding disk space or bandwidth.

However, if you don't recommend a specific VRML tool for browsing, you will have to be careful about what tricks you use to reduce file size. For example, many browsers do not accept zipped VRML files. If you do not have a tool that includes VRML browsing, you need to be prepared for a lot of testing and switching between your browser and your authoring application to be sure the links work, the navigation is comfortable and all the objects look right. You might also have to switch to a separate browser to see if in-lines load as intended and if objects that contain levels of detail are displayed properly.

When recommending browsers to visitors of your site, you should check how each of them perform on a similar system. The differences in speed can be quite dramatic. Some browsers are already set up to take advantage of a new breed of 3D acceleration chips. Other factors to consider are ease of use and stability. Many of the newer browsers have not been tested adequately, so it is safer to recommend a browser that has been thoroughly debugged.

Ease of use is to a certain extent a matter of taste. Some people prefer to use extensive navigation controls, and others feel more at home just using the mouse and keyboard shortcuts. A good browser gives you lots of choices for navigating around. If you do decide to recommend a VRML tool for browsing, you should check with the developer of the tool to see if you can make it available for downloading from your site. Many developers will be honored that you chose their tool and will allow you to distribute it free of charge. If the tool you distribute also includes authoring capabilities, you might find that your visitors will want to add to your VRML site or make improvements. In this case, you should let them know ahead of time what your policy is regarding VRML scenes uploaded to your server.

Mainstream Internet Case Histories

Jessica Keyes

West Virginia University

The Computing Services department at West Virginia University, located 70 miles south of Pittsburgh, is just like any other IT department. It's got computers and its got users. "Servicing over 22,000 students and 5000 employees requires a mixed bag of computers," according to Lew McDaniel, Director of Computing Services.

McDaniel's job is to keep West Virginia University's IBM mainframes, DEC Vaxes, PCs and various LANs running smoothly. And like most people in his position, McDaniel finds this a tough task. Of all the problems he faces, the one that, up until now, has caused the most problems is McDaniel's ability to stay current with the technology. "We're a rural state and we tend to get things last. But the ability to access these things is critical. Access to information is a real big problem," according to McDaniel.

McDaniel's solution, and increasing the solution of other savvy IT managers, is to go online with the Internet. His use of the Internet is twofold. Explains McDaniel, "I keep a watch on the federal government on subjects that I am interested in. For example, the government provides access to its documents concerning the national information infrastructure (i.e., Al Gore's information superhighway), which I find interesting for the purposes of long-range planning. If this information wasn't on-line I would have to get it on paper and that's a real bear to do." But aside from keeping track of the government, McDaniel and his staff also use the Internet to stay in touch with, as he puts it, "other folks like himself around the country."

How West Virginia Uses the Internet

McDaniel claims to have found a pot of gold on the Internet. "I've watched the federal government add a lot of information on the Internet. In the past two years, the Feds have gone from three to 50 to 60 sources of information." Information ranges from the Securities and Exchange Commission's EDGAR system, which stores over 32,000 documents from thousands of different companies, to the Department of Commerce's Economic Bulletin Board, to the full-text report on the federal government's proposed National Information Infrastructure. Table One provides a flavor of what's available, as well as its Internet address.

Thousands of information sources are on the Internet. The front cover of the over-700-page *Internet Directory* edited by Eric Braun and published in 1994 by Fawcett Columbine, New York, touts over 100 FTP servers and 300 Gopher services. Everyone from the Federal Government to most computer companies provides information—free for the asking.

This is perhaps the key difference between the Internet and other information services, such as America Online, CompuServe, and Prodigy. Where these companies do provide access to some of the same information, time-access charges can be quite steep precluding bottom-line weary organizations (like McDaniel's) from effective utilization. The tradeoff, according to McDaniel, is ease of use.

There is a wide diversity of resources, and hence access mechanisms, on the Internet. Where CompuServe (note: CompuServe is representative of all the other pay-for-use information providers; therefore, it is used throughout this section to represent all pay-for-use information providers) provides an easy-to-use Windows (or Mac or UNIX) interface, Internet users currently enter at their own risk. Table Two provides a quick guide to "net" terminology that will assist the reader in successfully navigating the Internet.

"The Internet is not easy to keep track of," according to McDaniel. "Gopher itself lets you maintain a list, a sort of bookmark that you can use to go directly to the things I am interested in. With the Internet becoming more and more loaded with information, things like bookmarks are a good way to manage the Net."

Currently, there is no one GUI-oriented product to manage access to the entire spectrum of Internet offerings. FTP is separate from Telnet, which is separate from the World Wide Web. In this last data-access service, however, a GUI-based interface is available. Netscape, available from a variety of sources, is a full-screen Web-browser that it, and its predecessor Mosaic, has developed the reputation of being the Internet's "Killer App."

Developed by the National Center for Supercomputer Applications (NCSA) at the University of Illinois, Mosaic is a multi-platform hypermedia browser. Some 50,000 copies of the shareware version of Mosaic are downloaded monthly, according to the NCSA. But the NCSA has also licensed Mosaic to VARs, such as O'Reilly & Associates, who make it available for a fee.

Most recently the original developers of Mosaic have left the University of Illinois and set up shop as Mosaic Communications. They have completely revamped Mosaic and offer it, at about $5000 a pop, to organizations who want to set up shop on the Internet.

Aside from "gophering" and e-mailing around Internet, McDaniel and his staff are big users of Internet e-mail and Usenet discussion groups. Responsible for networking, consulting, training, and operations, McDaniel personally stays in touch with others with common interests in such diverse areas as help desk, networking, and technology trends.

Representative of this genre of lists is one called *Adv-Info*, which tracks advances in the computer industry. The way mailing lists work is that the Internet user creates an e-mail message to subscribe to the list. In this case, sending the following message, which is contained in the body of the e-mail and not the subject, to listserv@utfsm.bitnet accomplishes this feat: SUB ADV-INFO your full name, where your full name is your real name and not your login ID. Astute readers can see the possibilities of using the net for more than just IT trends and issues. It can also be used to great advantage in gathering information about the business domains for which they are charged with developing application systems.

Another good technology source is Edupage, which is a summary of news items on information technology. It is provided three times each week as a service by Educom—a consortium of leading colleges and universities seeking to transform education through the use of information technology. To subscribe to Edupage, send an e-mail to: listproc@educom.edu and in the body of the message type subscribe edupage <your full name>.

Keeping track of and locating interesting Internet mailing lists can be akin to finding a needle in a haystack. Directories like Braun's Internet Directory are a good start, but the best way is from the source itself. You can obtain a list of mailing lists by sending e-mail to listserv@bitnic.bitnet with the message body containing the words list global. However, with 20,000,000 Internet users, there are many mailing lists, so be prepared to download a very large file (some 400,000 bytes).

Setting Up a Gopher Server

Some organizations see the value of providing access to its information through the Internet. West Virginia University is one of them. Basically organizations who wish to do so decide just how they want to present their information. For example, WWW information requires much effort in that hyermedia links need to be created. On the other hand, providing a gopher server is as easy as, according to McDaniel, "putting out a file."

The way McDaniel does this is intriguing because he is using one of West Virginia University's IBM mainframes for this purpose. "Our systems programmers have put together a way where e-mail messages are interpreted by our mainframe, which retrieves information and sends it back to the end-user," explains McDaniel.

According to McDaniel a mainframe approach to Gopher does require the person providing the information to understand a bit about the operating system, but that said, the rest is "essentially using a word processor to create an ASCII file."

But once you connect your site to the Internet, a whole set of new issues raises itself. One of these is security. There is no lack of news articles about people "hacking" their way into an organization's computers. The Internet does indeed provide a formidable access route. Here, conventional mainframe-oriented IS shops might actually have an advantage over the more traditional workstation-based Internet shops.

"We rely on the normal security of the mainframe. We are using American Management Systems Top Secret to secure our location. By forcing Internet users through their security "firewall" (note: a firewall is an Internet term for a hardware/software solution to Internet security), the University of West Virginia ensures that its network and data are protected from intruders.

Aside from the security issue, the other issue that McDaniel is concerned about is access to the Internet itself. The Internet was created, and continues to grow, in a decentralized fashion. In other words, there is no single Internet manager. Therefore, users "surfing" the net get the sense that information is sometimes here today and gone tomorrow. At times, sites that have provided an information source pull the plug leaving users with error messages indicating an unavailable location.

"The problem that we're running into right now is that the pipeline between me and the information source is not controlled by me. It can break. Or intermediate points can decide to do maintenance at 10 a.m., which happens to be when my people want to use it," explains McDaniel. Another difficulty that McDaniel, as well as other users, have encountered is the lack of uniformity from one organization to another. If you're accessing a thousand sites, you have to understand the nuances of a thousand computer systems.

Lew McDaniel can be reached at West Virginia University, Computing Services Department, University Avenue, Morgantown, West Virginia 26505, phone: (304) 293-3011 x2125 fax: (304) 293-6726 Internet: mcdaniel@wvuadmin3.csc.wvu.edu.

A Sampling of Government Information Sources

Source Via	Access Location	
FedWorldNational	ftp	ftp.fedworld.gov
Library of Congress	Telnet	locis.loc.gov
		marbel.loc.gov
National Trade Data	ftp	ftp-stat-usa.gov
U.S. Gov't gophers	gopher	peg.cwis.uci.edu
U.S. Gov't Publications	Telnet	database.carl.org
Zip Codes	telnet	gopher.uoregon.edu
Census	gopher	riceinfo.rice.edu

Public Opinion Index	telnet	uncvm1.oit.unc.edu
Information Superhighway	gopher	gopher.hpcc.gov
Economic Data	gopher	gopher.lib.umich.edu
EDGAR	ftp	town.hall.org
GATT	gopher	ace.esusda.gov

A Quick Guide to the Internet

E-mail

Internet e-mail spans the globe. Most universities, public institutions, and now large organizations have (or soon will) connected to the net. Internet e-mail works the same way as other e-mail, the only difference being the way mail is addressed. For example, Clinton's address is President@Whitehouse.gov.

.gov   Designates an e-mail address located in a government institution

.com   Designates an e-mail address located in a commercial organization

.edu   Designates an e-mail address located in an educational institution

Mailing lists

There are thousands of special interest groups that use mailing addresses to carry out their discussions. Subscribing to a mailing list makes you privy to a continuous stream of mail about that topic. For example, there are mailing lists for CICS, software engineering, software standards—and UFOs.

Usenet

Similar to mailing lists, but more robust because it really serves as a forum for discussion groups.

Internet Relay Chat (IRC)

Enables communication across the Internet in real time.

Telnet

Often described as a "virtual terminal," telnet provides terminal emulation on remote hosts. Essentially, you are logging onto an organization's providing, using the interface (teletype-oriented), they provide, to access that organization's information.

FTP

File Transfer Protocol (FTP) is probably the most frequently used data-access service on the Internet. It is a network-wide client/server standing for sending files from one computer to another. Using FTP, you can call up hundreds of FTP sites and download a huge range of files, from computer programs to IBM's recent announcements on PCs.

Archie

Archie accesses an index of FTP information and returns a list of descriptions and locations of materials that match your query.

Gopher

Provides an easy-to-use, menu-driven way to access the Internet. Essentially provides a more natural way to browse through particular gopher servers.

Veronica

Provides an indexing service for the many Gophers available on the Internet. Like Archie, you type in a word or a phrase and Veronica goes out to search its list of gophers. It returns a list of gopher sites that are of interest.

WAIS

Wide Area Information Server is another mode of Internet data-access service. WAIS automatically indexes the information stored on its servers.

WWW (or W3)

World Wide Web is perhaps the most popular of all the Internet services. Newer than FTP, telnet, or WAIS, it has attributes of all three. It links transparently to a list of servers. Once a server is picked, its interface is not a menu, but a hypertext page of text or graphics with "life" cross-links.

FAQ

Frequently asked questions. These are stored in abundance on the net. The reader is advised to always download this first in doing research because FAQs inevitably answers the questions they are searching for.

Whois

This utility helps you determine whether or not a particular person or entity is on the Internet.

Netiquette

The proper behavior on the net. The Internet grew up as a noncommercial enterprise and most denizens of the net still subscribe to that notion. Crass commercialism (i.e., advertising through mailing lists) is met swiftly with what is know as a "flame," which is a rather tart response to the indiscretion. On the other hand, :-) indicates good will on the net. If you can't figure out what this means, turn your head sideways (It's a happy face).

Network Software Associates

Network Software Associates is a hardware and software research and development lab that supports the federal government. With offices on both the East and West coast this Arlington, Virginia-based company manages a diversity of computers including IBM mainframes, UNIX RS/6000s, midrange AS400's, and a plethora of personal computers.

In business since 1981, Network Software Associates needed to find a way to communicate with their staff and their customers, as well as find a better way to keep up to date with the proliferation of software updates and fixes that a shop of their caliber requires.

According to Stan King, Director of R&D for Network Software Associates, the Internet began to be used heavily by his company about a year ago. Because Network Software Associates writes much of the software for the government and the government is not located on-site at NSA's offices, the Internet is a most valuable tool for user-developer communications.

Most of NSA's development projects are large and require the resources of many of its 128 employees. For a company that is spread across two coasts, the logistics of groupware are formidable. Users of both Da Vinci e-mail software and Lotus notes, King is presently looking for a way to integrate these two popular groupware packages with the power of Internet communications—at a reasonable cost.

It might be the NSA's Internet connection to Microsoft and IBM that will be of the most interest to IS/Analyzer readers. As the developer of critical government software, NSA is in the league that can claim partnership privileges with IBM, Microsoft and a host of others. What is worthwhile to note is that a vast majority of leading-edge software and hardware vendors are taking the Internet route. Gopher or WWW servers are sprouting up everywhere, offering up everything from FAQs to software updates to technical support. It is this last category that NSA takes advantage. Explains King, "This is a fantastic tool. For example, IBM provides technical support notes, as well as problem reports. In addition, we can communicate with the specific people concerned with a particular IBM product. We communicate with the CICS BTAM folks in Germany, as well as England."

King has also been able to extend his network to communicate with the academics, who are often on the leading edge of technology. "We communicate almost daily with the people at Princeton University. They have set up a Personal 370 lab. Personal 370 is a new technology that we are using from IBM. Because the use of this technology is limited to only a few places, we use the Internet to share thoughts back and forth with users of the product with Princeton being the moderator of that user group," says King.

How NSA communicates with the Internet

There are two ways to e-mail using the Internet. One is a personal message sent from one person to another. For example, when King communicates with

IBM's German CICS group, he is really communicating with one person. Hence, he addresses his e-mail to that particular person. Although there are assorted "White Page" directories that provide an alphabetical list of individuals and their associated Internet e-mail address, for the most part the best way to find out someone's address is to ask him/her.

The alternative to individual messaging is the Internet Usenet group or mailing list. Here, a moderator is a centralized company or person who maintains the subscription list. The subscription or mailing list address is used by others when they want to automatically send messages to the entire group. Although the majority of Internet users are content with subscribing to and then reading the messages of others, more active Internet users message frequently.

NSA is one of many who have also opted to start their own Usenet group. On the Internet, unlike services like CompuServe, you don't need anyone's permission to start your own discussion group. But it does require some special intelligence and some computer resources.

In the tradition of the Internet, the software to manage the mailing list is provided free of charge from the Internet itself. Listserv software can be downloaded via FTP in the /pub/listserv directory on cs.bu.edu.

Majordomo software, another mailing list administrative program, can be obtained via FTP in the/pub directory on ftp.GreatCircle.com. Once you've created your group, you can announce it to the world by sending a message containing the list's description to interest-groups-request@sri.com and to new-list@vmi.nodak.edu.

King's discussion group is, of course, private. But that doesn't mean it is exclusive. Given the mailing list's name mostly anyone can gain access to the messages in that list. According to King, this lack of security is not hampering. "Nothing we send as a message is proprietary and we always have the ability to go off and use the phone to talk confidentially," he says. One of the more popular uses of the Internet in the computer industry is the job search. "We place online ads when we try to hire people. Even if we're not hiring, the Internet provides a tremendous networking opportunity. It gives us an opportunity to establish rapport for a future relationships," explains King.

From a pure systems support perspective, King believes that the Internet provides unlimited advantages over the traditional way of supporting his installation. "Our productivity has improved a good 20% since we've been on the Internet. We've even done benchmark studies to see the difference between traditional telephone support and Internet support," says King.

The NSA has done side by side comparisons of supporting their IBM systems via the Internet. IBM has a support line for the 390 line of computers, where you pay approximately $400 a month for the ability to ask a question of their experts. IBM promises to respond within 24 hours with their expert advice.

"We sent the same question to IBM and to one of the IBM user groups. We got more answers, and more accurate answers, back faster from the IBM users group than from IBM. IBM's answer was ridiculous for this particular problem. We had to go back and forth with them to get the right answer. It took seven days to get the right answer from IBM, but only four hours from the IBM user group," says King.

NSA's Internet connection

The NSA provides a FTP server that provides tech support to its customers. Government users merely use the Internet to gain access to NSA's FTP server and download files and fixes. IS managers searching for a better way to provide upgrade information to its PC-based customers might want to consider NSA's approach as a model of efficient customer support.

But, according to King, connecting to the Internet is not as straightforward as it would be if you were dealing with a centralized organization, complete with tech support personnel. When connecting to the Internet, you are essentially on your own.

"The way we were able to connect our FTP server to the Internet was to hire someone with Internet experience," says King. The Internet, according to King, is pretty much ad-hoc, "We needed this person to understand the policies and procedures and the various standards."

King claims that the task of connecting to the net was difficult and time-consuming. More so because they have a high-speed link (65 KB) line. "We also made one minor mistake in starting out small. We had our server upload mail on an hourly basis. We outgrew that virtually overnight and had to go through that enormous process again."

That this was so difficult a task is the result of the Internet relying on physical numerical addresses called *IP addresses*. IP or Internet Protocol is the network layer for the TCP/IP Protocol Suite. It is a connectionless, best-effort packet switching protocol. For example, a server that we know logically as ns.uu.net has actually an IP address of 137.39.1.3. Because getting a new line also requires a new address, there is a big conversion effort that must be undertaken to change the mapping between logical and physical addresses.

There are a variety of connection options. Factors besides costs might be used to select the appropriate option or a series of options. These factors include size and projected use (traffic) of the connection, nature of the use and purpose of the enterprise driving the effort.

Three basic categories of IP service connection are available at this time. All three categories support essentially the same set of functions. They support a variety of line speeds (which affects total capacity of the connection) and will run on a variety of hardware platforms. Performance depends on the line speed, the hardware and software used, and the use.

The three basic connection categories are:

1. Dedicated connection

2. Dialup connection

3. Dialup access to a connection service

A dedicated connection requires a dedicated, point-to-point telecommunications circuit and an IP router (a dedicated networking device), linking the organization to the Internet. Line speeds range from 9.6 KB to 45 MB, with the most common connection speeds being 56 KB and 1.54 MB. A dedicated connection to the Internet most commonly connects to a campus-wide network with several hosts and workstations.

A dialup connection requires a workstation, which might or might not be dedicated to networking, with appropriate networking software and an attached modem. It uses a regular phone line. When a network connection is needed, the workstation is used to establish a connection over the modem and phone line. At the end of use, the connection is broken. Line speeds range from 9.6 KB to 56 KB, with lower speeds being most common. It can be used to connect a single workstation or a LAN. However, if it is used to connect a LAN, the workstation must provide some routing functionality.

However powerful the computer on your desktop might be, it becomes a dumb terminal on the Internet unless you provide a high-speed connection. The two types of high-speed IP connections are SLIP (Serial Line IP) and PPP (Point-to-Point Protocol). Both access methods require not only more physical resources, but more financial resources as well.

An organization contemplating a connection to the Internet should be careful to consider not only the physical connection and startup costs, but also the costs of supporting the resulting service infrastructure. This infrastructure includes the development and continued support of a network. In some organizations, this network might only support data, but at many other organizations, the development of a network must evolve to consider data, voice, and video as the applications and requirements of information technologies supported by internetworking technologies expand.

The Internet provides access to a wide variety of resources and a broad set of functions and services, which might or might not have been available locally. Support staff will require education and training to support and in turn train the faculty, other staff, and students in the use of the new technology and new resources made available.

This training might mean strategic re-orientation and deployment of networking information services. The costs of such added-value services should be planned for in advance.

Increased use of the Internet will make additional demands on existing network technical staff. Areas of the organization not currently participating in data network services will want to participate. Although not all of these services can be exactly quantified in terms of costs, they must be anticipated and incorporated into Internet planning.

Every organization connecting to the network must have a unique identifier. This identifier is known as the *campus IP network address*. In addition to a numerical identifier, most organizations also get what is known as a *domain name* (i.e., whitehouse.gov). It is through the numerical address and the domain name that the organization's hosts will become known throughout the Internet.

An organization must register with the authority that assigns IP addresses and for a domain name. The IP address is assigned by the Internet Address Naming Authority (IANA). The Domain Name is picked by the organization. A domain name is simply a character string that maps to the IP address. It makes it easier for humans to remember than a unique set of numbers.

There are different classes of Internet addresses, which correspond to the number of hosts an organization anticipates connecting to its networks. Thus, the campus should carefully consider the planned growth of its own network in applying for the appropriate class of membership. The IP service provider is an excellent source of advice in choosing a membership class.

Costs Associated with the Internet

What King found is that, on the whole, access to the Internet is far less expensive than access to information through other services, such as CompuServe. Although CompuServe charges a flat fee (somewhere around $9 a month), the extra charges incurred by "extended services" can easily run to over $40 a month.

Signing up for the Internet through a service provider should only incur a flat fee, although new service providers are springing up daily and taking advantage of naive Internet users by charging a per minute cost. The Internet service providers that are listed in Table 68.4 all charge a flat rate that averages approximately $250 per year per user.

Of course, setting up your own server negates sending out checks to an information provider, but the cost in hardware/software and human resources to support the connection can be quite expensive:

UNIX Workstation (server)	$5000 to $10,000
Phone line installation for T-1 line	$2500
Routers	$5000 to $6000 a year
Programmer	$60,000 a year

Some Internet experts claim that you can get a server up and running for as little as $14,000 in setup costs and $1000 a month in operating costs.

Summary

King equates the Internet to power. "Information is power and the Internet provides access to that information." But while utilizing, the Internet offers positive competitive advantages, there is a downside as well. Although access is free (unless a service provider is being used), there is still a cost associated with hardware/software/telecommunications, which, when supporting a large number of people, can be quite expensive.

In addition, the Internet is difficult to use and even more difficult to support. In terms of support, King recommends hiring someone with previous Internet experience, "Someone who understands the logical, physical and virtual connections that need to be made and support. Someone who understands that the Internet is a very loose aggregation of different nodes and protocols."

Finally, while King insists that the productivity of his staff has been boosted by at least 20%, there is a downside to using the Internet. It's known as *surfing*. Says King, "People tend to waste an awful lot of time looking at everything on the Internet."

References

Discussion GROUPS
Discussions about IBM 3090   listserve@trearn.bitnet
body = SUBSCRIBE YARDIMCI   your fullname

IBM mainframes   listserv@ualvm.ua.edu
body = SUBSCRIBE IBM-MAIN   your fullname
IBM mainframes and networks   listserv@bitnic.educom.edu
body = SUBSCRIBE IBM-NETS   your fullname

TCP/IP list   listserv@pucc.princeton.edu
body = SUBSCRIBE IBMTCP-L   your fullname

IBM's application system   listserv@vma.cc.nd.edu
body = SUBSCRIBE IBMAS-L   your fullname

IBM hardware upgrades   listserv@ipfwvm.bitnet
body = SUBSCRIBE UPGRADE   your fullname

ISPF   listserv@vm.usc.edu
body = SUBSCRIBE ISPF-L   your fullname

CICS   listserv@vm.ucs.ualberta.ca
body = SUBSCRIBE CICS-L   your fullname

ACM   listserv@kentvm.kent.edu
body = SUBSCRIBE ACM-L   your fullname

Partial Lists of IP Service Providers

ANS
Joel Maloff
Vice President Client Services

Advanced Network and Services
2901 Hubbard Rd.
Ann Arbor, MI 48105
(313) 663-7610
maloff@nis.ans.net
BARRNET
William Yundt

Pine Hall Rm. 115
Stanford, CA 94305-4122
(415) 723-3104
gd.why@forsythe.stanford.edu
Fax: (415) 723-0010

CERFnet
Susan Estrada
San Diego Supercomputer Center
P.O. Box 85608
San Diego, CA 92186-9784
(619) 534-5067
estradas@sdsc.edu
Fax: (619) 534-5167

CICnet
Michael Staman
President
ITI Building
2901 Hubbard Dr. Pod G
Ann Arbor, MI 48105
staman@cic.net
(313) 998-6101
Fax: (313) 998-6105

Colorado Supernet
Ken Harmon
CSM Computing Center
Colorado School Mines
1500 Illinois
Golden, CO 80401
(303) 273-3471
kharmon@csn.org
Fax: (303) 273-3475

CONCERT
Joe Ragland
CONCERT (Communications for NC
Education, Research, and Technology)
P.O. Box 12889
3021 Cornwallis Rd.
Research Triangle Park, NC 27709
(919) 248-1404
jrr@concert.net
Fax: (919) 248-1405
CREN

Jim Conklin
EDUCOM
1112 16th St. NW
Washington, DC 20036
(202) 872-4200
conklin@bitnic.bitnet
Fax: (202) 872-4318

CSUNET
Chris Taylor
Manager, Network Technology
Office of the Chancellor
Information Resources and Technology
P.O. Box 3842
Seal Beach, CA 90740-7842
(213) 985-9669
chris@calstate.edu
Fax: (213) 985-9400

JVNCnet
Sergio Heker
6 von Neumann Hall
Princeton University
Princeton, NJ 08544
(609) 258-2411
heker@jvnc.net
Fax: (609) 258-2424

LOS NETTOS
Ann Cooper
USC/Information Sciences Institute
4676 Admiralty Way
Marina del Rey, Ca 90292
(310) 822-1511
Fax: (310) 823-6714

Merit
Eric Aupperle
Merit Network
2200 Bonisteel Blvd.
Ann Arbor, MI 48109-2112
(313) 764-9423
ema@merit.edu
Fax: (313) 747-3745

MIDnet
Dale Finkelson
29 WSEC
University of Nebraska
Lincoln, NE 68588
(402) 472-5032
dmf@westie.unl.edu
Fax: (402) 472-5280
MRNET

Dennis Fazio
Executive Director
The Minnesota Regional Network
511 11th Ave. S., Box 212
Minneapolis, MN 55415
(612) 342-2570
dfazio@mr.net
Fax: (612) 344-1716

NCAR
Joseph H. Choy
P.O. Box 3000
Boulder, CO 80307-3000
(303) 497-1222
choy@ncar.ucar.edu
Fax: (303) 497-1137

NEARnet
John Rugo
Accounts Manager
BBN Systems and Technologies
10 Moulton St.
Cambridge, MA 02138
(617) 873-2935
jrugo@nic.near.net

NETILLINOIS
Ed Krol
University of Illinois
Computing Services Office
1304 W. Springfield
Urbana, IL 61801
(217) 333-7886
e-krol@uiuc.edu

NevadaNet
University of Nevada System
Computing Services
4505 Maryland Pkwy.
Las Vegas, NV 89154
(702) 739-3557

NorthWestNet
Eric S. Hood
Executive Director
NorthWestNet
2435 233rd Place NE
Redmond, WA 98053
(206) 562-3000
ehood@nwnet.net
NYSERnet

Jim Luckett
NYSERNET, Inc.
111 College Place
Room 3-211
Syracuse, NY 13244
(315) 443-4120
luckett@nysernet.org
Fax: (315) 425-7518

OARnet
Alison A. Brown
Ohio Supercomputer Center
1224 Kinnear Rd.
Columbus, OH 43085
(614) 292-9248
alison@osc.edu
Fax: (614) 292-7168

Onet
Eugene Siciunas
4 Bancroft Ave., Rm. 116
University of Toronto
Toronto, ON M5S 1A1
Canada
(416) 978-5058
eugene@vm.utcs.utoronto.ca
Fax: (416) 978-6620

PREPnet
Thomas W. Bajzek
530 North Neville St.
Pittsburgh, PA 15213
(412) 268-7870
twb+@andrew.cmu.edu
Fax: (412) 268-7875

PSCnet
Eugene F. Hastings, II
Pittsburgh Supercomputing Center
4400 5th Ave.
Pittsburgh, PA 15213
(412) 268-4960
hastings@psc.edu
Fax: (412) 268-5832
PSINet

William L. Schrader
President & CEO
11800 Sunrise Valley Dr.
Ste. 1100
Reston, VA 22091
(703) 620-6651
wls@psi.com
Fax: (703) 620-4586

SDSCnet
E. Paul Love, Jr.
San Diego Supercomputer Center
P.O. Box 85608
San Diego, CA 92186-9784
(619) 534-5043
loveep@sdsc.edu
Fax: (619) 514-5152

Sesquinet
Farrell Gerbode
Office of Networking and
Computing Systems
Rice University
Houston, TX 77251-1892
(713) 527-4988
farrell@rice.edu
Fax: (713) 527-6099

SURAnet
Jack Hahn
1353 Computer Science Center
University of Maryland
College Park, MD 20742-2411
(301) 454-5434
hahn@umd5.umd.edu

THEnet
Tracy LaQuey Parker
Computation Center
University of Texas
Austin, TX 78712
(512) 471-5046
tracy@utexas.edu

Beth Israel Hospital

Beth Israel Hospital, which is affiliated with Boston-based Harvard University, has all the same problems in supporting its computer installation as any other enterprise organization.

With two data centers running ES9000s, a host of applications programs written in Cobol, PL1, and CICS, Rocky Grasso, Beth Israel's technical support manager, needed a way to manage the rapid pace of change in the software that he supports while protecting his environment from outside interlopers.

"I use the Internet to communicate with people both inside and outside of my organization. I subscribe to various mailing lists such as ones on CICS and TCP/IP," explains Grasso.

Grasso's method of accessing the Internet is through a protocol called *TN3270* (note: TN3270 is available from a variety of sources. Spry, located in Seattle, Washington, sells a version called *Air tn3270*. Spry can be reached at (800)-777-9638 or on the net at info@spry.com). Essentially, this permits Grasso and his staff to emulate an IBM 3270 terminal to access IBM or other vendor information. But instead of a direct tie, or a telephone hookup into the vendor, Grasso uses the Internet as his network. "I use TN3270 instead of the Internet's Telnet. It enables me to emulate a 3270 display by executing it under Windows on my PC," he says.

Beth Israel is representative of those organizations who are utilizing the Internet for messaging and research without necessarily hooking a server onto the Net. However, according to Grasso, even this level of Internet activity requires an organization to formulate a security plan.

Explains Grasso, "When we first got onto the Internet we noticed that from time to time people would try to get into our system." What Grasso is referring to is the propensity of hackers to program their computers to randomly select Internet Protocol (IP) addresses in an attempt to break into an organization's (any organization's) computers.

Grasso found that many of these attempts were being made by students in such faraway places as Scotland and Austria. The Internet originated as a research and academic oriented network, so you can understand why a large number of students are on the network in the first place. If even only a few of these students have hacking on their mind, then the security-conscious organization moving onto the Internet should plan accordingly.

Those that think that the Internet poses minimal security risk to e-mail users is only fooling himself, according to Grasso. He reminds us that the Internet was designed for maximum flexibility and interoperability. Hence, the Internet evolved into a decentralized system spread out across thousands of computers worldwide. And each might have its own security procedures. As a result, security breaches should be expected.

Most of us can remember the case of Cornell University graduate student Robert Morris, Jr. who programmed an Internet worm that single-handedly brought down 6000 machines. In November 1991, the United States General

Accounting Office reported that computer hackers from the Netherlands broke into military computers, and, more recently, a group of students known as The Posse have been taking down systems just for the thrill of it. But according to officials, these hacking students are being quickly replaced by industrial spies.

Organizations that connect their computer system to the Internet put themselves at risk in two ways:

- E-mail might be intercepted and read.

- The business records stored on their computer system might be viewed, altered, or even destroyed.

Building a firewall

Internet security is a hot topic. "At this past IBM SHARE meeting there were quite a few sessions about Internet security and the building of firewalls," according to Grasso.

The hardware and software that sits between the computer operation and the Internet is colloquially known as a *firewall*. Its specific mission is to examine Internet traffic and allow only approved data to pass through.

One type of firewall is to use a software-driven filter in the organization's network connection. It is possible to program a packet router to instruct it to discard any packets requesting information or services that might pose a security threat.

A second approach to building a firewall is to use computers as routers and gateways. For example, Digital Equipment Corporation's SEAL product uses a physical workstation to monitor a network's connections. In this way, there is no direct connection between the internal network and the Internet, enabling all network traffic to be monitored before it is passed through to the internal network.

Beth Israel has created a software and procedural firewall solution to the Internet security problem. Rocky Grasso has provided IS/Analyzer with a copy of a memo that describes the procedures Beth Israel put into place: Network Services has been asked to provide protection to sensitive corporate data such as personnel information, payroll, and patient account information that reside on the network. In order to limit the potential for attacks from our exposure to the Internet, we are implementing a security system that will screen all inbound Internet traffic. This system is also referred to as a "bastion host" or firewall.

1. All outbound connections from BI (Beth Israel) will still be permitted without restriction (e-mail, ftp, telnet, etc.).

2. To maintain uniformity in username conventions, we will be performing all aliasing for BI on the bastion host machine.

3. Inbound mail will be permitted. However, as part of securing hosts internal to BI, we will strip all host names out of the address before they are

sent out of BI. Doing this will require changes to people's sendmail.cf file, as well as a few changes to some other system files. Network Services will be creating a generic sendmail.cf file that will work with the bastion host. This will not prevent mail from arriving into the institution addressed with a host name, but over time, we will encourage people to use the user-name@bih.harvard.edu standard.

4. We will permit in-bound telnet, ftp, and netnews. These services will be running on a bastion host and will act as a point of authentication for any inbound traffic. For any other inbound traffic, please contact Network Services so that we can determine if it can be added as a service on the bastion host. Please notice that some services will not be offered, such as Mosaic, until software has been written for them to be implemented in a secure manner.

5. If an individual has the need to transfer files into BInet, we will provide a host with one secure, but unrestricted, account. That machine will be the bastion host and will have an account where you can place files for immediate retrieval. We wish to emphasize that this will be only a temporary place for files; therefore, a program will delete all files each evening at midnight.

6. We will not permit disk mounts, fingering (i.e., an Internet program that displays information about a particular user, or all users, logged on the local system or on a remote system. It typically shows full name, last login time, idle time, terminal line, and terminal location. It might also display plan and project files left by the user), file transfer or remote logins from outside of BI to any BInet connected host.

Using Encryption

Organizations requiring an extremely stringent amount of security, says Grasso, should use encryption—both in e-mail and the data that is stored on disk. Most commercial messaging products, such as Lotus cc:Mail incorporate encryption, but there is nothing so exotic built into the Internet itself. That might change in the future, however. A new technology, called *Secure HTTP*, developed by Enterprise Integration Technologies Corp. of Palo Alto, is designed to bring data encryption, authentication, and digital signature technologies to the Internet.

But until this becomes publicly available, the organization needs to investigate available alternatives. One of these is a system called *PGP (Pretty Good Encryption)*. It works by combining two keys to encrypt and decrypt data. Readers who want to find out more about PGP should connect to ftp.netcom.com. In the directory /pub/gbe are five files named pgpfaq-1.asc, pgpfaq-2.asc, etc. These files are the text of the most frequently asked questions about PGP.

Internet Sources

The Internet Business Journal. Strangelove Press.
(613) 747-6106
mstrange@fonorola.net

The Internet Letter. Net Week, Inc.
(800) Net-Week
netweek@access.digex.net

The Internet Business Report. CMP Publications.
(800) 340-6485

Internet World. MecklerMedia.
(800) MECKLER
meckler@jvnc.net

The Internet Business Report. CMP Publications.
(800) 340-6485
ibr-august@ost.com

Morph's Outpost on the Digital Frontier. Morph's Outpost.
(510) 238-4545
doug_millison@morph.com

Internet Development in the Financial Services Community

Jessica Keyes

Before the "information highway" became synonymous with the brave new world of video-on-demand, high-powered multimedia and 24-hour home shopping, it was a road well traveled by those needing an efficient and productive way to keep on top of their business.

For those in the financial services area, the information highway, or "information services," as it was known pre-Al Gore, offer a wealth of information that will help you do your job faster, better, and smarter. And in spite of all the hubbub about it, it has been easily accessible for more than a decade.

The difference is that today it's no secret anymore. Although not everyone knows how to get to it, everyone at least knows it's out there. Most organizations are quickly realizing that they simply don't have a choice any longer. Not hitching a ride on the information highway (IH) is becoming a distinct competitive disadvantage.

The IH is really a misnomer (at least for now). Look at a map of the US and you'll see what I mean. Although there are some major arteries criss-crossing the country, the map is really a spider's web of roads, all connected together, to enable you to go from any one point in the US to any other point in the US.

It's the same with the IH. Really a collection of interconnected networks, understanding how to navigate it enables you to get from any one point in the IH to any other point in the IH.

Although the IH probably has more information nuggets tucked into its hard disks than the New York Public Library, for some strange reason it's e-mail that seems to have captured everyone's attention. The ability to communicate with millions of people across thousands of computers across seven continents is no mean feat. It's also a productivity booster.

Of course, the IH is far more than e-mail. It's also a series of databases and bulletin boards. Both provide sources of information that are worth looking into. Bulletin boards are exactly what they sound like, places to post information. Public forums are open to anyone who has a urge to take a look-see. For example, many of the software companies have bulletin boards that enable users to file trouble reports and/or download "fixes" to those troubles.

The most interesting of bulletin boards are those that are maintained by the various special interest groups that have sprung up on the IH. Sometimes referred to as *forums*, these are veritable goldmines of camaraderie and information. For example, CompuServe has a legal forum where I've been able to get assistance that would have cost me thousands of dollars if I had spoken to a non-digitized attorney.

CompuServe's finance forums are similarly well-endowed. The Investors Forum's libraries, for example, include such esoteric items of interest as stocks/bonds, fixed income, option trading, futures, commodities, newsletters, theories, charting, and technical analysis.

There's also all that shareware. CompuServers are a "sharing" lot, so there's quite a bit of "free" software (Shareware is, for all intents and purposes, free. However, you are often asked to make a donation of a rather nominal sum for the care and feeding of the developer of the program you are using. Payment is optional, but always appreciated). If you were to access the Charting and technical analysis library of the aforementioned Investors Forum, you could download QCharter 1.3, which is a shareware program for historical quote charting. Similarly, you could download useful ratios, macros, and text files, such as an index of the SEC's EDGAR database.

Although shareware software and databases dominate the forums, the database research services the IH are the real prize here. Knowledge-Index (KI), the night-owl version of Dialog's very expensive professional research database service, is a veritable gold-mine of financial information. For a paltry $16/hour (after 6 p.m. and all weekend), you get access to dozens of databases including: Books in Print, Business Dateline, BusinessWire, Pr NewsWire, Harvard Business Review, practically all of the computer, news and business publications (including Pravda) as well as Standard & Poor's Daily News and Corporate Descriptions.

If you recall the earlier comparison of the IH to a network of interconnected roads, you'll begin to understand how it works in relation to the services on CompuServe. When you sign on to CompuServe, you log on to CompuServe's computers, but when you request access to KI, CompuServe actually passes your request across a bridge to Dialog's own computer, hence the accurate analogy of a series of connecting roadways.

CompuServe offers numerous other financially oriented services (i.e., bridges). Basic Quotes provides delayed quotes for items, such as stocks, options, indexes, exchange rates, and mutual funds. Citibank's Global Report, which happens to be the primary information resource for many large corporations, integrates and organizes news and financial data, including real-time foreign exchange rates, spot commodity prices, and industry news. Commodity Markets and Pricing offers exactly what its title says it offers.

Company Analyzer provides public company information, including an income statement, balance sheet, and ownership information from Disclosure (which is also available), and an S&P estimate on future earnings. All you need is the company name, ticker symbol, or CUSIP number.

It wouldn't be feasible to describe the myriad of other services offered on CompuServe. They run the gamut from D&B's Business Directory to FundWatch Online to Thomas Register Online to TRW Business Profiles to Investext, which is a full-text on-line version of all the research reports done in the last two years.

America Online and Prodigy all offer commensurate services. Of course, Financial services firms will benefit from providing information on services, such as CompuServe, Prodigy, and American On-line. As shown, Citibank, S&P, D&B, and a host of others have already made an investment in just such an undertaking. Today, it is possible to use these non-Internet service providers to provide services to existing customers, to market to prospective customers, and to even provide information for a fee to whomever wants it.

For the most part, systems development in this venue is surprisingly easy and affordable. For example, CompuServe provides free access to an on-line area where the organization can develop its service as well, as access documentation for software with which to build the service. The developing organization is merely responsible for the time and labor necessary for creating, maintaining, and promoting its database, including transmitting and reformatting the product during the developmental stages.

CompuServe, and other proprietary service providers (i.e., America Online) approaches all information provider relationships as a partnership. They provide sufficient training, documentation, connect time, and disk storage for product development at no cost. They also provide the full support of their marketing and technical staff to assist in developing the organization's product to its full potential.

Interestingly, programming knowledge is not necessary, though it is helpful to be familiar with videotext services and menu-driven formats. The actual format for the product will depend on the nature of the information. CompuServe makes available, at their cost, several programs to facilitate the service's delivery:

- *Menu-Driven Display.* This program can be likened to an electronic magazine, whereby menus serve as the table of contents and lead the user to articles of information. This works well for concise factual information.

- *Keyword Search.* This program enables the developer to assign keywords to each entry and allows the user to enter the word(s) that he or she wants to find. It is particularly appropriate for dictionaries, access to information by state, date, or special interest, and other reference material.

- *Gateway Arrangement.* This is where information resides on the organization's host computer and the user is "transferred" to the host computer to access the information. It is particularly appropriate for information that requires immediate responses or minute to minute updating, such as stock prices.

- *Wire Service.* This CompuServe program gathers a continuous stream of information and makes the information available to users as soon as it is received. Information is dynamically added to menus in reverse chronological order. This continuous updating is typically used for news wires, which require timely processing of large amounts of data.

Developers can transmit information to CompuServe by various means. With a terminal and a modem, it can dial CompuServe's network and directly type the information into a CompuServe database using a CompuServe word processing program. Other means available are uploading and submission of diskettes and tapes to CompuServe's computer center.

A host of savvy financial services organizations have been using these Information Superhighway service providers for years for a definite competitive advantage. But with the thousands of articles and growing interest in the Internet, most of these organizations are looking to the Net as well. But what they're finding is that the Internet is as different from the proprietary service providers as night is from day from a development perspective.

Where CompuServe and its competitors work as partners to help the organization deploy its serve—going as far as providing access time and disk space—development on the Internet means going it alone. As you'll see in the rest of this chapter, there are many choices and issues that need to be grappled with if the financial services organization is to use the Internet successfully.

Using the Internet

A commonly asked question is "What is the Internet?" This question gets asked so often because there's no agreed-upon answer that neatly sums up the Internet. The Internet can be thought about in relation to its common protocols, as a physical collection of routers and circuits, as a set of shared resources, or even as an attitude about interconnecting and intercommunication. Some common definitions given in the past include:

- a network of networks based on the TCP/IP protocols

- a community of people who use and develop those networks

- a collection of resources that can be reached from those networks.

Today's Internet is a global resource connecting millions of users that began as an experiment over 20 years ago by the U.S. Department of Defense. Although the networks that make up the Internet are based on a standard set of protocols (a mutually agreed-upon method of communication between parties), the Internet also has gateways to networks and services that are based on other protocols.

In many ways, the Internet is like a church: it has its council of elders, every member has an opinion about how things should work, and you can either take part or not. It's your choice. The Internet has no president, chief operating officer, or Pope. The constituent networks might have presidents and CEOs, but that's a different issue; there's no single authority figure for the Internet as a whole.

The ultimate authority for where the Internet is going rests with the Internet Society (ISOC). ISOC is a voluntary membership organization whose purpose is to promote global information exchange through Internet technology.

The council of elders is a group of invited volunteers called the *Internet Architecture Board (IAB)*. The IAB meets regularly to "bless" standards and allocate resources, like addresses. The Internet works because there are standard ways for computers and software applications to talk to each other. This allows computers from different vendors to communicate without problems. It's not an IBM-only, Sun-only, or Macintosh-only network. The IAB is responsible for these standards; it decides when a standard is necessary, and what the standard should be. When a standard is required, it considers the problem, adopts a standard, and announces it via the network.

No one pays for the Internet. Instead, everyone pays for their part. The National Science Foundation pays for NSFNET. NASA pays for the NASA Science Internet. Networks get together, decide how to connect themselves together, and fund these interconnections. A college or corporation pays for their connection to some regional network, which in turn pays a national provider for its access.

Many big corporations have been on the Internet for years. Up until now, their participation has been limited to their research and engineering departments. Businesses are just now discovering that the Internet can provide many advantages to their bottom line:

1. Providing information to end-users is less expensive than with the proprietary networks, such as CompuServe, which normally charge a royalty on profits made.

2. There are many more users of the Internet than on all the proprietary networks combined. At last count, there are 22 million users of the Internet compared to less than five million on proprietary networks.

3. Advances in technology have provided the ability to build visual storefronts, which include liberal use of images and even video and sound. This is made possible through deployment of the Mosaic and Netscape graphical user interface and use of the Hypertext Markup Language (HTML), which has quickly become an Internet standard.

The glossary at the end of this chapter demonstrates the great variety of capabilities that the Internet provides organizations looking to it to provide information. Although Mosaic interfaces currently dominate the press, the readers should be aware that the Internet was successfully disseminating information long before Mosaic was developed.

Essentially, the Internet is being used by organizations in five venues:

- *E-mail.* Organizations are making good use of e-mail to correspond to clients and staff members. Updates and notices can be inexpensively and quickly routed to all four corners of the world.

- *FTP.* One of the oldest of the Internet technologies, File Transfer Protocol, enables organizations to provide databases of files (i.e., text files or programs) that others can download to their personal computers.

- *Gopher.* A distributed information service that makes available hierarchical collections of information across the Internet. It uses a simple protocol that allows a single Gopher client to access information from any accessible Gopher server, providing that the user with a single "Gopher space" of information. Public-domain versions of the client and server are available.

- *Telnet.* This technology enables those outside of the organization to remotely login to a host computer as a guest to access information that resides on that host.

- *World Wide Web.* The newest of Internet technologies. When used in conjunction with the Mosaic or Netscape graphical interfaces, it provides the ability to store hypertext and images for use by current and future customers.

Financial Services firms are using all of these technologies to take advantage of what is, for now at least, a practically free worldwide network.

Using FTP and e-mail for support

Network Software Associates (NSA) is a consulting firm that supports the government and industry—including financial services. With offices on the West and East coasts, NSA needed to find a way to better support their customer base. For NSA, the solution turned out to be the Internet.

NSA found that a large percentage of customer support traffic comes from the user requesting help in locating information or help in performing a certain function. The other important task in customer support was in providing timely software updates and fixes.

If the request is not time-critical, the user can be trained to e-mail a request for help to the customer service group or, alternatively, to other users. This second option is a form of e-mail known as *Usenet*.

Both the IS organization and the user community can greatly benefit from setting up Usenet discussion groups. In essence, Usenet is Internet e-mail with a twist: It is a mailing list to which users subscribe where a message is sent not to one individual, but to the entire mailing list of individuals.

Starting a Usenet. NSA is one of many who have opted to start its own Usenet group on the Internet. Although an organization doesn't require permission to start a discussion group, it does require some special intelligence and some computer resources.

In the tradition of the Internet, the software to manage the Usenet mailing list is provided on the Internet itself. The software, known as *Listserv*, can be downloaded free of charge using the Internet's File Transmission Protocol (FTP).

Usenet enables NSA customers to solve some of their own problems. Responding to questions and problems from the user community is only half of NSA's customer support problem; the other is providing fixes, patches, and software updates. NSA feels that there is no reason to use sneakernet anymore when you can distribute software to users through the network. (*Sneakernet* is the network created by physically walking from location to location to deliver software to users.)

Using FTP. To use FTP, the NSA decided to implement an FTP (File Transfer Protocol) server. The support of NSA users is handled using FTP for file transfers. NSA places the files in a common access location, then sends users an e-mail to inform them of the latest release, thereby giving them the option to obtain it or not.

According to NSA, becoming an FTP server is not as straightforward as it would be if you were dealing with a centralized organization complete with tech support personnel. Connecting to the net is no easy task and requires developing a careful plan. NSA didn't, and, as a result, suffered from it. For example, NSA did not accurately predict the high level of customer usage of its Internet-based services. As a result, they had to increase capacity by installing a higher-speed line.

This was such a difficult task because the Internet relies on physical numerical addresses called *IP addresses*. IP (Internet Protocol) is the network layer for the TCP/IP Protocol Suite. It is a connectionless, best-effort packet-switching protocol. For example, a server that we know as ns.uu.net has a physical address of 137.39.1.3. Because getting a higher-speed line also requires a new address, a big conversion effort must be undertaken to change the mapping between logical and physical addresses.

NSA had to consider a plethora of implementation issues when opting to create an FTP server:

- *Hardware.* The first decision was to consider the type of hardware to be used as the FTP server. Most organizations opt for high-powered, Unix-based workstations because the higher the number of users, the more powerful the machine must be.

  NSA opted for a Sparcstation and the Unix operating system because the number of users was large. However, most companies starting out can get by with a 486-based PC-compatible systems.

- *Software.* Unix is the operating system of choice for most servers because most of the software running on the Net (i.e., FTP itself) is Unix-based. In addition, of all the server-based operating systems, Unix is the most robust in the client/server arena.

  In addition to the operating system, the organization must also ensure that telnet and FTP software is available on that server. Although telnet is your basic remote telecommunications software readily available from a variety of sources, FTP comes in a couple of flavors. The traditional flavor of FTP is simply a series of Unix commands. This can be confusing to non-Unix users. Vendors have recently come out with a more graphical form of FTP. But there is a high financial cost associated with it. So, NSA decided that, although difficult to use, a bit of training and support would go a long way toward alleviating the problem of dealing with the Unix shell.

- *Phone line.* The organization must order, install, and test the circuit or phone line that is connected to the server. Before this can be accomplished, however, a model of the expected usage of the Internet must be developed to accurately determine line capacity. Model variables include number of users, number and type of services being used, and amount of data being uploaded and downloaded.

  NSA uses a dedicated connection to hook the FTP server to the Internet. This requires a dedicated, point-to-point telecommunications circuit and an IP router, which is a dedicated networking device, linking the organization to the Internet. Line speeds usually range from 9.6 KB to 45 MB, with the most common connection speeds being 56 KB and 1.54 MB. NSA ultimately required a 65-KB line to ensure good response time for its users.

  An alternative is to use a dialup connection. This method uses a regular phone line and a workstation. When a network connection is needed, the workstation is used to establish a connection over the modem and phone line. At the end of use, the connection is broken. Line speeds range from 9.6 KB to 56 KB, with lower speeds being most common. Obviously slower than a dedicated connection, this solution is used by organizations with fewer users dialing into the network. The trade-off here is increased response time versus lower costs.

- *Costs.* Depending on the number of users and the hardware configuration, the cost of implementing an FTP server ranges from $1000 to $5000 per month, with a one-time hardware and phone-line installation cost averaging $13,000.

  The actual cost really depends on the number of servers that you use, the number of customers you have, what they're doing and the amount of time they spend on the net, the type of software you're running, and the speed of your line.

Internet Security Considerations

Ten of the largest buy- and sell-side firms—including Scudder, Salomon, and Goldman Sachs & Co.—have joined together to establish the Financial Information Exchange (FIX). FIX is a common protocol for sending and receiving equity trading information, including orders, execution details, fill reports, and account allocations.

With the goal of eliminating the proliferation of proprietary order routing systems, one standard industry protocol means that brokers will be able to reach multiple clients while buyside traders can reach multiple brokers.

Since April of 1994, Fidelity has been communicating with Goldman Sachs and Salomon Brothers using the FIX protocol. According to all indications, these firms are experiencing a tremendous surge in productivity because these brokers no longer have to manually key in the information. From a liquidity point of view, sells and buys can be more quickly matched.

FIX allows customers to see on-screen, multiple inbound indications from different brokers on the same stock, and fill information coming back on multiple orders.

The most intriguing aspect of FIX is that the protocol, to enable open communication between firms, has been written to allow messages—including equity trade orders—to be sent over the Internet.

Wary of Internet hackers, those participating in FIX over the Internet have deployed stringent security measures, including data encryption, as well as strong firewalls. Internet subscribers can receive FIX information over the Net at fix@world.std.com. Included are the FIX protocol specification, FIX committee meeting minutes, application notes, and the FAQ (frequently asked questions).

The Internet poses a particularly high level of security risk. Few need to be reminded of the case of Cornell University graduate student Robert Morris, Jr. who programmed an Internet worm that single-handedly brought down 6000 machines. In November of 1991, the United States General Accounting Office reported that computer hackers from the Netherlands broke into military computers. More recently, a group of students known by the name The Posse have been taking down systems just for the thrill of it.

Setting security policies and procedures really means developing a plan for how to deal with computer security. A procedure for creating a security plan includes the following steps:

- Look at what you are trying to protect.

- Look at what you need to protect it from.

- Determine how likely the threats are.

- Implement measures that will protect your assets in a cost-effective manner.

- Review the process continuously, and improve things every time a weakness is found.

Most organizations utilize several methods to ensure security:

- *Passwords.*   Many organizations are lax in enforcing password assignment and maintenance for users of their mainframes and other in-house servers. Shadow passwords, which mean that no public password files are available for the casual browser, is the preferred method.

  Of course, all of this is worth nothing if security isn't an intrinsic part of the corporate mindset. Security begins with the individual. There has been more than one instance of employees giving out Internet IDs and passwords to friends—incidents usually immediately followed by a few break-in attempts.

- *Data encryption.*   Encryption is perhaps the most popular method of security for financial firms using the Internet. But it comes with its own set of problems.

  Other than a lack of standards in the industry, the problem is that people need to have some way of decrypting the message. If the messaging is done internally (i.e., over the organization's own network), or between two or more cooperating organizations (e.g., securities firms transmitting buy and sell information between each others' computers), then a private encryption key can be used. But if you're messaging on the Internet and a customer needs to transmit private financial information, a public key needs to be sent along with the message. The problem is that this public key needs to be decrypted at the receiving end of the message.

- *Firewalls.*   The hardware and software that sits between the computer operation and the Internet is colloquially known as a *firewall.* Its specific mission is to examine Internet traffic and allow only approved data to pass through.

  One type of firewall is a software-driven filter in the network connection. An organization might have 60 machines handling Internet e-mail; however, the use of a software filter makes it appear to the outside world that they only have one. It is also a good idea to strip the organization's host address. In this way, it is possible to lock out those who would attempt to get into a system through e-mail.

  A second approach to building a firewall is to use computers as routers or gateways. The main thrust of this solution is to route all Internet traffic through what is sometimes referred to as a *bastion* (i.e., *bastion* meaning *wall,* as in a wall between the main computer and the Internet) host. Essentially, this technique is simple. The bastion host is a server that is connected both to the Internet and the organization's main computer installation. Only users and/or information with the proper security clearance is routed through the bastion host to the organization's computers.

Using Mosaic-Type Interfaces

A variety of organizations are using a combination of the World Wide Web and a Mosaic interface to do everything from providing information to enabling catalog shopping.

The World Wide Web is a hypertext-based, distributed information system created by researchers at CERN in Switzerland. Users can create, edit, or browse hypertext documents—either in a text-based format or using a graphical user interface. As with most Internet technologies, software (to run a Web site as well as develop graphical user interfaces) is freely available on the Internet itself.

First Union Corporation, with headquarters in Charlotte, North Carolina, is a bank holding company made up of eight financial institutions, which is seriously interested in contributing to the free flow of information on the Internet.

First Union's vision of the future lies in our commitment to the delivery of, what they refer to as, Cyberbanking(sm) to its customers and strategic partners. Although, like most financial services firms, First Union is just getting started. They plan to enable their customers to buy products and services over the Web without worrying about security issues and having the money directly debited from the customer's checking or credit card account.

First Union has created the First Access Network. Although today it contains information solely about the bank, First Union soon hopes to provide its commercial customers the ability to build virtual storefronts. Even without these virtual storefronts, First Union's Web network is impressive for the amount of information it provides. This includes:

- Corporate Mission
- History of First Union Corporation
- Financial Information
- Investor Relations
- Stockholder Account
- Stock Listings
- News Media Contact
- Career Opportunities
- Products and Services
- Checking Accounts
- Savings Accounts 24-Hour Service
- Credit Solutions
- Loans and Leasing
- Buying and Refinancing Your Home
- Mortgages
- Equity Loans
- Relocation Services
- Investing for the Future

- Brokerage Services
- Estate Planning
- Retirement Services
- Insurance Services
- Business Services
- Consumer Reference Library
- Career Opportunities
- The Consumer's Guide to Credit
- Using Credit
- Basics of Credit
- What Every Consumer Needs to Know about Credit Cards
- VISA Home Page
- History of the Credit Card
- History of the Banking Industry
- First Union and the Community

Each of these items, which appears on First Union's Mosaic Home Page, is a link to a separate hypertext document, which contains information about the titled subject.

Creating a Mosaic document requires marketing and artistic skills, as well as technical skills. Because a Mosaic document is hypertext-linked, developers often have to draw a storyboard to keep track of where there are going.

Mosaic document designers really have to understand the ramifications of designing a document that will be displayed in a networked environment. The general rule is to keep documents relatively small and uncluttered. You don't put large images in the document because it would take a long time to download these images over a slow link, although the text comes very fast.

The major impediment to using the Mosaic/Web combination is speed. Most users of the Internet are accessing it using fairly slow 2400 bps modems, so downloading images that are typically 200 KB can be painstakingly slow. But although the Mosaic Web browser opens a connection to the server, requests a document, scans the document and then does the same for the next page, Netscape (a second-generation Mosaic tool) does this in a parallel fashion. Unfortunately, not everyone has Netscape (or even the slower Mosaic). The point here for developers is to be well aware of what your prospective users will be using as their graphical user interface.

Most developers limit their use of graphics to thumbnail images with the ability for the user to request a full-screen image. Because these images are stored on the organization's host (unless this work is contracted out to one of the many Internet service providers) careful deployment of imagery will prevent a network disaster. If you have a large document with many, many images, you can take a major hit on the net by requesting these images all at once.

Programming the Web is really a misnowmer. Developing a Mosaic document is more akin to word processing than programming. In fact, major vendors such as Microsoft have provided HTML extensions to their word processing packages at no additional cost.

HTML (Hypertext Markup Language) is really a rich text-formatted document that looks like the following example (from First Union):

```
<li> <a href="#mission">Corporate Mission</a>
<li> <a href="history.html">History of First Union Corporation</a>
<li> <a href="financial.html">Financial Information</a>
<li> <a href="financial.html#investor">Investor Relations</a>
<li> <a href="financial.html#account">Stockholder Account</a>
<li> <a href="financial.html#stock">Stock Listings</a>
<li> <a href="financial.html#media">News Media Contact</a>
<li> <a href="careers.html">Career Opportunities</a>
```

HTML enables the developer to embed images, as well as provide for hypertext links to other documents and even other Web sites, such as the Visa Home page.

There are really two halves to creating an on-line presence on the World Wide Web. You have to create one or more documents using HTML and then you have to develop a way to present those documents to someone looking for them on the Internet. In other words, you have to become a Web server.

Becoming a Web server requires some careful planning. Additional software, itself available free on the Internet, needs to be obtained and configured. In addition, the organization needs to estimate the bandwidth of the telecommunications line, as well as the required capacity of the hardware. This all depends on the amount of information to be disseminated and the number and workload of the users using the system.

Proprietary Service Providers

CompuServe. 800-525-0095. The Basic price here is $8.95 per month with lots of extra surcharges. Forums are an extra $8 per hour and database surcharges vary considerably.

Prodigy. 800-PRODIGY. $14.95 per month, with free access to forums, Prodigy is trying to be a contender to the venerable CompuServe. With so many people lusting after the IH, Prodigy is doing well.

America Online. 800-827-6364. You get five hours of free time for $9.95 per month, but every hour after that costs $3.50.

Internet Users' Glossary

address. The three types of addresses in common use within the Internet are e-mail address, IP (Internet or Internet address), and hardware or MAC address.

anonymous FTP.   Anonymous FTP allows a user to retrieve documents, files, programs, and other archived data from anywhere in the Internet without having to establish a userid and password. By using the special userid of "anonymous," the network user will bypass local security checks and will have access to publicly accessible files on the remote system.

archie.   A system to automatically gather, index, and serve information on the Internet. The initial implementation of archie provided an indexed directory of filenames from all anonymous FTP archives on the Internet.

archive site.   A machine that provides access to a collection of files across the Internet. An "anonymous FTP archive site," for example, provides access to this material via the FTP protocol.

Cyberspace.   A term coined by William Gibson in his fantasy novel Neuromancer to describe the "world" of computers, and the society that gathers around them.

dialup.   A temporary, as opposed to dedicated, connection between machines established over a standard phone line.

Electronic Mail (e-mail).   A system whereby a computer user can exchange messages with other computer users (or groups of users) via a communications network.

e-mail address.   The domain-based or UUCP address that is used to send electronic mail to a specified destination.

encryption.   Encryption is the manipulation of a packet's data in order to prevent any, but the intended recipient, from reading that data. There are many types of data encryption, and they are the basis of network security.

File Transfer Protocol (FTP).   A protocol that allows a user on one host to access and transfer files to and from another host over a network. Also, FTP is usually the name of the program the user invokes to execute the protocol.

Gopher.   A distributed information service that makes available hierarchical collections of information across the Internet. Gopher uses a simple protocol that allows a single Gopher client to access information from any accessible Gopher server, providing the user with a single "Gopher space" of information.

internet.   Although an internet is a network, the term *internet* is usually used to refer to a collection of networks interconnected with routers.

Internet.   (note the capital "I") The Internet is the largest internet in the world. It is a three-level hierarchy composed of backbone networks (e.g., NSFNET, MILNET), mid-level networks, and stub networks. The Internet is a multiprotocol internet.

Internet Relay Chat (IRC). A world-wide "party line" protocol that allows one to converse with others in real time.

Internet Society (ISOC). The Internet Society is a non-profit, professional membership organization that facilitates and supports the technical evolution of the Internet, stimulates interest in and educates the scientific and academic communities, industry, and the public about the technology, uses and applications of the Internet, and promotes the development of new applications for the system. The Society provides a forum for discussion and collaboration in the operation and use of the global Internet infrastructure. The Internet Society publishes a quarterly newsletter, the *Internet Society News*, and holds an annual conference, INET.

Point-to-Point Protocol (PPP). The Point-to-Point Protocol provides a method for transmitting packets over serial point-to-point links.

Serial Line IP (SLIP). A protocol used to run IP over serial lines, such as telephone circuits or RS-232 cables, interconnecting two systems.

Telnet. Telnet is the Internet standard protocol for remote terminal connection service.

Wide Area Information Servers (WAIS). A distributed information service that offers simple natural language input, indexed searching for fast retrieval, and a "relevance feedback" mechanism, which allows the results of initial searches to influence future searches.

World Wide Web (WWW or W3). A hypertext-based, distributed information system created by researchers at CERN in Switzerland. Users can create, edit, or browse hypertext documents.

Keyes' Annotated Resource Guide

There's a plethora of multimedia and Internet products out there. There's also a plethora of guides that list each of these products in painful detail. What I've done here, at the risk of incurring the wrath of literally hundreds of multimedia and Internet vendors, is list the ones that were most interesting to me. Because I have the same background as most of you, I think you'll find these products to be interesting as well. But, buyer beware. The field is ever changing. What's in business today, might not be in business tomorrow.

One more note! There is a big overlap between the Internet and multimedia, so look at all the listings.

Multimedia

Authoring

Compel. A simple, easy-to-use business multimedia presentations kit. You can choose from many backgrounds and even use a menu to create buttons.

Asymetrix Corporation
110 110th Ave. NE
Ste. 700
Bellevue, WA 98004
206-462-0501

Strata Media Forge. A high-powered DOS authoring system that provides any features you might need to develop interactive multimedia applications. Powerful object editors and form-based scripting capabilities are but a few of the tools at your command.

Strata Inc.
2 W. Street George Blvd., Ste. 2100
St. George, UT 84770
800-6STRATA

GameWare. This game-authoring tool sizzles. It's super fast and features the latest technology such as NURBS, Metaballs, etc. It also provides an open architecture option.

Wavefront Worldwide Headquarters
    530 E. Montecito St.
    Santa Barbara, CA 93103
    800-545-WAVE

Quest 5.0. The new standard for multimedia authoring on Windows. A breakthrough tool that allows creation of dynamic, highly interactive training courses, educational titles, etc. It's object-oriented, thus surpassing icon-driven authoring systems.

Allen Communications
    5225 Wiley Pkwy., Ste. 140
    Salt Lake City, UT 84116
    800-325-7850

OPEN!Info Manager 2.0. Create powerful and dramatic multimedia presentations with this multimedia authoring and database tool. Learning is a snap. It has never been easier to create, publish, and distribute your presentations.

Horizons Technology, Inc.
    3990 Ruffin Rd.
    San Diego, CA 92123
    800-828-3808

Authorware. For Macintosh or Windows, this authoring software offers hypermedia linking, integrated text handling, and dynamic search and retrieval. Instantaneous Mac-to-Windows and Windows-to-Mac conversions.

Macromedia
    600 Townsend
    San Francisco, CA 94103
    800-303-2196

Course Builder. Whether your delivery system is a MAC or Windows, this package creates programs speedily and efficiently. Some of the unique features: visual application development, built-in question templates, automatic reporting, etc.

Discovery Systems International, Inc.
    7325 Oak Ridge Hwy., Ste. 100
    Knoxville, TN 37931
    615-690-8829

Power Media. Able to run on all major computing platforms (Windows, Macintosh, UNIX), this object-oriented drag-and-drop authoring kit gives you all the power you need without complex flowcharts and graphs. Also, its total Internet connectivity provides all the global access you might require.

RAD Technologies
  745 Emerson St.
  Palo Alto, CA 94301
  415-617-9430

Kodak Photo CD Access Developer Toolkit. Available for Mac, IBM, and Sun, this kit lets developers build a flexible user interface to images stored on Photo CD discs.

Eastman Kodak Co.
  343 State St.
  Rochester, NY 14650
  800-242-2424

Scala MM200. Limitless multimedia capabilities according to its users. MIDI, laserdisc imagery, video, still photos, backgrounds, fonts, symbols, captions, scrolling, interactive, hot keys, wipes. For the Amiga.

Scala, Inc.
  12110 Sunset Hills Rd.
  Ste. 100
  Reston, VA 22090
  703-709-8043

MPower. Not exactly an authoring tool, but an enabler. Hewlett Packard's tool provides not only the ability to add video, audio, and graphics but also provides the ability to do real-time collaborative multimedia. In other words, two people separated by 5000 miles can work (and even annotate) the same screen. A UNIX-based product.

Hewlett-Packard
  4 Choke Cherry Rd.
  Rockville, MD 20850
  301-670-4300

Passport Producer. Creates audio and visual presentations on the Macintosh. Synchronizes QuickTime movies, animation, graphics, sound and music. Selected as "Best New Software" by *Keyboard Magazine*.

Passport
  100 Stone Pine Rd.
  Half Moon Bay, CA 94019
  415-726-0280

MediaMogul 1.1. CD-I authoring system. Lets you combine audio, video, sounds, images, drawings, and animations. What you create runs on a CD-I authoring player with a 650-MB hard disk.

Optimage Interactive Services
  1501 50th St.
  Ste. 100
  W. Des Moines, IA 50266
  515-225-7000

Quest Authoring System. Multimedia training/courseware generating software. Has some nice features, such as Flow-Chart, Search and Replace, Spell Checker, and Screen Capture.

Allen Communication, Inc.
  5225 Wiley Post Way
  Salt Lake City, UT 84116
  801-537-7800

PictureLink. An authoring system for interactive presentations. Controls video window functions, audio, laser disc, and NEC PC-VCR.

Multi-Media Productions, Inc.
  1855 Interrech Dr.
  Fenton, MO 63026
  314-349-4444

HyperWriter. HyperWriter offers a DOS/Windows hypermedia and multimedia authoring system. It includes full hypermedia, multimedia objects, powerful navigation, royalty-free runtime. Supports: Videodisc players, Video for Windows, Intel DVI, MCI command strings, animation, DDE, object-oriented screen painting, multiple word processing file formats, multiple graphics file formats.

NTERGAID, Inc.
  2490 Black Rock Tnpke.
  Ste. 337
  Fairfield, CT 06430
  203-380-1280

ProScribe. ProScribe offers an IBM/DOS solution for creating networked and single workstation multimedia applications. Using an object-oriented menuing system ProScribe provides: full motion 30 frame/sec. digital video, 16-bit photographs, dynamic text displays, crystal-clear stereo audio, and animation.

Dataseek, Inc.
  7500 San Felipe
  Ste. 525
  Houston, TX 77063
  713-975-5175

Hyperties. Hyperties is an easy-to-use DOS-based software package for creating hypertext based materials. In a Hyperties knowledgebase text, graphics and video are linked together. Features include: unlimited articles, external interfaces, scripting language, and unlimited fonts.

Cognetics Corp.
  55 Princeton-Hightstown Rd.
  Princeton, NJ 08550
  609-799-5005

IconAuthor. IconAuthor combines high-resolution graphics, full motion video, text, animation, and audio: enabling you to build interactive multimedia applications for the IBM platform. IconAuthor is a visual programming tool using the concept of the structure as its building metaphor. Content, including objects, text, graphics, etc., is added to the icon structure using dialog boxes.

AimTech Corp.
    20 Trafalgar Sq.
    Nashua, NH 03063
    603-883-0220

HSC InterActive. HSC InterActive is a Windows multimedia product that incorporates graphics, images, animation, live video, music, and voice.

HSC Software
    1661 Lincoln Blvd.
    Ste. 101
    Santa Monica, CA 90404
    301-392-8441

Guide. Guide is an authoring system that enables users to republish existing information as interactive multimedia documents. Can combine formatted text, color, graphics, sound, animation and full-motion video.

OWL International, Inc.
    2800 156th Ave. S.E.
    Bellevue, WA 98007
    800-344-9737

ToolBook. ToolBook is a high-level object-oriented software construction kit for Windows. Used as an example in this book.

Asymetrix Corp.
    110 110th Avenue N.E.
    Bellevue, WA 98004
    206-637-1594

Q/Media. This integrated tool suite enables developers to create Windows multimedia shows with video, animation, graphics, and audio.

Q/Media Software Corp.
    312 East 5th Ave.
    Vancouver, BC, V5T 1H4
    800-444-9356

Storyboard Live! 2.0. IBM's slick, DOS-based multimedia tool offers video, audio, as well as animation.

IBM
    P.O. Box 1328
    Boca Raton, FL 33429

StudioXA. A complete toolset that lets users create interactive CD-ROM XA titles with full use of video and audio. Enables creation of interleaved multimedia files, called streams, for playback on CD-ROM XA-capable platforms.

Mammoth Micro Productions
  1700 Westlake Ave. N.
  Ste. 702
  Seattle, WA 98109
  206-281-7500

Virtual BASIC. Although not a multimedia authoring package, it includes support for multimedia devices. Its object-oriented approach makes it popular with the professional programming crowd.

Microsoft Corp.
  One Microsoft Way
  Redmond, WA 98052
  206-882-8080

Multimedia Viewer. Those of you familiar with Windows will also be familiar with the Windows Help feature. Viewer enables you to author multimedia titles that have the look and feel of Microsoft Windows help applications. Hypertext oriented, you can also add sound, video, and animation.

Microsoft Corp.
  One Microsoft Way
  Redmond, WA 98052
  206-882-8080

Multimedia Studio. Multimedia presentation system for use in creating presentations that incorporate audio, video, video-in-a-window, and graphics.

Vision Imaging
  10231 Slater Ave.
  Ste. 112
  Fountain Valley, CA 92708
  714-965-7122

ScriptMotion. A DOS-based DVI authoring language.

In Motion
  Digital Interactive Media
  62 rue des Chantiers
  78000 Versaille, France
  33-1-39-53-67-88

Microsoft Multimedia Development Kit. MDK enables you to create diagrams that move, jumps to related text and objects, displays that talk and other multisensory experiences.

Microsoft Corp.
  One Microsoft Way
  Redmond, WA 98052
  800-426-9400

Multimedia Make Your Point. Easy-to-use end-user application for creating graphics-rich presentations that can incorporate multimedia effects.

Asymetrix Corp.
  110 110th Avenue NE
  Ste. 700
  Bellevue, WA 98004
  206-462-0501

CD Author. This professional toolkit consists of a suite of menu-driven modules for conversion, indexing and optimization of data. CD Answer, a companion product, is the retrieval software for information prepared with CD-Author. This software is especially popular with those organizations that need to disseminate huge amounts of information (i.e., magazines and corporate databases).

Dataware Technologies
  222 Third St.
  Ste. 3300
  Cambridge, MA 02142
  617-621-0820

Special Delivery. This media integration and delivery tool for the Mac enables a user to quickly and easily build an interactive multimedia presentation. The product uses the concept of an interactive slide and features a simple graphical technique for creating interactivity. Can combine buttons, text, pictures, movies, and sound.

Interactive Media Corp.
  P.O. Box 0089
  Los Altos, CA 94023
  415-948-0745

PCPresents/MacPresents. For both PC and Mac platforms, this tool combines photographs, diagrams, 3D graphics, QuickTime movies, and animations. Also includes a videodisc controller.

EMC, Ltd.
  7110 Ohms Ln.
  Edina, MN 55439
  612-831-1344

Audio Visual Connection (AVC). Runs under DOS and OS/2. Enables multimedia presentations to integrate images, sound, animation, and video.

IBM
  Multimedia Information Center
  P.O. Box 2150
  Atlanta, GA 30301
  800-IBM-9402

LinkWay/LinkWay Live! This is a simple, easy-to-use package popular in the education arena. Can integrate multimedia objects, such as motion video, digital sound buttons, and digital movies.

IBM
  Multimedia Information Center
  P.O. Box 2150
  Atlanta, GA 30301
  800-IBM-9402

Hybrid Formatter. Sony has come up with a way for a multimedia producer to create a single application that lets both Mac and PC users access it.

Sony Electronics
  9 W. 57 St.
  New York, NY 10019
  212-418-9439

Action! 3.0. Action! lets users quickly create dazzling multimedia presentations combining sound, motion, text, graphics, animation, digital video, and interactively. Its professional template libraries do all the design work.

Macromedia
  600 Townsend St.
  San Francisco, CA 94103
  800-288-4197

AT&T Multimedia Designer. AT&T Multimedia Designer for Windows NT is a full-color imaging solution that creates graphics for multimedia presentation, and photographic applications. Advanced features include: radial and rotatable linear gradients with multiple and repeating colors.

AT&T Multimedia Software Solutions
  12701 Maitland Center Pkwy.
  Maitland, FL 32751
  800-448-6727

Charisma 4.0. Charisma lets users create powerful presentations simply and easily. Based on a 32-bit engine, Charisma includes 3D drawing capabilities that let users extrude, blend, shade, etc.

Micrografx, Inc.
  1303 E. Arapaho
  Richardson, TX 70581
  800-326-3576

Curtain Call 2.0. Curtain Call is a multimedia video titling and presentation software for Windows. Features include: support for playback of Video for Windows AVI file format, support of FLI and FLC animations with synchronized sound, etc.

Zuma Group, Inc.
   6733 N. Black Canyon Hwy.
   Phoenix, AZ 85015
   800-332-3492

MediaBlitz! 3.0. MediaBlitz enables users to easily create powerful multimedia scores consisting of any combination of audio, video, animation, and graphics synchronized over time. Features include object linking and embedding. Media-Blitz consists of three applications: ClipMaker, ScoreMaker, and ScorePlayer.

Asymetrix Corp.
   110th Ave. NE, Ste. 700
   Bellevue, WA 98004
   800-448-6543

Multimedia Scrapbook. Multimedia Scrapbook is a tool for creating multimedia presentations under Windows. Users can effortlessly create presentations in minutes using pictures, sounds, CD-ROM, or laserdisc—without the need for any scripting languages.

Educational Renaissance, Inc.
   2474 Woodchuck Way
   Sandy, UT 84093
   801-943-0841

Photo Theatre. Photo Theatre is an authoring tool that enables users to create high-quality presentations easily and inexpensively on CD-ROM in Photo CD Portfolio format.

Incat Systems Software USA, Inc.
   1684 Dell Ave.
   Campbell, CA 95008
   408-379-2400

SuperLink for Windows. SuperLink is a professional-level development tool for creating multimedia presentations under Windows. It provides a complete development environment for the creation and assembly of multimedia applications to be delivered from sources, such as CD-ROM, laserdisc, etc.

Educational Renaissance, Inc.
   2474 Woodchuck Way
   Sandy, UT 84093
   801-943-0841

Authority. Authority is a visual system for building interactive DOS software without having to write code. Users just click and drag with the mouse to create educational software or multimedia presentations.

Interactive Image Technologies, Ltd.
   700 King St. W. Ste. 815
   Toronto, ON MTV 2Y6
   800-263-5552

Balboa. By merging the powerful capabilities of event-driven programming and high degree of data object abstraction, Balboa acts as an effective link to the demanding CD-RTOS environment. The Balboa Runtime Environment is an API toolbox of ready-to-use CD-I runtime libraries expressly created to reduce the prerequisite of skill and experience and allow a production team to concentrate on the creative aspects of CD-I programming.

Optimage
   7185 Vista Dr. W.
   Des Moines, IA 50266
   800-234-5484

Cast. Cast is a powerful, flexible, fully open, multipurpose multimedia authoring software solution for applications development, solution prototyping, process simulation, etc. Developers use a highly productive English language-based 4½ GL augmented with objects, subroutines, and menus.

Master Class Corp.
   Parkway 2 Ste. 10
   2697 International Pkwy.
   Virginia Beach, VA 23452
   804-427-5090

OPEN!Info Manager 2.0. A multimedia authoring and database tool that anyone can use. It eliminates the steep learning curve of complex authoring software. Pull-down menus and pre-defined templates speed you along. Absolutely no programming or scripting language to learn.

Horizons Technology Inc.
   3990 Ruffin Rd.
   San Diego, CA 92123
   800-828-3808

CB Cross Platform. CB Cross Platform transforms Course Builder modules for playback on Windows with the click of a button. Users can create an application on the Macintosh, use the CB Cross Platform to convert application files to a PC-compatible format.

Discovery Systems International, Inc.
   7325 Oak Ridge Hwy., Ste. 100
   Knoxville, TN 37931
   615-690-8829

CBT Express. CBT Express is an easy, fast course development system that allows users to create engaging and effective CBT courses—no programming, scripting, or flowcharting required.

AimTech Corp.
   20 Trafalgar Sq.
   Nashua, NH 03063
   800-289-2884

CD Author. CD Author is a complete system for CD-ROM database applications. CD Author is intended for use in information distribution applications that contain structured data, such as catalogs, directories, bibliographies, and indexes.

Dataware Technologies Inc.
22 Third St., Ste. 3300
Cambridge, MA 02142
800-229-8055

Conversion Artist. Conversion Artist converts image formats from more than 35 different sources. Its features include batch conversion of multiple files, color conversion between 1-bit, 16-color, 256-color, and 24-bit, on-line help, etc.

North Coast Software, Inc.
P.O. Box 459
Barrington, NH 03825
603-664-6000

Creative Voice Assist. A premiere speech-recognition system, Creative Voice Assist enables users to quickly and effortlessly customize up to 30 Windows applications with personal voice commands. It features an extensive, flexible command library.

Creative Labs, Inc.
1901 McCarthy Blvd.
Milpitas, CA 95035
800-998-5227

Disc-To-Disk. Disc-To-Disk is a simple, affordable method of getting CD-Audio content onto a hard disk in different file formats without a sound board. Users select the portion of the CD to capture; preview selections through the CD-ROM drive's audio outputs or the computer speaker; and then select the Windows file formats and sampling characteristics.

Optical Media International
180 Knowles Dr.
Los Gatos, CA 95030
800-347-2664

Everest Authoring System. The Everest Authoring System is an interactive multimedia development tool for computer-based training, performance support, information kiosks, and CD projects. Screen creation is easily created by simply dragging object icons from a Toolset and dropping them on either the VisualScreen or IconScript flowchart editors.

Intersystem Concepts Inc.
P.O. Box 041
Columbia, MD 20144
410-730-2840

Guide Author. Guide is a comprehensive authoring environment that enables users to create and distribute interactive documents optimized for computer screen display. Document layout tools and user interface configuration gives complete control over the appearance of documents.

InfoAccess
  2800 156th Ave. SE
  Bellevue, WA 98007
  206-747-3203

Guide Professional Publisher. Guide Professional Publisher is a complete system for electronic publication development and distribution that include a comprehensive set of tools to manage high-volume production of interactive publications. It includes both the software and support necessary to automate the conversion of existing documents while creating a custom interactive environment for the user.

InfoAccess
  2800 156th Ave. SE
  Bellevue, WA 98007
  206-747-3203

ImageKnife/VBX. ImageKnife/VBX is a data-aware custom control for Visual Basic and Visual C++ to provide simple, but comprehensive, image handling, including, display (with pan and zoom), format conversion (TIFF, BMP, DIB, PCX, GIF, and TARGA), image processing, color reduction, etc.

Media Architects Inc.
  7320 SW Hunziker Rd., Ste. 305
  Portland, OR 97223
  503-639-2505

ImageQ. ImageQ is a multimedia authoring tool that enables users to create a dynamic interactive multimedia application that can be run on the creation system, mastered to CD or multiple floppies, or saved as a multimedia screen saver.

Image North Technologies
  180 King St., Ste. 360
  Waterloo, ON N2J 1P8
  800-363-3400

KPWin. Knowledge Pro for Windows is a high-level object-oriented environment for developing Windows applications. KPWin uniquely integrates visual design tools, a full-featured OOP language, hypertext, multimedia, and expert systems capabilities with an easy-to-use tool.

Knowledge Garden, Inc.
  12-8 Technology Dr.
  Setauket, NY 11733
  516-862-0600

LEADTools. LEADTools is a complete imaging development tool designed to easily integrate images into an application or system. More than 145 functions are provided to read, write, convert, display, scroll, zoom, dither, color reduction, process, print, scan, and compress all standard image file formats available.

LEAD Technologies
900 Baxter St.
Charlotte, NC 28204
800-637-4699

Lotus ScreenCam for Windows. Lotus ScreenCam for Windows is a multimedia tool that allows users to capture application screen activity; cursor movements, and sound into an integrated screen movie that can be distributed and shared with workgroups of all sizes to improve learning, etc.

Lotus Development Corp.
55 Cambridge Pkwy.
Cambridge, MA 02142
800-343-5414

MediaDB. MediaDB is a multimedia database management system that manages information in the form of images, sound, and video, as well as text and numbers. It allows users to develop serious business applications that handle information in its most natural forms. Features include: object-oriented database management system; rich collection class library, etc.

MediaWay, Inc.
3080 Olcott St., Ste. 220C
Santa Clara, CA 95054
800-632-7401

Advanced Turbo Browser. Advanced Turbo Browser provides an integrated approach to viewing, searching, and controlling all types of files. It instantly views a gamut of program and data files (i.e., fonts, documents, spreadsheets, codes, graphics, etc.).

Pacific Gold Coast Corp.
15 Glen St., Ste. 201
Glen Cove, NY 11542
800-732-3002

MediaRecorder Toolkit. MediaRecorder Toolkit enables developers to build applications that perform video capture. Developers can build applications or databases that create digital video files and graphic files from any analog video source with any Windows-compatible capture card.

Lenel Systems International, Inc.
290 Woodcliff Office Park
Fairport, NY 14450
716-248-9720

Media Wrangler. Media Wrangler Provides a simple way to make and view multimedia interactive presentations. Users just drag and drop, point and click to combine audio, video, pictures, and text.

AltaVista Technology
   1671 Dell Ave., Ste. 209
   Campbell, CA 95008
   408-364-8777

MPC Wizard 3.0. PC Wizard enables users to test, tune and troubleshoot their multimedia PCs. Diagnostic tests check out sound, video, graphics, etc.

SoftKey International, Inc.
   201 Broadway
   Cambridge, MA 02139
   617-494-1219

Multimedia Grasp. Multimedia Grasp enables users to create animated presentations, point-of-sale demonstrations, interactive, tutorials and engineering simulations. It includes a rapid prototyping tool, as well as a toolbox of new and revised multimedia-authoring programs and utilities.

Paul Mace Software, Inc.
   400 Williamson Way
   Ashland, OR 97250
   800-944-0191

Multimedia WinHelp. Multimedia WinHelp allows users to visually and quickly integrate multimedia into any Windows Help system by adding video, sound and more to hotspot text, buttons, graphical pushbuttons or graphical 3D buttons. It works with all available Help development environments.

Blue Sky Software Corp.
   7486 La Jolla Blvd., Ste. 3
   La Jolla, CA 92037
   800-677-4946

NeoBook Professional. NeoBook can quickly and easily produce interactive multimedia applications—without programming experience or complicated scripting. Files might be imported from existing word processors, image editors, animation packages and audio software. NeoBook and created publications run under DOS or as a DOS application under Windows, OS/2, etc.

NeoSoft Corp.
   354 NE Greenword Ave., Ste. 108
   Bend, OR 97701
   800-545-1392

NewWorld Development Kit. This is a C/C++ programmer's toolkit containing a collection of linkable libraries, header files and tools that unleash the entire power and flexibility of Intel's I750 chip set.

Digital Video Arts, Ltd.
   715 Twining Rd., Ste. 107
   Dresher, PA 19025
   215-576-7932

Overtext. Overtext is a multimedia-authoring and management system that enables users to speedily create multimedia applications, without scripting or programming knowledge. Its speed is accomplished by generating all multimedia elements with any software users already own and use every day (i.e., word processors, etc.).

Protobyte, Inc.
   6050 Peachtree Pkwy., Ste. 340
   Norcross, GA 30092
   800-491-1119

PICPress. PICPress is a Windows image compression and viewing program. It allows user to access color and gray scale images and the ability to quickly compress BMP, PCX, and TGA files.

Pegasus Imaging Corp.
   4350 W. Cypress St., Ste. 908
   Tampa, FL 33607

RavenWrite 1.0. RavenWrite is a reusable object allowing Visual Basic C++ or Novell/Series programmers to incorporate hypermedia text objects into their applications. The RavenWrite object incorporates high-end word processing capabilities, plus advanced hyperlinking techniques to allow users to create and play back full-color hypermedia interactive presentations that incorporate video, graphics, text, and audio.

Looking Glass Software, Inc.
   11222 La Cienga Blvd., Ste. 305
   Inglewood, CA 90304
   310-348-8240

script2disc. script2disc is used to automatically build a fully functional "disc image"—the actual data that is recorded on a CD-I disc—after users have created and tested their application using MediaMogul.

Optimage
   7185 Vista Dr. W.
   Des Moines, IA 50266
   800-234-5484

SMILE 100/Pro. Fast and easy to use, users can develop multimedia with SMILE, SciApp's Multimedia Interactive developing Environment. There is no waiting, users can edit multimedia files on the fly. There also is no programming. With SMILE Pro, only the computer limits the size of a multimedia application.

SciApp Corp.
  6278 Songbird Cir., Ste. B
  Boulder, CO 80303
  303-442-0250

Strata Media Forge. The Media Forge authoring system for DOS provides a versatile authoring environment with powerful object editors and scripting capabilities. Media Forge provides robust hyperlinking support, as well as the ability to launch other software packages.

Strata Inc.
  2 W. St. George Blvd., Ste. 2100
  St. George, UT 84770

Summit Authoring System. The Summit Authoring System for DOS is a tool for creating interactive multimedia applications. Authors can quickly design text and graphics in a WYSIWYG form with help from pull-down menus. Users use the built-in A-pex programming language to develop simulations. Features include match spelling allowance, word search, sound alike, and more.

Intersystem Concepts, Inc.
  P.O. Box 1041
  Columbia, MD 21044
  410-730-2840

Syllabus. Syllabus is a CBT authoring system featuring an author friendly outliner, the ability to simulate GUI applications an multimedia support, answer analysis, and branching.

Legent Corp.
  7965 N. High St.
  Columbus, OH 43214
  800-829-9000

Teamworker Scholar. Teamworker Scholar is a highly sophisticated and intuitive authoring package that joins the power of multimedia with interactive group support technology. It allows an author/trainer to create attention-getting presentations to groups of up to 500 people.

Teamworker L.C.
  2469 E. Fort Union Blvd.
  Salt Lake City, UT 84121
  801-943-0160

TourGuide. A full-featured multimedia authoring system that allows users to create professional-quality interactive training and marketing applications. This package's intuitive icons and visual map graphically illustrate an entire application and help users author easily and quickly. There is no programming, no command line, no complex commands.

American Training International
    12638 Beatrice St.
    Los Angeles, CA 90066

ViperWrite 2.0. A Windows-based hypermedia text processor that uses high-end word processing capabilities, plus advance hyperlinking techniques to allow users to create and play back full-color interactive presentations. Features include editing tools to stylize hyperlink characters, words or phrases to other text, graphics, audio, or even video files.

Looking Glass Software, Inc.
    11222 La Cienga Blvd., Ste. 305
    Inglewood, CA 90304

VoiceSqueeze. VoiceSqueeze is a voice file-compression program that compresses voice files up to 50 times, without forsaking good communication-reproduction quality.

Interactive Products, Inc.
    1600 Valley River Dr.
    Ste. 170
    Eugene, OR 97401
    503-341-4964

WinMaker Pro 6.0. WinMaker Pro is as visual and easy to use as Visual Basic, but provides developers with C and C++ code instead of Basic. Features include Project Manager that allows users to instantly access and edit all objects and resources.

Blue Sky Software
    7486 La Jolla Blvd.
    Ste. 3
    La Jolla, CA 92037
    800-677-4946

WRAP. This program lets Windows developers maintain text, image, sound, and binary data in highly compressed form. Designed for use with KPWin, Visual Basic, Toolbook, or any other Windows development tool that can access Dynamic Link Libraries, WRAP provides a comprehensive set of functions for compressing and decompressing data on the fly directly from within the application.

Knowledge Garden, Inc.
    12-8 Technology Dr.
    Setauket, NY 11733
    516-862-0600

Projection

3M 9550 Enhanced Illumination Overhead Projector. This enhanced overhead projector provides the following features: 4000 lumens of light, allowing the room to stay light enough for note taking; images never go out of focus between use, ultra cool, ultra quiet, and much more.

3M Visual Systems
   6801 River Place Blvd.
   1145-5N
   Austin, TX 78726

Apollo Vision 16.7 LCD Projection Panel. This multimedia projection panel enlarges and projects both computer and video-generated images in up to 16.7 million true, vibrant colors. Dramatic multimedia presentations are a snap.

Apollo Presentation Products
   60 Trade Zone Ct.
   Ronkonkoma, NY 11779
   800-777-3750

Desktop Projector 2700 and 2800. These are completely self-contained personal computer peripherals for projecting computer or video images onto a large screen. Intuitive easy-to-use controls and portability are a few of its strong selling points.

Proxima Corp.
   9440 Caroll Park Dr.
   San Diego, CA 92121
   800-447-7694

Polaroid Polaview 300 Multimedia LCD Panel. It's 24-bit color capability enables it to project high-quality visuals and an integral video adapter allows direct input from a variety of video sources. Additionally, a stereo sound system allows the integration of music and pre-taped audio into presentations.

Polaroid Corp.
   575 Technology Sq.
   Cambridge, MA 02139
   800-225-1619

ShowStar. A high-brightness, video and data LCD projector that is designed for use in large audience venues. It's eight times as bright as that of traditional LCD and CRT-based projections.

Electrohome, Ltd.
   809 Wellington St. N.
   Kitchener, ON N26 4J6
   800-265-2171

Scanners

Kodak Professional RFS 2035 Plus Film Scanner. The Kodak Professional RFS 2035 Plus Film Scanner is an ultra-fast, 200 dpi, 12-bit per color area-array scanner for 35-mm slides and negatives. The scanner provides adjustable scanning resolutions, auto exposure, auto color balance, etc.

Eastman Kodak Co., Professional Imaging
    343 State St.
    Rochester, NY 14650
    800-242-2424

Polaroid CS-500i Digital Photo Scanner.   A high-speed, high-resolution digital scanner that along with its accompanying software scans and manipulates reflective images up to 4 × 6 inches. Scanned images can be stored in industry-standard file formats.

Polaroid Corp.
    575 Technology Sq.
    Cambridge, MA 02139
    800-225-1618

ScanMan Color.   A 24-bit color hand-held scanner that captures up to 16.8 million colors, as well as true 256 gray-scale data. It is bundled with FotoTouch Color Image Editing Software.

Logitech, Inc.
    6505 Kaiser Dr.
    Fremont, CA 94556
    800-231-7717

Digital video

928Movie.   A single-slot ISA or VL bus Windows and multimedia accelerator that delivers up to six times the performance of ordinary VGAs and visibly improves the quality of CD multimedia titles by scaling up video clips to full-color, full-screen movies.

VideoLogic Inc.
    2245 First St.
    Cambridge, MA 02142
    617-494-0530

Rapier 24.   A two-page graphics processor that brings workstation-class 24-bit true color performance to Windows Autodesk and TIGA applications. It provides resolutions from 640 × 480 to 1152 × 882 and allows user to select from a wide range of third-party multisync VGA and Apple monitors.

VideoLogic Inc.
    245 First St.
    Cambridge, MA 02142
    617-494-0530

SynchroMaster 300AV.   A synchronizer, switcher, fader, and dissolve unit for data display projectors. It provides instantaneous clean cuts between two computer sources of up to 1280-×-1024 pixel resolution, as well as fade and dissolves.

RGB Spectrum
    950 Marina Village Pkwy.
    Alameda, CA 94501
    510-814-7000

Vivid 3D. A sound-enhancement system for video games and multimedia. It creates dynamic 3D sound from only two speakers.

NuReality
    2907 Damier St.
    Santa Ana, CA 92705
    714-442-1080

DigiTracker. This uncomplicated digital tracker combines a multiple-sensor motion tracker up to 30 sensors-with a 3D digitizer that allows for easy creation of 3D models. Mesh files can be created by simply positioning the stylus on any point on a model and pressing a button to enter the coordinate.

Visual Circuits
    3309 83rd Ave. N.
    Brooklyn Park, MN 55443
    612-560-6205

LiveWindows. A collection of routines to provide real-time display and scaling of live video within a window or multiple windows on the VGA screen. The card plugs into a 16-bit slot and connects to a VGA card with a feature connector.

Software Interphase
    82 Cucumber Hill Rd.
    Ste. 258
    Foster, RI 02825
    800-542-2742

Super Video Windows (ISA). A professional-quality frame grabber and video windowing board that accepts up to three composite or S-VHS inputs from camera, VCR, or videodisc and displays full-motion video in a scalable window.

New Media Graphics Corp.
    780 Boston Rd.
    Billerica, MA 01821
    800-288-2207

Video-It!. A high-performance video capture card, featuring real-time capture and compression. Available in ISA, CPI, and VESA Local Bus version, it can display live video-in-a-window at any graphics resolution.

ATI Technologies, Inc.
    33 Commerce Valley Dr. E.
    Thornhill, ON L3T 7N6
    905-882-2600

VideoSurge.   A full-motion, 24-bit color video display and capture board that has the ability to do chroma-key and luma-key effects and forms the basis of any video-processing studio. Features include three independent audio and video sources, audio pass-through, and optimal support for 24-bit VGA color.

AITech International
   47971 Fremont Blvd.
   Fremont, CA 94538
   800-882-8184

Encoders/Decoders and Scan Converters

Audio/Video Key-PC Presentation Kit.   This add-on comprises two external interfaces that connect a DOS computer to a wide range of audio/visual hardware. With the included presentation software, HSC Interactive, AudioVideo Key, a portable multimedia presentation system.

Comedge, Inc.
   2211 S. Hacienda Blvd. #100
   Hacienda Heights, CA 91745
   818-336-7522

Chroma Gold.   This is a HiColor, 32,768-color VGA display adapter with NTSC composite output. It supports all VGA and SuperVGA modes with standard VGA outputs.

Ventura Technologies
   4820 Adhor Ln. Ste. M
   Camarillo, CA 93012

CVC.   The CVC converts interfaced 15-Hz RGB analog video to studio-quality component video in selectable Betacam or MlI formats.

Visual Circuits
   3309 83rd Ave. N.
   Brooklyn Park, MN 55443
   612-560-6205

Delta VC.   An integrated, PC solution for creating interactive and linear-play video program. It combines real-time MPEG video and audio compression technology with powerful interactive design and mastering tools.

Optimage
   7185 Vista Dr. W.
   Des Moines, IA 50266
   800-234-5484

Genie Scan Converter.   Genie is an external portable box that converts PC graphics to TV video. Genie is a true 100-percent hardware scan converter; it requires no software and is truly plug and play.

Jovian Logic Corp.
   47929 Fremont Blvd.
   Fremont, CA 94538
   510-651-4823

TV Link.   TV Link delivers precision computer images to any standard TV system. It handles VGA resolution up to 640 × 480 with as many as 16 million colors.

KDI/Precision Products, Inc.
   60 S. Jefferson Rd.
   Whippany, NJ 07981
   201-887-5700

Captivator ProTV.   Coupled to VESA Media Channel VMC-graphics systems, Captivator ProTV for VMC displays crystal-clear TV pictures on a PC screen. The user has total control of the picture attributes (brightness, contrast, etc.) through an easy-to-use control panel. The live-video window can be set to stay on top of the display, enabling the user to monitor the TV while working with another application. It's simple to install and use thus making it ideal for home use.

VideoLogic
   245 First St.
   Ste. 1403
   Cambridge, MA 02142
   617-494-0530
   usa@videologic.com

MPEG Player for VMC.   Using VideoLogic's PowerStream video processor and associated proprietary SmoothScale algorithms to deliver sensational-quality video, this peripheral equips today's PCs to take advantage of MPEG, the dominant standard for exceptionally high-quality digital video and audio. It features the highest-quality video playback, full support for application developers, outstanding CD audio, and easy installation.

VideoLogic
   245 First St.
   Ste. 1403
   Cambridge, MA 02142
   617-494-0530
   usa@videologic.com

MovieLine.   Full-featured, low-cost, MovieLine enables users to create dynamic presentations, etc., with digital effects and animation. MovieLine includes Movie Machine Pro with Motion-JPEG Option, Adobe Premiere, Animator Pro and XingCD MPEG encoding.

Fast Electronic
   393 Vintage Dr.
   Foster City, CA 94404
   800-864-MOVIE

Alladin Media Printer. Alladin integrates a seven-input digital switcher, fully programmable 3D DVE and bundles a graphics software package for paint, character generation, 3D modeling and animation. The open architecture enables user to customize the product to meet specific needs.

Pinnacle Systems, Inc.
   870 W. Maude Ave.
   Sunnyvale, CA 94086
   408-720-9669

Asii Switcher. This is a broadcast-quality plug-in switcher that utilizes the latest technology to provide various digital effects. PC control allows users to set up multiple events, allowing the editor to pre-select and store a series of digital effects.

Hotronic, Inc.
   1875 S. Winchester Blvd.
   Campbell, CA 95008
   408-378-3883

AmiLink CIP Desktop Video Editing Systems. This editing tool allows uses true A/B roll editing with consumer industrial level video equipment and lets users upgrade to professional editing and still use their CIP equipment. It comes with extensive edit list tools.

RGB Computer & Video, Inc.
   4152 Blue Heron Blvd. W.
   Ste. 118
   Riviera Beach, FL 33404
   808-5635-7876

Edit-San/Edit-San. This low-cost A/B roll system provides the professional features requested by most editors. It lets users create tape logs right from the editing software, then build edit decision lists directly from the tape logs.

TAO Inc.
   P.O. Box 1254
   Roll, MO 65401
   800-264-1121

The Executive Librarian. This system features multiuser access for fast, full text searches of thousands of records. Pull lists are generated from query results and might be further editing, saved, or e-mailed.

Imagine Products, Inc.
   581 S. Rangeline Rd., Ste. B3
   Carmel, IN 46032
   317-843-0706

Matrox Studio. The Matrox Studio PC-based video editing suite combines the productivity of nonlinear editing with the quality and versatility of linear tape-based online production.

Media Merge.   This video editing software is designed to edit video in Windows. It enables users to choose source material from popular video, paint, spreadsheet, animation, presentation, word processing, or desktop publishing packages and combine it into a new video presentation.

ATI Technologies
   33 Commerce Valley Dr. E.
   Thornhill, ON L3T 7N6
   905-882-2600

Scene Stealer.   Scene Stealer is a PC/AT circuit board and software for automatic scene detection and video logging, saving hours of logging drudgery. The on-board frame grabber examines incoming video to determine when a cut takes place.

Dubner International, Inc.
   13 Westervelt Pl.
   Westwood, NJ 07675
   201-664-6434

Strassner SES-2000 Through 3000.   An editors wish list of artistic tools. These features provide the ultimate in off-line and online editing applications, and every Strassner system has, built in, the capacity for upgrading and adding new features.

Strassner Editing Systems
   104-19 McCormick St.
   North Hollywood, CA 91601
   800-836-3348

Studio Magic.   Enables users to display VGA output on any TV screen. Second, it can capture full-size, full-color video images and store them on disk for later use. The heart is an on-line video production studio.

Studio Magic Corp.
   1690 Dell Ave.
   Campbell, CA 95008
   408-378-3638

U-Edit.   A very affordable news and video magazine edit controller. Based on the PC platform, U-Edit converts a user-supplied 286 or better into a frame-accurate 99 event editor.

Editing Technologies Corp.
   11992 Challenger Ct.
   Moorpark, CA 93021
   805-529-7074

Video Clipboard.   Video Clipboard provides the ideal method for using standard Windows graphics applications in a video environment. It stays resident during a Windows session and outputs to video any image users cut or copy into the shared Windows clipboard.

ScreenPlay 2.2.   A audio/video editing package that offers 24-bit true-color playback and is able to run on Windows-based applications as well as Apple's Quicktime applications. It's fully licensed to allow people the right to distribute the ScreenPlay 2.2 Viewer and ScreenPlay formatted movies over the Internet.

RAD Technologies
  745 Emerson St.
  Palo Alto, CA 94301
  415-617-9430

MediaSpace.   A cost-effective means to add video wherever needed, this digital video board allows you to record, edit and playback in real-time. It includes Adobe Premiere and works with more than 100 video for Windows compatible applications.

VideoLogic, Inc.
  245 First St.
  Ste. 1403
  Cambridge, MA 02142
  617-494-0530

Captivator: Video Capture Card.   A low-cost video capture card that brings desktop video to office and home PCs. Easily installed, this card enables high-quality video to be displayed in any size and in 8, 16 or 24-bit color.

VideoLogic, Inc.
  245 First St.
  Ste. 1403
  Cambridge, MA 02142
  617-494-0530

CD-ROMs

CD 4000.   This expansion cabinet can supply up to eight CD-ROM drives and/or hard drives. It's a cost-effective path for providing additional drives to a CD-ROM network.

Logicraft
  22 Cotton Rd.
  Nashua, NH 03063
  800-880-5644

CD-R Cube.   A desktop processing system for CD replication. It creates CD-ROM discs from files and scanned images for archiving, imaging, multimedia, etc.

Todd Enterprises, Inc.
  224-49 67th Ave.
  Bayside, NY 11364
  800-445-8633

CD/Maxtet.   Designed for sharing CD-ROM based information over a network, this tower might hold up to seven CD-ROM discs, allowing a file server to share them over a network.

Optical Access International, Inc.
   500 W Cummings Park Dr.
   Woburn, MA 01801
   800-433-5133

Philips CDD522.   This CD recorder supports all CD formats and includes such in-demand features as write-once CD format, data addition to recorded discs, double- or single-speed recording and playback, and a motorized tray for ease of loading.

Philips Laser Magnetic Storage
   4425 Arrows West Dr.
   Colorado Springs, CO 80907
   800-777-5674

PxCDS/PiCDS.   Two multisession Photo-CD, MPC and XA compatible drives. Both with an average access time of 490 ms. Tray-loading, 3-way eject, internal and external versions, accepts 12-cm or 8-cm diameter CDs, plays CD audio, stereo headphones jack with volume control.

Procom Technology
   2181 Dupont Dr.
   Irvine, CA 92715
   800-800-8600

CDR100.   Read and record faster than ever—4× as fast! Space efficient easily takes up the same amount of space as a 5.25-inch disk drive bay.

Yamaha
   100 Century Center Ct.
   San Jose, CA 95112
   800-543-7457

JVC CD Recording System.   Totally integrated CD recording solutions. This leading technology firm both manufactures CD-recording drives and designs software to work effortlessly with the most technologically developed drives.

JVC Information Products Company of America
   17811 Mitchell Ave.
   Irvine, CA 92714
   714-261-1292

Technicolor Optical Media Services.   This service provider will master your CDs, pack, ship and distribute them.

Technicolor Optical Media Services
   3301 E. Mission Oaks Blvd.
   Camarillo, CA 93012
   800-656-8667

Master CD. This desktop recorder/player allows the user to create his/her own CDs. Save up to 650 MB of data (including audio and video). It works with either a Macintosh or PC.

MicroNet Technology, Inc.
   80 Technology
   Irvine, CA 92718
   1-800-650-DISK

MultiSpin. NEC offers a series of high-quality CD-ROMs. What makes them unique is their multispin technology, which makes them exceptionally fast—about 280 ms. Compare this to the 800 ms of a typical, low-cost, catalog-quality CD-ROM drive and you'll immediately see the difference.

NEC Technologies, Inc.
   1255 Michael Dr.
   Wood Dale, IL 60191
   800-NEC-INFO

Chinon 435. MPC and Quicktime compatible
150 KB/sec sustained transfer rate
Data buffer: 64 KB
Built-in RCA jacks for stereo audio output
Headphone jack with volume control
Daisychain connection up to 7 drives

Chinon America
   615 Hawaii Ave.
   Torrance, CA 90503
   800-441-0222

MacCD Station. Quicktime compatible
SCSI interface
380-ms seek time
150-KB/sec sustained transfer rate
Stereo audio output
amplified speakers included
lightweight headphone included

Procom Technology, Inc.
   2181 Dupont Dr.
   Irvine, CA 92715
   800-800-8600

CD Porta-Drive. This is a CD-ROM drive for laptop, portable, and desktop computers.
Interfaces through SCSI
200-ms average access time
330-KB transfer rate
3.0 pounds in weight
Dual RCA phono/headphone jack
Uses a Toshiba XM-3401 drive

CD Technology, Inc.
766 San Aleso Ave.
Sunnyvale, CA 94086
408-752-8500

LapDrive.   Portable lightweight CD-ROM drive with a rechargeable battery providing up to 4 hours of use.

TACSystems
P.O. Box 650
Meridianville, AL 35759
205-828-6920

CD-ROM

Personal RomMaker CD-Recording System.   Get the most from your Macromedia programs with a JVC Personal RomMaker CD-Recording system. It provides Red Book audio recording mixed mode, CD-I, CD-ROM XA, and a unique hybrid dual-platform disc formatting.

JVC
17811 Mitchell Ave.
Irvine, CA 92714
714-261-1292

Rimage CD-R Printer.   The world's first silk-screen quality CD-R printer that offers versatility on-demand. Silk-screen quality printing (300 dpi); fast print speed (4 CDs per minute), and it uses standard CD-R media.

Rimage
7725 Washington Ave. S.
Minneapolis, MN 55439
612-944-8144

CD Recording System.   Copy files to a mounted recordable CD, mount and use discs in standard CD-ROM drives, add additional data at any time with this remarkable CD recording system. This system is ideal for storing, archiving, and distributing data.

Optima Technology
714-476-0515 ext. 244

CDD 521CW Desktop CD Recorder.   Philips Consumer Electronics' entry into the make-your-own CD arena. Comes bundled with CD-WRITE publishing software. Can also create your own audio discs.

Philips Consumer Electronics Company
One Philips Dr.
P.O. Box 14810
Knoxville, TN 37914
615-521-4316

CD Studio. For the RS/6000, CD Studio is a combination of hardware and software that enables organizations to master their own CD-ROMs. Consists of Makedisc, which is premastering software; CD Studio Controller, which is proprietary hardware, software, and dedicated hard drive; and the Philips CDD 521 CD-WO product.

Young Minds
   P.O. Box 7399
   Redlands, CA 92375
   714-335-1350

Personal RomMaker/Mixed Mode RomMaker. JVC's personal solution for in-house CD-ROM mastering. Mixed Mode enables you to mix data (Yellow Book) with audio (Red Book).

JVC
   19900 Beach Blvd.
   Ste. 1
   Huntington Beach, CA 92648
   714-965-2610

RCD-202. An affordable (less than $4,000), recordable CD-ROM drive for MAC and PC computers. Enables you to create your own HFS, ISO 9660 or audio CDs within minutes.

Pinnacle Micro
   19 Technology
   Irvine, CA 92718
   714-727-1913

Personal Scribe. Probably the cheapest and easiest way of making your own ISO 9660-compatible CD-ROMs. All you have to do is pick the directories and files you're interested in and hit the enter key. Another advantage is that you don't need excessive hard disk space. Prices start at less than $3000.

Meridian Data, Inc.
   5615 Scotts Valley Dr.
   Scotts Valley, CA 95066
   408-438-3100

TOPiX. Supports all CD-ROM standards. Basically a desktop mastering system that is affordable and easy to use.

Optical Media International
   180 Knowles Dr.
   Los Gatos, CA 95030
   408-376-3511

PCD LAN Writer 200. This package bundles Kodak's writable CD products with Netscribe Access Client Software from Meridian Data. The net result is a turnkey system that lets any DOS or Windows user on a Novell network to produce CD-ROM discs.

Eastman Kodak
343 State St.
Rochester, NY 14650
800-242-2424 X 52

Monitors and Other Input Devices

TruePoint.   Just plug and play; it has never been easier to add touch input to your multimedia system. This product is extremely durable and responds to even the lightest touch. It supports Windows, CD-I, OS/2, Macintosh, and UNIX.

MicroTouch
300 Griffin Park
Methuen, MA 01844
1-800-642-7686

Elo TouchSystems.   A touch screen system that will not drift. It features the trademarked IntelliTouch. This systems provides stable calibration.

Elo TouchSystems, Inc.
105 Randolph Rd.
Oak Ridge, TN 37830
800-356-8682

AccuTouch Touchscreens.   This touchscreen consists of two primary elements: a glass substrate covered with a tight-fitting plastic coversheet. It can be activated by a finger, gloved hand, or stylus.

Elo TouchSystems, Inc.
105 Randolph Rd.
Oak Ridge, TN 37830
800-356-8652

ProPoint.   A new world of interactivity—the freedom to sit back from the desk, stand up, and move around while using the computer. Its ergonomic shape fits comfortably into the palm of the hand and allows 360° cursor control with just a touch of the thumb.

Interlink Electronics
546 Flynn Rd.
Camarilo, CA 93012
805-484-1331

Speech Recognition Family.   A highly-accurate speech recognition facility that has an active vocabulary of more than 20,000 words. It analyzes a user's spoken words and displays them on the computer.

IBM Speech Information Support
Rt. 100, Mail Drop 2239
Somers, NY 10589
800-825-5263

Photo CD

Kodak Photo CD.   Although targeted primarily for consumers, where instead of developing your trip to the beach on paper, you develop it on a CD, Photo CD offers opportunities to businesses as well.

Eastman Kodak
    343 State St.
    Rochester, NY 14650
    716-724-6404

Compression

A compression driver that permits users of Stacker to write the compressed volumes to a CD-ROM and then access the compressed volumes from the CD-ROM discs.

CD-ROM USA, Inc.
    603 Park Point Dr., Ste. 110
    Golden, CO 80401

Graphics Pro Turbo.   Designed for professional true-color graphics applications and for users who want more colors under Windows and other GUI applications.

ATI Technologies, Inc.
    33 Commerce Valley Dr.
    East Thonhill, ON L3T 7N6
    905-882-2600

Hornet.   The ultimate true-color graphics accelerator. It's capable of displaying up to 256 colors at 1280 × 1024, up to 64K colors at 1024 × 768, and 16.8 million colors at 800 × 600.

Genoa Systems Corp.
    75 E. Trimble Rd.
    San Jose, CA 95131
    800-934-3662

PC Motion.   PCMotion is a PC board to decompress and display MPEG digital video. The card supports Microsoft's Video for Windows and Optibase's extended feature set of Motion Tools SDK.

Optibase, Inc.
    4006 Beltinline Rd., Ste. 200
    Dallas, TX 75244
    800-451-5101

Poem ColorBox III.   A software developer's kit SDK-that includes Dynamic Link Libraries for compression and decompression, sample programs with source code, 20 run-time licenses, and more. It features Fractal Transform Template technology and FIF Archiving to improve image quality while reducing file size by 20 percent or more.

Iterated Systems, Inc.
  5550-A Peachtree Pkwy.
  Norcross, GA 30092
  800-437-2285

Digital Cameras

Canon Still Video Camera/RC-360/RC-570.   Records color images on small floppy disks instead of using film. Using a separately purchased video card, you can input these images directly into your computer.

Canon USA
  One Canon Plaza
  Lake Success, NY 11042
  615-488-6700

FlexCam.   FlexCam is a small, flexible camera with built-in stereo microphones. Having the same quality as a Sony camcorder, the FlexCam looks somewhat like a desktop high intensity light. It can be directly hooked up to the PC through any video board. By pointing down at a desk, the FlexCam can also be used as a scanner.

VideoLabs
  612-897-1995

DS-100 Memory Card Camera.   Cardinal Technologies and Fuji Photo Film have combined forces to create this PC-ready digital camera. 21 photos can be stored on a reusable memory card. Capabilities include: auto flash/focus/exposure and 3× zoom.

Cardinal Technologies, Inc.
  1827 Freedom Rd.
  Lancaster, PA 17601
  800-722-0094

FotoMan Plus.   This is a 10-ounce, pocket-size portable camera that lets you take gray-scale digital photos. Costing about $800 retail, FotoMan is a one-button camera that holds up to 32 images and downloads those images through a serial interface. Bundled software completes the package.

Logitech, Inc.
  6505 Kaiser Dr.
  Fremont, CA 94555
  510-795-8500

Audio/Video Controllers

AC10 Computer Audio Controller.   This Control System is designed to manage and manipulate audio. An interface makes the AC10 the first audio product that allows full integration of the telephone into computers.

Altec Lansing Multimedia
   P.O. Box 277
   Millford, PA 18337-0277

AniMaster 1.0.   AniMaster is a full-featured animation controller for serial tape decks and laserdisc recorders that allows frame-by-frame output of rendered images without the need for additional hardware.

ICV, Inc.
   1020 Serpentine Ln., Ste. 114
   Pleasonton, CA 94556
   510-426-8320

Animax.   Animax puts the industry-standard V-LAN control inside an IBM compatible or Amiga computer. Available in two configurations, the Animax controller provides a solution for single-frame animation control of one serial videotape/disc/recorder.

Videomedia, Inc.
   175 Lewis Rd. #23
   San Jose, CA 95111

Audio Advantage.   With this PCMICA type-II sound device, it's easy to add sound to any notebook presentation. Users simply snap the card into place, plug in suitable speakers and the presentation is ready to go.

Turtle Beach Systems
   52 Grumbacher Rd.
   York, PA 17402
   800-645-5640

Bravado 8 & 16.   The Truevision Bravado boards provide total integration of computer technology with full audio/video presentation capabilities. It is the single-slot solution for creating multimedia presentations, etc. Features include 8- or 16-bit/pixel SuperVGA, NTSC, or PAL, video-in-a-window etc.

Truevision, a RasterOps Company
   7340 Shadeland Stn.
   Indianapolis, IN 46256
   800-933-8865

Express.   Express is a V-LAN compatible controller for single-VTR applications. Express uses the V-LAN 3.0 protocol to frame to accurately control a single RS-232 or RS-422 video device for use in animation recording, presentation, and authoring applications.

Videomedia, Inc.
   175 Lewis Rd. #23
   San Jose, CA 95111
   800-937-8526

The Ferel Effect. This TBC/Synchronizer features the ability to compress video both vertically and horizontally using line and pixel interpolatich. It features digital comb filtering and true 8-bit 4:2:2 processing for high-band-width, high-resolution picture play back.

James Grunder & Associates
9204 Bond St.
Overland Park, KS 66214
800-331-2019

MegaMotion. MegaMotion is a multimedia desktop video card that enables users to use two separate, full-motion video inputs, one live and one com-pressed.

ASL, Inc.
2361 McGaw Ave.
Irvine, CA 92714
800-576-4275

Monte Carlo. A 100-percent gam-compatible 16-bit sound card that includes Sierra Audio Rack, V-Synth software, and a games CD.

Turtle Beach Systems
52 Grumbacher Rd.
York, PA 17402
800-645-5640

RealMagic. A MPEG multimedia playback controller that allows ordinary PC systems to deliver full-screen, full-motion, full-color video combined with 16-bit CD quality stereo sound—all from a standard CD-ROM drive.

Sigma Designs, Inc.
46501 Landing Pkwy.
Fremont, CA 94538
510-770-0100

Series II. An external rack-mount animation controller that interfaces with any computer platform using RS-232C serial communication.

Diaquest, Inc.
1440 San Pablo Ave.
Berkeley, CA 94702
510-526-7167

SoftVTR. SoftVTR is a software-based animation controller for use on PCs and UNIX workstations. SoftVTR provides precision control of commercial and broadcast-quality videotape recorders (VTRs) and laserdiscs. It brings the VTR control panel to the computer screen.

Moonlight Computer Products, Inc.
5965 Pacific Center Blvd., Ste. 711
San Diego, CA 92121
619-625-0300

Clip art

Artmaker's MegaRom.   For Mac and PCs over 1000 top-quality clip art and graphics on CD-ROM.

The Artmaker Company
   1420 N. Claremont Blvd., #205-D
   Claremont, CA 91711
   Credit Card Orders: 909-626-8065

Encyclopedia of Stock Photography CD-ROM Vol. 6.   Contains over 21,000 professional stock photographs from over 40 diverse subject categories. Subjects include business and industry, science and backgrounds, etc.

Comstock, Inc.
   The Comstock Building
   30 Irving Place
   New York, NY 10003
   800-225-2727

Signature Series.   Transcend the boundaries of traditional stock photography with this collection of stunning photos from world renowned photographers. Each disc features a single photographer with 100 thematic images and all photos are drumscanned for incredible resolution.

PhotoDisc, Inc.
   2013 4th Ave.
   Seattle, WA 98121
   800-528-3472

Ad Art: Logos & Trademarks CD-ROM 3.0.   A collection of the most popular corporate symbols and service marks used to advertise and display products and services. This CD-ROM contains more than 1200 encapsulated PostScript images, representing organizations, manufacturers, and corporations. All trademarks represented in this collection are registered by their respective owners and are designed for editorial and advertising use.

Innovation Advertising & Design
   41 Mansfield Ave.
   Essex Junction, VT 05452
   800-255-0562

Corel Stock Photo Library.   200 CD-ROMs, 20,000 Photographs, all royalty free, high-resolution for use in everything from newsletters to T-shirts. This Kodak Photo CD is PC & Mac compatible and also includes such utilities as Corel Photo CD Lab, Corel Mosaic Visual File Manager, Corel Artview Screen Saver.

Corel
   1-613-728-0826 X 3080

Archive Films/Archive Photos.   A historical image library of more than 14,000 hours of historical stock footage drawn from newsreels, TV news, Hollywood feature films, silent films, historical documentaries, etc. All footage is shot and listed on a computer database for quick retrieval.

Archive Films/Archive Photos
    530 W. 25th St.
    New York, NY 10001
    800-876-5115

Backgrounds for Multimedia.   8- and 24-bit high-quality, full-screen images specifically designed with video, slide, animation, and texture-mapping applications in mind. Extras include tips, on-screen examples, and instructions for use in many software applications.

Airbeats
    P.O. Box 709
    Myrtle Creek, OR 97457
    800-444-9392

CD Link Volume 1.   A CD-ROM designed to be used with multimedia authoring tools, such as IBM's LinkWay, Storyboard Live and Windows. It includes 300 sound effects and music clips that can be used by educators and students to add pizzazz to their presentations. License rights to use the clip sounds are also included.

Educational Renaissance, Inc.
    2474 Woodchuck Way
    Sandy, UT 84093
    801-943-0841

Corel Gallery 2.   Able to work with all Windows-based application, this CD-ROM clip-art library provides 15,000 clip art images, 500 fonts, 500 photos, 75 sound clips, and 10 video clips, as well as a powerful multimedia file manager.

Corel
    613-728-0826

Video

Adobe Premier.   The hot-ticket for Macs—was even profiled on the Discovery channel.

Adobe Systems, Inc.
    1585 Charleston Rd.
    P.O. Box 7900
    Mountain View, CA 94039
    800-833-6687

CameraMan.   CameraMan is a screen movie-capture utility for Windows computers. Unlike screen capture utilities that can only capture static pictures of the screen, CameraMan records everything that takes place on the screen in real time to a standard movie file.

Motion Works USA
   524 Second St.
   San Francisco, CA 94107
   800-800-8476

D/Vision.   Enables you to produce edited videotapes and multimedia video. Uses Intel's i750/Indeo digital video board. Enables instant revision and playback of editorial decisions. Good price for the power. Touts SupeRTV which is an enhancement of Intel's RTV (real-time video); lets you "print" high-quality, full-screen video directly to videotape. There's actually two versions of this software. The basic system, which retails for under $500, is touted as being the lowest cost non-linear editing software on the market. The Pro version, retailing for slightly under $4000, turns your PC into a professional video production studio. It even stores over 70 hours of accessible, on-line digital video.

TouchVision Systems, Inc.
   1800 Winnemanc Ave.
   Chicago, IL 60640
   312-989-2160

VGA Producer Pro.   A VGA-to-NTSC genlockable encoder that enables you to transfer your multimedia work of art to videotape. Promises to be flicker-free.

Magni Systems, Inc.
   9500 SW Gemini Dr.
   Beaverton, OR 97005
   503-626-8400

DVA-4000.   A family of full-motion digital video adapters for IBM PC/AT, PS/2, or Mac computers.

VideoLogic, Inc.
   245 First St.
   Cambridge, MA 02142
   617-494-0530

Mediator.   High-quality computer graphics-to-video conversion system for Mac and VGA displays.

VideoLogic, Inc.
   245 First St.
   Cambridge, MA 02142
   617-494-0530

Pro Movie Spectrum.   This is a playback, capture, and editing add-in board with bundled software. Enables user to bring synchronized, full-motion video sequences to the PC.

Media Vision
   3185 Laurelview Ct.
   Fremont, CA 94538
   800-845-5870

Bandit. Bandit simplifies the process of transferring images between your computer and VCR or video camera. Bandit is a peripheral device, which works in the Mac and PC environments by connecting to either a SCSI or serial port.

Fast Forward Video
    18200-C W. McDurmott
    Irvine, CA 92714
    714-852-8404

Bravado. Combines full-featured, on-board VGA with live NTSC or PAL video-in-a-windows and controllable pass-through audio in one board. Apparently, a single-board multimedia presentation engine.

Truevision
    7240 Shadeland Stn.
    Indianapolis, IN 46256
    317-841-0332

Super Still-Frame Compression. Reduces storage requirements for captured video through JPEG 8:1 to 75:1-compression.

New Media Graphics
    780 Boston Rd.
    Billerica, MA 01821
    800-288-2207

VideoSpigot for Windows. Captures digital video from cameras, VCRs, laser discs, etc. Includes Microsoft Video for Windows, which enables editing of motion video sequences for embedding in any application that supports Object Linking and Embedding (OLE). CinePak software compression lets you stores AVI files at a fraction of their original size.

Creative Labs
    1901 McCarthy Blvd.
    Milpitas, CA 95035
    800-428-6600

Videovue. Ability to extract images from motion or still-frame video. Incoming video can be PAL, NTSC, composite or S-video.

Video Associates Labs
    4926 Spicewood Springs Rd.
    Austin, TX 78759
    800-331-0547

Intel Smart Video Recorder. One-step recording and Indeo compression allows a 50-MB 60-second clip to be stored in a relatively small 9 MB.

Intel Corp.
    2200 Mission College Blvd.
    Santa Clara, CA 95052
    800-538-3373

DigiTV. Built-in 122-channel cable-ready TV tuner, on-board 4-W stereo audio amplifier lets you watch TV through your PC.

Videomail, Inc.
568-4 Weddell Dr.
Sunnyvale, CA 94089
408-747-0223

Video Machine. Enables broadcast-quality video editing right on the desktop.

Fast Electronics
5 Commonwealth Rd.
Natick, MA 01760
508-655-FAST

TelevEyes. An inexpensive tool for converting computer VGA-to-recordable composite video. Allows displaying computer screens on any standard composite video monitor or recording VGS screens to video tape.

Digital Vision, Inc.
270 Bridge St.
Dedham, MA 02026
617-329-5400

WatchIT. This is an add-on board that allows you to watch TV on your PC. It runs under DOS or Windows using a pop-up remote control for TV adjustment.

New Media Graphics
780 Boston Rd.
Billerica, MA 01821
509-663-0666

PC Tele-VISION PLUS. This board allows an IBM-PC compatible computer to display NTSC or composite video in a window of variable size on a VGA or Super VGA monitor.

50/50 Micro Electronics
1249 Innsbruck Dr.
Sunnyvale, CA 94089
408-720-5050

TapeIT. An inexpensive video encoding board that converts VGA signals to NTSC or PAL.

New Media Graphics
780 Boston Rd.
Billerica, MA 01821
800-288-2207

The Indy Workstation. I haven't listed any multimedia PCs here because all vendors seem to be offering them. This is, however, unique. Silicon Graphics is now offering a workstation with a built-in color video camera for under $4995. Given the price of a multimedia-enabled PC nowadays, this workstation is worth a look-see. Remember, Silicon Graphics are the guys who brought you the special effects for Jurassic Park.

Silicon Graphics
   800-800-7441

Media add-in boards

ViVA.   This is truly a super board. It provides a low-cost multimedia solution by combining audio, video, and VGA—all on one board.

Omnicorp
   713-464-2990

MediaTime Adapter.   A NuBus adapter that combines CD-quality audio with 24-bit real-time digital video and graphics display for the MAC.

RasterOps
   2500 Walsh Ave.
   Santa Clara, CA 95051
   408-562-4200

Super VideoWindows.   Enables playing full-motion video and stereo audio from a TV camera, VCR, still-frame camera, videodisc, computer hard disk. Allows scalability, freeze or frame/grab, combination of audio/video, and VGA graphics.

New Media Graphics
   780 Boston Rd.
   Billerica, MA 01821
   800-288-2207

Super Motion Compression.   Captures clips of high-quality video and stereo audio, compresses and stores them to hard disk and allows instant playback.

New Media Graphics
   780 Boston Rd.
   Billerica, MA 01821
   800-288-2207

Video Blaster.   Integrates video and audio from a wide range of sources: cameras, VCRs, and video discs, then combines them with VGA graphics. Cropping, scaling, masking, and zooming capabilities. Includes a copy of Microsoft Video for Windows.

Creative Labs
   1901 McCarthy Blvd.
   Milpitas, CA 95035
   800-428-6600

Upgrade kits

Enables you to upgrade your PC for multimedia.

Sound Blaster Discovery CD 8 Upgrade Kit/Sound Blaster Discovery CD 16 Upgrade Kit. Includes sound card, stereo speakers, CD-ROM drive, and bundled software. The difference between two kits is the sound card; 16 is the higher quality. In both cases, the CD-ROM exceeds MPC specifications.

Creative Labs
　　1901 McCarthy Blvd.
　　Milpitas, CA 95035
　　800-428-6600

Media Vision Upgrades. Media Vision has several different upgrades. The CDPC is a unit that contains everything from a Sony CD-ROM drive, Pro AudioSpectrum audio digitizer, MIDI port, and amplifier. The Pro 16 MultiMedia System includes the Pro AudiSpectrum 16 sound card, a NEC SCSI CD-ROM, Windows 3.1, Lotus 1-2-3 on CD-ROM, Compton's Encyclopedia, Nautilus Multimedia Magazine on CD-ROM, MacroMind Action! on CD-ROM. This kit also includes a joystick port, and a stereo amplifier. The PC Upgrade Kit Plus is similar to the one just described, but instead of a 16-bit sound card, it has an 8-bit sound card. It also has a less-expensive CD-ROM drive.

Media Vision
　　47221 Fremont Ave.
　　Fremont, CA 94538
　　510-770-8600

MediaSonic Super Professional Deluxe. Upgrade either Mac or PC. Includes a pair of high-quality speakers; double-speed CD-ROM drive. Also includes a collection of titles.

April One Peripherals
　　4192 Fools Dr.
　　San Mateo, CA 94404
　　415-573-5170

Turtle Beach MultiSound MPC Upgrade Kit. This upgrade kit includes a MultiSound sound board and a CD-ROM drive.

Turtle Beach Systems
　　Cyber Center #33
　　1600 Pennsylvania Ave.
　　York, PA 17404
　　717-843-6916

Creative Omni4X Upgrade Kit. Designed for use in systems with or without a sound card, the Creative Omni4X Upgrade Kit features a quad-speed, internal CD-ROM drive that provides a transfer rate of 600 KB/s, 240-ms access time, 256-KB buffer memory, multisession Photo CD etc.

Creative Labs, Inc.
　　1901 McCarthy Blvd.
　　Milpitas, CA 95035
　　800-998-5227

Diamond Multimedia Kit 1000. The Multimedia Kit 100 contains everything users need to create their own affordable multimedia entertainment center: a fast double-speed CD-ROM drive with an access time of 250 ms, a WaveTable upgradeable 16-bit sound card, a pair of stereo speakers, and much more.

Diamond Multimedia Systems, Inc.
   1130 E. Arques Ave.
   Sunnyvale, CA 94086
   408-736-2000

Digital Schoolhouse. Turn your PC into a multimedia educational center with this exciting new product. It features Sound Blaster, double-speed internal CD-ROM drive, and much more.

Creative Labs, Inc.
   1901 McCarthy Blvd.
   Milpitas, CA 94035
   800-998-5227

Harmony Multimedia Power Kit II. Harmony's multimedia products re-designed to combine the latest in CD-ROM and audio technology. The Multimedia Power Kit II includes the Sound Blaster Pro, Panasonic CD-ROM drive, five CD titles, and five software programs.

WinSound 16 CD-ROM Kit. Gives multimedia aficionados the WinSound 16 sound-board capability, as well as a CD-ROM drive, computer speakers, joystick, and more than $1200 in free software.

Sigma Designs, Inc.
   46501 Landing Pkwy.
   Fremont, CA 94538
   510-770-0100

Laser disc players

Teac America, Inc. Makers of several high-end RS-232 controllable laser disc players for user in multimedia applications. The high-end of the product line enables WORM recordable.

Teac America, Inc.
   213-726-0303 X 659

Pioneer. RS-232 controllable laser disc players for use in multimedia applications.

Pioneer Communications 800-527-3766

Sony. Manufactures a series of RS-232 controllable laser disc players for use in multimedia applications.

Sony Multimedia Marketing Group
   Northeast 201-833-5200

Mid-Atlantic 301-577-4850
Southeast 404-263-9888
Southwest 214-550-5200
Midwest 708-773-6110
Northwest 408-944-4717
Western 714-229-4267

Networking

The following companies make devices and/or software that fit this tall order.

Fluent, Inc.
One Apple Hill
594 Worcester Rd.
Natick, MA 01760
508-651-0911

Starlight Networks
325 E. Middlefield Rd.
Mountain View, CA 94043
415-967-2774

Virtual MicroSystems
1825 S. Grant St.
Ste. 700
San Mateo, CA 94402
415-573-9596

Todd Enterprises
224-49 67th Ave.
Bayside, NY 11364
800-445-TODD

Artisoft
691 E. River Rd.
Tucson, AZ 85704
800-TINY-RAM ext. 600

CD-I players

CDI 350.   This is a portable CD-I player that sports a 6-inch active-matrix color LCD screen, NTSC or PAL compatibility, built-in pointing device, stereo speakers, etc.

Philips Consumer Electronics
1 Philips Dr.
P.O. Box 14810
Knoxville, TN 37914
800-835-3506

Kiosks

These are standalone units. You've seen them in museums, airports, and now even shopping centers.

ServiceTouch Kiosk.   Fully integrated self-service kiosk. Combines performance of a 486 computer, printer, speakers, and credit card reader with simplicity of a touch-screen interface.

MicroTouch Systems, Inc.
   55 Jonspin Rd.
   Wilmington, MA 01887
   508-694-9900

Touch Activity Center.   The IBM Ultimedia Touch Activity Center is a suite of multimedia kiosk solutions. Each of the solutions is a stand-alone cabinet-like enclosure kiosk-housing variations of IBM multimedia products.

IBM Multimedia Information Center
   P.O. Box 2150
   Atlanta, GA 30301
   800-IBM-9402 X 157

SmartTouch.   Touchscreen displays let you create your own kiosk solution.

Supermac
   485 Potrero Ave.
   Sunnyvale, CA 94086
   800-334-3005

Sound

20-20 Sound Editor.   A Windows program designed to deal with the audio part of multimedia presentation. Features include: fast, non-destructive waveform editing; powerful 8-tract audio file mixer, versatile multimedia browser, etc.

MKS Compu-Group, Inc.
   1730 Cunard St.
   Lava, PQ H7S 2B2
   514-332-4110

Ballade for Windows.   Record, play back, and print out sheet music with this production package. Pick and choose from a variety of musical sounds and sound effects contained in the computer sound card.

Dynaware
   950 Tower Ln., Ste. 1150
   Foster City, CA 94404
   415-349-5700

Cakewalk Home Studio.   Your PC can be turned into a multitrack recording studio with this innovative software package. Features include a virtual piano to record music with the keyboard or mouse.

Twelve Tone Systems
   P.O. Box 760
   Watertown, MA 02272
   800-234-1171

The Editor Plus.   Record one stereo sound file while listening to another with this software helpmate. It plays the file in the bottom waveform display window and records the new sound in the top window.

Digital Audio Labs
    114505 21st Ave., Ste. 202
    Plymouth, MN 55447
    612-473-7626

Knowledge Media Audio Plus.   Audio contains public domain, freeware, and shareware applications and data files, covering hundreds of sounds, sound effects, and MOD files.

Knowledge Media, Inc.
    436 Nunneley, Ste. B
    Paradise, CA 95969
    800-782-3766

MIDI Programmer's ToolKit for Windows.   The MIDI Programmer's ToolKit provides tools and documentation to assist Windows programmers in developing MIDI applications. All ToolKit features are found in a dynamic link library, which provides functions to easily access Standard MIDI files.

Music Quest, Inc.
    214-881-7408

Power Tracks Pro.   A full-featured, integrated 48-track MIDI sequencer and music notation program for Window 3.1. Power Tracks Pro can record, play back, and edit MIDI data.

P.G. Music, Inc.
    266 Elmwood Ave., Ste. 111
    Buffalo, NY 14222
    800-268-6272

MusicPrinter Plus.   A notation-based sequencer program that's chock full of such features as page view, automatic measure numbering, extended print to print, PCX files, accurate performance of artistic notation-rubato markings and more.

Temporal Acuity Products
    300 120th Ave. NE, Bldg. 1, Ste. 200
    Bellevue, WA 98005
    800-426-2673

Sound Impression.   Manage MIDI data, Waveform audio data (WAV files) and CD audio with this full-featured program. Among its attributes are the ability to create scores for multimedia presentation using WAV, CD and MIDI audio, and interface that appears and operates like a stereo component rack, extensive OLE support, etc.

Midisoft Corp.
   15379 NE 90th St.
   Redmond, WA 98052
   800-776-6434

AudioMan.   A portable hand-held device with a built-in microphone, speaker, and 8-bit sound digitizer. Really built to let you add verbal notes to your work, rather than handwritten notes.

Logitech, Inc.
   6505 Kaiser Dr.
   Fremont, CA 94555
   510-795-8500

PortAble Sound.   A parallel-port portable sound device with bundled DOS and Windows software.

Digispeech, Inc.
   550 Main St.
   Ste. J
   Placerville, CA 95667
   916-621-1787

SoundXchange.   Business-level audio solution using a telephone instead of a microphone.

Interactive
   204 N. Main
   Humboldt, SD 57035
   800-292-2112

Sound Blaster Deluxe/Sound Blaster Pro Deluxe/Sound Blaster 16 ASP.   A variety of cards for every need. Creative Labs creates sound cards for those interested in gaming (Sound Blaster Deluxe), as well as those interested in 16-bit, CD-quality sound (Sound Blaster 16 ASP).

Creative Labs
   1901 McCarthy Blvd.
   Milpitas, CA 95035
   800-428-6600

Wave Blaster.   A MIDI add-on daughter board to the Sound Blaster 16 card. Wave Blaster provides realistic instrument sounds, instead of FM synthesized sound.

Creative Labs
   1901 McCarthy Blvd.
   Milpitas, CA 95035
   800-428-6600

Audioport/Microkey.   Two products that let you take sound on the road. With Audioport, you can both record play sound; with Microkey, you can only play sound. Both devices are tiny and fit into the parallel port of your laptop computer. Uses 12-bit sampling and a 3:1 compression ratio for storage.

Video Associates Labs
    4926 Spicewood Springs Rd.
    Austin, TX 78759
    800-331-0547

Audioport.   Antex's Audioport (not to be confused with Creative Labs' product of the same name) is an external device that offers broadcast-quality digital audio. It interfaces with PCs via the parallel port and records or plays digital audio direct-to-disk.

Antex Electronics Corp.
    16100 South Figueroa St.
    Gardena, CA 90248
    310-532-3092

AdLib Gold.   This board is one of the standards in multimedia sound. Roughly equivalent to Creative Labs' Sound Blaster. Both of these boards are popular on the gaming side of the industry. Quality might not be what you're looking for in the professional arena.

AdLib Multimedia
    800-463-2686

Port Blaster.   A portable solution for "on-the-road" business or multimedia presentations. Works with a parallel port.

Creative Labs
    1901 McCarthy Blvd.
    Milpitas, CA 95035
    800-428-6600

UltraSound.   Can perform mixing of CD-audio, digital audio, synthesizers, a microphone, and line input.

Advanced Graphics Computer Technology
    604-431-5020

Microsoft Sound System.   Built primarily to add verbal notes to Windows applications, such as your spreadsheet or word processing document. Also has ProofReader, which provides an audible proofing of numbers and Voice Pilot, which enables users to execute commands by voice.

Microsoft Corp.
    One Microsoft Way
    Redmond, WA 98052
    206-882-8080

Roland SCC-1 Sound Card.   This card seems to be quite popular with those interested in recording high-fidelity music.

Roland Corp.
7200 Dominion Circle
Los Angles, CA 90040
213-685-5141

Audio Solution Board. Basically available through OEMs, IBM's Audio Solution Board supports Windows, OS/2, and DOS. Available either in ISA (Industry Standard Architecture) or Micro Channel bus versions for IBM's own PS/2 series. This board enables 16-bit audio.

IBM
800-426-3333

Sound Galaxy. Offers 8- or 16-bit sounds cards, as well as multimedia upgrade kits.

Aztech Labs, Inc.
46707 Fremont Blvd.
Fremont, CA 94538
510-623-8988

Midisoft Studio for Windows. MIDI recording/editing software that delivers the power of a professional music studio to your multimedia PC.

Midisoft Corp.
15513 NE 52nd St.
Redmond, WA 98052
206-881-7176

Trax. Easy-to-use software for the MIDI beginner.

Passport Designs, Inc.
100 Stone Pine Rd.
Half Moon Bay, CA 94019
415-726-0280

Wave for Windows. Professional audio software for Windows.

Turtle Beach Systems
P.O. Box 5074
York, PA 17405
717-843-6916

Monologue. A software product for Windows that adds speech to your applications.

First Byte
19840 Pioneer Ave.
Torrance, CA 90503
800-545-7677

IBM Speech Recognition Family. Brings the power of speech to AIX and OS/2 workstations. Has an active vocabulary of over 20,000 words and a sophisticated language model.

IBM Multimedia Information Center
  P.O. Box 2150
  Atlanta, GA 30301
  800-772-2227

20-20 Sound Editor.   An audio editing toolset for the IBM platform. Provides cut, paste, copy, an 8-track audio mixer, and special effects.

MKS Compu-Group, Inc.
  1730 Cunard St.
  Laval, PQ H7S 2B2
  514-332-4110

Read My Lips.   Not a George Bush record, but software for the Mac that lets users record voice or sounds and attach digitized audio clips to documents.

Praxitel
  Box 452
  Pleasanton, CA 94566
  510-846-9380

MCS Stereo.   The complete interface to your computer's audio capability. Controls CD-ROMs, plays, records, and edits WAV files, and has an integrated database for all of your audio sources.

Animotion Development
  3720 4th Ave. S. #205
  Birmingham, AL 35222
  205-591-5715

FluentLinks.   This NetWare Loadable Module enables multiple users to retrieve and play motion video and audio segments over industry-standard networks.

Fluent, Inc.
  One Apple Hill
  594 Worcester Rd.
  Natick, MA 01760
  508-651-0911

ACS300.1 Computer Speaker System.   Lets users hear digital audio sound with their computers. Users can plug this computer speaker system into any audio or video card to vastly enhance any business presentation (etc.) with the same level of recording quality as a music CD.

Altec Lansing Multimedia
  P.O. Box 277
  Milford, PA 18337-0277
  800-648-6663

AudioPrisma.   A professional digital audio workstation integrated onto a single system board. Contains everything needed for complete audio editing and production for multimedia applications.

Spectral Synthesis
    19501 144th Ave. NE, Ste. 100A
    Woodville, WA 98072
    206-487-2931

The CardD Plus. Specifically created for professional recording applications, this product delivers sonic performance that is equal to none. It comes complete with a Windows 3.1 driver and can be used with any Windows-compatible sound-editing software.

Digital Audio Labs
    14502 21st Ave., Ste. 202
    Plymouth, MN 55447
    612-473-7626

SoundMan Wave. SoundMan Wave is a wave table synthesis board coupled with up-to-the-minute 16-bit stereo. Audio will no longer sound computer-generated, but like real instruments.

Logitech, Inc.
    65505 Kaiser Dr.
    Fremont, CA 94555
    800-231-7717

Animation

Photorealism. That's what Strata calls their series of packages for the Mac. There's a bunch of them. Stratavision 3D is a 3D animation program; Stratatextures are collections of realistic-looking materials that can be applied to objects.

Strata
    2 W. Saint George Blvd.
    Ste. 2100
    St. George, UT 84770
    801-628-5218

DPS Personal Animation Recorder. This IBM-PC compatible recorder compliments all 3D applications, including 3D Studio and TOPAS Professional. Record your animations onto a dedicated hard drive and play them back in real time—3D animations without the expense of single-frame tape decks!

ElectriImage Animation System Version 2.5. Speed and quality. The color jumps and shouts; images that can make you forget you're watching Macintosh generated computer graphics. This package is the only per-frame render anywhere.

Electric Image, Inc.
    818-577-1627, ext. 224
    sales@electricimg.com

Real3D. A full-featured 3D animation, modeling, and rendering program for the Amiga. Enables objects to "rock and roll" and react to their environment with "intelligence."

RealSoft
    544 Queen St.
    Chatham, ON N7M 2J6
    407-539-0752

Animator Pro. This software has won a bunch of awards. It's a high-resolution, 2D paint, and animation software program for the PC. Provides a repertoire of special effects, such as tweening and color cycling.

Autodesk, Inc.
    2320 Marinship Way
    Sausalito, CA 94965
    415-332-2344

3D Studio. The superb animation product that made Autodesk a household name. Comes with over 500 MB of 3D objects, textures, and animation. Not cheap, though.

Autodesk, Inc.
    2320 Marinship Way
    Sausalito, CA 94965
    415-332-2344

Cyberspace Developer Kit. One of Autodesk's superb animation products. It's a complete toolset for 3D visualization and simulation. In other words, it lets you create virtual-reality applications.

Autodesk, Inc.
    2320 Marinship Way
    Sausalito, CA 94965
    415-332-2344

Animation Works Interactive. Sophisticated animation system with interactivity support, multimedia extensions support, and MCI support.

Gold Disk, Inc.
    5155 Spectrum Way, Unit 5
    Mississauga, ON L4W 5A1
    310-320-5080

Creative Toonz 2D CEL. This is animation software for Silicon Graphics workstations. Enables animators to experiment with up to 32 different fill colors, add 3D animations, build a picture base of images, use scanner input, etc.

Softimage, Inc.
    660 Newton-Yardley Rd.
    Ste. 202
    Newton, PA 18940
    215-860-5525

Liberty. A UNIX-based high-end graphics package coupled with animation tools.

Softimage, Inc.
   660 Newton-Yardley Rd.
   Ste. 202
   Newton, PA 18940
   215-860-5525

3D Choreographer.   3D Choreographer is a model-based 3D animation program for Windows. Users create animated sequences with pre-drawn people, 3D shapes, etc. Each character is customizable and has an extensive library of predefined actions.

AniCom, Inc.
   P.O. Box 428
   Columbia, MD 21045
   800-949-4559

Animation Gallery.   Animation Gallery contains more than 100 3D animations for use with any presentation manager that handles Audodesk 3D studio FLI-files.

Wizardware Multimedia, Ltd.
   918 Delaware Ave.
   Bethlehem, PA 18015
   800-548-5969

Animation How-To CD.   This intermediate-level book offers hands-on explanations that show users how to create dynamic moving objects. Each animation idea is explained, then the steps required to produce it are presented.

Waite Group Press
   200 Tamai Plaza Ct.
   Madera, CA 94925
   800-368-9369

Animation Paint Box.   Animation Paint Box for Windows offers exceptional productivity tools for 8-bit animators. Features include the ability to resize frames, extensive file conversion, ability to load a portion of a large animation, etc.

Azeena Technologies, Inc.
   P.O. Box 29169
   Long Beach, CA 90806
   310-981-2771

Animation Master.   Animation Master, the three-dimensional motion picture studio, is a powerful and affordable spline-based modeling and animation program specifically designed for classic character animation. Features include: inverse kinematics, time-based materials, image mapping, etc.

Hash, Inc.
   2800 E. Evergreen Blvd.
   Vancouver, WA 98661
   206-750-0042

Caligari trueSpace.   Caligari trueSpace for Windows enables users to easily create advanced 3D graphics. In a real-world 3D perspective, users can twist and bend simple cylinders and spheres into sophisticated, organic shapes with free-form deformation and point-editing.

Caligari Corp.
   1955 Landings Dr.
   Mountain View, CA 94043
   800-351-7620

Frame By Frame Graphic Animation System.   Frame By Frame Graphic Animation Systems enable producers to capture VFW or Quick Time movies and computer graphics directly to Panasonic videodisc recorders for instant playback or full-screen, full-resolution video and animation.

Image Management Systems
   239 W. 15th St.
   New York, NY 10011
   212-741-8765

MicroScribe-3D.   Compatible with most currently available 3D graphics packages including AutoCAD, 3D Studio, Wavefront, SoftImage, Alias and Form-Z. This tool enhances 3D animations without heavy out-of-pocket expenses.

Immersion Corp.
   2158 Paragon Dr.
   San Jose, CA 95131
   800-893-1160
   immersion@starconn.com

3D

Crystal Kaleidoscope.   This 3D animation suite answers all of your dreams and desires—multimedially speaking. It features Crystal TOPAS Professional 5.1, an extremely user-friend 3D animation software.

CrystalGraphics
   3110 Patrick Henry Dr.
   Santa Clara, CA 95054
   800-TOPAS-3D

Viewpoint Data Labs.   The world's largest 3D library available at one low price per title; no royalties, just one low, flat fee.

Viewpoint Data Labs
   625 S. State St.
   Orem, UT 84058
   800-328-2738

Photographic

Adobe Photoshop.   Perhaps the most popular product in the photo manipulation market. Enables user to retouch scanned photo and add significant amounts of creativity. Can make a photo look like original artwork. Runs under MAC or Windows.

Adobe Systems, Inc.
   1585 Charleston Rd.
   P.O. Box 7900
   Mountain View, CA 94039
   800-833-6687

Aldus PhotoStyler.   A close second to Adobe's product, but cheaper. Has all the quality and functionality you'd expect an Aldus product to have.

Aldus Corp.
   411 First Ave. S.
   Seattle, WA 98104
   206-622-5500

Video

PrimeTime.   Broadcast-quality character generation for the PC.

InnoVision Technology
   1933 Davis St.
   Ste. 238
   San Leandro, CA 94577
   800-238-8838

VideoFusion.   A complete software solution for QuickTime post-production. Create an MTV-style video that combines video, text, and graphics. Provides: 2D warps, morphing, transitions, and color transformations.

VideoFusion
   1722 Indian Wood Circle
   Ste. H
   Maumee, OH 43537
   800-638-5253

Splice.   Originally a DVI, ActionMedia II-based video editor, Splice now supports Microsoft's Video for Windows. Allows for full editing for AVS, AVI, and WAV files, as well as conversion and mixing.

Digital Media International
   352 Arch St.
   Ste. B
   Sunbury, PA 17801
   717-286-6068

Adobe Premier.   A MAC tool for creating high-quality Quicktime digital movies and videotapes. Premier is a powerful editing program that lets users combine video, audio, animation, still images, and graphics.

Adobe Systems, Inc.
    1585 Charleston Rd.
    P.O. Box 7900
    Mountain View, CA 94039
    800-833-6687

VideoShop.   VideoShop enables the development of digital movies or video-tapes on the MAC platform. The system provides the ability to combine video, graphics, PhotoCD, text, and CD-quality audio. VideoShop features include: 75 digital effects and filters, resizing any movie, layering of movies, graphics and titling, editing playout window, movie manager, and full-screen recording.

Diva 222
    Third St.
    Cambridge, MA 02142
    800-FYI-DIVA

Media Suite Pro.   This beginner's or non-professional video presentation suite runs on the MAC. An easy-to-use interface permits simple and rapid editing of video sequences, making you look like an expert.

Avid Technology, Inc.
    One Metropolitan Park W.
    Tewksbury, MA 01876
    800-949-AVID

Video Toaster 4000.   The Video Toaster reportedly replaces approximately $100,000 of broadcast production equipment. Running on the Amiga platform, the Video Toaster enables users to make broadcast-quality production videos.

NewTek, Inc.
    215 SE 8th St.
    Topeka, KS 66603
    900-847-6111

After Effects.   A special-effects application for QuickTime, designed to enable the MAC-based video producer to create the high-quality video productions. Enables composite layering of moving video and animation, generation of moving mattes and fading, rotating, and repositioning of images.

COSA
    14 Imperial Place
    Ste. 203
    Providence, RI 02903
    401-831-2672

Video For Windows.   A major extension to the Windows operating system, along with a series of utilities for creating and editing digital movies. These digital movies can be played back on any standard MPC compliance PC.

Utilities shipped with the product allow users to create, edit, and playback VRW clips in the AVI format. This product is shipped with most video add-in-boards.

Microsoft Corp.
   One Microsoft Way
   Redmond, WA 98052
   206-936-4423

QuickTime for Windows.   The Apple leader goes Windows. This is the preferred choice of experts.

Apple Computer
   20525 Mariani Ave.
   Cupertino, CA 95014
   408-996-1010

FluentLinks.   This NetWare-loadable module enables multiple users to retrieve and play motion video and audio segments over industry-standard networks.

Fluent, Inc.
   One Apple Hill
   594 Worcester Rd.
   Natick, MA 01760
   508-651-0911

Morphing

If you've seen Terminator 2, you know what morphing is. Basically, you have a starting point and an ending point; then the computer makes the gradual transition between the two. You've also seen this done in one too-many music videos.

Morph

Gryphon Software Corp.
   7720 Trade St.
   Ste. 120
   San Diego, CA 92121
   619-536-8815

HSC Digital Morph

HSC Software
   1661 Lincoln Blvd.
   Ste. 101
   Santa Monica, CA 90404
   310-392-8441

Graphics

addDepth for Windows.   A graphics application tool that adds 3D impact to type and line art. Users enter text or choose their artwork and depth and perspective are added automatically.

Ray Dream, Inc.
    1804 N. Shoreline Blvd.
    Mountain View, CA 94043
    800-846-0111

Color Tools.   Color Tools is a complete graphics solution for multimedia presentation. Color Tools provides a comprehensive set of line drawing tools, paint and effects brushes, and enhancement capabilities for all types of presentation screens, information displays, training applications, and more.

Time Arts, Inc.
    1425 Corporate Center Pkwy.
    Santa Rosa, CA 95407
    707-576-7722

Creative License.   Users can create and edit images, textures, and backgrounds with this affordable graphics package. It contains a broad range of pressure-sensitive drawing and painting tools.

Time Arts, Inc.
    1425 Corporate Center Pkwy.
    Santa Rosa, CA 95407

Designer 4.0.   Featuring a 32-bit graphics engine, this tool allows users unequaled precision, power, and performance for illustration on a PC. Features include streamlined interface, precision symbol creation, and editing with 29 drawing tools.

Micrografx, Inc.
    1303 E. Arapaho
    Richardson, TX 75081
    800-326-3576

Lumena.   Lumena is a powerful raster paint, vector draw, animation and videographics software package for DOS-based systems.

Time Arts, Inc.
    1425 Corporate Center Pkwy.
    Santa Rosa, CA 95407
    707-576-7722

Professional Ddraw.   Professional Ddraw is a precision illustration program with built-in desktop publishing and high-end color control. A snap-top modifier palette allows precise sizing and placement of objects on the fly.

Gold Disk, Inc.
    3350 Scott Blvd., Bldg. 14
    Santa Clara, CA 95054
    800-465-3375

Altamira Composer 1.01.   A revolutionary image-composition application for Windows that allows image elements to be automatically masked and anti-aliased through Dynamic Alpha technology and float as independent objects in an infinite stack.

Altamira Software Corp.
150 Shoreline Hwy.
Ste. B-27
Mill Valley, CA 94941
800-425-8264

Chroma Tools. This is a file-conversion utility for TARGA users. It converts TGA, PCX, GIF, TIF, BMP, MAC TIF, and VST images to TGA, PCX, GIF, TIF, VST, BMP, MAC TIF, and color/black and white PostScript. It supports all screen modes and includes multiple color-reduction algorithms.

Videotex Systems, Inc.
214-231-9200

EasyCopy/X. This package offers an X Window-based tool for capture and production of high-quality, full-color images. It works independently of any application and provides an OSF/Motif-based user interface, which permits users to work directly from the command line. It also allows direct printing of images.

Image-in. A Windows-based editing tool that provides utilities for drawing, painting and editing, or manipulating color, black and white, or gray-scale images.

CPI, Inc.
1820 Gateway Dr., Bldg. 3, Ste. 370
San Francisco, CA 94404
800-345-3540

"Pixel Perfect" Graphics. A CD-ROM that contains more than 2000 images in 11 formats in 300 dpi (high resolution). Categories include Animals, Business, Computers, Food, High Tech, Holidays, States, Countries, etc.

Wizardware Multimedia, Ltd.
918 Delaware Ave.
Bethlehem, PA 18015
610-866-9613

Digital Morph. With an easy-to-use image manipulation tool, users can now add exciting visual impact to their presentations with this sophisticated morphing tool. Users can morph from one still image to another or between moving images.

HSC Software
6303 Carpinteria Ave.
Carpinteria, CA 93013
805-566-6200

Image Partner. A full-featured image processing and analysis program that offers high resolution with up to $1,024 \times 768 \times 256$ gray-scale imaging displayable on Super/Extended VGA PC systems. One unique capability includes video camera characterization, which permits users to understand and quantify the systematic errors in imaging systems.

Image Automation
    7 Henry Clay Dr.
    Merimack, NH 03054
    603-598-3400

JAG for Windows. Concerned with the quality of digital images, JAG can be used to smooth out the stair-stepped edges in color and gray-scale graphics. It works with the popular paint, graphics, and image editing packages.

Ray Dream, Inc.
    1804 N. Shoreline Blvd.
    Mountain View, CA 94043
    800-846-0111

Picture Publisher 5.0. Picture Publisher is a professional image editing program that provides a combination of speed, functionality, and ease of use. Features include: object layers, intuitive interface, image browser, etc.

Micrografx, Inc.
    1303 E. Arapaho
    Richardson, TX 75081
    800-326-3576

3D Modeling Lab. Crystal-clear, hands-on examples enables users to learn 3D modeling, rendering and animation for the PC. They can design 3D images and animation for products, presentations, etc.

Waite Group Press
    200 Tamal Plaza Ct.
    Madera, CA 94925
    800-368-9369

Cheetah 3D. Render and animate complex 3D images with this powerful multimedia tool. Standard rendering features include up to 10 parallel light sources with spectacular and ambient light controls. High-end features include multiple area rendering, bit-map textures, etc.

Looking Glass Software
    11222 La Cienga Blvd, Ste. 305
    Inglewood, CA 90304
    310-348-8240

Envision. With unparalleled realism and rendering quality, this tool allows users to see their finished designs in photorealistic detail and 24-bit color. It renders any image and applies surface details, textures, or finishes on any background image.

ModaCAD
    1954 Cotner Ave.
    Los Angeles, CA 90025
    310-312-6632

Fractals for Windows. With a zoom box and menus, mouse users can create new Fractals and control more than 85 different fractal types. Bundled with WinFract, this package speedily computes mind-bending Fractals.

Waite Group Press
200 Tamal Plaza Ct.
Madera, CA 94925
800-368-9369

Imagine. A 3D image processing program that lets users create any kind of character with numberless effects applied to that character. Once users have snared the look that they have imagined, they can make those characters live through the extensive use of Imagine's animation capabilities.

Impulse, Inc.
8416 Xerxes Ave. N.
Brooklyn Park, MN 56544
800-328-0184

MacroModel. This package enables users to twist or bend 3D objects. Because there is a version for the Mac as well as for the IBM PC platforms, images created on one can be easily transferred to the other.

Macromedia, Inc.
600 Townsend St.
San Francisco, CA 94103
800-288-8229

223: The Stereo Paint System. A paint system that provides the ability to create true 3D, stereoscopic images. Also permits conversion of pre-existing 2D images into 3D images.

Latent Image Development Corp.
Digital Media Group
111 Fourth Ave.
New York, NY 10003
212-388-0122

Adobe Illustrator. A powerful professional design tool. Enables designers to draw from scratch or work with existing images. Supports: 16.7 million colors, text, generate separations, custom views and page sizes, objects manipulation (such as dividing, slicing, and combining), etc.

Adobe Systems, Inc.
1585 Charleston Rd.
P.O. Box 7900
Mountain View, CA 94039
800-833-6687

Painterly Effects. UNIX-based set of filters that let you turn boring images into classic art.

Softimage, Inc.
   660 Newton-Yardley Rd.
   Ste. 202
   Newton, PA 18940
   215-860-5525

Players

MultiMedia Works.   A universal player that supports 40 file formats including AVI, Quicktime, DVI, FLC, FLI, CD-Audio, WAV, and MIDI. Can embed into any Windows application.

Lenel Systems International, Inc.
   19 Tobey Village Office Park
   Pittsford, NY 14534-1763
   716-248-9720

PACo.   An audio/visual playback system. Platform-independent. Included is PACo Producer, which creates and presents animations, digital videos, visualizations and audio files in conjunction with MAC applications.

COSA
   14 Imperial Place
   Ste. 203
   Providence, RI 02903
   401-831-2672

Virtual reality

Because this is a category unto itself, I've decided to lump hardware and software together.

Mandala.   Almost impossible to explain. Using a video camera, this software puts you in your own virtual world. It is currently used by the Nickelodeon Channel.

 The Vivid Group
   317 Adelaide St. W.
   Ste. 302
   Toronto, ON M5V 1P9
   416-340-9290

Head-mounted displays.   Optics for head-mounted displays; cyberface head-mounted displays; other stereo optical equipment (cameras, etc.).

Leep Systems
   241 Crescent St.
   Waltham, MA 02154
   617-647-1395

WorldToolKit. WorldToolKit is a virtual-reality applications development toolkit that runs on a variety of robust hardware platforms. Basically, World Toolkit is a rendering, or visualization, software package that makes the impossible possible.

SENSE8 Corp.
4000 Bridgeway, Ste. 101
Sausalito, CA 94965
415-331-6318

ADL-1 Tracker. A sophisticated and inexpensive 6D tracking system that converts position and orientation information into computer-readable form. The ADL-1 calculates head/object position with six degrees of freedom by use of a lightweight, multiple-jointed arm. Sensors mounted on the arm measure the angles of the joints. The microprocessor-based control unit uses these angles to compute position-orientation information in a user-selectable coordinate system, which is then transmitted to the host computer.

Shooting Star Technology
1921 Holdon Ave.
Burnaby, BC V4B 3W4
604-298-8574

Spaceball 2003. The Spaceball 2003 is a 3D control device. With six simultaneous degrees of freedom control, users are able to manipulate 3D screen models or conduct virtual scene walkthroughs or flythroughs, as easily and intuitively, as if they performed these tasks in the real world. The spaceball consists of a tennis ball-sized sphere fixed on a stand. Users place their wrist on the stand and grasp the ball with their fingertips. They gently push, pull, or twist the ball to move the 3D screen object, in corresponding directions and speeds, in real time. Screen object or screen movement is smooth and dynamic. The Spaceball is supported on major workstation and person computer platforms and in a host of applications—from mechanical CAD to virtual reality.

Spaceball Technologies, Inc.
600 Suffolk St.
Lowell, MA 01854
508-970-0330

Flight Helmet. A head-mounted display.

Virtual Research
408-748-8712

Grip Master. A force sensor.

EXOS, Inc.
8 Blanchard Rd.
Burlington, MA 01803
617-229-2075

Cyberspace Developer Kit.   One of Autodesk's superb animation products. It's a complete toolset for 3D visualization and simulation. In other words, lets you create virtual-reality applications.

Autodesk, Inc.
  2320 Marinship Way
  Sausalito, CA 94965
  415-332-2344

Distant Suns/VistaPro.   Use your PC to simulate the night sky (Distant Suns) or create electronic landscapes. I heard that Arthur Clarke (author of 2001) is using this software to get "images" for his next book.

Virtual Reality Laboratories
  2341 Ganador Ct.
  San Luis Obispo, CA 93401
  805-545-8515

EYEGEN 3.   A head-mounted display that uses monochrome CRTs and color wheels to improve resolution and decrease weight. EYEGEN 3 has a screen resolution of 369,750 color elements. Adjustments include Inter-Pupilary Distance (IPD), focus, display release, and double ratchet headband.

Virtual Research
  3193 Belick St. Ste. #2
  Santa Clara, CA 95054
  408-748-8712

Smart 3D.   This 3D rendering system lets both Mac and Windows users manipulate objects in real-time. The nice thing about this package is that the images take up little space, about 200 KB to 500 KB, compared to 100 MB in other packages.

Macromedia, Inc.
  600 Townsend St.
  San Francisco, CA 94103
  800-288-8229

Catalogs

The following mail-order companies specialize in multimedia hardware/software.

Tiger Software
  800 Douglas Entrance
  Executive Tower
  7th Fl.
  Coral Gables, FL 33134
  800-888-4437

DAK Industries Inc.
 8200 Remmet Ave.
 Canoga Park, CA 91304
 919-888-8220

Conversion

Windowcraft. Converts Mac HyperCard stacks into Windows execute-only files.

Windowcraft Corp.
 1000 Main St.
 Acton, MA 01720
 508-263-7674

Media clips. Wallace Music & Sound, Inc., provides original music and sound effects for software developers and publishers.

Wallace Music & Sound, Inc.
 6210 West Pershing Ave.
 Glendale, AZ 95304
 602-979-6201

MusicBytes gives you access to dozens of exciting and dynamic production tunes ranging from rock to classical and from industrial to novelty. No licensing problems.

Soundtrack Express. Compatible with all authoring and presentation tools, is an unlimited source of professional-quality music for multimedia.

BlueRibbon Soundtracks, Ltd.
 P.O. Box 8689
 Atlanta, GA 30306
 800-226-0212

Multimedia Music Library. Multimedia Music Library is a collection of more than 100 pop and orchestral musical sequences. Royalty-free.

Midisoft Corp.
 P.O. Box 1000
 Bellevue, WA 98009
 206-881-7176

Killer Tracks. Killer Tracks is a series of music selections.

Killer Tracks
 6534 Sunset Blvd.
 Hollywood, CA 90028
 800-877-0078

HyperClips for Windows. HyperClips for Windows is a CD-ROM volume that contains hundreds of high-quality animation and sound clips to accent business, sales, and technical presentations.

The HyperMedia Group
  5900 Hollis St.
  Ste. O
  Emeryville, CA 94608
  510-601-0900

The DigiSound Audio Library. The DigiSound Audio Library brings exciting, full-fidelity sound to multimedia with professionally produced MIDI music, sound effects, and DigiVoice clips.

Presentation Graphics Group
  270 N. Canon Dr.
  Ste. 103
  Beverly Hills, CA 90210
  310-277-3050

Aris Entertainment. Aris Entertainment offers several sets of CD-ROMs for Windows, MAC, and PCs that contain a combination of sound effects, full-color photographs, and/or video clips. Under the trade name of MediaClips, the following sets illustrate the Aris offerings: Worldview: space images and sounds; Wild Places: North American photos and audio clips; Majestic Places: nature photos and audio clips; Business Background: photos, audio clips, and sound effects.

Aris Entertainment, Inc.
  4444 Via Marina, Ste. 811
  Marina del Rey, CA 90292
  310-821-0234
  800-228-2747

Digital Zone. Digital Zone hires professional photographers to take stunning photos. The photos are then stored on Kodak's Photo CD and are free to use for purchasers of one of the collections.

Digital Zone, Inc.
  P.O. Box 5562
  Bellevue, WA 98006
  800-538-3113

Archive Films/Archive Photos. Archive Films/Archive Photos contain thousands of hours of historical and entertainment footage and stills produced from 1894 until the present. Includes: Albert Einstein, Jacob Astor, Hollywood, presidents, kings, the Depression, etc.

Archive New Media
  530 W. 25th St.
  New York, NY 10001
  212-620-3980

CBS News Archives.   CBS News Archives offers just that.

CBS
   524 W. 57 St.
   New York, NY 10019
   212-975-2875

Buyout Music Library.   Buyout Music Library offers hours of royalty-free original music on CD.

Musi-Q
   305-572-9276

Station Break.   Station Break contains collections of license-free music. Pick by theme, such as Crime, Haunted, etc.

Station Break Music
   40 Glen St.
   Ste. 1
   Glen Cove, NY 11542
   800-ON-AIR-99

Video Tape Library.   Video Tape Library offers news clips, such as the LA Riot, gang shootings, sports, etc.

VTL
   1509 N. Crescent Heights Blvd.
   Ste. 2
   Los Angles, CA 90046
   213-656-4330

PhotoDisc.   PhotoDisc contains, on each CD, 336 multipurpose images on CD-ROM from award-winning photographers of landscapes, rain forests, deserts, animals, etc. Arranged in a user-friendly slide show.

PhotoDisc
   2013 4th Ave.
   Seattle, WA 98121
   206-441-9355

Clipper.   Clipper is a monthly clip art subscription service. You have choice of medium: paper, floppy, or CD-ROM. Each month, subscribers get a variety of themed images from leading artists.

Dynamic Graphics, Inc.
   6000 N. Forest Park Dr.
   P.O. Box 1901
   Peoria, IL 61656
   800-255-8800

Masterclips.   Masterclips has a collection of 6000 images on 60 different categories.

Masterclips, Inc.
    5201 Ravenswood Rd.
    Ste. 111
    Ft. Lauderdale, FL 33312
    800-292-2547

Magazines/Journals

Advanced Imaging.   Covers all facets of imaging including video. Monthly and free.

PTN Publishing
    445 Broad Hollow Rd.
    Melville, NY 11747
    516-845-2700

Interactivity.   All the info you need (and then some) on multimedia. Departments include Case Studies, Authoring Tools, etc.

Miller Freeman
    411 Borel Ave.
    Ste. 100
    San Mateo, CA 94402

AmigaWorld.   Amiga gets short shrift most of the time. But it's a great multimedia platform. The magazine is published monthly for $19.97/year.

AmigaWorld
    P.O. Box 595
    Mt. Morris, IL 61054
    800-827-0877

AVC Presentation.   Magazine geared for those involved in visual communications. Published monthly and free.

PTN Publishing
    445 Broad Hollow Rd.
    Melville, NY 11747
    516-845-2700

Boardwatch Magazine.   Actually directed to on-line users of bulletin boards, but a good source of information.

5970 South Vivian St.
    Littleton, CO 80127
    800-933-6038

Business Publishing.   Specifically for those interested in corporate publishing. Information on desktop publishing and electronic delivery. Published monthly. $24 per year.

Hitchcock Publishing Co.
   191 S. Gary Ave.
   Carol Stream, IL 60188
   800-234-0733
   708-665-1000

CD-I World.   Bi-monthly CD-I magazine on paper and disk.

Parker Taylor & Company, Inc.
   49 Bayview, Ste. 200
   Camden, ME 04843
   207-236-8524

CD-ROM Professional.   Monthly journal covering CD-ROM and optical publishing industries. $86 per year.

Pemberton Press, Inc.
   11 Tannery Ln.
   Weston, CT 06883
   203-227-8466

CD-ROMWORLD.   Information on new titles and techniques in the ever-expanding world of CD-ROM. Published monthly. $87 per year.

Meckler Corp.
   11 Ferry Ln. W.
   Westport, CT 06880
   203-226-6967

Computer Pictures.   Wonderful bi-monthly graphics publication. $40 per year.

Montage Publishing, Inc.
   Knowledge Industries Publications, Inc.
   701 Westchester Ave.
   White Plains, NY 10604
   914-328-9157

Consumer Multimedia Report.   Oriented toward gaming, interactive video, etc. Monthly. $395 per year.

Warren Publishing, Inc.
   2115 Ward Ct. NW
   Washington, DC 20037
   202-872-9200

Desktop Video World.   Similar to Digital Video magazine. Bi-monthly. $19.97/year.

Desktop Video World
   P.O. Box 594
   Mt. Morris, IL 61054

Digital Media.   A monthly publication that provides the usual high level of Seybold insight. $395 per year.

Seybold Publications
   428 E. Baltimore Pike
   P.O. Box 644
   Media, PA 19063
   215-565-2480

Digital Publishing Business.   Newsletter published for Optical Publishing Association members. Edited by Richard Bowers.

Optical Publishing Association
   P.O. Box 21268
   Columbus, OH 43221
   614-442-8805

Digital Technology Report.   Bi-weekly report on digital publishing in the consumer arena. $395 per year.

Digital Technology Report
   102-30 67th Ave.
   Forest Hills, NY 11375
   718-997-1581

Digital Video.   Bi-monthly magazine published by the mega-technology publishing group IDG. Very oriented toward experts. $24 per year.

TechMedia Publishing
   80 Elm St.
   Peterborough, NH 03458
   603-924-0100

Information Today.   Monthly magazine about information resources. $41.95 per year.

Learned Information, Inc.
   143 Old Marlton Pike
   Medford, NJ 08055
   609-654-6266

Interactive Age.   A magazine that deals with doing business via the Internet.

Interactive Age
   P.O. Box 1194
   Skokie, IL 60076
   708-647-6834

Interactive PR.   A newsletter on new media for public relations executives.

Interactive PR Group
   310-442-9149
   inteactive@deltanet.com
   interactpr@aol.com

The Interactive Engineer.   Publication about CD-I software engineering.

Philips Interactive Media of America
    11050 Santa Monica Blvd.
    Los Angeles, CA 90025
    310-444-6519

Information Standards Quarterly. A National Information Standards Organization NISO; Quarterly; $40 per year.

National Information Standards Organization (NISO)
    P.O. Box 1056
    Bethesda, MD 20827
    301-975-2814

The International CD-ROM Report. Bi-monthly report on what's new and what's not in CD-ROMs. $72 per year.

Innotech
    110 Silver Star Blvd., Unit #107
    Scarborough, ON M1V 5A2
    416-321-3838

Link-UP. A newspaper for users of online services and CD-ROMs. Encompasses information of interest to business, education, and personal. Published bi-monthly. $26.50 per year.

Learned Information, Inc.
    143 Old Marlton Pike
    Medford, NJ 08055
    609-654-6266

Multimedia Business Report. This newsletter is published 24 times per year. Covers interactive CDs, online services, audiotex, software interactive television, videogames, integrated learning systems. $449 year.

SIMBA Information, Inc.
    P.O. Box 7430
    Wilton, CT 06897
    203-834-0033

Multimedia-CD Publisher. Newsletter with a multimedia publisher's orientation. $147 per year for 12 issues.

Meckler Publishing
    11 Ferry Ln.
    Westport, CT 06880
    203-226-6967

Multimedia Networking Newsletter. Specifically deals with the issues of networked multimedia. Published monthly. $495 per year.

Publications Research Group
    P.O. Box 765
    North Adams, MA 01247
    413-664-6185

Multimedia Review.   Quarterly academic-oriented journal. $97 per year.

Meckler Publishing
  11 Ferry Ln.
  Westport, CT 06880
  203-226-6967

Multimedia Monitor.   Probably the best newsletter on the market. Filled with latest news, plus contacts and their phone numbers. $357 per year.

Future Systems, Inc.
  P.O. Box 26
  Falls Church, VA 22040
  703-241-1799

Multimedia Week.   An executive report on business opportunities in the multimedia marketplace.

Phillips Business Information, Inc.
  7811 Montrose Rd.
  Potomac, MD 20854
  301-424-3338

Nautilus.   The first magazine for multimedia published on CD-ROM. Not only does it provide latest news, it also provides demos of latest products in the field. Well worth the money.

Nautilus Metatec Corp.
  7001 Discovery Blvd.
  Dublin, OH 43017
  800-637-3472
  614-766-3165

Multimedia: nuts and bolts.   Quarterly CD-ROM journal that covers new products, technology, applications, "how-to," trends, and case histories.

115 Bloomingdale Ln.
  Woodbridge, ON L4L 6X8
  800-363-3227

New Media.   Slick, enjoyable magazine. Great ads. A bargain.

Hypermedia Communications, Inc.
  901 Mariner's Island Blvd.
  Ste. 365
  San Mateo, CA 94404
  415-573-5170

New Media News.   If you're a member of the Boston Computer Society, you're in luck.

Boston Computer Society
  One Kendall Sq., Bldg. 100
  Cambridge, MA 02139
  617-252-0600

Online & CD-ROM Review.   An international journal of information sciences concentrating on on-line and optical information sources, systems, and services. Published every two months.

Learned Information, Ltd.
   Woodside, Hinksey Hill
   Oxford OX1 5AU
   United Kingdom
   44-0-865-730275

PC Presentations-Productions Magazine.   A new magazine focusing on the use of PC technology for better business presentations. Magazine focuses on using products to get the job done. Easy, conversational style.

PCPP Magazine
   Pisces Publishing Group
   417 Bridgeport Ave.
   Devon, CT 06460
   203-877-1927

Ultimedia Solutions.   Ignore the IBM marketing pitch and concentrate on the case histories of multimedia uses. Bi-monthly. Free.

IBM Multimedia Solutions
   4111 Northside Pkwy. #HO4L1
   Atlanta, GA 30327

Virtual Reality Report Magazine.   A must have if you're into VR. Another of the fine Meckler publications.

Meckler Corp.
   11 Ferry Ln. W.
   Westport, CT 06880
   203-226-6967

Wolf World.   A lightly written monthly newsletter that covers multimedia issues relevant to PC Sound Card users. Available both in paper format and in electronic format on CompuServe via GO WESTPOINT.

Westpoint Creative
   Delta House
   264 Monkmoor Rd.
   Shrewsbury SY2 5ST
   United Kingdom
   44-0-743-248590

Books

A Guide to Multimedia, Victoria Rosenborg. New Riders Publishing; 1993.
Apple CD-ROM Handbook, Joel Nagy. Addison-Wesley Publishing Co.; 1992.
The Brady Guide to CD-ROM, L. Buddine and E. Young. Brady Books; 1987.

Building Hypermedia Applications: A Software Developer's Guide, Gary Thomas Howell. McGraw-Hill; 1992.

CD-I and Interactive Videodisc Technology, S. Lambert and J. Sallis. Howard W. Sams & Co.; 1987.

CD-I Design Handbook, Philips IMS. Addison-Wesley; 1992.

CD-I Designer's Guide, Signe Hoffos, Graham Sharpless, Philip Smith, Nicholas Lewis. McGraw-Hill UK; 1992.

The CD-I Production Handbook, Philips IMS, Philips Electronics UK Ltd. Addison Wesley; 1992.

CD-ROM 2: Optical Publishing, S. Ropiquet. Microsoft Press; 1987.

CD-ROM Applications and Markets, J.P. Roth. Meckler Publishing; 1988.

CD-ROM: Facilitating Electronic Publishing, Linda Helgerson. Van Nostrand Reinholt; 1992.

CD-ROM Directory, Bi-yearly. Wilton, CT: Pemberton Press.

CD-ROM Finder, James Shelton, ed. Medford, NJ: Learned Information; 1993, 5th ed.

CD-ROM Handbook, Chris Sherman. McGraw-Hill; 1989.

CD-ROM Market Place 1993, Westport, CT: Meckler Publishing; 1993.

CD-ROM Standards: The Book, Julie B. Schwerin. Learned Information Ltd.; 1986.

CD-ROM: Facilitating Electronic Publishing, Linda Helgerson. Van Nostrand Reinhold; 1992.

CD-ROM: The New Papyrus, S. Lambert and S. Ropiquet. Microsoft Press; 1986; $24.95.

CD-ROMs: Breakthrough in Information Storage, Frederick Holtz. TAB Books; 1988.

The CD-ROM Handbook, Chris Sherman, ed. McGraw-Hill; 1988.

CD-ROMs in Print, Norman Desmaris. Westport, CT: Meckler; Yearly.

Compact Disc Interactive: A Designer's Overview, Philips International, eds. McGraw-Hill; 1988.

Digital Video in the PC Environment, Arch C. Luther. McGraw-Hill; 1989.

Discovering CD-I, Eric Miller, Walden Microware Systems Corporation; 1991.

Essential Guide to CD-ROM, J.P. Roth. Westport, CT: Meckler Publishing; 1986.

Guide to CD-ROM, Dana Parker & Bob Starrett. New Riders Publishing; 1992.

A Guide to Optical Storage Technology, John A. McCormick. Dow Jones-Irwin; 1990.

IBM LinkWay: Hypermedia for the PC, R. Harrington, B. Fancher, and P. Black. John Wiley & Sons; 1990.

Interactive Multimedia, Sueann Ambron and Kristina Hooper. Microsoft Press; 1988.

Introducing CD-I, Philips IMS, Philips Electronics UK Ltd. Addison Wesley, 1992.

Learning with Interactive Multimedia, Sueann Ambron and Kristina Hooper. Microsoft Press; 1990.

Managing Interactive Video-Multimedia Projects, R. E. Bergman and T. V. Moore. Educational Technology Publications; 1990.

Mapping Hypertext, Robert E. Horn. Lexington, MA: The Lexington Institute; 1989.

Microsoft Windows Multimedia Authoring and Tools Guide, Microsoft Press.

Multimedia Applications Development: Using DVI Technology, Mark Bunzel & Sandra Morris. McGraw-Hill; 1992.

Multimedia Interface Design, M. Blattner and R. Dannenberg. ACM Press- Addison-Wesley; 1992.

Multimedia Madness, Ron Wodaski. SAMS Publishing. 1992.

Multimedia: Making It Work, Tay Vaughan. Osborne/McGraw-Hill; 1993.

The Multimedia Producer's Survival Guide, Stephan Ian McIntosh. Campbell, CA: Multimedia Computing Corp.

NonLinear: A guide to electronic film and video editing, Michael Rubin. Triad Publishing Co.; 1992.

OS-9 INSIGHTS: An advanced programmer's Guide to OS-9, 2nd Ed., Peter Dibble.

Publish Yourself on CD-ROM, D. Straughan and F. Caffarelli. Random House; 1992.

Scripting for New AV Technologies, 2nd Ed., Dwight V. Swain and Joye R. Swain. Focal Press; 1991.

Selected Resources for CD-ROM and New Media Publishers, Richard A. Bowers. Information Arts; 1992.

SGML Backgrounder for CD-ROM Publishers, Richard A. Bowers. Optical Publishing Association; 1992.

The SGML Handbook: The annotated full text of ISO 8879 - Standard Generalized Markup Language, Charles F. Goldfarb. Oxford University Press; 1990.

Text, Context, and Hypertext: Writing with and for the computer, Edward Barrett. MIT Press; 1988.

Video Engineering. Andrew Inglis. McGraw-Hill; 1993.

The Whole Internet: User's Guide & Catalog, Ed Krol. O'Reilly & Associates, Inc.; 1992.

On-line forums

CompuServe.   The multimedia forums on CompuServe, operated by Multimedia Computing Corp. under contract to Simba Information, are the leading on-line information exchanges for multimedia. Topics range from audio and video to Photo CD and CD-I. About 20 vendors offer support in the Multimedia Vendor Forum. The forums libraries offer a wide variety of information, programs, hardware drivers and other useful files.

CompuServe
   800-848-8199
   operator 228

Image scanning and Slide creation

Show&Tell
   39 West 38th St.
   New York, NY 10018
   212-840-2912

Digicolor 1300
   Dexter Ave. N.
   Seattle, WA 98109
   800-967-3714

Slide Services, Inc.
   2537 25th Ave. S.
   Minneapolis, MN 55406
   612-721-2434

CD-ROM mastering

Northeastern Digital Recording, Inc.
   2 Hidden Meadow Ln.
   Southborough, MA 01772
   508-481-9322

MultiMedia PC Enterprises, Inc.
   3 Hanover Sq.
   Ste. 19A
   New York, NY 10004
   212-509-9636

Electronic Publishers International Corp.
   P.O. Box 17006
   Winston-Salem, NC 27116
   800-258-4423

International Teleproduction Society
350 Fifth Ave.
Ste. 2400
New York, NY 10118
212-629-3265

Technidisc
2250 Meijer Dr.
Troy, MI 48084
313-435-7430

3M Prerecorded Optical Media
3M Center Blvd., 223-5N-01
St. Paul, MN 55144
612-733-2142

Packaging

Ames Specialty Packaging
21 Properzi Way
P.O. Box 120
Somerville, MA 02143
617-776-3360

Legal

Elman Wilf & Fried
20 W. Third St.
P.O. Box 703
Media, PA 19063
215-892-9580

Conferences

MacWorld Exposition
Mitch Hall Associates
P.O. Box 4010
Dedham, MA 02026
617-361-0817

Video Expo Image World
Jacob K. Javits Convention Center
New York City, NY
800-800-5474

The Networked Economy Conference
Communications Week Interactive Age
600 Community Dr.
Manhasset, NY 11030
1-800-266-9335

The Interactive Services Industry 10th Annual Conference
  ISA
  1-800-883-8817
  http://www.isa.net./isa
  isa@aol.com

EMail World and Internet Expo
  DCI
  http://www.dciexpo.com
  508-470-3880

Intermedia
  Moscone Convention Center
  San Francisco, CA
  203-840-5484

Orlando Multimedia'95 SALT
  Hyatt Orlando Hotel
  Kissimmee, FL
  800-457-6812

High Tech Direct 2000
  High Tech Direct 2000
  Santa Clara Convention Center
  Santa Clara, CA
  800-808-3976

New Media Expo'95
  Los Angeles Convention Center
  Los Angeles, CA
  617-449-6600

VideoCom'95
  Capital Hilton
  Washington, DC
  800-822-6338

NAB-Multimedia World'95
  Las Vegas Convention Center
  Las Vegas, NV

DigMedia Geneva
  Geneva, Switzerland
  41-22-730-5969-730-5192

Comdex/Spring and Windows World
  Georgia World Congress Center
  Atlanta, GA
  617-449-6600

Electronic Entertainment Expo
  Los Angeles Convention Center
  Los Angeles, CA
  800-800-5474

Winter Consumer Electronics Show
  Electronic Industries Association
  2001 Pennsylvania Ave. NW
  Washington, DC 20006-1813
  202-457-8700

IMEX/NOTA
  ICM (Imaging Conference Management)
  Bay Colony Corporate Center
  1000 Winter St., Ste. 3700
  Waltham, MA 02154
  617-487-7934

Image World West Knowledge
  Industry Publications, Inc.
  701 Westchester Ave.
  White Plains, NY 10604
  914-328-9157

Interact
  Interactive Services Association
  8403 Colesville Rd., Ste. 865
  Silver Spring, MD 20910
  301-495-4955

Annual Document & Image Management Systems Conference
  BIS Strategic Decisions
  One Longwater Circle
  Norwell, MA 02061
  617-982-9500

Montage
  International Festival of the Image
  31 Prince St.
  Rochester, NY 14607
  716-442-6722

TechDoc
  GCA
  100 Daingerfield Rd.
  Alexandria, VA 22314-2888
  703-519-8160

Government Imaging Conference
USPDI, Inc.
1734 Elton Rd., Ste. 200
Silver Spring, MD 20903-1724
301-445-4405

CONCEPTS

Graphic Arts Show Co.
1899 Preston White Dr.
Reston, VA 22091-4367
703-264-7200

Quicktime and Multimedia Conference
Sumeria, Inc.
329 Bryant St., Ste. 3D
San Francisco, CA 94107
415-904-0800

Home Media Expo
American Expositions, Inc.
The Soho Bldg.
110 Greene St., #703
New York, NY 10012
212-226-4141

Image World
Knowledge Industry Publications, Inc.
701 Westchester Ave.
White Plains, NY 10604
914-328-9157

Intermedia
Reed Exhibition Company
P.O. Box 3833
999 Summer St.
Stamford, CT 06905-0833
203-352-8254

FOSE
National Trade Productions, Inc.
313 S. Patrick St.
Alexandria, VA 22314-3567
800-638-8510

The Seybold Conference
Seybold Seminars
P.O. Box 6710
Malibu, CA 90264
800-433-5200

CDISC-4
  Philips Interactive Media of America
  11050 Santa Monica Blvd.
  Los Angeles, CA 90025
  310-444-6519

NAB Multimedia World Conference
  National Association of Broadcasters
  1771 N. St., NW
  Washington, DC 20036-2891
  202-429-5346

Digital Video New York
  American Expositions, Inc.
  The Soho
  Bldg. 110 Greene St., #703
  New York, NY 10012
  212-226-4141

MultiMedia Expo
  American Expositions, Inc.
  The Soho Bldg.
  110 Greene St., #703
  New York, NY 10012
  212-226-4141

TED4KOBE
  TED Conferences, Inc.
  59 Wooster St.
  New York, NY 10012
  212-219-8993

Virtual Reality
  Meckler
  11 Ferry Ln. W.
  Westport, CT 06880
  800-635-5537

Summer Consumer Electronics Show (CES)
  Consumer Electronics Shows
  2001 Pennsylvania Ave. NW
  Washington, DC 20006-1813
  202-457-8700

REPLItech International
  Knowledge Industry Publications, Inc.
  701 Westchester Ave.
  White Plains, NY 10604
  914-328-9157

Image World New York
Knowledge Industry Publications, Inc.
701 Westchester Ave.
White Plains, NY 10604
914-328-9157

CDROM Expo
Mitch Hall Associates
P.O. Box 4010
Dedham, MA 02026
617-361-0817

Online/CD-ROM
Multimedia & CD-ROM Seminar
462 Danbury Rd.
Wilton, CT 06897
203-761-1466

CD-ROM Expo
Mitch Hall Associates
260 Milton St.
Dedham, MA 02026
617-361-2001

Comdex
Interface Group
300 First Ave.
Needham, MA 02194-2722
617-449-6600

Internet World/Document Delivery World
Meckler
11 Ferry Ln. W.
Westport, CT 06880
800-635-5537

Milia
International Exhibition Organization
475 Park Ave. S.
New York, NY 10016
212-689-4220

Media Summit Strategic Forum for New Business Alliances ACCU-Reg
1420 MacArthur Drive
Ste. 104
Carrollton, TX 75007
203-352-8302

Associations

CD-I Association. A professional association for developers of CD-I or for those interested in developing CD-I. Members receive a quarterly newsletter, *Inside CD-I*, and other publications.

CD-I Association of North America
    Attn.: Laura Foti Cohen
    11111 Santa Monica Blvd., Ste. 700
    Los Angeles, CA 90025
    310-444-6619

European CD-I Association
    Attn.: Julien Lynn-Evans
    188 Tottenham Court Rd.
    London W1P 9LE
    United Kingdom

Interactive Multimedia Association
    3 Church Circle
    Ste. 800
    Annapolis, MD 21401
    410-626-1380

International Interactive Communications Society
    IICS
    P.O. Box 1862
    Lake Oswego, OR 97035
    503-649-2065

Multimedia PC Marketing Council, Inc.
    1730 M St. NW
    Ste. 707
    Washington, DC 20036
    202-331-0494

Optical Publishing Association
    P.O. Box 21268
    Columbus, OH 43221
    614-442-8805

Consulting

Quest. Rex Allen runs a mean multimedia shop. Hitched to their Quest authoring tool, Allen Communication is a good consulting bet.
Allen Communication, Inc.
    5225 Wiley Post Way
    Salt Lake City, UT 84116
    801-537-7800

Corporate Media Communications. Corporate Media Communications specializes in multimedia applications. It specializes in creative communications, including large and small business meetings, multi-image slides, video and print materials, for both marketing and training.

Corporate Media Applications
   1530 Cooledge Rd.
   Atlanta, GA 30085
   404-491-6300

OnTape Multimedia. OnTape Multimedia makes affordable and effective videotapes of PC-related products for marketing and educational purposes. OnTape Multimedia also provides consulting and purchasing advice for those interested in desktop video and PC-based multimedia.

OnTape Multimedia
   1509 S. Azalea
   Columbia, MO 65201
   314-874-5191

Optibase. Optibase is a world leader in ISO implementations of MPEG, full-motion digital video, and audio products.

Optibase
   4006 Beltline Rd.
   Ste. 200
   Dallas, TX 75244
   214-386-2040

NuMedia Corporation. NuMedia Corporation specializes in the implementation of large multimedia networks that distribute multimedia presentations nationwide. These networks use LANs, telephone lines, and satellites to facilitate the production, delivery, and presentation of multimedia. NuMedia's family of multimedia products include options for desktop VGA presentations or scheduled presentations playing over cable or in-house TV networks.

NuMedia Corp.
   201 N. Union
   Ste. 400
   Alexandria, VA 22314
   703-684-9000

Wallace Music & Sound, Inc.. Wallace Music & Sound, Inc., provides original music and sound effects for software developers and publishers.

Wallace Music & Sound, Inc.
   6210 W. Pershing Ave.
   Glendale, AZ 95304
   602-979-6201

Multimedia Computing Corp.   Multimedia Computing Corp. is a leading multimedia strategic consulting firm. The company was founded in 1988 by Nick Arnett and Tim Bajarin, two of the top computer industry analysts. Clients have included Apple Computer, IBM, Microsoft, Hitachi, Wherehouse, and many others in computing, telecommunications, entertainment, consumer electronics, and publishing.

Multimedia Computing Corp.
  2105 S. Bascom Ave.
  Ste. 300
  Campbell, CA 95008
  408-369-1233

The Multimedia Department.   The Multimedia Department provides corporate communications services including: strategic video and multimedia consulting; audio, video and interactive video production, duplication, packaging, direct mail, and order fulfillment.

The Multimedia Department
  140 West 69th St.
  Ste. 45A
  New York, NY 10023
  212-721-6117

Performance Software, Inc.   Performance Software, Inc. is a consultancy in starting and using multimedia.

Performance Software, Inc.
  100 Shield St.
  West Hartford, CT 06110
  800-348-1377

Technology Helping People, Inc.   Technology Helping People, Inc. does exactly what its name implies. But it specializes in the implementation of multimedia.

Technology Helping People, Inc.
  404-499-9800

In Motion.   In Motion offers consulting digital interactive media, training, applications tools development.

In Motion
  Digital Interactive Media
  62 rue des Chantiers
  78000 Versaille France
  31-1-39-53-67-88

Centrimedia.   Centrimedia Company offers consulting services, as well as production services for the creation of applications for marketing, training, education, and consumer markets.

Centrimedia
3964 26th St.
San Francisco, CA 94131
415-282-7875

Dataware Technologies.   Dataware Technologies works with organizations to index and store data on CD-ROM. They use their own software tools, CD Author and CD Answer, which can be purchased separately.

Dataware Technologies
222 Third St.
Ste. 3300
Cambridge, MA 02142
617-621-0820

RR Donnelley & Sons.   RR Donnelley & Sons Company, a heavy-hitter in the traditional print world, is even bigger in the CD-ROM world. They will, according to their promo, "take the information you already have and target it, translate it, move it around the world, customize it, personalize it, give it more impact, make it interactive, compact it, CD-ROM it, floppy disk-it, multimedia it, on-line it."

RR Donnelley & Sons Company
77 W. Wacker Dr.
Chicago, IL 60601
800-438-0223 (for free CD-ROM)
312-326-8000

Sasha Lewis.   Sasha Lewis specializes in networking and multimedia products. The author of six books, she also produces multimedia videos.

Sasha Lewis
715 Piercy Rd.
San Jose, CA 95138
408-629-0755
1-800-60 MEDIA.

Internet

Internet authoring

Power Media.   Able to run on all major computing platforms (Windows, Macintosh, Unix), this object-oriented drag-and-drop authoring kit gives you all the power you need without complex flowcharts and graphs. Also, its total Internet connectivity provides all the global access you might require.

RAD Technologies
745 Emerson St.
Palo Alto, CA 94301
415-617-9430

Internet Publishing Kit.   For Windows or Macintosh, it's a complete publishing toolkit, featuring HotMetal Pro and Netscape Navigator, plus text, sound, and graphics editing tools, Web-page templates, and much more.

Ventana Communications
   800-743-5369
   http://www.vmedia.com

AnchorPage.   Fully automates concept extraction and hypertext anchoring of HTML documents. Offers end users four different methods of referencing document content.

ICONOVEX Corp.
   7900 Xerxes Ave. S., Ste. 550
   Bloomington, MN 55431
   1-800-943-0292
   http://www.iconovex.com

HTML.edit.   For the MAC, it does an excellent job of putting a friendlier face on top of HTML. Nearly every feature of HTML is accessible from easy-to-use dialog boxes and pop-up menus.

Murray Altheim
http://www.metrics.nttc.edu/tools/htmledit/htmledit.html

Site Writer Pro.   For the MAC, this tool splits the edit window into three panes for the header, body, and footer of a document. It supports even the most recent extension to the HTML tag set.

Rik Jones
http://www.ric.dccd.edu/human/swpro.htm

Web Weaver.   For Macs only, it's one of the category of "paste attribute" editors that help isolate the user from the need to know HTML tags.

Robert Best
   http://www.potsdam.edu/web.weaver/about.htm

Simple HTML Editor.   For Macs only, it's a very basic text editor with only the barest of HTML editing tools.

Eric Morgan
http://www.lib.ncsu.edu/staff/morgan/simple.html

HTML Editor.   A Mac-based utility, it provides a good basic environment in which to work. It offers the most commonly used HTML through pop-up menus and buttons.

Rick Giles
http://dragon.acadiau.ca/~giles/html editor/documentation.html

BBEdit/HTML Tools/Lindsay Davies
http://www.york.ac.uk/~idn/BBEditTools.html

HTML Extensions/Carles Bellver
http://www.uji.es/bbedit/html/extensions.html

Beyond Press (for Quark users)

Astrobyte
303-534-6344
support@astrobyte.com
http://www.astrobye.com

XPress to HTML Converter/Jeremy Hylton

http://the-tech.mit.edu/~jerremy/qtzwww.html

HTML Xport

Eric Knudsstrup

ftp://mars.aliens.com/pub/Macintosh/HTML Xport.sit
These Quart XPress extensions map Quark styles to HTML tags.

WebSucker (for PageMaker)

Mitch Cohen
http://www.iii.net/users/mcohen/websucker.html

Web-It (for Claris)

University of Michigan
http://www.umich.edu/~demonner/Primer_main/primer_main.html

HTML+

Leonard Rosenthol
leonard@netcom.com

XL2HTML.XLS (for Microsoft Excel)

Jordan Evans
http://www710.gsfc.nasa.gov/704/dgd/xlzhtml.html

This Visual Basic macro for Excel helps turn Excel 5.0 data into HTML tables, maintaining simple text formatting.

1-Way.   Author hyperlinked information on a PC, Mac, or UNIX workstation without dealing with HTML syntax. Information readily available for net surfers without file conversion and transport.

ForeFront Group, Inc.
   1360 Post Oak Rd.
   Ste. 1660
   Houston, TX 77056
   800-867-1101
   info@ffg.com

InContext Spider.   A HTML editor and Web browser, a package that allows you to create dynamic and imaginative pages without muss and fuss. It speaks directly to the browser; there's no limit to what you can produce.

InContext Corp.
   2 St. Clair Ave. W.
   16th Fl.
   Toronto, ON M4V 1L5
   http://incontext.ca
   800-263-1027

HTML.edit.   For the Mac, it does an excellent job of putting a friendly face on top of HTML. Nearly every feature of HTML is accessible from easy-to-use dialog boxes and pop-up menus.

Murray Altheim
   http://www.metrics.nttc.edu/tools/htnledit.html

Arachnid.   Features on-screen support for most HTML tags. Shines in the creation of forms. For the MAC only.

Robert McBurney
http://sec/look.uowa.edu/about/projects/arachmin/page.html

HotMetal.Pro.   For use with Windows, Mac, or UNIX; it provides useful features, such as spell checker, search-replace, and thesaurus.

SoftQuad Corp
   http://www.wq.com/hmpro.html

InContext Spider.   An HTML editor and Web browser that speaks directly to the Web, thus allowing dynamic home page creation and Web cruising.

InContext Systems
   800-263-0127
   http://www.incontext.ca

HTML Pro.   A great environment for both novices and expert Mac users. Two editable windows allow the novice users to begin in the preview window and watch the HTML representation being built as they work.

Niklas Frykholm
   http://www.ts.umu.se:80/~rad/shareware/htmlpro_help.html

Webtor (Web Editor).   A great tool for beginners, it does a good job of isolating the author from the complexities of HTML. It displays text, URLs, and in-line graphics on screen.

Jochen Schales
   http://www.igd.fhg.de/~neuss/webtor/webtor.html

Internet access providers

America Online. Very user-friendly, this online service provides excellent Internet access, as well as ease of e-mail and downloading of files.

America Online
8619 Westwood Center Dr.
Vienna, VA 22182-9806
800-827-6364

Prodigy. At a recent trade show, this on-line service out-ranked its leading competitors by 58.8 points to their 26 and 10.2. Software can be downloaded directly from their web site.

Prodigy
800-PRODIGY, Ext. 481
http://www.astranet.com

Delphi. This on-line service offers host-to-host connections (Telnet), file transfers (FTP), internet relay chat (IRC), and other valuable and useful services.

Delphi Internet Services
1030 Massachusetts Ave.
Cambridge, CA 02138
1-800-695-4005

Telephone

Internet Phone. A software package that allows the user to talk for free via the Internet. Free demo copy can be downloaded from: http://www. vocaltec.com/it.html.

VocalTec, Inc.
157 Veterans Dr.
Northvale, NJ 07647
201-768-9400
info@vocaltec.com

Digiphone. This software package allows users natural two-way conversations, and offers such services as conference calling, caller ID, call screening, and voice mail. It includes an interface for connecting to the Internet and other on-line services.

Third Planet Publishing
Camelot Place
17770 Preston Rd.
Dallas, TX 75652
214-713-2607

Firewall

SmartWall. A smart card provides one of the most secure rides through the Internet. Electronic commerce, digital signature, encryption for files sessions; it's all available now.

Virtual Open Network Environment
  12300 Twinbrook Pkwy.
  Rockville, MD 20852
  800-881-7090
  http://www.v-one.com

BorderWare Firewall Server.   Easy to install, easy to use, this secure Internet gateway is unique among firewalls in that it integrates packet filters and circuit-level gatways with application servers into a single highly secure, self-contained system.

Border Network Technologies, Inc.
  20 Toronto St.
  Toronto, ON M5C 2B8
  http://www.border.com
  info@border.com

The Black Hole.   A highly effective firewall, invisible within the Internet, this private network protects your data from cyber criminals.

Milkyway Networks Corp.
  255-265 Queensview Dr.
  Ottawa, ON K2B 8H6
  613-596-5549

Sidewinder.   Featuring a patented-type enforcement mechanism, this internetwork (including the Internet) security technology prevents unauthorized access to your data. It actually traps intruders, going beyond the capabilities of traditional passive firewalls.

Secure Computing Corp.
  2675 Long Lake Rd.
  Roseville, MN 55113
  800-692-LOCK

Web server

Website.   A new server software kit for NT3.5 and Windows 95 users to publish, at very low-cost, via the Internet. Easy training is provided by a complete tutorial and on-line help.

O'Reilly & Associates, Inc.
  103A Morris St.
  Sebastopol, CA 95472
  800-998-9938
  catalog@online.ora.com

Explore OnNet.   A package that enables Internet access in as little as 5 minutes. Windows-based, it features an enhanced NCSA Mosaic Internet browser, Gopher+ information retriever, e-mail, etc.

FTP Software
  100 Brickstone Sq.
  Andover, MA 01810
  800-282-4FTP, ext. 455
  http://www.ftp.com
  Info@ftp.com

Purveyor.   Point-and-click graphical interface allows easy access to the Web. It also features sample home pages, hot-links to registration and support, sample forms, report generators, and excellent security and password protection.

Process Software Corp.
  959 Concord St.
  Framingham, MA 01701
  1-800-722-7770
  info@process.com
  http://www.process.com

Sun Netra Internet Server.   Just plug it in and quick as can be your PC LANs can be on the Internet. All the system software, application software, and administration tools have already been installed.

Sun Microsystems, Inc.
  2550 Garcia Ave.
  Mountain View, CA 94043
  800-786-0785 ext. 110

Apple Internet Server.   Installed with a simple click of a mouse, this server makes creating a web site a sail of calm seas. It comes bundled with Adobe Acrobat Pro.

Apple 800-538-9696, ext. 830
  http://abs.apple.com

BSDI Internet Server.   An affordable, easy-to-set up and administer Internet package. Even novices can get running and set up a home page in record time.

Berkeley Software Design, Inc.
  7759 Delmonico Dr.
  Colorado Springs, CO 80919
  800-800-4273
  info@bsdi.com
  http://www.bsdi.com

Publications

Webweek.   I read it each and every week. Good stuff!

Mecklermedia Corp.
  20 Ketchum St.
  Westport, CT 06880

InterAd Monthly.   Every month, the publication provides competitive monitoring, trends and statistics, and relevant news. Everything one needs to in terms of on-line corporate marketing and communications.

Webtrack
  9 E. 38th St.
  8th Fl.
  New York, NY 10016-0003
  212-725-5328
  info@webtrack.com

Internet Business Report.   A newsletter centered on doing business on the Internet.

Jupiter Communications
  627 Broadway
  New York, NY 10012
  212-780-6060
  http://www.jup.com

Internet World.   A glossy magazine that covers the consumer side of the Internet.

Internet World
  P.O. Box 713
  Mt. Morris, IL 61054
  iwsubs@kable.com

Associations

Internet Business Association
  1160 S. Lakes Dr., Ste. 348
  Reston, VA 22081
  800-779-1323

Conferences

E-Mail World and Internet Expo.   Held November 28-30, 1995, Boston, MA. This conference featured the Internet, The Web, messaging, and electronic commerce.

DCI
  http://www.dciexpo.com
  508-470-3880

Online Marketplace. Held April 1995, Chicago, IL. Featured how-to market on line.

Jupiter Communications
  800-481-1212
  info@jup.com

Spring Internet World 95

Mecklermedia
  1-800-Meckler
  http://www.mecklerweb.com-iwconf
  iwconf@mecklermedia.com

Contributors' Biographies

Phil Abram, Product Manager, Portfolio Authoring Products, CD Imaging, Eastman Kodak Company, has worked in the field of desktop electronic printing and publishing since joining Kodak nearly 10 years ago. He holds a Bachelor of Science degree in Electrical Engineering, and a master's degree in finance and accounting, from the University of Rochester (NY).

Rex J. Allen is president and cofounder of Allen Communication, Inc., a highly successful multimedia software and courseware development company. Dr. Allen has been immersed in multimedia for the past 14 years, having designed and directed dozens of multimedia training applications for clients such as IBM, Xerox, AT&T, Union Pacific Railroad, and Ford Motor. Most recently, Dr. Allen has led efforts to apply cognitive-task-analysis to multimedia training in troubleshooting skills for the U.S. Air Force. Dr. Allen received a bachelor's degree from Brigham Young University in advertising, and his MS and Ph.D. degrees at Florida State University in Instructional Design and Organizational Development, respectively.

Chris Ammen has been involved in video production technology for his entire 25-year professional career. Mr. Ammen has pioneered technological developments in analog and digital video production. He was awarded the prestigious Joey Award for New Technologies for his work in Synchronization Services. Mr. Ammen has continued to expand his expertise into the computer-to-video scan conversion process.

Mr. Ammen is Vice President of Engineering for Television Associates (TVA) of Mountain View, CA. TVA is one of Silicon Valley's leading video production facilities. Television Associates is known for its commitment to serve the communications needs of corporate communicators, independent producers, broadcasters, and the training community. Mr. Ammen is responsible for assembling and perfecting TVA's Digital Bridge technologies, which include multimedia presentations, MPEG and QuickTime encoding, and other digital video services.

Asymetrix Corporation is a software company based in Bellevue, Washington. It is the leading provider for Windows-based tools for multimedia development, creative content, and client-server solutions.

Barbara Baker has been with Starlight Networks for two years as Marketing Manager. Ms. Baker has extensive experience marketing applications in emerging markets. Her background includes marketing OEM voice-processing products for Voysys Corporation, and development of vertical market voice applications through VAR channels for Octel Communications. She also has worked in the electronics practice for McKinsey and Company. Ms. Baker received her MBA from Harvard Business School, and a BA in Computer Science from the University of California, Berkeley.

Mel Baiada has been president of Bluestone since founding the company in 1989. Prior to Bluestone, Mr. Baiada worked in the Aerospace and Financial industries after graduating from Drexel University with a BS and Masters in Electrical Engineering. Mr. Baiada attributes his and Bluestone's success to several key factors: maintaining the utmost respect for customers and employees, alike; maintaining lead-edge industry knowledge through the hiring and ongoing education of employees; and enabling and empowering employees to act in the best interest of both the customer and the company. Regularly reading over 20 industry and business periodicals and books per month, Mr. Baiada is known as one of the industries "most well-read" figures.

Glenn Becker is the Vice President of Research and Development for the NuMedia Corporation of Alexandria, VA, where he has been since 1987. He has been closely involved with the design and implementation of large multimedia networks that distribute multimedia presentations nationwide. These networks use LANs, telephone lines, and satellite broadcast to facilitate the production, delivery, and presentation of multimedia. NuMedia's family of multimedia products includes options for desktop VGA presentations or scheduled presentations playing over cable or in-house TV networks. Mr. Becker also is working on his Ph.D. in Computer Science at The George Washington University in Washington, D.C. He has received an MS in Computer Science and a BS in Electrical Engineering, also from GWU.

Bob Bennett is a senior product manager for Autodesk's Multimedia Division. Bennett has played an active role in the computer graphics industry for most of his professional life, from developing computer-aided mapping systems to managing oil and gas lease information on Alaska's North Slope to developing state-of-the-art rendering and animation software packages. He has been with Autodesk, Inc. as a product manager for over four and a half years.

Since joining Autodesk in early 1988, Bennett has been instrumental in gaining the company's support for multimedia application development. Starting as the AutoShade product manager, Mr. Bennett then became product manager for Autodesk's award-winning software product, Autodesk Animator. Under Mr. Bennett's direction, Autodesk Animator won the PC Magazine Award for Technical Excellence in Graphics for 1989, and the Most Valuable Product Award from *PC Computing* magazine. Since receiving those honors, Mr. Bennett has had responsibility for Autodesk 3D Studio.

Educated at the University of Washington, Mr. Bennett was awarded a Bachelor of Arts degree in Urban Planning from the university's School of Architecture and Urban Planning in 1978. He is a frequent speaker at industry conferences on the topics of multimedia and animation.

Pam Berger is a Library Media Specialist at the Byram Hills High School located in Armonk, New York, as well as a library technology consultant for the DataSearch Group, Inc. She also is the publisher and editor of Information Searcher. Berger currently is the Conference Chair for the Databases in Schools conference. She is the coauthor of *CD-ROM in Schools: The Definitive Handbook* (Eight Bit Books, 1994) and *Guide to Information Sources in Public and Academic Media Centers* (Gale Research, 1981).

Peter B. Blakeney, employed by IBM since 1967, is an expert in the field of multimedia computing. As Manager of U.S. Operations, Mr. Blakeney is responsible for a wide variety of functions relative to the development, introduction, and marketing of IBM's multimedia products, as well as strategic planning for the organization.

Mr. Blakeney joined IBM's multimedia organization as a marketing support manager in 1986, after serving in a variety of field sales, headquarters staff, and management positions.

Mr. Blakeney received his graduate degree in Economics from the University of Cincinnati. Upon graduation, he joined IBM in Cincinnati, OH, in a sales capacity. Mr. Blakeney resides in Atlanta, GA.

Jesse Bornfreund recently joined Advantis, an IBM company. He wrote his contribution to this book while the Director of Desktop Marketing at UNIX International. Before coming to UNIX International, Mr. Bornfreund was Product Marketing Manager, UNIX, for Commodore Business Machines, Inc., and responsible for product management and marketing programs for the Commodore UNIX Amiga product line, including product launches, distribution programs, and sales and marketing programs.

Before joining Commodore, Mr. Bornfreund was Marketing Manager of UNIX Products for Rabbit Software, and Director of Operations for Telexpress, Inc. He has been involved in the UNIX industry since 1979. He is a frequent panelist/speaker at industry events, has published several articles in the trade press, and is author of UNIX International's White Paper "Desktop UNIX System V and Microsoft's Windows NT: A Functional Comparison."

Alan Briggs is a portrait painter, collector of tape recorders, record-sleeve artist, recording-studio owner, record-company owner, tour and concert promoter, music-video maker, concert-hall owner, film maker.

Computers: a long and varied route to bring me to where I am today. At art school I began to collect tape recorders, at one time I had nearly 200 different machines. In the '60s I started painting portraits of the pop music stars and celebrities of "Swinging London." Most of my friends were also up-and-coming musicians, who frequently borrowed my tape recorders to record rehearsals or songs. Eventually, this somehow developed into my first recording studio, and I wound up with seven around the UK.

Most of the young bands who used the studios needed work, so I started promoting them and this grew into promoting bigger acts, until I was doing UK, Europe, and world tours. For the benefit, originally, of my musician clients, I established the first of three record companies, where we also designed record sleeves. I wound up owning my own Venue in London, where I recorded artists in the 48-track studio, and shot my first videos in the 20-camera studio.

Recording music, recording pictures, painting pictures: this was everything I needed to start making movies, so I made my first in 1984. By 1987, I was living in Jamaica, shooting videos, and making another movie.

In 1989, I was living in San Francisco, where I began my long-lasting love-affair with computers. In one place I can write my script, draft my storyboard, store my audio, process and edit them, and produce all my special effects, before exporting the finished product to film or video. I have written a book explaining the techniques for the creative user, the *Digital Movie/Video Maker*, and which is about to become the manual for three training centers, which are to be funded by the European Governments and the UK government. It should open in 1996.

Tim Brock is a computer graphics specialist in Instructional Technology at St. Petersburg Junior College. His work includes multimedia-based project support for faculty and staff. He received his Masters of Communication at Pratt Institute. He currently is an artist of computer-based media, and has created virtual environments and numerous computer animations. He has exhibited and presented both non-sequential and temporal works in the United States and Canada. His newest animations, "Making Bread" and "Psalm 22," completed while in residency at the Banff Centre for The Arts, premiered in early 1993 at the Florida Film Festival.

John F. Buford is Director of the Interactive Media Group at the University of Massachusetts, Lowell, and a full-time faculty member in the Department of Computer Science. He serves as U.S. Head of Delegation to ISO MHEG, and has served as a consultant on multimedia standards and technology to DOD DISA, UNIX International, Siemens Nixdorf, and others. Dr. Buford is a frequent panelist on multimedia standards and has published over 20 papers. He holds a Ph.D. in Computer Science from Technische Universitaet Graz, Austria, and a BS and MS from MIT.

Red Burns is chair and a professor of the Tisch School of the Arts' Interactive Telecommunications Program at New York University. The focus of this graduate department is on the production of electronic multimedia and telecommunications. She is currently a coprincipal investigator of an interactive cable/telephone project. She is also the Director of the Alternate Media Center, a research and implementation center for new technologies that she co-founded in 1971.

During the 1970s and 1980s, Burns was the Director of Implementation of a series of projects such as two-way television for senior citizens, developing telecommunications uses to serve the developmentally disabled (a field trial of Teletext), media programs for drug abusers, an electronic community service on cable television, and an experimental videotex data base. Professor Burns teaches in the graduate program at NYU and has served on many committees, attended numbers of working meetings, and spoken publicly on new communications technologies.

Steven Bussard has unique experiences, which have let him observe firsthand how products are developed for different media. He worked on an Academy Award winning film, "All the President's Men," and a number-one TV show, "Charlie's Angels." These experiences gave him insights into two different approaches for creating filmed materials.

Steve was assistant to Mike Medavoy, head of production at United Artists. There he learned how films make the journey from initial idea to final cut. He saw the impact that each department in a motion-picture studio has on the final product. In the computer area, Steven Bussard was a member of the design team for dBASE IV. He watched four versions of the product go through their complete development cycles. As a liaison between different departments, he saw what each contributed to the overall process.

Steve has also worked on numerous writing and design projects—each of which had their own development history and production structure. He foresaw interactive entertainment's potential back in 1983, and he looks forward to using his skills to establish a development department for one of the major studios.

Julie Capsambelis has been designing and developing training programs in a variety of formats for more than 10 years. She has developed particular expertise with Instructional Systems Design (ISD) methodology, applying it to self-instructional, classroom, and video training programs.

She is Instructional Designer for St. Petersburg Junior College's Corporate Training Services Division, for which she designs customized instructional programs for area businesses and industry. Julie also has worked as an instructional designer for a national retailer, writing and producing instructional video; as manager of Training and Development for a major ground transportation company in Dallas; and independently, as a consultant in both Dallas and the Tampa Bay Area.

Alton Christensen is a New York-and-Washington-based freelancer working on several motion graphics projects. He uses Grass Valley Group Kadenza, Quantel Harry, and, more often these days, animation software on Mac-based systems. His experience includes graphic and animation design for a variety of clients in the United States, Europe, and the United Kingdom. Alton was the senior animator in the acclaimed graphics department of the Grant Tinker/Gannett project, USA Today: The Television Show. He also was the design director for the Audio Video Design Group. He worked with NBC Sports as an animation designer for the Games of the XXV Olympiad in Barcelona, Spain, and was awarded a Sports Emmy for his work as part of the Olympics design team.

John Colligan is President and Chief Operating Officer of Macromedia, a company he joined in January 1989. Colligan previously worked for Apple Computer's Macintosh Division as International Product Marketing Manager for Macintosh and later as head of the higher-education marketing and sales department. He was instrumental in launching HyperCard, producing the Knowledge Navigator video, and defining Apple's initial thrust into multimedia.

Colligan graduated from Georgetown University in 1976 with a Bachelor of Science degree in International Economics, and from the Stanford Graduate School of Business in 1983 with an MBA.

The Cross-Industry Working Team (XIWT) is a membership organization consisting of a diverse group of communications, computer system, information, and service providers who have joined together to develop a common technical vision for the National Information Infrastructure (NII).

Among our activities, XIWT publishes White Papers intended to improve the quality and accelerate the evolution of the NII by establishing common understanding about technical issues among those involved with its development and use.

XIWT activities have a technical focus, which might have broader implications. Hence, we expect this series of papers will be of interest to policy makers, to others contemplating activity in the NII, and to the general public.

Cross-Industry Working Team, Corporation for National Research Initiatives, 1895 Preston Dr., Ste. 100, Reston, VA 22091-5434. Tel: 703-620-8990, E-mail: info-xiwt-info@cnri.reston.va.us.

Kevin N. Daniel was born in 1955 in Cincinnati, Ohio. Kevin's educational background focused on Fine Arts and History. Since 1976, he has made his home near the city of Bend in the mountains of Central Oregon.

In the late 1970s, he began working with customer support for vertical-market CP/M systems. Through the 1980s, he held a series of positions in the software industry, beginning with technical writing and progressing through developing marketing support materials, designing consumer interfaces, product package design, advertising and administration. Kevin joined NeoSoft Corp. in 1992 as Director of Marketing and oversees marketing efforts and production of documentation and support materials.

Kevin's interest in history has led to publication of several of his works, including the book *Reinventing the Truth*. He has also authored several electronic titles currently available through on-line services and on the Internet, and has served as editor for publishing projects that range from books to periodicals.

Joan Davies is the Director of Communications for Mathematica, Inc., in Lakeland, Florida. She has coordinated marketing, press, technical documentation, training, and graphic production for the TEMPRA products since February 1991. She has an extensive desktop publishing background, and finds the transition from paper marketing to electronic marketing to be creatively exciting and potentially rewarding. She has totally "electronized" her marketing department, with all advertising and product materials developed on the computer desktop.

Davies is a Floridian who has lived in Turkey and Colorado, where she headed publicity, video production, and publication departments, before moving back to her native state. She holds a bachelor of arts degree in communication/multimedia (minor, PR) and a master's degree in interpersonal communication/theatre. She is a member of the National Association for Female Executives and the Society of Professional Journalists. She is Executive Secretary for the Deaf Service Center of Polk County, where she volunteers her desktop publishing and PR services for the deaf and hearing-impaired community.

Davies enjoys her work at Mathematica, Inc., because the company is so close to the cutting edge, it has to be careful not to fall off. She sincerely believes that no other industry can offer the technological advancements of the computer industry, and that multimedia is the "tool" that will make computers more friendly and accessible to the masses.

Mark Doran recently joined Intel Corporation. He wrote his contribution to this book while at UNIX International. Prior to joining UNIX International, Mark was a technical consultant with the Hoskyns Group Plc (formerly The Instruction Set), based in London, England. While at Hoskyns, Mark worked on a number of UNIX development projects as well as standards-related activities, notably with IEEE and X/Open. Mark has published a number of articles in the trade press and is the author of a book on the ANSI C programming language standard. Mark holds a Joint Honors degree in Computer Science and Electronics Engineering from University College, London.

L. W. (Les) Dunaway is Vice President, Multimedia, at Technology Helping People, Inc., a multimedia systems house. Les joined THP in July 1992 after 28 years with IBM. Les was part of the original team hired to set up the IBM Multimedia Division. While at IBM, Les developed the distributed multimedia architecture.

Joseph Dunn is Vice President of Product Development at Macromedia, which he joined in January 1991. Dunn is responsible for the development, documentation, and QA for the entire Macromedia software product line. Prior to joining Macromedia, Dunn was Director of Software Development at Frame Technology in Santa Clara, CA, where he managed the software group and succeeded in shipping two major FrameMaker versions on the SUN platform. In addition he was responsible for the development of FrameMaker as a portable application, with versions shipping on UNIX, Macintosh, and NeXT platforms.

At Acorn Computers in the UK and Palo Alto, Dunn held a variety of technical and management positions in the development of system software for personal computers. He graduated with a BS degree in Computer Science from Cambridge University in 1980.

Dr. Schahram Dustdar is head of the Department of Informatics (ZID) at the University of Art at Linz-Austria. He also heads the Austrian National Support Center for MICE (Multimedia Integrated Conferencing for Europe), an EU-project, which supports the implementation and use of MBone multimedia conferencing tools. He is member of the editorial board of *Multimedia Tools and Applications* (Kluwer Academic Publishers) and on the international programme committee of the European Conference on Information Systems (ECIS). During 1996, he will be a visiting fellow at the MIS-Department, University of Arizona.

Mike Evans is Director of Applications for the Corporate Technology Group at National Semiconductor. He manages several communications technology areas, including product development for the isoLan program. He is responsible for the Hong Kong design center, which recently has been incorporated into the Applications Technology Group. In 1985, Evans was instrumental in ushering National Semiconductor into the networking market through the development of Ethernet chip sets, and inventing the definition of today's industry-standard Ethernet controller.

Mike obtained his Bachelor of Science degree in Electrical Engineering from Manchester University, UK, and has designed many avionics systems. Since joining National Semiconductor Corporation in 1979, he has been responsible for developing a number of new areas for the company, including its industry leading Ethernet chip set. Presently he is concentrating on multimedia communications.

Joseph Fantuzzi joined Macromedia in February 1990 as Vice President of Marketing. Before that he was Director of International Marketing at Interleaf, Inc., and project engineer at Analogic Corporation. He now holds a joint patent on 3M's laser imager. Fantuzzi received a BS in Electrical Engineering from Bucknell University in 1980, and an MS in Computing Engineering from Tufts University in 1985.

Jeffrey P. Geibel is the Managing Partner of GEIBEL Marketing Consulting, which helps technology vendors and resellers to improve their sales and marketing effectiveness by diagnosing and improving their sales successes. He is a widely published author, and has written frequently on the implementation of innovative sales and marketing tools, including on-line services. He is the creator of the Sales Autopsy methodology, Solution Marketing programs, the seminar *How to Develop a Vertical Marketing Program for Software and Systems* and the book *Applications Software Marketing: A Field Manual for Success*. He can be reached at P.O. Box 611, Belmont, MA 02178-0005 Tel: 617-484-8285, Fax: 617-489-3567, E-mail: 74752.3072@compuserve.com.

Ken Gerlach is Marketing Programs Manager of Hewlett-Packard's Distance Learning Systems Operation. He manages activities for the planning and introduction of integrated products and services for delivering interactive distance-learning training and education. Products include multimedia computing integrated with HP-IN (Hewlett-Packard Interactive Network), one of the most advanced interactive distance-learning television broadcast production and telecommunications services in the world. HP-IN incorporates HP's global business television network for interactive technical programming, utilizing 3 broadcast host sites and 177 remote downlink receiving sites in North America and Europe.

Ken's 12 years of experience at Hewlett-Packard have also spanned engineering project and marketing program management of computer hardware and software applications that include emerging datacom, remote conferencing, and graphic presentation technologies.

Formerly, Ken provided project leadership as a Management Consultant at SRI International on techno-economic and market feasibility studies of computer automation and telecommunications for business and institutional clients in the United States, Europe, and Asia. His early career began in project-engineering design with the world's two largest engineering consulting firms, Skidmore, Owings and Merrill in the United States and Ove Arup and Partners in London.

Ken holds an MBA in marketing from Santa Clara University, as well as an MS and BS in mechanical engineering from Pennsylvania and Portland State universities, respectively. Currently he is a part-time instructor of graduate and undergraduate business courses at the U.C. Berkeley Extension and other extended education programs. He is a member of numerous engineering and trade associations and a Chartered Engineer (Europe).

Lewis Gruskin joined IBM in 1968 as a systems engineer. He then became a marketing representative, with clients in the retail, apparel, and process industries. Staff and management positions followed in strategy, marketing, and channels development. In 1986, Lew joined the IBM multimedia organization, helping to develop marketing strategy, industry applications, business-partner strategy, and multimedia strategy. Currently he is Worldwide Practice Leader for Multimedia Consulting, a unit of the IBM Consulting Group.

Lew was born in New York. He and his family now reside in Atlanta, Georgia.

Konstantin Guericke resides in Los Altos Hills, CA and is currently employed as Executive Vice President at Caligari Corp., maker of trueSpace and Fountain. At Caligari, he spends most of his time on strategic partnerships and new business development. Lately, his emphasis has been on shepherding Caligari's VRML efforts. Mr. Guericke is a German national, who has also lived, worked, and studied in Japan. He started the Central European office for Roykore, a graphics start-up that was acquired by Micrografx in the spring of 1992. He stayed on with Micrografx, where he held a variety of management positions in sales, marketing, and development. He is a frequent speaker at trade show panels, holds a BS and MS from Stanford University and enjoys the outdoors.

Satiah Gupta is Vice President of Strategic Marketing at Media Vision. He is responsible for product strategy and for developing strategic technologies and alliances with businesses and universities. Formerly he held various technical and management positions in nearly all aspects of the IBM business, the most recent of which included managing multimedia products and DVI technology partnerships between IBM and Intel. Gupta holds a Master of Science degree in Engineering and Economic Systems from Stanford University.

Harry Hallman entered the U.S. Air Force at the age of 18 and was trained as a photographer with emphasis on aerial photographic recon. After four years of service, two in Vietnam, he returned to Philadelphia and continued his education while working as Head Medical Photographer at the University of Penn. Vet School.

During the year 1970 Hallman founded (with a partner) Photo Communications Corp., an audiovisual production company located in Philadelphia. The firm was an early pioneer in the creation of multi-image slide programs for use in marketing and motivational meetings. While associated with PCC, Hallman worked at a variety of jobs including writing/producing, marketing, and general management.

In 1981, Hallman sold his interest in PCC and moved to Atlanta to form a new company called Corporate Media Communications, Inc. CMC created all forms of creative communications including large and small business meetings, multi-image slides, video and print materials, for both marketing and training. Clients included AT&T, IBM, BellSouth, Texaco, and numerous other Fortune 500 companies.

In 1987, CMC opened a Philadelphia branch that provides similar service. As new media such as computer-based presentations, multimedia, CD-I, and CDROM became viable, both offices offered these services. Current CMC clients include Pep Boys, Educational Testing Services, Siemens, and many other organizations in diverse industries.

Hallman recently has formed a new venture: Hallman Electronic Publishing, a company devoted to producing and distributing video, CD-I, and other print forms of communications to the general and professional consumer.

Hallman has contributed writings to professional publications and newsletters, written for video and other media, and is coauthor of a training program currently used in industry to teach customer service. The program title is "Through The Customer's Eyes™."

Dr. Guy Hancock graduated from the Ohio State University College of Veterinary Medicine in 1973 and worked in small animal practices as staff member or owner until 1983, when he became Director of the Veterinary Technology Program at St. Petersburg (FL) Junior College. He served as President-elect (1992-93) of the Association of Veterinary Technician Educators and as Assistant Director of the Veterinary Technology Interactive Technologies Consortium. He is doing graduate study in Instructional Technology at the University of South Florida College of Education. Publications and presentations include the subjects human/animal bond, pet loss and bereavement, animal-assisted therapy, dental radiology, and client relations for geriatric pets.

Ray Harris is a Senior Vice President of North America at Optibase. Mr. Harris has over 14 years experience in marketing and selling leading-edge technology products through OEM, system-integrator, and reseller channels. The technologies with which he has been involved include PCs, laser printers, multiuser UNIX super-micro computers, document image-processing, and multimedia full-motion digital video.

Prior to joining Optibase in 1991, Mr. Harris was Western Regional Manager for Kofax Image products, the leading developer of tools for the document image-processing markets.

Mr. Harris has delivered information presentations to numerous groups over the years. Most recently he has made presentations on MPEG and/or full-motion video to the Electronic Imaging Show, the DSP Expo, and the Digital Video/Multimedia Expo East.

Optibase is a world leader in ISO implementation of MPEG, full-motion, digital video, and audio products.

David E. Hartman is an Assistant Professor of English at St. Petersburg Junior College, where he teaches English Composition and Greek Mythology. He received his bachelor's degree from Eckerd College and his master's from The University of South Florida. His hypertext prototype, "The Labyrinth," has been published on the Apple Community College Alliance CD-ROM.

Donna Hefner joined Macromedia in January 1993. As Corporate Writer, Hefner is responsible for the research and development of corporate positioning papers and other marketing materials. Hefner received a BA in Journalism from California State University, Long Beach, in 1990.

Christine Hemrick is the Director of Cisco IOS Product Marketing at Cisco Systems, Inc. Her group is responsible for product planning and marketing of software for Cisco's entire family of multiprotocol routers, including routing and bridging support, and wide-area networking. Prior to this position at Cisco, she was Manager of Software Product Marketing. Before joining Cisco, Ms. Hemrick was with Bell Communications Research (BELLCORE) as District Manager for Broadband Data Services Planning. In this capacity, she was one of the original designers of the broad-band Switched Multimegabit Data Service (SMDS), and led a group responsible for developing SMDS service requirements and plans.

Josh Hendrix is a user-interface designer and quality assurance specialist. He currently works for CoSA, a Providence, RI-based software developer, where he code-signed the user interface for the company's flagship product, CoSA After Effects. He also was project manager for the company's CD-ROM-based interactive brochure, The Art of Visual Computing. He is a graduate of Brown University with a degree in Cognitive Science.

Jeff Hooks is an assistant professor at St. Petersburg (FL) Junior College, where he teaches literature, humanities, and creative writing. An SPJC graduate, he obtained his bachelor's degree and his MA in English and American Literature at the University of South Florida. His composition students have collaborated long-distance in real time between SPJC Macintosh labs and Jackson (MI) Community College. Students in his literature classes have studied *King Lear* with a HyperCard application he developed that keyed scenes from the play to corresponding sequences on the videodisc version of Sir Laurence Olivier's performance.

Using the Library of Congress's American Memory Project, his humanities students have created projects that displayed digitized photographs, texts, films, and recordings from the library's William McKinley-era archives. His creative writing students electronically published stories and poems by posting them to Usenet conferences on the Internet. For a year (1992-93), Mr. Hooks was on professional leave, teaching at a small college in the interior of China where his only classroom tools were books and chalkboard. Fascinated as he was by Chinese culture, and grateful for the time he had to reflect, he returned to St. Petersburg media-starved for his Macintosh and cable TV!

Lynn Jones, Product Manager for Digital Equipment Corporation's Video and Interactive Information Services (VIIS), is responsible for media server products that enable corporate, educational, healthcare, and government users to harness the power of video in the workplace.

Previously, Lynn was a Product Manager for the ChannelWorks Internet Brouter and new business development for Internet access via cable TV. She authored and presented a paper on Internet Access via Cable TV published by The National Cable Television Association (NCTA). As a Business Development Manager for Data Communications Products and Services for the cable television industry with Digital's Cable Television group, she was an early proponent of Ethernet via cable television and was responsible for the introduction of the ChannelWorks bridge. Lynn was also product manager for Digital's first multivendor network management platform, the DECmcc Management Station for ULTRIX (MSU).

Prior to joining Digital in 1988, Lynn worked for Bolt, Beranek, and Newman (BBN), where she was a Project Engineering Group Leader for government Internet networks and a Senior Project Engineer for international X.25 packet switch networks. She was Primary Project Engineer for worldwide data networks for Kokusai Denshin Denwa (KDD) and Barclays Bank. She also worked for Distribution Management Systems, a leading supplier of international distribution management systems.

Lynn received an Executive MBA from Boston University in 1991, and is a Phi Beta Kappa, Magna Cum Laude graduate of the University of Massachusetts, with a BA in Psychology.

Roger Karr founded the Integrated Multimedia Solutions group at Digital Equipment Corporation. He has program-managed several multimedia-based executive information applications. He has consulted on the applicability of multimedia solutions in a number of domains, including the utilities industry, education, federal, state, and local government agencies, and the retail industry. His work focuses on application design and implementation. Roger's current work is in the area of point-of-information kiosk applications for multimedia-based, corporate communications applications, executive-profiling and succession-planning applications, and information kiosks for state and local government agencies.

Michael Kellner, previously of Apple Computer Inc., was responsible for the integration of QuickTime into A/UX, Apple's UNIX product. He was a contributing factor in creating an easier-to-use UNIX. Michael currently is employed by IBM's Advanced Workstation Division in Austin, TX. There, he is involved in the PowerOpen effort and in the use of multimedia on workstations.

Richard V. Kelly, Jr. founded and runs the Artificial Life and Virtual Reality Applications Group at Digital Equipment Corporation. He has built commercial applications in advanced technologies with and for dozens of U.S., Asian, and European corporations, and he has taught extensively in the United States and Japan. His current research and application development work is focused on the conjoining of artificial life to virtual reality in order to enliven virtual universes. Currently he is working on biomedical, telecomm, utilities, pharmaceutical, training, entertainment, and financial-services VR applications. His latest book, presently in production, will be entitled *The Future of Virtual Reality: Unexpected Consequences of a New Technology*.

Jessica Keyes is president of Techinsider/New Art Inc., a technology consultancy/research firm specializing in productivity and high-technology applications. She is publisher of *Techinsider Reports* as well as *Computer Market Letter*. Organizer and leader of Techinsider seminars, Keyes has given seminars for such prestigious universities as Carnegie Mellon, Boston University, University of Illinois, James Madison

University, and San Francisco State University. Prior to founding Techinsider, Keyes was Managing Director of Technology for the New York Stock Exchange and has been an officer with Swiss Bank Co. and Banker's Trust, both in New York City. She has over 15 years of technical experience in such diverse areas as AI, multimedia, CASE, and reengineering. She holds an MBA from New York University.

A noted columnist and correspondent, with over 150 articles published in such journals as *Software* magazine, *Computerworld*, *AI Expert*, and *Datamation*, Keyes also is the author of four books including *Infatrends: The Competitive Use of Information* (McGraw-Hill, 1992), which was chosen as one of the best business books of 1992 by the *Library Journal*. She is currently working on her sixth book, *The Productivity Paradox* (McGraw-Hill).

Susan Kinnell currently divides her time between being the Custom Publishing Manager at the UCSB Bookstore in Santa Barbara, California; an instructor in the Computer Division at Santa Barbara City College; and an education/computer consultant with Carty Graphics, Santa Barbara. She is the coauthor of *CD-ROM in Schools: The Definitive Handbook* (Eight Bit Books, 1994), as well as *Hypertext / Hypermedia in Schools: A Resource Book* (ABCCLIO, 1990).

Paulina Knibbe is Product Manager at Cisco Systems, Inc., where she is responsible for key technologies, such as IP Multicasting and Resource Reservation. Paulina's previous positions at Cisco were as Manager of Protocol Software Group and, previously, Software Engineer for OSI. Prior to joining Cisco, Paulina was Manager, Network Development at David Systems. She also held this position at Ungermann Bass, where she was involved with routing protocol development. She attended the University of Michigan and received an MS in Computer Information and Control Engineering.

Cliff Kondratiuk holds a Bsc. in Electrical Engineering from the University of Alberta, and he is currently a design engineer with Sierra Semiconductor of Canada. He is responsible for the research and development of DSP operating systems and firmware for the Aria line of multimedia audio chipsets. Aria-based sound cards are designed around an open architecture utilizing a custom Texas Instruments TMS320C25 DSP. The Aria chipset is a 16-bit sound device that offers Soundblaster Rev. 1.5 compatibility, a 32-voice wavetable music synthesizer, four channels of sample playback, ADPCM compression, up to 44.1-kHz recording and playback, and firmware-based, speaker-independent speech recognition. Aria's open architecture has allowed for the recent additions of reverb and Qsound™ 3D audio algorithms as DSP tasks downloaded from the PC. His work has included the design of a DSP-based Soundblaster/Adlib emulation, audio compression and effects processing algorithms, as well as the joint development of a digital wavetable/sample-based synthesizer. He recently was awarded a patent for the development of a digital music-synthesis technique.

Lucy Lediaev, Manager of Developer Services at Philips Interactive Media in Los Angeles, brings to her position almost 10 years of experience in software support and CAD/CAM and in multimedia. Ms. Lediaev is a liberal arts graduate of The University of Iowa. She has been involved in the production of user-documentation, engineering-documentation, and technical-marketing support activities, and customer and engineering support services. Her current position involves the day-to-day supervision of engineering support and test personnel, who provide telephone and e-mail support to those engaged in CD-I software engineering; editing and production of *The Interactive Engineer*, a bimonthly technical newsletter for CD-I software engineers;

editing and dissemination of technical notes and production notes for the CD-I community; and planning and execution of the annual Compact Disc Interactive Software Conference (CDISC). She also participates actively in CD-I support via the CompuServe Multimedia forum.

Claude Leglise was appointed Director of Video Brand Marketing at Intel in January 1993. He joined the firm in 1982 and has held a variety of marketing and management positions. In 1985, as the i386 marketing manager, he directed the introduction of Intel's first 32-bit microprocessor. In 1987 he was appointed director of marketing of the Microprocessor Division. In 1989 he became director of the i860 Focus Group, and in 1990 was promoted to the position of General Manager of the Supercomputing Components Operation. In 1992, as Director of Marketing for the Multimedia and Supercomputing Components Group, he managed the team that launched the Indeo Video technology.

Mr. Leglise received his MS degree in Electrical Engineering from ENSAM, Paris, France, and his MBA from Stanford University.

James Long, President of Starlight Networks, founded the company with Charlie Bass in early 1990 in order to develop products to enable digital-video networks and servers. In the previous 10 years, Long worked as a venture capitalist with Fred Adler and with a number of high-technology start-up companies both as a founder and in positions such as President or Vice President of Marketing. Much of his work has been in the area of real-time voice and data management, and graphics software. Affiliations include Ready Systems, Manageware, Veritas, and Unix International. Long began his career at Hewlett-Packard, where he was responsible for software development and product marketing. He holds a BS degree in Electrical Engineering and Computer Science from the University of California at Berkeley, and an MBA degree from Harvard Business School.

Kirk Mahoney is a winner of an Interactive Advertising and Media Award. His formal education includes art design, photography, neurophysiology, nuclear medicine, and computer science, and he has been developing custom software since 1980 in more than 20 programming languages.

Author of more than 15 peer-reviewed scientific articles, he has earned seven degrees, beginning with an A.A.S. in Instructional Media Technology and concluding with a Ph.D. in Biomathematics from UCLA School of Medicine. He also is a graduate of the University of Houston's world-renowned Accelerated Language Program in Spanish.

Prior to founding Engaging Media, Mahoney was founding Co-Director of the Communication Sciences Division of the UCLA Crump Institute for Biological Imaging, where he produced and commercialized a CD-ROM, sold worldwide, that teaches the basic science and clinical applications of positron emission tomography.

Having spoken at several business and scientific seminars, Mahoney has delivered speeches for such organizations as Siemens Medical Systems and New Media Expo.

Perhaps the only individual to hold California Community College Instructor Credentials in the three fields of Computer and Related Technologies, Biological Sciences, and Mathematics, Mahoney has taught at the community-college, graduate-school, and continuing-medical-education levels. He also has been a statistical consultant and the medical photographer for a county hospital.

Mahoney is Founding Treasurer of the Houston chapter of the International Interactive Communications Society. He also has served IICS/Houston as President, Electronic Information Officer, and Showcase Publicity Chair.

Mahoney's interactive-media productions have appeared on a CD-ROM for the book *Multimedia Madness, Deluxe Edition* (published by Sams Publishing) and on the videotapes *Brain Mapping: New Tools for the Clinical Neuroscientist* in the 1990s (published by the American Academy of Neurology) and *InterAction 1994: The Best Interactive Advertising & Media This Year* (published by *Advertising Age*). Mahoney can be reached by e-mail at kmahoney@engaging.com. His company's URL on the Web is http://www.engaging.com.

Mike McGonagle is Manager of Workstation Development at Computer Corporation of America. Mike has 19 years of experience in the software development field. He has been involved in the development of distribution and manufacturing applications, as well as systems and communications software. This work was done at companies such as Keydata, Distribution Management Systems (DMS), Cullinet, Atex, and now at Computer Corp. of America. He first got involved with voice-recognition and -response systems in the early eighties at DMS, where several prototype systems were built to demonstrate the potential of these systems in the distribution industry. This work led to the integration of voice response into Cullinet's expert system product, Application Expert.

Mike is currently in charge of Workstation Development for CCA, where his research into the commercial use of this technology continues. He has one bachelor's degree in Mathematics from Lowell Technical Institute and another in Pure Mathematics from Brown University.

Rob Morris, President of V-Graph, holds a degree in Broadcasting and Film from Boston University, and a graduate degree in Computer Science from Villanova University. His family has deep roots in American history. One of his ancestors came to America with William Penn, and another was a member of the Jamestown colony. His namesake signed the Declaration of Independence and Constitution. This Robert Morris was the financier of the Revolution, nominated Washington for President in addition to starting the Navy, commissioning the flag, and personally underwriting the battle of Yorktown, which ended the war.

The present Robert Morris worked as an independent film producer at Harvard University and in the promotion department at WGBH, the public broadcasting station in Boston, before he became involved with interactive video in 1979. In 1979 he proposed a TV show that included an adventure game, where the participants moved in a variety of real-time 3D graphic worlds. They said it couldn't be done. Now we know it as *virtual reality*.

From 1981 to 1984, Mr. Morris worked in Philadelphia at Interactive Video Concepts, Inc. with Peg Callahan working on a variety of laser-disk based projects from Health Care database programs, to Level 2 videodisk applications, to designing an authoring package, called *Pharos*. He developed interactive video programs for RCA, the Franklin Institute, Smith Kline & French International, AT&T, Bell Atlantic, the National Institute of Health, and others.

In 1985, he started a long-time association with Trip Denton, who was destined to become co-founder of V-Graph Inc. a year or so later. Their first project was a promo disk where the user could build and operate a local area network in one of three environments. This project for Bell of PA was an interactive 4-color graphic application that fit on a 360K floppy and ran on a 512K PC (Not even an XT). It took users 45 minutes to run through the 95+ graphic screens and it was so successful that it was sent to all the telecommunications managers in the Bell Atlantic region.

V-Graph Inc. was founded in 1986 to create, use, and market the first digital video, digital audio commercial authoring software, VirtualVideo. VirtualVideo was shipped before Apple shipped Hypercard and before the Amiga was delivered. VirtualVideo also included speech recognition as an input source. A year later, motion digital video was added. It was called *VirtualVideo* because the term *multimedia* was being used to describe slide shows at that time.

In 1991, Rob Morris met with the president of Mathematica Inc., a paint program company, and convinced him that by shipping the VirtualVideo authoring software with this Tempra paint software, they could be the first to provide an integrated solution to multimedia developers. VirtualVideo became Tempra Show and was bundled with the Video Blaster, Genoa video boards, a multimedia book, and the Snap Plus. Over 200,000 copies were delivered around the world. A more powerful version was made called *Tempra Media Author*, and was shipped with Tempra Pro. Just as the market was starting to build, Windows came along and people became convinced that Windows was necessary for multimedia. This was a big surprise because VirtualVideo was working just fine without it. The multimedia market became very confusing to people as a result of the plethora of exaggerated and conflicting claims being made by a variety of vendors. This required Mathematica to spend large sums in promotion. Unfortunately, Mathematica spent more money than they made and the company went into bankruptcy. Mr. Morris's company took possession of the Tempra product line to supply those users with software and continuity of support.

Now Mr. Morris and his partner have developed another new software system. This system, OZONE (The Object Zone), lets people construct all kinds of applications using authoring-style techniques. Mr. Morris explains the benefits of OZONE as a system where projects can be delivered in 15% of the time they would take using conventional technology because the programming is 100% visual. OZONE uses a standard software plug-in as its primary object so that users can add their own objects simply by purchasing them on the market.

Inventor, businessman, part-time historian, husband, and dad, Rob Morris toils away in relative obscurity, creating new ways for people to improve their lives. Surfing on the bleeding edge of the technology curve, Rob Morris shows the world how to make the future come to life.

Glenn K. Morrissey manages Asymetrix's growing multimedia business. He played a key role in developing Multimedia ToolBook, and he continues to work closely with customers in pioneering multimedia Windows applications. Morrissey is a former writer, producer, director, and musician with many years of experience in the entertainment industry.

Asymetrix Corp. is a privately held, employee-owned software company based in Bellevue, WA, committed to a mission of bringing pioneering productivity to all levels of Windows users with affordable, easy-to-use software.

Ken Morse received his B.Eng. in Electronic Engineering from the University of Liverpool, England, in 1986, and his Ph.D. in Electronic Engineering also at the University of Liverpool in 1992.

Since graduating, he has formed three companies. MTL was founded in 1982 to provide software security and delivery systems for cassette and floppy disk-based software in the home computer market.

Ultra Digital Systems was founded in 1986 to market digital signal-processor development systems based on the Texas Instruments TMS320 family Multimedia Consultants was founded in 1992 as a multimedia software and hardware consultancy.

Dr. Morse has also worked as consultant at IBM Hursley, England. Currently he is working as a consultant at Kaleida Labs.

Kurt Mueller is founder and president of Dataware Technologies, Inc. Previously he served as general manager for the Lotus Development Corporation in Germany and Austria. He has served as a management consultant with Bain and Company in the United States and in Europe. Mr. Mueller holds a BA in Computer Science from Northwestern University and an MBA from the University of Chicago, and he has studied law at Harvard Law School.

Jim Murray is a former technical writer and former U.S. Navy carrier aviator, who now has a real job as Senior Technical Information Engineer at Gateway 2000. Jim was the force behind Gateway's Online Guides, which were the PC industry's first interactive user guides. He wrote all the text, created the 3D art and animations, designed the interface, and did the programming as well, leaving no one else to blame when things went wrong. Educated in mathematics and project management, Jim spends his time these days developing content for Gateway's World Wide Web site, gw2k.com.

Eric R. Nahm is Vice President, Marketing and Sales for Verbex Voice Systems, Inc., of Edison, New Jersey. His background includes sales, marketing, management and executive positions at IBM and AT&T.

Jeffrey V. Nickerson is a Technical Director at Coopers & Lybrand L.L.P. As part of the National Client/Server Practice, he provides management consulting services in object-oriented technology, client/server system design, and information architectures. Most recently, he has helped companies use multimedia tools to visualize the contents of their data warehouses. His multimedia background includes computer graphics and image processing work in the areas of computer games, computer-aided design, image recognition, and visual programming. He has appeared on CNBC's Technology Edge and was featured on the cover of Information Week. He holds an M.F.A. in Graphic Design from Rhode Island School of Design and a Ph.D. in Computer Science from New York University.

Michael O'Berry has over 20 years of visual communications experience. He has taught for Pinellas County schools, Sarasota's nationally renowned Ringling College of Art and Design, and currently teaches computer graphic applications for St. Petersburg Junior College's Corporate Training Services. As Director of Training for one of the nation's largest graphic arts firms, he has participated in software beta testing for several national computer graphic software companies, including Adobe Systems and QuarkXPress. He has also provided computer graphics consulting for Harvard University, Time-Life Books, and Smithsonian's *Air and Space Magazine*. Most recently, he has lectured for Kodak on PhotoCD, CD-ROM based imaging, and for Adobe Systems on Photoshop imaging software.

Amy Pearl has been at Sun Microsystems since 1986. She runs the Enterprise Communication Initiative (ECI), a cross-functional collaboration between Sun's MIS department, Sun's training organization, Sun Laboratories, and SunSoft. The ECI is developing opportunities for multimedia communication to increase corporate productivity. While in Sun Microsystems' laboratories, she developed Videoconf, an integrated desktop videoconferencing prototype as part of a collaborative-computing research project.

Pearl received her BA in Computer Science from Mills College in Oakland in 1983. After a brief stint at Zilog, she attended Stanford University, where she received an MS in Computer Science in 1986. At Stanford she developed a protocol for automatic screen-sharing in an early network window system.

Her professional interest is in using networked computers to support people working together. At Sun she designed and developed the Link Service, an interapplication communication support service for large-scale software development. She is now involved in the design and development of network services to support distributed multimedia. She has been on the board of USACM, the ACM's Public Policy Committee, and has also been on the national executive committee of Computer Professionals for Social Responsibility.

Tim Picraux is Program Marketing Manager for Unisys' Imaging Systems Group. He is responsible for the definition of product requirements to incorporate imaging technologies into Unisys solutions for the commercial and manufacturing sectors.

Picraux has 10 years of experience in the automotive industry, applying computer technologies to solve engineering and manufacturing problems. He has 15 years of experience in the development and marketing of engineering systems, including CAD/CAM and document-imaging.

He holds a master's degree in Systems Engineering from Oakland University in Rochester, Michigan, as well as a management degree from the University of Michigan.

Marco Pinter received a bachelor's degree in Computer Science from Cornell University, and did his graduate work at the University of California. He has also served on the Computer Science faculty of Bucknell University. Pinter founded Digital Media International in the fall of 1990, and has led a number of multimedia projects, including DVI-based instructional programs for GPU Nuclear Corporation. Pinter also has led the development of several video-editing tools in the PC environment.

Rudy Prokupets, Vice President of R&D for Lenel Systems International, was born and educated in the former Soviet Union. He holds two master's degrees, one in Electrical Engineering from the prestigious Electrotechnical Institute of Leningrad and the other in Applied Mathematics from the University of Leningrad. He immigrated to the United States in 1978. He worked for Bausch and Lomb and subsequently the Eastman Kodak Company, where he held positions as Senior Research Scientist and Senior Software Designer.

In 1985 Mr. Prokupets and his wife, Elena, founded Edicon, a Kodak venture company, with a focus on electronic identification and photodatabase security systems. The most successful and profitable Kodak venture company, Edicon achieved Division status in 1990.

Mr. and Ms. Prokupets left Edicon in 1990 to found Lenel Systems International, Inc. In the two years since its inception, Lenel has become a leading developer of object-oriented multimedia software and has forged development and business alliances with such companies as Microsoft, Borland, Sony, Panasonic, and Intel.

Steven L. Raber joined IBM in Charleston, South Carolina, in 1976 as a sales trainee. He held different marketing and staff positions until his appointment into management in 1985 in Atlanta, Georgia. Subsequently he became Southern Area Manager of Large Systems Marketing.

In 1989 Steve was named Marketing Branch Manager in Nashville, Tennessee. While in Nashville he was active in community affairs, including serving on the Board of Directors of the United Way, the Nashville Symphony, and Junior Achievement.

In January 1992, Steve was named Administrative Assistant in the office of the Chairman of the Board, and in March 1993 he was announced as Director of Multimedia Marketing.

Steve was born in Kansas and raised in southern Illinois. He attended Florida State University, where he graduated with a degree in finance.

Bruce A. Rady is the President and CEO of TouchVision Systems, Inc., the developer of D/Vision: The Digital Video Editor. It is a nonlinear capture/edit tool for the PC/Intel platform.

Mr. Rady has been a pioneer in the development of nonlinear video editing for over a decade. He spent 10 years as an engineering and marketing manager at Bell and Howell, where he worked in new product development. There, he headed the team that began development of the TouchVision nonlinear editing system for film production.

In 1983, Bell and Howell spun off its professional division and the TouchVision project, resulting in the creation of BHP, Inc. Rady was co-owner and head of BHP's Editing Systems Division.

Six years later, TouchVision was being used by Hollywood filmmakers for films starring the likes of Madonna and Sylvester Stallone. Development then began on the product known today as D/Vision, a digital-video version of TouchVision. Shortly thereafter, TouchVision split from BHP, and Rady began to concentrate his efforts on making D/Vision available to a wider market.

Rady holds an MBA from the University of Chicago and a BS in Electrical Engineering from the University of Kentucky. He is married and the father of three children.

Gary Robbins has been an officer with the St. Petersburg (FL) Police Department for almost 51 years. The department's 500+ sworn officers serve a population of about 250,000 residents, as well as numerous visitors at any given time. Since 1986, he also has been an adjunct instructor at St. Petersburg Junior College's Criminal Justice Institute, in generalized instruction (Report Writing, Patrol Procedures, and Officer Safety) and in high-liability instruction (Defensive Tactics, Firearms, and Driving). Most of his law-enforcement experience has been as a Field Training Officer, whose responsibility is to teach new police officers how to apply their fundamental academy knowledge "on the street in real-life situations." Gary also has considerable tactical experience as a SWAT team member and leader for more than 10 years. In addition, he is currently a sergeant in the Field Training Unit.

John Sievel is President and co-founder of Gnomon Inc., a software development company specializing in interactive 3D graphics. He is the author of FlashRender, a high-speed cross-platform rendering software library. Prior to founding Gnomon, Sievel consulted for companies in the publishing, communications, brokerage, and scientific research areas, in New York, Miami, and Connecticut. He holds a B.S.E.E. from the University of Connecticut, with honors.

Deborah M. Slater is Inside Sales Manager for Verbex. Her background includes writing and editing positions in the publishing industry.

Lex van Sonderen, Manager of Knowledge Transfer at Philips Interactive Media in Los Angeles, has as his mission the dissemination of information and training in CD-I software development. Mr. van Sonderen, who holds a master's degree in Industrial Design Engineering from the Technical University of Delft in the Netherlands, is applying his extensive experience in software engineering to the design of a CD-I training program and a CD-I developer support program under the umbrella of the worldwide Philips Interactive Media organization.

Mr. van Sonderen also is responsible for the technical component of the activities of the engineering support, text, and training personnel in the Los Angeles organization. He also is contributing editor to *The Interactive Engineer* and is a frequent contributor to the CompuServe Multimedia forum and libraries. In addition, he acts as a technical liaison between the activities in the Los Angeles organization and the Philips organization in the Netherlands.

Lawrence Strickland has more than 15 years of experience in computer training at the college level or higher. In addition, he has more than 20 years of experience in general technology and in programming in UNIX, DOS, and Macintosh environments. Larry is the Coordinator for Instructional Computing for St. Petersburg Junior College.

Valerie Taylor's 20 years of data processing and multimedia experience include a comprehensive background in high-technology product development, management, customer service, and marketing. Ms. Taylor has a proven track record in multimedia production, product design, and management for a variety of products and services from CD-ROM titles and educational software to Internet information publishing and World Wide Web promotional services.

Ms. Taylor directed the development and marketing of multimedia projects for clients that included Amdahl, Montparnasse Multimedia, NASA Ames Research Center, Syntex Laboratories, Sun Microsystems, and The Tech Museum of Innovation.

Serge Timacheff is Senior Manager of Public Relations for Logitech Inc., and formerly a senior reviews editor for *InfoWorld* magazine. He is the author of two books, including *InfoWorld: Understanding Windows* (Brady Books, 1990) and *The Personalized PC* (Random House, 1993). He speaks and represents Logitech frequently on computer-related topics such as multimedia, giving senses to computers, computer personalization, business presentations, and the development of the PC industry.

Logitech manufactures and markets Senseware—products designed to give "senses" such as sight, sound, and touch to the computer, making human-to-computer communication more intuitive and natural. Retail and OEM products of the company and its affiliates include pointing devices (such as mice and trackballs), hand-held scanners, digital cameras, pen digitizers, joysticks, sound products, and related software applications for IBM, Macintosh, and other platforms. Logitech International, the financial holding company for the Logitech Group, is traded publicly in Switzerland on the Zurich and Geneva exchanges. With operational headquarters in Fremont, CA, the group maintains manufacturing facilities in Fremont; Hsinchu, Taiwan; Shanghai, China; and Cork, Ireland, and offices in major cities in the United States, Europe, and the Far East.

Bill Tonnies has more than 16 years of computer systems and programming experience. His primary field of expertise is application development using high-level programming languages, such as C and C++. He has also developed computer-based training using authoring systems that vary from mainframe-based to multimedia.

Currently, he is employed by an international training corporation that specializes in training for large corporations and government agencies. He was brought on to the BEAT project as a consultant and Lingo programmer.

Prem Uppaluru is Vice President of Engineering and Product Marketing at Fluent in Natick, MA. Before joining Fluent, Dr. Uppaluru was Vice President of Engineering at Samsung Software America, where he participated in the development of advanced networked imaging products. Prior to that he was with Bellcore and Bell Laboratories. His areas of technical expertise include network computing, object-oriented systems, operating systems, databases, parallel processing, and computer architecture. He received his Ph.D. in Computer Science and Engineering from the University of Texas at Austin.

Verbex Voice Systems, Inc. develops and manufactures continuous speech recognition systems that enable people to control computers with voice. The company builds products that respond to continuous speech. Verbex's goal is to improve the way that people interact with their computers by providing a natural and efficient means of communication and data entry.

Vince Walisko has been involved in the satellite communications industry for 12 years, and in radio and television broadcasting for 20. He also spent several years working with NuMedia Corporation on the issues of communications in the multimedia computing environment. He worked extensively on the development of satellite news-gathering while at GTE Spacenet and with GEC McMichael and as a principal of Spectra Communications, Inc. Most recently Mr. Walisko has focused on the international satellite communications area while working at both PanAmSat and INTELSAT. He also is a principal in The Walisko Group, located in Washington, D.C., and Lieberman and Walisko. He has been involved in the design, implementation, and operation of satellite systems from compressed digital video and VSAT networks to shipboard television transmissions for a U.S. television network. He has tested satellite power and receiver sensitivity in various parts of the world. He has taught an undergraduate course in television technology at The American University in Washington, D.C. He studied Electrical Engineering at Rensselaer Polytechnic Institute, and Television/Radio Communications at Syracuse University.

Rob Wallace is codeveloper and MIDI author of "Multimedia Kaleidosonics," a popular CD-ROM and DOS interactive graphic-and-music product. Wallace Music & Sound, Inc. provides original music and sound effects for software developers and publishers. Rob's credits include the musical arrangements in the Miracle Piano Teaching System for The Software Toolworks, and original music for the following: Mig 29 by Spectrum Holobyte; Snoopy's Game Club, for Accolade; Monster Bash, for Apogee; Wayne's World, for Capstone; Eagle Eye Mysteries, for Electronic Arts; Tom Landry Strategic Football, for Merit Software; and Video Poker for Windows, for Masque Publishing.

Besides dozens of other musical scores for Games and educational products, Wallace lends his character-voice acting abilities and stable of actors for complete digital voice tracks. Among them is Mario's Missing Deluxe (CD-ROM version), which contains over 2000 speeches from 57 separate roles, of which Rob voiced 15. Wallace Music & Sound, Inc. has been operating since 1989.

Joseph Weintraub is President of Thinking Software, a small creative software development firm in Woodside, New York; he was the first winner of the Loebner Prize Competition, held at the Boston Computer Museum in 1991. The winning software program was called PC Therapist III, and is available for the IBM/PC.

Joseph has been a Data Processing instructor at New York University and at Pace University. He is a graduate of the City College of the City University of New York, and is a member of Mensa. He has been Senior Programmer for Time Magazine in New York, and has authored articles for *AI Expert*, *AI magazine*, *PC/AI* magazine and a book for the Rosen Publishing Group (NYC) called *Exploring Careers in the Computer Field*. He is a certified member of the exclusive Developer Programs both at IBM Small Systems Division and Creative Labs.

Weintraub's current areas of research and interest include multimedia and virtual reality.

J. Alan Whiteside, Ph.D., is Senior Instructional Designer at Multimedia Learning, Inc., in Irving, Texas. He received his doctorate in instructional design from The Pennsylvania State University and has over 14 years of experience in designing, developing, and delivering effective instruction. Dr. Whiteside has been involved as a project manager and instructional designer of computer-based training in two large Air Force projects. In addition he has managed the development of "conventional" and multimedia projects in the financial, manufacturing, transportation, and energy sectors. Dr. Whiteside's areas of emphasis include effective integration of visuals with text and sound in multimedia, and the application of sound instructional strategies in technology-based instruction.

Mary F. Whiteside, Ph.D., is Director of the Media Development graduate studies program and assistant professor in the Office of Medical Education at The University of Texas Southwestern Medical Center at Dallas. Dr. Whiteside received her doctorate in instructional design from The Pennsylvania State University. She also consults with a variety of commercial firms on instructional design issues. Dr. Whiteside has managed the development of interactive videodisc and multimedia education and training programs. Currently she is project manager for an innovative performance support system designed for third-year medical students. Dr. Whiteside's interests are the integration of technology-based instruction into curricula and training programs, and the use of effective design techniques to produce multimedia.

Frederic M. Wilf is special counsel with the Philadelphia law firm of Saul, Ewing, Remick, & Saul. The 150-lawyer general practice firm maintains its home page on the World Wide Web at http://www.saul.com. Mr. Wilf is resident in the firm's Berwyn office, where he practices technology and intellectual property law, with an emphasis on the computer industry. Mr. Wilf's clients included multimedia and software developers, vendors, and consultants, as well as writers, artists and photographers. Mr. Wilf may be reached via the Internet at fwilf@saul.com, on CompuServe at 72300, 2061 and at the following address: Saul, Ewing, Remick & Saul, 1055 Westlakes Drive, Suite 150, Berwyn, PA 19312, U.S.A.

Les Wilson is Marketing Manager of Multimedia Communications Development for the Systems Application Technology group at National Semiconductor Corporation in Santa Clara, CA. He is responsible for providing future visions of markets and their technology requirements. Wilson currently is doing end-user market research, and for the last two years has planned the development of worldwide video networking systems that use compression, LANs, WANs, and new protocols. Wilson has over ten years' experience in developing communications architecture.

Before joining National, Wilson was involved in the development of state-of-the-art critical-care biomedical-monitoring systems that networked important physiological information, real-time, from the bedside to doctors and nurses. These graphical display instruments were designed for reliability, accuracy, and ease of use. In addition Wilson spent two years in the typesetting industry, which supplies typesetting systems to publishers.

Wing F. Wong is a Technical Director of the National Client/Server Practice at Coopers & Lybrand L.L.P. He provides management consulting services in internetworking design and planning, large scale client/server systems integration and capacity planning, and Internet information architecture. He has designed and supported world-wide distributed networks and has in-depth experience in client/server information retrieval systems on the Internet. Most recently, he helped design and implement World-Wide Web technology for an on-line and real-time document publishing system. He is a regular contributor of the *Coopers & Lybrand View* from Summit newsletter and has been frequently quoted in *Client/Server Computing Magazine* and *Software Magazine*. He presented the topic "UNIX Internet Tools and Services" at the 1994 Enterprise Computing Solutions Conference in Chicago. He holds an MBA from the William E. Simon Graduate School of Business Administration and a BS in Computer Science from the University of Iowa. He graduated with a Phi Beta Kappa.

Andrew Young is well known within the Unix industry for developing new directions for CD-ROM and multimedia standards. He is the principal author of two innovative Unix/CD-ROM proposals: the Rock Ridge Interchange Protocol and the Systems Use Sharing Protocol. He is currently the Chairman of the IEEE CD-ROM File System Format Working Group. Mr. Young is President and cofounder of Young Minds, Inc., a company that provides CD-ROM and CD-recordable solutions. He holds a master's degree in Mathematics from the University of California at San Diego.

He is a frequent speaker for industry meetings and conferences such as SIGCAT, CD-ROM Expo, Intermedia, UniForum, OnLine Multimedia, and the SCO Forum. He authored articles for *SurWorld*, *SunExpert*, *DISC*, and *CD-ROM Professional*. He also wrote the first monthly Unix column for a CD-ROM industry magazine.

U

ABOUT THE EDITOR

Jessica Keyes is president of Techinsider/New Art, Inc., a technology consulting and research firm specializing in productivity and high-technology applications. Formerly managing director of technology for the New York Stock Exchange and an officer with Swiss Bank Co. and Banker's Trust, she publishes *Techinsider Reports* and *Computer Market Letter*. Keyes is a frequent contributor to such well-known publications as *Software Magazine* and *Computerworld*, and is the author of several best-selling books, including *Infotrends*, *Software Engineering Productivity*, and *Solving the Productivity Paradox*.